New Perspectives on

JavaScript

Comprehensive

New Perspectives on

JavaScript

Comprehensive

Patrick Carey

Carey Associates, Inc.

Frank Canovatchel

Champlain College

COURSE TECHNOLOGY
CENGAGE Learning

Australia • Brazil • Japan • Korea • Mexico • Singapore • Spain • United Kingdom • United States

COURSE TECHNOLOGY
CENGAGE Learning™

New Perspectives on JavaScript—Comprehensive
Patrick Carey, Frank Canovatchel

Senior Managing Editor: Rachel Goldberg

Product Managers: Katherine T. Pinard,
  Karen Stevens

Associate Product Manager: Shana Rosenthal

Editorial Assistant: Janine Tangney

Marketing Manager: Joy Stark

Developmental Editor: Sasha Vodnik

QA Manuscript Reviewers: Chris Carvalho,
  Ashlee Welz Smith

Production Editor: Danielle Slade

Copy Editor: Mark Goodin

Proofreader: John Bosco

Indexer: Alexandra Nickerson

Composition: GEX Publishing Services

Text Designer: Steve Deschene

Cover Designer: Nancy Goulet

Cover Artist: Helmick & Schechter Sculpture
  www.handsart.net

ISBN-13: 978-0-619-26797-1

ISBN-10: 0-619-26797-6

Course Technology
20 Channel Center Street
Boston, MA 02210
USA

Cengage Learning is a leading provider of customized learning solutions with
office locations around the globe, including Singapore, the United Kingdom,
Australia, Mexico, Brazil, and Japan. Locate your local office at
www.cengage.com/global

Cengage Learning products are represented in Canada by Nelson Education, Ltd.

To learn more about Course Technology, visit
www.cengage.com/coursetechnology

Purchase any of our products at your local bookstore or at our preferred online
store **www.ichapters.com**

Printed in the United States of America
  6 7 8 9 10   13 12 11 10 09

ED258

Preface

Real, Thought-Provoking, Engaging, Dynamic, Interactive—these are just a few of the words that are used to describe the New Perspectives Series' approach to learning and building computer skills.

Without our critical-thinking and problem-solving methodology, computer skills could be learned but not retained. By teaching with a case-based approach, the New Perspectives Series challenges students to apply what they've learned to real-life situations.

Our ever-growing community of users understands why they're learning what they're learning. Now you can too!

See what instructors and students are saying about the best-selling New Perspectives Series:

"First of all, I just have to say that I wish that all of my textbooks were written in the style of the New Perspectives Series. I am using these titles for all of the courses that I teach that have a book available."
— Diana Kokoska, University of Maine at Augusta

"The New Perspectives format is a pleasure to use. The Quick Checks and the tutorial Review Assignments help students view topics from a real-world perspective."
— Craig Shaw, Central Community College—Hastings

"We have been using the New Perspectives Series for several years and are pleased with it. Step-by-step instructions, end-of-chaper projects, and color screenshots are positives."
— Michael J. Losacco, College of DuPage

...and about New Perspectives on JavaScript:

"The excellent, step-by-step, hands-on approach combined with the figures interspersed throughout make it easy for students to compare their code to that in the text and be certain they have completed each snippet properly before advancing to the next portion of the application."
— Mike Michaelson, Palomar College

www.cengage.com/ct/newperspectives

Why *New Perspectives* will work for you

Context

Each tutorial begins with a problem presented in a "real-world" case that is meaningful to students. The case sets the scene to help students understand what they will do in the tutorial.

Hands-on Approach

Each tutorial is divided into manageable sessions that combine reading and hands-on, step-by-step work. Screenshots—now 20% larger for enhanced readability—help guide students through the steps. **Trouble?** tips anticipate common mistakes or problems to help students stay on track and continue with the tutorial.

Review

In New Perspectives, retention is a key component to learning. At the end of each session, a series of Quick Check questions helps students test their understanding of the concepts before moving on. And now each tutorial contains an end-of-tutorial summary and a list of key terms for further reinforcement.

Assessment

Engaging and challenging Review Assignments and Case Problems have always been a hallmark feature of the New Perspectives Series. Now we've added new features to make them more accessible! Colorful icons and brief descriptions accompany the exercises, making it easy to understand, at a glance, both the goal and level of challenge a particular assignment holds.

Reference

While contextual learning is excellent for retention, there are times when students will want a high-level understanding of how to accomplish a task. Within each tutorial, Reference Windows appear before a set of steps to provide a succinct summary and preview of how to perform a task. In addition, each book includes a combination Glossary/Index to promote easy reference of material.

Student Online Companion

This book has an accompanying online companion Web site designed to enhance learning. Go to www.course.com/carey to find:

- Additional content for further exploration
- List of URLs from the book
- Student Data Files
- Student Edition Labs—These online interactive labs offer students hands-on practice and reinforcement of skills and concepts relating Web and Internet topics.
- Information about other Patrick Carey products

www.cengage.com/ct/newperspectives

New Perspectives offers an entire system of instruction

The New Perspectives Series is more than just a handful of books. It's a complete system of offerings:

New Perspectives catalog
Our online catalog is never out of date! Go to the catalog link on our Web site to check out our available titles, request a desk copy, download a book preview, or locate online files.

Coverage to meet your needs!
Whether you're looking for just a small amount of coverage or enough to fill a semester-long class, we can provide you with a textbook that meets your needs.
- Brief books typically cover the essential skills in just 2 to 4 tutorials.
- Introductory books build and expand on those skills and contain an average of 5 to 8 tutorials.
- Comprehensive books are great for a full-semester class, and contain 9 to 12+ tutorials.
- Power Users or Advanced books are perfect for a highly accelerated introductory class or a second course in a given topic.

So if the book you're holding does not provide the right amount of coverage for you, there's probably another offering available. Go to our Web site or contact your Course Technology sales representative to find out what else we offer.

Instructor Resources
We offer more than just a book. We have all the tools you need to enhance your lectures, check students' work, and generate exams in a new, easier-to-use and completely revised package. This book's Instructor's Manual, ExamView testbank, PowerPoint presentations, data files, solution files, figure files, and a sample syllabus are all available on a single CD-ROM or for downloading at www.course.com.

How will your students master Computer Concepts and Microsoft Office?
Add more muscle and flexibility to your course with SAM (Skills Assessment Manager)! SAM adds the power of skill-based assessment and the award-winning SAM classroom administration system to your course, putting you in control of how you deliver exams and training.

By adding SAM to your curriculum, you can:
- Reinforce your students' knowledge of key computer concepts and application skills with hands-on exercises.
- Allow your students to "learn by listening," with access to rich audio in their training.
- Build hands-on computer concepts exams from a test bank of more than 200 skill-based concepts, windows, and applications tasks.
- Schedule your students' training and testing exercises with powerful administrative tools.
- Track student exam grades and training progress using more than one dozen student and classroom reports.

Teach your introductory course with the simplicity of a single system! You can now administer your entire Computer Concepts and Microsoft Office course through the SAM platform. For more information on the SAM administration system, SAM Computer Concepts, and other SAM products, please visit samcentral.course.com.

Distance Learning
Enhance your course with any of our online learning platforms. Go to www.course.com or speak with your Course Technology sales representative to find the platform or the content that's right for you.

www.cengage.com/ct/newperspectives

About This Book

This book provides comprehensive instruction in basic to advanced concepts of JavaScript, teaching students how to apply JavaScript to create real-world applications using a practical, step-by-step approach.

- Step-by-step instructions help students create animated text, image rollovers, pull-down menus, pop-up windows, interactive forms, and drag and drop objects.
- Includes detailed coverage of foundation concepts such as objects, expressions, arrays, and loops.
- Two review tutorials help students review HTML, XHTML, and CSS concepts.
- Students use cookies to build an online shopping cart.
- Includes a tutorial on web forms with coverage of regular expressions and passing data between Web forms.
- Students learn JavaScript interactively with demo pages.
- Coverage of string objects, including number formatting, and form validation and validating credit card data, is included.
- Students create a dynamic Table of Contents using nodes and the node tree.
- An appendix on common JavaScript mistakes, capturing errors, and debugging code is included.
- Robust Student Online Companion with additional material is available.

Acknowledgments

We would like to thank the people who worked so hard to make this book possible. Special thanks to Sasha Vodnik for his excellent suggestions and ideas in developing this material and to Kitty Pinard, Karen Stevens, and Donna Gridley, the Product Managers who worked so hard in overseeing this project, keeping it on task and on target. Other people at Course Technology who deserve credit are Rachel Goldberg, Managing Editor; Shana Rosenthal, Associate Product Manager; Danielle Slade, Production Editor; and Quality Assurance Testers Chris Carvalho and Ashlee Welz Smith.

Feedback is an important part of writing any book, and thanks go to the following reviewers for their ideas and comments: Mike Michaelson, Palomar College; Sally Catlin, Indiana University - Purdue University; Sandi Watkins, Foothill College; LeShawn Roberts, Florida Career College; George Jackson, Collin County Community College; Allen Schmidt, Madison Area Technical College; Dorothy Harman, Tarrant County College; Cheryl Jordan, San Juan College; Lisa Friedrichsen, Johnson County Community College; and Mary Lee Herrmann, Hagerstown Community College.

Special thanks also go to the members of our New Perspectives HTML Advisory Committee: Dr. Nazih Abdallah, University of Central Florida; Liz Drake, Santa Fe Community College; Ric Heishman, Northern Virginia Community College, Manassas Campus; George Jackson, Collin County Community College District; David Jampole, Bossier Parrish Community College; Eric Kisling, Indiana University; Diana Kokoska, University of Maine Augusta; William Lomerson, Northwestern State University—Natchitoches; Lisa Macon, Valencia Community College; David Ray, Jones County Junior College; Lo-An Tabar-Gaul, Mesa Community College; Sandi Watkins, Foothill College; and Zachary Wong, Sonoma State University.

I want to thank my wife Joan for her love and encouragement, and my six children: John Paul, Thomas, Peter, Michael, Stephen, and Catherine, to whom this book is dedicated. In memory of my brother, Kevin.

—Patrick Carey

I want to thank God, my wife Patti, and my children, Justin, James, Maureen, Matthew, Christopher, David, and Daniel, for their encouragement and support.

—Frank Canovatchel

www.cengage.com/ct/newperspectives

Table of Contents

New Perspectives on
JavaScript

Read This Before You Begin

To the Student

Data Files

To complete the tutorials, you need the starting student Data Files. Your instructor will either provide you with these Data Files or ask you to obtain them yourself.

The JavaScript Tutorials require the folders shown to complete the Tutorials, Review Assignments, and Case Problems. You will need to copy these folders from a file server, a standalone computer, or the Web to the drive and folder where you will be storing your Data Files.

Your instructor will tell you which computer, drive letter, and folder(s) contain the files you need. You can also download the files by going to www.course.com; see the inside back or front cover for more information on downloading the files, or ask your instructor or technical support person for assistance.

▼ **JavaScript**

Tutorial.01	Tutorial.05	Tutorial.09
Tutorial.02	Tutorial.06	Tutorial.10
Tutorial.03	Tutorial.07	
Tutorial.04	Tutorial.08	

Student Online Companion

The Student Online Companion can be found at www.course.com/carey. It contains additional information to supplement what you are learning in the text, as well as links to downloads and other tools.

Steps and solutions in this text have been verified for the following browsers:

• Windows's Internet Explorer version 6.0 and above

• Firefox 1.0

• Opera 7

• Netscape Navigator 6 and above

• Safari for the Macintosh

The steps and solutions in this book do not support Netscape 4 or Internet Explorer 5 for the Macintosh and we do not recommend the use of those browsers in completing the exercises in this book.

To the Instructor

The Data Files are available on the Instructor Resources CD for this title. Follow the instructions in the Help file on the CD to install the programs to your network or standalone computer. See the "To the Student" section above for information on how to set up the Data Files that accompany this text.

You are granted a license to copy the Data Files to any computer or computer network used by students who have purchased this book.

System Requirements

If you are going to work through this book, using your own computer, you need:

• **System Requirements** A text editor and a Web browser that supports the current standards for HTML and either the W3C or Internet Explorer Document Object Model. Browsers meeting these requirements include the 6.0 (and higher) versions of Internet Explorer, Netscape, and Opera, and the 1.0 (and higher) versions of Safari for Macintosh and Firefox.

We do not recommend use of a Netscape 4 level browser or Internet Explorer 5 for the Macintosh, as both browsers have compatibility issues with current standards. Users who wish to understand how to write code for Netscape 4 level browsers can review the material in Appendix E.

• **Data Files** You will not be able to complete the tutorials or exercises in this book using your own computer until you have the necessary starting Data Files.

www.cengage.com/ct/newperspectives

Objectives

- Understand the history of the Web and HTML
- Study the basic syntax for creating elements and attributes
- Learn to create block-level and inline elements
- Understand how to insert nontextual objects such as inline images into a Web page
- Study how to create and populate Web tables
- Learn how to work with Web forms and their content
- Understand how to create Web frames and inline frames

Introducing HTML and XHTML

Creating Web Pages with HTML

Introducing the World Wide Web and HTML

One of the most significant communications innovations in the past 50 years is the development of the Internet. In its early days in the late 1960s, the Internet was called the ARPANET and consisted of two network nodes, located at UCLA and Stanford, that were connected by a land line. Since then, the Internet has grown to include hundreds of millions of interconnected computers, cell phones, PDAs (personal digital assistants), televisions, and networks. The physical structure of the Internet uses fiber-optic cables, satellites, phone lines, and other telecommunications media to enable a worldwide community to communicate and share information.

Most early Internet tools required mastery of a bewildering array of terms, acronyms, and commands. Even navigating the network required users to be well versed in both computers and network technology. Before the Internet could be accessible to the general public, it needed to have a simple interface, which arrived in the form of the World Wide Web. The foundations for the **World Wide Web**, or **Web**, were laid in 1989 by Timothy Berners-Lee and other researchers at the CERN nuclear research facility near Geneva, Switzerland. They needed an information system that made it easy for their researchers to locate and share data and required minimal training and support. To meet this need, they developed a system of interconnected documents using hypertext. In this system, documents were stored on network computers called **servers**, which made them accessible to users running computers known as **clients**.

Hypertext is a technology that allows users to click items called **links** to open documents and other information sources. A link can open another document on your computer or, using the World Wide Web, a document on another computer located almost anywhere in the world.

The hypertext approach was just what was needed to make the Internet accessible to the general public. An end user didn't need to know exactly where in the world a linked document was located; instead, the user could simply click a mouse to open the document from the server. This approach puts any online document at a user's fingertips. It is a testament to the success of this approach that the Internet and the World Wide Web are synonymous in many users' minds.

Student Data Files

There are no Student Data Files needed for this review.

Web Pages, Servers, and Browsers

Documents on the Web are known as **Web pages**. In addition to text, Web pages can contain images, video and sound clips, and even programs that users can run remotely from their computers. A Web page is stored on a **Web server**, which makes it available to the entire World Wide Web. To view a Web page, a user runs a software program called a **Web browser**, which retrieves the page from the server and displays it (see Figure 1-1).

| Figure 1-1 | Viewing a document on the World Wide Web |

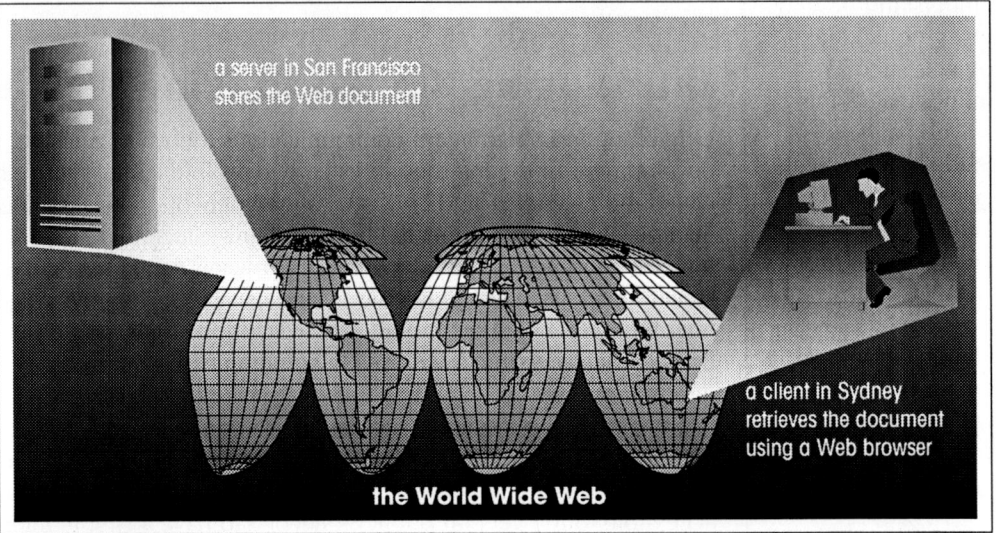

The earliest browsers were text based and incapable of displaying images. Today, however, most computers support graphical browsers, which can display images, video, sound, animations, and a variety of other graphical features. Cell phones can also connect to the Web to display the latest sports scores, stock market tickers, and even rudimentary Web pages. In addition, browsers can run on teletype machines, PDAs, Braille machines, and even information devices within a car. How does a Web page work with so many combinations of browsers, clients, and devices? To understand, you have to look at how Web pages are created.

HTML: The Language of the Web

A Web page is simply a text file that is written in a language called **Hypertext Markup Language**, or **HTML**. A **markup language** describes the structure and the content of a document. Each item within such a document is set off using a **markup tag**. If the content of this review were stored using a markup language, markup tags would identify whether a particular block of text represented the review's title, a paragraph, a figure caption, and so forth.

In the early years after HTML was created, no single organization was responsible for the language. Web browser developers were free to define and modify HTML in whatever ways they thought best. Although many rules were common, competing browsers, seeking to dominate the market, introduced some differences in the language. Such changes to the language were called **extensions**. The two major browsers during the 1990s, Netscape Navigator and Microsoft Internet Explorer, added the most extensions to HTML. These extensions were providing Web page authors with more options but at the expense of complicating Web page development. The challenge for Web designers was to determine which browser or browser version supported a particular extension and tocreate a workaround for browsers that did not. Extensions, while often useful and often needed, diminished the promise of simplicity that made HTML so attractive in the first place.

Ultimately, a group of Web developers, programmers, and analysts formed the **World Wide Web Consortium**, or **W3C**, to create a set of standards for all browser manufacturers to follow. The W3C has no enforcement power, but because agreeing on a uniform approach to Web page creation is in the best interests of everyone, the W3C's recommendations are usually followed (though not always right away). The W3C also provides online tutorials, documentation, and quizzes that allow users to test their knowledge of HTML and other languages. For more information on the W3C and the services it offers, see its Web site at www.w3c.org.

Figure 1-2 summarizes the various versions of HTML that the W3C has released over the past decade. Don't worry if you don't understand all of the details of these versions yet—the important thing to understand is that HTML doesn't come in only one flavor and that as a Web page author you may need to support a wide variety of HTML versions.

Versions of HTML and XHTML ◄ **Figure 1-2**

Version	Date	Description
HTML 1.0	1989–1994	The first public version of HTML, which included browser support for inline images and text controls.
HTML 2.0	1995	The first version supported by all graphical browsers. It introduced interactive form elements such as option buttons and text boxes. A document written to the HTML 2.0 specification is compatible with almost all browsers on the World Wide Web.
HTML 3.0	1996	A proposed replacement for HTML 2.0 that was never widely adopted.
HTML 3.2	1997	This version included additional support for creating and formatting tables and expanded the options for interactive form elements. It also supported limited programming using scripts.
HTML 4.01	1999	This version added support for style sheets to give Web designers greater control over page layout. It added new features to tables and forms and provided support for international features. This version also expanded HTML's scripting capability and added increased support for multimedia elements.
XHTML 1.0	2001	This version is a reformulation of HTML 4.01 in XML and combines the strength of HTML 4.0 with the power of XML. XHTML brings the rigor of XML to Web pages and provides standards for more robust Web content on a wide range of browser platforms.
XHTML 1.1	2002	A minor update to XHTML 1.0 that allows for modularity and simplifies writing extensions to the language.
XHTML 2.0	2004	The latest version, designed to remove most of the presentational features left in HTML.

You also have to stay familiar with which versions of HTML are actually supported in the browser market. This may mean dealing with a collection of approaches: some that are new and meet the latest specifications and some that are older but still widely supported. Older features of HTML are often **deprecated** by the W3C, meaning that they might not be supported in current or future browsers, and you should use caution in applying them. Even though deprecated features are in the process of being phased out, this doesn't mean that you can't continue to use them; indeed, if you are supporting older browsers, you may need to. Because it's hard to predict how quickly deprecated features will disappear from common usage on the Web, knowledge of them is crucial.

Although HTML has been instrumental in making the Web popular and accessible, the future of Web development focuses more on two other languages: XML and XHTML. **XML (Extensible Markup Language)** is another markup language used to create documents that must adhere to specific rules for content and structure. XML contrasts sharply with a language such as HTML, which allows for a wide variety of rules without a built-in mechanism for enforcing them. XML can be used to define other markup languages, and one of its applications is a stricter version of HTML called **XHTML (Extensible Hypertext Markup Language)**. XHTML is designed to confront some of problems associated with the different and competing versions of HTML and to better integrate HTML with XML.

Even though XHTML shows great promise for the Web, HTML will not become obsolete anytime soon. In addition to the considerable overlap between HTML and XHTML, the World Wide Web is full of old HTML documents and some users are still running older versions of Web browsers that may not recognize some of the features of XHTML. Where does all of this leave you as a potential Web page author? A few guidelines are helpful:

- **Become well versed in the history of HTML:** Unlike other programming and markup languages, the history of HTML plays a major role in the choices you make in writing your code.
- **Know your market:** Do you have to support older browsers, or have your clients standardized on a particular browser or browser version? The answer affects how you design your pages. Become familiar with what different browsers can and cannot do.
- **Test:** If you have to support several types of browsers and several types of devices, acquire them and use them to view your document. Don't assume that if your page works in one browser it will work in an older version of that same browser. The same browser version might even act differently on different operating systems.

Creating an HTML Document

When you consider creating an HTML document, it's useful to think of it in terms of elements. An **element** is a distinct feature of a document, such as a paragraph, a heading, or the page's title. Even a whole document itself can be considered an element. Each element is marked within the HTML file with a **tag**. Tags can be either two sided or one sided. A two-sided tag contains some document content. The general syntax of a two-sided tag is

```
<element>content</element>
```

where *element* is the name of the HTML element and *content* is any content it contains. For example, the following code marks the text "Welcome to Pixal Products" with the <p> tag. As you'll learn later, this directs browsers to treat the text as a paragraph element.

```
<p>Welcome to Pixal Products</p>
```

The terms "tag" and "element" are sometimes used interchangeably, but this book uses the term "element" to refer to an element itself, and "tag" to refer to that part of the HTML code that marks an element for a browser. Thus, you would mark the p element in a Web page by inserting a <p> tag in an HTML file.

The scope of a two-sided tag is identified by its **opening tag** (<p>) and its **closing tag** (</p>), with the content ("Welcome to Pixal Products") placed between them. Web browsers often allow you to omit a closing tag if the surrounding code clearly indicates the tag's content, but this practice is not recommended. XHTML requires both an opening and a closing tag.

HTML does not distinguish between uppercase and lowercase letters. Thus, you can type either <p> or <P> to mark a paragraph element. However, because XHTML strictly requires lowercase tag names, this book follows that convention, and it is strongly recommended that you do likewise to ensure that your code is consistent with current and future standards.

Unlike a two-sided tag, a **one-sided tag** contains no content. The general syntax for a one-sided tag is

```
<element />
```

where *element* is once again the element name. HTML also allows you to enter one-sided tags using the syntax *<element>* (omitting the space and the closing slash); however, because XHTML does not support this form, it is also strongly recommended that you include the space and the closing slash at all times. Elements that employ one-sided tags are called **empty elements** because they contain no content. One example of an empty element is a line break, which forces the browser to place the content that follows on a new line. To create a line break, you use the one-sided tag

```
<br />
```

Inserting Two-sided and One-sided Tags

- To create a two-sided tag, use the syntax
  ```
  <element>content</element>
  ```
  where *element* is the name of the HTML element and *content* is any content that it contains. Element names should be in lowercase.
- To create a one-sided tag, use the syntax
  ```
  <element />
  ```

A third type of tag is a comment tag. Comment tags are used to add notes to your HTML code. Comments are not required and are ignored by Web browsers, but they are useful in documenting your HTML code for yourself and others. The syntax of the comment tag is

```
<!-- comment -->
```

where *comment* is the text of your note. The following is an example of a comment tag:

```
<!-- Home page for Pixal Products -->
```

A comment can also be spread over several lines as follows:

```
<!-- Home page for
     Pixal Products
-->
```

Inserting a Comment

- To insert a comment anywhere within your HTML file, enter

  `<!-- comment -->`

  where `comment` is the text of your comment. Comments can extend over several lines.

White Space and HTML

The fact that comments can be spread over several lines brings up an important point concerning how you enter your HTML code. As simple text files, HTML documents are composed of text characters and **white space**, which are the blank spaces, tabs, and line breaks within the file. A browser reading an HTML file treats all consecutive occurrences of white space as a single blank space. Thus, so far as a browser is concerned, there is no difference between a blank space, a tab, and a line break—or indeed between two blank spaces and a single blank space. When a browser encounters consecutive occurrences of white space, it collapses them into a single occurrence. The following code samples are equivalent so far as a browser is concerned:

```
<p>This is an example of White Space</p>
<p>This is an example   of    White      Space</p>
<p>This is an example
   of    White
   Space</p>
```

Even though browsers ignore extra white space, careful application of white space can make your HTML code more readable—for example, by indenting lines or by separating blocks of code from one another.

Element Attributes

Elements also have attributes that provide browsers with additional information about how to treat them. Attributes are inserted into the element's opening tag using the following syntax:

`attribute1="value1" attribute2="value2"`

where `attribute1`, `attribute2`, and so forth are the names of the attributes and `value1`, `value2`, and so on are the values associated with those attributes. For example, you can use attributes to align the content of an element. The following code aligns the paragraph "Pixal Products" with the right page margin:

`<p align="right">Pixal Products</p>`

Attributes can be listed in any order, but they must be separated from one another in the opening tag by white space. As with element names, you should enter attribute names in lowercase letters and enclose attribute values within quotation marks. Although many browsers still accept attribute values without quotation marks, you can ensure maximum compatibility with all the different versions of HTML and XHTML by always including them. XHTML requires quotation marks for all attribute values.

Inserting Attributes

• To add attributes to an element, insert the following into the element's opening tag:
```
attribute1="value1" attribute2="value2"
```
where `attribute1`, `attribute2`, and so forth are the names of the attributes and `value1`, `value2`, and so on are the values associated with each of those attributes.

The Structure of an HTML File

Any markup document must include a **root element**, which contains all other elements in the document. For an HTML document, the root element is the html element. Thus, the basic structure of an HTML document is

```
<html>
    content
</html>
```

where `content` is any content included within the document. The content is divided into two sections: the head and the body. The **head element** contains information about the document, such as the document's title or keywords that a search engine on the Web might use to locate the document for others to use. The content of the head element is not displayed within the Web page, but browsers may use it in other ways—for example, the document's title is usually displayed in a browser's title bar. The **body element** contains all of the content to be displayed in the Web page. It can also contain code that tells browsers how to render that content. To mark the head and body elements, you use the <head> and <body> tags as follows:

```
<html>
    <head>
        head content
    </head>
    <body>
        body content
    </body>
</html>
```

Note that the body element is always placed after the head element.

The technique of placing one element within another is called **nesting**. When one element contains another element, you must close the inside element before closing the outside element. Thus, the following code sample is incorrect because it closes the html element before the nested body element is closed:

```
<html><head>head content</head><body>body content</html></body>
```

To correct this, you must ensure that the body element is closed before the containing element—in this case the html element—is closed. The correct form is

```
<html><head>head content</head><body>body content</body></html>
```

Working with the Document Head

The head element also contains its own collection of nested elements. One required element is the title element, which specifies the page title that is displayed in the title bar of a user's Web browser. For example, the following code adds the page title "Pixal Products" to a document. Note that a Web document can contain only one title element.

```
  <head>
    <title>Pixal Products</title>
</head>
```

The head element can also contain meta elements, which store information about the document that may be of use to programs running on Web servers. A meta element is created using the one-sided <meta /> tag as follows:

```
<meta name="text" content="text" scheme="text" http-equiv="text" />
```

where the name attribute specifies the name of a property for the page, the content attribute provides a property value, and the scheme attribute provides the format of the property value; the http-equiv attribute takes the place of the name attribute for some Web servers. For example, the following <meta /> tag stores the name of a Web page's author:

```
<meta name="author" content="Lisa Burkett" />
```

Some Web sites use search engines to create lists of Web pages devoted to particular topics. You can give extra weight to a Web page by including a description of the page and a list of keywords in <meta /> tags such as the following:

```
<meta name="description" content="Pixal Products" />
<meta name="keywords" content="digital imagining, scanning, graphics" />
```

Note that while a Web document can contain only one title element, it can contain several meta elements. The use of meta tags to aid search engines is somewhat controversial, however. Some Web page authors have used meta tags to manipulate search engine cataloging by repeating keywords to give their pages a higher ranking. In response, many search engines have stopped reviewing meta tags entirely.

Working with Block-level Elements

Within a document's body element, page content is marked as either a block-level element or an inline element. A **block-level element** contains content displayed in a separate section within the page, setting it off from other blocks. One common block-level element is the paragraph. **Inline elements**, on the other hand, are placed within block-level elements and are not separated from other page content as paragraphs are. In the next sections, you'll examine some of the more common block-level elements, starting with headings.

Creating Headings

Headings are titles placed within the page body, usually to mark different topics appearing on the page. HTML supports six heading elements, numbered h1 through h6. The h1 heading is reserved for the largest and most prominent headings, whereas the h6 element indicates a minor heading. The syntax to mark a heading element is

```
<hy>content</hy>
```

where y is a heading number 1 through 6 and content is the content of the heading. Figure 1-3 illustrates the general appearance of the six heading elements. Because there is no set method for displaying heads, your browser might use slightly different fonts and sizes.

HTML headings   Figure 1-3

This is an h1 heading

This is an h2 heading

This is an h3 heading

This is an h4 heading

This is an h5 heading

This is an h6 heading

Inserting a Heading

Reference Window

- To define a heading, use the syntax
  ```
  <hy>content</hy>
  ```
  where *y* is a heading number 1 through 6 and *content* is the content of the heading.

Creating Paragraphs

As noted earlier, paragraphs are another popular block-level element. To mark content as a paragraph, use the following tag:

```
<p>content</p>
```

where *content* is the content of the paragraph. When a browser encounters the opening <p> tag, it starts the enclosed content on a new line with blank space above it, separating the new paragraph from the preceding element. In earlier versions of HTML when standards were not firmly fixed, Web authors would often include only the opening <p> tag, omitting the closing tag entirely. Although many browsers still allow this, your Web pages display more reliably if you consistently use the closing tag. Additionally, if you wish to write code compliant with the standards of XHTML, you must include the closing tag.

Creating a Paragraph

Reference Window

- To create a paragraph, use the syntax
  ```
  <p>content</p>
  ```
  where *content* is the content of the paragraph.

Creating Lists

Another block-level element is the list. HTML supports three kinds of lists: ordered, unordered, and definition. You use an **ordered list** for items that have a prescribed sequential order. Ordered lists are created using the ol element in the following form:

```
<ol>
    <li>item1</li>
    <li>item2</li>
...
</ol>
```

where *item1*, *item2*, and so on are items in the list. Each <li> tag marks the content for a single list item. For example, if you wanted to enter shopping items in an ordered list, the code might look as follows:

```
<ol>
    <li>Milk</li>
    <li>Celery</li>
    <li>Bagels</li>
</ol>
```

By default, a browser displays an ordered list with numeric markers as follows:

1. Milk
2. Celery
3. Bagels

For lists in which the items do not need to be placed in any special order, you can create an **unordered list**. An unordered list has the same structure as an ordered list except that the content of the list is contained within a <ul> tag:

```
<ul>
    <li>item1</li>
    <li>item2</li>
    ...
</ul>
```

By default, list items in an unordered list are displayed as bulleted text. Thus, the code

```
<ul>
    <li>Milk</li>
    <li>Celery</li>
    <li>Bagels</li>
</ul>
```

is displayed by a browser as

• Milk
• Celery
• Bagels

One list can also contain another list. The following combination of ordered and unordered lists

1. Dairy
    • Milk
    • Sour cream

    2. Produce
       • Celery
       • Lettuce
    3. Bakery
       • Bagels
       • Bread

is created using the following HTML code:

```
<ol>
    <li>Dairy
        <ul>
            <li>Milk</li>
            <li>Sour cream</li>
        </ul>
    </li>
    <li>Produce
        <ul>
            <li>Celery</li>
            <li>Lettuce</li>
        </ul>
    </li>
    <li>Bakery
        <ul>
            <li>Bagels</li>
            <li>Bread</li>
        </ul>
    </li>
</ol>
```

Note that in this code some of the list items themselves contain lists.

A third list element supported by HTML is a **definition list**, which contains a list of definition terms with each term followed by a definition description. The syntax for creating a definition list is

```
<dl>
    <dt>term1</dt>
    <dd>definition1</dd>
    <dt>term2</dt>
    <dd>definition2</dd>
</dl>
```

where *term1*, *term2*, and so on are the terms in the list and *definition1*, *definition2*, and so on are the definitions of the terms. For example, the following code creates a definition list of computer terms:

```
<dl>
    <dt>server</dt>
    <dd>A device that makes a resource available on a network</dd>
    <dt>client</dt>
    <dd>A device on a network that requests the resources stored on a
        server</dd>
</dl>
```

Web browsers typically display the definition description slightly indented from the definition term. A browser would display the above definition list as

   server
     A device that makes a resource available on a network
   client
     A device on a network that requests the resources stored on the server

Creating Lists

- To create an ordered list, use the syntax
  ```
  <ol>
      <li>item1</li>
      <li>item2</li>
      ...
  </ol>
  ```
  where *item1*, *item2*, and so on are items in the list.
- To create an unordered list, use the syntax
  ```
  <ul>
      <li>item1</li>
      <li>item2</li>
      ...
  </ul>
  ```
- To create a definition list, use the syntax
  ```
  <dl>
      <dt>term1</dt>
      <dd>definition1</dd>
      <dt>term2</dt>
      <dd>definition2</dd>
      ...
  </dl>
  ```
  where *term1*, *term2*, and so on are the terms in the list and *definition1*, *definition2*, and so on are the definitions of the terms.

Creating a Generic Block

HTML and XHTML also support a block-level element called the **div element**, which is a generic container for any block-level content. The syntax of the div element is

```
<div>
    content
</div>
```

where *content* is any page content you want to enclose and mark as a block-level element. Browsers display the content in a block but usually do not apply any other formatting.

Using Other Block-level Elements

HTML supports several other block-level elements that you may find useful in your Web pages. For example, the address element is used to mark contact information. Most browsers display the content of address elements in an italicized font. Long quotes can be indicated by applying the blockquote element. A browser encountering this element typically indents the quoted text. Figure 1-4 shows a fuller list of block-level elements and the typical visual appearance of each.

Block-level elements ◄ Figure 1-4

Block-Level Element	Description	Visual Appearance
<address> ... </address>	Identifies contact information	*Italicized text*
<blockquote> ... </blockquote>	Identifies a long quotation	Plain text indented from the left and the right
<center> ... </center>	Centers content horizontally within a block. **Deprecated**	Plain text, centered
<dd> ... </dd>	Identifies a definition description	Plain text
<dir> ... </dir>	Identifies a multicolumn directory list; superseded by the ul element. **Deprecated**	Plain text
<div> ... </div>	Identifies a generic block-level element	Plain text
<dl> ... </dl>	Identifies a definition list	Plain text
<dt> ... </dt>	Identifies a definition term	Plain text
<hy> ... </hy>	Identifies a heading, where y is a value from 1 to 6	**Boldfaced text of various font sizes**
<li> ... </li>	Identifies a list item in an ordered or unordered list	Bulleted or numbered text
<menu> ... </menu>	Identifies a single-column menu list; superseded by the ul element. **Deprecated**	Plain text
<ol> ... </ol>	Identifies an ordered list	Plain text
<p> ... </p>	Identifies a paragraph	Plain text
<pre> ... </pre>	Retains all white space and special characters in preformatted text	`Fixed-width text`
<ul> ... </ul>	Identifies an unordered list	Plain text

Working with Inline Elements

Now that you've examined block-level elements, let's turn to the inline elements. One type of inline element is the **character-formatting element**, which is used to define the appearance or format of text within a block. Figure 1-5 describes some character-formatting elements supported by HTML.

| Figure 1-5 | **Character-formatting elements** |

Character-formatting Element	Identifies	Visual Appearance
<abbr> ... </abbr>	an abbreviation	Plain text
<acronym> .. </acronym>	an acronym	Plain text
<b> ... </b>	boldface text	**Boldface text**
<big> ... </big>	big text	Larger text
<cite> ... </cite>	a citation	*Italicized text*
<code> ... </code>	program code text	`Fixed-width text`
<del> ... </del>	deleted text	~~Strikethrough text~~
<dfn> ... </dfn>	a definition term	*Italicized text*
<em> ... </em>	emphasized content	*Italicized text*
<i> ... </i>	italicized text	*Italicized text*
<ins> ... </ins>	inserted text	Underlined text
<kbd> ... </kbd>	keyboard-style text	`Fixed-width text`
<q> ... </q>	quoted text	"Quoted text"
<s> ... </s>	strikethrough text. **Deprecated**	~~Strikethrough text~~
<samp> ... </samp>	sample computer code text	`Fixed-width text`
<small> ... </small>	small text	Smaller text
<span> ... </span>	a generic inline element	Plain text
<strike> ... </strike>	strikethrough text. **Deprecated**	~~Strikethrough text~~
<strong> ... </strong>	strongly emphasized content	**Boldface text**
_{...}	subscripted text	Subscripted text
^{...}	superscripted	Superscripted text
<tt> ... </tt>	teletype text	`Fixed-width text`
<u> ... </u>	underlined text. **Deprecated**	Underlined text
<var> ... </var>	programming variables	*Italicized text*

For example, if you wanted to mark a section of boldface text within a paragraph, you could enter the following HTML code:

```
<p>Welcome to the <b>Home Page</b></p>
```

This code results in the following paragraph on the Web page:

Welcome to the **Home Page**

To mark those same words as italicized text, you would use

```
<p>Welcome to the <i>Home Page</i></p>
```

If you wanted the phrase "Home Page" to be marked as both boldface and italics, you could use the code

```
<p>Welcome to the <b><i>Home Page</i></b></p>
```

which would be displayed as

Welcome to the ***Home Page***

As you examine the tag list in Figure 1-5, you may notice some overlap in the way the content appears in a browser. For example, if you wanted to display italicized text, you could use the <dfn>, <em>, <i>, or <var> tag (or even the <address> tag if you want to italicize a block of text). Why does HTML support so many different ways of formatting text?

The main purpose of HTML is not to format text but rather to create a structure for the content of the document. Page elements are therefore often organized into two types: logical elements and physical elements. A **logical element**, created with tags like <cite> and <code>, describes the nature of the enclosed content but not necessarily how that content should appear. A **physical element**, created with tags such as <b> and <i>, describes how text should appear, but it doesn't indicate the nature of the element's content.

While it can be tempting to use logical and physical elements interchangeably, your Web pages benefit in several ways when you respect the distinction. For one, different browsers can and do display logical elements differently. For example, both Netscape's browser and Internet Explorer display text created with the <cite> tag in italics, but the text-based browser Lynx displays citation text using a fixed-width font. Some browsers, such as those that display Braille or convert HTML code into speech, don't display formatted text at all. An aural browser might increase the volume when it encounters emphasized text. Web programmers can also use logical elements to extract content information from a page—for example, a program could automatically generate a bibliography from all of the citations listed within a Web site.

In general, you should use a logical element whenever that element accurately describes the content it encloses, and use physical elements only for general content.

Working with IDs and Classes

As you add more elements to your Web page, you may find the need to identify distinct elements or groups of elements. You can do this using the id attribute (to identify a distinct element) and the class attribute (to mark a group of elements). The syntax of the id attribute is

```
id="text"
```

where *text* is the unique name of the id value. For example, the following code gives a paragraph the id value of "leading", which a programmer might use to indicate that this paragraph represents a leading paragraph on the page:

```
<p id="leading">Welcome to Pixal Products.</p>
```

A particular id value is associated with only one element and thus can be used only once in an HTML file. To mark several elements as related, use the class attribute with the syntax

```
class="text"
```

where *text* is the name of the element class. For example, the following code uses the class attribute to indicate groupings of elements in an unordered list:

```
<ul>
   <li class="Dairy">Milk</li>
   <li class="Dairy">Sour cream</li>
   <li class="Produce">Celery</li>
   <li class="Produce">Lettuce</li>
   <li class="Bakery">Bagels</li>
   <li class="Bakery">Bread</li>
</ul>
```

The class attribute becomes useful in page design when you want to create a common format for elements that belong to the same class. This topic is examined further in the next review.

Creating Links

One of the great advantages of HTML is the ease of creating links to other documents and resources. To change content into a link, you mark the content with a two-sided <a> tag:

```
<a href="url">content</a>
```

where *url* is the address or URL of the linked resource and *content* is the page content that you want to act as a link. For example, the following code marks the text "Pixal Products" as a link pointing to the URL www.pixalproducts.com:

```
<a href="http://www.pixalproducts.com">Pixal Products</a>
```

By default, a browser opens a linked file at the top of the document; in some cases, though, you may want to link to a location farther down. To do this, you have to first mark a location within the document to which you want to be able to link. This can be done either by adding the id attribute to the element at that location in the document or by using the <a> tag to create an **anchor** at that location. The syntax for creating an anchor is

```
<a name="id"></a>
```

where *id* is the name of the anchor. Using the <a> tag to create anchors is currently being phased out in favor of the use of the id attribute; however, use of the <a> tag is still supported by older browsers that might not recognize the id attribute. Whichever method you use, you link to the anchor or element id using the URL

```
file#id
```

where *file* is the location and file name of the linked resource and *id* is an anchor or id within the file. For example, to link to an anchor in the home.htm file with the id or name value of "leading", you use the URL

```
home.htm#leading
```

Working with Images and Other Nontextual Content

Because HTML files are simple text files, nontextual objects must be stored in separate files and loaded by the browser when the page is rendered. The most common nontextual object is the graphic image, which is placed within a Web page as an **inline image**. Inline images are another example of an inline element and thus must be placed within a block-level element such as a paragraph. Inline images are most widely viewable in one of two file formats: GIF (Graphics Interchange Format) or JPEG (Joint Photographic Experts Group). To mark an inline image, you use the img element:

```
<img src="url" alt="text" />
```

where *url* is the location and the the name of the image file and *text* is an alternative text string that browsers can use in place of an image. It's important to include a value for the alt attribute with all of your inline images. Because many users run browsers that do not display images, any information conveyed by the image needs to be duplicated in text. Although HTML does not require that you use an alt attribute with your inline images, XHTML does.

Reference Window

Inserting an Inline Image

- To insert an inline image, use the tag
  `<img src="url" alt="text" />`
  where *url* is the location and the name of the image file and *text* is alternative text that browsers can use in place of the image.

If the image file is located in the same folder as the HTML file, you do not need to include any file location path information along with the file name. However, if the image file is located in another folder or on another computer, you need to include the full location path along with the file name in the src attribute.

Creating Horizontal Lines

Another graphic object that you can add to a Web page is a horizontal line. The syntax to create a horizontal line is

`<hr />`

There is no accepted default for the rendering of a horizontal line. Typically, the line extends across the complete width of the page with a height of 1 pixel. Some graphical browsers display the line in a solid black color; others apply a chiseled or embossed effect to the line. Text-based browsers display the line using dashes or underscores.

Working with Special Characters

Occasionally, you want to include special characters in your Web pages that do not appear on your keyboard. For example, a page might require mathematical symbols such as Σ or π, or you might need to include the copyright symbol © to show that the text or image is copyrighted. HTML supports the use of character symbols that are identified by a code number or name. The syntax for creating a special character is

`&code;`

where *code* is either a code name or a code number. Code numbers are preceded by a pound symbol (#). Figure 1-6 shows some HTML symbols and the corresponding code numbers and names. Note that some older browsers support only code numbers, not code names.

| Figure 1-6 | ▶ | Special characters and codes |

Symbol	Code	Name	Description
©	©	©	Copyright symbol
®	®	®	Registered trademark
•	·	·	Middle dot (bullet)
°	°	°	Degree symbol
			Nonbreaking space, used to insert consecutive blank spaces
<	<	<	Less-than symbol
>	>	>	Greater-than symbol
&	&	&	Ampersand

Embedding Media Clips

In recent years, as home computers have improved in speed and power and faster connections to the Web have become more readily available, it has become more practical to place video and audio clips within Web pages. Multimedia clips can be embedded within a Web document using the one-sided tag

```
<embed src="url" width="value" height="value" autostart="type" />
```

where url is the URL of the media clip, the width and height attributes specify the width and the height of the clip and its controls as it is rendered on the page, and the autostart attribute specifies whether to start the clip automatically when the page loads ("true") or only when the user clicks a start button on the clip's controls ("false"). Note that although the embed element is supported by most browsers, it is not part of the official HTML specifications and its support may be discontinued in the future. It is also not supported by XHTML.

In place of the embed element, the current specifications for HTML and XHTML call for the use of the object element, which is a two-sided tag with the form

```
<object data="url" type="mime-type">
   page content
</object>
```

where url is the URL of the file containing the multimedia object, $mime$-$type$ is a text string that defines the type of data contained in the object, and $page$ $content$ is alternate content that should be displayed in place of the object if a browser does not support the object element or the data type of the object. Figure 1-7 lists the different MIME types supported by the object element.

| Figure 1-7 | ▶ | MIME types |

Audio		Text		Image		Video	
Object	MIME Type	Object	MIME Type	Object	MIME Type	Object	MIME Type
aiff	audio/aiff	HTML file	text/html	gif	image/gif	asf	video/x-ms-asf
au	audio/basic	Plain text file	text/plain	jpg	image/jpeg	avi	video/x-msvideo
midi	audio/mid			png	image/png	mpeg	video/mpeg
mp3	audio/mpeg					quicktime	video/quicktime
wav	audio/wav						

For example, to insert a graphic image, you can use either the inline image

```
<img src="logo.jpg" alt="Pixal Products" />
```

or, equivalently, the object element

```
<object data="logo.jpg" type="image/jpeg">
   <h2>Pixal Products</h2>
</object>
```

If you wanted to embed a video clip in a Web page, you could use the following code:

```
<object data="trailer.avi" type="video/x-msvideo">
   Movie Trailer
</object>
```

Alternatively, you could use the embed element as described above. Be aware that at present the object element is not well supported by most browsers. Thus, you may need to use a combination of the embed element and the object element if you need to support multimedia clips in your Web pages.

Creating Web Tables

Tables are an important feature in Web page design. Tables are marked using the two-sided <table> tag. Nested within the table element is the tr element, which encloses the content of each table row. The td element, which encloses the content of each table cell, is nested within each tr element. Thus, the general structure of a Web table is

```
<table>
   <tr>
      <td>content</td>
      <td>content</td>
      . . .
   </tr>
   <tr>
      <td>content</td>
      <td>content</td>
      . . .
   </tr>
   . . .
</table>
```

where *content* is the content of an individual table cell. For example, the code

```
<table>
   <tr>
      <td>First Cell</td>
      <td>Second Cell</td>
   </tr>
   <tr>
      <td>Third Cell</td>
      <td>Fourth Cell</td>
   </tr>
</table>
```

creates a table with two rows and two columns (see Figure 1-8). You may have noticed that HTML includes no tag for table columns. This is because the number of columns is determined by the size of the longest row in the table. If the longest row in a table contains four td elements, the table has four columns.

Figure 1-8   A simple Web table

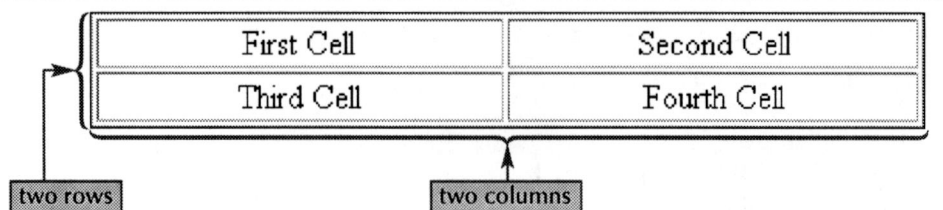

The "td" in the <td> tag stands for "table data". You can also place cell content within a th element, which marks the content as a table heading. The difference is that the contents of a th element is usually centered and displayed in a boldface font by browsers.

Defining the Table Structure

- To mark a table, use the tag
  ```
  <table>content</table>
  ```
  where *content* includes the table's rows, headings, and cells.
- To create a table row, use the tag
  ```
  <tr>content</tr>
  ```
  where *content* includes the table's cells and headings.
- To create a table cell that contains a row or column heading, use the tag
  ```
  <th>content</th>
  ```
  where *content* is the content of the heading. Table headings are usually displayed in a centered, bold font.
- To create a table cell that contains table data, use the tag
  ```
  <td>content</td>
  ```
  where *content* is the cell content.

Creating Row Groups

To indicate the role that each table row plays in the table, you can organize the rows into **row groups**. HTML supports three types of row groups, identifying the table head, table body, and table footer. Because order is important in an HTML file, the table header must be listed first, followed by the table footer, and finally the table body. To mark the rows that belong to the table head, you use the syntax

```
<thead>
    table rows
</thead>
```

where `table rows` are rows of the table. Note that a table can contain only one row group for the table head. To mark the rows of a table footer, use the syntax

```
<tfoot>
    table rows
</tfoot>
```

As with the table head, a table can contain only one row group for the footer. Finally, to mark the rows of the table body, use the syntax

```
<tbody>
    table rows
</tbody>
```

A table can contain multiple table body sections. Row groups are sometimes used when tables draw their data from external sources such as databases or XML documents. In those cases, scripts can be written in which the content of the table body rows spans several different Web pages, with the content of the table header and footer repeated on each page. Not all browsers support this capability, however.

Creating a Table Caption

Table captions provide descriptive information about a table's content. The syntax for creating a caption is

```
<caption>content</caption>
```

where *content* is the content of the caption. The <caption> tag must appear directly after the opening <table> tag. By default, a caption appears centered above a table. However, you can change the placement of a caption using the align attribute, as follows:

```
<caption align="position">content</caption>
```

where *position* equals

- "bottom" to place the caption centered below the table
- "top" to place the caption centered above the table
- "left" to place the caption above the table, aligned with the left table margin
- "right" to place the caption above the table, aligned with the right table margin

Spanning Rows and Columns

By default, a table cell occupies the intersection of a single row and a single column; however, in some cases you may want a table cell to cover more than one row or column. Figure 1-9 shows an example of table cells that need to cover several rows and/or columns.

Spanning cells | **Figure 1-9**

Such cells are called **spanning cells** and are created by applying the rowspan attribute, the colspan attribute, or both attributes to a <td> or <th> tag. The syntax for these attributes is

```
<td rowspan="value" colspan="value"> ... </td>
```

or

```
<th rowspan="value" colspan="value"> ... </th>
```

where *value* is the number of rows or columns that the cell spans in the table. The direction of the spanning is downward and to the right of the cell containing the rowspan and colspan attributes. For example, to create a cell that spans two columns in a table, you enter the <td> tag as

```
<td colspan="2"> ... </td>
```

For a cell that spans two rows, the tag is

```
<td rowspan="2"> ... </td>
```

and to span two rows and two columns at the same time, the tag is

```
<td rowspan="2" colspan="2"> ... </td>
```

It's important to remember that when a table includes a cell that spans multiple rows or columns, you must adjust the number of cell tags used in the other table rows to compensate for the additional space taken up by the spanning cell. For example, if a row contains five columns but one of the cells in the row spans three columns, you need only three <td> tags within the row: two <td> tags for each of the cells that occupy a single column and a third for the cell spanning three rows.

When a cell spans several rows, you need to adjust the number of cell tags in the rows below the spanning cell. Consider the table shown in Figure 1-10, which contains three rows and four columns. The first cell in the first row is a spanning cell that spans three rows. You need four <td> tags for the first row but only three <td> tags for rows two and three. This is because the spanning cell from row one occupies the cells that would normally appear in those rows.

| Figure 1-10 | A row-spanning cell |

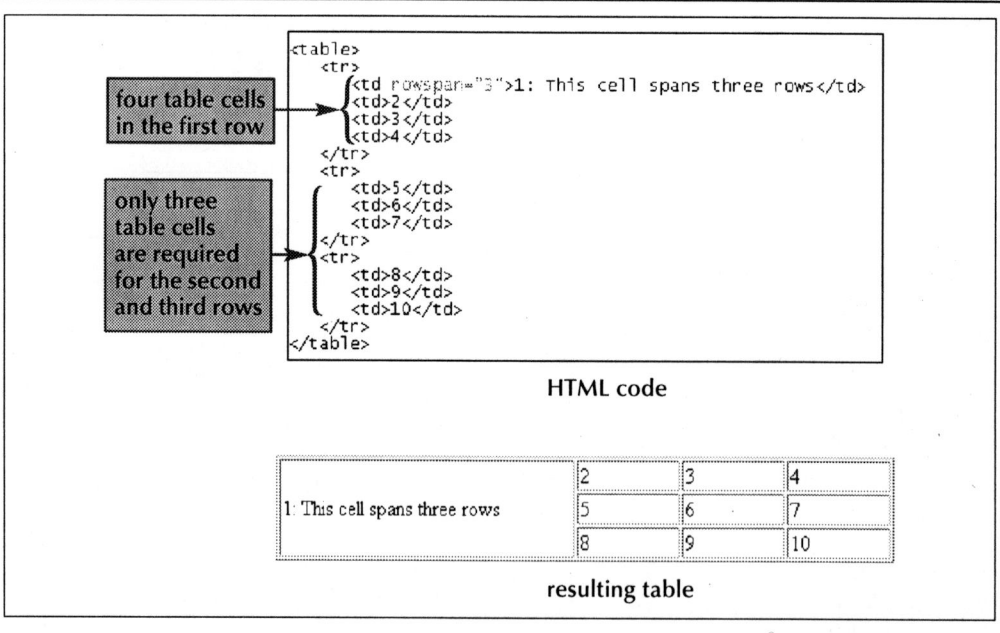

```
<table>
  <tr>
    <td rowspan="3">1: This cell spans three rows</td>
    <td>2</td>
    <td>3</td>
    <td>4</td>
  </tr>
  <tr>
    <td>5</td>
    <td>6</td>
    <td>7</td>
  </tr>
  <tr>
    <td>8</td>
    <td>9</td>
    <td>10</td>
  </tr>
</table>
```

four table cells in the first row

only three table cells are required for the second and third rows

HTML code

1: This cell spans three rows	2	3	4
	5	6	7
	8	9	10

resulting table

Reference Window

Creating a Spanning Cell

- To create a column-spanning cell, add the following attribute to the td or th element:
    `colspan="value"`
  where `value` is the number of columns to be spanned.
- To create a row-spanning cell, add the following attribute to the td or th element:
    `rowspan="value"`
  where `value` is the number of rows to be spanned.

Setting the Border, Spacing, and Padding Size

Most browsers automatically render a table to take up the least amount of space on the page. This is done by fitting the largest amount of text into each column with the least amount of line wrapping across the columns. There are several attributes you can use to override the default table size, however. These include attributes to set the size of the table border, the space between the table cells, and the space within the table cells.

By default, browsers display tables without borders. You can create a table border by adding the border attribute to the <table> tag. The syntax for creating a table border is

```
<table border="value"> ... </table>
```

where `value` is the width of the border in pixels. Figure 1-11 shows the effect of different border sizes on a table's appearance. Note that unless you specify a border size of 0 pixels, the size of the internal borders (also called gridlines) is not affected by the border attribute.

Tables with different border sizes ◄ Figure 1-11

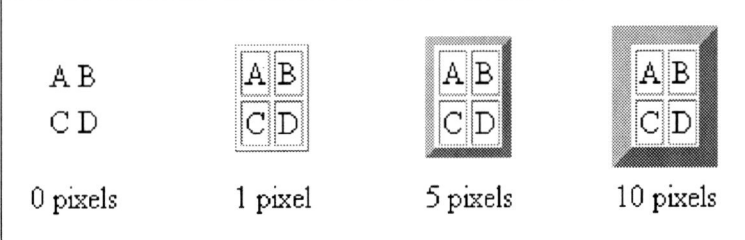

To change the amount of space between table cells, which is known as the **cell spacing**, use the cellspacing attribute:

```
<table cellspacing="value"> ... </table>
```

where `value` is the size of the cell spacing in pixels. If you have applied a border to your table, changing the cell-spacing value also affects the size of the interior borders. By default, the size of the cell spacing is set to 2 pixels. Figure 1-12 shows how different cell-spacing values affect the appearance of these gridlines.

Figure 1-12 | Tables with different cell-spacing values

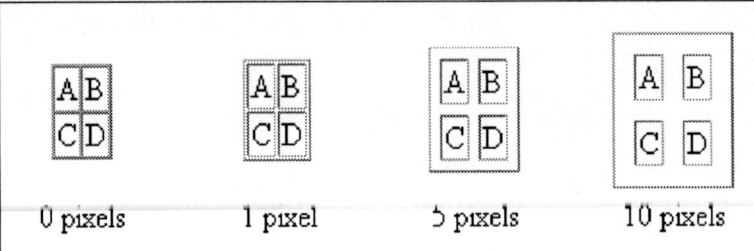

The space between the content of each table cell and the cell's border is known as **cell padding**. The default cell-padding value is 1 pixel; to set a different value for the cellpadding attribute, use

```
<table cellpadding="value"> ... </table>
```

where *value* is the size of the cell padding in pixels. Figure 1-13 shows how different cell-padding values affect the appearance of the text within a table.

Figure 1-13 | Tables with different cell-padding values

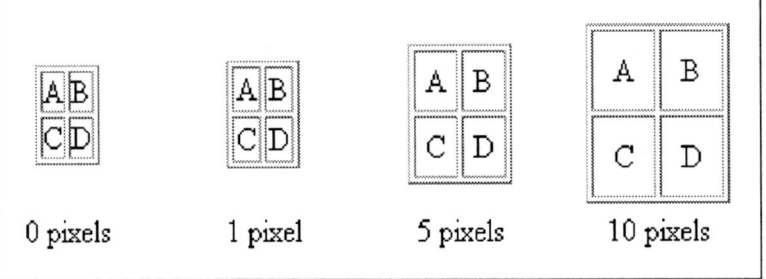

As discussed earlier, the overall size of a table is largely determined by its content. A table expands in width to match the content of its cells. If you want to set a table width to a fixed value, you use

```
<table width="value"> ... </table>
```

where *value* is the width either in pixels or as a percentage of the width of the containing element. If you specify a fixed width, the table remains constant but the table height increases to match the content. You can set a table to fill the entire width of a page by specifying a width value of 100%. Note that a browser never displays a table with a width smaller than that required to display the content. If table content requires a width of 100 pixels, for example, a browser ignores an attribute value that sets the width at 50 pixels.

The width attribute can also be applied to individual cells within a table, using the form

```
<td width="value"> ... </td>
```

or

```
<th width="value"> ... </th>
```

where *value* is the cell's width either in pixels or as a percentage of the width of the entire table. You can set the width of a column by setting the width of the first cell in the column; when you do, the remaining cells in the column adopt that width. If the content of one of the other cells exceeds that width, however, the browser expands the size of all cells in the column to match the width required to display that content. If you set different widths for two cells in the same column, a browser applies the larger value to the column.

Sizing a Table

- To set the size of a table, add the following attributes to the table element:
    `width="value" height="value"`
  where *value* is the size either in pixels or as a percentage of the containing element.
- To set cell spacing, add the following attribute to the table element:
    `cellspacing="value"`
  where *value* is the gap between adjacent cells in pixels. The default spacing is 2 pixels.
- To set cell padding, add the following attribute to the table element:
    `cellpadding="value"`
  where *value* is the size of the gap between the cell content and the cell border. The default padding is 1 pixel.

Creating Frames and Rules

By default, the table border surrounds the entire table and each of the cells within the table. You can modify this by applying the frame and rules attributes to the table element. The frame attribute defines which sides of a table have borders (the default is to apply the border to all sides). The syntax of the frame attribute is

```
<table frame="type"> ... </table>
```

where *type* is "box" (the default), "above", "border", "below", "hsides", "vsides", "lhs", "rhs", or "void". Figure 1-14 shows the effect of each of these values on the appearance of the table border.

Figure 1-14 ▶ **Frame values**

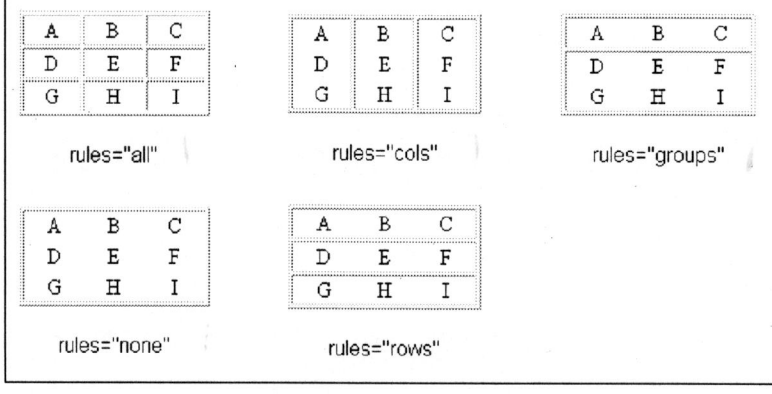

The rules attribute lets you define how gridlines are drawn within the table. By default, gridlines are placed around each table cell. The syntax of the rules attribute is

```
<table rules="type"> ... </table>
```

where *type* is "all" (the default), "cols", "groups", "none", or "rows". Figure 1-15 shows the impact of each of these attribute values.

Figure 1-15 ▶ **Rules values**

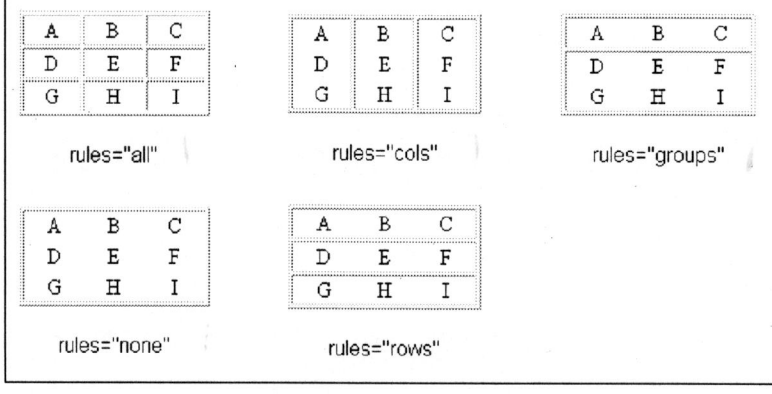

Creating Frames and Rules

- To change the frame style of a table border, add the following attribute to the table element:

    `frame="type"`

  where `type` is "box" (the default), "above", "border", "below", "hsides", "vsides", "lhs", "rhs", or "void".
- To change the rules style of the internal gridlines, add the following attribute to the table element:

    `rules="type"`

  where `type` is "all" (the default), "cols", "groups", or "none".

Working with Column Groups

Although there are no elements to create table columns, you can organize the columns that are generated by the browser into **column groups**, which allow you to format the appearance of every cell in a column. To define a column group, insert the following element after the opening <table> tag (unless there is a table caption, in which case it should follow the caption element):

```
<colgroup span="value" />
```

where `value` is the number of columns in the group. For example, you could use the following tags to organize a table with five columns into two groups: one group for the first three columns and a second group for the last two:

```
<colgroup span="3" />
<colgroup span="2" />
```

If you wanted to set the width of the first four columns to 50 pixels and the next two columns to 100 pixels, the tags for the column groups would appear as

```
<colgroup span="4" width="50" />
<colgroup span="2" width="100" />
```

The colgroup element can also be expressed as a two-sided element, using the syntax

```
<colgroup>
        columns
</colgroup>
```

where `columns` are elements that define the properties for individual columns within the group. To define a single column within the group, you use the one-sided col element. The col element is useful when individual columns within a group need to have slightly different formats. For example, if you want to define a different width for each column within a column group, you could do the following:

```
<colgroup span="3">
      <col width="50" />
      <col width="100" />
      <col width="150" />
</colgroup>
```

In this case, the first column is 50 pixels wide, the second column is 100 pixels wide, and the third column in the group has a width of 150 pixels. The col element can also be used along with the span attribute to format several columns within a group, as in the following example:

```
<colgroup span="5">
      <col span="2" width="50" />
      <col width="100" />
      <col span="2" width="150" />
</colgroup>
```

In this sample, the column group consists of five columns: the first two columns are 50 pixels wide, the middle column is 100 pixels wide, and the last two columns have a width of 150 pixels each.

Creating Web Forms

One of the most important uses of the Web is to collect information from users to order items, register products, or complete surveys and questionnaires. This is often done using Web forms. The data from these forms can then be sent to a program running on a Web server or client for processing. Elements of a form in which a user can enter information or otherwise interact are called **control elements**. The following are the control elements supported by Web forms:

- **input boxes** for text and numerical entries
- **selection lists** for long lists of options, usually appearing in **list boxes**
- **option buttons** (also called **radio buttons**) to select a single option from a predefined list
- **check boxes** to specify an item as either present or absent
- **group boxes** to organize form elements
- **text areas** for extended entries that can include several lines of text
- **form buttons** that can be clicked to start processing the form

A control element in which a user can enter information is also called a **field**. The information entered into a field is referred to as the **field value**. In some fields, users are free to enter anything they choose. Other fields, such as selection lists, limit the user to a predefined list of options. Figure 1-16 shows a sample Web form containing different control elements and fields.

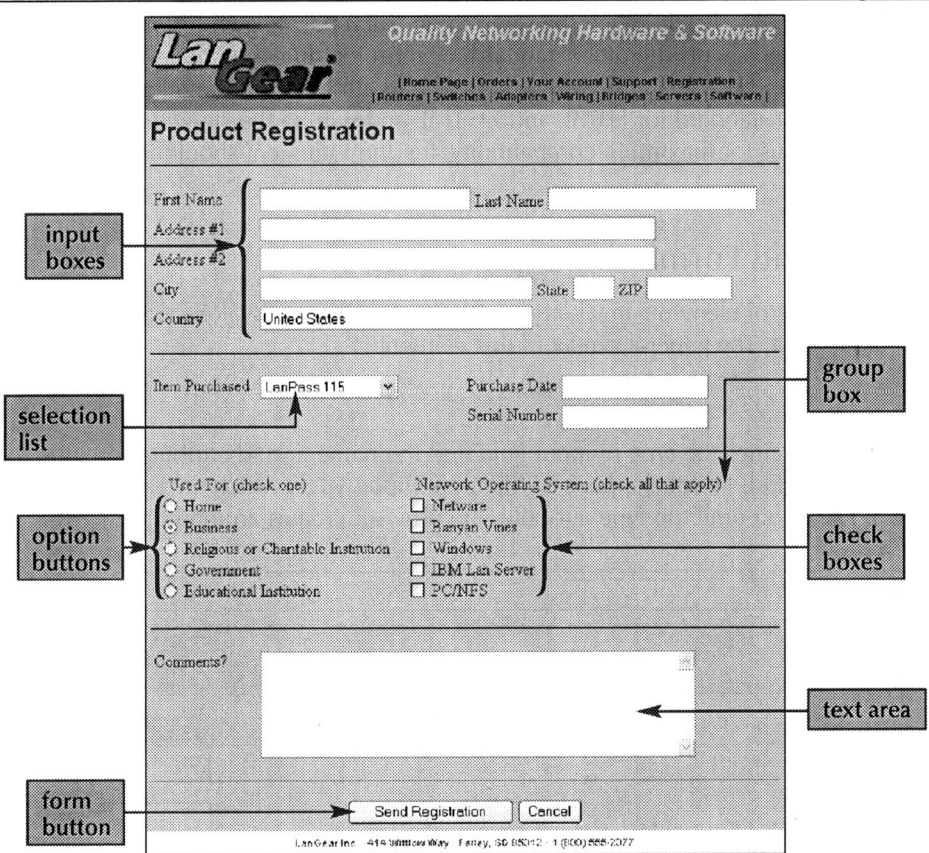

Creating a Form Element

Forms are created using the form element, using the following structure:

```
<form attributes>
     page elements
</form>
```

where *attributes* are the attributes that control how the form is processed and *page elements* are elements placed within the form. Forms typically contain many of the control elements shown in Figure 1-16 but can also contain page elements such as tables, paragraphs, inline images, and headings.

Form attributes usually tell browsers the location of the server-based program to be applied to the form's data, how that data is to be transferred to the script, and so forth. In addition to not needing these attributes when first designing the form, it's also useful to omit them at first. This prevents you from accidentally running the program on an unfinished form, causing the program to process incomplete information. After you've finalized the form's appearance, you can add the final features required by the server program.

You should always specify an id or a name for a form. This is useful in situations where a page contains multiple forms and you need to differentiate one form from another. In addition, it is often required for programs that retrieve values from the form. Two attributes are available to identify a form: the id attribute and the name attribute. The syntax of these attributes is

```
<form name="name" id="id"> ... </form>
```

where `name` is the name of the form and `id` is the id of the form. Although these two attributes may appear to do much the same thing, each has its own history and role. The name attribute represents the older standard for form identification and thus is often required for older browsers and Web servers. The id attribute, on the other hand, represents the current standard for HTML and XHTML and will be the standard for all future applications. Thus for maximum compatibility, the form element should include both attributes.

Creating and Formatting Input Boxes

Most of the control elements in which users are asked to insert values are marked with an input element. The general syntax of this element is

```
<input type="type" name="name" id="id" />
```

where `type` specifies the type of input field and the name and id attributes provide the field's name and id. HTML supports 10 different input types, which are described in Figure 1-17. If you omit the type attribute, the browser creates an input box.

Figure 1-17   **Input types**

Type	Description	
type="button"	Display a button that can be clicked to perform an action from a script	button
type="checkbox"	Display a check box	☑
type="file"	Display a browse button to locate and select a file	Browse...
type="hidden"	Create a hidden field, not viewable on the form	
type="image"	Display an inline image that can be clicked to perform an action from a script	👤
type="password"	Display an input box that hides text entered by the user	********
type="radio"	Display an option button	⊙
type="reset"	Display a button that resets the form when clicked	reset
type="submit"	Display a button that submits the form when clicked	submit
type="text"	Display an input box that displays text entered by the user	LanGear

By default, an input box displays 20 characters of text on a single line (though the actual amount of text entered into the box may be longer). To change the width of an input box, you use the size attribute:

```
<input size="value" />
```

where `value` is the size of the input box in characters. Setting the width of an input box does not limit the number of characters the box can hold. If a user tries to enter text longer than a box's width, the text scrolls to the left, hiding a portion of the field value. Although a user would not be able to see the entire text in such a case, all of it would still be sent to the server for processing.

There are times when you want to limit the number of characters a user can enter to reduce the chance of erroneous data entry. For example, if you have a Social Security number field, you know that only nine characters are required and that any attempt to enter more than nine characters is a mistake. The syntax for setting the maximum length for field input is

```
<input maxlength="value" />
```

where *value* is the maximum number of characters that can be stored in the field.

If most people enter the same value in a field, it may make sense to define a default value for that field. Default values can save time and increase accuracy for users of your Web site. To define a default value, use the syntax

```
<input value="value" />
```

where *value* is the default text or number that is displayed in the field when the Web form is opened. Even though you specify a default value, users are usually still able to enter their own values if they wish.

Creating Option Buttons

Option buttons, or radio buttons, confine users to making a selection from a list of predetermined choices. A user can select only one option button at a time from a group. The syntax to create an option button is

```
<input type="radio" name="name" id="id" value="value" />
```

where *name* identifies the field containing the collection of option buttons, *id* identifies the specific option, and the value attribute indicates the value of the selected option. Note that in the case of option buttons, the name and id attributes are not redundant as they are with input boxes. In fact, the id attribute is required only if you intend to use a field label with the option button.

Although the id attribute is optional, you *must* include the name attribute because it groups distinct option buttons together. Within a group, selecting one option button automatically deselects all of the others.

There is no text attribute for an option button, so for users to understand the purpose of an option button, you must insert descriptive text next to it. If you enclose the descriptive text within a label tag, users can select the option button by clicking either the button or the label.

Figure 1-18 shows an example of HTML code that creates option buttons for party affiliations.

Figure 1-18 | **Creating option buttons**

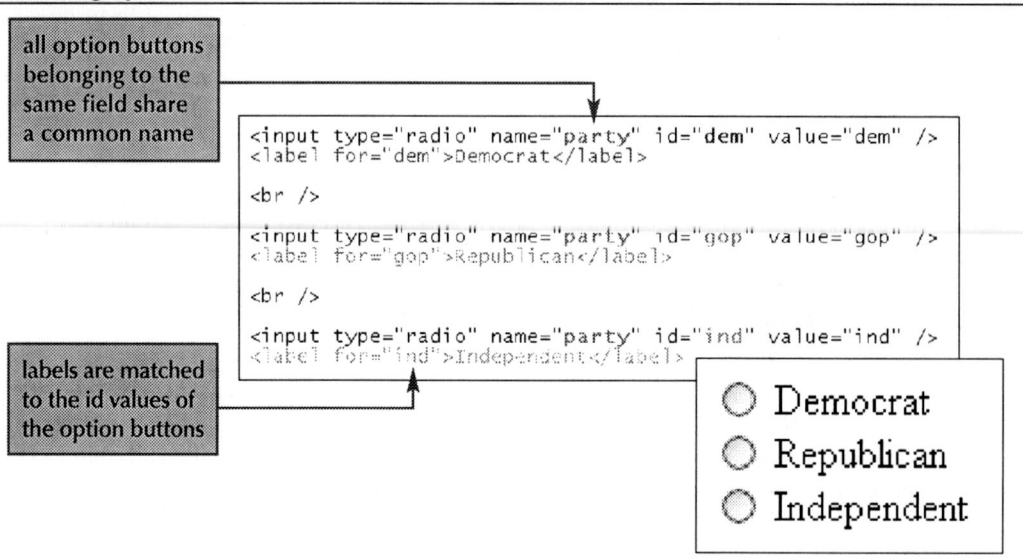

all option buttons
belonging to the
same field share
a common name

labels are matched
to the id values of
the option buttons

```
<input type="radio" name="party" id="dem" value="dem" />
<label for="dem">Democrat</label>

<br />

<input type="radio" name="party" id="gop" value="gop" />
<label for="gop">Republican</label>

<br />

<input type="radio" name="party" id="ind" value="ind" />
<label for="ind">Independent</label>
```

    Note that in this sample code, the value sent to the server does not match the field label. For example, if a user selects the Republican option button, the value "gop" is sent to the server, paired with the field name "party". By default, no option buttons are selected. If you want an option button to be selected when the form opens, you add the checked attribute to the <input> tag:

```
<input type="radio" checked="checked" />
```

Reference Window | **Creating an Option Button**

- To create an option button, use the following HTML tag:
  ```
  <input type="radio" name="name" id="id" value="value" />
  ```
  where *name* identifies the field containing the option button, *id* identifies the specific option value, and *value* specifies the value sent to the server when the option button is selected. The id attribute is not required unless you intend to use a field label with the option button. The value attribute is required.
- To make a particular option button the default option, use the attribute
  ```
  <input type="radio" checked="checked" />
  ```
  Most browsers also accept the syntax
  ```
  <input type="radio" checked />
  ```
  though this does not follow the syntax guidelines of HTML or XHTML.

Creating Check Boxes

Check boxes are similar to option buttons except that they limit the user to only one of two possible choices. The syntax to create a check box is

```
<input type="checkbox" name="name" id="id" value="value" />
```

where the name and id attributes identify the check box and the value attribute specifies the value that is sent to the server if the check box is selected. Unlike for input boxes, the value attribute is required for every check box; unlike option buttons, the name and id attributes should both be included even though they usually contain the same information. For example, the following code assigns the value "democrat" to the party field if the check box is selected:

```
<input type="checkbox" name="party" id="party" value="democrat" />
```

As with input boxes and option buttons, check boxes do not display any text. You add text or a label next to a check box using a separate tag. By default, a check box is not selected. To have a Web form open with a check box already selected, use the checked attribute as follows:

```
<input type="checkbox" checked="checked" />
```

Reference Window

Creating a Check Box

- To create a check box, use the following HTML tag:
  ```
  <input type="checkbox" name="name" id="id" value="value" />
  ```
  where the name and id attributes identify the check box field and the value attribute specifies the value sent to the server if the check box is selected.
- To specify that a check box be selected by default, use the checked attribute as follows:
  ```
  <input type="checkbox" checked="checked" />
  ```
  Most browsers also accept the syntax
  ```
  <input type="checkbox" checked />
  ```
  though this does not follow the syntax guidelines of HTML or XHTML.

Creating a Selection List

A selection list is a list box from which a user selects a particular value or set of values. Selection lists are a good idea when a field's input is a fixed set of possible responses; in such a case, a selection list helps prevent spelling mistakes and erroneous entries. You create a selection list using the <select> tag, and you specify each individual selection item with the <option> tag. The general syntax for the select and option elements is

```
<select name="name" id="id">
   <option>item1</option>
   <option>item2</option>
   .
   .
   .
</select>
```

where the name and id attributes identify the selection field, and each option element represents an individual item in the selection list. Users see the text *item1*, *item2*, and so forth as the options in the selection list. By default, a select element displays one option from the selection list along with a list arrow to view additional selection options. You can change the number of options displayed by modifying the size attribute. The syntax of the size attribute is

```
<select size="value"> ... </select>
```

where *value* is the number of items that the selection list displays in the form. By specifying a value greater than 1, you change the selection list from a list box to a list box with a scroll bar that allows a user to scroll through the selection options. If you set the size attribute to be equal to the number of options in the selection list, the scroll bar either is not displayed or is dimmed. See Figure 1-19.

Figure 1-19	Size values of the selection list

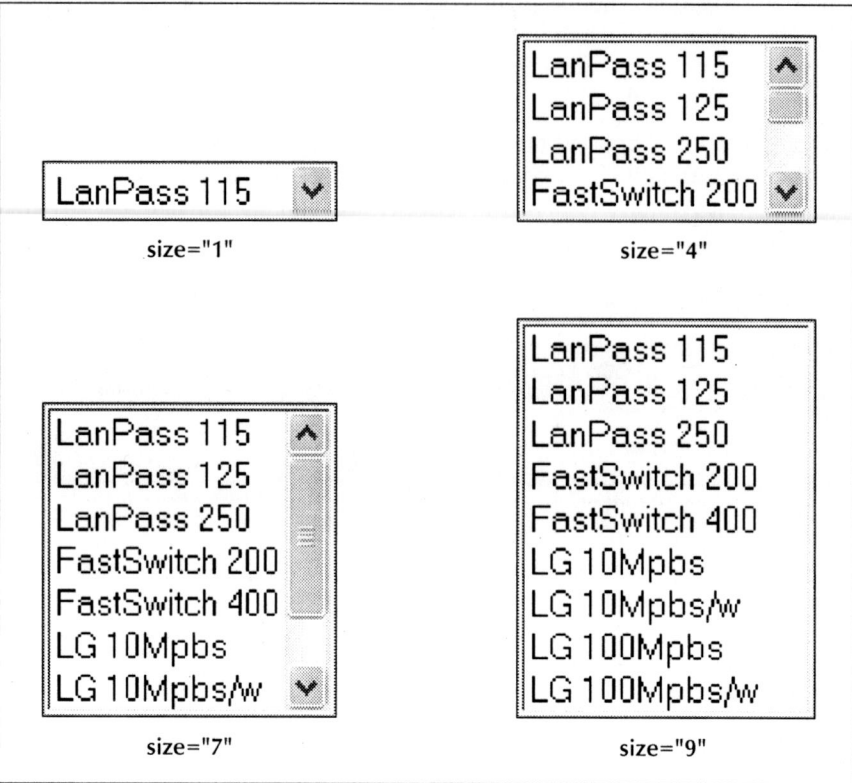

Users are not limited to a single selection from a selection list. Adding the multiple attribute to the select element enables multiple selections from the list. The syntax for this attribute is

```
<select multiple="multiple"> ... </select>
```

To make multiple selections from a selection list, a user must hold down an **access key** while making selections. The Windows operating system offers two different access keys:

• For noncontiguous selections, press and hold the Ctrl key while you make your selections.

• For a contiguous selection, select the first item, press and hold the Shift key, and then select the last item in the range. This selects the two items as well as all the items between them.

By default, a form sends the value displayed in the list for each selected item to the server. For example, if a user selects the first option from a selection list, the text string of that option is sent to the server. Sometimes, however, you may want to send an abbreviation or a code to the server instead of the entire text string; for example, you may display descriptive text for each option in a selection list to help users make an informed choice but require only an abbreviated version for your records. You can specify the value that is sent to the server with the value attribute. The syntax is

```
<option value="value">item</option>
```

where `value` is the value associated with the selection item. You can also specify which item in the selection list is selected, or highlighted, when the form is initially displayed.

The first option in the list is highlighted by default, but you can specify a different value using the following attribute:

```
<option selected="selected">item</option>
```

where the selected attribute indicates that the item is the default item in the selection list.

Creating a Selection List

- To create a selection list, use the following code:
    ```
    <select name="name" id="id">
        <option>item1</option>
        <option>item2</option>

          .
          .
          .

    </select>
    ```
    where the name and id attributes identify the selection field.
- To set the size of a selection list, use the size attribute:
    ```
    <select size="value"> ... </select>
    ```
    where value is the number of items to display in the selection list at once. The default is "1".
- To allow multiple selections from the list, use the multiple attribute:
    ```
    <select multiple="multiple"> ... </select>
    ```
- To associate a value with a selection option, use the value attribute:
    ```
    <option value="value">item</option>
    ```
    where value is the value associated with the selection item.
- To define the default selected item, use the selected attribute:
    ```
    <option selected="selected">item</option>
    ```

Creating a Text Area Box

An input box is limited to a single line of text. To allow users to insert several lines of text, you can instead create a text area box. The syntax to create a text area box is

```
<textarea name="name" id="id" rows="value" cols="value">
   default text
</textarea>
```

where the rows and cols attributes define the dimensions of the input box. The rows attribute indicates the number of lines in the input box—though some early browser versions show more lines than indicated by the rows attribute—and the cols attribute specifies the number of characters in each line. Though not required, you can specify default text that appears in a text area box when a form is initially displayed.

Reference Window | **Creating a Text Area Box**

- To create a text area for extended text entry, use the following tag:
  ```
  <textarea name="name" id="id" rows="value" cols="value">
      default text
  </textarea>
  ```
  where *default text* is the text that is displayed in the text area (optional) and the rows and cols attributes specify the number of lines in the text area and the number of characters in each line, respectively.

Creating a Form Button

A Web form usually contains push buttons that users can click to run a program, submit the form data for processing, or reset the form. The syntax to create a form button is

```
<input type="type" value="text" />
```

where *type* is the button type and *text* is the text that appears on the button. To create a button to submit a form to a script for processing, the type value should be set to "submit". To reset the form to its default values, the type value is "reset". For buttons that run programs or scripts when clicked, the type value is "button".

Aside from the text that a form button displays, its appearance is determined by the Web browser. For greater artistic control over the appearance of your form buttons, you can use the button element, which has the syntax

```
<button name="name" id="id" value="value" type="type">
    content
</button>
```

where the name and value attributes specify the name of the button and the value sent to a server-based program, the id attribute specifies the button's id, the type attribute specifies the button type (submit, reset, or button), and *content* is page content displayed within the button. The page content can include formatted text, inline images, and other design elements supported by HTML.

Reference Window | **Creating Form Buttons**

- To create a button to submit form input to a program, use the following tag:
  ```
  <input type="submit" name="name" id="id" value="text" />
  ```
  where the value attribute defines the text that appears on the button and is also sent to the program to indicate which button on the form has been clicked.
- To create a button that cancels or resets a form, set the value of the type attribute to "reset":
  ```
  <input type="reset" name="name" id="id" value="text" />
  ```
- To create a generic button to perform an action within a Web page, set the value of the type attribute to "button":
  ```
  <input type="button" name="name" id="id" value="text" />
  ```
- To create a button that can contain other Web page elements, use the code
  ```
  <button name="name" id="id" value="value">content</button>
  ```
  where the value attribute provides an initial value for the button and *content* consists of the page element(s) you want displayed in the button.

Creating a Hidden Field

In some cases, you may want to insert a field in your form to store information that you do not want displayed on the page. To do this, you can create a **hidden field**. The syntax for creating a hidden field is

```
<input type="hidden" name="name" id="id" value="value" />
```

Because the field is hidden, you can place it anywhere within the form element. A common practice is to place all hidden fields in one location, usually at the beginning of the form, to make it easier to read and interpret your HTML code. You should also include a comment describing the purpose of the field.

Working with Form Attributes

When a form is submitted, the action performed on the form values is specified by the form's action, method, and enctype attributes. The syntax of the form attributes is

```
<form action="url" method="type" enctype="type"> ... </form>
```

where *url* specifies the file name and the location of the program that processes the form, the method attribute specifies how the Web browser sends data to the server, and the enctype attribute specifies the format of the data stored in the form's fields.

There are two possible values for the method attribute: get or post. The **get method** is the default, and it appends the form data to the end of the URL specified in the action attribute. The **post method** sends form data in a separate data stream, allowing the Web server to receive the data through what is called "standard input." Because it is more flexible, most Web designers prefer the post method for sending data to the server. Because some Web servers limit the length of URLs, the post method is also safer, avoiding the possibility of data attached to a long URL being truncated by the server.

Working with Frames

Typically, as a Web site grows in size and complexity, each page is dedicated to a particular topic or group of topics: one page might contain a list of links, another page might display contact information for the company or organization, and another page might describe the business philosophy. As more pages are added to the site, the designer might wish for a way to display information from several pages at the same time.

One solution is to duplicate that information across the Web site, but this strategy presents problems. It requires a great deal of time and effort to repeat (or copy and paste) the same information over and over again. Also, each time a change is required, you need to repeat your edit for each page in the site—a process that could easily result in errors.

Such considerations contributed to the development of frames. A **frame** is a section of the browser window capable of displaying the content of an entire Web page. Figure 1-20 shows an example of a browser window containing two frames. The frame on the left displays the content of a Web page containing a list of links; the frame on the right displays a second Web page showing a list of products. These two pages come from an old version of the NEC Web site that once utilized frames.

Figure 1-20 ▶ **Frame example**

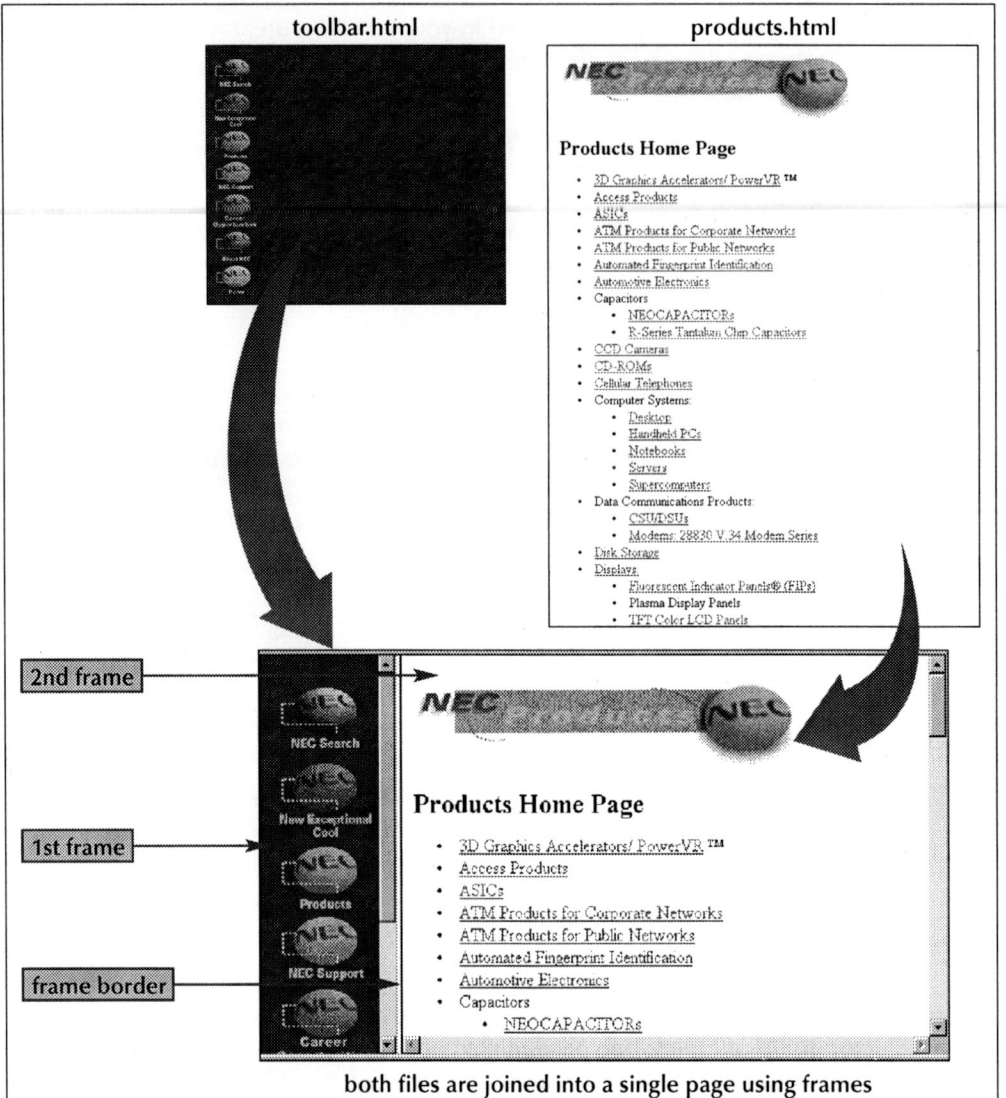

both files are joined into a single page using frames

This example illustrates a common use of frames: displaying a list of links in one frame while showing individual pages from the site in another. Figure 1-21 illustrates how a list of links can remain on the screen while the user navigates through the content of the site. Using this layout, a designer can easily update the list of links because it is stored on only one page rather than having to update the link list through every page in the Web site.

Activating a link within a frame ◀ Figure 1-21

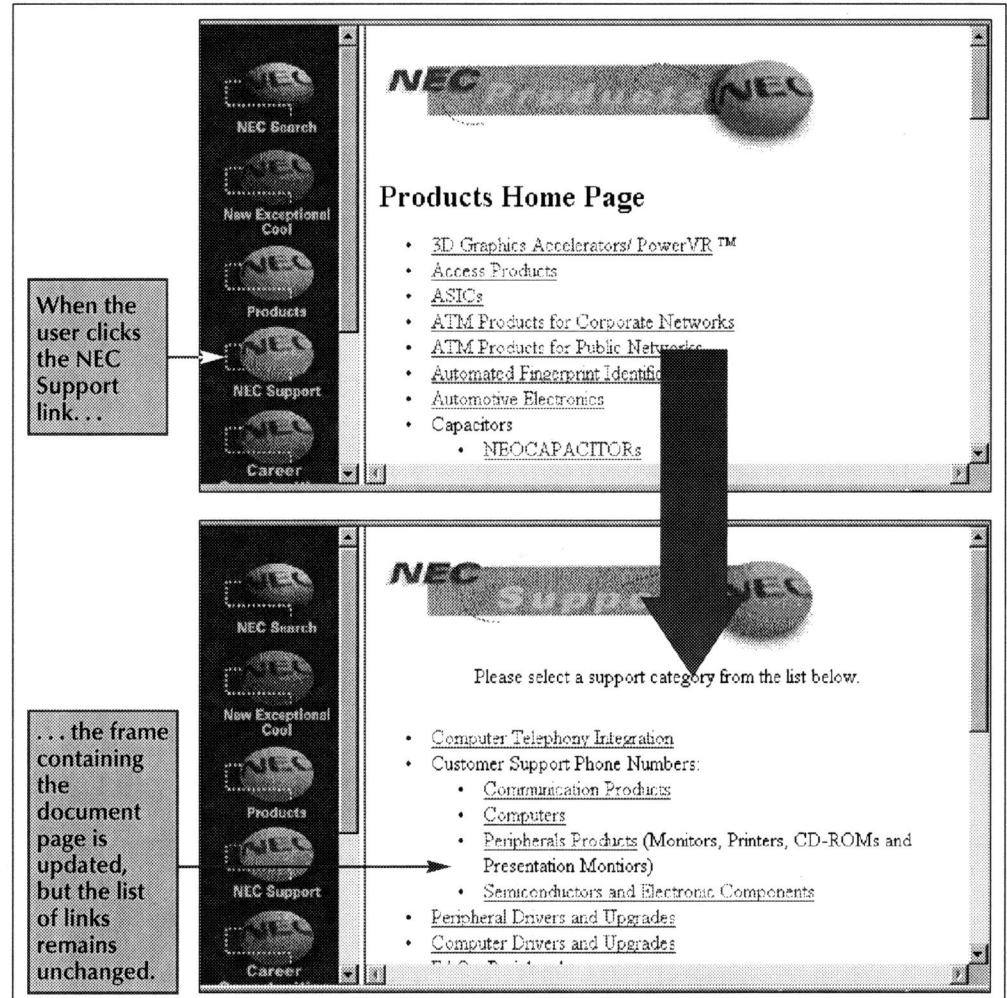

Creating a Frameset

Within the browser window, frames are arranged in a **frameset**. The general syntax for creating a frameset is

```
<html>
<head>
<title>title</title>
</head>
<frameset>
    frames
</frameset>
</html>
```

where *frames* are the individual frames within the frameset. You'll explore how to create these frames shortly.

Note that the frameset element replaces the body element in this HTML document. Because this HTML file displays the content of other Web pages, it is not technically a Web page and thus does not include a page body. A frameset is laid out in either rows or columns but not both. Figure 1-22 shows two framesets: one in which the frames are laid out in three columns and the other in which they are placed in three rows.

Figure 1-22 ▶ **Frame layouts in rows and columns**

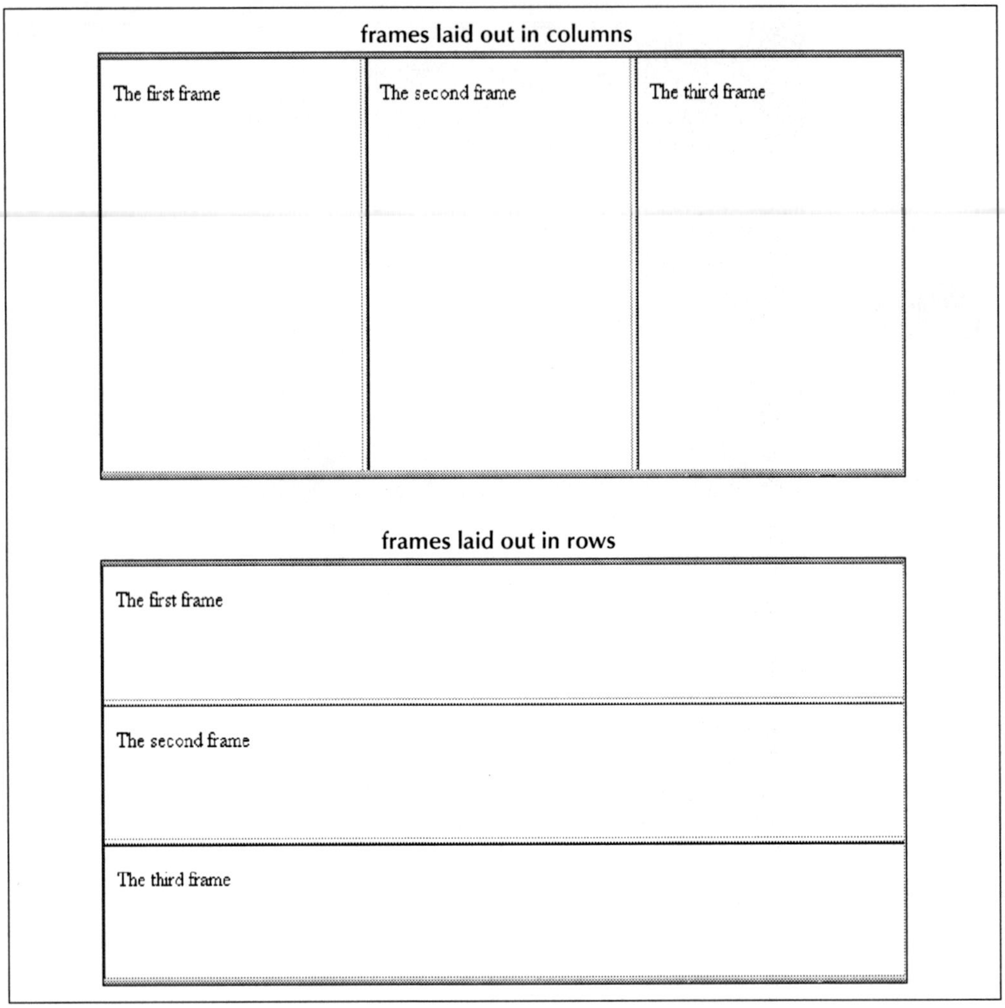

frames laid out in columns

The first frame	The second frame	The third frame

frames laid out in rows

The first frame

The second frame

The third frame

The syntax for defining the row or column frame layout is

```
<frameset rows="row1,row2,row3,...">  ...  </frameset>
```

or

```
<frameset cols="column1,column2,column3,...">  ...  </frameset>
```

where *row1*, *row2*, *row3*, and so on are the heights of the frame rows and *column1*, *column2*, *column3*, and so forth are the widths of the frame columns. There is no limit to the number of rows or columns you can specify for a frameset.

The row and column sizes can be specified in three ways: in pixels, as a percentage of the total size of the frameset, or by an asterisk (*). The asterisk instructs the browser to allocate any unclaimed space in the frameset to the given row or column. For example, the tag <frameset rows="160,*"> creates two rows of frames. The first row has a height of 160 pixels, and the height of the second row is equal to whatever space remains in the browser window. You can also combine the three methods within a single frameset. The tag <frameset cols="160,25%,*"> lays out the frames in the columns shown in Figure 1-23. The first column is 160 pixels wide, the second column is 25% of the width of the display area, and the third column covers whatever space is left.

Sizing frames ◀ Figure 1-23

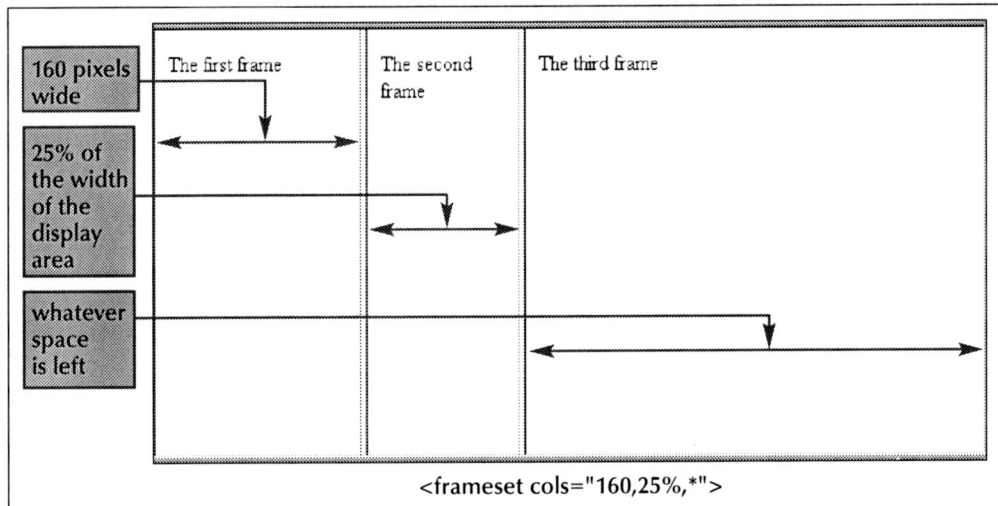

<frameset cols="160,25%,*">

It is a good idea to specify at least one of the rows or columns of your frameset with an asterisk to ensure that the frames fill up the screen regardless of the size of the browser window. You can also use multiple asterisks, which cause browsers to allocate the remaining display space equally among the frames with no defined size. For example, the tag <frameset rows="*,*,*"> creates three rows of frames of equal height.

Creating a Frameset

Reference Window

- To create frames laid out in rows, enter the following tags:
  ```
  <frameset rows="row1,row2,row3,...">
      frames
  </frameset>
  ```
  where *row1*, *row2*, *row3*, and so on are the heights of the frame rows and *frames* defines the frames within the frameset.
- To create frames laid out in columns, enter the following tags:
  ```
  <frameset cols="column1,column2,column3,...">
      frames
  </frameset>
  ```
  where *column1*, *column2*, *column3*, and so on are the widths of the frame columns.

A frameset places frames in either rows or columns but not both. Thus, if you wish to create a layout containing frames in rows and columns, you must nest one frameset within a frame in another frameset. When you use this technique, the interpretation of the rows and cols attributes changes slightly. For the nested frameset, a row height of 25% does not mean 25% of the browser window but rather 25% of the height of the frame in which that frameset has been placed.

Specifying a Frame Source

Frames are marked using the one-sided <frame /> tag. Within the frame element, you use the src attribute to define which document that frame should display. The syntax is

```
<frame src="url" />
```

where `url` is the URL of the document. The following code creates three rows of frames displaying the documents home.htm, main.htm, and footer.htm:

```
<frameset rows="100, *, 100">
   <frame src="home.htm" />
   <frame src="main.htm" />
   <frame src="footer.htm" />
</frameset>
```

Note that frame elements can be placed only within a frameset.

Reference Window

Creating a Frame

- To create a frame element, use the following HTML tag:
  ```
  <frame src="url" />
  ```
  where `url` is the URL of the document you wish to display within the frame.

Formatting Frames

You can control several attributes of your frames: the appearance of scroll bars, the size of the margin between the source document and the frame border, and whether or not users are allowed to change the frame size. By default, a scroll bar is displayed when the content of the source page does not fit within a frame. You can override this setting using the scrolling attribute. The syntax for this attribute is

```
scrolling="type"
```

where `type` can be either "yes" (to always display a scroll bar) or "no" (to never display a scroll bar). If you don't specify a setting for the scrolling attribute, the browser displays a scroll bar when necessary. When working with frames, keep in mind that you should remove scroll bars from a frame only when you are convinced that the entire Web page will be visible in the frame. To do this, you should view your Web page using several different monitor settings. Few things are more irritating to Web site visitors than to discover that some content is missing from a frame and no scroll bars are available to reveal the missing content.

When a user's browser retrieves a frame's Web page, it determines the amount of space between the content of the page and the frame border. Occasionally, the browser sets the margin between the border and the content too large. Generally, you want the margin to be big enough to keep the source's text or images from running into the frame's borders. However, you do not want the margin to take up too much space because you typically want to display as much of the source as possible. The attribute for specifying margin sizes for a frame is

```
marginheight="value" marginwidth="value"
```

where marginheight specifies the amount of space, in pixels, above and below the frame source and marginwidth specifies the amount of space to the left and the right of the frame source. You do not have to specify both the margin height and the margin width. However, if you specify only one, the browser assumes that you want to use the same value for both. Setting margin values is a process of trial and error as you determine what combination of margin sizes looks best. By default, users can resize frame borders in a browser by simply dragging a frame border. However, some Web designers prefer to freeze, or lock, frames so that users cannot resize them. The attribute for preventing frame resizing is

```
noresize="noresize"
```

Formatting a Frame

Reference Window

- To control whether a frame contains a scroll bar, add the following attribute to the frame element:
  ```
  scrolling="type"
  ```
  where *type* is either "yes" (scroll bar) or "no" (no scroll bar). If you do not specify the scrolling attribute, a scroll bar appears only when the content of the frame source cannot fit within the boundaries of the frame.
- To control the amount of space between frame content and the frame boundary, add the following attribute to the frame element:
  ```
  marginwidth="value" marginheight="value"
  ```
  where the width and height values are expressed in pixels. The margin width is the space to the left and the right of the frame source. The margin height is the space above and below the frame source. If you do not specify a margin height or width, the browser assigns dimensions based on the content of the frame source.
- To keep users from resizing frames, add the following attribute to the frame element:
  ```
  noresize="noresize"
  ```

Working with Frames and Links

Clicking a link within a frame opens the linked file inside the same frame; however, you can specify a different location by assigning a name to each frame and then pointing the link to one of the other named frames. To assign a name to a frame, add the name attribute to the frame element. The syntax for this attribute is

```
<frame src="url" name="name" />
```

where *name* is the name assigned to the frame. Case is important in assigning names: "information" is considered a different name than "INFORMATION". Also, frame names cannot include spaces. To point the link to a specific frame, add the following attribute to the link tag:

```
target="name"
```

where *name* is the name you've assigned to a frame in your Web page. For example, you can name a frame "main" using the following code:

```
<frame src="home.htm" name="main" />
```

If you want a link's target to appear within the main frame, apply the target attribute as follows:

```
<a href="gloss.htm" target="main">Display the glossary</a>
```

In addition to frame names, you can also specify **reserved target names**, which cause a linked document to appear within a specific location in the browser. Figure 1-24 lists the reserved target names supported by HTML.

Figure 1-24	Reserved target names

Reserved Target Name	Function in a Frameset
_blank	Loads the target document into a new browser window
_self	Loads the target document into the frame containing the link
_parent	Loads the target document into the parent of the frame containing the link
_top	Loads the document into the full display area, replacing the current frame layout

For example, if you want a link target to appear in a new browser window, you could enter the following code:

```
<a href="gloss.htm" target="_blank">Display the glossary</a>
```

All reserved target names begin with the underscore character (_) to distinguish them from other target names. Note that reserved target names are case sensitive, so you must enter them in lowercase.

Reference Window

Directing a Link to a Frame

- To assign a name to a frame, insert the following attribute:
  ```
  <frame name="name" />
  ```
  where name is the name of the frame.
- To point the target of a link to a named frame, use the target attribute:
  ```
  target="name"
  ```
  where name is the name you assigned to the frame.
- To use the same target for all links, add the target attribute to the base element in the document head.

Using the noframes Element

To make your Web site viewable with browsers that do not support frames (known as **frame-blind browsers**) as well as by those that do, you can use the noframes element to mark a section of your HTML file for code that browsers incapable of displaying frames can use. The noframes element is nested within the frameset element as follows, and it uses the syntax shown:

```
<html>
<head>
<title>title</title>
</head>
<frameset>
   frames
   <noframes>
      <body>
         page content
      </body>
   </noframes>
</frameset>
</html>
```

where *page content* is the content that you want the browser to display in place of the frames. A document can contain only one noframes element. When a browser that supports frames processes this code, it ignores everything within the <noframes> tag and concentrates solely on the code to create the frames. When a browser that doesn't support frames processes this HTML code, however, it doesn't know what to do with the <frameset> and <noframes> tags, so it ignores them. It does know how to render whatever appears within the <body> tags, though. Using this setup, both types of browsers are supported within a single HTML file. Note that when you use the <noframes> tag, you must enclose the page content within a body element.

Reference Window

Supporting Frame-blind Browsers

- To create a version of your page that does not use frames, insert the following tags within the frameset element:

```
<noframes>
    <body>
        page content
    </body>
</noframes>
```
where *page content* is the content of the page you want displayed in place of the frames.

Creating Inline Frames

Another way of using frames is to create a floating frame. Introduced by Internet Explorer 3.0 and added to the HTML 4.0 specifications, a **floating frame**, or **inline frame**, is displayed as a separate box or window within a Web page in much the same way as inline images are placed within a page. The syntax for creating an inline frame is

```
<iframe src="url">
   alternate content
</iframe>
```

where *url* is the URL of the document you want displayed in the inline frame and *alternate content* is the content you want displayed by browsers that don't support inline frames. The following code displays the content of the bio.htm file within an inline frame; for browsers that don't support inline frames, it displays a paragraph containing a link to the file:

```
<iframe src="bio.htm">
     <p>
     View the online <a href="bio.htm">bio</a> of Jeff Bester
     </p>
</iframe>
```

Figure 1-25 shows an example of how such an inline frame might be rendered by a Web browser.

| Figure 1-25 | An example of an inline frame |

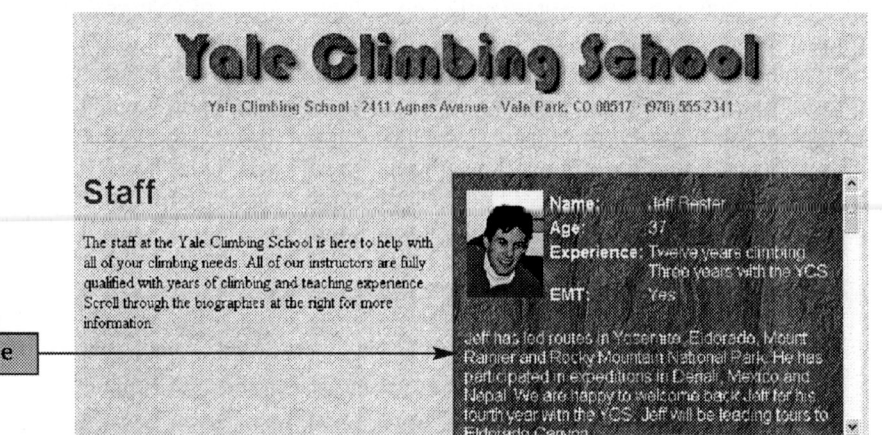

Frame-based Web sites have drawbacks that have led many Web sites to discontinue their use. A browser that opens a framed site has to load multiple HTML files before the user can view any of them, resulting in increased waiting time for potential customers. It is also very difficult to bookmark pages within a frames-based Web site or to make their content available to Internet search engines that create content-based catalogs. (In other words, if you want your content to be easily found by the world, don't use frames.) Some browsers also have difficulty printing the pages within individual frames, although this is less of a problem than it once was. Finally, some users simply prefer layouts where the entire browser window is devoted to a single page. For these reasons, many Web designers suggest that if you still want to use frames, you should create both framed and non-framed versions for a Web site and give users the option of which one to use.

Review Summary

In this review, you learned about the history and syntax of HTML. The review started with a discussion of the history of HTML and the Web. You then learned about the basic syntax requirements of HTML and how to insert elements and attributes. The review then examined block-level elements and inline elements, showing how to use those objects within a Web page. This review also covered the elements used to display nontextual objects such as inline images. The review then looked at how to create and use Web tables and Web forms. The review concluded with a discussion of frames and inline frames.

Key Terms

access key
anchor
block-level element
body element
cell padding
cell spacing
character-formatting
    element
check box
client
closing tag
column group
control element
definition list
deprecated
div element
element
empty element
Extensible Hypertext
    Markup Language
Extensible Markup
    Language
extension
field
field value

floating frame
form button
frame
frame-blind browser
frameset
get method
group box
head element
hidden field
HTML
Hypertext Markup
    Language
inline element
inline frame
inline image
input box
link
list box
logical element
markup language
markup tag
nesting
one-sided tag
opening tag
option button

ordered list
physical element
post method
radio button
reserved target name
root element
row group
selection list
server
spanning cell
tag
text area
unordered list
W3C
Web
Web browser
Web page
Web server
white space
World Wide Web
World Wide Web
    Consortium
XHTML
XML

Review

Review Questions

1. What are servers? What are clients?
2. What is hypertext?
3. What is a markup language? What is a markup tag?
4. Why was the World Wide Web Consortium created?
5. What is a deprecated feature?
6. What is XHTML? What is the relationship between HTML and XHTML?
7. What is the general syntax of a two-sided tag? Give an example of a two-sided tag.
8. What is the general syntax of a one-sided tag? Give an example of a one-sided tag.
9. What is the general syntax of a comment tag? Give an example of a comment tag.
10. What is white space? How do browsers handle occurrences of white space within an HTML file?
11. What is the root element of an HTML file? What are the two elements it contains?
12. What code would you add to an HTML file to set the Web page title to "Pixal Products Home Page"? Where should the code be placed?
13. What is a block-level element? What is an inline element?
14. What code would you use to create an h1 heading containing the text "Pixal Products"?
15. What code would you enter to create an ordered list containing the items Planes, Trains, and Automobiles?

16. What code would you enter to place the text "Pixal Products" in a generic block-level element?

17. What is a character formatting element? Provide two examples of a character formatting element.

18. What is a logical element? What is a physical element?

19. What code would you enter to create an inline image containing the image file logo.jpg with the alternate text "Pixal Products"?

20. What is general code you would enter to create a table containing two rows and three columns?

21. What is a spanning cell? What code would you enter to create a table cell that spans two rows and three columns?

22. What code would you enter to create a form with the id and name "orderForm"?

23. What code would you enter to create an input box field named "zipCode" with a size of 9 characters?

24. What code would you enter to create an option button belonging to a collection of option buttons named "gender"?

25. What code would you enter to create a checkbox with an id and name of "isMember" and a value of "yes"?

26. What code would you enter to create a selection list named "transport" containing the options Planes, Trains, and Automobiles?

27. What attribute would you add to a selection list to allow for multiple selections?

28. What code would you enter to create a submit button containing the text "Submit Order"?

29. Describe the difference between the get and post methods when submitting a form to be processed.

30. What is a frame? What is a frameset?

31. What code would you enter to display the file "pixal.htm" in a frame?

32. What code would you enter to create a link whose destination is the frame named "topFrame"?

33. What code would you enter to create an inline frame displaying the file "pixal.htm"?

Objectives

- Understand the history of Cascading Style Sheets
- Study how to apply inline, embedded, and external style sheets
- Understand how style definitions are inherited and cascade through a Web site
- Learn how to
  - Work with font and text styles
  - Understand how to apply image and color styles
  - Study how to size and position elements on a page
  - Learn how to work with ids, classes, pseudoelements, and pseudoclasses
  - Understand how to create style sheets for different media types
  - Study how to create styles for printed output

Introducing Cascading Style Sheets

Formatting Web Pages with CSS

Introducing CSS

The primary purpose of HTML and XHTML is to create structured documents but not necessarily to describe how such documents should be rendered by Web browsers. In theory, this focus on structure ensures that HTML files are accessible by a wide variety of devices and output media. However, as HTML developed and the Web expanded worldwide, Web page authors demanded elements and attributes that would give them many of the same formatting tools found in word-processing programs. After all, for most Web pages, appearance is just as important as content. This demand resulted in the introduction of several HTML attributes and elements that describe how browsers should render a document. This development was not true to the original vision of a markup language, however; as a result, many of these elements have now been deprecated in favor of style sheets.

A **style sheet** is a collection of properties that describes how elements within a document should be rendered by the device presenting the document. The advantage of style sheets is that they separate document content from document presentation. Thus, by applying different style sheets, the same document can be rendered on different types of devices—from computer monitors to printers to speech-synthesized browsers—without having to alter the content or structure of the original document.

Student Data Files

There are no Student Data Files needed for this review.

Although several style sheet languages exist, by far the most commonly used on the Web is the **Cascading Style Sheets** language, also known as **CSS**. Like HTML and XHTML, the specifications for CSS are maintained by the World Wide Web Consortium, and, like those languages, several versions of CSS exist with varying levels of browser support. The first version of CSS, called **CSS1**, was introduced in 1996 but was not fully implemented by any browser for another three years. CSS1 introduced styles for the following document features:

- **Fonts:** Setting font size, type, and other properties
- **Text:** Controlling text alignment and applying decorative elements such as underlining, italics, and capitalization
- **Color:** Specifying background and foreground colors of different page elements
- **Backgrounds:** Setting and tiling background images for any element
- **Block-level elements:** Controlling margins and borders around blocks, setting the padding space within a block, and floating block-level elements on a page as is done with inline images

The second version of CSS, **CSS2**, was introduced in 1998. It expanded the language to support styles for the following controls:

- **Positioning:** Placing elements at specific coordinates on a page
- **Visual formatting:** Clipping and hiding element content
- **Media types:** Creating styles for different output devices, including printed media and aural devices
- **Interfaces:** Controlling the appearance and behavior of system features such as scrollbars and mouse cursors

At present, browser support for CSS2 is mixed. Most of the styles for positioning and visual formatting are supported, but many of the other CSS2 styles are not. An update to CSS2, **CSS2.1**, was introduced by the W3C in April 2002. Although the update did not add any new features to the language, it cleaned up some minor errors that were introduced in the original specification.

Even though browsers are still trying to catch up to all of the features of CSS2, the W3C has pressed forward with the next version, **CSS3**. Still in development as of this writing, CSS3 is being designed in individual modules. This approach should make it easier for software developers to design applications that support only those features of CSS that are relevant to their products. For example, an aural browser might not need to support the CSS styles associated with printed media, so the browser's developers could concentrate only on the CSS3 modules that deal with aural properties. This setup promises to make browser development easier and the resulting browser products more compact in size and therefore more efficient. This is an especially important consideration in trying to fit a browser into a small handheld device such as a PDA or cell phone. CSS3 will also expand the range of styles supported by the language:

- **User interfaces:** Adding dynamic and interactive features
- **Accessibility:** Supporting users with disabilities and other special needs
- **Columnar layout:** Giving Web authors more page layout options
- **International features:** Providing support for a wide variety of languages and typefaces
- **Mobile devices:** Supporting the device requirements of PDAs and cell phones
- **Scalable vector graphics:** Making it easier for Web authors to add graphic elements to their Web pages

As with HTML and XHTML, the applicability of these features depends on the support of the browser community. Because CSS2 is still not completely supported, it is unclear how long it will take after the W3C releases the final specification for CSS3 styles before they are adopted. In addition, individual browsers have introduced their own extensions to CSS. For example, Internet Explorer has introduced styles to format inline images and to add slideshow effects to Web pages. This means that once again Web page designers need to be aware of compatibility issues not just between different versions of CSS but also between different versions of each browser.

Applying a Style Sheet

There are three ways of applying a style to an HTML or XHTML document:

- **Inline styles:** Each style is applied to a specific element through the use of the style attribute in the element's tag.
- **Embedded styles:** A style sheet is placed in a document's head, setting the style definitions for the document's elements.
- **External styles:** A style sheet is saved in a separate document and is applied to a group of pages in a Web site.

Each approach has its own advantages and disadvantages, and you'll probably use some combination of all three in developing your Web sites.

Using Inline Styles

An **inline style** is applied to an element by adding the style attribute to the element's markup tag. The syntax of the style attribute is

```
<element style="style1: value1; style2: value2; style3: value3; ...">
```

where `element` is the name of the element, `style1`, `style2`, `style3`, and so forth are the names of the styles, and `value1`, `value2`, `value3`, etc. are the values associated with each style. For example, the inline style in the following code instructs browsers to display the h1 heading "Pixal Products" in a red font:

```
<h1 style="color: red">Pixal Products</h1>
```

Inline styles are easy to use and interpret because they are applied directly to the elements they affect. However, there are also some problems with their use. The main complication is that an inline style applies only to the specific element that it modifies. With inline styles, if you wanted all of your headings to be rendered in a sans-serif font, you would have to locate all of the h1 through h6 tags in the Web site and apply the same font-family style to them. This is no small task in a large Web site with hundreds of headings spread through dozens of pages.

Using Embedded Styles

The power of style sheets becomes evident as you move the style definitions farther away from the document content. One way of doing this is to use **embedded style** definitions within the head element of a Web document using the style element. The syntax of the style element is

```
<style>
   style declarations
</style>
```

where *style declarations* are the declarations of the different styles to be applied to the document. Each style declaration is applied to a group of elements within the document called the *selector*. The style declaration has the syntax

```
selector {style1: value1; style2: value2; style3: value3; ...}
```

where *selector* identifies an element or elements within the document and the *style: value* pairs follow the same syntax that you use to apply inline styles to elements. For example, to render all h1 headings in a red font, you use the selector h1 and insert the following style declaration in the documents head:

```
<head>
<title>Web Page Title</title>
<style>
    h1 {color: red}
</style>
</head>
```

Later in this review, you'll look at different ways of expressing the selector value to select wide-ranging groups of elements.

The style element supports several attributes that define the type of style sheet language to be used, the type of output media for which the style is designed, and a name or id that identifies the style element. The syntax of these attributes is

```
<style type="mime_type" media="media_type" title="text" id="text">
    style declarations
</style>
```

where the type attribute indicates the style sheet language, the media attribute identifies the output media, and the title and id attributes provide a label for the set of style declarations in the style element. For style declarations written in CSS, you set the *mime_type* value to "text/css".

The media attribute indicates the output media for which a style sheet is written. For example, you can create different style sheets for printed output and output directed toward a computer screen. Figure 2-1 describes the different values of the media attribute.

Figure 2-1 ▶ **Values of the media attribute**

Media	Used for
all	All output devices (the default)
aural	Speech and sound synthesizers
braille	Braille tactile feedback devices
embossed	Paged Braille printers
handheld	Small or handheld devices with small screens, monochrome graphics, and limited bandwidth
print	Printers
projection	Projectors
screen	Computer monitors
tty	Fixed-width devices such as teletype machines and terminals
tv	Television-type devices with low resolution, color, and limited scrollability

For example, if you wanted to create a style sheet specifically for printed output, you would use an embedded style sheet similar to the following in your HTML or XHTML file:

```
<style type="text/css" media="print">
   h1 {color: red}
</style>
```

Under this style sheet, the h1 heading is displayed in red for printed output. Note that this style sheet doesn't apply to other output media such as computer monitors. In a different medium, an h1 heading would still have the default appearance defined by that device, or it would have its appearance defined by another style sheet written for that medium. The media attribute is discussed in more detail later in this review.

Finally, because a single HTML file can contain several embedded style sheets, the id and title attributes provide a means of distinguishing one style sheet from another. This can be useful in a script that loads different style sheets in response to requests from users. The id and title attributes are optional; unless you need to use multiple style sheets on a particular page, you probably will not have to use them.

Creating an Embedded Style Sheet

Reference Window

- To create an embedded style sheet, enter the following tags within a document's head element:

  ```
  <style type="mime-type" media="type" title="text" id="text">
    style declarations
  </style>
  ```
  where the type attribute specifies the MIME type of the style sheet language, the media attribute specifies the output type, the title and id attributes provide labels for the style sheet, and style declarations are the individual style declarations applied to elements in the document. For CSS style sheets, use a type value of "text/css". The default media value is "all", which applies the style sheet to all output media.

Using an External Style Sheet

An **external style** sheet is a simple text file that contains only style declarations. The file can be linked to any page in a Web site, allowing the same styles to be applied to the entire site at once. Thus, to make all of the h1 headings in a Web site appear in a red font, you could simply add the following text to the external style sheet

```
h1 {color: red}
```

and then link that style sheet to each page. To link an external style sheet to a Web page, you add the following link element to the head element of the HTML or XHTML file:

```
<link href="url" rel="stylesheet" type="mime-type" media="media type"
   id="text" title="text" />
```

where url is the URL of the external style sheet, and the remaining attributes have the same meanings as they did for an embedded style sheet. An external style sheet written in the CSS language should have the file name extension ".css". Thus, to link a Web page to a style sheet named "styles.css", you would enter the following link in the head element of the Web document:

```
<link href="styles.css" rel="stylesheet" type="text/css" />
```

You can include several link elements within a single file, allowing your Web page to retrieve styles from different style sheets. This method allows you to link a Web page to separate style sheets for printed output, computer monitors, and so forth (see Figure 2-2).

Figure 2-2 ▶ **Applying multiple style sheets to a single document**

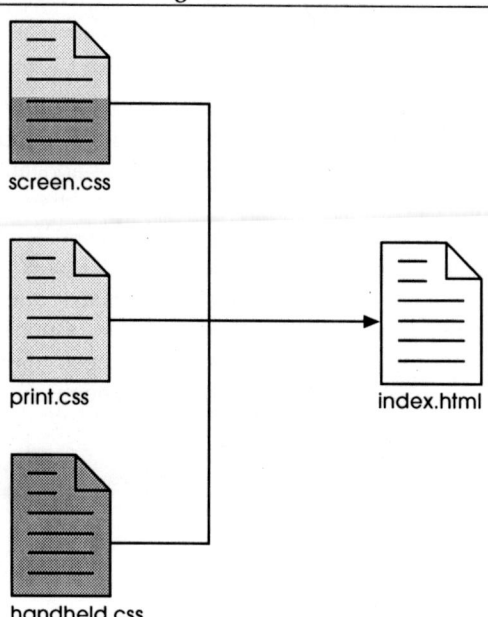

In addition, the same style sheet can be linked to several different Web pages, giving all of the pages in the Web site a common look and feel. If you make a change to the style sheet, the change is automatically reflected across the Web site (see Figure 2-3).

Figure 2-3 ▶ **Applying a single style sheet to multiple documents**

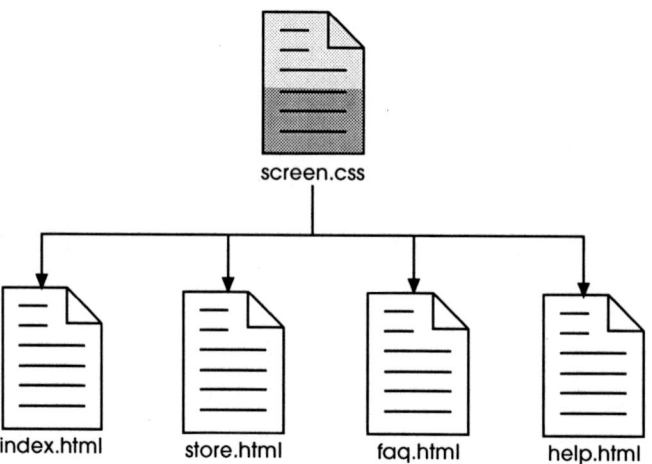

Style Comments

In addition to style declarations, an embedded or external style sheet can also contain comments that document important information about the style sheet. To add a comment, use the form

```
/* comment */
```

where *comment* is the text of the comment. For example, the following line inserts the comment "Pixal Products Style Sheet" into a style sheet:

```
/* Pixal Products Style Sheet */
```

Understanding Style Precedence

You've seen how styles can be applied inline with individual elements, how they can be embedded within a single file, and how an external style sheet can be applied to an entire Web site. With so many potential sources of styles for a single document, how does a browser determine what takes precedence when styles conflict? When styles come from several sources, they are weighted as follows (in order of increasing importance):

1. External style sheet
2. Embedded styles
3. Inline styles

Thus, an inline style takes precedence over an embedded style, which has precedence over an external style sheet. If two styles have the same weight, the one declared last has precedence. For example, in the embedded style

```
<style type="text/css">
    h1 {color: orange}
    h1 {color: blue}
</style>
```

the blue font color is applied to the h1 heading because it is declared last, overriding the orange color style. You can override the precedence rules by adding the !important property to the style declaration. The style sheet

```
<style type="text/css">
    h1 {color: orange !important}
    h1 {color: blue}
</style>
```

results in h1 headings being rendered in an orange font, as the orange style is given a higher weighting than the blue style. The !important property is useful in situations when you want to ensure that a particular style is always enforced no matter what its location in the order of precedence.

Note that any style can still be overridden by users who have set up their own style sheets for use with their browsers. This is often done by people with disabilities who have unique needs (such as the need for text to be displayed in large fonts with highly contrasting colors). The styles in these style sheets take precedence over a browser's default styles and the styles specified by a Web page author. Thus, you should make sure that your Web pages are still readable even when a user does not adopt your style sheets. The ability to view the content of your Web pages should not depend on the ability to access your style sheets.

Understanding Style Inheritance

If a style for an element is not specified, the element adopts the style of its parent element. This effect, known as **style inheritance**, causes style declarations to cascade down through the document hierarchy. For example, if you want to set the text color of every element on a page to blue, you could use the declaration

```
body {color: blue}
```

Every element within the body element (which is to say, every element that is displayed on the page) inherits this style. To override style inheritance, you specify an alternate style for one of the descendant elements of the parent. Together, the styles

```
body {color: blue}
p {color: red}
```

change the text color to blue for every element on the page except for paragraphs and any element contained within a paragraph. As with style precedence, you can override style inheritance by using the !important property.

Working with Text Styles

Now that you've learned how to apply a style to a document, you'll next examine some of the specific styles supported by CSS, starting with a look at text styles.

Choosing a Font

By default, browsers apply a single font face to Web page text—usually Times New Roman. You can specify a different font for any page element using the style

```
font-family: fonts
```

where *fonts* is a comma-separated list of specific or generic font names. A **specific font** is a font such as Times New Roman, Arial, or Garamond that is actually installed on a user's computer. A **generic font** is a name for the general description of the font's appearance. Browsers recognize five generic font names: serif, sans-serif, monospace, cursive, and fantasy. Figure 2-4 shows examples of each. Note that each generic font can represent a wide range of designs.

Figure 2-4 **Generic fonts**

	font samples		
serif	defg	defg	defg
sans-serif	defg	defg	defg
monospace	defg	defg	defg
cursive	defg	defg	defg
fantasy	defg	defg	DEFG

When you specify a generic font, you cannot be exactly sure how the text is rendered by a given user's browser—this depends on how the browser has been configured to deal with generic fonts. This is one reason why CSS allows you to specify a list of fonts, rather than just one. You list the specific fonts you want browsers to try first, in order of preference, and then end the list with the generic font. If a browser cannot find any of the specific fonts listed, it uses the generic font as the final choice. For example, to apply a sans-serif font to the text within an element, you could use the following style:

```
font-family: Arial, Helvetica, sans-serif
```

This style tells the browser to first try to apply the Arial font. If Arial is not available, it tells the browser to look for Helvetica. If neither of those is installed, it tells the browser to use the generic sans-serif font (whatever that may be).

Choosing a Font

• To choose a font for an element's text, use the style
    `font-family: fonts`
  where *fonts* is a comma-separated list of font names, starting with the most specific and desirable fonts and ending with a generic font name.

Setting the Font Size

As with font faces, font sizes are largely determined by a user's Web browser but can be overridden by style sheets. The style to change the font size used in an element is

`font-size: length`

where *length* is a length measurement. Lengths can be specified in four different ways:

• With a unit of measurement
• With a keyword description
• As a percentage of the size of the containing element
• With a keyword expressing the size relative to the size of the containing element

If you choose to specify lengths using measurement units, you can use absolute units or relative units. Because absolute and relative units are options for a lot of other styles as well, it's worthwhile to spend some time understanding them. **Absolute units** define a font size using one of the following standard units of measurement: mm (millimeter), cm (centimeter), in (inch), pt (point), or pc (pica).

Relative units express the font size relative to the size of a standard character in the output device (whatever that may be). The two common typesetting standards are referred to as "em" and "ex". The **em unit** is equal to the width of the capital letter "M". The **ex unit** is equal to the height of a lowercase "x" (see Figure 2-5).

The em and ex units ◀ Figure 2-5

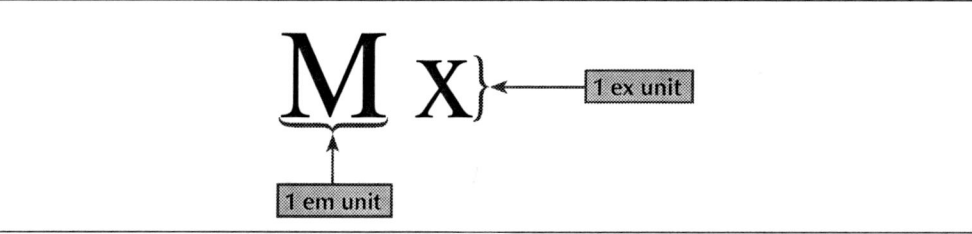

For example, to set the font size about 50% larger than the width of a capital "M" in the default font, you could set the font size as

`font-size: 1.5em`

You can use relative units to make a page **scalable**, allowing the page to be rendered in the same way no matter how a particular browser has been configured. For example, one user may have a large monitor and have set the default font size for body text to 18pt. Another user may have a smaller monitor and have set the default font size to 12pt. You want your heading text to be about 50% larger than the body text for either user. You can't specify the default font size for each user's browser, but if you use a value of 1.5em for the heading, it is sized appropriately on either monitor. Note that you can achieve the same effect by expressing a font size as a percentage of an element's default font size. For example, the style

```
font-size: 150%
```

causes the heading to appear 50% larger than the default size. Because of the advantages of scalability, Web designers often opt for the em unit over an absolute unit such as point size (even though point size is the most commonly used unit in desktop publishing).

The final unit of measurement you need to examine is the **pixel**, which represents a single dot on the output device. Because a pixel is the most fundamental unit, for most length measurements browsers assume that length is expressed in pixels if no unit is specified. Thus, to set the font size to 20 pixels, you could use either of the following styles:

```
font-size: 20px
font-size: 20
```

In general, it's best to include the measurement unit to ensure that your style declaration is unambiguous.

Finally, you can express font sizes using seven descriptive keywords: xx-small, x-small, small, medium, large, x-large, or xx-large. Each browser is configured to display text at a particular size for each of these keywords, thus enabling you to achieve some uniformity across browsers.

Reference Window

Setting the Font Size

- To set the font size, use the style
  ```
  font-size: value
  ```
  where `value` is either a unit of length (specified in mm, cm, in, pt, pc, em, or ex units), a keyword (xx-small, x-small, small, medium, large, x-large, or xx-large), a percentage of the default font size, or a keyword describing the size relative to the size of the containing element (smaller or larger). The default font size unit is the pixel (px).

Controlling Spacing and Indentation

CSS support styles that allow you to perform some basic typographic tasks, such as setting the **kerning** (the amount of space between letters) and **tracking** (the amount of space between words). The styles to control an element's kerning and tracking are

```
letter-spacing: value
word-spacing: value
```

where `value` is the size of space between individual letters or words. You specify these sizes with the same units that you use for font sizing. As with font sizes, the default unit of length for kerning and tracking is the pixel (px). The default kerning and tracking value is 0 pixels each. A positive value increases the letter and word spacing. A negative value reduces the space between letters and words.

Another typographic feature that you can set is **leading**, which is the space between lines of text. The style to set the leading for the text within an element is

```
line-height: length
```

where `length` is a specific length or a percentage of the font size of the text on the affected lines. If no unit is specified, a browser interprets the number as the ratio of the line height to the font size. The standard ratio is 1.2:1, meaning that the line height is 1.2 times the font size. To create double-spaced text, you use the style

```
line-height: 2
```

The final way to control the spacing of your text is to set the indentation used in the first line. The style is

```
text-indent: value
```

where `value` is either a length expressed in absolute or relative units or a percentage of the width of the text block. For example, an indentation value of 5% indents the first line by 5% of the width of the block. The indentation value can also be negative, extending the first line to the left of the text block to create a hanging indent.

Setting Text Spaces

Reference Window

- To set the space between letters (kerning), use the style
  ```
  letter-spacing: value
  ```
  where `value` is the space between individual letters. The default is 0 pixels.
- To set the space between words (tracking), use the style
  ```
  word-spacing: value
  ```
  where `value` is the space between individual words. The default is 0 pixels.
- To set the vertical space between lines of text (leading), use the style
  ```
  line-height: value
  ```
  where `value` is either the length between the lines, a percentage of the font size, or the ratio of the line height to the font size. The default is a ratio of 1.2:1.
- To set the indentation of the first line, use the style
  ```
  text-indent: value
  ```
  where `value` is the length of the indentation expressed either as a length or as a percentage of the width of the text block. The default is 0 pixels.

Setting Font Styles, Weights, and Other Decorative Features

Browsers often apply default font styles to particular types of elements. For example, text marked with an <address> tag usually appears in italics. You can specify font styles yourself using the style

```
font-style: type
```

where `type` is normal, italic, or oblique. The italic and oblique styles are similar in appearance but may differ subtly depending on the font in use.

You have also seen that browsers render certain elements in heavier fonts. For example, most browsers render headings in a boldface font. You can control the font weight for any page element using the style

```
font-weight: weight
```

where `weight` is the level of bold formatting applied to the text. You express weights as values ranging from 100 to 900, in increments of 100. In practice, however, most browsers cannot render nine different font weights. For practical purposes, you can assume that 400 represents normal (unbolded) text, 700 is bold text, and 900 represents extrabold text. You can also use the keywords "normal" or "bold" in place of a weight value, or you can express the font weight relative to the containing element, using the keywords "bolder" or "lighter".

Another style you can use to change the appearance of text is

```
text-decoration: type
```

where `type` is none (for no decorative changes), underline, overline, line-through, or blink. You can apply several decorative features to the same element. For example, the following style:

```
text-decoration: underline overline
```

places a line under and over the text in the element: note that the text-decoration style cannot be applied to nontextual elements, such as inline images.

To control the case of the text within an element, you use the style

```
text-transform: type
```

where `type` is capitalize, uppercase, lowercase, or none (to make no changes to the text case). For example, if you wanted to capitalize the first letter of each word in an element, you could use the style

```
text-transform: capitalize
```

To display every letter in lowercase, you use the text-transform value "lowercase". Similarly, the setting "uppercase" displays every letter in uppercase.

Finally, you can display text in uppercase letters and a small font, using the style:

```
font-variant: type
```

where `type` is normal (the default) or small-caps (small capital letters). Small-caps are often used in legal documents, such as software agreements, where the capital letters indicate the importance of a phrase or point, but the text is made small so as not to detract from other elements in the document.

Setting Font Styles

- To set a font's appearance, use the style
    ```
    font-style: type
    ```
    where `type` is either normal, italic, or oblique.
- To set a font's weight, use
    ```
    font-weight: value
    ```
    where `value` is either a value from 100 to 900 in increments of 100, or the keyword "normal" or "bold". To increase the weight of the font relative to its containing element, use the keywords "bolder" or "lighter".
- To decorate text, use the style
    ```
    text-decoration: type
    ```
    where `type` equals underline, overline, line-through, blink, or none.
- To change the case of the text in an element, use the style
    ```
    text-transform: type
    ```
    where `type` equals capitalize, lowercase, uppercase, or none.
- To display a variant of the current font, use the style
    ```
    font-variant: type
    ```
    where `type` equals normal or small-caps.

Aligning Element Content

CSS provides two styles for aligning the content of an element. To align text horizontally, use the style

```
text-align: type
```

where `type` is left, right, center, or justify (which spaces out the content to touch both the left and the right margins of the element). To vertically align an element's content, use the style

```
vertical-align: type
```

where `type` is one of the keywords described in Figure 2-6.

Values of the vertical-alignment style ◄ **Figure 2-6**

Vertical Alignment	Description
baseline	Aligns the element with the bottom of lowercase letters in surrounding text. (the default)
bottom	Aligns the bottom of the element with the bottom of the lowest element in surrounding content
middle	Aligns the middle of the element with the middle of the surrounding content
sub	Subscripts the element
super	Superscripts the element
text-bottom	Aligns the bottom of the element with the bottom of the font of the surrounding content
text-top	Aligns the top of the element with the top of the font of the surrounding content
top	Aligns the top of the element with the top of the tallest object in the surrounding content

Instead of using keywords, you can specify a length or a percentage for an element to be aligned relative to the surrounding content. A positive value moves the element up, and a negative value lowers the element. For example, the style

```
vertical-align: 50%
```

raises the element by half of the line height of the surrounding content, whereas the style

```
vertical-align: -100%
```

drops the element an entire line height below the baseline of the current line.

Combining All Text Formatting in a Single Style

This review has covered a lot of different text and font styles. You can combine most of them into a single style declaration, using the form:

```
font: font-style font-variant font-weight font-size/line-height
    font-family
```

where *font-style* is the font's style, *font-variant* is the font variant, *font-weight* is the weight of the font, *font-size* is the size of the font, *line-height* is the height of the lines, and *font-family* is the font face. For example, the style

```
font: italic small-caps bold 16pt/24pt Arial, sans-serif
```

displays the text of the element in an italic bold Arial or sans-serif font. The font size is 16pt and the space between the lines is 24pt. The text appears in small capital letters. You do not have to include all of the properties of the font style. The only required properties are size and font-family. A browser assumes the default value for any omitted property. However, you must place any properties that you do include in the order indicated above. For example, the following is a correct style declaration to specify a 16pt bold monospace font:

```
font: bold 16pt monospace
```

However, it would *not* be correct to switch the order, placing the font-family property before the style and weight properties, as in

```
font: monospace bold 16pt
```

Although some browsers would be able to correctly interpret this style, others would reject it because of the flawed syntax.

Working with Color and Image Styles

CSS provides several different styles for adding color and images to your Web pages. You can define the foreground and background color for each element on a page. The foreground color is usually the color of the text in an element, although in the case of horizontal lines it defines part of the line's color. The style to define an element's foreground color is

```
color: color
```

where *color* is either a color value or a color name. Color values are entered in the form rgb (red, green, blue) where red is the red component of the color, green is the green component, and blue is the blue component. Component values range from 0 (no intensity) to 255 (highest intensity). The style to define an element's background color is

```
background-color: color
```

If you do not define an element's color, the color is taken from the containing element. For example, if you specify red text on a gray background for a Web page's body, all elements within the page inherit that color combination unless you specify a different style. For example, if you want to display all paragraphs in white text on a black background, the style is

```
p {color: white; background-color: black}
```

Reference Window

Setting Foreground and Background Colors

- To set an element's foreground color, use the style
    ```
    color: color
    ```
  where color is either a color name or a color value.
- To set an element's background color, use the style
    ```
    background-color: color
    ```

Setting a Background Image

Almost any element can be displayed with a background image. You can set four properties on a background image:

- The source of the image file
- Where the image is placed in the background of the element
- How the image is repeated across the background of the element
- Whether the image scrolls with the display window

To apply a background image, use the style

```
background-image: url(url)
```

where url is the location and the name of the image file.

Controlling Image Placement

By default, background images are tiled both horizontally and vertically until they occupy the background of the entire element. You can control how browsers tile a background image using the style

```
background-repeat: type
```

where type equals repeat, repeat-x, repeat-y, or no-repeat. Figure 2-7 shows an example of each of these repeat types. The default type value is "repeat", which causes the tiling to occur in both the vertical and the horizontal directions.

Figure 2-7   **Values of the background-repeat style**

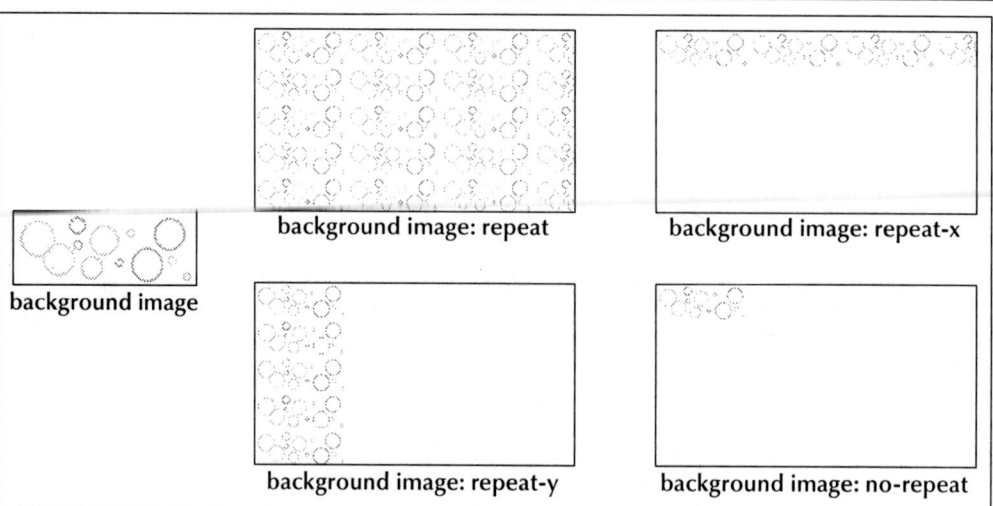

background image

background image: repeat

background image: repeat-x

background image: repeat-y

background image: no-repeat

By default, background images are placed in the upper-left corner of the space occupied by an element and then repeated from there if tiling is in effect. You can place a background image in a different location using the style

```
background-position: horizontal_position vertical_position
```

where `horizontal_position` and `vertical_position` are the horizontal and vertical coordinates of the upper-left corner of the image. For example, the style

```
background-position: 30 50
```

places the image 30 pixels to the right and 50 pixels down from the upper-left corner of the element space. If you specify only one value, a browser applies it to both the horizontal and the vertical coordinates.

To describe image position more generally, you can use a combination of six keywords: left, center, right (for the horizontal position) and top, center, bottom (for the vertical position). You can also define the position of a background image as a percentage of the width and the height of the element. For example, the style

```
background-position: 50% 50%
```

places the background image at the center of the element. By default, a background image moves with the element as the page is scrolled through the browser display window. You can change this behavior using the style

```
background-attachment: attachment
```

where `attachment` is either "scroll" (the default) to scroll the image with the page, or "fixed" to place the image at a fixed location in the display window. Fixed background images are often used to create the illusion of a **watermark**, mimicking a translucent graphic impressed into the very fabric of paper and often used in specialized stationery.

Like the font style, all of the various background image styles can be combined into a single style:

```
background: color url(url) repeat attachment position
```

where `color` is the color name or color value of the element background, `url` is the URL of the background image file, `repeat` specifies how the image is tiled in the background, `attachment` specifies whether the image scrolls with the page, and `position` provides the coordinates of the background image. For example, the declaration

```
body {background: yellow url(paper.gif) no-repeat fixed center center}
```

displays the image file "paper.gif" on the page body's background. The image file is centered on the page, fixed in position (so that it doesn't scroll), and is not repeated or tiled across the page body. In places where the background image is not displayed, a background color of yellow is displayed.

Inserting a Background Image

- To insert a background image behind an element, use the style
     `background-image: url(url)`
  where `url` is the file name and the location of the image file.
- To control the tiling of the background image, use the style
     `background-repeat: type`
  where `type` is repeat (the default), repeat-x, repeat-y, or no-repeat.
- To place the background image in a specific position behind the element, use the style
     `background-position: horizontal vertical`
  where `horizontal` is the horizontal position of the image and `vertical` is the vertical position. You can specify a position as the distance from the top-left corner of the element, a percentage of the element's width and height, or by using a keyword. Keyword options are top, center, or bottom for vertical position and left, center, or right for horizontal placement.
- To control whether the background image scrolls, use the style
     `background-attachment: attachment`
  where `attachment` is scroll (the default) or fixed.
- To place all of the background options in a single declaration, use the style
     `background: color image repeat attachment position`
  where `color` is the background color, `image` is the image file, `repeat` is the method of tiling the image, `attachment` defines whether the image scrolls or is fixed, and `position` defines the position of the image within the element.

Sizing Elements

By default, the size of each element is determined either by its content or by the size of its containing element. For example, the width of a paragraph expands to match the width of its containing element, and the paragraph's height is determined by its content. You can use CSS to override these default settings, specifying a different width or height for any element on a page.

Setting an Element's Width

To set the width of an element, apply the following style:

```
width: value
```

where `value` is expressed as a percentage of the width of the parent element or in absolute units. For example, to set the width of all paragraphs on a page to 4 inches, you use the following style declaration:

```
p {width: 4in}
```

If you do not specify a unit of measurement, browsers assume that the width is set in pixels. For example, the style

```
p {width: 250}
```

sets the width of all paragraphs to 250 pixels.

Setting an Element's Height

To set the height of an element, use the style

```
height: value
```

where `value` is the height of the element specified as a percentage of the parent element or in absolute units. If you do not specify a height, browsers expand the height of the element until all of the content is visible.

Handling Content Overflow

If you do specify a height for an element, you run the risk of not being able to fit its content into a defined space. In that case, you can control how the browser handles the extra content by applying the style

```
overflow: type
```

where `type` is visible (the default), hidden, scroll, or auto. A value of "visible" instructs browsers to increase the height of the element to fit the extra content. A value of "hidden" hides the extra content. Both the "scroll" and "auto" values instruct browsers to display scroll bars that enable users to view the extra content. The "auto" option adds scroll bars only when needed, whereas the "scroll" option adds scroll bars whether they are needed or not (see Figure 2-8).

| Figure 2-8 | Values of the overflow style |

overflow: visible

overflow: hidden

overflow: scroll

overflow: auto

Clipping Content

Another attribute related to overflow is the clip attribute. The clip attribute allows a Web designer to define a rectangular area through which the content of an element can be viewed. Any content that falls outside of the clip area is hidden. The syntax for the clip attribute is

```
clip: rect(top, right, bottom, left)
```

where *top*, *right*, *bottom*, and *left* define the coordinates of the rectangular region. For example, a clip value of rect(10, 175, 125, 75) defines a clip region whose top and bottom edges are 10 and 125 pixels from the top of the element and whose right and left edges are 175 and 75 pixels from the left side of the element (see Figure 2-9).

Clipping an element ◄ **Figure 2-9**

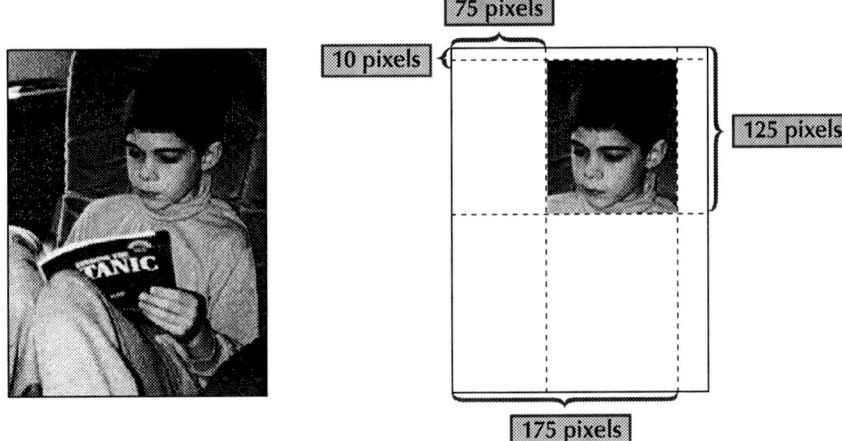

75 pixels

10 pixels

125 pixels

175 pixels

full element   clip: rect(10, 175, 125, 75)

The *top*, *right*, *bottom*, and *left* values can also be set to "auto", which shifts the clipping region to the edge of an element. For example, a clip value of rect(10, auto, 125, 75) creates a clipping rectangle whose right edge matches the right edge of the element while the rest of the edges are clipped.

Working with Borders, Margins, and Padding

For each page element, CSS defines a **box model** that identifies the different parts of the element. The box model describes four aspects of an element (see Figure 2-10):

- The margin between the box and the other elements
- The border of the box
- The padding between the element's content and the border
- The element's content

Figure 2-10 ▶ **Parts of the box model**

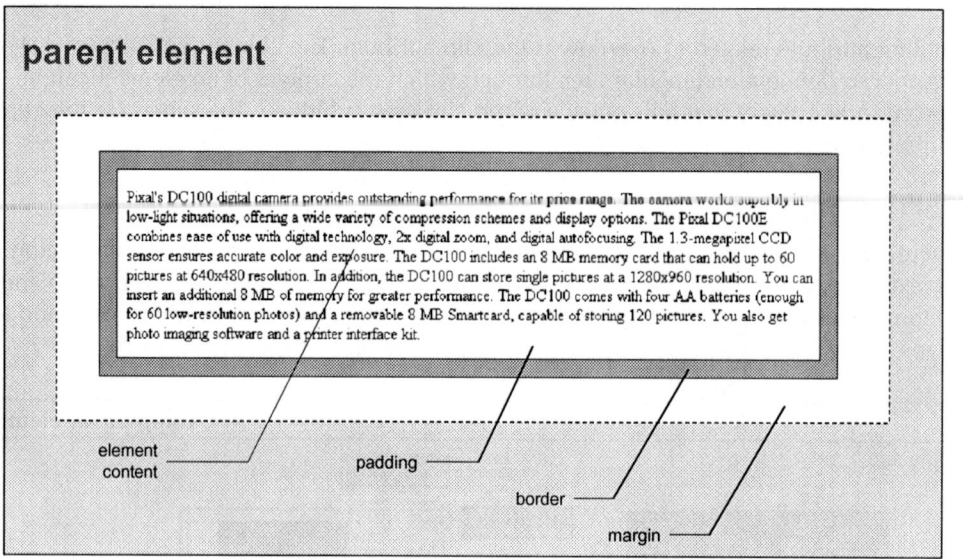

CSS provides styles to work with the margins, borders, and padding of any page element.

Working with Margins

CSS supports four styles that can be used to control the size of the margin of a page element. These attributes are

```
margin-top: value
margin-right: value
margin-bottom: value
margin-left: value
```

where *value* is the size of the margin expressed in absolute units or as a percentage of the width of the parent element. You can also use the value "auto", which instructs browsers to determine the margin size. For example, to create margins of 10 pixels on each side and 5 pixels above and below every h1 element, you use the following style:

```
h1 {margin-top: 5; margin-right: 10; margin-bottom: 5; margin-left: 10}
```

Margin sizes can also be negative, which you can use to crowd or overlap elements on a page. The four margin styles can also be combined into a single style:

```
margin: top right bottom left
```

where *top*, *right*, *bottom*, and *left* are sizes of the corresponding margins. If you include only three values in the combined attribute, they are interpreted as top, right, and bottom, and browsers match the size of the left and right margins. If only two values are specified, they are applied to the top and right margins, and browsers match the bottom and left margins to those two values. If only one value is entered, browsers apply that size to all four margins.

Setting the Margin Size

- To set the size of the margins around an element, use the styles

    ```
    margin-top: length
    margin-right: length
    margin-bottom: length
    margin-left: length
    ```
    where *length* is a unit of length, a percentage of the width of the containing element, or the keyword "auto" (the default), which enables browsers to set the margin size.
- To combine all margin styles in a single style, use

    ```
    margin: top right bottom left
    ```
    where *top*, *right*, *bottom*, and *left* are the margins of the top, right, bottom, and left edges. If you include only three values, the margins are applied to the top, right, and bottom, and the left value matches the right one. If you specify only two values, the first value is applied to the top and bottom edges, and the second value is applied to the right and left edges. If you specify only one value, it is applied to all four edges.

Working with Borders

You can create a border around any element and define its thickness, color, and style. You can apply styles to individual border sides or to all four sides at once. Figure 2-11 describes the various CSS border attributes.

Border styles ◄ **Figure 2-11**

Border Style	Description	Notes
border-top-width: *value*	Width of the top border	Where *value* is the width of the border in absolute or relative units or defined with the keyword "thin", "medium", or "thick"
border-right-width: *value*	Width of the right border	
border-bottom-width: *value*	Width of the bottom border	
border-left-width: *value*	Width of the left border	
border-width: *top right bottom left*	Width of any or all of the borders	
border-top-color: *color*	Color of the top border	Where *color* is a color name or color value
border-right-color: *color*	Color of the right border	
border-bottom-color: *color*	Color of the bottom border	
border-left-color: *color*	Color of the left border	
border-color: *top right bottom left*	Color of any or all of the borders	
border-top-style: *type*	Style of the top border	Where *type* is one of the nine border styles: solid, dashed, dotted, double, outset, inset, groove, ridge, or none
border-right-style: *type*	Style of the right border	
border-bottom-style: *type*	Style of the bottom border	
border-left-style: *type*	Style of the left border	
border-style: *top right bottom left*	Style of any or all of the borders	

Border widths can be expressed using units of length or with the keywords "thin", "medium", or "thick". Border color is defined using a color name or value. For border style, CSS supports the nine different types described in Figure 2-12.

Figure 2-12 ▶ **Border style types**

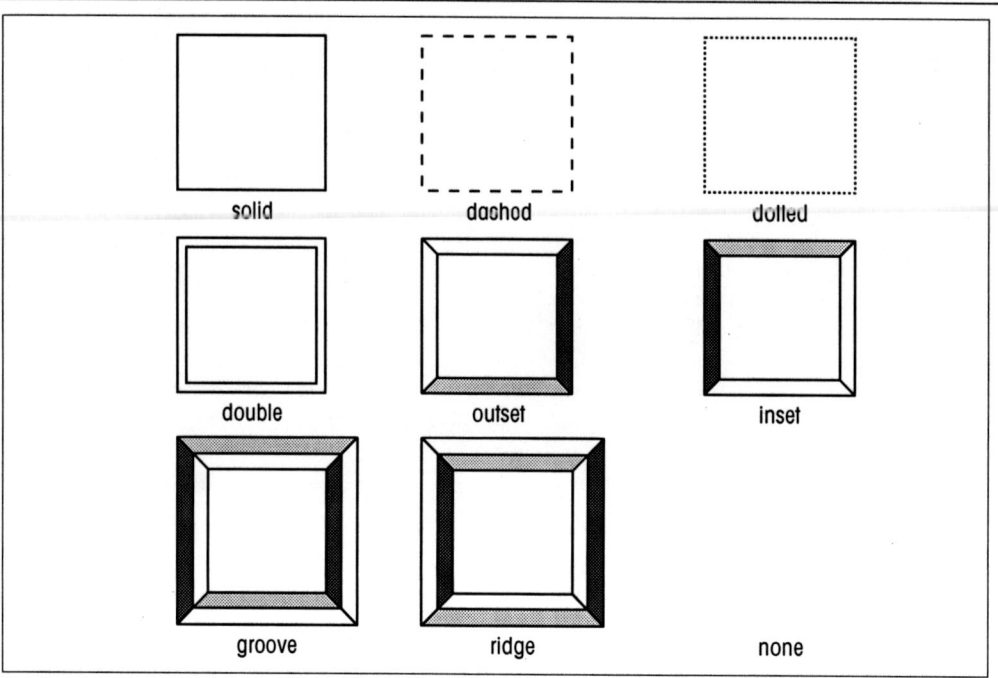

For example, to place a double border around an entire Web page, you could use the style

```
body {border-style: double}
```

All of the border attributes can be combined into a single style declaration using the style

```
border: width style color
```

To create a 5pt blue dotted border around h1 headings, you could use the style declaration

```
h1 {border-width: 5pt; border-style: dotted; border-color: blue}
```

or you could combine the attributes into the style declaration

```
h1 {border: 5pt dotted blue}
```

To work with individual borders, you can identify specific borders to format using the styles

```
border-top: width style color
border-right: width style color
border-bottom: width style color
border-left: width style color
```

There are several methods of formatting the border for a block element, but support for the different methods is inconsistent across browsers and browser versions. As always, be sure that the styles you use are supported by the browsers your audience is likely to be using.

Setting the Border Style

- To set the width of an element's border, use the style
  ```
  border-width: top right bottom left
  ```
  where *top*, *right*, *bottom*, and *left* are the widths of the top, right, bottom, and left borders. To define the border width for individual sides, use the styles border-top-width, border-right-width, border-bottom-width, and border-left-width.
- To set the border color, use the style
  ```
  border-color: top right bottom left
  ```
  where *top*, *right*, *bottom*, and *left* are the colors of the top, right, bottom, and left borders. To define the border color for individual sides, use the styles border-top-color, border-right-color, border-bottom-color, and border-left-color.
- To set the border style, use
  ```
  border-style: top right bottom left
  ```
  where *top*, *right*, *bottom*, and *left* are the styles of the top, right, bottom, and left borders. Possible border style values are solid, dashed, dotted, double, outset, inset, groove, ridge, and none. To define the border style for individual sides, use the styles border-top-style, border-right-style, border-bottom-style, and border-left-style.
- To format the entire border, use the style
  ```
  border: width style color
  ```
  where *width* is the border width, *style* is the border style, and *color* is the border color. To define the border appearance for individual sides, use the styles border-top, border-right, border-left, and border-bottom.

Working with Padding

To increase the space between element content and its border, you increase the size of the padding for the block. You can do this using any of the following styles:

```
padding-top: value
padding-right: value
padding-bottom: value
padding-left: value
padding: top right bottom left
```

where the padding values can be expressed in absolute units or as a percentage of the width of the block-level element. As with the combined margin style discussed earlier, if you enter fewer than four of the values for top, right, bottom, and left, browsers match the opposite sides. For example, to set the padding of all sides to 5 millimeters, you could use the style

```
padding: 5mm
```

Setting Padding Size

- To set the size of the internal padding, use the style
  ```
  padding: top right bottom left
  ```
  where *top*, *right*, *bottom*, and *left* are the top, right, bottom, and left padding sizes. To define the padding size for only one side of an element, use the styles padding-top, padding-right, padding-bottom, and padding-left.

Positioning Elements

Each page element is placed using the default settings of a user's Web browser. You can override these settings, however, and place elements at specific coordinates on the page. The style to set the position of an element is

```
position: type; top:value; right:value; bottom:value; left:value
```

where $type$ indicates the type of positioning applied to the element and the top, right, bottom, and left styles indicate the coordinates of the top, right, bottom, and left edges of the element. In practice, only the top and left coordinates are used because the bottom and right coordinates can be inferred given the element's height and width. Coordinates can be expressed in the usual CSS measurement units.

The position style has five possible values: static, absolute, relative, fixed, and inherit. The default position is static, which allows browsers to place an element based on where it flows in a document. This is essentially the same as not using any CSS positioning at all. When the position is static, any values specified for the top or left styles are ignored by the browser.

Reference Window

Positioning an Object with CSS

- To place an object at a specific location, use the style

```
position: type; top: value; right: value; bottom: value; left:
    value
```

where $type$ indicates the type of positioning applied to the element (absolute, relative, static, fixed, or inherit), and the top, right, bottom, and left styles indicate the coordinates of the top, right, bottom, and left edges of the element.

Absolute Positioning

Absolute positioning places an element at defined coordinates within its parent element. In most cases, the parent element is the document window itself, meaning that the absolute position coordinates refer to the coordinates within the window. The coordinates are specified with respect to the upper-left corner of the parent element. A positive top value places the object down from the top edge; a negative value moves the object above the top edge of the parent. Similarly, a positive left value moves the element to the right of the left edge, and a negative value moves the element to the left of the parent.

Figure 2-13 shows an object that has been placed at the coordinates (100, 150)—that is, 100 pixels to the right and 150 pixels down from the upper-left corner of its containing element. Absolute positioning essentially takes the object out of the document flow. Note that the other elements in the document move up in the flow of the document, occupying the space previously taken by the absolutely positioned object.

Absolute positioning ◄ **Figure 2-13**

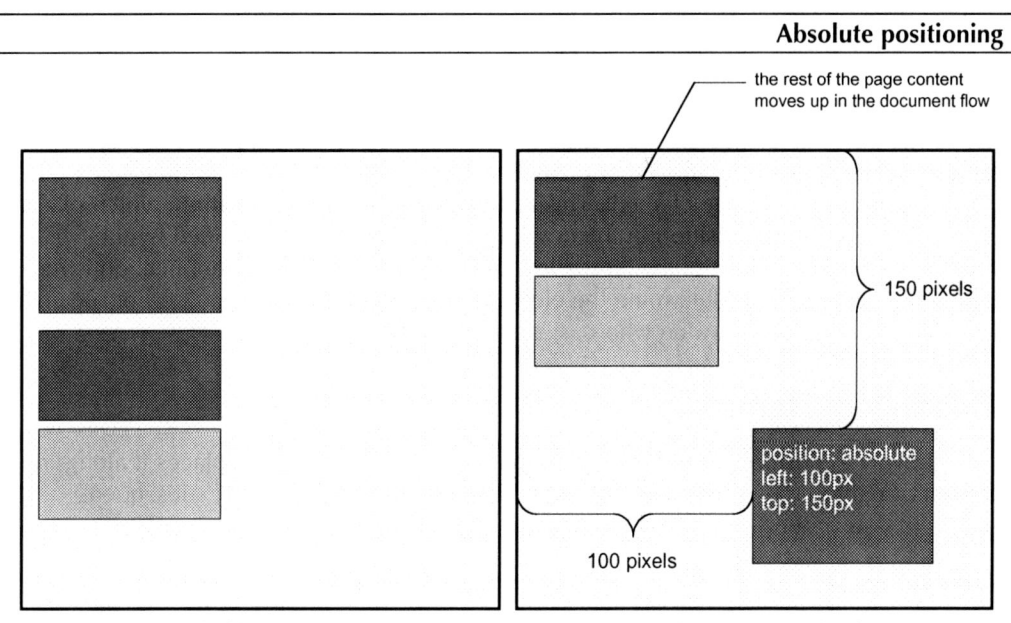

the rest of the page content
moves up in the document flow

150 pixels

position: absolute
left: 100px
top: 150px

100 pixels

original layout   layout with absolute positioning

Relative Positioning

An alternative approach is to offset an element by using **relative positioning**. This approach moves an element a specific distance from where the browser would have placed it. For example, the element shown in Figure 2-14 is offset 50 pixels to the left and 75 pixels down from its original location on the page. Unlike absolute positioning, relative positioning does not affect the placement of subsequent objects on the page. Other objects are placed at their original locations just as if no relative positioning had taken place. Relative positioning affects only the object being moved.

Relative positioning ◄ **Figure 2-14**

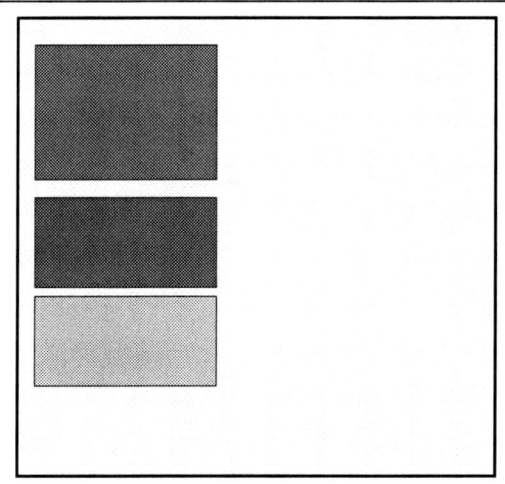 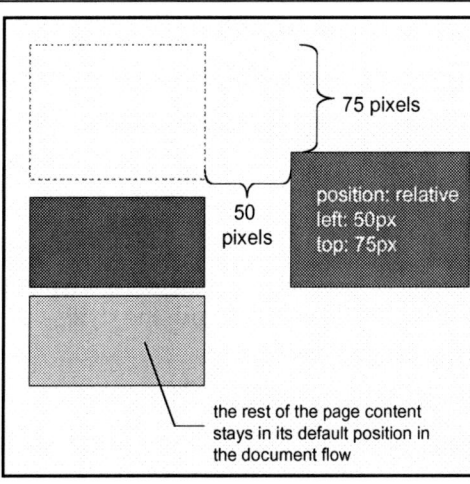

75 pixels

50
pixels

position: relative
left: 50px
top: 75px

the rest of the page content
stays in its default position in
the document flow

original layout   layout with relative positioning

Fixed and Static Positioning

A **fixed position** places an element at a fixed location in the display window. The element remains in that location and does not scroll with other elements on the page. Similar to absolute positioning, the other elements in the document move into the space previously occupied by the element. This is different from a **static position**, which places an object in its natural position in the flow of the document as determined by the browser. Using static positioning, you allow the browser, or whatever application is rendering the document, to determine the element's location. Therefore you do not specify a top, right, bottom, or left value when using static positioning.

Floating an Element

Another way to position an element is to float it. Floating an element places it alongside the left or right margin of the page or the containing element, allowing subsequent blocks to flow around it. The style to float an element is

```
float: margin
```

where `margin` is either left or right. Figure 2-15 shows an example of an element that has been resized and is floating on the right margin of the page.

| Figure 2-15 | The float style |

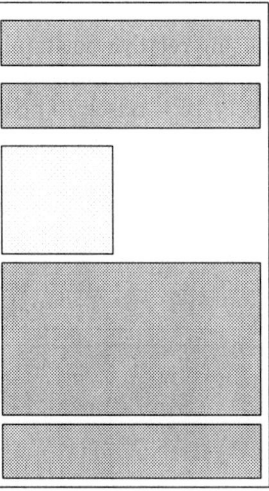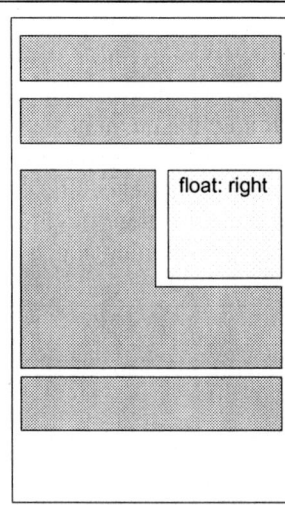

original layout

element is floated on the right margin, and the subsequent content wraps around it

You can prevent an element from wrapping around a floating element by clearing it. To clear an element, you use the style

```
clear: margin
```

where `margin` is left, right, or both. For example, if the value of the clear style for an element is set to "right", the element is not rendered on the page until the right margin is clear of all floating elements. A clear value of "both" requires both margins to be clear. Figure 2-16 illustrates the flow of an element when both the float and the clear attributes are used.

The clear style ◀ Figure 2-16

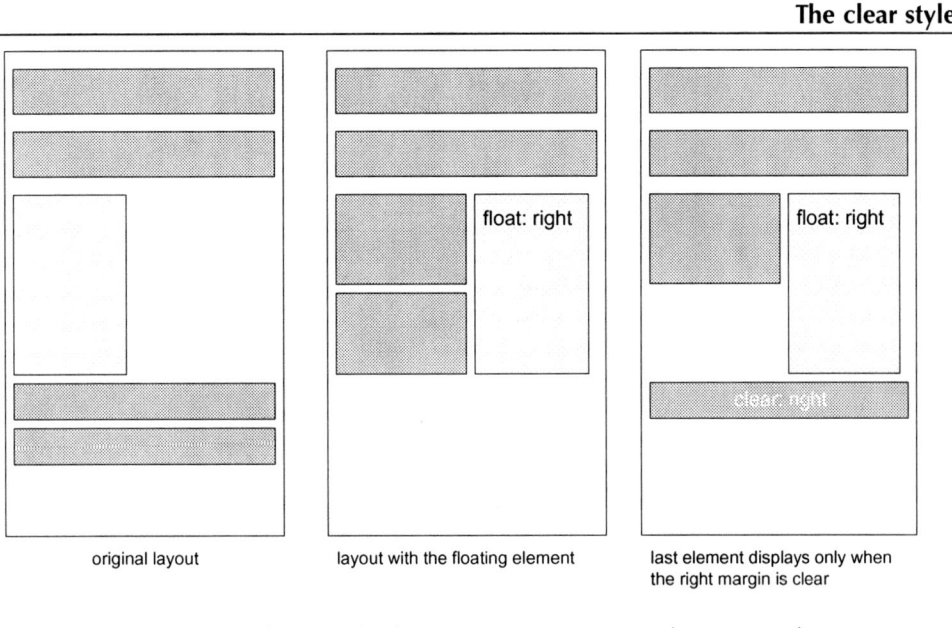

original layout   layout with the floating element   last element displays only when the right margin is clear

The clear style is most often used when you want to ensure that a page footer is always placed at the bottom of the page after all other page content has been displayed.

Floating and Clearing an Element

Reference Window

- To float an element on the left or right margin, use the style
    ```
    float: position
    ```
  where *position* is none (the default), left, or right.
- To display an element in the first available space where the specified margin is clear of floating elements, use the style
    ```
    clear: position
    ```

Stacking Elements

The ability to move elements to different locations on a page can lead to elements overlapping each other. By default, elements that are defined later in a document are placed on top of earlier elements. To specify a different stacking order, use the style

```
z-index: value
```

where *value* is a positive or negative integer or the value "auto". Elements are stacked based on their z-index values, with the highest z-index values placed on top. A value of "auto" uses the default stacking order. Figure 2-17 shows the effect of the z-index attribute on the stacking of several different elements.

Figure 2-17 | Using the z-index style

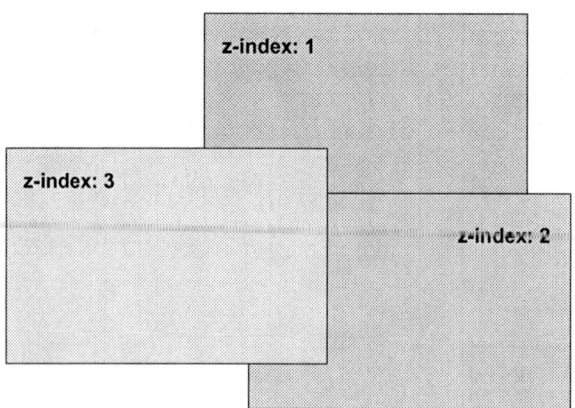

Note that the z-index attribute is applied only when elements share the same parent, and it has no effect on elements with different parent elements.

Setting the Element Display Style

Most page elements are classified as either inline elements or block-level elements. You can use CSS to change the display style applied to any element, allowing you to make inline elements appear as block-level elements and vice versa. The syntax of the display style is

```
display: type
```

where *type* is one of the CSS display types described in Figure 2-18.

Figure 2-18 | Setting the display style

Display	Description
block	Display as a block-level element
inline	Display as an inline element
inline-block	Display as an inline element with some of the properties of a block (much like an inline image or a frame)
inherit	Inherit the display property of the element's parent
list-item	Display as a list item
none	Do not display the element
run-in	Display as either an inline or a block-level element, depending on the context
table	Display as a block-level table
inline-table	Display as an inline table
table-caption	Treat as a table caption
table-cell	Treat as a table cell
table-column	Treat as a table column
table-column-group	Treat as a group of table columns
table-footer-group	Treat as a group of table footer rows
table-header-group	Treat as a group of table header rows
table-row	Treat as a table row
table-row-group	Treat as a group of table rows

For example, to display an element as a block, you can use the style

```
display: block
```

Reference Window

Setting the Display Style

- To define the display style of an element, use the style
    ```
    display: type
    ```
  where *type* is the display. Use a *type* value of "block" to format an element as a block, and use "inline" to format it is an inline element.

Hiding Elements

You can also use CSS to prevent elements from being displayed on a rendered Web page. This is useful in situations where you want one element to be displayed in a particular output medium (such as the computer screen) but not displayed in another medium (such as printed output). There are two ways of hiding an element. One is to set the value of the display style to "none", as in the following style declaration:

```
address {display: none}
```

which turns off the display of the address element. Alternatively, you can use the visibility style, which has the syntax

```
visibility: type
```

where *type* is visible, hidden, collapse, or inherit (the default). A value of "visible" makes an element visible; the "hidden" value hides the element; a value of "collapse" is used with the tables to prevent a row or column from being displayed; and the "inherit" value causes an element to inherit the visibility style from its parent. Unlike the display style, the visibility style hides an element, but does not remove it from the flow of elements in a page. As shown in Figure 2-19, setting the display style to "none" not only hides an element, but also removes it from the page flow.

Comparing the visibility and display styles ◄ **Figure 2-19**

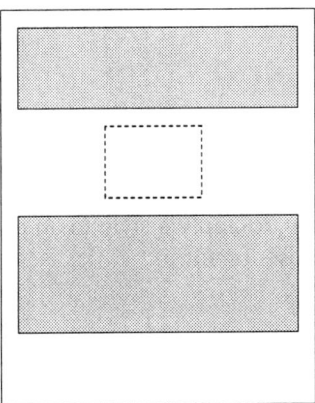

visibility: hidden

object is hidden but still
is part of the page flow

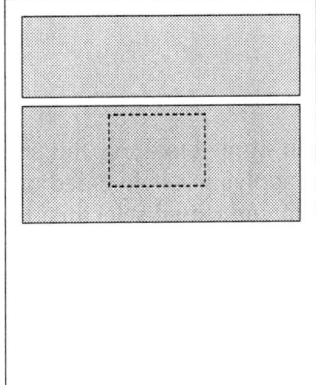

display: none

object is hidden and is
removed from the page flow

The display: none style is more appropriate for hiding elements in most cases. Use of the visibility: hidden style is usually reserved for scripts in which an element is alternatively hidden and made visible in order to create an animated effect.

Working with Selectors

Now that you've learned about some of the important styles, next you'll look at how you can apply those styles to your Web sites. So far you've looked only at styles applied to individual elements. However, CSS also allows you to work with selectors that match different combinations of elements. For example, if you want to apply the same style to a collection of elements, you can group them by entering the elements in a comma-separated list. This feature allows you to replace a set of repetitive declarations, such as

```
h1 {font-family: sans-serif}
h2 {font-family: sans-serif}
h3 {font-family: sans-serif}
h4 {font-family: sans-serif}
h5 {font-family: sans-serif}
h6 {font-family: sans-serif}
```

with a single declaration, such as

```
h1, h2, h3, h4, h5, h6 {font-family: sans-serif}
```

You can also combine grouped and ungrouped selectors. In the following example, the h1 headings are displayed in a red sans-serif font, while the h2 headings are displayed in a blue sans-serif font.

```
h1, h2 {font-family: sans-serif}
h1 {color: red}
h2 {color: blue}
```

Placing common styles in a single declaration is a useful way of simplifying your style sheets.

Contextual Selectors

Sometimes you want to apply styles to elements depending on how those elements are used in a document. For example, the following style causes all boldfaced text to appear in a blue:

```
b {color: blue}
```

However, if you wanted to apply this style only to boldfaced text within lists, you would need a way of applying a style based on the context in which an element is used. You can do this with **contextual selectors**. For example, to apply a style to an element only when it is descended from another element, you use the form

```
parent descendant {styles}
```

where *parent* is the parent element, *descendant* is a descendant of the parent, and *styles* are the styles to be applied to the descendant element. Thus, to apply a blue color only to boldfaced text found in lists, you use the style

```
li b {color: blue}
```

In this case li is the parent element and b is the descendant element. Any boldfaced text not contained in a list item is not affected by this style. Note that the descendant element does not have to be direct child of the parent element. In the code

```
<li><span><b>Special</b> Orders</span> this month!</li>
```

the boldfaced text is a descendant of the list item, but it is a direct child of the span element.

Contextual selectors can also be grouped with other selectors. The following style applies a blue font to h2 headings and to boldfaced list items, but nowhere else:

```
li b, h2 {color: blue}
```

The parent/descendant form is only one example of a contextual selector. Figure 2-20 shows some of the other contextual forms supported by CSS.

Simple and contextual selectors ◄ | **Figure 2-20**

Selector	Description
*	Matches any element in the hierarchy
e	Matches any element, e, in the hierarchy
e1, e2, e3, ...	Matches the group of elements e1, e2, e3, ...
e f	Matches any element, f, that is a descendant of an element, e
e > f	Matches any element, f, that is a direct child of an element, e
e + f	Matches any element, f, that is immediately preceded by a sibling element, e

To illustrate just how versatile these patterns can be, Figure 2-21 shows six selector patterns applied to the same document tree. Selected elements are highlighted in red for each pattern. Remember that because of style inheritance, any style applied to an element is passed down the document tree.

Examples of selector patterns ◄ | **Figure 2-21**

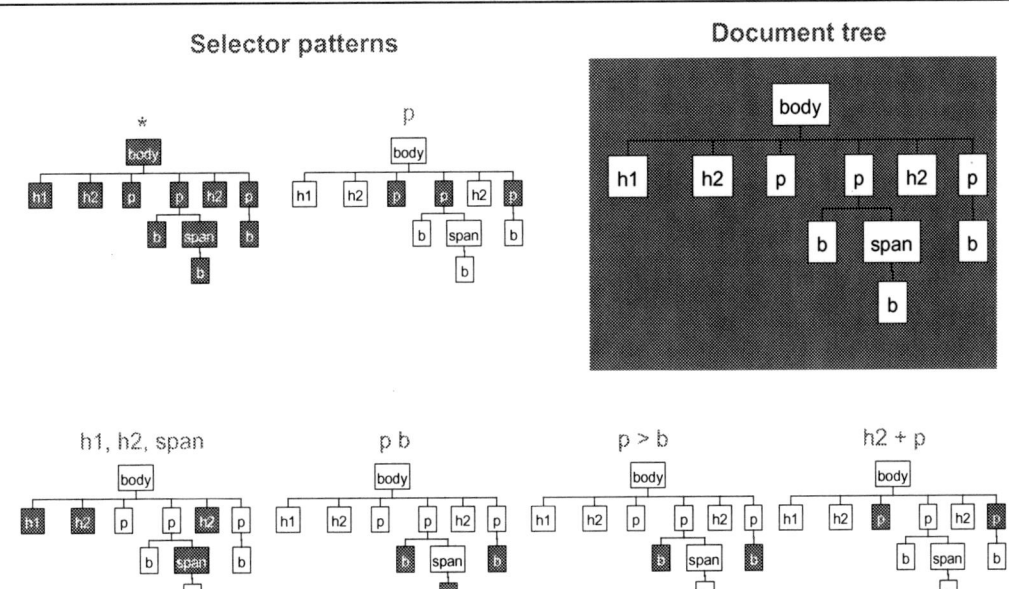

While the contextual selectors listed in Figure 2-20 are part of the specifications for CSS2, they may not be well supported by many browsers. The *e* > *f* and *e* + *f* contextual selectors in particular should be used with caution.

Attribute Selectors

On occasion, you might also need to select elements based on their attribute values. For example, if you want to display link text in a blue font, you can use the following declaration:

```
a {color: blue}
```

However, this declaration makes no distinction between <a> tags used to mark links and <a> tags used to mark document anchors. HTML makes this distinction based on the presence or absence of the href attribute. To select an element based on the element's attributes you can create an **attribute selector**. For example, the selector

```
element[att] {styles}
```

selects all elements named *element* which contain an attribute named `att` and applies the `styles` in the list to them. Thus, to apply a blue font to link text, you use the declaration

```
a[href] {color: blue}
```

Any <a> tag used to mark anchors does not contain the href attribute, and thus is not affected by this style. Figure 2-22 describes some of the other attribute selectors supported by CSS.

| Figure 2-22 | Attribute selectors |

Selector	Description	Example	Interpretation
[att]	The element contains the *att* attribute	a[href]	Matches a elements containing the href attribute
[att="val"]	The element's *att* attribute equals "val"	a[href="gloss.htm"]	Matches a elements whose href attribute equals "gloss.htm"
[att~="val"]	The element's *att* attribute value is a space-separated list of words, one of which is exactly "val"	a[rel~="glossary"]	Matches a elements whose rel attribute contains the word "glossary"
[att|="val"]	The element's *att* attribute value is a hyphen-separated list of words, beginning with "val"	p[id|="first"]	Matches paragraphs whose id attribute starts with the word "first" in a hyphen-separated list of words
[att^="val"]	The element's *att* attribute begins with *val* (CSS3)	a[rel^="prev"]	Matches a elements whose rel attribute begins with "prev"
[att$="val"]	The element's *att* attribute ends with *val* (CSS3)	a[href$="org"]	Matches a elements whose href attribute ends with "org"
[att*="val"]	The element's *att* attribute contains the value *val* (CSS3)	a[href*="faq"]	Matches a elements whose href attribute contains the text string "faq"

As with contextual selectors, browser support for attribute selectors is mixed. For this reason, you should use attribute selectors with caution. Note that some of the attribute selectors listed in Figure 2-22 are part of the proposed specifications for CSS3 and have very little browser support at the present time.

Applying Styles to IDs and Classes

CSS provides selectors to apply styles to elements based on their id and class values. To apply a style to an element based on the value of its id attribute, use the form

`#id {styles}`

where *id* is the id value of an element in the document. For example, if you want to center the text in the following h1 heading:

`<h1 id="company">Pixal Products</h1>`

you use the following style declaration in the embedded or external style sheet:

`#company {text-align: right}`

Recall that each id is unique and cannot be applied to more than one element. To identify a group of elements you use the class attribute. To apply a style to a group of elements based on the value of their class attribute, use the selector

`.class {styles}`

where *class* is the value of the class attribute for the group. Figure 2-23 shows how applying a style based on class values can be used to apply the same style to a group of elements.

Applying a style to a class ◄ Figure 2-23

```
<ul>
  <li class="fruit">Apples</li>
  <li class="vegetable">Carrots</li>
  <li class="fruit">Grapes</li>
  <li class="vegetable">Lettuce</li>
  <li class="fruit">Melons</li>
  <li class="vegetable">Onions</li>
</ul>
```

elements

```
.fruit {color: red}
.vegetable  {color: green}
```

styles

. Apples
. Carrots
. Grapes
. Lettuce
. Melons
. Onions

rendered content

If you want to apply a style to a class of elements of a particular type, include the element name along with the class value using the form

`element.class {styles}`

where *element* and *class* are the element and class names, respectively. Figure 2-24 demonstrates how to use the class value along with an element name to format the h1 and h2 headings described above. Note that the sans-serif font is applied to any element of the title class, but the italic font style is only applied to h2 headings in the title class.

| Figure 2-24 | Applying a style to a class and element |

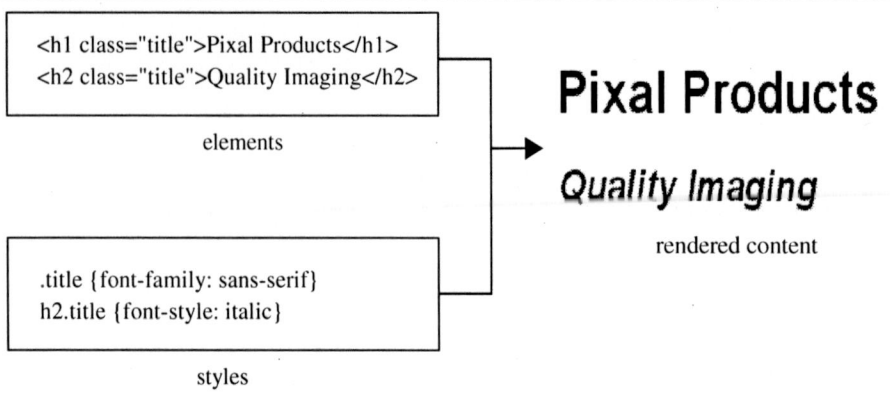

Reference Window

Applying Styles to ids and Classes

- To apply styles to an element with an id, use the form
    `#id {styles}`
  where `id` is the value of the id attribute for the element.
- To apply styles to a class of elements, use the form
    `.class {styles}`
  where `class` is the value of the class attribute for the elements.
- To apply styles to a class of elements of a particular type, use the form
    `element.class {styles}`
  where `element` is the name of the element.

Applying Styles to Pseudoclasses and Pseudoelements

Another selector form is based on pseudoclasses. A **pseudoclass** is a classification of an element based on its status, position, or current use in a document. For example, one pseudoclass indicates whether a user has previously visited a link. Another pseudoclass indicates whether the links is currently being activated or clicked. To create a style for a pseudoclass, use the style

`selector:pseudoclass {styles}`

where `selector` is an element or group of elements within the document, `pseudoclass` is the name of a pseudoclass, and `styles` are the styles you want to apply. Figure 2-25 lists some of the pseudoclasses supported by CSS.

Pseudo classes | Figure 2-25

Pseudo class	Description	Example
link	The link has not yet been visited by the user	a:link {color: red}
visited	The link has been visited by the user	a:visited {color: green}
active	The link is in the process of being activated by the user	a:active {color: yellow}
hover	The mouse pointer is hovering over the link (CSS2)	a:hover {color: blue}
focus	The element has received the focus of the keyboard or mouse pointer (CSS2)	input.focus {background-color: yellow}
first-child	The element is the first child of its parent (CSS2)	p:first-child {text-indent: 0}
lang	The language to be used with the element (CSS2)	q:lang(FR) {quotes: '«' '»'}

If you wanted to change the font color of all previously visited links to red, for example, you could use the style declaration

```
a:visited {color: red}
```

Pseudoclasses are often used to create **rollover effects**, in which effects are applied to elements when a user's mouse pointer hovers over them. For example, the following styles remove the underlining from all links in a document *except* when a user hovers the mouse pointer over a link, in which case an underline appears:

```
a {text-decoration: none}
a:hover {text-decoration: underline}
```

In some cases, two or more pseudoclasses can apply to the same element—for example, a link can be both previously visited and hovered over. In such situations, the standard cascading rules apply: the style that is more heavily weighted or declared last is applied to the element. Because of the cascading rules, order is important. The hover pseudoclass is used only if it is listed after the link and visited pseudoclasses. Similarly, the active pseudoclass should be listed last in preference to the link, visited, and hover pseudoclasses.

Thus far all of the selectors have been based on elements that exist somewhere in the document hierarchy. However, you can also define selectors that are not actual elements, but are instead abstracted from what you know of an element's content, use, or position. For example, a paragraph element is part of a document, but the first letter of that paragraph is not (there is no "first letter" element). You can work with this kind of abstracted element by treating it as a **pseudoelement**.

CSS supports a wide variety of pseudoelements, including those that select the first letter or first line of an element's content. The syntax for creating a style declaration for a pseudoelement is similar to that for a pseudoclass:

```
selector:pseudoelement {styles}
```

where *selector* is an element or group of elements within a document, *pseudoelement* is an abstract element based on the selector, and *styles* are the styles that you want to apply to the pseudoelement. Figure 2-26 lists some of the pseudoelements supported by CSS.

Figure 2-26 **Pseudoelements**

Pseudoelement	Description	Example
first-letter	The first letter of the element text	p:first-letter {font-size: 14pt}
first-line	The first line of the element text	p:first-line {text-transform: uppercase}
before	Content to be placed directly before the element (CSS2)	p:before {content: "Special!"}
after	Content to be placed directly after the element (CSS2)	p:after {content: "eof"}

For example, to display the first letter of every paragraph in a gold fantasy font, you use the declaration

```
p:first-letter {font-family: fantasy; color: gold}
```

You can use pseudoelements to create drop-caps. To create a dropped cap, you increase the font size of an element's first letter and float it on the left margin. Dropped caps also generally look better if you decrease the line height of the first letter, enabling the surrounding content to better wrap around the letter.

Reference Window

Working with PseudoClasses and PseudoElements

- To create a style for a pseudoclass, use the style
     selector:pseudoclass {styles}
  where selector is an element or group of elements within the document, pseudoclass is the name of a pseudoclass, and styles are the styles you want to apply to the selector. Some useful pseudoclasses are the link, visited, hover, and active pseudoclasses; these are applied to the a element to format linked, visited, hovered, and active hyperlinks.
- To create a style for a pseudoelement, use the style
     selector:pseudoelement {styles}
  where selector is an element or group of elements within the document, pseudoelement is the name of a pseudoelement, and styles are the styles you want to apply to the pseudoelement. Some useful pseudoelements are the first-line and first-letter pseudoelements, which represent the first line or first letter of an element's content.

Working with Different Media

By default, a style sheet is applied to all devices, and each device must determine how best to match the styles specified to its own requirements. For example, when you print a Web page, a Web browser and its built-in styles prepare the document for the printer. A user has some control over that process—for example, determining the size of the page margins or the content of the printout's header or footer.

You can use the media attribute in either the link or style element to define the output device for a specific style sheet. For example, to specify that an external style sheet named "sounds.css" should be used for aural browsers, you enter the following link element in your HTML or XHTML document:

```
<link href="sounds.css" type="text/css" media="aural" />
```

In the same way, you use the media attribute in an embedded style sheet to indicate that its styles are intended for aural devices:

```
<style type="text/css" media="aural">
...
</style>
```

The media attribute can also contain a comma-separated list of media types. The following link element links to a style sheet designed for both print and screen media:

```
<link href="output.css" type="text/css" media="print, screen" />
```

Style sheets cascade through different media types in the same way they cascade through a document tree. A style sheet in which the output device is not specified is applied to all devices, unless it is superseded by a style designed for a particular device. In the following set of embedded style sheets, h1 headings are displayed in a sans-serif font for all devices; however, text color is red for computer screens and black for printed pages:

```
<style type="text/css">
   h1 {font-family: sans-serif}
</style>
<style type="text/css" media="screen">
   h1 {color: red}
</style>
<style type="text/css" media="print">
   h1 {color: black}
</style>
```

The @media Rule

You can also specify the output media within a style sheet using the following rule:

```
@media type {style declarations}
```

where *type* is one of the supported media types and *style declarations* are the styles associated with that media type. For example, the following declarations set the font size of body text and h1 headings for a variety of different output media:

```
@media screen {body {font-size: 1em} h1 {font-size: 2em}}
@media print {body {font-size: 12pt} h1 {font-size: 16pt}}
@media handheld {body {font-size: 8pt} h1 {font-size: 12pt}}
@media tv {body {font-size: 16pt} h1 {font-size: 24pt}}
```

In this style sheet the font size is smallest for a handheld device (which presumably has a limited screen area), and largest for a television (which is usually viewed from a greater distance). Similar to the media attribute, the @media rule also allows you to place media types in a comma-separated list:

```
@media screen, print, handheld, tv {h1 {font-family: sans-serif}}
```

Both the media attribute and the @media rule come with their own benefits and disadvantages. The @media rule allows you to consolidate all of your styles within a single style sheet; however, this consolidation can result in larger and complicated files. The alternative, placing media styles in different sheets, can make those sheets easier to maintain; however, if you change the design of your site, you may have to duplicate your changes across several style sheets.

Creating Styles for Different Media

- To create a style sheet for a specific media, add the following attribute to either the link element or the style element:
  ```
  media="type"
  ```
  where *type* is one or more of the following: aural, braille, embossed, handheld, print, projection, screen, tty, tv, or all. If you don't specify a value for the media attribute, the style sheet is applied to all media. Multiple types should be entered in a comma-separated list.
- To create style declarations for a specific media within a style sheet, use the form
  ```
  @media type {style declarations}
  ```

Supporting Older Browsers

Many older browsers do not support the media attribute, the @media rule, or many CSS2 styles. For these older browsers, the most common practice for formatting output for different media is to link each page to a **printer-friendly version** of the document, which is formatted specifically for printing. While this approach comes with the drawback of forcing you to create and maintain duplicate copies of your pages, it provides users a choice of printed styles. They can print from the page as it appears on the computer screen or use the specially formatted print style that you design.

Media Groups

Despite the differences among various types of output media, they do share some common properties. The computer screen and the printed page are both visual media. A sound recording is not visual but aural. Output sent to a television might be both visual and aural. CSS2 organizes these different basic properties into **media groups**. There are four media groups that describe a basic facet of the output. The output media can be:

- Continuous or paged
- Visual, aural, or tactile
- Grid (for character grid devices) or bitmap
- Interactive (for devices that allow user interaction) or static (for devices that allow no interaction)

Figure 2-27 shows how each output media is categorized based on the four media groups. A printout is paged (because the output comes in discrete units or pages), visual, bitmap, and static (you can't interact with it). A computer screen is continuous, visual, bitmap, and can be either static or interactive.

Media groups ◀ Figure 2-27

Media Types	Media Groups			
	continuous/ paged	visual/aural/ tactile	grid/ bitmap	interactive/ static
aural	continuous	aural	N/A	both
braille	continuous	tactile	grid	both
embossed	paged	tactile	grid	both
handheld	both	visual	both	both
print	paged	visual	bitmap	static
projection	paged	visual	bitmap	static
screen	continuous	visual	bitmap	both
tty	continuous	visual	grid	both
tv	both	visual, aural	bitmap	both

Media groups are important because the CSS2 specifications indicate which media group a particular style belongs to rather than the specific media device. For example, the font-size style belongs to the visual media group, meaning that you should be able to use it with handheld, print, projection, screen, tty, and tv media. The pitch style, used to define the pitch or frequency of a speaking voice, belongs to the aural media group, which means that it should be supported by aural and tv devices. Studying the media groups can help you choose the styles that apply to a given output device.

Using Print Styles

CSS2 defines printed pages by extending the box model described earlier to incorporate the entire page in a **page box**. As with other objects in the box model, you can specify the size of a page, the page margins, the internal padding, and so on. Although a page box specifies how a document should be rendered within the rectangular area of the page, it is the browser's responsibility to transfer that model to the printed sheet. The general rule to create and define a page box is

```
@page {styles}
```

where `styles` are the styles you want applied to the page. For example, the following embedded style sets the page margin for the printed output to 5 inches and displays the page's body text in a 12pt serif font:

```
<style type="text/css" media="print">
   @page {margin: 5in}
   body {font-size: 12pt; font-family: serif}
</style>
```

A page box does not support all of the measurement units you've used with the other elements. For example, pages do not support the em or ex measurement units.

Page Pseudoclasses and Named Pages

In some cases you may need to define multiple page styles within the same document. You can do this through pseudoclasses or page names. The syntax to apply a pseudoclass to a page is

```
@page:pseudoclass {styles}
```

where *pseudoclass* is one of the three following supported types:

- **first**: For the first page of the printout
- **left**: For pages that appear on the left in double-sided printouts
- **right**: For pages that appear on the right in double-sided printouts

For example, if you are doing two-sided printing, you may wish to mirror the margins of the left and right pages of the printout. The following styles result in pages in which the inner margin is set to 5 centimeters and outer margin is set to 2 centimeters:

```
@page:left {margin: 3cm 5cm 3cm 2cm}
@page:right {margin: 3cm 2cm 3cm 5cm}
```

To format specific pages other than the first, left, or right pages, you can create a named label for a page style and then apply that page to particular elements in your document. The syntax to create a page name is

```
@page name {styles}
```

where *name* is the label assigned to the page style. To access a named page, use the page style in a style declaration as follows:

```
selector {page: name}
```

For example, the following styles define a page named "large_margins" and then indicate that this page should be used for every instance of a table in a document:

```
@page large_margins {margin: 10cm}
table {page: large_margins}
```

Note that named pages can be applied only to block-level elements, meaning that you cannot apply them to inline elements. Also, if two consecutive block-level elements are assigned different page names, browsers automatically insert a page break between the elements.

Setting the Page Size

The size of the output page can be defined using the size style. With this style, Web authors can define the dimensions of the printed page, as well as whether pages should be printed in portrait or landscape orientation. The syntax of the size style is

```
size: width height orientation
```

where *width* and *height* are the width and height of the page, and *orientation* is the orientation of the page (portrait or landscape). If you don't specify the orientation, browsers assume a portrait orientation. To format a page as a standard-size page in landscape orientation with a 1-inch margin, you could use the style

```
@page {size: 8.5in 11in landscape; margin: 1in}
```

If you remove the orientation value, as in the style

```
@page {size: 8.5in 11in; margin: 1in}
```

browsers default to an orientation setting of portrait. You can also replace the width, height, and orientation values with the keyword "auto" (to let the browser determine the page dimensions and orientation) or "inherit" (to inherit the page size and orientation from the parent element). If a page does not fit into the dimensions specified by the style, browsers either rotate the page box 90 degrees or scale the page box to fit the sheet size.

Displaying Crop Marks

In high-quality printing, crop marks are used to define where a page should be trimmed before binding. CSS2 supports the marks property, which adds crop marks to a printed sheet. The syntax of the marks style is

```
marks: type
```

where *type* is crop, cross, inherit, or none. Figure 2-28 shows examples of the crop and cross values.

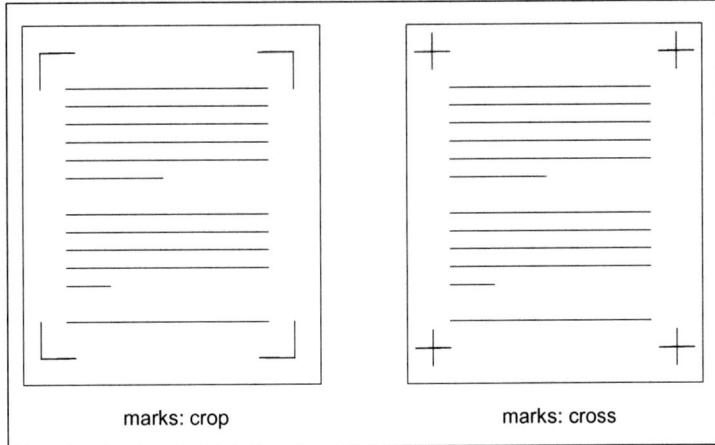

marks: crop   marks: cross

The size, style, and position of the crop marks depend on the browser.

Working with Page Breaks

CSS supports three styles that determine where page breaks should be placed in relation to the elements in a page. The page-break-before and page-break-after styles are used to place page breaks before or after a given element. The syntax of the page-break-before and page-break-after styles is

```
page-break-before: type
page-break-after: type
```

where *type* is always (to always place a page break), avoid (to never place a page break), left (to force a page break where the succeeding page is a left page), right (to force a page break where the succeeding page is a right page), auto (to allow the browser to determine whether or not to insert a page break), or inherit (to inherit the page break style of the parent element). For example, if you want tables to always appear on their own pages, you can place a page break before and after each table using the following style:

```
table {page-break-before: always; page-break-after: always}
```

You can also prevent the insertion of a page break using the page-break-inside style with the following syntax:

```
page-break-inside: type
```

where *type* is auto, inherit, or avoid. If you wanted to avoid placing a page break inside of a table, you use the following style:

```
table {page-break-inside: avoid}
```

Note that the avoid type does not guarantee that there will not be a page break within the element. If the content of an element exceeds the dimensions of the sheet, the browser may be forced to insert a page break.

You can combine the various page styles to provide greater control over printed output. For example, if your document contains several wide tables, you can place the tables on separate pages in landscape orientation using the following style declarations:

```
@page table_page {8.5in 11in landscape}
table {page: table_page; page-break-before: always; page-break-inside:
avoid; page-break-after: always}
```

Finally, you can use CSS2 to control the sizes of the widows and orphans that appear when a page break is inserted within an element. A **widow** refers to the final few lines of an element's text when they appear at the top of a page, while most of the element's text appears on the previous page. The term **orphan** describes the first few lines of an element's text when they appear at the bottom of a page, with the bulk of the element's text appearing on the next page. The styles to control widows and orphans are

```
widow: value
orphan: value
```

where value is the number of lines that must appear within the element before a page break is inserted. The default value is 2, which means that widows and orphans must both contain at least two lines of text. If you wanted to increase the size of widows and orphans to three lines for the paragraphs of your document, you use the following style declaration:

```
p {widow: 3; orphan: 3}
```

It's important to note that browsers might not always implement the widow and orphan values that you specify. Browsers attempt to use page breaks that obey the following guidelines:

- Insert all of the manual page breaks as indicated by the page-break-before, page-break-after, and page-break-inside styles.
- Avoid inserting page breaks where indicated in the style sheet.
- Break the pages as few times as possible.
- Make all pages that don't have a forced page break appear to have the same height.
- Avoid page breaking inside of a block-level element that has a border.
- Avoid breaking inside of a table.
- Avoid breaking inside of a floating element.

Only after attempting to satisfy these constraints are the recommendations of the widow and orphan styles applied.

Working with Print Styles

- To define a page box for a printout that indicates the page size, margins, and orientation, use the declaration
    `@page {styles}`
  where *styles* are the styles you want used to define the page.
- To apply a style to a particular page, use the declaration
    `@page:pseudoclass {styles}`
  where *pseudoclass* is first (for the first page), left (for pages that appear on the left), or right (for pages that appear on the right).
- To set the page size and orientation use the style
    `size: width height orientation`
  where *width* and *height* are the width and height of the page, and *orientation* is the orientation of the page (portrait or landscape).
- To display crop marks, use the style
    `marks: type`
  where *type* is crop, cross, inherit, or none.
- To format the page break before an element, use the style
    `page-break-before: type`
  where *type* is always (to always place a page break), avoid (to never place a page break), left (to force a page break where the succeeding page is a left page), right (to force a page break where the succeeding page is a right page), auto (to allow the browser to determine whether or not to insert a page break), or inherit (to inherit the page break style of the parent element).
- To format the page break after an element, use the style
    `page-break-after: type`
  where *type* has the same values as for the page-break-before style.
- To apply a page break inside an element, use the style
    `page-break-inside: type`
  where *type* is auto, inherit, or avoid.

Review Summary

In this review you learned about the history and syntax of Cascading Style Sheets. You saw how to apply style sheets to a Web page using inline styles, embedded styles, and external style sheets. You also saw how style definitions are inherited and cascade through the contents of a given document, as well as all of the documents in a Web site. This review also covered the different styles supported by CSS. You learned about the different styles that apply to fonts, text, colors, and images. You also learned how to create styles to resize elements, apply borders, and set the margin and padding size. The review also discussed how to use CSS to position elements on a page. In the later part of the review you learned about different selector forms and how to apply styles to elements based on their uses in documents, their id values, and their class values. The review also covered how to work with pseudoclasses and pseudoelements to create effects such as rollovers and dropped caps. The review concluded with a discussion of style sheets designed for different media output, as well as specific styles designed for printed output.

Key Terms

absolute position	external style	relative position
absolute unit	fixed position	relative unit
attribute selector	generic font	rollover effect
box model	inline style	scalable
Cascading Style Sheets	kerning	selector
contextual selector	leading	specific font
CSS	media group	static position
CSS1	orphan	style inheritance
CSS2	page box	style sheet
CSS2.1	pixel	tracking
CSS3	printer-friendly version	watermark
em unit	pseudoclass	widow
embedded style	pseudoelement	
ex unit		

Review Questions

1. What is a style sheet?
2. What is CSS?
3. What are the three ways of applying a style sheet to a document?
4. What is the syntax for applying an inline style?
5. What inline style would you add to an h1 heading to change the color of the text "Pixal Products" to blue?
6. What is the syntax for creating an embedded style sheet?
7. What is the syntax of a style declaration within an embedded or external style sheet?
8. What code would you enter to create an embedded style sheet that sets the color of all h1 headings to blue?
9. What attribute would you add to the style element to indicate that a style sheet is designed for printed media?
10. What code would you enter to create a link to the external style sheet file "styles.css"? Assume that the style sheet is designed for printed media.

11. What code would you add to a style sheet to insert the comment "printed styles"?
12. What style would you enter to apply the fonts Arial, Helvetica, or sans-serif to every h3 heading in the document?
13. What are absolute units and relative units?
14. What style would you enter to increase a font size 50% from its default size?
15. What are kerning, tracking, and leading? What are the styles to set the kerning, tracking and leading values for an element?
16. What style would you use to display text in italics?
17. What single style would you enter to display text in a bold 12pt Arial font?
18. What style declaration would you enter to change the background color of a page to the color value (212, 255, 155)?
19. What style declaration would you enter to change the background image to the image file paper.jpg?
20. What style declaration would you enter to set the width and height of the element with the id "logo" to 250 pixels wide by 100 pixels high?
21. What style declaration would you enter to add a 10 pixel blue border around the logo element, displayed in the outset border style?
22. What are absolute and relative positioning?
23. What style do you enter to float an element on a page's left margin?
24. What two styles can you enter to prevent a browser from displaying an object?
25. What selector would you enter to match all bold elements placed within address elements?
26. What selector would you use to match all elements belong to the class "links"?
27. What is a pseudo-class? Give two examples of a pseudo-class.
28. What is a pseudo-element? Give two examples of a pseudo-element.
29. What style would you enter to define a page box with a 5-inch margin?
30. What style declaration would you enter to set the margins of the right page in a double-sided printout to 3 inches?
31. What style declaration would you enter to insert a page break before every h1 heading?

Objectives

Session 1.1
- Understand the history and theory of JavaScript
- Create a script element
- Understand and use basic JavaScript syntax
- Write text to a Web document using a JavaScript command

Session 1.2
- Understand the different data types supported by JavaScript
- Declare a variable and assign it a value
- Reference a variable in a JavaScript statement
- Create and call a JavaScript function
- Access functions from an external JavaScript file
- Document code with multiline and single-line comments
- Understand basic techniques for debugging JavaScript code

Introducing JavaScript

Hiding E-Mail Addresses from Spammers

Case

Monroe Public Library

Kate Howard is the head of technical services at Monroe Public Library. One of her jobs is to maintain the library's Web site. In previous years, the library has made its staff directory, including all e-mail links to library employees, available online. Kate thinks that this is an important part of making the library more accessible to everyone. However, Kate has become concerned about the security issues involved with making the staff's e-mail addresses so accessible. Kate is aware that e-mail addresses can be scanned from an HTML file and used to send junk mail to the recipients.

She would like to have some way of scrambling the e-mail addresses within the HTML code while still making them viewable when the page is rendered by a Web browser. Kate has approached you for help in writing a program to accomplish this.

Student Data Files

▼tutorial.01

▽ **tutorial folder**
mpltxt.htm
spam.js
mplstyles.css
mpl.jpg

▽ **review folder**
mpl2txt.htm
random.js
mplstyles.css
+ 11 graphic files

▽ **case1 folder**
skymaptxt.htm
datetime.js
skyweb.css
+ 26 graphic files

▽ **case2 folder**
fronttxt.htm
ads.js
random.js
styles.css
+ 7 graphic files

▽ **case3 folder**
todaytxt.htm
functions.js
back.jpg
+ 7 HTML files
+ 2 style sheets

▽ **case4 folder**
birthstxt.htm
functions.js
styles.css
logo.jpg

Session 1.1

Introduction to JavaScript

You meet with Kate to discuss her problems with Monroe library's staff directory page. She's shows you the content and page layout she has created.

To view the staff directory page:

▶ 1. Use your text editor to open **mpltxt.htm** from the tutorial.01/tutorial folder. Enter *your name* and *the date* in the comment section at the top of the file and save the file as **mpl.htm**.

▶ 2. Take some time to scroll through the file to become familiar with its contents.

▶ 3. Open **mpl.htm** in your Web browser. Figure 1-1 shows Kate's design of the staff directory.

Note that the staff directory table contains a column in which Kate wants to insert links to each employee's e-mail address; however, at present, the column is empty.

Figure 1-1 ▶ **The staff directory at the Monroe Public Library Web page**

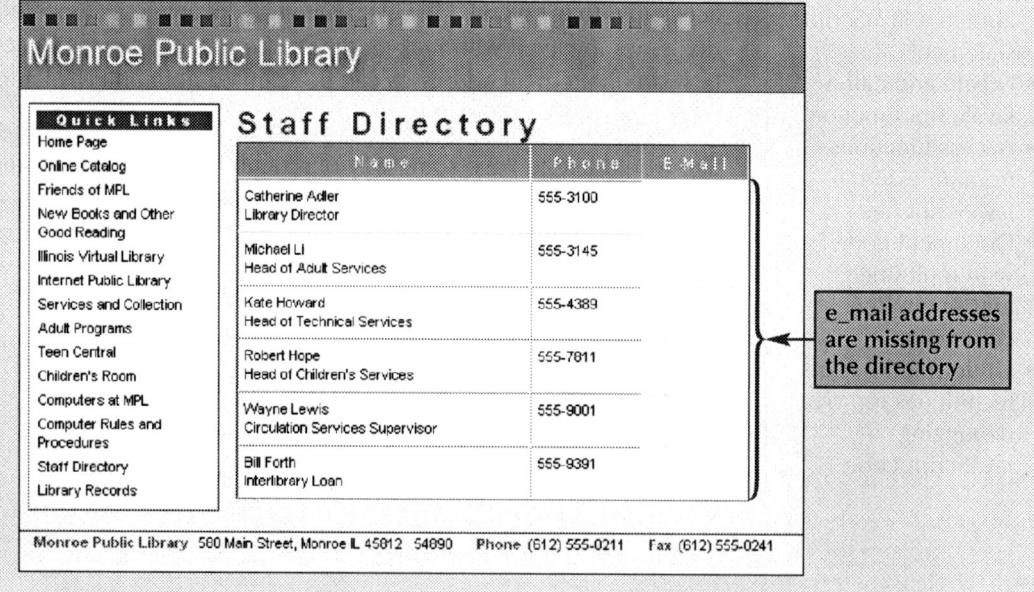

While the staff directory page has proven invaluable in making library employees more responsive to the needs of the public, Kate is concerned with the security risks of putting e-mail addresses in that directory. Kate is most concerned about spam. **Spam** is essentially junk e-mail, advertising products and services not requested by the recipient. A **spammer** is a person who sends spam—sometimes in bulk e-mailings involving tens of thousands of e-mail recipients. Aside from the annoyance of receiving unsolicited e-mail, spam costs companies thousands, and sometimes millions, of dollars each year by consuming valuable resources on mail servers and other devices forced to process bulk e-mailings. Spam also reduces productivity by forcing employees to wade through numerous spam messages every day to find those messages that are truly relevant.

One way that spammers collect e-mail addresses is through the use of e-mail harvesters. An **e-mail harvester** is a program that scans documents, usually Web pages, looking for e-mail addresses. Any e-mail address the harvester finds within the document code is added to a database, which can then be used for sending spam. Kate's main concern is that by putting the staff's e-mail addresses in the HTML code for the staff directory, she is also making them available to e-mail harvesters (see Figure 1-2).

Harvesting e-mail addresses ◄ **Figure 1-2**

```
<tr>
    <td>Catherine Adler<br />Library Director</td>
    <td>555-3100</td>
    <td>
        <a href="mailto:cadler@mpl.gov">cadler@mpl.gov</a>
    </td>
</tr>
<tr>
    <td>Michael Li<br />Head of Adult Services</td>
    <td>555-3145</td>
    <td>
        <a href="mailto:mikeli@mpl.gov">mikeli@mpl.gov</a>
    </td>
</tr>
<tr>
    <td>Kate Howard<br />Head of Technical Services</td>
    <td>555-4389</td>
    <td>
        <a href="mailto:khoward@mpl.gov">khoward@mpl.gov</a>
    </td>
</tr>
<tr>
    <td>Robert Hope<br />Head of Children's Services</td>
    <td>555-7811</td>
    <td>
        <a href="mailto:rhope@mpl.gov">rhope@mpl.gov</a>
    </td>
</tr>
<tr>
    <td>Wayne Lewis<br />Circulation Services Supervisor</td>
    <td>555-9001</td>
    <td>
        <a href="mailto:wlewis@mpl.gov">wlewis@mpl.gov</a>
    </td>
</tr>
<tr>
    <td>Bill Forth<br />Interlibrary Loan</td>
    <td>555-9391</td>
    <td>
        <a href="mailto:bforth@mpl.gov">bforth@mpl.gov</a>
    </td>
</tr>
```

Ah! E-mail addresses!

e-mail addresses in the staff directory

Kate would like you to scramble the e-mail addresses so they don't appear within the Web page code, but when a browser loads and renders the page for a user, the e-mail addresses are unscrambled (see Figure 1-3). This mechanism will thwart most e-mail harvesters examining the document's HTML code while still making the addresses available to users who are viewing the page on the Web. Note that some e-mail harvesters can view both the underlying code and the page as it's rendered by a browser, meaning that the proposed scrambling method is not 100% effective. However, since this technique will thwart many e-mail harvesters in use, Kate accepts it as a compromise solution.

Figure 1-3	Scrambling e-mail addresses

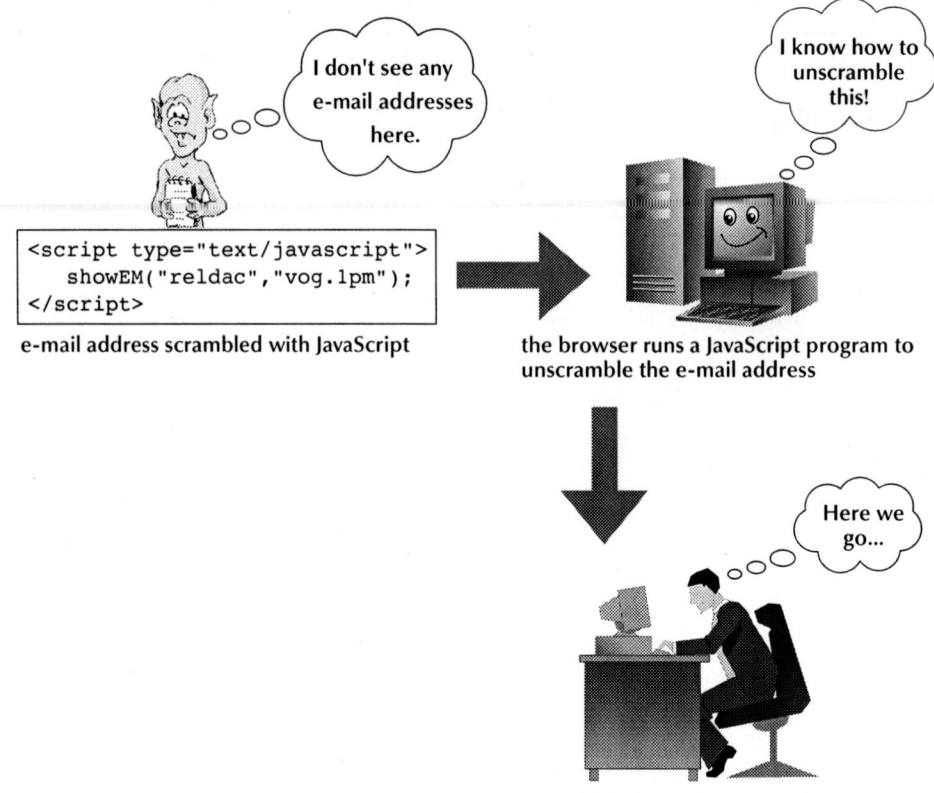

```
<script type="text/javascript">
   showEM("reldac","vog.1pm");
</script>
```

e-mail address scrambled with JavaScript

the browser runs a JavaScript program to unscramble the e-mail address

which the end user can view

You tell Kate that you'll have to write a program to scramble and unscramble the e-mail addresses from her staff directory as this is neither a feature offered by HTML or XHTML nor a standard function of Web browsers. Kate doesn't want to force library patrons to download any special applications to perform this operation. After some discussion you decide that JavaScript is well suited to this task. You'll start on this project by first finding out just what JavaScript is and how to use it.

Server-Side and Client-Side Programming

Programming on the Web comes in two types: server-side programming and client-side programming. In **server-side programming**, a program is placed on the server that hosts a Web site. The program is then used to modify the contents and structure of Web pages. In some cases, users can interact with the program, requesting that specific information be displayed on a page (see Figure 1-4), but all interaction is done remotely—from the user to the server.

Server-side programming | Figure 1-4

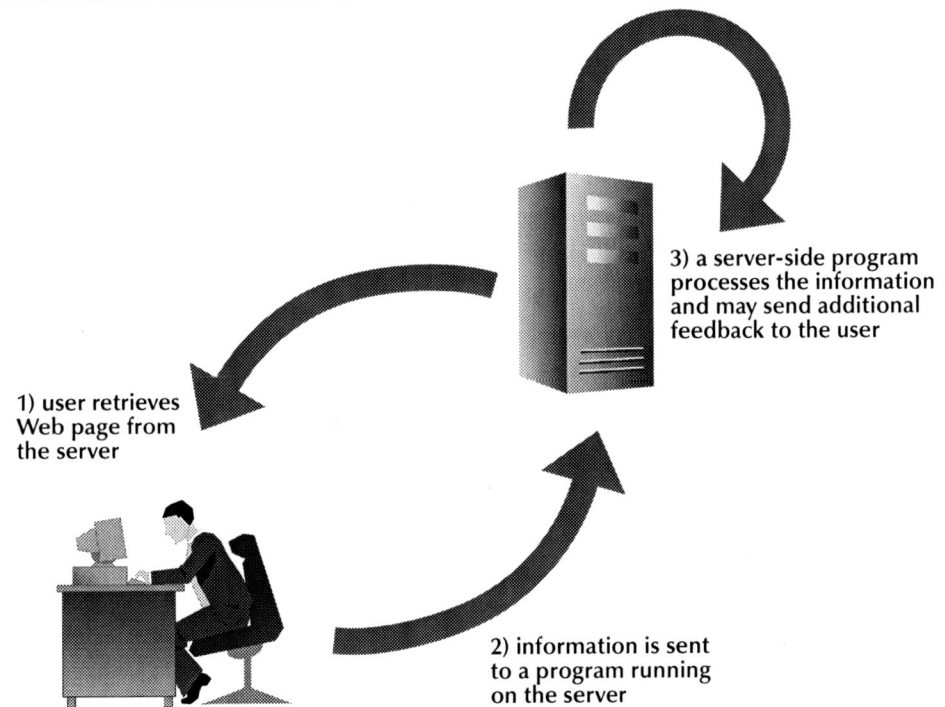

3) a server-side program processes the information and may send additional feedback to the user

1) user retrieves Web page from the server

2) information is sent to a program running on the server

There are advantages and disadvantages to this approach. A program running on a server can be connected to a database containing information not usually accessible to end users, allowing them to perform tasks not available on the client side. This enables Web pages to support such features as online banking, credit card transactions, and discussion groups. However, server-side programs use Web server resources, and in some cases a server's system administrator might place limitations on access to server-side programs to prevent users from continually accessing the server and potentially overloading the system. If the system is overloaded, an end user might have to sit through long delays as the server-side program handles multiple requests for information and action.

Client-side programming solves many of these problems by running programs on each user's own computer rather than remotely off the server (see Figure 1-5). Computing is thus distributed so that the server is not overloaded with program-related requests. Client-side programs are also likely to be more responsive to users, because users do not have to wait for data to be sent over the Internet to a Web server. However, client-side programs can never completely replace server-side programming. If you need to run a search form or process a purchase order, for example, these types of jobs must be run from a central server, because only the server contains the database needed to complete these types of operations.

Figure 1-5 ▷ **Client-side programming**

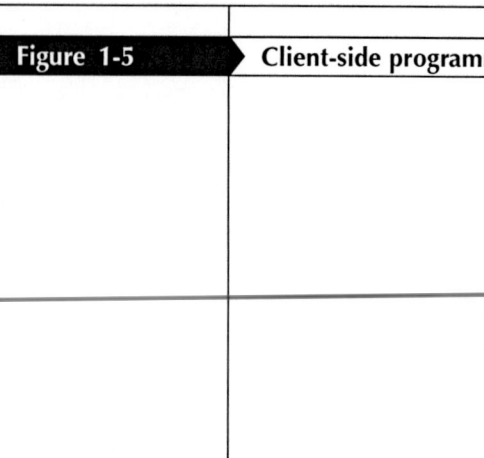

1) user retrieves
Web page from
the server

2) user runs the program
locally, receiving instant
feedback

In many cases, you use a combination of both server-side and client-side programming. For example, Web forms typically use client-side programs to validate a user's entries (such as ensuring that all address information has been completely entered) and server-side programs to submit the validated form for further processing (such as sending a purchase order to a central database). See Figure 1-6.

Figure 1-6 ▷ **Combining client-side and server-side programming**

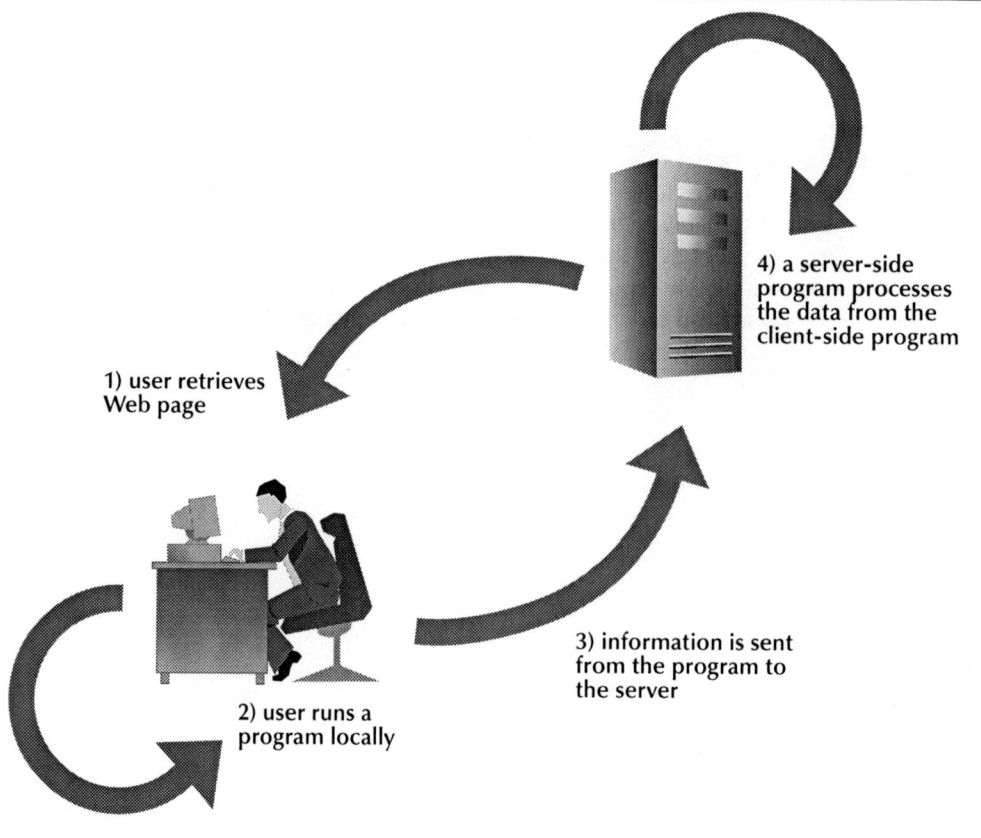

4) a server-side
program processes
the data from the
client-side program

1) user retrieves
Web page

3) information is sent
from the program to
the server

2) user runs a
program locally

In this book we'll concern ourselves only with client-side programming. However, it's important to be aware that, in many cases, a completed Web application includes both client-side and server-side elements.

The Development of JavaScript

Several programming languages can be run on the client side. One client-side programming language that has gained popular support is **Java**, which was developed by Sun Microsystems in the 1990s. Java programs are designed to be run within applications called **Java interpreters**. Because Java interpreters can be created for different operating systems, any Java program should be able to be run within a wide variety of operating systems and environments, including UNIX, Windows, and the Macintosh operating system. Just as HTML was designed to be platform independent, so was Java. Java programs that run within an interpreter are called **applets**, since they are not stand-alone applications but rely on the interpreter to run. A Java applet is downloaded along with a Web page from a Web server, but the applet itself is run on the user's computer. This frees up the Web server for other purposes.

When Java was introduced, its advantages were quickly apparent and it was soon in wide use. Netscape incorporated a Java interpreter into Netscape Navigator version 2.0, and Microsoft wasted little time including its own Java interpreter with Internet Explorer version 3.0. However, one early problem with Java was that nonprogrammers found it difficult to learn and use, and creating an executable Java applet required access to the Java Developer's Kit (JDK).

To simplify this process, a team of developers from Netscape and Sun Microsystems created a subset of Java called **JavaScript**, which was different from Java in several important ways. Java is an example of a **compiled language**, meaning that the program code must be submitted to a compiler that manipulates it, translating the code into a more basic language that machines can understand. For Java, this compiled code is the Java applet. Thus, to create and run a program written in a compiled language you need both the compiler and an application or operating system that can run the compiled code.

On the other hand, JavaScript is an **interpreted language**, meaning that the program code is executed directly without compiling. You only need two things to use JavaScript: 1) a text editor to write the JavaScript commands, and 2) a Web browser to run the commands and display the results. JavaScript code can be inserted directly into an HTML or XHTML file or placed in a separate text file that is linked to the Web page. JavaScript is not as powerful a computing language as Java, but it is simpler to use and meets the needs of most users who want to create programmable Web pages. Figure 1-7 highlights some of the key differences between Java and JavaScript.

Comparing Java and JavaScript | Figure 1-7

Java	JavaScript
A compiled language	An interpreted language
Requires the JDK (Java Developer's Kit) to create the applet	Requires a text editor
Requires a Java virtual machine or interpreter to run the applet	Requires a browser that can interpret JavaScript code
Applet files are distinct from the HTML and XHTML code	JavaScript programs are integrated with HTML and XHTML code
Source code is hidden from the user	Source code is accessible to the user
Powerful, requiring programming knowledge and experience	Simpler, requiring less programming knowledge and experience
Secure. Programs cannot write content to the hard disk	Secure. Programs cannot write content to the hard disk; however, there are more security holes than in Java
Programs run on the client side	Programs run on the client side

Through the years, JavaScript has undergone several revisions. Internet Explorer actually supports a slightly different version of JavaScript called **JScript**. While JScript is almost identical to JavaScript, some JavaScript commands are not supported in JScript, and vice versa. In addition, although it is tempting to use commands available in the latest JavaScript or JScript versions, these commands might prevent your programs from running on older browsers. For these reasons, you should always test your JavaScript programs on a variety of Web browsers.

Because of the proliferation of competing versions and revisions of scripting languages, the responsibility for the development of a scripting standard has been transferred to an international body called the **European Computer Manufacturers Association (ECMA)**. The standard developed by the ECMA is called **ECMAScript**—though browsers still refer to it as JavaScript. Figure 1-8 lists the versions of JavaScript or JScript and their corresponding browser support.

Figure 1-8	Versions of JavaScript and JScript

Version	Browser	Year
JavaScript 1.0	Netscape Navigator 2.0	1995
JScript 1.0	Internet Explorer 1.0	1996
JavaScript 1.1	Netscape Navigator 3.0	1996
JavaScript 1.2	Netscape Navigator 4.0	1997
JScript 3.0	Internet Explorer 4.0	1997
JavaScript 1.3	Netscape Navigator 4.5	1998
JScript 5.0	Internet Explorer 5.0	1999
JavaScript 1.5	Netscape Navigator 6.0	2001

Other client-side programming languages are also available to Web page designers, such as the Internet Explorer scripting language **VBScript**. However, because of the nearly universal support for JavaScript, you'll use this language for your work on the library Web site.

Working with the Script Element

JavaScript programs can either be placed directly in an HTML file or saved in an external text file. Placing JavaScript code in a Web page file means that users need only retrieve one file from the server. In addition, because the code and the page it affects are both within the same file, it may be easier to locate and fix programming errors. However, if you place the code in a separate file, the programs you write can be shared by the different pages in your Web site. In this tutorial, you'll work with JavaScript code entered into an HTML file as well as code stored in an external file. You'll first examine how to insert JavaScript code directly into an HTML file.

Creating a Script Element

Scripts are entered into an HTML or XHTML file using the script element. The syntax of the script element is

```
<script type="mime-type">
    script commands
</script>
```

where *mime-type* defines the language in which the script is written and *script commands* are commands written in the scripting language. The type attribute is required for XHTML documents and should be used for HTML documents as well. The MIME type for JavaScript programs is "text/javascript", meaning that, for JavaScript programs, you would use the form

```
<script type="text/javascript">
   JavaScript commands
</script>
```

You may see other ways of entering script elements into Web page code. In earlier versions of HTML, the language attribute was used in place of the type attribute to indicate the script language. For older browsers, you indicate that the scripting language is JavaScript using the form

```
<script language="JavaScript">
   JavaScript commands
</script>
```

The language attribute has been deprecated and is not supported by strict applications of XHTML. Thus, you should use the type attribute in its place if you want to conform to current standards.

Note that the script element can be used with programming languages other than JavaScript. Other client-side scripting languages are identified by using a different value for the type attribute. For example, if you use VBScript from Microsoft, the MIME type is "text/vbscript". We won't be discussing VBScript in this book.

Creating a Script Element

- To place a script element into a Web page, insert the following two-sided tag:
    ```
    <script type="mime-type">
      script commands and comments
    </script>
    ```
  where *mime-type* is the MIME type of the script language. To create a script element for JavaScript, set *mime-type* to "text/javascript". The script element may be placed within either the head or body section of the document.

Placing the Script Element

When a browser encounters a script element within a file, it knows to treat any lines within the element as commands to be run. There is no limit to the number of script elements that you can use within a Web page. Script elements are processed in the order in which they appear within a file. Scripts can be placed in either the head section or body section of a document. When placed in the body section, a browser interprets and runs them as it loads the different elements of the Web page. While a single page may contain many script elements, the browser is still able to work with them as a single unit. Thus, JavaScript commands that are created in one script element can be referenced by commands in other script elements.

Creating a Statement

Now that you've reviewed some of the basics involved in entering JavaScript into your HTML files, you'll write your first piece of JavaScript code. JavaScript code consists of a series of statements. Each **statement**—also known as a **command**—is a single line that indicates an action for the browser to take. A statement should end in a semicolon as follows:

```
JavaScript statement;
```

where *JavaScript statement* is the code that the browser runs. The semicolon is the official way of notifying the browser that it has reached the end of the statement. Most browsers are very forgiving and still interpret most statements correctly if you neglect to include the ending semicolon. However, it is good programming practice to include the semicolons, and some browsers do require them.

Writing Output to a Web Document

The first piece of code you'll add to Kate's document will be to write the text of an e-mail address into the Web page. While you could enter the e-mail address directly, you'll use this opportunity to experiment with JavaScript. You'll also build on this simple statement as you progress through the rest of the tutorial. You'll insert the e-mail address for Catherine Adler as the first entry in the staff directory. Her e-mail address is

cadler@mpl.gov

To write this text to the Web document, you'll insert the statement

```
<script type="text/javascript">
   document.write("cadler@mpl.gov");
</script>
```

This document.write() statement tells the browser to send the text string "cadler@mpl. gov" to the Web page. To see how your browser would apply this command, enter the script element and command into Kate's mpl.htm file.

To write text to your Web document with JavaScript:

1. Return to **mpl.htm** in your text editor.

2. Locate the table cell after the entry for Catherine Adler and insert the following code (see Figure 1-9):

```
<script type="text/javascript">
   document.write("cadler@mpl.gov");
</script>
```

Figure 1-9 | **Inserting a script element**

```
<tr>
   <td>Catherine Adler<br />Library Director</td>
   <td>555-3100</td>
   <td>
      <script type="text/javascript">
         document.write("cadler@mpl.gov");
      </script>
   </td>
</tr>
```

← script to write content to the Web document

3. Save your changes to the file and then reload **mpl.htm** in your Web browser. As shown in Figure 1-10, the text of Catherine's e-mail address should appear in the staff directory.

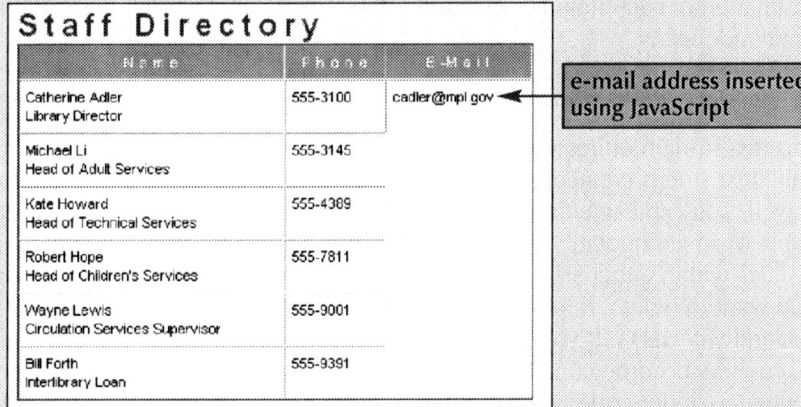

Trouble? If you are running Netscape, you may have to reopen the Web page rather than refresh it in your browser window.

Trouble? Internet Explorer may display a yellow alert bar at the top of the Web document with the warning that it has restricted access to active content for security reasons. This is done to allow users to prevent their browsers from running unwanted scripts. To run the script, click the information bar and choose **Allow Blocked Content** from the pop-up menu, and then click **Yes** in the dialog box that follows.

Note that the placement of the script element tells the browser where to place the new text. Since the script element is placed between the opening and closing <td> tags, the text generated by the script is placed there as well. Kate is pleased with the new entry, but she would like it to appear as a link.

The document.write() Method

The document.write() method is one of the basic ways in JavaScript to send output to the Web document. Why do we call it a method? In JavaScript, many commands involve working with objects in the Web page and browser. An **object** can be any item from the browser window to a document displayed in the browser to an element displayed within the document. Even the mouse pointer, the window scrollbars, or the browser application itself can be treated as an object. A **method** is a process by which JavaScript manipulates or acts upon the features of an object. In this case, you've used the write() method to write new text into the document object. You'll learn about other objects and methods in greater detail in upcoming tutorials. For now, you'll focus only on the document object and the write() method.

The document.write() method has the general syntax

```
document.write("text");
```

where *text* is a string of characters that you want written to the Web document. The text string can also include HTML tags. For example, the following statement writes the text "Monroe Public Library" marked as an h1 heading into a document:

```
document.write("<h1>Monroe Public Library</h1>");
```

When a browser encounters this statement it places the text and the markup tags into the document and renders that text as if it had been entered directly into the HTML file.

Kate wants the e-mail addresses in the staff directory to appear as links. This requires placing the e-mail addresses within <a> tags and adding the href attribute value indicating the destination of each link. For example, the code to create a link for Catherine Adler's e-mail address is

```
<a href="mailto:cadler@mpl.gov">cadler@mpl.gov</a>
```

Writing this text string requires you to include quotation marks around the href attribute value. While text strings created with the document.write() method must be enclosed in quotes as well, you can use either double or single quotation marks. The option to use either double or single quotation marks allows you to write text strings that contain attribute values within either single or double quotation marks, such as e-mail address links. If you want to write a double quotation mark, you enclose the text string in single quotations, and vice versa. If you try to enclose double quotes within double quotes, for example, browsers become confused as to when the quoted text string begins and ends. The following JavaScript code writes Catherine Adler's e-mail address as a link, placing the href attribute value in single quotes:

```
document.write("<a href='mailto:cadler@mpl.gov'>");
document.write("cadler@mpl.gov");
document.write("</a>");
```

Note that this example places the entire code into three separate document.write() commands for clarity. While you could use one long text string, it might be more difficult to read and to type without making a mistake. A browser treats these consecutive commands as one long string of text to be written into the document.

To write the e-mail link for Catherine Adler:

1. Return to **mpl.htm** in your text editor.

2. Directly after the opening <script> element, insert the command

   ```
   document.write("<a href='mailto:cadler@mpl.gov'>");
   ```

3. Directly before the closing </script> element, insert the command

   ```
   document.write("</a>");
   ```

   Figure 1-11 shows the revised code in the file.

Figure 1-11	Inserting several document.write() commands

```
<tr>
    <td>Catherine Adler<br />Library Director</td>
    <td>555-3100</td>
    <td>
        <script type="text/javascript">
            document.write('<a href="mailto:cadler@mpl.gov">');
            document.write("cadler@mpl.gov");
            document.write("</a>");
        </script>
    </td>
</tr>
```

writing HTML tags with attribute values to the Web document

4. Save your changes and then reopen **mpl.htm** in your Web browser.

   The e-mail address for Catherine Adler now appears as a link.

5. Verify that the Catherine Adler entry contains an e-mail link by hovering your mouse pointer over the e-mail address; the link to the e-mail address should appear in the window's status bar (see Figure 1-12).

Viewing an e-mail link

Figure 1-12

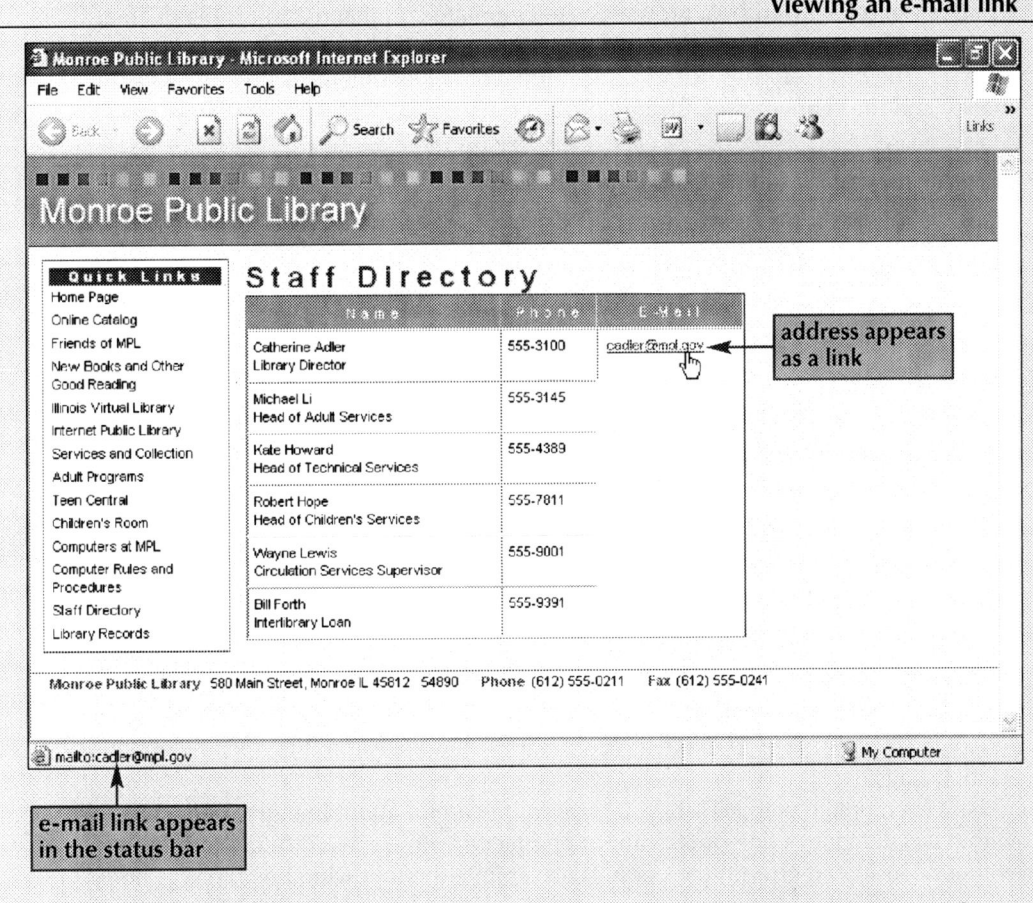

Trouble? If the link does not appear, verify that you included the opening and closing quotation marks in the JavaScript commands you just entered.

Writing Output to the Web Page

Reference Window

- To write text to your Web page, use the JavaScript command

  ```
  document.write("text");
  ```
  where *text* is the HTML content to be written to the page.

Understanding JavaScript Rules and the Use of White Space

Besides the use of semicolons, there are some other syntax rules you should keep in mind when writing JavaScript statements. JavaScript is case sensitive, which means that you must pay attention to whether letters are capitalized or not. For example, the following statements are *not* equivalent as far as JavaScript is concerned:

```
document.write("</a>");
Document.write("</a>");
```

The first command writes the HTML tag </a> to a Web page document. The second command is not recognized by a browser as a legitimate command and results in an error message. Figure 1-13 shows the error message generated by the Internet Explorer browser. The browser does not recognize the word "Document" (as opposed to "document") and thus cannot process the command.

Figure 1-13 ▶ **An error message resulting from improper case**

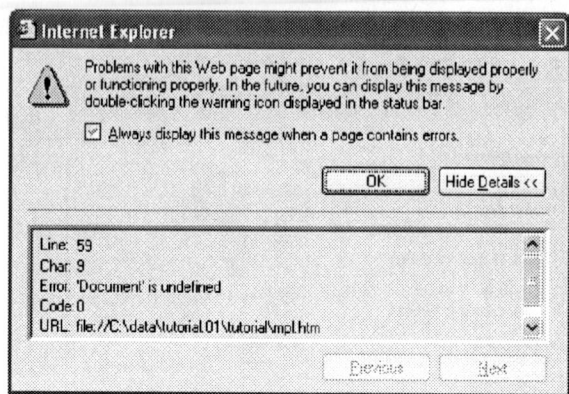

Like HTML, JavaScript ignores most occurrences of extra white space. This means that you can add extra spaces around your code to make it easier to read. You can see examples of this in Figure 1-9 and Figure 1-11, where the newly entered statements are indented several spaces to make the commands stand out from the opening and closing <script> tags.

However, unlike with HTML, you have to be careful about line breaks occurring within a statement. A line break cannot be placed within a word or quoted text string without causing an error in the code. For example, the following line break is not allowed:

```
document.write("<a href='mailto:cadler@mpl.gov'>
   cadler@mpl.gov
   </a>");
```

It is good practice to not break a statement into several lines if you can possibly avoid it. If you have to break a long statement into several lines, you can indicate that the statement continues on the next line using a backslash, as follows:

```
document.write("<a href='mailto:cadler@mpl.gov'> \
   cadler@mpl.gov \
   </a>");
```

If the line break occurs within a quoted text string, you can also break the string into several distinct text strings placed over several lines by adding a plus symbol (+) at the end of each line:

```
document.write("<a href='mailto:cadler@mpl.gov'>" +
   "cadler@mpl.gov" +
   "</a>");
```

The plus symbol (+) used in this command combines several text strings into a single text string. You'll explore other ways to use this symbol in the next session. However, breaking a single statement into several lines is usually not recommended because of the possibility of introducing error into the code. It should be done only with very long and complicated statements.

Supporting Non-JavaScript Browsers

For browsers that don't support scripts or that have their support for client-side scripts disabled, you can specify alternative content using the noscript element. The syntax of the noscript element is

```
<noscript>
    alternative content
</noscript>
```

where *alternative content* is the content a browser should display in place of accessing and running the script. For example, the following code displays a text message indicating that the page requires the use of JavaScript:

```
<script type="text/javascript">
    JavaScript statements
</script>
<noscript>
    <p>This page requires JavaScript. Please turn on JavaScript if your
browser supports it and reload the page.</p>
</noscript>
```

Browsers that support client-side scripts and have that support enabled ignore the content of the noscript element.

Using JavaScript code within an XHTML file can also lead to problems because XHTML parsers attempt to process the symbols in JavaScript code. Because character symbols such as angle brackets (< >) and the ampersand (&) are often used in JavaScript programs, this can lead to a page being rejected by an XHTML parser. To avoid this problem, you can place your JavaScript code within a CDATA section as follows:

```
<script type="text/javascript">
<![cdata[
    JavaScript code
]]>
</script>
```

The CDATA section marks the text of the JavaScript code as data that should not be processed by XHTML parsers. Unfortunately, the CDATA section is not well supported by current browsers. A third alternative is not to embed your scripts within XHTML files at all, but instead to always place them in external files. This practice has the added advantage of separating program code from page content. If you need to create valid XHTML documents, this is probably the best solution.

You've completed the first phase of creating a script to scramble e-mail addresses in Kate's staff directory. At this point you've worked on learning how to create and run JavaScript code to write text to a Web document. In the next session you'll add to this the ability to create and work with variables and functions. If you intend to take a break before the next session, you may close any open files now.

Session 1.1 Quick Check

Review

1. What is a client-side program? What is a server-side program?
2. What tag do you enter in your HTML code to create a script element for the JavaScript programming language?
3. What JavaScript command writes the text "Public Library" as an h2 heading to a Web document?
4. What JavaScript command would you enter to write the tag <h2 id="sub">Public Library</h2> to a Web document?
5. How do you enter a single JavaScript statement on two lines?

6. Why would the following command produce an error message?

```
document.Write("Monroe Public Library");
```

7. What code should you enter in an HTML file to display the following paragraph for browsers that don't support JavaScript?

```
<p><i>JavaScript required.</i></p>
```

Session 1.2

Working with Variables

In the previous session you learned how to write page content to a Web page using the document.write() method. Because you used this method to specify a text string explicitly, the code did little more than what you could have accomplished by entering the e-mail link directly into an HTML tag. However, the document.write() method is much more powerful and versatile when used in conjunction with variables. A **variable** is a named item in a program that stores information. Most JavaScript programs use variables to represent values and text strings. Variables are useful because they can store information created in one part of a program and use that information elsewhere. Variable values can also change as the program runs, allowing the program to display different values under varying conditions.

Declaring a Variable

It's common practice to introduce variables in your code by declaring them. **Declaring** a variable tells a JavaScript interpreter to reserve memory space for the variable. The statement to declare a variable is

```
var variable;
```

where `variable` is the name assigned to the variable. For example, the following statement creates a variable named emLink:

```
var emLink;
```

You can also declare multiple variables by entering the variable names in a comma-separated list. The following statement declares three variables named emLink, userName, and emServer:

```
var emLink, userName, emServer;
```

JavaScript imposes some limits on variable names:

- The first character must be either a letter or an underscore character (_).
- The remaining characters can be letters, numbers, or underscore characters.
- Variable names cannot contain spaces.
- You cannot use words that JavaScript has reserved for other purposes. For example, you cannot name a variable "document.write".

Like other aspects of the JavaScript language, variable names are case sensitive. The variable names emLink and emlink represent two different variables. One common programming mistake is to forget this important fact and to use uppercase and lowercase letters interchangeably in variable names.

Assigning a Value to a Variable

Once a variable has been created or declared, you can assign it a value. The statement to assign a value to a variable is

```
variable = value;
```

where *variable* is the variable name and *value* is the value assigned to the variable. For example, the following statement assigns the value "cadler" to a variable named userName:

```
userName = "cadler";
```

You can combine the variable declaration and the assignment of a value in a single statement. The following statements both declare the userName and emServer variables and set their initial values:

```
var userName = "cadler", emServer = "mpl.gov";
```

Note that declaring a variable with the var keyword is not required in JavaScript. The first time you use a variable, JavaScript creates the variable in memory. The following statement both creates the directory variable (if it has not already been declared in a previous statement) and assigns it an initial value:

```
director = "Catherine Adler";
```

Though it's not required, it's considered good programming style to include the var command whenever you create a variable. Doing so helps you keep track of the variables a program uses and also makes it easier for others to read and interpret your code. Many Web designers place all of their variable declarations at the beginning of their programs along with comments describing the purpose of each variable in a program.

Working with Data Types

The examples so far have looked at variables that store text strings. However, JavaScript variables can store different types of information. The type of information stored in a variable is referred to as its **data type**. JavaScript supports the following data types:

- numeric value
- text string
- Boolean value
- null value

A **numeric value** is any number, such as 13, 22.5, or -3.14159. Numbers can also be expressed in scientific notation, such as 5.1E2 for the value 5.1×10^2 (or 510). Numeric values are specified without any quotation marks. Thus, if you wished to store the value 2007 in the year variable, you would use the statement

```
year = 2007;
```

rather than

```
year = "2007";
```

A **text string** is any group of text characters, such as "Hello" or "Happy Holidays!" Strings must be enclosed within either double or single quotation marks, but not both; the string value 'Hello' is acceptable, but the string value "Hello' is not.

A **Boolean value** indicates the truth or falsity of a statement. There are only two Boolean values: true and false. For example, the following statement sets the value of the useNetscape variable to true and the value of the useIE variable to false:

```
useNetscape = true;
useIE = false;
```

Boolean values are most often used in programs that have to act differently based on different conditions. The useNetscape variable cited above might be used in a program that tests whether a user is running the Netscape browser. If the value is set to true, the program might be written to run differently for the user than if the value were set to false. Note that, if a Boolean variable's value is left undefined, it is interpreted by JavaScript as having a value of false for any operations that involve Boolean values. You'll learn more about working with Boolean values in the next tutorial.

Finally, a **null value** indicates that no value has yet been assigned to the variable. This can also be done explicitly using the keyword "null" in assigning a value to the variable, as in the following statement:

```
emLink = null;
```

or implicitly by simply declaring the variable without assigning it a value:

```
var emLink;
```

In either case, the emLink variable would have a null value until it was assigned a value using one of the other data types.

In JavaScript a variable's data type is always determined by the context in which it is used. This means that a variable can switch from one data type to another within a single program. In the following two statements, the variable Month starts out as a numeric variable with an initial value of 5, but then becomes a text string variable with a value of "March".

```
Month = 5;
Month = "March";
```

Programmers refer to JavaScript as a **weakly typed language** because variables are not strictly tied to specific data types. Other programming languages are **strongly typed languages**, forcing the programming to explicitly identify a variable's data type. In those languages the above code would result in an error because a given variable cannot store more than one type of data. A weakly typed language such as JavaScript relieves the programmer from the task of assigning a data type to a variable. However, this can lead to unpredictable results if you aren't careful.

For example, in JavaScript the plus symbol (+) has two purposes: it adds two numeric values together, and it combines two text strings into a single string. What would happen if you combined a numeric value and a text string using the plus symbol (+), as in the following set of code?

```
x = 5;
y = "4";
z = x + y;
```

Whenever you use a plus symbol (+) to combine a numeric and a text string variable, the result is always a text string. Thus, in the example above, the value of the variable z is the text string "54", rather than the numeric value 9. However this result is not readily apparent from the code without a prior understanding of how JavaScript handles text and numeric values. This is one of the limitations of a weakly typed language in which data types are inferred by the rules of the language and not by the programmer.

In future tutorials you'll look more closely at JavaScript commands to manipulate the values and properties of text strings and numbers. For now, understand that, because JavaScript is a weakly typed language, the data type of a variable can change based on how you use the variable in a program.

Writing a Variable Value to a Web Document

After a variable has been created it can be used in JavaScript statements in place of the value it contains. The following code writes the text string "Monroe Public Library" to a Web page:

```
var libName = "Monroe Public Library";
document.write(libName);
```

You can also use the plus symbol (+) to combine a variable with a text string and then write the combined text string to the document. The following statements send the text string <p>Welcome to the Monroe Library</p> to the Web document:

```
var libName = "Monroe Library";
document.write("<p>Welcome to the "+libName+"</p>");
```

You decide to create two variables to store Catherine Adler's e-mail address. One advantage of putting the e-mail address in variables is that it reduces the risk of typing the e-mail address wrong as it is repeated several times in the program code. Placing it in two variables will also help confuse e-mail harvesters, which typically look for a single text string containing an e-mail address.

The first variable, userName, stores the account name of Catherine Adler's e-mail address. The second variable, emServer, stores the name of the e-mail server. The commands to create the two variables for Catherine Adler's e-mail address are:

```
var userName = "cadler";
var emServer = "mpl.gov";
```

You'll then use the plus symbol (+) to combine these two variables into a text string that contains the complete e-mail address along with the at symbol (@), storing the text string in a third variable named emLink:

```
var emLink = userName+"@"+emServer;
```

In this case, the emLink variable stores the text string "cadler@mpl.gov." Finally, you'll write the value of the emLink variable to the Web document as an e-mail link. The complete code is

```
var userName = "cadler";
var emServer = "mpl.gov";
var emLink = userName+"@"+emServer;
document.write("<a href='mailto:"+emLink+"'>")
document.write(emLink);
document.write("</a>");
```

When run by a browser, this code writes the following text to the Web document:

```
<a href='mailto:cadler@mpl.gov'>cadler@mpl.gov</a>
```

Revise the script you created in the last session, using the emLink variable in the above code.

To create and use a JavaScript variable:

1. If necessary, reopen **mpl.htm** in your text editor.

2. Locate the script element you created in the last session and directly below the opening <script> tag, insert the following code:

```
var userName = "cadler";
var emServer = "mpl.gov";
var emLink = userName+"@"+emServer;
```

3. Replace the first two document.write() commands with the following code:

```
document.write("<a href='mailto:"+emLink+"'>");
document.write(emLink);
```

Figure 1-14 shows the new and revised code in the mpl.htm file.

Figure 1-14	Declaring variables

```
<tr>
   <td>Catherine Adler<br />Library Director</td>
   <td>555-3100</td>
   <td>
      <script type="text/javascript">
         var userName = "cadler";
         var emServer = "mpl.gov";
         var emLink = userName+"@"+emServer;
         document.write("<a href='mailto:"+emLink+"'>");
         document.write(emLink);
         document.write("</a>");
      </script>
   </td>
</tr>
```

creating the three variables

4. Save your changes to the file.

5. Refresh or reopen **mpl.htm** in your Web browser. The e-mail link for Catherine Adler should remain unchanged from that shown earlier in Figure 1-12.

Reference Window | **Declaring a JavaScript Variable**

- You can create (declare) variables with either of the following JavaScript commands:
  ```
  var variables;
  var variable = value, variable = value ...;
  ```
  where *variables* is a comma-separated list of the variables, and *value* is the initial value of the variable. The first command creates variables without assigning them values; the second command both creates variables and assigns them values.

Creating a Function to Perform an Action

So far, in writing code for the staff directory page, you've focused on the e-mail address of only one person. However, five other individuals are listed in the staff directory. If you wanted to use JavaScript to write the e-mail links for the rest of the directory, you could repeat the code you used for Catherine Adler's entry five more times. However, JavaScript provides a simpler way of doing this.

When you want to reuse JavaScript commands repeatedly within a program, you store the commands in a function. A **function** is a collection of commands that performs an action or returns a value. Every function includes a **function name**, which identifies it, and a set of commands that are run when the function is called. Some functions also require **parameters**, which are variables defined to be used in the function. The general syntax of a JavaScript function is

```
function function_name(parameters){
    JavaScript commands
}
```

where *function_name* is the name of the function, *parameters* is a comma-separated list of variable names used in the function, and *JavaScript commands* are the statements in the command block run by the function. Function names, like variable names, are case sensitive. For example, weekDay and WEEKDAY are treated as different function names. A function name must begin with a letter or underscore (_) and cannot contain any spaces. The following is an example of a function named showMsg() that writes a paragraph to a Web document:

```
function showMsg() {
    document.write("<p>Welcome to the Monroe Library</p>");
}
```

There are no parameters to this function. If you had stored the name of the library in a parameter named libName, the showMsg() function would look as follows:

```
function showMsg(libName) {
    document.write("<p>Welcome to the" + libName +"</p>");
}
```

If the libName parameter had the value "Monroe Public Library", then the paragraph "<p>Welcome to the Monroe Public Library</p>" would be sent to the Web document.

Calling a Function

When a browser encounters a function, it bypasses it without executing any of the code it contains. The function is executed only when called by another JavaScript command. Calling a function also defines the values of any parameters in the function. The expression to call a function (and run the commands it contains) has the following form:

```
function_name(parameter values)
```

where *function_name* is the name of the function and *parameter values* is a comma-separated list of values that match the parameters of the function. For example, to call the showMsg() function using the text string "Monroe Public Library" as the value of the libName parameter, you would run the command

```
showMsg("Monroe Public Library");
```

and the text string "<p>Welcome to the Monroe Public Library</p>" would be written to the document.

Parameter values can also themselves be variables. The following commands store the library name in a text string variable named libText and call the showMsg() function using that variable as the parameter value. The result is that the paragraph "<p>Welcome to the Cutler Public Library</p>" is written to the Web document.

```
var libText="Cutler Public Library";
showMsg(libText);
```

Functions can be called repeatedly with different parameter values to achieve different results. For example, the following code calls the showMsg() function twice with different parameter values to display two welcome paragraphs for the Monroe and Cutler Public Libraries:

```
var libText = "Monroe Public Library";
showMsg(libText);
var libText2 = "Cutler Public Library";
showMsg(libText2);
```

ewrite the code for generating the e-mail link for each person in the staff
u'll put the commands in a function named showEM(). The code for the

```
howEM(userName,emServer) {
ink = userName+"@"+emServer;
t.write("<a href='mailto:"+emLink+"'>");
t.write(emLink);
t.write("</a>");
```

e code for this function to the script you created in Figure 1-14. Rather than
explicitly entering the values of the userName and emServer variables, they're placed as
parameters of the showEM() function. You can call the function using values from Figure
1-14 in place of the parameter values. The command to call the function for Catherine
Adler's e-mail address is

```
showEM("cadler","mpl.gov");
```

This gives the same result as the code you used earlier, writing the e-mail link to the Web
page; however, the great advantage is that you can reuse this function for other e-mail
addresses in the staff directory by simply changing the parameter values.

The showEM() function can be placed anywhere within the mpl.htm file as long as it is
placed before any command that calls it. This is to ensure that a command does not try
to call the function before the browser encounters the function code. Note that any function placed within one script element can be accessed by the commands in another
script element. By convention, functions are usually placed within a script element in the
document head. This organizes all of the functions used by a document in one central
location. Next you'll add the showEM() function to the document head of the
mpl.htm file.

To create the showEM() function:

1. Return to the **mpl.htm** file in your text editor.

2. Directly above the closing </head> tag, insert the following script element and
   function (see Figure 1-15):

```
<script type="text/javascript">
function showEM(userName,emServer) {
    var emLink = userName+"@"+emServer;
    document.write("<a href='mailto:"+emLink+"'>");
    document.write(emLink);
    document.write("</a>");
}
</script>
```

Figure 1-15 Creating the showEM() function

```
<title>Monroe Public Library</title>
<link href="mplstyles.css" rel="stylesheet" type="text/css" />

<script type="text/javascript">
function showEM(userName,emServer) {
    var emLink = userName+"@"+emServer;
    document.write("<a href='mailto:"+emLink+"'>");
    document.write(emLink);
    document.write("</a>");
}
</script>

</head>
```

3. Save your changes to the file.

   Next, you'll replace the commands you inserted earlier to generate the e-mail link for
Catherine Adler with a single command that calls the showEM() function.

To call the showEM() function:

1. Locate the script element that writes the e-mail address for Catherine Adler.

2. Replace the commands within the script element with the following single command (see Figure 1-16):

```
showEM("cadler","mpl.gov");
```

Calling the showEM() function ◄ **Figure 1-16**

```
<tr>
   <td>Catherine Adler<br />Library Director</td>
   <td>555-3100</td>
   <td>
     <script type="text/javascript">
       showEM("cadler","mpl.gov");
     </script>
   </td>
</tr>
```

3. Save your changes to the file, and refresh **mpl.htm** in your Web browser. The link
to Catherine Adler's e-mail address should appear unchanged in the Web page.

   Finally, you'll insert the remaining five entries in the staff directory with script elements
that automatically generate the e-mail links.

To insert the remaining staff entries:

1. Return to the **mpl.htm** file in your text editor.

2. Locate the entry for Michael Li. His e-mail address is mikeli@mpl.gov. Add the following script element to the empty table cell that directly follows the entry for
Michael Li:

```
<script type="text/javascript">
    showEM("mikeli","mpl.gov");
</script>
```

(*Hint*: You may want to use the copy and paste features of your text editor, as the
changes you'll make to the file in these steps are so similar.) If you're not sure
where to place the script element for Michael Li, refer to Figure 1-17.

3. Kate Howard's e-mail address is khoward@mpl.gov. Insert the following script element in the empty table cell for her entry in the staff directory:

```
<script type="text/javascript">
    showEM("khoward","mpl.gov");
</script>
```

4. Robert Hope's e-mail address is rhope@mpl.gov. Enter the following script element
for him:

```
<script type="text/javascript">
    showEM("rhope","mpl.gov");
</script>
```

5. Wayne Lewis's e-mail address is wlewis@mpl.gov. Enter the following script element in the empty table cell for him:

```
<script type="text/javascript">
   showEM("wlewis","mpl.gov");
</script>
```

6. Bill Forth's e-mail address is bforth@mpl.gov. Enter the following code in his empty table cell:

```
<script type="text/javascript">
   showEM("bforth","mpl.gov");
</script>
```

Figure 1-17 shows the revised code in the mpl.htm file.

| Figure 1-17 | Inserting the remaining e-mail addresses |

```
<tr>
    <td>Michael Li<br />Head of Adult Services</td>
    <td>555-3145</td>
    <td>
       <script type="text/javascript">
          showEM("mikeli","mpl.gov");
       </script>
    </td>
</tr>
<tr>
    <td>Kate Howard<br />Head of Technical Services</td>
    <td>555-4389</td>
    <td>
       <script type="text/javascript">
          showEM("khoward","mpl.gov");
       </script>
    </td>
</tr>
<tr>
    <td>Robert Hope<br />Head of Children's Services</td>
    <td>555-7811</td>
    <td>
       <script type="text/javascript">
          showEM("rhope","mpl.gov");
       </script>
    </td>
</tr>
<tr>
    <td>Wayne Lewis<br />Circulation Services Supervisor</td>
    <td>555-9001</td>
    <td>
       <script type="text/javascript">
          showEM("wlewis","mpl.gov");
       </script>
    </td>
</tr>
<tr>
    <td>Bill Forth<br />Interlibrary Loan</td>
    <td>555-9391</td>
    <td>
       <script type="text/javascript">
          showEM("bforth","mpl.gov");
       </script>
    </td>
</tr>
```

7. Save your changes to the file and reload **mpl.htm** in your Web browser. Figure 1-18 shows the complete list of e-mail addresses in the staff directory. Verify that each address is a link by hovering your mouse pointer over the address text and viewing the destination of the link in the browser's status bar.

Functions and Variable Scope

As you've seen, the commands within a function are run only when called. This has an impact on how variables within the function are treated. Every variable you create has a property known as its **scope**, which indicates where and how the variable can be used in your application. A variable's scope can be either local or global. A variable created within a JavaScript function has **local scope** and can be used only within that function. Variables with local scope are sometimes referred to as **local variables**. In the function you just created, the emLink variable has local scope and can be used only within the showEM() function. Parameters such as the userName and emServer parameters from the showEM() function also have local scope and are not recognized outside of the function in which they're used. When the showEM() function stops running, those variables and their values disappear and can no longer be accessed. The only exception to this rule is when one function calls another function; in this case, any variable from the first function can be used in commands in the second function.

Variables not declared within functions have **global scope** and are accessible to all code in a page (including any code within a function). This is true even for variables defined within different script elements—a variable defined in one script element is accessible to code within another script element. Variables with global scope are often referred to as **global variables**.

Creating a Function to Return a Value

The showEM() function was created to perform the action of writing a text string to your Web document. The other use of functions is to return a calculated value. For a function to return a value, it must include a return statement. The syntax of a function that returns a value is

```
function function_name(parameters){
    JavaScript commands
    return value;
}
```

where `value` is the calculated value that is returned by the function. For example, the following Area() function calculates the area of a rectangular region by multiplying the region's length and width:

```
function Area(length, width) {
   var size = length*width;
   return size;
}
```

In this function, the area is stored in a variable named size, which is then returned by the function. You can then call the function to retrieve this value. The following code uses the function to calculate the area of a rectangle whose dimensions are 8 by 6 units:

```
var x = 8;
var y = 6;
var z = Area(x,y);
```

The first two commands assign the values 8 and 6 to the x and y variables, respectively. The values of both of these variables are then sent to the Area() function as the values of the length and width parameters. The Area() function uses these values to calculate the area, which it then returns, assigning that value to the z variable. As a result of these commands, a value of 48 is assigned to the z variable.

Functions that return a value can be placed within larger expressions. For example, the following code calls the Area() function within an expression that multiples the area value by 2:

```
var z = Area(x,y)*2;
```

When this command is run, the value of the Area() function is returned, multiplied by 2, and then stored in the z variable. Using the above parameter values, the value of the z variable would be equal to 96.

Reference Window | Creating and Calling a JavaScript Function

- To create a function that performs an action, use the structure
    ```
    function function_name(parameters){
       JavaScript commands
    }
    ```
    where `function_name` is the name of the function, `parameters` are the parameters of the function separated by commas, and the opening and closing braces enclose the `JavaScript commands` used by the function.
- To create a function that returns a value, use the structure
    ```
    function function_name(parameters){
       JavaScript commands
       return value;
    }
    ```
    where `value` is the value returned by the function.
- To call a function, use the command
    ```
    function_name(values);
    ```
    where `function_name` is the name of the function, and `values` is the list of values substituted for each of the function parameters. Depending on the function, calling a function either runs the actions of the function or accesses the value returned by the function.

Accessing an External JavaScript File

You show your work on the staff directory to Kate. She's happy that you were able to use JavaScript to generate the e-mail addresses, but she's still concerned that the text of each employee's username and mail server are present in the document as parameter values of the showEM() function. She would like to have those values further hidden from any e-mail harvesters that may be scanning the document code. You discuss the issue with some other programmers. One of them sends you a file containing the following function:

```
function stringReverse(textString) {
    if (!textString) return '';
    var revString='';
    for (i = textString.length-1; i>=0; i--)
        revString+=textString.charAt(i);
    return revString;
}
```

Interpreting the code contained within this function is beyond the scope of this tutorial, but for now it is sufficient to know in general what the function does. The function has a single parameter named textString, which stores a string of characters. The function then creates a variable name revString that stores the characters from textString in reverse order, and that reversed text string is returned by the function. For example, if you called the function in the statements

```
userName = stringReverse("reldac");
emServer = stringReverse("vog.lpm");
```

the userName variable would have the value "cadler", and the emServer variable would have the value "mpl.gov" (the text strings "reldac" and "vog.lpm" in reverse order). You show this function to Kate and she agrees that this will be sufficient to hide the actual username and server name from most e-mail address harvesters.

The stringReverse() function has already been entered for you and stored in a file named spam.js. To access JavaScript code and functions placed in external files, you can use the same script element you've been using to insert script commands into the staff directory document. The HTML element to access an external script file is

```
<script type="mime-type" src="url"></script>
```

where *mime-type* is the language of the code in the external script file and *url* is the URL of the external document. For example, to access the code in the spam.js file, you would add the following script element to your Web document:

```
<script type="text/javascript" src="spam.js"></script>
```

It's a common practice for JavaScript programmers to create libraries of functions located in external files, which are easily accessible to pages in the entire Web site. Any new functions added to the external file are then instantly accessible to each Web page without having to edit the contents of those pages. In general, script elements that point to external files are placed in a document's head section. This enables browsers to load all of the external script commands and functions before processing the body of the page. External files containing JavaScript commands and functions always have the file extension ".js" to distinguish them from files containing script commands from other languages.

When a browser encounters a script element that points to an external file, it loads the contents of the external file into the Web document just as if the programmer had entered the code from the external file directly into the Web file (see Figure 1-19).

| Figure 1-19 | Using an external script |

```
function stringReverse(textString) {
    if (!textString) return '';
    var revString='';
    for (i = textString.length-1; i>=0; i--)
        revString+=textString.charAt(i)
    return revString;
}
```

spam.js

```
<title>Monroe Public Library</title>
<link href="mplstyles.css" rel="stylesheet" type="text/css" />

<script type="text/javascript" src="spam.js"></script>

<script type="text/javascript">
function showEM(userName,emServer) {
    var emLink = userName+"@"+emServer;
    document.write("<a href='mailto:"+emLink+"'>")
    document.write(emLink);
    document.write("</a>");
}
</script>

</head>
```

Insert a script element into the staff directory page to access the code from the spam.js file.

To access the code in the spam.js file:

1. Return to the **mpl.htm** file in your text editor.

2. Directly above the script element in the head section, insert the following code (see Figure 1-20):

```
<script type="text/javascript" src="spam.js"></script>
```

| Figure 1-20 | Inserting a link to an external script file |

```
<title>Monroe Public Library</title>
<link href="mplstyles.css" rel="stylesheet" type="text/css" />

<script type="text/javascript" src="spam.js"></script>

<script type="text/javascript">
function showEM(userName,emServer) {
    var emLink = userName+"@"+emServer;
    document.write("<a href='mailto:"+emLink+"'>");
    document.write(emLink);
    document.write("</a>");
}
</script>
```

3. Save your changes to the file.

Next you want to confirm that the stringReverse() function from the spam.js file is working correctly. To test the function, call it to reverse the text string values of the user-Name and emServer parameters from the showEM() function.

To apply the stringReverse() function:

1. Go to the **showEM()** function.

2. Insert the following two lines at the top of the function, as shown in Figure 1-21:

```
userName = stringReverse(userName);
emServer = stringReverse(emServer);
```

| Figure 1-21 | Calling the stringReverse() function |

```
function showEM(userName,emServer) {
    userName = stringReverse(userName);
    emServer = stringReverse(emServer);
    var emLink = userName+"@"+emServer;
    document.write("<a href='mailto:"+emLink+"'>");
    document.write(emLink);
    document.write("</a>");
}
```

3. Save your changes to the file and then reload **mpl.htm** in your Web browser. As shown in Figure 1-22, the username and mail server portions of each person's e-mail address now appear reversed on the Web page.

Staff Directory

Name	Phone	E-Mail
Catherine Adler Library Director	555-3100	reldac@vog.lpm
Michael Li Head of Adult Services	555-3145	ilekim@vog.lpm
Kate Howard Head of Technical Services	555-4389	drawohk@vog.lpm
Robert Hope Head of Children's Services	555-7811	epohr@vog.lpm
Wayne Lewis Circulation Services Supervisor	555-9001	siwelw@vog.lpm
Bill Forth Interlibrary Loan	555-9391	htrofb@vog.lpm

username and e-mail server names appear reversed

The stringReverse() function appears to be working correctly. Of course, you don't want the e-mail addresses to be reversed in the rendered document; you want those addresses to appear correctly. Instead, you want the code *within* the document reversed in order to thwart e-mail harvesters. Thus, you need to enter the username and e-mail server names in reverse order.

To change the username and e-mail server names:

1. Return to **mpl.htm** in your text editor.

2. Go down to the script element for Catherine Adler's e-mail address and change the value of the userName parameter from cadler to **reldac**. Change the value of the emServer parameter from mpl.gov to **vog.lpm**.

3. Change the parameter values for Michael Li's e-mail address to **ilekim** and **vog.lpm**.

4. Change the parameter values for Kate Howard's e-mail address to **drawohk** and **vog.lpm**.

5. Change the parameter values for Robert Hope's e-mail address to **epohr** and **vog.lpm**.

6. Change the parameter values for Wayne Lewis's e-mail address to **siwelw** and **vog.lpm**.

7. Change the parameter values for Bill Forth's e-mail address to **htrofb** and **vog.lpm**.

Figure 1-23 shows the revised code in the mpl.htm file.

Entering the reversed username and e-mail server names

```
<tr>
   <td>Catherine Adler<br />Library Director</td>
   <td>555-3100</td>
   <td>
      <script type="text/javascript">
         showEM("reldac","vog.lpm");
      </script>
   </td>
</tr>
<tr>
   <td>Michael Li<br />Head of Adult Services</td>
   <td>555-3145</td>
   <td>
      <script type="text/javascript">
         showEM("ilekim","vog.lpm");
      </script>
   </td>
</tr>
<tr>
   <td>Kate Howard<br />Head of Technical Services</td>
   <td>555-4389</td>
   <td>
      <script type="text/javascript">
         showEM("drawohk","vog.lpm");
      </script>
   </td>
</tr>
<tr>
   <td>Robert Hope<br />Head of Children's Services</td>
   <td>555-7811</td>
   <td>
      <script type="text/javascript">
         showEM("epohr","vog.lpm");
      </script>
   </td>
</tr>
<tr>
   <td>Wayne Lewis<br />Circulation Services Supervisor</td>
   <td>555-9001</td>
   <td>
      <script type="text/javascript">
         showEM("siwelw","vog.lpm");
      </script>
   </td>
</tr>
<tr>
   <td>Bill Forth<br />Interlibrary Loan</td>
   <td>555-9391</td>
   <td>
      <script type="text/javascript">
         showEM("htrofb","vog.lpm");
      </script>
   </td>
</tr>
```

8. Save your changes to the file and then reload **mpl.htm** in your Web browser. As shown in Figure 1-24, the e-mail addresses of all the staff members should now appear correctly.

Figure 1-24   The final staff directory page

Monroe Public Library

Quick Links

Home Page
Online Catalog
Friends of MPL
New Books and Other Good Reading
Illinois Virtual Library
Internet Public Library
Services and Collection
Adult Programs
Teen Central
Children's Room
Computers at MPL
Computer Rules and Procedures
Staff Directory
Library Records

Staff Directory

Name	Phone	E-Mail
Catherine Adler Library Director	555-3100	cadler@mpl.gov
Michael Li Head of Adult Services	555-3145	mikeli@mpl.gov
Kate Howard Head of Technical Services	555-4389	khoward@mpl.gov
Robert Hope Head of Children's Services	555-7811	rhope@mpl.gov
Wayne Lewis Circulation Services Supervisor	555-9001	wlewis@mpl.gov
Bill Forth Interlibrary Loan	555-9391	bforth@mpl.gov

Monroe Public Library   580 Main Street, Monroe IL 45812 54890   Phone (612) 555-0211   Fax (612) 555-0241

Commenting JavaScript Code

You review your progress with Kate Howard. As she scans through the code in the HTML file, she's pleased to note that none of the e-mail addresses for the six staff members appears in any readable form. By breaking the e-mail addresses into two parts (the user-Name and the emServer parts) and entering the text in reverse order, you have effectively hidden the actual addresses from harvesting programs. Kate is pleased to see how JavaScript is able to unscramble the e-mail addresses and present them to users in a readable form. However, she is concerned that she may forget how this program is designed to work in the months and years to come. She would like you to add some commentary to the code you created.

Inserting Single- and Multiline Comments

Commenting your code is an important programming practice. It helps other people who examine your code to understand what your programs are designed to do and how they work. It can even help you in the future when you return to edit the programs you've written and need to recall the programming choices you made. In JavaScript, comments can be added to script elements on either single or multiple lines. The syntax of a single-line comment is

```
// comment text
```

where *comment text* is the JavaScript comment. Single-line comments can be placed within the same line as a JavaScript command, making it easier to interpret each command in your code. The following is an example of a JavaScript statement that includes a single-line comment:

```
document.write(emLink); // write e-mail address to the Web page
```

For more extended comments, you place the comment text on several lines using the syntax

```
/*
   comment text spanning
   several lines
*/
```

The following is an example of a multiline comment applied to a JavaScript program:

```
/*
   The showEM() function displays a link to the user's e-mail address.
   The username and e-mail server name are entered in reverse order
   to thwart e-mail harvesting programs
*/
```

Add comments to the showEM() function you created.

To add comments to the showEM() function:

1. Return to the **mpl.htm** file in your text editor.

2. Add the following multiline comment at the start of the showEM() function (see Figure 1-25).

```
/*
The showEM() function displays a link to the user's e-mail
address. The username and e-mail server name are entered in
reverse order to thwart e-mail harvesting programs.
*/
```

3. Add the following single-line comment to the line that applies the stringReverse() function to the userName parameter:

`// undo the reversed username`

4. Add the following comment to the line that applies the stringReverse() function to the emServer parameter:

`// undo the reversed server name`

5. Add the following comment to the line that creates the emLink variable:

`// combine the username and server name`

Figure 1-25 highlights the single- and multiline comments added to the showEM() function.

Figure 1-25 ▶ **Adding comments to the showEM() function**

```
function showEM(userName,emServer) {
/*
   The showEM() function displays a link to the user's e-mail address.
   The username and e-mail server name are entered in reverse order
   to thwart e-mail harvesting programs.
*/

   userName = stringReverse(userName); // undo the reversed username
   emServer = stringReverse(emServer); // undo the reversed server name
   var emLink = userName+"@"+emServer; // combine the username and server name
   document.write("<a href='mailto:"+emLink+"'>");
   document.write(emLink);
   document.write("</a>");
}
```

6. Close the **mpl.htm** file, saving your changes.

7. Reopen **mpl.htm** in your Web browser and verify that you have not introduced any errors by adding comments to the showEM() function. Close the Web page when finished.

You show the commented version of the showEM() function to Kate Howard. She agrees that it will help her better remember the purpose of the function, as well as how the function works.

Using Comments to Hide JavaScript Code

Comments have another purpose besides documenting the code used in a JavaScript application. Older browsers that do not support JavaScript can present a problem for Web designers. If such browsers encounter JavaScript commands, they may display the program code as part of the Web page body. To avoid this problem, you can hide a script from these browsers using both HTML and JavaScript comment lines. The syntax for doing this is

```
<script type="text/javascript">
<!-- Hide from non-JavaScript browsers
   JavaScript commands
// Stop hiding from older browsers -->

</script>
```

When a Web browser that doesn't support scripts encounters this code, it ignores the <script> tag, as it does any tag it doesn't recognize. The next line it sees is the start of the HTML comment tag, which doesn't close until the arrow symbol (-->)in the second-to-last line. This means that the browser ignores the entire JavaScript program. It similarly ignores the final </script> tag.

On the other hand, a browser that *does* support JavaScript recognizes the <script> tag and ignores any HTML tags found between the <script> and </script> tags. Therefore, in this example, it bypasses the comment tag in the second line and processes the JavaScript program as written. The JavaScript comment, which starts with the double slash symbol (//) in the second-to-last line, is included to help other users understand and interpret your code.

Hiding JavaScript code from older browsers is not as important as it once was, so you will not add this feature to the application you created for the staff directory page.

Debugging Your JavaScript Programs

As you work with JavaScript, you will inevitably encounter scripts that fail to work because of an error in the code. There are three types of errors: load-time errors, run-time errors, and logical errors. A **load-time error** occurs when a script is first loaded by a Java-Script interpreter. As the page loads, the browser reads through the code looking for mistakes in syntax. For example, suppose you had neglected to include the closing parenthesis in the following command from the showEM() function:

```
document.write("</a>";
```

In this case, you would be making a mistake in the syntax of the document.write() method. When a load-time error is uncovered, the JavaScript interpreter halts loading the script. Depending on the browser, an error message may also appear. Figure 1-26 shows the message generated by the above error in Internet Explorer. An error message typically includes the line number and character number of the error. This does not mean that the error occurred at this location in the document—the source of the trouble could be much earlier in the script. The message simply indicates the location at which the JavaScript interpreter was forced to cancel loading the script.

Reporting a load-time error  Figure 1-26

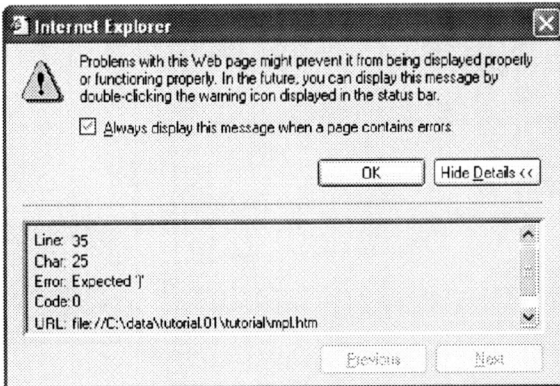

A **run-time error** occurs after a script has been successfully loaded and is being executed. In a run-time error, the mistake occurs when the browser is unable to complete a line of code. One common source of a run-time error is mislabeling a variable name. For example, the following line of code in the showEM() function:

```
document.write(emlink);
```

would result in the run-time error shown in Figure 1-27.

| Figure 1-27 | Reporting a run-time error |

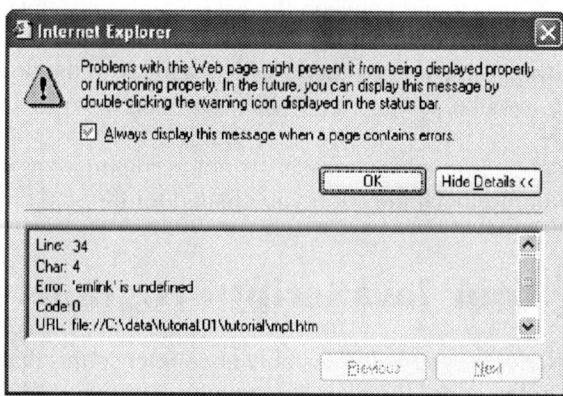

The mistake in this line of code is that there is no variable named "emlink" in the showEM() function—the variable name should be "emLink" (recall that variable names are case sensitive). When a browser attempts to write the contents of the emlink variable to the Web document, it discovers that no such variable exists and thus reports the run-time error. When a JavaScript interpreter catches a run-time error, it halts execution of the script and displays an error message indicating the location where it was forced to quit.

Logical errors are free from syntax and structural mistakes, but result in incorrect results. A logical error is often the hardest to fix and may require you to meticulously trace every step of your code to detect the mistake. Suppose you had incorrectly entered the line of code to create the emLink variable, placing the server name before the username:

```
var emLink = emServer + "@" + username;
```

In this case, a browser would display the list of e-mail addresses as shown in Figure 1-28.

| Figure 1-28 | Displaying a logical error |

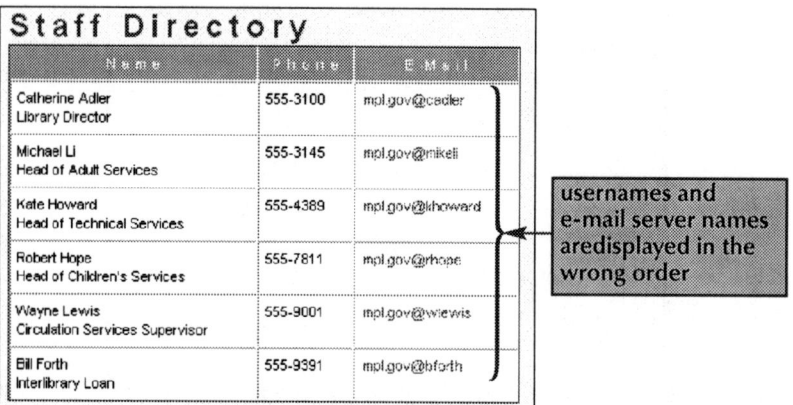

While the browser did not report any mistakes, this is obviously not the way Kate wants e-mail addresses displayed!

Common Mistakes

To fix a problem with a program, you need to debug it. **Debugging** is the process of searching code to locate a source of trouble. The following are common errors that may creep into your scripts:

- Misspelling a variable name: For example if you named a variable "ListPrice", then misspellings or incorrect capitalization, such as "listprice", "ListPrices", or "list_price", would result in the program failing to run correctly.
- Mismatched parentheses or braces: The following code results in an error because the function lacks the closing brace:

```
function Area(width, height) {
    var size = width*height;
```

- Mismatched quotes: If you neglect the closing quotes around a text string, JavaScript treats the text string as an object or variable, resulting in an error. The following code results in an error, because the closing double quote is missing from the firstName variable:

```
var firstName="Sean';
var lastName="Lee";
document.write(firstName+" "+lastName);
```

- Missing quotes: When you combine several text strings using the plus symbol (+), you may neglect to quote all text strings. For example, the following code generates an error because of the missing quotes around the <br /> tag:

```
document.write("MidWest Student Union"+<br />);
```

Debugging Tools and Techniques

There are several techniques you can employ to avoid making mistakes and to quickly locate the mistakes you do make. One is to write **modular code**, which entails breaking up a program's different tasks into smaller, more manageable chunks. A common strategy when creating modular code is to use functions that perform a few simple tasks. The different functions can then be combined and used in a variety of ways.

If you do encounter a logical error in which the incorrect results are displayed by the browser, you can monitor the changing values of your variables using an alert dialog box. An **alert dialog box** is a dialog box generated by JavaScript that displays a text message with an OK button. Clicking the OK button closes the dialog box. The command to create an alert dialog box is

```
alert(text);
```

where *text* is the text string that you want displayed in the dialog box. You can also use a variable name in place of a text string. For example, the command

```
alert(emLink);
```

displays the current value of the emLink variable. Figure 1-29 shows the appearance of this dialog box for the first entry in the library staff directory. Alert dialog boxes are useful in determining what is happening to your variable values while a program is running.

| Figure 1-29 | Displaying a variable value in an alert dialog box |

value of the emLink variable

You can also use different tools for debugging a program. Microsoft offers the **Microsoft Script Debugger** for use with its Internet Explorer browser. The debugger can help you to easily create and debug your JavaScript programs. The Microsoft Script Debugger is available for free from the Microsoft Web site and is also included with the Microsoft Office suite. When the Microsoft Script Debugger is installed you are prompted when a load-time or run-time error is encountered in one of your scripts (see Figure 1-30).

| Figure 1-30 | Microsoft Script Debugger Error message |

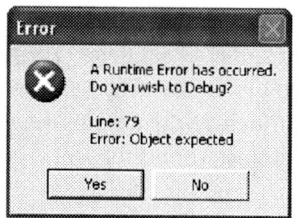

Clicking the Yes button opens the Microsoft Script Debugger window, highlighting the source of the error. As shown in Figure 1-31, the source of this particular error is that the showEM() function was referenced as showem(). Because function names are case sensitive, the browser was unable to locate the function and reported an error. You can learn more about the script debugger using the online help provided with the Microsoft Script Debugger or at the Microsoft Web site.

| Figure 1-31 | Microsoft Script Debugger window |

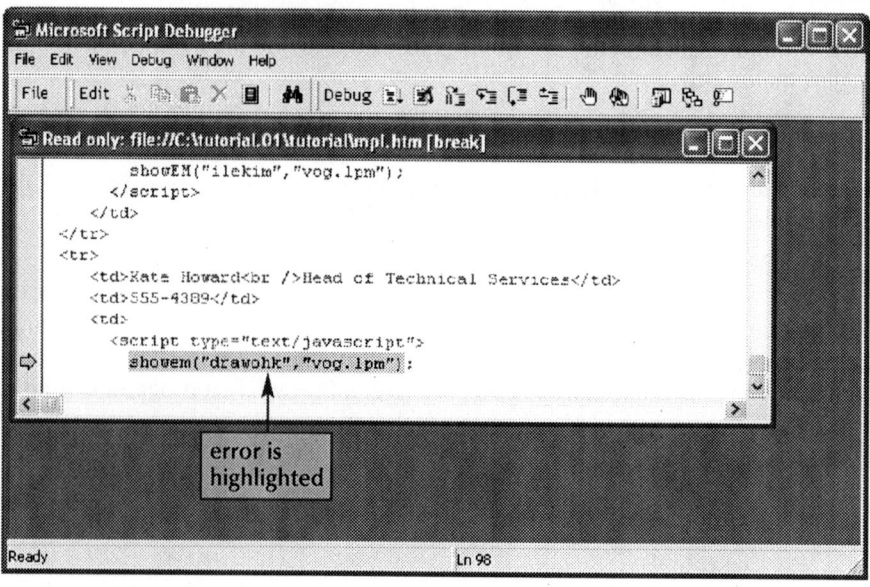

error is highlighted

Netscape also provides its own debugger called the **Netscape JavaScript Console**. The console displays a list of all script errors generated by the current document. To open the console, you type "javascript:" in Netscape's address bar (see Figure 1-32).

Accessing the Netscape JavaScript Console | **Figure 1-32**

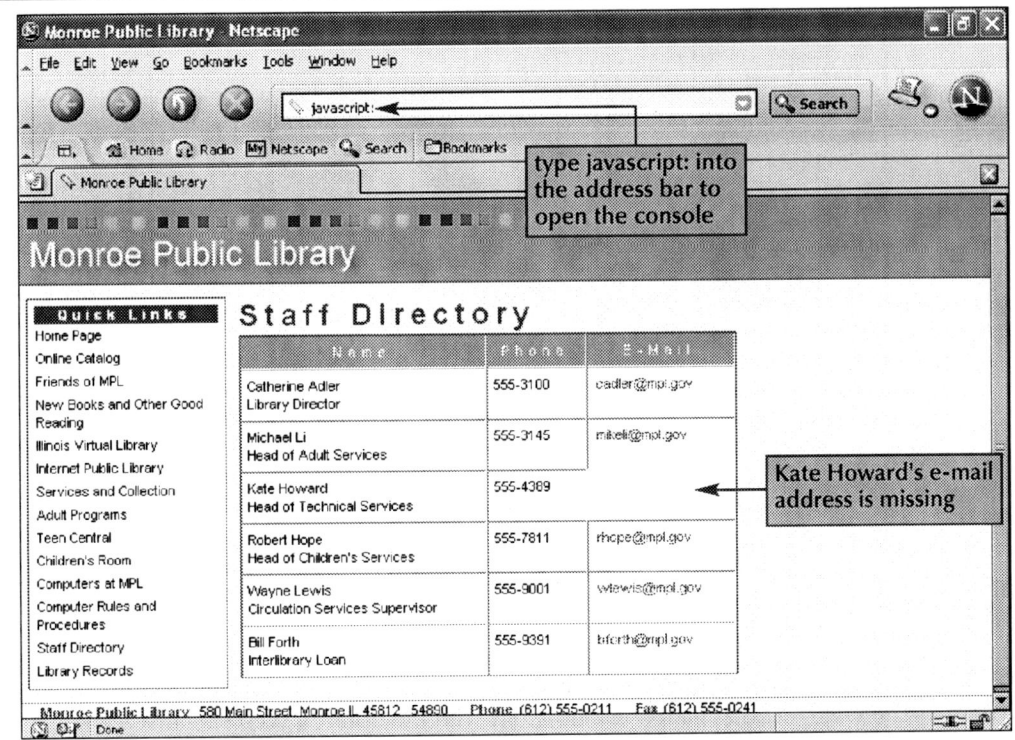

The console appears as another Netscape browser window (see Figure 1-33). Within the console is an Evaluate box in which you can insert JavaScript code commands to evaluate your code and variable values at the point at which the error occurred. The console also includes a link to another Netscape window that displays the code for the source file. The point at which the error was detected is highlighted in this window (see Figure 1-34).

The Netscape JavaScript Console | **Figure 1-33**

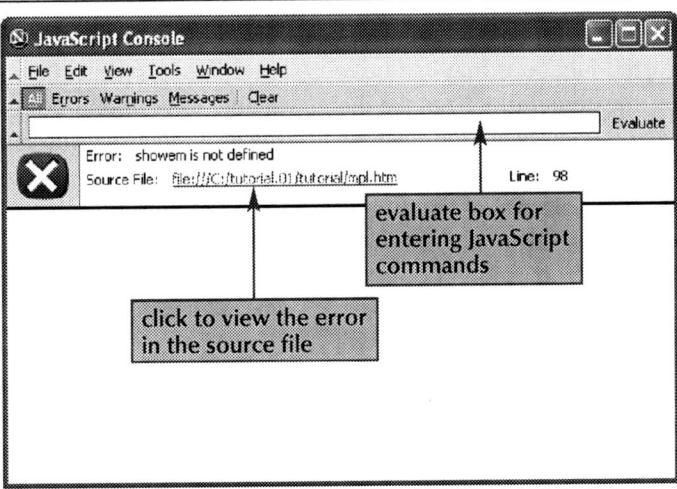

Figure 1-34 **Highlighting the source of the error**

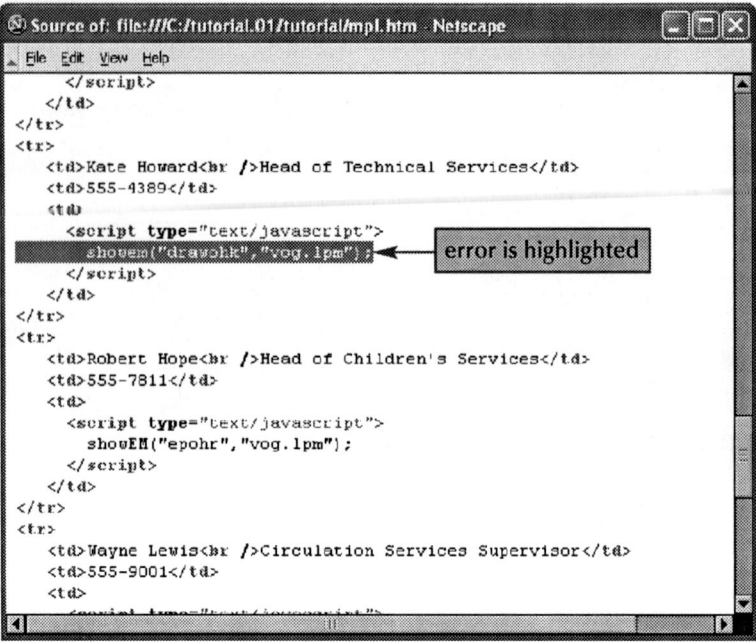

You can learn more about the Netscape JavaScript Console by using the online help in the console window. Because errors inevitably creep into any programming task you undertake, becoming familiar with the different debugging tools available to you is essential.

At this point you've completed your work on the staff directory for the Monroe Public Library. Kate will call you again as other issues with the library's Web site arise.

Tips for Writing Good JavaScript Code

- Apply layout techniques to make your code more readable. For example, indent statements to set them off from other code.
- Use descriptive variable names to indicate the purpose of each variable.
- Because JavaScript is case sensitive, be consistent in how you apply uppercase and lowercase letters to your variable names.
- Add comments to your code to document the purpose of your commands, variables, and functions.
- Create customized functions that can be reused in different scripts. Place your customized functions in external files to make them available to your entire Web site.
- Break up long and complicated functions into smaller functions, with each function performing a specific and easily defined task.
- Use the debugging tools available in the Netscape and Internet Explorer browsers to quickly correct coding errors.
- In case of a logical error, use alert boxes to check on the progress of variable values as the browser executes the script.

Session 1.2 Quick Check

1. What are the four data types supported by JavaScript?
2. What JavaScript command declares a variable named weekDay with an initial value of "Friday"?
3. What are the two purposes of a JavaScript function?
4. Describe the two types of variable scope. Variables declared within a function have what type of scope?
5. What is the general syntax of a JavaScript function that returns a value?
6. What code would you enter to insert a multiline comment containing the following comment text:
   This function displays the current date in the format
   month day, year
7. What command would you run to display the value of the userName variable in an alert dialog box?
8. Your code has a misspelled variable name. What type of error will result from this mistake?

Tutorial Summary

In this tutorial you learned how to create and run Web page programs written in the JavaScript language. In the first session, you learned about the history of JavaScript and how it compares to Java. You then studied how to create a script element and how to use JavaScript to write text to a Web document. In the second session, you learned how to create and use variables. The second session also introduced the concept of functions, showing how functions can be used to run tasks or calculate values. You learned how to access code stored in external JavaScript files. The session then demonstrated how to document your code with comments. The tutorial concluded with a discussion of common scripting errors and an overview of some tools and techniques you can use to ensure that your code is error free.

Key Terms

alert dialog box	function name	Netscape JavaScript Console
applet	global scope	null value
Boolean value	global variable	numeric value
client-side programming	human input validation	object
command	interpreted language	parameter
compiled language	Java	run-time error
data type	Java interpreter	scope
debugging	JavaScript	server-side programming
declaring	JScript	spam
ECMA	load-time error	spammer
ECMAScript	local scope	statement
e-mail harvester	logical error	strongly typed language
European Computer	local variable	text string
Manufacturers	method	variable
Association	Microsoft Script Debugger	VBScript
function	modular code	weakly typed language

Review Assignments

Data files needed for this Review Assignment: 0.jpg through 9.jpg, mpl2txt.htm, mpl.jpg, mplstyles.css, random.js

Kate has a new assignment for you. One of the pages in the Monroe Library Web site is the library records page; it contains sensitive information on the library patrons and the books they have checked out. Kate has already created a Web form in which a staff member must enter a username and password before getting access to the library records. However, she has heard that some hackers create programs that search for Web forms that open confidential pages. One technique of these hackers is to have automated programs that submit thousands of username/password combinations, hoping to break into the system. Kate has heard that some sites use human input validation to thwart these programs.

Human input validation is a technique that requires the entry of some piece of information that humans can easily enter, but automated programs cannot. One approach is to display a series of images containing numbers or letters and request the user to enter the numbers or letters being displayed. Since most automated programs can't "see" images, they cannot answer this question; most humans, on the other hand, can enter the requested information without trouble. Kate suggests you write a program that shows five images, each displaying a random number between 0 and 9. In addition to entering a username and password, users will be required to enter the numbers they see on the screen. Figure 1-35 shows a preview of the completed Web page.

Figure 1-35

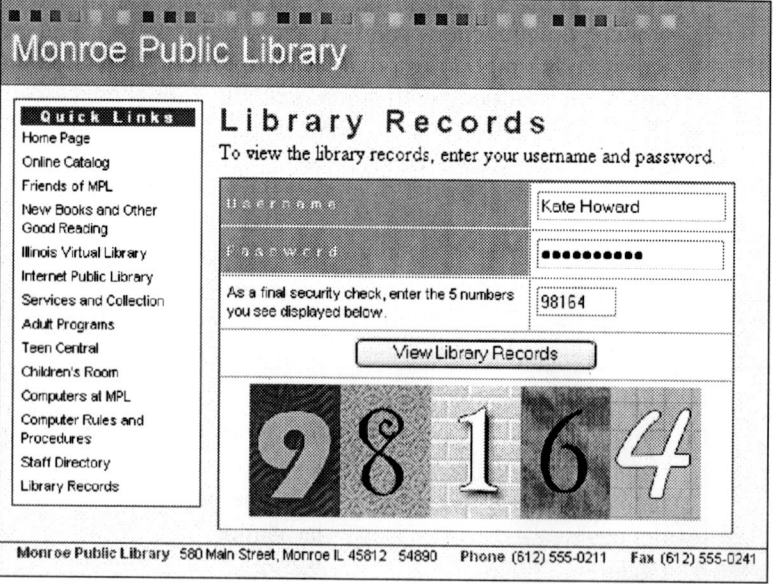

Your job is to write a script to display the random images. The images have been stored in files named 0.jpg through 9.jpg. To help you, Kate has located a file that contains a JavaScript function to return a random integer from 0 to *size*, where *size* is the largest integer to be returned. To call the function, you use the command

```
randomInteger(size)
```

The randomInteger() function has been stored in the random.js file.

To complete this Web page:

1. Using your text editor, open **mpl2txt.htm** from the tutorial.01/review folder. Enter *your name* and *the date* in the head section and save the file as **mpl2.htm**.
2. In the head section, just above the closing </head> tag, insert a script element that accesses the code in the random.js file. ✓
3. Add a second script element for code to be placed in the mpl2.htm page.
4. Within the second script element, create a function named showImg(). The purpose of this function is to write an inline image into the current document. The function has no parameters. Add the following statements to the function:
   a. Add the following multiline comment to the start of the showImg() function:
   The showImg() function displays a random image from the 0.jpg through 9.jpg files. The random image is designed to thwart hackers attempting to enter the library records database by requiring visual confirmation.
   b. Declare a variable named imgNumber equal to the value returned by the randomInteger() function. Use 9 as the value of the size parameter in the randomInteger() function.
   c. Append the statement that creates the imgNumber variable with the following single-line comment:
   Return a random number from 0 to 9
   d. Insert a command that writes the following text to the document:
   ```
   <img src='imgNumber.jpg' alt='' />
   ```
   where *imgNumber* is the value of the imgNumber variable.
5. Scroll down to the bottom of the file and locate the last table cell in the document. Within this empty table cell, insert a script element.
6. Within the script element, call the showImg() function five times.
7. Save your changes to the file.
8. Open **mpl2.htm** in your Web browser. Verify that, each time you refresh the Web page, a different sequence of five image numbers appears at the bottom of the Web form. Debug your code as necessary using any of the tools or techniques described in this tutorial.
9. Submit the completed Web site to your instructor.

Case Problem 1

Data files needed for this Case Problem: datetime.js, mask.gif, sky0.jpg through sky23.jpg, skymaptxt.htm, skyweb.css, skyweb.jpg

SkyWeb Astronomy Dr. Andrew Weiss of Central Ohio University maintains an astronomy page called SkyWeb for his students. On his Web site he discusses many aspects of astronomy and stargazing. One of the tools of the amateur stargazer is a planisphere, which is a handheld device composed of two flat disks: one disk shows a map of the constellations, and the other disk contains a window corresponding to the part of the sky that is visible at a given time and date. When a user rotates the second disk to the current date and time, the constellations that appear in the window correspond to the constellations currently visible in the nighttime sky.

Dr. Weiss has asked your help in constructing an online planisphere for his Web site. He has created 24 different sky charts, named sky0.jpg through sky23.jpg, that represent 24 different rotations of the nighttime sky. He has also created an image containing a transparent window through which a user can view a selected sky chart. A preview of the completed Web page is shown in Figure 1-36.

Figure 1-36

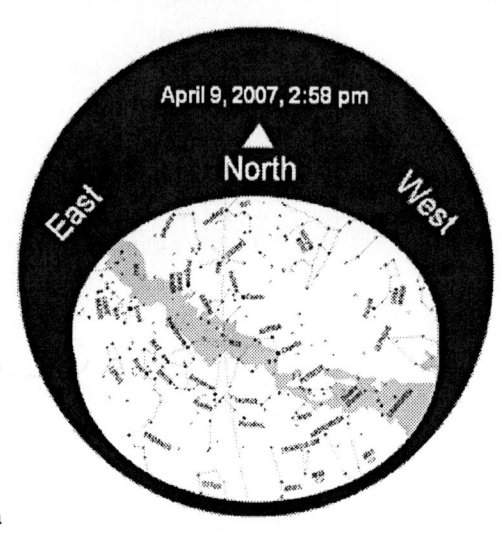

Dr. Weiss has already designed the page layout but he needs your help in entering JavaScript code to display the current date and time and to display the correct sky chart for that date and time. To do this, you've been provided with two functions:

- The showDateTime() function, which returns the current date and time in the following text string:

  Month Day, *Year*, *hour:time* am/pm

  where *Month* is the name of the current month, *Day* is the current day, *Year* is the current year, *hour* is the current hour, *minute* is the current minute, and am/pm changes based on the current time.

- The getMap() function, which returns a number from 0 to 23. The number matches the number of the sky map image to show the current date and time.

Both functions have been placed in an external JavaScript file named datetime.js.

To complete this Web page:

1. Using your text editor, open **skymaptxt.htm** from the tutorial.01/case1 folder. Enter *your name* and *the date* in the head section and save the file as **skymap.htm**.

2. Directly below the link element in the head section, insert a script element accessing the datetime.js file.

3. Below that script element, insert another script element that contains the following statements:
   a. Declare a variable named timeStr equal to the value returned from the showDateTime() function.
   b. Declare a variable named mapNum equal to the value returned from the getMap() function.
   c. Above the two variable declarations, insert the following multiline JavaScript comment:
      ```
      timeStr is a text string containing the current date and time
      mapNum is the number of the map to display in the planisphere
      ```
4. Scroll down the file to the div element with id value "maps" and replace the line
   <img id="sky" src="sky0.jpg" alt="" /> with a script element that writes the following HTML code:
   ```
   <img id='sky' src='skymapNum.jpg' alt='' />
   ```
   where *mapNum* is the value of the mapNum variable.
5. Scroll down a few lines and replace the date/time value "January 1, 2007, 12:00 am" with a script element that writes the value of the timeStr variable to the Web page.
6. Save your changes to the file and then open **skymap.htm** in your Web browser. Verify that the planisphere displays the current date and time. If you're able to modify the date/time settings on your computer, change the date and time and then reload or refresh the page to verify that the date/time value changes and that the map also changes. Debug your code as necessary.
7. Submit the completed Web site to your instructor.

Apply

Use JavaScript to display random banner ads

Case Problem 2

Data files needed for this Case Problem: ad1.jpg through ad5.jpg, ads.js, fp.jpg, fronttxt.htm, logo.jpg, random.js, styles.css

Ridgewood Herald Tribune Maria Ramirez manages advertising accounts for the Ridgewood Herald Tribune. Recently, the paper has put more of its content online. To offset the cost of the Web site, Maria is selling ad space on the company's home page. She is looking at creating banner ads to be displayed on the paper's masthead, with each ad linked to the advertiser's Web site. Because ad space on the paper's home page is the most valuable, Maria has decided to sell space to five companies, with the selection of the banner ad determined randomly each time a user opens the page.

Maria has asked your help in writing the JavaScript code to display banner ads randomly. She has provided a collection of functions that will be useful to you:
- The randInt() function, which returns a random integer from 1 to n. To call the randInt() function, use the expression
  ```
  randInt(n)
  ```
- The adDescription() function, which returns the description of the nth ad of a collection of ad descriptions. To call the function, use the expression
  ```
  adDescription(n)
  ```
- The adLink() function, which returns the URL of the nth ad of the collection. To call the function, use the expression
  ```
  adLink(n)
  ```

The random.js file contains the randInt() function. The ads.js file contains the adDescription() and adLink() functions. Figure 1-37 shows a preview of the completed Web page.

Figure 1-37

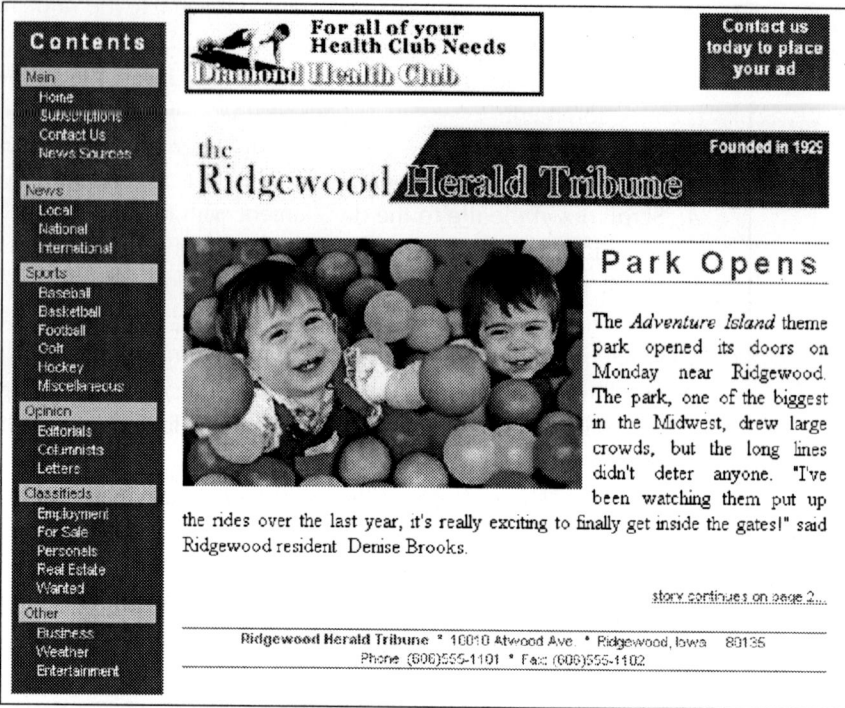

To complete this Web page:

1. Using your text editor, open **fronttxt.htm** from the tutorial.01/case2 folder. Enter *your name* and *the date* in the head section and save the file as **front.htm**.

2. After the link element in the head section, insert a script element accessing the functions in the random.js file. ✓

3. Insert another script element accessing the functions in the ads.js file. ✓

4. Scroll down the document to the div element with the id value "ads". Replace the content of the div element with a script element containing the following commands:

   a. Declare a variable named rNumber equal to the value returned from the randInt() function using 5 as the parameter value. Append the following comment to the statement: "generate a random integer from 1 to 5"

   b. Declare a variable named rAd equal to the text string returned from the adDescription() function using rNumber as the parameter value. Append the following comment to the statement: "description of the random ad".

   c. Declare a variable named rLink equal to the URL returned from the adLink() function using rNumber as the parameter value. Append the comment "URL of the random ad".

   d. Insert a command to write the following text to the Web document:
   ```
   <a href="URL">
      <img src="adn.jpg" alt="description" />
   </a>
   ```

where *URL* is the value of the rLink variable, *n* is the value of the rNumber variable, and *description* is the value of the rAd variable.

5. Save your changes to the file.

6. Open **front.htm** in your Web browser. Refresh or reload the Web page multiple times, verifying that different banner ads appear as the page is refreshed or reloaded. Debug your code as necessary.

7. Submit the completed Web site to your instructor. ✔

Challenge

Write a script to display the daily calendar of events at a student union

Case Problem 3

Data files needed for this Case Problem: back.jpg, friday.htm, functions.js, monday.htm, mw.css, saturday.htm, schedule.css, sunday.htm, thursday.htm, todaytxt.htm, tuesday.htm, wednesday.htm

Sean Lee manages the Web site for the student union at MidWest University. The student union provides daily activities that enrich the lives of the students on campus. As Web site manager, part of Sean's job is to keep the Web site up to date on the latest activities sponsored by the union. At the beginning of each week, she revises a set of seven Web pages, each detailing the events for one day in the upcoming week.

Sean would like the Web site to display the current day's schedule in an inline frame within the Web page named "Today at the Union". To do this, her Web page needs to be able to determine the day of the week and then load the appropriate file into the frame. She would also like the "Today at the Union" page to display the current day and date. Figure 1-38 shows a preview of the page she wants you to create.

Figure 1-38

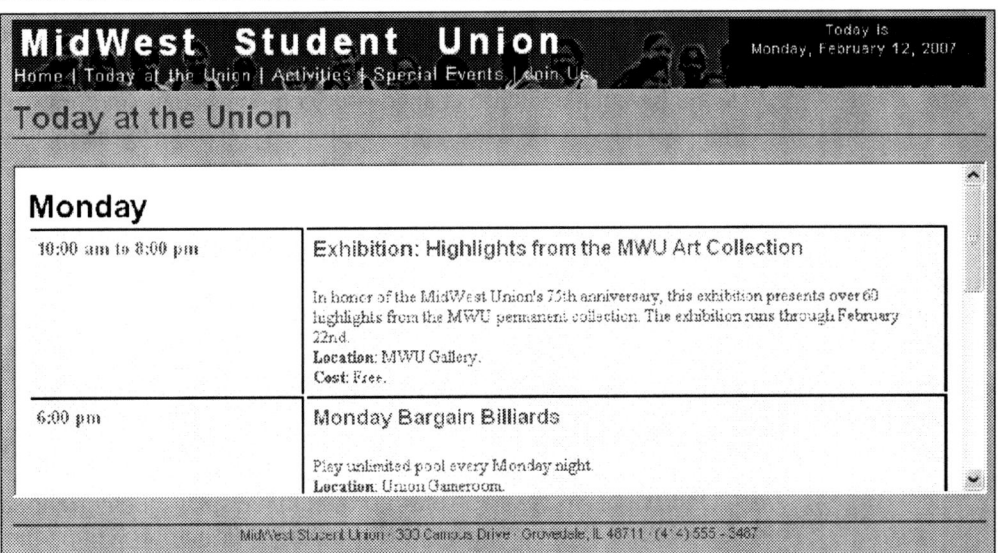

Sean has already created the layout of the page, and she needs you to write the scripts to insert the current date and the calendar of events for the current day. To assist you, she has located two functions:

• The showDate() function, which returns a text string containing the current date in the format *Weekday, Month Day, Year*. The function has no parameter values.

- The weekDay() function, which returns a text string containing the name of the current weekday, from "sunday" through "saturday".

The two functions have been stored in an external JavaScript file named functions.js. The daily schedules have been stored in files named sunday.htm through saturday.htm.

To complete this Web page:

1. Using your text editor, open **todaytxt.htm** from the tutorial.01/case3 folder. Enter *your name* and *the date* in the head section and save the file as **today.htm**.
2. In the head section just above the </head> tag, insert a script element accessing the functions.js file.
3. Scroll down the file and locate the div element with the id "dateBox". Within this element, insert a script element. The script element should run the following two commands:
    a. Write the HTML code "Today is
" to the Web document.
    b. Write the text string returned by the showDate() function to the Web document.

Explore

4. Scroll down the file and locate the h2 heading, "Today at the Union". Within the empty paragraph that follows this heading, insert another script element. Within the script element, do the following:
    a. Insert this multiline comment:
       Display the daily schedule in an inline frame.
       Daily schedules are stored in the files sunday.htm through saturday.htm.

Explore

    b. Insert a command to write the following text to the Web document:
       `<iframe src='weekday.htm'></iframe>`
       where *weekday* is the text string returned by the weekDay() function.
5. Save your changes to the document.
6. Open **today.htm** in your Web browser. Verify that it shows the current date and that the daily schedule matches the current weekday.
7. If you have the ability to change your computer's date and time, change the date to different days of the week and refresh the Web page. Verify that the date and daily schedule change to match the new date you selected. Debug your code as necessary.
8. Submit the completed Web site to your instructor.

Create

Test your knowledge of JavaScript by creating an opening screen displaying famous birthdays

Case Problem 4

Data files needed for this Case Problem: birthstxt.htm, functions.js, logo.jpg, styles.css

HappyBirthday.com   Linda Chi is the owner of a Web site called HappyBirthday.com that specializes in birthday gifts and memorabilia. To make her site more interesting for users, Linda wants to create a splash screen that displays the current date and a famous birthday occurring on that date. She has asked your help in writing the JavaScript code to generate the welcoming message. She has already designed the page's style and content and has also located the following JavaScript functions:

- The showDate() function, which returns the current date in the text string "*Weekday, Month Day, Year*" where *WeekDay* is the day of the week, *Month* is the name of the month, *Day* is the day of the month, and *Year* is the four-digit year value. The showDate() function has no parameters.

- The dayNumber() function, which returns the day number of the current date, ranging from 1 (the first day of the year) to 366 (the last day of the year). The dayNumber() function has no parameters.
- The showBirthDay() function, which returns a text string describing a famous birthday on the given date. The function has a single parameter, day, which is equal to the day number of the famous birthday you want to view.

The three functions have already been saved for you in a file named functions.js. You do not have to edit this file. Figure 1-39 shows a preview of the completed Web page.

Figure 1-39

To complete this assignment

1. Using your text editor, open **birthstxt.htm** from the tutorial.01/case4 folder. Enter *your name* and *the date* in the head section and save the file as **births.htm**.
2. Open **births.htm** in your Web browser to become familiar with the opening screen's appearance.
3. Use your knowledge of JavaScript to replace the content of the welcome box with generated text that displays the current date and the name of a famous person born on that date. Include comments that describe each of the variables you use in writing this code and the functions that the code accesses.
4. Save your changes to the file and then reopen it in your Web browser. Verify that the page displays the current date and a birthday for that date. If you are able to change the date on your computer's clock, change the date and refresh the Web page. Verify that the page displays the new date and a new famous birthday. Debug your code as necessary
5. Submit the completed Web site to your instructor.

Quick Check Answers

Session 1.1

1. A client-side program is a program that is run on a user's computer, usually with a Web browser. A server-side program runs off of a Web server.

2. <script type="text/javascript"> ... </script>
   Note that older browsers might use:
   <script language="JavaScript"> ...</script>

3. document.write("<h2>Public Library</h2>");

4. document.write('<h2 id="sub">Public Library</h2>');

5. Place the backslash (\ ) symbol at the end of the line to indicate that the statement continues on the next line.

6. JavaScript is case sensitive, so this command should read:
   document.write("Monroe Public Library");

7. <noscript>
       <p><i>JavaScript required.</i></p>
   </noscript>

Session 1.2

1. numeric value, text string, Boolean value, and null value

2. var weekDay = "Friday";
   or
   weekDay = "Friday";

3. to perform an action or to return a value

4. Local and global. A variable with local scope is defined within a function and accessible only within that function. A variable with global scope is not declared within a function and is accessible to all code in the page. Variables within functions have local scope.

5. ```
   function function_name(parameters) {
       JavaScript commands
       return value;
   }
   ```

6. ```
   /*
   This function displays the current date in the format
   month day, year
   */
   ```

7. alert(userName);

8. run-time error

Objectives

Session 2.1
- Work with event handlers
- Insert a value into a Web form field
- Create and work with date objects
- Extract information from date objects

Session 2.2
- Work with arithmetic, unary, conditional, and logical operators
- Understand the properties and methods of the Math object
- Understand how JavaScript works with numeric values
- Run time-delayed and timed-interval commands

Working with Operators and Expressions

Creating a New Year's Day Countdown Clock

Case

Dixon's New Year's Bash

Every year on December 31st, Dixon, Oklahoma, rings in the New Year with a daylong celebration. The New Year's Bash includes races, jugglers, tasting booths, live bands, and dances, and is capped by fireworks at midnight. The bash has become so big that partygoers come from miles away to join in the fun, and planning for the celebration starts early.

Hector Sadler manages promotion for the New Year's Bash. One of his responsibilities is to maintain a Web site that advertises the event and builds up anticipation for it. Hector would like to include a countdown clock on the site's home page displaying the current date and the number of days, hours, minutes, and seconds remaining before the fireworks go off. Hector has asked your help in writing JavaScript code to create this clock.

Student Data Files

▼tutorial.02

▽ **tutorial folder**

clocktxt.htm
functxt.js
+ 1 style sheet
+ 3 graphic files

▽ **review folder**

eventstxt.htm
datestxt.js
+ 1 style sheet
+ 1 graphic file

▽ **case1 folder**

oaetxt.htm
functions.js
+ 1 style sheet
+ 6 graphic files

▼**tutorial.02 continued**

▽ **case2 folder**

hometxt.htm
randtxt.js
tips.js
+ 1 style sheet
+ 2 graphic files

▽ **case3 folder**

worldtxt.htm
zonestxt.js
+ 1 style sheet
+ 2 graphic files

▽ **case4 folder**

malltxt.htm
timetxt.js
mall.txt
+ 4 graphic files

Session 2.1

Working with onEvent Processing

The New Year's Bash is still half a year away, but it's not too soon to sit down with Hector to discuss creating the countdown clock for the Web site. Hector envisions a clock that updates itself every second to add a dynamic effect to the site's home page. Hector has already created a Web page displaying a static value for the date, time, and amount of time left until the new year. Open this file now.

To view the Web page:

1. Use your text editor to open **clocktxt.htm** from the tutorial.02/tutorial folder. Enter *your name* and *the date* in the comment section at the top of the file and save the file as **clock.htm**.

2. Scroll through the file to become familiar with its contents.

3. Open **clock.htm** in your Web browser. Figure 2-1 shows the initial version of the Web page.

The initial clock page ◄ **Figure 2-1**

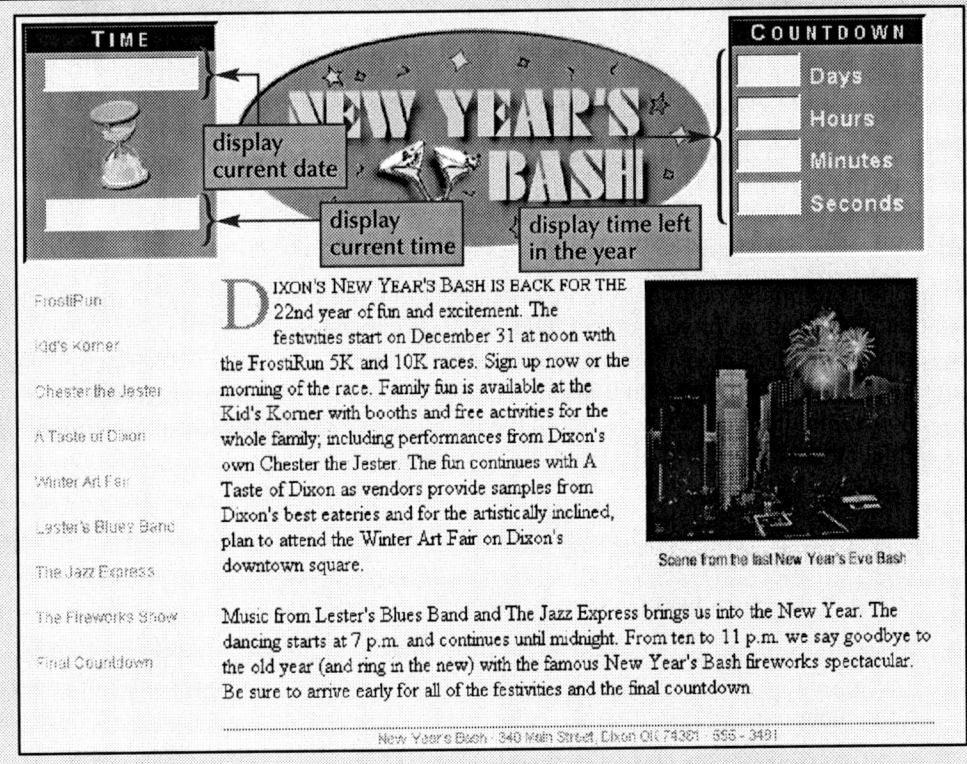

At the top of the Web page are Web form fields in which the current date, time, and countdown clock will appear. The form's name is "clockform". Figure 2-2 shows the names of the fields within the form along with sample values for each field.

Form field names ◄ **Figure 2-2**

Hector wants these values to be constantly updated. To do this, you'll write a JavaScript function that calculates the current date and time and the time remaining until New Year's Day, and then run that function once every second. You'll start creating this function by writing sample text into the different fields of the clockform Web form. To set the value of a form field, you use the JavaScript command

```
document.form.field.value = field_value;
```

where *form* is the name of the form, *field* is the name of the field, and *field_value* is the value you want to place into the field. For example, in Hector's Web page the current date is stored in the dateNow field of the clockform Web form. To set this value to the text string "2/24/2007", you would use the JavaScript command

```
document.clockform.dateNow.value = "2/24/2007";
```

In the same way, to display the text "2:35:05 pm" in the timeNow field, you would use the JavaScript command

```
document.clockform.timeNow.value = "2:35:05 pm";
```

In upcoming tutorials you'll learn more about how to work with forms and fields, but this is enough information for you to start work on Hector's Web page. You'll begin by placing sample date and time values into the clockform Web form using a JavaScript function named NYClock(). For now, you'll insert placeholding values of "99" in the fields for days, hours, minutes, and seconds left in the year. Later in this tutorial you'll learn how to calculate these values and place the results into the form.

To create the NYClock() function:

1. Return to the **clock.htm** file in your text editor.

2. Above the closing </head> tag, insert the following embedded script, as shown in Figure 2-3 (the single-line comments will make it easier to interpret the commands in the function):

```
<script type="text/javascript">
function NYClock() {
// display the current date and time
   document.clockform.dateNow.value = "2/24/2007";
   document.clockform.timeNow.value = "2:35:05 pm";

// calculate the time left until the New Year's Bash
   document.clockform.daysLeft.value = "99";
   document.clockform.hrLeft.value = "99";
   document.clockform.minLeft.value = "99";
   document.clockform.secLeft.value = "99";
}
</script>
```

| Figure 2-3 | Inserting the NYClock function |

```
<title>Dixon's New Year's Bash</title>
<link href="newyear.css" rel="stylesheet" type="text/css" />
<script type="text/javascript">
function NYClock() {
// display the current date and time
   document.clockform.dateNow.value = "2/24/2007";
   document.clockform.timeNow.value = "2:35:05 pm";

// calculate the time left until the New Year's Bash
   document.clockform.daysLeft.value = "99";
   document.clockform.hrLeft.value = "99";
   document.clockform.minLeft.value = "99";
   document.clockform.secLeft.value = "99";
}
</script>
</head>
```

3. Save your changes to the file.

Since these values are to be updated constantly while the page is displayed by a user's browser, it's clear that the NYClock() function will have to run when the page is initially loaded, and then repeatedly run thereafter. This is in contrast to the code you wrote in the last tutorial, which ran only once when the page was loaded by the browser. In that tutorial, the code was run either when it was encountered within a script element or called as part of a function. For the NYClock() function, you need to run code in response to events that occur after the page is loaded.

Understanding Event Handlers

An **event** is an action that occurs within a Web browser or Web document. Most objects have specific events associated with them. For example, one event associated with a Web form button is the action of being clicked by a user. Another event occurs when a user hovers the mouse pointer over the button without clicking it. A Web document itself has associated events such as the action of being loaded or unloaded by a browser. Each action that occurs provides an opportunity to run a program in response to it.

To attach a program to an event, you add an event handler to an object. An **event handler** is a statement that tells browsers what code to run in response to the specified event. For a Web page element, event handlers can be added directly to the element's tag as an attribute of the element. The syntax to insert an event handler as an attribute is

```
<element onevent="script" ...> ...
```

where `element` is the name of the element, `event` is the name of an event, and `script` is a command or collection of commands to be run in response to the event. If you intend to run several commands in response to an event, it's easiest to place them within a function and run the function using a single command. One commonly used event handler, onclick, runs a program in response to a user clicking an element with the mouse button. For example, the event handler in the following element runs the calcTotal() function when a user clicks the input button:

```
<input type="button" value="Total Cost" onclick="calcTotal()" />
```

Figure 2-4 lists some other event handlers you can use on the elements in your Web page. You can also view an extended list of event handlers in the appendices.

Figure 2-4   JavaScript event handlers

Category	Event Handler	Description
Window and document event handlers	onload	The browser has completed loading the document
	onunload	The browser has completed unloading the document
	onerror	An error has occurred in the JavaScript program
	onmove	The user has moved the browser window
	onresize	The user has resized the browser window
	onscroll	The user has moved the scrollbar within the browser window
Form event handlers	onfocus	The user has entered an input field
	onblur	The user has exited an input field
	onchange	The content of an input field has changed
	onselect	The user has selected text within an input or text area field
	onsubmit	The user has submitted the Web form
	onreset	The user has reset the Web form
Mouse and keyboard event handlers	onkeydown	The user has pressed a key
	onkeypress	The user has pressed and released a key
	onclick	The user has clicked the mouse button
	ondblclick	The user has double-clicked the mouse button
	onmousedown	The user has pressed down the mouse button
	onmouseup	The user has released the mouse button
	onmousemove	The user has moved the mouse pointer over the element
	onmouseout	The user has moved the mouse pointer off of the element

For the clock Web page, you want to run the NYClock() function when the page is loaded. Loading is one of the events associated with the Web page, and thus can be handled by adding the following event handler to the <body> tag:

```
<body onload="NYClock()">
```

Add this event handler to the clock.htm file.

To insert the onload event handler:

1. Within the <body> tag, insert the attribute **onload="NYClock()"** as shown in Figure 2-5.

Figure 2-5   Inserting the onload event handler

```
<script type="text/javascript">
function NYClock() {
// display the current date and time
    document.clockform.dateNow.value = "2/24/2007";
    document.clockform.timeNow.value = "2:35:05 pm";

// calculate the time left until the New Year's Bash
    document.clockform.daysLeft.value = "99";
    document.clockform.hrLeft.value = "99";
    document.clockform.minLeft.value = "99";
    document.clockform.secLeft.value = "99";
}
</script>
</head>

<body onload="NYClock()">
<form name="clockform" id="clockform" action="">
```

event handler to run the NYClock() function when the page is loaded

2. Save your changes to the file and then reload **clock.htm** in your Web browser.

The page opens displaying the field values, as shown in Figure 2-6.

Field values inserted into the clockform Web form ◀ Figure 2-6

Trouble? If you receive an error message when loading the page, check the code in the NYClock() function and the onload event handler. Some common programming errors that might have occurred within the NYClock() function include mismatching uppercase and lowercase letters, misspelling variable names, forgetting to close up double quotes, and forgetting to enclose command blocks and functions within curly braces.

Running JavaScript Commands as Links

Another way to run a JavaScript command is as a link. This method is akin to running the command in response to a click event within an element. The syntax for doing this is

```
<a href="javascript:script">content</a>
```

where `script` is the command (or commands) you want to run when a user clicks the link. For example, the following code runs the calcTotal() function when a user clicks the link:

```
<a href="javascript:calcTotal()">
   Calculate total cost
</a>
```

You do not need to use this technique in Hector's Web page. However, it is often used for older browsers that don't support event handlers, or for elements that do not support the onclick event handler. This is a less important issue than it once was when event handlers were a new feature of HTML.

Reference Window

Running Scripts in Response to Events

- To insert an event handler as an element attribute, use
    ```
    <element onevent = "script"> ...
    ```
  where `element` is the Web page element, `event` is the name of an event associated with the element, and `script` is the command (or commands) to be run in response to the event.
- To run a JavaScript command as a link, use the code
    ```
    <a href="javascript:script">content</a>
    ```
  where `script` is the command (or commands) you want to run when a user clicks the link.

Working with Dates

Now that you've created the initial form of the NYClock() function, you need some way of generating the date and time information rather than typing the values directly into the JavaScript code. To work with dates, JavaScript supports a **date object**, which contains information about a specified date and time. Date objects are created using the following command:

```
variable = new Date("month day, year hours.minutes.seconds");
```

where *variable* is the name of the variable that contains the date object, and *month*, *day*, *year*, *hours*, *minutes*, and *seconds* indicate the date and time to be stored in the object. Time values are entered using 24-hour time; thus, a time of 2:35 pm would be entered as 14:35. For example, the following command stores a date object in a variable named thisDate corresponding to a date of February 24, 2007, and a time of 2:35:05 pm:

```
thisDate = new Date("February 24, 2007 14:35:05");
```

If you omit the hours, minutes, and seconds values, JavaScript assumes that the time is 0 hours, 0 minutes, and 0 seconds—in other words, midnight of the specified day. If you omit both the date and time information, JavaScript returns the current date and time, which it gets from the system clock on the user's computer. For example, the following command creates a variable named thisDate containing the current date and time:

```
thisDate = new Date();
```

You can also create a date object using the form

```
variable = new Date(year, month, day, hours, minutes, seconds)
```

where *year*, *month*, *day*, *hours*, *minutes*, and *seconds* are the values of the date and time. In this form, the *month* value is an integer from 0 to 11, where 0 = January, 1 = February, and so forth. Time values are once again expressed in 24-hour time. Thus, to create a date object for February 24, 2007, at 2:35:05 pm, you would use the command

```
thisDate = new Date(2007, 1, 24, 14, 35, 5);
```

Now that you've seen how to store date and time information in a variable, you'll create a variable named today that stores a date object. You'll use February 24, 2007, as your initial date and 2:35:05 pm as your initial time. Later in the tutorial you'll set the value of the today variable to the current date and time (whatever that may be); for now, though, using a preset date and time will allow you to check that any calculations done using this date are correct. Add this variable to the NYClock() function you just created.

To create the today variable:

1. Return to **clock.htm** in your text editor.

2. Insert the following lines at the beginning of the NYClock() function, as shown in Figure 2-7:

```
// the today variable contains the current date and time
   var today=new Date("February 24, 2007 14:35:05");
```

Creating a date object ◄ **Figure 2-7**

```
function NYClock() {
// the today variable contains the current date and time
   var today=new Date("February 24, 2007 14:35:05");

// display the current date and time
   document.clockform.dateNow.value = "2/24/2007";
   document.clockform.timeNow.value = "2:35:05 pm";

// calculate the time left until the New Year's Bash
   document.clockform.daysLeft.value = "99";
   document.clockform.hrLeft.value = "99";
   document.clockform.minLeft.value = "99";
   document.clockform.secLeft.value = "99";
}
```

variable storing the date object

3. Save your changes to the file.

Retrieving the Date, Month, and Hour Values

A date object is really just a numeric value equal to the number of milliseconds between the specified date and time and January 1, 1970; however, you rarely see dates expressed in that way. For your sample date and time of February 24, 2007, at 2:35:05 pm the date object has a hidden value equal to 1,172,349,305,000 milliseconds. Fortunately, you don't have to work with this value. Instead, JavaScript provides **date methods**, which are methods you can use to retrieve information from a date object or to change a date object's value.

If you're given a date object, you may want to extract only the day of the month from it. To get that information, JavaScript provides the getDate() method. The syntax to apply the getDate() method is

```
DateObject.getDate()
```

where *DateObject* is a date object (or a variable that contains a date object). For example, the following code extracts the day value from the thisDate variable, storing the result in the thisDay variable:

```
thisDate = new Date("February 24, 2007 14:35:05");
thisDay = thisDate.getDate();
```

After running these commands, the value of the thisDay variable is "24".

A similar method exists for extracting the value of the current month. This method is named getMonth(). Note that, because JavaScript starts counting the months with 0 for January, you must add 1 to the month number returned by the getMonth() method to translate the value to the commonly used system of numbering months from 1 to 12. The following JavaScript code extracts the current month number, increases it by 1, and stores it in a variable named thisMonth:

```
thisDate = new Date("February 24, 2007 14:35:05");
thisMonth = thisDate.getMonth()+1;
```

In this code sample, the value of the thisMonth variable is "2".

Another method you'll be using in your program is the getFullYear() method. As the name suggests, the getFullYear() method extracts the 4-digit year value from the date object. The following code shows how you would store the value of the current year in a variable you name thisYear:

```
thisDate = new Date("February 24, 2007 14:35:05");
thisYear = thisDate.getFullYear();
```

As you would expect, the value of the thisYear variable would be "2007". Notice that the method name is getFullYear(), rather than simply getYear(). This is because a separate get-Year() method exists, which returns only the last two digits of the year for years prior to 2000. For example, instead of 1999, a date of 99 would be returned. As shown in Figure 2-8, the getYear() method runs into difficulty beyond the year 1999.

Figure 2-8 ▸ **Values of the getYear() method from 1998–2001**

Year	getYear() value Internet Explorer	Netscape / Opera
1998	98	98
1999	99	99
2000	2000	100
2001	2001	101

The getYear() date method returns a value of 2000 for the year 2000 for Internet Explorer, but 100 for the Netscape and Opera browsers. If you use this method with Internet Explorer to calculate the number of years between 1998 and 2000, you would come up with an answer of 1902 years! Netscape and Opera would give the correct answer but at the expense of incorrectly displaying the date for years after 1999. This is a classic example of the Y2K bug that caused so much concern in the late 1990s. The bottom line is that you should use the getFullYear() method when you need to work with calendar years, and you should avoid the getYear() method.

Retrieving the Hour, Minute, and Second Values

JavaScript supports similar methods for extracting the hours, minutes, and seconds values from a date object. These are

```
DateObject.getSeconds()
DateObject.getMinutes()
DateObject.getHours()
```

where *DateObject* is once again a date object or a variable containing a date object. Hours are expressed in 24-hour time, meaning that the code

```
thisDate = new Date("February 24, 2007 14:35:05");
thisHour = thisDate.getHours();
```

stores the value "14" in the thisHour variable. Figure 2-9 summarizes the methods for retrieving date and time values from date objects.

	Extracting date and time values from date objects		Figure 2-9

Method	Retrieves	Value
The sample data in the Value column assumes that the variable thisDate stores the date object for the date "June 15, 2007 14:35:28".		
thisDate.getSeconds()	Retrieves the seconds value	28
thisDate.getMinutes()	Retrieves the minutes value	35
thisDate.getHours()	Retrieves the hours value (in military time)	14
thisDate.getDate()	Retrieves the day of the month value	15
thisDate.getDay()	Retrieves the day of the week (0 = Sunday, 1 = Monday, 2 = Tuesday, 3 = Wednesday, 4 = Thursday, 5 = Friday, 6 = Saturday)	5
thisDate.getMonth()	Retrieves the month value (0 = January, 1 = February, 2 = March, etc.)	5
thisDate.getFullYear()	Retrieves the four-digit year value	2007
thisDate.getTime()	Retrieves the time value, as expressed in milliseconds, since January 1, 1970	1,181,936,128,000

Retrieving Date and Time Values

Reference Window

- To retrieve the year value from a date object named *DateObject*, use the command
    `Year = DateObject.getFullYear();`
- To retrieve the month value, use the command
    `Month = DateObject.getMonth();`
  A *Month* value of 0 equals the first month of the year, or January; a *Month* value of 1 equals the second month of the year or February; and so forth.
- To retrieve the day of the month value, use
    `Day = DateObject.getDate();`
- To retrieve the day of the week value, use
    `DayofWeek = DateObject.getDay();`
  A *DayofWeek* value of 0 equals the first weekday, or Sunday; a *DayofWeek* value of 1 equals the second weekday, or Monday; and so forth.
- To retrieve the hours value, use
    `Day = DateObject.getHours();`
- To retrieve the minutes value, use
    `Day = DateObject.getMinutes();`
- To retrieve the seconds value, use
    `Day = DateObject.getSeconds();`

Setting Date and Time Values

In addition to retrieving date and time values, you can also use JavaScript to set these values. This is most often used in programs where you have to change the value of a date object from one particular date or time to another. For example, the following code uses the setFullYear() method to change the date stored in the thisDate variable from February 24, 2007, to February 24, 2008:

```
thisDate = new Date("February 24, 2007");
thisDate.setFullYear(2008);
```

Figure 2-10 summarizes the other methods supported by JavaScript for setting date and time values.

Figure 2-10 ▶ **Setting date and time values for date objects**

Method	Description
DateObject.setSeconds(*value*)	Sets the seconds value of *DateObject* to *value*
DateObject.setMinutes(*value*)	Sets the minutes value of *DateObject* to *value*
DateObject.setHours(*value*)	Sets the hours value of *DateObject* to *value*
DateObject.setDate(*value*)	Sets the day of the month value of the *DateObject* to *value*
DateObject.setMonth(*value*)	Sets the month number of *DateObject* to *value* (U=January, 1=February, etc.)
DateObject.setFullYear(*value*)	Sets the four-digit year value of *DateObject* to *value*
DateObject.setTime(*value*)	Sets the time of *DateObject* in milliseconds since January 1, 1970

You'll create a function that uses the setFullYear() method in the next session.

Creating a Date and Time Function

Now that you've seen some of the methods associated with date objects, you'll use those methods to create functions that extract the date and time values from a date object, returning those values in formatted text strings. The first function you'll create is named showDate() and has the following code:

```
function showDate(dateObj) {
    thisDate = dateObj.getDate();
    thisMonth = dateObj.getMonth()+1;
    thisYear = dateObj.getFullYear();
    return thisMonth + "/" + thisDate + "/" + thisYear;
}
```

The showDate() function has a single parameter named dateObj, which stores the date object to be evaluated. The function extracts the day of the month, the month number, and the 4-digit year value and returns a text string combining all of the values in the format

month/day/year

where *month* is the value of the thisMonth variable, *day* is the value of the thisDate variable, and *year* is the value of the thisYear variable. You'll call this function by placing the generated text string into the dateNow field of the Web form in Hector's Web page.

The code for the showTime() function is similar:

```
function showTime(dateObj) {
    thisSecond=dateObj.getSeconds();
    thisMinute=dateObj.getMinutes();
    thisHour=dateObj.getHours();
    return thisHour + ":" + thisMinute + ":" + thisSecond;
}
```

The showTime() function extracts the hours, minutes, and seconds values from the date object, returning the text string

hour:minute:second

where *hour* is the value of the thisHour variable, *minute* is the value of the thisMinute variable, and *second* is the value of the thisSecond variable.

To create the showDate() and showTime() functions:

1. Use your text editor to open the **functxt.js** file located in the tutorial.02/tutorial folder. Enter *your name* and *the date* in the comment section at the top of the file and save the file as **functions.js**.

2. Below the comment section, insert the following two functions, as shown in Figure 2-11:

```
function showDate(dateObj) {
    thisDate = dateObj.getDate();
    thisMonth = dateObj.getMonth()+1;
    thisYear = dateObj.getFullYear();
    return thisMonth + "/" + thisDate + "/" + thisYear;
}
function showTime(dateObj) {
    thisSecond=dateObj.getSeconds();
    thisMinute=dateObj.getMinutes();
    thisHour=dateObj.getHours();
    return thisHour + ":" + thisMinute + ":" + thisSecond;
}
```

Creating the showDate() and showTime() functions ◀ Figure 2-11

```
function showDate(dateobj) {
    thisDate = dateobj.getDate();
    thisMonth = dateobj.getMonth()+1;
    thisYear = dateobj.getFullYear();
    return thisMonth + "/" + thisDate + "/" + thisYear;
}

function showTime(dateobj) {
    thisSecond=dateobj.getSeconds();
    thisMinute=dateobj.getMinutes();
    thisHour=dateobj.getHours();
    return thisHour + ":" + thisMinute + ":" + thisSecond;
}
```

3. Save your changes to the file

Next you'll add a link to this external script to the clock.htm file and call the two functions, placing their values in the appropriate fields of the Web form.

To call the showDate() and showTime() functions:

1. Return to the **clock.htm** file in your text editor.

2. Directly above the opening <script> tag, insert the following external script element:

```
<script type="text/javascript" src="functions.js"></script>
```

3. In the embedded script element, replace the command that stores the date value in the dateNow field with

```
document.clockform.dateNow.value = showDate(today);
```

4. Replace the command that stores the time value in the timeNow field with

```
document.clockform.timeNow.value = showTime(today);
```

Figure 2-12 shows the revised code for the clock.htm file.

Figure 2-12   **Calling the showDate() and showTime() functions**

```
<script type="text/javascript" src="functions.js"></script>
<script type="text/javascript">
function NYClock() {
// the today variable contains the current date and time
   var today=new Date("February 24, 2007 14:35:05");

// display the current date and time
   document.clockform.dateNow.value = showDate(today);
   document.clockform.timeNow.value = showTime(today);

// calculate the time left until the New Year's Bash
   document.clockform.daysLeft.value = "99";
   document.clockform.hrLeft.value = "99";
   document.clockform.minLeft.value = "99";
   document.clockform.secLeft.value = "99";
}
</script>
```

5. Save your changes to the file and then reopen or refresh **clock.htm** in your Web browser. Figure 2-13 shows the current values in the page's Web form.

Figure 2-13   **Revised countdown clock values**

You show the current output from the countdown clock to Hector. He sees two things that he would like changed. First, he wants the time values displayed in 12-hour time rather than 24-hour time. In addition, a minute or second value less than 10 should have a zero placed before its value as a placeholder. In other words, instead of displaying
   14:35:5
Hector wants the time to read
   2:35:05 pm
In the next session you'll learn how to add these features to the countdown clock as well as how to create functions to calculate the number of days, hours, minutes, and seconds remaining in the year. For now, if you wish to take a break you can close your open files.

Review

Session 2.1 Quick Check

1. What is an event handler?
2. What attribute would you add to a button element to run the showImage() function when the button is clicked?
3. What HTML code would you enter to create a link that runs the showImage() function when the link is clicked?
4. What JavaScript command would you enter to create a variable named examDate storing the following date and time: May 8, 2007, at 6:55:28 pm?
5. What command would you use to extract the month value from the examDate variable? What value would be returned by this method?
6. What command would you use to extract the 4-digit year value from the examDate variable?

7. What command would you use to change the day of the month value in the exam-Date variable from 8 to 9 (while leaving all of the other date and time values unchanged)?

8. What command would you use to create a variable named currentTime that stores the current date and time (whatever that may be)?

Session 2.2

Working with Operators

In the previous session you learned how to work with date objects to display specified dates and times in your Web page. In this session you'll learn how to perform calculations with dates and JavaScript variables. To perform a calculation, you need to insert a JavaScript statement containing an operator. An **operator** is a symbol used to act upon an item or a variable within a JavaScript expression. The concept of an operator is a very basic concept. In fact, you've already been using operators throughout this tutorial. For example, you've been using the "+" operator to combine text strings and add numeric values. The following statement from the showDate() function uses the + operator to increase the value of dateObj.getMonth() by 1:

```
thisMonth = dateObj.getMonth()+1;
```

You have also used the + operator to combine text strings, as in the following statement from the showDate() function:

```
thisMonth + "/" + thisDate + "/" + thisYear;
```

This statement displays dates in the format *month/date/year*.

Arithmetic Operators

The + operator belongs to a group of operators called **arithmetic operators** that perform simple mathematical calculations. Figure 2-14 lists some of the arithmetic operators and gives examples of how they work.

Arithmetic operators | Figure 2-14

Operator	Description	Example
+	Combines or adds two items	Men = 20; Women = 25; Total = Men + Women;
-	Subtracts one item from another	Income = 1000; Expense = 750; Profit = Income - Expense;
*	Multiplies two items	Width = 50; Length = 20; Area = Width * Length;
/	Divides one item by another	Persons = 50; Cost = 200; CostPerPerson = Cost / Persons
%	Calculates the remainder after dividing one value by another	TotalEggs = 64; CartonSize = 12; EggsLeft = TotalEggs % CartonSize;

The arithmetic operators shown in Figure 2-14 are also known as **binary operators** because they work with two items in an expression. JavaScript also supports **unary operators**, which work on only one item. Unary operators can make your code more compact and efficient, but they're easy to misuse if you're not careful. One of the unary operators is the **increment operator**, which is used to increase the value of an expression by 1. The increment operator is indicated by the ++ symbol and can be placed either before or after an expression. With the increment operator, the following three expressions are equivalent:

```
x = x + 1;
x++;
++x;
```

You need to use care with using unary operators to assign values to other variables. For example, if $x = 5$ then the statement

```
y = x++;
```

assigns a value of 5 to y and 6 to x. While the result may seem counterintuitive, this single command actually contains two distinct operations performed in a specific order:

```
y = x;
x = x+1;
```

The first operation assigns a value of 5 to y, and the second increases x by 1, changing its value to 6. On the other hand, if you place the increment operator before x as in the statement

```
y = ++x;
```

you are telling JavaScript to run the commands in the following order:

```
x = x + 1;
y = x;
```

This expression increases the value of x by 1, changing its value to 6, and then sets y equal to 6 as well. As you can see, while using a unary operator allows you to create compact expressions that assign values to several variables, such operators can become complicated and difficult to interpret.

The two other unary operators are the **decrement operator**, which decreases an item's value by 1, and the **negation operator**, which changes the sign of (or negates) an item's value. Figure 2-15 summarizes the three unary operators.

Figure 2-15   **Unary operators**

Operator	Description	Example	Equivalent To
++	Increases the item's value by 1	x++	x = x + 1
--	Decreases the item's value by 1	x--	x = x - 1
-	Changes the sign of the item's value	-x	x = 0 - x

Assignment Operators

Operators are also used when assigning values to items within a JavaScript statement. These types of operators are called **assignment operators**. The most common assignment operator is the equal sign (=), which assigns the value of one item to another. JavaScript provides additional assignment operators to assign values and change values within a single operation. One of these is the += operator. In JavaScript, the following two expressions create the same result:

```
x = x + y;
x += y
```

In both expressions, the value of the x variable is added to the value of the y variable, and then the new value is stored back into the x variable.

An assignment operator also can be used with numbers to increase a variable by a specific amount. For example, to increase the value of the x variable by 2, you can use either of the following two expressions:

```
x = x + 2;
x += 2
```

A common use of the += operator is to create extended text strings. In this case, the operator appends one text string to another. For example, if you have a text string that covers several lines, you may find it difficult to store that text in a variable using a single statement. However, you can use the += operator to do so in the following manner:

```
quote = "To be or not to be: ";
quote +="That is the question. ";
quote +="Whether 'tis nobler in the mind to suffer "
quote +="the slings and arrows of outrageous fortune, ";
quote +="Or to take arms against a sea of troubles";
quote +="And by opposing end them. ";
...
```

Continuing in this fashion, the quote variable eventually contains the complete text of Hamlet's soliloquy, but it does so using a series of short, simple expressions rather than a single long and cumbersome one. This technique is often used to store long text strings within a variable. Other assignment operators are discussed in Figure 2-16.

Assignment operators | **Figure 2-16**

Operator	Description	Example	Equivalent To
=	Assigns the value of the expression on the right to the expression on the left	x = y	
+=	Adds two expressions	x += y	x = x + y
-=	Subtracts the expression on the right from the expression on the left	x -= y	x = x - y
*=	Multiplies two expressions	x *= y	x = x * y
%=	Calculates the remainder from dividing the expression on the right from the expression on the left	x %= y	x = x % y

As you can see, once you master the syntax, assignment operators allow you to create expressions that are both efficient and compact. As you start learning JavaScript, you might prefer using the longer form for such expressions. However, if you study the code of other JavaScript programmers, you will certainly encounter programs that make substantial use of assignment operators to reduce program size.

Calculating the Days Left in the Year

You'll use what you've learned about operators and date objects to create a function that calculates the number of days remaining in the year. This function, which you'll name calcDays(), has a single parameter named currentDate that contains a date object for the current date and time (whatever that may be). The function needs to do the following:

```
function calcDays(currentDate) {
    create a date object for January 1 of the next year
    calculate the difference between currentDate and January 1
}
```

Add this function structure to the function.js file.

To create the calcDays() function:

▶ 1. If necessary, use your text editor to reopen the **functions.js** file.

▶ 2. At the bottom of the file, insert the following function (see Figure 2-17):

```
function calcDays(currentDate) {
// create a date object for January 1 of the next year
// calculate the difference between currentDate and January 1
}
```

Figure 2-17 ▶ Creating the calcDays() function

```
function calcDays(currentDate) {
// create a date object for January 1 of the next year
// calculate the difference between currentDate and January 1
}
```

▶ 3. Save your changes to the file.

Next you will enter the commands for the calcDays() function. The first line creates the January 1 date object. Since you need to specify a year value, you'll use the year 2007:

```
newYear = new Date("January 1, 2007");
```

The value "2007" for the year is only temporary. What you really want is the value of the current year (whatever that may be) plus 1. You can determine this value by extracting the year value from the currentDate parameter and adding 1 to it using the command

```
nextYear = currentDate.getFullYear()+1;
```

Next you use the setFullYear() method to set the year value of the newYear date object:

```
newYear.setFullYear(nextYear);
```

To calculate the time difference between New Year's Day and the current day, you subtract one date object from the other:

```
days = newYear - currentDate;
```

However, you need to remember that JavaScript measures time in terms of milliseconds, not days. Thus, this difference tells you the number of milliseconds between the current date and time and New Year's Day. If you want to express this value in days, you need to divide the difference by the number of milliseconds in one day. The revised expression is

```
days = (newYear - currentDate)/(1000*60*60*24);
```

because there are 1000 milliseconds in one second, 60 seconds in one minute, 60 minutes in one hour, and 24 hours in one day. Putting all of these commands together, the complete calcDays() function is

```
function calcDays(currentDate) {
// create a date object for January 1 of the next year
   newYear = new Date("January 1, 2007");
   // insert a temporary date for January 1
   nextYear = currentDate.getFullYear()+1;
   // the year value of the next year
   newYear.setFullYear(nextYear);
   // change newYear to the next year

// calculate the difference between currentDate and January 1
   days = (newYear - currentDate)/(1000*60*60*24);
   // convert milliseconds to days
   return days;
}
```

Add these commands and comments to the calcDays() function.

To add commands to the calcDays() function:

1. Below the first comment line in the calcDays() function, add the following lines:

```
newYear = new Date("January 1, 2007");
// insert a temporary date for January 1
nextYear = currentDate.getFullYear()+1;
// the year value of the next year
newYear.setFullYear(nextYear);
// change newYear to the next year
```

2. Add the following lines below the next comment line (see Figure 2-18):

```
days = (newYear - currentDate)/(1000*60*60*24);
// convert milliseconds to days
return days;
```

Adding commands to the calcDays() function   Figure 2-18

```
function calcDays(currentDate) {
// create a date object for January 1 of the next year
   newYear = new Date("January 1, 2007");   // insert a temporary date for January 1
   nextYear = currentDate.getFullYear()+1; // the year value of the next year
   newYear.setFullYear(nextYear);          // change newYear to the next year

// calculate the difference between currentDate and January 1
   days = (newYear - currentDate)/(1000*60*60*24); // convert milliseconds to days
   return days;
}
```

3. Save your changes to the file.

   Now call the function from the clock.htm file and display the value returned by the function in the daysLeft field of the clockform Web form.

4. If necessary, reopen the **clock.htm** file in your text editor.

5. Directly above the line that sets the value of the daysLeft field, insert the following line:

```
var days = calcDays(today);
```

6. Change the line that sets the value of the daysLeft field to

```
document.clockform.daysLeft.value = days;
```

Figure 2-19 shows the revised code for the clock.htm file.

Figure 2-19	Calling the calcDays() function

```
function NYClock() {
// the today variable contains the current date and time
   var today=new Date("February 24, 2007 14:35:05");

// display the current date and time
   document.clockform.dateNow.value = showDate(today);
   document.clockform.timeNow.value = showTime(today);

// calculate the time left until the New Year's Bash
   var days = calcDays(today);
   document.clockform.daysLeft.value = days;
   document.clockform.hrLeft.value = "99";
   document.clockform.minLeft.value = "99";
   document.clockform.secLeft.value = "99";
}
```

7. Save your changes to the file.

8. Reload or refresh the **clock.htm** file in your Web browser. Figure 2-20 shows the field values in the Web page.

Figure 2-20	Displaying the days left until New Year's Day

Trouble? If no value appears in the Days field, check the code in the calcDays() function against the code shown in Figure 2-18.

The value displayed in the daysLeft field is 310.3923... The fractional part of the value represents the hours, minutes, and seconds until midnight on New Year's Eve. You need to display only the days value and then convert the fractional part of this value into the hours, minutes, and seconds values. To do this you'll have to use some of the Math methods supported by JavaScript.

Working with Math Methods and Constants

Another way of performing a calculation is to use JavaScript's Math object. The **Math object** is an object used in JavaScript for performing mathematical tasks and storing mathematical values.

Math Methods

The Math object supports several different **Math methods**, which are methods for performing advanced calculations such as generating random numbers, extracting square roots, and calculating trigonometric values. The syntax for applying a Math method is

```
Math.method(expression)
```

where `method` is the method you'll apply to an expression. To calculate the square root of a number, you can use the sqrt method, which has the syntax

```
Math.sqrt(expression)
```

For example, the following commands result in the value "4" being stored in the y variable:

```
x = 16;
y = Math.sqrt(x);
```

Figure 2-21 lists the JavaScript Math methods and describes how to apply them. Case is important in applying the Math object, meaning that you cannot use "math" instead of "Math" for the object name.

Math methods ◄ **Figure 2-21**

Math Method	Description
Math.abs(x)	Returns the absolute value of x
Math.acos(x)	Returns the arc cosine of x in radians
Math.asin(x)	Returns the arc sine of x in radians
Math.atan(x)	Returns the arc tangent of x in radians
Math.atan2(x, y)	Returns the angle between the x-axis and the point (x, y)
Math.ceil(x)	Returns x rounded up to the next highest integer
Math.cos(x)	Returns the cosine of x
Math.exp(x)	Returns e^x
Math.floor(x)	Returns x rounded down to the next lowest integer
Math.log(x)	Returns the natural logarithm of x
Math.max(x, y)	Returns the larger of x and y
Math.min(x, y)	Returns the smaller of x and y
Math.pow(x, y)	Returns x^y
Math.random()	Returns a random number between 0 and 1
Math.round(x)	Returns x rounded to the nearest integer
Math.sin(x)	Returns the sine of x
Math.sqrt(x)	Returns the square root of x
Math.tan(x)	Returns the tangent of x

Math Constants

There are several mathematical constants, such as π and e, that you may want to include in a JavaScript function. Rather than entering these values directly into a variable, you can use the Math object to generate these values. The syntax to access one of these mathematical constants is

```
Math.CONSTANT
```

where *CONSTANT* is the name of the mathematical constant supported by the Math object. Figure 2-22 lists the Math object constants.

Figure 2-22 ▶ **Math constants**

Math Constant	Description
Math.E	The natural logarithm base, e (approximately 2.7183)
Math.LN10	The natural logarithm of 10 (approximately 2.3026)
Math.LN2	The natural logarithm of 2 (approximately 0.6931)
Math.LOG10E	The base 10 logarithm of e (approximately 0.4343)
Math.LOG2E	The base 2 logarithm of e (approximately 1.4427)
Math.PI	The value π (approximately 3.1416)
Math.SQRT1_2	The value of 1 divided by the square root of 2 (approximately 0.7071)
Math.SQRT2	The value of the square root of 2 (approximately 1.4142)

For example, the formula to calculate the area of a circle is πr^2, where r is the radius of the circle. You can create a function to calculate a circle's area using the following code:

```
function circle_area(radius) {
   area = Math.PI*Math.pow(radius, 2);
   return area;
}
```

For the countdown clock, you need to display only the integer portion of the days left in the year. You can calculate this value using the Math.floor() method, which rounds a value down to the next lowest integer. For a value of 310.39, this method returns the value 310. Apply this method to the value displayed in the daysLeft field.

To apply the Math.floor() method:

▶ **1.** Return to the **clock.htm** file in your text editor.

▶ **2.** Change the statement that sets the value of the daysLeft field to the following two lines (see Figure 2-23):

```
// display days rounded to the next lowest integer
document.clockform.daysLeft.value = Math.floor(days);
```

Figure 2-23 ▶ **Using the Math.floor() method**

```
function NYClock() {
// the today variable contains the current date and time
   var today=new Date("February 24, 2007 14:35:05");

// display the current date and time
   document.clockform.dateNow.value = showDate(today);
   document.clockform.timeNow.value = showTime(today);

// calculate the time left until the New Year's Bash
   var days = calcDays(today);

   // display days rounded to the next lowest integer
   document.clockform.daysLeft.value = Math.floor(days);
   document.clockform.hrLeft.value = "99";
   document.clockform.minLeft.value = "99";
   document.clockform.secLeft.value = "99";
}
```

3. Save your changes to the file and reopen or refresh **clock.htm** in your Web browser. As Figure 2-24 shows, the daysLeft field now displays the daysLeft value as an integer.

Calculating the Hours, Minutes, and Seconds Left in the Year

Next you want to calculate the hours, minutes, and seconds left in the year. Using the Math.floor() function, you know that the number of whole days left in the year is 310. The difference between this number and 310.3923... is 0.3923... The 0.3923... represents the fractional part of the current day remaining. You need to convert this value to hours. You can do this by multiplying 0.3923... by 24 (because there are 24 hours in a single day.) Thus, the JavaScript command to calculate the number of hours remaining in the current day is

```
var hours = (days - Math.floor(days))*24;
```

For a value of 0.3923, the value of the hours variable is 9.4152 hours. The fractional part of this value represents the minutes and seconds left within the current hour. You first need to round the hours value down to the next lowest integer, like you did with the daysLeft field value.

To calculate the hours left in the day:

1. Return to the **clock.htm** file in your text editor.

2. Insert the following two lines below the statement that sets the value of the daysLeft field value:

```
// calculate the hours left in the current day
var hours = (days - Math.floor(days))*24;
```

3. Change the statement that sets the value of the hoursLeft field to

```
// display hours rounded to the next lowest integer
document.clockform.hrLeft.value = Math.floor(hours);
```

See Figure 2-25.

Figure 2-25 **Creating the hours variable**

```
function NYClock() {
  // the today variable contains the current date and time
  var today=new Date("February 24, 2007  14:35:05");

  // display the current date and time
  document.clockform.dateNow.value = showDate(today);
  document.clockform.timeNow.value = showTime(today);

  // calculate the time left until the New Year's Bash
  var days = calcDays(today);

  // display days rounded to the next lowest integer
  document.clockform.daysLeft.value = Math.floor(days);

  // calculate the hours left in the current day
  var hours = (days - Math.floor(days))*24;

  // display hours rounded to the next lowest integer
  document.clockform.hrLeft.value = Math.floor(hours);
  document.clockform.minLeft.value = "99";
  document.clockform.secLeft.value = "99";
}
```

4. Save your changes to the file and reopen or refresh **clock.htm** in your Web browser. As shown in Figure 2-26, the hoursLeft field now displays hours left in the current day.

Figure 2-26 **Hours left in the current day**

The technique to calculate the minutes left in the current hour is similar. Once again, you multiply the difference between the hours value and whole hours value by 60 to express the fractional part in terms of minutes. The command is

```
var minutes = (hours - Math.floor(hours))*60;
```

Finally, to calculate the seconds left in the current minute, you multiply the fractional part of the minutes variable by 60.

```
var seconds = (minutes - Math.floor(minutes))*60;
```

As with the days and hours variables, you display only the integer part of the minutes and seconds variables. Add these commands to the NYClock() function.

To calculate the minutes and seconds left:

1. Return to the **clock.htm** file in your text editor.

2. Insert the following lines below the statement that sets the value of the hrLeft field value:

```
// calculate the minutes left in the current hour
var minutes = (hours - Math.floor(hours))*60;
```

3. Change the statement that sets the value of the minLeft field to

```
// display minutes rounded to the next lowest integer
document.clockform.minLeft.value = Math.floor(minutes);
```

4. Insert the following lines below the statement that sets the value of the minLeft field value:

```
// calculate the seconds left in the current minute
var seconds = (minutes - Math.floor(minutes))*60;
```

5. Change the statement that sets the value of the secondsLeft field to:

```
// display seconds rounded to the next lowest integer
document.clockform.secLeft.value = Math.floor(seconds);
```

See Figure 2-27.

Creating the minutes and seconds variables ◀ **Figure 2-27**

```
function NYClock() {
// the today variable contains the current date and time
    var today=new Date("February 24, 2007 14:35:05");

// display the current date and time
    document.clockform.dateNow.value = showDate(today);
    document.clockform.timeNow.value = showTime(today);

// calculate the time left until the New Year's Bash
    var days = calcDays(today);

    // display days rounded to the next lowest integer
    document.clockform.daysLeft.value = Math.floor(days);

    // calculate the hours left in the current day
    var hours = (days - Math.floor(days))*24;

    // display hours rounded to the next lowest integer
    document.clockform.hrLeft.value = Math.floor(hours);

    // calculate the minutes left in the current hour
    var minutes = (hours - Math.floor(hours))*60;

    // display minutes rounded to the next lowest integer
    document.clockform.minLeft.value = Math.floor(minutes);

    // calculate the seconds left in the current minute
    var seconds = (minutes - Math.floor(minutes))*60;

    // display seconds rounded to the next lowest integer
    document.clockform.secLeft.value = Math.floor(seconds);
}
```

6. Save your changes to the file and reopen or refresh **clock.htm** in your Web browser. As shown in Figure 2-28, the Web form now displays the time left in the current year in days, hours, minutes, and seconds.

Displaying the time left in terms of days, hours, minutes, and seconds ◀ **Figure 2-28**

In some cases, your countdown value may show an extra (or missing) hour, minute, or second. Why is that? There are several factors involved. One is the presence of daylight savings time, in which the clock is moved forward (or backward) one hour. If your time interval crosses this event, the hour value will appear off as an extra hour is added to or subtracted from the time interval. Another factor is that the day is not evenly divided into seconds (hence the reason why JavaScript measures time in milliseconds). There is always a fraction of a second left over each day. As the days accumulate, these fractions of a second add up. Most time devices, such as atomic clocks, account for this accumulation by adding a "leap second" on certain days of the year. The effect of adding these leap seconds is included in any time calculations you make with JavaScript. Thus, there is more going on in calculating the time difference between one date and another than it may appear at first glance.

Controlling How JavaScript Works with Numeric Values

As you perform mathematical calculations using JavaScript, you'll run into situations in which you need to work with the properties of numeric values themselves. JavaScript provides several methods that allow you to examine the properties of numbers and specify how they're displayed on a Web page.

Handling Illegal Operations

Some mathematical operations can return results that are not numeric values. For example, you cannot divide a number by a text string. If you attempted to perform the following operation in your script:

```
var x = 5/"A";
document.write(x);
```

your Web page would display the value "NaN", which stands for "Not a Number". Essentially, this is JavaScript's way of telling you that you are attempting an operation that you think uses a numeric value, but doesn't. You can check for the presence of this particular error using the function isNaN(). The syntax of the function is

```
isNaN(value)
```

where *value* is the value or variable you want to test for being numeric. The isNaN() function returns a Boolean value: true if the value is not numeric (i.e., NaN) and false if otherwise. The use of the isNaN() function is one way of locating illegal operations in your code.

Attempting to divide a number by 0 is another illegal operation. The code

```
var x = 5/0;
document.write(x);
```

results in the value "Infinity" being written to the Web page. The Infinity value indicates that you've attempted a numeric calculation whose result is greater than the largest numeric value supported by JavaScript. There is also an Infinity value for operations whose result is less than the smallest numeric value. JavaScript is limited to numeric values that fall between approximately 1.8×10^{-308} and 1.8×10^{308}. Any operation that would exceed those bounds, such as dividing a number by zero, causes JavaScript to assign a value of Infinity to the result. You can check for this outcome using the function

```
isFinite(value)
```

where *value* is the value you want to test for being finite. Like the isNaN() function, the isFinite() function returns a Boolean value: true if *value* is a finite number falling within JavaScript's acceptable range, and false if the numeric value falls outside that range or if *value* is not a number at all.

Specifying the Number Format

When JavaScript displays a numeric value, it displays all of the calculated digits in that value. This can result in long numeric strings of digits. For example, the code

```
var x = 1/4;
var y = 1/3;
document.write("x = " + x);
document.write("y = " + y);
```

causes the following two text strings to be written to the Web page:

```
x = 0.25
y = 0.3333333333333333
```

In most cases, you don't need to display a calculated value to 16 digits. With currency values, you usually want to display results only to two decimal places. To control the number of digits displayed by the browser, you can apply the following function:

```
value.toFixed(n)
```

where *value* is the value or variable and *n* is the number of decimal places that should be displayed in the output. The following examples show the toFixed() function applied to different numeric values:

```
testValue = 2.835;
testValue.toFixed(0)   // returns "3"
testValue.toFixed(1)   // returns "2.8"
testValue.toFixed(2)   // returns "2.84"
```

Note that the toFixed() function not only limits the number of decimals displayed by a value, but also converts that value into a text string. Also, the toFixed() function rounds the last digit in an expression rather than truncating it. Older browsers do not support the toFixed() method. If you need to round a number to a certain number of digits, you must create your own custom function. You'll look at examples of customized math functions at the end of this tutorial.

Converting Between Numbers and Text Strings

You may also come across situations in your code when you need to convert a number to a text string and vice versa. One way to convert a number to a text string is by using the + operator to add a text string to a number. For example

```
testNumber = 123;            // numeric value
testString = testNumber + ""; // text string
```

To go in the other direction, converting a text string to a number, you can apply an arithmetic operator (other than the + operator) to the text string. For example:

```
testString = "123";          // text string
testNumber = testString*1;   // numeric value
```

Another approach is to use the parseInt() function, which extracts the leading integer value from a text string. The syntax of the parseInt() function is

```
parseInt(text)
```

where `text` is the text string or variable from which you need to extract the leading integer value. The parseInt() function determines whether the first nonblank character in the text string is a number. If it is, it then parses the text string from left to right until the end of the number or a decimal point is encountered. Any characters in the string after that are discarded. Only the first integer in the string is returned, and the parseInt() function does not return either decimal points or numbers to the right of a decimal. If a text string does not begin with a number, the parseInt() function returns the value NaN, indicating that there is no accessible number in the text string. The following are some sample values returned by the parseInt() function:

```
parseInt("120 lbs")                 // returns 120
parseInt("206.58 lbs")              // returns 206
parseInt("weight equals 55 lbs")    // returns NaN
```

The other function you can use is the parseFloat() function, which has the syntax

```
parseFloat(text)
```

where, once again, `text` is a text string or variable containing a text string. The parseFloat() function works like the parseInt() function except that it retrieves both integers and numbers with decimals. The following are sample values returned by the parseFloat() function:

```
parseFloat("120 lbs")               // returns 120
parseFloat("206.58 lbs")            // returns 206.58
parseFloat("weight equals 55 lbs")  // returns NaN
```

Since the countdown clock is not performing any calculations on values within the Web form, you don't need to use the parseInt() or parseFloat() functions in your code. However, you will have an opportunity to use these functions in the case problems at the end of the tutorial. Figure 2-29 summarizes the different JavaScript methods and functions used to work with numeric values.

Figure 2-29 **Numeric functions and methods**

Method	Description
isFinite(*value*)	Returns a Boolean value indicating whether *value* is finite and a legal number
isNaN(*value*)	Returns a Boolean value, which has the value true if *value* is not a number
parseFloat(*string*)	Extracts the first numeric value from a text string
parseInt(*string*)	Extracts the first integer value from a text string
value.toExponential(*n*)	Returns a text string displaying *value* in exponential notation with *n* digits to the right of the decimal point
value.toFixed(*n*)	Returns a text string displaying *value* to *n* decimal places
value.toPrecision(*n*)	Returns a text string displaying *value* to *n* significant digits either to the left or to the right of the decimal point

Using Numeric Methods and Functions

- To display a numeric value to a set number of digits, use the function
  ```
  value.toFixed(n)
  ```
  where *value* is the numeric value and *n* is the number of digits to the right of the decimal place to be displayed. The toFixed() method converts the numeric value to a text string.
- To extract an integer from the beginning of a text string, use
  ```
  parseInt(string)
  ```
  where *string* is a text string that starts with an integer value.
- To extract a numeric value from the beginning of a text string, use
  ```
  parseFloat(string)
  ```
  where *string* is a text string that starts with a numeric value.
- To test whether a value represents a number, use
  ```
  isNaN(value)
  ```
  where *value* can be either a text string, numeric value, or other data type. The isNaN() function returns the Boolean value true if *value* is not a number, and false if it is.

Working with Conditional Operators

Recall that Hector wanted the countdown clock to display the current time using the 12-hour format rather than the 24-hour format. In the 24-hour format, the hour values go from 0 hours (representing 12 am) up to 23 hours (representing 11 pm); thus, a time of 14:35 in the 24-hour format is equivalent to 2:35 pm in the 12-hour format. To convert from 24-hour time to 12-hour time, your code needs to apply the following rules:

1. If the hour value is less than 12, display the time as "a.m."; otherwise, display the time as "p.m."
2. If the hour value is greater than 12, subtract 12 from the value.
3. If the hour value is equal to 0, change it to 12.

Thus, your code needs to run different operations based on the hours value. You can specify these options through the use of a conditional operator. A **conditional operator** is an operator that tests whether a certain condition is true or not. If the condition is true, one value is returned, but if the condition is not true, a different value is returned. The syntax of a conditional operator is

```
(condition) ? trueValue : falseValue
```

where *condition* is an expression that is either true or false, *trueValue* is the value returned if the condition is true, and *falseValue* is the value returned if the condition is false. You can use a conditional operator to assign a value to a variable using the following statement:

```
variable = (condition) ? trueValue : falseValue
```

where *variable* is the variable to which the resulting value is assigned.

To create expressions that have true or false values, you use comparison operators. A **comparison operator** is an operator that compares the value of one expression to another. One commonly used comparison operator is the less than operator (**<**), which is used to determine whether one value is less than another. The following expression demonstrates the use of the less than (<) comparison operator:

```
x < 100
```

If *x* is less then 100, then this expression is true, but if *x* is greater than or equal to 100, the expression is false. Figure 2-30 lists the comparison operators supported by JavaScript.

Figure 2-30 ▶ **Comparison operators**

Operator	Description	Example
==	Returns true if the values are equal	x == y
!=	Returns true if the values are not equal	x != y
>	Returns true if the value on the left is greater than the value on the right	x > y
<	Returns true if the value on the left is less than the value on the right	x < y
>=	Returns true if the value on the left is greater than or equal to the value on the right	x >= y
<=	Returns true if the value on the left is less than or equal to the value on the right	x <= y

Note that, when you want to test whether two values are equal, you use a double equal sign (==) rather than a single equal sign. The single equal sign (=) is an assignment operator and is reserved only for that purpose. Thus, to test whether *x* is equal to 100, you would use the expression

```
x == 100
```

JavaScript also supports **logical operators** that allow you to connect several expressions. One such operator is && which returns a value of true only if both of the expressions are true. For example, the statement

```
(x < 100) && (y == 100)
```

is true only if *x* is less then 100 *and y* is equal to 100. Figure 2-31 lists the logical operators supported by JavaScript.

Figure 2-31 ▶ **Logical operators**

Operator	Description	Example	Value
In the following examples, assume that x = 20 and y = 25			
&&	Returns true when both expressions are true	(x == 20) && (y == 25)	true
||	Returns true when at least one expression is true	(x == 20) || (y < 10)	true
!	Returns true if the expression is false and false if the expression is true	!(x == 20)	false

Now that you've seen how to work with comparison and logical operators, you'll use them to write code for the three rules described above to convert from 24-hour time to 12-hour time. First you need a variable named "ampm" that indicates whether the time is am or pm. Recall that the value of the current hour is stored in the thisHour variable. If the value of the thisHour variable is less than 12, the value of the "ampm" variable is "am"; otherwise, its value is "pm". The conditional operator for this rule is therefore

```
ampm = (thisHour < 12) ? "am" : "pm";
```

The second rule should check if the thisHour value is greater than 12. If so, the rule should subtract 12 from the thisHour value; otherwise, it should leave the value unchanged. You can accomplish this using the command

```
thisHour = (thisHour > 12) ? thisHour - 12 : thisHour;
```

Finally, the third rule should check if thisHour is equal to 0. If so, the rule should change the value of thisHour to 12; otherwise, it should leave it unchanged. The code for this rule is

```
thisHour = (thisHour == 0) ? 12 : thisHour;
```

Add these commands to the showTime() function you created in the last session.

To modify the showTime() function:

1. If necessary, reopen the **functions.js** file in your text editor.

2. Within the showTime() function, insert the following commands below the statement that creates the thisHour variable:

   ```
   // change thisHour from 24-hour time to 12-hour time by:
   // 1) if thisHour < 12 then set ampm to " am" otherwise set it
   to " pm"
   var ampm = (thisHour < 12) ? " am" : " pm";

   // 2) subtract 12 from the thisHour variable
   thisHour = (thisHour > 12) ? thisHour - 12 : thisHour;

   // 3) if thisHour equals 0, change it to 12
   thisHour = (thisHour == 0) ? 12 : thisHour;
   ```

   Next you need to modify the text string returned by the function so that it displays the am/pm value at the end of the text string.

3. Change the return statement to:

   ```
   return thisHour + ":" + thisMinute + ":" + thisSecond + ampm;
   ```

   Figure 2-32 shows the revised code in the showTime() function.

Changing the time to 12-hour format — **Figure 2-32**

```
function showTime(dateObj) {
    thisSecond=dateObj.getSeconds();
    thisMinute=dateObj.getMinutes();
    thisHour=dateObj.getHours();

    // change thisHour from 24-hour time to 12-hour time by:
    // 1) if thisHour < 12 then set ampm to " am" otherwise set it to " pm"
    var ampm = (thisHour < 12) ? " am" : " pm";

    // 2) subtract 12 from the thisHour variable
    thisHour = (thisHour > 12) ? thisHour - 12 : thisHour;

    // 3) if thisHour equals 0, change it to 12
    thisHour = (thisHour == 0) ? 12 : thisHour;

    thisMinute = thisMinute < 10 ? "0"+thisMinute : thisMinute;
    thisSecond = thisSecond < 10 ? "0"+thisSecond : thisSecond;

    return thisHour + ":" + thisMinute + ":" + thisSecond + ampm;
}
```

4. Save your changes to the file.

5. Reload or refresh **clock.htm** in your Web browser. Figure 2-33 shows the revised clock, displaying time in a 12-hour format.

Figure 2-33	Displaying the time in 12-hour format

The final change you have to make to the time value is to display minutes and seconds values with a leading zero if they are less than 10. In other words, Hector wants the clock to display 2:35:05 pm, not 2:35:5 pm. You can make this change by adding another conditional operator to the showTime() function. Incorporating this final modification, the statement to change the displayed value of the thisMinute variable would appear as

```
thisMinute = thisMinute < 10 ? "0"+thisMinute : thisMinute;
```

Note that you enclose the value 0 in quotes, which causes JavaScript to treat the 0 as a text string rather than a numeric value. Also note that if the value of the thisMinute variable is not less than 10, you leave it unchanged. The code to change the display of the thisSecond variable is similar:

```
thisSecond = thisSecond < 10 ? "0"+thisSecond : thisSecond;
```

Add these two commands to the showTime() function and then reload the Web page.

To change the minutes and seconds format:

1. Return to the **functions.js** file in your text editor.

2. Add the following commands as shown in Figure 2-34:

```
// add leading zeros to minutes and seconds less than 10
thisMinute = thisMinute < 10 ? "0"+thisMinute : thisMinute;
thisSecond = thisSecond < 10 ? "0"+thisSecond : thisSecond;
```

Figure 2-34	Changing format of the minutes and seconds values

```
function showTime(dateObj) {
    thisSecond=dateObj.getSeconds();
    thisMinute=dateObj.getMinutes();
    thisHour=dateObj.getHours();

    // change thisHour from 24-hour time to 12-hour time by:
    // 1) if thisHour < 12 then set ampm to " am" otherwise set it to " pm"
    var ampm = (thisHour < 12) ? " am" : " pm";

    // 2) subtract 12 from the thisHour variable
    thisHour = (thisHour > 12) ? thisHour - 12 : thisHour;

    // 3) if thisHour equals 0, change it to 12
    thisHour = (thisHour == 0) ? 12 : thisHour;

    // add leading zeros to minutes and seconds less than 10
    thisMinute = thisMinute < 10 ? "0"+thisMinute : thisMinute;
    thisSecond = thisSecond < 10 ? "0"+thisSecond : thisSecond;

    return thisHour + ":" + thisMinute + ":" + thisSecond + ampm;
}
```

3. Save your changes and close the **functions.js** file.

4. Reload or refresh **clock.htm** in your Web browser. Figure 2-35 shows the revised clock with the formatted minutes and seconds values.

Minutes and seconds values in the revised format ◄ Figure 2-35

You've completed work on the showTime() and showDate() functions. Since your purpose is to display the current date and time (and the time remaining in the year), replace the test date of February 24, 2007, with the current date and time. Recall that a date object stores the current date and time when you do not specify a value.

To display the current date and time:

1. Return to the **clock.htm** file in your text editor.

2. Change the command to create the today variable to:

```
var today = new Date();
```
See Figure 2-36.

Using the current date and time in the NYClock() function ◄ Figure 2-36

inserts the current date and time

```
function NYClock() {
// the today variable contains the current date and time
    var today=new Date();◄

// display the current date and time
    document.clockform.dateNow.value = showDate(today);
    document.clockform.timeNow.value = showTime(today);

// calculate the time left until the New Year's Bash
    var days = calcDays(today);

    // display days rounded to the next lowest integer
    document.clockform.daysLeft.value = Math.floor(days);

    // calculate the hours left in the current day
    var hours = (days - Math.floor(days))*24;

    // display hours rounded to the next lowest integer
    document.clockform.hrLeft.value = Math.floor(hours);

    // calculate the minutes left in the current hour
    var minutes = (hours - Math.floor(hours))*60;

    // display minutes rounded to the next lowest integer
    document.clockform.minLeft.value = Math.floor(minutes);

    // calculate the seconds left in the current minute
    var seconds = (minutes - Math.floor(minutes))*60;

    // display seconds rounded to the next lowest integer
    document.clockform.secLeft.value = Math.floor(seconds);
}
```

3. Save your changes and then reload or reopen **clock.htm** in your Web browser. The Web page should now display the current date and time as well as the time remaining in the year.

Running Timed Commands

You've completed work on the functions required for the countdown clock, but one problem remains: the clock is largely static, changing only when the page is loaded by the browser. Hector wants the clock to be constantly updated so that it always shows the current time and the time remaining until the New Year's Bash. To do this, you need to run the function at certain times. JavaScript provides two methods for doing this: time-delayed commands and timed-interval commands.

Working with Time-Delayed Commands

A **time-delayed command** is a JavaScript command that is run after a particular amount of time has passed. The syntax to run a time-delayed command is

```
setTimeout("command", delay);
```

where `command` is a JavaScript command and `delay` is the delay time in milliseconds before the browser runs the command. Note that the command must be placed within either double or single quotes. For example, to set a 5 millisecond delay before the browser runs the showClock() function, you would use the command

```
setTimeout("showClock()", 5);
```

In some cases, you may need to cancel a time-delayed command before it is actually run. To cancel the command, you use the method

```
clearTimeout();
```

There is no limit to the number of time-delayed commands a browser can process. This could cause some confusion if you wanted to be able to access one of those time-delayed commands (perhaps to cancel it before it actually is run). If that's the case, you need a way of separating one time-delayed command from another. A browser does this by assigning each command a unique ID. You can store the value of this id in a variable using the form

```
timeID = setTimeout("command",delay);
```

Once you've assigned an ID to a time-delayed command, you can cancel it using the clearTimeout method

```
clearTimeout(timeID);
```

where `timeID` is the ID of the command (or a variable that contains that ID value).

Running Commands at Specified Intervals

The other alternative for timing your commands is to instruct the browser to run the same command repeatedly at specified intervals. The method to run such a command, known as a **timed-interval command**, is

```
setInterval("command",interval);
```

where once again `command` is the JavaScript command that is to be run repeatedly, and `interval` is the interval, in milliseconds, before the command is run again. To instruct the browser to stop running the command, you use the method

```
clearInterval();
```

As with time-delayed commands, you may have several timed-interval commands running simultaneously. To separate one from another, you store the time ID value for a command using the form

```
timeID = setInterval("command",interval);
```

where *timeID* is the variable containing the ID for the timed-interval command. To halt the repeating command, you use the clearInterval() method with the *timeID* variable:

```
clearInterval(timeID);
```

An important point to remember about the setTimeout() and setInterval() methods is that after a browser processes a request to run a command at a later time, it doesn't stop; it proceeds to any other commands running in your script and processes those commands without delay. For example, you might try to run three functions at 50 millisecond intervals using the following structure:

```
setTimeout("function1()",50);
setTimeout("function2()",50);
setTimeout("function3()",50);
```

However, a browser would execute this code by running all three functions almost simultaneously 50 milliseconds later. To run the functions with a separation of about 50 milliseconds between one function and the next, you would need to use three different delay times, as follows:

```
setTimeout("function1()",50);
setTimeout("function2()",100);
setTimeout("function3()",150);
```

In this case, a user's browser would run the first function after 50 milliseconds, the second function 50 milliseconds after that, and the third function after an additional 50 milliseconds has passed.

You have only one function to run for Hector's Web page: the NYClock() function. You want the function to run once every second. Thus, you would use the command:

```
setInterval("NYClock()", 1000)
```

You can replace the event handler in the <body> tag with this setInterval method. The revised event handler is

```
onload="setInterval('NYClock()', 1000)"
```

This causes a browser displaying the page to run the NYClock() function one second after loading and then every second thereafter. Note that since the event handler is enclosed in double quotes, you must use single quotes to enclose the name of the function.

To run the NYClock() function every second:

1. Return to the **clock.htm** file in your text editor.
2. Change the attribute of the onload event handler in the <body> tag to
   ```
   onload="setInterval('NYClock()',1000)"
   ```
   See Figure 2-37.

Figure 2-37 | **Running a function at timed intervals**

run the NYClock() function every
second after the page loads

```
<body onload="setInterval('NYClock()',1000)">
<form name="clockform" id="clockform" action="">

<div id="clock">
    <h4>Time</h4>
    <p>
        <input size="12" id="dateNow" name="dateNow" /><br />
        <img src="clock.jpg" alt="" /><br />
        <input size="12" id="timeNow" name="timeNow" />
    </p>
</div>
```

3. Close the file, saving your changes.

4. Reload or reopen **clock.htm** in your Web browser. The countdown clock should appear 1 second after the page loads, and both the countdown clock and the current time should be updated continually as the NYClock() function is run again and again.

Reference Window | **Running Timed Commands**

- To run a command after a delay, use the method
    ```
    timeID = setTimeout("command", delay)
    ```
  where *command* is the command to be run, *delay* is the delay time in milliseconds, and *timeID* is a variable that stores the ID associated with the time-delayed command.
- To repeat a command at set intervals, use the method
    ```
    timeID = setInterval("command", interval)
    ```
  where *interval* is the time, in milliseconds, between repeating the command.
- To cancel a time-delayed command, use
    ```
    clearTimeout(timeID)
    ```
  where *timeID* is the ID of the time-delayed command. To clear all time-delayed commands, use the method clearTimeout().
- To cancel a repeated command, use
    ```
    clearInterval(timeID)
    ```
  where *timeID* is the ID of the repeated command. To clear all repeated commands, use the method clearInterval().

You've completed your work on the countdown clock for the New Year's Bash. Hector will continue to work on the event's Web site and get back to you with any new projects or concerns.

Performing Special Mathematical Tasks

While JavaScript offers many of the tools needed for doing mathematical calculations, it is not always easy to perform operations in JavaScript that are simple tasks in other programming languages. Rounding a number to two digits and generating random integers are two examples of such tasks. In this concluding section you'll look at these two common mathematical tasks and explore how to perform them with JavaScript.

Rounding a Value to a Specified Number of Digits

Because online ordering is one of the most common uses of the Web, you may find a need to use JavaScript to perform calculations on monetary values. For example, suppose you needed to calculate a 5% tax on a customer's purchase of a $25.49 item. One way of doing this is to use the following code:

```
var price = 25.49;
var taxrate = 0.05;
var tax = price*taxrate;
document.write("$"+tax);
```

When running these commands, however, you would discover that the value written to the Web page would be $1.2745. You could use the toFixed() function discussed earlier to display the result to only two decimal places; however, recall that the toFixed() function doesn't change a variable's value, only how it is displayed. An additional concern is that the toFixed() method is not supported by older browsers.

    Instead, you need to round the actual value of the tax variable to the hundredths digit. The only Math methods available for rounding are the Math.floor(), Math.ceil(), and Math.round() methods used to round values to the next highest, next lowest, and nearest integer; there are no Math methods for rounding values to decimals. If you want to round a currency value to two digits, you must first multiply the value by 100, apply the Math.round() method to round the value to the nearest integer, and then divide that result by 100. For the tax rate example, 1.2745 multiplied by 100 is 127.45; that value rounded to the nearest integer is 127; dividing that number by 100 results in a currency value of $1.27. In JavaScript this sequence of operations can be placed in a single expression as follows:

```
var roundedtax = Math.round(100*tax)/100;
document.write("$"+roundedtax);
```

If you wanted to round a number to one decimal place, you would multiply the value by 10, round it, and then divide that integer by 10. To round a number to three decimal places, you would multiply and divide by 1000. Thus, the formulas for rounding to one, two, and three decimal places are:

```
Math.round(10*value)/10;      // round to tenths
Math.round(100*value)/100;    // round to hundredths
Math.round(1000*value)/1000;  // round to thousandths
```

where $value$ is the numeric value or variable to be rounded. In general, if n is the number of decimal places you want to round the value to, you want to multiply and divide by 10^n. You could use this fact to create your own custom function to round values to a specified number of decimal places. Recall from Figure 2-21 that you can use the Math.pow(x, y) method to calculate the value of x^y. For example, 100 is equal to 10^2 or Math.pow(10,2). The following code uses this method of the Math object to create a general rounding function that rounds values to "n" decimal places:

```
function roundValue(value, n) {
    return Math.round(Math.pow(10,n)*value)/Math.pow(10,n);
}
```

The following code shows how you can call the roundValue() function to simplify the code for displaying the 5% sales tax:

```
var price = 25.49;
var taxrate = 0.05;
var tax = price*taxrate;
document.write("$"+roundValue(tax,2));
```

You can also specify a negative value for the "n" parameter in the roundValue() function. This has the effect of rounding a value to the nearest ten, hundred, thousand, and so forth. For example roundValue(238414, -3) returns a value of 238,000.

Generating Random Numbers

One of the most useful applications of JavaScript is to create dynamic pages that can change in a random fashion. A commercial Web site might need to display banner ads in a random order so that customers see a different ad each time they access the page. To create these kinds of effects, you need a script that generates a random value. JavaScript accomplishes this using the Math.random() method. In the following statement, a random number between 0 and 1 is stored in the randValue variable:

```
var randValue = Math.random();
```

You can enlarge the random number range by multiplying the random value by the desired size of the range. For example, to generate a random number between 0 and 10, the statement is

```
var randValue = 10*Math.random();
```

To move the range, you add the lower boundary to the random number. Thus, to generate a random number from 20 to 30, the operation is

```
var randValue = 20 + 10*Math.random();
```

To force the random number to be an integer, you apply either the Math.ceil() method to round the value to the next highest integer or the Math.floor() method to round the value to the next lowest integer. You should not use the Math.round() method. While the Math.round() method would round the random value to the nearest integer within the defined range, it would not do so evenly: the range's lower and upper value would appear less often than the other integers, and thus each integer would not have an equal chance of being selected. To generate a random integer from 20 to 30, you can use the Math.floor() method as follows:

```
var randValue = Math.floor(20 + 11*Math.random());
```

Note that this expression multiplies the random value by 11, not 10. This is because there are 11 integers in the range from 20 to 30. You can combine all of these operations in a customized function that returns a random integer for a specified range and lower boundary. The code for the function is

```
function randInt(lower, size) {
   return Math.floor(lower + size*Math.random());

}
```

With this function you can generate a random integer from 1 to 10 using the function call

```
var randValue = randInt(1, 10);
```

Once you've generated the random integer, you can use it in your scripts to display randomized images, banner ads, and text on the Web page.

Tips for Working with Operators and Expressions

- Use unary and assignment operators to create compact code.
- Use constants from the Math object when performing advanced mathematical calculations involving such values as π and e.
- Never apply mathematical operations to text strings. Extract numeric values from text strings using the parseInt() or parseFloat() functions.
- In the case of a logical error involving a mathematical operation, use the isFinite() and isNaN() functions to determine the state of your data values.
- Use the toFixed() method to format numeric output. If you need to support older browsers, use a customized function to round the values to a specific number of digits.

Review

Session 2.2 Quick Check

1. How do you use a unary operator to increase the value of the thisMonth variable by 1?
2. How do you use an assignment operator to increase the value of the thisMonth variable by 1?
3. What command would you use to round the value of the thisMonth variable to the nearest integer?
4. What conditional operator would you use to change the value of the thisMonth variable to 12 if it equals 11 but otherwise leave the value unchanged?
5. What function would you use to test whether the value of the thisMonth variable is a number or not?
6. What command would you use to display the value of the thisDay variable with no decimal places?
7. What statement would you use to run the function calcMonth() after a 0.5 second delay?
8. What statement would you use to run the function calcMonth() every 0.5 seconds?

Review

Tutorial Summary

In this tutorial you learned how to work with date objects, math functions, and timed commands to create a countdown clock. The first session discussed how to create event handlers that allow you to run functions in response to particular events occurring within a Web page and Web browser. You also saw how to set the values of fields within a Web form. The rest of the first session introduced the date object and discussed how to work with the properties and methods of dates in order to display a specified date in a Web form. In the second session you worked with JavaScript operators to calculate the amount of time left in the year from a specified date. You then used a Math object to convert this value into days, hours, minutes, and seconds. The second session then discussed how to work with numeric values in JavaScript. The session also covered how to use comparison operators to apply different possible values to a single variable. The countdown clock task concluded with a discussion of timed commands, which were used to run a function at a specified time interval.

Key Terms

arithmetic operator	decrement operator	negation operator
assignment operator	event	operator
binary operator	event handler	time-delayed command
comparison operator	increment operator	timed-interval command
conditional operator	logical operator	unary operator
date method	Math methods	
date object	Math object	

Practice

Practice the skills you learned in the tutorial using the same case scenario.

Review Assignments

Data files needed for this Review Assignment: datestxt.js, dixon.css, eventstxt.htm, logo.jpg

Hector has now been promoted to general manager of promotion for all of Dixon's special events. He remembers the work you did on the countdown clock for the New Year's Bash and would like you to create something similar for all of the events sponsored by the city. Hector envisions a Web page displaying a list of special events. The list would include each event's name, the date that it occurs, and the time remaining until the event (in days, hours, minutes, and seconds). Hector wants the following events listed on the Web page:

* Heritage Day on January 14 at 10:00 am
* Spring Day Rally on May 21 at 12:00 pm
* July 4th Fireworks on July 4 at 9:00 pm
* Summer Bash on September 1 at 12:00 pm
* Holiday Party on December 1 at 11:30 am
* New Year's Bash on December 31 at 3:30 pm

Like the countdown clock, the contents of the Web site should be constantly updated by a user's browser. Hector has already created the Web page's design and layout, but he needs your help in writing the JavaScript program to run the clocks. Figure 2-38 shows a preview of the completed Web page.

Figure 2-38

To complete this Web page:

1. Using your text editor, open **eventstxt.htm** from the tutorial.02/review folder. Enter *your name* and *the date* in the head section and save the file as **events.htm**. Use your text editor to open **datestxt.js**, enter *your name* and *the date* in the comment section, and save the file as **dates.js**. ✓

2. Go to the dates.js file in your text editor. The file contains a single function named showDateTime() that displays the date and time of a date object in a formatted text string. Below this function, insert a function named changeYear(). The purpose of this function is to change a date's year value if the date has already been passed in the current calendar year. To create the changeYear parameter, do the following:

   a. Specify two parameters for the changeYear function: today and holiday. The today parameter is used to store a date object representing the current date. The holiday parameter is used to store a date object representing one of the events in Hector's list.

   b. In the first line of the function, use the getFullYear() date method to extract the 4-digit year value from the today variable and store the value in a variable named year.

   c. In the second line, use the setFullYear() date method to set the full year value of the holiday date object to the value of the year variable. This changes the date of the holiday event to whatever the current year might be.

   d. In the third line, use a conditional operator on the year variable. The test condition is whether the value of the holiday date object is less than the today date object. If it is, this means that the event has already passed in the current year and the value of the year variable should be increased by 1. If it is not, the event has not yet occurred and the year value should remain unchanged.

   e. In the fourth line of the function, once again set the full year value of the holiday date object to the value of the year variable.

3. Below the changeYear() function, create another function named countdown(). The purpose of the countdown() function is to return a text string displaying the number of days, hours, minutes, and seconds between a starting date and a stopping date. Create the function as follows:

   a. Specify two parameters for the function: start and stop. The start parameter will contain a date object for the starting date. The stop parameter will contain a date object for the stopping date.

   b. In the first line of the function, calculate the time difference between stop and start, storing the difference in a variable named time.

   c. Convert the time difference into days, hours, minutes, and seconds and return the text string:

      days days, *hours* hrs, *minutes* mins, *seconds* secs

      where *days*, *hours*, *minutes*, and *seconds* are variables that store the integer values of the days, hours, minutes, and seconds. (*Hint*: Use the commands in the NYClock() function from the tutorial as a guide for converting the time difference into days, hours, minutes, and seconds.)

4. Close the file, saving your changes.

5. Go to the **events.htm** file in your text editor. Above the closing </head> tag, insert an external script element to access the code in the dates.js file; then, below that element, insert a second script element for code to be embedded in the events.htm file.

6. Within the embedded script element, create a function named showCountdown(). The showCountdown() function has no parameters. Within the function, do the following:

   a. Create a variable named today containing a date object. Use the date and time shown in Figure 2-38 (December 1, 2007 6:31:45). Create six additional date objects in variables named Date1 through Date6. Assign the dates and times from the six events in Hector's list to the Date1 through Date6 variables. Use a year value of "2007" for these six dates (you'll set the current year value in a later step).

   b. Using the today variable as the parameter value, call the showDateTime() function and store the value returned by the function in the thisDay field of the eventform Web form.

   c. Using today as the first parameter value and Date1 as the second parameter value, call the changeYear() function. Calling this function sets the correct year value for the first event in Hector's list. Repeat this step for the Date2 through Date6 variables.

   d. Call the countdown() function using the today variable as the first parameter value and the Date1 variable as the second. Display the result returned by this function in the count1 field of the eventform Web form. Running this command displays the time remaining until the first event in Hector's list. Repeat this step for the other five events.

7. Add an event handler to the <body> tag that runs the showCountdown() function when the page is loaded by the browser.

8. Save your changes to the file.

9. Open **events.htm** in your Web browser. Verify that it shows the same date, time, and countdown values shown in Figure 2-38.

10. Return to the **events.htm** file in your text editor. Modify the initial value of the today variable so that it always uses the current date and time (whatever that may be).

11. Modify the event handler in the <body> tag so that it runs the showCountdown() function every tenth of a second after the page is loaded.

12. Close the file, saving your changes.

13. Reload or refresh the **events.htm** file in your Web browser and verify that it now shows a countdown clock with the current date and time.

14. Submit the completed Web site to your instructor.

Apply

Jse JavaScript to create
nd run an exam timer.

Case Problem 1

Data files needed for this Case Problem: figa.jpg, figb.jpg, figc.jpg, figd.jpg, figures.jpg, functions.js, oae.jpg, oaetxt.htm, quiz.css

Online Aptitude Exams Grunwald Testing Inc. creates and administers a series of aptitude tests for schools, government agencies, and private firms. The company has been exploring the feasibility of putting some of its tests online. John Paulson is directing the effort and has asked you to help design a sample test page. The company's tests are graded on two measures: the number of correct answers by the respondents and the time required to complete the exam. John wants you to work on creating an online timer that starts the moment users begin work on an exam and stops once users have submitted their answers. The exam questions will be hidden from users until the clock starts. Once users submit their answers, the exam questions will close and an alert box will appear showing the number of correct answers and the time, in seconds, taken to complete the exam. John has already collected some of the functions you'll need for this page in a separate file named functions.js. The file contains three functions:

- The showQuiz() function displays the quiz questions on the Web page.
- The gradeQuiz() function returns the number of correct answers of a submitted quiz, highlights the correct answers in the page, and disables the quiz, preventing users from changing their answers.

Your job will be to write the code to start and stop the quiz timer as well as to call the functions to show and grade a completed quiz. Figure 2-39 shows a preview of the exam page in action.

Figure 2-39

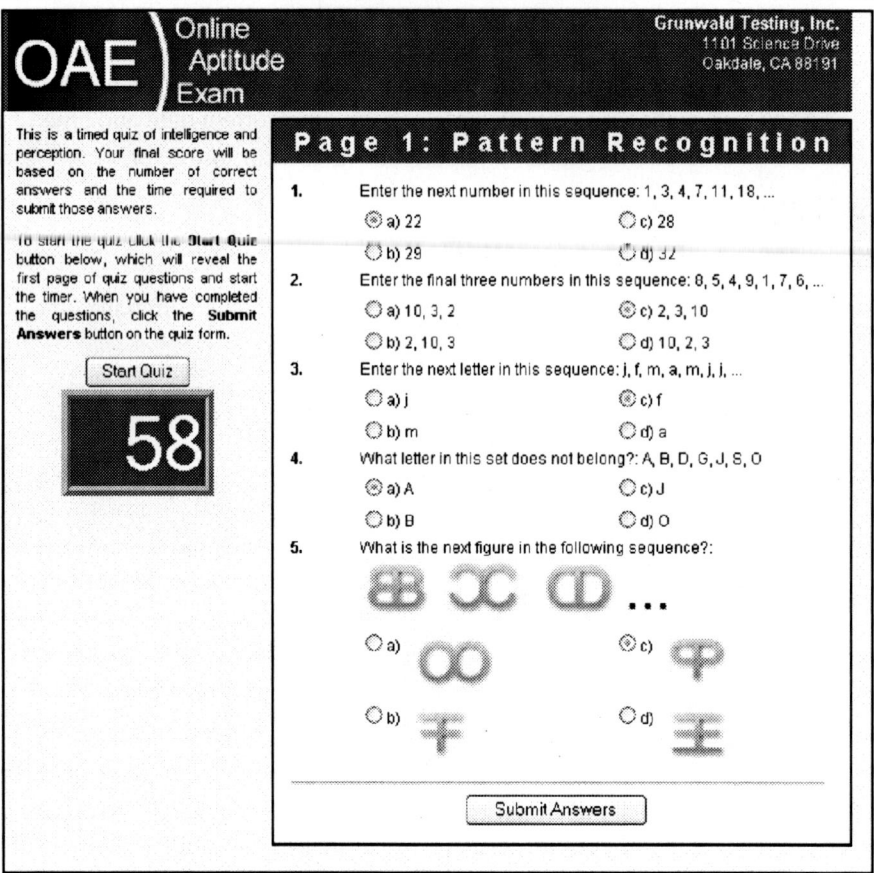

To complete this Web page:

1. Using your text editor, open **oaetxt.htm** from the tutorial.02/case1 folder. Enter **your name** and **the date** in the head section and save the file as **oae.htm**

2. Above the closing </head> tag, insert an external script element that points to the functions contained in the functions.js file.

3. Below this script element, insert another script element. Within the script element, declare two variables. The first variable is named seconds and will store the current elapsed time that the user has worked on the exam. The second variable, clockId, will be used to reference the commands used to repeatedly update the clock value. Set the initial value of the seconds variable to 0. Do not set an initial value for the clockId variable.

4. Create a function named runClock(). The purpose of this function is to update the time value in the Web page's clock. There are no parameters. Add the following commands to the function:

   a. Use a unary operator to increase the value of the seconds variable by 1.

   b. Change the value of the quizclock field in the quiz form to the value of the seconds variable.

5. Create a function named startClock(). The purpose of the startClock() function is start the Web page clock and then to repeatedly update elapsed time displayed in the clock. There are no parameters to this function. Add the following commands:
   a. Call the showQuiz() function to display the questions in the online exam.
   b. Call the runClock() function every second, storing the ID of this timed-interval command in the clockId variable.

6. Create a function named stopClock(). The purpose of this function is to stop the timer, display the user's score, and disable the exam to prevent further entry. There are no parameters to this function. Add the following commands:

Explore

   a. Halt the repeated calls to the runClock() function. (*Hint*: Use the clearInterval() method.)
   b. Call the gradeQuiz() function, storing the value returned by the function in a variable named correctAns.
   c. Display an alert box containing the following text string:
      You have *correctAns* correct of 5 in *timer* seconds.
      where *correctAns* is the value of the correctAns variable and *timer* is the value of the quizclock field in the quiz form.

Explore

7. Locate the input button for the Start Quiz button. Add an event handler attribute that runs the startClock() function when the button is clicked.

8. Go to the bottom of the file and locate the input button for the Submit Answers button. Add an event handler attribute that runs the stopClock() function when the button is clicked.

9. Save your changes to the file.

10. Open **oae.htm** in your Web browser. Verify that by clicking the Start Quiz button the quiz questions are made visible and the timer starts running. Further verify that clicking the Submit Answers button stops the timer, disables the exam, and displays an alert box with the number of correct answers and the elapsed time to complete the exam. Note that to restore the timer and the Web form to its original state, you will have to reload the page in the browser. Clicking the browser's Refresh button will not remove the Web form values or zero the timer.

11. Submit the completed Web site to your instructor.

Apply

Use JavaScript to display a random text box.

Case Problem 2

Data files needed for this Case Problem: hometxt.htm, logo.jpg, randtxt.js, styles.css, tips.js, work.jpg

The Home Center Tom Vogel manages The Home Center, a Web site for do-it-yourself enthusiasts. The site contains articles, forums, and products for home repair and maintenance. Tom thinks it would be useful for users to see a short home repair tip on the site's home page. He would like to have a different tip appear each time a user loads the page. To this end he has created a collection of 10 tips that he would like displayed randomly on the page. Tom has already obtained two functions to display the tip title and text:

- The tipTitle() function returns the title of the nth tip title. The value of *n* is entered as a parameter of the function.
- The tipText() function returns the text of the nth tip of the tip collection. The value of *n* is entered as a parameter of the function.

The tipTitle() and tipText() functions have been stored in the tips.js file. Your job is to create a function that randomly selects a tip from this collection and then writes the title and text of that tip to an appropriate spot on the Web page. A preview of the completed Web page is shown in Figure 2-40.

Figure 2-40

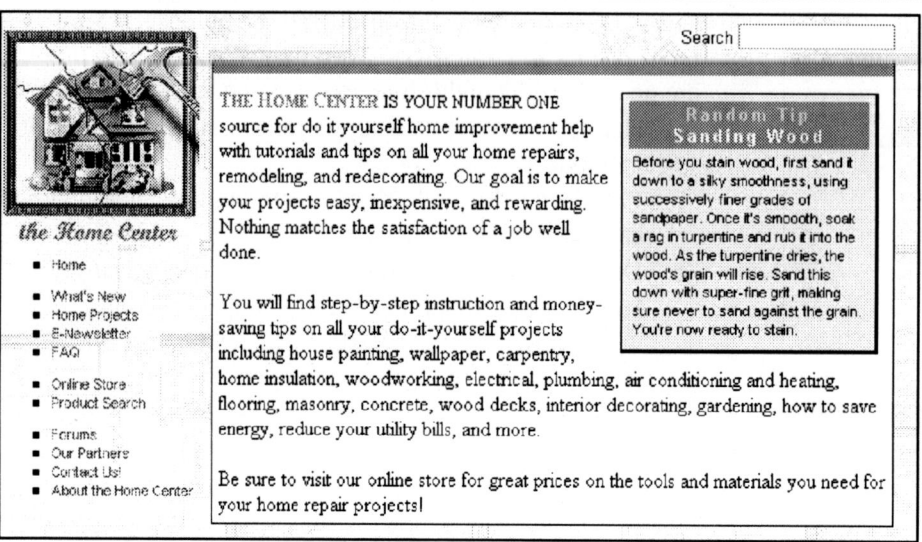

To complete this Web page:

1. Using your text editor, open **hometxt.htm** from the tutorial.02/case2 folder. Enter *your name* and *the date* in the head section and save the file as **home.htm**. Open **randtxt.js** using your text editor. Enter *your name* and *the date* in the comment section and save the file as **random.js**. ✓

Explore

2. Within the random.js file, create a function named randInt(). The purpose of this function is to generate a random integer within a given range. The function has two parameters: lower and upper, where lower is the lowest integer in the range and upper is the highest integer in the range. Add the following commands to the function:

   a. Declare a variable named size equal to the number of integers in the given range. (*Hint*: The size of the range is one more than the difference between the highest and lowest integer.)

   b. Use the Math.floor() and Math.random() methods as well as the lower parameter and size variable to generate a random integer. (*Hint*: See the section on generating a random integer in this tutorial for guidance.) ✓

3. Close the file, saving your changes.

4. Go to the **home.htm** file in your text editor. Above the closing </head> tag, insert two external script elements: one that links to the tips.js file and the other that links to the random.js file you just created. ✓

5. Scroll down the document to the div element with an ID value of "tip". Replace the contents of this element with an embedded script element. Within the script element do the following:

   a. Declare a variable named tipNum equal to a random integer between 1 and 10 returned by the randInt() function you created in the random.js file.

b. Use a series of document.write() methods to the write the following HTML code to the Web page:

```
<h1>Random Tip<br />title</h1>
<p>tip</p>
```

where *title* is the title of the random title as generated by the tipTitle() function and *tip* is the text of the random tip as generated by the tipText() function.

6. Save your changes to the file.

7. Open **home.htm** in your Web browser and verify that a random tip appears in the floating tip box each time you reload or refresh the Web page.

8. Submit the completed Web site to your instructor.

Challenge

Explore how to use JavaScript to create a world clock.

Case Problem 3

Data files needed for this Case Problem: je.css, logo.jpg, map.jpg, worldtxt.htm, zonestxt.js

Jackson Electronics Jackson Electronics is a worldwide company that manufactures and sells quality electronic equipment and components. The company has six corporate offices at different locations on the globe and the employees of the company have to keep in constant communication with the different offices. David Lin maintains the corporate Web site and has come to you for help with a problem. He would like to augment the Web page that displays the location of the corporate offices to display the local time at each location. This will give employees important information when they want to call or fax data from one office to another. To create this world clock, David needs to know how JavaScript's date object works with different time zones.

The Earth is divided into 24 time zones. Each time zone is referenced in comparison to the time kept in Greenwich, England, which is known as **standard time** or **Greenwich Mean Time** (**GMT**). You can determine how many minutes Greenwich time differs from your local time using the getTimezoneOffset() method. For example, if the today variable contains a date object and is run on a computer in New York, the expression

```
today.getTimezoneOffset()
```

returns the value 300 because Greenwich Mean Time is 300 minutes or five hours ahead of New York. With this information, you can determine the time in Greenwich by adding the offset value to your computer's local time. Since JavaScript measures time in milliseconds, you have to multiply the offset by the number of milliseconds in one minute. Thus, the code to calculate the number of hours using this function would be

```
today.getTimezoneOffset()*60*1000
```

You can determine the time anywhere in the world if you know Greenwich's time and the other location's offset from GMT. David has compiled a list of the six corporate offices and the time difference in minutes between each of those cities and GMT. The offices are:

*   Office 1: Houston (-360)
*   Office 2: London (0)
*   Office 3: New York (-300)
*   Office 4: Seattle (-480)
*   Office 5: Sydney (660)
*   Office 6: Tokyo (540)

The number in parentheses indicates the number of minutes the city is offset from GMT. A negative value indicates that the city is behind Greenwich Mean Time, while a positive value indicates that it is ahead of Greenwich. Tokyo, for example, is 540 minutes or 9 hours ahead of Greenwich.

David has already designed the contents of the world map Web page, but he needs your help in programming the times for the six offices. Figure 2-41 shows a preview of the completed Web page.

Figure 2-41

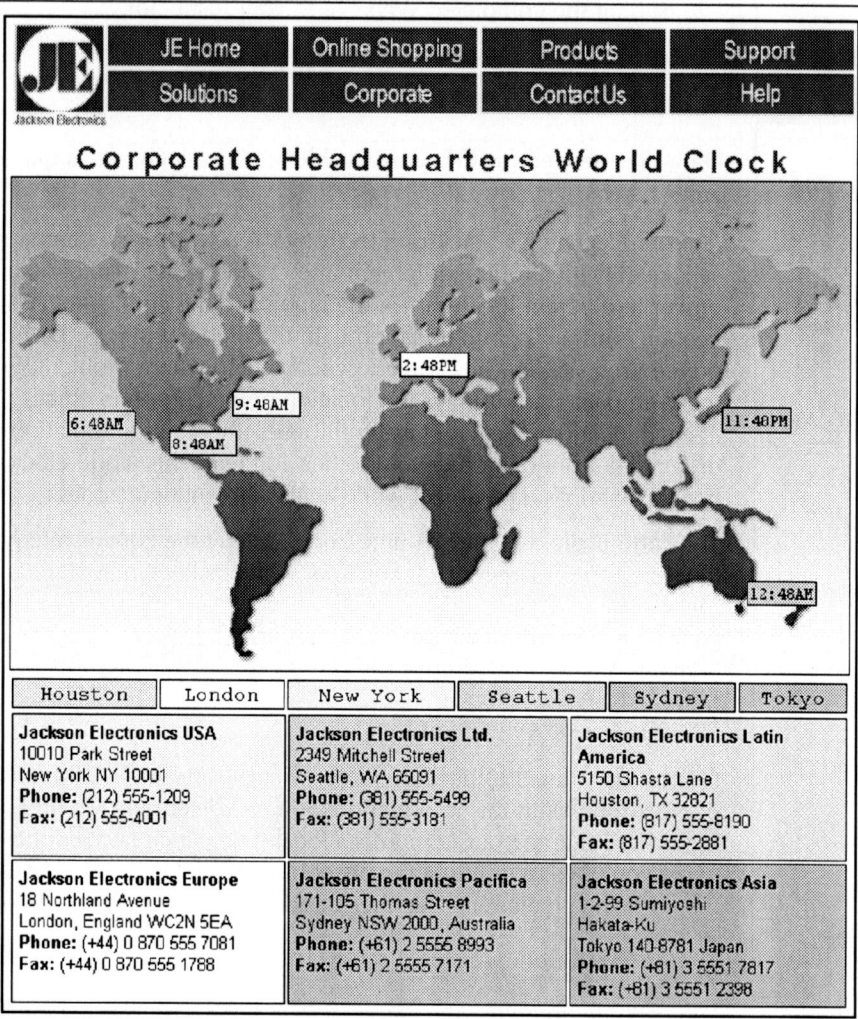

To complete this Web page:

1. Using your text editor, open **worldtxt.htm** from the tutorial.02/case3 folder. Enter *your name* and *the date* in the head section and save the file as **world.htm**. Use your text editor to open **zonestxt.js**, enter *your name* and *the date* in the comment section, and save the file as **zones.js**.

2. Within the **zones.js** file, create a function named addTime(). The purpose of the addTime() function is to create a new date object by adding a specified number of milliseconds to an initial time value. The function has two parameters, named oldTime and milliSeconds. The oldTime parameter stores a date object representing an initial time value. The milliSeconds parameter stores the amount of time, in milliseconds, that should be added to the oldTime parameter. Add the following commands to the function:

   a. Create a date object named newTime, but do not specify a value for its date or time.

   Explore

   b. Using the getTime() method, extract the number of milliseconds contained in the oldTime parameter and add this to the milliSeconds parameter. Store the sum in a variable named newValue.

   Explore

   c. Using the setTime() method, set the time value of the newTime date object to the value of the newValue variable.

   d. Return the newTime date object from the function.

3. Below the addTime() function, create a function named showTime(). The purpose of this function is to return a text string showing the time in a 12-hour format. The function has a single parameter named time, which contains the date and time that you want displayed. Using the showTime() function from the tutorial as a guide, have this function return the following text string:

   hour:minute AM/PM

   where *hour* is the hour value in the 12-hour format, *minute* is the minute value, and AM/PM is either "AM" or "PM" depending on the time of day.

4. Save your changes to the **zones.js** file.

5. Go to the **world.htm** file in your text editor. Above the closing </head> tag, insert an external script element to access the functions you created in the zones.js file and then insert a second embedded script element.

6. Within the embedded script element, create a function named worldClock(). The purpose of this function is to calculate the time in different time zones. Within this function, do the following:

   a. Create a date object variable named today equal to the current date and time.

   Explore

   b. Apply the getTimeZoneOffset() method to the today variable to calculate the offset of your computer's clock from GMT in minutes. Change this value to milliseconds by multiplying the value by 60 and then by 1000. Store the result in a variable named offSet.

   c. Call the addTime() function using today as the first parameter value and offSet as the second. Store the value returned by this function in a variable named GMT. The GMT variable represents the current date and time in Greenwich.

   Explore

   d. Calculate the current date and time at Jackson Electronics' first office (Houston). To calculate this value, call the addTime() function with GMT as the first parameter and the second parameter equal to the number of milliseconds that Houston is offset from GMT. (*Hint*: Since Houston is 360 minutes behind Greenwich, the offset from GMT is equal to (-360)*60*1000.) Store the date object returned by the addTime() function in a variable named time1. Repeat this step to create variables named time2 through time6 for the other five office locations using the offset values that David has indicated in the list above.

e. The current times for the six office locations are to be displayed in input fields named place1 through place6 in the zones Web form. To display the value of the place1 field, call the showTime() function using the time1 variable as the parameter value. Repeat this step for the five remaining input fields.

7. Add an event handler attribute to the <body> tag to run the worldClock() function when the page is loaded by the browser and every second thereafter.

8. Close the file, saving your changes.

9. Open **world.htm** in your Web browser. Verify that it shows the current time for the six office locations and that these times are correctly offset from Greenwich.

10. Submit the completed Web site to your instructor.

Note: This is a simplified example of what is a very complicated problem. Different countries apply time zones in different ways. For example, China spans several time zones but applies a uniform time throughout the country. Some countries also shift their time(s) twice a year during daylight savings time (otherwise known as summer time) while others do not apply daylight savings time at all. For example, the reported times in the case problem will be off by 1 hour during daylight savings time for the Seattle, Houston, and New York clocks. To create a truly accurate world clock, you would have to take into account all the various idiosyncrasies of global timekeeping.

Create

Test your knowledge of JavaScript by creating a countdown clock for the opening of a shopping mall.

Case Problem 4

Data files needed for this Case Problem: logo.jpg, mall1.jpg, mall2.jpg, mall3.jpg, mall.txt, malltxt.htm, timetxt.js

The Cutler Mall Alice Samuels is the director of promotion for the Cutler Shopping Mall, a large new mall opening on March 23 in Cutler, Iowa. She has asked you to work on the design of the Web page announcing the mall's opening. She's provided you with the text of the page as well as several graphic images; however, she would also like you to program a countdown clock that displays the days, hours, and minutes until the mall opens. The final design of the site is up to you, and you may supplement the provided material with your own.

To complete this assignment

1. Using your text editor, open **malltxt.htm** from the tutorial.02/case4 folder. Enter *your name* and *the date* in the head section and save the file as **mall.htm**.

2. Insert a Web form named mallclock in the Web page that has the following fields:
   - A dayNow field that displays the current date in the format month/day/year
   - A timeNow field that displays the time in a 12-hour format
   - A days field that displays the number of days until the mall opens
   - An hours field that displays the number of hours left in the current day
   - A minutes field that displays the number of minutes left in the current hour; round this value to the nearest minute.

3. Add the remaining content to the Web page. Refer to the mall.txt text file for the content that Alice would like to see in the Web page.

4. Open the **timetxt.js** file in your text editor and enter *your name* and *the date* in the comment section. Save the file as **time.js**. In the file, add the following functions:
   - A dayDiff() function that calculates the number of days, rounded down to the next lowest integer, between a starting date and a stopping date.
   - An hoursLeft() function that calculates the number of hours left in the current day rounded down to the next lowest integer.

- A minutesLeft() function that calculates the number of minutes left in the current hour rounded down to the next lowest integer.
- A showDate() function that displays the value of a date object in the format *month/day/year*.
- A showTime() function that displays the value of a date object in the format *hour:minute* am/pm.

5. Insert an external script element to access the functions in the time.js script file from the mall.htm file.
6. Add an embedded script to the mall.htm file to use the functions from the time.js file to display the current date and time in the document as well as the days, hours, and minutes remaining until the mall opening. Assume an opening date of March 23, and a time of 11 am.
7. Have the countdown clock updated every 10 seconds on the Web page.
8. Submit your completed Web site to your instructor.

Quick Check Answers

Session 2.1

1. An event handler is an attribute added to an element that instructs Web browsers to run a script command or commands when an event (such as a mouse click) occurs within the element.
2. onclick = "showImage()"
3. <a href="javascript:showImage()"> ... </a>
4. var examDate = new Date("May 8, 2007 18:55:28");
5. examDate.getMonth() // the value returned would be 4.
6. examDate.getFullYear()
7. examDate.setDate(9);
8. currentTime = new Date();

Session 2.2

1. thisMonth++
2. thisMonth += 1;
3. Math.round(thisMonth)
4. thisMonth = (thisMonth == 11) ? 12 : thisMonth;
5. IsNan(thisMonth)
6. thisDay.toFixed(0);
7. setTimeout("calcMonth", 500);
8. setInterval("calcMonth", 500);

Objectives

Session 3.1
- Create an array
- Populate and reference values from an array
- Work with array methods

Session 3.2
- Work with For loops
- Work with While loops
- Loop through the contents of an array
- Work with If, If... Else, and multiple conditional statements

Session 3.3
- Use arrays, loops, and conditional statements to create a table
- Work with break, continue, and label commands

Working with Arrays, Loops, and Conditional Statements

Creating a Monthly Calendar

Case

The Chamberlain Civic Center

With first-class concerts, performances from Broadway touring companies, and shows from famous comics, singers, and other entertainers, the Chamberlain Civic Center (CCC) is a popular attraction in southwest Missouri. Maria Valdez is the new publicity director for the center. Part of her job is to oversee the development of the center's Web site, which you maintain. After reviewing the Web site, Maria sees a few changes she would like you to make.

In addition to links connecting visitors to the site's main features, the CCC home page provides a brief description of the events for the current month. Maria thinks it would be useful if a monthly calendar could be placed at the top of the home page so that visitors could quickly see what day each event is held. However, Maria does not want staff members to have to construct the calendar manually each month; instead, she would like to add a program to the site that displays the monthly calendar for the current date. She asks for your help in writing a program to automatically generate the calendar.

Student Data Files

▼**tutorial.03**

▽ **tutorial folder**
  ccctxt.htm
  caltxt.js
  calendar.css
  ccc.css
  + 3 graphic files

▽ **review folder**
  caltxt.htm
  yeartxt.js
  + 2 style sheets
  + 3 graphic files

▽ **case1 folder**
  clisttxt.htm
  list.js
  lhouse.css
  logo.jpg

Session 3.1

Introducing the Monthly Calendar

You go to the publicity director's office early one morning to discuss with her the plans for the Chamberlain Civic Center's home page. Maria has a printout of the CCC home page on her desk and has drawn out her idea for creating the monthly calendar. The printout shows the events from the previous month, May 2007. The main text of the page contains a description of May events at the CCC. Maria would like the monthly calendar for May to appear in the upper-right corner of the page so that users can relate the events to the dates on the calendar. Figure 3-1 shows how Maria envisions the calendar appearing on the Web page.

Figure 3-1 | Inserting a monthly calendar

Maria wants the program you write to be easily usable on other Web pages. She envisions placing the entire JavaScript code for the calendar in an external file named calendar.js and running it from a single function. The styles for the calendar should also be placed in a single external file named calendar.css (see Figure 3-2). Accessing and displaying the monthly calendar table should require only a minimal amount of recoding within any page at the CCC Web site.

Creating and formatting the monthly calendar | **Figure 3-2**

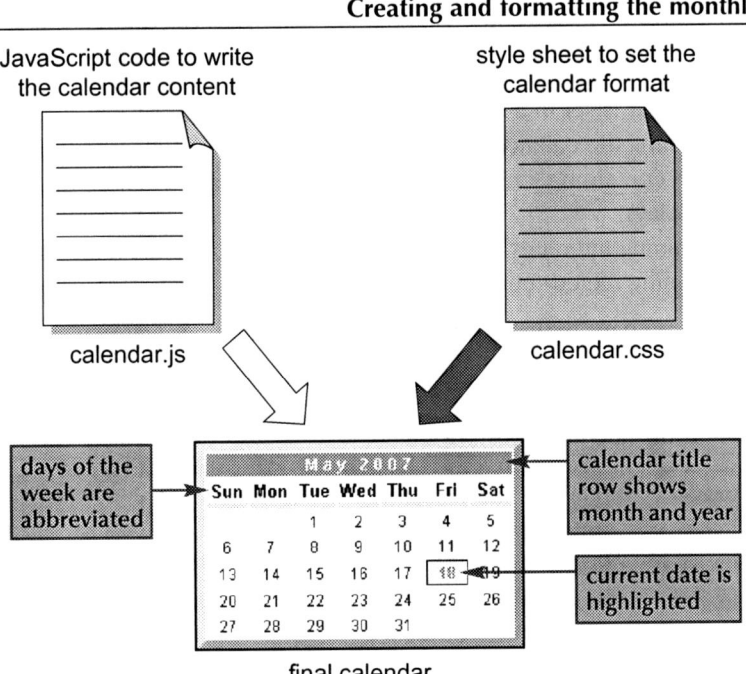

JavaScript code to write the calendar content

style sheet to set the calendar format

calendar.js

calendar.css

days of the week are abbreviated

calendar title row shows month and year

current date is highlighted

final calendar

Maria has already created the styles required for the calendar table, but has left the coding to you. Add links to both the calendar.js and calendar.css files to the Chamberlain Civic Center's home page.

To access the CCC files:

1. Use your text editor to open **caltxt.js** from the tutorial.03/tutorial folder. Enter **your name** and **the date** in the comment section at the top of the file and save the file as **calendar.js**.

2. Open the **ccctxt.htm** file in your text editor. Once again, enter **your name** and **the date** in the comment section at the top of the file and save the file as **ccc. htm**.

3. Add the following code above the closing </head> tag to create links to both the calendar.css style sheet and the calendar.js JavaScript file (see Figure 3-3):

```
<link href="calendar.css" rel="stylesheet" type="text/css" />
<script src="calendar.js" type="text/javascript"></script>
```

Linking to the JavaScript and stylesheet files | **Figure 3-3**

```
<title>The Chamberlain Civic Center</title>
<link href="ccc.css" rel="stylesheet" type="text/css" />
<link href="calendar.css" rel="stylesheet" type="text/css" />
<script src="calendar.js" type="text/javascript"></script>
</head>
```

4. Save your changes to the file.

The Calendar Style Sheet

Before you start writing the code to create the monthly calendar, you should take a quick look at the styles in the calendar.css style sheet. Maria has assigned class names and id names to different parts of the table. There are five class or id names you'll use in creating the monthly calendar:

- The entire calendar is set in a table with the id **calendar_table**.
- The cell containing the calendar title has the id **calendar_head**.
- The seven cells containing the days of the week abbreviations all belong to the class **calendar_weekdays**.
- The cells containing the dates of the month all belong to the class **calendar_dates**.
- The cell containing the current date has the id **calendar_today**.

For each of these parts, calendar.css has a style declaration. Figure 3-4 shows the style sheet contained in the calendar.css file.

Figure 3-4 ▶ **The contents of the calendar.css style sheet**

```
#calendar_table     {float: right; background-color: white; font-size: 9pt;
                     font-family: Arial, Helvetica, sans-serif;
                     border-style: outset; border-width: 5px; margin: 0px 0px 5px 5px}

#calendar_head      {background-color: orange; color: ivory; letter-spacing: 4}

.calendar_weekdays  {width: 30px; font-size: 10pt; border-bottom-style: solid}

.calendar_dates     {text-align: center; background-color: white}

#calendar_today     {font-weight: bold; color: orange; background-color: ivory;
                     border: 1px solid black}
```

As you create the code that writes this table, you need to make sure that you add the id and class attributes to the appropriate table and cell tags. One of the advantages of placing this information in a separate style sheet is that you can easily modify the table's appearance without having to rewrite the code that generates the table.

The calendar() Function

Because Maria wants the calendar application to be available to any page in the CCC Web site, you'll place all of the commands in a single function named calendar(). The first commands you'll add to the function use the document.write() method to write the HTML code for a table element with an id of 'calendar_table'. The initial code for the calendar() function is

```
function calendar() {
   document.write("<table id='calendar_table'>");
   document.write("</table>");
}
```

You'll call this function by adding the command in a script element within the ccc.htm file. Add this code to the calendar.js and ccc.htm files now.

To begin work on the calendar() function:

1. Return to the **calendar.js** file in your text editor. At the bottom of the file, add the following code (see Figure 3-5):

```
function calendar() {
    document.write("<table id='calendar_table'>");
    document.write("</table>");
}
```

Creating the calendar() function ◄ Figure 3-5

```
function calendar() {
    document.write("<table id='calendar_table'>");
    document.write("</table>");
}
```

2. Save your changes to the file.

3. Return to the **ccc.htm** file in your text editor. Locate the div element with the id "head". The calendar should be placed as a table element within this section of the page. To run the calendar() function to create the table, insert the following code, as shown in Figure 3-6:

```
<script type="text/javascript">
    calendar();
</script>
```

Calling the calendar() function ◄ Figure 3-6

```
<body>
<div id="head">
    <script type="text/javascript">
        calendar();
    </script>
    <img src="logo.gif" alt="Chamberlain Civic Center" />
</div>
```

4. Close the file, saving your changes.

5. Open **ccc.htm** in your Web browser. Verify that the browser does not report any coding errors. You will not see a calendar table in the Web page because you haven't created any content for the table yet.

At this point you've completed all of the coding you have to do within the ccc.htm file. You will do all of the remaining work to build the calendar() function within the calendar.js file. Creating the calendar table can be broken into three main tasks:

- Creating the table header row
- Creating the table row containing the names of the days of the week
- Creating the rows containing the days of the month

In this first session of this tutorial you'll look at how to create the header row for the calendar table.

Working with Arrays

Maria wants the header row of the calendar table to display the text *Month, Year* where *Month* is the name of the month and *Year* is the four-digit year value. In the previous tutorial you learned that date objects support methods that allow you to extract the date's month number. For example, a date object storing the date "May 18, 2007" has a month value of 4 (recall that month values start with 0 for the month of January). Maria wants the month name to appear in the table, rather than the month number, but no date method exists that returns the name of the month. Instead, you will have to write code to associate each month number with a month name. One way of doing this is through an array.

An **array** is a collection of data values organized under a single name. Each individual data value has a number or **index** that distinguishes it from other values in the array. The general form of an array value is

```
array[i]
```

where `array` is the name of the array and `i` is the index of a specific value in the array. The first item in any array has an index value of 0, the second item has an index value of 1, and so forth. For example, the expression

```
monthName[4]
```

references the fifth (not the fourth) item in the monthName array.

Creating and Populating an Array

To create an array, you run the following command:

```
var array = new Array(length);
```

where `array` is the name of the array and `length` is the number of items in the array. The `length` parameter is not required. If you omit the `length` parameter, the array expands to match the number of items defined for it. Arrays without a defined length can take up more memory. When the length of an array is defined, JavaScript allots only the amount of memory needed to generate the array, making your code run more efficiently. To create an array named monthName for the twelve month names, you can enter the command

```
var monthName = new Array(12);
```

or, omitting the array length,

```
var monthName = new Array();
```

Once you create an array, you can populate it with values using the same commands you use for any variable. The only difference is that you must specify both the array name and index number of the array item. The command to set the value of a specific item in an array is

```
array[i] = value;
```

where *i* is the index of the array item and *value* is the value assigned to the item. For example, to insert the month names into the monthName array, you could run the following commands:

```
monthName[0] = "January";
monthName[1] = "February";
monthName[2] = "March";
. . .
monthName[10] = "November";
monthName[11] = "December";
```

A more compact way of creating and populating an array is to specify the array values when the array is first created. The syntax for this statement is

```
var array = new Array(values);
```

where *values* is a comma-separated list of values. The command to create and populate the monthName array in a single statement would be

```
var monthName = new Array("January", "February", "March", "April", "May",
"June", "July", "August", "September", "October", "November",
"December");
```

A final way of creating an array is with an **array literal**, in which the array values are entered into a bracketed list. The expression to create an array literal is

```
var array = [values];
```

where once again, *values* is a comma-separated list of item values. The command to create an array literal of month names therefore appears as

```
var monthName = ["January", "February", "March", "April", "May", "June",
"July", "August", "September", "October", "November", "December"];
```

Because the array literal is not supported by some older browsers, it's customary to use the other two forms to create and populate arrays. Note that there is no requirement for array values to be all of the same data type. You can mix numeric values, text strings, and other data types within a single array, as in the following statement:

```
var x = new Array("JavaScript", 3.14, true, null);
```

Now that you've seen how to create and populate an array, you'll create an array of month names that can be used in creating the calendar application. You'll insert the array in a function named writeCalTitle() that you'll use to write the header row of the calendar table. The function has a single parameter named calendarDay that will store a date object containing the date to be highlighted in the calendar. The initial code for the writeCalTitle() function is

```
function writeCalTitle(calendarDay) {
   var monthName = new Array("January", "February", "March", "April",
   "May", "June", "July", "August", "September", "October", "November",
   "December");
}
```

Add this function to the calendar.js file.

To create the writeCalTitle() function:

1. Return to the **calendar.js** file in your text editor.

2. At the bottom of the file, insert the following code, as shown in Figure 3-7:

```
function writeCalTitle(calendarDay) {
    var monthName = new Array("January", "February", "March",
    "April", "May", "June", "July", "August", "September",
    "October", "November", "December");
}
```

Figure 3-7 Creating the monthName array

```
function calendar() {
    document.write("<table id='calendar_table'>");
    document.write("</table>");
}

function writeCalTitle(calendarDay) {
    var monthName = new Array("January", "February", "March", "April", "May",
    "June", "July", "August", "September", "October", "November", "December");
}
```

Trouble? Make sure that you enclose each array item value within a set of double quotes and that the line does not wrap within a quoted text string.

Next the function needs to extract the month value and year value from the calendarDay parameter using the getMonth() and getFullYear() date methods introduced in Tutorial 2. You'll store the values in variables named thisMonth and thisYear as follows:

```
var thisMonth=calendarDay.getMonth();
var thisYear=calendarDay.getFullYear();
```

Finally, the function will write the HTML code for the first table row of the monthly calendar. The monthly calendar will have seven columns, so the row containing the calendar title has to span seven columns. Recall that the heading row will also have the id calendar_head. The HTML code for the heading row has the following form:

```
<tr>
   <th id='calendar_head' colspan='7'>
      Month Year
   </th>
</tr>
```

where *Month* is the month name and *Year* is the four-digit year value. The year value is simply the value of the thisYear variable. The thisMonth variable tells you the month value, and you can use that as the index value from which to extract the corresponding month name in the monthName array. You'll use the expression

```
monthName[thisMonth]
```

Recall that, like the indices in the monthName array, the values of the thisMonth variable start with 0 for the first month of the year and go up to 11. Thus, the code to write the first row of the calendar table is

```
document.write("<tr>");
document.write("<th id='calendar_head' colspan='7'>");
document.write(monthName[thisMonth]+" "+thisYear);
document.write("</th>");
document.write("</tr>");
```

Complete the writeCalTitle() function by adding the commands to create the thisMonth and thisYear variables and to write the HTML code for the first table row.

To complete the writeCalTitle() function:

1. Insert the following commands into the writeCalTitle() function, as shown in Figure 3-8:

```
var thisMonth=calendarDay.getMonth();
var thisYear=calendarDay.getFullYear();

document.write("<tr>");
document.write("<th id='calendar_head' colspan='7'>");
document.write(monthName[thisMonth]+" "+thisYear);
document.write("</th>");
document.write("</tr>");
```

The completed writeCalTitle() function ◀ **Figure 3-8**

```
function writeCalTitle(calendarDay) {
    var monthName = new Array("January", "February", "March", "April", "May",
    "June", "July", "August", "September", "October", "November", "December");

    var thisMonth=calendarDay.getMonth();
    var thisYear=calendarDay.getFullYear();

    document.write("<tr>");
    document.write("<th id='calendar_head' colspan='7'>");
    document.write(monthName[thisMonth]+" "+thisYear);
    document.write("</th>");
    document.write("</tr>");
}
```

2. Save your changes to the file.

Creating and Populating Arrays

Reference Window

- To create an array, run the command
    ```
    var array = new Array(length);
    ```
    where `array` is the name of the array and `length` is the number of items in the array. The `length` parameter is not required unless you want to limit the array to a specific size to save space.
- To set a value of an item within an array, use
    ```
    array[i] = value;
    ```
    where `i` is the index of the array item and `value` is the value assigned to the item.
- To create and populate an array, use the command
    ```
    var array = new Array(values);
    ```
    where `values` is a comma-separated list of values.
- To create an array literal, use
    ```
    var array = [values];
    ```

Next you have to specify a date for the calendar to display. To have a common date, you'll add a date object named calDate to the calendar() function that stores the date "May 18, 2007". You'll then call the writeCalTitle() function using this date as the value for the calendarDay parameter.

To revise the calendar() function:

1. Insert the following statement at the beginning of the calendar() function to create the calDate variable:

```
var calDate = new Date("May 18, 2007");
```

2. Insert the following command to call the writeCalTitle() function, as shown in Figure 3-9:

```
writeCalTitle(calDate);
```

Figure 3-9 | **Calling the writeCalTitle() function**

```
function calendar() {
    var calDate = new Date("May 18, 2007");

    document.write("<table id='calendar_table'>");
    writeCalTitle(calDate);
    document.write("</table>");
}

function writeCalTitle(calendarDay) {
    var monthName = new Array("January", "February", "March", "April", "May",
    "June", "July", "August", "September", "October", "November", "December");

    var thisMonth=calendarDay.getMonth();
    var thisYear=calendarDay.getFullYear();

    document.write("<tr>");
    document.write("<th id='calendar_head' colspan='7'>");
    document.write(monthName[thisMonth]+" "+thisYear);
    document.write("</th>");
    document.write("</tr>");
}
```

3. Save your changes to the file.

4. Reopen or refresh **ccc.htm** in your Web browser. As shown in Figure 3-10, the calendar table should now appear in the upper-right corner of the page, displaying only the title "May 2007".

Figure 3-10 | **Displaying the calendar title**

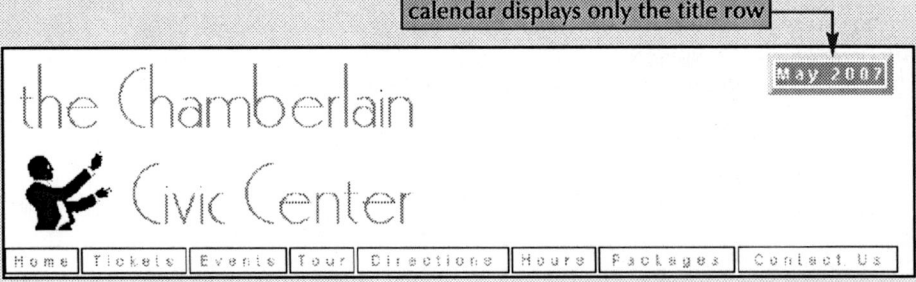

calendar displays only the title row

May 2007

the Chamberlain Civic Center

Home | Tickets | Events | Tour | Directions | Hours | Packages | Contact Us

Working with Array Length

To increase the size of an array, you can simply add more items to it. Unlike other programming languages, JavaScript arrays are not required to stay at a fixed size, even if you defined a value for the *length* parameter when an array was declared. In addition, you do not have to define a value for every item in an array. The following commands create an array of 100 items even though only the first and last items actually have defined values. The other array items have null values and are not stored in memory:

```
var x = new Array();
x[0] = "start";
x[99] = "stop";
```

Arrays like the x array with several missing or null items are called **sparse arrays**. To determine the size of an array, you can use the length property, which has the syntax

```
array.length
```

where *array* is the name of the array. The value of the length property is always equal to one more than the highest index number in the array. For the sparse array defined above, the length is 100, even though there are only two items in the array with defined values.

You change the value of the length property to either increase or decrease the size of an array. Increasing the array length adds more items to an array, but until they are defined, the items have a null value. Decreasing the array length truncates an array, removing any defined items whose indexes are not included in the new length. For example, if you ran the following command on the monthName array:

```
monthName.length = 3;
```

the array would be reduced to three items: "January", "February", and "March".

<table>
<tr><td>**Array Length**</td><td>Reference Window</td></tr>
</table>

- To determine the size of an array, use the property
     `array.length`
  where `array` is the name of the array and `length` is one more than the highest index in the array.
- To add more items to an array, run the command
     `array[i] = value;`
  where `i` is an index value higher than the highest index currently in the array.
- To remove items from an array, run the command
     `array.length = value;`
  where `value` is an integer that is smaller than highest index currently in the array.

Reversing an Array

Arrays are associated with a collection of methods that allow you to change their contents, order, and size. You can also use these methods to combine different arrays into a single array and to convert arrays into text strings. Though you will not need to use these methods with the calendar() function, you'll examine them for future projects. Each method is applied using the syntax

```
array.method()
```

where *array* is the name of an array and *method* is the name of the method. Some array methods have parameter values that control how they are applied to an array. You'll examine a few of these array methods.

By default, array items are placed in an array either in the order in which they're defined, or explicitly using the index numbers of the array. JavaScript supports two methods for changing the order of array items after an array is created: reverse() and sort(). The reverse() method, as the name suggests, reverses the order of items in an array. In the following set of commands, the reverse() method is used to change the order of the values in the weekDay array:

```
var weekDay = new Array("Sun", "Mon", "Tue", "Wed", "Thu", "Fri", "Sat");
weekDay.reverse();
```

After running the reverse() method, the weekDay array contains the items in the following order: "Sat", "Fri", "Thu", "Wed", "Tue", "Mon", and finally, "Sun".

Sorting an Array

The sort() method sorts array items in alphabetical order. Applying the command

```
weekDay.sort();
```

to the weekDay array causes the array to store the weekday abbreviations in the order "Fri", "Mon", "Sat", "Sun", "Thu", "Tue", "Wed". Note that if you apply the sort() method to numeric values, the method treats the values as text strings and sorts them in order by their first digits, rather than by their true numerical values. This sorting, which is analogous to arranging words in alphabetical order, can lead to some unexpected results. For example, the following commands create and sort an array named x:

```
var x = new Array(3, 45, 1234, 24);
x.sort();
```

The sorted x array will store items in the order 1234, 24, 3, 45, because this is the order of those numbers when sorted by their first digits. To correctly sort nontextual data, you have to create a **compare function** that compares the values of two adjacent items in the array at a time. The items are indicated by two parameters in the compare function.

The two items are sorted based on the value returned by the compare function. If the value is 0, the order of the two items remains unchanged. If the value is positive, the first of the two items is sorted to a higher index than the second. If the value is negative, the second of the two items is sorted to a higher index than the first. The following code shows a compare function you can use to sort array items in increasing numeric order:

```
function numSort(a, b) {
    return a-b;
}
```

The "a" parameter in the function represents the first of two adjacent items in the array; the "b" parameter represents the second of the two adjacent items. The value returned by the numSort() function is either positive, negative, or 0. To apply a compare function to the sort() method, you use the expression

```
array.sort(function)
```

where *function* is the name of the compare function. To use the numSort() compare function in sorting the x array in numeric order, you would run the following command:

```
x.sort(numSort)
```

The values of the resulting x array would be sorted in the following order: 3, 24, 45, 1234. To sort the array in decreasing numeric order, you would need a different compare function. The following function can be used to sort numeric values in decreasing order. Note that in this function, the comparison process returns the value (b-a) rather than (a-b).

```
function numSortDesc(a, b) {
    return b-a;
}
```

Extracting and Inserting Array Items

In some scripts you want to extract a section of an array, known as a **subarray**. For example, you might want to extract only the names of the summer months—June, July, and August—from the monthName array. To create a subarray you can use the slice() method, which extracts a part of an array. The original contents of the array are unaffected, but the extracted items can be stored in another array. The syntax of the slice() method is

```
array.slice(start, stop)
```

where `start` is the index of the array item at which the slicing starts and `stop` is the index before which the slicing ends. The `stop` value is optional. If no `stop` value is provided, the array is sliced to the end of the array. For example, if you wanted to slice the monthName array, extracting only the summer months, you would use the following command:

```
summerMonths = monthName.slice(5, 8);
```

The summerMonths array will contain the values "June", "July", and "August". Remember that arrays start with the index value 0, so the sixth month of the year (June) has an index value of 5 and the ninth month of the year (September) has an index of 8. Related to the slice() method is the splice() method, which is a general purpose method for extracting and inserting array items. The syntax of the splice() method is

```
array.splice(start, size)
```

where `start` is once again the index of the array item at which to start extracting items from the array and `size` is the number of items to extract. If no `size` value is specified, items are removed up through the end of the array. For example, to extract the summer months from the monthName array using the splice() method, you could run the command:

```
summerMonths = monthName.splice(5, 3);
```

One of the important differences between the slice() and splice() methods is that the splice() method not only extracts the selected items, but also removes them from the original array. Thus, applying the splice() method to the monthName array above would create a subarray of the summer months as well as removing those three months from the monthName array. This is not true of using the slice() method, which leaves the contents of the monthName array unaffected.

You can also use the splice() method to insert new items into an array. To insert new array items, you use the expression

```
array.splice(start, size, values)
```

where `values` is a comma-separated list of new values to replace the old values in the array. If you wanted to replace the first three month names with their first letters, for example, you could apply the following splice() method to the monthName array:

```
monthName(0, 3, "J", "F", "M");
```

The values in the monthName array would now be J, F, M, April, May, and so on.

In some cases you want to work only with items at the beginning or end of an array. The most efficient methods to insert or remove those items are the push(), pop(), unshift(), and shift() methods. The push() method appends new items to the end of an array and has the syntax

```
array.push(values)
```

where *values* is a comma-separated list of values to be appended to the end of the array. To remove the last item from an array, use the method

```
array.pop()
```

The push() and pop() methods are often used with item lists that follow the "first-in, last-out" principle The following set of commands demonstrates how to use the push() and pop() methods to expand and contract an array of values. Note that the most recent additions to the array are popped out first, since recent additions are added to the end of an array by default.

```
var x = new Array("a", "b", "c");
x.push("d", "e"); // x now contains ["a", "b", "c", "d", "e"]
x.pop();           // x now contains ["a", "b", "c", "d"]
x.pop();           // x now contains ["a", "b", "c"]
```

The unshift() method is similar to the push() method except that it inserts new items at the start of the array. In the same fashion, the shift() method is akin to the pop() method except that it removes the first, not the last, array item.

Reference Window | Array Methods

- To reverse the order of items in an array, use the method
    ```
    array.reverse()
    ```
  where *array* is the name of the array.
- To sort an array in alphabetical order, use
    ```
    array.sort();
    ```
- To sort an array in any order, use
    ```
    array.sort(function);
    ```
  where *function* is the name of a compare function that returns a positive, negative, or zero value.
- To extract items from an array without affecting the array contents, use
    ```
    array.slice(start, stop);
    ```
  where *start* is the index of the array item at which the slicing starts and *stop* is the index before which the slicing ends. If no *stop* value is provided, the array is sliced to the end of the array.
- To add or remove items in an array, use
    ```
    array.splice(start, size);
    ```
  where *start* is the index of the array item at which the splicing starts and *size* is the number of items to splice from or into the array. If no *splice* value is specified, the array is spliced to its end.
- To add new items to the end of an array, use
    ```
    array.push(values)
    ```
  where *values* is a comma-separated list of values.
- To remove the last item from an array, use
    ```
    array.pop()
    ```

Figure 3-11 summarizes several of the other methods that can be applied to arrays. Arrays are a very powerful and useful feature of the JavaScript language and the methods associated with arrays can be used to simplify and expand the capabilities of your Web page scripts. Note, however, that older browsers do not support many of these array methods and thus you should use them with caution if you want to support a wide range of browser versions.

Array methods | Figure 3-11

Array Method	Description
array.concat(*array1, array2, ...*)	Joins *array* to two or more arrays, creating a single array containing the items from all the arrays
array.join(*separator*)	Joins all items in *array* into a single text string. The array items are separated using the text in the *separator* parameter. If no *separator* is specified, a comma is used.
array.pop()	Removes the last item from *array*
array.push(*values*)	Appends *array* with new items, where *values* is a comma-separated list of item values
array.reverse()	Reverses the order of items in *array*
array.shift()	Removes the first item from *array*
array.slice(*start, stop*)	Extracts the *array* items starting with the *start* index up to the *stop* index, returning a new subarray
array.splice(*start, size, values*)	Extracts *size* items from *array* starting with the item with the index *start*. To insert new items into the array, specify the array item in a comma-separated *values* list.
array.sort(*function*)	Sorts *array* where *function* is the name of a function that returns a positive, negative, or zero value. If no *function* is specified, *array* is sorted in alphabetical order.
array.toString()	Converts the contents of *array* to a text string with the array values in a comma-separated list
array.unshift(*values*)	Inserts new items at the start of *array*, where *values* is a comma-separated list of new values

You've completed your work in this session on setting up the first parts of the online calendar. If you plan on taking a break before starting the next session you may close any open files or Web pages. In the next session you'll complete the monthly calendar by working with loops and conditional statements.

Session 3.1 Quick Check

Review

1. What is an array?
2. What command would you use to create an array named dayNames?
3. What command would you use to both create and populate the dayNames array with the abbreviations of the seven days of the week? (Start with "Sun" going through "Sat".)
4. What expression do you use to return the third value from the array dayNames?
5. What command would you enter to create the dayNames array as an array literal?
6. What command would you enter to sort the dayNames array in alphabetical order?
7. What command would you enter to extract the middle five values from the dayNames array?
8. What command would you enter to convert the contents of the dayNames array to a text string with each value separated by a comma?

Working with Program Loops

Now that you're familiar with the properties and methods of arrays, you'll continue your work on the calendar() function. So far you've created only the header row, which displays the calendar's month and year. The next row of the table will contain the three-letter abbreviations of the seven days of the week, starting with "Sun" and continuing through "Sat". Each abbreviation needs to be placed within a th element with the class name "calendar_weekdays". Using a document.write() command for each line of HTML, you could generate this table row with the following code:

```
document.write("<tr>");
document.write("<th class='calendar_weekdays'>Sun</th>");
document.write("<th class='calendar_weekdays'>Mon</th>");
document.write("<th class='calendar_weekdays'>Tue</th>");
document.write("<th class='calendar_weekdays'>Wed</th>");
document.write("<th class='calendar_weekdays'>Thu</th>");
document.write("<th class='calendar_weekdays'>Fri</th>");
document.write("<th class='calendar_weekdays'>Sat</th>");
document.write("</tr>");
```

This code contains a lot of repetitive text. Imagine if you had to repeat essentially the same string of code dozens, hundreds, or thousands of times. The code would become so long it would be unmanageable. Programmers deal with this kind of situation by creating program loops. A **program loop** is a set of commands that it is executed repeatedly until a stopping condition has been met. Two commonly used program loops in JavaScript are the For and While loops.

The For Loop

In a For loop, a variable known as a **counter variable** is used to track the number of times a set of commands is run. Each time through the loop, the value of the counter variable is increased or decreased by a set amount. When the counter variable reaches a specified value, the For loop stops. The general structure of a For loop is

```
for (start; continue; update) {
    commands
}
```

where *start* is an expression that sets the initial value of a counter variable, *continue* is a Boolean expression that must be true for the loop to continue, *update* is an expression that indicates how the value of the counter variable should change each time through the loop, and *commands* is the JavaScript commands that are run each time through the loop.

For example, suppose you wanted to set a counter variable to range in value from 0 to 3 in increments of 1. You could use the following expression to set the initial value of the variable:

```
var i = 0;
```

The name of the counter variable here is i, which is a common variable name often applied in program loops. The next expression in the For loop structure defines the stopping condition for the program loop. The following expression sets the loop to continue as long as the value of the counter variable is less than 4:

```
i < 4;
```

Finally, the following update expression uses the increment operator (introduced in the last tutorial) to indicate that the value of the counter variable increases by 1 each time through the program loop:

```
i++;
```

Putting all of these expressions together, the For loop would look as follows:

```
for (var i=0; i < 4; i++) {
    commands
}
```

The collection of commands that is run each time through a loop is collectively known as a **command block**, a feature that you've already worked with in functions. Command blocks are easily distinguished by their opening and closing curly braces { }. If a For loop contains only a single command, however, you don't need the command block and can dispense with the curly braces.

The following is an example of a For loop that writes the value of the counter variable to a table cell on the Web page. As shown in Figure 3-12, each time through the loop, the value displayed in the table cell is changed by 1.

```
for (var i=0; i < 4; i++) {
    document.write("<td>"+i+"</td>");
}
```

Running a For loop ◄ **Figure 3-12**

```
<table border="2">
<tr>

    <script type="text/javascript">
      for (var i=0; i < 4; i++) {
        document.write("<td>"+i+"</td>");
      }
    </script>

</tr>
</table>
```

For loop

Parts of the For Loop	Expressions	Counter Values	Code Written to the Page
start	var i=0	0	<td>0</td>
continue	i < 4	1	<td>1</td>
		2	<td>2</td>
update	i ++	3	<td>3</td>

Values during the For loop

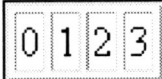

resulting table

For loops can be nested inside one another. Figure 3-13 shows code used to create a table containing three rows and four columns. This example uses two counter variables, named rowNum and colNum. The rowNum variable loops through the values 1, 2, and 3. In addition, for each value of the rowNum variable, the colNum variable loops through the values 1, 2, 3, and 4. Each time the value of the colNum variable changes, a new cell is added to the table. Each time the value of the rowNum variable changes, a new row is added to the table.

Figure 3-13 ▶ Running a nested For loop

```
<table border="2">

  <script type="text/javascript">
    for (var rowNum=1; rowNum < 4; rowNum++) {
      document.write("<tr>");

      for (var colNum=1; colNum < 5; colNum++) {
        document.write("<td>"+rowNum+", "+colNum+"</td>");
      }

      document.write("</tr>");
    }
  </script>

</table>
```

nested For loops

```
1,1 1,2 1,3 1,4
2,1 2,2 2,3 2,4
3,1 3,2 3,3 3,4
```

resulting table

rowNum Values	colNum Values	Code Written to the Page
1		<tr>
1	1	<td>1,1</td>
1	2	<td>1,2</td>
1	3	<td>1,3</td>
1	4	<td>1,4</td>
1		</tr>
2		<tr>
2	1	<td>2,1</td>
2	2	<td>2,2</td>
2	3	<td>2,3</td>
2	4	<td>2,4</td>
2		</tr>
...		
3	4	<td>3,4</td>
3		</tr>

The update expression is not limited to increasing the counter by 1. You can use the other operators introduced in Tutorial 2 to create a wide variety of increment patterns. Figure 3-14 shows a few of the many different ways of updating the value of the For loop's counter variable.

Figure 3-14 ▶ Counter values in the For loop

For Loop	Counter Values
for (i=1; i <=5; i++)	i = 1, 2, 3, 4, 5
for (i=5; i > 0; i--)	i = 5, 4, 3, 2, 1
for (i=0; i <= 360; i+=60)	i = 0, 60, 120, 180, 240, 300, 360
for (i=1; i <= 64; i*=2)	i = 1, 2, 4, 8, 16, 32, 64

For Loops and Arrays

For loops are often used to cycle through the different values contained within an array. The general structure of accessing each value from an array is

```
for (var i=0; i < array.length; i++) {
   commands involving array[i]
}
```

where *array* is the array containing the values to be looped through and *i* is the counter variable used in the loop. The counter variable in this case represents the **index** number of an item from the array. Note that the length property is used to determine the size of the array. Since the last item in the array has an index value one less than the array's length (because array indices start with zero), you only continue the loop when the array index is less than the length value.

You now have enough information to create a function that employs arrays and a For loop to create a row displaying the names of the seven days of the week. First you need to create an array named dayName containing the three letter abbreviations of each day. You'll use the following code to do this:

```
var dayName = new Array("Sun", "Mon", "Tue", "Wed", "Thu", "Fri", "Sat");
```

You'll then loop through the values of the dayName array, displaying each value in a header cell with the class name calendar_weekdays:

```
document.write("<tr>");
for (var i=0;i<dayName.length;i++) {
    document.write("<th class='calendar_weekdays'>"+dayName[i]+"</th>");
}

document.write("</tr>");
```

Add these commands to a new function named writeDayNames(), and then apply the function to your monthly calendar.

To create the writeDayNames() function:

1. If necessary, reopen the **calendar.js** file in your text editor.

2. At the bottom of the file, insert the following function:

```
function writeDayNames() {
    var dayName = new Array("Sun", "Mon", "Tue", "Wed", "Thu", "Fri",
        "Sat");
    document.write("<tr>");
    for (var i=0;i<dayName.length;i++) {
        document.write("<th class='calendar_weekdays'>
"+dayName[i]+"</th>");
    }
    document.write("</tr>");
}
```

3. Scroll up to the calendar() function and insert **writeDayNames()** below the command that calls the writeCalTitle() function. (See Figure 3-15).

Creating the writeDayNames() function | **Figure 3-15**

4. Save your changes to the file.

5. Reopen **ccc.htm** in your Web browser. As shown in Figure 3-16, the monthly calendar should now show a second row containing the abbreviations of the seven days of the week.

Figure 3-16 | Calendar with day names

The While Loop

The For loop is only one way of creating a program loop in JavaScript. Before continuing with the calendar() function, you'll investigate a few others. Similar to the For loop is the While loop, in which a command block is run as long as a specific condition is met. However, unlike the For loop, the condition in a While loop does not depend on the value of a counter variable. The general syntax of the While loop is

```
while (continue) {
    commands
}
```

where *continue* is any Boolean expression. The Boolean expression is tested before each time through the program loop. If the expression returns a value of true, the command block is run; otherwise, the command block is not run and the program loop ends. Every While loop includes a condition under which the loop stops; if a While loop didn't include this, the loop would run without end, causing users' browsers to crash.

The following code shows how you would create the table shown earlier in Figure 3-12 as a While loop. In this loop, the command block is run as long as the value of the i variable remains less than 4. Each time through the command block, the loop writes the value of the i variable into a table cell and then increases the value of the i variable by 1.

```
var i = 0;
while (i < 4) {
    document.write("<td>"+i+"</td>");
    i++;
}
```

Like For loops, While loops can be nested within one another. The following code demonstrates how you would create the 3 × 4 table shown earlier in Figure 3-13 using nested While loops. Once again, the initial values of the counter variables are set before the While loops are run and are updated within the command blocks.

```
rowNum = 1;
while (rowNum < 4) {
    document.write("<tr>");
    colNum = 1;
    while (colNum < 5) {
        document.write("<td>"+rowNum+","+colNum+"</td>");
        colNum++;
    }
    document.write("</tr>");
    rowNum++;
}
```

Because For loops and While loops share many of the same characteristics, which one you choose for a given application is often a matter of personal preference. In general, For loops are used whenever you have a counter variable, and While loops are used for conditions that don't easily lend themselves to using counters.

The Do/While Loop

In the For and While loops, the test to determine whether to continue to loop is made before the command block is run. JavaScript also supports a program loop called Do/While that tests the condition to continue the loop right after the latest command block is run. The structure of the Do/While loop is

```
do {
    commands
}
while (continue);
```

For example, to create the table shown in Figure 3-12 as a Do/While loop, you would enter the following code:

```
var i = 0;
do {
    document.write("<td>"+i+"</td>");
    i++;
}
while (i < 4);
```

The Do/While loop is only used in those situations where you are always sure that the program loop should run at least once. However, because of its similarity to the While loop, you rarely see the Do/While loop used in scripts.

Program Loops

Reference Window

- To create a For loop, use the syntax
```
for (start; continue; update) {
    commands
}
```
where *start* is an expression that sets the initial value of a counter variable, *continue* is a Boolean expression that must be true for the loop to continue, *update* is an expression that indicates how the value of the counter variable should change each time through the loop, and *commands* are the JavaScript commands that are run each time through the loop.
- To create a While loop, use the syntax
```
while (continue) {
    commands
}
```
- To create a Do/While loop, use the syntax
```
do {
    commands
}
while (continue);
```
- To loop through the contents of array, enter the For loop
```
for (var i=0; i < array.length; i++) {
    commands involving array[i]
}
```
where *i* is a counter variable representing the indices of the array items and *array* is the array to be looped through.

Working with Conditional Statements

Your next task in the calendar application is to enter the table rows containing month dates. Each table cell within those rows will contain a number for the day of the month. When you reach the last day, you'll stop writing table cells and rows. Obviously, this process needs to involve some kind of program loop. The number of times this loop runs will depend on the number of days in the current month. Because months have differing numbers of days, you'll need to create an array containing the length of each month to use in conjunction with the loop. The array will look as follows:

```
var dayCount = new Array(31,28,31,30,31,30,31,31,30,31,30,31);
```

You'll create this array within a function named daysInMonth(). Like the writeCalTitle() function you created earlier, the daysInMonth() function has a single parameter, calendarDay, representing a date object. The function creates two variables, thisYear and thisMonth, containing the four-digit year value and month value. The thisMonth variable is used to supply the index from which the number of days in the month is returned by the function.

To start creating the daysInMonth() function:

1. Return to the **calendar.js** file in your text editor.

2. At the bottom of the file, insert the following code (see Figure 3-17):

```
function daysInMonth(calendarDay) {
    var thisYear = calendarDay.getFullYear();
    var thisMonth = calendarDay.getMonth();
    var dayCount = new Array(31,28,31,30,31,30,31,31,30,31,30,31);
    return dayCount[thisMonth]; // return the number of days in the
        month
}
```

Figure 3-17	The initial daysInMonth() function

```
function writeDayNames() {
    var dayName = new Array("Sun", "Mon", "Tue", "Wed", "Thu", "Fri", "Sat");
    document.write("<tr>");
    for (var i=0;i<dayName.length;i++) {
        document.write("<th class='calendar_weekdays'>"+dayName[i]+"</th>");
    }
    document.write("</tr>");
}

function daysInMonth(calendarDay) {
    var thisYear = calendarDay.getFullYear();
    var thisMonth = calendarDay.getMonth();
    var dayCount = new Array(31,28,31,30,31,30,31,31,30,31,30,31);
    return dayCount[thisMonth]; // return the number of days in the month
}
```

There is one problem with the dayCount array you've created: February sometimes has 29, not 28, days. Figure 3-18 shows the general process to determine whether a particular year is a leap year or not.

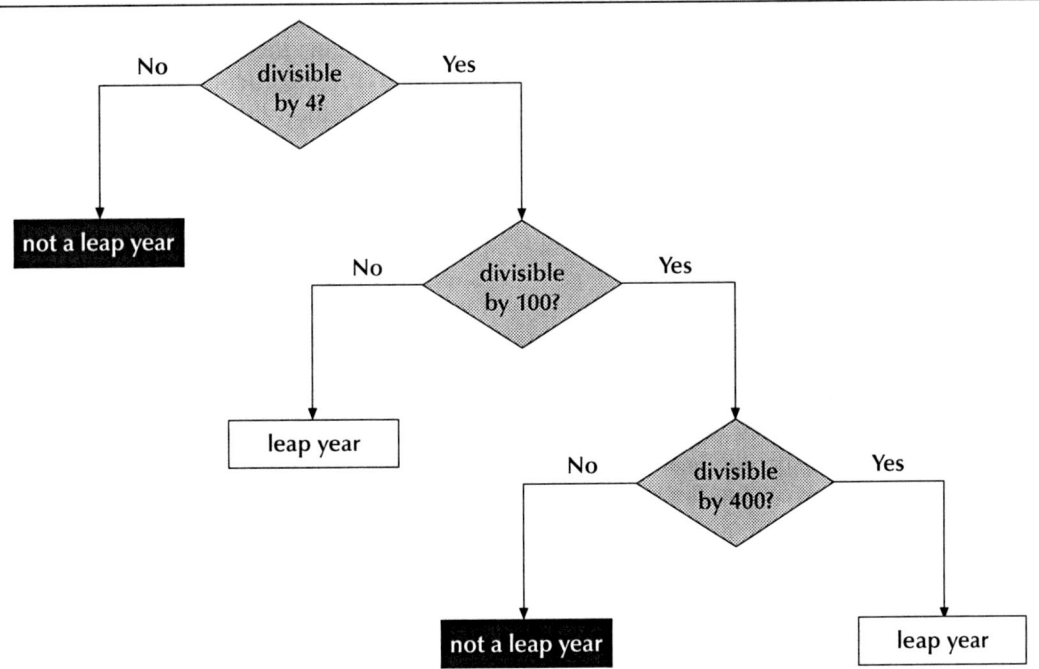

For example, any year that is not divisible by 4, is not a leap year. Thus, a year like 2007 is not a leap year since it is not divisible by 4. Beyond that, the situation is a little more complicated. In most cases, a year that is divisible by 4 is a leap year. The only exception are years that occur at the turn of the century that are divisible by 100. Such a year is not a leap year unless it is also divisible by 400. Thus, years like 1800, 1900 and 2100 are not leap years, even though they are divisible by 4. Years like 2000 and 2400, however, are leap years because they are divisible by 400.

For your function to determine whether February has 28 or 29 days, you have to examine the year value and then set the value for the number of days in February to either 28 or 29 based on the year value. You can do this through a conditional statement. A **conditional statement** is a statement that runs a command or command block only when certain conditions are met. The most common conditional statement is the If statement.

The If Statement

The syntax of the If statement is

```
if (condition) {
    commands
}
```

where `condition` is a Boolean expression that is either true or false, and `commands` is the command block that is run if `condition` is true. If only one command is run, you can dispense with the command block and enter the If statement as

```
if (condition) command;
```

The `condition` expression uses the same comparison and logical operators you've used in the conditional operator from Tutorial 2. The main difference between a comparison operator and a conditional statement is that, instead of changing the value of a variable based on a condition, you are choosing whether or not to run a particular command or command block. For example, the following If statement sets the value of the dayCount array for February to 29 if the year value is 2008 (a leap year):

```
if (thisYear == 2008) {
    dayCount[1] = 29;
}
```

Note that the conditional expression in this example uses the == operator, which tests whether two items are equal. One common error is to use the = symbol, which should be used only in assigning values to variables and objects.

For the calendar application, you need to create a conditional expression that indicates whether the current year is a leap year (not just 2008). Start by looking at methods of determining whether the year is divisible by 4. One way is to use the % operator, which is also known as the modulus operator. The **modulus operator** returns the integer remainder after dividing one integer by another. For example, the expression

```
2009 % 4
```

returns the value 1 because 1 is the remainder after dividing 2009 by 4. To test whether a year value is divisible by 4, you use the conditional expression

```
thisYear % 4 == 0
```

where the thisYear variable contains the four-digit year value. The complete If statement to change the value of the dayCount array for the month of February is

```
if (thisYear % 4 == 0) {
    dayCount[1] = 29;
}
```

Nesting If Statements

The above If statement works as a simple approximation, but it is not completely accurate because it doesn't take into account century years. You need to include a second test to account for the different leap year rules during century years. The general structure of this nested If statement is

```
if (thisYear % 4 == 0) {
    if statement for century years
}
```

The nested If statement needs to test for two conditions: (1) the year is not divisible by 100, and (2) the year is divisible by 400. The two expressions are

```
thisYear % 100 != 0
thisYear % 400 == 0
```

If either of those two conditions is true for a year evenly divisible by 4, then the year is a leap year. Note that you use the != operator to test for an inequality in the first expression. You then combine these two expressions into a single expression using the or operator (||), which was introduced in Tutorial 2. The combined expression is

```
(thisYear % 100 != 0) || (thisYear % 400 == 0)
```

Finally, you place this conditional expression in a nested If statement. The complete code is therefore

```
if (thisYear % 4 == 0) {
   if ((thisYear % 100 !=0) || (thisYear % 400 == 0)) {
      dayCount[1] = 29;
   }
}
```

Under this set of nested If statements, the number of days in February is 29 only if the thisYear variable is divisible by 4 *and* only if it also divisible by 400 or *not* divisible by 100. Take some time to compare this set of nested If statements with the chart shown earlier in Figure 3-18 to confirm that it satisfies all possible conditions for leap years. Putting this nested If statement into the daysInMonth() function, you can return the number of days for any month in any given year.

By adding this nested If statement to the daysInMonth() function, you arrive at the final version of the function, shown below:

```
function daysInMonth(calendarDay) {
   var thisYear = calendarDay.getFullYear();
   var thisMonth = calendarDay.getMonth();
   var dayCount = new Array(31,28,31,30,31,30,31,31,30,31,30,31);
   if (thisYear % 4 == 0) {
      if ((thisYear % 100 !=0) || (thisYear % 400 == 0)) {
         dayCount[1] = 29; // this is a leap year
      }
   }
   return dayCount[thisMonth]; // return the number of days in the
      month
}
```

You can now complete the daysInMonth() function in the calendar.js file.

To create the daysInMonth() function:

1. Before the final return statement in the daysInMonth() function, insert the following nested If structure (see Figure 3-19):

```
if (thisYear % 4 == 0) {
   if ((thisYear % 100 !=0) || (thisYear % 400 == 0)) {
      dayCount[1] = 29; // this is a leap year
   }
}
```

The complete daysInMonth() function   **Figure 3-19**

```
function daysInMonth(calendarDay) {
   var thisYear = calendarDay.getFullYear();
   var thisMonth = calendarDay.getMonth();
   var dayCount = new Array(31,28,31,30,31,30,31,31,30,31,30,31);
   if (thisYear % 4 == 0) {
      if ((thisYear % 100 !=0) || (thisYear % 400 == 0)) {
         dayCount[1] = 29; // this is a leap year
      }
   }
   return dayCount[thisMonth]; // return the number of days in the month
}
```

2. Close the file, saving your changes.

The If...Else Statement

The If statement runs a command or a command block only if the conditional expression returns the value true; it does nothing if a value of false is returned. However, on some occasions, you may want to choose between two alternate sets of commands. In those cases you would use an If...Else structure, in which one set of commands is run if the conditional expression is true and a different set is run if the expression is false. The general structure of an If...Else statement is

```
if (condition) {
   commands if true
} else {
   commands if false
}
```

If only a single command is run in response to the conditional expression, you can use the abbreviated form

```
if (condition) command if true
else command if false;
```

The following example of an If...Else statement runs one of two possible document. write() commands:

```
if (day == "Friday") document.write("Thank God It's Friday")
else document.write("Today is "+day);
```

In this statement, the text "Thank God It's Friday" is written to the document if the value of the day variable is "Friday". Otherwise, the text string "Today is *day*" is written to the document, where *day* is the value of the day variable.

Like the If statement, If...Else statements can be nested. With a nested If...Else statement, you place the inner statements within command blocks. The following nested If... Else statement chooses between three possible text strings to write to a document:

```
if (day == "Friday") document.write("Thank God It's Friday")
else {
   if (day == "Monday") document.write("Blue Monday")
   else document.write("Today is "+day);
}
```

As you nest more and more If...Else statements within one another, you may end up confused as to which Else clause belongs with which If statement. One way of avoiding this problem is to always indent nested If...Else statements, allowing you to visually line up matching statement lines. Another technique is to always use curly braces even if a command block contains only a single command. This practice tends to separate one Else clause from another. Finally, when reading through nested statements, it can be helpful to remember that an Else clause usually pairs with the nearest preceding If statement.

Using Multiple Else...If statements

For more complicated scripts, you may need to choose between several alternatives. In these cases, you can specify multiple Else clauses, each with its own If statement. This is not a new type of conditional structure, but rather a way of taking advantage of the syntax rules inherent in the If...Else statement. The general structure for choosing between several alternatives is

```
if (condition 1) {
    first command block
}
else if (condition 2) {
    second command block
}
else if (condition 3) {
    third command block
}
...
else {
    default command block
}
```

where *condition 1*, *condition 2*, *condition 3*, and so on, are the different conditions to be tested. This construction should always include a final Else clause that is run by default if none of the previous conditional expressions return the value true. When a browser runs this series of statements, it stops examining the remaining Else clauses when it encounters the first true Else clause (since there no longer is an Else condition to investigate.) The following example is a structure that employs multiple Else...If conditions:

```
if (day == "Friday") {
    document.write("Thank God It's Friday");
}
else if {day == "Monday") {
    document.write("Blue Monday");
}
else if {day == "Saturday") {
    document.write("Sleep in today");
}
else {
    document.write("Today is "+day);
}
```

Conditional Statements

- To test a single condition, use the construction

```
if (condition) {
   commands
}
```

where *condition* is a Boolean expression and *commands* is a command block run if the conditional expression is true.
- To test between two conditions, use

```
if (condition) {
   commands if true
} else {
   commands if false
}
```

- To test multiple conditions, use

```
if (condition 1) {
   first command block
}
else if (condition 2) {
   second command block
}
else if (condition 3) {
   third command block
}
...
else {
   default command block
}
```

where *condition 1*, *condition 2*, *condition 3*, and so on, are the different conditions to be tested. If no conditional expressions return the value true, the default command block is run.

The Switch Statement

When you have to choose between several possible conditions, you may find a series of Else...If statements to be cumbersome to work with. A simpler structure is the Switch statement (otherwise known as the Case statement), in which different commands are run based upon different possible values of a variable. The syntax of a Switch statement is

```
switch (expression) {
   case label1: commands1
   break;
   case label2: commands2
   break;
   case label3: commands3
   break;
...
   default: default commands
}
```

where *expression* is an expression that returns a value other than a Boolean value; *label1*, *label2*, *label3*, and so on are possible values of that expression; *commands1*, *commands2*, *commands3*, and so on are the commands to run for each matching label; and *default commands* are the commands to be run if no label matches the value returned by *expression*. The previous Else...If statement could be rewritten as a Switch statement as follows:

```
switch (day) {
   case "Friday": document.write("Thank God It's Friday"); break;
   case "Monday": document.write("Blue Monday"); break;
   case "Saturday": document.write("Sleep in today"); break;
   default: document.write("Today is "+day);
}
```

As the browser moves through the different case values, it executes any command or command block in which the label matches the expression's value. The break statement is optional and is used to halt the execution of the Switch statement once a match has been found. If you omit the break statements, then browsers continue moving through the Switch statements, running all matching commands, which always includes the default statement.

The Switch Statement

Reference Window

- To create a Switch statement to test for different values of an expression, use the structure
  ```
  switch (expression) {
     case label1: commands1
     break;
     case label2: commands2
     break;
     case label3: commands3
     break;
  ...
     default: default commands
  }
  ```
  where *expression* is an expression that returns a value, other than a Boolean value; *label1*, *label2*, *label3*, and so on are possible values of that expression; *commands1*, *commands2*, *commands3*, and so on are the commands to run for each matching label; and *default commands* are the commands to be run if no label matches the value returned by *expression*.

At this point you've become familiar with all of the tools you'll need for completing the calendar() function. In the next session, you'll enter the code to create a monthly calendar for any date you choose. If you want to take a break before the next session, you may close any open files or pages.

Session 3.2 Quick Check

Review

1. What is a program loop? Name three types of program loops supported by JavaScript.
2. What expressions would you place in a For statement to use a counter variable named i that starts with the value 0 and continues up to 100 in increments of 10?

3. What For statement would you enter to create a table row consisting of five table cells? Assume the table cells display the text "Column *i*" where *i* is the value of the counter variable and the value of the counter variable ranges from 1 to 5 in increments of 1.

4. What is a conditional statement? What is the most commonly used conditional statement?

5. What code would you enter to write the text "Internet Explorer Browser" to the document if the Boolean variable WebBrowser equals true?

6. The WebBrowser variable has been changed to a text string variable which can equal either "IE" or "Netscape". Write an If...Else statement to display the text "Internet Explorer Browser" if WebBrowser equals "IE" and "Netscape Browser" otherwise.

7. Now the WebBrowser variable can equal "IE", "Netscape", "Safari", or "Firefox". Write a series of Else...If statements that write the name of the browser to the document. If WebBrowser equals none of the four text strings listed above, write the text "Generic Browser" to the document.

8. Repeat the previous steps using a Switch statement. Use a break statement to break off from processing the Switch statement once a match has been found.

Session 3.3

Creating the calendar() Function

You are now ready to complete the calendar application. You've already written the code that writes the calendar title and the row of abbreviated day names. In this session you'll combine all you've learned about arrays, loops, and conditional statements to create the part of the calendar() function that writes the actual calendar dates. This will involve the following steps:

1. Calculating the day of the week in which the month starts
2. Preceding the first day of the month with blank table cells.
3. Looping through all of the days of the month, writing each date in a different table cell, starting a new table row on each Sunday, and ending the table rows after each Saturday.
4. Highlighting the current date in the calendar.

Figure 3-20 shows the monthly calendar for a date of May 18, 2007, applying the steps described above.

| Figure 3-20 | **Building the monthly calendar** |

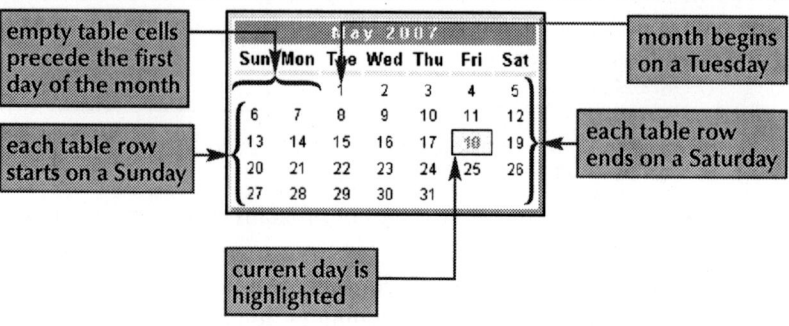

You'll place these commands in a function named writeCalDays(). The function will have a single parameter named calendarDay. As in the other functions in the calendar.js file, the parameter for the writeCalDays() function contains a date object. You'll create the basic structure of the different tasks within the writeCalDays() function using single-line comments. Add this function to the calendar.js file now.

To insert the writeCalDays() function:

1. If necessary, reopen the **calendar.js** file in your text editor.

2. At the bottom of the file, insert the following function (see Figure 3-21):

```
function writeCalDays(calendarDay) {
    // determine the starting day of the week
    // write blank cells preceding the starting day
    // write cells for each day of the month
}
```

Starting the writeCalDays() function   **Figure 3-21**

```
function daysInMonth(calendarDay) {
    var thisYear = calendarDay.getFullYear();
    var thisMonth = calendarDay.getMonth();
    var dayCount = new Array(31,28,31,30,31,30,31,31,30,31,30,31);
    if (thisYear % 4 == 0) {
        if ((thisYear % 100 !=0) || (thisYear % 400 == 0)) {
            dayCount[1] = 29; // this is a leap year
        }
    }
    return dayCount[thisMonth]; // return the number of days in the month
}

function writeCalDays(calendarDay) {
    // determine the starting day of the week
    // write blank cells preceding the starting day
    // write cells for each day of the month
}
```

3. Save your changes to the file.

Setting the First Day of the Month

To loop through all of the days of the month, you'll need to keep track of the day currently being written to the calendar table. You'll store this information in a variable named dayCount. The initial value of the dayCount variable will be set to 1 and will increase up to the total number of days in the month. You can determine the total days in the month by calling the daysInMonth() function you created in the last session. The first two lines of the writeCalDays() function are therefore

```
var dayCount = 1;
var totalDays = daysInMonth(calendarDay);
```

Next you reset the value of the calendarDay variable so that it is equal to the first day of the month. This is done using the setDate() method. The command is

```
calendarDay.setDate(1);
```

Finally, your code has to determine on which day of the week this date falls. The getDay() method returns this information, with values ranging from 0 (Sunday) to 6 (Saturday). You'll store this value in a variable named weekDay. The command to declare the week-Day variable is

```
var weekDay = calendarDay.getDay();
```

Add these commands to the writeCalDays() function.

To declare the initial variables in the writeCalDays() function:

1. Below the first comment line in the writeCalDays() function, insert the following commands (see Figure 3-22):

```
var dayCount = 1;
var totalDays = daysInMonth(calendarDay);
calendarDay.setDate(1);              // set the date to the first
   day of the month
var weekDay = calendarDay.getDay();  // the day of week of the
   first day
```

Figure 3-22 | Setting the first day of the month

```
function writeCalDays(calendarDay) {
   // determine the starting day of the week
   var dayCount = 1;
   var totalDays = daysInMonth(calendarDay);
   calendarDay.setDate(1);              // set the date to the first day of the month
   var weekDay = calendarDay.getDay();  // the day of week of the first day

   // write blank cells preceding the starting day
   // write cells for each day of the month
}
```

2. Save your changes to the file.

Placing the First Day of the Month

Prior to the first day of the month, the calendar table should show only empty table cells. The value of the weekDay variable indicates how many empty table cells you need to create. For example, if the value of the weekDay variable is 4 (Thursday), you know that there are four blank table cells—corresponding to Sunday, Monday, Tuesday, and Wednesday—that need to be written at the start of the first table row. The loop to create the blank table cells is therefore

```
document.write("<tr>");
for (var i=0; i < weekDay; i++) {
   document.write("<td></td>");
}
```

Note that if weekDay equals 0—indicating that the month starts on a Sunday—then no blank table cells will be written because the value of the counter variable, i, is never less than the value of the weekDay variable. Insert these commands into the writeCalDays() function.

To write the initial blank cells of the first table row:

1. Below the second comment line, insert the following For loop (see Figure 3-23):

```
document.write("<tr>");
for (var i=0; i < weekDay; i++) {
   document.write("<td></td>");
}
```

Writing the preceding blank table cells | Figure 3-23

```
function writeCalDays(calendarDay) {
    // determine the starting day of the week
    var dayCount = 1;
    var totalDays = daysInMonth(calendarDay);
    calendarDay.setDate(1);              // set the date to the first day of the month
    var weekDay = calendarDay.getDay();  // the day of week of the first day

    // write blank cells preceding the starting day
    document.write("<tr>");
    for (var i=0; i < weekDay; i++) {
        document.write("<td></td>");
    }

    // write cells for each day of the month
}
```

2. Save your changes to the file.

3. Reopen the **ccc.htm** file in your Web browser and verify that no run-time errors have been introduced by incorrectly typing any of the code in this or the previous step. The appearance of the page should be unchanged from what was shown earlier in Figure 3-16.

Writing the Calendar Days

Now that the code has determined into which table cell the initial date is placed, the rest of the function will be devoted to inserting the remaining dates. This is done using a While loop. Each time through the loop, the function should write the table cells containing the calendar dates, and, if necessary, add new rows to the table. At the end of the command block, the dayCount variable should be increased, moving to the next day in the month. The general structure of the While loop is

```
while (dayCount <= totalDays) {
    write the table rows and cells
    move to the next day
}
```

Add this While loop to the writeCalDays() function.

To insert the While loop:

1. Below the last comment line in the writeCalDays() function, insert the following While loop:

```
while (dayCount <= totalDays) {
    // write the table rows and cells
    // move to the next day
}
```

Figure 3-24 shows the new code in the writeCalDays() function.

Figure 3-24 **The While loop for adding the calendar days**

```
function writeCalDays(calendarDay) {
    // determine the starting day of the week
    var dayCount = 1;
    var totalDays = daysInMonth(calendarDay);
    calendarDay.setDate(1);              // set the date to the first day of the month
    var weekDay = calendarDay.getDay();  // the day of week of the first day

    // write blank cells preceding the starting day
    document.write("<tr>");
    for (var i=0; i < weekDay; i++) {
        document.write("<td></td>");
    }

    // write cells for each day of the month
    while (dayCount <= totalDays) {
        // write the table rows and cells
        // move to the next day
    }
}
```

2. Save your changes to the file.

Each new table row in the calendar table starts with a Sunday; thus, the first command in the While loop's command block needs to determine whether the value of the week-Day variable corresponds to a Sunday. If so, the function will write the opening <tr> tag for the table row. The If statement appears as follows:

```
if (weekDay == 0) document.write("<tr>");
```

This expression uses the same weekDay variable you used previously to determine the day on which the month started. As you proceed through the While loop, the value of this variable is constantly updated to reflect the current calendar date being written. The next step is to write a table cell containing the date. Because every date belongs to the class calendar_dates (see Figure 3-4), the code is

```
document.write("<td class='calendar_dates'>"+dayCount+"</td>");
```

Because every table row ends with a Saturday, you also must test whether the day being written falls on a Saturday. If this is the case, you need to write a </tr> to end the table row. The command to do this is

```
if (weekDay == 6) document.write("</tr>");
```

In the final part of the command block for the While loop, you update the values of the dayCount, calendarDay, and weekDay variables so that the next time through the loop they point to the next day in the calendar. The commands are similar to what you used to set the initial values of these variables before the While loop, except that you increase the dayCount variable by 1 using the ++ increment operator:

```
dayCount++;
calendarDay.setDate(dayCount);
weekDay = calendarDay.getDay();
```

The complete code for the While loop is

```
while (dayCount <= totalDays) {
   // write the table rows and cells
   if (weekDay == 0) document.write("<tr>");
   document.write("<td class='calendar_dates'>"+dayCount+"</td>");
   if (weekDay == 6) document.write("</tr>");

   // move to the next day
   dayCount++;
   calendarDay.setDate(dayCount);
   weekDay = calendarDay.getDay();
}
```

After the While loop is finished running, you'll write a closing </tr> tag to ensure that the table row is closed off if the last day of the month does not fall on a Saturday. You do not need to write blank table cells at the end of the month like you did at the beginning, because browsers will simply ignore any missing table cells at the end of a table row.

To insert the While loop:

▶ 1. Below the first comment line within the While loop, insert the commands

```
if (weekDay == 0) document.write("<tr>");
document.write("<td class='calendar_dates'>"+dayCount+"</td>");
if (weekDay == 6) document.write("</tr>");
```

▶ 2. Below the second comment line within the While loop, insert the commands

```
dayCount++;
calendarDay.setDate(dayCount);
weekDay = calendarDay.getDay();
```

▶ 3. Below the While loop insert the command:

```
document.write("</tr>");
```

Figure 3-25 shows the revised code for the writeCalDays() function.

Adding commands to the While loop　　Figure 3-25

```
// write cells for each day of the month
while (dayCount <= totalDays) {
   // write the table rows and cells
   if (weekDay == 0) document.write("<tr>");
   document.write("<td class='calendar_dates'>"+dayCount+"</td>");
   if (weekDay == 6) document.write("</tr>");

   // move to the next day
   dayCount++;
   calendarDay.setDate(dayCount);
   weekDay = calendarDay.getDay();
}

document.write("</tr>");
}
```

Next, you have to run the writeCalDays() function from the calendar() function. You can then test the monthly calendar to verify that it correctly lays out the dates in the calendar.

To test the calendar() function:

1. Scroll up to the calendar() function and insert the following command, as shown in Figure 3-26:

```
writeCalDays(calDate);
```

Figure 3-26	Calling the writeCalDays() function

```
function calendar() {
    var calDate = new Date("May 18, 2007");

    document.write("<table id='calendar_table'>");
    writeCalTitle(calDate);
    writeDayNames()
    writeCalDays(calDate);
    document.write("</table>");
}
```

2. Save your changes to the file.

3. Reload **ccc.htm** in your Web browser. As shown in Figure 3-27, the monthly calendar should now show all of the dates laid out in different table cells and rows.

Figure 3-27	The monthly calendar table

the Chamberlain Civic Center

	May 2007					
Sun	Mon	Tue	Wed	Thu	Fri	Sat
		1	2	3	4	5
6	7	8	9	10	11	12
13	14	15	16	17	18	19
20	21	22	23	24	25	26
27	28	29	30	31		

Home   Tickets   Events   Tour   Directions   Hours   Packages   Contact Us

Highlighting the Current Date

You show the current form of the calendar to Maria. She likes the calendar's appearance but reminds you that the calendar should also highlight the current date. To indicate the current date, the corresponding table cell should have the id "calendar_today". As shown earlier in Figure 3-4, a different style is applied to the table cell with this id. As you loop through each day in the calendar, you need to insert an If statement that tests whether the day being written to the table represents the current date. If it does, you write the HTML code

```
<td class='calendar_dates' id='calendar_today'> day </td>
```

where *day* is the day number; otherwise, the script should write

```
<td class='calendar_dates' > day </td>
```

omitting the id attribute. To do this test, you'll create a new variable named currentDate, setting it equal to the date value returned by applying the getDate() date object method to the calendarDay parameter. You need to create this variable before the While loop because the While loop alters the value of the calendarDay parameter as it moves through the calendar rows and cells.

To highlight the current date:

1. Return to the **calendar.js** file in your text editor and scroll down to the writeCalDays() function.

2. Insert the following line of code as the first command in the function:

```
var currentDay = calendarDay.getDate();
```

3. In the While loop, replace the command that writes the table cell for each day with the following If structure:

```
if (dayCount == currentDay) {
   // highlight the current day
   document.write("<td class='calendar_dates' id='calendar_
   today'>"+dayCount+"</td>");
} else {
   // display the day as usual
   document.write("<td class='calendar_dates'>"+dayCount+"</td>");
}
```

Figure 3-28 shows the final version of the writeCalDays() function:

Highlighting the current day | Figure 3-28

```
function writeCalDays(calendarDay) {
   var currentDay = calendarDay.getDate();

   // determine the starting day of the week
   var dayCount = 1;
   var totalDays = daysInMonth(calendarDay);
   calendarDay.setDate(1);           // set the date to the first day of the month
   var weekDay = calendarDay.getDay();  // the day of week of the first day

   // write blank cells preceding the starting day
   document.write("<tr>");
   for (var i=0; i < weekDay; i++) {
      document.write("<td></td>");
   }

   // write cells for each day of the month
   while (dayCount <= totalDays) {
      // write the table rows and cells
      if (weekDay == 0) document.write("<tr>");

      if (dayCount == currentDay) {
         // highlight the current day
         document.write("<td class='calendar_dates' id='calendar_today'>"+dayCount+"</td>");
      } else {
         // display the day as usual
         document.write("<td class='calendar_dates'>"+dayCount+"</td>");
      }

      if (weekDay == 6) document.write("</tr>");

      // move to the next day
      dayCount++;
      calendarDay.setDate(dayCount);
      weekDay = calendarDay.getDay();
   }

   document.write("</tr>");
}
```

4. Save your changes to the file and then reload **ccc.htm** in your Web browser.

As shown in Figure 3-29, May 18 should now be highlighted in the calendar as this is the date specified in the calendar() function.

Figure 3-29 | **The completed home page for the CCC**

Setting the Calendar Date

Maria is pleased with the calendar application, but asks how you would use it to display dates other than May 18, 2007. You respond that you would have to change the value of the calDate variable in the calendar() function. Maria thinks that the date value should be included as a parameter value in the calendar() function, allowing the calendar() function to be easily used for any date. You agree that this would be an improvement and set to work on making the change.

It would be ideal if the calendar() function worked like the JavaScript new Date() command, creating a monthly calendar for a specified date with the command

```
calendar("May 18, 2007")
```

but producing the calendar for the current month if no date is specified, for example

```
calendar()
```

To test for the presence or absence of a parameter value, you simply insert an If condition that tests whether the parameter value is null or not. If it is null, the value of the calDate variable is set to the current date; otherwise, the calDate variable is set to the date specified in the calendarDay parameter. The revised calendar() function would appear as follows:

```
function calendar(calendarDay) {
   if (calendarDay == null) calDate=new Date()
   else calDate = new Date(calendarDay);
...
```

Edit the calendar() function to add this feature and then retest the calendar() function using both the current date and a date that you specify.

To complete and test the calendar() function:

1. Return to the **calendar.js** file in your text editor.

2. Go to the calendar() function and add the parameter **calendarDay** to the function line.

3. Replace the first line of the calendar() function with the following If statement:

```
if (calendarDay == null) calDate=new Date()
else calDate = new Date(calendarDay);
```

Figure 3-30 highlights the revised code of the calendar() function.

The final calendar() function ◄ Figure 3-30

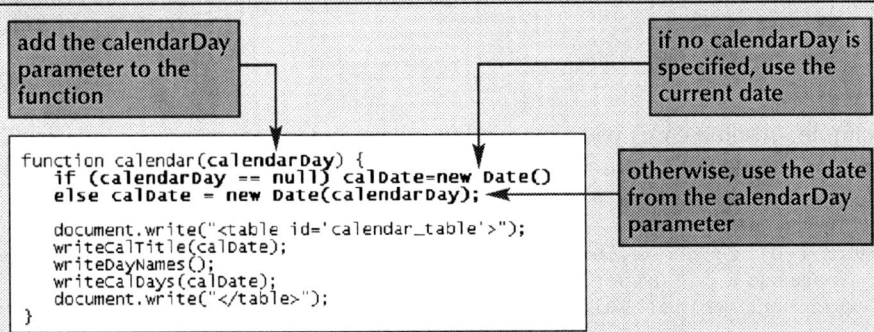

add the calendarDay parameter to the function

if no calendarDay is specified, use the current date

otherwise, use the date from the calendarDay parameter

```
function calendar(calendarDay) {
    if (calendarDay == null) calDate=new Date()
    else calDate = new Date(calendarDay);

    document.write("<table id='calendar_table'>");
    writeCalTitle(calDate);
    writeDayNames();
    writeCalDays(calDate);
    document.write("</table>");
}
```

4. Close the **calendar.js** file, saving your changes.

5. Reopen the **ccc.htm** file in your Web browser. Verify that it shows the monthly calendar for the current date (whatever that may be).

6. Return to the **ccc.htm** file in your text editor and change the statement that runs the monthly calendar to **calendar("May 25, 2007");** (see Figure 3-31).

Displaying the monthly calendar for May 25, 2007 ◄ Figure 3-31

```
<body>
<div id="head">
    <script type="text/javascript">
        calendar("May 25, 2007");
    </script>
    <img src="logo.gif" alt="Chamberlain Civic Center" />
</div>
```

7. Close the **ccc.htm** file, saving your changes. Reopen the file in your Web browser and verify that it now displays the monthly calendar for May 25, 2007. Close your Web browser.

Maria is happy with the final version of the calendar() function. Because of how the function and style sheets were designed, she can use this utility in many of the other pages on the CCC Web site with only a minimal amount of recoding in the Web documents. Maria will contact you if she has more tasks for you in the future.

Managing Program Loops and Conditional Statements

While you are finished with the calendar() function, there are still some features of program loops and conditional statements that you should become familiar with for your future work with these important JavaScript structures. You'll examine three features in more detail: the break, continue, and label commands.

The break Command

You briefly saw how to use the break command in creating a Switch statement, but the break command can actually be used anywhere within your program code. The purpose of the break command is to terminate any program loop or conditional statement. When a browser runs a break command, it passes control to the statement immediately following it. The break statement is most often used to exit a program loop without waiting for the loop to end when the stopping condition is met. The syntax of the break command is simply

```
break;
```

For example, in some cases you may need to create a loop that examines an array for the presence or absence of a particular value such as a customer id number or name. The code for the loop might look as follows:

```
for (var i=0; i< names.length; i++) {
   if (names[i] = "Valdez") {
      document.write("Valdez is in the list");
   }
}
```

Although this loop indicates whether the names array contains the text string "Valdez", what would happen if the array had tens of thousands of entries? It would be wasteful to keep examining the array if "Valdez" was encountered within the first few array items. This is where the break command can be useful to avoid wasting processing time. The following For loop breaks off when it encounters the "Valdez" text string, thus keeping the browser from needlessly examining the rest of the array:

```
for (var i=0; i< names.length; i++) {
   if (names[i] = "Valdez") {
      document.write("Valdez is in the list");
      break;  // stop processing the For loop
   }
}
```

The continue Command

The continue command is similar to the break command except that, instead of stopping the program loop altogether, the continue command stops processing the commands in the current iteration of the loop and jumps to the next iteration. For example, you could create a For loop to add up the values from an array. The code for this For loop would be

```
var total = 0;
for (var i=0; i < data.length; i++) {
   total += data[i];
}
```

Each time through the loop, the value of the current entry in the data array is added to the totals variable. When the For loop is finished, the total variable is equal to the sum of the values in the data array. However, what would happen if this were a sparse array containing several empty entries? In that case, when a browser encountered a missing or null value, that value would be added to the total variable; this would result in the value of the total variable also being equal to missing or null. One way to fix this problem would be to use the continue statement, jumping out of the loop if a missing or null value were encountered. The revised code would look as follows:

```
var total = 0;
for (var i=0; i < data.length; i++) {
   if (data[i]==null) continue;  // continue with the next iteration
   total += data[i];
}
```

In this code, the value of the total variable is not updated if a null value is encountered. In those cases, the loop continues at the next step in the iteration.

Statement Labels

Labels are used to identify statements in your JavaScript code so that you can reference those statements elsewhere in a program. The syntax of the label is

```
label: statement
```

where `label` is the text of the label and `statement` is the statement identified by the label. You've already seen labels in use with the Switch statement, but they can also be used with other program loops and conditional statements to provide more control over how your statements are processed. Labels are often used with break and continue commands to direct a program to the statement that it should go to if it needs to break off or continue a program loop. The syntax to reference a label in such cases is simply:

```
break label;
```

or

```
continue label;
```

For example, the following nested For loop contains two labels: one for the outer loop, and the other for the inner loop. The program breaks to the outer loop when the variable i is equal to the variable j.

```
outer_loop:
for(i=1; i<4; i++) {
   document.write("<br />"+"outer "+i+": ");
   inner_loop:
   for(j=1; j<4; j++) {
      document.write("inner "+j+" ");
      if(j==x) break outer_loop;
   }
}
```

As the code is run, it writes the following text to the document:

```
<br />outer 1: inner 1
<br />outer 2: inner 1
<br />outer 2: inner 2
<br />outer 3: inner 1
<br />outer 3: inner 2
<br />outer 3: inner 3
```

Some programmers discourage the use of break, continue, and label statements because they create confusing code as a script jumps in and out of loops. Most of the tasks you perform with these statements can also be performed by carefully setting up the conditions for your program loops. For example, to create the same output from the above code without labels or the break command, you could define the counter variable used in the inner loop so that it is always less than or equal to the counter value of the outer loop. The following code demonstrates how this might be done:

```
for(i=1; i<4; i++) {
    document.write("<br />"+"outer "+i+": ");
    for(j=1; j<=i; j++) {
        document.write("inner "+j+" ");
    }
}
```

You've completed your work on conditional statements and program loops. In the case problems that follow, you'll have a chance to apply them to a variety of problems and exercises.

Tips for Arrays, Program Loops, and Conditional Statements

- Save space in your program code by declaring and populating each array in a single new Array() declaration. If your target browsers support it, consider using an array literal to further simplify your code.
- Use array methods like sort() and reverse() to quickly rearrange the contents of your arrays.
- Use a For loop when your loop contains a counter variable. Use a While loop for a more general stopping condition.
- To simplify your code, avoid nesting too many levels of If statements when possible.
- Use the Switch statement for conditional statements that involve variables with several different possible values.
- Avoid using break and continue statements to cut off loops unless necessary. Instead, set break conditions in the conditional expression for a loop.

Review

Session 3.3 Quick Check

1. What command would you use to extract the day of the week value from a date object variable named thisDate?
2. What day of the week value is returned for a date occurring on a Friday?
3. What command would you run to change the thisDate variable to the fifth day of the month?
4. A function named showDate() has an optional parameter named thisDate. What expression would you enter to test whether the showDate() function was called with a value set for the thisDate parameter?
5. What command would you enter to break out of a program loop?
6. What command would you enter to force the script to go to the next iteration of the current program loop?

Review

Tutorial Summary

In this tutorial you learned how work with arrays, program loops, and conditional statements to create an application that produces a monthly calendar for any given date. In the first session, you were introduced to arrays. You learned how to create and populate arrays, and you also learned some of the JavaScript methods available to sort and modify arrays. The second session dealt with program loops and conditional statements. You learned how to repeat sections of code multiple times in either For or While loops. Using the If statement, you saw how to run commands only when certain conditions are met. In the third session, you applied what you learned about program loops and conditional statements to complete the calendar application. The third session concluded with a discussion of the break, continue, and label commands.

Key Terms

array	conditional statement	program loop
array literal	counter variable	sparse array
command block	index	subarray
compare function	modulus operator	

Practice

Practice the skills you learned in the tutorial using the same case scenario.

Review Assignments

Data files needed for this Review Assignment: back.jpg, caltxt.htm, ccc.jpg, logo.gif, styles.css, yearly.css, yeartxt.js

Maria has had some time to work with the calendar() function you created for her. She finds it an incredibly useful feature for the CCC Web site. However, she would like you to create a new calendar application that displays monthly calendars for the entire year on a single page. The calendar would still highlight the current date (or a date specified by the user) within the table. Figure 3-32 shows a preview of the yearly calendar that you'll create for Maria.

Figure 3-32

Maria has already created the Web page layout and a style sheet for both the Web page and the yearly calendar. Your job is to create the functions that generate the yearly calendar.

To complete this assignment:

1. Using your text editor, open **caltxt.htm** from the tutorial.03/review folder. Enter *your name* and *the date* in the head section and save the file as **calendar.htm**. Use your text editor to open **yeartxt.js**, enter *your name* and *the date* in the comment section, and save the file as **yearly.js**.

2. Go to the **yearly.js** file in your text editor. Many of the functions to create the individual monthly calendars have already been created for you. To combine all of the monthly calendars into a single calendar, you create a larger 3 x 4 table in which each table cell contains a monthly calendar.

3. Insert a function named writeMonthCell(). The purpose of this function is to place a monthly calendar within a larger table cell. The function has two parameters: calendarDay and currentTime. The calendarDay parameter contains a date object for the first day of the month to be displayed in the monthly calendar. The currentTime parameter contains the time value of the date that should be highlighted in the yearly table. Add the following commands to the writeMonthCell() function:

   a. Write the following HTML code to the document:
   ```
   <td class='yearly_months'>
   ```
   b. Call the writeMonth() function using calendarDay and currentTime as the parameter values. The purpose of the writeMonth() function is to write a monthly calendar into the table cell.
   c. Write a closing </td> tag to the document.

4. Insert a function named yearly(). The purpose of this function is to write the entire yearly calendar containing all of the separate monthly calendars as cells within the larger table. The function has a single parameter named calDate. Add the following commands:

   a. If calDate equals null, set the calendarDay variable equal to a date object pointing to the current date and time; otherwise, calendarDay equals a date object using the text string in the calDate parameter.
   b. Create a variable named currentTime equal to the time value of the calendarDay variable. (*Hint*: Use the getTime() date object method to extract the time value from calendarDay.)
   c. Create a variable named thisYear equal to the four-digit year value from the calendarDay variable.
   d. Write the following HTML code to the document:
   ```
   <table id='yearly_table'>
   <tr>
      <th id='yearly_title' colspan='4'>
         thisYear
      </th>
   </tr>
   ```
   where *thisYear* is the value of the thisYear variable.
   e. Create a variable named monthNum, setting its initial value equal to -1. The purpose of the monthNum variable is to keep track of the month value of the current month being written in the calendar.
   f. Create a For loop that writes the rows of the yearly table. Create a counter variable named i that goes from 1 to 3 in increments of 1. The first command within the For loop should write the opening <tr> tag to the document.
   g. Within the For loop you just created, add a nested For loop that writes the individual cells of the yearly table. The counter variable, j, of the nested For loop should go from 1 to 4 in steps of 1. In this nested For loop, add the following commands: (1) increase the value of monthNum by one; (2) use the setDate() date object method to change the day value of calendarDay to 1 (the first day of the month); (3) use the setMonth() date object method to change the month value of calendarDay to monthNum; and (4) call the writeMonthCell() function using calendarDay and currentTime as the parameter values.
   h. After the nested For loop, but still within the outer loop, write a closing </tr> tag to the document.
   i. After the nested loops, write a closing </table> tag to the document.

5. Locate the writeDayNames() function in the document. Within this function, change the values of the dayName array from three letter abbreviations of the day names to the one-letter abbreviations S, M, T, W, R, F, and S.

6. Close yearly.js, saving your changes.

7. Go the **calendar.htm** file in your text editor. In the head section of the document, add links to both the yearly.css style sheet and the yearly.js external script file.

8. Scroll down the document and locate the div element with the id "main". After the h1 heading in this element, insert an embedded script element. Within the script, run the command yearly() using the date "June 7, 2007" as the parameter value.

9. Save your changes to the file.

10. Open **calendar.htm** in your Web browser. Verify that the yearly calendar shown in Figure 3-32 is displayed on the Web page.

11. Return to **calendar.htm** in your text editor. Change the yearly() function so that no parameter value is specified (so that the function uses the current date, whatever that may be). Save your changes and reload **calendar.htm** in your Web browser. Verify that the calendar for the current year is displayed and that the current date is the only one highlighted in the calendar.

12. Close any open files and then submit your completed Web site to your instructor.

Apply

Use the skills you learned in this tutorial to create a list of contributors

Case Problem 1

Data files needed for this Case Problem: clisttxt.htm, lhouse.css, list.js, logo.jpg

The Lighthouse   The Lighthouse is a charitable organization located in central Kentucky that matches donors with needy groups. The fundraising coordinator for The Lighthouse is Aaron Kitchen. On a Web page available only to Lighthouse staff, Aaron wants to display a list of recent donations including the name and address of the donor, the amount donated, and the date of the donation. A list of donations from the last month has been downloaded from an external database and stored in a collection of arrays named firstName, lastName, street, city, state, zip, amount, and date. Aaron needs your help in displaying the data from those arrays in a Web table. He also wants a summary table that displays the total number of contributors and the total contribution amount. Figure 3-33 shows a preview of the Web page you'll create.

Figure 3-33

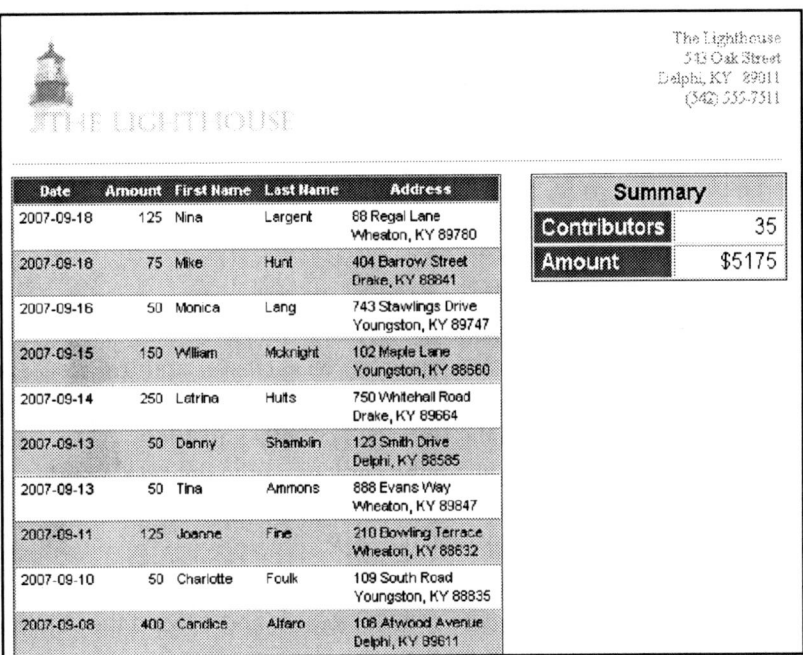

To complete this assignment:

1. Using your text editor, open **clisttxt.htm** from the tutorial.03/case1 folder. Enter *your name* and *the date* in the head section and save the file as **clist.htm**.

2. The firstName, lastName, street, city, state, zip, amount, and date arrays have already been created and populated for you in the list.js file. In the head section of the document, insert a script element that points to this file.

3. Below the script element you just created, insert another script element that contains the function amountTotal(). The purpose of the amountTotal() function is to return the sum of all of the values in the amount array. There are no parameters for this function. Add the following commands to the function:

    a. Declare a variable named total, setting its initial value to 0.

    b. Create a For loop that loops through all of the values in the amount array. At each iteration of the loop, add the current value of the array item to the value of the total variable.

    c. After the For loop is completed, return the value of the total variable.

4. Scroll down the document and locate the div element with the id "data_list". Within the div element, add a script element that contains the following commands:

    a. Write the following code to the document:
    ```
    <table border='1' rules='rows' cellspacing='0'>
       <tr>
          <th>Date</th><th>Amount</th><th>First Name</th>
          <th>Last Name</th><th>Address</th>
       </tr>
    ```

    b. Create a For loop in which the counter variable starts at 0 and, while the counter is less than the length of the amount array, increase the counter in increments of 1.

c. Aaron wants every other row in the data list to be displayed with a yellow background; to do this, within the For loop insert an If condition that tests whether the counter variable is divisible evenly by 2 (*Hint*: Use the % modulus operator). If the counter variable is divisible by 2, write the following HTML tag:

```
<tr>
```

Otherwise write the tag

```
<tr class='yellowrow'>
```

d. Next, within the For loop, write the following HTML code to the document:

```
<td>date</td>
<td class='amt'>amount</td>
<td>firstName</td>
<td>lastName</td>
```

where `date`, `amount`, `firstName`, and `lastName` are the values of the date, amount, firstName, and lastName arrays for the index indicated by the current value of the For loop's counter variable.

e. Finally, within the For loop, write the HTML code

```
<td>street<br />
    city, state zip
</td>
</tr>
```

where `street`, `city`, `state`, and `zip` are the values of the street, city, state, and zip arrays for the current index value.

5. Go to the div element with the id "totals". Insert a script element that writes the following HTML code to the document:

```
<table border='1' cellspacing='1'>
    <tr>
        <th id='sumTitle' colspan='2'>
            Summary
        </th>
    </tr>
    <tr>
        <th>Contributors</th>
        <td>contributions</td>
    </tr>
    <tr>
        <th>Amount</th>
        <td>$total</td>
    </tr>
</table>
```

where `contributions` is the length of the amount array and `total` is the value returned by the amountTotal() function you created earlier.

6. Close the file, saving your changes:

7. Open **clist.htm** in your Web browser and verify that a list of 35 contributions totaling $5175 is displayed on the table, and that alternate rows of the contributor list are displayed with a yellow background.

8. Submit the completed Web site to your instructor.

Apply

Use the skills you earned in this tutorial to create a horizontal bar chart

Case Problem 2

Data files needed for this Case Problem: back.jpg, electtxt.htm, logo.jpg, results.css, votes.js

ElectionWeb ElectionWeb is an online source for election news and results from national, state, and local races. Faye Summerall is one of the managers of the Web site development team. Faye would like to add horizontal bar charts to the Web pages displaying election results. The length of each bar should correspond to the percentage of votes that the corresponding candidate receives in a given race. She has asked your help in developing a JavaScript program to automatically write the bar chart. Figure 3-34 shows a preview of the Web page for a series of Congressional races.

Figure 3-34

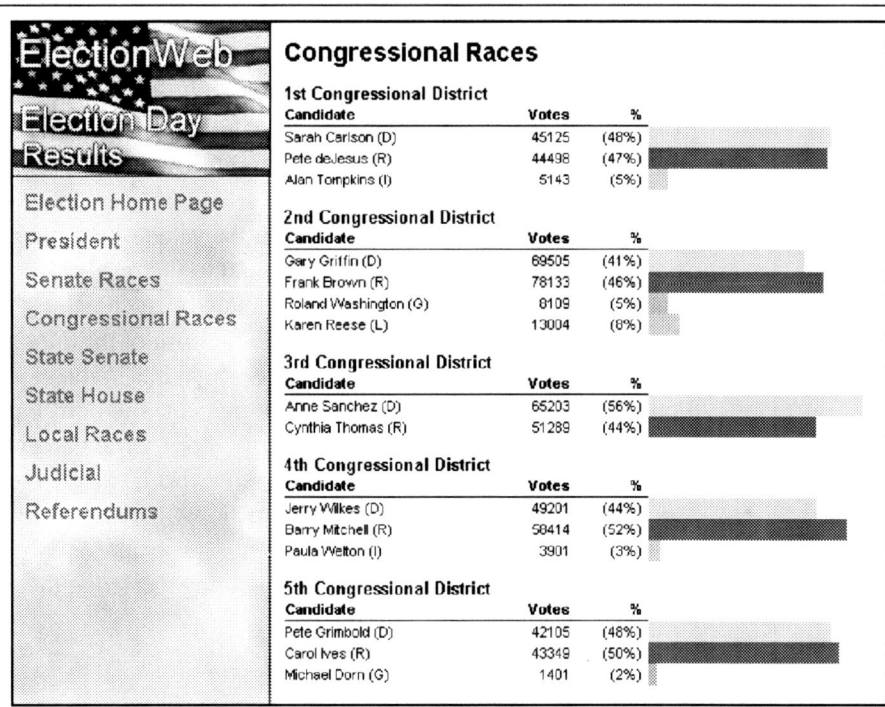

The horizontal bar charts will be created within table rows. The length of each bar will be determined by the number of blank table cells it contains. For example, to display a horizontal bar representing 45% of the vote, you'll write 45 blank table cells. The color of each bar is determined by the background color of its table cells. To apply the background color, you'll add class attributes to the blank table cells. A style in the results.css style sheet determines the background color for each class of table cells.

The data for each election has been stored in arrays in an external file named votes.js. The file includes data from five elections for different Congressional seats. The names of the races have been stored in an array named race. The name1 array contains the candidate names for the first race, the name2 array contains the candidate names for the second race, and so on through the name5 array. The party affiliations for each candidate in the first race have been stored in the party1 array, for the second race in the party2 array, and so forth. The votes1 through votes5 arrays store the votes for each candidate in each of the five races.

To complete this assignment:

1. Using your text editor, open **electtxt.htm** from the tutorial.03/case2 folder. Enter *your name* and *the date* in the head section and save the file as **election.htm**.

2. Take some time to study the contents of the **votes.js** file in your text editor to become familiar with the different arrays and their contents; then return to the **election.htm** file in your text editor and add a script element to the head section of the file that points to the **votes.js** file.

3. Insert another script element in the head section. In this script element, insert a function named totalVotes(). The purpose of this function is to calculate the sum of all the values within an array. The function has a single parameter, votes, which represents one of the five vote arrays (vote1 through vote5). Add the following commands to the function:

   a. Declare a variable named total, setting its initial value to 0.

   b. Create a For loop that loops through each of the items in the votes array, adding that item's value to the total variable.

   c. After the For loop is completed, return the value of the total variable.

4. Insert another function named calcPercent(). The purpose of this function is to calculate a percentage, rounded to the nearest integer. The function has two parameters: item and sum. Have the function return the value of the item variable divided by sum, multiplied by 100, and then rounded to the nearest integer. (*Hint*: Use the Math.round() method to round the calculated percentage.)

5. Insert a function named createBar(). The purpose of this function is to write the blank table cells that make up each horizontal bar in the election results. The function has two parameters: partyType and percent. The partyType parameter stores the party affiliation of the candidate (D, R, I, G, or L). The percent parameter stores the percentage the candidate received in the election, rounded to the nearest integer. Add the following commands to the function:

Explore

   a. Create a Switch statement that tests the value of the partyType parameter. If partyType equals "D", store the following text string in a variable named barText:
   ```
   <td class='dem'> </td>
   ```
   If partyType equals "R", barText should equal
   ```
   <td class='rep'> </td>
   ```
   If partyType equals "I", barText should equal
   ```
   <td class='ind'> </td>
   ```
   If partyType equals "G", barText should equal
   ```
   <td class='green'> </td>
   ```
   Finally, if partyType equals "L", barText should equal
   ```
   <td class='lib'> </td>
   ```
   Make sure that you add break commands after each case statement so that the browser does not attempt to perform additional cases after it has found a match.

   b. Create a For loop in which the counter variable goes from 1 up through the value of the percent parameter in increments of 1. At each iteration, write the value of the barText variable to the Web document.

6. Insert a function named showResults(). The purpose of this function is to show the results of a particular race. The function has four parameters: race, name, party, and votes. The race parameter contains the name of the race. The name parameter contains the array of candidate names. The party parameter contains the array of party affiliations. Finally, the votes parameter contains the array of votes for each candidate in the race. Add the following commands to the function:
   a. Declare a variable named totalV equal to the value returned by the totalVotes() function using votes as the parameter value.
   b. Write the following HTML code to the document:

```
<h2>race</h2>
<table cellspacing='0'>
   <tr>
      <th>Candidate</th>
      <th class='num'>Votes</th>
      <th class='num'>%</th>
   </tr>
```
   where race is the value of the race parameter.
   c. Create a For loop in which the counter variable starts at 0 and, while the counter is less than the length of the name array, increase the counter in increments of 1. At each iteration of the For loop, run the commands outlined in the following five steps.
   d. Write the following HTML code:

```
<tr>
   <td>name (party)</td>
   <td class='num'>votes</td>
```
   where name, party, and votes are the entries in the name, party, and votes arrays for the index indicated by the counter variable.
   e. Create a variable named percent equal to the value returned by the calcPercent() function. Use the current value from the votes array for the value of the item parameter, and totalV for the value of the sum parameter.
   f. Write the following HTML code:

```
<td class='num'>(percent%)</td>
```
   where percent is the value of the percent variable.
   g. Call the createBar() function using the current value of the party array and percent as the parameter values.
   h. Write a closing </tr> tag to the document.
   i. After the For loop has completed, write a closing </table> tag to the document.
7. Scroll down the document. After the h1 heading, "Congressional Races", insert a script element containing the following commands:
   a. Call the showResults() function using race[0], name1, party1, and votes1 as the parameter values.
   b. Repeat the previous command for the remaining four races, using race[1] through race[4] as the parameter value for the race parameter, party2 through party5 for the party parameter, name2 through name5 for the name parameter, and votes2 through votes5 for the votes parameter.
8. Save your changes to the file and open **election.htm** in your Web browser. Verify that the correct percentages for each candidate are shown and that a horizontal bar chart representing that percent value is displayed next to each candidate.
9. Submit the completed Web site to your instructor.

Challenge

Explore how to use JavaScript to create an auction log

Case Problem 3

Data files needed for this Case Problem: aucttxt.htm, logo.jpg, styles.css

Schmitt AuctionHaus   David Schmitt owns Schmitt AuctionHaus, an auction center located in rural Indiana that specializes in estate and farm sales and auctions. Recently David has been looking at the ways to improve the bidding process for silent auctions in which applicants enter their name and bid for various items. David would like to create a Web page containing bidding information on various items at the auction center. The bidding could be displayed on a kiosk or terminal in the auction center, giving customers a quick look at the current status of different items for sale. David has asked for your help in designing a Web form to track bids for a sales item. The form should include the name of the item, the current highest bid, a list of the bidding history for the item, and a form in which new bids can be entered. Since mistakes are sometimes made in entering a bid, David wants the ability to remove the last bid from the list. Figure 3-35 shows a preview of a sample page you'll create for David.

Figure 3-35

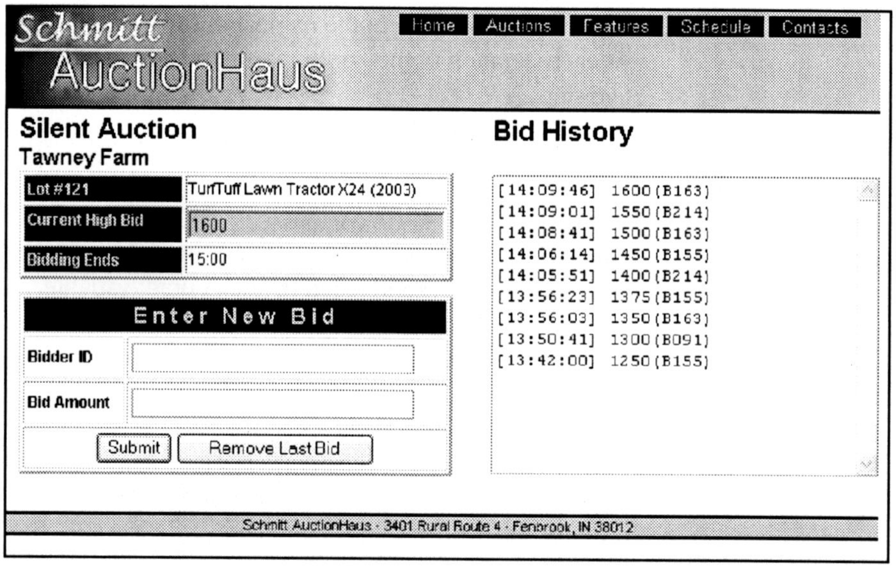

The layout and styles used in the page have already been created for you. Your job is to program the script that enters new bids and updates the box displaying the bid history and the highest current bid. You need to collect three pieces of information from each bid: the bid amount, the bidder id, and the time when the bid was placed. You'll record this information in three arrays named bids, bidders, and bidTime, respectively.

(*Note:* Older browsers do not support the array methods used in this Case Problem. In particular, Internet Explorer for the Macintosh does not support the required array methods. To complete the case problem you will have to use an up-to-date version of your browser.)

To complete this assignment:

1. Using your text editor, open **aucttxt.htm** from the tutorial.03/case3 folder. Enter *your name* and *the date* in the head section and save the file as **auction.htm**.
2. In the head section of the file, insert an embedded script element. Within the script element, create three new arrays named bids, bidders, and bidTime. Do not populate these arrays with any values.

3. Insert a function named writeBid(). The purpose of this function is to write the bidding history and highest current bid to the Web page. There are no parameters for this function. Add the following commands to the function:

   a. Declare a variable named historyText, setting its initial value to an empty text string. This variable will be used to record the bidding history.

   Explore

   b. Insert a For loop in which the counter variable goes from 0 through the length of the bids array in increments of 1. Each time through the loop, append the following text string to the historyText variable:

   `bidTime bids (bidders) \n`

   where `bidTime`, `bids`, and `bidders` are the current items in the bidTime, bids, and bidders array based on the value of the counter variable. Note that \n is an escape character indicating a new line, and causes the next entry to the historyText variable to be placed on a new line.

   Explore

   c. After the For loop finishes, write the value of the historyText variable to the text area box with the name bidList. (*Hint*: To write text into a form field, use the expression document.*form.field*.value = *text*, where *form* is the name of the form, *field* is the name of the form field, and *text* is the text string to be written to the field. In this example, the name of the form is bidForm and the name of the field is bidList.)

   d. Write the value of the first item in the bids array to the highBid field.

   e. Set the values of the bidId and bidAmount fields to empty text strings.

4. Create a function named addBid(). The purpose of this function is to add a bid to the start of the bids, bidders, and bidTime arrays. Add the following commands:

   Explore

   a. Using the unshift() array method, insert the current value of the bidId field to the start of the bidders array.

   b. Use the unshift() array method to insert the current value of the bidAmount field at the start of the bids array.

   c. Declare a variable named now containing a date object for the current date and time.

   d. Extract the hours, minutes, and seconds values from the now variable, storing these values in variables named hours, minutes, and seconds.

   e. Use a conditional operator to insert leading zeroes in the minutes and seconds values if they are less than 10. (*Hint*: See Tutorial 2 for an example of inserting leading zeroes in minutes and seconds values.)

   f. Create a variable named timeText equal to the text

   `[hours:minutes:seconds]`

   where *hours*, *minutes*, and *seconds* are the values of the hours, minutes, and seconds variables.

   g. Using the unshift() array method, insert the value of the timeText variable at the start of the bidTime array.

   h. Call the writeBid() function.

5. Create a function named removeBid(). The purpose of this function is to remove the first entry from the bids, bidders, and bidTime arrays. Add the following commands:

   Explore

   a. Using the shift() array method, remove the first entry from the bids array.

   b. Repeat the previous step to remove the first entry from the bidders and bidTime arrays.

   c. Call the writeBid() function.

6. Scroll down the document to the Submit input button. Add an event handler attribute to run the addBid() function when the button is clicked.

7. Add an event handler attribute to the Remove Last Bid button to run the removeBid() function when the button is clicked.

8. Save your changes to the file.

9. Open the **auction.htm** file in your Web browser. Enter new bids in the Bidder Id and Bid Amount input fields. Click the Submit button to update the bidding history and Current High Bid field. Verify that the newest bid entries are placed at the top of the bidding history. Click the Remove Last Bid button and verify that the latest bid is removed from the list.

10. Submit the completed Web site to your instructor.

Assess

Test your knowledge of arrays, loops, and conditional statements by creating a lunar calendar

Case Problem 4

Data files needed for this Case Problem: astro.css, caltxt.css, lunartxt.htm, lunartxt.js, moonfunc.js, phase0.jpg through phase15.jpg, skyweb.jpg

SkyWeb Dr. Andrew Weiss of the SkyWeb astronomy Web site is working on a Web page describing the phases and properties of the moon. He has contacted you for help in completing the page. Dr. Weiss would like the page to contain a table describing the current conditions of the Moon, including the Moon phase, age (days since the last new moon), distance from the Earth, and position in the nighttime sky. He would also like the page to contain a lunar calendar for the current month. A lunar calendar is a calendar that displays the phases of the Moon on each day of the month. A preview of the page that Dr. Weiss would like you to create is shown in Figure 3-36.

Figure 3-36

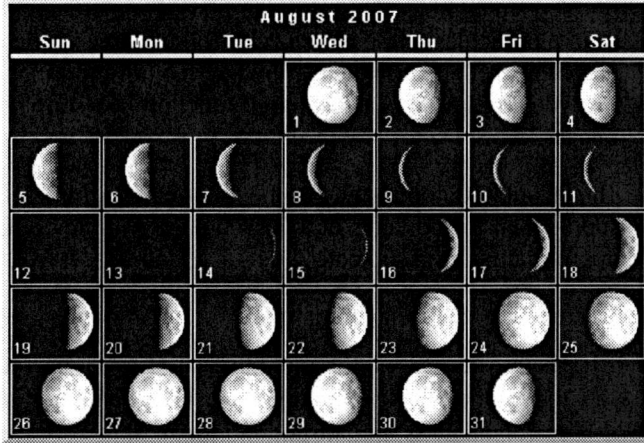

Dr. Weiss has already designed the basic layout for the page. He needs you to write scripts to generate the lunar calendar as well as to insert data on the current lunar conditions in a summary table located at the top of the page. To aid you in creating this page, Dr. Weiss has supplied a file named moonfunc.js containing the functions described in Figure 3-37.

Figure 3-37

Function	Description
calcMPhase(cDay)	Returns the phase number (from 0 to 15) of the moon for the date stored in cDay
calcMAge(cDay)	Returns the age of the moon for the date stored in cDay
calcMDist(cDay)	Returns the distance in earth radii between the earth and the moon on the date stored in cDay
calcMDec(cDay)	Returns the declination (latitude on the nighttime sky) of the moon on the date stored in cDay
calcMRA(cDay)	Returns the right ascension (longitude on the nighttime sky) of the moon on the date stored in cDay
calcMZodiac(cDay)	Returns the name of the constellation or sign of the zodiac in which the moon resides on the date stored in cDay

Each function has a date object parameter named cDay that you can use to return information on the Moon's status for that day. Dr. Weiss has also supplied a collection of 16 images named phase0.jpg through phase15.jpg. Each file contains an image of the Moon from a particular phase in its cycle. The file phase0.jpg contains an image of the new moon, phase8.jpg contains an image of a full moon, and so forth. Dr. Weiss points out that you can use the calcMPhase() function he's supplied to determine which of the 16 images to display for any given day.

The layout and appearance of the lunar calendar are left up to you. You are also free to supplement the contents of this Web page with any other material you think would be appropriate for the subject.

To complete this assignment

1. Using your text editor, open the **caltxt.css**, **lunartxt.htm**, and **lunartxt.js** files from the tutorial.03/case4 folder. Enter *your name* and *the date* in each file. Save the files as **calendar.css**, **lunar.htm**, and **lunarcal.js** respectively. The **calendar.css** file will be used to store the style sheet for the lunar calendar you'll create. The **lunar.htm** file contains the Web page that Dr. Weiss wants to display on the SkyWeb Web site. The **lunarcal.js** file will contain the functions required to create the lunar calendar.

2. Go to the **lunar.htm** file in your text editor. In the head section, add links to the **calendar.css** style sheet, the **moonfunc.js** JavaScript file, and the **lunarcal.js** JavaScript file.

3. Insert a script element in the head section containing the following:

   a. A variable named calendarDay containing a date object with the date set to August 8, 2007.

   b. A function named writeDate(). The purpose of this function is to display a date in the format *Month Day, Year*, where *Month* is the name of the month, *Day* is the day of the month, and *Year* is the four-digit year value. The function has a single parameter, calendarDay, which contains the date object to be formatted.

4. Scroll down to the summary table in the body of the document. Add the following to the table:

   a. In the table's title cell, display the text Today: *today*, where *today* is the date from the calendarDay variable formatted using the writeDay() function.

   b. In the lunarimg cell, display the lunar image for the date in calendarDay. (*Hint:* Use the calcMPhase() function to return the phase number of the image.)

    c. In the cell next to the Moon's Age label, display *age* days, where *age* is the age of the moon on calendarDay.

    d. In the cell next to the Right Ascension label, display *ra*°, where *ra* is the right ascension of the moon on calendarDay.

    e. In the cell next to the Declination label, display *dec*°, where *dec* is the declination of the moon on calendarDay.

    f. In the cell next to the In Constellation label, insert *zodiac*, where *zodiac* is the constellation that the moon resides in on calendarDay.

    g. In the cell next to the Distance label, insert *distance*, where *distance* is the distance from the Earth to the Moon in Earth radii on calendarDay.

5. Scroll down to the lunar_cal div element. Within this element, insert a script that calls the function lunar_calendar() for the date in calendarDay.

6. Save your changes to the **lunar.htm** file.

7. Go to the **lunarcal.js** file in your text editor. Create a function named lunar_ calendar() that displays a lunar calendar. The function should have a single parameter named calendarDay that contains the date you want to use for the calendar. You may use the calendar() function created in the tutorial as a model for your function and any supporting functions required to complete the calendar. The calendar does not have to highlight the current date.

8. Go to the **calendar.css** file in your text editor and create the styles required for your lunar calendar. You may use the calendar.css file from the tutorial as a model, but you may also create a layout of your choosing.

9. After completing your work in the **lunarcal.js** and **calendar.css** files, open **lunar.htm** in your Web browser. Verify that the lunar calendar and the Moon data follow the information shown in Figure 3-37.

10. Submit the completed Web site to your instructor.

Review

Quick Check Answers

Session 3.1

1. An array is a collection of data values organized under a single name with each value referenced by an index number.

2. var dayNames = new Array();

3. var dayNames = new Array("Sun", "Mon", "Tue", "Wed", "Thu", "Fri", "Sat");

4. dayNames[2]

5. var dayNames = ["Sun", "Mon", "Tue", "Wed", "Thu", "Fri", "Sat"];

6. dayNames.sort();

7. dayNames.slice(1,6);

8. dayNames.toString();

Session 3.2

1. A program loop is a set of commands that is executed repeatedly until a stopping condition has been met. Three program loops supported by JavaScript are the For, While, and Do/While loops.

2. for (var i=0; i<=100; i+=10)

3. ```
document.write("<tr>");
for (var i=1; i<=5; i++) {
  document.write("<td>Column "+i+"</td>");
}
document.write("</tr>");
```

4. A conditional statement is a statement that runs a command block only when certain conditions are met. The most commonly used conditional statement is the If statement.

5. ```
if (WebBrowser) document.write("Internet Explorer Browser");
```
   or
   ```
if (WebBrowser == true) document.write("Internet Explorer Browser");
```

6. ```
if (WebBrowser == "IE") document.write("Internet Explorer Browser")
else document.write("Netscape Browser");
```

7. ```
if (WebBrowser=="IE") document.write("Internet Explorer Browser")
else if (WebBrowser=="Netscape") document.write("Netscape Browser")
else if (WebBrowser=="Safari") document.write("Safari Browser")
else if (WebBrowser=="Firefox") document.write("Firefox Browser")
else document.write("Generic Browser");
```

8. ```
switch (WebBrowser) {
case "IE": document.write("Internet Explorer Browser"); break;
case "Netscape": document.write("Netscape Browser"); break;
case "Safari": document.write("Safari Browser"); break;
case "Firefox": document.write("Firefox Browser"); break;
default: document.write("Generic Browser");
}
```

## Session 3.3

1. thisDate.getDay();
2. 5
3. thisDate.setDate(5);
4. if (thisDate != null) ...
5. break;
6. continue;
```

Objectives

Session 4.1
- Define DHTML and describe its uses
- Understand objects, properties, methods, and the document object model
- Distinguish between different object models
- Work with object references and object collections
- Modify an object's properties
- Apply a method to an object
- Create a cross-browser Web site using object detection

Session 4.2
- Work with the style object to change the styles associated with an object
- Write functions to apply positioning styles to an object

Session 4.3
- Place a JavaScript command in a link
- Run timed-delay and timed-interval commands
- Work with the properties of the display window
- Describe the techniques of linear and path animation
- Create customized objects, properties, and methods

Working with Objects

Creating an Animated Web Page

Case

Avalon Books

Avalon Books is a popular bookstore chain, with several stores scattered throughout the western United States and Canada. In recent years, Avalon Books has begun to make its products available online. You've been hired as part of the Web site development team.

Your supervisor, Terry Schuler, wants you to create the opening screen for the company's Web site. The page should be visually interesting, with eye-catching motion and graphics. Some of this can be done with animated GIFs and Java applets, but Terry doesn't want too many of these kinds of elements because they take longer to load. If the browser doesn't promptly display the page, potential customers might be unlikely to wait, and will do their shopping elsewhere. Terry doesn't want the total size of the page and associated elements to be more than 40 KB.

You can add animation to a page without the overhead of extra applets or large graphics by using JavaScript to move, hide, and re-display the objects in the page. You decide to investigate how to use JavaScript to create these effects.

Student Data Files

▼tutorial.04

▽ tutorial folder	▽ review folder	▽ case1 folder
abtxt.htm	abtxt2.htm	golftxt.htm
scripttxt.js	indextxt.htm	golftxt.js
styles.css	script2txt.js	ballpath.txt
+ 1 demo file	styles2.css	styles.css
+ 4 graphic files	+ 5 graphic files	+ 3 graphic files

Student Data Files	▼tutorial.04 continued		
	▽ case2 folder	▽ case3 folder	▽ case4 folder
	ccctxt.htm	trailtxt.htm	bug.txt
	ccctxt.js	trail.js	bug.jpg
	styles.css	trail.css	bugdead.jpg
	+ 2 graphic files	path.txt	shoe.jpg
		+ 19 graphic files	

Session 4.1

Introduction to DHTML

Early in the development of HTML, Web page authors were limited to creating completely static Web pages—pages whose content and layout were fixed after being downloaded from their Web servers. As the Web became an increasingly important vehicle for sharing information, Web page authors and Web browser developers began to look for ways to create dynamic pages—pages whose content and style could be modified after being loaded, in response to events such as a reader's actions. Some early attempts involved the use of applets that the Web browser would retrieve and install along with the Web page.

The 4.0 and later versions of Netscape and Internet Explorer allowed for a new approach, in which the HTML code itself supported dynamic elements. Unlike applets, no additional software was needed to create and display dynamic Web pages—only browsers capable of working with JavaScript. These enhancements were known collectively as **dynamic HTML**, or **DHTML**. DHTML involves the interaction of three aspects of Web design:

- A page's HTML/XHTML code
- A style sheet that defines the styles used in the page
- A script, usually written in either JavaScript or VBScript, to control the behavior of elements on the page

DHTML is not a separate language. Instead, it can be thought of as a collection of programming techniques that use the scripting language to modify a Web page's contents or styles after the page is initially rendered by the browser. In this way, the Web page author can create documents that dynamically interact with users. Some uses for DHTML that you may have seen include:

- Animated text that moves and changes in response to user action
- Pop-up menus that provide users with quick access to other pages in a Web site without devoting valuable screen space to a long, complicated list of links
- Rollovers in which images and text change in response to mouse pointer movement
- Web pages that retrieve their content from external data sources, giving Web page authors more freedom in the types of materials they can display in their pages
- Elements that can be dragged from one location on the page and dropped at another

In the following tutorials, you'll examine how to create these effects and more. In the current tutorial, you'll study how to add animated effects to the Avalon Books Web site. Let's first look at the opening page of the Avalon Books Web site.

To open the Web page:

1. Use your text editor to open **abtxt.htm** from the tutorial.04/tutorial folder. Enter *your name* and *the date* in the comment section and save the file as **avalon.htm**.

2. Scroll through the contents of the file and familiarize yourself with the page's elements.

3. Open **avalon.htm** in your Web browser. Figure 4-1 shows the current appearance of the page.

The Avalon Books opening page | Figure 4-1

The page contains five different items placed in separate div elements. These items and their id values are:

- An image of Avalon Books' best-selling fiction book (id="fiction")
- An image of Avalon Books' best-selling nonfiction book (id="nfiction")
- An image of a person reading a book, which contains a link to the rest of Avalon Books' Web site (id="ab")
- The text string "Avalon" (id="avalon")
- The text string "Books" (id="books")

The position of each item on the page is set using absolute positioning with an external style sheet. Terry wants you to change this page from a static layout to a dynamic one by adding the following animated effects (see Figure 4-2):

- The word "Avalon" should appear near the top of the document window and then drop vertically down the page.
- After "Avalon" has dropped down the page, the word "Books" should appear from behind it moving from left to right.
- After the word "Books" has finished moving, the other three items should appear on the screen in sequence.

Figure 4-2 ▶ Terry's plan for animating the Avalon Books opening page

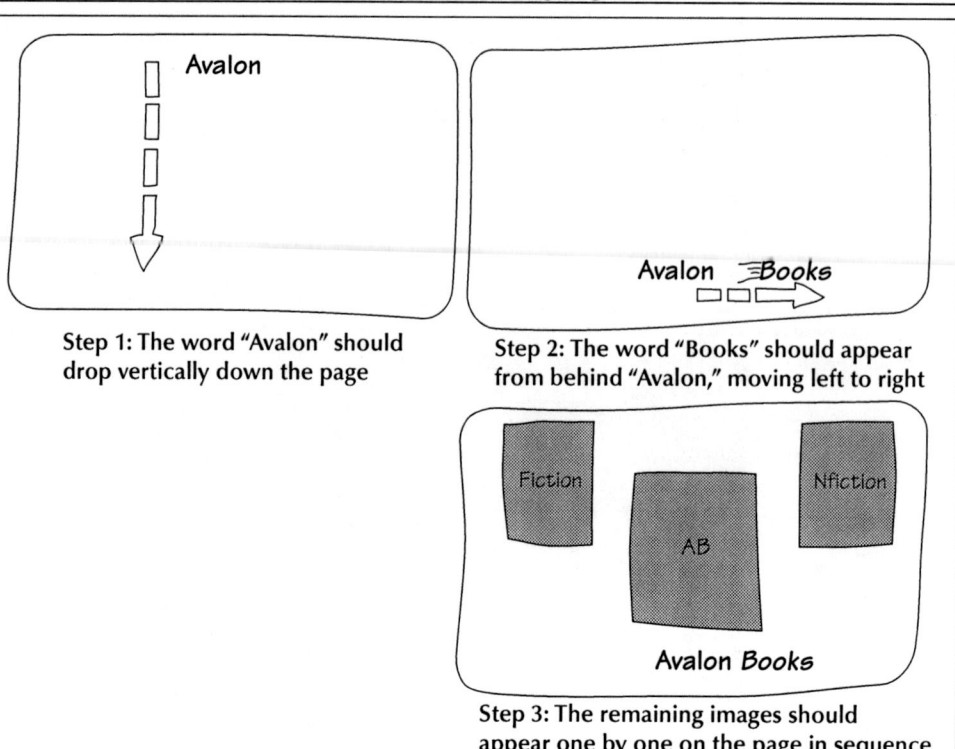

Step 1: The word "Avalon" should drop vertically down the page

Step 2: The word "Books" should appear from behind "Avalon," moving left to right

Step 3: The remaining images should appear one by one on the page in sequence

To create these effects, you first need to know how to use JavaScript to work with different page objects. We've been working with several different objects in the last three tutorials. Let's look at a more formal definition of what we mean by the term "object."

Understanding JavaScript Objects

JavaScript is an **object-based language**, which means that it is based on manipulating objects by modifying their properties or by applying methods to them. That definition might sound complex, but the concept is simple. An **object** is any item associated with a Web page or Web browser. Each object has **properties** that describe its appearance, purpose, or behavior. Each object also has **methods**, which are actions that can be performed with the object or to it.

JavaScript objects are similar to most everyday objects you come into contact with. Take an oven as an example. It has certain properties, such as model name, age, size, and temperature. There are certain methods you can perform with the oven, such as turning on the grill or the self-cleaner. Some of these methods change the properties of the oven, such as the oven's temperature when you're preheating it.

Similarly, your Web browser has its own set of objects, properties, and methods. The Web browser itself is an object, and the page you're viewing is also an object. If the page contains frames, each frame is an object, and if the page contains a form, the form and any fields it contains are objects. A paragraph is also an object, and the text within that paragraph can be considered its own object.

Each of these objects has its own set of properties. The browser object has a property that indicates its type, such as Netscape or Internet Explorer, and another that indicates its version. A form object has a name or id property that distinguishes it from other forms. An object that has been placed on a page has properties for its page coordinates. Most objects also have methods. You apply a method to the browser when you open it, close it, reload its contents, or move back and forth in its history list. You apply a method to a Web form when you submit it to a program on a Web server for processing.

We can create a program in JavaScript to alter object properties or apply methods to an object. Thus, we could use a program to apply methods to reload a Web page or to submit a Web form. For the Avalon Books page, we can create an animation by altering the position properties of the various elements. We'll learn more about properties and methods later in this session. First, though, we'll examine the different objects available to us.

Exploring the Document Object Model

All of the objects within documents and browsers need to be organized in a systematic way in order for programming languages like JavaScript to be able to work with them. The organized structure of objects and events is called the **document object model**, or **DOM**. In theory, every object related to documents or to browsers should be part of the document object model and thus accessible to a scripting language like JavaScript or VBScript. However, in practice, browsers—and sometimes even different versions of the same browser—differ in the objects that their document object models support. Some DOMs only support a few Web page or browser objects. In other cases, every single item is part of the DOM, including individual lines of text. The fact that we can encounter different DOMs depending on which browser a user is running makes it difficult to write code that satisfies all browsers and browser versions. In order to appreciate the complexity of the different document object models, we need to briefly review the history of their development.

Development of a Common DOM

The first document object model for the Web was introduced in Netscape Navigator 2.0. This is often referred to as the **basic model**, or in some cases, the **DOM Level 0**. The basic model supported the common objects used in many JavaScript programs, such as the browser window, the Web document, and the browser itself. Using the basic model, a programmer could reference these objects in the scripting language, but in most cases could not modify their properties once the page was loaded by the browser. Only form elements could be modified after the page was loaded; the rest of the page was static and could not be changed. Internet Explorer 3.0 was the first version of Internet Explorer to support the basic model.

However, like the development of HTML, the development of a more comprehensive DOM followed two paths: one adopted by Netscape and the other adopted by Internet Explorer. Unfortunately, differences between the two browsers' DOMs have proved more difficult to reconcile than their differences in introducing HTML.

The next objects to be added to the DOM were inline images. Netscape 3.0 introduced the ability to create image rollovers, in which the source of an inline image could be switched in response to a mouse pointer hovering over the image. This effect made Web pages more interesting and dynamic; however, since earlier browser versions did not support rollovers, programmers who wanted to avoid error messages from other browsers had to write scripts that would detect which browser was in use before attempting to implement a rollover effect. Internet Explorer eventually supported rollovers in version 4.0.

Netscape 4 further expanded the scope of its document object model by adding the ability to capture mouse and keyboard events occurring within the browser. Thus, a script could be run in response to a user pressing a particular key, clicking a mouse button, or dragging the mouse pointer across the document window. Netscape 4 also introduced the concept of layers, allowing page content to be isolated in containers whose properties could be manipulated almost as if they were separate documents. While layers were a great innovation, they were not supported by Internet Explorer; the layer concept is no longer being developed by Netscape, and support for layers was dropped by later Netscape versions.

Internet Explorer 4.0 introduced perhaps the most sweeping extension to the document object model. In Internet Explorer 4.0, all Web page elements were added to the DOM. CSS attributes also became part of the DOM. This meant you could write a program that could modify objects such as the text of a heading, a page's background image, text color, and even the font face used by a browser. Moreover, because all of the elements became dynamic, they could be modified even after a page was loaded by the browser. The Internet Explorer DOM also provided a technique for responding to—or **capturing**—events occurring within the browser. Unfortunately, the approach adopted by Internet Explorer was incompatible with the approach of Netscape 4.

Thus, the browser wars had reached a stage at which two fundamentally incompatible document object models were in use, and programmers who wanted to create dynamic Web pages had major headaches trying to reconcile the differences. At this point, the World Wide Web Consortium (W3C) stepped in—much like it did with HTML—to develop specifications for a common document object model.

The first specification, **DOM Level 1**, was released in October 1998 and provided support for all elements contained within HTML and XML documents. An update to this specification was released in September 2000 and fixed some errors from the earlier release. DOM Level 1 enjoys nearly universal support in current browser versions.

The second specification, **DOM Level 2**, was released in November 2000. This specification enhanced the document object model by providing an event model in which programs could be written to capture and respond to events occurring within a browser. DOM Level 2 also added a style model to work with CSS style sheets, and a range model to allow programmers to manipulate sections of text within a document. The DOM Level 2 specifications were also placed within six different modules, allowing browser developers to support those sections of the DOM of importance to them. Current browsers support many, but not all, of the features of DOM Level 2.

The most recent specification is **DOM Level 3**, released in April 2004. DOM Level 3 provides a framework for working with document loading and saving, as well as for working with DTDs and document validation. Few browsers support the DOM Level 3 specifications at the time of this writing.

Figure 4-3 summarizes the different DOMs and indicates their support in different versions of Internet Explorer, Netscape, and Opera.

Document Object Models ◄ Figure 4-3

DOM	Description	Netscape	Internet Explorer	Opera
DOM Level 0 (Basic Model)	The basic DOM that supported few page and browser objects and allowed dynamic content only for form elements	NS2, NS3, NS4, NS6, NS7	IE3, IE4, IE5, IE6	OP3, OP4, OP5, OP6, OP7
DOM Level 0 + Images	The basic DOM with added support for image rollovers	NS3, NS4, NS6, NS7	IE3 (Macintosh), IE4, IE5, IE6	OP3, OP4, OP5, OP6, OP7
Netscape 4 (layers)	The basic DOM with support for the Netscape 4 layer element and the ability to capture events within the browser	NS4		
Internet Explorer 4	An expanded DOM allowing dynamic content for most page elements		IE4, IE5, IE6	OP6, OP7
Internet Explorer 5	The IE 4 DOM with additional refinements and enhancements		IE5, IE6	OP6, OP7
W3C DOM Level 1	The first DOM specification by the W3C, which supported all page and browser elements and handled all events occurring within the browser	NS6, NS7	IE5, IE6	OP6, OP7
W3C DOM Level 2	The second DOM specification, allowing for the capture of events, manipulation of CSS styles, working with element text, and document subsets	NS6, NS7	IE6	OP6, OP7
W3C DOM Level 3	The third DOM specification provides a framework for working with document loading and saving, as well as working with DTDs and document validation			

Be aware that within each DOM, particular features may not be supported by every browser. With so many DOMs, writing a dynamic Web page that accommodates all browsers, all browser versions, and all operating systems is not a simple task, and the conscientious programmer should be ready to do a lot of testing. Generally if you want to ensure the widest compatibility across browsers, your code should be compatible with the following DOMs:

- Netscape 4
- Internet Explorer 5
- W3C DOM Level 1 and 2

The Netscape 4 DOM refers to the document object model used in the fourth-generation Netscape browsers (4.0 and 4.7). You may be tempted to think that you could use the Netscape 4 DOM for all subsequent versions of Netscape, but this is not the case. The DOM supported by Netscape version 6 and above is not backward-compatible with the Netscape 4 DOM. For the purposes of creating dynamic Web pages, you should treat Netscape 4 and Netscape 6 as totally different browsers instead of different versions of the same browser. The number of users running Netscape 4 has dwindled considerably in recent years, so supporting the Netscape 4 DOM is not as essential as it once was. For more information about the Netscape 4 DOM and how to write code for it, see Appendix J.

For the Avalon Books Web page, we'll concentrate on Level 1 and Level 2 of the W3C DOM; however we'll also examine the features of the Internet Explorer 5 DOM when circumstances warrant. In the text that follows, you should assume that any code samples refer to the Level 1 and Level 2 W3C DOMs unless otherwise noted.

The Document Tree

Each DOM organizes objects into a hierarchy known as a document tree. Figure 4-4 shows part of this hierarchy.

Figure 4-4	The object hierarchy

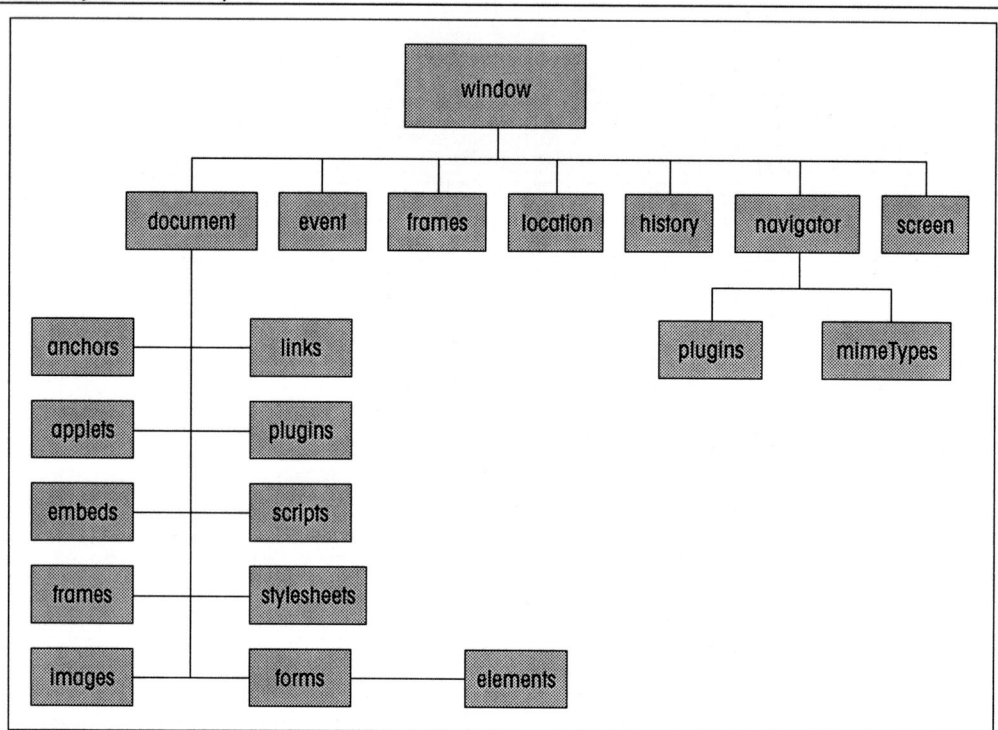

The topmost object in the hierarchy is the window object, which represents the browser window. Within the browser window are objects for the Web page document, each frame, the history of Web pages visited, and even the browser itself. Those objects can themselves contain yet another level of objects. For example, the document object contains objects for Web forms, images, applets, inline frames, and links. Obviously as document object models encompass more objects, the tree structure itself became more elaborate, including more of the objects within the window, browser, and document. The object hierarchy for the W3C Level 1 and Level 2 DOMs even includes a structure for individual tags, tag attributes, and text strings within an HTML file.

Referencing Objects

A DOM defines how the objects and events for browsers and documents are organized; it can be used by any scripting language, such as JavaScript. Thus, once you understand how to work with a document object model, you can often apply the lessons you learn to several programming languages. In this case we'll look at how to work with a DOM using JavaScript. We'll start by examining how to reference particular elements or groups of elements within a document object model.

Object Names

In JavaScript each object is identified by an **object name**. Figure 4-5 lists the object names for some of the objects at the top of the hierarchy.

Object Name	Description
window	The browser window
document	The Web document displayed in the window
document.body	The body of the Web document displayed in the browser window
event	Events or actions occurring within the browser window
history	The list of previously visited Web sites within the browser window
location	The URL of the document currently displayed in the browser window
navigator	The browser itself
screen	The screen displaying the document

For example, in the previous three tutorials you used the document object when writing content to the Web page. To indicate the location of an object within the hierarchy, you separate different levels using a dot. The general form is

```
object1.object2.object3. ...
```

where `object1` is at the top of the hierarchy, `object2` is a child of `object1`, `object3` is a child of `object2`, and so forth. Thus, to reference the history of Web pages visited within the browser window, you would use the form

```
window.history
```

However, in some cases you do not have to indicate an object's location in the hierarchy. For example, when you simply use the object name "document", JavaScript automatically assumes that it is located within the browser window. Thus, if you wanted to work with the body part of a document (that is, the part of the document displayed in the browser window), you could use the object reference

```
document.body
```

Working with Object Collections

When more than one of the same type of object exists, these objects are organized into arrays called **object collections**. This occurs chiefly within Web page documents that include several objects of the same type. To reference a particular collection within the document, JavaScript uses the form

```
document.collection
```

where `collection` is the name of the object collection. Figure 4-6 displays a list of the different object collections along with the browser support information for each. Not all collections are supported by all browsers or browser versions. In addition, the Netscape 4 DOM has its own object collections, which are discussed in Appendix J.

Figure 4-6	Object collections

Object Collection	Description	Netscape	Internet Explorer	Opera
document.all	All elements		IE4, IE5, IE6	OP6, OP7
document.anchors	All anchors	NS2, NS3, NS4, NS6	IE3, IE4, IE5, IE6	OP4, OP5, OP6, OP7
document.applets	All applets	NS3, NS4, NS6, NS7	IE4, IE5, IE6	OP4, OP5, OP6, OP7
document.embeds	All embed elements	NS3, NS4, NS6, NS7	IE4, IE5, IE6	OP4, OP5, OP6, OP7
document.forms	All Web forms	NS2, NS3, NS4, NS6, NS7	IE3, IE4, IE5, IE6	OP4, OP5, OP6, OP7
document.*form*.elements	All elements within a specific *form*	NS3, NS4, NS6, NS7	IE4, IE5, IE6	OP5, OP6, OP7
document.frames	All inline frames		IE4, IE5, IE6	OP4, OP5, OP6, OP7
document.images	All inline images	NS3, NS4, NS6, NS7	IE4, IE5, IE6	OP4, OP5, OP6, OP7
document.links	All links	NS2, NS3, NS4, NS6, NS7	IE3, IE4, IE5, IE6	OP4, OP5, OP6, OP7
document.namespaces	All namespaces defined in the document		IE6	
document.plugins	All plug-ins in the document	NS4, NS6, NS7	IE5, IE6	OP5, OP6, OP7
document.scripts	All script elements		IE4, IE5, IE6	OP6, OP7
document.styleSheets	All style sheet elements	NS6, NS7	IE4, IE5, IE6	
document.all.tags	All tags defined in the document		IE4, IE5, IE6	OP6, OP7
navigator.plugins	All plug-ins supported by the browser	NS4, NS6, NS7	IE5, IE6	OP5, OP6, OP7
navigator.mimeTypes	All mime-types supported by the browser	NS6, NS7	IE5, IE6	OP6, OP7
window.frames	All frames within the browser window	NS4, NS6, NS7	IE4, IE5, IE6	OP4, OP5, OP6, OP7

To reference a specific object within a collection, you can use either of the following forms:

```
document.collection["idref"]
document.collection.idref
```

where `idref` is either an index number representing the position of the object in the array or the value of the id or name attribute assigned to that element. As with other arrays, the first object in the collection has an index number of 0. For example, if the first form element in the HTML file is

```
<form id="Survey"> ... </form>
```

you can reference the form using any of the following expressions:

```
document.forms[0]
document.forms["Survey"]
document.forms.Survey
```

Like arrays, you can create a For loop to loop through each item in an object collection. The general form to loop through an object collection is:

```
for (var i=0; i<collection.length; i++) {
    commands on collection[i];
}
```

where *collection* is the object reference to the object collection. Note that, like arrays, object collections support the length property, so you can always determine the number of elements in any object by using the expression

```
collection.length
```

Using document.all and document.getElementById

Not all elements are associated with an object collection. For example, in Terry's HTML file, she has placed much of the content within div elements. Although JavaScript does not support a div collection, she can reference these objects using their id values. The Internet Explorer and W3C DOMs provide different methods for doing this. In the Internet Explorer DOM, you can use the document.all collection to reference all elements in a document. Thus, to reference a specific element by its id, you can use either of the following forms:

```
document.all["id"]
document.all.id
```

where *id* is the id value of the element. Alternatively, you can omit "document.all" from the reference and simply use

```
id
```

as the object reference. Using the Internet Explorer DOM, any of the following could be used to reference an element whose id value is "Greetings":

```
document.all["Greetings"]
document.all.Greetings
Greetings
```

In the W3C DOMs, you use the getElementById method to reference a specific element. The syntax is

```
document.getElementById("id")
```

Thus, the reference for an element with an id of "Greetings" would be

```
document.getElementById("Greetings")
```

Case is important when using the getElementById method. A common mistake is to enter the code as getElementByID; however, because the final letter is incorrectly capitalized, this code would result in an error. Internet Explorer also supports the getElementById method.

Referencing Tags

You can also create object collections based on HTML tag names. In the Internet Explorer DOM, you would use the form

```
document.all.tags(tag)
```

where *tag* is the name of the HTML tag. For example, the reference

```
document.all.tags(p)
```

returns an object collection of all of the paragraph tags in the document. To reference the first paragraph, you would use the expression

```
document.all.tags(p)[0]
```

In the W3C DOMs, you reference tags using the getElementsByTagName method. The syntax is

```
document.getElementsByTagName("tag")
```

Thus, the expression to access a document's first paragraph would be

```
document.getElementsByTagName("p")[0]
```

We'll explore other methods for accessing specific elements and objects within an HTML document in a later tutorial.

Reference Window | **Referencing Objects**

- To reference an object as part of the collection in a document, use the syntax
  ```
  document.collection[idref]
  ```
  where `idref` is either an index number representing the position of the object in the collection or the value of the id or name attribute assigned to that element.
- To reference a document object based on its id, use
  ```
  document.getElementById(id)
  ```
- To reference a document object based on its element tag, use
  ```
  document.getElementsByTagName(tag)
  ```
  where `tag` is the name of the element tag. Note that this returns a collection of elements with that tag name rather than a single item.

Working with Object Properties

Each object in JavaScript has properties associated with it. The number of properties depends on the type of object: some objects have only a few properties, while others have many. The syntax for setting the value of an object property is

```
object.property = expression
```

where `object` is the JavaScript name of the object you want to manipulate, `property` is a property of that object, and `expression` is a JavaScript expression that assigns a value to the property. For example, one of the properties of a document is the document title. If you want to set the document title using JavaScript instead of using the HTML title element, you could run the following command:

```
document.title = "Avalon Books"
```

The text "Avalon Books" would then appear in the title bar of a Web browser displaying the document. Figure 4-7 presents other examples of setting object properties using JavaScript. To make it easier to separate the object names, properties, and expressions, the object names are displayed in red, the properties are displayed in blue, and the values of the expressions are displayed in green.

Setting object property values   Figure 4-7

Expression	Description
document.bgColor="black"	Sets the background color of the document to black
document.fgColor="white"	Sets the foreground color of the document to white
document.links[0].href="http://www.avalon.com"	Sets the URL of the document's first link to "http://www.avalon.com"
document.images[2].src="avalon.gif"	Sets the source of the document's third inline image to "avalon.gif"
document.getElementById("books").style.fontWeight="bold"	Sets the font weight of the element with the id "books" to bold
document.getElementsByTagName("p")[0].style.fontSize="16pt"	Sets the font size of the document's first paragraph to 16pt
document.forms[1].action="http://www.avalon.com/mailer"	Sets the action of the second Web form to "http://www.avalon.com/mailer"
location.href="http://www.avalon.com"	Sets the page displayed by the browser to the URL "http://www.avalon.com"
window.status="Page Loaded"	Displays the text "Page Loaded" in the browser window's status bar

We'll explore additional objects and their properties throughout the next four tutorials; you can review the list of these objects and properties in Appendix G. Figure 4-7 gives you an idea of the scope of what you can do by modifying the property values of objects in your document and browser.

Not all properties can be changed. Some properties are **read-only**, meaning that you can read the property value, but you cannot modify it. One such property is the appVersion property of the navigator object, which identifies the version of the user's Web browser. Although it could come in handy to be able to upgrade a user's browser by running a simple JavaScript command, this value is not changeable. Figure 4-8 describes some of the other properties that provide information about your browser and its operating environment.

Browser properties   Figure 4-8

Browser Property	Description
navigator.appName	The name of the browser
navigator.appVersion	The major version number of the browser (may also include a compatibility value and the name of the operating system)
navigator.appMinorVersion	The minor version number of the browser
navigator.appCodeName	The name of the browser's code
navigator.userAgent	The name of the browser-associated user agent
navigator.platform	The operating system under which the browser is running
navigator.cpuClass	The type of CPU in use with the browser
navigator.systemLanguage	The language used by the browser
navigator.cookieEnabled	A Boolean value indicating whether cookies are enabled

Storing a Property in a Variable

Although you cannot change the value of read-only properties, you can assign a value to a variable in a JavaScript program. The syntax for assigning a property value to a variable is

```
variable = object.property
```

where *variable* is the variable name, *object* is the name of the object, and *property* is the name of the property. For example, to store the name of a user's browser in a variable, you could use the command

```
BrowserName = navigator.appName
```

Using Properties in Conditional Expressions

Sometimes you need to work with properties in conditional statements, which change how a Web page behaves based on the value of certain object properties. The following JavaScript code shows how you can incorporate object properties into a simple conditional expression:

```
if(document.bgColor=="black") {
   document.fgColor="white";
} else {
   document.fgColor="black";
}
```

In this example, JavaScript first checks the background color of the Web page. If the background color is black, JavaScript changes the color of the text on the page to white, using the page's fgColor property. If the background color is not black, then the text color is changed to black. As you can see, using objects, properties, and conditional statements provides you with a great deal of control over the appearance of your Web pages.

Reference Window | **Working with Object Properties**

- To set the value of an object property, use
    ```
    object.property = expression
    ```
  where *object* is the object reference, *property* is the object property, and *expression* is the value you want to assign to the property.
- To store an object property value, use
    ```
    variable = object.property
    ```
  where *variable* is the variable that will store the property value.

Working with Object Methods

You can also manipulate objects by applying methods to them. The syntax for applying a method is

```
object.method(parameters)
```

where *object* is the name of the object, *method* is the method to be applied, and *parameters* is a comma-separated list of parameter values used with the method. In the previous tutorial you applied the "write" method to a document in order to write content to the page. In that case, the parameter value was the text of the content to be written. Figure 4-9 lists some other examples of applying methods to objects. In the figure, object names are highlighted in red, methods are displayed in blue, and parameter values are displayed in green. Not every method requires parameter values.

Browser methods ◄ Figure 4-9

Expression	Action
location.reload()	Reload the current page in the browser
document.forms[0].reset()	Reset the first form in the Web page
document.forms[0].submit()	Submit the first form in the Web page
document.write("Avalon Books")	Write "Avalon Books" to the Web page
history.back()	Go back to the previous page in the browser's history list
thisDay.getFullYear()	Return the four-digit year value from the thisDay date object
Math.rand()	Return a random value using the Math object
navigator.javaEnabled()	Return a Boolean value indicating whether Java is enabled in the browser
window.close()	Close the browser window
window.print()	Print the contents of the browser window
window.scroll(x, y)	Scroll the browser window to the (x, y) coordinate

Working with Object Methods — Reference Window

- To apply a method to an object, use

  `object.method(parameters)`

  where `object` is the object reference, `method` is the method to be applied, and `parameters` is a comma-separated list of parameter values used by the method.

Creating a Cross-Browser Web Site

As you learned earlier, different browsers can support different document object models. Current browsers all do a good job of supporting Level 1 and Level 2 of the W3C DOM. However, if you need to support older browsers your code must be able to accommodate different DOMs. You can create this kind of code, known as **cross-browser** code, using two different approaches: browser detection or object detection.

Using Browser Detection

Using **browser detection**, your code determines which browser (and browser version) a user is running. In some cases, the code may even have to establish which operating system a browser is running under. After collecting this information, the program then runs code tailored for the user's system. Successfully using browser detection requires that you do your homework and map out the requirements of each browser, browser version, and perhaps even operating system. This is no small task!

Recall that information about a browser is stored in the navigator object. To retrieve a browser's name, you use the property

`navigator.appName`

For Netscape, this expression returns the value "Netscape." For Internet Explorer, the value would be "Microsoft Internet Explorer." However, for Opera, the value of the appName property is often listed as "Microsoft Internet Explorer". This is because Opera supports many of the features of the Internet Explorer DOM. If you need to determine whether a user is running the Opera browser, you can test whether the browser supports the window.opera property. We'll examine how to perform object detection in the next section.

No property returns the browser version in an easy-to-read text string. The expression navigator.appVersion returns both the version number and additional text that describes features of the version. Unfortunately, this text is usually not reliable in determining the version number. For example, the following values of the appVersion property correspond to the listed versions of Netscape, Internet Explorer, and Opera:

- Netscape 7.1 for Windows: 5.0 (Windows; en-US)
- Internet Explorer 6.0 for Windows: 4.0 (compatible; MSIE 6.0; Windows NT 5.1)
- Opera 7.51 for Windows: 4.0 (compatible, MSIE 6.0; Windows NT 5.1)

Additional information about the browser is stored in the navigator.userAgent property, and most browser detection scripts—commonly known as **browser sniffers**—use this property to extract information about the version number. Because these programs can be long and complicated, we won't go into the details here. However, you can find a number of browser detection scripts of varying degrees of sophistication through a simple Web search. In summary, while it is relatively easy to determine which browser a user is running, it is not so easy to extract detailed information about the browser version.

Using Object Detection

Most Web page developers recommend bypassing browser detection entirely, and relying instead on object detection. With **object detection**, you determine which document object model a browser supports by testing which object references it recognizes. For example, only the Netscape 4 DOM recognizes the document.layers object collection, only the Internet Explorer DOM uses the document.all reference, and only the W3C DOM recognizes the document.getElementById object reference.

We can use this information to construct three Boolean variables whose values are true if a user's browser supports the Netscape 4, Internet Explorer, or W3C document object models, respectively. The code is:

```
var NS4DOM = document.layers ? true:false;
var IEDOM = document.all ? true:false;
var W3CDOM = document.getElementById ? true:false;
```

This code uses the comparison operator to test whether the browser recognizes each object reference. If a browser understands a given object reference, then we can assume that the browser supports the document object model associated with that object reference. For example, if the browser recognizes the document.all reference, the IEDOM variable returns a value of true, indicating that the browser supports the Internet Explorer DOM; otherwise the IEDOM variable returns a value of false.

One advantage of the object detection approach is that it can work for any object and any browser. You can also use it to test for support of earlier versions of the document object model. For example, the expression

```
var BasicDOM = document.forms ? true:false;
var ImagesDOM = document.images ? true:false;
```

creates two variables that we can use to test whether the browser supports DOM Level 0 or DOM Level 0 plus image rollovers. To demonstrate these concepts, a demo page has been prepared for you to display the properties of your browser and the objects that it supports. Open this page now.

To view supported objects and browser properties:

1. Use your browser to open **demo_browser.htm** from the tutorial.04/tutorial folder.

2. Study the tables on the page to learn about the properties of your browser and the supported objects.

   You can also enter your own object name to test whether it is supported by your browser. Try this now to see whether your browser supports the document.all object reference (necessary for browsers that support the Internet Explorer DOM).

3. Type **document.all** in the Enter an object name text box at the bottom of the page and click the **test** button.

   Figure 4-10 shows the content of the page for the Internet Explorer 6.0 browser for Windows.

Browser properties and supported objects ◄ Figure 4-10

Navigator Object Properties	
navigator.appName	Microsoft Internet Explorer
navigator.appVersion	4.0 (compatible; MSIE 6.0; Windows NT 5.1)
navigator.appMinorVersion	;SP1;Q822925;Q330994;Q824145;Q832894;Q837009;Q831167;
navigator.appCodeName	Mozilla
navigator.userAgent	Mozilla/4.0 (compatible; MSIE 6.0; Windows NT 5.1)
navigator.platform	Win32
navigator.cpuClass	x86
navigator.systemLanguage	en-us
navigator.cookieEnabled	true

Supported Objects			
document.all	yes	document.images	yes
document.anchors	yes	document.layers	no
document.applets	yes	document.links	yes
document.childNodes	yes	document.namespaces	yes
document.classes	no	document.plugins	yes
document.embeds	yes	document.scripts	yes
document.forms	yes	document.styleSheets	yes
document.frames	yes	document.tags	no
document.getElementById	yes	navigator.plugins	yes
document.getElementsByName	yes	navigator.mimeTypes	yes
document.getElementsByTagName	yes	window.frames	yes
document.ids	no		

Enter an object name: documentall [test] yes

4. Close the page and any other files you've opened in this session.

Employing Cross-Browser Strategies

Once you settle on a mechanism to determine the capabilities of your users' browsers (by either browser or object detection), your next task is to choose a cross-browser strategy for your Web site. One strategy, called **page branching**, creates separate pages for each browser (and, if you need to get really detailed, for each browser version) along with an initial page. When a user opens the initial page, a script determines the capabilities of the user's browser and automatically loads the appropriate page. See Figure 4-11. The initial page itself can be used for browsers that don't support a scripting language or any of the document object models.

Figure 4-11	Page branching

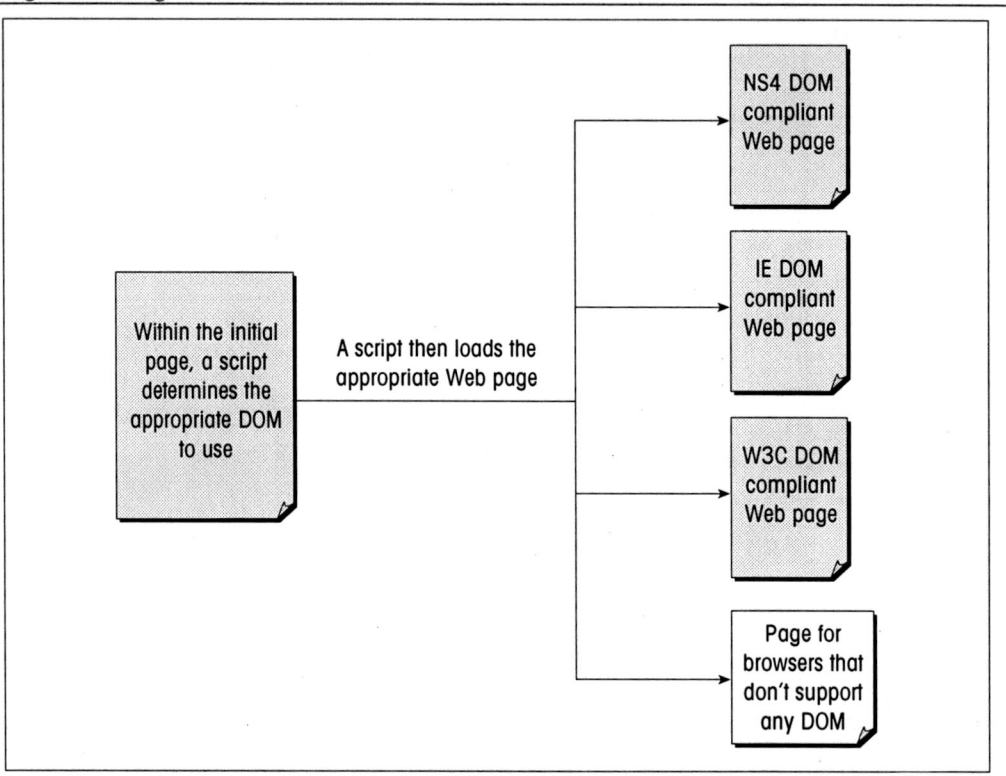

To automatically load a page into a browser based on the type of browser detected, use the command

```
location.href=url;
```

where `url` is the URL of the new page to be loaded. The page branching commands should be placed in the header section of the HTML file to ensure that the script is run before the initial page is loaded.

The following example shows code for a page that loads the page_ns4.htm page if the user's browser works with the Netscape 4 DOM. If the browser doesn't support that model, the code then tests for support of the Internet Explorer DOM and loads the page_ie.htm page if appropriate. Finally, if the browser doesn't support either of those DOMs, the code tests for support of the W3C DOM, loading the page_w3c.htm file if it is supported. If none of these DOMs are supported, the browser continues to open the current file.

```
<html>
   <head>
   <title>Avalon Books</title>
   <script language="JavaScript">
      if (document.layers) location.href="page_ns4.htm"
      else if (document.all) location.href="page_ie.htm"
      else if (document.getElementById) location.href= "page_w3c.htm"
   </script>
   </head>
   <body>
   <h1>Welcome to Avalon Books!</h1>
   </body>
</html>
```

Page branching requires you to maintain several versions of the same page. In a Web site containing many pages, this means a lot of extra work keeping all of the pages consistent.

A second cross-browser strategy is to use internal branching, in which each piece of JavaScript code is enclosed in an if...else statement. The general syntax is:

```
if (document.layers) {
   JavaScript commands for the Netscape 4 DOM;
   } else if (document.all) {
   JavaScript commands for the Internet Explorer DOM;
   } else if (document.getElementById) {
   JavaScript commands for the W3C DOM;
   }
}
```

This construction would have to be repeated every time you run a set of JavaScript commands. Internal branching works well for pages that do not employ a lot of JavaScript code. However, pages that contain a lot of JavaScript code quickly become unwieldy and prone to errors if you use internal branching.

Many Web developers apply a third cross-browser strategy: they create an application programming interface. An **application programming interface** or **API** is an external text file that contains custom commands and functions. These customized functions are written to resolve any cross-browser differences. When you create a Web page, you link it to the API and use commands from the API file in your Web page (see Figure 4-12) rather than placing the code within the HTML file on your page.

Using an API file  Figure 4-12

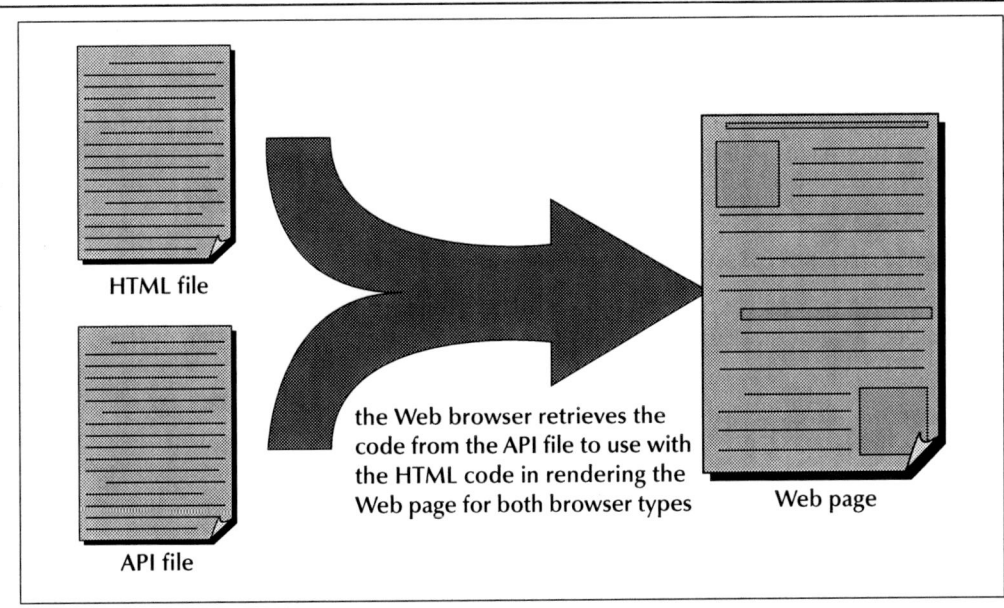

HTML file

API file

the Web browser retrieves the code from the API file to use with the HTML code in rendering the Web page for both browser types

Web page

You've completed your work reviewing the concepts behind objects, properties, methods, and the document object model. In the next session, you'll put what you've learned to work in creating an animated page for the Avalon Books Web site.

Session 4.1 Quick Check

1. What is the document object model? What are three DOMs that you should write code for if you wish to support the widest range of browsers and browser versions?
2. What object would you use to write a program to access the pages previously visited in a user's browser?
3. What object collection would you use to access a Web form?
4. How do the IE DOM and the W3C DOMs differ in referencing objects by their id value?
5. What command could you run to change the source of the first inline image in a document to the file logo.jpg?
6. What object and property should you use to retrieve the name of the browser in use?
7. What object and method would you use to print the contents of the browser window?
8. What is object detection and how could you use it to determine which DOM a user's browser supports?

Session 4.2

Creating Custom Functions for Avalon Books

You and Terry determine that you'll need the following functions to create the animation for the Avalon Books Web page:

- A function that returns an object's left coordinate
- A function that returns an object's top coordinate
- A function to place an object at specific coordinates on the page
- A function to move an object a certain distance from its current location
- A function to hide an object
- A function to unhide an object

You'll put these functions in a separate file named scripts.js so that they can be used again by other pages in the Avalon Books Web site if Terry chooses.

To create the scripts.js file:

1. Use your text editor to open the **scripttxt.js** file from the tutorial.04/tutorial folder, and enter *your name* and *the date* in the comment section at the top of the file.

2. Save the file as **scripts.js**.

Working with the Style Object

To create the animation effect that Terry wants, you have to be able to place each of the five div elements from the avalon.htm file at specific locations on the page. Positioning is done using CSS positioning styles, so you have to apply one of those styles to each of the elements. JavaScript treats the styles associated with an element as an object. The syntax for applying a style is:

```
object.style.attribute = value
```

where *object* is a reference to an object in the Web document, *attribute* is one of the CSS styles that apply to that object, and *value* is the value of the style. The style attribute is converted to a JavaScript style value by removing any dashes in the style name and capitalizing the first letter following each removed dash. For example, the CSS style

```
background-image
```

becomes

```
backgroundImage
```

in JavaScript. Thus, to change the font size of the first paragraph in a document to 16 points, you could use the following JavaScript command:

```
document.getElementsByTagName("p")[0].style.fontSize="16pt"
```

Figure 4-13 lists some other applications of the style object.

Using the style object ◀ **Figure 4-13**

Expression	Description
document.getElementById("logo").style.color="black"	Sets the foreground color of the logo element to black
document.getElementById("logo").style.fontWeight="bold"	Displays the text in the logo element in a boldfaced font
document.getElementById("logo").style.fontStyle="italic"	Displays the text in the logo element in italics
document.getElementById("logo").style.margin="10px"	Sets the margin around the logo element to 10 pixels
document.getElementById("logo").style.fontFamily ="Arial"	Sets the font of the logo element to Arial
document.getElementById("logo").style.width="100px"	Sets the width of the logo element to 100 pixels
document.getElementById("logo").style.textAlign="center"	Horizontally centers the contents of the logo element
document.getElementById("logo").style.backgroundImage="url(paper.gif)"	Sets the background image of the logo element to paper.gif

Setting an Object's Style Attribute

Reference Window

- To change the value of a style associated with an object, use
    object.style.attribute = value
  where *object* is the object reference, *attribute* is one of the style attributes associated with the object, and *value* is the value assigned to the style attribute.

Note that the style object references only styles created either using a JavaScript command or as inline styles added directly to an element's markup tag. Styles defined in embedded or external style sheets are not treated as part of the style object for an element.

Setting an Element's Position

JavaScript uses the same positioning style values as CSS. Thus, you can set an element's top and left coordinates, specify its z-index value (for stacked elements), and hide or re-display it using the display or visibility styles. Figure 4-14 describes the positioning styles we'll use in the Avalon Books Web page.

Figure 4-14	Positioning properties

Positioning Property	Sets
object.style.position="*value*"	the position type of the *object*, where *value* is absolute, relative, fixed, static, or auto
object.style.left="*value*"	the left coordinate of the *object*
object.style.top="*value*"	the top coordinate of the *object*
object.style.right="*value*"	the right coordinate of the *object*
object.style.bottom="*value*"	the bottom coordinate of the *object*
object.style.zIndex="*value*"	the z-index value of the *object*
object.style.visibility="*type*"	the visibility of the *object* where *type* is either hidden or visible
object.style.width="*value*"	the width of the *object*
object.style.height="*value*"	the height of the *object*
object.style.overflow="*type*"	the type of overflow applied to the *object* where *type* is auto, visible, hidden, or scroll
object.style.clip="*value*"	the size of the clipping rectangle where *value* is a text string containing the clipping rectangle values

For example, if you wanted to set the left coordinate of an object with the id "avalon" to 100 pixels you would enter the following JavaScript command:

```
document.getElementById("avalon").style.left="100px"
```

Note that coordinate values also contain the unit of length. If you need to add to or subtract from a coordinate (in order to move an object on the page), you have to first extract the numeric value. This can be done using the parseInt() method, which extracts a numeric value from a text string. For example, the expression

```
leftpos=parseInt("100px")
```

stores the numeric value 100 in the leftpos variable. At that point you could apply any mathematical operation to change the position value, and then store the new coordinate in the left style object for the element. The following code moves the avalon object 5 pixels to the left:

```
leftpos=parseInt(document.getElementById("avalon").style.left);
leftpos=leftpos+5;
document.getElementById("avalon").style.left=leftpos+"px";
```

Note that when the code updates the left position of the object it also appends the unit "px" to indicate to the browser that the unit of length is pixels.

Positioning Properties in the IE DOM

The Internet Explorer DOM supports the style object described above, as well as some additional properties that can be used to position objects on the Web page. Figure 4-15 describes the Internet Explorer DOM positioning properties.

IE DOM positioning properties

Figure 4-15

Positioning Property	Sets
object.style.pixelLeft="*value*"	The position of the left edge of the *object* in pixels
object.style.pixelTop="*value*"	The position of the top edge of the *object* in pixels
object.style.posLeft="*value*"	The position of the left edge of the *object* in the specified unit of length
object.style.posTop="*value*"	The position of the top edge of the *object* in the specified unit of length

The posLeft and posTop properties are equivalent to the left and top properties in the W3C DOM. The pixelLeft and pixelTop properties assume that the unit of length is the pixel and thus use only numeric values with no length unit. Thus the expressions

```
parseInt(object.style.left)
parseInt(object.style.posLeft)
object.style.pixelLeft
```

return the same value in a browser supporting the IE DOM when pixels are the unit of the length.

Creating the Positioning Functions for Avalon Books

Now that you've reviewed some of the issues associated with positioning objects with JavaScript, you're ready to create the functions for the Avalon Books Web site. Each function will take as an input value the id of an object in the Web page, and will then set the positioning property values for the object. When the animation runs, the code will need the current location of the objects on the page, so the first two functions we'll create will return the values of the left and top coordinates. The code for the first two functions is

```
function xCoord(id) {
    object=document.getElementById(id);
    xc=parseInt(object.style.left);
    return xc;
}
function yCoord(id) {
    object=document.getElementById(id);
    yc=parseInt(object.style.top);
    return yc;
}
```

The xCoord() function returns the position of the object's left edge. Note that the parseInt() method is used to return only the numeric value and not the unit. For this project we'll assume that all coordinates are expressed in pixels. The yCoord() function returns the position of the object's top edge.

To insert the xCoord() and yCoord() functions:

1. Return to the **scripts.js** file in your text editor.

2. Below the comment section, insert the following code:

```
function xCoord(id) {
    object=document.getElementById(id);
    xc=parseInt(object.style.left);
    return xc;
}
```

```
function yCoord(id) {
    object=document.getElementById(id);
    yc=parseInt(object.style.top);
    return yc;
}
```

The next function places an object at specific coordinates on the page. The full text of the function is

```
function placeIt(id, x, y) {
    object=document.getElementById(id);
    object.style.left=x+"px";
    object.style.top=y+"px";
}
```

The placeIt() function takes three parameters: the id name of the object, and the x and y coordinates at which we want to place it. The function first uses the id value to create a reference to the appropriate object in the document, and then places the object by modifying the values of the left and top style properties. For example, if we call the function using the command

```
placeIt("avalon", 100, 50)
```

the browser places the avalon object at the coordinates (100, 50).

To insert the placeIt() function:

1. Below the yCoord() function, insert the following code:

   ```
   function placeIt(id, x, y) {
       object=document.getElementById(id);
       object.style.left=x+"px";
       object.style.top=y+"px";
   }
   ```

Next, we need a function that moves an object a specified distance in the x and y directions from its current location. We will use this function when we create the animation that moves the words "Avalon" and "Books" across the Web page. This function, which we will call shiftIt(), will have three parameters, named id, dx, and dy. The id parameter contains the id value of the object. The dx and dy parameters contain the distance, in pixels, to move the object to the right and down. The code for the complete shiftIt() function is

```
function shiftIt(id, dx, dy) {
    object=document.getElementById(id);
    object.style.left=xCoord(id)+dx+"px";
    object.style.top=yCoord(id)+dy+"px";
}
```

In this function we use the xCoord() and yCoord() functions we created earlier to retrieve the current coordinates of the object. The shiftIt function then adds the value of the dx and dy parameters to those coordinates and appends these values with the "px" text string to indicate that coordinate values are in pixels.

To insert the shiftIt() function:

▶ **1.** Below the placeIt() function, insert the following code:

```
function shiftIt(id, dx, dy) {
    object=document.getElementById(id);
    object.style.left=xCoord(id)+dx+"px";
    object.style.top=yCoord(id)+dy+"px";
}
```

In the final part of Terry's proposed animation, images will appear to "pop up" on the Web page. To achieve that effect, we need to create functions both to hide objects and to unhide previously hidden objects. The functions are

```
function hideIt(id) {
    object=document.getElementById(id);
    object.style.visibility="hidden";
}
function showIt(id) {
    object=document.getElementById(id);
    object.style.visibility="visible";
}
```

To add the hideIt() and showIt() functions:

▶ **1.** Below the shiftIt() function, insert the following code:

```
function hideIt(id) {
    object=document.getElementById(id);
    object.style.visibility="hidden";
}

function showIt(id) {
    object=document.getElementById(id);
    object.style.visibility="visible";
}
```

▶ **2.** Figure 4-16 shows the completed functions for the scripts.js file. You should check the code you entered against this figure. Make sure that the text matches exactly, including the use of uppercase and lowercase letters and quotation marks.

Figure 4-16	Functions in the scripts.js file

```
function xCoord(id) {
    object=document.getElementById(id);
    xc=parseInt(object.style.left);
    return xc;
}

function yCoord(id) {
    object=document.getElementById(id);
    yc=parseInt(object.style.top);
    return yc;
}

function placeIt(id, x, y) {
    object=document.getElementById(id);
    object.style.left=x+"px";
    object.style.top=y+"px";
}

function shiftIt(id, dx, dy) {
    object=document.getElementById(id);
    object.style.left=xCoord(id)+dx+"px";
    object.style.top=yCoord(id)+dy+"px";
}

function hideIt(id) {
    object=document.getElementById(id);
    object.style.visibility="hidden";
}

function showIt(id) {
    object=document.getElementById(id);
    object.style.visibility="visible";
}
```

3. Close **scripts.js**, saving your changes.

You've completed inserting the functions in the scripts.js file. In the next session, you'll create a link to this file and use the functions you created to animate the Avalon Books Web page.

Review

Session 4.2 Quick Check

1. What JavaScript command increases the z-index value of the Logo object by 1?
2. What JavaScript commands would place the Logo object at the coordinates (150, 350)? Assume that the unit of measure is pixels.
3. What JavaScript command would you use to hide the Logo object?
4. What JavaScript command would you use to set the width of the Logo object to 100 pixels?
5. What JavaScript command would you use to set the size of the clipping rectangle around the Logo object to (10, 210, 150, 10)?
6. What JavaScript command would you use to display scrollbars if the contents of the Logo object overflow its boundaries?
7. If you were supporting the IE DOM, what JavaScript command would you enter to place the Logo object at the coordinates (150, 350). Assume that the unit of measure is pixels.

Session 4.3

Applying an Event Handler

You can now use the functions that you entered to animate the contents of Terry's Web page. Recall from Figure 4-12 that Terry first wants the single word "Avalon" to appear near the top of the page and then drop vertically down the page. At a certain point, "Avalon" should stop dropping, and the word "Books" should appear, moving to the right from behind the word "Avalon." After that, the three other images should appear on the screen in sequence.

To create this animation, you'll place the words "Avalon" and "Books" near the top of the page, with "Avalon" stacked on top of "Books" to hide it. You'll also place the three images in the appropriate locations on the page, but hidden. While some of these tasks (such as placing the objects on the page) can be performed with CSS style attributes, you can use this opportunity to test the functions you created by performing the tasks with JavaScript instead.

First you'll set the initial places for the five objects. The coordinates for the ab, fiction, and nfiction objects should remain unchanged, but the avalon and books objects should be placed at new coordinates: 175 pixels to the left and 10 pixels down from the upper-left corner of the window. Because the avalon object has a higher z-index value than the books object, it will appear on top of the books object. The coordinates for the five objects are therefore

- "avalon": (175, 10)
- "books": (175, 10)
- "ab": (230, 40)—as before
- "fiction": (5, 5)—as before
- "nfiction": (475, 5)—as before

You'll also hide the ab, fiction, and nfiction objects. You'll place all of these actions within a single file named placeObjects(), which you'll add to the avalon.htm file. The initial code for the placeObjects() function is

```
function placeObjects() {
    placeIt("avalon", 175,10);
    placeIt("books",175,10);
    placeIt("ab",230,40);
    placeIt("fiction",5,5);
    placeIt("nfiction",475,5);
    hideIt("ab");
    hideIt("fiction");
    hideIt("nfiction");
}
```

Because the placeObjects() function calls the functions we added to the scripts.js file, we also need to add a link to that file. Revise the avalon.htm file now.

To edit the avalon.htm file:

1. Reopen **avalon.htm** in your text editor.

2. Directly above the </head> tag insert the following line:

   ```
   <script src="scripts.js" type="text/javascript"></script>
   ```

3. Below this link insert the following script element:

   ```
   <script type="text/javascript">
   function placeObjects() {
       placeIt("avalon",175,10);
   ```

```
        placeIt("books",175,10);
        placeIt("ab",230,40);
        placeIt("fiction",5,5);
        placeIt("nfiction",475,5);
        hideIt("ab");
        hideIt("fiction");
        hideIt("nfiction");
    }
    </script>
```

▶ **4.** Figure 4-17 shows the newly added code.

Figure 4-17	Inserting the placeObjects() function

```
<title>Avalon Books</title>
<link href="styles.css" rel="stylesheet" type="text/css" />
<script src="scripts.js" type="text/javascript"></script>
<script type="text/javascript">
function placeObjects() {
    placeIt("avalon",175,10);
    placeIt("books",175,10);
    placeIt("ab",230,40);
    placeIt("fiction",5,5);
    placeIt("nfiction",475,5);
    hideIt("ab");
    hideIt("fiction");
    hideIt("nfiction");
}
</script>
</head>
```

Next you need to run this function when the page is initially loaded by a browser. You can do this using an onload event handler in the <body> tag of the avalon.htm file (for a discussion of the onload event handler, see Tutorial 2).

To add the onload event handler:

▶ **1.** Within the <body> tag, insert the attribute **onload="placeObjects()"** as shown in Figure 4-18.

Figure 4-18	Inserting the onload event handler

```
<script type="text/javascript">
function placeObjects() {
    placeIt("avalon", 175,10);
    placeIt("books",175,10);
    placeIt("ab",230,40);
    placeIt("fiction",5,5);
    placeIt("nfiction",475,5);
    hideIt("ab");
    hideIt("fiction");
    hideIt("nfiction");
}
</script>
</head>

<body onload="placeobjects()">
```

▶ **2.** Save your changes to the file and then load **avalon.htm** in your Web browser.

▶ **3.** The page opens as shown in Figure 4-19. Since the three images are hidden, they do not appear in the page. In addition, the word "Books" is hidden behind the word "Avalon."

Trouble? If you receive an error message when loading the page, check the code in the scripts.js file. Some common programming errors include mismatching uppercase and lowercase letters, misspellings of variable names, forgetting to close up double-quote-marked text, and forgetting to enclose command blocks and functions within curly braces.

Animating an Object

The first piece of animation you'll add to the Avalon Web page will be the word "Avalon" dropping down the page. The initial position of the word is at the coordinates (175, 10). Terry suggests dropping it down to the coordinates (175, 270). This means that while moving the object, the function will need to monitor the value of the y-coordinate and stop moving the word when that value exceeds 260 (note that the x-coordinate does not change). Once the function stops moving the word "Avalon," the browser should then run a function that moves the word "Books" to the right. The initial form of the moveAvalon() function will appear as follows:

```
function moveAvalon() {
   var y=yCoord("avalon");
   if (y <=260) {
      shiftIt("avalon",0,10);
      shiftIt("books",0,10);
      moveAvalon();
   } else {
      // run moveBooks function;
   }
}
```

There are a couple of important things to notice about this function. First, it retrieves the current y-coordinate from the yCoord() function you entered into the API. Second, it uses the shiftIt() function you created in the last session to move both the word "Avalon" and the word "Books" down 10 pixels at a time. Remember, you want the word "Books" to remain behind "Avalon" as it moves down the page. Once it has moved those two words, the function calls itself to start the moving process all over again. Finally, when the y-coordinate exceeds 260, the function then runs the moveBooks() function (which you haven't written yet) to begin moving the word "Books" out from behind "Avalon." For now we'll mark that spot with a comment.

The only thing missing from the function is a way to control the timing. Because a Web browser will run this function in a millisecond, from the viewpoint of a user the word "Avalon" will jump down the page in a blink of an eye. We'll slow down this process by using a time-delayed command. Recall from Tutorial 2 that we can delay when a browser runs a command using the setTimeout() method. In this case we'll use setTimeout() to repeat the moveAvalon() function after a delay of 30 milliseconds. The command is

```
setTimeout("moveAvalon()",30);
```

The entire moveAvalon() function is therefore

```
function moveAvalon() {
   var y=yCoord("avalon");
   if (y <= 260) {
      shiftIt("avalon",0,10);
      shiftIt("books",0,10);
      setTimeout("moveAvalon()",30);
   } else {
      // run moveBooks function;
   }
}
```

The function now moves the words "Avalon" and "Books" down 10 pixels every 30 milliseconds until the avalon object is 260 pixels from the top of the page. Generally, when you do animation, you have to experiment with several different movement and time-delay values before you arrive at a combination that creates a smooth motion. The value of 30 milliseconds was chosen after some experimentation.

To insert the moveAvalon() function:

1. Return to the **avalon.htm** file in your text editor.

2. After the placeObjects() function, insert the following code:

```
function moveAvalon() {
   var y=yCoord("avalon");
   if (y <= 260) {
      shiftIt("avalon",0,10);
      shiftIt("books",0,10);
      setTimeout("moveAvalon()",30);
   } else {
      // run moveBooks function;
   }
}
```

You also need to call the moveAvalon() function from within the placeObjects() function.

3. At the end of the placeObjects() function, directly after the command to hide the nfiction object, insert the command

```
moveAvalon();
```

Your script should resemble the code shown in Figure 4-20.

The moveAvalon() function | Figure 4-20

```
<script type="text/javascript">
function placeobjects() {
    placeIt("avalon", 175,10);
    placeIt("books",175,10);
    placeIt("ab",230,40);
    placeIt("fiction",5,5);
    placeIt("nfiction",475,5);
    hideIt("ab");
    hideIt("fiction");
    hideIt("nfiction");
    moveAvalon();
}

function moveAvalon() {
    var y=yCoord("avalon");
    if (y <= 260) {
        shiftIt("avalon",0,10);
        shiftIt("books",0,10);
        setTimeout("moveAvalon()",30);
    } else {
        // run moveBooks function;
    }
}
</script>
```

run moveAvalon() after placing the objects

4. Save your changes and reopen or refresh the **avalon.htm** file in your Web browser.

   The text "Avalon" should now move down the page once, and "Books" should move with it, hidden behind it.

   Next, your script needs to move the books object out from behind the avalon object. The moveBooks() function will resemble the moveAvalon() function, except that it will move only the books object and will move it from the left to the right. Terry used trial and error to determine that you should move "Books" from the coordinates (175, 270) to (330, 270). Once the text is in this location, the script should unhide the remaining figures; for now you'll just add a comment to the script indicating this. Following is the moveBooks() function that you'll use:

```
function moveBooks() {
   var x=xCoord("books");
   if (x <= 320) {
      shiftIt("books",10,0);
      setTimeout("moveBooks()",50);
   } else {
   // display the hidden images;
   }
}
```

Instead of using the yCoord() function from the API, moveBooks() uses the xCoord() function to track the object as it moves in the horizontal direction. Also, the second and third parameters of the shiftIt() function are switched so that the books object moves 10 pixels to the right every 50 milliseconds.

To insert the moveBooks() function:

1. Return to the **avalon.htm** file in your text editor.

2. After the moveAvalon() function, insert the following code:

```
function moveBooks() {
   var x=xCoord("books");
   if (x <= 320) {
      shiftIt("books",10,0);
      setTimeout("moveBooks()",50);
   } else {
```

```
        // display the hidden images;
      }
  }
```

Next you need to revise the moveAvalon() function so that it calls moveBooks() when it finishes.

▶ 3. Scroll up to the moveAvalon() function and replace the comment text "// run move-Books function;" with

```
moveBooks();
```

Figure 4-21 shows the revised text.

Figure 4-21 ▶ The moveBooks() function

run moveBooks() after
moving the avalon object

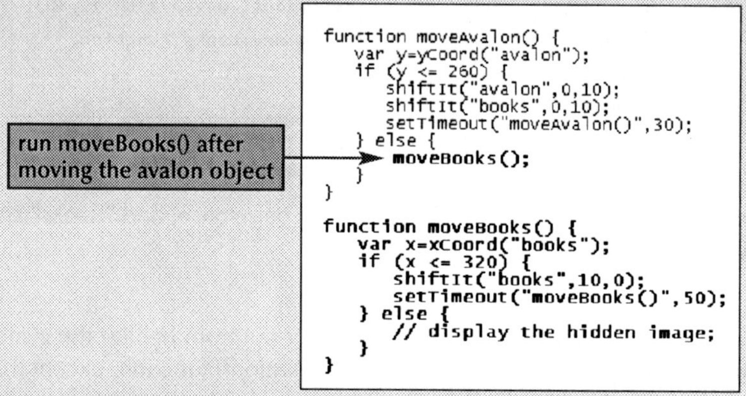

```
function moveAvalon() {
   var y=yCoord("avalon");
   if (y <= 260) {
      shiftit("avalon",0,10);
      shiftit("books",0,10);
      setTimeout("moveAvalon()",30);
   } else {
      moveBooks();
   }
}

function moveBooks() {
   var x=xCoord("books");
   if (x <= 320) {
      shiftit("books",10,0);
      setTimeout("moveBooks()",50);
   } else {
      // display the hidden image;
   }
}
```

▶ 4. Save your changes to the file and then reload or refresh **avalon.htm** in your Web browser.

The text "Avalon" should move down the page and after it stops the text "Books" should move from behind it.

The last step in the animation is to unhide the three images: ab, fiction, and nfiction. You decide to unhide each image at half-second intervals. The function to do this is

```
function showObjects() {
   setTimeout("showIt('ab')",500);
   setTimeout("showIt('fiction')",1000);
   setTimeout("showIt('nfiction')",1500);
}
```

Notice that you insert the object names in single quotes rather than double quotes, because you have to enclose the entire command in double quotes. Also notice that in order to unhide the images at half-second intervals, you specify 500 milliseconds, then 1000 milliseconds, and finally 1500 milliseconds for the delay times.

To insert the showObjects() function:

▶ 1. Return to the **avalon.htm** file in your text editor.

▶ 2. After the moveBooks() function, insert the following code:

```
function showObjects() {
   setTimeout("showIt('ab')",500);
   setTimeout("showIt('fiction')",1000);
   setTimeout("showIt('nfiction')",1500);
}
```

3. Replace the comment in the moveBooks() function with:

```
showObjects();
```

Figure 4-22 shows the revised code.

The showObjects() function ◀ Figure 4-22

```
function moveBooks() {
    var x=xCoord("books");
    if (x <= 320) {
        shiftIt("books",10,0);
        setTimeout("moveBooks()",50);
    } else {
        showObjects();
    }
}

function showObjects() {
    setTimeout("showIt('ab')",500);
    setTimeout("showIt('fiction')",1000);
    setTimeout("showIt('nfiction')",1500);
}
</script>
```

run showObjects() after
moving the books object

4. Save your changes to the file and then reload or refresh **avalon.htm** in your Web browser.

You should see the complete animation, ending with the three images appearing in sequence.

You may have noticed that, in creating this animation, each function called the next one in sequence after it was finished. This is a common technique when creating animation with JavaScript. By calling the next function only after the current function is finished, you ensure that your effects are presented in the proper order. In this example, this technique ensures that the "Books" text doesn't come out from behind the "Avalon" text until after they are both at the correct location near the bottom of the screen, and that the three images don't appear until the "Books" text has moved out from behind the "Avalon" text.

Controlling Layout for Different Monitor Resolutions

Terry is pleased with the opening screen you've designed. She notices, however, that you've created the page based on a monitor resolution of 640 x 480 pixels. What happens, she wonders, when users view the page at other resolutions? After experimenting, she shows you your page viewed at three different, but commonly used, resolutions (see Figure 4-23).

Figure 4-23   **The Avalon Books Web page at different monitor resolutions**

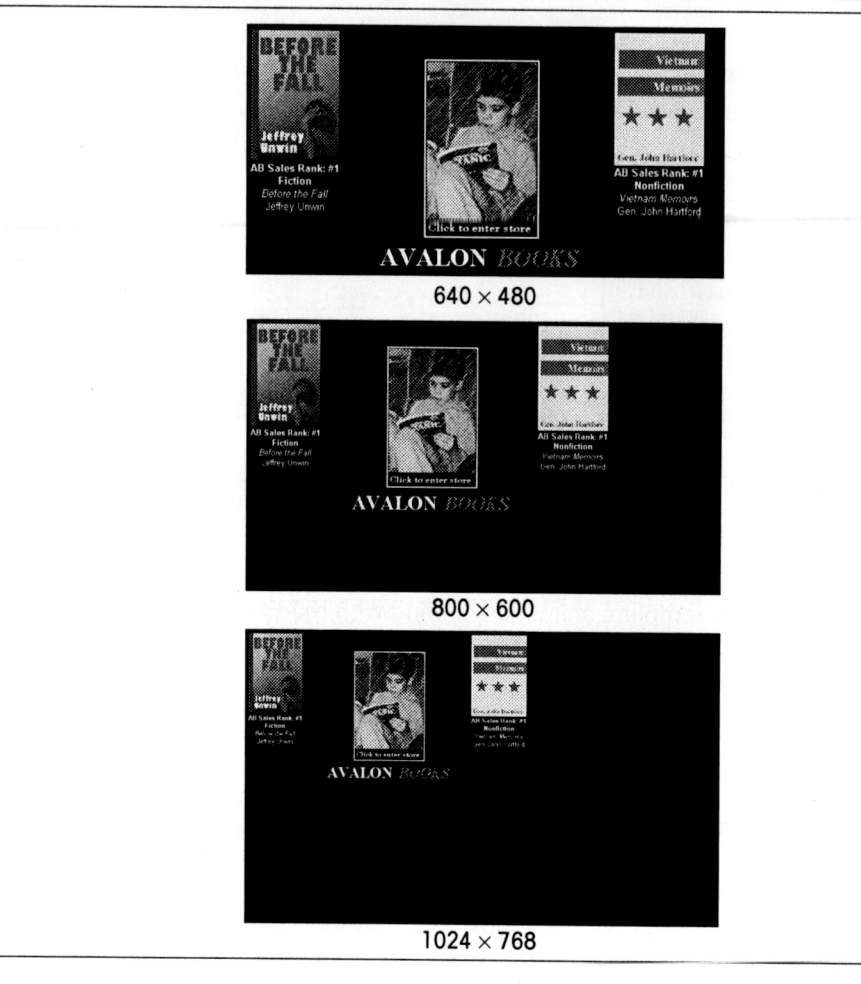

At sizes larger than 640 x 480, the images and text move progressively toward the upper-left corner of the display window. Terry would like to see the images remain in the center of the display window, both horizontally and vertically. Rather than create a different page for each monitor resolution, Terry suggests that you think of the objects as existing on a canvas that is 620 pixels wide by 300 pixels high. Every object would then be offset from the left and top edges of the window by a distance equal to the size of the border around this imaginary canvas. For example, if the dimensions of the display window are 760 x 560 pixels, the border width would be (760 – 620)/2 or 70 pixels, and the border height would be (560 – 300)/2 or 80 pixels (see Figure 4-24).

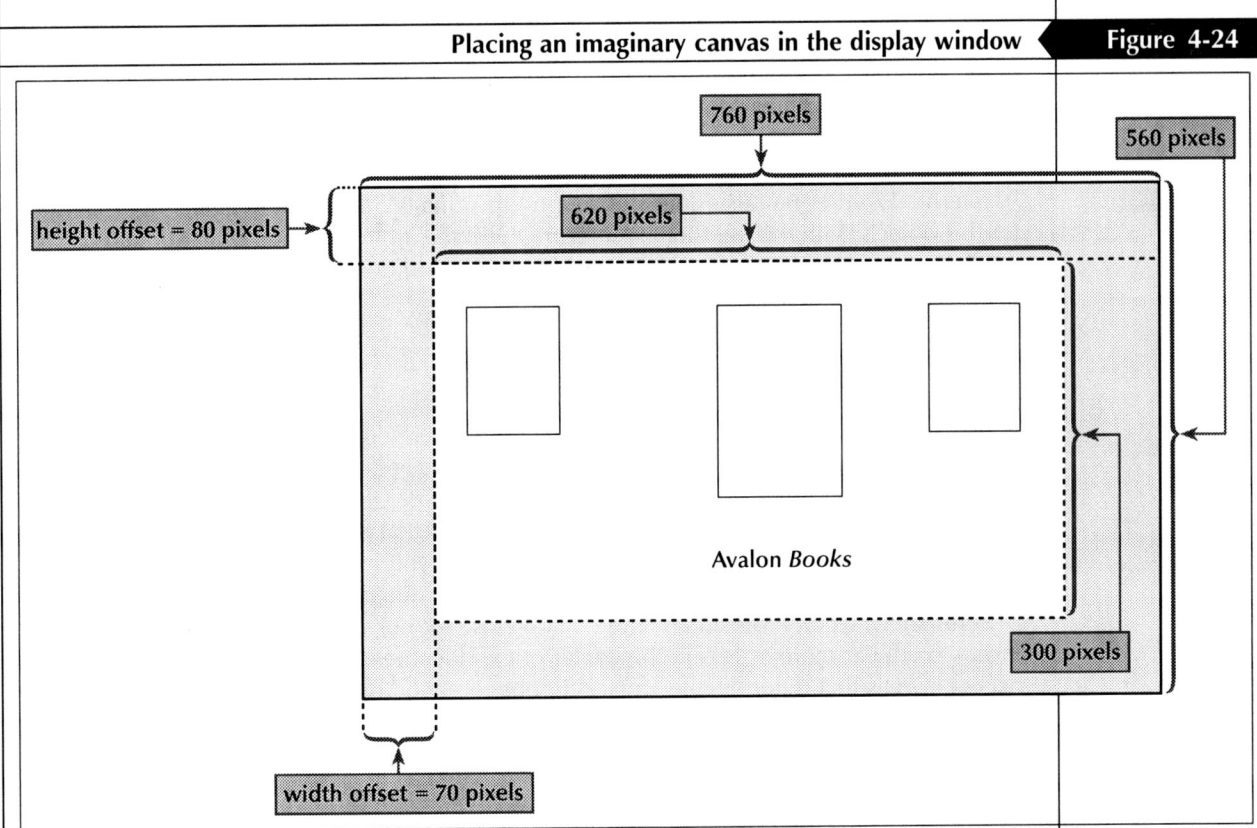

Placing an imaginary canvas in the display window **Figure 4-24**

Under Terry's proposal, if the width of the display window is W, then the space in the horizontal direction would be (W – 620)/2. If the height of the window is H, the space in the vertical direction would be (H – 300)/2. By adding these spaces to the current coordinates of each object, the display would be centered at any monitor resolution. However, to use this calculation, you first need to determine the width (W) and height (H) of the user's display window.

Calculating the Size of the Display Window

For the Level 1 and Level 2 W3C DOMs, the width and height of the browser window are stored in the properties

```
window.outerWidth
window.outerHeight
```

These values include the display window and the browser's toolbars, menus, and status bars. For our calculations, we want to exclude those elements. To determine the size of only the display window, without any other browser features, we can use the properties

```
window.innerWidth
window.innerHeight
```

However, no version of Internet Explorer supports these properties. For Internet Explorer 4.0 or Internet Explorer 5.0, the closest approximation is

```
document.body.clientWidth
document.body.clientHeight
```

The document.body reference is used in Internet Explorer 4.0 and 5.0 to refer to the size of the Web page body. In this case, the clientWidth and clientHeight properties return the document's width and height in pixels. However, the document.body reference is no longer supported in Internet Explorer 6.0 and has been replaced by the object reference document.documentElement.

Internet Explorer 6.0 also does not support the clientWidth and clientHeight properties for this object. With the Internet Explorer 6 DOM, the approximation of the document window size that gives the most reasonable answer and doesn't cause an error message in other browsers comes from the properties

```
document.documentElement.offsetWidth
document.documentElement.offsetHeight
```

In general, the values returned by the innerWidth/innerHeight properties in Netscape and the values returned by the offsetWidth/offsetHeight properties do not agree, although they are close. Currently, this is one of the headaches of DHTML for which there is no easy way of resolving the conflicts. The bottom line is that if you need to do precise work involving the dimensions of your document window, you must create a complicated script that accounts for cross-browser differences and quirks.

Fortunately, we don't need anything that precise for our page. Terry simply wants the layout to appear more or less in the center of the document window, and she's willing to accept layouts that differ by a few pixels in one direction or the other. With this in mind, you and Terry decide to add functions to the scripts.js file named winWidth() and winHeight() that calculate the size of the document window using the following approach:

1. If the window.innerWidth and window.innerHeight properties are supported, return those values.
2. Otherwise, if the browser supports the document.documentElement object, return the value of the document.documentElement.offsetWidth and document.documentElement.offsetHeight properties.
3. Otherwise, use the document.body.clientWidth and document.body.clientHeight properties, if they are supported.

You can be confident that this approach will return an acceptable answer in all browsers. The functions to calculate the window's width and height are therefore

```
function winWidth() {
    if (window.innerWidth) return window.innerWidth;
    else if (document.documentElement) return document.documentElement.
offsetWidth;
    else if (document.body.clientWidth) return document.body.
clientWidth;
}

function winHeight() {
    if (window.innerHeight) return window.innerHeight;
    else if (document.documentElement) return document.documentElement.
offsetHeight;
    else if (document.body.clientHeight) return document.body.
clientHeight;
}
```

Add these functions to the scripts.js file now.

To insert the winWidth() and winHeight() functions:

1. Open **scripts.js** in your text editor.

2. At the bottom of the file, insert the following code (see Figure 4-25):

```
function winWidth() {
    if (window.innerWidth) return window.innerWidth;
    else if (document.documentElement) return document.
 documentElement.offsetWidth;
    else if (document.body.clientWidth) return document.body.
clientWidth;
}


function winHeight() {
    if (window.innerHeight) return window.innerHeight;
    else if (document.documentElement) return document.
documentElement.offsetHeight;
    else if (document.body.clientHeight) return document.body.
clientHeight;
}
```

Trouble? Make sure that each else if statement is on a single line.

Inserting the winWidth() and winHeight() functions | **Figure 4-25**

```
function winwidth() {
    if (window.innerwidth) return window.innerwidth;
    else if (document.documentElement) return document.documentElement.offsetwidth;
    else if (document.body.clientwidth) return document.body.clientwidth;
}

function winHeight() {
    if (window.innerHeight) return window.innerHeight;
    else if (document.documentElement) return document.documentElement.offsetHeight;
    else if (document.body.clientHeight) return document.body.clientHeight;
}
```

3. Close the file, saving your changes.

Now you'll be able to use the winWidth() and winHeight() functions in your avalon.htm file. To calculate the values of the W and H variables, use the following code:

```
W=(winWidth()-620)/2;
H=(winHeight()-300)/2;
```

Declaring the W and H variables outside the functions gives them global scope, making them available for use within any of the functions that follow.

To modify the avalon.htm file:

1. Return to **avalon.htm** in your text editor.

2. Directly above the placeObjects() function, insert the following code (see Figure 4-26):

```
W=(winWidth()-620)/2;
H=(winHeight()-300)/2;
```

Figure 4-26 | **Creating the W and H variables**

```
W=(winWidth()-620)/2;
H=(winHeight()-300)/2;

function placeObjects() {
    placeIt("avalon", 175,10);
    placeIt("books",175,10);
    placeIt("ab",230,40);
    placeIt("fiction",5,5);
    placeIt("nfiction",475,5);
    hideIt("ab");
    hideIt("fiction");
    hideIt("nfiction");
    moveAvalon();
}
```

Next you have to add the W and H values to each coordinate in the placeObjects() function so that objects are placed in appropriate locations for all display windows.

To modify the coordinate values in the placeObjects() function:

1. In the placeObjects() function directly below the code you just entered, change the coordinates from (175, 10) to **(W+175, H+10)** for the avalon and books objects.

2. Change the coordinates for the ab object to **(W+230, H+40)**.

3. Change the coordinates for the fiction object to **(W+5, H+5)**.

4. Change the coordinates for the nfiction object to **(W+475, H+5)**.

   Figure 4-27 shows the revised placeObjects() function.

Figure 4-27 | **Final placeObjects() function**

```
function placeObjects() {
    placeIt("avalon", W+175,H+10);
    placeIt("books",W+175,H+10);
    placeIt("ab",W+230,H+40);
    placeIt("fiction",W+5,H+5);
    placeIt("nfiction",W+475,H+5);
    hideIt("ab");
    hideIt("fiction");
    hideIt("nfiction");
    moveAvalon();
}
```

You also need to change the value of the coordinates used to determine where to stop moving the Avalon and Books text.

To modify the moveAvalon() and moveBooks() functions:

1. Scroll down to the moveAvalon() function.

2. Change the text, "y <= 260" to **y <= H+260**.

3. Scroll down to the moveBooks() function.

4. Change the text, "x <= 320" to **x <= W+320**.

   Figure 4-28 shows the revised code in these functions.

Final moveAvalon() and moveBooks() functions ◄ Figure 4-28

```
function moveAvalon() {
    var y=yCoord("avalon");
    if (y <= H+260) {
        shiftIt("avalon",0,10);
        shiftIt("books",0,10);
        setTimeout("moveAvalon()",30);
    } else {
        moveBooks();
    }
}

function moveBooks() {
    var x=xCoord("books");
    if (x <= W+320) {
        shiftIt("books",10,0);
        setTimeout("moveBooks()",50);
    } else {
        showObjects();
    }
}
```

5. Close **avalon.htm**, saving your changes, and then reload the file in your browser and verify that the animation still works correctly.

6. If you have the capability of changing the resolution of your monitor, view the page under different screen sizes and verify that the page objects appear approximately in the center of the page each time. If you are using a large or high-resolution monitor, you can simply reduce the size of the browser window and reload the page to verify that the page contents recenter themselves.

Using Path Animation

The animation you created for the Avalon Books page is an example of **linear animation**, meaning that the animation takes place over a straight line, going from one point to the next (either down or to the right). Another type of animation is **path animation**, in which each set of coordinates in the path is entered into an array, and the animation moves from point to point. The path can be any shape, as shown in Figure 4-29.

Linear and path animations ◄ Figure 4-29

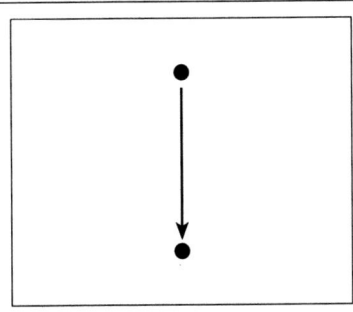

Linear animation proceeds in a straight line

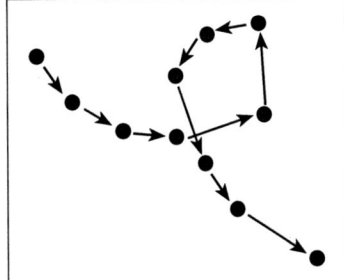

Path animation can jump to any coordinate on the page

To use path animation, you store the x- and y-coordinate values in arrays. This means you need to do the work of calculating all of the coordinate positions in your path. Once you enter the values into two arrays, you can retrieve the coordinates from the arrays, one coordinate at a time, until both arrays have been entirely read. The following sample shows code for a path animation:

```
x=new Array(0,40,80,120,200,300,400,300,150);
y=new Array(0,20,40,120,120,80,60,30,0);
index = 0;

function moveObject() {
    if (index <= x.length-1) {
        shiftIt("path_object", x[index], y[index]);
        index++;
        setTimeout("moveObject()", 10);
    }
}
```

In this example, an object named "path object" is moved from point to point following the x- and y-coordinate values in the x and y arrays. The index value is initially set to 0, to point to the first item in each array. Each time the object moves to a new location, the index value is increased by one using the increment operator (++). When the value of the index exceeds the length of the array minus one, as indicated by the property x.length-1, the path animation stops.

Why use the length of the array minus one, rather than the length of the array? Recall that the first array element has an index value of zero; therefore for an array with a length of n, the last array element has the array value n − 1.

For more interesting path animations, you can add a third array containing the delay times between each movement, rather than using the same delay time throughout.

You've completed your work on the Avalon Books opening Web page. Terry is going to have some other people in the design team review your work. She'll get back to you with any changes she wants you to make. You can close any open files now.

Working with Custom Objects

In this tutorial we learned how to work with some of JavaScript's built-in objects. However, JavaScript's support for objects, properties, and methods goes beyond what is found within your Web browser or Web page. You can also create your own class of objects. In some cases, creating an object to handle particular tasks or calculations can greatly expand your code's flexibility and power.

The new Operator

Objects can be created and defined using the **new operator**. The general syntax of the new operator is:

```
var obj = new object();
```

where *object* is the name of the object and *obj* is a variable that contains a specific example of the object. We refer to specific objects as **instances** of an object, while the general object itself is the object **class**. You've already worked with the new operator in previous tutorials where you created date objects and arrays using statements like:

```
var thisDate = new Date();
```

and

```
var monthName = new Month();
```

In those examples, thisDate and monthName were instances of the Date and Array class of objects. You can also create your own class of objects using the same new operator. For example, to create a class of objects for rectangles, you could enter the following statement:

```
var rectangle1 = new rect();
```

In this case, rect is the object class and rectangle1 is a particular instance of that object. Once an object has been created using the new operator, we can define properties and use those property values in our scripts.

Customized Properties

Properties are defined by using the same syntax we've used for JavaScript's built-in objects. Thus, to define the width and height of our rectangle object, we could run the following commands:

```
rectangle1.width = 6;
rectangle1.height = 4;
```

and the width and height properties would be added as a property of the rectangle1 object. We could use this property as we would any of the built-in JavaScript object properties. For example, to calculate the area of rectangle1, we could run the following command:

```
var area1 = rectangle1.width*rectangle1.height;
```

To display the width value in a Web page, we could run the command:

```
document.write("The width is: "+rectangle1.width);
```

and the text string "The width is: 6" would be written to the document. To change the value of rectangle1's width, you would just run another command referencing the width property, and so forth.

However, it is important to note that the width and height properties have only been defined for one instance of the rect object—the rectangle1 object. If you created a second rectangle object, rectangle2, it would not have either of those properties defined for it until you explicitly defined them in expressions like those used for rectangle1.

Object Constructors

For a more general class of objects that have built-in object properties, we have to create an object constructor. An **object constructor** is a function that defines the properties of a class of objects. The structure to create an object constructor is

```
var obj = new Object();

function Object() {
    properties
}
```

where *Object* is the name of the new object class and *properties* are commands which set the names of properties associated with the object class. Note that the name of the new object class is the same as the function which defines it. To set the object properties within the function, we use the JavaScript keyword this. The **this keyword** refers to the current object in the script, whatever that may be. In the case of object constructors, the current object is the object being created.

For example, to construct a customized rectangle object, we could run the following commands:

```
var rectangle1 = new rect();

function rect() {
    this.width;
    this.height;
}
```

Note that we haven't defined a value for the width and height properties, but that can be done after a specific instance of the rect object is created. So, to create a second rectangle, we would run the commands:

```
var rectangle2 = new rect();
rectangle.width = 5;
rectangle.height = 6;
```

We can also add parameters to the constructor function to both create the object and define its property values. For the rect object, this would appear as

```
function rect(w, h) {
    this.width = w;
    this.height = h;
}
```

Now, to define the dimensions of our rectangle, we could run the single command

```
var rectangle1 = new rect(6,4);
```

and the values of rectangle1.width and rectangle1.height would be automatically set by the object constructor.

Customized Methods

As you've seen in this tutorial, methods are actions associated with objects. Another way to say this is that methods are functions associated with objects. However, in JavaScript, functions are themselves considered objects (remember that *everything* is an object to JavaScript). Thus, to create a method for an object, we can associate a function with the object. The general syntax for associating a function with an object is

```
object.method = function;
```

where *object* is an object, *method* is the name of a method, and *function* is the name of a function. Once a method has been associated with an object, we can run it in the usual way:

```
object.method();
```

For example, let's create a function named calcArea() that calculates the area of an object given its width and height. The function is

```
function calcArea() {
    return this.width*this.height;
}
```

Note that this function once again uses the this keyword to refer to the current object being processed (whatever that may be). Now, let's associate this method with the rectangle1 object to create a method named "area":

```
rectangle1.area = calcArea;
```

Defining the area method doesn't run it, so we'll next apply the method, storing the calculated area in a variable:

```
var area1 = rectangle1.area();
```

If rectangle1 has the dimensions 6x4, the area1 variable will store the value 24. Once again, this method is only defined for the rectangle1 instance, not for the general class of rect objects. To make the area method a method for all rect objects, we have to add it to the constructor function. The complete code for the rect constructor function would look as follows:

```
function rect(w, h) {
    this.width = w;
    this.height = h;
    this.area = calcArea;
}
function calcArea() {
    return this.width*this.height;
}
```

Now we can use the rect object with a new rectangle. The following code creates a 7x4 rectangle object and calculates the area using the customized area method.

```
var rectangle3 = new rect(7, 4);
var area3 = rectangle3.area();
```

As you can see, by defining our own customized objects, properties, and methods, we've simplified our code greatly. We can also add to the constructor functions method to calculate the rectangle's perimeter or increase the rectangle's width or height by set amounts. While the rectangle object is a simple application of this technique, the general approach can be used for a wide range of complicated objects and features.

Tips for Working with JavaScript Objects

- If your code reuses the same object reference, store the object in a variable.
- Place your customized functions in external files so that they can be reused throughout your Web site.
- Use object detection to test the capabilities of browsers running your code. Provide workarounds for browsers that do not support your objects.
- Use path animation and create interesting visual effects by varying the path coordinates and delay times.
- Break up your animated effects into separate functions that call one another, preserving the sequence.
- Consider customized objects, properties, and methods to simplify your code.

Session 4.3 Quick Check

Review

1. What command would you enter to run the function moveGraphic() after a tenth-of-a-second delay?
2. What command would you enter to run the function moveGraphic() every tenth of a second, saving the time id for the command in a variable named "mg"?
3. What command would you enter to stop running the function you started in Question 2?
4. What W3C object property returns the height of the entire browser window?

5. What W3C object property returns the height of the browser window excluding the toolbars, menus, and status bars?
6. What is the difference between linear animation and path animation?
7. Provide the commands you would enter to construct an object class named circle. Provide the class of circle objects with a property named radius and a method named circum() that returns the circle's circumference (equal to 2*pi*radius.) Assume that the circle's radius can be set as a parameter named r of the constructor function.
8. Using the object constructor you defined in the previous question, create an instance of the circle object named circle1 with the circle's radius set to 5. Store the circumference in a variable named circum1.

Review

Tutorial Summary

In this tutorial you **were** introduced to the principles of DHTML and the document object model. The first session covered the history of the document object model and discussed the different types of DOMs supported by the browser market. The session then examined how objects are organized within the DOM and you can use JavaScript to access those objects. The session also examined how to work with object properties and object methods and showed how they can be used in a JavaScript program to apply different effects to a Web page and a user's browser. The second session introduced the style object and showed how you can apply CSS styles using JavaScript. The session then showed how to use this information to create simple functions for applying positioning styles to the objects on a Web page. In the third session, these functions were used to add a simple animation to a Web page. The session also covered how to work with event handlers and discussed the different types of event handlers available to programmers. In creating the animation, you learned how to work with timed-interval and time-delay commands, and you learned how to work with the width and height properties of the browser display window. The discussion on animation concluded with a look at linear and path animation. The tutorial finished with an overiew of customized objects, properties, and methods.

Key Terms

API	DOM	object class
application	DOM Level 0	object collection
programming	DOM Level 1	object constructor
interface	DOM Level 2	object detection
basic model	DOM Level 3	object instance
browser detection	dynamic HTML	object name
browser sniffer	linear animation	page branching
capture	method	path animation
cross-browser	new operator	property
DHTML	object	read-only
document object model	object-based language	this keyword

Review Assignments

Data files needed for this Review Assignment: ab.gif, ablogo.gif, abtxt2.htm, fiction.jpg, indextxt.htm, kids.jpg, nfiction.jpg, script2txt.js, styles2.css

Terry's design team has reviewed your page and recommended the following changes:

- Add a page, named index.htm, that supports older browsers. If a browser that doesn't support the W3C DOM is detected, this page should be loaded.
- Replace the animation on the Avalon Books page with one that moves the title "Avalon Books" from the left edge of the page to the center when the page opens. Also, the text "Books" should appear in a red italic font below and overlapping the text "Avalon," rather than appearing from behind.
- After moving the title, display the three image files kids.jpg, fiction.jpg, and nfiction.jpg in rotation below the title. The images should be stacked on top of each other, and every two seconds the top image in the stack should be moved to the bottom, and the other images should be moved up in the stack. This causes the images to appear to rotate, allowing viewers to see one at a time.

Figure 4-30 shows a preview of the page you'll create for Terry.

Figure 4-30

To create the new opening page for Avalon Books:

1. Use your text editor to open the **indextxt.htm** file from the tutorial.04/review folder. Enter *your name* and *the date* in the comment section and save the file as **index.htm**. Open the **script2txt.js** file from the same folder and enter *your name* and *the date* in the comment section. Save the file as **scripts2.js**. Open the **abtxt2.htm** file and enter *your name* and *the date* in the comment section. Save the file as **avalon2.htm**.
2. Go to the **index.htm** file. Below the title element, insert an embedded script that uses an if statement to test whether the browser supports the W3C DOM. (*Hint*: Use object detection with the document.getElementById object.) If the browser does support the DOM, have the browser load the avalon2.htm file using the href property of the location object.

3. Save your changes and close the file.

4. Go to the **scripts2.js** file and create a new function named setZ(). The function should have two parameters: id and z. The function should use the value of the id parameter to select the object in the document with that id value. It should then set the z-index of the object to the value of the z parameter.

5. Create a new function named swapIt(). The purpose of the swapIt() function is to swap the order of three overlapping objects on the page, moving the object on top to the bottom of the stack and then moving the other two objects up. The function should be created as follows:

   • The function should have three parameters named id1, id2, and id3 that contain the id values of the three objects.

   • Use the getObject() function to create three variables named object1, object2, and object3 that reference objects with id values of id1, id2, and id3.

   • Create three variables named z1, z2, and z3, setting these variables equal to the z-index values of object1, object2, and object3.

   • Change the z-index value of object1 to z3 (thus moving it to the bottom of the stack). Change the z-index value of object2 to z1 (moving it the top of the stack) and finally change the z-index value of object3 to z2 (moving it to the middle of the stack).

6. Save your changes to the file and close it.

7. Go to the **avalon2.htm** file in your text editor and, directly below the link to the styles2.css stylesheet, place a link to the **scripts2.js** file.

8. Below the link to the scripts2.js file, insert an embedded script.

9. Within the embedded script, insert a function named placeObjects(). The purpose of this function is to set the initial placement of the objects on the page. Have the function do the following:

   • Declare a variable named "W" that is equal to half of the value returned by the winWidth() function.

   • Use the placeIt() function to place the "avalon" object at the coordinates (0, 0).

   • Place the "kids", "fiction", and "nfiction" objects at the coordinates (W-75, 100).

   • Use the setZ() function to set the z-index value of the "kids" object to 3.

   • Set the z-index value of the "fiction" object to 2.

   • Set the z-index value of the "nfiction" object to 1.

   • Call the moveAvalon() function. (You'll create this function in the next step.)

10. Below the placeObjects() function, insert the moveAvalon() function. The purpose of the moveAvalon() function is to move the text "Avalon Books" across the page. Create the function as follows:

   • Create a variable named "x" that is equal to the x-coordinate of the "avalon" object. (*Hint*: Use the xCoord() function from the scripts2.js file.)

   • If x is less than or equal to the value of W minus 125, then do the following: (a) use the shiftIt() function from the scripts2.js file to move the "avalon" object 10 pixels to the right, and (b) call the moveAvalon() function again after a delay of 50 milliseconds.

   • If x is greater than W − 125, then run the swapImages() function. (You'll create this function next.)

11. Below the moveAvalon() function, insert the swapImages() function. The purpose of the swapImages() function is to change the stacking order of the three image objects. The function should do the following:
    - Use the showIt() function to unhide the "kids", "fiction", and "nfiction" objects.
    - Every two seconds, have the browser run the swapIt() function from the scripts2.js file to change the stacking order of the "kids", "fiction", and "nfiction" objects.
12. Add an onload event handler to the body element to run the placeObjects() function when the page is loaded.
13. Save your changes to **avalon2.htm**.
14. Load the **index.htm** file in your Web browser. Verify that the following occurs:
    - The page automatically loads the avalon2.htm file.
    - The avalon2.htm file starts with the text "Avalon Books" on the left edge of the page.
    - The text "Avalon Books" moves to the center of the page.
    - After "Avalon Books" reaches the center, the image file kids.jpg appears along with its caption.
    - Every two seconds thereafter, the image file is swapped with the next image file in the stack.
15. If you can, test the layout of your page at various monitor resolutions. Verify that the content appears horizontally centered at each resolution.
16. Submit the completed Web site to your instructor.

Case Problem 1

Data files needed for this Case Problem: ball.gif, ballpath.txt, clouds.jpg, golfer.gif, golftxt.htm, golftxt.js, styles.css

The Golf Page   Mark Reim, the owner of an online golf store called "The Golf Page," has asked you to create an animated opening screen for his Web site. Mark envisions a golf ball flying across the screen, from the top left down to the bottom of the screen, bouncing once, and then landing in the middle of the company name, taking the place of the letter "o" in "Golf."

Mark also wants the text "Your Online Source of Golf Equipment" to appear after the ball has landed. The text should appear with a font size of 0 points and then increase up to 20 points.

Functions that you can use in this Web page are stored in the golf.js file. One of the functions is named placeIt() and is used to place an object at a specified page coordinate. A second function named showIt() unhides a hidden object. Another text file available to you is the ballpath.txt file, which contains the coordinates of the flying ball relative to its final location on the page. Figure 4-31 shows a preview of the page you'll work with.

Apply

Use the skills you learned to create a Web page employing path animation

Figure 4-31

To create the animation for The Golf Page:

1. Use your text editor to open the **golftxt.htm** file from the tutorial.04/case1 folder. Enter *your name* and *the date* in the comment section and save the file as **golfpage.htm**. Take some time to study the contents of the file to become familiar with the objects and id values. Note that the company's slogan is located in a span element with the id name "slogan" and the image of the golf ball is located in a span element with the id name "Ball". Next, open the **golftxt.js** file from the same folder and enter *your name* and *the date* in the comment section. Save the file as **golf.js**.

2. Go to the **golf.js** file in your text editor. At the bottom of the file create a function named getFontSize(). The function should only have one parameter named "id" which represents the id value of an object in the document. Within the function, create a variable named object that represents the object with the specified id value; then, return the font size of the text in that object. Use the style object to retrieve the font size and use the parseInt() function to extract the numeric value of the font size only.

3. Below the getFontSize() function insert another function named setFontSize(). The purpose of this function is to set the font size for an object. We'll assume that all font sizes are expressed in points. The function should have two parameters: id (for the id value of the object) and fs (for the font size you want to apply to the object). In the first step of the function, create a variable named object that represents the object with the specified id value. In the second step of the function, set the font size of the object to the value of fs appended by the text string "pt" (to represent points).

4. Below the setFontSize() function insert a third function named changeFontSize(). The purpose of this function is to increase the font size by a specified amount. There are two parameters for this function: id and dfs. The id parameter contains the object's id value and the dfs parameter contains the amount by which the font size should be increased. In the function's first step, use the id parameter to call the getFontSize() function and retrieve the current font size of the object. Store the value in a variable named "fs". In the second step, use the id parameter again to call the setFontSize() function and set the new font size of the object to the value fs+dfs.

5. Close **golf.js**, saving your changes.

6. Go to the **golfpage.htm** file in your text editor. Directly below the link to the styles.css style sheet, create a link to the golf.js file.

7. Below the link to the golf.js script, insert an embedded script. Within the embedded script, paste the code found in the ballpath.txt file. The x array contains the x-coordinates of the flying ball. The y array contains the y-coordinates.

8. Below the array declaration, create a variable named "index", setting the initial value of the index to 0.

9. Below the index variable, create a function named "moveBall()". The purpose of the moveBall() function is to move the golf ball across the page until it stops at the location of the letter "o" in the word "golf." The moveBall() function should do the following:

   • Create an if statement to test whether the value of the index variable is less than or equal to the length of the x array minus 1. (*Hint:* The length of the x array can be determined using the expression: x.length.)

   • If the condition of the if statement is met, then (a) use the placeIt() function from the golf.js file to place the "Ball" object at the coordinates (x[index], y[index]); (b) increase the value of the index variable by 1; and (c) run the moveBall() function again after a five-millisecond delay.

   • Otherwise, do the following: (a) Use the setFontSize() function to set the font size of the "slogan" object to 0, (b) use the showIt() function to display the "slogan" object, and (c) run the growText() function. (You'll create this function next.)

10. Below the moveBall() function, insert the growText() function. The purpose of this function is to grow the text in the "slogan" object from 0 points up to 21 points. The function should contain the following steps:

    • Call the getFontSize() function using "slogan" as the parameter value to retrieve the current font size of the "slogan" object. Store the value in a variable named "fs".

    • Create an if statement that tests whether the value of the fs variable is less than or equal to 20.

    • If the condition is met, then (a) call the changeFontSize() function to increase the font size of the "slogan" object by 1, and (b) rerun the growText() function after a delay of 20 milliseconds.

11. Add an event handler to the body element to run the moveBall() function when the page is loaded.

12. Save your changes to the file.

13. Open the **golfpage.htm** file in your Web browser and verify that the ball flies across the page, landing in the title, appearing as the letter "o". Also verify that the slogan "Your Online Source of Golf Equipment" appears after the golf ball has landed and steadily grows in size. (Note: The animation will not run if you are using Internet Explorer for the Macintosh.)

14. Submit the completed Web site to your instructor.

Apply

Use the skills you earned to create a scrolling marquee

Case Problem 2

Data files needed for this Case Problem: back.jpg, ccc.gif, ccctxt.htm, ccctxt.js, styles.css

The Chamberlain Civic Center Laura Bromquist, the director of the Chamberlain Civic Center, has asked you to design a page listing the upcoming events at the center. Laura would like the page to display a marquee in which event names automatically scroll for the user. She would also like to give the user the ability to start and stop the marquee. A preview of the page you'll create is shown in Figure 4-32.

Figure 4-32

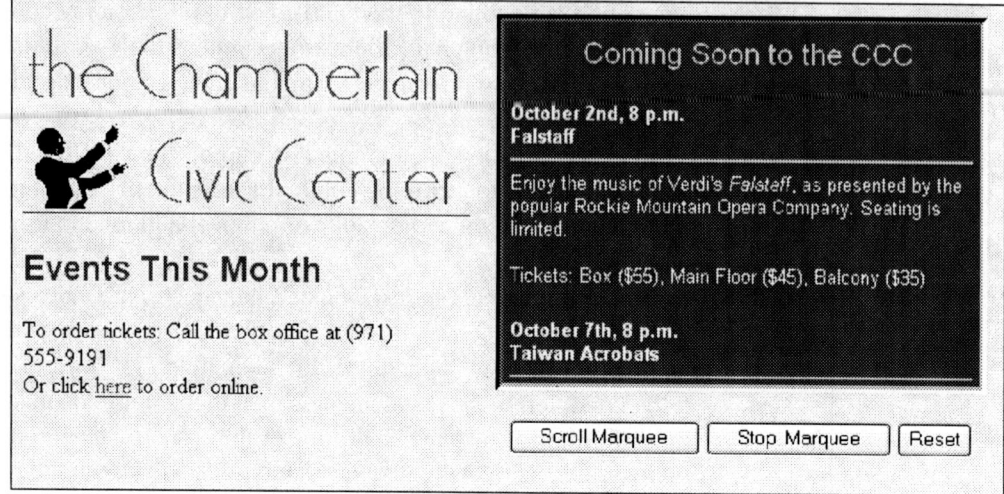

Much of the work in setting up the page has already been done for you. Your remaining task is to program the movements of the marquee.

To create the scrolling marquee:

1. Use your text editor to open the **ccctxt.js** file from the tutorial.04/case2 folder. Enter **your name** and **the date** in the comment section and save the file as **ccc.js**. Also open the **ccctxt.htm** file with your text editor. Enter **your name** and **the date** in the comment section and save the file as **ccc.htm**.

   Take some time to study the contents of the ccc.htm file to become familiar with the objects and id values. Note that the text of the marquee has been stored in a div element with the id "BOX" and that the marquee text is divided into six separate div elements with ids from "Text1" through "Text6". Each of the six div Text elements is positioned using absolute positioning and has a different value for the top coordinate. You'll change this value to create the marquee effect.

2. Go to the **ccc.js** file in your text editor. Create the following functions: placeIt() to place objects at a specified coordinate given the object's id, and values for the x and y coordinate (assume coordinates are measured in pixels); shiftIt() to shift an object a specified distance given the object's id and the distance to be shifted in the x and y direction; and yCoord() to return the numeric value of an object's top coordinate given the object's id (assume that coordinate is measured in pixels).

3. Close the file, saving your changes.

4. Go to the **ccc.htm** file in your text editor and insert a link to the ccc.js file directly below the link to the styles.css style sheet.

5. Below the link to the ccc.js file, insert an embedded script. Within the embedded script, create a function named moveIt(). The purpose of this function is to move an object vertically within the marquee. The moveIt() function should have a single parameter named "id" that indicates the id value of the object to be moved. Write the moveIt() function as follows:

   • Use the yCoord() function from the ccc.js file to retrieve the current y-coordinate of the id object. Store this coordinate value in a variable named "y".

- If the value of y is less than –100, use the placeIt() function from the ccc.js file to place the id object at the page coordinate (5, 750). This has the effect of dropping the id object back down to the beginning of the marquee.
- If the value of y is greater than or equal to –100, use the shiftIt() function from the ccc.js file to move the id object up 5 pixels. This has the effect of moving the object back up the marquee.

6. Above the moveIt(id) function, create a function named "Marquee()". This function will be used to start the marquee text moving for all six text objects. The Marquee() function should do the following:

- Run the moveIt() function every 130 milliseconds with the value of the id parameter set to "Text1". This has the effect of continuously moving the text contained in the Text1 object. Store the time id for this command in a variable named "t1".
- Also run the moveIt() function every 130 milliseconds for the objects "Text2" through "Text6". Store the value of the time ids for these commands in variables named "t2" through "t6".

7. Below the Marquee() function, create a function named Stop(). This function should halt the marquee text by clearing the time interval commands for the time ids t1 through t6.

8. Locate the button labeled Scroll Marquee and add an onclick event handler to run the Marquee() function when the button is clicked.

9. Locate the button labeled Stop Marquee and add an onclick event handler to run the Stop() function when it's clicked.

10. Locate the reset button and add an onclick event handler to reload the current page when the button is clicked. (*Hint*: Use the reload() method of the location object.)

11. Save your changes to the file and open the page in your Web browser. Verify that when you click the Scroll Marquee button, the marquee starts scrolling vertically from bottom to top; when you click the Stop Marquee button, the movement stops; and when you click the Reset button, the scrolling stops and the listings return to their original position.

12. Submit the completed Web site to your instructor.

Challenge

Explore how to create an animated trail map using object properties and methods

Case Problem 3

Data files needed for this Case Problem: button.gif, path.txt, photo2.jpg-photo8.jpg, redball.gif, text1.gif-text9.gif, trail.css, trail.gif, trail.js, trailtxt.htm

Chiricahua National Monument Located in southeastern Arizona, the Chiricahua National Monument is a wilderness area containing the remnants of volcanic mountains rising between 5000 and 8000 feet above the surrounding grasslands. The park's unusual rock formations and beautiful spires make it a favorite spot of hikers and birders. The rangers at the Chiricahua National Monument have asked you to help them create an animated trail map that will highlight some of the most striking features of the area. They hope that by creating an animated map, more people will be encouraged to visit and enjoy the trails at Chiricahua. When completed, the map will be made available on the Web and at kiosks in the visitors' center. Figure 4-33 shows a preview of the map that you'll work on.

Figure 4-33

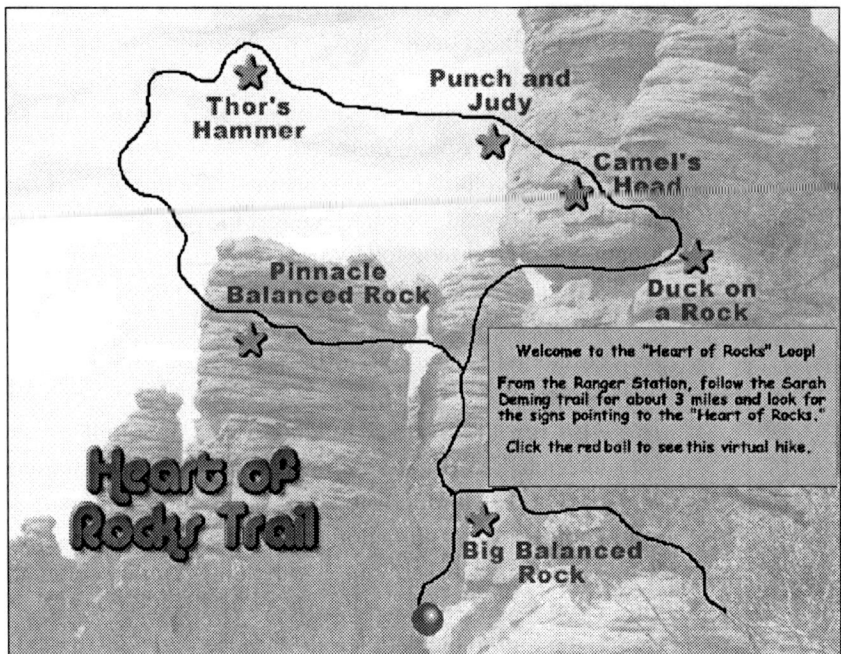

Much of the design work on the map has already been done. Another employee at Chiricahua has created all of the graphic images required for the map, including image files that display text descriptions of nine landmarks along the trail. For six of these landmarks, the employee has also scanned a photo of a rock formation or spire. The text descriptions are stored in graphic files named "text1.gif" through "text9.gif". The corresponding photo images are stored in files named "photo2.jpg" through "photo8.jpg" (there are no photos for the first and ninth landmarks).

For the animated map, the rangers would like a red ball to move along the Heart of Rocks Trail, stopping at each of the nine landmarks. At each landmark, the browser should display the corresponding text description and, if one exists for that landmark, the corresponding photo. Clicking the red ball should cause it to start moving again to the next landmark. After the red ball has reached the last landmark, the page should reload back to its original conditions after a delay of seven seconds.

A script file has already been created for you that contains functions for moving and placing an object on the Web page. The coordinates of the trail have been stored in two arrays in a text file. Your job is to write the program code that uses the functions and these coordinates to create the red ball animation.

To create the animated trail map:

1. Use your text editor to open the **trailtxt.htm** file from the tutorial.04/case3 folder. Enter *your name* and *the date* in the comment section and save the file as **trail.htm**. Take some time to study the contents of the file. There are nine landmarks on the trail with each trail description and photo located in a separate div element. Figure 4-34 lists the div elements for the photos, along with the text description of each landmark. Note that some landmarks contain only text descriptions and not photos. Also take some time to study the contents of the trail.js file. Note that it includes three functions: placeIt(), showIt(), and hideIt(). You should now be familiar with the purpose of these functions.

Figure 4-34

Landmark	Text	div Elements
1	A Welcome Message	text1
2	The Big Balanced Rock	text2, photo2
3	Duck on a Rock	text3, photo3
4	The Camel's Head	text4, photo4
5	Punch and Judy	text5, photo5
6	Thor's Hammer	text6, photo6
7	The Pinnacle Balanced Rock	text7, photo7
8	The Big Balanced Rock	text8, photo8
9	An Exit Message	text9

2. Below the link to the trail.css style sheet, insert a link to the trail.js script file.

3. Below the link to the trail.js script file, insert an embedded script element. Copy and paste the arrays in the path.txt file into this script element. The xArray contains the x-coordinates of the trail path and the yArray contains the y-coordinates. Each array contains a total of 270 values, marking out 270 distinct points along the trail.

4. Directly below the yArray variable, declare a variable named "index". The index variable will be used to track the position of the red ball as it moves through the trail. Set the initial value of the index variable to 1.

5. Directly below the statement that declares the index variable, create the hideAll() function. The hideAll() function will ensure that all text and photo objects on the screen are hidden as the red ball travels around the trail. To create this effect, have the function hide each of the div elements with ids text1 through text9 and photo2 through photo8. (*Hint*: Use the hideIt() function from the trail.js file.)

Explore

6. Below the hideAll() function, create the describeIt() function, which will display the text description and photo for a given landmark. The describeIt() function should have two parameters, named text and photo, containing the id values of the text and photo to be displayed. Use the showIt() function from the trail.js file to display the text object. Since not every landmark has a photo, use object detection to determine whether a div element with the value of the photo parameter exists and if it does call the showIt() function to display the photo.

Explore

7. Below the describeIt() function, create the runPath() function. The runPath() function will move the red ball along the hiking trail, stopping if the red ball encounters one of the nine landmarks. The runPath() function should do the following:

   • Call the hideAll() function to ensure that all text and photos are hidden on the page.

   • Increase the value of the index variable by 1.

   • Use the placeIt() function to place the "redBall" object at the (xArray[index], yArray[index]) coordinate.

   • Use a switch statement to test the different values of the index variable. If the index variable equals 0, call the describeIt() function with the text parameter equal to "text1". This causes the red ball to stop and display the text description for the first landmark. You do not have to supply a value for the photo parameter. Be sure to include a break statement so that the program stops after running this command. If the index variable equals 16, call the describeIt() function with the text parameter equal to "text2" and the photo parameter equal to "photo2".

- Continue adding case statements for the remaining landmarks. The third landmark should be displayed when the index variable equals 68. The fourth landmark corresponds to an index value of 82. The fifth landmark matches an index value of 97. The sixth landmark corresponds to an index value of 130. The seventh landmark appears when the index value equals 188. The eighth landmark is displayed when the index value equals 231. Make sure that you include a break statement after each case statement.
- If the index variable equals 269, do the following in the case statement: (a) call the describeIt() function with "text9" as the parameter value, (b) set the value of the index variable to 0, and (c) reload the Web page after a seven-second delay. Be sure to place a break at the end of this case statement.
- If the value of the index variable matches none of the case statements, the default behavior is to call the runPath() function again after a tenth-of-a-second delay. This will have the effect of continuing the red ball's trip through the hiking trail until it reaches one of the nine landmarks.

Explore

8. Locate the div element for the red ball. Mark the redball.gif inline image as a link and set the href attribute of the link to run the runPath() function when the ball is clicked.
9. Save your changes to the file.
10. Open the Web page in your browser and click on the red ball image. The red ball should move to the Big Balanced Rock landmark and display a text description and photo of the formation. There should be no descriptions or photos displayed as the red ball moves. To move to the next landmark on the trail, click the red ball again. Verify that the red ball traverses the entire trail, displaying photos and descriptions at each landmark. When you reach the end of the trail, the page should reload after a delay of seven seconds. (Note: If you are using Internet Explorer for the Macintosh you will see a blue border around the red ball image.)
11. Submit the completed Web site to your instructor.

Create

Test your knowledge of objects and animation by creating an animated Web page

Case Problem 4

Data files needed for this Case Problem: bug.jpg, bug.txt, bugdead.jpg, shoe.jpg

The Exterminators   The Exterminators is a pest control company that specializes in the removal of insects, rodents, and small animals from urban homes and offices. Bruce Feinman has asked you to create a Web site for his company. He would like to have an opening screen in which a small bug flies around the page, only to be squashed. After the opening animation, he would like information about the company to appear on the page. Bruce provides you with the following files:

- bug.jpg, a clip art image of a bug
- bugdead.jpg, a clip art image of a squashed bug
- shoe.jpg, a clip art image of a giant shoe print
- bug.txt, a text file describing Bruce's company

You may supplement these files with any additional materials available to you. The final design of the Web site is up to you, but it must include the following features:

1. If a viewer's browser doesn't support DHTML, an index.htm file should appear that is static but informative.
2. If a customer's browser supports DHTML, use page branching to send the user from the index.htm file to an animated page named bug.htm.

3. Integrate at least one example of each of the following techniques into the bug.htm file:
   - Positioning with JavaScript
   - Linear animation
   - Path animation
   - Unhiding objects
   - The setTimeout or the setInterval method
4. Submit the completed Web site to your instructor.

Quick Check Answers

Session 4.1

1. The document object model is the organized structure of objects and events within a document. The three main DOMs used by the browser market are the W3C DOMs, the Internet Explorer DOM, and the Netscape 4 DOM.
2. the history object
3. document.forms
4. The IE DOM uses the document.all.*id* object and the W3C DOMs use document.getElementById("*id*") where *id* is the id value.
5. document.images[0].src="logo.jpg"
6. navigator.appName
7. window.print()
8. Object detection tests whether the browser supports a particular object. If the browser supports the object reference, then it most likely supports the DOM. You can test for support of the Netscape 4 DOM using the document.layers object reference. To test for support of the IE DOM, use document.all. To test for support of the W3C DOMs, use document.getElementById.

Session 4.2

1. getElementById("Logo").style.zIndex = getElementById("Logo").style.zIndex+1;
2. getElementById("Logo").style.left = "150px";
3. getElementById("Logo").style.top = "350px";
4. getElementById("Logo").style.visibility = "hidden";
5. getElementById("Logo").style.width = "100px";
6. getElementById("Logo").style.clip = "rect(10 210 150 10)";
7. getElementById("Logo").style.overflow = "auto";
8. document.all("Logo").style.pixelLeft=150;
9. document.all("Logo").style.pixelTop=350;

Session 4.3

1. setTimeout("moveGraphic()", 100);
2. mg = setInterval("moveGraphic()", 100);
3. clearInterval(mg);
4. window.outerHeight
5. window.innerHeight
6. In linear animation, you add or subtract a fixed value to change the coordinates of the object. In path animation, the coordinates are retrieved from an array of coordinate values.

```
7. function circle(r) {
       this.radius = r;
       this.circum = calcCircum;
   }

   function calcCircum() {
       return 2*Math.Pi*this.radius;
   }
8. var circle1 = new circle(5):
   var circum1 = circle1.circum();
```

Objectives

Session 5.1
- Understand how to work with the JavaScript document. images collection
- Create image objects and image object arrays
- Set the properties of image objects
- Create image rollovers with image objects and the document.images collection
- Understand how to create text rollovers

Session 5.2
- Understand how to work with pop-up, pull-down, tabbed, and sliding menus
- Hide and unhide objects in a Web page

Session 5.3
- Understand and implement Internet Explorer's filter styles
- Understand and apply Internet Explorer's transition styles
- Create an interpage transition using the meta element

Working with Special Effects

Creating Rollovers, Menus, Filters, and Transitions

Case

The World of Shakespeare

Clare Daynes is a professor of English literature at MidWest University. One of Clare's areas of research is the writings of William Shakespeare. In conjunction with her work, Clare is creating a site on the World Wide Web containing the complete works of Shakespeare. The site will include several tools of interest to researchers, including a search engine to locate particular words or phrases from Shakespeare's plays.

Clare has asked for your help in designing the Web site. She wants the site to have a user-friendly interface, and also some visual impact. She has seen sites on the Web that employ special effects such as rollovers and pop-up menus to aid in navigation. She would like to see these elements added to her site. She also wonders whether there are other special effects that can be added to her site.

Clare wants the page to load quickly, so she doesn't want any large multimedia files or applets attached to the site. Thus, she hopes you can create an interesting site using only JavaScript.

Student Data Files

▼tutorial.05

▽ **tutorial folder**

    playstxt.htm
    wstxt.htm
    scripts.js
    styles1.css
    styles2.css
    + 2 demo files
    + 17 graphic files

▽ **review folder**

    temptxt.htm
    linktest.htm
    scripts.js
    plays.css
    + 14 graphic files

▽ **case1 folder**

    housetxt.htm
    premier.css
    + 18 graphic files

Student Data Files

▼**tutorial.05 continued**

▽case2 folder
- tilestxt.htm
- tiles.js
- games.css
- + 10 graphic files

▽case3 folder
- printtxt.htm
- je.css
- + 28 graphic files

▽case4 folder
- lp.txt
- ps.txt
- sm.txt
- + 7 graphic files

Session 5.1

Working with Image Objects

You and Clare sit down to discuss the current state of her Web site. She shows you the opening page, shown in Figure 5-1. This page contains graphical links to five different pages, covering the following topics: Shakespeare's plays, his sonnets, his biography, the Globe Theatre, and the town of Stratford-upon-Avon. Open this page now.

To open the Shakespeare Web page:

1. Use your text editor to open **wstxt.htm** from the tutorial.05/tutorial folder. Enter ***your name*** and ***the date*** in the comment section and save the file as **ws.htm**.
2. Scroll through the document to familiarize yourself with its layout and its HTML code.
3. Open **ws.htm** in your Web browser. Figure 5-1 shows the current appearance of the page.

Figure 5-1 The World of Shakespeare opening page

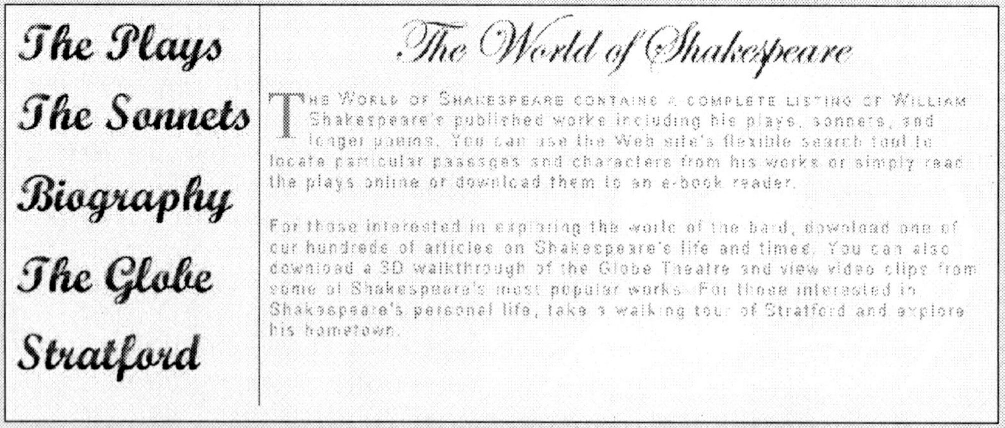

The first addition that Clare would like you to create is a rollover effect, so that as users move the pointer over each of the five links, the graphic image changes. Clare suggests that you add a red drop shadow to each graphic image as the pointer moves over the link (see Figure 5-2). She feels that the addition of this effect will give the page visual interest, as well as give a tangible clue that the pointer is currently over a link.

Using a rollover effect | Figure 5-2

as the pointer moves over the image, the image changes to one containing a colored drop shadow

To create a rollover effect for Clare's page, you first have to study how JavaScript can be used to create and manage images.

Referencing an Inline Image

Support for images is one of the oldest technologies in JavaScript, incorporated in the Level 0 document object model. (For a discussion of the different DOMs, see Tutorial 4.) Each inline image is part of an array of images in the document called the **image collection**. The image collection follows the same reference syntax used for other object collections. To reference a particular image in the document you can use either of the following forms:

```
document.images[idref]
document.images.idref
```

where *idref* is either an index number representing the position of the image in the array of all images in the document, or the text of the id or name attribute assigned to the image. As with arrays, the first image in the document has an index number of 0. For example, if the first inline image is

```
<img name="logo" id="logo" src="logo.jpg" alt="WS Page" />
```

you can reference this image using any of the following:

```
document.images[0]
document.images["logo"]
document.images.logo
```

Note that the id or name attribute must be placed in quotes. You can also bypass the document.images collection entirely and rely solely on the id attribute using the getElementById() method, which was discussed in the previous tutorial. In that case you could reference this image using the form

```
document.getElementById("logo")
```

Finally, many browsers also recognize the form

```
document.name
```

where *name* is the value of the name attribute for the inline image. However, since the name attribute has been deprecated in favor of the id attribute, it's generally safer to use the document.images object collection.

While the id and name attributes may seem to serve the same function of providing a unique identifier for an image, you should still use both of them in your HTML code (with their attribute values set to the same value). This is to provide backward-compatibility with earlier browser versions, which may not recognize the id attribute, but will recognize the name attribute. If you're writing code to be compliant with strict XHTML, you should use only the id attribute.

Reference Window

Referencing an Inline Image

- To reference an inline image, use the object collection
  ```
  document.images[idref]
  ```
  where *idref* is either the index number of the image object, or the text of its id or name attribute (enclosed in quotes). Note that the first inline image in the document has an index number of 0.
- You can also reference an inline image using the form
  ```
  document.getElementById(id)
  ```
  where *id* is the value of the id attribute for the inline image.
- Other browsers also support the reference form
  ```
  document.name
  ```
  where *name* is the value of the name attribute for the inline image.

Figure 5-3 shows the object references for the five inline images on the Shakespeare page. You'll be using this image collection to refer to individual images when you create the image rollovers later, so you'll need to keep this information in mind. Background images are not part of the images collection because they are not treated as inline images in the document. Also note that the index numbers refer to the order in which the <img> tags appear in an HTML file, not how the images are presented on the rendered Web page.

Figure 5-3   Images in the Shakespeare page

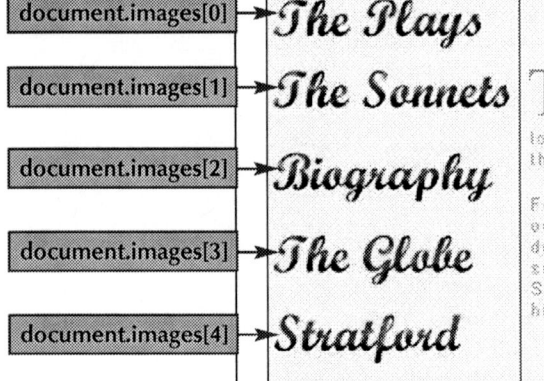

document.images[0] → *The Plays*
document.images[1] → *The Sonnets*
document.images[2] → *Biography*
document.images[3] → *The Globe*
document.images[4] → *Stratford*

Creating an Image Object

JavaScript treats all inline images as objects known as **image objects**. You can also use JavaScript to create new image objects that are not part of a document but can be stored in the browser memory for use in your program. The syntax to create a new image object is

```
image = new Image(width, height);
```

where *image* is the variable that you'll use to store in the image object, and *width* and *height* are optional values specifying the width and height of the image in pixels. If you don't specify a width and height, the image object is sized to match the dimensions of whatever graphic file is stored in the image. Notice that the image object does not support a parameter for specifying the source of the image object. To provide this information you need to modify the properties of the image object itself.

Creating an Image Object

Reference Window

- To create an image object, use the syntax
    ```
    image = new Image(width, height);
    ```
  where *image* is the variable name you give the image object, and *width* and *height* are optional values specifying the width and height of the image in pixels. If you don't specify a width and height, the image object is sized to match the dimensions of the graphic file.
- To specify the source for an image object, use the property
    ```
    image.src = "url";
    ```
  where *image* is the image object and *url* is the URL of the image's graphic file.

Properties of Image Objects

Like all objects, image objects have properties that determine how they appear and how they are used by the browser. Most of these properties will be very familiar to you since they are derived from the attributes associated with inline images in HTML. Figure 5-4 summarizes some of the properties of image objects.

Figure 5-4	Properties of the image object

Property	Description	Example
alt	Alternate text displayed by non-graphical browsers	document.images[5].alt = "The World of Shakespeare";
border	The size of the image border in pixels	document.images.[0].border = 0;

complete	A Boolean value indicating whether the image has been completely loaded by the browser	if (document.images[0].complete) {
		    commands to run
		}

height	The height of the image in pixels	document.images[0].height = 50;
hspace	The horizontal space around the image in pixels	document.images[0].hspace = 10;
id	The id of the image object	document.images[5].id = "logo";
lowsrc	The URL of a low resolution version of the image	document.images[5].lowsrc = "logo_small.jpg";
name	The name of the image object	document.images[5].name = "logo";
src	The URL of the graphic image to be displayed in the image object	document.images[5].src = "logo.jpg";
vspace	The vertical space around the image in pixels	document.images[0].vspace = 10;
width	The width of the image in pixels	document.images[0].width = 100;

For example, to create an image object and then define its source, you would use the src property, as in the following set of commands:

```
var newImage = new Image();
newImage.src = "logo.jpg";
```

When run, these commands create the newImage image object and then store the source file, logo.jpg, as part of its definition. In addition to the properties listed in Figure 5-4, you can also use the style property discussed in Tutorial 4 to modify the appearance of an image object as it appears in your Web browser. Thus, if you wanted to set the border size around the image to 5 pixels, you could use either of the following JavaScript commands:

```
newImage.border = "5px";
newImage.style.borderWidth = "5px";
```

Because the border property is derived from HTML's deprecated border attribute, you may wish to use the style property to keep your code consistent with current HTML and XHTML standards.

Note that older browsers such as Netscape 4 do not allow you to modify the appearance of an inline image once your browser has loaded it. For example, you cannot change the dimensions of an image by modifying its height and width properties. Netscape 4 allows you to do this only before the page has been loaded. Current browsers, on the other hand, make all of the attributes of an inline image available to you to modify at any time. Thus, if you're writing a script in which the appearance of an inline image is to be modified by the users' browsers, you should be aware that your code might not work correctly for users of older browser versions.

Detecting Image Objects

It is possible (though not likely) that your users will be running a very early browser version that does not support JavaScript's treatment of image objects. If this is a concern, you can use object detection to determine each user's level of browser support. The following structure tests for support of the document.images object and then runs a command block if that support is detected:

```
if (document.images) {
    Command block to create and modify images
}
```

If a user is running an older browser that doesn't support the images object collection, the value of document.images is false, and the command block that follows is skipped. Such users will still be able to use the Web site, but they won't see the image rollovers. Browsers that do support the document.images object collection will run the command block.

Creating an Image Rollover

An **image rollover** is created when you change the source of an inline image from one graphic file to another, usually in response to the mouse pointer hovering over and then leaving the image. Clare shows you a collection of images and alternate images to be used in the Web page, as shown in Figure 5-5. When the user hovers the mouse pointer over an image, the browser should load the corresponding image from the right column in Figure 5-5. When the mouse pointer moves off the image, the corresponding image from the left column in Figure 5-5 should be redisplayed.

Rollover images — Figure 5-5

image	rollover image
The Plays plays_out.jpg	*The Plays* plays_over.jpg
The Sonnets son_out.jpg	*The Sonnets* son_over.jpg
Biography bio_out.jpg	*Biography* bio_over.jpg
The Globe globe_out.jpg	*The Globe* globe_over.jpg
Stratford strat_out.jpg	*Stratford* strat_over.jpg

Preloading the Images

Performance is an important consideration when creating a rollover effect. You do not want users to have to wait while their browsers download the new images. To avoid this problem, you can preload all of the image objects a user may need, storing the images in the browser's memory. When the browser invokes the rollover effect, the new image file is then quickly retrieved from memory rather than going through a process of loading the graphic file. Thus, all of the loading of image objects is done when the document is initially loaded by the browser.

In cases where you apply rollover effects to several images on a page, it is often more efficient to store your image objects in arrays. The following is a typical example:

```
var ImgOver = new Array();
ImgOver[0] = new Image();
ImgOver[1] = new Image();
ImgOver[2] = new Image();
```

With the image objects in arrays, you can reference them in your program using their array index numbers rather than with distinct variable names. In Clare's page, you need to create five pairs of image objects. Place these images in two image object arrays, named ImgOver and ImgOut. In addition, add an object test to ensure that the browser supports the document.images object collection.

To create the ImgOver and ImgOut image arrays:

1. Above the closing </head> tag, insert the following embedded script (see Figure 5-6):

```
<script type="text/javascript">
if (document.images) {
    var ImgOver = new Array();
    ImgOver[0] = new Image();
    ImgOver[1] = new Image();
    ImgOver[2] = new Image();
    ImgOver[3] = new Image();
    ImgOver[4] = new Image();


    var ImgOut = new Array();
    ImgOut[0] = new Image();
    ImgOut[1] = new Image();
    ImgOut[2] = new Image();
    ImgOut[3] = new Image();
    ImgOut[4] = new Image();
}
</script>
```

Creating the ImgOver and ImgOut arrays ◄ Figure 5-6

```
<link href="styles1.css" rel="stylesheet" type="text/css" />
<script type="text/javascript">
if (document.images) {
   var ImgOver = new Array();
   ImgOver[0] = new Image();
   ImgOver[1] = new Image();
   ImgOver[2] = new Image();
   ImgOver[3] = new Image();
   ImgOver[4] = new Image();

   var ImgOut = new Array();
   ImgOut[0] = new Image();
   ImgOut[1] = new Image();
   ImgOut[2] = new Image();
   ImgOut[3] = new Image();
   ImgOut[4] = new Image();
}
</script>
</head>
```

► **2.** Save your changes to the file.

Next, you have to specify the graphic file for each of these image objects. For the objects in the ImgOver array, you'll use the graphic files specified in the right column of Figure 5-5. For objects in the ImgOut array, you'll use the graphic files from the left column in Figure 5-5.

To populate the ImgOver and ImgOut arrays:

► **1.** Before the command to create the ImgOut array, insert the following commands to specify the source for the ImgOver objects:

```
ImgOver[0].src = "plays_over.jpg";
ImgOver[1].src = "son_over.jpg";
ImgOver[2].src = "bio_over.jpg";
ImgOver[3].src = "globe_over.jpg";
ImgOver[4].src = "strat_over.jpg";
```

► **2.** Before the closing curly brace, insert the source for the ImgOut objects.

```
ImgOut[0].src = "plays_out.jpg";
ImgOut[1].src = "son_out.jpg";
ImgOut[2].src = "bio_out.jpg";
ImgOut[3].src = "globe_out.jpg";
ImgOut[4].src = "strat_out.jpg";
```

Figure 5-7 shows the revised ws.htm file.

Figure 5-7

Specifying sources for the ImgOut and ImgOver arrays

```
if (document.images) {
    var ImgOver = new Array();
    ImgOver[0] = new Image();
    ImgOver[1] = new Image();
    ImgOver[2] = new Image();
    ImgOver[3] = new Image();
    ImgOver[4] = new Image();
    ImgOver[0].src = "plays_over.jpg";
    ImgOver[1].src = "son_over.jpg";
    ImgOver[2].src = "bio_over.jpg";
    ImgOver[3].src = "globe_over.jpg";
    ImgOver[4].src = "strat_over.jpg";

    var ImgOut = new Array();
    ImgOut[0] = new Image();
    ImgOut[1] = new Image();
    ImgOut[2] = new Image();
    ImgOut[3] = new Image();
    ImgOut[4] = new Image();
    ImgOut[0].src = "plays_out.jpg";
    ImgOut[1].src = "son_out.jpg";
    ImgOut[2].src = "bio_out.jpg";
    ImgOut[3].src = "globe_out.jpg";
    ImgOut[4].src = "strat_out.jpg";
}
```

Swapping Image Objects

Once the images are preloaded, you can use JavaScript to swap the source for one image with the source for another. When you place image objects in arrays, you can match the array of image objects with the array of inline images in the document.images collection. For example, the command

```
document.images[0].src = ImgOver[0].src
```

replaces the source of the first inline image in the document with the source of the first image object in the ImgOver array. A more general function to do this would be

```
function RollOver(i) {
    if (document.images) document.images[i].src = ImgOver[i].src;
}
```

where the i parameter indicates which objects in the two arrays should be swapped. Note that you use object detection again to verify that the browser supports image objects before attempting to do the swap. A similar function would swap the images in the document.images collection with the images in the ImgOut array:

```
function RollOut(i) {
    if (document.images) document.images[i].src = ImgOut[i].src;
}
```

Add these two functions to the embedded script element in Clare's Web page.

To add the RollOver() and RollOut() functions to the file:

1. Before the closing </script> tag, enter the following commands (see Figure 5-8):

```
function RollOver(i) {
    if (document.images) document.images[i].src = ImgOver[i].src;
}
function RollOut(i) {
    if (document.images) document.images[i].src = ImgOut[i].src;
}
```

The RollOver() and RollOut() functions | Figure 5-8

```
function RollOver(i) {
    if (document.images) document.images[i].src = ImgOver[i].src;
}

function RollOut(i) {
    if (document.images) document.images[i].src = ImgOut[i].src;
}

</script>
</head>
```

2. Save your changes to the file.

Running the Image Rollover

To run the two functions you just created you'll use event handlers. Recall from Tutorial 2 that event handlers specify the commands that should be run in response to an event occurring within an element. In this case, you'll use two event handlers: onmouseover and onmouseout. When the mouse pointer hovers over the image, the onmouseover event handler is used to run the RollOver() function. When the mouse pointer moves off of the image, the onmouseout event handler is used to run the RollOut() function. You'll attach these two event handlers to each of the five images in the list of links on the Shakespeare home page. The parameter values for the RollOver() and RollOut() functions will be based on the image being rolled over. For example, because the image displaying the "The Plays" graphic is the first inline image in the document, you'll add the following event handlers to that image:

```
onmouseover = "RollOver(0)" onmouseout = "RollOut(0)"
```

Remember that the DOM numbers elements starting from 0 rather than 1. Thus, because this is the first inline image, the index number sent to the RollOver() and RollOut() functions is 0. The other images will have index values of 1, 2, 3, and 4, corresponding to the locations of those images in both the document.images collection and the image object arrays.

To call the RollOver() and RollOut() functions:

1. Scroll down the file until you locate the inline image element for the plays_out.jpg graphic image.

2. Add the following attributes to the <img /> tag for that inline image:

```
onmouseover="RollOver(0)" onmouseout="RollOut(0)"
```

Now add the onmouseover and onmouseout event handlers for the rest of the inline images in the list of links (again, you can use the copy and paste features of your text editor to make this task easier).

3. Locate the inline image for the son_out.jpg graphic and insert the event handlers:

```
onmouseover="RollOver(1)" onmouseout="RollOut(1)"
```

4. Within the <img /> tag for the bio_out.jpg graphic insert:

```
onmouseover="RollOver(2)" onmouseout="RollOut(2)"
```

5. Insert the following within the <img /> tag for the globe_out.jpg graphic:

```
onmouseover="RollOver(3)" onmouseout="RollOut(3)"
```

6. Finally, locate the inline image for the strat_out.jpg graphic and insert the event handlers:

```
onmouseover="RollOver(4)" onmouseout="RollOut(4)"
```

Your revised code should match that shown in Figure 5-9.

Figure 5-9   **Running the image rollover functions**

```
<div id="links">
<a href="plays.htm">
   <img src="plays_out.jpg" alt="The Plays" onmouseover="RollOver(0)" onmouseout="RollOut(0)" />
</a>

<a href="sonnets.htm">
   <img src="son_out.jpg" alt="The Sonnets" onmouseover="RollOver(1)" onmouseout="RollOut(1)" />
</a>

<a href="bio.htm">
   <img src="bio_out.jpg" alt="Biography" onmouseover="RollOver(2)" onmouseout="RollOut(2)" />
</a>

<a href="globe.htm">
   <img src="globe_out.jpg" alt="The Globe" onmouseover="RollOver(3)" onmouseout="RollOut(3)" />
</a>

<a href="stratford.htm">
   <img src="strat_out.jpg" alt="Stratford" onmouseover="RollOver(4)" onmouseout="RollOut(4)" />
</a>
</div>
```

Note that you also could have produced the same rollover effect by adding these event handlers to the <a> tags that surround the inline images. You can now test the page to see the effects of the rollover functions.

To test the rollovers:

1. Save your changes to the **ws.htm** file and close your text editor.

2. Reopen or refresh **ws.htm** in your Web browser.

3. Move your mouse cursor over each of the five linked images and verify that a red drop shadow appears as a rollover image is swapped with the original image. (Note that Clare hasn't created the other five Web pages yet, so if you test the links you will get an error message from your browser.)

   Trouble? If the rollover effect does not work, check your code against the code shown in Figures 5-6 to 5-9. Pay close attention to the use of uppercase and lowercase letters.

4. Close your Web browser.

Creating a Text Rollover

While the Shakespeare page employs rollovers only of graphical images, the rollover effect can also be applied directly to text. This is usually done with linked text, but can also be applied to other elements in a Web document. Note that older browsers such as Netscape 4.7 or earlier and versions of Internet Explorer prior to 5.0 do not support text rollovers.

Using the Hover Pseudo-Class

If you are creating a rollover effect for linked text, the simplest approach is to use a style declaration for the <a> tag that employs the hover pseudo-class. The general syntax is

```
a:hover {styles}
```

where *styles* are the styles you want applied to the linked text when the mouse hovers over the link. For example, to change your links to a bold red font in response to the hover event, apply the style

```
a:hover {color:red; font-weight:bold}
```

This approach allows you to create a rollover effect without writing JavaScript code.

General Text Rollovers

A more general approach is to modify the style properties of an element in response to the rollover event. The following code shows how you would change the appearance of a bulleted list item:

```
<script type="text/javascript">
function RollOver() {
   this.style.color="red";
   this.style.fontWeight = "bold";
}
function RollOut() {
   this.style.color = "black";
   this.style.fontWeight = "normal";
}
</script>
<ul>
   <li onmouseover="RollOver()" onmouseout="RollOut()">
      The Globe
   </li>
</ul>
```

As the mouse pointer passes over the list item, the font color of the text "The Globe" changes to a boldfaced red, and then changes to a normal black when the pointer moves off of the item. Note that, to apply the style to the list item, the RollOver() and RollOut() functions use the "this" keyword, which is an object name that refers to whatever the current object is. When the RollOver() and RollOut() functions are called in response to the onmouseover and onmouseout events, the current object is the list item containing the text "The Globe".

You've completed your work with rollovers for Clare. She's pleased with the visual interest it adds to her page. She now has some other work she wants you to do on her Web site. In the next session, you'll learn how to use DHTML to create a menu system for a page listing Shakespeare's plays.

Session 5.1 Quick Check

Review

1. The second inline image on your Web page has the name "Links". What are two ways of referencing this image in JavaScript?
2. What code would you enter to change the dimensions of an inline image named "Links" to 150 pixels wide by 200 pixels high?
3. What code would you enter to change the source of the Links image to "links2.jpg"?
4. What code would you use to create an image object named "LinksOver" that is 75 pixels wide and 100 pixels high?

5. What code would you enter to create an array of image objects named LinksArray, containing image objects pointing to graphic files image1.jpg, image2.jpg, and image3.jpg?
6. What "if" condition must you use to determine whether a browser supports the image collection?

Session 5.2

Working with Menus

Clare is pleased with your modifications to the opening page. She wants you to work next on a page that contains links to all of Shakespeare's plays. Shakespeare wrote almost 40 plays, and Clare is concerned that a page with so many links will be cumbersome. Ideally, she would like all of the links to fit within the space of a single screen.

Clare wonders whether you can create a series of menus containing links to each of the plays. She envisions four menus, one for each of the four types of Shakespeare's plays: comedies, histories, tragedies, and romances. Clare sketches out her idea for you, as shown in Figure 5-10.

| Figure 5-10 | Menus for the Plays page |

Clare suggests placing five headers at the top of the page: one for each of the four types of plays, and a fifth box that is linked to the opening page. When a user moves the mouse pointer over one of the four play type headers, a menu box should appear, listing all of Shakespeare's plays of that type. The user can then click one of the plays from the list to go to a Web page containing the text of that play. If the user moves the mouse pointer off of the list, the list of plays should disappear, leaving just the five headers at the top of the page.

Creating a Pop-Up Menu

Menus fall into four general classes: pop-ups, pull-downs, sliding, and tabbed. In a **pop-up menu**, a user clicks an object on the page and the menu appears, sometimes elsewhere on the page. To close a pop-up menu, a user clicks either the menu itself or another item on the page.

One common way to create a pop-up menu for the Web is to place the menu contents within a set of <div> container tags, hidden on the page using the visibility style attribute. When a user clicks an object on the page, a JavaScript program is run that unhides the menu (see Figure 5-11). To rehide the menu, a second JavaScript program is run that changes the menu's visibility property back to hidden.

Creating a pop-up menu   **Figure 5-11**

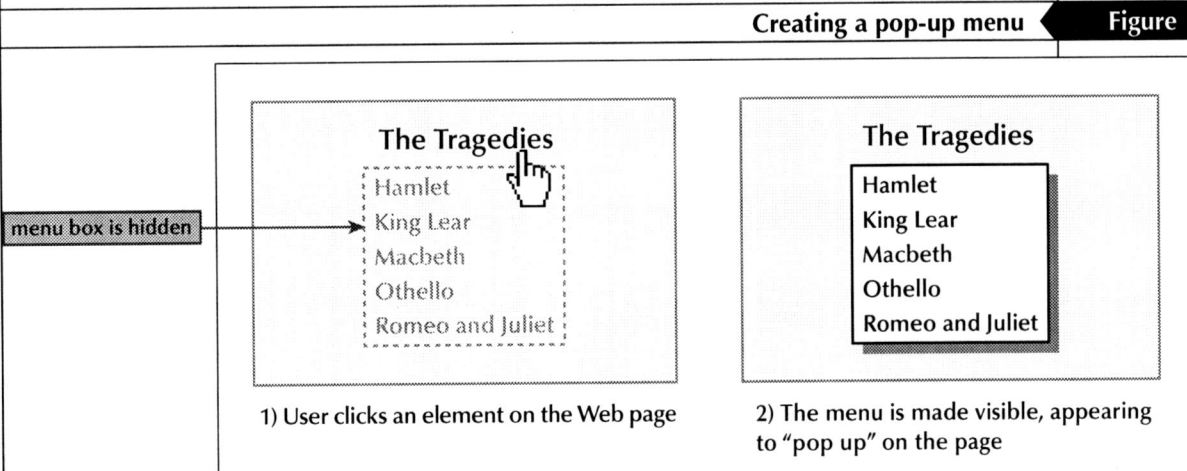

1) User clicks an element on the Web page

2) The menu is made visible, appearing to "pop up" on the page

Creating a Pull-Down Menu

In a **pull-down menu**, part of the menu—usually a header for the title—is visible. When a user clicks the visible part (or moves the mouse pointer over it), the rest of the menu is revealed. This creates the illusion that the rest of the menu is being "pulled down" from the visible part.

To create a pull-down menu, you again place the contents within a set of <div> tags, but this time you use the clip style attribute to "cut off" part of the menu. The part of the menu that is still visible usually contains a title describing the menu's contents. When a user either clicks the title or moves the mouse pointer over it, a JavaScript command is run that displays the hidden section (see Figure 5-12). Clicking another title on the page or moving the pointer off of the title pulls the menu back up. To change the size of the clipping rectangle, you modify the value of the clip property.

Creating a pull-down menu   **Figure 5-12**

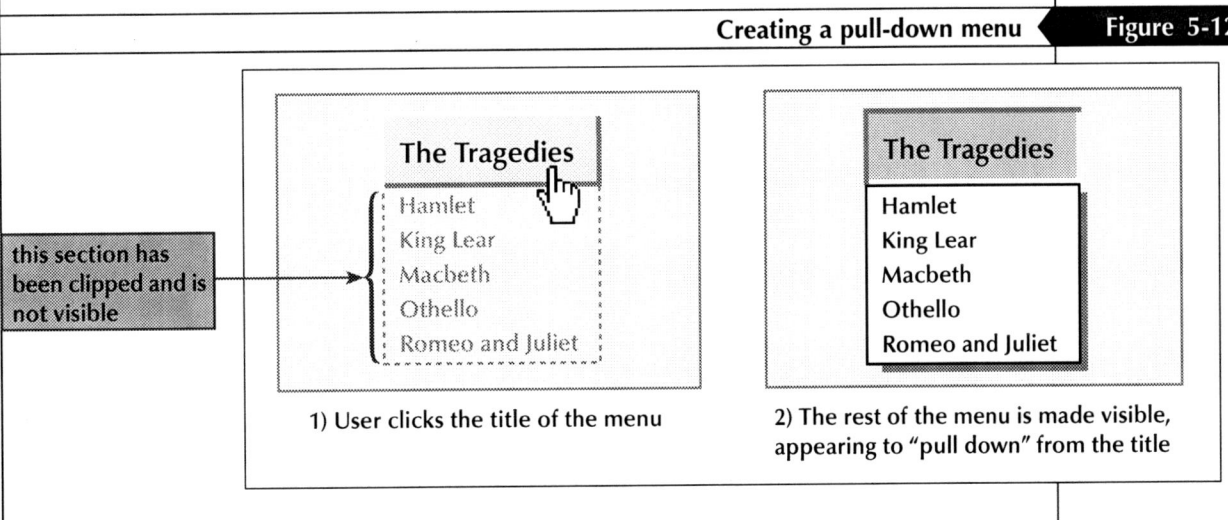

1) User clicks the title of the menu

2) The rest of the menu is made visible, appearing to "pull down" from the title

Creating a Sliding Menu

In a **sliding menu**, a menu is partially hidden either off the Web page or behind another object on the page. When the user clicks the visible part of the menu, the menu "slides" into a fully visible position (see Figure 5-13).

Figure 5-13 **Creating a sliding menu**

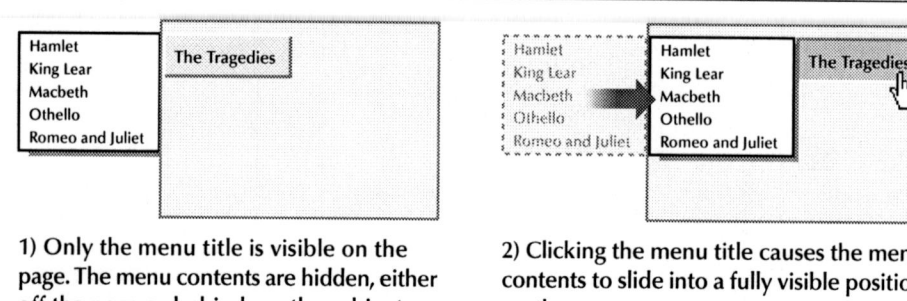

1) Only the menu title is visible on the page. The menu contents are hidden, either off the page or behind another object

2) Clicking the menu title causes the menu contents to slide into a fully visible position on the page

To create a sliding menu, use the positioning styles of the object to place it in a location where it is partially obscured. To place the object off the page, use absolute positioning and set the top and left styles to negative values. For example, the following style declaration:

```
position: absolute; top: -50px; left: -10px;
```

will set the object 50 pixels above and 10 pixels to the left of the visible browser window. To place your sliding menu behind another object, use the z-index style to set it below the other image on the page.

Once the sliding menu has been partially obscured, you can use the animation techniques used in Tutorial 4 to move the menu from its original location to a more visible spot. To hide the menu, use animation to move it back to its original location.

Creating a Tabbed Menu

In a **tabbed menu**, several menus are stacked on the page with one part of each menu visible to the user. When you click the visible part of a menu, the selected menu moves to the top of the stack, making its contents visible to the user (see Figure 5-14).

Creating a tabbed menu   Figure 5-14

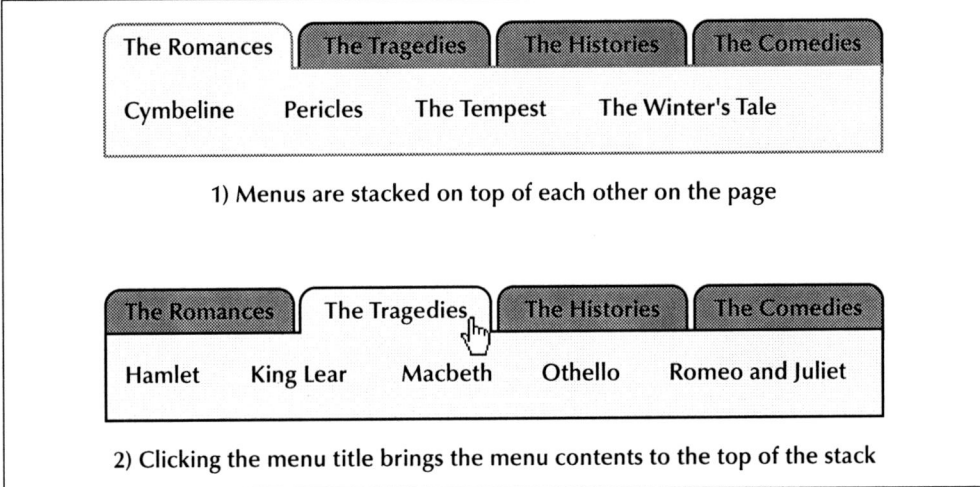

1) Menus are stacked on top of each other on the page

2) Clicking the menu title brings the menu contents to the top of the stack

To create a tabbed menu system, you need to ensure that part of each menu is always visible, no matter where it is located in the stack. To move items to the top of the stack, you can simply change the value of the z-index style for the selected menu, setting the value to one higher than the z-index value of the menu currently on top of the stack. For example if menu3 is on top of the stack and you want to move menu5 to the top, you could run the following set of commands:

```
menu3 = document.getElementById("menu3");
menu5 = document.getElementById("menu5");
maxZ = menu3.style.zIndex;
menu5.style.zIndex = maxZ+1;
```

and menu5 will now be displayed on top of menu3.

Clare decides to use a pop-up for the menu system on the Plays page. Most of the work of setting up the contents of the menus and their positions on the page has already been done for you. The Plays page is in the playstxt.htm file. Open this file now.

To open the Plays Web page:

1. Use your text editor to open **playstxt.htm** from the tutorial.05/tutorial folder. Enter *your name* and *the date* in the comment section and save the file as **plays.htm**.

2. Scroll through the code for the document to familiarize yourself with its content.

3. Open **plays.htm** in your Web browser. Figure 5-15 shows the current appearance of the page.

| Figure 5-15 | The menus for the Plays page |

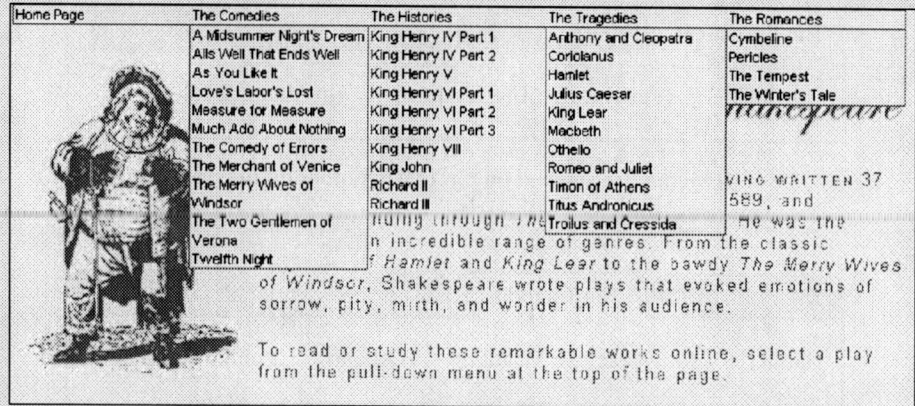

Trouble? Different browsers might display the Web page slightly differently. Figure 5-15 shows how the page appears in the Internet Explorer 6.0 browser for Windows.

The menu contains five submenu titles, created using <div> tags and given the id values "Home", "Comedy", "History", "Tragedy", and "Romance". The contents of the Comedy, History, Tragedy, and Romance menus are placed in their own div elements with the ids "ComedyMenu", "HistoryMenu", "TragedyMenu", and "RomanceMenu". Within each menu box is a list of all the plays of that genre, linked to individual pages for each play. The rest of the page is contained in a div element named "main".

As the page stands, the menu boxes hide most of the page, so you'll start editing Clare's page by hiding the menus using the visibility style. The menus all belong to the same class, which is named "Menu", so you'll add an embedded style sheet to the plays.htm file to hide this class of elements.

To hide the menus:

1. Return to the **plays.htm** file in your text editor.

2. Add the following embedded style above the closing </head> tag, as shown in Figure 5-16:

```
<style type="text/css">
   .Menu {visibility: hidden}
</style>
```

| Figure 5-16 | Hiding the menus |

```
<title>Shakespeare's Plays</title>
<link href="styles2.css" rel="stylesheet" type="text/css" />
<style type="text/css">
   .Menu {visibility: hidden}
</style>

</head>
```

3. Save your changes to the file.

4. Refresh or reopen **plays.htm** in your Web browser. As shown in Figure 5-17, the menus should now be hidden.

The Plays page with hidden menus ◀ **Figure 5-17**

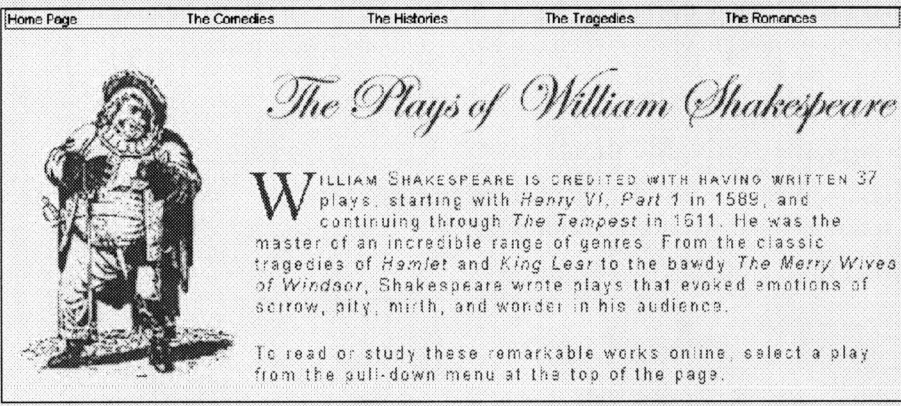

Creating Pop-Up Menu Functions

You discuss with Clare exactly how she wants the menus to work. Clare outlines the following behaviors:

- The contents of only one pop-up menu should be displayed at a time.
- If a user clicks a menu title, the corresponding menu should be displayed, and any other menu should be hidden.
- If a user clicks the page content that appears below the menus, any active menu should be hidden.

To perform these tasks, you need some functions to hide and unhide elements on the page. Two functions named hideIt() and showIt() have already been created for you and stored in the scripts.js file. Figure 5-18 shows the code for these two functions.

The functions in the scripts.js file ◀ **Figure 5-18**

```
function hideIt(object) {
    object.style.visibility="hidden";
}

function showIt(object) {
    object.style.visibility="visible";
}
```

Both functions have a single parameter named "object" which represents an object on the page that you want to either hide or show. Add a link to this file's functions in the plays.htm file.

To link to the scripts.js file:

▶ **1.** Return to the **plays.htm** file in your text editor.

▶ **2.** Add the following external script element directly above the closing </head> tag:

   `<script src="scripts.js" type="text/javascript"></script>`

▶ **3.** Save your changes to the file.

To create Clare's pop-up menus, you need a way to track which menu, if any, is currently visible. You'll do this by creating a global variable named "ActiveMenu" that stores an object representing the current menu. The initial value of this variable will be null, because no menus are visible when a browser initially loads the page.

To create the ActiveMenu variable:

▶ 1. Above the external script element you just inserted, add the following embedded script element, as shown in Figure 5-19:

```
<script type="text/javascript">
   var ActiveMenu = null;
</script>
```

Figure 5-19 Creating the ActiveMenu variable

```
<script type="text/javascript">
   var ActiveMenu = null;
</script>
<script src="scripts.js" type="text/javascript"></script>
</head>
```

▶ 2. Save your changes to the file.

Displaying Menu Contents

Next, you need to create two functions: one to display one of the hidden menus, and the other to hide the visible menu. The first function you'll create will hide the currently active menu. The code for the hideActive() function is

```
function hideActive() {
   if (ActiveMenu !== null) {
      hideIt(ActiveMenu);
      ActiveMenu = null;
   }
}
```

The function first has to test whether there is an active menu to hide (to avoid generating an error message if there is not). It does this by testing whether the value of the ActiveMenu variable has been set to null. If the variable is not null, the function calls the hideIt() function from the scripts.js file to hide the active menu, and then resets the value of the ActiveMenu variable to null to indicate that no menu is now actively displayed on the Web page.

To insert the hideActive() function:

▶ 1. Insert the following code below the declaration that creates the ActiveMenu variable as shown in Figure 5-20:

```
function hideActive() {
   if (ActiveMenu !== null) {
      hideIt(ActiveMenu);
      ActiveMenu = null;
   }
}
```

Inserting the hideActive() function

Figure 5-20

```
<script type="text/javascript">
    var ActiveMenu = null;

    function hideActive() {
        if (ActiveMenu !== null) {
            hideIt(ActiveMenu);
            ActiveMenu = null;
        }
    }
</script>
```

2. Save your changes to the file.

Next you'll create a function named popMenu() to display a menu. This function will perform three actions:

1. Hide the active menu
2. Set the menu selected by the user as the new active menu
3. Display the menu selected by the user

The code for the popMenu() function is

```
function popMenu(M) {
    hideActive();
    ActiveMenu = document.getElementById(M);
    showIt(ActiveMenu);
}
```

The popMenu() function has one parameter, M, which is the id of the menu that will be displayed on the page. The first line of the function calls the hideActive() function to hide the previous menu. The second line sets the ActiveMenu variable to the menu selected by the user. The third line of the function uses the showIt() function from the scripts.js file to display the newly selected menu. For example, to display the contents of the Comedy menu, you would use the command

```
popMenu("ComedyMenu");
```

and the browser would hide the active menu (if one exists), and then display the Comedy menu, making it the new active menu. Add the popMenu() function to the plays.htm file now.

To insert the popMenu() function:

1. Insert the following code below the hideActive() function, as shown in Figure 5-21:

```
function popMenu(M) {
    hideActive();
    ActiveMenu = document.getElementById(M);
    showIt(ActiveMenu);
}
```

Figure 5-21	Inserting the popMenu() function

```
<script type="text/javascript">
   var ActiveMenu = null;

   function hideActive() {
      if (ActiveMenu !== null) {
         hideIt(ActiveMenu);
         ActiveMenu = null;
      }
   }

   function popMenu(M) {
      hideActive();
      ActiveMenu = document.getElementById(M);
      showIt(ActiveMenu);
   }
</script>
```

2. Save your changes to the file.

Calling the Menu Functions

You want to run the popMenu() function when the user clicks one of the menu titles. Each of the menu titles is enclosed within <a> tags. For example, the code for the Comedy Menu title is

```
<div id="Comedy" class="MenuTitle">
   <a href="#">The Comedies</a>
</div>
```

The link currently points to "#", which causes the page to reload. However, you want to change this so that the menu title runs the popMenu() function when clicked. You can do this by changing the target of the link to the JavaScript function. The revised HTML code is

```
<div id="Comedy" class="MenuTitle">
   <a href="JavaScript:popMenu('ComedyMenu')">The Comedies</a>
</div>
```

When a user clicks the Comedy menu title, the contents of the Comedy menu are displayed. Make this change for the Comedy menu title and the other menu titles on Clare's page.

To call the popMenu() function:

1. Scroll down the plays.htm file and locate the <div> tag for the Comedy element.

2. Change the target of the link from "#" to **"JavaScript: popMenu('ComedyMenu')"**.

3. Change the target of the History link from "#" to **"JavaScript: popMenu('HistoryMenu')"**.

4. Change the target of the Tragedy link from "#" to **"JavaScript: popMenu('TragedyMenu')"**.

5. Change the target of the Romance link from "#" to **"JavaScript: popMenu('RomanceMenu')"**.

Figure 5-22 shows the revised HTML code for the menu titles.

```
<div id="Home" class="MenuTitle">
   <a href="ws.htm">Home Page</a>
</div>
<div id="Comedy" class="MenuTitle">
   <a href="JavaScript:popMenu('ComedyMenu')">The Comedies</a>
</div>
<div id="History" class="MenuTitle">
   <a href="JavaScript:popMenu('HistoryMenu')">The Histories</a>
</div>
<div id="Tragedy" class="MenuTitle">
   <a href="JavaScript:popMenu('TragedyMenu')">The Tragedies</a>
</div>
<div id="Romance" class="MenuTitle">
   <a href="JavaScript:popMenu('RomanceMenu')">The Romances</a>
</div>
```

If a user clicks in the main body of the Web page, you want to hide the active menu. You can do this by adding an onclick event handler to the div element for the main page content, running the hideActive() function in response.

To call the hideActive() function:

► 1. Scroll down the file and locate the <div> tag for the main element.

► 2. Add the event handler **onclick="hideActive()"** to the <div> tag, as shown in Figure 5-23.

```
<div id="main" onclick="hideActive()">
   <p id="falstaff"><img src="falstaff.jpg" alt="" /></p>
   <p id="title"><img src="theplays.jpg" alt="The Plays of Shakespeare" /></p>
   <p id="firstp">
William Shakespeare is credited with having written 37 plays,
starting with <i>Henry VI, Part 1</i> in 1589, and continuing through
<i>The Tempest</i> in 1611. He was the master of an incredible range of
genres. From the classic tragedies of <i>Hamlet</i> and <i>King Lear</i>
to the bawdy <i>The Merry Wives of Windsor</i>, Shakespeare wrote plays
that evoked emotions of sorrow, pity, mirth, and wonder in his audience. </p>
   <p>To read or study these remarkable works online, select a play
from the pull-down menu at the top of the page.</p>
</div>
```

► 3. Close the file, saving your changes.

► 4. Reload or refresh **plays.htm** in your Web browser. Verify that as you click the menu titles, the menu contents appear on the page and that when you click the rest of the page contents the active menu is hidden. Figure 5-24 shows the pop-up menu in action.

Figure 5-24 | **The pop-up menu for the Plays Web page**

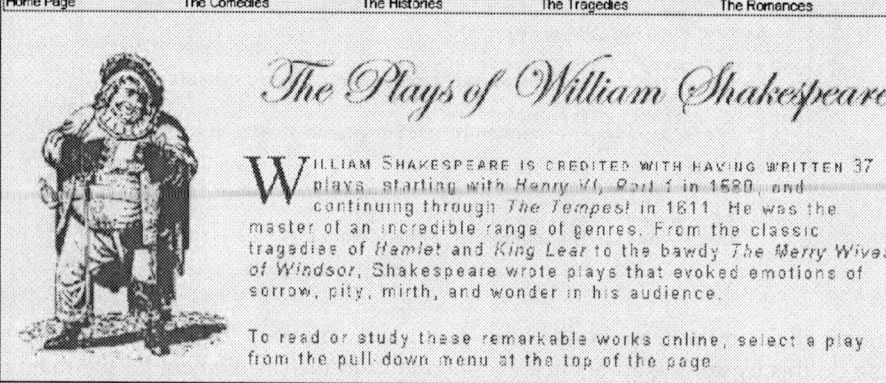

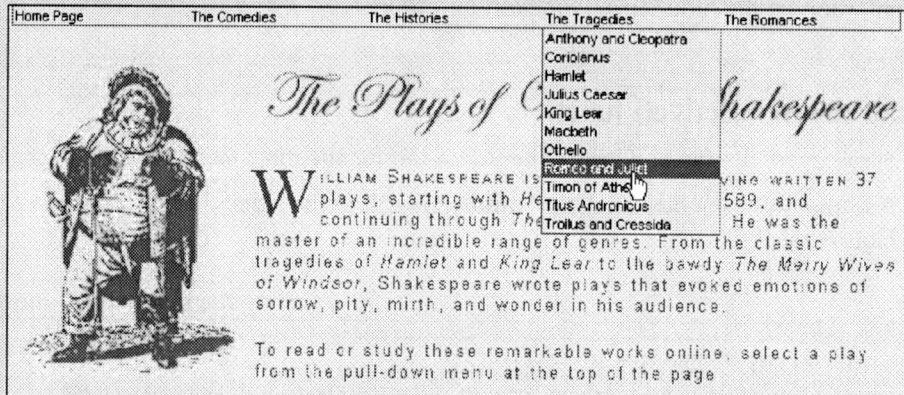

Trouble? At this point, the Web pages for the individual plays have not been created, so you will receive an error message if you click the links in the pop-up menus.

Trouble? If you click a blank area of the document window outside of the page content, the pop-up menu will not close.

5. After you are finished viewing the Web page, close your Web browser.

Clare is pleased with the Web page. She feels that the pop-up menus you created will give her users quick access to the rest of her Web site, while leaving the page simple and easy to use. She has a few other features that she wants you to add to the page. You'll discuss those changes in the next session.

Review

Session 5.2 Quick Check

1. What is a pop-up menu?
2. What is a pull-down menu?
3. What JavaScript command would you use to hide an object with the id "main"?
4. What JavaScript command would you use to unhide an object with the id "main"?

Session 5.3

Working with Internet Explorer Filters

You've employed two special effects for Clare's Web site: an image rollover and a pop-up menu. Clare would like you to investigate another type of special effect supported by Internet Explorer, called a filter. A **filter** is an effect that is applied to an object or page to change its appearance. Using Internet Explorer filters, you can make text or images appear partially transparent, add a drop shadow, or make an object appear to glow. Filters were introduced in Internet Explorer version 4.0 and are not supported by other browsers, so you have to use them with caution.

Filters cannot be applied to every element on a page. In Internet Explorer 4.0, filters can be applied only to the following elements:

• div and span elements with a defined height, width, or absolute position
• inline images and marquees
• form buttons, input fields, and text area fields
• table headings, rows, and cells

If you want to apply a filter to a div or span element in Internet Explorer 4.0, you must define an absolute position for the element, or set its height or its width; otherwise, Internet Explorer will generate an error message. In Internet Explorer 5.5 and above, any element that has a defined height and width can be filtered.

A filter is applied either by adding a filter style to the Web page's style sheet or by running a JavaScript command that applies a filter to an object in the document. Let's first look at how to create a filter using styles.

Applying Filters by Using Styles

The syntax that Internet Explorer uses to employ the filter style differs between browser versions. In version 4.0, the filter style is expressed as

```
filter: filter_name(params)
```

where `filter_name` is the name of one of the many Internet Explorer 4.0 filters, and `params` are the parameter values (if any) that apply to the filter. The syntax for filter styles employed in Internet Explorer 5.5 and above is

```
filter: progid:DXImageTransform.Microsoft.filter_name(params)
```

Besides the syntactical differences between the two versions, there are some differences in how different versions of Internet Explorer apply the filter style. In Internet Explorer 4.0, the filter effect is clipped when it is set too close to an object's boundary; with Internet Explorer 5.5 and above, the filter effect extends beyond an object's boundary.

Figure 5-25 lists some of the filter names and parameters supported by Internet Explorer 5.5 and above.

Figure 5-25 ▶ **Internet Explorer 5.5 filters**

Filter Name	Parameters	Description
Alpha	style=0, 1, 2, 3 opacity=1–100 finishOpacity=1–100 startX=1–100 finishX=1–100 startY=1–100 finishY=1–100	Applies a transparency filter. A low opacity value makes the object transparent, while a high value makes the object opaque. The style parameter is used to indicate the direction of the transparency effect. The rest of the parameters control where in the element the transparency is applied
BasicImage	rotation=0, 1, 2, 3 opacity=0–1 mirror=0, 1 invert=0, 1 xRay=0, 1 grayscale=0,1	Modifies the appearance of the object. The rotation parameter rotates the object (0=0 deg., 1=90 deg., 2=180 deg., 3=270 deg.). The opacity parameter sets the opacity of the object. The remaining parameters, if their values are set to "1," create a mirror image, invert the object, apply an "x-ray" effect, or display the object in grayscale
Blur	pixelRadius=*value* makeShadow=true, false shadowOpacity=0–1	Blurs the object. The pixelRadius parameter determines the amount of the blurring. The makeShadow and shadowOpacity parameters apply shadowing to the blur effect
Chroma	color=#*rrggbb*	Makes a specified color in the object transparent
DropShadow	color=#*rrggbb* offX=*value* offY=*value*	Creates a drop shadow of the specified color with a length of offX in the x-direction and offY in the y-direction
Emboss		Applies an embossing effect to the object
Engrave		Applies an engraving effect to the object
Glow	color=#*rrggbb* strength=1–255	Applies a glowing border around the object with the size of the glow determined by the strength parameter and the glow's color determined by the color parameter
Gradient	gradientType=0, 1 startColorStr=#*rrggbb* endColorStr=#*rrggbb*	Applies a color gradient to the object. The gradientType parameter determines the direction of the gradient, either vertical (0) or horizontal (1). The startColorStr and endColorStr parameters indicate the starting and ending colors. Intermediate colors are supplied by the filter
MotionBlur	direction=*angle* strength=1–255	Applies a motion blur effect. The direction parameter provides the angle of the motion, and the strength parameter indicates the length of the motion lines
Pixelate	maxSquare=*value*	Pixelates the object, where maxSquare is the size of the pixel
Shadow	direction=*angle* color=#*rrggbb* strength=1–255	Applies a simple drop shadow to the object with the angle of the shadow specified by the direction parameter, the color by the color parameter, and the size of the shadow determined by the strength parameter
Wave	freq=*value* lightStrength=*value* phase=*value* strength=*value*	Applies a sine-wave distortion to the object; the appearance of the wave is determined by the four parameters

For example, to apply a drop shadow filter in Internet Explorer 5.5 or above, you would add the following filter style to the element:

```
filter: progid:DXImageTransform.Microsoft.
dropShadow(color=#FF0000, offX=5, offY=10)
```

With this filter style, the element will appear with a red drop shadow (since #FF0000 is the hexadecimal color value for red), offset 5 pixels to the right and 10 pixels down.

Internet Explorer 5.5 supports a wider range of filter effects than version 4.0. Figure 5-26 describes how some of the version 4.0 filters are matched with their 5.5 forms.

Internet Explorer 4.0 and 5.5 filters | Figure 5-26

IE 4.0 Filter	IE 5.5 Filter
Alpha	progid:DXImageTransform.Microsoft.Alpha
Blur	progid:DXImageTransform.Microsoft.MotionBlur
Chroma	progid:DXImageTransform.Microsoft.Chroma
DropShadow	progid:DXImageTransform.Microsoft.dropShadow
FlipH	progid:DXImageTransform.Microsoft.BasicImage(rotation=2, mirror=1)
FlipV	progid:DXImageTransform.Microsoft.BasicImage(mirror=1)
Glow	progid:DXImageTransform.Microsoft.Glow
Gray	progid:DXImageTransform.Microsoft.BasicImage(grayscale=1)
Invert	progid:DXImageTransform.Microsoft.BasicImage(invert=1)
Light	progid:DXImageTransform.Microsoft.Light
Mask	progid:DXImageTransform.Microsoft.MaskFilter
Shadow	progid:DXImageTransform.Microsoft.Shadow
Wave	progid:DXImageTransform.Microsoft.Wave
Xray	progid:DXImageTransform.Microsoft.BasicImage(xray=1)

The Internet Explorer 4.0 filters are supported in version 5.5, so you may prefer to use them for greater compatibility. If compatibility is not an issue, however, you should take advantage of the greater power and flexibility offered by the 5.5 filters. Filters are difficult to understand and appreciate without actually working with them. To better understand how filters work, a demonstration page has been created for you. Open it now.

To view the filters demo:

1. Open the **demo_filter.htm** file from the tutorial.05/tutorial folder in your Internet Explorer browser.

2. Select a filter type from the **Filter Type** drop-down list box.

3. If the filter uses parameters, select values for each of the parameters.

   As you select the filter and parameter values, the object on the right side of the page is modified. The code for filter style is shown at the bottom of the page (see Figure 5-27). Note that the filter is applied to the entire object, which consists of an inline image and text, all contained within a <div> tag.

Figure 5-27 Running the filter demo

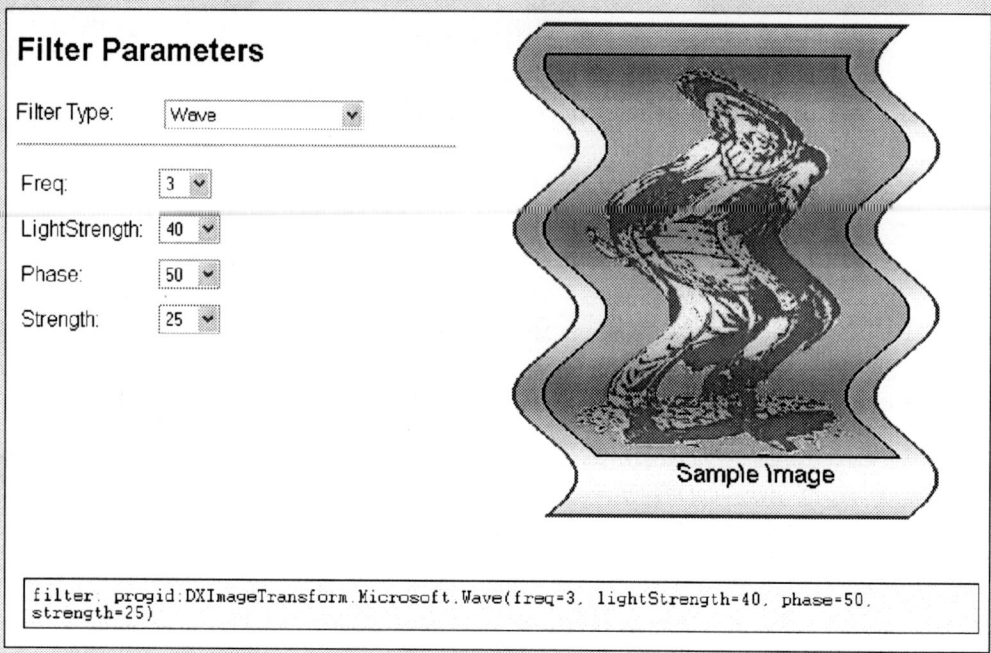

Filter Parameters

Filter Type: Wave

Freq: 3
LightStrength: 40
Phase: 50
Strength: 25

Sample Image

```
filter: progid:DXImageTransform.Microsoft.Wave(freq=3, lightStrength=40, phase=50,
strength=25)
```

Trouble? If you're not running Internet Explorer 4.0 or above, you will not be able to see any of these filter effects.

4. Continue going through the list of filters and parameter values and close the Web page when finished.

Reference Window | **Creating a Filter Style**

- To create a filter style in Internet Explorer 4.0, use the style attribute
    filter: *filter_name (params)*
  where *filter_name* is the name of one of the Internet Explorer 4.0 filters, and *params* are the parameter values (if any) that apply to the filter.
- To create a filter style in Internet Explorer 5.5 and above, use the style attribute
    filter: progid:DXImageTransform.Microsoft.*filter_name(params)*

Filters can also be combined to create interesting visual effects. The effects are added in the order in which they are entered into the style declaration. To combine the alpha filter with a drop shadow, for example, you would enter the following set of filters:

```
filter: progid:DXImageTransform.Microsoft.Shadow(direction=135,
color=#0000FF strength=5)
progid:DXImageTransform.Microsoft.Alpha(style=0, opacity=30)
```

This code applies a drop shadow to the object and then changes the opacity value to 30. If you switch the order of the filters, the drop shadow is added after the object is made transparent, meaning that the shadow itself is not made transparent (see Figure 5-28). You can also apply the same filter several times. For example, you can add two drop shadows to the same object by applying two shadow filters.

Shadow filter applied first and then the Opacity filter

Opacity filter applied first and then the Shadow filter

Most browsers do not support the Internet Explorer filter styles, and they are not part of the official specifications for CSS. When other browsers encounter a style sheet that employs the filter style, they usually ignore those particular styles while processing the other styles in the sheet. One exception is Netscape 4. If Netscape 4 encounters an unknown style attribute, such as the filter style, it can cause the browser to ignore *all* of the style declarations for that object. One way to avoid this problem is to place the filter styles in a separate declaration, away from the other, more standard, style attributes. Another option is to apply the filter style using a JavaScript program instead of a style sheet.

Running Filters with JavaScript

As with other style attributes, the filter style can be applied in JavaScript using the style property. The syntax for applying a filter style is

```
object.style.filter = "filter text";
```

where `object` is an object in the Web page, and `filter text` is the text of the filters applied to the object. As in a style sheet, the text string can contain multiple filters separated by spaces. For example, to apply the alpha filter to the first inline image in a document, you could use the following JavaScript command:

```
document.images[0].style.filter = "progid:DXImageTransform.Microsoft.
Alpha(style=0, opacity=30)";
```

Internet Explorer's version of JavaScript also recognizes the **filter collection**, which is the collection of all filters associated with a particular object. The reference syntax of the filter collection is

```
object.filters[idref]
```

where `object` is an object that has some filters applied to it, and `idref` is either the index number or the name of a filter within that collection. As with other arrays, the index numbering starts at 0. For example, the expression

```
document.images[0].filters[1]
```

references the second filter associated with the first inline image in the document. If you want to reference the filter by its name, you would use a reference like the following:

```
document.images[0].filters["DXImageTransform.Microsoft.Alpha"]
```

where Internet Explorer's Alpha filter is one of the filters applied to the first inline image in the document. One of the purposes of using JavaScript to work with filter styles is to modify the parameter values. You can reference specific parameters within each filter using the syntax

```
filter.param
```

where *filter* is a specific filter in an object's filters collection, and *param* is the name of a parameter associated with the filter. For example, to change the opacity value of the Alpha filter for the first inline image, you could run the expression

```
document.images[0].filters["DXImageTransform.Microsoft.Alpha"].
opacity=25;
```

Note that this command only works if the Alpha filter has already been defined for the inline image.

Reference Window	**Working with Filters in JavaScript**

- To apply a filter to an object, use the JavaScript expression
  ```
  object.style.filter = "filter text";
  ```
  where *object* is an object in the Web document, and *filter text* is the filter name (or names) and the filter parameters.
- To access a particular filter associated with an object, use the reference
  ```
  object.filters[idref]
  ```
  where *object* is an object that has a set of filters defined for it and *idref* is either the index number or name of a filter in the collection.
- To access a parameter associated with a filter, use the syntax
  ```
  filter.param
  ```
  where *filter* is a filter in the object's filter collection and *param* is one of the parameters associated with the filter.

If your users' browsers support them, you can use filters to create the same kind of rollover effects you worked with in the last session. Rather than creating two versions of the same image, you can use JavaScript to apply a filter effect in response to the onmouseover event, and then remove that filter in response to the onmouseout event. The following functions show how the RollOut() and RollOver() functions might look if you wanted to apply a drop shadow to an inline image in a document:

```
function RollOver(i) {
    document.images[i].style.filter=
    "progid:DXImageTransform.Microsoft.DropShadow(color=#DDDDDD,
    offX=10, offY=10)";
}

function RollOut(i) {
    document.images[i].style.filter="";
}
```

Adding a Filter Effect to the Plays Page

You discuss the Internet Explorer filters capability with Clare. She's intrigued by the idea and suggests that you add a filter to the Plays page. Clare suggests you add a drop shadow to the menus. To add the drop shadow, you'll insert another style declaration in the embedded style sheet. Since all of the menus belong to the Menu class, you can apply the drop shadow style using the declaration

```
.Menu {filter: progid:DXImageTransform.Microsoft.DropShadow
(color=#999999, offX=3, offY=3)}
```

This drop shadow will appear in a medium shade of gray offset 3 pixels to the right and below each of the menus. Add this filter style to Clare's page.

To add the drop shadow filter style to the menu items:

1. Open the **plays.htm** file in your text editor.

2. Within the embedded style sheet, insert the following style declaration (see Figure 5-29):

```
.Menu {filter:progid:DXImageTransform.Microsoft.DropShadow
(color=#999999, offX=3, offY=3)}
```

Adding the drop shadow filter style ◄ **Figure 5-29**

```
<style type="text/css">
   .Menu {visibility: hidden}
   .Menu {filter:progid:DXImageTransform.Microsoft.DropShadow(Color=#999999, offX=3, offY=3)}
</style>
```

3. Save your changes to the file.

4. Open **plays.htm** in Internet Explorer. Access the menus and verify that the menus now appear with a gray drop shadow located to the right and below the menu box. (See Figure 5-30.)

Viewing the drop shadow filter ◄ **Figure 5-30**

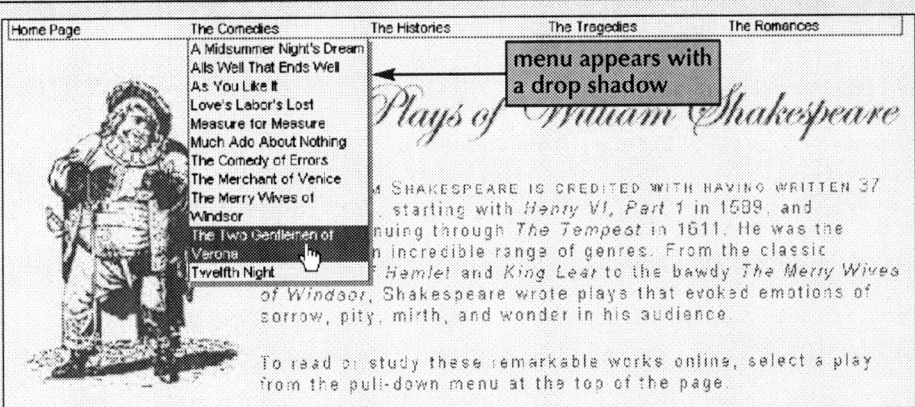

Trouble? If you're running a browser other than Internet Explorer 4.0 or later, you will not see any drop shadow effect, but the page should still be rendered correctly.

Using a Light Filter

Another popular filter that can add visual interest to your Web pages is the Light filter, which creates the illusion of a light (or multiple lights) illuminating an object. Much like a drop shadow, adding a light source can give your page elements a dynamic 3D effect. The style to create a Light filter in Internet Explorer 4.0 is:

```
filter: Light()
```

In Internet Explorer 5.5 and above, the style is:

```
filter: progid:DXImageTransform.Microsoft.Light()
```

Once you've created the Light filter, the next step is to define a light source for the object. This is done not with a style declaration, but with a JavaScript command. There are three methods for creating a light source: addAmbient(), addPoint(), and addCone(). The addAmbient() method applies an overall or ambient light to the object. The syntax of the method is

```
object.filters.Light.addAmbient(red, green, blue, strength)
```

where *object* is the object being illuminated; *red*, *green*, and *blue* are the RGB color values of the light; and *strength* is the strength of the light source, expressed as a number from 0 to 100. For example, the following statement adds a red light source at highest intensity on the document's first inline image:

```
document.images[0].filters.Light.addAmbient(255,0,0,100)
```

The addAmbient() method doesn't assume a specific location for the light source. To specify a location for the light, you can use the addPoint() method, which creates a point light source hovering above the object. The syntax to add a point light source to the Light filter is

```
object.filters.Light.addPoint(x, y, z, red, green, blue, strength)
```

where *x* and *y* are the horizontal and vertical coordinates of the light source, and *z* is the height, in pixels, of the light source above the object. For example, to create a high-intensity red light source 50 pixels above the object at the (x,y) coordinates (50, 75), you would use the following expression:

```
document.images[0].filters.Light.addPoint(50,75,50,255,0,0,100)
```

The addPoint() method assumes that the light is shone directly down on the object. If you want the light source to shine at an angle, you need to use the addCone() method. The syntax of the addCone() method is

```
object.filters.Light.addCone(x, y, z, x2, y2, red, green, blue,
strength, spread)
```

where *x*, *y*, *z* are once again the coordinates of the light source and *x2*, *y2* are the coordinates of the focus of the light—where the light actually "hits" the object. The spread parameter indicates the angle (or spread) of the light between the light source and the surface of the object. The spread parameter varies from 0 to 90 degrees. The other parameters have the same meanings as those used with the addAmbient() and addPoint() methods. If all this seems confusing to you, you can explore the parameter values of the Light filter in more detail using the Filter Demo Web page.

You can create up to 10 light sources for a particular object. Internet Explorer assigns each light source a number. The first light source you define has a light number of 0; the second light source has a value of 1, and so forth. Once a light source has been created, Internet Explorer provides several methods to manipulate it. You can move the light source to a new location, change its color, change its intensity, or remove the light altogether. To move the light source to another location, use the method

```
object.filters.Light.moveLight(light, x, y, z, absolute)
```

where *light* is the light source's light number; *x*, *y*, and *z* are the new coordinates of the light source; and *absolute* is a Boolean value that has the value true when the new coordinates are expressed in absolute terms, and has the value false when the coordinates are expressed relative to the present coordinates of the light source.

To change the color of the light, use the method

```
object.filters.Light.changeColor(light, red, green, blue, absolute)
```

where *red*, *green*, and *blue* are the new RGB color values of the light source; and *absolute* is a Boolean value that is true when the color values are expressed as absolute values, and false when the color values are to be added to the light source's current color values. You can use negative color values if the absolute parameter is set to false.

To change the intensity of the light source, use the method

```
object.filters.Light.changeStrength(light, strength, absolute)
```

where *strength* is the new strength of the light source, and *absolute* is a Boolean value that is set to true if the strength parameter is expressed in absolute terms, and false if the value of the strength parameter is to be added to the light source's current strength. Once again, the strength parameter can be negative if the value of the absolute parameter is set to false.

As you create light sources, you can remove the effect of a particular light source by setting its strength parameter back to 0. You can remove all of the light sources applied to a particular object by using the method

```
object.filters.Light.clear()
```

Internet Explorer does not provide a method of removing a specific light source while keeping all of the others. Clare does not need to use the light filter in her Web page.

Working with Transitions

A second type of special effect supported by Internet Explorer is the transition. A **transition** is a visual effect that is applied to an object over an interval of time. For example, instead of having a pop-up menu disappear instantaneously, you can apply a transition that makes the pop-up menu appear to gradually blend into the background until it disappears.

Applying Transition Styles

As with the filter style, the transition you use depends on the version of Internet Explorer you're trying to support. Internet Explorer 4.0 supports two kinds of transitions: blend and reveal. A **blend transition** is a transition in which one object is blended into another. The style to create a blend transition is

```
filter: blendTrans(duration = value)
```

where *value* is the amount of time, in seconds, for the blending transition to take place. Two separate objects need not be used. You can apply a blend transition on a single object by initially making the object invisible (using the visibility style) and then applying the blendTrans() filter to move it to a visible state.

A **reveal transition** is a more general transition in which a visual effect is applied as one object is changed into another. The style for the reveal transition is

```
filter: revealTrans(duration = value, transition = type)
```

where *type* is a number from 0 to 23, specifying the transition effect. The various transition effects and their numeric values are listed in Figure 5-31.

Figure 5-31

Internet Explorer 4.0 revealTrans types

Transition	Numeric Code	Transition	Numeric Code
Box In	0	Random Dissolve	12
Box Out	1	Split Vertical In	13
Circle In	2	Split Vertical Out	14
Circle Out	3	Split Horizontal In	15
Wipe Up	4	Split Horizontal Out	16
Wipe Down	5	Strips Left Down	17
Wipe Right	6	Strips Left Up	18
Wipe Left	7	Strips Right Down	19
Vertical Blinds	8	Strips Right Up	20
Horizontal Blinds	9	Random Bars Horizontal	21
Checkerboard Across	10	Random Bars Vertical	22
Checkerboard Down	11	Random	23

In Internet Explorer 5.5, the blendTrans() and revealTrans() transitions were replaced by a whole library of transition effects. The style is similar to the syntax Internet Explorer 5.5 uses for applying filters:

```
filter: progid:DXImageTransform.Microsoft.transition(param)
```

where *transition* is the name of the transition and *param* is parameters of the transition that define how the transition operates. Figure 5-32 describes some of the Internet Explorer 5.5 transitions and their parameters. In addition to the parameters listed in Figure 5-32, each transition also supports the duration parameter, which indicates how many seconds the transition lasts.

Internet Explorer 5.5 transitions | Figure 5-32

Transition Name	Parameters	Description
Barn	motion=out, in orientation=horizontal, vertical	Applies a "barn door" transition
Blinds	bands=value direction=up, down, left, right	Applies a "window blinds" effect
Checkboard	direction=up, down, left, right squaresX=value squaresY=value	Creates a checkboard transition. The size of the checkboard is determined by the squaresX and squaresY parameters
Fade	overlap=0–1	Fades one object into another. The overlap parameter controls the degree of overlap as the fade occurs
GradientWipe	gradientSize=0–1 wipeStyle=0, 1 motion=forward, reverse	Wipes one object into another. The gradientSize parameter controls the blurring effect. The wipeStyle parameter indicates whether to wipe left to right (0) or up to down (1)
Inset		Applies an inset transition
Iris	irisStyle=multiple motion=out, in	Applies an iris-opening transition effect. The style of the iris is determined by the irisStyle parameter
Pixelate	maxSquare=value	Applies a pixelate transition, where maxSquare is the size of the pixel
RadialWipe	wipeStyle=clock, wedge, radial	Applies a radial wipe transition
RandomBars	orientation=horizontal, vertical	Applies a random bars transition
RandomDissolve	duration=value	Dissolves one object into another. The duration parameter indicates the dissolve time in seconds
Slide	slideStyle=hide, push, swap bands=value	Slides one object over or into another
Spiral	gridSizeX=value gridSizeY=value	Spirals one object into another
Stretch	stretchStyle=hide, push, spin	Stretches one object into another
Strips	motion=left-up, left-down, right-up, right-down	Wipes one object over another in a diagonal direction
Wheel	spokes=value	Applies a wheel transition
ZigZag	gridSizeX=value gridSizeY=value	Applies a zig-zag transition

Creating Transition Styles

- To create a blend transition in Internet Explorer 4.0, use the style
    `filter: blendTrans(duration = value)`
  where *value* is the amount of time, in seconds, for the blending process to take place.
- To create a reveal transition in Internet Explorer 4.0, use the style
    `filter: revealTrans(duration = value, transition = type)`
  where *type* is a number from 0 to 23, specifying the transition effect.
- To create a transition in Internet Explorer 5.5 and above, use the style
    `filter: progid:DXImageTransform.Microsoft.transition(param)`
  where *transition* is the name of the transition, and *param* is parameters used with that transition.

Figure 5-33 shows how some of the version 4.0 transitions are translated into their 5.5 forms.

Figure 5-33 ▶ **Comparison of Internet Explorer 4.0 and 5.5 transitions**

IE 4.0 Transition	IE 5.5 Transition
blendTrans()	DXImageTransform.Microsoft.Fade()
revealTrans(0)	DXImageTransform.Microsoft.Iris(irisStyle="square", motion="in")
revealTrans(1)	DXImageTransform.Microsoft.Iris(irisStyle="square", motion="out")
revealTrans(2)	DXImageTransform.Microsoft.Iris(irisStyle="circle", motion="in")
revealTrans(3)	DXImageTransform.Microsoft.Iris(irisStyle="circle", motion="out")
revealTrans(4)	DXImageTransform.Microsoft.Blinds(direction="up", bands="1")
revealTrans(5)	DXImageTransform.Microsoft.Blinds(direction="down", bands="1")
revealTrans(6)	DXImageTransform.Microsoft.Blinds(direction="right", bands="1")
revealTrans(7)	DXImageTransform.Microsoft.Blinds(direction="left", bands="1")
revealTrans(8)	DXImageTransform.Microsoft.Blinds(direction="right")
revealTrans(9)	DXImageTransform.Microsoft.Blinds(direction="down")
revealTrans(10)	DXImageTransform.Microsoft.Checkerboard(direction="right")
revealTrans(11)	DXImageTransform.Microsoft.Checkerboard(direction="down")
revealTrans(12)	DXImageTransform.Microsoft.RandomDissolve()
revealTrans(13)	DXImageTransform.Microsoft.Barn(orientation="vertical", motion="in")
revealTrans(14)	DXImageTransform.Microsoft.Barn(orientation="vertical", motion="out")
revealTrans(15)	DXImageTransform.Microsoft.Barn(orientation="horizontal", motion="in")
revealTrans(16)	DXImageTransform.Microsoft.Barn(orientation="horizontal", motion="out")
revealTrans(17)	DXImageTransform.Microsoft.Strips(motion="leftdown")
revealTrans(18)	DXImageTransform.Microsoft.Strips(motion="leftup")
revealTrans(19)	DXImageTransform.Microsoft.Strips(motion="rightdown")
revealTrans(20)	DXImageTransform.Microsoft.Strips(motion="rightup")
revealTrans(21)	DXImageTransform.Microsoft.RandomBars(orientation="horizontal")
revealTrans(22)	DXImageTransform.Microsoft.RandomBars(orientation="vertical")

To better understand these various transition effects, a demo of transition effects has been prepared for you. Open it now.

To view the transitions demo:

1. Open the **demo_transitions.htm** file from the tutorial.05/tutorial folder in Internet Explorer.

2. Select a filter type from the **Transition Type** drop-down list box.

3. Select a duration value from the **Duration** drop-down list box.

4. Select parameter values for the selected transition.

   As you change the transition type, duration, and transition parameter values, the object on the right displays the transition effect for the parameters you've entered. The style for the selected transition is shown in the box at the bottom of the page. See Figure 5-34.

Running the transition demo | Figure 5-34

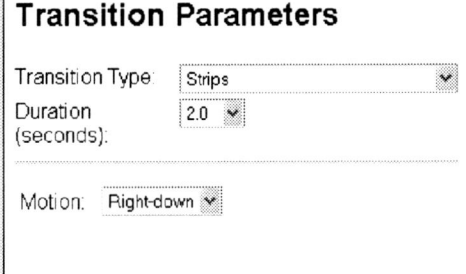

Transition Parameters

Transition Type: Strips

Duration (seconds): 2.0

Motion: Right-down

Second Sample Image

```
filter:progid:DXImageTransform.Microsoft.Strips(Motion=rightdown)
```

Trouble? If you're not running Internet Explorer 4.0 or above, you will not be able to see any of these transition effects.

5. Continue going through the list of transition effects and parameter values.

6. Close the Web page when finished.

Scripting Transitions

The code for scripting a transition follows the same syntax you used earlier for filters. For example, the code to apply the RadialWipe transition with a WipeStyle value of "clock" to an object is:

```
object.style.filter =
"progId:DXImageTransform.Microsoft.RadialWipe(WipeStyle=clock)"
```

You can also use the filters collection to modify the parameter value of a selected transition:

```
object.filters["DXImageTransform.Microsoft.RadialWipe"].
WipeStyle="clock";
```

Once again, if you use a filters collection, you must define a filter style in the style sheet for the object.

Running a Transition

If you want to see the effect of a transition style on your object, you have to run it using a series of JavaScript commands. Running a transition involves four steps:

1. Setting the initial state of the object
2. Applying a transition to the object
3. Specifying the final state of the object
4. Playing the transition

The initial state of the object is the status of the object before the transition. This includes such things as the visibility property of the object, the source of the inline image, or the HTML code applied to the object. Once the initial state of the object has been determined, you apply the transition by using the apply() method as follows:

```
object.filters[idref].apply();
```

where *object* is the object that you want to apply the transition and *idref* is either the index number or the text of the transition name. Applying the transition does not actually run the transition, because the final state of the object has not been determined yet. At this point, it simply "freezes" the object in its initial state. Once the transition has been applied, you can write code to modify the appearance of the object, but since the object is frozen, these changes will not appear in the Web page.

After you've defined the final state of the object, you use the play() method to "unfreeze" the object and run the transition effect, moving the object from its initial state to its final state. The syntax for playing a transition is

```
object.filters[idref].play(duration);
```

where *duration* is the time, in seconds, for the transition to run. Note that for IE 4.0 transitions, the duration of the transition is entered as a parameter of the transition. The following code demonstrates how to create a transition between two sources for an inline image:

```
<style type="text/css">
#Img1 {filter: progid:DXImageTransform.Microsoft.
Slide(slideStyle=push,Bands=1)}
</style>
<script type="text/javascript">
function newSlide() {
    document.getElementById("Img1").filters[0].apply();
    document.getElementById("Img1").src = "slide2.jpg";
    document.getElementById("Img1").filters[0].play(2);
}
</script>
<img id="Img1" src="slide1.jpg" onclick="newSlide()" alt="" />
```

The object in this case is an inline image named "Img1." Initially, the image uses the slide1.jpg source file. When a user clicks the inline image, the newSlide() function is called. The apply() method applies the Slide transition to the image and freezes it. The source of the inline image is changed to a new file. The play() method is then invoked, running the Slide transition for two seconds. After the transition is complete, the Img1 object is left displaying a new inline image.

To create a Fade-in or Fade-out transition, you use the same basic structure, except that the initial and final states are based on the object's visibility. The following is an example of a transition that is applied to the text "The Rest is Silence":

```
<style type="text/css">
#Hamlet {visibility: visible}
#Hamlet {filter: progid:DXImageTransform.Microsoft.Fade(overlap=1)}
</style>
<script type="text/javascript">
function fadeOut() {
   Hamlet.filters[0].apply();
   Hamlet.style.visibility="hidden";
   Hamlet.filters[0].play();
}
</script>
<div id="Hamlet" onclick="fadeOut()">
   <h1>The Rest is Silence</h1>
</div>
```

In this example, the text string will fade out when the user clicks on it, changing its state from visible to hidden. You also could have used the blendTrans() method from Internet Explorer 4.0 if you wanted to ensure compatibility across browsers. Because this is a div element, you have to define an absolute position before the transition can be applied. The span element has a similar requirement.

Running a Transition

Reference Window

- To play a transition, first set the initial state of the object.
- Next, apply the transition effect to the object using the syntax
    `object.filters[idref].apply();`
  where `object` is the object that the transition is applied to, and `idref` is either the index number or name of a transition defined in the object's style sheet.
- Then specify the final state of the object after the transition.
- Finally, play the transition, using the syntax
    `object.filters[idref].play(duration);`
  where `duration` is the duration of the transition in seconds.

Adding a Transition to the Plays Page

You discuss the use of transition effects in Internet Explorer with Clare. Clare wonders whether you can use a Wipe Down transition when the user selects a menu from the page. Clare's idea is that when the menu is displayed, the transition will be invoked, giving the illusion of a menu unwrapping. Figure 5-35 demonstrates Clare's idea. Users of other browsers won't be able to see this effect, but they will still be able to use the menus as before.

Figure 5-35 **Applying a transition to a menu**

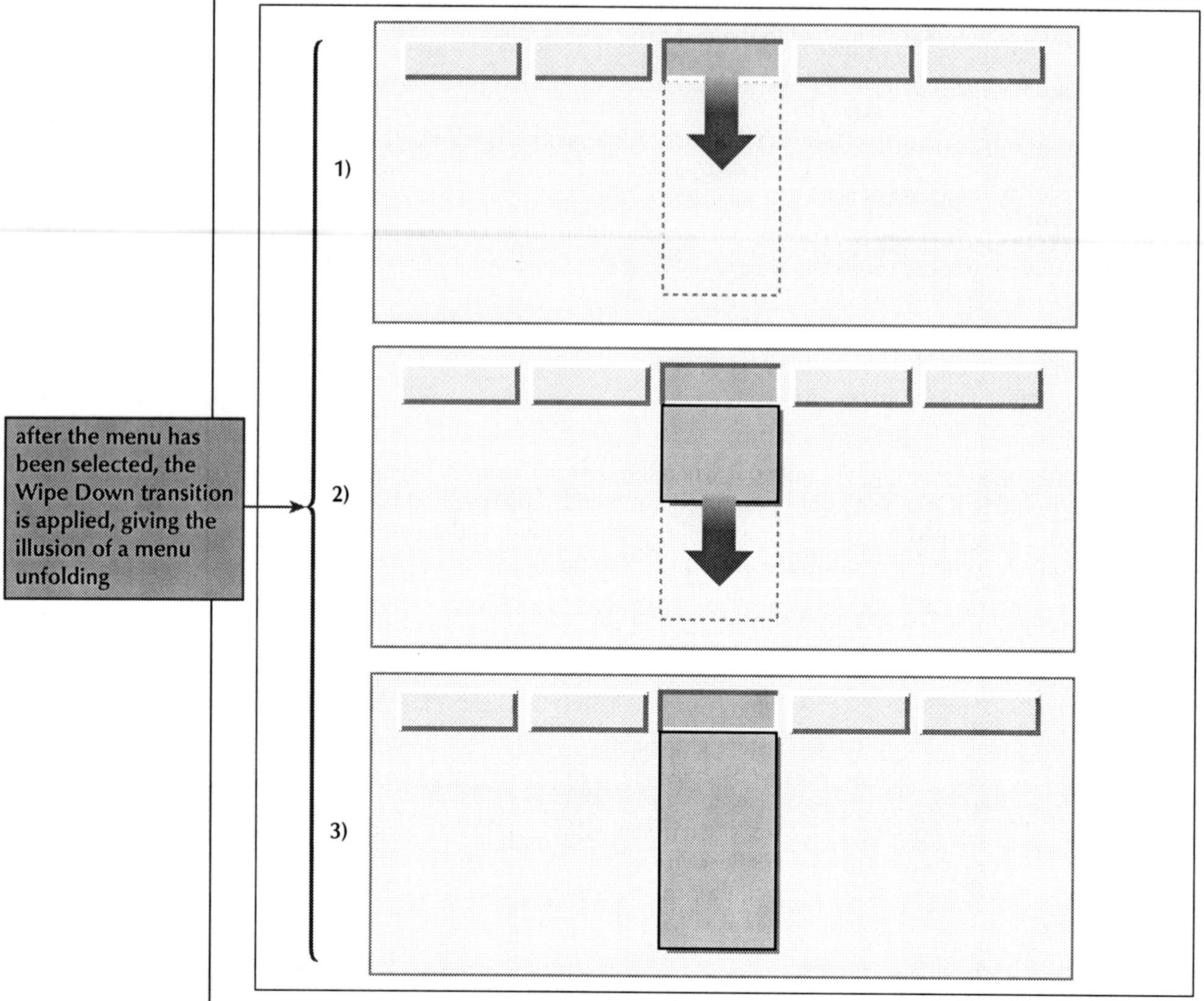

after the menu has been selected, the Wipe Down transition is applied, giving the illusion of a menu unfolding

To create this effect, you can use either the Internet Explorer 4.0 transition

```
revealTrans(transition=5)
```

or the Internet Explorer 5.5 transition

```
progId:DXImageTransform.Microsoft.Blinds(direction=down, bands=1)
```

Clare asks you to use the Internet Explorer 5.5 transition. Add this style to the style declaration for the menus in Clare's Web page.

To add the transition filter:

1. Return to the **plays.htm** file in your text editor.

2. Add the following style to the style declaration for the Menu class (see Figure 5-36):

```
progid:DXImageTransform.Microsoft.Blinds(direction=down, bands=1)
```

Adding the transition filter style   Figure 5-36

```
<style type="text/css">
   .Menu {visibility: hidden}
   .Menu {filter:progid:DXImageTransform.Microsoft.DropShadow(Color=#999999, offX=3, offY=3)
              progid:DXImageTransform.Microsoft.Blinds(direction=down, bands=1)}
</style>
```

Next you have to run the transition on the active menu. Since the transition style is supported only by Internet Explorer, you have to include object detection to determine whether the browser supports transitions before attempting to run it. You'll add the transition commands to the popMenu() function. The revised popMenu() function looks as follows:

```
function PopMenu(M) {
   hideActive();
   ActiveMenu = document.getElementById(M);
   if (ActiveMenu.filters) ActiveMenu.filters[1].apply();
   showIt(ActiveMenu);
   if (ActiveMenu.filters) ActiveMenu.filters[1].play(0.5);
}
```

In the revised function, after the ActiveMenu variable is set to the new menu, you apply the transition filter to it. Note that you first verify that the browser supports the ActiveMenu.filters object before attempting to apply the transition. In the next step you use the showIt() function to show the contents of the active menu; however, since you've applied the transition filter to this object, the active menu is not shown until the transition is run. In the next step you run the transition with a duration of 0.5 seconds. Revise the popMenu() function now.

To revise the popMenu() function:

1. Go to the popMenu() function and add the following statement after the second step in the function:

   ```
   if (ActiveMenu.filters) ActiveMenu.filters[1].apply();
   ```

2. Add the following statement as the last line in the popMenu() function:

   ```
   if (ActiveMenu.filters) ActiveMenu.filters[1].play(0.5);
   ```

   Figure 5-37 shows the revised popMenu() function.

Revising the popMenu() function   Figure 5-37

```
function popMenu(M) {
   hideActive();
   ActiveMenu = document.getElementById(M);
   if (ActiveMenu.filters) ActiveMenu.filters[1].apply();
   showIt(ActiveMenu);
   if (ActiveMenu.filters) ActiveMenu.filters[1].play(0.5);
}
```

3. Close the **plays.htm** file, saving your changes.

4. Reopen or refresh the **plays.htm** file in your Web browser.

5. Click the menus and verify that they appear using the unfolding transition effect.

   Trouble? If you are using a browser other than Internet Explorer, you will not see any Wipe Down effect in the menus.

Using Interpage Transitions

You can also create transitions between one Web page and another. These transitions, known as **interpage transitions**, involve effects applied to a page when a browser either enters or exits the page. Interpage transitions are created using the meta element within the head section of the HTML file. The meta element specifies the type of transition, the duration, and whether it's applied on entering or exiting the page. There are four types of transitions, which are run when a user initially enters the Web page, exits the page, enters the Web site, or exits the site, respectively. The syntax for each of the four different interpage transitions is

```
<meta http-equiv = "Page-Enter" content = "type" />
<meta http-equiv = "Page-Exit" content = "type" />
<meta http-equiv = "Site-Enter" content = "type" />
<meta http-equiv = "Site-Exit" content = "type" />
```

where `type` is one of the transitions supported by Internet Explorer and the `http-equiv` attribute specifies when the transition should be applied. The syntax for the transition type is the same for interpage transitions as it is for an object within a page. These transitions appear only when you go from one page to another or from one Web site to another. A user does not see a Page-Enter transition if the page is the first file the user opens when starting a Web browser.

Reference Window

Creating an Interpage Transition

- To create an interpage transition when either entering or exiting a Web page, add one or more of the following meta elements to the document head:
  ```
  <meta http-equiv = "Page-Enter" content = "type" />
  <meta http-equiv = "Page-Exit" content = "type" />
  <meta http-equiv = "Site-Enter" content = "type" />
  <meta http-equiv = "Site-Exit" content = "type" />
  ```
  where `type` is one of the transitions supported by Internet Explorer.

For example, to display an inset transition with a duration of 3 seconds when a user enters the page, you would apply the following meta element:

```
<meta http-equiv="Page-Enter" content="progid:DXImageTransform.
Microsoft.Inset(duration=3)" />
```

To apply a 2-second Wheel transition upon exiting the page, you would use the meta element:

```
<meta http-equiv="Page-Exit" content="progid:DXImageTransform.
Microsoft.Wheel(Spokes=8, duration=2)" />
```

Clare suggests that you modify the ws.htm file so that it runs a 3-second Wipe Up transition whenever the user exits the page. You'll use the Internet Explorer 4.0 form of this transition.

To insert the Wipe Up interpage transition:

1. Reopen the **ws.htm** file in your text editor.

2. After the title element, insert the following meta element, as shown in Figure 5-38:

   ```
   <meta http-equiv="Page-Exit" content="revealTrans(duration=3,
   transition=4)" />
   ```

Creating an interpage transition | Figure 5-38

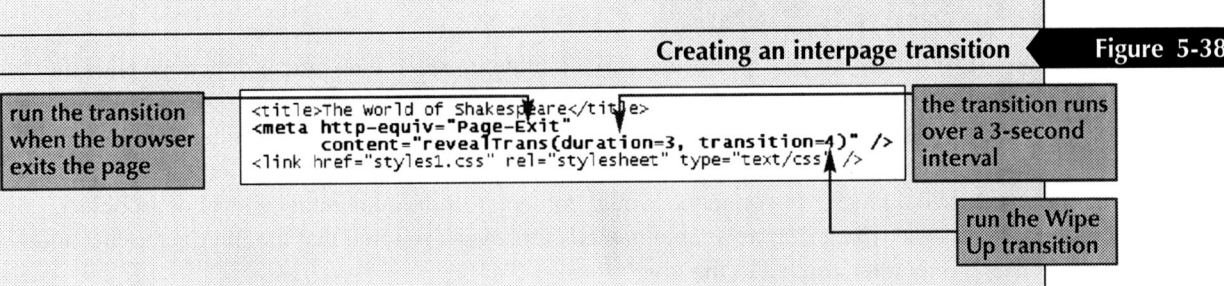

run the transition when the browser exits the page

```
<title>The World of Shakespeare</title>
<meta http-equiv="Page-Exit"
      content="revealTrans(duration=3, transition=4)" />
<link href="styles1.css" rel="stylesheet" type="text/css" />
```

the transition runs over a 3-second interval

run the Wipe Up transition

3. Close the file, saving your changes.

4. Reopen **ws.htm** in your Web browser.

5. Click the **The Plays** link and verify that, as the browser exits the home page, the Wipe Up transition is played (see Figure 5-39).

Running an interpage transition | Figure 5-39

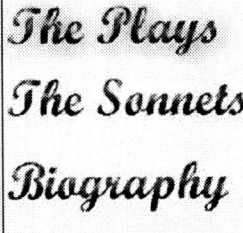

Trouble? If you are using a browser other than Internet Explorer, you will not see the interpage transition effect.

6. Close your Web browser.

You've completed your work on Clare's Web site for now. Clare is pleased with the special effects that you've created for her. She feels that they add a lot of visual interest to the page. As she adds more pages to her Web site, she'll get back to you for further assistance.

Tips for Working with Special Effects

- Preload all images used in image rollovers to speed up the rollover effect
- Place rollover images in image arrays to make it easier to write programs that swap the images
- Place long lists of links into pop-up or pull-down menus to save screen space
- Place filter styles in separate style declarations to avoid problems with older browsers
- If you use filter or transition styles, test your Web site on non-Internet Explorer browsers to ensure that their use does not cause problems for those browsers

Review

Session 5.3 Quick Check

1. What style would you use to flip an inline image in the vertical direction? Give the answer for both Internet Explorer 4.0 and Internet Explorer 5.5.
2. What JavaScript command would you enter to apply the emboss filter to an object named "Logo"? Give the answer for Internet Explorer 5.5.
3. What JavaScript command would you enter to store the opacity level of an object named "Logo" in a variable named "OpLevel"? Assume that the filter is the first and only filter applied to the object.
4. Describe the two types of transitions supported by Internet Explorer 4.0.
5. What transition would you use in Internet Explorer 5.5 to duplicate the effect of the blendTrans() method?
6. What JavaScript command would you use to store the duration of the Logo object's first transition in a variable named "DLevel"?
7. What HTML tag would you enter to create a Random transition effect lasting 2 seconds, whenever the HTML file is opened by the browser?

Review

Tutorial Summary

In this tutorial you learned how to add special visual effects to a Web site. The first session explored how to create image rollovers by working with image objects and the document.images collection. In this session you learned how to preload images and how to place those images in an image array. The session concluded with a brief discussion of text rollovers and uses of the hover class. The second session looked at techniques to create pop-up, pull-down, sliding, and tabbed menus. In this session you learned how to use the visibility style to alternately hide and unhide an object on the page. The third session focused on styles supported by Internet Explorer to add visual effects to a Web page. You learned how to use the filter style to modify the appearance of objects in a Web document and you saw how to create a transition effect from one object to another. The session concluded with a discussion of interpage transitions that run when a browser switches from one page to another.

Key Terms

blend transition	image rollover	reveal transition
filter	interpage transition	sliding menu
filter collection	pop-up menu	tabbed menu
image collection	pull-down menu	transition
image object		

Practice

Practice the skills you learned in the tutorial using the same case scenario.

Review Assignments

Data files needed for this Review Assignment: bio_out.jpg, bio_over.jpg, caliban.gif, globe_out.jpg, globe_over.jpg, linktest.htm, menu1.jpg, menu2.jpg, plays.css, plays_out. jpg, plays_over.jpg, scripts.js, son_out.jpg, son_over.jpg, strat_out.jpg, strat_over.jpg, tempest.jpg, temptxt.htm

Clare is pleased with the work you did on the two Shakespeare pages. She now wants you to work on the design for the opening screen for a page on Shakespeare's play *The Tempest*. In this page, you'll employ some of the features you used in the ws.htm and plays.htm files.

Your job will include the following tasks:

- Create a rollover effect for a list of graphic links at the top of the page, so that when a user passes the mouse pointer over one of the five links, a drop shadow appears.
- Add a drop shadow to the graphic image of Caliban, located on the right side of the page.
- Create separate pop-up menus that appear when a user clicks the graphic images "The Play" or "Dramatis Personae." Have the pop-up menus disappear when the user clicks anywhere within the description of the play.
- Add a Wipe Right transition effect that plays when the pop-up menu is displayed on the page.
- Add a Box Out interpage transition, to be run when the user initially enters the page.

A preview of the page you'll create is shown in Figure 5-40.

Figure 5-40

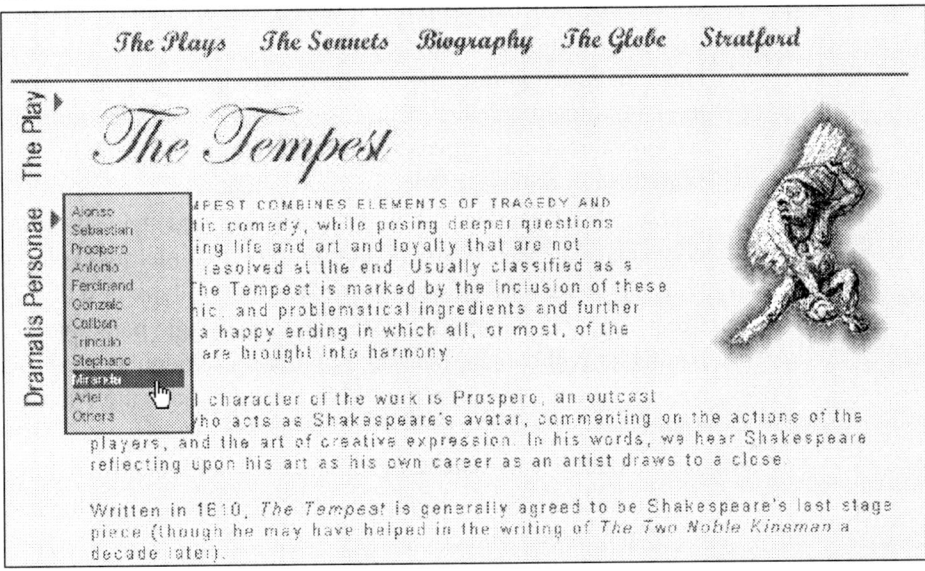

Much of the work in setting up the page has been done for you. Text for the two pop-up menus is located within <div> tags with the id names "ThePlay" and "Dramatis". You'll use these id names to identify which pop-up menu to display. The HTML file also contains a link to an external JavaScript file named scripts.js. This file contains the functions hideIt() and showIt(), which can be used to hide and show the pop-up menus.

To create the Web page for *The Tempest*:

1. Use your text editor to open the **temptxt.htm** file from the tutorial.05/review folder. Enter *your name* and *the date* in the comment section and save the file as **tempest.htm**.
2. Add an embedded script element to the head section of the document. Within the embedded script, create two image arrays named ImgOver and ImgOut. Populate the ImgOver array with the following images: plays_over.jpg, son_over.jpg, bio_over.jpg, globe_over.jpg, and strat_over.jpg. Populate the ImgOut array with the following image files: plays_out.jpg, son_out.jpg, bio_out.jpg, globe_out.jpg, and strat_out.jpg. Use the arrays created in the first session of this tutorial as your model.

3. Create a function named RollOver() with a single parameter named "i". Have the function test whether the user's browser supports the document.images() collection, and if so, swap the image whose index value is i between the document.images collection and the ImgOver array. Create a similar function named RollOut() that swaps images between the document.images() collection and the ImgOut array.

4. Add onmouseover and onmouseout event handlers to the <a> tags for the plays_out.jpg, son_out.jpg, bio_out.jpg, globe_out.jpg, and strat_out.jpg inline images. When the user passes the mouse over these images, run the RollOver() function, using the image's index number from the document.images() collection. Similarly, when the user's mouse cursor leaves each image, run the RollOut() function with the appropriate index number.

5. The two pop-up menus belong to the Menu class. Add an embedded style sheet to the document's head section and, within the style sheet, create a style for objects belonging to the Menu class, setting their visibility style to "hidden".

6. Within your embedded script element, create a variable named ActiveMenu that will contain the active pop-up menu object. Set the initial value of ActiveMenu to null.

7. Create a function named HideMenu(), whose purpose is to hide the active menu. Have the function test whether the ActiveMenu variable is not equal to null. If that is the case, hide the active menu (using the hideIt() function from the scripts.js file) and set the value of the ActiveMenu variable to null. (*Hint*: Use the hideActive() function from this tutorial as a model for your function.)

8. Add another style declaration to your embedded style sheet for objects in the Menu class. Have all Menu class objects employ the Internet Explorer 4.0 revealTrans filter with a duration of 0.5 seconds and a transition type of 6 (the Wipe Right transition).

9. Create a function named PopMenu() with a single parameter variable, M. The M parameter will contain the name of a pop-up menu to be displayed. Using the popMenu() function from the tutorial as a model, have the PopMenu() function do the following:

   a. Hide the active menu by calling the HideMenu() function you just created.
   b. If the user's browser supports transition filters, apply the first transition filter for the ActiveMenu object.
   c. Call the showIt() function from the scripts.js file to show the contents of the ActiveMenu object.
   d. If the user's browser supports filters, play the first transition filter for the ActiveMenu object.

10. Change the href attributes of the links around the menu1.jpg and menu2.jpg inline images so that the browser runs the PopMenu() function when the user clicks the images. For the menu1.jpg image, use the parameter value "ThePlay" for the value of the M parameter. For the menu2.jpg image, use the parameter value "Dramatis".

11. Add an event handler to the div element with the id "main" that runs the HideMenu() function when a user clicks within this object.

12. Add an Internet Explorer 5.5 glow filter style to the caliban.gif graphic. Set the color parameter to #40853D and the strength parameter to 15.

13. Add an interpage transition to the Web page, running the Internet Explorer 5.5 Slide transition over an interval of 2 seconds whenever a user enters the page. Set the slideStyle parameter to "push" and the bands parameter to 1.

14. Close the file, saving your changes.

15. Open the **linktest.htm** file in your Web browser. Click the Tempest link and verify that the browser runs the Slide transition (for users of Internet Explorer 5.5 and above). In the tempest.htm page, verify that, as you pass the mouse pointer over the list of links at the top of the page, a red drop shadow appears behind the link names. Also test that, as you click the graphic images "The Play" and "Dramatis Personae," menus pop up with links for the individual scenes and characters from the play. Verify that these pop-up menus disappear whenever you click the description of the play.

16. If you are running Internet Explorer, verify that a green glow effect appears behind the inline image of Caliban, located at the right edge of the page. Test whether the Wipe Right transition is run when you open the pop-up menus.

17. Submit the completed Web site to your instructor.

Apply

Use the skills you earned to create a Web slide show

Case Problem 1

Data files needed for this Case Problem: housetxt.htm, ldown.gif, lup.gif, pback.jpg, pr.gif, premier.css, rdown.gif, rup.gif, slide00.jpg through slide11.jpg

Premier Realty Connie Peres of Premier Realty in Vale Park, Colorado, has asked you to help her with the design of Web pages detailing the company's listings. Each listing will have its own page with a brief introductory paragraph, a table of specific information, and a collection of photos of the property.

Connie would like to see the photos organized in a slide show. Potential buyers would click buttons to move forward and backward through the slide show. Connie thinks it would be great if you could add some transitional effects to the slide show to increase the visual impact. A preview of the page you'll create is shown in Figure 5-41.

Figure 5-41

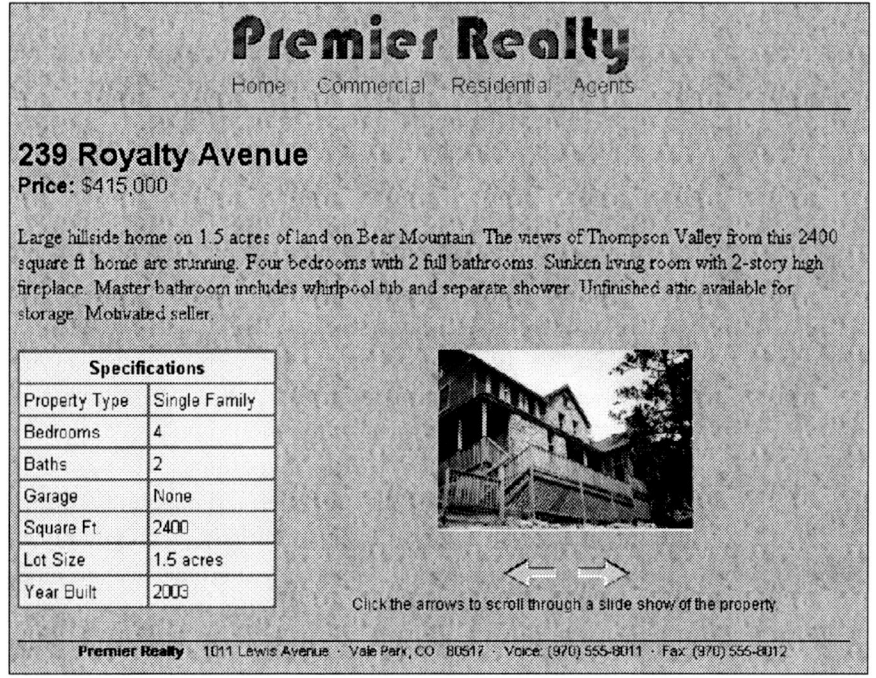

The photos for the slide show are stored in 12 JPEG files, named in consecutive order, starting with slide00.jpg and finishing with slide11.jpg. The initial photo displayed in the page is slide00.jpg. The name assigned to the inline image in the HTML file is "Photo".

In addition, graphic images for the left and right arrow buttons are provided. The graphic files ldown.gif and lup.gif display the left arrow button when it is pressed down and released back up. Similarly, the down and up positions of the right arrow button are stored in the rdown.gif and rup.gif files. The names of these two inline images in the HTML file are LeftArrow and RightArrow.

When a user clicks the left arrow in the slide show, the page should display the previous graphic image in the list. For example, if the user is viewing slide05.jpg, clicking the left arrow should open slide04.jpg. When the beginning of the list is reached, the slide show should jump to the end of the list. Clicking the right arrow moves the user up in the list of images. When the user reaches the end of the slide show, the first slide should be displayed.

When Internet Explorer users click the left or right arrow buttons, an Internet Explorer 5.5 GradientWipe transition should be played as the page swaps the image files. Users of other browsers will not see these transition effects.

To create the slide show:

1. Use your text editor to open the **housetxt.htm** file from the tutorial.05/case1 folder. Enter *your name* and *the date* in the comment section and save the file as **house.htm**.

2. Add an embedded script element to the head section of the document. Within the script element create four image objects named RUp, RDown, LUp, and LDown. Set the source of these four image objects to the graphic files rup.gif, rdown.gif, lup.gif, and ldown.gif respectively.

3. Create four functions named LIn(), LOut(), RIn(), and ROut(). The purpose of these functions is to change the images used for the left and right arrows. The functions should do the following:

   a. The LIn() function should set the source of the LeftArrow inline image to the source of the LDown image object.

   b. The LOut() function should set the source of the LeftArrow inline image to the source of the LUp image object.

   c. The RIn() function should set the source of the RightArrow inline image to the source of the RDown image object.

   d. The ROut() function should set the source of the RightArrow inline image to the source of the RUp image object.

4. Add event handlers to the <a> tag that surrounds the LeftArrow inline image. Run the LIn() function when the user presses the mouse button down. Run the LOut() function when the user releases the mouse button. Make similar changes to the <a> tag that surrounds the RightArrow inline image.

5. Save your changes to the file and open the page in your browser. Verify that the left and right arrows change appearance briefly when you click them.

Explore

6. Return to the **house.htm** file in your text editor. Add an embedded style sheet to the head section of the document. Within the style sheet apply the Internet Explorer 5.5 GradientWipe transition filter to the Photo image. (*Hint*: The Photo image has an id value of "Photo".) Set the gradientSize parameter to 0.5, the wipeStyle parameter to 0, and the motion parameter to forward.

7. Within the embedded script element, create an image array named "Slides" that contains image objects for each of the 12 slide graphic files. Start your array with an index value of 0, and continue up through an index value of 11.

8. Create a variable named SlideNum. The purpose of the SlideNum variable is to store the number of the currently displayed slide. Set the initial value of SlideNum to 0.

Explore

9. Create a function named SlideShow(). The function has a single parameter named direction, which will be used to indicate the direction of the slide show (either "forward" or "reverse"). The purpose of this function is to move the house image slide show either forward or backward by swapping in the correct image from the list of slide show images. Add the following commands to the SlideShow() function:

   a. Set the value of the SlideNum variable by creating a conditional structure that tests whether the value of the direction parameter is equal to "forward" or "reverse". If the value of the direction parameter is "forward", use a conditional operator that tests whether the current value of the SlideNum variable is equal to 11 (the last slide in the list). If SlideNum is equal to 11, set its new value to 0 (bringing it back to the first slide in the list); otherwise increase the value of SlideNum by 1. If the value of the direction parameter is "reverse", use a conditional operator that tests whether SlideNum is equal to 0 (the first slide), in which case set the new value of SlideNum to 11 (the last slide); otherwise decrease the value of the SlideNum variable by 1.

   b. Determine whether to apply an Internet Explorer transition to the slide show by creating a conditional structure to test whether the user's browser supports transitions. (*Hint*: Use object detection with the object document. images["Photo"].filters as the object in the conditional statement.) If a user's browser doesn't support transitions, set the source of the Photo inline image to the image in the Slides image array with the index value equal to SlideNum. If the user's browser does support transitions, run a function named TransSlide() with the direction variable as the parameter value. You'll create this function next.

Explore

10. Create a function named TransSlide(). The purpose of this function is to run the slide show for Internet Explorer users with a gradient wipe transition applied to the moving images. The function has a single parameter named direction, which indicates the direction of the gradient wipe. Add the following commands to the TransSlide() function:

    a. Set the value of the motion parameter for the Photo image's filter to the value of the direction parameter. (*Hint*: Use the object document.images["Photo"]. filters[0].motion to reference the motion parameter.)

    b. Apply the transition to the Photo inline image.

    c. Change the source of the Photo inline image to the image in the Slides image array with the index value equal to SlideNum.

    d. Play the transition for the Photo inline image over a duration of 2 seconds.

11. Add event handlers to run the slide show functions you just created. Go to the <a> tag for the LeftArrow image, and change the href attribute so that it runs the Slide-Show() function when clicked. Set the parameter value of the SlideShow() function to "reverse".

12. Go to the <a> tag for the RightArrow image, and change the href attribute so that it also runs the SlideShow() function when clicked. Use a parameter value of "forward".

13. Save your changes to the file.

14. Reopen **house.htm** in your Web browser and verify that, when you click the left arrow button under the house image, the browser scrolls back through the slide show. Also verify that, when you click the right arrow button, the browser moves forward through the slide show.

15. If you are running Internet Explorer 5.5 or later, verify that, when you move forward and backward through the slide show, the GradientWipe transition is applied to the photos.

16. Submit the completed Web site to your instructor.

Apply

Use the skills you learned to create a matching game

Case Problem 2

Data files needed for this Case Problem: games.css, image1.jpg through image8.jpg, logo.jpg, tile.jpg, tiles.js, tilestxt.htm

Games, Etc. Games, Etc. is a company that specializes in games and puzzles. Part of the company's Web site includes online games for customers to enjoy while shopping around. Pete Burdette, the supervisor of the Web site development team, has asked you to help create a Concentration game. In Concentration, images are turned over on a table, and the object is to turn over matched pairs of images until all of the images have been turned over. Pete has set up a board with eight pairs of images laid out in a four-by-four grid. The eight images for the game are stored in JPEG files with the names image1.jpg through image8.jpg. An additional image file, tile.jpg, represents the tile when an image is hidden. A preview of this page is shown in Figure 5-42.

Figure 5-42

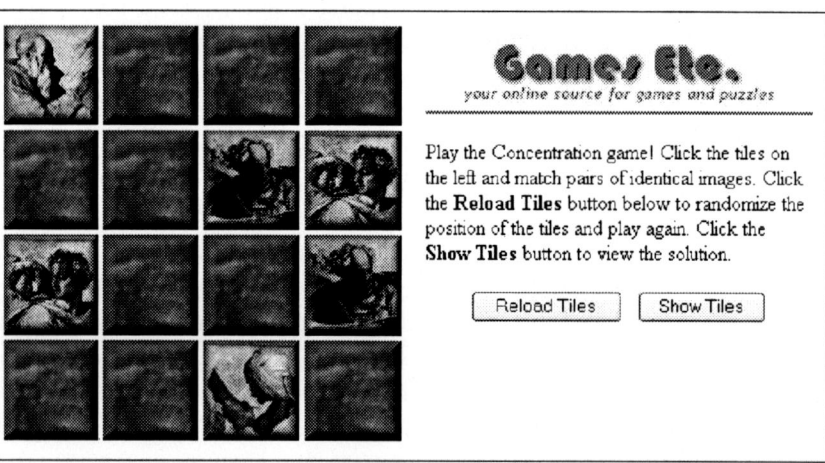

Pete wants you to program part of this page. Some of the programming has already been done for you and is stored in the file tiles.js. The tiles.js file contains code that creates an image array named Tiles containing 16 image objects, representing the 16 possible tile images. The first image object in the array is Tiles[0], which stores the image hidden under the tile located in the first row and first column of the game board. The last image object is Tiles[15], which stores the image for the tile in the last row and column. The source for each of the 16 image objects is randomly assigned and will change each time the page is reopened.

Your job is to program the action of the game. The rules are as follows:

- A tile is turned over by clicking the tile image with the mouse.
- If a player turns over two tiles with the same image, the tiles remain face up on the board.
- If the player turns over tiles with different images, the tiles are flipped over after 8/10 of a second.
- A player can view the complete solution to the puzzle at any time by clicking the Show All button on the page.
- A player can reload the page—and thus scramble the tiles—by clicking the Reload Tiles button.

To create the Concentration game:

1. Use your text editor to open the **tilestxt.htm** file from the tutorial.05/case2 folder. Enter *your name* and *the date* in the comment section and save the file as **tiles.htm**.
2. Within the head section of the HTML file, create an external script element pointing to the **tiles.js** file. This provides access to the code that creates and populates the Tiles image array.
3. Below the external script element, insert an embedded script. In the embedded script create three global variables named FlipCount, Tile1, and Tile2. The FlipCount variable will be used to count the number of tiles that have been previously flipped in the current turn (either 0 or 1). Set the initial value of the FlipCount variable to zero. The Tile1 variable will be used to store the board location of the first tile flipped during the current turn. The Tile2 variable records the location of the second tile flipped. Board locations are represented by index numbers from 0 to 15. Do not set initial values for the Tile1 and Tile2 variables.
4. Create a function named ShowAll(). The purpose of the ShowAll() function is to display all of the hidden tiles on the board. There are no parameters for this function. To complete this function, add a For loop with an index number "i" that runs from 0 to 15. The value of the i variable represents each of the 16 images in the document. images collection and the Tiles image array. For each value of i, swap the source of the image in the document.images collection whose index value is i with the source of the corresponding image object in the Tiles image array.
5. Create a function named FlipBack(), used to rehide the images of the two flipped tiles. The FlipBack() function will be run whenever a player flips two tiles containing different images. There are no parameters for the FlipBack() function. Add the following commands to the function:
   a. Set the source of the inline image document.images[Tile1] to the tile.jpg file. This has the effect of hiding the image under the tile.
   b. Set the source of the inline image document.images[Tile2] to the tile.jpg file.
   c. Change the value of the FlipCount variable to 0, indicating that a new turn is about to begin.
6. Create a function named CheckTiles(). The purpose of the CheckTiles() function is to check whether the images of the two flipped tiles is the same. There are no parameters for this function. Add the following commands to the function:
   a. Insert an if condition that tests whether the source of the document.images[Tile1] inline image is different from the source for the document.images[Tile2] image.
   b. If the images are different, run the FlipBack() function after an interval of 0.8 seconds. (*Hint*: Use the setTimeout() method discussed in the previous tutorial.)

c. If the images are the same, set the value of the FlipCount variable back to 0. This has the effect of leaving the matching tiles flipped and prepares the board for the user's next turn.

7. Create a function named Flip(). The purpose of the Flip() function is to flip a single tile, displaying the image underneath and then checking whether the user has flipped a matching tile. The Flip() function has a single parameter "i" representing the location of the tile to be flipped. Add the following commands to the Flip() function:

   a. Set the source of the ith image in the document.images collection to the source of the ith image in the Tiles image array (thus displaying the hidden image under the tile).

   b. Create an if condition that tests whether the current value of the FlipCount variable is 0. This test indicates whether the first tile or the second tile in the current turn has been flipped.

   c. If FlipCount equals 0 (meaning that the first tile has been flipped): 1) Set the value of the Tile1 variable to i (storing the location of the first flipped tile), and 2) Set the value of the FlipCount variable to 1 (indicating that 1 tile has been flipped in the current turn).

   d. Otherwise: 1) Set the value of the Tile2 variable to i (storing the location of the second flipped tile), and 2) Run the CheckTiles() function you created earlier to test whether the two flipped tiles have the same image.

8. Locate the 16 inline images for the Concentration board. For each <a> tag surrounding those inline images, change the href attribute so that the browser runs the Flip() function whenever the user clicks the tile. The Flip() function should have a single parameter value—the index number of the tile image in the document.images collection. (*Hint*: The first tile will have a parameter value of 0, the second will have a parameter value of 1, and so forth.)

9. Locate the Reload Tiles button at the bottom of the HTML file. When this button is clicked, have the browser reload the page. (Run the location.reload() method.)

10. Locate the Show All button. When this button is clicked, have the browser run the ShowAll() function.

11. Close the file, saving your changes.

12. Open **tiles.htm** in your Web browser. Play the game and test whether pairs of unlike tiles are automatically flipped after a brief interval. Verify that pairs of like tiles remain face up. Click the Show Tiles button and confirm that it displays the location of all of the tiles. Click the Reload Tiles button and verify that it randomizes the order of the tiles on the game board.

13. Submit the completed Web site to your instructor.

Challenge

Explore how to use JavaScript to create tabbed and sliding menus

Case Problem 3

Data files needed for this Case Problem: back.jpg, je.css, logo.jpg, main1 through main6.jpg, main1_over.jpg through main6_over.jpg, mainmenu1.jpg through mainmenu6.jpg, printer.jpg, printtxt.htm, side1.jpg through side6.jpg, sidemenu.jpg

Jackson Electronics   Tara Dawson is in charge of Web site development for the product portion of the Jackson Electronics (JE) Web site. Recently the company has begun an overhaul of the site's design. One of the goals of the overhaul is to improve navigation of the site by placing links to different pages within a system of online menus. Tara has asked you to work on the design of the home page describing JE's printer products.

The printer products page will display two types of menus. A tabbed menu at the top of the page will direct customers to the main sections of the JE Web site. This menu appears on every page in the site. A sliding menu located on the page's left margin will display links to pages directly related to the different JE printer products when the user clicks a link. Figure 5-43 shows a preview of the page's Supplies menu after the user clicked the Supplies link.

Figure 5-43

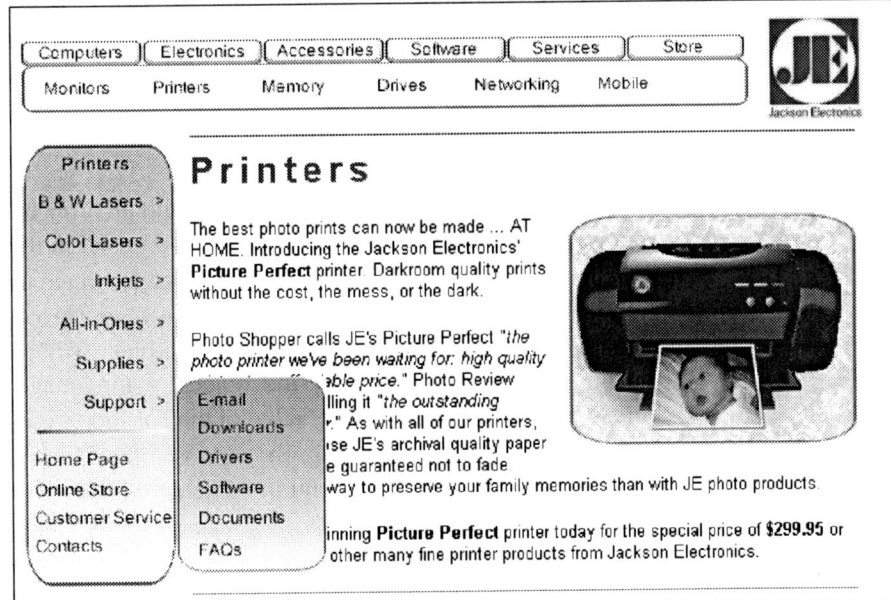

Tara has already started work on the printer products page and has given it to you in the file printtxt.htm. In that file, the menu boxes have been placed within image files. In the tabbed menu, the image files have been stacked. In the side menu, the image files for each sub menu need to be hidden behind the main side menu to create a sliding menu. Figure 5-44 describes the different image files in this Web site.

Figure 5-44

Files	Description
main1.jpg – main6.jpg	The menu titles for the six tabbed menus
main1_over.jpg – main6_over.jpg	The image displayed when the mouse pointer hovers over the tabbed menu title
mainmenu1.jpg – mainmenu6.jpg	The contents of the six tabbed menus
sidemenu.jpg	The side menu containing links to the six submenus
side1.jpg – side6.jpg	The six submenus hidden behind the main side menu

Your job will be to program the actions of the tabbed and sliding menus. To aid in creating the sliding menu effect, use the following functions:

- xCoord()   Returns the x-coordinate of the active sliding menu
- shiftMenu(dx, dy)   Shifts the active sliding menu dx pixels to the right and dy pixels down

To complete this assignment:

1. Using your text editor, open **printtxt.htm** from the tutorial.05/case3 folder. Enter *your name* and *the date* in the head section and save the file as **printer.htm**.

2. Scroll down the document and locate the div elements named mainMenu1 through mainMenu6. Within each div element, insert an inline style setting the z-index value of mainMenu1 to 6, mainMenu2 to 5, mainMenu3 to 4, mainMenu4 to 3, main-Menu5 to 2, and mainMenu6 to 1.

3. Scroll down to the submenus of the sliding menu, contained within div elements named sideMenu1 through sideMenu6. For each of these div elements, change the value of the left style from 125px to 10px. This has the effect of moving the sub-menu behind the main side menu.

4. Return to the document's head section and add another script element. Within this script element, insert the following commands:

   a. Create two arrays: an array named image and an array named image_over. These arrays will be used to store the image objects used in the tabbed menu titles.

   b. Create a For loop in which the counter variables range from 1 to 6 in increments of 1. Each time through the loop, store an image object in the image and image_over arrays. Set the source of the object in the image array to the file main*i*.jpg and the source of the object in the image_over array to the file main*i*_over.jpg, where *i* is the value of the For loop's counter variable.

   c. Create a variable named maxZ. The purpose of this variable is to store the z-index of the currently displayed menu in the tabbed menu system. Set the initial value of this variable to 6.

   d. Create a variable named activeMenu. The purpose of this variable is to store the submenu currently displayed in the sliding menu. Set the initial value of this variable to null.

5. Create a function named swapIn(). The purpose of this function is to create a rollover effect for the menu titles in the tabbed menu. The function has a single parameter named num that indicates the index number of the inline image and image object to swap. Use the value of the num parameter to swap the source of an inline image in the document with the corresponding source of an image object in the image_over array.

6. Create a function named swapOut(). The purpose of this function is to restore the menu title image to its original appearance. Like swapIn(), this function has a single parameter named num representing the index of the inline images and image objects to swap. Use the num parameter to swap the source of the inline image with the corresponding source in the image array.

7. Create a function named showMain(). The purpose of this function is to move one of the tabbed menus to the top of the stack. The function has a single parameter, num, which represents the number of the menu to be displayed. Add the following com-mands to the function:

   a. Increase the value of the maxZ variable by 1.

   b. Set the z-index value of the element with the id mainMenu*num* to the value of the maxZ variable, where *num* is the value of the num parameter. (*Hint*: Use the getElementById() method to reference the main menu element.)

8. Create a function named hideActive(). The purpose of this function is to hide one of the sliding submenus behind the main side menu. There are no parameters for this function. Within the function, run a command to change the value of the left style property of the activeMenu object to "10px".

9. Create a function named slideMenu(). The purpose of this function is to slide the active menu across the page until it reaches an x-coordinate of 126 pixels. Add the following commands to this function:
   a. Create a variable named x equal to the value returned by the xCoord() function.
   b. Insert an If condition that tests whether the value of the x variable is less than 126. If so, then do the following: 1) Call the shiftMenu() function using the parameter values 2 and 0 to shift the activeMenu 2 pixels to the right; 2) Call the slideMenu() function again after a delay of 10 milliseconds.

10. Create a function named startSlide(). The purpose of this function is to hide the currently displayed submenu and then to start sliding the selected submenus out from behind the side menu. The function has a single parameter, num, indicating the number of the submenu to slide. Add the following commands:
    a. Insert an If condition that tests whether the value of the activeMenu variable is not equal to null. If it is not equal to null, run the hideActive() function to hide the currently displayed submenu.
    b. Point the activeMenu variable to the object whose reference is sideMenu*num*, where *num* is the value of the num parameter. (*Hint*: Use the document. getElementById() method to reference the sideMenu object.)
    c. Call the slideMenu() function.

11. Scroll down the document and locate the <a> tag surrounding the inline image main1.jpg. Change the href attribute of this inline image from "#" to a link that calls the showMain() function using 1 as the parameter value. (*Hint*: See Tutorial 2 for a discussion of running JavaScript commands as hyperlinks.)

12. Add an onmouseover event handler to the main1.jpg inline image to run the swapIn() function. Use 1 as the parameter value. Then add an onmouseover event hander to the main1.jpg inline image, running the swapOut() function. Once again use the value 1 as the parameter value.

13. Repeat Steps 11 and 12 for the main2.jpg through main6.jpg inline images, setting the values of the parameters in the showMain(), swapIn(), and swapOut() functions from 2 through 6.

14. Scroll down to the linkmap image map. Within the hotspot for the first area element, change the href attribute from "#" to a link that calls the startSlide() function using 1 as the parameter value. Repeat for the remaining 5 hotspots, increasing the value of the parameter value from 2 through 6.

15. Add an onclick event handler to the main div element, calling the hideActive() function.

16. Save your changes to the file.

17. Open **printer.htm** in your Web browser and verify that the image in the six tabbed menu titles changes in response to a mouse rollover; clicking one of the six tabbed menu titles displays the menu for that option; clicking one of the six menu titles in the side menu causes the submenu menu for that option to slide out into view while hiding the previously displayed submenu; and clicking the main section of the document hides the active sub menu.

18. Submit your completed Web site to your instructor.

Create

Test your knowledge of special effects by adding them to a Web page

Case Problem 4

Data files needed for this Case Problem: jackson.jpg, lp1.gif, lp2.gif, lp.txt, ps1.gif, ps2.gif, ps.txt, sm1.gif, sm2.gif, sm.txt

Jackson Electronics You work for Paul Reichtman of Jackson Electronics. Paul has asked you to update some Web pages that describe three of the company's products: the Scan-Master, the LaserPrint 5000, and the Print/Scan 150. Information on these three products can be found in the files sm.txt, lp.txt, and ps.txt respectively.

Paul would like you to insert graphical links between these three pages. He's supplied you with three graphic files named sm1.gif, lp1.gif, and ps1.gif. He's also supplied "rollover" versions of these files, named sm2.gif, lp2.gif, and ps2.gif.

To create the Web site for Jackson Electronics:

1. Create three files named **scanner.htm**, **printer.htm**, and **ps150.htm**, containing the information on the ScanMaster, the LaserPrint 5000, and the Print/Scan 150. The layout and design of the pages are up to you. You may supplement the material provided with any other additional resources you think will help the Web site. Save these files in the tutorial.05/case4 folder.
2. Each page should have graphical links to the other files, with rollover effects.
3. Add an Internet Explorer 5.5 interpage transition effect to each page; display another Internet Explorer 5.5 transition whenever the user exits the site.
4. Submit the completed Web site to your instructor.

Review

Quick Check Answers
Session 5.1

1. document.images["Links"]
   document.images[1]
   document.images.Links
   document.getElementById["Links"]
   document.Links
2. document.images["Links"].width = 150;
   document.images["Links"].height = 200;
3. document.images["Links"].src = "links2.jpg";
4. LinksOver = new Image(75, 100);
5. LinksArray = new Array();
   LinksArray[0] = new Image();
   LinksArray[1] = new Image();
   LinksArray[2] = new Image();
   LinksArray[0].src = image1.jpg;
   LinksArray[1].src = image2.jpg;
   LinksArray[2].src = image3.jpg;
6. if (document.images)

Session 5.2

1. In a pop-up menu, a user clicks an object on the page and the menu appears, sometimes elsewhere on the page.
2. In a pull-down menu, part of the menu is visible. When a user either clicks the visible part or moves a mouse pointer over it, the rest of the menu is revealed.
3. document.getElementById("main").visibility="hidden";
4. document.getElementById("main").visibility="visible";

Session 5.3

1. Internet Explorer 4.0: FlipV();
   Internet Explorer 5.5: progid:DXImageTransform.Microsoft.BasicImage(mirror=1)
2. document.getElementById("Logo").style.filter =
   "progid:DXImageTransform.Microsoft.Emboss()";
3. OpLevel = document.getElementById("Logo").filters[0].opacity;
4. A blend transition is a transition in which one object is blended into another. A reveal transition is a more general transition in which a visual effect is applied as one object is changed into another.
5. DXImageTransform.Microsoft.Fade()
6. DLevel = document.getElementById("Logo").filters[0].duration;
7. <meta http-equiv = "Page-Enter"
   content = "revealTrans (Transition=23, Duration=2)" />

Objectives

Working with Windows and Frames

Enhancing a Web Site with Interactive Windows

Case

iMusicHistory

Teresa Jenner, a professional musician and college instructor, started a music history Web site two years ago to supplement the university courses she teaches. Since she and her students found it to be so helpful, Teresa decided to expand the site further, create a new name for it, and market it as an online course. Last month Teresa bought a new domain name for the Web site, iMusicHistory, so that she can take it off her university's server. Teresa has hired you to add interactive features to her online music history course Web site.

Because this is a new site, she needs you to create scripts to redirect users automatically to the new URL from the old university one. Beyond that, Teresa wants to have more control over the interaction between users' browsers and her Web site. For example, she would like to create her own customized status bar messages. She would also like to add pop-up windows to her Web site for use in an online quiz, and add a glossary of musical terms.

Finally, because part of her Web site uses frames, she would like you to write some scripts to control their appearance and behavior. Teresa hopes that any solutions you create will be cross-browser compatible.

Student Data Files

▼**tutorial.06**

▽ **tutorial folder**

concertotxt.htm
defaulttxt.htm
indextxt.htm
lesson3txt.htm
navtxt.htm
quiztxt.htm
sonatatxt.htm
symphonytxt.htm
+ 13 HTML files
+ 2 style sheets
+ 7 graphic files
+ 1 text file

▽ **review folder**

atempotxt.htm
bottomtxt.htm
defaulttxt.htm
maintxt.htm
quiz2txt.htm
+ 11 HTML files
+ 2 style sheets
+ 7 graphic files

▽ **case1 folder**

covertxt.htm
cwjtxt.htm
formtxt.htm
+ 2 style sheets
+ 4 graphic files

▽ **case2 folder**

braintxt.htm
+ 2 style sheets
+ 1 graphic file

▽ **case3 folder**

titletxt.htm
+ 3 HTML files
+ 2 style sheets
+ 1 graphic file
+ 2 text files

▽ **case4 folder**

allentxt.htm
birdtxt.htm
boottxt.htm
corraltxt.htm
courthousetxt.htm
indextxt.htm
schieftxt.htm
+ 1 style sheet
+ 14 graphic files

Session 6.1

Working with the Window Object

At your first meeting with Teresa, she shows you the current status of her music Web site, and discusses the changes she wants you to make. You'll start by examining the work she's done already.

To open the iMusicHistory home page:

1. In your text editor, open the **defaulttxt.htm** file located in the tutorial.06/tutorial folder. Enter *your name* and *the date* in the comment section and save the file as **default.htm**.

2. Open the **default.htm** page in your Web browser (see Figure 6-1).

The iMusicHistory home page | **Figure 6-1**

iMusicHistory
i n t e r a c t i v e

Music History
An Interactive Online Approach

Welcome to iMusicHistory, an interactive approach to music history.

Based on the widely used text *A History of Western Music* by Donald Jay Grout and Claude V. Palisca, this resource offers a motivating, interactive environment for exploring, reviewing, listening to, and learning about music history.

Contact us with any questions you may have about our interactive music history course. We look forward to hearing from you.

Features include:

- Study quizzes with immediate interactive responses.

- Hypertext music terms throughout the Web site with unobtrusive, convenient pop-up windows that open and close, supplementing the lessons.

  Click here for a sample: *a tempo*

- Glossary of Music Terms.

Coming Soon:

- Listening samples.
- Links to further resources.
- Public and private message boards.
- The entire Web site will be available for electronic download or via CD-ROM.

To top

iMusicHistory

Home - Lessons - Quiz - Glossary

Contact: Teresa Jenner, Ph.D., 123 March Lane, San Rafael, CA 12345

Trouble? Some of the links in the Web page will not work yet, since you haven't created the required files.

As you can see from the links on the home page, the iMusicHistory Web site has four main pages:

- A home page, describing the purpose and features of the site
- A Lessons page, containing an interactive lesson on music history
- A Quiz page, containing an online quiz for students to review
- A Glossary page, containing definitions of musical terms

The first changes that Teresa wants you to make to her Web site involve the text that appears in the Web browser's status bar. Teresa would like a status bar message welcoming visitors to the site to appear as soon as the home page of the Web site loads. She would also like a description of each navigational link to appear in the status bar whenever someone moves the mouse pointer over a navigation link.

To create the messages in the status bar that Teresa wants, you'll need to manipulate the appearance of the browser window. JavaScript considers the browser window an object, which it calls the **window object**. Thus, many features of the browser window, including the text in the status bar, are properties of the window object. Figure 6-2 lists some of the other properties of the window object.

Figure 6-2 ▷ **Properties of the window object**

Property	Description
closed	Returns a Boolean value indicating whether the window has been closed
defaultStatus	Defines the default message displayed in the status bar
document	The document object displayed in the window
frames	The collection of frames within the window
history	The history object, containing a list of Web sites visited within that window
innerHeight	The inner height of the window excluding all toolbars, scrollbars, and other features (Netscape only)
innerWidth	The inner width of the window excluding all toolbars, scrollbars, and other features (Netscape only)
location	The location object containing the URL of the current Web document
name	The name of the window
opener	The source browser window, which opened the current window
outerHeight	The outer height of the window including all toolbars, scrollbars, and other features (Netscape only)
outerWidth	The outer width of the window including all toolbars, scrollbars, and other features (Netscape only)
scrollbars	The scrollbar object contained in the browser window
status	The temporary or transient message displayed in the status bar
statusbar	The status bar object used for displaying messages in the browser window
toolbar	A Boolean value indicating whether the window's toolbar is visible

The syntax to set a property of the window object is

```
windowObject.property = "value"
```

where `windowObject` is a browser window, `property` is a property of the window, and `value` is the value that we assign to the property. Note that you can have more than one browser window open during a session, and you can use JavaScript to work with the properties and content of those different windows. We'll discuss how to work with multiple windows later in this tutorial. If you're only working with the properties of the current browser window, you don't need to specify the browser window and can instead use the object name "window", or in some cases leave the window object reference out entirely. For example, to set the value of the inner height of the current browser window to 300 pixels, you would use the command

```
window.innerHeight = "300";
```

If the property of the window object is itself an object, you can drop the reference to the window object. Thus, the following object reference

```
window.location
```

which references the location bar, is equivalent to

```
location
```

as long as you are looking at the properties and objects of the current browser window. If you want to reference the objects and properties of another window, you then need to include the reference to that window object in the command.

Working with Status Bars

The borders of a browser window, including items such as the toolbars and scrollbars, are collectively referred to as the window's **chrome**. One part of the chrome that is common to all browsers is the **status bar**, used to display messages to the user about actions occurring within the window. These messages can be either permanent or transient. Let's look first at how to work with permanent status bar messages.

Setting the Default Status Bar Message

The **permanent status bar message** is the message that appears in the status bar by default when no actions are occurring with the browser window. The syntax for setting the permanent status bar message is

```
windowObject.defaultStatus="text"
```

where *text* is the message that will appear by default in the browser window's status bar. Note that this message is only permanent for the current document. Once the browser loads a different page, the permanent status bar message returns to either the browser default or a permanent message specified for the new page.

Teresa asks you to set the permanent message of the browser window's status bar for the iMusicHistory home page to "Welcome to iMusicHistory".

To change the default status bar message:

1. Return to the **default.htm** file in your text editor.

2. Add the following event handler to the body element as shown in Figure 6-3.

   ```
   onload="window.defaultStatus='Welcome to iMusicHistory'"
   ```

Setting the default status bar message **◄** Figure 6-3

```
<title>Teresa Jenner's iMusicHistory course</title>
<link href="main.css" rel="stylesheet" type="text/css" />
</head>

<body onload="window.defaultStatus='Welcome to iMusicHistory'">
```

status bar message

3. Save your changes.

4. Reload **default.htm** in your Web browser and verify that the welcome message appears in the status bar (see Figure 6-4).

Figure 6-4

The modified status bar text

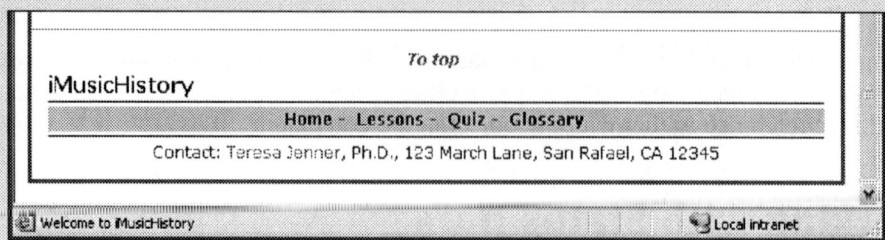

Trouble? Some browsers, such as Firefox, do not allow JavaScript to modify the status bar message by default. See your browser's documentation to learn if this feature can be enabled.

Creating a Transient Status Bar Message

The iMusicHistory home page contains several links at the bottom of the page. By default, most browsers display the URL of a link in the status bar when a user passes the pointer over the link. However, Teresa would like the message "Learn more about iMusicHistory" to appear in the status bar when users pass the pointer over the Home link. This message is an example of a **transient status bar message** because it appears only temporarily in response to an event occurring within the browser. Once the event is over the transient message should disappear, being replaced by the permanent message.

To create a transient status bar message, you need to run the following two lines of code:

```
windowObject.status="text";
return true;
```

where *text* is the text that will appear as a transient message in the status bar. The first line sets the transient message in the status bar. The second line returns the Boolean value "true" to the browser. Recall that the return keyword essentially tells a browser to stop running a process and return the indicated value. You have already used this keyword to stop a function; however, it can also apply to other types of processes. Remember that, by default, a browser generates its own transient message for the action of hovering over a link: it displays the URL of the link. In this case, you need to stop that default action from happening, because you want to display your own message instead. Running the return command stops that process before it occurs, thereby keeping the browser from displaying its own transient message.

To change the transient status bar message for the Home link, you'll add the following onmouseover event handler to the link:

```
onmouseover = "window.status='Learn more about iMusicHistory';
return true"
```

When the user moves the pointer off the link, you want the status bar to become blank. However, by default transient status bar messages remain until some other event replaces them. In order to remove your message, you need to also add an onmouseout event handler that changes the transient message to an empty text string. The event handler for this action is

```
onmouseout = "window.status='';return true"
```

When the browser encounters a blank transient message, it understands that it as a signal to display no message, or to redisplay the permanent status bar message if one exists.

To add a status bar message to the Home link:

1. Return to the **default.htm** file in your text editor.

2. Scroll down to the bottom of the file and locate the Home link.

3. Insert the following event handlers into the link as shown in Figure 6-5:

   ```
   onmouseover = "window.status='Learn more about iMusicHistory';
   return true"
   onmouseout = "window.status='';return true"
   ```

Setting the transient status bar message	**Figure 6-5**

```
<!-- Begin navigation text cell -->
<tr>
<td valign="middle" bgcolor="#99CC99" align="center" class="nav">
<a class="nav" href="default.htm"
   onmouseover="window.status='Learn more about iMusicHistory';return true"
   onmouseout="window.status='';return true">Home</a> - 
<a class="nav" href="lesson3.htm">Lessons</a> - 
<a class="nav" href="quiz.htm">Quiz</a> - 
<a class="nav" href="terms.htm">Glossary</a><br />
<img src="dotclear.gif" border="0" alt="" /></td>
</tr>
```

4. Save your changes.

5. Reload **default.htm** in your Web browser and pass the mouse pointer over the **Home** link at the bottom of the page. Verify that the text "Learn more about iMusicHistory" appears in the status bar (see Figure 6-6).

Viewing the transient status bar message	**Figure 6-6**

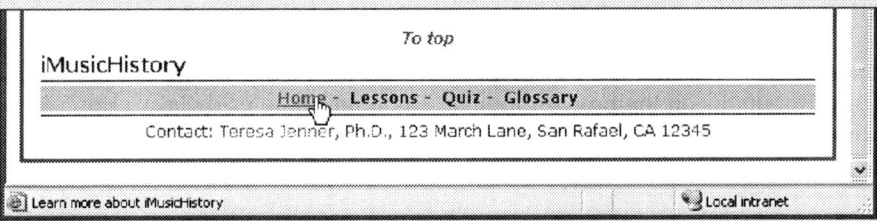

Trouble? Some browsers, such as Opera, will not override the default transient status bar message for this link, and the permanent message you entered earlier will still appear.

Setting the Status Bar Message

Reference Window

- To set the permanent message displayed in the browser window's status bar, use the JavaScript command

  windowObject.defaultStatus="*text*";

  where *windowObject* is the browser window and *text* is the new default message.
- To create a transient status bar message, use the commands

  windowObject.status="*text*";
  return true;

Recently, some browser developers have begun disabling the ability of JavaScript programs to modify permanent and transient status bar messages because of potential security issues. Modifying status bar messages can be used as part of an overall process of creating counterfeit Web sites that resemble real, legitimate sites. Counterfeit sites are sometimes created in order to trick unsuspecting users into revealing personal information such as contact information, passwords, and credit card numbers. Because it's possible that a user's browser won't display your customized status bar messages, you should never put essential information into a status bar message.

You've completed your work for now on the status bar messages. Later you'll have to apply the techniques you just learned to the other links and pages in the Web site. For now, however, Teresa wants you to work more with the main browser window.

Working with the History and Location Objects

Previously, the iMusicHistory Web site was stored on the servers at Teresa's university and the home page was located in a file named index.htm (rather than default.htm). Teresa still wants to include the index.htm page in her site since some users will still have links or bookmarks that point to it; however, she wants that page to alert users about the changes and provide a link to default.htm. Teresa would also like a link on the old home page that, when clicked, takes users back to the previous page they visited. This will make it easier for users to notify the authors of pages linked to the iMusicHistory Web site that the link should be updated. Finally, if a user does nothing, Teresa would like the browser to load the new site automatically after a brief interval.

Browsers maintain information about where users have been and the pages they're currently visiting within each window. You can access this information through the location and history objects. The **location object** contains information about the page that is currently displayed in the window. The **history object** holds a list of the sites the Web browser has displayed before reaching the current page in the window.

Moving Forward and Backward in the History List

In a browser window, you usually navigate through the history list by clicking the Back and Forward buttons on the browser toolbar. To do the same using JavaScript, you use the following methods of the history object:

```
history.back();
history.forward();
```

The back() method causes the window to load the page prior to the current page in the history list; in other words, it changes the page visible in the window to the page the user was previously viewing. If a user is at the beginning of the history list, there is no page to go back to, and the current page is not replaced. The forward() method loads the next page in the history list after the current page. If you're at the end of the history list, there is no page to go to, and the current page remains in the browser. Note that both of the above commands access the history object within the current browser window. If you want to use history objects in other browser windows, you have to specify the window object as follows:

```
windowObject.history.back();
```

where *windowObject* is a reference to the browser window. You can also navigate to a particular page in the history object using the method

```
history.go(integer)
```

where *integer* can be a positive or negative number or zero, and represents how many pages the browser should move through in the history list. For example, the command history.go(-1) moves the user back one page in the history list. The command history.go(1) moves the user to the next page in the list, and the command history.go(0) keeps the user at the current page.

A common way to implement the back() and forward() methods is as links with the following structure:

```
<a href="javascript:history.back()">Back</a>
```

and

```
<a href="javascript:history.forward()">Forward</a>
```

You'll implement this approach in Teresa's old home page. Much of the content of the revised index.htm page has been created for you and stored in the index.htm file. Your first task will be to create a link on the index.htm page that points to the page previously visited by the user.

To create a link to the previously visited page:

1. Open **indextxt.htm** from the tutorial.06/tutorial folder in your text editor. Enter *your name* and *the date* in the comment section and save the file as **index.htm**.

2. Locate the word "return" in the third paragraph in the document body and link it to the following target (see Figure 6-7).

   ```
   javascript:history.back()
   ```

Creating a link to the previously visited page ◀ Figure 6-7

```
<p>If a link has led you erroneously to this page, <br />
   please click <a href="javascript:history.back()">return</a>
   to go back to the previous page,<br />
   and notify the page's author of the outdated link.</p>
```

3. Save your changes to the file.

4. Return to your current browser window and use it to open the **index.htm** page shown in Figure 6-8.

   Trouble? In some browsers you have to insert the URL of the index.htm file in the browser's address bar in order to open it in the current browser window.

Figure 6-8 The index page with a link to the previously visited page

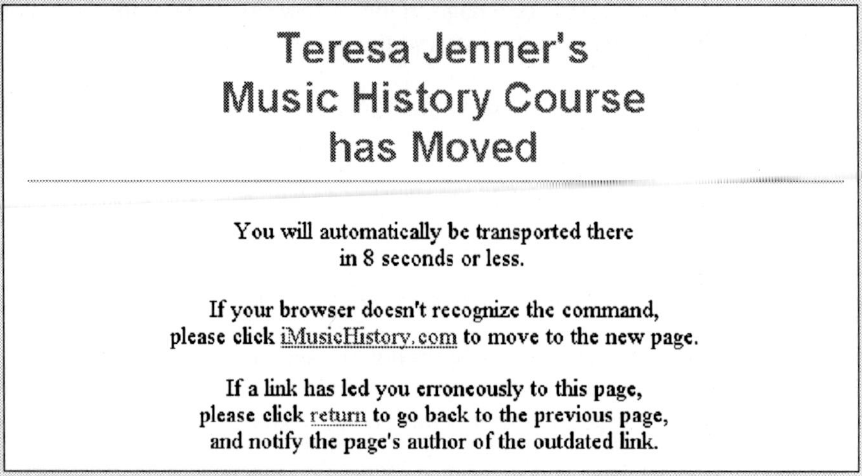

Teresa Jenner's
Music History Course
has Moved

You will automatically be transported there
in 8 seconds or less.

If your browser doesn't recognize the command,
please click iMusicHistory.com to move to the new page.

If a link has led you erroneously to this page,
please click return to go back to the previous page,
and notify the page's author of the outdated link.

5. Verify that when you click **return** on the page, the browser reloads the previous page you opened (in this case, the default.htm file).

With the link to the previous page taken care of, your next task is to redirect users' browsers to the new Web site automatically, so that if users don't click any of the links or their Back or Forward buttons, the new default.htm file will be loaded.

Automatic Page Navigation

There are two ways to redirect the user to another Web page automatically. One way is to add a command to the <meta> tag located in the Head section of an HTML file. The other is to create a JavaScript program that runs when the page is loaded and opens the new page automatically. Since some browser versions do not support JavaScript, you'll employ both methods in the index.htm file.

The syntax to redirect a browser to a new page using the meta element is

```
<meta http-equiv="Refresh" content="sec;URL=url" />
```

where *sec* is the amount of time in seconds that will elapse before the new page opens, and *url* is the new page to be loaded. For example, to load the default.htm page automatically after 8 seconds, you would add the following tag to the index.htm file:

```
<meta http-equiv="Refresh" content="8;URL=default.htm" />
```

Setting the time value to zero causes the redirection to occur almost instantaneously, so that often users are not even aware that a redirection has taken place. However, for Teresa's site you want users to have time to read the text notifying users that they need to update their links to iMusicHistory.

The other approach to redirecting a browser to another page, using the location object, employs the following syntax:

```
windowObject.location.href = "url";
```

where *url* is the new page to be loaded. To redirect the current browser window to the default.htm page, you would add the following JavaScript command to the index.htm file:

```
location.href="default.htm";
```

To add a delay, you can run this command with the setTimeout() method, setting a delay time of 8000 milliseconds (8 seconds):

```
function redirect() {
    setTimeout("location.href='default.htm'",8000);
}
```

To ensure maximum compatibility with all browsers, use both techniques in the outdated home page for iMusicHistory.

To add automatic redirection to the index.htm page:

1. Return to the **index.htm** file in your text editor.

2. Add the following meta element to the head section of the document:

   ```
   <meta http-equiv="Refresh" content="8;URL=default.htm" />
   ```

3. Add the following embedded script to the head section:

   ```
   <script type="text/javascript">
   function redirect() {
       setTimeout("location.href='default.htm'",8000);
   }
   </script>
   ```

4. Add the following event handler to the body element so that the redirect() functions runs when the page is loaded:

   ```
   onLoad="redirect()"
   ```

   Figure 6-9 shows the revised code.

Adding automatic redirection to the index.htm file ◀ **Figure 6-9**

```
<title>iMusicHistory has moved</title>
<meta http-equiv="Refresh" content="8;URL=default.htm" />

<script type="text/javascript">
function redirect() {
    setTimeout("location.href='default.htm'",8000);
}
</script>

<style>
body {text-align: center; background-color: white}
h1 {color:red; font-family:Arial, Helvetica, sans-serif}
p {font-size:medium}
</style>
</head>

<body onload="redirect()">
<h1>Teresa Jenner's<br />
    Music History Course<br />
    has Moved<hr /></h1>
```

5. Close the file, saving your changes.

6. Reopen the **index.htm** file in your browser window. Verify that, after about 8 seconds, the window opens the default.htm file.

Reference Window

Automatically Redirecting Web Pages

- To redirect visitors automatically from one page to another, add the following meta element to the document's head:

  ```
  <meta http-equiv="Refresh" content="sec;URL=url" />
  ```
  where *sec* is the amount of time in seconds that will elapse before opening the new page, and *url* is the new page to be loaded.
- To redirect to a new page using JavaScript, run the command:

  ```
  setTimeout("location.href='url'", msec);
  ```
  where *msec* is the delay time in milliseconds.

Security Issues

In Netscape, the history object also supports the properties current, next, and previous, which contain the URLs of the previous, current, and next page in a user's history list. However, use of these properties is restricted to prevent Web page authors from creating scripts to record what sites their users have been visiting. Most people would consider such tracking an invasion of privacy.

Netscape (version 4.0 and above) uses signed scripts to request permission to access restricted information such as the current, next, and previous properties. The process of creating a signed script involves acquiring digital certification of your identity as a legitimate developer or organization. Digital certification can come from a variety of sources on the Web including www.thawte.com and www.verisign.com. Signed scripts are not available in Internet Explorer, however, and prior to Netscape version 4 these properties were not available at all from a script.

Another way of retrieving this information is through the document.referrer property, which records the URL of the page from which the current page was accessed. The following code uses the document.referrer property to write the name of the page from which the current page was loaded. Note that the document.referrer property works only when the current page is accessed via a link, and that some browsers disable this property for security reasons:

```
if (document.referrer) {
    document.write('You came from: ' + document.referrer);
}
```

Teresa has finished examining your work and is pleased with the messages you created for the status bar, as well as your solution to redirecting visitors from her old domain to her new one. In the next session you'll work on her online music history glossary terms, which will require creating new windows with JavaScript.

Review

Session 6.1 Quick Check

1. Explain the difference between permanent and transient status bar messages.
2. What single JavaScript command would you enter to move a user two places backward in the history list?
3. What JavaScript command(s) would you enter to change the transient status bar message to "View News page"?

4. Describe at least two methods (a JavaScript method and a non-JavaScript method) of redirecting visitors from a Web site or Web page to its new location.

5. What is the document.referrer property used for? What are two limitations of this property?

Session 6.2

Creating New Browser Windows

The iMusicHistory Web site contains a glossary of musical terms. When a user clicks a linked term, its definition on the glossary page is displayed. See Figure 6-10.

Accessing the music glossary ◄ Figure 6-10

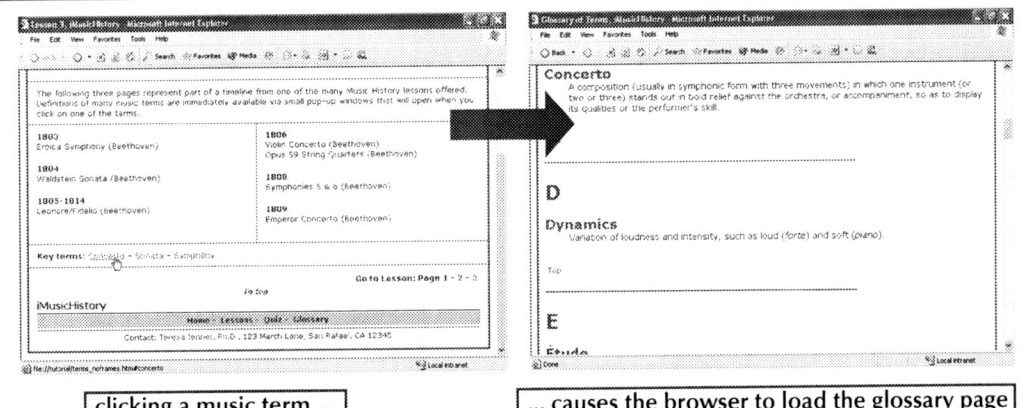

clicking a music term ...

... causes the browser to load the glossary page

Teresa is concerned that jumping from one page to another to view definitions is inconvenient and distracting. As a user goes back and forth between the two windows, it's easy to get lost. She would much rather see a smaller window containing the definition of the clicked word appear alongside the main window. A user could then quickly read the definition without losing contact with the main window. Figure 6-11 shows a preview of the system Teresa would like you to create.

Viewing a definition in a pop-up window ◄ Figure 6-11

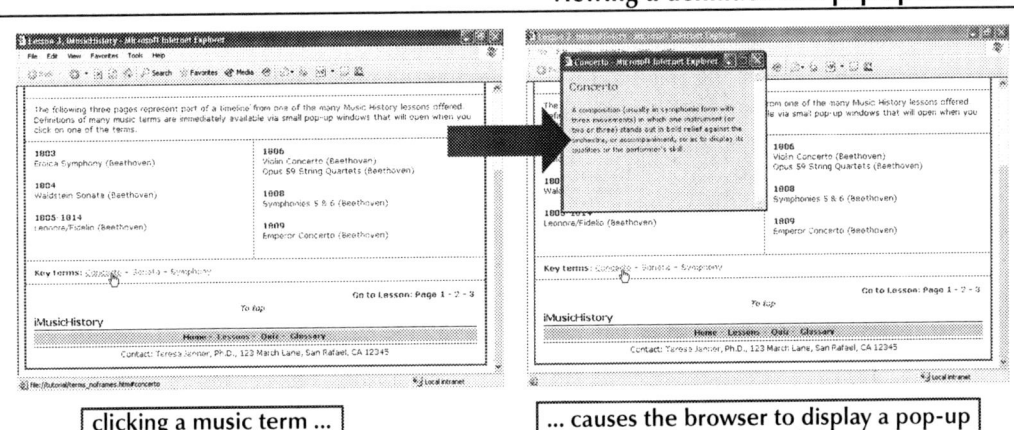

clicking a music term ...

... causes the browser to display a pop-up window containing the definition

Windows that open in addition to the main browser window are called **secondary windows** or **pop-up windows**. Teresa wants you to add pop-up windows to her Web site.

Opening New Windows with HTML

By default, each new Web page that a user opens appears in the main browser window. As users move from one page to another, the contents of the browser window change accordingly. If you want one of your links to open the target document in a new window, you specify the window name using the target property. The general syntax is

```
<a href="url" target="name">link text</a>
```

where `url` is the URL of the target document, and `name` is the name of the secondary browser window in which the document should appear. The value of the target attribute doesn't affect the appearance or content of the new window. In fact, you need to keep track of the target attribute's value only if you intend to use the same window for other links. For example, Teresa's Web site could open a secondary window that displays biographies of the great composers. HTML tags for links to that window could appear as follows:

```
<a href="Wagner.htm" target="Composer">View Wagner's biography</a>
<a href="Mozart.htm" target="Composer">View Mozart's biography</a>
```

Clicking either link would open a secondary window with the target name "Composer". If the Composer window were already open, its contents would be replaced with the new page.

You can give a new window any name, except one that is reserved by HTML for other purposes. For example, if your Web page contains frames, you can't give the new window the name assigned to one of your frames, because the page will appear in the frame rather than in a separate window.

Opening New Windows with JavaScript

You can also use JavaScript to create new windows. JavaScript offers more control and many more options for creating new windows than the target property does. For example, you can control the contents of a window you create; the window size (height and width properties); its position on the screen; and whether the new window has toolbars (and which ones), a menu bar, and a status bar. In contrast, any new windows created using the target property draw their appearance (toolbars, menu bars, scroll bars, etc.) from the appearance of the main browser window.

The JavaScript command to create a new browser window is

```
window.open("url","name","features")
```

where `url` is the URL of the page to be displayed in the new window, `name` is the target name assigned to the window, and `features` is a comma-separated list of features that control the appearance and behavior of the window. If you don't need to specify a target name for the new window, you can specify an empty text string for the `name` value. The features list can include the size and width of the window, as well as whether the window's scroll bar, toolbar, status bar, and menu bar are to be displayed.

You can store a new window as an object in a JavaScript program. This is useful if your script will be modifying the appearance or content of the window later. To store a new window as an object, you use the syntax

```
windowObject = window.open("url","name","features")
```

where *windowObject* is the object representing the new browser window you open.

Reference Window

Creating a Pop-up Window

- To create a pop-up window, use the JavaScript command
    ```
    window.open("url","name","features")
    ```
  where *url* is the URL of the document to be displayed in the window, *name* is the target name assigned to the window, and *features* is a comma-separated list of the features of the window.
- To assign a pop-up window to an object, use the command
    ```
    windowObject = window.open("url","name","features")
    ```
  where *windowObject* is the name of the window object representing the pop-up window.

Before creating a window for Teresa's glossary, let's examine the features list in more detail.

Setting the Features of a Pop-up Window

The features list obeys the following syntax:

```
"feature1=value1,feature2=value2,...featureN=valueN"
```

where *feature1, feature2,* . . . are the names of the different window features, and *value1, value2,* . . . are the values associated with those features. Figure 6-12 describes these features and their values.

Figure 6-12 ▷ **Feature list values**

Feature	Description	Value
alwaysLowered	Sets the window below all other windows (Netscape only)	yes/no
alwaysRaised	Sets the window above all other windows (Netscape only)	yes/no
dependent	Window is a dependent of the parent window that created it and closes when it closes (Netscape only)	yes/no
fullscreen	Displays the window in full screen mode (Internet Explorer only)	yes/no
height	Window height, in pixels	integer
hotkeys	Disables keyboard hotkeys in the window (Netscape only)	yes/no
innerHeight	Inner height of the window, in pixels (Netscape only)	integer
innerWidth	Inner width of the window, in pixels (Netscape only)	integer
left	Sets the screen coordinate of the left edge of the window, in pixels (Internet Explorer only)	integer
location	Displays the location bar in the window	yes/no
menubar	Displays the menu bar in the window	yes/no
outerHeight	Outer height of the window, in pixels (Netscape only)	integer
outerWidth	Outer width of the window, in pixels (Netscape only)	integer
resizable	Allows users to resize the window	yes/no
screenX	Sets the screen coordinate of the left edge of the window, in pixels (Netscape only)	integer
screenY	Sets the screen coordinate of the top edge of the window, in pixels (Netscape only)	integer
scrollbars	Displays scrollbars in the window	yes/no
status	Displays the status bar in the window	yes/no
top	Sets the screen coordinate of the top edge of the window, in pixels (Internet Explorer only)	
titlebar	Displays the title bar (Netscape only)	yes/no
toolbar	Displays the window's toolbar	yes/no
width	Sets the width of the window, in pixels	integer
z-lock	Prevents the window from rising above other windows (Netscape only)	yes/no

For example, to create a browser window that is resizable, but without the menu bar, location box, and toolbar, you would use the following features list:

```
"resizable=yes,menubar=no,location=no,toolbar=no"
```

You can substitute the numbers "1" for "yes" and "0" for "no" in your features list; thus, you could also enter the above features list as:

```
"resizable=1,menubar=0,location=0,toolbar=0"
```

A features list is not required. If you don't specify a features list, the new window adopts the characteristics of the browser window that created it. However, once you start applying a features list, the new window follows these rules:

- If you don't specify a width or height, the width or height of the original browser window is used.
- If you don't include a particular feature in the list, that feature will not appear in the window.

For example, if the features list appears as

```
"width=300,height=200,resizable=yes"
```

the new window will have a width of 300 pixels, a height of 200 pixels, and will be resizable; however, none of the other objects of the window (toolbars, status bar, scroll bars, etc.) will appear.

By default, a pop-up window will appear in the upper-left corner of your screen; however you can specify a different location in the window.open() method. Internet Explorer and Netscape use different features for this. Internet Explorer uses features named left and top, while Netscape uses screenX and screenY (Netscape 4.0 and above also supports the left and top feature names). By default, a pop-up window appears near the upper-left corner of the screen. If you instead wanted to place a window at the screen coordinates (200, 250)—200 pixels from the left edge and 250 pixels down—you would specify the features as follows:

```
"left=200,top=250,screenX=200,screenY=250"
```

To see how JavaScript can be used to define the properties of the pop-up window, a demo page has been prepared for you.

To open the pop-up window demo:

1. Use your Web browser to open the **demo_popup.htm** file from the tutorial.06/ tutorial folder.

2. In the Web page form, enter **400** in the Left edge box.

   Note that, as you change values and select check boxes from the form, a box at the bottom of the page showing the JavaScript code to create the pop-up window changes in response.

3. Enter **35** in the Top edge box.

4. Set the width and height values to **200** and **150**, respectively.

5. Click the **Display status bar** check box to select it.

6. Click the **Show pop-up window** button on the form.

   Your browser displays a pop-up window (see Figure 6-13).

Figure 6-13 ▶ Running the pop-up demo

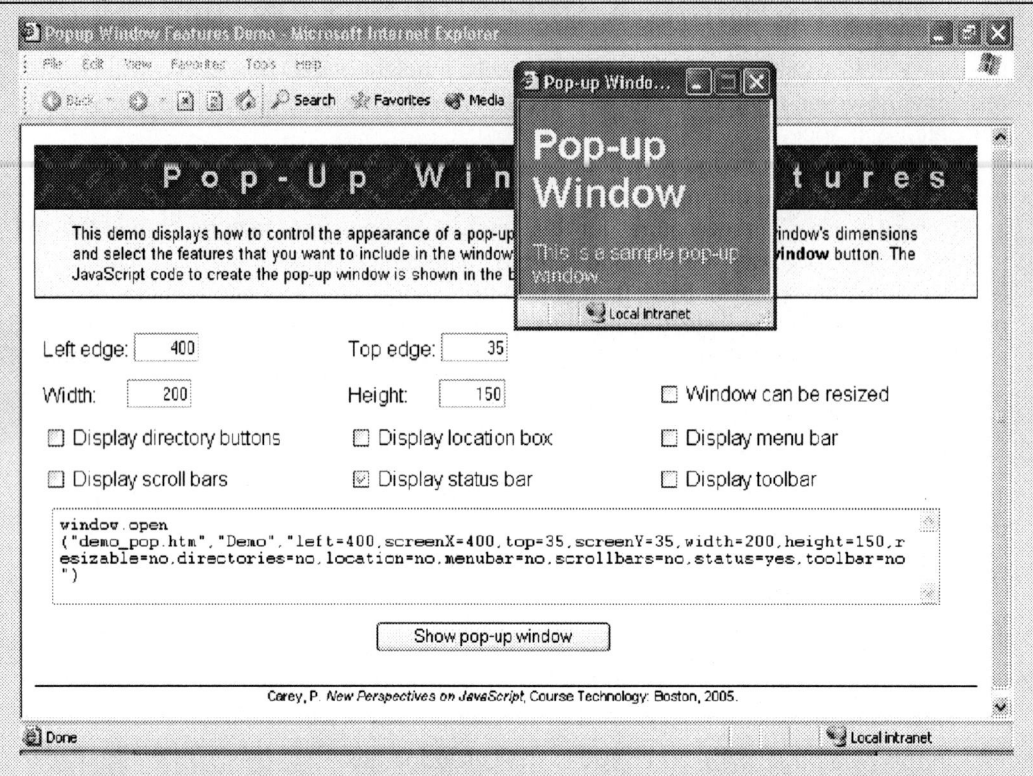

Trouble? Depending on your browser, your window will look slightly different. If you are running a pop-up blocker, you may have to turn it off to run this demo.

7. Close the pop-up window.

8. Continue generating pop-up windows with different features.

9. Close the demo page when finished.

Controlling Pop-up Window Features   Reference Window

- To define the width and height of the pop-up window, add the following to the features list in the window.open() method:

      `width=x,height=y`
  where x and y are the width and height of the window, in pixels.
- Internet Explorer: To set the screen position of a pop-up, add the features

      `left=x,top=y`
  where x is the coordinate of the left edge, in pixels, and y is the coordinate of the window's top edge.
- Netscape: To set the screen position of a pop-up, add the features

      `screenX=x,screenY=y`
- To display the directory buttons, location box, menu bar, scroll bar, status bar, or toolbar, add the features

      `directories=value,location=value,menubar=value,`
      `scrollbars=value,status=value,toolbar=value`
  where value is either "yes" (to show the feature) or "no" (to hide the feature). You can also substitute the values "1" for "yes" and "0" for "no."

Working with Pop-up Blockers

In recent years, pop-up windows have become a common and often annoying feature of the World Wide Web. In general, pop-ups come in two types: those that users open by clicking a link, and those that open automatically whether users want to see them or not. Many Web sites, eager to generate commercial revenue, have incorporated automated pop-ups to display sponsors' advertisements. On some sites, a user can be inundated with so many commercial pop-up windows that it can be difficult to view the contents of the Web site itself! In response to the proliferation of pop-ups, browser and third-party software developers have created **pop-up blockers** that prevent pop-up windows from opening. There are a variety of pop-up blockers on the market. Some make a distinction between automated pop-ups and pop-ups opened by users, and others do not.

There's not a lot you can do to override pop-up blockers—and this is not something you should do anyway, if you wish to create a user-friendly Web site that respects each user's preferences regarding pop-ups. However, you can work to ensure that any failure to open a pop-up window is dealt with constructively by a user's browser. You can have the browser check whether the pop-up window has been opened or not. If it hasn't, you can then open the linked file in the current browser window. A function to test whether a pop-up window has failed to open has the general form

```
function popWin(url) {
 winObj = window.open("url","name","features")
 test=(winObj == null || typeof(winObj) == "undefined") ? true: false;
 return test;
}
```

The important variable in this function is test, which has a value of true if the pop-up fails to open and a value of false if the pop-up opens normally. You use a conditional operator to test whether the pop-up opens. You know that the pop-up did not open if either winObj is null (which means that it was not created) or the type of the winObj variable is undefined. Note that popWin uses the typeof() function to determine the variable type of the object. The popWin() function then returns the value of the test variable. You call the popWin() function from a link on the page using the following code:

```
<a href="url" onclick="return(popWin('url'))">link text</a>
```

If the popWin() function returns the Boolean value true, then the link code processes the onclick event, thus overriding the normal action of the browser to process the href attribute in response to a mouse click. However, if the popWin() function returns the value false, it cancels the click event and the browser opens the link via the href attribute in the usual way—but not as a pop-up window. Thus, in either case, a user sees the contents of the pop-up window—in one case as a pop-up, and in the other in the current browser window. Note that the return keyword has the same purpose here as it did in creating a transient status bar message in the last session: it breaks the normal behavior of the Web browser and allows us to ensure that the linked page is available to the user.

If pop-up windows are an important part of your Web site, you should test your code against various pop-up blockers and under a variety of conditions. You need to ensure that the contents of your Web site are always accessible to your users, no matter what browser and pop-up blocker they may be using. Keep in mind that most pop-up blockers block only automated pop-ups and not those activated by a user clicking a link to a pop-up window.

Adding a Pop-up Window to the iMusicHistory Site

Teresa has begun the process of copying the musical definitions into their own separate HTML files for use as pop-up windows. She has already created three HTML files for the musical terms concerto, sonata, and symphony. The links for these three definitions are stored in the lesson3.htm file. Since you'll be modifying the contents of these files later, open and save them under different names now.

To open and view Teresa's files:

1. In your text editor, open the **concertotxt.htm**, **sonatatxt.htm**, **symphonytxt.htm**, and **lesson3txt.htm** files. Enter *your name* and *the date* in the comment section of each file. Save the files as **concerto.htm**, **sonata.htm**, **symphony.htm**, and **lesson3.htm** respectively.

2. Open **lesson3.htm** in your Web browser.

3. Go the bottom of the page and click the **Concerto**, **Sonata**, and **Symphony** links to verify that the links open the corresponding definitions on the glossary page.

Teresa would like the pop-up window for the definitions to be fairly small, perhaps containing a link or button to close it, and without any features other than the scroll bar. To avoid retyping the same commands for each definition, you'll create the following function, named popWin(), to display each Web page as a pop-up window:

```
function popWin(url) {
    defwin=window.open(url,"pop","width=330,height=220,scrollbars=yes");
    testpop=(defwin==null || typeof(defwin)=="undefined") ? true: false;
    return testpop;
}
```

In this function, the url parameter contains the URL of the document appearing in the pop-up window. Of the different features of the window, only the scroll bar will be displayed. Since the other features are not included in the list, they will not be applied to the pop-up window. As discussed earlier, this function checks if the pop-up window has been blocked and returns a value of true if the pop-up window is blocked.

To add the popWin() function to the lesson3 page:

1. Return to **lesson3.htm** in your text editor.

2. Insert an embedded script in the document's head and add the following function, as shown in Figure 6-14:

```
function popWin(url) {
    defwin=window.open(url,"pop","width=330,height=220,
    scrollbars=yes");
    testpop=(defwin==null || typeof(defwin)=="undefined") ? true:
    false;
    return testpop;
}
```

The popWin() function   Figure 6-14

```
<title>Lesson 3, iMusicHistory</title>
<link href="main.css" rel="stylesheet" type="text/css" />
<script type="text/javascript">
function popWin(url) {
    defwin=window.open(url,"pop","width=330,height=220,scrollbars=yes");
    testpop=(defwin==null || typeof(defwin)=="undefined") ? true: false;
    return testpop;
}
</script>
</head>
```

Next you need to call the function from the three links on the lesson3 page.

To call the popWin() function:

1. Scroll to the Key Terms section of the lesson3.htm file (located near the midpoint of the file).

2. In the code for the link for the Concerto definition, add the event handler

   `onclick="return(popWin('concerto.htm'))"`

3. Add the following event handler to the sonata definition link:

   `onclick="return(popWin('sonata.htm'))"`

4. Finally add the same event handler to the symphony.htm file:

   `onclick="return(popWin('symphony.htm'))"`

   Figure 6-15 shows the revised code for the three links.

Calling the popWin() function   Figure 6-15

```
<!--- Key Terms --->
    <tr>
    <td colspan="2" bgcolor="white" class="body">
    <p><b>Key terms:</b>
    <a href="terms_noframes.htm#concerto"
       onclick="return(popWin('concerto.htm'))">Concerto</a> -
    <a href="terms_noframes.htm#sonata"
       onclick="return(popWin('sonata.htm'))">Sonata</a> -
    <a href="terms_noframes.htm#symphony"
       onclick="return(popWin('symphony.htm'))">Symphony</a><br />
    </p>
    </td>
    </tr>
```

5. Save your changes to the file and then reopen or refresh the file in your Web browser.

6. Verify that when you click the **Concerto** link located near the bottom of the page, the Concerto pop-up window appears (see Figure 6-16).

Figure 6-16 Viewing the definition pop-up window

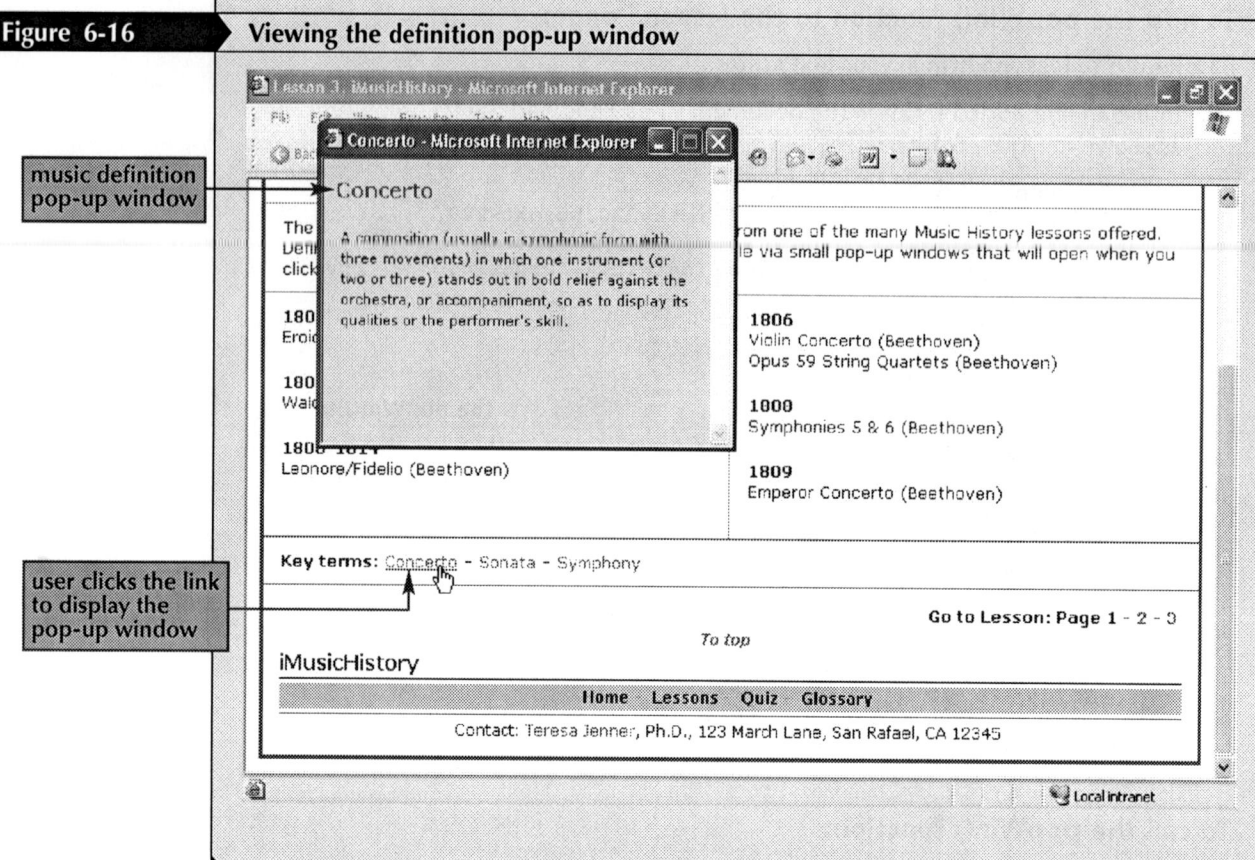

music definition pop-up window

user clicks the link to display the pop-up window

7. Close the Concerto definition window and verify that the two other music definition links display pop-up windows.

Window Security Issues

A browser's ability to open new windows on a user's computer raises some security issues. For example, you cannot create a new window with a width and height less than 100 pixels. This restriction is designed as a precaution to prevent the creation of windows that might be invisible or almost invisible to the visitor.

Working with Window Methods

Teresa likes the work you've done on the pop-up definitions, but she is concerned that users will not like extra windows cluttering their desktops. She wonders if there's a way the pop-up window can be automatically closed once a user is done looking at it—perhaps when the user returns to the Lesson 3 page.

You can use JavaScript to control the interaction between your various browser windows. You can specify which browser window has the focus (is active) on your desktop. You can remove the focus from one window and give it to another. You can also allow users to move windows to different locations on the screen and resize them, and you can automatically close windows that are no longer needed. Most of these features are controlled by methods applied to the window object.

Window Methods

Figure 6-17 describes some of the methods you can use to manipulate your windows once they're created.

Methods of the window object — Figure 6-17

Method	Description
blur()	Removes the focus from the window
close()	Closes the window
focus()	Gives the window the focus
moveBy(dx, dy)	Moves the window dx pixels to the right and dy pixels down
moveTo(x, y)	Moves the top left corner of the window to the screen coordinates (x, y)
print()	Prints the contents of the window
resizeBy(dx, dy)	Resizes the window by dx pixels to the right and dy pixels down
resizeTo(x, y)	Resizes the window to x pixels wide and y pixels high
scrollBy(dx, dy)	Scrolls the document content in the window by dx pixels to the right and dy pixels down
scrollTo(x, y)	Scrolls the document in the window to the page coordinates (x, y)

Most of the time your scripts will be used to open and close browser windows or to add or remove the focus from a window. For example, you can create a window object named "PopWin" using the command

```
PopWin=window.open("pop.htm", "Demo", "width=200,height=150")
```

If you wanted to give PopWin the focus somewhere in a script, you would use the Java-Script command

```
PopWin.focus();
```

PopWin would then become the active window on your desktop. To remove the focus from PopWin, you would use the command

```
PopWin.blur();
```

Finally, if you wanted to close the window, you would run the JavaScript command

```
PopWin.close();
```

You can also use the resizeBy() and resizeTo() methods to change the dimensions of your browser windows, and the moveBy() and moveTo() methods to move windows around users' screens.

Reference Window

Applying Methods to a Window Object

- To give the focus to a window, use the command
  windowObject.focus()
  where *windowObject* is the window to receive the focus.
- To remove the focus from a window, use the command
  windowObject.blur()
- To close a window, use the command
  windowObject.close()
- To move a window, use either
  windowObject.moveBy(*dx*, *dy*)
  or
  windowObject.moveTo(*x*, *y*)
  where *dx* and *dy* are the distance in pixels to shift the window to the right and down, respectively, and *x* and *y* are the screen coordinates of the window's top-left corner.
- To resize a window, use either
  windowObject.resizeBy(*dx*, *dy*)
  or
  windowObject.resizeTo(*x*, *y*)
  where *dx* and *dy* are the number of pixels to increase the width and height of the window, respectively, and *x* and *y* are the width and height of the window in pixels.

To see how you can use these methods in your Web pages, a demo page has been prepared in which you use JavaScript to open a pop-up window on your desktop, move it and resize it, and then close it.

To run the pop-up demo:

1. In your Web browser, open **demo_popup2.htm** from the tutorial.06/tutorial folder on your Data Disk.

2. Click the **Show Pop-up Window** button to display the pop-up window.

3. Click the **Move Window** buttons to move the pop-up window around your screen.

4. Click the **Resize Window** buttons to expand and contract the width and height of the pop-up window (see Figure 6-18).

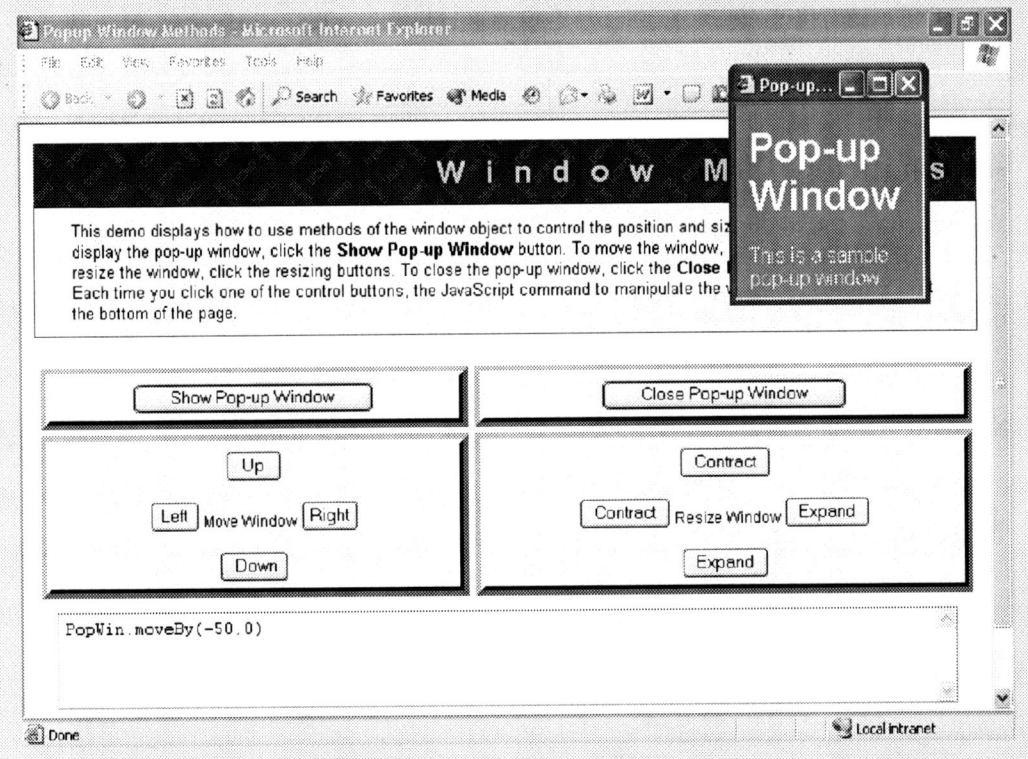

Trouble? You cannot reduce the width or height of the pop-up window to below 100 pixels.

Trouble? As the focus shifts between the main browser window and the pop-up window, you may notice a bit of sluggishness in moving the window around your desktop.

▶ **5.** Click the **Close Pop-up Window** button to close the pop-up window.

▶ **6.** Continue experimenting with the demo page and then close the file when finished.

The self and opener Keywords

If your script opens several windows, it can be confusing for users to keep track of them. There are several ways of identifying the different windows. One way is through the object name you assign to each window as you create it, as in the PopWin example above. JavaScript also provides two keywords: self and opener.

The **self keyword** refers to the current window. The self keyword is synonymous with the window keyword, but you may see it used to improve clarity when a script refers to many different windows and frames. This means that to close the current window, you can use either the command

```
self.close();
```

or

```
window.close();
```

The **opener keyword** refers to the window or frame that used the window.open() method to open the current window. For example, when a secondary window is spawned from another window, the secondary window can close the original window with the command

```
opener.close();
```

Automatically Closing the Definition Window

You now have the information to make the change to the pop-up window that Teresa requested. Recall that Teresa wants the pop-up window to close whenever it loses the focus. You can do this by adding the following onblur event handler to the body element of each pop-up definition window:

```
onblur="self.close()"
```

You have to make this change to all three of the files for the definitions.

To add the onblur event handler to the pop-up definitions:

1. If necessary, reopen **concerto.htm** in your text editor.

2. Add the following event handler to the body element, as shown in Figure 6-19.

```
onblur="self.close()"
```

Figure 6-19 Adding an onblur event handler

```
<body onblur="self.close()">
<h2>Concerto</h2>
<p>A composition (usually in symphonic form with three movements) in which
one instrument (or two or three) stands out in bold relief against the
orchestra, or accompaniment, so as to display its qualities or the
performer's skill.
</p>
</body>
```

3. Save your changes to the file and close it.

4. Return to **sonata.htm** in your text editor. Insert **onblur="self.close()"** into the <body> tag and then close the file, saving your changes.

5. Add the same onblur event handler to the <body> tag of the **symphony.htm** file, and then save and close the file.

6. Return to your Web browser and reopen the **lesson3.htm** file.

7. Click each of the definitions, and verify that when you click back anywhere on the Lesson3 page, the pop-up window closes automatically.

   Trouble? Some browsers do not support the onblur() event handler for the body element, so you may have to close the pop-up windows yourself.

Now that you have completed pop-up windows for some of the definitions, you can turn your attention to the changes Teresa wants you to make to her online quiz.

Creating Dialog Boxes

The next part of the iMusicHistory Web site that Teresa wants you to work on is a page containing a quiz about music history. The page consists of a series of multiple-choice questions in a Web form. Open this file now.

To open the Quiz page:

▶ **1.** In your text editor, open **quiztxt.htm** from the tutorial.06/tutorial folder. Enter *your name* and *the date* in the comment section of the file and save it as **quiz.htm**.

▶ **2.** Open **quiz.htm** in your Web browser. Do not attempt to answer the quiz questions yet.

There are four questions and four choices for each question. Teresa has already added event handlers to each of the radio buttons in the form to run a function named answer() when a user clicks one of the choices. For example, the HTML code for the four choices in the first question is:

```
<input type="radio" name="Q1"
 onclick="answer('Robert Minute',false)" />
<input type="radio" name="Q1"
 onclick="answer('Johannes Brahms',false)" />
<input type="radio" name="Q1"
 onclick="answer('Frederic Chopin',true)" />
<input type="radio" name="Q1"
 onclick="answer('None of the above',false)" />
```

The answer function has two parameters. The first parameter contains the text of the user's guess, and the second parameter contains a Boolean value indicating whether the guess is correct or not. Teresa wants the answer() function to display a window containing the text of the user's choice that indicates whether that choice is correct or not. Teresa has not written that function yet and has asked for your help.

A dialog box is a simple way to create a window containing customized text. JavaScript supports three types of customized dialog boxes: alert, prompt, and confirm. As you learned in Tutorial 1, an **alert dialog box** displays a message along with an OK button, which can be used to close the dialog box. A **prompt dialog box** displays both a message and a text box in which a user can enter text. A **confirm dialog box** displays a message along with OK and Cancel buttons. The syntax to create each of these dialog boxes is

```
alert("message")
prompt("message","default")
confirm("message")
```

where *message* is the text that appears in the dialog box, and *default* is the default text that appears in a prompt dialog box. Figure 6-20 shows examples of each type of dialog box. Note that different browsers display their dialog boxes with slight differences, but all browsers display dialog boxes with the common features of a title bar, a default value (in the case of prompt dialog boxes), an OK button, and a Cancel button (in the case of prompt and confirm dialog boxes).

Figure 6-20 | **Alert, prompt, and confirm dialog boxes**

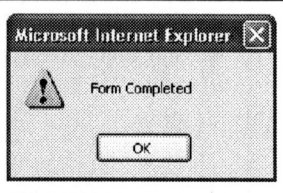

alert("Form Completed")

prompt("User Name", "Enter your name")

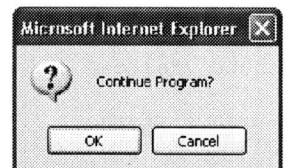

confirm("Continue Program?")

In addition to displaying messages, the prompt and confirm dialog boxes return a value indicating the action that the user took within the dialog box. For the prompt dialog box, the value returned is the value entered into the text box. For the confirm dialog box, the Boolean value "true" is returned if a user clicks the OK button, while the value "false" is returned if a user clicks the Cancel button.

Reference Window | **Creating Dialog Boxes**

- To create an alert box, use the window method
    alert("*message*")
  where *message* is the text that appears in the dialog box.
- To create a prompt box, use the window method
    prompt("*message*","*default*")
  where *message* is the text that appears in the dialog box, and *default* is the default text appearing in the text input box.
- To create a confirm box, use the window method
    confirm("*message*")
  where *message* is a statement that you want users to confirm or cancel.

For the Quiz page, you'll use an alert box that indicates whether a user has answered the question correctly. The text of the answer function is

```
function answer(choice, guess) {
   if (guess) {
      alert(choice + " is correct!");
   } else {
      alert(choice + " is incorrect. Try again");
   }
}
```

In this function, the guess parameter contains the Boolean value indicating whether the user responded correctly. If guess is true, the function displays an alert box containing the text of the answer followed by "is correct!" If guess is false, the alert box displays the text of the answer followed by "is incorrect. Try again." Add this function to the quiz.htm page and test the quiz form.

To create and run the answer() function:

1. Return to **quiz.htm** in your text editor.

2. Add the following embedded script in the head section of the document (see Figure 6-21):

   ```
   <script type="text/javascript">
   function answer(choice, guess) {
      if (guess) {
         alert(choice + " is correct!");
      } else {
         alert(choice + " is incorrect. Try again");
      }
   }
   </script>
   ```

Creating alert boxes with the answer() function   **Figure 6-21**

```
<title>iMusicHistory Quiz</title>
<link href="main.css" rel="stylesheet" type="text/css" title="General" />
<script type="text/javascript">
function answer(choice, guess) {
   if (guess) {
      alert(choice + " is correct!");
   } else {
      alert(choice + " is incorrect. Try again");
   }
}
</script>
</head>
```

3. Save your changes to the file.

4. Reopen **quiz.htm** in your Web browser.

5. Click the option button for **a) Robert Minute** below the first question. Your browser should display the first alert box shown in Figure 6-22.

6. Click the **OK** button and then click **c) Frederic Chopin** below the first question. The browser should display an alert indicating that your choice is correct (see Figure 6-22).

Figure 6-22 **Alert boxes from the answer() function**

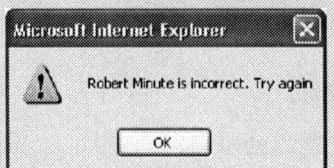
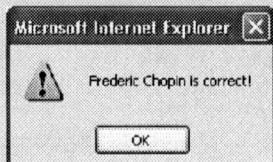

7. Verify that the rest of the quiz works as planned. The correct answers are: 1-c, 2-c, 3-c, and 4-b.

Working between Windows

You show the current state of the Quiz page to Teresa. While she's happy with the dialog boxes you've created, she feels that they're not visually interesting. Teresa wonders if you can add graphic images and formatted text. While it is not possible to do this with the alert() method, you can do it by creating a customized pop-up window. In order to change the message for each response, you need to either create a separate file for each possible response or write the HTML code directly into the pop-up window. You'll employ the latter method for Teresa's Web site.

Writing Content to a Window

To write content to a pop-up window, you use the document.write() method, specifying the window that will receive the new content. The syntax is

```
windowObject.document.write("Content");
windowObject.document.close();
```

where *windowObject* is the window object and *Content* is a text string containing the HTML code that will be placed in the window. The document.close() method is used to close the input stream to the window. Some browsers require you to close this input stream before they will write the window content. When you are writing the entire HTML code in the window, you usually want to break up the *Content* text string into smaller text strings. You can do this by using multiple write commands as follows:

```
windowObject.document.write("Content 1");
windowObject.document.write("Content 2");
  . . .
windowObject.document.write("Content N");
windowObject.document.close();
```

Alternatively, you can create a single variable containing part of the text string, and then use an assignment operator to add additional text strings to it.

```
textstring="String 1";
textstring+="String 2";
textstring+="String 3";
  ...
textstring+="String N";
windowObject.document.write(textstring);
windowObject.document.close();
```

In this case, *textstring* is a variable that contains all of the text contained in the text strings "*String 1*" to "*String N*". Which approach you take is a matter of personal preference.

Accessing an Object within a Window

The use of the document.write() method highlights an important point about working with the content of other browser windows. Once you specify a window object, you can work with the objects contained in the window's document. For example, to access a document object based on its id value, you can use the object reference

```
windowObject.document.getElementById(id)
```

where *id* is the id of the document object. Thus, you can run a script in one window that manipulates objects and properties in another window. These objects can also include the variables and functions defined in other browser windows, which JavaScript treats as objects within that window. To access a variable defined in another browser window, you use the object reference

```
windowObject.variable
```

where *variable* is the name of the JavaScript variable. To call a function from another browser window, you use the reference

```
windowObject.function()
```

where *function* is the name of a function defined in the *windowObject* window. Note that a document must be open in a browser window for you to access the variables and functions contained in that document. For example, if your primary window opens a pop-up window, the pop-up window can access a variable named "logoName" from the document in the primary window using the object reference

```
opener.logoName
```

Recall that opener is a special JavaScript keyword that refers to the window or frame that opened the current window. In the same way, you can run a function named "showLogo" contained in the original browser window using the command

```
opener.showLogo()
```

Working between Windows

- To write content to a pop-up window, use the commands
    `windowObject.document.write(content);`
    `windowObject.document.close();`
  where `windowObject` is the window that you wish to write to and `content` is a text string of HTML code to be written into the window.
- To access an object within a document window, use the object reference
    `windowObject.document.getElementById(id)`
  where `id` is the id of the object in the document.
- To access a variable within a document window, use the object reference
    `windowObject.variable`
  where `variable` is the name of a variable defined in the window.
- To run a function from another window, use the reference
    `windowObject.function()`
  where `function` is the name of a function in the window.

Creating the Quiz Pop-up Window

You'll write the following HTML code to create the answer window for Teresa's quiz:

```
<html>
<head>
   <title>iMusicHistory Quiz</title>
   <link rel="stylesheet" href="quiz.css" type="text/css" />
</head>
<body>
   <p>
   <img src="treble2.gif" alt="" />
   message
   <br />
   <input type="button" value="OK" onclick="self.close()" />
   </p>
</body>
</html>
```

where *message* is the message in the pop-up window that indicates whether a student's answer is correct or not. Figure 6-23 shows how this pop-up window will appear for incorrect and correct answers. Note that this window mimics an alert box by including a form button that uses the self.close() command to close the window.

Figure 6-23 | **Customized windows**

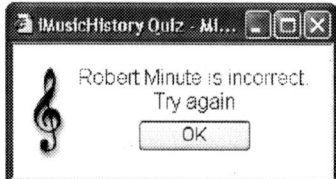 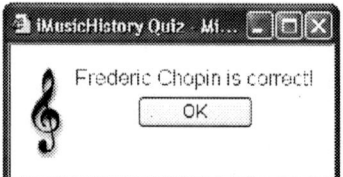

To write this content to the pop-up windows, you'll use the following function:

```
function writeContent(windowObj, choice, guess) {
   content="<html><head><title>iMusicHistory Quiz</title>";
   content+="<link rel='stylesheet' href='quiz.css'
   type='text/css' />";
   content+="</head><body><p><img src='treble2.gif' alt='' />";
   if (guess) {
      content += choice + " is correct!";
```

```
    } else {
        content += choice + " is incorrect. Try again";
    }
    content+="<br /><input type='button' value='OK'
        onclick='self.close()' />";
    content+="</p></body></html>";
    windowObj.document.write(content);
    windowObj.document.close();
}
```

The writeContent() function has three parameters. The windowObj parameter is the window object that will receive this HTML code. The choice and guess parameters have the same purpose and values as they did for the answer() function you just created. Due to the way browsers process white space in HTML code, you can insert several HTML tags on the same line, reducing the number of statements in the function. Additionally, while the HTML code is enclosed using double quotes, any attribute values within that code are enclosed in single quotes. Because this is a complicated function and it would be easy to make a typing mistake, the function code has been provided for you to copy and paste into the Quiz document.

To create the writeContent() function:

1. Use your text editor to open the **writeContent.txt** text file from the tutorial.06/ tutorial folder.

2. Copy the text of the function and then close the text file.

3. Return to **quiz.htm** in your text editor.

4. Below the answer() function, paste the code of the writeContent() function, as shown in Figure 6-24.

The writeContent() function ◀ Figure 6-24

```
<script type="text/javascript">
function answer(choice, guess) {
    if (guess) {
        alert(choice + " is correct!");
    } else {
        alert(choice + " is incorrect. Try again");
    }
}

function writeContent(windowobj, choice, guess) {
    content="<html><head><title>iMusicHistory Quiz</title>";
    content+="<link rel='stylesheet' href='quiz.css' type='text/css' />";
    content+="</head><body><p><img src='treble2.gif' alt='' />";
    if (guess) {
        content += choice + " is correct!";
    } else {
        content += choice + " is incorrect. Try again";
    }
    content+="<br /><input type='button' value='OK' onclick='self.close()' />";
    content+="</p></body></html>";
    windowobj.document.write(content);
    windowobj.document.close();
}
</script>
```

Your last task is to revise the answer() function to create the pop-up window. This involves three steps:

1. Use the window.open() method to open the pop-up window.

2. Test whether the pop-up window has been blocked or has otherwise failed to open.

3. If the pop-up window has failed to open, display alert dialog boxes as before (they are not blocked by pop-up blockers); otherwise, call the writeContent() function to display the pop-up window.

The revised code for the answer() function is as follows:

```
function answer(choice, guess) {
  ansWin=window.open("","","width=250,height=100,left=250,
  screenX=250,top=250,screenY=250");
  popfailed = (ansWin == null || typeof(ansWin) ==
  "undefined") ? true : false;
  if (popfailed) {
     if (guess) {
        alert(choice + " is correct!");
     } else {
        alert(choice + " is incorrect. Try again");
     }
  } else {
  writeContent(ansWin, choice, guess);
  }
 }
```

The answer() function first creates a window object named ansWin that is 250 pixels wide and 100 pixels high and placed 250 pixels to the right and below the upper-left corner of the screen. There is no URL or target name specified for this window because you will be writing the HTML directly into it. The next line of the function creates the popfailed variable to test whether the pop-up window opened. If the pop-up failed, you run the conditional statement you created earlier to display the appropriate alert dialog box; otherwise, the writeContent() function is run using the ansWin window as the window object and the choice and guess variables as the second and third parameter values.

To revise the answer() function and test it:

1. Revise the answer() function so that the code for the function reads as follows (you may wish to indent your code to make it easier to read):

```
function answer(choice, guess) {
  ansWin=window.open("","","width=250,height=100,left=250,
  screenX=250,top=250,screenY=250");
  popfailed = (ansWin == null || typeof(ansWin) ==
  "undefined") ? true : false;
  if (popfailed) {
     if (guess) {
        alert(choice + " is correct!");
     } else {
        alert(choice + " is incorrect. Try again");
     }
  } else {
  writeContent(ansWin, choice, guess);
  }
 }
```

Figure 6-25 shows the answer() function with the newly inserted code in bold type.

The final answer() function ◀ Figure 6-25

```
function answer(choice, guess) {
    answin=window.open("","","width=250,height=100,left=250,screenX=250,top=250,screenY=250");
    popfailed = (answin == null || typeof(answin) == "undefined") ? true : false;
    if (popfailed) {
        if (guess) {
            alert(choice + " is correct!");
        } else {
            alert(choice + " is incorrect. Try again");
        }
    } else {
        writeContent(answin, choice, guess);
    }
}
```

2. Close the file, saving your changes.

3. Reopen **quiz.htm** in your Web browser.

4. Click the various answers in the Web form and verify that a formatted pop-up window appears. Click the **OK** button to close each pop-up window before answering a different question from the form.

5. Close any open browser or editor windows.

Working with Modal and Modeless Windows

Dialog boxes and windows can either be modal or modeless. A **modal window** is a window that prevents users from doing work in any other window or dialog box until the window is closed. A **modeless window**, on the other hand, allows users to work in other dialog boxes and windows even as the window stays open. An alert box in a browser window is an example of a modal window, because you cannot do any other work in the browser window until you close the alert box. Pop-up windows, by contrast, are generally modeless. You can force a pop-up window to be modal, however, by adding the following event handler to the window's body element:

```
onblur = "self.focus()"
```

Starting with version 4.0, Internet Explorer introduced new methods to allow JavaScript to create modal and modeless windows. Internet Explorer 4 introduced the showModalDialog() method to create modal windows, and Internet Explorer 5 added the showModelessDialog() method for modeless windows. The syntax of the showModalDialog() method is

```
windowObject.showModalDialog("url", "arguments", "features")
```

where *url* is the URL of the file to display in the modal window; *arguments* is an optional parameter containing a value, variable, object, or array of values to pass to the window; and *features* is a comma-separated list of features that control the appearance of the window. The syntax to create a modeless dialog box is similar:

```
windowObject.showModelessDialog("url", "arguments", "features");
```

Both methods allow a dialog box to return values back to the browser window that called it. For example, you can create a modal or modeless dialog box containing a Web form, and then return values from that form to the original browser window. While both the showModalDialog() and showModelessDialog() methods are useful ways of creating specialized pop-ups and dialog boxes, they are not generally supported by browsers other than Internet Explorer.

Working with the Features List

The features list of the showModalDialog() and showModelessDialog() methods is similar to that used with the window.open() method. Figure 6-26 describes some of the features and their values.

Figure 6-26 ▷ **Features of Internet Explorer modal and modeless dialog boxes**

Feature	Value	Description
dialogHeight	Numeric	Sets the height of the dialog window; the default unit of measurement is "em" in Internet Explorer 4.0, and pixels in Internet Explorer 5.0
dialogLeft	Numeric	Specifies the screen coordinates of the left edge of the dialog box, in pixels
dialogTop	Numeric	Specifies the screen coordinates of the top edge of the dialog box, in pixels
dialogWidth	Numeric	Sets the width of the dialog window; the default unit of measurement is "em" in Internet Explorer 4.0, and pixels in Internet Explorer 5.0
center	yes, no	Specifies whether to center the dialog box on the desktop
dialogHide	yes, no	Specifies whether to hide the dialog box when printing or using print preview
edge	sunken, raised	Specifies the edge style of the window; the default is raised
help	yes, no	Specifies whether the window displays the context-sensitive Help icon in the title bar
resizable	yes, no	Specifies whether the window is resizable
scroll	yes, no	Specifies whether the window displays scroll bars
status	yes, no	Specifies whether the window displays a status bar
unadorned	yes, no	Specifies whether the window displays the browser chrome

For example, you could create a modal window with the following features list:

```
window.showModalDialog("name.htm","dialogHeight:150, dialogWidth:
300,edge:sunken,resizable:yes,scroll:yes,status:no,unadorned:no");
```

In this case, the name.htm file would be displayed in the modal window. The window would be 150 pixels high and 300 pixels wide. It would have sunken edges and scroll bars, but would not have a status bar or any other part of the browser chrome. The user would be able to resize the window, however. No *arguments* parameter is used in creating this window.

Exchanging Information between the Windows

Neither the showModalDialog() nor the showModelessDialog() methods allow direct interaction between the calling browser window and the pop-up window. Thus, you cannot use the document.write() method to write content directly to a new window created with either of these methods. If you need to send information, you must include that data in the *arguments* parameter for the method you're using. The value stored in this parameter can then be accessed within the pop-up window using the dialogArguments property of the window object. For example, if the *arguments* parameter contains an array of values, you can retrieve the first value of the array and store it in a variable using the command

```
data = window.dialogArguments[0];
```

You can then use the data variable in a program running within the pop-up. Since you also can't write information from a pop-up back to the original window, you store any information that you want returned using the following window property:

```
window.returnValue;
```

As with the *arguments* parameter, the returnValue property can store any type of information including a number, text string, array, or object. To access the returned value, simply use the showDialogModal() or showDialogModeless() methods in a statement that assigns a value. The syntax is

```
variable = windowObject.
showModalDialog("url", "arguments", "features")
variable = windowObject.showModelessDialog("url", "arguments",
"features");
```

Because these methods are not well supported by browsers other than Internet Explorer, you decide against using them in the iMusicHistory Web site.

You've now completed your work on creating a variety of new windows, closing windows, and writing to a window via script-generated HTML. In the next session, you'll learn how to enhance the Glossary section of Teresa's iMusicHistory Web site with interactive frames.

Session 6.2 Quick Check

Review

1. What HTML tag would you use to create a link that opens the file home.htm as a new window with the target name "HomePage"?
2. What JavaScript command would you run to open the file home.htm as a pop-up window that is 300 pixels wide and 150 pixels high? You do not have to specify a value for the window's target name, but can instead use an empty text string.
3. What JavaScript command would you enter to include scroll bars and a status bar in the pop-up window described in the previous question?
4. What JavaScript command would you enter to write the HTML tag <body bgcolor="yellow"> to a window object named "Home"?
5. What JavaScript command would you use to create an alert box containing the text "Script Finished"?
6. What JavaScript command would you use to create a confirm dialog box containing the text "Proceed"?
7. What is a modal window? What is a modeless window?

Session 6.3

Working with Frames

Frames are considered one of the most powerful features of HTML. They enable the division of the browser window into multiple panes, with each frame displaying a separate document. Recall that frames are organized into framesets, using the following HTML tag structure:

```
<frameset id="frameset">
    <frame id="fname1" name="fname1" src="url1" />
    <frame id="fname2" name="fname2" src="url2" />
```

```
    ...
        <frame id="fnameN" name="fnameN" src="urlN" />
    </frameset>
```

where each frame displays a separate URL. A single window can contain multiple framesets, and framesets can be nested inside each other. Each frame element in this example contains both an id value and a name value. The name attribute is used when creating links whose targets are designed to appear in specific frames. Thus, the syntax for linking content to a specific frame is

```
    <a href="url" target="fname"> content </a>
```

where *fname* is the name of a specific frame in the browser window. However, if you want to reference a specific frame in your JavaScript code, you need to use the id attribute rather than the name attribute. The current practice, therefore, is to use both the name and id attributes, setting them to the same value as in the following frame element:

```
    <frame id="top" name="top" src="home.htm" />
```

Teresa has decided to use frames in iMusicHistory's Glossary page. One of the files displayed in the frameset is nav.htm. The nav.htm file contains the iMusicHistory logo and some navigational text that you'll use in editing Teresa's page. Open this file now, and then use your Web browser to open the Glossary page.

To view the iMusicHistory glossary:

1. Use your text editor to open the **navtxt.htm** file from the tutorial.06/tutorial folder. Enter **your name** and **the date** in the comment section and save the file as **nav.htm**.

   The iMusicHistory Glossary frameset is stored in the terms.htm file. Open the glossary now.

2. Use your Web browser to open the **terms.htm** file from the tutorial.06/tutorial folder. Figure 6-27 shows the contents of the Glossary frameset.

Figure 6-27 **Customized windows**

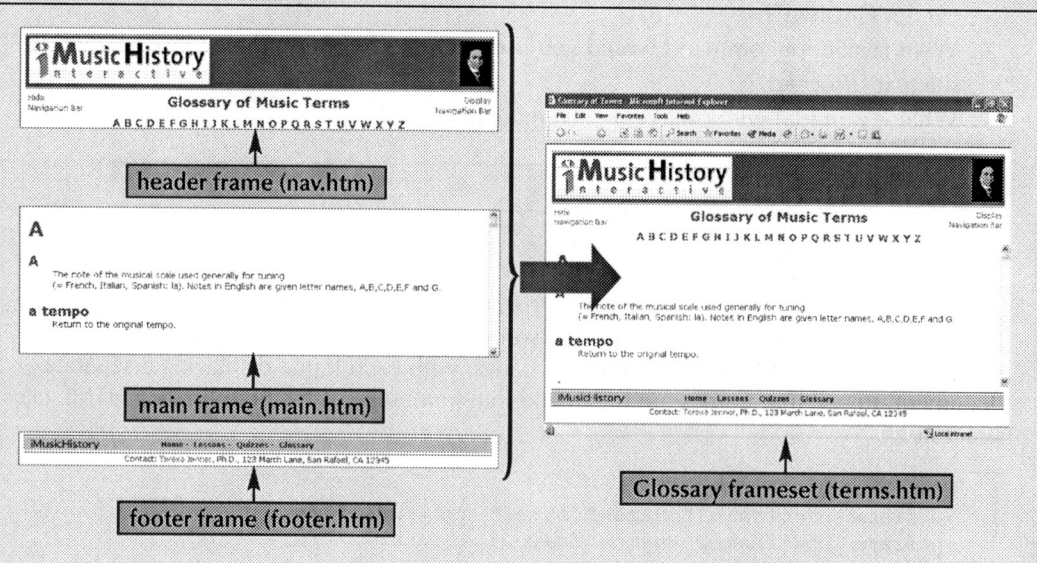

The Glossary frameset is composed of three frames. The header frame displays the contents of the nav.htm file, providing an alphabetic list of links to the glossary terms; the main frame displays the contents of the main.htm file, listing the glossary of musical terms; and the footer frame, drawn from the footer.htm file, displays a navigation bar with links to the other pages of the iMusicHistory Web site.

The following is the HTML code for the Glossary frameset:

```
<frameset rows="160,*,64" id="Glossary" frameborder="0" border="0">
    <frame name="header" id="header" src="nav.htm" scrolling="no" />
    <frame name="main" id="main" src="main.htm" />
    <frame name="footer" id="footer" src="footer.
htm" scrolling="no" />
</frameset>
```

One problem with frames is that they can take up valuable screen space. Teresa would like to give users the option of allocating more space to the list of the music terms shown in the main frame. As shown in Figure 6-28, Teresa envisions users clicking links in the header frame that alternately hide or display the footer frame, providing more screen space to the definition list.

Collapsing and expanding the footer frame Figure 6-28

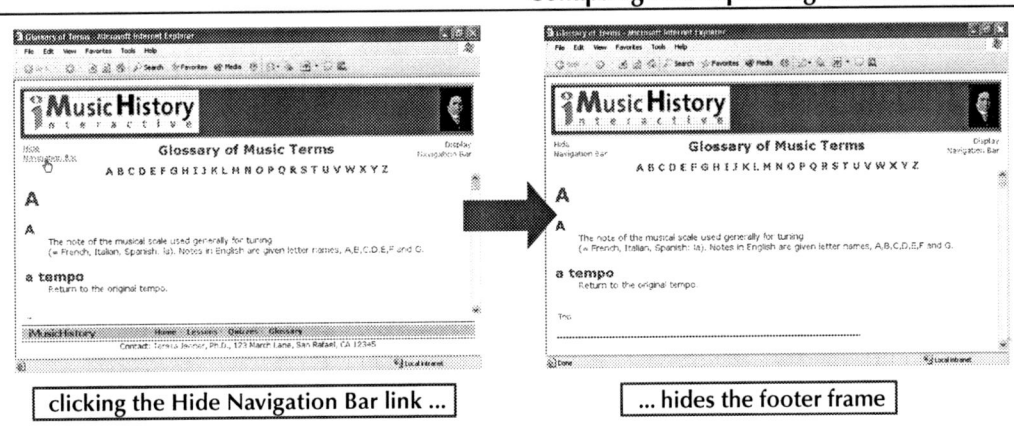

clicking the Hide Navigation Bar link ...   ... hides the footer frame

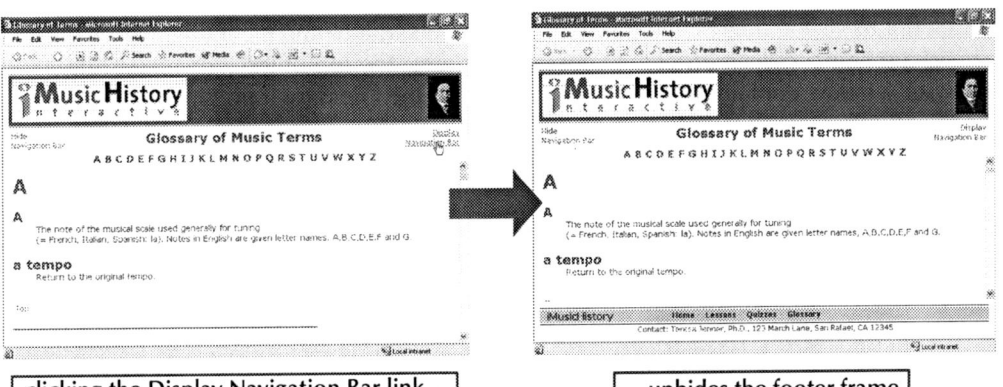

clicking the Display Navigation Bar link ...   ... unhides the footer frame

To create this effect, you first have to learn how JavaScript handles frames.

Working with the Frame and Frameset Objects

In the document object model, each frame in a frameset is part of the frames collection—an array of all of the frames within the browser window. The frames collection uses the following reference syntax:

```
windowObject.frames[idref]
```

where *windowObject* is the browser window containing the frames and *idref* is either the id or the index number of a frame in the collection. For example, to reference the header frame in the current browser window, you would use either of the following object references:

```
window.frames[0]
window.frames["header"]
```

There is no frameset object in JavaScript. If you need to reference the frameset element, you must provide an id for the frameset and then use the getElementById() method to reference the frameset element. For example, to reference the Glossary frameset from within the terms.htm file, you would use the object reference

```
document.getElementById("Glossary")
```

Reference Window

Referencing Frames and Framesets

- To reference a particular frame in a frameset, use
    ```
    windowObject.frames[idref]
    ```
  where *windowObject* is the browser window containing the frameset and *idref* is the id or index number of a frame in the frames collection.
- To reference a frameset element, use the reference
    ```
    document.getElementById(id)
    ```
  where *id* is the value of the id attribute in the <frameset> tag.

Navigating between Frames

JavaScript treats the frames in a frameset as elements in a hierarchical tree. Figure 6-29 shows a schematic diagram of the Glossary frameset. The top of the hierarchy is the browser window containing the terms.htm file and the Glossary frameset. At the second level of the tree are the nav.htm, main.htm, and footer.htm files, containing the header, main, and footer frames.

The frame hierarchy | Figure 6-29

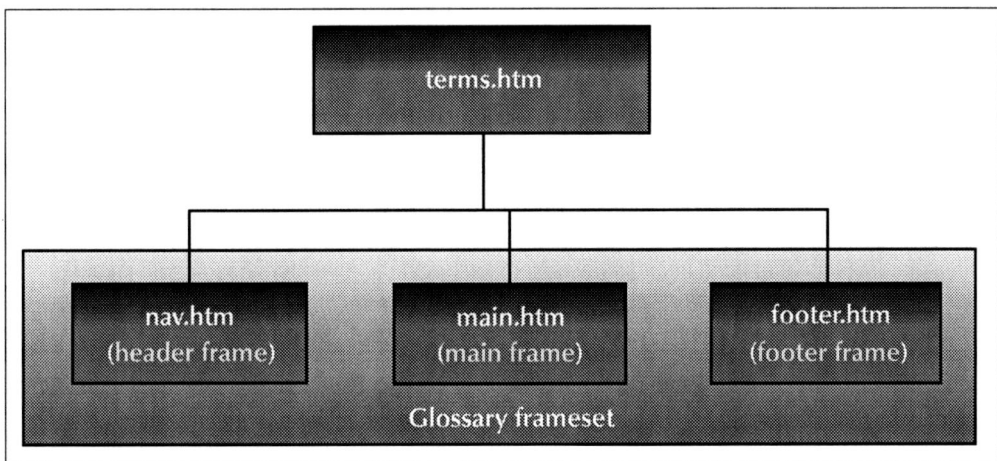

If you want to access the contents of one frame from another, you have to navigate through this hierarchy of objects. JavaScript provides two keywords to do this: parent and top. The **parent keyword** refers to any object that is placed immediately above another object in the hierarchy. The browser window containing the terms.htm file is the parent object of the three frames in the Glossary frameset. To reference one of the other frames, you first go up to the parent and then down the hierarchy. Thus, to reference the main frame from within the header frame you would use either of the following object references:

```
parent.frames[1]
parent.frames["main"]
```

If you have several levels of nested objects, you can stack parent references to go up through the different levels of the tree. The reference

```
parent.parent.parent.object
```

points to a child element of the parent object three levels up in the hierarchy.

If you want to go directly to the top of the hierarchy, you can use the **top keyword**. In the case of frames, the top keyword refers to the browser window that contains the frameset document and the frames within that frameset. When the frames are direct children of the browser window (as is the case with the Glossary frameset), the parent and top keywords are synonymous.

Note that the Glossary frameset itself is not a parent of the frames it contains. The Glossary frameset is an object within the document displayed in that window. If you need to reference the Glossary frameset directly, you have to go down the document hierarchy using the document object and the getElementById() method. The complete reference to the Glossary frameset from one of the child frames is therefore

```
parent.document.getElementById("Glossary")
```

Treating Frames as Windows

In most cases JavaScript treats a frame as a separate browser window, meaning that most of the properties and methods you've been applying to window objects can also be applied to frame objects. For example, if you want to write content into a frame, you would use the commands

```
frameObject.document.write(content)
frameObject.document.close()
```

where `frameObject` is the object reference to the frame. To change the source of the document displayed within a frame, you use the location property as follows:

`frameObject.location.href = "url"`

where `url` is the URL of the document to appear in the frame. The frame object also supports such window methods as setInterval() and setTimeout() for time-delayed commands, and alert() for displaying an alert box within a frame. However, you cannot close a frame the same way that you close a window. If you want to remove a frame from a frameset, you have to change the frameset layout.

Reference Window | **Changing the Content of a Frame Document**

- To change a frame's source document, use the command:
    `frameObject.location.href="url";`
  where `frameObject` is the frame object and `url` is the URL of the document to display in the frame.
- To write content into a frame, use the commands:
    `frameObject.document.write(content);`
    `frameObject.document.close();`
  where `content` is a text string of HTML code to be written into the frame.
- To reference the document displayed within a frame, use the object reference
    `frameObject.document.getElementById(id)`
  where `id` is the id of the object in the document.

Setting the Frameset Layout

Recall that a frameset is laid out in either rows or columns using the rows and cols attribute of the <frameset> tag. To do the same thing in JavaScript, you use the rows and cols properties of the frameset object. The syntax is

```
frameset.rows = "text"
frameset.cols = "text"
```

where `frameset` is an object reference to a frameset element and `text` is a text string specifying the frame layout. Currently, the value of the row attribute for the Glossary frameset is the text string "160,*,64". To change this to "180,*,64", for example, you would use the command

```
document.getElementById("Glossary").rows = "180,*,64";
```

To remove or hide a frame from a frameset, you set its height (or width) value to 0 pixels. Thus, to remove the footer frame from the Glossary frameset, you could use the command

```
document.getElementById("Glossary").rows = "160,*,0";
```

The footer frame would still be present in the frameset, but it would not be visible to users.

Collapsing and Expanding a Frame

You now have the information you need to create functions to collapse and expand the glossary's footer frame. You'll add two functions to the nav.htm file, named collapse() and expand(). The collapse() function reduces the height of the footer frame. The expand() function resets the footer frame's height to its original 64 pixels. Since you'll be running these functions from within the nav.htm file, you need to go up the object hierarchy to access the properties of the Glossary frameset. The code for the collapse() and expand() functions is

```
function collapse() {
    parent.document.getElementById("Glossary").rows = "160,*,1";
}
function expand() {
    parent.document.getElementById("Glossary").rows = "160,*,64";
}
```

Note that in the collapse() function, we set the height of the footer frame to 1 pixel rather than 0 pixels. For some browsers, like Netscape, setting the height to 0 pixels removes the frame entirely from the frameset. With the footer frame removed, you would not be able to re-display it later. To resolve this problem, you can set the height to 1 pixel, which preserves the footer frame in the layout, but essentially hides it from the user. You'll call the collapse() and expand() functions from links within the nav.htm file. Add these functions to the nav.htm file now.

To create and run the collapse() and expand() functions:

1. Return to **nav.htm** in your text editor.

2. Add the following embedded script to the head section of the document (see Figure 6-30):

```
<script type="text/javascript">
function collapse() {
    parent.document.getElementById("Glossary").rows = "160,*,1";
}
function expand() {
    parent.document.getElementById("Glossary").rows = "160,*,64";
}
</script>
```

The collapse() and expand() functions ◀ **Figure 6-30**

```
<title>Glossary of Terms, iMusicHistory</title>
<link href="main.css" rel="stylesheet" type="text/css" title="General" />
<script type="text/javascript">
function collapse() {
    parent.document.getElementById("Glossary").rows = "160,*,1";
}
function expand() {
    parent.document.getElementById("Glossary").rows = "160,*,64";
}
</script>
</head>
```

3. Scroll down the document to the <a> tag for the text "Hide Navigation Bar" and set the value of the href attribute to:

```
href="javascript:collapse()"
```

4. Set the value for the href attribute for the "Display Navigation Bar" link to:

`href="javascript:expand()"`

Figure 6-31 shows the revised HTML code for the two links.

Figure 6-31	Calling the collapse() and expand() functions

```
<!-- Place Display/Hide Navigation Bars Here -->
<tr>
<td width="100" align="left">
<p class="gloss">
<a href="javascript:collapse()">Hide Navigation Bar</a></p>
</td>

<td bgcolor="white" class="body" valign="top" align="center">
<a class="gloss" name="glossary">Glossary of Music Terms</a></td>

<td width="100" align="right">
<p align="right" class="gloss">
<a href="javascript:expand()">Display Navigation Bar</a></p>
</td>
</tr>
<!-- End of Navigation Bars --->
```

5. Save your changes to the file and reopen **terms.htm** in your Web browser.

6. Click the **Hide Navigation Bar** and **Display Navigation Bar** links and verify that they hide and redisplay the footer frame.

Next, Teresa would like you to control the interaction between the pages in her Web site and other sites on the Web. She's particularly concerned about the behavior of frames.

Controlling Frame Behavior

Many users don't like the effect that frames can have on Web sites that they view. For example, some Web site designers either aren't aware of or don't add code to prevent external Web sites from being caught inside their frames. This can confuse viewers by making it appear that an external Web site is actually part of the frameset. Additionally, a page designed to be viewed only within a frame might be mistakenly opened outside of its frameset. Without the context that the frameset provides, such a page can be meaningless or irritating to viewers.

The iMusicHistory Web site has experienced both problems in the past. Teresa has noticed that sometimes her Web site gets stuck inside another Web site's frameset, and search engines often bring visitors to the iMusicHistory site via one of the frames in the Glossary frameset. She would like you to control the behavior of her Web site's frames to prevent these two problems from happening.

Blocking an Unwanted Frame

When one of Teresa's Web pages gets stuck within another Web site's frame, her page in essence becomes a child of that browser window frameset. A demo page has been prepared for you to display this effect in action. Open the demo now.

To view the frame-blocking demo:

1. Open the **demo_frameblocker.htm** file from the tutorial.06/tutorial folder in your Web browser.

2. Click the **default.htm** link in the left frame.

   As shown in Figure 6-32, the default.htm file appears in the right frame of the browser window.

   Trouble? This demo might not work with the Safari browser.

Frame blocking demo page | Figure 6-32

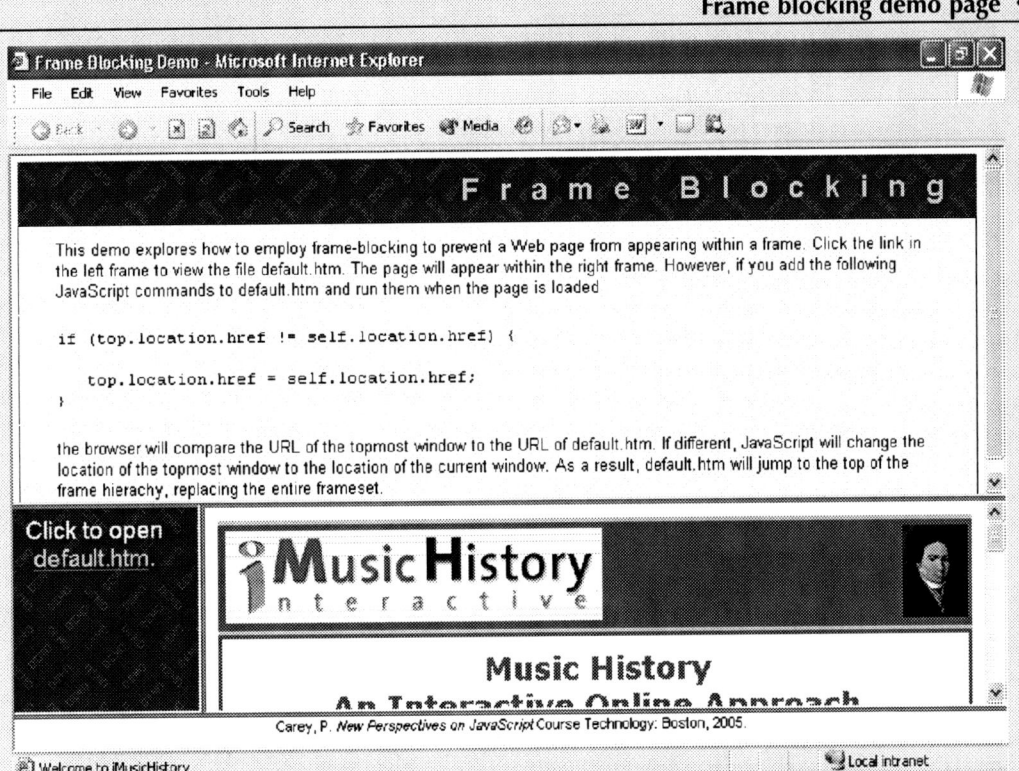

Carey, P. *New Perspectives on JavaScript* Course Technology: Boston, 2005.

When this happens to one of Teresa's pages, she would like the page to move out of the frame and occupy the browser window. To do this, you need to run a command testing whether the page is at the top of the window hierarchy when the browser loads the page. The condition to do this test is

```
if (top.location.href != self.location.href) {
   top.location.href = self.location.href;
}
```

In this code, JavaScript compares the URL of the document in the topmost window to the URL of the document in the current window or frame. If they're different, JavaScript changes the URL of the topmost window's document to the current window's document. As a result, the page cannot be forced into another site's frameset. It will always jump to the top of the hierarchy, occupying the browser window and replacing any frameset file. If the page is already at the top of the hierarchy, the code has no effect. Try this now by adding frame blocking to the default.htm file and then retesting the file in the demo page.

To add frame blocking to the iMusicHistory home page:

1. Reopen **default.htm** in your text editor.

2. Add the following embedded script to the document's head, as shown in Figure 6-33:

```
<script type="text/javascript">
    if (top.location.href != self.location.href) {
        top.location.href = self.location.href;
    }
</script>
```

Figure 6-33 ▶ Blocking a page from appearing in a frame

```
<title>Teresa Jenner's iMusicHistory course</title>
<link href="main.css" rel="stylesheet" type="text/css" />
<script type="text/javascript">
    if (top.location.href != self.location.href) {
        top.location.href = self.location.href;
    }
</script>
</head>
```

3. Close the file, saving your changes.

4. Reopen **demo_frameblocker.htm** in your Web browser.

5. Click the **default.htm** link in the left frame and verify that the document now jumps out of the frame to occupy the entire browser window.

Now Teresa can be confident that her home page won't get stuck within the frame of another Web site.

Forcing a Page into a Frameset

Teresa's second task involves the opposite problem: instead of forcing a page out of a frameset, she wants to ensure that the three files that compose the Glossary frameset (nav.htm, main.htm, and footer.htm) are always displayed within the frameset, and never as separate Web pages. This prevents visitors from inadvertently accessing one of those pages outside the context of the iMusicHistory Glossary.

Although the problem is different, the solution is similar. It involves verifying that whenever a browser opens the nav.htm, main.htm, or footer.htm files, the topmost window is always the browser window containing the terms.htm file. The code to make this happen is

```
if (top.location.href == self.location) {
    top.location.href="terms.htm";
}
```

Here, JavaScript checks whether the URL of the document in the topmost window is the same as that of the active window or frame. If this condition is true for a file like nav.htm, it means that the file is occupying the top browser window rather than a frame within that window. In that case, the script changes the URL of the top window so that it displays the frameset located in the terms.htm file. Apply this code to the nav.htm file now.

To force nav.htm to always appear in the Glossary frameset:

1. Return to **nav.htm** in your text editor.

2. Add the following commands to the embedded script element, as shown in Figure 6-34:

```
if (top.location.href == self.location.href) {
    top.location.href="terms.htm";
}
```

Forcing a file into a frameset ◄ **Figure 6-34**

```
<script type="text/javascript">
if (top.location.href == self.location.href) {
    top.location.href = "terms.htm";
}

function collapse() {
    parent.document.getElementById("Glossary").rows = "160,*,1";
}
function expand() {
    parent.document.getElementById("Glossary").rows = "160,*,64";
}
</script>
```

3. Close the file, saving your changes.

4. Open **nav.htm** in your Web browser and verify that the browser opens the entire Glossary frameset, not just the navigation bar.

5. Close your Web browser.

Reference Window

Blocking and Forcing Frames

- To prevent a document from appearing within a frame, run the following commands when a browser loads the page:
```
if (top.location.href != self.location.href) {
    top.location.href = self.location.href;
}
```
- To force a document to always appear within a frameset, run the following commands when the page is loaded:
```
if (top.location.href == self.location.href) {
    top.location.href = "url";
}
```
where *url* is the URL of the frameset document.

Working with Inline Frames

Another way to use frames in a Web site is by incorporating an inline frame, which appears as a separate window within the document. Recall that inline frames are created in HTML using the tag

```
<iframe src="url" id="text" name="text" width="value" height="value">
    alternate content
</iframe>
```

where *url* is the URL of the document that appears in the inline frame, the id and name attributes identify the frame, the width and height attributes specify the size of the frame in pixels, and *alternate content* is content that appears in the document window for browsers that don't support inline frames. As with other HTML elements, you should include both the name and id attributes to ensure maximum compatibility across browsers, setting those attributes to the same value.

JavaScript allows you to treat an inline frame either as an object in the current document or as a frame in the frames collection. For example, if you create the following inline frame:

```
<iframe src="logo.htm" id="logo" name="logo" width="300" height="200">
</iframe>
```

you can reference it from the current document window using the object reference

```
document.getElementById("logo")
```

or as a frame using the frames reference

```
window.frames["logo"]
```

To change the document displayed by the inline frame, you once again have two choices. You can either treat the frame as an object in the document and change the value of its src property, or you can treat it as a frame and change the value of the href property of its location object. Thus, to change the URL of the logo frame to point to the logo2.htm file, you could use either of the following commands:

```
document.getElementById("logo").src = "logo2.htm";
```

or

```
window.frames["logo"].location.href = "logo2.htm";
```

If you want to write content directly into an inline frame, you have to treat it as part of the frames collection. To write content into the logo inline frame, you would use the document.write() method as follows:

```
window.frames["logo"].document.write(content)
```

Treating inline frames as frame objects is more widely supported than treating them as document objects. Opera 6.0, for example, treats inline frames only as part of the frames collection and not as objects in the document (though this is not true of more recent releases of Opera). However, if you need to manipulate the appearance or placement of an inline frame within a document, you may find it easier to work with it as an object in the document and change its style values. For example, you could float the logo inline frame on the page's left margin by simply changing the value of the float property:

```
document.getElementById("logo").style.float = "left";
```

In the end, how you treat inline frames depends on the task you're trying to accomplish with your script. Fortunately, JavaScript and most browsers support either approach.

Since Teresa has not chosen to include inline frames in her Web site, your work on her project is finished. Teresa is excited about the progress you've made with her Web site. Later, she wants you to incorporate the work you've done on these pages into the rest of the iMusicHistory Web site.

Tips for Working with Windows and Frames

- If you use JavaScript to write a transient status bar message, be sure to properly erase the message when the action or event is finished, so that other messages your browser may wish to display are not prevented from displaying.
- Due to their unpopularity in the eyes of some users, keep the use of pop-up windows to a minimum, and forewarn your users if possible about the presence of a pop-up window.
- Include code to verify that a pop-up window has not been blocked and, if possible, provide alternative methods of displaying the same content if the pop-up is blocked.
- Include code that makes it easy for users to close your pop-up windows, in order to prevent those windows from cluttering a user's desktop.
- Allow your users to resize your pop-up windows to ensure that no content is hidden.
- If the existence of pop-up blockers poses a problem, consider using alert, prompt, and confirm dialog boxes in place of pop-up windows.
- If frames are a concern, add conditional statements to your documents to prevent them from appearing within the framesets of other Web sites.
- Add JavaScript code to your frame documents so that they always appear within the context of their framesets.

Session 6.3 Quick Check

Review

1. What reference name would you use to access a frame named "Logo" located in the topmost window of the browser window hierarchy?
2. What command would you use to change the source of the document in the Logo frame to "logo.html"?
3. What command would you use to write the text string "<html></html>" to the document in the Logo frame?
4. Assume that the Logo frame is part of a frameset with the id "Home". What command would you use to change the column widths of the frames in the Home frameset to "150,150,*"?
5. The Home frameset is saved in an HTML file named "home.htm." What JavaScript command(s) would you add to the logo.html file so that it always appears within the home.htm page?
6. A Web page contains an inline frame with the id "report". Provide two ways of changing the source of the inline frame to the document report.htm. Assume that you are running the command from within the document containing the inline frame.

Review

Tutorial Summary

In this tutorial you learned how to use JavaScript to create and format browser windows and frames. In the first session you learned how to work with the properties of the window's status bar, location object, and history objects. You also saw how to employ automatic page navigation using both the meta element and a JavaScript program. The second session focused on techniques to create and populate new browser windows. You first learned how to use the window.open() method to create a new browser window based on a pre-existing source document. You saw how to specify the properties of that window and how to work with methods of the window object to close a pop-up window and to set the focus on it. The second session also showed how to create alert, prompt, and confirm dialog boxes. The session then showed how to write content into a pop-up window using the document.write() method and discussed how to reference variables and functions in other browser windows. The second session concluded with a discussion of specialized Internet Explorer methods to create modal and modeless dialog boxes. The third session concerned working with frames and framesets. You learned how to navigate through the object hierarchy of a frameset and how to reference the contents of one frame from another. You also saw how to modify the layout of a frameset by changing the properties of the frameset object. The third session also provided a demonstration of how to use JavaScript to block frames and to force documents to remain within framesets. The tutorial concluded with a brief discussion of inline frames, showing how they can be treated either as frames in the frames collection or as objects within a document.

Key Terms

alert dialog box	opener keyword	self keyword
chrome	parent keyword	status bar
confirm dialog box	permanent status bar	top keyword
history object	message	transient status bar
location object	pop-up blocker	message
modal window	pop-up window	window object
modeless window	prompt dialog box	

Practice

Practice the skills you learned in the tutorial using the same case scenario.

Review Assignments

Data files needed for this Review Assignment: atempotxt.htm, bottomtxt.htm, concerto. htm, defaulttxt.htm, dotclear.gif, header.gif, index.htm, lesson3.htm, lesson3a.htm, lesson3b.htm, lvb.gif, main.css, maintxt.htm, nav.htm, navy8th.gif, quiz2.css, quiz2.gif, quiz2txt.htm, quiz.htm, sonata.htm, symphony.htm, terms.htm, terms_noframes.htm, treble2.gif, treble.gif

Teresa has reviewed your work on the iMusicHistory Web site. She's happy with your progress and wants you to apply the changes you've made so far to the rest of the Web site. Here are the tasks for your next assignment:

- Add transient status bar messages to the other three links at the bottom of the iMusicHistory home page.
- Add a pop-up window to the iMusicHistory home page that displays the definition of the term "a tempo", which appears on the page.
- Create a customized pop-up window and alert box for the questions on the Quiz 2 Web page.

- Prevent the Quiz 2 Web page from appearing within a frame.
- Write code to ensure that the contents of the bottom.htm and main.htm files always appear within the context of the Glossary frameset.

Make sure that any pop-up windows you create will behave nicely if they encounter pop-up blockers. Figure 6-35 shows a preview of the pop-up window you'll create for the new quiz page.

Figure 6-35

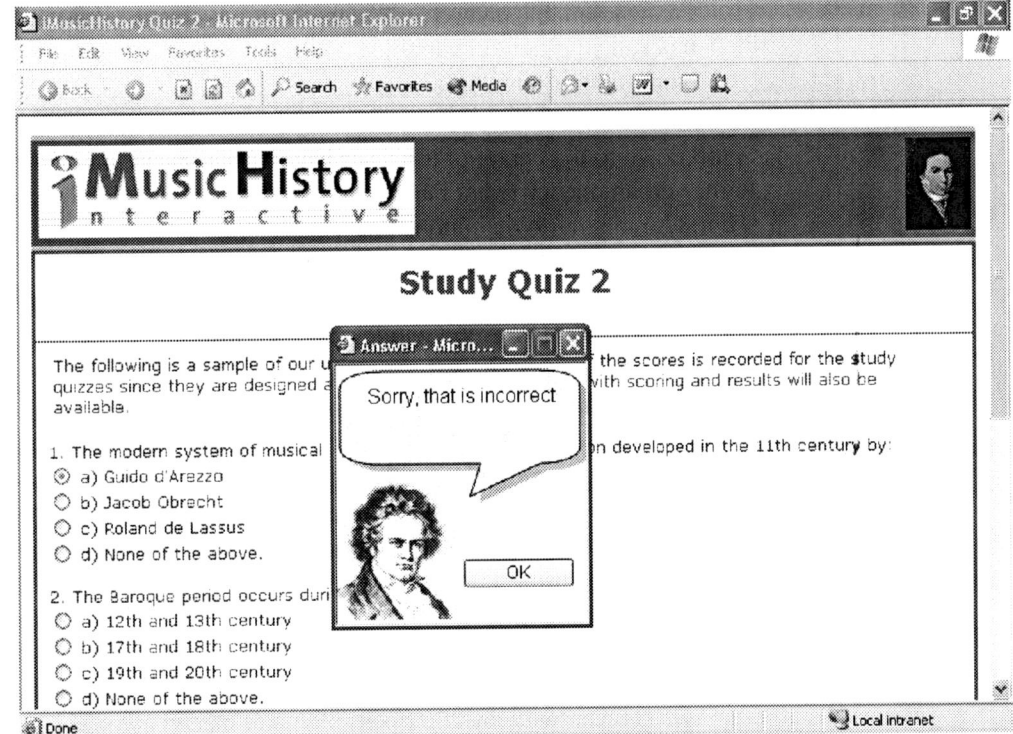

To revise the iMusicHistory Web site:

1. Go to the tutorial.06/review folder and use your text editor to open the **defaulttxt. htm, atempotxt.htm, quiz2txt.htm, maintxt.htm**, and **bottomtxt.htm** files. Within each file enter *your name* and *the date* in the comment section and save the files as **default.htm, atempo.htm, quiz2.htm, main.htm**, and **bottom.htm**, respectively.

2. Return to the **default.htm** file in your text editor and add transient status bar messages to the document as follows:

   a. Go to the navigation cell text near the bottom of the document and locate the link to the lesson3.htm file. Add an onmouseover event handler to this link that displays the message "Go to the Lessons page". Add an onmouseout event handler that removes the status bar message when the mouse leaves the link.

   b. Use an onmouseover event handler to change the transient status bar message for the quiz.htm link to "Go to the First Online Quiz". Be sure to remove this message using the onmouseout event handler.

   c. Repeat the process to change the transient status bar message for the terms.htm link to "View the Music Glossary".

3. In the embedded script at the top of the page, insert a function named showDef(). The purpose of this function is to display a pop-up window. The function has a single parameter named source that contains the URL of the document to be displayed. Add the following commands to the showDef() function:

   a. Use the window.open() method to open a window displaying a document with a URL equal to the value of the source parameter. Leave the target name as a blank text string. The window should be 200 pixels wide by 100 pixels high, displayed at the screen coordinates (100, 100). Store the window object in a variable named defWin.

   b. Create a variable named notPop that tests whether the defWin window object was blocked. The notPop variable should have a value of "true" if the window was blocked and "false" if otherwise.

   c. Return the value of the notPop variable.

4. Scroll down to the center of the document and locate the link for the "a tempo" term. Add an onclick event handler that returns the value of the showDef() function. (*Hint*: Use the music definitions pop-ups from the tutorial as an example.)

5. Close the **default.htm** file, saving your changes.

6. Go to the **atempo.htm** file in your text editor. Add an onblur event handler to the body element that closes the window when it loses the focus. Close the file, saving your changes.

7. Return to the **quiz2.htm** file in your text editor. Add an embedded script in the head section of the document, and within the script element insert a function named answer(). The purpose of the answer() function is to write a pop-up window telling the student whether he or she answered the quiz question correctly. The answer() function should have one parameter named "correct" used to store a Boolean value indicating whether the student's answer is correct or not. Appropriate parameter values for the answer() function have already been added to onclick event handlers for the radio buttons in the form. Complete the answer() function as follows:

   a. Use the window.open() method to create a pop-up window named popWin that is 200 pixels wide by 200 pixels high and placed at the screen coordinates (250, 250). Specify a blank text string for the window's URL and target name.

   b. Create a variable named notPop that has a value of true if the popWin window failed to open and a value of false if it opened without error.

   c. If the value of notPop is true (indicating that the pop-up window failed to open) create a conditional statement that tests whether the value of the correct parameter is true or false. If correct is true, display an alert box containing the text "Correct!" If correct is false, display an alert box with the text "Sorry, that is incorrect".

d. If the value of notPop is false (indicating that a pop-up window was generated) write the following HTML code into the popWin window:

```
<html>
<head>
<title>Answer</title>
<link rel='stylesheet' href='quiz2.css' type='text/css' />
</head>
<body>
message
<p><input type='button' value='OK' onclick='self.close()' /></p>
</body>
</html>
```

where *message* is either the text string "<p>Correct!</p>" if the correct parameter is true or the text string "<p>Sorry, that is incorrect</p>" if the correct parameter is false.

8. Add JavaScript commands to the **quiz2.htm** file so that the page cannot be placed in a frame. Close the file, saving your changes.

9. Go to the **bottom.htm** and **main.htm** files in your text editor. Add scripts to both files that force them to be displayed only within the Glossary frameset of the terms.htm file. Close both files, saving your changes.

10. Open **default.htm** in your browser. Verify that: a) Transient status bar messages appear for the Lessons, Quizzes, and Glossary links at the bottom of the page and b) Clicking the "a tempo" definition link displays a pop-up window showing the term's definition and that this pop-up window automatically closes when it loses the focus.

11. Open **quiz2.htm** in your browser. Verify that clicking the radio buttons in the quiz form displays an appropriate pop-up window indicating whether the answer is correct or not. Also verify that clicking the OK button within the pop-up window closes it.

12. Open **bottom.htm** and **main.htm** in your Web browser and verify that both files are opened within the context of the Glossary frameset.

13. Submit your completed Web site to your instructor.

Apply

Use the skills you learned to create a subscription pop-up window

Case Problem 1

Data files needed for this Case Problem: cover.css, cover.jpg, covertxt.htm, cwj.css, cwj.jpg, cwjtxt.htm, formtxt.htm, logo.gif, parch.jpg

The Civil War Journal Terrence Whyte is the editor of the online version of *The Civil War Journal*, a magazine for people interested in the Civil War. Terrence would like to have a small pop-up window appear when users open the home page of the online edition. The window will advertise the print version of the magazine and provide a link to a subscription form. Also, Terrence would like the status bar to display informative text for links on the page. Figure 6-36 shows a preview of the window you'll create.

Figure 6-36

To create the pop-up windows:

1. Use your text editor to open the **cwjtxt.htm**, **covertxt.htm**, and **formtxt.htm** files from the tutorial.06/case1 folder. Enter *your name* and *the date* in each file and save them as **cwj.htm**, **cover.htm**, and **form.htm** respectively.

2. Go to the **cwj.htm** file in your text editor. Locate the five links at the top of the page and create the following transient status bar messages for them:
   - Home Page: "Go to the Home Page"
   - News: "View Current Events"
   - Features: "Go to Feature Articles"
   - Forum: "Go to the Civil War Forum"
   - Subscriptions: "Subscribe Today!"

   Configure the messages to appear in response to the onmouseover event. Make sure the messages are removed in response to the onmouseout event.

3. In the head section of the document, insert an embedded script containing a function named subscribe(). The subscribe() function should open a new browser window containing the cover.htm document. Give the pop-up window a target name of "popWin". Set the width and height of the pop-up window to 125 pixels by 240 pixels. Open the window 10 pixels down and to the right of the upper-left corner of the screen. Since this pop-up window displays only an advertisement for the magazine and not critical content, Terrence has not requested that you check for the presence of pop-up blockers.

4. Add an event handler to the body element to run the subscribe() function when the page loads.

5. Close the file, saving your changes.

xplore

6. Return to the **cover.htm** file in your text editor. Within the head section, insert an embedded script containing the showForm() function. The purpose of this function is to display the contents of the form.htm file in the main browser window. Have the function do the following:

   a. Display the form.htm file in the browser window that was used to open the cover.htm file. (*Hint*: Use the "opener" keyword to reference the main browser window, and the location.href property to specify the document to be displayed in that window.)

   b. Close the current window.

7. Locate the linked text in the body of the document and change the value of the href attribute so that it runs the showForm() function when clicked.

8. Close the file, saving your changes.

9. Return to the **form.htm** file in your text editor and create the same set of transient status bar messages that you created for the cwj.htm file. Close the file, saving your changes.

10. Open **cwj.htm** in your Web browser. Verify that the status bar messages change in response to hovering the mouse pointer over the five links at the top of the page and verify that a subscription pop-up window appears on your screen.

11. Click the link in the subscription pop-up window. Verify that the pop-up closes and that the subscription form now appears in the original browser window.

12. Submit the completed Web site to your instructor.

Challenge

xplore how to write
ontent into an inline
ame

Case Problem 2

Data files needed for this Case Problem: brain.css, brain.jpg, braintxt.htm, frame.css

Anatomy 101   Jacob Terrell teaches Anatomy 101 at Thomas More College. He's asked for your help in creating a Web page on the brain. The page will display an inline image showing different parts of the human brain. As students move their mouse pointers over a section, he would like an inline frame to display a description of that part of the brain. Figure 6-37 shows a preview of the page he wants you to create for him.

Figure 6-37

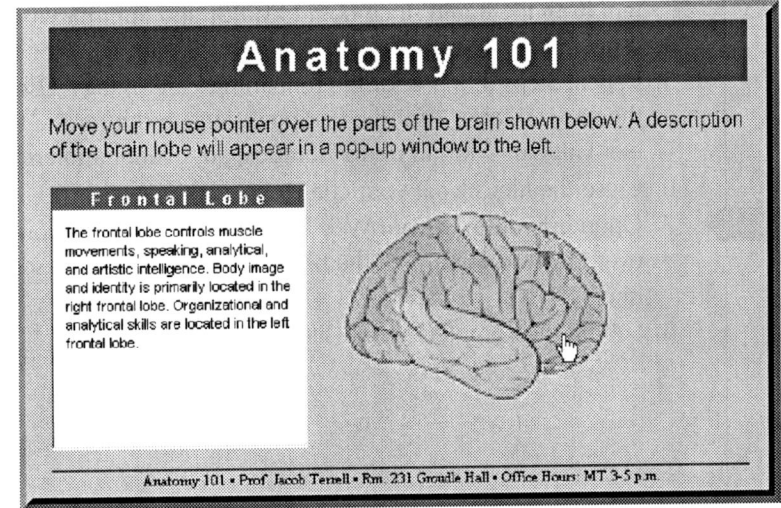

The text of the inline frame has already been entered for you and stored in two arrays. The Head array stores the names of four different brain lobes. The Summary array contains a brief description of each lobe. Your job is to insert the contents of these arrays into the inline frame.

To create Professor Terrell's Web page:

1. Use your text editor to open **braintxt.htm** from the tutorial.06/case2 folder. Enter *your name* and *the date* in the file and save it as **brain.htm**.

Explore

2. Within an embedded script element in the document's head section, create a function named writeFrame() that contains a single parameter named "i". The purpose of this function is to write the content that appears in the inline frame. The i parameter stores the index number of the entry from the Head and Summary arrays that should appear in the inline frame. The writeFrame() function should perform the following actions:

   a. Create a variable named frameWin that contains the object reference to the first frame in the current browser window.

   b. Write the following HTML code into frameWin:
```
<html>
<head>
<title>Head</title>
<link rel='stylesheet' href=frame.css' type='text/css' />
</head>
<body>
<h2>Head</h2>
<p>Summary</p>
</body>
</html>
```
   where *Head* is the text contained in the *i*th element in the Head array and *Summary* is the *i*th entry in the Summary array.

3. Add an onmouseover handler to the frontal lobe <area> tag to run the writeFrame() function, with a parameter value of 1. Running this function sets the content of the inline frame to describe information about the brain's frontal lobe.

4. Add an onmouseout handler to the frontal lobe <area> tag to run the writeFrame() function, with a parameter value of 0. Running this function removes the text content from the frame since both Head[0] and Summary[0] are empty elements in the array.

5. Repeat Steps 3 and 4 for the remaining <area> tags. Use a parameter value of 2 for the parietal lobe, 3 for the occipital lobe, and 4 for the temporal lobe. Use a parameter value of 0 for all of the onmouseout event handlers.

6. Close the file, saving your changes.

Explore

7. Open **brain.htm** in your Web browser. Verify that as you pass your mouse pointer over the various parts of the brain, the inline frame describes the part of the brain highlighted.

8. Submit the completed Web site to your instructor.

Challenge

*xplore how to write
ITML and CSS code
ito a frame*

Case Problem 3

Data files needed for this Case Problem: code.css, css.htm, css.txt, demo.gif, demo.htm, html.htm, html.txt, title.css, titletxt.htm

Web Designers Andrew Seaborn teaches a class in Web design. During the first few weeks of the course he teaches students the basics of HTML tags and CSS style sheets. Andrew thinks it would be useful for his students to have a demo page in which they can enter HTML and CSS code directly into one set of frames and then have that code rendered as a Web page in another frame. As one of his teaching assistants, you've been asked to create the demo page for him. Figure 6-38 shows a preview of the page you'll create.

Figure 6-38

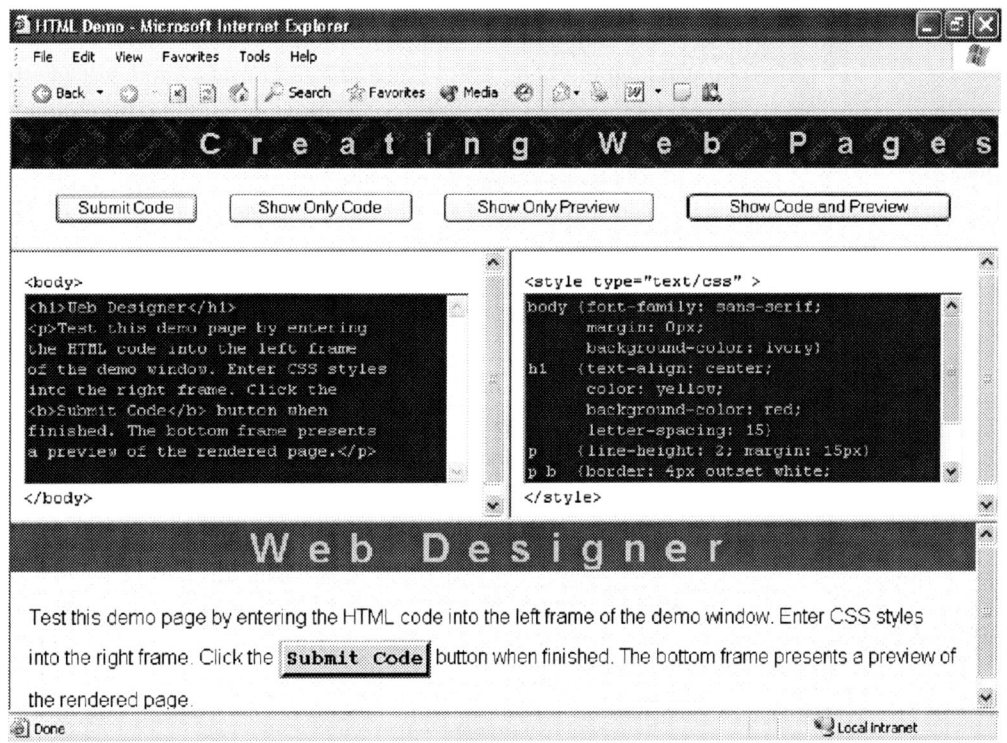

The demo is organized into four files. The demo.htm file displays a frameset named "demo" containing four frames named title, htmlcode, csscode, and preview. The title frame contains the contents of the title.htm file. You'll create the JavaScript programs in this file that you need to run the demo. The htmlcode frame contains the contents of the html.htm file. This file contains a textarea field with the id value inputhtml where you'll enter the HTML code that you want to display. The csscode frame contains the contents of the css.htm file. This file also contains a textarea field with the id value inputcss. You'll use this textarea field to enter the CSS styles that you want to apply to the elements in your HTML. The preview pane does not contain any document at all. Instead, you'll create the document content by writing the content of the two textarea boxes into the preview frame.

To create the demo page:

1. Use your text editor to open the **titletxt.htm** file from the tutorial.06/case3 folder. Enter *your name* and *the date* in the file and save it as **title.htm**.

2. Insert an embedded script element in the head section of the document. Within the script element, create a function named showPreview(). The purpose of this function is to hide the htmlcode and csscode frames, providing more screen space to the preview frame. To hide those two frames, change the value of the rows attribute for the demo frameset to "100,1,*". (*Hint*: You will have to go up to the parent element of the current document to access the frameset object. Remember that the id of the frameset object is "demo".)

3. Insert a function named showCode(). The purpose of this function is to hide the preview frame and to increase the size of the textarea fields in the html.htm and css.htm documents. Add the following commands to the function:
   a. Set the value of the demo frameset's row attribute to "100,*,1".
   b. Change the height of the textarea field in the html.htm file to 300 pixels. (*Hint*: Remember that you will have to move up to the parent object and then down to the second frame in the frames collection to reference the contents of the html.htm document. You can then use the document.getElementById() method to reference the textarea field and use the style.height property to set the textarea field's height to 300 pixels.)
   c. Change the height of the textarea field in the css.htm file to 300 pixels. Use the same techniques you employed for the textarea field in the html.htm file to reference this object. The css.htm file is stored in the third frame of the frames collection.

4. Insert a function named showBoth(). The purpose of this function is to show both the code and preview frames in the demo frameset. Add the following commands to the function:
   a. Set the value of the demo frameset's row attribute to "100,210,*".
   b. Set the height of the textarea field in the html.htm document to 150 pixels.
   c. Set the height of the textarea field in the css.htm document to 150 pixels.

5. Create a function named sendCode(). The purpose of this function is to extract whatever code has been entered into the two textarea boxes and write that code to the preview frame. To complete this function:
   a. Create a variable named previewFrame that references the fourth frame in the demo frameset.
   b. Create a variable named htmlCode that is equal to the value of the textarea field in the html.htm document. (*Hint*: The value of the textarea field can be extracted using the value property in the expression *object*.value, where *object* is the object reference to the textarea field. To reference the textarea field you will once again have to navigate through the frames hierarchy and then down through the contents of the html.htm document.)
   c. Create a variable named cssCode that is equal to the value of the textarea field in the css.htm document.
   d. Write the following code to the document within the previewFrame object:

```
<html>
<head>
<title></title>
<style type='text/css'>
    styles
```

```
    </style>
    </head>
    <body>
        html code
    </body>
    </html>
```

where *styles* is the value of the cssCode variable and *html code* is the value of the htmlCode variable.

6. Add an onclick event handler to the Submit Code button to run the sendCode() function. Add similar onclick event handlers to the other three buttons in the Web form to run the appropriate function when each button is clicked.

7. Close the file, saving your changes.

8. Open the **demo.htm** file in your Web browser. Copy the html code from the **html.txt** file and paste it into the textarea box in the left frame. Copy the css code from the **css.txt** file and paste it into the textarea box in the right frame. Click the Submit Code button and verify that the preview frame displays the elements and styles from the two code frames.

9. Click the Show Only Preview button. Verify that it hides the two code frames and increases the size of the preview pane.

10. Click the Show Only Code button. Verify that it hides the preview frame and increases the height of the code frames and the textarea boxes they contain.

11. Click the Show Code and Preview button. Verify that it restores the frameset layout, displaying all four frames with the textarea boxes back to their original heights.

12. Submit your completed Web site to your instructor.

est your knowledge of op-up windows by modifying a tourism Web site

Case Problem 4

Data files needed for this Case Problem: allen-img.jpg, allen-logo.gif, allentxt.htm, birdcage-img.jpg, birdcage-logo.gif, birdtxt.htm, boothill-img.jpg, boothill-logo.gif, boottxt.htm, corral-img.jpg, corral-logo.gif, corraltxt.htm, courthouse-img.jpg, courthouse-logo.gif, courthousetxt.htm, indextxt.htm, logo.gif, map.gif, schief-img.jpg, schief-logo.gif, schieftxt.htm, styles.css

Tombstone Chamber of Commerce The Tombstone, Arizona Chamber of Commerce has a small office in the main tourist area of Tombstone. Tony Diaz is in charge of designing a Web site that advertises the features of interest in the town. The Web site's home page will have a map of Tombstone with hot spots linked to different tourist attractions. When a user clicks a hot spot, a page describing the attraction is displayed. Tony would like your help in making the following changes to his Web site:

• Change the transient status bar message for each hot spot to a text string that describes the tourist attraction.

• Have each hot spot open a pop-up window describing the attraction.

• If a pop-up window loses the focus, have it close automatically.

• If a user is running a pop-up blocker, have links to the area attractions appear in the main browser window and not as a pop-up.

To complete this assignment:

1. Open the **allentxt.htm, birdtxt.htm, boottxt.htm, corraltxt.htm, courthousetxt.htm, indextxt.htm,** and **schieftxt.htm** files from the tutorial.06/case4 folder using your text editor. Enter *your name* and *the date* in the comment section of each file. Save the files as **allen.htm, bird.htm, boot.htm, corral.htm, courthouse.htm, index.htm,** and **schief.htm** respectively.

2. Go to the **index.htm** file and create a transient status bar message for the six hot spots in the image map. The text of the status bar messages is up to you, but it should include some brief description of the tourist attraction.

3. Create a permanent status bar message for the Tombstone home page. The text of the message is up to you, but it should convey a welcome greeting to the casual tourist.

4. Create a function named tourWin() that generates a pop-up window. The features of the pop-up window are up to you. Include code that verifies that the pop-up window has been properly opened. If it hasn't, have the browser open the target document within the main browser window.

5. Apply the tourWin() function to the six links in the image map.

6. Go to the six target documents in your text editor. Add event handlers to each of them so that if they lose their focus as pop-up windows, the browser closes them automatically.

7. Open **index.htm** in your Web browser and test the hot spot links. Verify that: a) each of your links has a customized status bar message, b) the home page has a permanent status bar message conveying a greeting, c) each hot spot link opens in a customized pop-up window, and d) each pop-up window closes automatically when it loses the focus.

8. Submit your completed Web site to your instructor.

Review

Quick Check Answers
Session 6.1

1. A permanent status bar message appears by default in the status bar. A transient status bar message only appears in response to a particular action or event.
2. history.go(-2)
3. window.status="View News page"
   return true;
4. One way is with the following meta element:
   <meta http-equiv="Refresh" content="*sec*;URL=*url*" />
   where *sec* is the amount of time in seconds that will elapse before opening the new page, and *url* is the new page to be loaded.
   Another way is to use the window.location.href property along with the setTimeout method.
5. The document.referrer property records the URL of the page from which the current page was accessed. However, this property only works when the current page is accessed via a link, and some browsers disable it for security reasons.

Session 6.2

1. <a href="home.htm" target="HomePage">*link text*</a>
2. window.open("home.htm","width=300,height=150");

3. window.open("home.htm","width=300,height=150,scrollbars=yes,status=yes");
   or
   window.open("home.htm","width=300,height=150,scrollbars=1,status=1");
4. Home.document.write("<body bgcolor='yellow'>");
5. alert("Script Finished");
6. confirm("Proceed?");
7. A modal window prevents users from doing anything outside the window until it is closed. A modeless window allows users to work in other windows while it's open.

Session 6.3

1. top.frames ["Logo"]
2. top.frames["Logo"].location.href="logo.html";
3. top.frames["Logo"].document.write("<html></html>");
4. top.document.getElementById("Home").cols="150,150,*";
5. if (top.location.href == self.location) {
       top.location.href = "home.htm";
   }
6. document.getElementById("report").src = "report.htm";
   or
   window.frames["report"].location.href = "report.htm";

Objectives

Session 7.1
- Understand how to reference form element objects
- Extract data from input fields, selection lists, and option button groups
- Create a calculated field

Session 7.2
- Understand the principles of form validation
- Perform a client-side validation
- Work with the properties and methods of string objects

Session 7.3
- Learn to create a regular expression
- Explore the properties and methods of the regular expression object
- Apply regular expressions to ZIP code fields
- Apply the Luhn Formula to validate credit card numbers
- Learn how to pass data from one form to another

Working with Forms and Regular Expressions

Validating a Web Form with JavaScript

Case

GPS-ware

GPS-ware is a company that specializes in mapping and global positioning software and hardware. The company is in the planning stages of making its products available online. Carol Campbell is heading the development effort and has asked for your help in developing a Web form for domestic sales.

A GPS-ware employee has already created three Web forms for the Web site. The forms include fields in which users enter the details of their purchases, delivery information, and credit card data. Carol would like the forms to automatically calculate the cost of a user's order and validate any data that the user has entered. All of this should be done before the form is submitted to the Web server for processing.

Student Data Files

▼tutorial.07

  ▽ **tutorial folder**

    form1txt.htm
    form2txt.htm
    form3txt.htm
    done.htm
    + 1 JavaScript file
    + 1 style sheet
    + 3 graphic files
    + 4 demo pages

  ▽ **review folder**

    ordertxt.htm
    done.htm
    + 1 JavaScript file
    + 1 style sheet
    + 2 graphic files

  ▽ **case1 folder**

    mpltxt.htm
    + 1 style sheet
    + 1 graphic file

Session 7.1

Working with Forms and Fields

You meet with Carol to discuss the forms she has created for online ordering. Figure 7-1 shows the three forms that you'll be working with. Customers enter order information in the first form, delivery information in the second form, and method of payment in the third form.

Figure 7-1 ▶ **The GPS-ware forms**

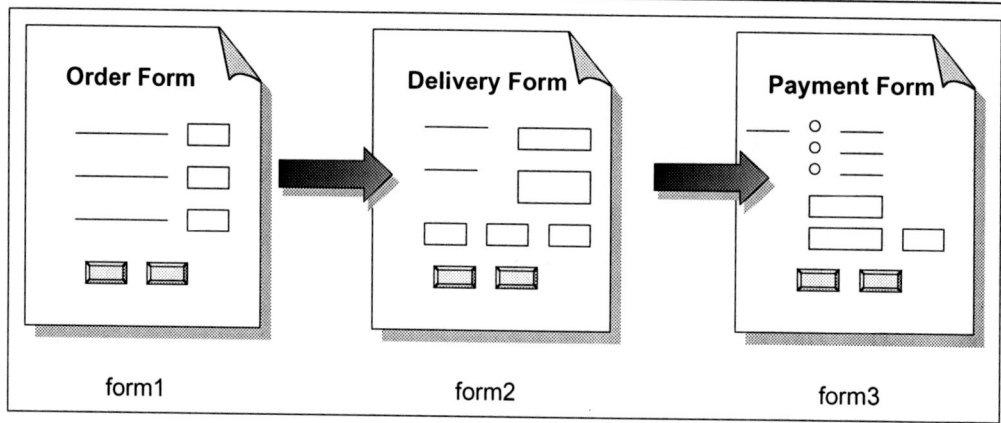

You'll start working on Carol's Web site by looking at the order form. Open this form now.

To open the page containing the order form:

1. In your text editor, open the **form1txt.htm**, **form2txt.htm**, and **form3txt.htm** files located in the tutorial.07/tutorial folder. Enter **your name** and **the date** in the comment section of each and save the files as **form1.htm**, **form2.htm**, and **form3.htm** respectively.

2. Close the form2.htm and form3.htm files. You will not be working with them in this session.

3. Take some time to review the HTML code in the form1.htm file, and then open **form1.htm** in your Web browser. Figure 7-2 displays the contents of the form1 form, including the names assigned to the different form elements.

◀ Figure 7-2

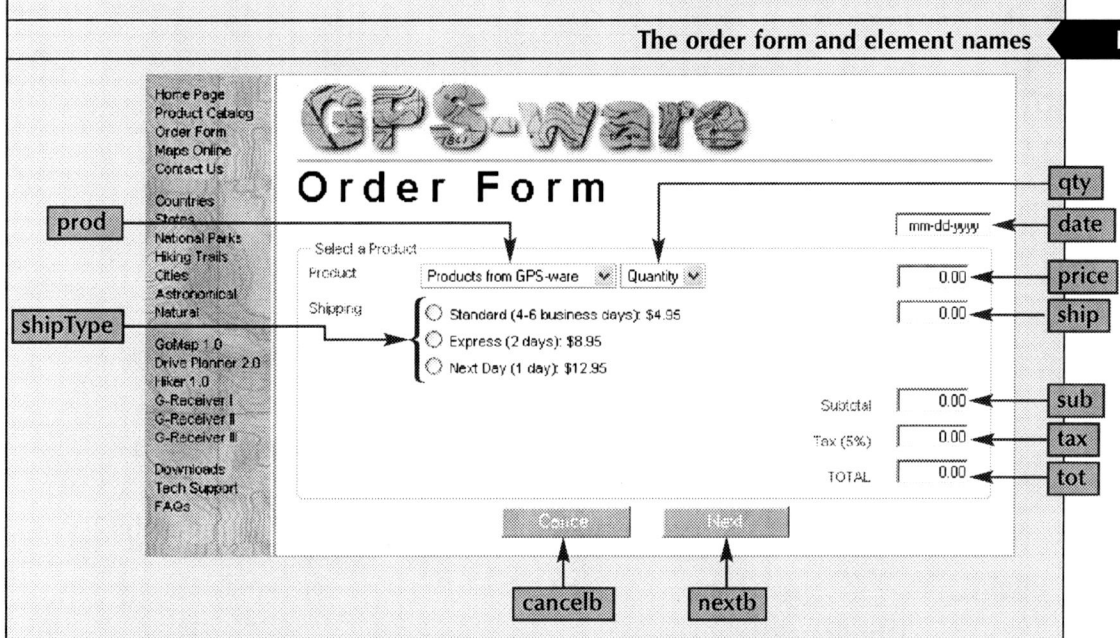

Trouble? You cannot enter data in either the date field or any of the fields that display the cost of the product, tax, or shipping. Carol has set these fields to read-only, and their values can only be set using JavaScript.

Customers use the order form to select a GPS-ware product to purchase, indicating the product name, quantity, and shipping method. Customers are given three choices for shipping: standard, which costs $4.95 and arrives in four to six business days; express, which costs $8.95 and arrives in two days; and overnight, which costs $12.95. There is also a 5% sales tax on all orders. Carol wants this form to automatically calculate the cost of the items purchased, add the cost of shipping, determine the sales tax, and then calculate the total order cost. All of these calculations should be done automatically by the browser. At the top of the form is a date field in which the current date should be displayed. Carol wants this information to be automatically entered by the Web browser as well.

Referencing a Web form

To program a Web form like this, you have to work with the properties and methods of the form object and the elements it contains. You've worked briefly in Web forms in Tutorial 2, but now it's time to look at the topic more formally. As shown in Figure 7-3, Web forms and their elements are part of the hierarchy of objects within a Web document.

Figure 7-3 The forms hierarchy

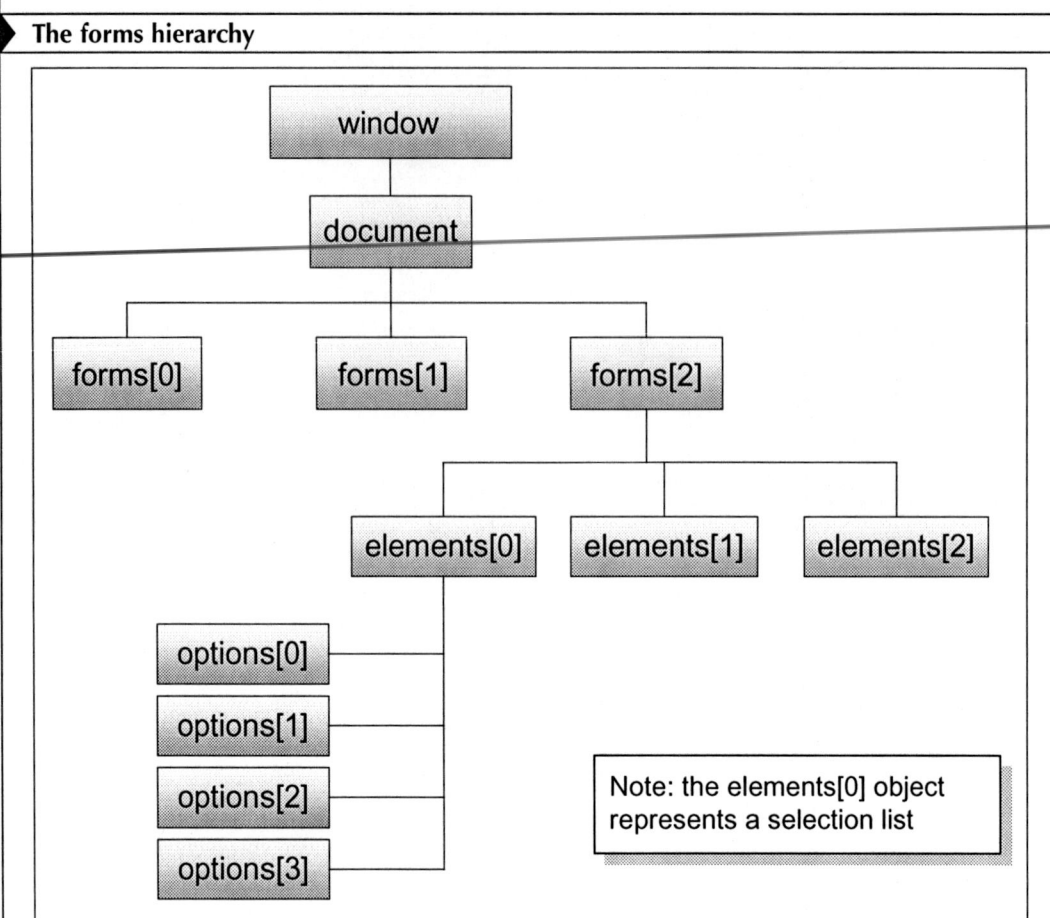

Since a Web page can contain multiple Web forms, JavaScript supports an object collection for forms. Thus, you can access a form within the current document using the object reference

```
document.forms[idref]
```

where *idref* is the id or index number of the form. JavaScript also allows you to reference a form by its name attribute, using the object reference

```
document.fname
```

where *fname* is the value of the name attribute assigned to the form. In addition, you can always use the document.getElementById() method to reference a form based on the value of its id attribute. Carol has named her order form "form1", and it is the first (and only) form in the Web page. Based on this information, you can access the form using either of the following object references:

```
document.forms[0]
document.form1
```

Referencing a form element

The elements within a form, including all input fields, buttons, and labels, are organized into an elements collection. You can reference a form element either by its position in the collection or by its name or id attributes. For example, the first element in Carol's order form is the date input box. To reference this object you use either

`formObject.elements[0]`

or

`formObject.date`

where `formObject` is the reference to the order form using one of the two methods described above. If the element is a selection list, it contains its own object collection consisting of the options within the list. Likewise, option buttons belonging to the same group have a unique syntax. You'll examine how to work with both selection lists and option buttons later in this session.

   Figure 7-4 lists the object references for the fields and buttons in Carol's order form. Note that the object references are drawn from the element names, which were displayed earlier in Figure 7-2.

Objects in the order form   **Figure 7-4**

Object	Reference
The order form	document.form1
The date field	document.form1.date
The product selection list	document.form1.prod
The quantity selection list	document.form1.qty
The price of the product field	document.form1.price
The group of shipping options	document.form1.shipType
The shipping cost field	document.form1.ship
The subtotal field	document.form1.sub
The tax field	document.form1.tax
The total field	document.form1.tot
The cancel button	document.form1.cancelb
The next button	document.form1.nextb

Referencing Form Objects

- To access a Web form, use the object reference
    ```
    document.forms[idref]
    ```
    where *idref* is the id or index number of the form. You can also use
    ```
    document.fname
    ```
    where *fname* is the name of the form.
- To reference an element within a form, use the object reference
    ```
    formObject.elements[idref]
    ```
    where *formObject* is the object reference to the form and *idref* is the id or index number of the form element. You can also use:
    ```
    formObject.ename
    ```
    where *ename* is the name of the form element.

Working with Input Fields

The first task on Carol's list is to have the current date displayed in the Web form. To change the value of the date field you need to work with the properties and methods of input fields.

Setting the field value

To set the value contained in a field such as an input box, you use the value property. The general syntax is

```
formObject.element.value = fieldvalue;
```

where *formObject* is a reference to the Web form, *element* is the object reference to the form element, and *fieldvalue* is the value you want placed in the field. For example, to have the date field display the text string "6-23-2006" you would run the command

```
document.form1.date.value = "6-23-2006";
```

The value property is one of many properties and methods associated with input fields. Figure 7-5 shows a few of the others.

Properties and methods of the input field ◀ | Figure 7-5

Property	Description
defaultvalue	The default value that is initially displayed in the field
form	References the form containing the field
maxlength	The maximum number of characters allowed in the field
name	The name of the field
size	The width of the input field in characters
type	The type of input field (button, check box, file, hidden, image, password, radio, reset, submit, text)
value	The current value of the field

Method	Description
blur()	Remove the focus from the field
focus()	Give focus to the field
select()	Select the field

Working with Fields

Reference Window

- To set the value of a form field, use the object property
  ```
  field.value = "value"
  ```
  where `field` is the reference to the form field and `value` is the value you want to assign to the field.
- To move the focus to a form field, use the method
  ```
  field.focus()
  ```

Navigating between fields

Carol also wants the product selection list to be selected automatically when the form opens, so it's ready for data entry. Like pop-up windows, form fields support the focus and blur events. The focus event occurs when a user's cursor moves to the field. The blur event occurs when the cursor moves away from the field. Thus, to place the cursor in a particular field on a form, you would use the following focus() method:

```
formObject.element.focus();
```

To remove the focus from this field, you would use the blur() method:

```
formObject.element.blur();
```

You now have enough information to write the first function to be used in the order form. Carol has created a function named todayTxt() that returns a text string with the current date in the format *mm-dd-yyyy*. She's stored this function in the external script file functions.js, which has already been linked to the files in her Web site. You'll use this function to set the value of the date field and then change the focus to the product selection list. The code appears as follows:

```
function startForm() {
   document.form1.date.value = todayTxt();
   document.form1.prod.focus();
}
```

Add the startForm() function to the form1.htm file and run it using an onload event handler applied to the document's body element.

To create and run the startForm() function:

▶ 1. Return to the **form1.htm** file in your text editor.

▶ 2. Insert the following embedded script element above the closing </head> tag in the document:

```
<script type="text/javascript">
function startForm() {
    document.form1.date.value = todayTxt();
    document.form1.prod.focus();
}
</script>
```

▶ 3. Add the event handler **onload="startForm()"** to the body element as shown in Figure 7-6.

Figure 7-6 | Creating the startForm() function

```
<title>Product Order Form 1</title>
<link href="gpsware.css" rel="stylesheet" type="text/css" />
<script type="text/javascript" src="functions.js"></script>
<script type="text/javascript">
function startForm() {
    document.form1.date.value = todayTxt();
    document.form1.prod.focus();
}
</script>
</head>

<body onload="startForm()">
<form name="form1" id="form1" method="post" action="form2.htm">
```

▶ 4. Save your changes to the file and then reopen or refresh the **form1.htm** file in your Web browser.

As shown in Figure 7-7, the current date should now be displayed in the date field and the product selection list should be highlighted, ready for a customer to select a product to purchase.

Figure 7-7 | Displaying the current date

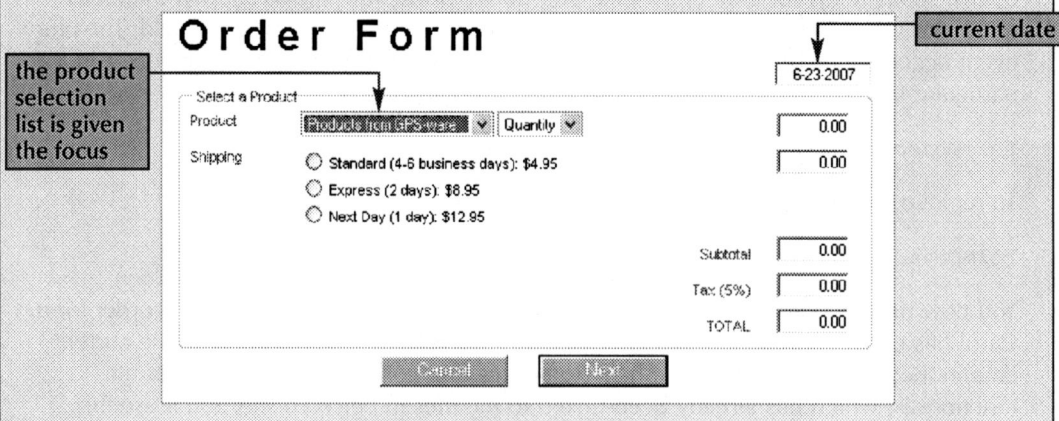

Working with Selection Lists

In the rest of the form you need to create functions to calculate the cost of a customer's order. This involves: 1) determining the price of the order (equal to the price of the product multiplied by the quantity ordered), 2) determining the cost of shipping, 3) calculating the cost of the sales tax, and 4) adding up all of these costs to arrive at the grand total. You'll start by creating a function to calculate the price of the order.

The product price and quantities have both been placed within selection lists. This is done to ensure that customers select only valid products and quantities. However, unlike an input box, there is no value property for an entire selection list, only for each option within the list. For example, the product selection list contains the following options and values:

```
<select name="prod" id="prod">
    <option value="0">Products from GPS-ware</option>
    <option value="19.95">GoMap 1.0 ($19.95)</option>
    <option value="29.95">Drive Planner 2.0 ($29.95)</option>
    <option value="29.95">Hiker 1.0 ($29.95)</option>
    <option value="149.50">G-Receiver I ($149.50)</option>
    <option value="199.50">G-Receiver II ($199.50)</option>
    <option value="249.50">G-Receiver III ($249.50)</option>
</select>
```

JavaScript organizes all of the options into an options collection contained within the selection list object. The syntax to reference a particular option in the collection is

```
element.options[idref]
```

where `element` is the reference to the selection list object and `idref` is the index number or id of the option. Each option in the selection list supports text and value properties specifying the text and value associated with the option. Figure 7-8 shows the text and value properties for the different options in the product selection list.

Properties in the products selection list ◀ **Figure 7-8**

object	object.text	object.value
document.form1.prod.options[0]	Products from GPS-ware	0
document.form1.prod.options[1]	GoMap 1.0 ($19.95)	19.95
document.form1.prod.options[2]	Drive Planner 2.0 ($29.95)	29.95
document.form1.prod.options[3]	Hiker 1.0 ($29.95)	29.95
document.form1.prod.options[4]	G-Receiver I ($149.50)	149.50
document.form1.prod.options[5]	G-Receiver II ($199.50)	199.50
document.form1.prod.options[6]	G-Receiver III ($249.50)	249.50

Figure 7-9 summarizes the properties of both selection list objects and selection list option objects.

| Figure 7-9 | | **Properties of selection list and option objects** |

selection list	Property	Description
	length	The number of options in the list
	name	The name of the selection list
	options	The collection of options in the list
	selectedIndex	The index number of the currently selected option in the list

selection list option	Property	Description
	defaultSelected	A Boolean value indicating whether the option is selected by default
	index	The index value of the option
	selected	A Boolean value indicating whether the option is currently selected
	text	The text associated with the option
	value	The value associated with the option

Since there is no value property for the entire selection list, you use the value or text of the selected option in any calculations you need to perform. To determine the currently selected option in a list, you use the selectedIndex property of the selection list object. The following code demonstrates how you would determine the price associated with a product selected by a customer:

```
product = document.form1.prod;
pindex = product.selectedIndex;
product_price = product.options[pindex].value;
```

In this code the product variable stores the object reference to the product selected in the form1 Web form. The pindex variable stores the index of the currently selected option (whatever that may be). Finally, the product_price variable stores the value of that selected option, which is the product's price. The code to determine the quantity ordered is similar:

```
quantity = document.form1.qty;
qindex = quantity.selectedIndex;
quantity_ordered = quantity.options[qindex].value;
```

To calculate the total price for a given product, you multiply the price of the product by the quantity ordered. The following calcPrice() function performs the necessary calculation to determine the price, and then displays the value in the price field of the Web form:

```
function calcPrice() {
   product = document.form1.prod;
   pindex = product.selectedIndex;
   product_price = product.options[pindex].value;
   quantity = document.form1.qty;
   qindex = quantity.selectedIndex;
   quantity_ordered = quantity.options[qindex].value;
   document.form1.price.value = product_price*quantity_ordered;
}
```

You want to run the calcPrice() function whenever a user selects a new option from either the product or the quantity selection lists. One way of doing this is to use the onchange event handler, which runs a command whenever the selected option in the list changes. Add the calcPrice() function and the onchange event handler to Carol's Web form.

To create and run the calcPrice() function:

1. Return to the **form1.htm** file in your text editor.

2. Add the following function to the embedded script element (see Figure 7-10):

```
function calcPrice() {
    product = document.form1.prod;
    pindex = product.selectedIndex;
    product_price = product.options[pindex].value;
    quantity = document.form1.qty;
    qindex = quantity.selectedIndex;
    quantity_ordered = quantity.options[qindex].value;
    document.form1.price.value = product_price*quantity_ordered;
}
```

Creating the calcPrice() function | **Figure 7-10**

```
function calcPrice() {
    product = document.form1.prod;
    pindex = product.selectedIndex;
    product_price = product.options[pindex].value;
    quantity = document.form1.qty;
    qindex = quantity.selectedIndex;
    quantity_ordered = quantity.options[qindex].value;
    document.form1.price.value = product_price*quantity_ordered;
}
</script>
```

3. Scroll down the document and add the following event handler to the select element for the "prod" selection list.

```
onchange = "calcPrice()"
```

4. Add the **onchange = "calcPrice()"** event handler to the <select> tag for the "qty" field as well (see Figure 7-11).

Calling the calcPrice() function | **Figure 7-11**

```
<td class="inputcell">
    <select name="prod" id="prod" onchange="calcPrice()">
    <option value="0">Products from GPS-ware</option>
    <option value="19.95">GoMap 1.0 ($19.95)</option>
    <option value="29.95">Drive Planner 2.0 ($29.95)</option>
    <option value="29.95">Hiker 1.0 ($29.95)</option>
    <option value="149.50">G-Receiver I ($149.50)</option>
    <option value="199.50">G-Receiver II ($199.50)</option>
    <option value="249.50">G-Receiver III ($249.50)</option>
    </select>

    <select name="qty" id="qty" onchange="calcPrice()">
    <option value="0">Quantity</option>
    <option value="1">1</option><option value="2">2</option><option value="3">3</option>
    <option value="4">4</option><option value="5">5</option><option value="6">6</option>
    <option value="7">7</option><option value="8">8</option><option value="9">9</option>
    <option value="10">10</option>
    </select>
</td>
```

5. Save your changes to the file and then reopen **form1.htm** in your Web browser.

6. Select **Hiker 1.0 ($29.95)** from the selection list for the product list box and **2** from the quantity list box. Notice that, as you select these options (changing the selected options in the list), the value in the price field is updated. See Figure 7-12.

Figure 7-12 **Calculating the price of an order quantity**

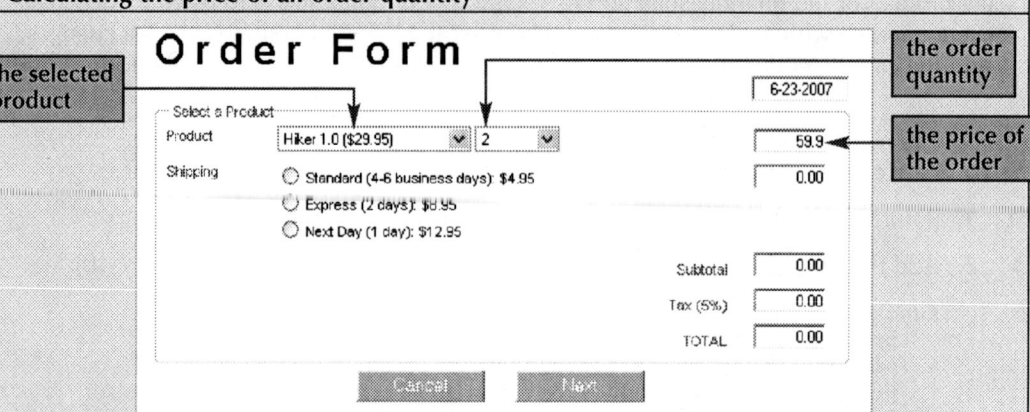

7. Select other product and quantity options and verify that the price field automatically changes in response.

Trouble? You will notice that for some product/quantity combinations the value in the price field is not displayed with a two-digit cents value. You'll learn to format the calculated output to always show the price in dollars and cents later in this session.

Some selection lists are set up to collect multiple selections. In those cases the selectedIndex property returns only the index number of the first selected item. If you wanted to determine the indices of all the selected items, you would have to create a For loop that would run through all of the options in the list, checking each to determine whether the selected property is true (indicating that the option was selected by the user). The selected options could then be added to an array from which further calculations and operations could be performed.

Reference Window **Working with Selection Lists**

- To determine which option in a selection list has been selected, use the object property
    `field.selectedIndex`
  where `field` is the selection list object.
- To extract the text of an option in a selection list, use the object reference
    `field.options[idref].text`
  where `idref` is the index number or id of the option.
- To extract the value of an option in a selection list, use the object reference
    `field.options[idref].value`

Working with Option Buttons and Checkboxes

Your next task is to display the cost of the shipping option that a user selects. Carol has placed the shipping options within a group of option buttons using the following HTML tags:

```
<input type="radio" name="shipType" id="ship1" value="4.95" />
<input type="radio" name="shipType" id="ship2" value="8.95" />
<input type="radio" name="shipType" id="ship3" value="12.95" />
```

You need to add event handlers to each of these buttons so that the value in the ship field reflects whatever option button has been clicked.

Using option buttons

Since each option button in a group shares a common name value, JavaScript places the individual buttons within that group into an array. Individual option buttons have the reference

```
element[idref]
```

where *element* is the reference to the group of option buttons and *idref* is either the index number or id of the individual option button within that group. In Carol's form, either of the following object references could be used for the first shipType option button:

```
document.form1.shipType[0]
document.form1.shipType["ship1"]
```

You can also reference an option button using the document.getElementById() method if an id has been assigned to it. Figure 7-13 describes some of the properties associated with option buttons.

Properties of option buttons — Figure 7-13

Property	Description
checked	A Boolean value indicating whether the option button is currently selected
defaultChecked	A Boolean value indicating whether the option button is selected by default
name	The name of the option button
value	The value associated with the option button

Thus, to extract the value of the first shipType option button, you would use the expression

```
document.form1.shipType[0].value
```

Reference Window

Working with Option Button Groups

- To reference a specific option button within a group, use the object reference
  ```
  element[idref]
  ```
  where *element* is the reference to the option button group, and *idref* is the id or index number of the option button.
- To determine whether an option button is currently checked, use the object property
  ```
  element[idref].checked
  ```
  which returns the Boolean value true if the button is checked.
- To determine which button in the option button group is checked, create a For loop that examines each option button's checked property, returning the index of the checked button.

Using the "this" keyword

To calculate the cost of shipping, you want to use the following function, which displays the cost of the selected shipping option in the ship field:

```
function calcShipping(shipOption) {
    document.form1.ship.value = shipOption.value;
}
```

In this function the shipOption parameter represents the shipping option button selected by a customer. But how do you determine which option button is selected? Unfortunately, there is no selectedIndex property for option buttons as there is for selection lists. However, other methods are available to determine which option button a customer clicked. One technique is to loop through all of the option buttons in the group and use the checked property, described in Figure 7-13, to determine which button the user clicked.

Another approach is to use the "this" keyword. Recall from Tutorial 4 that the "this" keyword is a JavaScript object reference that refers to the currently selected object, whatever that may be. The keyword is particularly useful in situations when a function might be called from several different objects and you need a way to work with the object that called the function. Indeed, that is the situation you are currently in. To use the "this" keyword with the calcShipping() function, you add the following onclick event handlers to the tags for the three option buttons:

```
<input type="radio" name="shipType" id="ship1" value="4.95"
    onclick="calcShipping(this)" />
<input type="radio" name="shipType" id="ship2" value="8.95"
    onclick="calcShipping(this)" />
<input type="radio" name="shipType" id="ship3" value="12.95"
    onclick="calcShipping(this)" />
```

When a customer clicks one of the shipType option buttons, the calcShipping() function is called. The object indicated by the "this" keyword is stored in the shipOption parameter, which is then used in determining the cost of the selected shipping option.

To create and run the calcShipping() function:

1. Return to the **form1.htm** file in your text editor.

2. Add the following calcShipping() function to the embedded script element, as shown in Figure 7-14.

```
function calcShipping(shipOption) {
    document.form1.ship.value = shipOption.value;
}
```

Figure 7-14

Creating the calcShipping() function

```
function calcshipping(shipoption) {
        document.form1.ship.value = shipoption.value;
}
</script>
</head>
```

3. Scroll down the document and add the event handler
onclick="calcShipping(this)" to each of the shipType option buttons. (See Figure 7-15.)

Figure 7-15

Calling the calcShipping() function

```
<td class="labelcell">Shipping</td>
<td>
    <p><input type="radio" name="shipType" id="ship1" value="4.95"
        onclick="calcshipping(this)" />
        <label for="ship1">Standard (4-6 business days): $4.95</label>
    </p>
    <p><input type="radio" name="shipType" id="ship2" value="8.95"
        onclick="calcshipping(this)" />
        <label for="ship2">Express (2 days): $8.95</label>
    </p>
    <p><input type="radio" name="shipType" id="ship3" value="12.95"
        onclick="calcshipping(this)" />
        <label for="ship3">Next Day (1 day): $12.95</label>
    </p>
</td>
```

4. Save your changes to the file and then reload **form1.htm** in your Web browser.
Verify that each time you click one of the three shipping options, the shipping cost
appears in the ship field on the right edge of the form.

Working with check boxes

Carol's order form contains no check boxes, which work the same way as option buttons.
Like an option button, a check box supports the checked property, indicating whether the
box is checked or not. In addition, the value associated with a check box is stored in the
value property of the check box object. However, this value is applied only when the
check box is checked; if a check box is not checked, its field has no value assigned to it.
As with option buttons, you can run a function in response to a user clicking a check box
by applying the onclick event handler. However, unlike option buttons, there is only one
check box for each entry field.

Creating Calculated Fields

To complete Carol's Web form, you need to calculate the form's remaining values: the
subtotal (the product price plus the shipping cost), the sales tax, and the total cost of the
order (the subtotal plus the sales tax). JavaScript treats the contents of input fields as
text strings. This means you cannot simply add the input field values together, because
JavaScript would append the text strings rather than add the values they represent. For
example, if the value displayed in the price field is "39.9" and the value in the ship field
is "9.95", then the expression

```
document.form1.price.value + document.form1.ship.value
```

returns the text string "39.99.95" (adding the two text strings together). If you want to treat the contents of input fields as numeric values, you must first convert them from text strings to numbers.

One way of converting a text string to a numeric value, discussed earlier in Tutorial 2, is to use the parseFloat() method. Recall that the parseFloat() method extracts the leading numeric value from a text string, returning a number instead of a text string in the process. The following set of commands uses the parseFloat() method to add the numeric values stored in the price and ship fields, storing the result in the sub field:

```
priceVal = parseFloat(document.form1.price.value);
shipVal = parseFloat(document.form1.ship.value);
document.form1.sub.value = priceVal+shipVal;
```

You'll use these commands in a function named calcTotal() that calculates the values of the subtotal, tax, and total fields. The text of the calcTotal() function is

```
function calcTotal() {
    priceVal = parseFloat(document.form1.price.value);
    shipVal = parseFloat(document.form1.ship.value);
    taxVal = 0.05*(priceVal+shipVal);
    document.form1.sub.value = priceVal+shipVal;
    document.form1.tax.value = taxVal;
    document.form1.tot.value = priceVal+shipVal+taxVal;
}
```

You want to run the calcTotal() function whenever a customer makes a selection on the form. This occurs when a product or quantity is picked from a selection list, or when a shipping option is selected. Since you've already created event handlers for each of those actions to run the calcPrice() and calcShipping() functions, you can simply add a command to the end of those functions to run calcTotal().

To create and run the calcTotal() function:

1. Return to the **form1.htm** file in your text editor.

2. Add the following calcTotal() function to the embedded script element:

```
function calcTotal() {
    priceVal = parseFloat(document.form1.price.value);
    shipVal = parseFloat(document.form1.ship.value);
    taxVal = 0.05*(priceVal+shipVal);
    document.form1.sub.value = priceVal+shipVal;
    document.form1.tax.value = taxVal;
    document.form1.tot.value = priceVal+shipVal+taxVal;
}
```

3. Go to the calcPrice() and calcShipping() functions and add a line to the end of each function calling the calcTotal() function. See Figure 7-16.

Creating the calcTotal() function | **Figure 7-16**

```
function calcPrice() {
    product = document.form1.prod;
    pindex = product.selectedIndex;
    product_price = product.options[pindex].value;
    quantity = document.form1.qty;
    qindex = quantity.selectedIndex;
    quantity_ordered = quantity.options[qindex].value;
    document.form1.price.value = product_price*quantity_ordered;
    calcTotal();
}

function calcShipping(shipoption) {
    document.form1.ship.value = shipoption.value;
    calcTotal();
}

function calcTotal() {
    priceVal = parseFloat(document.form1.price.value);
    shipVal = parseFloat(document.form1.ship.value);
    taxVal = 0.05*(priceVal+shipVal);
    document.form1.sub.value = priceVal+shipVal;
    document.form1.tax.value = taxVal;
    document.form1.tot.value = priceVal+shipVal+taxVal;
}
</script>
</head>
```

▶ **4.** Save your changes to the file and reload **form1.htm** in your Web browser.

▶ **5.** Select **Drive Planner 2.0 ($29.95)** from the product selection list, **2** from the quantity selection list, and click the **Standard (4–6 business days): $4.95** option button.

▶ **6.** As you select each of these options, the subtotal, tax, and total values should be automatically updated in the Web form. See Figure 7-17.

Calculating the total cost of an order | **Figure 7-17**

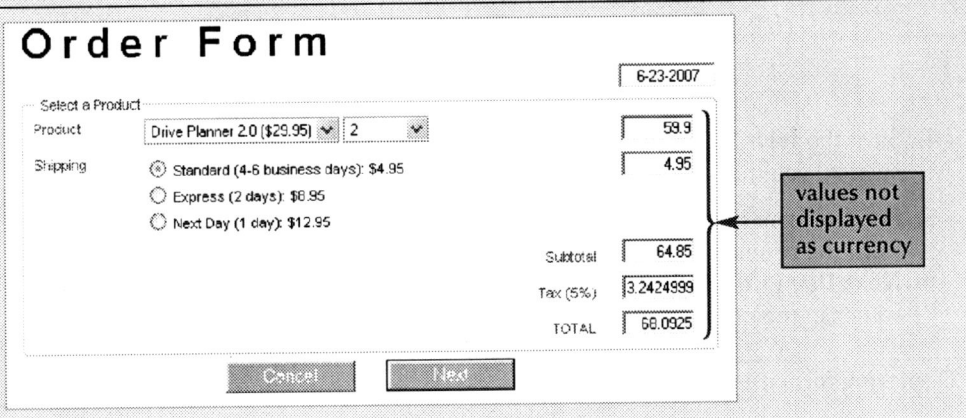

Using the options you selected, the form automatically calculates the subtotal value to be $64.85, the tax value to be approximately $3.24, and the total cost of the order to be about $68.09. All of these monetary values need to be displayed in dollars and cents, rounded to two decimal places. Our next task is to round these figures to currency values. To do this, we can use the toFixed() method. As discussed earlier in Tutorial 2, the toFixed() method converts a number to a text string, displaying the value to a specified number of digits.

To apply the toFixed() method:

▶ **1.** Return to the **form1.htm** file in your text editor.

2. Go to the calcPrice() function and change the statement that sets the value of the price field to the following:

```
document.form1.price.value =
(product_price*quantity_ordered).toFixed(2);
```

3. Go to the calcTotal() function and change the statements that set the values of the sub, tax, and tot fields to the following:

```
document.form1.sub.value = (priceVal+shipVal).toFixed(2);
document.form1.tax.value = taxVal.toFixed(2);
document.form1.tot.value = (priceVal+shipVal+taxVal).toFixed(2);
```

You do not have to make any changes to the calcShipping() function since the three shipping values are stored in the selection list already in currency format. Figure 7-18 shows the revised code in the document.

Figure 7-18	Applying the toFixed() method

```
function calcPrice() {
    product = document.form1.prod;
    pindex = product.selectedIndex;
    product_price = product.options[pindex].value;
    quantity = document.form1.qty;
    qindex = quantity.selectedIndex;
    quantity_ordered = quantity.options[qindex].value;
    document.form1.price.value = (product_price*quantity_ordered).toFixed(2);
    calcTotal();
}

function calcShipping(shipoption) {
    document.form1.ship.value = shipoption.value;
    calcTotal();
}

function calcTotal() {
    priceval = parseFloat(document.form1.price.value);
    shipval = parseFloat(document.form1.ship.value);
    taxval = 0.05*(priceval+shipval);
    document.form1.sub.value = (priceval+shipval).toFixed(2);
    document.form1.tax.value = taxval.toFixed(2) ;
    document.form1.tot.value = (priceval+shipval+taxval).toFixed(2);
}
</script>
</head>
```

4. Save the **form1.htm** file. If you plan on taking a break before starting the next session, you may also close the file.

5. Reopen **form1.htm** in your Web browser and select **G-Receiver I ($149.50)** from the product selection list, **3** from the quantity selection list, and click the **Next Day (1 day): $12.95** shipping option button. Figure 7-19 shows the resulting values in the order form.

Figure 7-19	Displaying formatted currency values

Order Form

Trouble? If you are using an older browser, it may not support the toFixed() method. In this case, you can instead use the customized function toFixed2(*value*) where *value* is the value you want formatted to two decimal places. You'll learn about the toFixed2() function shortly.

6. Continue to experiment with different order options to verify that the form works as expected. Close the Web page when you're finished.

You've completed your work on creating a Web form to perform automatic calculations and correctly format values. Carol will look over your work and get back to you with further tasks in the next session.

Working with Older Browsers

Before going on to the next session, it's important to note that the toFixed() method was introduced in JavaScript 1.5, and thus is not supported by older browsers. Specifically, it is not supported in browser versions earlier than Internet Explorer 5.5, Netscape 6.0, and Opera 6.02. If you need to support those browsers, you must format your output using a JavaScript program. Let's consider a few examples.

When you want to limit your output to a certain number of decimal places, you have to round the value to those decimal places. JavaScript does not support a generalized rounding function. The only built-in rounding functions are the Math.floor(), Math.ceil(), and Math.round() methods used to round a number to the next highest, next lowest, and closest integer, respectively. If you need to round a number to a specified number of decimals, you can use the following customized function:

```
function roundValue(value, n) {
    return Math.round(Math.pow(10,n)*value)/Math.pow(10,n);
}
```

where the *value* parameter is the number to be rounded and the *n* parameter is the number of digits the value can be rounded to. The value of the *n* parameter must be an integer, but it can be either positive or negative; a negative *n* parameter has the effect of rounding a value to the nearest ten, hundred, thousand, and so forth. The following code shows how the roundValue() function can be used to round the same number to different decimal places:

```
roundValue(45.783,2)   // returns 45.78
roundValue(45.783,1)   // returns 45.8
roundValue(45.783,0)   // returns 46
roundValue(45.783,-1)  // returns 50
```

The roundValue() function returns a numeric value, but not a text string with a value displayed to a set number of decimals as the toFixed() method does. To simulate the toFixed() method for currency values displayed with two decimal places, you can use the following function:

```
function toFixed2(value) {
    n = Math.round(value*100)/100;
    if (n == Math.round(n)) return n+".00";
    else if (n*10 == Math.round(n*10)) return n+"0";
    else return String(n);
}
```

The following are the text strings returned by this function for a set of numeric values:

```
toFixed2(45.783) // returns "45.78"
toFixed2(45.787) // returns "45.79"
toFixed2(45.8)   // returns "45.80"
toFixed(45)      // returns "45.00"
```

These two functions and a few other number formatting functions have been placed in the functions.js file for your use in your own Web site. If you are using an older browser, you can use these functions in place of the more recent JavaScript methods.

For example, to display the sales tax value from the form1.htm file using the toFixed() method, you can enter the following command:

```
document.form1.tax.value = taxVal.toFixed(2);
```

Using the toFixed2() function, this should be written as:

```
document.form1.tax.value = toFixed2(taxVal);
```

At this point you've completed your work in creating calculated fields for Carol's Web form. In the next session, you'll explore how to ensure that a Web form is correctly filled out.

Review

Session 7.1 Quick Check

1. Specify the object reference to the second Web form in a document.
2. Specify the object reference to the lastname input field found in a Web form named "register".
3. What command would change the value of the lastname field to "Carol Campbell"? What command would move the cursor to the lastname field?
4. Specify the object reference to the fourth option in the statename selection list. Assume that the name of the Web form is "register".
5. What expression would return the index number of the selected option from the statename selection list?
6. What expression would indicate whether the contactme check box field in the register Web form is selected?
7. What expression would you use to convert the value 3.14159 to a text string displaying the value rounded to 2 decimal places? What problems might old browsers encounter in using this expression?

Session 7.2

Working with Form Validation

Carol has now had some time to work with your changes to her order form. While she appreciates the form's ability to automatically calculate the different costs associated with an order, she's concerned that the form contains nothing to prevent customers from filling it out incorrectly. She points out that users could submit an order without specifying a shipping option. Carol would like to see the form contain some checks on whether a customer has correctly filled it out.

Carol's request is an example of **form validation**, a process by which the server or a user's browser checks a form for data entry errors. On the Web, validation can occur on the client side or the server side. As shown in Figure 7-20, with **server-side validation**, a form is sent to the Web server for checking. If an error is found, the user is notified and asked to resubmit the form. In **client-side validation**, the Web browser checks the form, which is not submitted to the server until it passes inspection.

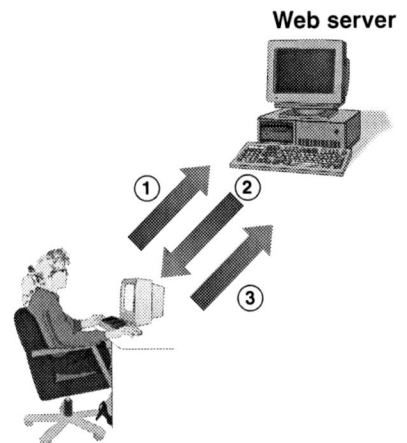

Web server

Web server

Server-side validation

1) The user submits the form to the Web server.

2) The Web server validates the user's responses and, if necessary, returns the form to the user for correction.

3) After correcting any errors, the user resubmits the form to the Web server for another validation.

Client-side validation

1) The user submits the form, and validation is performed on the user's computer.

2) After correcting any errors, the user submits the form to the Web server.

In practice, server-side and client-side validation are commonly used together. Client-side validation provides immediate feedback to users and lessens the load on servers by distributing some of the validation tasks to users' computers. The server then has the task of performing a final check on submitted data before processing it. Carol is aware that GPS-ware's Web server might handle hundreds of orders per hour on a good business day, and anything that can be done to reduce the load on the server helps. Carol would like you to ensure that, before her form can be submitted to the server, a customer has done the following:

1. selected a GPS-ware product
2. selected a quantity of the product to order
3. selected a shipping option

If these conditions are not met, Carol would like the user's browser to alert the customer of the problem and refuse to submit the form to the server.

Submitting a Form

When a user completes a form and then clicks the submit button, the form initiates a submit event. By default, the browser initiates the action indicated in the form's action and method attributes. As you may have already discovered by working with the form1. htm file, submitting Carol's first order form causes a user's browser to open the second of her three Web forms. The submit button is the button labeled "Next" on the Web form.

To control this submission process, JavaScript provides the onsubmit event handler that can be added to the form element. The syntax used with the onsubmit event handler is

```
<form onsubmit="return function()"> ... </form>
```

where *function* is a function that returns the Boolean value true or false. As you saw in the previous tutorial when working with pop-up windows and transient status bar messages, you can use such a function to prevent a browser's default behavior in response to an event. In this case, if the function returns a value of false, the submit event is cancelled, while a value of true allows the submit event to continue unabated.

For the first of Carol's three Web forms, you'll create a function named checkForm1() that tests whether the selected index of the product or quantity selection lists is equal to zero (indicating that no product or quantity was selected), or if the cost of shipping is equal to "0.00" (indicating that no shipping option was selected). If the function identifies any of these problems, it means that the form has not been properly completed. In this case, the function will display an alert box specifying the problem to the user, and return a value of false. If the function does not identify any of these problems, it will return a value of true and allow the form to be submitted. The complete code of the checkForm1() function is

```
function checkForm1() {
    if (document.form1.prod.selectedIndex == 0)
       {alert("You must select a GPS-ware product");
        return false;}
    else if (document.form1.qty.selectedIndex == 0)
       {alert("You must select a quantity to order");
        return false;}
    else if (document.form1.ship.value == "0.00")
       {alert("You must select a shipping option");
        return false;}
    else return true;
}
```

Note that the return keyword ends this function when one of the conditions is met. Thus, only one alert box will be displayed at a time, even if more than one error is present in the form.

To create and apply the checkForm1() function:

1. If necessary, reopen the **form1.htm** file in your text editor.

2. Add the following function to the embedded script element in the document's head section:

```
function checkForm1() {
    if (document.form1.prod.selectedIndex == 0)
       {alert("You must select a GPS-ware product");
        return false;}
    else if (document.form1.qty.selectedIndex == 0)
       {alert("You must select a quantity to order");
        return false;}
    else if (document.form1.ship.value == "0.00")
       {alert("You must select a shipping option");
        return false;}
    else return true;
}
```

3. Scroll down the file and add the following event handler to the form element:

```
onsubmit = "return checkForm1()"
```

Figure 7-21 shows the new code in the form1.htm file.

Creating the checkForm1() function | Figure 7-21

```
function checkForm1() {
    if (document.form1.prod.selectedIndex == 0)
        {alert("You must select a GPS-ware product");
         return false;}
    else if (document.form1.qty.selectedIndex == 0)
        {alert("You must select a quantity to order");
         return false;}
    else if (document.form1.ship.value == "0.00")
        {alert("You must select a shipping option");
         return false;}
    else return true;
}
</script>
</head>

<body onload="startForm()">
<form name="form1" id="form1" method="post" action="form2.htm"
      onsubmit="return checkForm1()">
```

▶ **4.** Save your changes to the file.

▶ **5.** Reopen **form1.htm** in your Web browser.

▶ **6.** Click the **Next** button without selecting any products, quantities, or shipping options from the form.

   As shown in Figure 7-22, the browser displays an alert box indicating that you have not selected a product to order (the first mistake found in the form).

Validating the Web form | Figure 7-22

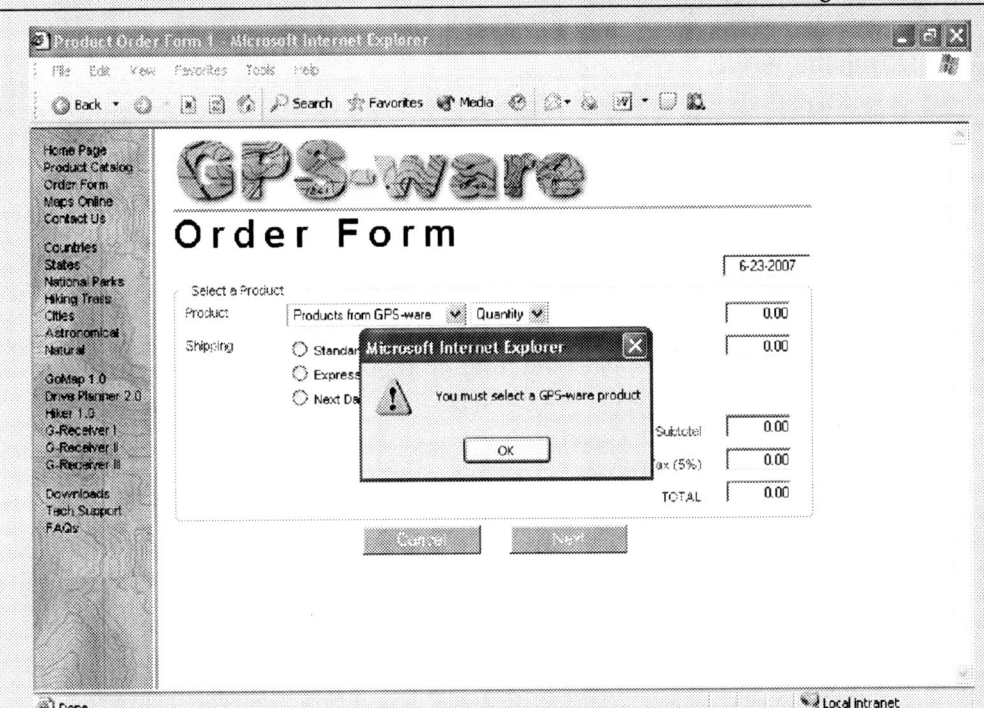

▶ **7.** Click **OK** to close the alert box and then continue to test the form by omitting one of three required pieces of information when you submit the form. Verify that the browser fails to accept the form.

▶ **8.** Correctly complete the order form and then click the **Next** button. Verify that the browser has accepted the completed form and displayed the contents of the second of Carol's three Web forms.

Resetting a Form

The other event associated with Web forms is the reset event, which occurs when a user clicks a reset button within the form. Clicking the reset button has the effect of resetting all form fields to their default values. You can control how the reset event is handled by adding an onreset event handler to the form element in the same way that you add the onsubmit event handler to manage form submission.

In Carol's order form, the Cancel button plays the role of the reset button. However, Carol wants to modify what happens when the form is reset. Recall that the first action this form takes is to insert the current date into the date field. Thus, Carol wants the reset button to both reset the fields to their default values and to rerun the startForm() function which inserts the current date into the date field. You can perform both of these actions by having the browser reload the document when the reset event is initiated. When the page is reloaded, the startForm() function runs automatically and the fields return to their default values. To reload the page, you use the reload() method of the location object.

To apply the onreset event handler:

1. Return to the **form1.htm** file in your text editor.

2. Add the following event handler to the form element, as shown in Figure 7-23:

   ```
   onreset = "location.reload()"
   ```

Figure 7-23 ▶ **Working with the onreset event handler**

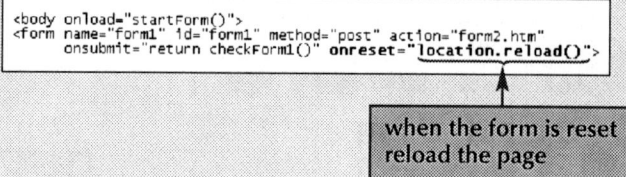

Note that you are not using the return keyword in this event handler. This is because you don't want to cancel the reset event, but simply to change what actions are caused by the occurrence of a form reset.

3. Close the **form1.htm** file, saving your changes.

4. Reopen **form1.htm** in your Web browser.

5. Select a product to order, a quantity, and a shipping option and then click the **Cancel** button at the bottom of the form. Verify that the page reloads, setting the fields to their default values and displaying the current date in the date field. The product selection list should be the selected field in the form.

Validating a Web Form

- To validate a Web form when it is submitted, add the following event handler to the form element:

    `<form onsubmit="return function()"> ... </form>`

    where *function* is a function that returns a Boolean value. A value of false cancels the submission of the form, while a value of true allows the form to be submitted.
- To control the resetting of a form, add the event handler

    `<form onreset="function"> ... </form>`

    where *function* is a function that is run when the reset event is initiated.

Working with Text Strings

You've completed your work on the first of Carol's Web forms. The second form, shown in Figure 7-24, contains fields for collecting a customer's contact and delivery information.

The delivery form   Figure 7-24

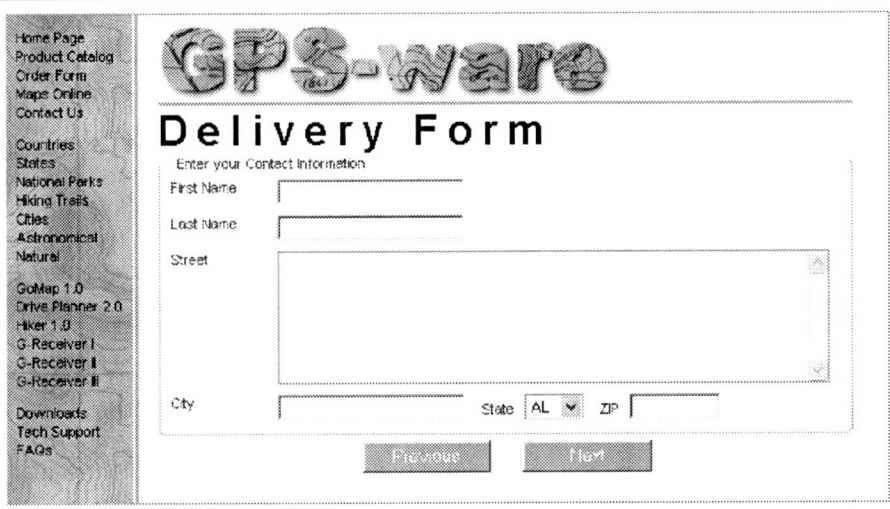

Figure 7-25 lists the object references for each of the elements in the form.

Objects in the delivery form   Figure 7-25

Object	Reference
The first name field	document.form2.fname
The last name field	document.form2.lname
The street text area box	document.form2.street
The city field	document.form2.city
The state selection list	document.form2.state
The ZIP code field	document.form2.zip
The previous button	document.form2.prevb
The next button	document.form2.nextb

While this form requires no calculations, Carol would like you to implement the following validation checks before the form is accepted by the browser:

1. A customer must specify a first name, last name, street address, and city.
2. If a ZIP code is entered, it should consist of five digits with no non-numeric characters.

Since you need to apply these validation checks to text strings, you'll now take a deeper look at the properties and methods of text strings.

The string object

JavaScript treats each text string as an object called a **string object**. The most common way to create a string object is to assign a text string to a variable. You can also create a string object using the object constructor

```
stringVariable = new String("text");
```

where *stringVariable* is a variable that stores the text string, and *text* is the text of the string. This approach has the advantage of explicitly identifying a variable as containing a text string, rather than having JavaScript implicitly create a string object based on the content of a variable.

Calculating the length of a text string

Only a few properties are associated with string objects. Of chief interest to us is the length property, which returns the number of characters in the text, including all whitespace characters and nonprintable characters. The following code calculates the number of characters in the stringVar variable, storing the value 17 in the lengthValue variable:

```
stringVar = "GPS-ware Products";
lengthValue = stringVar.length;
```

The length property is commonly used for functions that process a text string character by character, and need some way of knowing when to stop. You can also use the length property to validate the entries in Carol's delivery form. Her first requirement is that customers enter a first and last name, a street address, and a city. Thus, for each of those fields the length of the text string must be greater than zero. You'll use the length property to verify this condition for each of these fields in your first set of validation checks for the delivery form, which will be stored in a function called checkForm2(). As with the earlier checkForm1() function, you'll have the browser display an appropriate alert dialog box the first time it encounters an invalid field. The initial code for the checkForm2() function is

```
function checkForm2() {
   if (document.form2.fname.value.length == 0)
      {alert("You must enter a first name");
       return false;}
   else if (document.form2.lname.value.length == 0)
      {alert("You must enter a last name");
       return false;}
   else if (document.form2.street.value.length == 0)
      {alert("You must enter a street address");
       return false;}
   else if (document.form2.city.value.length == 0)
      {alert("You must enter a city name");
       return false;}
   else return true;
}
```

Notice that since JavaScript treats field values as text strings—that is to say, string objects—you can use the length property to determine whether a customer has entered a value. You will not be checking whether those values make any sense, but simply verifying that the customer has entered something. Add this function to the form2.htm file and then call it by adding an onsubmit event handler to the form element.

To create and apply the checkForm2() function:

1. Open the **form2.htm** file in your text editor. Take some time to review its contents to understand the HTML code.

2. Directly above the closing </head> tag, insert the following embedded script element and function:

```
<script type="text/javascript">
function checkForm2() {
    if (document.form2.fname.value.length == 0)
        {alert("You must enter a first name");
         return false;}
    else if (document.form2.lname.value.length == 0)
        {alert("You must enter a last name");
         return false;}
    else if (document.form2.street.value.length == 0)
        {alert("You must enter a street address");
         return false;}
    else if (document.form2.city.value.length == 0)
        {alert("You must enter a city name");
         return false;}
    else return true;
}
</script>
```

Since this is a long piece of code, take some time to ensure that you have correctly entered the code. Make sure that you enclose all command blocks within curly braces {} and that you use the == symbol rather than a single = symbol in a conditional statement.

3. Scroll down the file and add the following event handler to the form element:

```
onsubmit = "return checkForm2()"
```

Figure 7-26 shows the new code in the form2.htm file.

Adding the checkForm2() function ◀ **Figure 7-26**

```
<script type="text/javascript">
function checkForm2() {
    if (document.form2.fname.value.length == 0)
        {alert("You must enter a first name");
         return false;}
    else if (document.form2.lname.value.length == 0)
        {alert("You must enter a last name");
         return false;}
    else if (document.form2.street.value.length == 0)
        {alert("You must enter a street address");
         return false;}
    else if (document.form2.city.value.length == 0)
        {alert("You must enter a city name");
         return false;}
    else return true;
}
</script>

</head>

<body>
<form name="form2" id="form2" method="post" action="form3.htm"
      onsubmit="return checkForm2()">
```

4. Save your changes to the file and open **form2.htm** in your Web browser.

As with the previous form, the Next button submits this form for processing. In this case, submitting the form will cause the browser to load the form3.htm file.

5. Click the **Next** button without entering any contact information in the first name, last name, street, or city fields.

   The browser displays an alert box indicating that you have not specified a first name.

6. Click **OK** to close the alert box, and then continue to test the form by omitting different required fields and then clicking the **Next** button. Verify that you have to type in all the required information before the browser accepts the completed form.

Working with string object methods

Carol's second validation check involves examining the digits in the ZIP field. This field should be five characters long and should consist only of numeric characters (you'll look at how to validate extended ZIP codes that include a dash and additional digits in the next session).

   To validate the ZIP code, you'll create a function called checkZip(). The initial version of this function will check only the length of the ZIP code. Since a ZIP code is not required for delivery, you'll allow valid ZIP codes to contain either 0 or 5 digits; any other length will be invalid. The initial code for the checkZip() function is

```
function checkZip(zip) {
   if (zip.length != 0 && zip.length != 5) return false;
   return true;
}
```

Add this function to the form2.htm file.

To create the checkZip() function:

1. Return to the **form2.htm** file in your text editor.

2. Add the following function to the embedded script (see Figure 7-27):

```
function checkZip(zip) {
   if (zip.length != 0 && zip.length != 5) return false;
   return true;
}
```

Figure 7-27 The initial checkZip() function

```
function checkZip(zip) {
   if (zip.length != 0 && zip.length != 5) return false;
   return true;
}
</script>
```

3. Save your changes to the file.

   The checkZip() function can confirm that the ZIP code contains five characters, but does not check whether each of those characters are digits. To do that, you'll use some of the JavaScript methods associated with string objects.

JavaScript supports methods that allow you to examine the individual characters within a text string. A character is identified by its placement in the text string. Like arrays and object collections, the first character has an index value of 0, the second has an index value of 1, and so forth. If you want to reference a character with a particular index, use the method

```
string.charAt(i)
```

where *string* is the string object and *i* is the index of the character. For example, the expression

```
"GPS-ware".charAt(2)
```

returns the third character from the text string, which in this case is an uppercase "S". The charAt() method extracts only a single character. To extract longer text strings, known as **substrings**, use the slice() method:

```
string.slice(start, end)
```

where *start* is the starting index and *end* is the index at which the slicing stops. If you do not specify an *end* value, the substring is extracted to the end of the text string. For example, the statement

```
"GPS-ware Products For Sale".slice(9,17)
```

returns the substring "Products", since it starts at index number 9 and ends right before index 17. You can also extract substrings based on their length using the method

```
string.substr(start, length)
```

where *length* is the number of characters in the substring. If you do not specify a *length* value, JavaScript extracts the substring to the end of the string. Thus, to extract the word "Products" from the previous text string, you can also use

```
"GPS-ware Products For Sale".substr(9,8)
```

Both the slice() and substr() methods are limited in that they create only a single substring. In some cases, you may need to break a text string into several substrings. For example, you may need to break a long sentence into individual words. Another common use would be to break a field in which customers enter both their first and last names into two strings. Rather than run the substr() or slice() methods several times on the same text string, you can create an array of substrings in a single expression using the method

```
strArray = string.split(str)
```

where *strArray* is the array that will store the substrings and *str* is a text string that marks the break between one substring and another, which is known as a **delimiter**. For example, the command

```
words = "GPS-ware Products For Sale".split(" ")
```

splits the text string at each occurrence of a blank space, storing the substrings in the words array. The substrings stored in the words array are

```
words[0] = "GPS-ware"
words[1] = "Products"
words[2] = "For"
words[3] = "Sale"
```

Note that the characters specified in the delimiter are not placed in the substrings. This is one technique you can use to remove character strings from a large text string.

Other string object methods are used to search for the occurrence of particular substrings within larger text strings. The most often used method is

```
string.indexOf(str, start)
```

which returns the index value of the first occurrence of the substring *str* within *string*. The *start* parameter is optional, and indicates from which character to start the search. The default value of the *start* parameter is 0, indicating that the search should start with the first character. For example, the expression

```
"GPS-ware Products For Sale".indexOf("P")
```

returns the value 1 since that is the index number of the first occurrence of an uppercase "P" in the text. To locate the next occurrence of "P", you can set the *start* value to 2 so that the search starts with the third character in the string. The expression

```
"GPS-ware Products For Sale".indexOf("P",3)
```

returns the value 9. Note that if there is no occurrence of the substring, the indexOf() method returns the value −1. For this reason, the indexOf() method is often used to test whether a text string contains a particular substring.

Reference Window

Working with String Objects

- To determine the number of characters in a text string, use the object property
  ```
  string.length
  ```
  where *string* is a text string object.
- To extract a character from a text string, use the method
  ```
  string.charAt(i)
  ```
  where *i* is the index of the character. The first character in the text string has an index number of 0.
- To extract a substring from a text string, use the method
  ```
  string.slice(start, end)
  ```
  where *start* is the starting index and *end* is the index at which the substring stops. If you do not specify an *end* value, the substring is extracted to the end of the string.
- To split a string into several substrings, use the command
  ```
  strArray = string.split(str)
  ```
  where *strArray* is the array that will store the substrings and *str* is a text string that marks the break between one substring and another.
- To search a string, use the method
  ```
  string.indexOf(str, start)
  ```
  where *str* is the substring to search for within the larger string and *start* is the index of the character from which to start the search. If you do not specify a *start* value, the search starts with the first character in the string.

Figure 7-28 summarizes the different string object methods used to extract information from text strings.

String extracting methods | Figure 7-28

Method	Description	Example(text= "GPS-ware Products")
string.charAt(*i*)	Returns the *i*th character from *string*	text.charAt(4);// returns "w"
string.charCodeAt(*i*)	Returns the *i*th character's Unicode value from the *string*	text.charCodeAt(4);// returns 119
string.concat(*str2, str3, ...*)	Appends *string* with the text strings *str2, str3*, etc.	text.concat(" Sale"); // returns "GPS-ware Products Sale"
String.fromCharCode(*n1, n2, ...*)	Returns a text string consisting of characters whose Unicode values are *n1, n2*, etc.	String.fromCharCode(71,80,83); // returns "GPS"
string.indexOf(*str, start*)	Searches *string*, beginning at the *start* index number, returning the index number of the first occurrence of *str*; if no *start* value is specified, the search begins with the first character	text.indexOf("P",5);// returns 9
string.lastIndexOf(*str,start*)	Searches *string*, beginning at the *start* index number, returning the index number of the last occurrence of *str*; if no *start* value is specified, the search begins with the first character	text.lastIndexOf("P");// returns 9
string.slice(*start, end*)	Extracts a substring from *string*, between the *start* and *end* index values; if no *end* value is specified, the substring extends to the end of the string	text.slice(4,8);// returns "ware"
string.split(*str*)	Splits *string* into array of string characters at each occurrence of *str*	word=text.split(" "); // word[0] = "GPS-ware" // word[1] = "Products"
string.substr(*start, length*)	Returns a substring from *string* starting at the *start* index value and continuing for *length* characters; if no *length* value is specified, the substring continues to the end of *string*	text.substr(9,4);// returns "Prod"
string.substring (*start, end*)	Extracts a substring from *string*, between the *start* and *end* index values; if no *end* value is specified, the substring extends to the end of the string (identical to the slice() method)	text.substring(4,8);// returns "ware"

You'll use the charAt() and indexOf() methods to determine whether a customer has entered 5 digits in the ZIP code. First you'll create a string object named validchars that stores the digits from 0 to 9. Then you loop through the ZIP code string, extracting the character at each index using the charAt() method. For each character you'll use the indexOf() method to check whether it can be found in the validchars text string. If it can't be found in that text string, the indexOf() method will return the value –1, and you'll know that the ZIP code contains a non-numeric character. The complete code is

```
validchars = "0123456789";
for (i=0; i<5; i++) {
   zipchar=zip.charAt(i);
   if (validchars.indexOf(zipchar) == -1) return false;
}
```

You'll add these commands to the checkZip() function, running them as another condition in the structure you created earlier.

To modify the checkZip() function:

1. Return to **form2.htm** in your text editor.

2. Add the following code to the checkZip() function, as shown in Figure 7-29:

```
else {
   validchars = "0123456789";
   for (i=0; i<5; i++) {
      zipchar=zip.charAt(i);
      if (validchars.indexOf(zipchar) == -1) return false;
   }
}
```

Figure 7-29   **Checking for valid characters in the zip code**

```
function checkZip(zip) {
   if (zip.length != 0 && zip.length != 5) return false;
   else {
      validchars = "0123456789";
      for (i=0; i<5; i++) {
         zipchar=zip.charAt(i);
         if (validchars.indexOf(zipchar) == -1) return false;
      }
   }
   return true;
}
</script>
```

Next you'll call the checkZip() function from the checkForm2() function in order to add this validation check to the others.

3. Add the following code to the checkForm2() function as shown in Figure 7-30:

```
else if (checkZip(document.form2.zip.value) == false)
   {alert("You must enter a valid zip code");
   return false;}
```

Calling the checkZip() function | Figure 7-30

```
function checkForm2() {
    if (document.form2.fname.value.length == 0)
        {alert("You must enter a first name");
         return false;}
    else if (document.form2.lname.value.length == 0)
        {alert("You must enter a last name");
         return false;}
    else if (document.form2.street.value.length == 0)
        {alert("You must enter a street address");
         return false;}
    else if (document.form2.city.value.length == 0)
        {alert("You must enter a city name");
         return false;}
    else if (checkZip(document.form2.zip.value) == false)
        {alert("You must enter a valid zip code");
         return false;}
    else return true;
}
```

4. Save your changes to the file, then reload **form2.htm** in your browser.

5. Enter text into the first name, last name, street, and city fields, and then click the **Next** button to submit the delivery form.

   Your browser should display the contents of Carol's third Web form.

6. Return to the **form2.htm** page. Enter the value **ZIP1** into the ZIP field and click the **Next** button. Repeat for the values **123**, **1234a**, and **12345**. Your browser should display an alert box and fail to accept the form except for the ZIP code value of 12345.

7. If you want to take a break before starting the next session, close your browser and editor.

Formatting text strings

Another set of JavaScript methods allows you to format a text string's appearance. For example, to display a text string in all uppercase letters you would use the method

```
string.toUpperCase()
```

where *string* is the string object. Thus, to change the text "GPS-ware" to all uppercase letters you would use the JavaScript expression

```
"GPS-ware".toUpperCase()
```

Figure 7-31 lists other formatting methods for string objects along with their equivalent HTML tags. Note that running these methods does not add the HTML tags to the object, but rather achieves the same effects that you would get if you applied those formatting tags to the text string.

Figure 7-31   **String formatting methods**

Method	Description	HTML Equivalent
string.anchor(*text*)	Creates an anchor with the anchor name *text*	`<a name="text">string</a>`
string.big()	Changes the size of the *string* font to big	`<big>string</big>`
string.blink()	Changes *string* to blinking text	`<blink>string</blink>`
string.bold()	Changes the font weight of *string* to bold	`<bold>string</bold>`
string.fixed()	Changes the font of *string* to a fixed width font	`<tt>string</tt>`
string.fontcolor(*color*)	Changes the color of *string* to the hexadecimal *color* value	`<font color="color">string</font>`
string.fontsize(*value*)	Changes the font size of *string* to *value*	`<font size="value">string</font>`
string.italics()	Changes *string* to italics	`<i>string</i>`
string.link(*url*)	Changes *string* to a link pointing to *url*	`<a href="url">string</a>`
string.small()	Changes the size of the *string* font to small	`<small>string</small>`
string.strike()	Adds strikethrough characters to *string*	`<strike>string</strike>`
string.sub()	Changes *string* to a subscript	`<sub>string</sub>`
string.sup()	Changes *string* to a superscript	`<sup>string</sup>`
string.toLowerCase()	Changes *string* to lower-case letters	
string.toUpperCase()	Changes *string* to upper-case letters	

You may have noticed that many of the HTML tags shown in Figure 7-31 have been deprecated in favor of style sheets. In the same way, the string formatting methods are not often used in preference to formatting text strings using the style object. The most often used formatting methods are the toUpperCase() and toLowerCase() methods. At this point you don't have to do any text formatting for Carol's Web forms, but you'll keep these methods in mind for future tasks.

Review

Session 7.2 Quick Check

1. What is server-side validation? What is client-side validation?
2. You've written a function named testForm() that validates your Web form. What event handler should you add to the form element to run the validation before the form is submitted?
3. What expression returns the number of characters in the username string object?
4. What expression returns the first character from the username string? What expression returns the last character from the string?

5. What expression returns the first five characters from the username string?
6. E-mail addresses are usually written in the format *username@domain*. Write code that breaks an e-mail variable into two text strings: one containing *username*, and the other containing *domain*.
7. Government e-mail addresses will often end with ".gov". What expression tests whether the e-mail string object contains the ".gov" substring?
8. What expression would change the username string object to uppercase letters?

Session 7.3

Introducing Regular Expressions

Carol is finished examining your work on the delivery form. While she likes the form validation functions you created, she is concerned about the function that validates the ZIP code. Domestic ZIP codes commonly come in two forms: five digits (*nnnnn*), and five digits followed by a dash and four more digits (*nnnnn-nnnn*). In recent years, the second version has become more prevalent and Carol wants your validation functions to support either format. While you could revise the checkZip() function to accommodate the extended ZIP code format, a much quicker and easier approach is to use a regular expression.

A **regular expression** is a text string that defines a character pattern. One use of regular expressions is **pattern-matching**, in which a text string is tested to see whether it matches the pattern defined by a regular expression. In our ZIP code example, you might create a regular expression for the pattern of five digits followed by a dash and another four digits, and then verify that a customer's ZIP code matches that pattern. Pattern matching is just one use of regular expressions. They can also be used to extract substrings, insert new text, or replace old text. The greatest advantage of regular expressions is that the code is compact and powerful, so that what might take several lines of code using other methods can be done in a single line with a regular expression. However, with this power comes complexity: the syntax of regular expressions can be intimidating to new programmers, taking time and practice to master.

Creating a regular expression

You create a regular expression in JavaScript using the command

```
re = /pattern/;
```

where `pattern` is the text string of the regular expression and `re` is the object that stores the regular expression. This syntax for creating regular expressions is sometimes referred to as a **regular expression literal**. A regular expression is treated by a JavaScript interpreter as an object with a collection of properties and methods that can be applied to it. You'll explore some of those properties and methods later in this session. For now you'll work on understanding the language of regular expressions. To help you understand regular expressions, a demo page has been created in which you can enter a regular expression and apply pattern matching against a sample text string. Open this page now.

To view the regular expressions demo:

1. Open the **demo_regexp.htm** file from the tutorial.07/tutorial folder in your Web browser.

The demo page contains a text box in the upper-left corner in which you enter your sample text. Below the text box you can either enter a predefined regular expression or type one of your own. To match the regular expression against the sample text, you click the Pattern Test button.

2. Type the following text into the text box in the upper-left corner of the page (see Figure 7-32):

```
GPS-ware Products Are Prepared With Care
```

Figure 7-32	The regular expression demo page

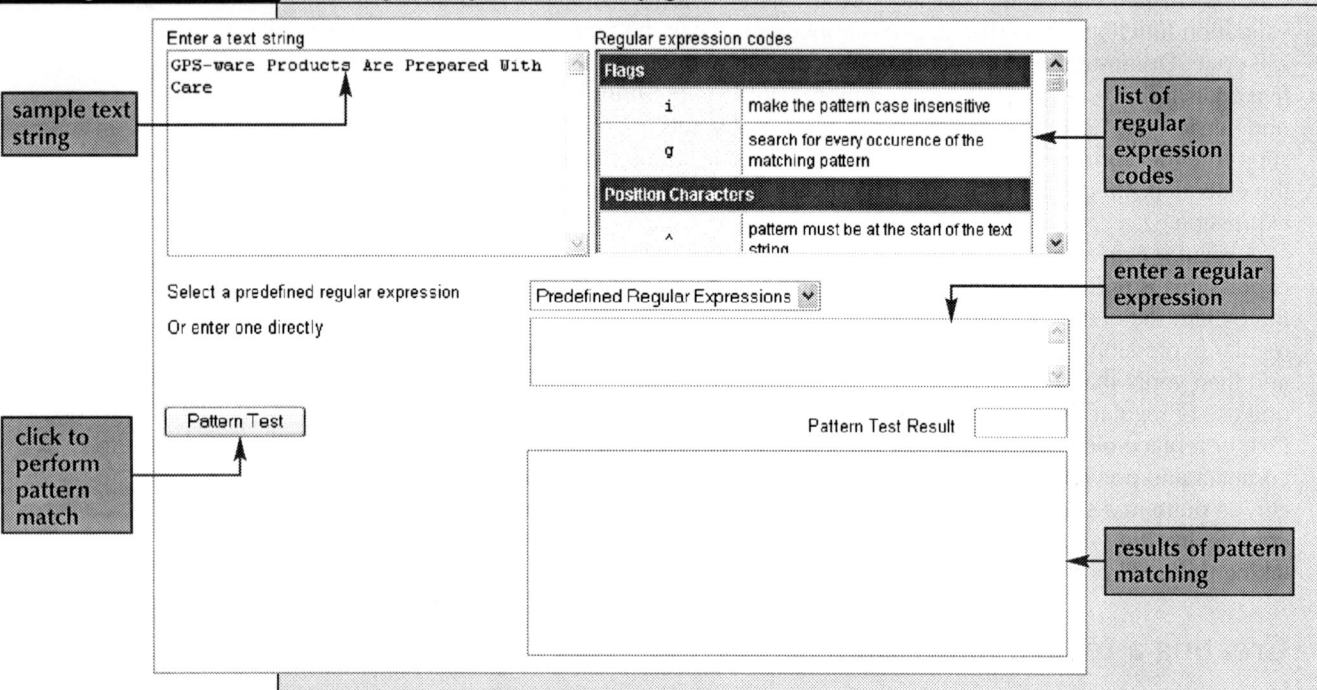

Matching a substring

The most basic regular expression consists of a substring that you want to locate in the text string. The regular expression to match the first occurrence of a substring is

/chars/

where *chars* is the text of the substring. Regular expressions are case sensitive, so *chars* must match the uppercase and lowercase letters of the substring you're searching for. To see how this applies to the text string you've already entered in the demo page, create regular expressions to locate the occurrences of the substrings "are" and "Are".

To match a simple substring:

▶ **1.** Click the text area box for the regular expression (located directly below the drop-down list box) and type **/are/**.

▶ **2.** Click the **Pattern Test** button.

As shown in Figure 7-33, the first occurrence of the "are" substring is highlighted and the Pattern Test Result field displays the word "match", indicating that a matching pattern has been found in the test string.

Matching a substring ◀ **Figure 7-33**

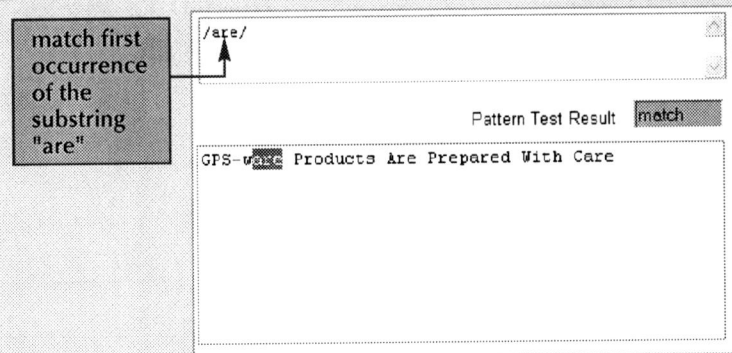

match first
occurrence
of the
substring
"are"

/are/

Pattern Test Result match

GPS-ware Products Are Prepared With Care

▶ **3.** Change the regular expression to **/Are/** and click the **Pattern Test** button.

The pattern now matches the word "Are" occurring later in the test string.

Before continuing, it's important to note that spaces are considered characters in a regular expression pattern. While JavaScript allows some flexibility in the use of white space, regular expressions do not. The patterns / GPS / and /GPS/ are considered two totally different regular expressions: in one, the substring "GPS" is surrounded by blank spaces; in the other, it is not. While you might be tempted to insert spaces to make a regular expression more readable, adding spaces changes the regular expression.

Setting regular expression flags

By default, pattern matching stops after the first match is discovered, and the match is case sensitive. You can override both of these behaviors by adding flags to a regular expression. To make a regular expression not sensitive to case, use the regular expression literal

```
/pattern/i
```

To allow a global search for all matches in a test string, use the regular expression literal

```
/pattern/g
```

To apply both at the same time, simply apply both flags to the regular expression:

```
/pattern/ig
```

Try this now on the demo page.

To set the global and case-insensitive flags:

▶ **1.** Change the regular expression to **/are/ig**.

▶ **2.** Click the **Pattern Test** button. As shown in Figure 7-34, all examples of the "are" substring are highlighted, regardless of case.

Figure 7-34	Matching a substring using the g and i flags

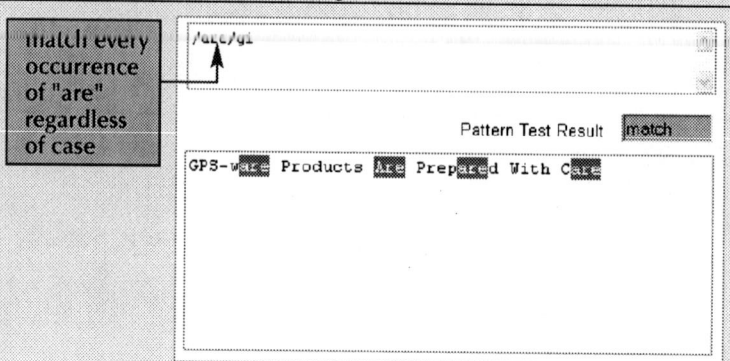

Defining character positions

So far you've only used regular expressions to match simple text strings, which is not much more than you could have accomplished using the string object methods from the last session. The true power (and complexity!) of regular expressions comes with the introduction of special characters that allow you to match text based on the type, content, and placement of the characters in the text string. The first such characters you'll consider are positioning characters. The four positioning characters are described in Figure 7-35.

Figure 7-35	Positioning characters

Character	Description	Example
^	Indicates the beginning of the text string	/^GPS/ matches "GPS-ware" but not "Products from GPS-ware"
$	Indicates the end of the text string	/ware$/ matches "GPS-ware" but not "GPS-ware Products"
\b	Indicates the presence of a word boundary	/\bart/ matches "art" and "artists" but not "dart"
\B	Indicates the absence of a word boundary	/art\B/ matches "dart" but not "artist"

Regular expressions recognize the beginning and end of a text string, indicated by the ^ and $ character respectively. The following pattern uses the ^ character to mark the start of the text string:

```
/^GPS/
```

In this pattern, any text string starting with the substring "GPS" would be matched; however, the expression would not match the GPS substring occurring elsewhere in the text string. In the same way, the end of the text string is indicated with the $ character. Thus, the following expression matches any text string that ends with the characters "-ware":

```
/-ware$/
```

The ^ and $ characters are often used together to define a pattern for the complete text string. For example, the pattern

```
/^GPS-ware$/
```

would match only a string containing the text "GPS-ware" and nothing else.

The other positioning characters are used to locate words within a text string. The term "word" has a special meaning in regular expressions. Words are composed of word characters, where a **word character** is any letter, numeral, or underscore. Symbols like *, &, and - are not considered word characters, nor are spaces, periods, or tabs. Thus, the string "R2D2" is considered a single word, but "R2D2&C3PO" is considered two words, with the & symbol acting as a boundary between the words. In a regular expression, the presence of a word boundary is indicated with the \b symbol. Thus, the pattern

```
/\bart/
```

matches any word that starts with the characters "art", but does not match "art" found in other locations. For example, this pattern would match the word "artist", but not the word "dart". The \b symbol can also indicate a word boundary at the end of a word. For example, the pattern

```
/art\b/
```

matches any word that ends in "art"—such as "dart" or "heart"—but not "artist". By using the \b symbol at both the beginning and the end of a pattern, you can define a complete word. The pattern

```
/\bart\b/
```

would match only the word "art" and nothing else. In some cases, you want to match substrings only within words. In these situations you use the \B symbol, which indicates the absence of a word boundary. For example, the pattern

```
/\Bart\B/
```

matches the substring "art" only when it occurs within a word like "hearts" or "darts".

The \b and \B symbols illustrate a common element of syntax in regular expression symbols: many regular expression symbols have opposite meanings in uppercase letters. Thus, \B means the opposite of \b. You'll see this pattern in some of the other regular expression characters that you'll be examining shortly.

To view the effect of word boundaries on regular expressions:

1. Return to the demo page and change the regular expression to **/\bare\b/gi**.

2. Click the **Pattern Test** button. As shown in Figure 7-36, only the word "Are" is highlighted, since it is the only occurrence of the substring "are" as a complete word.

Figure 7-36 ▶ Matching a whole word

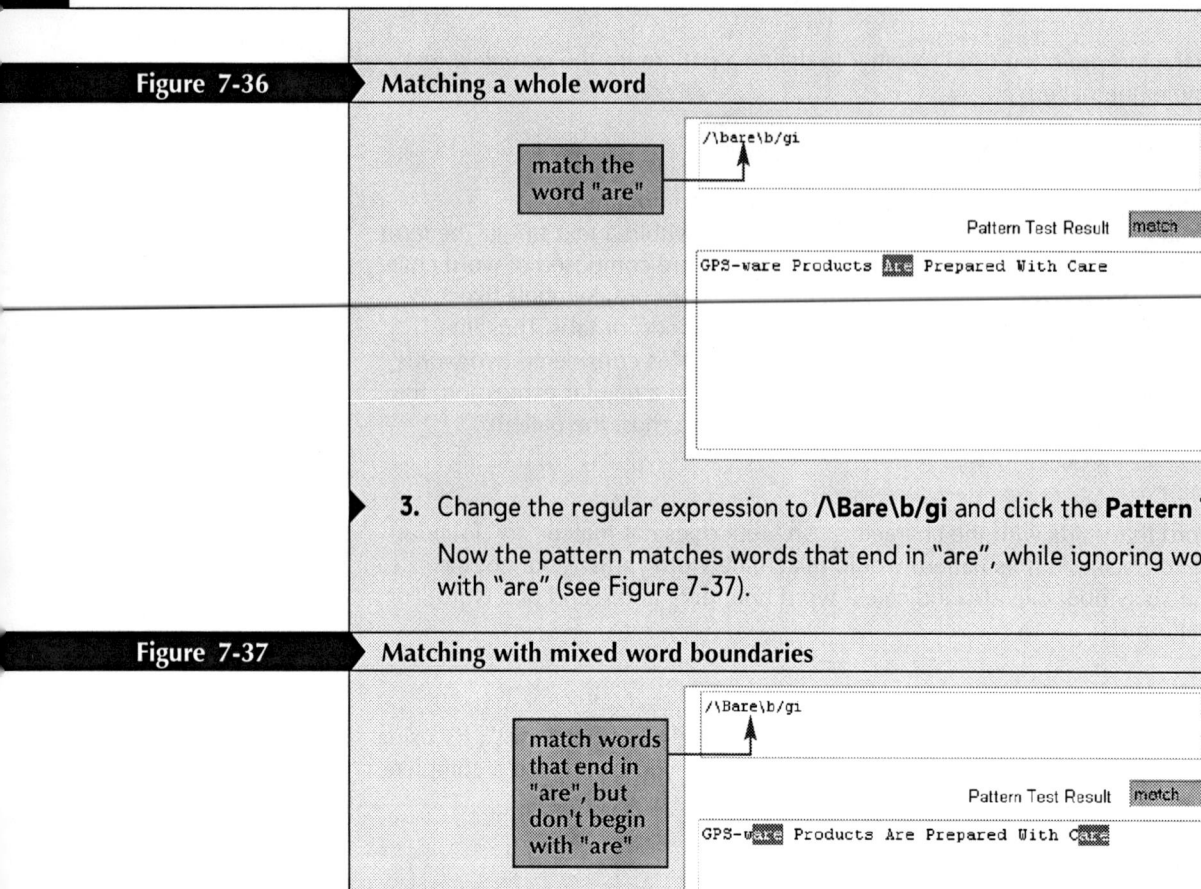

3. Change the regular expression to **/\Bare\b/gi** and click the **Pattern Test** button.

   Now the pattern matches words that end in "are", while ignoring words that start with "are" (see Figure 7-37).

Figure 7-37 ▶ Matching with mixed word boundaries

4. Change the regular expression to **/\Bare\B/gi** and click the **Pattern Test** button to locate all instances of the substring "are" that occur within a word.

   The pattern now matches only the substring "are" found within the word "Prepared".

Defining character types and character classes

Another class of regular expression characters indicates character type. There are three general types of characters: word characters, digits (numeric characters from 0 to 9), and white space characters (blank spaces, tabs, and new lines). Figure 7-38 describes the regular expression symbols for these character types.

Character classes ◀ Figure 7-38

Character	Description	Example
\d	A digit (from 0 to 9)	/\dth/ matches "5th" but not "ath"
\D	A non-digit	/\Ds/ matches "as" but not "5s"
\w	A word character (an upper- or lower-case letter, a digit, or an underscore)	/\w\w/ matches "to" or "A1" but not "$x" or " *"
\W	A non-word character	/\W/ matches "$" or "&" but not "a", "B", or "3"
\s	A white space character (a blank space, tab, new line, carriage return, or form feed)	/\s\d\s/ matches " 5 " but not "5"
\S	A non-white space character	/\S\d\S/ matches "345" or "a5b" but not "5"
.	Any character	/./ matches anything

For example, digits are represented by the \d character. To match any occurrence of a single digit, you would use the regular expression

/\d/

This would find matches in such text strings as "105", "6", or "U2", since all of these contain an instance of a single digit. If you want to match several consecutive digits, you can simply repeat the \d symbol. The regular expression

/\d\d\d/

matches the occurrence of any three consecutive digits. It would find matches in strings like "105", "1250", or "EX500". If you want to limit yourself only to words consisting of three digit numbers, you can use the \b character to mark the boundaries around the digits; thus, the pattern

/\b\d\d\d\b/

would match strings like "105" or "229", but not "1250" or "EX500".

At this point you've barely scratched the surface of regular expressions, but you already have enough information to create a regular expression for a five-digit ZIP code. The pattern is

/^\d\d\d\d\d$/

This regular expression matches only a text string that contains five digits and no other characters (recall that the ^ and $ symbols mark the beginning and end of the entire text string). Test this pattern now in the demo page.

To test the ZIP code pattern:

▶ 1. Change the text in the sample text string box to **12345**.

▶ 2. Change the regular expression in the Pattern input box to **/^\d\d\d\d\d$/** and click the **Pattern Test** button.

The Pattern Test Result box displays the result "match".

3. Continue experimenting with the pattern, trying sample text strings of **1**, **123**, and **1234a**. Verify that you receive a valid match only if you enter a five-digit value and no other characters or numbers.

You have now achieved with a single regular expression what took several lines of code to do in the previous session. This should give you some idea of the power of regular expressions in detecting character patterns.

For more general character matching you can use the \w symbol, which matches any word character, or the \s symbol, which matches any white space character. For example, the pattern

```
/\s\w\w\w\s/
```

matches any three-letter word surrounded by white space. Remember, however, that a word character can be a letter, digit, or the underscore character. Thus, this pattern would match a text string like " car " as well as " 123 ". There is no character type that matches only letters. However, you can specify a collection of characters known as a **character class** to limit the regular expression to only a select group of characters. The syntax to define a character class is

```
[chars]
```

where `chars` are characters in the class. To create a negative character class that matches any character not in the class, you use the syntax

```
[^chars]
```

Note that the negative character set uses the same ∧ symbol that you used to mark the beginning of a text string. While the symbol is the same, however, the meaning is very different in this context. To explore working with a character class, you'll create character classes for vowels and consonants.

To create a character class:

1. Change the sample text to **GPS Products For Sale**.

2. Change the regular expression in the Pattern input box to **/[aeiou]/gi** and click the **Pattern Test** button.

As shown in Figure 7-39, every vowel in the sample text string is highlighted.

Figure 7-39	Matching a character set

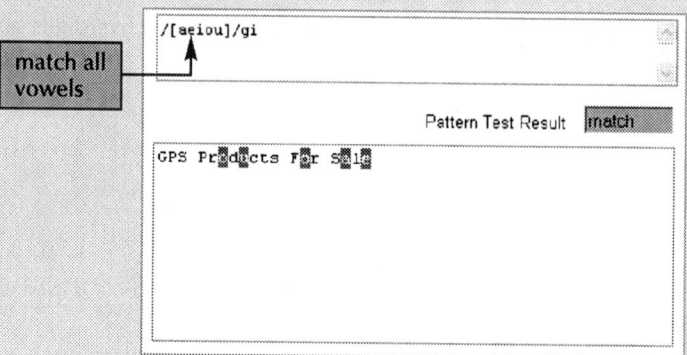

Next, create a character class for all of the consonants.

3. Change the regular expression in the Pattern input box to **/[^aeiou\s]/gi** and click the **Pattern Test** button again.

By including the \s symbol in your negative character class, you prevent the pattern from matching white space characters like blank spaces. Figure 7-40 shows the revised pattern match as it applies to the text string.

Matching a negative character set | Figure 7-40

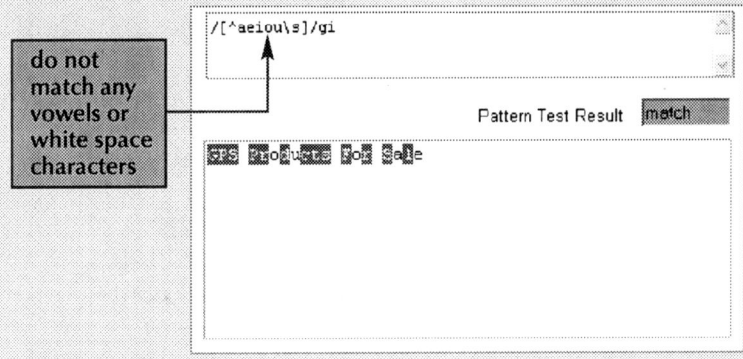

For a larger character class, you can define a range of characters by separating the starting and ending characters in the range with a dash. Since characters are arranged in sequential and alphabetical order, to create a character class for all lowercase letters you would use

`[a-z]`

For uppercase letters, you would use

`[A-Z]`

For both uppercase and lowercase letters, you would use

`[a-zA-Z]`

You can continue to add ranges of characters to a character class. The following character class matches only uppercase and lowercase letters and digits:

`[0-9a-zA-Z]`

Figure 7-41 summarizes the syntax for creating regular expression character classes.

Figure 7-41 | **Character classes**

Character	Description	Example
[chars]	Match any character in the list of characters, chars	/[dog]/ matches "god" and "dog"
[^chars]	Do not match any character in chars	/[^dog]/ matches neither "god" nor "dog"
[char1-charN]	Match characters in the range char1 through charN	/[a-c]/ matches the lowercase letters a through c
[^char1-charN]	Do not match characters in the range char1 through charN	/[^a-c]/ does not match the lowercase letters a through c
[a-z]	Match lowercase letters	/[a-z][a-z]/ matches any two consecutive lowercase letters
[A-Z]	Match uppercase letters	/[A-Z][A-Z]/ matches any two consecutive uppercase letters
[a-zA-Z]	Match letters	/[a-zA-Z][a-zA-Z]/ matches any two consecutive letters
[0-9]	Match digits	/[1][0-9]/ matches the numbers "10" through "19"
[0-9a-zA-Z]	Match digits and letters	/[0-9a-zA-Z][0-9a-zA-Z]/ matches any two consecutive letters or numbers

Repeating characters

So far our regular expression symbols have applied to single characters. Regular expressions also include symbols that indicate the number of times a particular character should be repeated. To exactly specify the number of times to repeat a character, you append the character with the symbols

$\{n\}$

where n is the number of times to repeat the character. For example, to specify that a text string contain only five digits, like a ZIP code, you could use either

```
/^\d\d\d\d\d$/
```

or the more compact form

```
/^\d{5}$/
```

If you don't know exactly how many times to repeat a character you can use the symbol * (for 0 or more repetitions), + (for 1 or more repetitions), or ? (for 0 or 1 repetition). Figure 7-42 describes these and other repetition characters supported by regular expressions.

Repetition characters | Figure 7-42

Repetition Character(s)	Description	Example
*	Repeat 0 or more times	/\s*/ matches 0 or more consecutive white space characters
?	Repeat 0 or 1 time	/colou?r/ matches "color" or "colour"
+	Repeat 1 or more times	/\s+/ matches 1 or more consecutive white space characters
{n}	Repeat exactly n times	/\d{9}/ matches a nine digit number
{n, }	Repeat at least n times	/\d{9,}/ matches a number with at least nine digits
{n,m}	Repeat at least n times but no more than m times	/\d{5,9}/ matches a number with 5 to 9 digits

Now practice using some of the repetitive symbols to create a regular expression in the demo page.

To apply a repetition pattern:

▶ 1. Change the sample text to **To be or not to be. That is the question.**

Next you'll create a regular expression for all words that begin with the letter t followed by any number of uppercase or lowercase letters.

▶ 2. Change the regular expression in the Pattern input box to **/\bt[a-zA-Z]*\b/gi** and click the **Pattern Test** button. As shown in Figure 7-43, words of varying length beginning with the letter t are selected.

Using repetitive characters | Figure 7-43

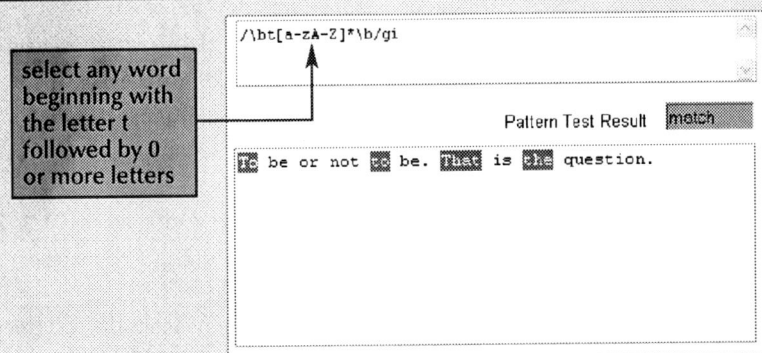

select any word beginning with the letter t followed by 0 or more letters

```
/\bt[a-zA-Z]*\b/gi
```

Pattern Test Result   match

To be or not to be. That is the question.

Next you'll revise the pattern so that it selects only three-letter words beginning with the letter t. You'll do this by limiting the number of letters after the t to two.

▶ 3. Change the regular expression to **/\bt[a-zA-Z]{2}\b/gi** and click the **Pattern Test** button. Now only the word "the" is highlighted.

Escape sequences

Many regular expression symbols are reserved. For example, the forward slash symbol / is reserved to mark the beginning and end of a regular expression literal. The ?, +, and * symbols are used in specifying the number of times a character may be repeated. What if you need to use one of these characters in your regular expression? For example, how would you create a regular expression matching the date pattern *mm/dd/yyyy* when the / symbol is already used to mark the boundaries of the regular expression?

In these cases, you use an escape sequence. An **escape sequence** is a special command inside a text string that tells the JavaScript interpreter not to interpret what follows as a character. The character that indicates an escape sequence in a regular expression is the backslash character \. You've actually been using escape sequences for several pages now—for example, you've used the characters "\d" to represent a numeric digit, while "d" simply represents the letter d. The \ character can also be applied to reserved characters to indicate their use in a regular expression. For example, the escape sequence \$ represents the $ character while the escape sequence \\ represents a single \ character. Figure 7-44 provides a list of escape sequences for other special characters.

| Figure 7-44 | Escape sequences |

Escape sequences

Escape Sequence	Represents	Example
\/	The / character	/\d\/\d/ matches "5/9" "3/1" but not "59" or "31"
\\	The \ character	/\d\\\d/ matches "5\9" or "3\1" but not "59" or "31"
\.	The . character	/\d\.\d\d/ matches "3.20" or "5.95" but not "320" or "595"
*	The * character	/[a-z]{4}*/ matches "help*" or "pass*"
\+	The + character	/\d\+\d/ matches "5+9" or "3+1" but not "59" or "39"
\?	The ? character	/[a-z]{4}\?/ matches "help?" or "info?"
|	The	character	/a|b/ matches "a|b"
\(\)	The (and) characters	/\(\d{3}\)/ matches "(800)" or "(555)"
\{ \}	The { and } characters	/\{[a-z]{4}\}/ matches "{pass}" or "{info}"
\^	The ^ character	/\d+\^\d/ matches "321^2" or "4^3"
\$	The $ character	/\$\d{2}\.\d{2}/ matches "$59.95" or "$19.50"
\n	A new line	/\n/ matches the occurrence of a new line in the text string
\r	A carriage return	/\r/ matches the occurrence of a carriage return in the text string
\t	A tab	/\t/ matches the occurrence of a tab in the text string

Enter an escape sequence in the demo page to create a regular expression for the date pattern.

To use an escape sequence:

1. Change the sample text to the date **5/21/2007**

   You'll create a regular expression for a text string that starts with one or two digits followed by a forward slash, then another one or two digits followed by a forward slash, followed by four digits.

2. Change the regular expression in the Pattern input box to **/^\d{1,2}\/\d{1,2}\/\d{4}$/** and click the **Pattern Test** button. As shown in Figure 7-45 the test date you entered matches the regular expression pattern.

Using an escape sequence

Figure 7-45

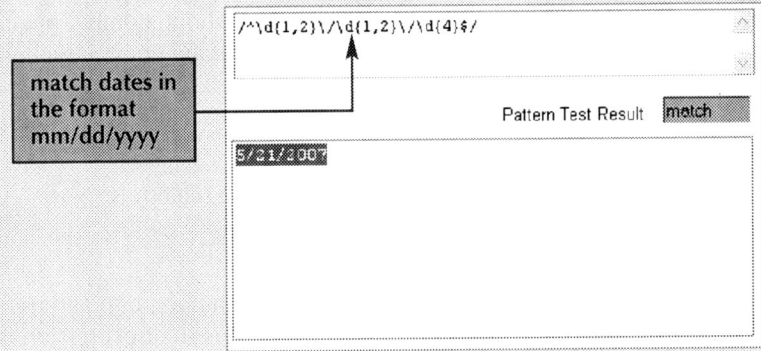

match dates in the format mm/dd/yyyy

`/^\d{1,2}\/\d{1,2}\/\d{4}$/`

Pattern Test Result | match

5/21/2007

3. Test the regular expression pattern against other possible dates and verify that it matches any date in the format mm/dd/yyyy.

Note that the regular expression you used for the date format also matches some invalid date patterns such as 23/99/0007 or 0/0/0000. It does not check that the month values go from 1 to 12 or that the day values always range from 1 to 31. You can explore the date expressions available from the selection list on the demo page to learn more about writing expressions that control for these factors.

Alternate Patterns and Grouping

The final aspects of regular expression patterns that you'll examine are alternate patterns and grouping. In some regular expressions you may want to define two possible patterns for the same text string. The syntax for creating alternate patterns is to use the alternation character | with the syntax

`pattern1|pattern2`

where `pattern1` and `pattern2` are two distinct patterns. For example, the expression

`/^\d{5}$|^$/`

matches a text string that either contains only five digits or is empty. Explore how to use the alternate character in the demo page by creating a regular expression that matches the honorifics Mr., Mrs., or Miss.

To choose between alternate patterns:

1. In the regular expression demo, change the sample text to **Mr.**

2. Change the regular expression pattern to **/Mr\.|Mrs\.|Miss/** and click the **Pattern Test** button. The pattern test result shows a match.

3. Change the sample text to **Mrs.** and then to **Miss**, and verify that the text string matches the pattern in both cases.

Another useful technique in regular expressions is to group character symbols. Once you create a group, the symbols within that group can be treated as a single unit. The syntax to create a group is

```
(pattern)
```

where `pattern` is a regular expression pattern.

Groups are often used with the alternation character to create regular expressions that match different variations of the same text. For example, a phone number might be entered with an area code or without. The pattern for the phone number without an area code, matching such numbers as 555-1234, is

```
/^\d{3}-\d{4}$/
```

If an area code is included in the format 800-555-1234, the pattern is

```
/^\d{3}-\d{3}-\d{4}$/
```

To allow the area code to be added or not, you place it within a group and use the ? repetition character applied to the entire area code group. The regular expression is therefore:

```
/^(\d{3}-)?\d{3}-\d{4}$/
```

which matches either 555-1234 or 800-555-1234. Test this now in the demo page.

To create a pattern group:

1. Go back to the regular expression demo and change the text string to **555-1234**

2. Change the regular expression pattern to **/^(\d{3}-)?\d{3}-\d{4}$/** and click the **Pattern Test** button. The pattern test result shows a match (see Figure 7-46).

Figure 7-46 ▶ **Creating a group**

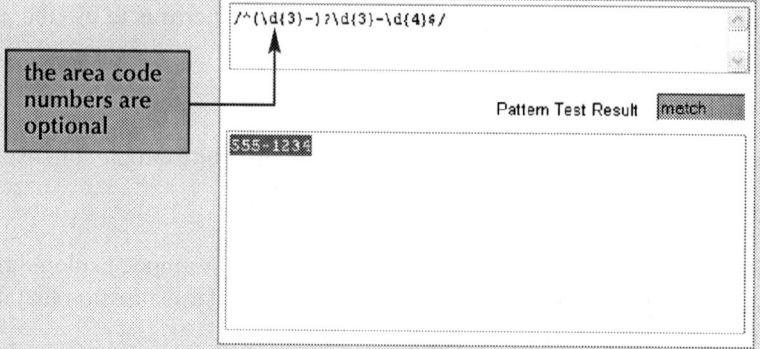

3. Change the phone number to **800-555-1234** and click the **Pattern Test** button again to verify that this form of the phone number also matches the regular expression.

Another benefit of grouping is that the captured groups can be referenced as distinct entities within the regular expression. This is known as creating a **back-reference**. Groups are referenced using the expression

`\group`

where *group* is the number of the group in the regular expression. The first group has a back-reference of \1, the second group has the back-reference \2, and so forth. For example, you could use back-referencing to create a regular expression that searches for consecutive occurrences of the same word (a common typing mistake). First you would create a regular expression to match a single word of one or more characters, placing that word within a group. The pattern would be

`/(\b\w+\b)/`

Next you would add a back-reference to match that group. Since you are looking for consecutive words separated by a space, you would add the space character to the pattern as well. The regular expression would be

`/(\b\w+\b)\s\1/`

Remember that the \1 symbol is the back-reference for the first group in the regular expression, indicating that you are looking for a repeat of the characters in the first group. Now enter this expression in the demo page to test it against consecutive occurrences of the same word.

To match multiple occurrences of the same word:

1. Go back to the regular expression demo and change the text string to **GPS-ware products for for sale**

2. Change the regular expression pattern to **/(\b\w+\b)\s\1/** and click the **Pattern Test** button. The pattern test result matches the two consecutive occurrences of the word "for" (see Figure 7-47).

Matching consecutive occurrences of the same word | Figure 7-47

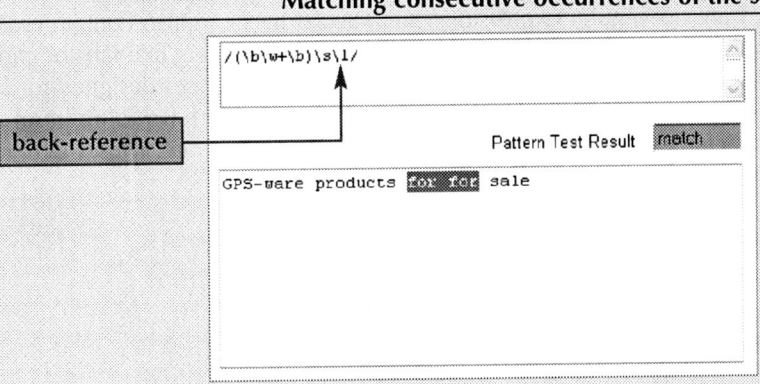

3. Close the demo page.

The ( ) group is only one type of group used in regular expressions. You can also create groups that do not allow for back-referencing (which reduces the process time required to run the regular expression). Figure 7-48 summarizes the character codes for grouping and performing alternate matching.

Figure 7-48   **Alternation and grouping characters**

Characters	Description	Example
pattern1|pattern2	Matches either pattern1 or pattern2	/color|colour/ matches either "color" or "colour"
(pattern)	Treats pattern as a single group and allows a back-reference to the captured group	/(Mr\.\s)?\w+/ matches either "Mr. Smith" or "Smith"
\n	Back-reference to group n in the regular expression	/(\s)\1/ matches consecutive occurrences of white space
(?pattern)	Treats pattern as a single group, but does not allow for back-referencing	

The regular expression object constructor

The regular expression literal that you've been using so far in this session is only one way of creating a regular expression in JavaScript. Another approach is to create a regular expression object using the following object constructor:

```
re = new RegExp(pattern, flags)
```

where `re` is the regular expression object, `pattern` is a text string of the regular expression pattern, and `flags` is a text string of the regular expression flags. The following two commands are equivalent as far as JavaScript is concerned:

```
var re = /GPS-ware/ig;
var re = new RegExp("GPS-ware","ig");
```

While JavaScript treats both commands the same, there are some important differences between them. For one, the regular expression literal is already compiled, which means that it is ready to perform pattern matching and other regular expression tasks. The new RegExp() object, on the other hand, must be compiled before it can be used. (You'll learn how to compile a regular expression in the next section.) The other important difference is that the new RegExp() constructor takes a text string for its parameter value. Even though they are not regular expressions, such text strings can also contain escape sequences, which may be used to insert non-textual characters like tabs or carriage returns. As a result, to avoid conflict between escape sequences designed for text strings and escape sequences designed for regular expressions, you have to insert an additional escape character \ for each regular expression escape sequence. Thus, the regular expression literal

```
/\b\w*\b\s\d{3}/
```

would appear in the new RegExp() operator as

```
new RegExp("\\b\\w*\\b\\s\\d{3}")
```

In most cases you'll use the regular expression literal form in your code. The new RegExp() operator is most often used when your script needs to retrieve the regular expression text string from another source, such as a data entry field.

Creating a Regular Expression

- The syntax to create a regular expression literal is
  ```
  re = /pattern/flags
  ```
  where `re` is the regular expression object, `pattern` is the regular expression pattern and `flags` are the flags assigned to the regular expression.
- The syntax to create a regular expression with the object constructor is
  ```
  re = new RegExp(pattern, flags)
  ```
  where `pattern` is the text string of the regular expression and `flags` is the text string of the regular expression flags.

Working with the Regular Expression Object

Now that you've looked at the syntax involved in writing a regular expression, you can use regular expressions in your JavaScript programs. As noted earlier, a regular expression is treated as an object with its own collection of properties and methods. Before implementing regular expressions for Carol's Web forms, familiarize yourself with some of the methods associated with regular expressions.

Regular Expression methods

One method associated with regular expressions is the test() method, which is used to determine whether a text string contains a substring that matches the pattern defined by a regular expression. The syntax of the test() method is

```
re.test(text)
```

where `re` is a regular expression object and `text` is the text string you want to test. The test() method returns the Boolean value true if a match is located and false otherwise. For example, the following code tests whether a given text string matches a five-digit ZIP code:

```
zipstring = "12345";
reg = /^\d{5}$/;
testvalue = reg.test(zipstring);
```

If zipstring matches the pattern of the reg regular expression, then the testvalue variable will have the Boolean value true; otherwise, it will have the value false.

Sometimes you need to know where in a text string a pattern match has been found. In such a case, you can apply the search() method, which has the syntax

```
re.search(text)
```

The search() method returns the index of the first matching substring from `text`. If no match is found, it returns the value –1, just like the indexOf() method discussed in the last session. The search() method starts with the first character in `text` and locates the first match. Unlike the indexOf() method, there is no way to start the search() method at a location other than the start of the text string.

You can also use regular expression methods that extract substrings from a text string. The match() method creates an array of substrings from a text string that match the pattern defined in a regular expression. The syntax of the match() method is

```
results = re.match(text)
```

where *results* is an array containing each matched substring. For example, the following set of commands extracts the individual words from the text string, placing each word in the words array:

```
re = /\b\w+\b/g;
words = "GPS-ware Products For Sale".split(re);
```

Note that the global flag has to be set to locate all matches in the text string. If you neglect to include the g flag, only the first match is returned. Similar to the match() method is the split() method, which splits the text string at each location where a pattern match is found. You saw how to use the split() method in the last session when it was applied to string objects. It can likewise be used with regular expressions. The following code shows how to split a text string at each word boundary followed by a white space character:

```
re = /\b\s*/g;
words = "GPS-ware Products For Sale".split(re);
```

In this example each element in the words array contains a word from the larger text string.

Besides pattern matching and extracting substrings, regular expressions can also be used to replace text. The syntax of the replace method is

```
text.replace(re,newsubstr)
```

where *text* is a text string containing text to be replaced, *re* is a regular expression defining the substring to be replaced, and *newsubstr* is the replacement substring. The following code shows how to apply the replace() method to change a text string:

```
oldtext = "<h1>GPS-ware Products</h1>";
reg = /h1/g;
newtext = oldtext.replace(reg,"h2");
```

The *newtext* variable now contains the text string "<h2>GPS-ware Products</h2>". Thus, this code replaces every occurrence of the substring "h1" with the substring "h2". A program that utilizes regular expressions can be very useful in revising HTML code. Note that if you neglect to include the "g" flag, only the first occurrence of the substring is replaced.

Working with Regular Expressions

- To test whether a text string matches a regular expression, use the method
    ```
    re.test(text)
    ```
    where `re` is the regular expression object and `text` is the text string to be tested. The test() method returns a Boolean value.
- To search a text string, use
    ```
    re.search(text)
    ```
    The search() method returns the index of the first matching substring from the text string.
- To create an array of the matching substrings from a text string, use
    ```
    results = re.match(text)
    ```
    where `results` is an array containing each matched substring.
- To split a string into substrings, use
    ```
    results = text.split(re)
    ```
    where `results` is an array containing the substrings, `text` is the original text string, and `re` is a regular expression that indicates the splitting points in the text string.
- To replace a substring with a new substring, use
    ```
    text.replace(re, newsubstr)
    ```
    where `text` is the text string containing the text to be replaced, `re` is a regular expression defining the substring to be replaced, and `newsubstr` is the replacement substring.

Figure 7-49 summarizes the methods associated with the regular expression object.

Methods of the regular expression object

Figure 7-49

Method	Description
re.compile(*pattern,flags*)	Compiles or recompiles a regular expression *re*, where *pattern* is the text string of the new regular expression pattern and *flags* are flags applied to the *pattern*
re.exec(*text*)	Executes a search on *text* using the regular expression *re*; pattern results are returned in an array and reflected in the properties of the global RegExp object
re.match(*text*)	Performs a pattern match in *text* using the *re* regular expression; matched substrings are stored in an array
text.replace(*re, newsubstr*)	Replaces the substring defined by the regular expression *re* in the text string *text* with *newsubstr*
text.search(*re*)	Searches *text* for a substring matching the regular expression *re*; returns the index of the match, or -1 if no match is found
text.split(*re*)	Splits *text* at each point indicated by the regular expression *re*; the substrings are stored in an array
re.test(*text*)	Performs a pattern match on the text string *text* using the regular expression *re*, returning the Boolean value true if a match is found and false otherwise

Validating a ZIP code

You'll now use what you've learned of regular expressions to create a new function to validate customers' entries in the ZIP field. In the first line of the function, you'll create a regular expression that matches either a five-digit or a nine-digit ZIP code or an empty text string (since the ZIP code is not required for delivery). The regular expression is

```
/^\d{5}(-\d{4})?$|^$/
```

This regular expression matches ZIP codes in the form ddddd or ddddd-dddd, and also uses the alternation character | to allow for empty text strings. Take some time to study this regular expression so that you understand how it works. The second line of the function uses the test() method to determine whether a customer's ZIP code matches that pattern, returning the test result as a Boolean value. The complete code of the checkZip2() function is

```
function checkZip2(zip) {
    re = /^\d{5}(-\d{4})?$|^$/;
    return re.test(zip);
}
```

Compared to the checkZip() function you created in the last session, this is a more compact function that still manages to test for more variation in ZIP code patterns than the original function did. Add this function to the validation tests for Carol's delivery form now.

To create the checkZip2() function:

1. Reopen **form2.htm** in your text editor.

2. Add the following function to the embedded script in the head section of the file:

```
function checkZip2(zip) {
    re = /^\d{5}(-\d{4})?$|^$/;
    return re.test(zip);
}
```

3. Change the checkForm2() function so that it calls the **checkZip2()** function to validate the ZIP code field. Figure 7-50 shows the new and revised code in the file.

| Figure 7-50 | The checkZip2() function |

```
function checkForm2() {
    if (document.form2.fname.value.length == 0)
        {alert("You must enter a first name");
        return false;}
    else if (document.form2.lname.value.length == 0)
        {alert("You must enter a last name");
        return false;}
    else if (document.form2.street.value.length == 0)
        {alert("You must enter a street address");
        return false;}
    else if (document.form2.city.value.length == 0)
        {alert("You must enter a city name");
        return false;}
    else if (checkZip2(document.form2.zip.value) == false)
        {alert("You must enter a valid zip code");
        return false;}
    else return true;
}

function checkZip(zip) {
    if (zip.length != 0 && zip.length != 5) return false;
    else {
        validchars = "0123456789";
        for (i=0; i<5; i++) {
            zipchar=zip.charAt(i);
            if (validchars.indexOf(zipchar) == -1) return false;
        }
    }
    return true;
}

function checkZip2(zip) {
    re = /^\d{5}(-\d{4})?$|^$/;
    return re.test(zip);
}
</script>
```

4. Save your changes to **form2.htm** and close the file.

5. Reopen **form2.htm** in your Web browser. Enter some sample text in the first name, last name, street, and city fields.

6. Enter **12345-1234** in the ZIP field and click the **Next** button. Verify that your browser opens the third of Carol's Web forms, indicating that the delivery form passed the validation test.

7. Return to **form2.htm** in your Web browser and verify that the form validates only when a proper ZIP code (or no ZIP code at all) is entered in the ZIP field.

You've completed your validation checks for the delivery form. Now you'll look at the last of Carol's forms.

Validating Financial Information

The final of Carol's three forms is the payment form, in which customers enter the credit card information that indicates how they will pay for their order. Figure 7-51 shows the contents of the payment form.

The payment form ◄ **Figure 7-51**

Figure 7-52 lists the object reference for each element in the form.

Objects in the payment form ◄ **Figure 7-52**

Object	Reference
The American Express radio button	document.form3.ccard[0]
The Diners Club radio button	document.form3.ccard[1]
The Discover radio button	document.form3.ccard[2]
The MasterCard radio button	document.form3.ccard[3]
The Visa radio button	document.form3.ccard[4]
The credit card name field	document.form3.cname
The credit card number field	document.form3.cnumber
The credit card month selection list	document.form3.cmonth
The credit card year selection list	document.form3.cyear
The previous button	document.form3.prevb
The next button	document.form3.nextb

A user's credit card data will eventually be validated on the Web server against an online database containing valid credit card numbers and customer names; however, you can do some validation checks on the client side in order to weed out problems before they get to the server. One such validation check is to ensure that each customer selects a credit card type and enters the name and number appearing on the card. The following two functions have already been entered into the form3.htm file to perform these three validation checks:

```
function checkForm3() {
   if (selectedCard() == -1)
      {alert("You must select a credit card");
       return false;}
   else if (document.form3.cname.value.length == 0)
      {alert("You must enter the name on your credit card");
       return false;}
   else if (document.form3.cnumber.value.length == 0)
      {alert("You must enter the number on your credit card");
       return false;}
   else return true;
}
function selectedCard() {
   card=-1;
   for (i=0; i<5; i++) {
      if (document.form3.ccard[i].checked) card=i;
   }
   return card;
}
```

The first function, checkForm3(), verifies that: 1) the customer has selected a credit card, 2) the customer has entered the name on the card, and 3) the customer has entered the number on the card. While you have no way of knowing whether the name and number represent real credit card accounts, you're using the checkForm3() function to verify that each customer enters something in those fields. The checkForm3() function tests whether one of the five credit cards on the payment form has been selected by calling the selectedCard() function. The selectedCard() function goes through all of the option buttons from the ccard field and returns the index number (from 0 to 4) of the checked option button. If no option button is checked (meaning that the customer has not selected a credit card from the list), then it returns a value of −1 and the form is not validated. Verify that these functions are working correctly by attempting to submit the form without entering any of the required financial information.

To test the payment form:

1. Open **form3.htm** in your Web browser.

2. Click the **Next** button without filling in different parts of the Web form or without selecting option buttons from the form. Verify that the form is accepted by the browser only when you have entered all of the financial information.

Removing blank spaces from credit card numbers

Beyond verifying that a customer has entered something for each field, you can also check whether a user has entered a legitimate credit card number. Credit card numbers often appear on credit cards broken up by spaces in order to make it easier for cardholders to read off the card numbers. Therefore, before you examine the actual card numbers you have to remove any blank spaces that a customer may have entered into the credit card number field. You can do this by creating a regular expression that searches for any occurrence of white space in the credit card number field, and then applying the replace() method to replace each occurrence of white space with an empty text string. The regular expression to match all occurrences of white space in a text string is

```
wsre = /\s/g
```

Note that you add the "g" flag so that the regular expression searches the entire text string, instead of stopping at the first occurrence of white space. The command to remove the white space from the credit card number field is

```
cnum = document.form3.cnumber.value.replace(wsre,"");
```

Now add both of these commands to a function named checkNumber() that you'll build upon to validate your customers' credit card numbers.

To insert the checkNumber() function:

1. Open **form3.htm** in your text editor.

2. Within the embedded script element, insert the following function, as shown in Figure 7-53:

```
function checkNumber() {
    wsre = /\s/g
    cnum = document.form3.cnumber.value.replace(wsre,"");
}
```

Removing white space from the credit card numbers ◀ **Figure 7-53**

```
function selectedcard() {
    card=-1;
    for (i=0; i<5; i++) {
        if (document.form3.ccard[i].checked) card=i;
    }
    return card;
}

function checkNumber() {
    wsre = /\s/g
    cnum = document.form3.cnumber.value.replace(wsre,"");
}
</script>
```

match all white space in the text string

Validating credit card number patterns

Each credit card has a certain pattern to its numbers that uniquely identifies it. GPS-ware accepts five different credit cards: American Express, Diners Club, Discover, MasterCard, and Visa. Figure 7-54 lists the number pattern for each card, along with a regular expression that matches the described pattern.

Figure 7-54	Credit card number patterns

Credit Card	Number Pattern	Regular Expression
American Express	Starts with 34 or 37 followed by 13 other digits	`/^3[47]\d{13}$/`
Diners Club	Starts with 300-305 followed by 11 digits, or starts with 36 or 38 followed by 12 digits	`/^30[0-5]\d{11}$|^3[68]\d{12}$/`
Discover	Starts with 6011 followed by 12 other digits	`/^6011\d{12}$/`
MasterCard	Starts with 51, 52, 53, 54, or 55 followed by 14 other digits	`/^5[1-5]\d{14}$/`
Visa	Starts with a 4 followed by 12 or 15 other digits	`/^4(\d{12}|\d{15})$/`

To validate the credit card number entered by a customer, you can use the test() method with the regular expressions indicated in Figure 7-54. Recall from the earlier code that the selectedCard() function returns the index number of the selected option button, where 0=American Express, 1=Diners Club, 2=Discover, 3=MasterCard, and 4=Visa. The following code uses a switch statement to test each of the five card patterns based on the credit card type selected by a user in the Web form:

```
switch (selectedCard()) {
    case 0: re=/^3[47]\d{13}$/;break;
    case 1: re=/^30[0-5]\d{11}$|^3[68]\d{12}$/;break;
    case 2: re=/^6011\d{12}$/;break;
    case 3: re=/^5[1-5]\d{14}$/;break;
    case 4: re =/^4(\d{12}|\d{15})$/;break;
}
pattern = re.test(cnum);
return pattern;
```

Based on the value returned by the selectedCard() function, the switch statement applies the appropriate regular expression pattern to the card number. The results of the pattern match are placed in the pattern variable. A value of true indicates that a customer's credit card number matches the selected pattern, and a value of false means that the number does not match and is thus invalid. Add this switch statement to the checkNumber() function.

To add the credit card number patterns:

1. Add the following commands to the checkNumber() function (see Figure 7-55):

```
switch (selectedCard()) {
    case 0: re=/^3[47]\d{13}$/;break;
    case 1: re=/^30[0-5]\d{11}$|^3[68]\d{12}$/;break;
    case 2: re=/^6011\d{12}$/;break;
    case 3: re=/^5[1-5]\d{14}$/;break;
    case 4: re =/^4(\d{12}|\d{15})$/;break;
}
pattern = re.test(cnum);
return pattern;
```

Checking credit card number patterns ◀ **Figure 7-55**

```
function checkNumber() {
    wsre = /\s/g
    cnum = document.form3.cnumber.value.replace(wsre,"");

    switch (selectedCard()) {
        case 0: re=/^3[47]\d{13}$/;break;
        case 1: re=/^30[0-5]\d{11}$|^3[68]\d{12}$/;break;
        case 2: re=/^6011\d{12}$/;break;
        case 3: re=/^5[1-5]\d{14}$/;break;
        case 4: re =/^4(\d{12}|\d{15})$/;break;
    }
    pattern = re.test(cnum);
    return pattern;
}
```

▶ **2.** Save your changes to the file.

Next, call this function from the checkForm3() function to add it to the list of validation checks already present in the payment form.

To check for valid credit card number patterns:

▶ **1.** Add the following command to the checkForm3() function, as shown in Figure 7-56:

```
else if (checkNumber() == false)
    {alert("Your card number is not valid");
    return false;}
```

The final checkForm3() function ◀ **Figure 7-56**

```
function checkForm3() {
    if (selectedCard() == -1)
        {alert("You must select a credit card");
        return false;}
    else if (document.form3.cname.value.length == 0)
        {alert("You must enter the name on your credit card");
        return false;}
    else if (document.form3.cnumber.value.length == 0)
        {alert("You must enter the number on your credit card");
        return false;}
    else if (checkNumber() == false)
        {alert("Your card number is not valid");
        return false;}
    else return true;
}
```

▶ **2.** Save your changes to the file.

▶ **3.** Reopen **form3.htm** in your Web browser.

Now test the form to confirm that the browser accepts the completed form only when a valid credit card number is entered.

▶ **4.** Enter sample text in the name field so that the form is not invalidated for lack of a credit card name.

▶ **5.** Click each of the credit card option buttons and enter the corresponding sample credit card numbers displayed in Figure 7-57. Verify that the form accepts the valid numbers and rejects the invalid ones.

Figure 7-57 | **Valid and invalid credit card number patterns**

Credit Card	Valid	Invalid
American Express	34 12345 67890 123	35 12345 67890 123
Diners Club	303 12345 67890 1	310 12345 67890 1
Discover	6011 12345 67890 12	6012 12345 67890 12
MasterCard	51 12345 67890 1234	59 12345 67890 1234
Visa	4 12345 67890 12345	8 12345 67890 12345

▶ **6.** Continue testing other combinations of credit card numbers to verify that only numbers that match the card patterns described in Figure 7-54 are accepted by the browser.

The Luhn Formula

There is one last test you can do on the client side to weed out mistakes that a customer might make in entering his or her credit card number. All credit card numbers must satisfy the **Luhn Formula**, or **Mod10 algorithm**, which is a formula developed by a group of mathematicians in the 1960s to provide a quick validation check on an account number by adding up the digits in the number. Almost all institutions that employ unique account or identification numbers, including credit card companies, use numbers that satisfy the Luhn Formula. The following steps are used to determine whether a particular number satisfies the Luhn Formula (see Figure 7-58):

1. Starting from the second to the last digit in the account number, separate every other digit into two groups, moving to the left.
2. Double the value of each digit in the first group (the group containing the first digit you selected).
3. Calculate the sum of the digits (not the numbers) in both groups.
4. Add the values of the two sums together.
5. If the total sum is evenly divisible by 10, then the number satisfies the Luhn Formula.

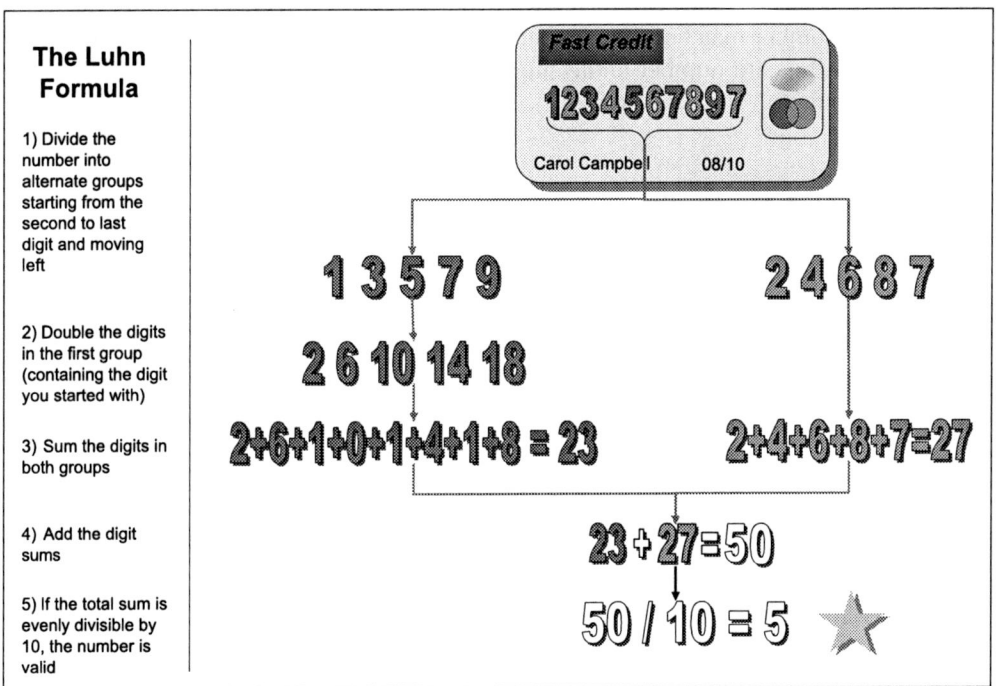

The Luhn Formula

1) Divide the number into alternate groups starting from the second to last digit and moving left

2) Double the digits in the first group (containing the digit you started with)

3) Sum the digits in both groups

4) Add the digit sums

5) If the total sum is evenly divisible by 10, the number is valid

A function to calculate the Luhn Formula has been created for you and is stored in the functions.js file. The code for the luhn() function is

```
function luhn(num) {
   var luhnTotal=0;
   for (i=num.length-1; i>=0; i--) {
      luhnTotal += parseInt(num.charAt(i));
      i--;
      num2 = new String(num.charAt(i)*2);
      for (j=0; j < num2.length; j++) {
         luhnTotal += parseInt(num2.charAt(j));
      }
   }
   return (luhnTotal % 10 == 0);
}
```

The luhn() function has a single parameter, num, which contains the text string of the account number to be validated. It assumes that all white space characters have already been removed from the text string. The function loops through each digit in the text string, adding up the digit sums. Each time it encounters a digit that should be doubled, it stores the doubled digit in a string object named num2, which is then summed before continuing through the larger number string. A running total of the digit sum is stored in the luhnTotal variable. After the last digit has been added, the function then uses the % operator to test whether dividing luhnTotal by 10 results in a remainder of 0. If it does, a Boolean value of true is returned by the function; otherwise, it returns a Boolean value of false. Take some time to study the code in this function. While this function may seem daunting at first, it is composed entirely of string object methods and properties you learned earlier in this tutorial.

You can call the luhn() function from the checkNumber() function you just created. The checkNumber() function will then have two tests: first it will check whether the selected card number matches the number pattern of the credit agency, and then it will check whether the card number fulfills the criterion of the Luhn Formula. Add the test for the Luhn Formula to your code now.

To add the test for the Luhn Formula:

1. Return to **form3.htm** in your text editor.

2. Go to the checkNumber() function and insert the following line before the "return pattern" statement:

```
luhnCheck = luhn(cnum);
```

3. Change the statement "return pattern;" to **return (pattern && luhnCheck);**. Figure 7-59 shows the revised code of the checkNumber() function.

Figure 7-59 The final checkNumber() function

```
function checkNumber() {
    wsre = /\s/g
    cnum = document.form3.cnumber.value.replace(wsre,"");

    switch (selectedCard()) {
        case 0: re=/^3[47]\d{13}$/;break;
        case 1: re=/^30[0-5]\d{11}$|^3[68]\d{12}$/;break;
        case 2: re=/^6011\d{12}$/;break;
        case 3: re=/^5[1-5]\d{14}$/;break;
        case 4: re =/^4(\d{12}|\d{15})$/;break;
    }
    pattern = re.test(cnum);
    luhnCheck = luhn(cnum);
    return (pattern && luhnCheck);
}
```

Note that the checkNumber() function returns a value of true only if both the pattern and the luhnCheck variables are true. In other words, the credit card number must both match the specified pattern and fulfill the Luhn Formula.

4. Close the file, saving your changes.

5. Reopen **form3.htm** in your Web browser.

6. Click **American Express** from the list of credit cards. Enter a sample name in the Name field.

7. Enter **34 12345 67890 123** in the Number field and click the **Next** button. Your browser should alert you that the number is not valid.

8. Change the credit card number to **34 12345 67890 127** and click the **Next** button. This number is accepted and a Web page opens indicating that the order has been submitted successfully.

At this point the customer's order could be sent to the Web server for further processing and validation checks. Obviously the server would have to consult secure databases to verify that the credit card information represented a real account. By adding these validation checks on the client side, however, your program can weed out some errors that the company's server would otherwise have to deal with.

Passing Data Between Forms

To simplify form validation for the GPS-ware Web site, Carol broke up the data that she wanted collected into three separate forms. When customer input is spread out over several forms, you usually need some way of passing collected data along as customers move from one form to another. One way of doing this in JavaScript is by appending a data string to a URL.

Appending data to a URL

Text strings can be appended to any URL by adding the ? character to the Web address followed by the text string. For example, the link

```
<a href="form2.htm?GPS-ware">Go to form2</a>
```

opens the form2.htm file, passing along the substring "GPS-ware" as part of the URL. When a user clicks the above linked text, form2.htm opens in the Web browser displaying the URL

```
http://server/path/form2.htm?GPS-ware
```

where `server` and `path` are the server and path names in the Web address. How do you access the data appended to the URL from within the form2.htm page? Recall that the URL of the current Web page is stored in the location object. One property of the location object is the location.search property, which contains the text of any data appended to the URL, including the ? character. Thus, running the following command from within the form2.htm file:

```
document.write("Products from " + location.search);
```

causes the following text to be written to the document window:

```
Products from ?GPS-ware
```

You can remove the ? character by running the slice() or substring() methods (see Figure 7-28), extracting all of the characters from the second character forward. The expression to display only the data part of the URL is therefore

```
document.write("Products from " + location.search.slice(1));
```

which writes the following text to the document window:

```
Products from GPS-ware
```

There are several limitations to the technique of appending data to a URL. For one, URLs are limited in their length. Internet Explorer, for example, limits the length of a URL text string to 2083 characters. Thus, you cannot append huge amounts of data to a URL. In addition, characters other than letters and numbers cannot be passed in the URL without modification. Because URLs cannot contain blank spaces, for example, a blank space is converted to the character code %20. Thus, the link

```
<a href="form2.htm?GPS-ware Products">Go to form2</a>
```

would result in the URL

```
http://server/path/form2.htm?GPS-ware%20Products
```

Character codes like %20 can be removed from a text string and replaced with the characters they represent (such as blank spaces) by running the unescape() function on the text string. The syntax of the unescape() function is

```
unescape(text)
```

where *text* is the text string containing the character codes. Thus, the command

```
unescape("GPS-ware%20Products")
```

returns the text string

```
GPS-ware Products
```

JavaScript also supports the escape() function, which inserts character codes into text strings. You use this function when you need to convert a text string into a format that can be easily passed as a single text string with no white space or other unprintable characters.

Appending and retrieving form data

You can use the technique of appending data to the URL with Web forms, too. You do this by setting a form's action attribute to the URL of the page to which you want to pass the data, and setting the method of the form to "get". For example, the form element

```
<form action="form2.htm" method="get">
```

causes the form2.htm file to be opened when the form is submitted. When the browser opens the form2.htm file, it will have the URL

```
http://server/path/form2.htm?field1=value1&field2=value2& ...
```

where *field1*, *field2*, etc. are the names of the fields in the Web form and *value1*, *value2*, etc. are the corresponding values in each of those fields. For example, if your Web form contains fields named "firstname" and "lastname" with values of "Carol" and "Campbell", then the following URL is applied to the form2.htm file when it appears in the browser:

```
http://server/path/form2.htm?firstname=Carol&lastname=Campbell
```

Because URLs cannot contain blank spaces, any blank space in a field value is converted to a + symbol. If your Web form contains a single field named "username" with a field value of "Carol Campbell", the URL for the submitted form is

```
http://server/path/form2.htm?username=Carol+Campbell
```

As before, you can use the location.search property with the slice() method to extract only the part of the URL containing the field names and field values. For example, the expression

```
location.search.slice(1)
```

returns the text string

```
field1=value1&field2=value2& ...
```

Once you have the field names and values in this format, you can extract the form information using what you've learned about string methods and regular expressions. The four steps to extracting form data from a URL are therefore:

1. Use the location.search property and the slice() method to extract only the text string of the field names and values.
2. Use the unescape() function to remove any escape sequence characters from the text string.
3. Convert each occurrence of the + symbol to a blank space.
4. Split the text string at every occurrence of a = or & character, storing the substrings into an array.

The following code shows how these steps would appear in a function:

```
function retrieveData() {
    searchString = location.search.slice(1);
    searchString = unescape(searchString);
    formString = searchString.replace(/\+/g, " ");
    data = formString.split(/[&=]/g);
}
```

Note that you use the regular expression /\+/g to match all occurrences of the + symbol in a text string, and the regular expression /[&=]/g to match all occurrences of the & or = characters. After running this function, the data array contains a separate item for each field name and field value. Thus, data[0] stores the name of the first field, data[1] stores the value of the first field, and so forth.

To see how transferring data from one form to another works in practice, a demo page has been created for you. Open this page now.

To view the demo form:

1. Open **demo_form1.htm** from the tutorial.07/tutorial folder in your Web browser.

2. Enter *your name*, *your age*, and *your city* in the appropriate fields in the form (see Figure 7-60).

Entering form data ◄ **Figure 7-60**

3. Click the **Submit** button.

As shown in Figure 7-61, the values you entered in the first form are retrieved from the URL and displayed in the second form.

Figure 7-61 ▶ **Retrieving form data**

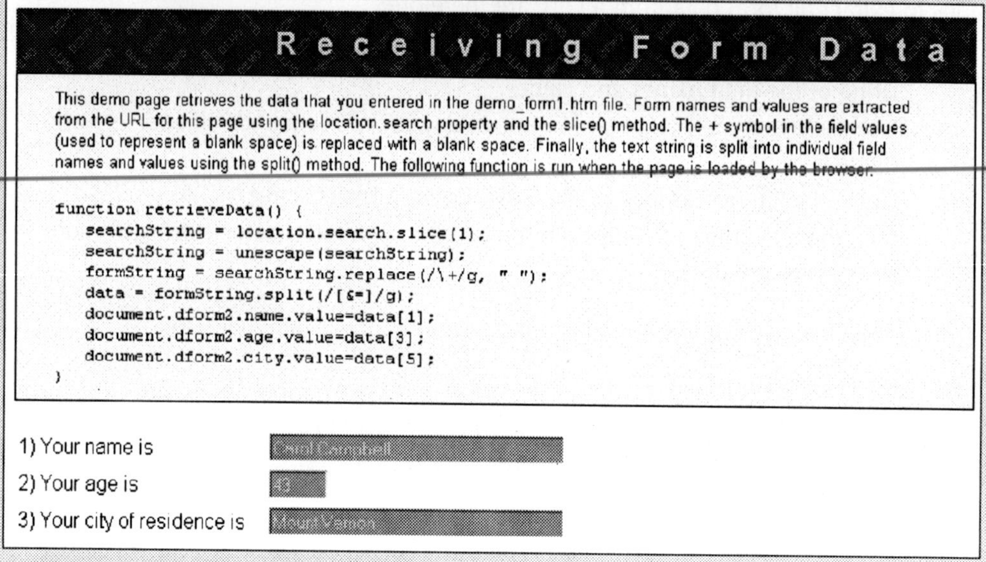

> ### R e c e i v i n g   F o r m   D a t a
>
> This demo page retrieves the data that you entered in the demo_form1.htm file. Form names and values are extracted from the URL for this page using the location.search property and the slice() method. The + symbol in the field values (used to represent a blank space) is replaced with a blank space. Finally, the text string is split into individual field names and values using the split() method. The following function is run when the page is loaded by the browser.
>
> ```
> function retrieveData() {
>     searchString = location.search.slice(1);
>     searchString = unescape(searchString);
>     formString = searchString.replace(/\+/g, " ");
>     data = formString.split(/[&=]/g);
>     document.dform2.name.value=data[1];
>     document.dform2.age.value=data[3];
>     document.dform2.city.value=data[5];
> }
> ```
>
> 1) Your name is   Carol Campbell
> 2) Your age is   43
> 3) Your city of residence is   Mount Vernon

▶ **4.** Close your Web browser.

Note that this script works only when all form fields are filled out. An empty field value causes the script to fail. At this point, you won't add the ability to pass form data to Carol's Web form. However, she will probably want you to add this in the future.

You've completed your work on Carol's order forms. She'll take some time to study your work and get back to you with future projects.

Tips for Validating Forms

- Use selection lists, option buttons, and check boxes to limit the ability of users to enter erroneous data.
- Indicate to users which fields are required, and if possible, indicate the format that each field value should be entered in.
- Use the maxlength attribute of the input element to limit the length of text entered into a form field.
- Format financial values using the toFixed() and toPrecision() methods. For older browsers use custom scripts to format financial data.
- Apply client-side validation checks to lessen the load of the server.
- Use regular expressions to verify that field values correspond to a required pattern.
- Use the length property of the string object to test whether the user has entered a value in a required field.
- Test credit card numbers to verify that they match the patterns specified by credit card companies.
- Test credit card numbers to verify that they fulfill the Luhn Formula.

Session 7.3 Quick Check

1. What is the regular expression to match every occurrence of the substring "GPS" in a text string, regardless of case?
2. What is the regular expression to match the first occurrence of the word "products"?
3. A social security number consists of nine digits. Write a regular expression to match this pattern.
4. Social security numbers can be entered either as dddddddd or ddd-dd-dddd. Write a regular expression to match either pattern.
5. Write a regular expression that matches any of the substrings "street", "avenue", or "lane". Make the match case insensitive and match every occurrence of the substring in the text string.
6. What JavaScript command would you enter to test whether the text string "username" matches the pattern specified in the regular expression object reuser?
7. What JavaScript command would you enter to split the text string "date" at every occurrence of the / character?
8. What is the Luhn Formula?
9. What object property would you use to extract any data appended to the URL of the current Web document?

Tutorial Summary

This tutorial explored how JavaScript can be used to validate Web forms. In the first session you learned how to reference different elements in a Web form, including input boxes, selection lists, and option button groups. You saw how to extract values from form fields and use them to create calculated fields. You also learned about some of the difficulties in displaying numeric values in a Web form and learned some of the techniques to create nicely formatted output. The second session introduced the concept of form validation: comparing the benefits and costs of client-side and server-side validation. You learned how to validate a form before allowing it to be processed, and you also learned about the properties and methods associated with string objects. The third session introduced the language of regular expressions. You learned how to create a regular expression to match a wide variety of patterns, and you learned about the properties and methods associated with regular expression objects. In the third session you employed regular expressions to validate both ZIP code and credit card data. You also learned about the Luhn Formula and saw how it could be used to validate credit card numbers before they're submitted to a Web server. The third session concluded with a discussion of passing data from one Web page to another, with a special emphasis on passing field names and values from one Web form to another.

Key Terms

back-reference
character class
client-side validation
delimiter
escape sequence

form validation
Luhn Formula
Mod10 algorithm
pattern matching
regular expression

regular expression literal
server-side validation
string object
substring
word character

Practice

Practice the skills you learned in the tutorial using the same case scenario.

Review Assignments

Data files needed for this Review Assignment: border.jpg, done.htm, functions.js, gps. css, gpsware.jpg, ordertxt.htm

After reviewing the first order form, Carol has a few changes she wants you to make. Rather than displaying the GPS-ware products in a selection list, Carol would like the product names to appear as separate fields. This allows customers to purchase more than one product without having to open a second form. Also, instead of displaying the quantity to order in a selection list, Carol wants the quantity value placed in an input field, so that customers can specify any quantity in their order. Figure 7-62 shows a preview of the new order form.

Figure 7-62

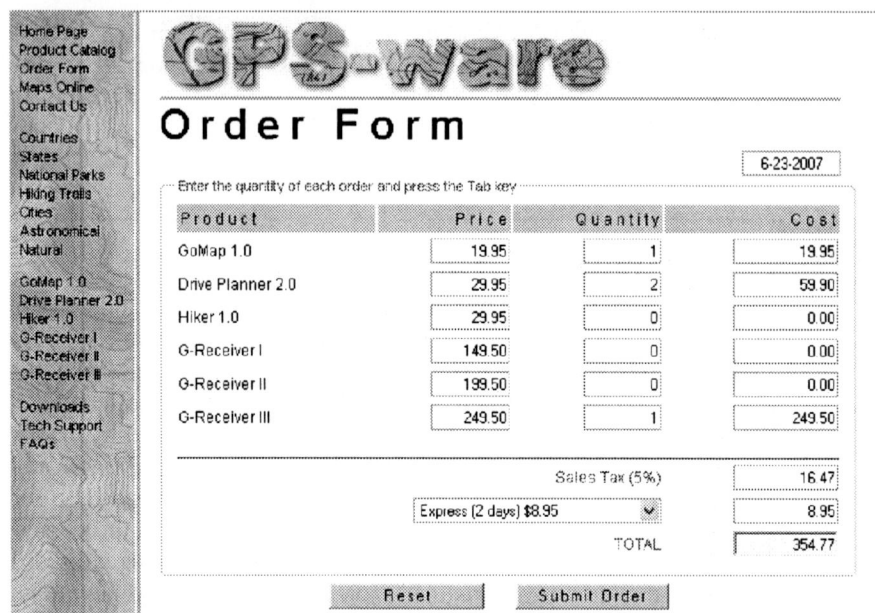

Carol wants the new form to include the following features:

- When a customer opens the form, the current date should appear in the date field.
- When a customer enters a new quantity in the Quantity column, the cost of the order should be automatically updated.
- Customers should be prevented from entering anything other than digits in the Quantity column. If a value other than a digit is entered, the customer should be notified of the error and the quantity value that was incorrectly entered should be reset to 0.
- When a customer selects a shipping option, the cost of the order should be automatically updated to reflect the price of shipping.
- The form should not be submitted unless a shipping option has been selected.

To complete this Web form:

1. Use your text editor to open the **ordertxt.htm** file from the tutorial.07/review folder. Enter *your name* and *the date* in the comment section and save the file as **order. htm**. Examine the contents of the file to become familiar with the order form and its elements.

2. The external script file functions.js contains a function named todayTxt() that returns the current date in the format *mm/dd/yyyy*. A link to the file has already been placed in the order.htm file. Below the script element for this external script, insert an embedded script element.

3. In the embedded script, add the function setDate(). The purpose of this function is to display the current date in the date field. There are no parameters to the function. Add the following commands to the function:

   a. Change the value of the date field to the value returned by the todayTxt() function.

   b. Move the focus to the qty1 field.

   c. Use the select() method to select the contents of the qty1 field.

4. Below the setDate() function, insert the productCosts() function. The purpose of the productCosts() function is to return the sum of the total costs of the six GPS-ware products in the order form. The costs of items are stored in input fields named cost1 through cost6. Have the function do the following:

   a. Create a variable named pc1 that is equal to the value of the cost1 field. Use the parseFloat() function to convert the field's value from a text string to a number.

   b. Use the same process to create variables pc2 through pc6, which are equal to the numeric values of the cost2 through cost6 fields.

   c. Return the sum of the pc1 through pc6 variables.

5. Create a function named shipExpense(). The purpose of the shipExpense() function is to return the cost of the selected shipping option. The shipping options are stored within a selection list named shipping. Have the function do the following:

   a. Create a variable named sindex equal to the selected index from the shipping selection list.

   b. Return the numeric value of the option from the shipping selection list whose index is equal to the sindex variable. Be sure to use the parseFloat() function to convert the option value from a text string to a number.

6. Create a function named calcTotal(). The purpose of the calcTotal() function is to display the cost of the sales tax and also the total cost of the order. Add the following commands to the function:

   a. Create a variable named ordercost equal to the value returned by the product-Costs() function. Create a variable named ordertax equal to 5% of the ordercost variable. Create a variable named ordership equal to the value returned by the shipExpense() function. Finally, create a variable named ordertotal equal to the sum of the ordercost, ordertax, and ordership variables.

   b. Store the value of the ordertax variable in the tax field. Display the value rounded to two decimal places. (*Hint*: Use the toFixed() method [or if you are using an older browser, the toFixed2() function] found in the function.js file.)

   c. Store the value of the ordertotal variable in the total field. Also display the value rounded to two decimal places.

7. Create a function named calcShipping(). The purpose of the function is to display the cost of the selected shipping option and to update the total order costs. Add the following commands to the function:

   a. Store the value returned by the shipExpense() function in the shipcost field.

   b. Run the calcTotal() function.

8. Create a function named calcCost(). The purpose of the calcCost() function is to display the cost of the quantity of items ordered by a customer and to update the total cost of the order. This function will also test whether a customer has correctly entered an integer in one of the quantity fields. The calcCost() function has a single parameter named item. The item parameter will store an integer from 1 to 6, representing one of the six items sold by GPS-ware. The purpose of the item parameter is to indicate which item the customer has ordered. Note that the price of each item is stored in the price*item* field where *item* is the item number. The cost of each item is stored in the cost*item* field. And the quantity ordered by each item is stored in the qty*item* field. To complete the calcCost() function, add the following commands:

   a. Create a variable named price which references the price*item* field where *item* is the value of the item parameter. (*Hint*: Use the document.orders.elements collection along with the field's name to reference the price*item* field.)

   b. Create a variable named qty which references the qty*item* field.

   c. Create a variable named cost which references the cost*item* field.

   d. Create a regular expression object named reqty for a text string containing 1 or more digits and no other characters.

   e. Still within the calcCost() function, test whether the value of the qty object matches the pattern defined by the reqty regular expression. If the pattern matches, then: 1) Set the value of the cost object equal to the value of the price object multiplied by the value of the qty object. Display the value of the cost object to two decimal places; 2) Run the calcTotal() function. If the pattern does not match (meaning that the customer has not entered a quantity value in integers), then: 1) Display the alert message "Please enter a digit greater than or equal to 0"; 2) Set the value of the qty object to 0; 3) Set the focus back to the qty object and use the select() method to select that object's value; 4) Rerun the calcCost() function using item as the parameter value.

9. Create a function named validateForm(). The purpose of this function is to ensure that the form has been filled out correctly before it is submitted. Add the following commands to the function:

   a. Test whether the selected index in the shipping field is equal to 0. If it is (meaning that no shipping method has been chosen by the customer), then: 1) Display the alert message "You must select a shipping option"; 2) Return the value false.

   b. Otherwise return the value true.

10. Add an event handler to the form element to run the validateForm() function whenever the form is submitted.

11. Add an event handler to the form element that reloads the Web page in response to the reset event.

12. Locate the input element for the qty1 field. Add an event handler to this element that runs the calcCost() function in response to the blur event. Use 1 as the value for the item parameter.

13. In the same fashion, run the calcCost() function in response to the blur event for the qty2 through qty6 input fields. Set the item parameter's value equal to the item number of each field.

14. Locate the shipping selection list. Add an event handler to the select element that runs the calcShipping() function whenever the value of the selected item in the list changes. (*Hint*: Use the onchange event handler.)

15. Close **order.htm**, saving your changes. Open the file in your Web browser and verify that it correctly updates the total cost of the order as you change the values in the quantity column. Also verify that the form will not accept any quantity values other than integers. Check that the cost of shipping changes to reflect the shipping method selected by the customer and that the form cannot be submitted unless a shipping method has been selected. Verify that clicking the Reset button reloads the Web page.

16. Submit the completed Web site to your instructor.

Case Problem 1

Data files needed for this Case Problem: mpl.jpg, mplstyles.css, mpltxt.htm

The Monroe Public Library   Denise Kruschev works at the Monroe Public Library on the library's Web site. One of her jobs is to add content to the site that will be of interest to the library's patrons. Denise's latest assignment is to create a Web page containing links to hundreds of government Web sites. She is aware that a long list of links will fill up the page, making the page difficult to use. Instead, Denise wants to use "select and go navigation," in which the links are placed within a selection list. When a user selects a link from the list, the linked page should open automatically. Denise has set up the selection lists, but she needs your help in writing the JavaScript program. Figure 7-63 shows a preview of the Web page.

Apply

Use the skills you learned to create a select and go navigation list

Figure 7-63

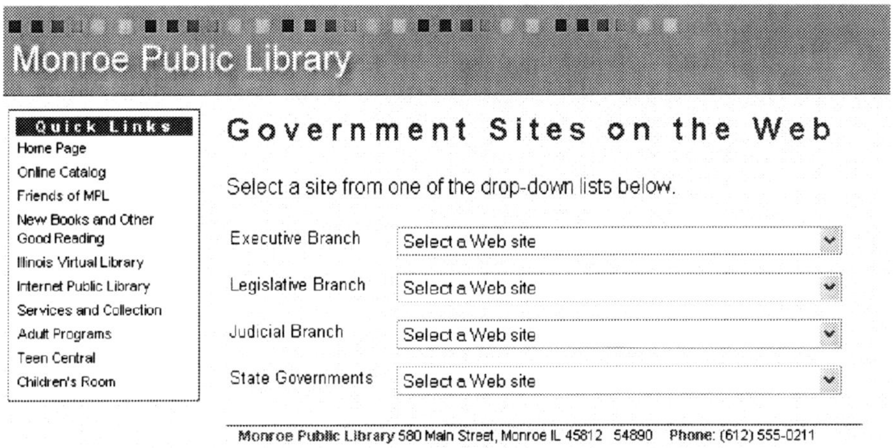

To create the select and go navigation list:

1. Open the **mpltxt.htm** file from the tutorial.07/case1 folder in your text editor. Enter *your name* and *the date* in the comment section and save the file as **mpl.htm**.

2. Insert an embedded script element in the head section of the document.

Explore

3. Each option in the selection matches the URL of a government Web site. Create a function named selectLink() whose purpose is to open the Web site specified by the option value. The selectLink() function has a single parameter named siteList, which references a selection list in the Web page. Add the following commands to the function:

   a. Create a variable named sindex equal to the index number of the selected option in siteList.

   b. Use the location.href property to open the Web site indicated in the value property of the selected option in siteList.

4. Locate the select element for the first selection list. Add an event handler to run the selectLink() function whenever the selected option in the list changes. Use the "this" keyword as the object specified in the siteList parameter.

5. Repeat step 4 for the three remaining selection lists.

6. Save your changes to the file and then open **mpl.htm** in your Web browser. Verify that each linked Web site that you select from the selection list opens in your Web browser.

7. Submit your completed Web site to your instructor.

Apply

Use the skills you learned to create an online travel expense report

Case Problem 2

Data files needed for this Case Problem: back.jpg, done.htm, exp.css, exptxt.htm, functions.js, links.jpg, logo.jpg

DeLong Enterprises Kay Ramirez is the payroll manager for DeLong Enterprises, a manufacturer of computer components. The company has been busy putting corporate information up on the company's intranet. Kay is heading a project to put all of the payroll-related forms and reports online. She has come to you for help in writing a program for the online travel expense form. The travel expense report form requires employees to itemize their various travel expenses for corporate trips. Kay would like scripts added to the form to ensure that all of the required data is entered in the correct format. If a required data field is left blank or if data is entered in an improper format, Kay would like the program to highlight the field in yellow and refuse submission of the form to the corporate Web server. Kay wants the form to support the following features:

- An employee must enter his or her last name, first name, social security number, an address for the reimbursement check, and a summary of the trip.

- The employee must enter the account ID number in the format ACTdddddd, the department ID number in the format DEPTdddddd, and the project ID number in the format PROJdddddd.

- For each day in which the employee has recorded an expense, the travel date must be entered.

- When the employee enters a travel, lodging, or meal expense, the subtotal of expenses for that day and the total cost of the trip should be automatically updated.

- Travel expenses must be entered as digits (either with or without the two-digit decimal place) and displayed to two digits.

A preview of the completed form (highlighting a few erroneous entries) is displayed in Figure 7-64.

Figure 7-64

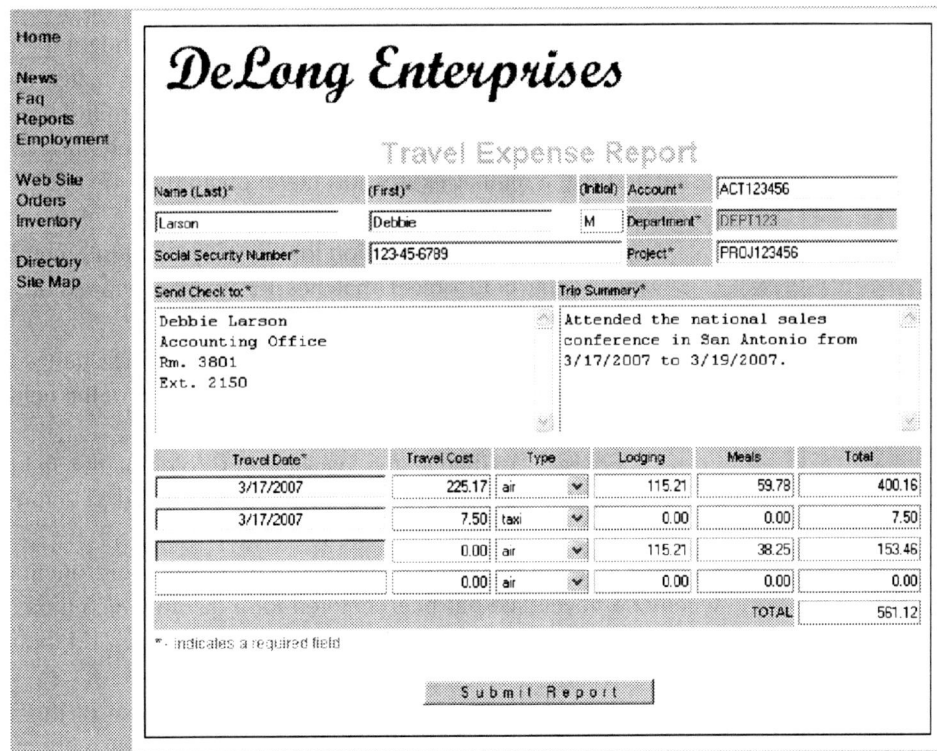

To complete this assignment:

1. Use your text editor to open the **exptxt.htm** file from the tutorial.07/case2 folder. Enter *your name* and *the date* in the comment section and save the file as **exp.htm**. Take some time to examine the contents of the file. Pay close attention to the field names and the organization of the form.

2. In the head section of the file, create an embedded script element and insert a function named testLength(). The purpose of the testLength() function is to test whether the user has entered any text in a required field. If no text has been entered, the function should highlight the field and return the value false. If any text has been entered, the function should remove any highlighting and return the value true. The function has a single parameter named "field" that represents the field object to be tested. To complete the function:

   a. Insert a conditional expression that tests whether the length of the field value is equal to 0.

   b. If the length is equal to 0, then: 1) Change the background color of the field object to yellow and 2) return the Boolean value false.

   c. Otherwise: 1) Change the background color of the field object to white and 2) return the Boolean value true.

3. Create a function named testPattern(). The purpose of this function is to compare the value of a field against a regular expression pattern. If the field's value does not match the regular expression, the function should highlight the field on the form and return the Boolean value false. If the field's value does match the regular expression, the function should remove any highlighting and return the Boolean value true. The function has two parameters: the field parameter representing the field object to be tested and reg, a regular expression literal containing the pattern used for the testing. To complete the testPattern() function:

   a. Insert a conditional expression that employs the test() method to test whether the value of the field object matches the regular expression contained in the reg parameter.

   b. If the test() method returns the value false, then: 1) Change the background color of the field object to yellow; 2) Change the color of the field object to red; and 3) Return the Boolean value false.

   c. Otherwise: 1) Change the background color of the field object to white; 2) Change the color of the field object to black; and 3) Return the Boolean value true.

4. Create a function named testDates(). The purpose of this function is to check whether a travel date has been entered for a day in which the employee has recorded an expense. The function has no parameters. Add the following commands to the function:

   a. Create a variable named dateExists. The purpose of this function is to record whether the employee recorded a traveling expense without entering the date. Set the initial value of this variable to true.

   b. Create a For loop that loops through integer values from 1 to 4. The purpose of this loop is to examine each of the four rows in the travel expense table. If the subtotal value in the row is greater than 0, there should be a date entered in the corresponding date field. The subtotal fields in the table are named sub1 through sub4. The date fields in the table are named date1 through date4.

   c. Within the For loop, insert a conditional statement that tests whether the value of sub*i* is not equal to "0.00", where *i* is the value of the counter in the For loop. (*Hint*: Use the object reference document.expform.elements["sub"+i].value where i is the counter in the For loop.)

   d. If sub*i* is not equal to "0.00" (indicating that an expense has been entered in that row of the travel expense table), do the following: 1) Call the testLength() function using the date*i* field as the parameter; 2) Store the value returned by the testLength() function in a variable named rowDateExists; and 3) If the value of the rowDateExists variable is false, set the value of the dateExists variable to false.

   e. After the For loop, return the value of the dateExists variable.

5. Create a function named validateForm(). The purpose of this function is to validate the form before it can be submitted to the server by calling the testPattern(), testLength(), and testDates() functions you just created. The function has no parameters. Add the following commands to the function:

   a. Create a variable named valid. The purpose of this variable is to record whether the form is valid or not. Set the initial value of the valid variable to true.

   b. Call the testLength() function with the lname field object as the parameter. (*Hint*: Use the object reference document.expform.lname.) If the value returned by the testLength() function is false, set the value of the valid variable to false. Repeat this step for the fname, address, and summary fields.

   c. Call the testPattern() function with the account field object for the field parameter. For the reg parameter insert a regular expression literal that matches a text string containing only the text "ACT" followed by 6 digits. If the value returned by the testPattern() function is false, set the value of the valid variable to false.

   d. Call the testPattern() function with the department field for the field parameter. The reg parameter should contain a regular expression literal for a text string containing only the characters "DEPT" followed by six digits. If the value of the testPattern() function is false, set the value of the valid variable to false.

   e. Repeat the previous step for the project field, using a regular expression that matches a text string containing only the characters "PROJ" followed by six digits.

   f. Call the testPattern() function for the ssn field (containing the social security number of the employee). The regular expression should match either a nine-digit number or a text string in the form ddd-dd-dddd. If the testPattern() function returns the value false, set the value of the valid variable to false.

   g. Call the testDates() function. If the function returns the value false, set the value of the valid variable to false.

   h. Insert a conditional statement that tests whether the value of the valid variable is false. If it is false then: 1) Display the following alert message: "Please fill out all required fields in the proper format."

   i. Return the value of the valid variable.

6. Locate the form element and add an event handler to run and return the value of the validateForm() function whenever the form is submitted.

7. Go back to the embedded script element and add a function named calcRow(). The purpose of this function is to return the subtotal of the expenses within a single row in the travel expense table. The function has a single parameter named row, which represents the number of the table row (from 1 to 4) to calculate from. Add the following commands to the function:

   a. Create a variable named travel equal to the numeric value of the travel*row* field, where *row* is the value of the row parameter. (*Hint*: Use the object reference document.expform.elements["travel"+row].value.) Be sure to use the parseFloat() function to convert the field value to a number. In the same fashion, create a variable named lodge equal to the numeric value of the lodge*row* field and a variable named meal equal to the numeric value of the meal*row* field.

   b. Return the sum of the travel, lodge, and row variables.

8. Create a function named calcTotal(). The purpose of this function is to return the total of all expenses in the travel expense table by calling the calcRow() function for each row in the table. The function has no parameters. Add the following commands to the function:

   a. Create a variable named totalexp and set its initial value to 0.

   b. Insert a For loop with a counter that runs from 1 to 4.

   c. Within the For loop, increase the value of the totalexp variable by the value returned by the calcRow() function using the value of the counter as the value of the row parameter.

   d. Return the value of the totalexp variable.

9. Create a function named update(). The purpose of this function is to update the expense values displayed in the table and to verify that the employee has entered a valid expense amount. The function will be called whenever the employee exits from one of the 12 expense fields in the table. The function has a single parameter named expense that represents the field object that called the function. Add the following commands to the function:

   a. Create a variable named numRegExp that contains the regular expression literal /^\d*(\.\d{0,2})?$/. This pattern matches any text string that only contains a number with or without two decimal place accuracy.

   b. Insert a conditional statement that tests whether the value property of the expense parameter matches the numRegExp pattern.

   c. If the condition is met (meaning that the employee has entered a valid expense amount), then run the following commands: 1) Display the value property of the expense parameter to two decimal places (*Hint*: Use the toFixed() method; if your browser does not support this method, use the toFixed2() function from the functions.js file.); 2) Insert a For loop with a counter that runs from 1 to 4. Within the For loop, set the value of the sub*i* field to the value returned by the calcRow() function, where *i* is the value of the For loop counter. Format the value to appear to two decimal places; and 3) Set the value of the total field equal to the value returned by the calcTotal() function. Display the total field value to two decimal places.

   d. If the condition is not met (meaning that the user has entered an invalid number), then: 1) Display the alert message "Invalid currency value"; 2) Change the value property of the expense parameter to "0.00"; and 3) Return the focus to the expense object.

10. Locate the HTML tag for the travel1 input field. Add an event handler that runs the update() function in response to the blur event. Use the "this" keyword for the expense object parameter. Add the same event handler to the travel2 through travel4 fields, the lodge1 through lodge4 fields, and the meal1 through meal4 fields.

11. Save your changes to the file. Open **exp.htm** in your Web browser. Test the operation of the travel expense table, verifying that it automatically updates the travel expenses as you add new values to the table.

12. Test the form validation commands by attempting to submit the form under the following conditions: 1) Without all of the required fields filled out; 2) With invalid entries for the account, department, project, and social security number fields; and 3) With travel expenses entered without corresponding dates in the travel expense table. The form should highlight the errors and alert you of the mistake.

13. Submit your completed Web site to your instructor.

Explore how to pass data from a Web form

Case Problem 3

Data files needed for this Case Problem: back.jpg, conf.css, conftxt.htm, edge.jpg, links.jpg, logo.jpg, summary.css, sumtxt.htm

The CGIP Conference   Rajiv Rammohan is a Web site consultant for the annual conference of Computer Graphics and Image Processing. This year the conference will be putting all of its registration forms and documents online. Rajiv is working on the form in which participants will enter their registration information. Rajiv wants the form to have the following features:

- The participant must enter his or her first and last name, address, e-mail address, and phone number.

- Phone numbers must follow the pattern ddd-ddd-dddd.

- The form should calculate the total registration fee. The fee is equal to $145 plus $30 for every person attending the conference banquet. CGIP members receive a $25 discount on the conference fee.

When a successful form is submitted, Rajiv wants the browser to display a page summarizing all of the registration information and choices made by the participant. Figure 7-65 shows a preview of both the registration form and the summary page.

Figure 7-65

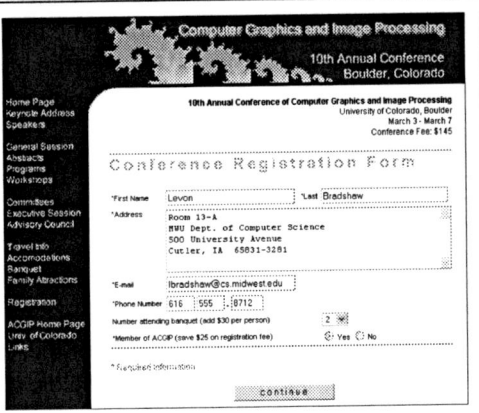 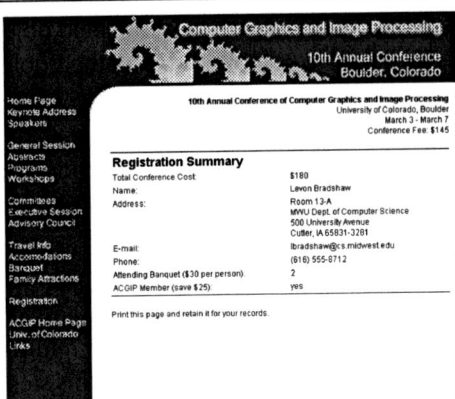

To complete this assignment:

1. Use your text editor to open the **conftxt.htm** and **sumtxt.htm** files from the tutorial. 07/case3 folder. Enter *your name* and *the date* in the comment section of each, and save the files as **conf.htm** and **summary.htm** respectively.

2. Go to the **conf.htm** file in your text editor. Examine the contents of the file and the Web form. Note that the form has a hidden field named total. In this field you'll store the total cost of the registration.

3. Insert a script element in the document head and create a function named calcCost(). The purpose of this function is to calculate the total registration fee. There are no parameters for this function. Add the following commands to the function:

   a. Create a variable named cost and set its initial value to 145, the default cost of the conference.

   b. Retrieve the value of the selected index property from the guests selection list. This value indicates the number of guests invited to the banquet. Multiply the selected index by 30 and add this to the cost variable.

   c. If the first member radio button is checked, subtract 25 from the value of the cost variable.

   d. Set the value of the total field equal to the value of the cost variable.

4. Create a function named testLength(). The purpose of the function is to test whether the user has entered any text in a required field. The function has a single parameter named field that represents the field object to be tested. To complete the function:

   a. Insert a conditional expression that tests whether the length of the field value is equal to 0.

   b. If the length is equal to 0, then: 1) Change the background color of the field object to yellow and 2) return the Boolean value false. Otherwise: 1) Change the background color of the field object to white and 2) return the Boolean value true.

5. Create a function named testPattern(). The purpose of this function is to compare the value of a field against a regular expression pattern. The function has two parameters: the field parameter representing the field object to be tested and reg, a regular expression literal containing the pattern used for the testing. To complete the testPattern() function:

   a. Insert a conditional statement that employs the test() method to test whether the value of the field object matches the regular expression contained in the reg parameter.

   b. If the test() method returns the value false, then: 1) Change the background color of the field object to yellow; 2) Change the color of the field object to red; and 3) return the Boolean value false. Otherwise: 1) Change the background color of the field object to white; 2) Change the color of the field object to black; and 3) return the Boolean value true.

6. Create a function named submitForm(). The purpose of this function is to validate the form and calculate the total registration fee. Add the following commands to the function:

   a. Create a variable named valid. Set the initial value of the variable to true.

   b. Call the testLength() function using the fname field as the parameter. If the function returns the value false, change the value of the valid variable to false. Repeat this step for the lname, address, and email fields.

   c. The phone number is divided into three fields named phone1, phone2, and phone3, representing the area code, exchange, and local number. The phone1 and phone2 fields should both contain only three digits. The phone3 field should contain only four digits. Call the testPattern() function for each field along with the appropriate regular expression literal. If the value returned by the testPattern() function is false for any of the fields, set the value of the valid variable to false.

   d. Insert a conditional statement that tests whether neither of the member radio buttons is checked. If neither has been checked then: 1) Change the background color of each member radio button to yellow, and 2) Set the value of the valid variable to false. (*Hint*: To test whether neither radio button has been checked, use the condition: ((`form.member[0].checked` || `form.member[1].checked`) == `false`) where `form` is the object reference to the registration form.)

   e. If the valid variable is false then display the alert message "Enter all required information in the appropriate format"; otherwise, run the calcCost() function.

   f. Return the value of the valid variable.

7. Add an event handler to the form element that runs and returns the value of the submitForm() function when the form is submitted.

8. Save your changes to **conf.htm**. Open the file in your Web browser and verify that the form cannot be submitted unless all of the required fields are filled out, the phone number is entered in the appropriate format, and the user has indicated whether or not he or she is a member of the CGIP. A valid form should open the summary.htm file with a list of field names and values appended to the URL. Note that browsers differ in how they change the background color of option buttons. If you are running Internet Explorer, the background color of the option buttons changes to yellow. If you are running Netscape, the background color of the option buttons does not turn yellow. If you are running Opera, the internal color of the option buttons changes color.

Explore

9. Open the **summary.htm** file in your text editor. Add an embedded script element to the head section of the document. Add the following commands to the script element:
    a. Create a variable named searchString equal to everything but the first character of the location.search object.
    b. Use the replace() method to replace every occurrence of the + character in the searchString variable with a blank space. Store the revised text string in a variable named formString.
    c. Apply the unescape() method to the formString variable to remove any escape characters from the string. Store the revised text string in a variable named dataString.
    d. Use the split() method to split the dataString at every occurrence of a & or = character. Store the substrings in an array named data.

Explore

10. Scroll down the file. Notice that embedded script elements have already been placed in the table. Your next task is to write the field values from the data array into the appropriate places in the table. Field values are stored in data[1], data[3], data[5], and so forth. The total cost of the conference is stored in data[1]. In the first script element, use the document.write() method to write the value of data[1] preceded by a $ symbol to the document. The participant's first and last name is stored in data[3] and data[5]. In the second script element, write the values data[3] and data[5], separated by a blank space.

Explore

11. The next row in the table displays the participant's address. This value is stored in data[7]. However, the value came from a textarea field that could contain multiple lines of text. Each line return has to be converted into <br /> tags to preserve the appearance of the address text. To write the participant's address, do the following:
    a. Create a regular expression literal named reg that matches the occurrence of every new line character. (*Hint*: Use the \n escape sequence.)
    b. Use the replace() method with the reg regular expression object to replace every occurrence of the new line character in the data[7] text string with the substring <br />. Store the revised text string in a variable named address.
    c. Write the address variable to the document.
12. Write the remaining field values to the remaining table cells. Use data[9] for the e-mail address; data[11], data[13], and data[15] for the phone number; data[17] for the number of banquet guests; and data[19] for whether the participant is an CGIP member.
13. Save your changes to the file.
14. Reopen **conf.htm** in your Web browser. Fill out the form correctly, including a multi-line address in the address field. Submit the form. Verify that the field values and total cost of the conference are written to the table cells in the summary page. Also verify that the summary page retains the line breaks present in the address field.
15. Submit the completed Web site to your instructor.

Create

Create an order form for a commercial Web site

Case Problem 4

Data files needed for this Case Problem: back.jpg, functions.js, info.txt, logo.jpg

Wizard Works   Wizard Works is a leading seller of customized and brand name fireworks in the United States. Roger Blaine supervises the company's Web site development team. He's asked you to work on the order form for the company's line of custom fountains. Roger wants the following elements to appear on the form:

- Data entry fields for the customer's first and last name, address, and phone number.
- Data entry fields for the customer's credit card type (Wizard Works accepts American Express, Diners Club, Discover, MasterCard, and Visa), name of the credit card, credit card number, and expiration date.
- Data entry fields from which the customer can select which item or items to order, and the quantity of each item.
- Data entry fields from which the customer can select a shipping option (standard for $4.95, express for $8.95, or next day for $12.95).

The final design of the order form is up to you. Roger has provided several files to aid you in creating the order form. You may supplement this material with material of your own. However, the order form needs to perform the following tasks:

- Automatically calculate the total cost of the order, including the cost of shipping. The cost of the order should be formatted to two decimal places.
- Confirm that the user has entered an integer quantity of items to order.
- Confirm that the customer has entered a first and last name, address, and phone number.
- Confirm that the phone number follows one of the following patterns: (ddd) ddd-dddd, ddd-ddd-dddd, or ddd ddd dddd.
- Confirm that the customer has selected a credit card type, entered a credit card name, and entered a credit card number that matches both the number pattern for the selected card and fulfills the Luhn Formula.

To complete this assignment:

1. Using the material found in the tutorial.07/case4 folder, create a Web form in a file named **works.htm**. The form should contain all of the entry fields specified by Roger.
2. Design the form so that it opens a file named done.htm using the post method when it is successfully submitted to the browser. Create the done.htm file, displaying a message that the order form has been correctly filled out.
3. Add scripts to the Web page to perform all of the necessary calculations and validation tasks.
4. Use regular expressions to test whether the credit card numbers match the card patterns specified by the card company. See the info.txt file for information on the appropriate number patterns for each card.
5. Test your Web form, verifying that it performs all calculations and validation tasks correctly.
6. Submit the completed Web site to your instructor.

Quick Check Answers

Session 7.1

1. document.forms[1]
2. document.forms["register"].elements["lastname"]

   or

   document.register.lastname
3. document.register.lastname.value = "Carol Campbell";
   document.register.lastname.focus();
4. document.register.statename.option[3]
5. document.register.statename.selectedIndex
6. document.register.contactme.checked
7. 3.14159.toFixed(2)

   This expression might not be supported by older browsers.

Session 7.2

1. Client-side validation is the validation of a data entry form that occurs on the user's Web browser. Server-side validation is validation that occurs on the Web server.
2. onsubmit = "return testForm()"
3. username.length
4. username.charAt(0)
   username.charAt(username.length-1)
5. username.slice(0,5)
6. words = email.split("@")
   words[0] contains the *username*; words[1] contains the *domain*
7. email.indexOf("gov")
8. username.toUpperCase()

Session 7.3

1. /GPS/gi
2. /\bproducts\b/
3. /^\d{9}$/
4. /^\d{9}$|^\d{3}-\d{2}-\d{4}$/

   or

   /^\d{3}-?\d{2}-?\d{4}$/

   Other solutions are also possible.
5. /(street|avenue|lane)/ig
6. reuser.test(username)
7. date.split(/\//g)
8. The Luhn Formula is a formula developed by a group of mathematicians in the 1960s to provide a quick validation check for a number string. It calculates the sum of digits in an account number to verify that the number is valid.
9. location.search

Objectives

Session 8.1
- Learn different methods for applying event handlers
- Study event propagation in the Internet Explorer event model
- Understand event propagation in the DOM event model
- Create functions that resolve the differences between the event models

Session 8.2
- Work with the properties of the event object under both models
- Identify the object that initiated an event
- Determine the coordinates of a mouse event
- Create objects that can be dragged and dropped

Session 8.3
- Work with cursor styles
- Create functions that respond to double-click events
- Determine which mouse button a user clicked
- Work with keyboard events, including determining which key a user pressed
- Understand how to work with modifier keys

Working with the Event Model

Creating a Drag-and-Drop Shopping Cart

Case

Games Etc.

Games Etc., a company that sells puzzles and games, recently decided to put its merchandise online. You have been hired to create a Web page for the company's monthly specials. Your supervisor, Pete Burdette, wants users to be able to select the specials they want to purchase from a list of items.

Because of the nature of the company, Pete also wants the page to have an interface that incorporates various elements of board games. For example, rather than clicking a check box to select an item, Pete would like to see users click and drag items into a shopping cart area, much as game pieces are moved on a game board. Thus, the elements on the page won't be fixed in one place; rather, users will be able to move them around.

To add this feature to the Games Etc. Web page, you have to work with the event models of Internet Explorer and the W3C, learning how to make the Web page respond to mouse and keyboard actions initiated by users. You will not be able to run the pages in this tutorial using Internet Explorer for the Macintosh due to the limitations of that browser in working with the attachEvent and detachEvent methods of the Internet Explorer event model.

Student Data Files

▼**tutorial.08**

▽ **tutorial folder**

gamestxt.htm
shoptxt.js
+ 1 style sheet
+ 3 graphic files
+ 2 demo files

▽ **review folder**

puzztxt.htm
+ 3 JavaScript files
+ 1 style sheet
+ 26 graphic files

▽ **case1 folder**

survtxt.htm
+ 1 JavaScript file
+ 1 style sheet
+ 3 graphic files

Session 8.1

Working with Events

You and Pete meet to discuss his idea for a shopping cart page. He has already designed the page layout. Open the file now to view the current page.

To open the Games Etc. Web page:

1. In your text editor, open the **gamestxt.htm** file from the tutorial.08/tutorial folder. Enter **your name** and **the date** in the comment section and save the file as **games.htm**.

2. Take some time to study the HTML code for this file, taking careful note of the div elements and their id values.

3. Open **games.htm** in your Web browser. Figure 8-1 shows the current appearance of the page.

Figure 8-1 | The Games Etc. Web page

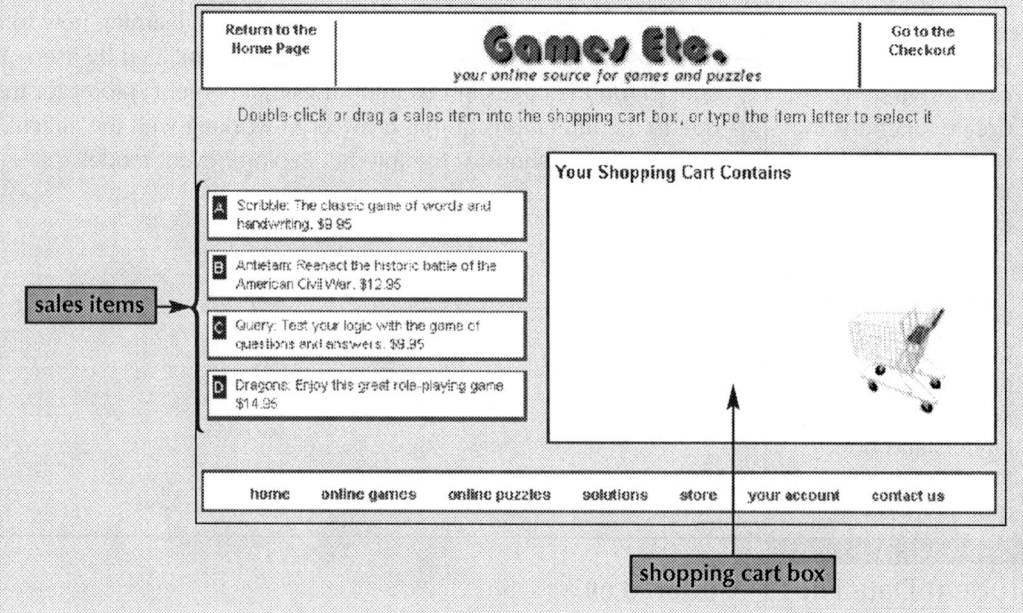

The Games Etc. page displays the four specials for the current month in separate boxes on the left side of the page. The box on the right acts as a shopping cart for prospective customers, displaying the items a user has decided to purchase. Many of the objects on the page have been stored within div elements and placed on the page using absolute positioning. In particular, each of the four monthly specials is entered as a separate div element, as is the shopping cart box. The id names for the four specials are item1, item2, item3, and item4. The id name for the shopping cart box is cartBox.

To assist you in programming this page, Pete has acquired an external JavaScript file containing several customized functions that will handle various tasks that you'll need to complete this project. Figure 8-2 describes the different functions available in the shop.js file. You'll be adding some additional functions to this file as you work on the Games Etc.page.

Functions in the shop.js file   Figure 8-2

Function	Description
placeIt(object, x, y)	Places object at coordinates (x, y)
getXCoord(object)	Returns the x-coordinate of object
getYCoord(object)	Returns the y-coordinate of object
withinIt(x, y, object)	Returns a Boolean value indicating whether the coordinates (x, y) lie within object's boundaries (true) or not (false)
colorIt(object, color)	Changes the font color and border color of object to "color"

Open the shop.js file now to familiarize yourself with these functions.

To open the shop.js file:

1. Use your text editor to open the **shoptxt.js** file from the tutorial.08/tutorial folder. Enter *your name* and *the date* in the comment section and save the file as **shop.js**.

2. Review the contents of the file.

For scripts you'll use in this tutorial, you'll need to create the following global variables:

• dragItem: Used to store a reference to the object being dragged
• shop1 - shop4: Used to store a reference to the four shopping cart items
• cart: Used to store a reference to the shopping cart box

Add these global variables to a script in the Web page. Then set the initial values for each of these variables in a function named setUp() that you'll run when the page is loaded by the browser. The initial value of the dragItem variable should be left null since no objects are being dragged when the page is loaded by the browser.

To create the global variables and the setUp() function:

1. Return to **games.htm** in your text editor and above the closing </head> tag insert an embedded script element containing the following global variables:

```
var dragItem, shop1, shop2, shop3, shop4, cart;
```

2. Below the global variables you just created, insert the following function to set the object references of these variables:

```
function setUp() {
    shop1 = document.getElementById("item1");
    shop2 = document.getElementById("item2");
    shop3 = document.getElementById("item3");
    shop4 = document.getElementById("item4");
    cart = document.getElementById("cartBox");
}
```

3. Add the event handler **onload = "setUp()"** to the body element. Figure 8-3 shows the new and revised code in the file.

Figure 8-3 ⟩ **Creating the setUp() function**

```
<script type="text/javascript">
var dragItem, shop1, shop2, shop3, shop4, cart;

function setUp() {
    shop1 = document.getElementById("item1");
    shop2 = document.getElementById("item2");
    shop3 = document.getElementById("item3");
    shop4 = document.getElementById("item4");
    cart = document.getElementById("cartBox");
}

</script>
</head>

<body onload="setUp()">
```

You may wonder why you were instructed to place the commands for setting up the object references in the setUp() function, rather than when you first declared the global variables. The reason is that when a browser encounters an embedded script element in the head section of a document, it has not yet processed the contents of the Web page body, and thus would not recognize references to elements in the page body. However, when the setUp() function is run in response to the onload event, the browser has already read in the complete contents of the HTML file and thus can assign those object references.

Event Handlers

Pete describes how he wants the page to operate. As shown in Figure 8-4, Pete wants to give customers the ability to drag and drop each of the four sales items into the shopping cart box. Then, when a user clicks the "Go to the checkout" link, a CGI script can be run that totals the cost of the selected items and prompts the user for additional purchase information. Your task is to program only the drag-and-drop aspect of this page. Someone else will create the rest of the shopping cart application for the company.

Dragging items into the shopping cart ◄ **Figure 8-4**

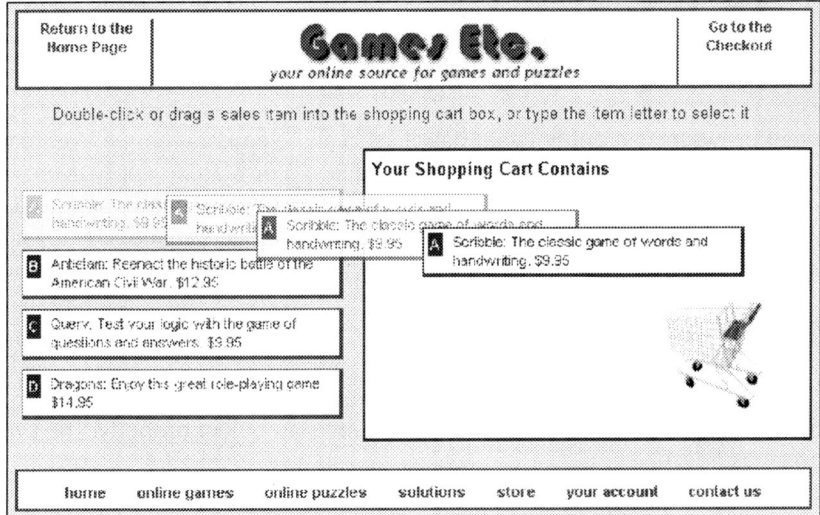

To complete the drag-and-drop part of this task, your script must be able to do the following:

- Select a sales item on the page when the customer depresses the mouse button on the object.
- Move the sales item along with the mouse pointer as it travels across the screen.
- Place the sales item in its new location when the customer releases the mouse button.

To create this effect, the browser needs to react to the actions of pressing the mouse button down, moving the mouse pointer, and finally releasing the mouse button. As each of these events occurs, you need to modify the page layout in response. As you've seen in previous tutorials, one common way of responding to an event is by adding an event handler attribute to an element's tag using the syntax:

```
<element onevent = "script" ...> ... </element>
```

where *element* is the document element, *event* is the name of the event, and *script* is a command or command block that the browser will run in response to the event occurring within the element. Figure 8-5 lists the event handlers associated with mouse events.

Mouse event handlers ◄ **Figure 8-5**

Event Handler	Description
oncontextmenu	The right (or secondary) mouse button has been clicked
onclick	A mouse button has been clicked
ondblclick	A mouse button has been double-clicked
onmousedown	A mouse button has been depressed
onmousemove	The mouse pointer has moved
onmouseout	The mouse pointer has moved off of the element
onmouseover	The mouse pointer has moved over the element
onmouseup	A mouse button has been released

For example, if you wanted to run a script named moveItem() in response to the mousemove event occurring within the first sales item, you could add the onmousemove event handler to that item's HTML tag, as follows:

```
<div id="item1" onmousemove="moveItem()" ...>
```

Most current browsers can apply event handlers to any element within a Web page or browser. However, older browsers such as Netscape 4.0 or 4.7 can apply event handlers only to a specific group of elements. (For a discussion of the elements supported by Netscape 4, see Appendix E.) Thus, if you're creating a Web site that needs to support older browsers, you will have to consider those browsers' limitations when scripting for events.

Event Handlers as Object Properties

Another way to apply an event handler is to treat it as an object property. The syntax of this approach is

```
object.onevent = function;
```

where `object` is the object that the event applies to, `onevent` is the event handler, and `function` is the name of the JavaScript function that is run in response to the event. For example, to run the moveItem() function whenever the mousemove event occurs within the item1 element, you could run the following JavaScript command:

```
document.getElementById("item1").onmousemove=moveItem;
```

Note that this form uses the name of the function as the property value; it does not call the function. It would not be correct syntax to use the construction

```
document.getElementById("item1").onmousemove=moveItem();
```

Also note that the name of the event handler must be in lowercase letters. For example, you can specify "onmouseover" as an event handler, but not "onMouseOver". Using an event handler as an object property provides programmers with greater flexibility in designing their scripts. For example, the function assigned to an event can be changed at one or more points in a program. The function name can also be passed as a variable. A programmer could write a script that prompts a user for the function the user wants to run in response to specific events. Finally, in a Web page that may contain dozens of elements that require event handlers, a programmer could write a program that assigns event handlers to the appropriate objects without having to go through the process of adding event handler attributes to each of the HTML tags.

One of the main disadvantages of handling events as object properties is the inability to include a function's parameter values in a property. In addition, you can assign only one function at a time to a particular object and event—although, as you'll see later, there are ways of working around this limitation. Another important consideration in using the object property method is that you must insert the event handler *after* an object has been loaded by the browser. You can do this either by placing the JavaScript commands at the bottom of the file or by running the commands in a function after the page is loaded.

Event Handlers as Script Elements

You can also invoke event handlers as attributes of the script element. The general syntax is

```
<script type="text/javascript" for="id" event="onevent">
```

where *id* is the id of an element in the Web page and *onevent* is the event handler. For example, the code

```
<script type="text/javascript" for="item1" event="onmousemove">
    commands
</script>
```

runs the *commands* in the embedded script when the mousemove event occurs within the item1 element. Note that this syntax can only be applied to elements with a specified id.

Reference Window

Using Event Handlers

- To add an event handler to an element, add the following attribute to the element's tag:
    `onevent="script"`
  where *event* is the name of the event and *script* is the command or commands run in response to the event occurring within the element.
- To apply an event handler as a property of an object, use the JavaScript command
    `object.onevent = function;`
  where *object* is the object in the Web page or browser and *function* is the name of the function to assign to *event*.
- To apply an event handler to a script element, create a script element like the following:
    ```
    <script type="text/javascript" for="id" event="onevent">
        commands
    </script>
    ```
  where *id* is the id of an element in the Web page and *commands* are the commands to be run in response to the event.

Using an Event Handler to Cancel an Action

As you've seen in previous tutorials, many events have default actions associated with them. Hovering a mouse pointer over a link changes the text of the window status bar; clicking a submit button in a Web form submits the contents of the form for processing. You've also seen that you can cancel the default action for any event by assigning a function to the event handler that returns the Boolean value false. For example, in the following sample code, the disableLink() function returns the Boolean value false. This has the effect of canceling the default action of the onclick event handler for the first link in the document.

```
document.links[0].onclick=disableLink;
function disableLink() {
    return false;
}
```

To restore the default action associated with clicking the link, you could run a second function that returns the Boolean value true:

```
document.links[0].onclick=enableLink;
function enableLink() {
    return true;
}
```

Canceling the default action associated with an event is most often used when you want to substitute your own actions for those usually undertaken by the browser. You'll use this technique later in the tutorial in creating the drag-and-drop script for Pete's Web page.

Assigning an Event Handler

For the task that Pete wants you to accomplish, you need to control the movements of the mouse as applied to several different objects on the Web page. While you could write a separate event handler for each object on the page, this would be a cumbersome process. Instead, you'll use the object property method to invoke your event handlers, which gives you more flexibility in writing your script. You'll start this task by creating event handlers that run a function named grabIt() whenever a customer depresses the mouse button in one of the shopping cart items. Because you'll be creating several event handlers in this tutorial and applying them to several objects, you'll place all of your event handlers for the sales items within a general function named assignF(). This saves you the effort of writing the same code four times for each of the four sales items. The initial code of the assignF() function is

```
function assignF(object) {
    object.onmousedown=grabIt;
}
```

Here the *object* parameter represents the object that receives the onmousedown event handler. You'll call this function for each of the shopping cart items from the setUp() function you created earlier. Recall that you've placed references to those shopping cart items in four global variables named shop1 through shop4.

To create the assignF() function:

1. Within the **games.htm** file in your text editor, insert the following function below the setUp() function:

   ```
   function assignF(object) {
       object.onmousedown=grabIt;
   }
   ```

2. Add the following commands to the setUp() function. Figure 8-6 shows the revised code.

   ```
   assignF(shop1);
   assignF(shop2);
   assignF(shop3);
   assignF(shop4);
   ```

Figure 8-6	Creating the assignF() function

```
function setUp() {
    shop1 = document.getElementById("item1");
    shop2 = document.getElementById("item2");
    shop3 = document.getElementById("item3");
    shop4 = document.getElementById("item4");
    cart = document.getElementById("cartBox");

    assignF(shop1);
    assignF(shop2);
    assignF(shop3);
    assignF(shop4);
}

function assignF(object) {
    object.onmousedown=grabIt;
}
```

3. Close the file, saving your changes.

With this new code, each of the shopping cart items will now run the grabIt() function when a customer depresses the mouse button in them. The purpose of the grabIt() function is to select the shopping cart item in preparation for dragging it across the Web page. Before you can create the grabIt() function, you need to look at how browsers handle events.

Introducing the Internet Explorer Event Model

Events, like other objects in a Web page, have their own properties and methods. The way that a browser works with events is called its **event model**. When you were creating event handlers in this and previous tutorials, you were working with an early version of an event model. Generally, this event model is considered part of the DOM Level 0 standard discussed in Tutorial 4. Since this model was created, more sophisticated event models have been developed. You'll consider two event models in this tutorial: the **Internet Explorer event model** developed for the Internet Explorer browser, and the **DOM event model** developed by the W3C for DOM Level 2. The Internet Explorer event model is supported by Internet Explorer version 5 and higher. The DOM event model is supported by Netscape 6 and 7, Firefox, and other Mozilla browsers. A third event model was developed for Netscape 4 and Netscape 4.7, but you won't consider it here. You can learn more about the Netscape 4 event model in Appendix E.

Eventually all browsers will likely support the DOM event model; however, for now you'll need to create code that accommodates both event models. The differences between the two lie in how they capture events within a Web page, how they refer to events, and the methods and properties that they associate with those events. We'll start with the Internet Explorer event model.

Event Bubbling

The first thing you'll examine for the Internet Explorer model is how events are captured and propagated through the browser. When a user performs an action such as clicking an element on a Web page, that event originates within the given element. If an event handler has been added to the element, a function may run in response to the event. However, elements are often nested within other elements; in addition, all page elements are ultimately nested within the document element itself, and the document is nested within the browser window. In the case of nested objects, how does a browser determine which object really initiated the event?

In the Internet Explorer event model, events are initiated at the bottom of the document tree and rise to the top of the object hierarchy in a process known as **event bubbling**. Thus, the event passes through the lowest object in the tree, though every object in the path to the top of the tree has an opportunity to respond to the event (see Figure 8-7).

Figure 8-7 Event bubbling in the IE Event Model

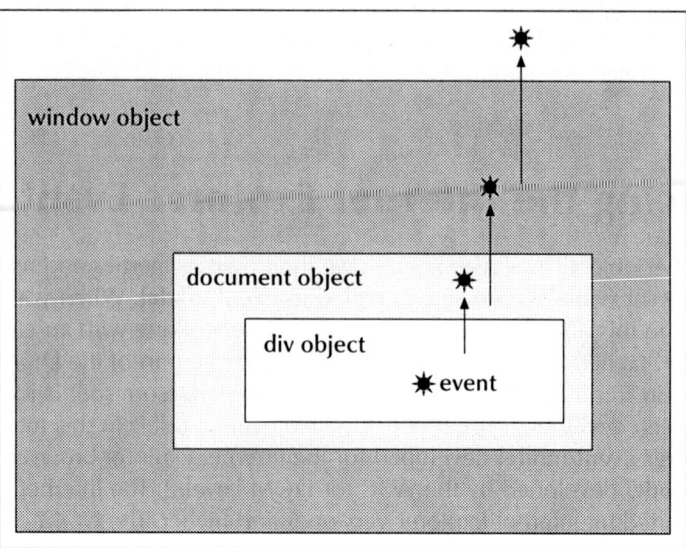

To see how event bubbling works in practice, a demo page has been prepared for you. Open this page now in a browser that supports the Internet Explorer event model.

To view the event bubbling demo:

1. With an Internet Explorer browser (or a browser such as Opera that supports the Internet Explorer event model), open the **demo_bubble.htm** file from the tutorial. 08/tutorial folder.

2. Click within the **Level 1** box on the Web page (see Figure 8-8).

Figure 8-8 Event bubbling

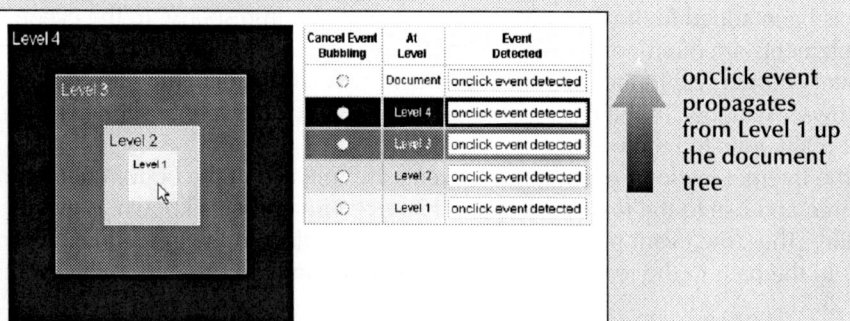

When you click within the Level 1 box (the lowest level on the document tree in this Web page), the onclick event bubbles up through the other three boxes and into the main document object. Note that the propagation is slowed down so that you can see it happen more clearly. In actual practice, the propagation of the event occurs almost instantaneously.

One of the advantages of event bubbling is that you can set up different functions to handle the event as it propagates up the document tree. One function can be run when the event is detected within a nested object, and another function can be run when the click event bubbles to the document object itself.

Canceling Event Bubbling

In some scripts you may want to prevent an event from propagating up the document tree. This would occur if you wanted an event like the onclick event to be noticed only by a nested object, but ignored by all of the parent elements of that object. To prevent event bubbling from occurring, run the following command when the event reaches the level at which you want the propagation to stop:

```
event.cancelBubble=true;
```

To turn event bubbling back on, run the command

```
event.cancelBubble=false;
```

The following set of commands illustrates this process:

```
document.getElementById("Level 3").onclick=clickMsg;
event.cancelBubble=true;
```

The first command runs the clickMsg() function when the onclick event is encountered in the Level 3 object. The second command cancels the event, preventing it from propagating up the object hierarchy to the next level. Thus, the onclick event is essentially hidden from objects higher up on the document tree. Return to the demo page to see this effect in action.

To cancel event bubbling:

1. Click the **Level 3 option** button to cancel event bubbling starting at that level in the demo page.

2. Once again, click within the **Level 1** box on the Web page (see Figure 8-9).

Canceling event bubbling ◄ **Figure 8-9**

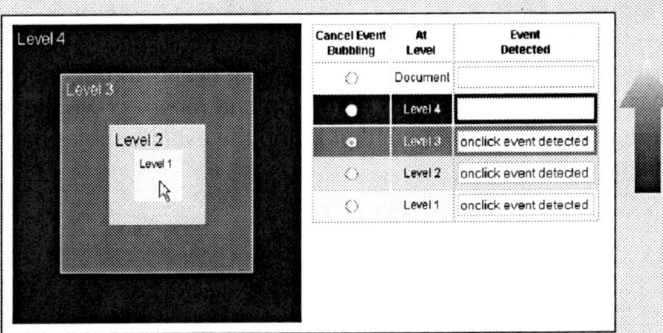

onclick event propagates until it reaches an event.cancelBubble command

The onclick event is recognized up to Level 3 in the demo page. After that, the event is not propagated to the upper levels in the object hierarchy, and thus no onclick event is detected.

3. Close **demo_bubble.htm**.

If you want to cancel an event at the current level as well as all levels above the object, run the command

```
event.returnValue = false;
```

This has the same effect as accessing a function that returns the Boolean value false to cancel any default actions associated with an event. Note that the returnValue property is supported only in the Internet Explorer event model.

Attaching and Detaching Events

One problem with the object.property method of attaching event handlers to objects is that you can assign only one function to a particular event. The Internet Explorer event model overcomes this limitation with the attachEvent() method. The syntax is

```
object.attachEvent(onevent, function);
```

where *object* is the object receiving the event, *onevent* is the text string of the event handler, and *function* is the function that runs in response to the event. For example, the following command runs both the Rollover() and showColor() functions when the mouse pointer is passed over the Logo object:

```
document.getElementById("Logo").attachEvent("onmouseover",Rollover);
document.getElementById("Logo").attachEvent("onmouseover",showColor);
```

If you then wanted to detach one of these functions from the mouseover event, you would use the detachEvent() method as follows:

```
document.getElementById("Logo").detachEvent("onmouseover",showColor);
```

Once a function is detached from an object, the event no longer triggers the function. Functions can be attached and detached multiple times, depending on the needs of a given program. It's important to stress that the attachEvent() and detachEvent() methods are supported only by Internet Explorer 5.0 and above, along with any other browser that supports the Internet Explorer event model. The attachEvent and detachEvent methods are not supported by Internet Explorer for the Macintosh.

Introducing the DOM Event Model

The DOM event model uses a different approach to propagating events through the document tree. In the DOM model, an event starts at the top and moves down the object hierarchy until it reaches the target of the event; at that point, the event bubbles back up the object hierarchy (see Figure 8-10).

Event propagation in the DOM event model | **Figure 8-10**

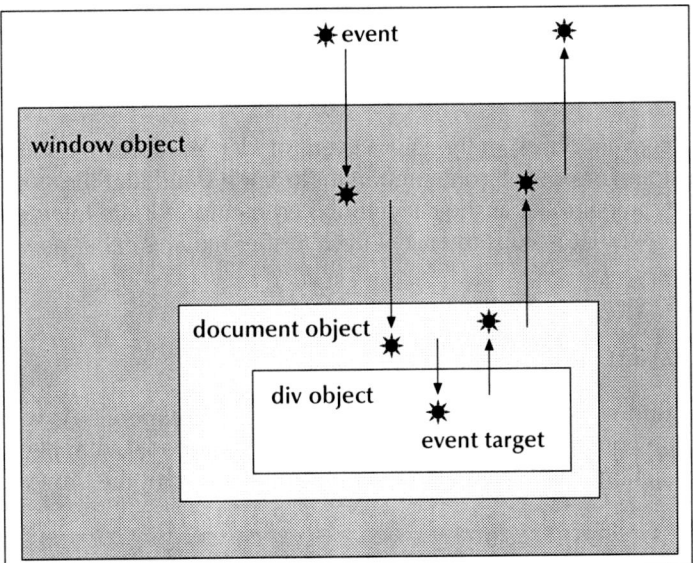

In the DOM model, an event is split into three phases:

1. A **capture phase** as the event moves down the object hierarchy
2. A **target phase** in which the event reaches the object from which the event originated
3. A **bubbling phase** in which the event moves back up the object hierarchy

The DOM event model is particularly powerful because it allows you to run a function that responds to an event at any phase in this process. To run a function, you create an **event listener** that detects when a particular event has reached an object in the document. The syntax for creating an event listener is

```
object.addEventListener(event, function, capture);
```

where `object` is the object receiving the event, `event` is the text string describing the event, `function` is the function that runs in response to the event, and `capture` is a Boolean variable that tells the browser when to apply the event handler. If `capture` is true, the function is executed in the capture phase as the event travels down the object hierarchy. If `capture` is false, the function is executed in the bubble phase. For example, to apply the RollOver() function to the Logo object during the bubble phase, you would use the following command:

```
document.getElementById("Logo").addEventListener("mouseover",
RollOver, false);
```

The addEventListener() method is similar to Internet Explorer's attachEvent() method. Like the attachEvent() method, you can use this method to attach several functions to the same event. Note that the addEventListener() method does not identify events using the "on" form. Thus, to respond to a click event, you would use "click" rather than "onclick" as you would with the attachEvent() method in the Internet Explorer event model.

To remove an event listener, use the command

```
object.removeEventListener(event, function, capture);
```

The three parameters have the same meaning as those in the addEventListener() method. Finally, you can prevent an event from propagating through the object hierarchy using the method

```
evt.stopPropagation();
```

where *evt* is the event object in the DOM event model. You'll learn about event objects in the next session. For now, it's only important to understand that the stopPropagation() method has the same impact as the cancelBubble() method for the Internet Explorer event model except that it stops the event from further moving either down or up the object hierarchy.

To cancel an event entirely, use the method

```
evt.preventDefault();
```

where once again *evt* is the event object in the DOM event model. As with the returnValue=false approach in the Internet Explorer event model, running this method cancels default actions associated with the event on the part of the browser.

Reference Window

Working with Event Propagation

Internet Explorer Event Model

- To prevent an event from bubbling up the document tree, run the command
  `event.cancelBubble = true;`
- To allow an event to continue bubbling up the document tree, run
  `event.cancelBubble = false;`
- To attach a function to an object, run
  `object.attachEvent(onevent, function);`
  where *object* is the object receiving the event, *onevent* is the text string of the event handler, and *function* is the function that runs in response to the event. Multiple functions can be attached to the same event in the same object.
- To detach a function, run
  `object.detachEvent(onevent, function);`
- To cancel an event, run
  `event.returnValue=false;`

DOM Event Model

- To prevent an event from propagating through the object hierarchy, run the command
  `evt.stopPropagation();`
  where *evt* is the event object that is propagating through the object hierarchy.
- To run a function when an event reaches an object, use
  `object.addEventListener(event, function, capture);`
  where *object* is the object receiving the event, *event* is the text string describing the event, *function* is the function to run in response to the event, and *capture* equals true if the event is moving down the document tree and false if the event is bubbling up the tree.
- To stop listening for an event, run
  `object.removeEventListener(event, function, capture);`
- To cancel the default action associated with an event, run
  `evt.preventDefault();`

Creating a Cross-Browser Event Model

Since two event models exist, with different approaches and syntax, you need to determine which event model a user's browser supports and then run commands appropriate for that model. Recall from Tutorial 4 that one way of working with different models is through object detection. In object detection, you find an object, property, or method that is unique for a particular model and create a Boolean variable that indicates whether the current browser supports that object, property, or method. For the IE and DOM event models, you can use the attachEvent and addEventListener methods as parts of the object detection. The code to employ object detection in this case is

```
var IE = document.attachEvent ? true:false;
var DOM = document.addEventListener ? true:false;
```

If a user's browser supports the IE model, the IE variable has the value true; otherwise it has the value false. Similarly, browsers that support the DOM model return a value of true for the DOM variable and false otherwise. Since you'll be doing a lot of object detection in this tutorial, add these two variables as global variables to the shop.js file. You can then use them whenever you need to determine which event model is being run by a user's browser.

To create the IE and DOM variables:

1. Go to the **shop.js** file in your text editor.

2. Directly before the placeIt() function, insert the following global variables, as shown in Figure 8-11:

```
var IE = document.attachEvent ? true:false;
var DOM = document.addEventListener ? true:false;
```

Performing object detection   Figure 8-11

```
var IE = document.attachEvent ? true:false;
var DOM = document.addEventListener ? true: false;

function placeIt(object, x, y) {
    object.style.left=x;
    object.style.top=y;
}
```

Next you'll need a cross-browser function to apply an event function to an object. Since the Internet Explorer event model uses the attachEvent() method and the DOM event model uses the addEventListener() method, you'll have to use the IE and DOM variables you created to determine which method to apply. The function will look as follows:

```
function applyEventF(obj,ename,fname,capture) {
    if (IE) obj.attachEvent("on"+ename, fname);
    else if (DOM) obj.addEventListener(ename,fname,capture);
}
```

The function has four parameters: obj represents the object that the event is applied to, ename is the event name, fname is the name of the function associated with the event, and capture indicates whether the event is traveling down the hierarchy or bubbling up. For example, if you call the function using the parameters

```
applyEventF(shop1,"click",grabIt,false)
```

browsers that support the Internet Explorer event model run the command

```
shop1.attachEvent("onclick",grabIt)
```

and browsers that support the DOM event model run

```
shop1.addEventListener("click",grabIt,false)
```

The cross-browser function to remove an event function from an object is similar.

```
function removeEventF(obj,ename,fname,capture) {
   if (IE) obj.detachEvent("on"+ename, fname);
   else if (DOM) obj.removeEventListener(ename,fname,capture);
}
```

Add these two functions to the shop.js file.

To create the applyEventF() and removeEventF() functions:

1. At the end of the **shop.js** file, insert the following functions (see Figure 8-12):

```
function applyEventF(obj,ename,fname,cap) {
   if (IE) obj.attachEvent("on"+ename, fname);
   else if (DOM) obj.addEventListener(ename,fname,cap);
}
function removeEventF(obj,ename,fname,cap) {
   if (IE) obj.detachEvent("on"+ename, fname);
   else if (DOM) obj.removeEventListener(ename,fname,cap);
}
```

| Figure 8-12 | Creating two custom functions |

```
function colorIt(object, color) {
   object.style.color=color;
   object.style.borderColor=color;
}

function applyEventF(obj,ename,fname,cap) {
   if (IE) obj.attachEvent("on"+ename, fname);
   else if (DOM) obj.addEventListener(ename,fname,cap);
}

function removeEventF(obj,ename,fname,cap) {
   if (IE) obj.detachEvent("on"+ename, fname);
   else if (DOM) obj.removeEventListener(ename,fname,cap);
}
```

2. Close the file, saving your changes.

You've completed the initial work on the shopping cart Web page. In the next session you'll work on creating the functions that will enable you to drag an item across the Web and drop it on a new location.

Review

Session 8.1 Quick Check

1. What JavaScript command would you enter to run the function CalcTotal when the user presses the mouse button down while the mouse pointer is in an object with the id "Total"?
2. What script element would you enter to run a script in response to the event described in the previous question?

3. How do events propagate through the document tree under the Internet Explorer event model?

4. What command would you run under the IE model to attach the function CalcTotal to the Total object in response to the click event?

5. What command would you enter to cancel event bubbling under the Internet Explorer event model?

6. Describe how events propagate under the DOM event model.

7. What command would you run under the DOM event model to apply the function CalcTotal to the Total object in response to the click event?

8. What command would you enter to cancel event propagation under the DOM event model?

Session 8.2

Working with Event Objects

In the last session you examined how the two main document object models detect and react to events; however, this is only part of what's involved with an event model. You also need to get information about an event itself. If a user has clicked a mouse button in a document, you may need to know where the mouse pointer was located when this happened. If the user has pressed a key on the keyboard, you may want to know which key was pressed. This type of information is stored in an **event object**. The two event models provide different means of working with event objects. Start by looking at the event object under the Internet Explorer event model.

The Internet Explorer Event Object

In the Internet Explorer event model, the event object has the object reference

```
windowObject.event
```

where `windowObject` is the browser window in which the event occurred. If you are dealing with events in the current browser window, you can drop the `windowObject` reference and reference the event object as simply

```
event
```

You may recognize the event object from the last session, when it was used in the command to cancel event bubbling or the default action associated with an event. Under the Internet Explorer model, the event object can be treated as a global variable—one that is never declared by you, but is accessible in any function you write. This system works because only one event is being processed at any given time; thus, there is no need to reference multiple event objects within a given function. The Internet Explorer event model always knows which event the event object is referencing based on the function that has been attached and called by the program.

The event object supports a wide variety of properties. A partial list is displayed in Figure 8-13. You may recognize some of these from the previous session.

| Figure 8-13 | Properties of the IE event object |

Property	Description
event.altKey event.ctrlKey event.shiftKey	Returns a Boolean value indicating whether the Alt, Ctrl, or Shift key was pressed down during the event
event.button	Returns the number of the button pressed by the user (1=left, 2=right, 4=middle)
event.cancelBubble	Set this property to true to cancel event bubbling; set it to false to continue event bubbling
event.clientX event.clientY	Returns the x- and y-coordinates of the event within the browser window
event.fromElement	For mouseover and mouseout events, returns the object from which the mouse pointer is moving
event.keyCode	Returns the Unicode character code of the key that was struck by the user
event.offsetX event.offsetY	Returns the x and y distances of the event from the object in which the event was initiated
event.returnValue	Set this property to false to cancel the default action of the event; set it to true to retain the default action
event.screenX event.screenY	Returns the x- and y-coordinates of the event within the computer screen
event.srcElement	Returns the object in which the event was generated
event.toElement	For mouseover and mouseout events, returns the object to which the mouse pointer is moving
event.type	Returns a text string indicating the type of event
event.X event.Y	Returns the x and y positions of the event relative to the element that initiated the event

One of the more important properties is srcElement, which returns the object that initiated the event. The srcElement property is akin to the "this" keyword discussed in the previous tutorial, allowing you to determine which of many possible objects on the page called the function that responded to the event. In the shopping cart example, you could store the object in the dragItem variable using the expression

```
dragItem = event.srcElement;
```

The other properties of immediate interest are the clientX and clientY properties, which return the (x, y) coordinates of the event within the browser window. You'll use these properties later to determine the location of the mouse pointer as it moves across the Web page.

The DOM Event Object

The DOM event model takes a different approach to referencing the event object. In the DOM event model, the event object is inserted as a parameter of whatever function responds to the event. You can give the event object any parameter name, but the standard practice is to name the parameter "e" or "evt". For example, if you wanted to run the grabIt() function when a user presses the mouse button down in a document, you could insert the JavaScript commands

```
document.onmousedown=grabIt;
function grabIt(e) {
    commands
}
```

The e parameter in the grabIt() function represents the mousedown event object, and contains information describing that event. As with the Internet Explorer event object, since functions are called by specific events, there is no confusion over which event a particular event object is referring to. Figure 8-14 lists the properties associated with the DOM event object.

Properties of the DOM event object ◄ Figure 8-14

Property	Description
evt.altKey *evt*.ctrlKey *evt*.shiftKey *evt*.metaKey	Returns a Boolean value indicating whether the Alt, Ctrl, Shift, or any meta key was pressed down during the event
evt.bubbles	Returns a Boolean value indicating whether *evt* can bubble
evt.button	Returns the number of the button pressed by the user (0=left, 1=middle, 2=right; in Netscape 6: 1=left, 2=middle, 3=right)
evt.cancelable	Returns a Boolean value indicating whether *evt* can have its default action canceled
evt.clientX *evt*.clientY	Returns the x- and y-coordinates of the event within the browser window
evt.currentTarget	Returns the object that is currently handling the event
evt.eventPhase	Returns the phase in the event propagation of *evt* (1=capture, 2=target, 3=bubbling)
evt.relatedTarget	For mouseover events, returns the object that the mouse left when it moved over the target of the event; for mouseout events, returns the object that the mouse entered when leaving the target
evt.screenX *evt*.screenY	Returns the x- and y-coordinates of the event within the computer screen
evt.target	Returns the object that initiated the event
evt.timeStamp	Returns the date and time that the event was initiated
evt.type	Returns a text string indicating the event type

For the DOM event model, the object currently responding to an event is returned using the currentTarget property. Thus, to set the object reference for the dragItem variable, you would use the command

```
dragItem = evt.currentTarget;
```

where *evt* is the parameter of the event function. The DOM event model also supports the target property, which returns a reference to the object that initiated the event. There is no matching property in the Internet Explorer event model. Finally, you can determine the (x, y) coordinates of an event within the browser window using the clientX and clientY properties just as you would with the Internet Explorer event model. To give you a feeling for the type of information that can be returned by the event object (under either event model), a demo page has been prepared for you.

To view the event demo page:

1. Use your Web browser to open the **demo_events.htm** file from your tutorial.08/ tutorial folder.

2. Move your mouse pointer over the page. As you move the pointer, the page displays the different event coordinates supported by the event model. In addition, the event type "mousemove" is displayed in the type field.

   Trouble? Only browsers that support the Internet Explorer event model display values for the offsetX and offsetY properties.

3. Click and hold down the left mouse button within the container element. The demo page indicates which button was clicked and provides the event coordinates within the container, on the page, and on the screen (see Figure 8-15).

Figure 8-15	Event object demo

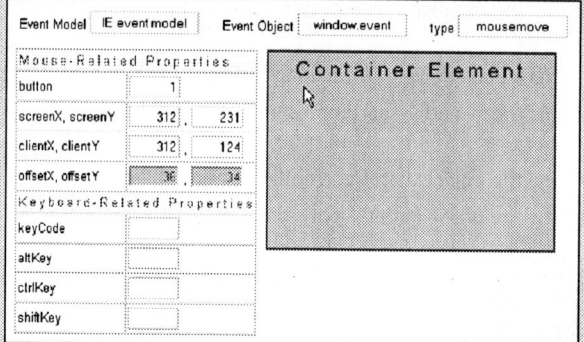

4. Close the demo page when finished.

Working with Event Objects

Internet Explorer Event Model

- To reference the event object, use the object reference
    `windowObject.event`
  where `windowObject` is the browser window in which the event occurred. For the current browser window, simply use
    `event`
- To return the object that initiated an event, use the property
    `event.srcElement`
- To return the (x,y) window coordinates that indicate where an event was initiated, use the properties
    `event.clientX`
    `event.clientY`

DOM Event Model

- To reference the event object, use
    `evt`
  where `evt` is the parameter of the function assigned to the event.
- To return the object that initiated an event, use the property
    `evt.target`
- To return the object that is currently handling an event, use the property
    `evt.currentTarget`
- To return the (x,y) window coordinates that indicate where an event was initiated, use the properties
    `evt.clientX`
    `evt.clientY`

Now that you know a little more about event objects, you are ready to create objects that users can drag and drop on the shopping cart Web page. Start with the grabIt() function.

Creating the grabIt() Function

Recall that you entered code in the last session to run the grabIt() function whenever a user depresses the mouse button while the mouse pointer lies within one of the four sales items. The purpose of this function is to prepare the sales item for being dragged across the page. To do so, the function has to perform the following tasks:

1. Identify the object that lies beneath the pointer.
2. Determine the page coordinates of the mouse pointer at the moment the user presses the mouse button down.
3. Calculate the difference between the coordinates of the mouse pointer and the coordinates of the selected object.
4. Assign functions to the object that run whenever the user moves the mouse pointer or releases the mouse button.

Determining the Event Source

Because you have two event models to accommodate, you'll create cross-browser functions that resolve the differences between the two models for each of these tasks, as you did in the last session. You can then call these functions in the grabIt() function without having to worry about which event model is supported by a customer's browser. The first function you'll create is the eventSource() function, which has the following code:

```
function eventSource(e) {
    if (IE) return event.srcElement;
    else if (DOM) return e.currentTarget;
}
```

In this function, you've named the event parameter used by the DOM event model "e". The function uses the object detection variables created in the last session to determine which event object property to return. If a user's browser supports the Internet Explorer event model, the function returns the property event.srcElement; if the browser supports the DOM event model, the function returns the e.CurrentTarget property. Add this function to the shop.js file.

To add the eventSource() function:

1. Open the **shop.js** file in your text editor.

2. At the end of the file, insert the following function (see Figure 8-16).

```
function eventSource(e) {
    if (IE) return event.srcElement;
    else if (DOM) return e.currentTarget;
}
```

Figure 8-16 The eventSource() function

```
function removeEventF(obj,ename,fname,cap) {
    if (IE) obj.detachEvent("on"+ename, fname);
    else if (DOM) obj.removeEventListener(ename,fname,cap);
}

function eventSource(e) {
    if (IE) return event.srcElement;
    else if (DOM) return e.currentTarget;
}
```

Determining the Event Coordinates

Next you need two cross-browser functions to determine the window coordinates of the mouse pointer when the mousedown event occurs. For this task you'll use the clientX and clientY properties of the event objects in both event models. You'll add the following two functions to the shop.js file:

```
function eventPositionX(e) {
    if (IE) return event.clientX;
    else if (DOM) return e.clientX;
}
function eventPositionY(e) {
    if (IE) return event.clientY;
    else if (DOM) return e.clientY;
}
```

Once again, you use "e" as the event parameter for the DOM event model.

To add the eventPositionX() and eventPositionY() functions:

1. At the end of the file, insert the following functions (see Figure 8-17).

```
function eventPositionX(e) {
    if (IE) return event.clientX;
    else if (DOM) return e.clientX;
}
function eventPositionY(e) {
    if (IE) return event.clientY;
    else if (DOM) return e.clientY;
}
```

The eventPosition() functions ◀ Figure 8-17

```
function eventSource(e) {
    if (IE) return event.srcElement;
    else if (DOM) return e.currentTarget;
}

function eventPositionx(e) {
    if (IE) return event.clientx;
    else if (DOM) return e.clientx;
}

function eventPositionY(e) {
    if (IE) return event.clienty;
    else if (DOM) return e.clienty;
}
```

2. Save your changes to the file.

Now you can return to the games.htm file and start using all of the cross-browser functions you've created. A script element linked to the shop.js file has already been created for you, so you don't have to add that to the file. The initial code for the grabIt() function is

```
function grabIt(e) {
    dragItem = eventSource(e);
    mouseX=eventPositionX(e);
    mouseY=eventPositionY(e);
}
```

The grabIt() function assigns the object returned by the eventSource() function to the dragItem variable you created in the last session. This should be the object in which the mousedown event was initiated. You've also stored the (x,y) coordinates of that event in the variables mouseX and mouseY. In addition, you have to include an event parameter in your functions to support the DOM event model. This allows the event object to be passed to the cross-browser functions you created in the shop.js file.

To create the grabIt() function:

1. Reopen the **games.htm** file in your text editor.

2. Below the assignF() function, insert the following code, as shown in Figure 8-18.

```
function grabIt(e) {
    dragItem=eventSource(e);
    mouseX=eventPositionX(e);
    mouseY=eventPositionY(e);
}
```

| Figure 8-18 | Determining the event source and coordinates |

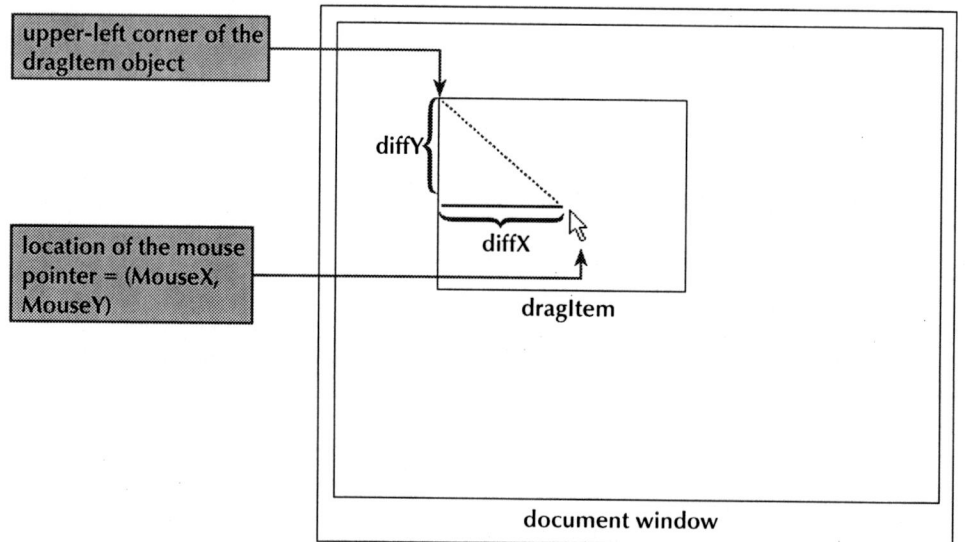

```
function grabIt(e) {
    dragItem=eventSource(e);
    mouseX=eventPositionX(e);
    mouseY=eventPositionY(e);
}

</script>
</head>

<body onload="setup()">
```

The next piece to add to the grabIt() function is code to calculate the distance between the mouse pointer and dragItem. You'll need this information later to keep drag-Item a constant distance away from the mouse as you move it across the page.

Calculating the Distance from the Pointer

The coordinates of an object are often expressed in relation to the object's upper-left corner. This means that you need to calculate the value of the variables diffX and diffY, which represent the horizontal and vertical distances between the mouse pointer and the object's upper-left corner (see Figure 8-19).

| Figure 8-19 | The diffX and diffY variables |

upper-left corner of the dragItem object

diffY

diffX

location of the mouse pointer = (MouseX, MouseY)

dragItem

document window

The coordinates of dragItem can be determined by using the getXCoord() and getYCoord() functions from the shop.js file. Thus, the values of diffX and diffY are

```
diffX=mouseX-getXCoord(dragItem);
diffY=mouseY-getYCoord(dragItem);
```

To create the diffX and diffY variables:

▶ **1.** In the grabIt() function, below the statement to create the mouseY variable, insert the following two lines:

```
diffX=mouseX-getXCoord(dragItem);
diffY=mouseY-getYCoord(dragItem);
```

▶ **2.** Save your changes to the file.

The final task in the grabIt() function is to assign functions to dragItem that will run whenever the user moves the mouse pointer or releases the mouse button. When the mouse pointer moves, you'll run a function named moveIt() that will be used to move dragItem across the page. When the mouse button is released, you'll run the dropIt() function that drops dragItem onto the page in a new location. To call these two functions, you'll use the applyEventF() function created in the last session. The code you need to add to the grabIt() function is

```
applyEventF(dragItem,"mousemove",moveIt,false);
applyEventF(dragItem,"mouseup",dropIt,false);
```

Recall that you created applyEventF() in the last session as a cross-browser function to accommodate the attachEvent() and addEventListener() methods of the Internet Explorer and DOM event models.

To call the applyEventF() function:

▶ **1.** Add the following commands to the grabIt() function (see Figure 8-20):

```
applyEventF(dragItem,"mousemove",moveIt,false);
applyEventF(dragItem,"mouseup",dropIt,false);
```

The grabIt() function ◀ Figure 8-20

```
function grabIt(e) {
    dragItem=eventSource(e);
    mouseX=eventPositionX(e);
    mouseY=eventPositionY(e);

    diffX=mouseX-getXCoord(dragItem);
    diffY=mouseY-getYCoord(dragItem);

    applyEventF(dragItem,"mousemove",moveIt,false);
    applyEventF(dragItem,"mouseup",dropIt,false);
}
```

▶ **2.** Save your changes to the file.

Now the grabIt() function is complete. Your next task is to create the moveIt() function, which will allow users to move items on the page from one location to another.

Creating the moveIt() Function

To move dragItem across the Web page, the moveIt() function needs to perform the following tasks:

1. Determine the current location of the mouse pointer.
2. Maintain dragItem at a constant distance from the mouse pointer.

By keeping an object a constant distance from the mouse pointer as it moves across the page, you create the illusion that the pointer is dragging the object (see Figure 8-21). You already know what that distance should be: it's the value of the diffX and diffY variables calculated in the dropIt() function.

Figure 8-21 ▷ **Maintaining a constant distance from the mouse pointer**

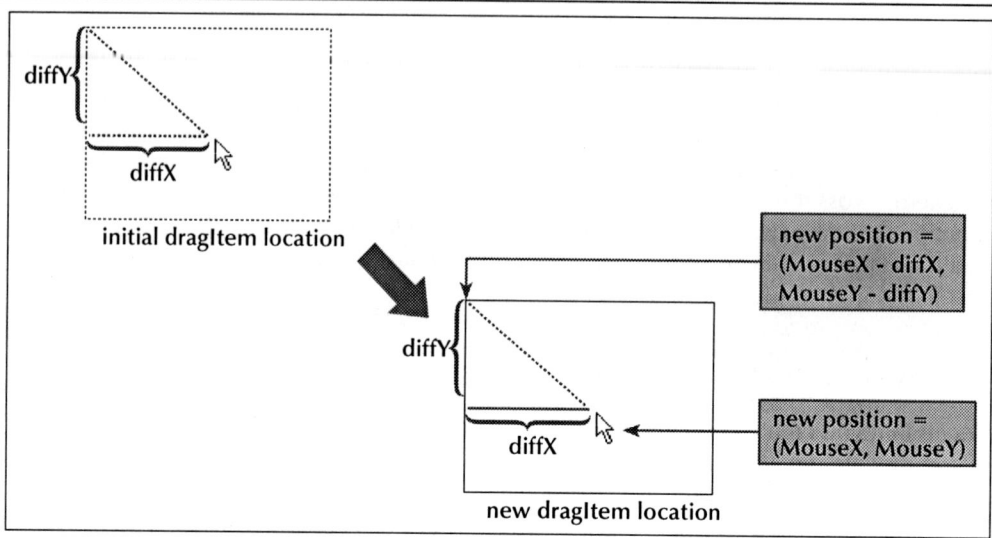

To place dragItem at specific page coordinates, you'll use the placeIt() function from the shop.js file, subtracting the values of the diffX and diffY variables from the current position of the mouse pointer. The code for the moveIt() function is therefore

```
function moveIt(e) {
   mouseX=eventPositionX(e);
   mouseY=eventPositionY(e);
   placeIt(dragItem, mouseX-diffX, mouseY-diffY);
}
```

To create the moveIt() function:

1. Directly below the grabIt() function, insert the following code (see Figure 8-22):

```
function moveIt(e) {
   mouseX=eventPositionX(e);
   mouseY=eventPositionY(e);
   placeIt(dragItem, mouseX-diffX, mouseY-diffY);
}
```

```
function grabIt(e) {
    dragItem=eventSource(e);
    mouseX=eventPositionX(e);
    mouseY=eventPositionY(e);

    diffX=mouseX-getXCoord(dragItem);
    diffY=mouseY-getYCoord(dragItem);

    applyEventF(dragItem,"mousemove",moveIt,false);
    applyEventF(dragItem,"mouseup",dropIt,false);
}

function moveIt(e) {
    mouseX=eventPositionX(e);
    mouseY=eventPositionY(e);
    placeIt(dragItem, mouseX-diffX, mouseY-diffY);
}
```

2. Save your changes to the file.

Creating the dropIt() Function

The next function to create for the Games Etc. drag-and-drop effect is the dropIt() function. The dropIt() function is run whenever the user releases the mouse button, initiating the mouseup event. In response, the dropIt() function causes the browser to stop running the function assigned to the mousemove event. With the moveIt() function no longer being called, dragItem ceases to follow the mouse pointer across the page, leaving it at the place where it was moved. To release the function assigned to the mousemove event, you'll use the removeEventF() function you created in the last session. The code for the dropIt() function is therefore

```
function dropIt(e) {
    removeEventF(dragItem, "mousemove",moveIt,false);
}
```

To create and test the dropIt() function:

1. Directly below the moveIt() function, insert the following code (see Figure 8-23):

```
function dropIt(e) {
    removeEventF(dragItem, "mousemove",moveIt,false);
}
```

```
function moveIt(e) {
    mouseX=eventPositionX(e);
    mouseY=eventPositionY(e);
    placeIt(dragItem, mouseX-diffX, mouseY-diffY);
}

function dropIt(e) {
    removeEventF(dragItem,"mousemove",moveIt,false);
}
```

2. Save your changes to the file.

3. Reload **games.htm** in your Web browser.

4. Move the mouse pointer over any of the four sales items, then click and hold the left mouse button. Verify that as you move the mouse pointer, the sales item moves across the page, following the mouse pointer, and that when you release the mouse button, the sales item is left at the new page location (see Figure 8-24).

Figure 8-24 ▶ Dragging the first sales item

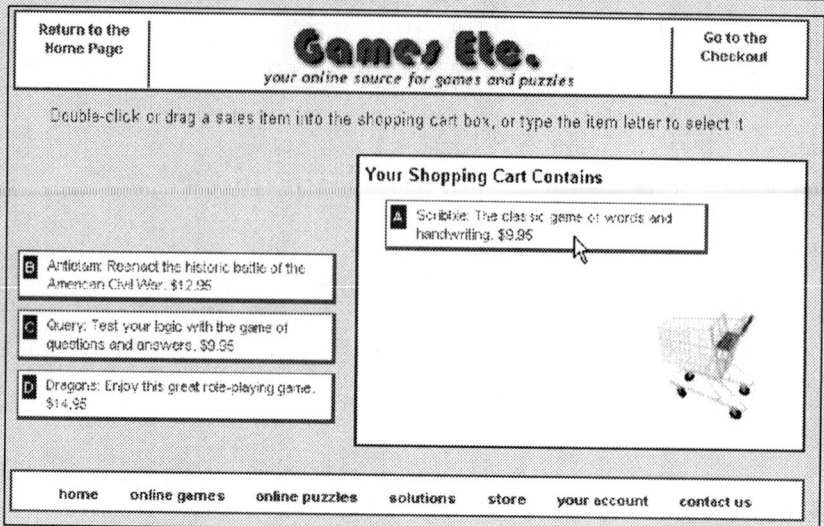

Trouble? If you click the blue highlighted letter within a sales item box, the sales item might not move across the page. This is because these letters are objects nested within each sales item and are not set up to capture the mouse events.

Refining the Drag-and-Drop Feature

You show the games.htm page to Pete. As Pete works with the page, he notices that in some instances, the object that is being moved "disappears" behind other objects on the page (see Figure 8-25). He'd like you to make sure the dragged item is always on top.

Figure 8-25 ▶ A dragged item hidden by another object on the page

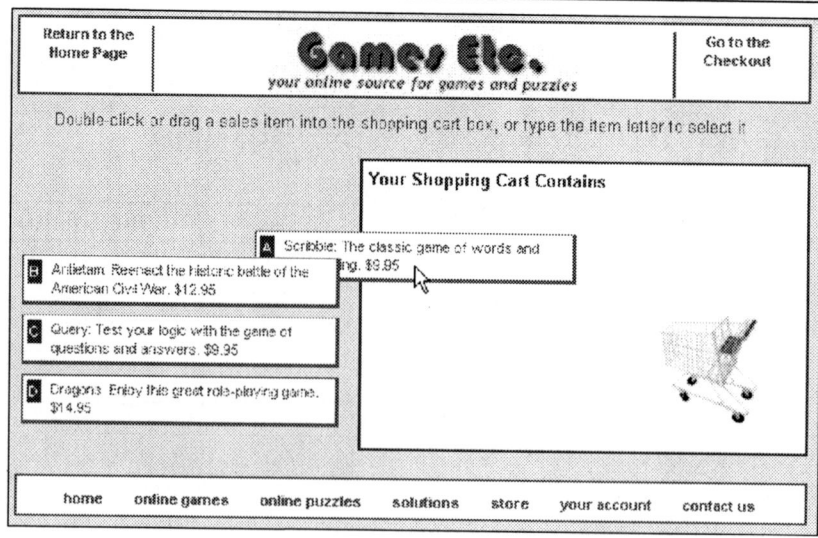

Keeping Dragged Items on Top

To do this, you'll create a global variable named maxZ, which stores the maximum value of the z-index style on the page. Each time you grab an item, the value of maxZ is increased by 1 and then applied to the z-index style of the grabbed item. Thus, when the grabbed item is dragged across the page, it will have the highest z-index of any object on the page and will always appear on top. Set the initial value of the maxZ variable to 1.

To create the maxZ variable:

1. Return to the **games.htm** file in your text editor.

2. Directly above the setUp() function, insert the following line:

   `var maxZ=1;`

3. Scroll down to the grabIt() function and insert the following two lines, as shown in Figure 8-26.

   ```
   maxZ++;
   dragItem.style.zIndex=maxZ;
   ```

Keeping dragged items on top ◄ **Figure 8-26**

```
function grabIt(e) {
    dragItem=eventSource(e);
    mouseX=eventPositionX(e);
    mouseY=eventPositionY(e);

    diffX=mouseX-getXCoord(dragItem);
    diffY=mouseY-getYCoord(dragItem);

    maxZ++;
    dragItem.style.zIndex=maxZ;

    applyEventF(dragItem,"mousemove",moveIt,false);
    applyEventF(dragItem,"mouseup",dropIt,false);
}
```

4. Save your changes to the file and reload **games.htm** in your Web browser. Verify that the sales items remain on top when they are dragged across the page.

Returning a Dragged Item to Its Starting Point

Another problem Pete notices is that users can drag an item from the list of specials and drop it anywhere on the page—not just in the shopping cart. He points out that the CGI script that you'll be using with the page expects that monthly specials stay either in the shopping cart box or back at their starting points on the page. Therefore, Pete wants you to add the following tasks to the dropIt() function:

1. Determine whether the dropped item lies within the boundaries of the shopping cart.
2. If the item does fall within the shopping cart's boundaries, leave it there.
3. If the item lies outside the cart's boundaries, it should snap back to its original location on the page.

To determine whether dragItem falls within the boundaries of the shopping cart, Pete suggests you use the same withinIt function that you used earlier. You'll add the following command block to the dropIt function:

```
dropPosX=getXCoord(dragItem);
dropPosY=getYCoord(dragItem);
if (!withinIt(dropPosX, dropPosY, cart)) snapBack();
```

Here dropPosX and dropPosY represent the (x, y) coordinates of the sales item as it is dropped onto the page. The "!" symbol is a negation operator and has the effect of switching the value of a Boolean variable. In this case it switches the value of the withinIt() function from false to true, and vice versa. Thus, if the expression !withinIt(dropPosX, dropPosY, cart) is true (in other words, if the coordinates are not inside the cart object), then the snapBack() function is run.

You'll create the snapBack() function shortly. For now, add the command block to the dropIt() function to determine whether dragItem is dropped in the shopping cart.

To test whether the item has been dropped into the shopping cart:

1. Return to the **games.htm** file in your text editor.

2. Add the following commands to the dropIt() function, as shown in Figure 8-27:

```
dropPosX=getXCoord(dragItem);
dropPosY=getYCoord(dragItem);
if (!withinIt(dropPosX, dropPosY, cart)) snapBack();
```

| Figure 8-27 | Revised dropIt() function |

```
function dropIt(e) {
    dropPosX=getXCoord(dragItem);
    dropPosY=getYCoord(dragItem);
    if (!withinIt(dropPosX, dropPosY, cart)) snapBack();
    removeEventF(dragItem,"mousemove",moveIt,false);
}
```

Finally, you need to create the snapBack() function, which should return the dragItem item to its original location. From the <div> tags in the games.htm file, you know that the original coordinates for the four monthly specials are:

- shop1 (Scribble): (10, 140)
- shop2 (Antietam): (10, 185)
- shop3 (Query): (10, 230)
- shop4 (Dragons): (10, 275)

The snapBack() function should therefore appear as follows:

```
function snapBack() {
    if (dragItem==shop1) placeIt(dragItem, 10, 140);
    else if (dragItem==shop2) placeIt(dragItem, 10, 185);
    else if (dragItem==shop3) placeIt(dragItem, 10, 230);
    else if (dragItem==shop4) placeIt(dragItem, 10, 275);
}
```

Add the above function to the games.htm file.

To create and test the snapBack() function:

1. Below the dropIt() function, insert the following code, as shown in Figure 8-28:

```
function snapBack() {
    if (dragItem==shop1) placeIt(dragItem, 10, 140);
    else if (dragItem==shop2) placeIt(dragItem, 10, 185);
    else if (dragItem==shop3) placeIt(dragItem, 10, 230);
    else if (dragItem==shop4) placeIt(dragItem, 10, 275);
}
```

The snapBack() function **Figure 8-28**

```
function dropIt(e) {
    dropPosX=getXCoord(dragItem);
    dropPosY=getYCoord(dragItem);
    if (!withinIt(dropPosX, dropPosY, cart)) snapBack();
    removeEventF(dragItem,"mousemove",moveIt,false);
}

function snapBack() {
    if (dragItem==shop1) placeIt(dragItem, 10, 140);
    else if (dragItem==shop2) placeIt(dragItem, 10, 185);
    else if (dragItem==shop3) placeIt(dragItem, 10, 230);
    else if (dragItem==shop4) placeIt(dragItem, 10, 275);
}
```

2. Save your changes to the file.

3. Reload **games.htm** in your Web browser and verify that you cannot drop any of the sales items anywhere but within the shopping cart box. If you drop an item elsewhere, it should jump back to its original location.

Trouble? If the monthly specials all jump to the fourth spot in the list, check the code for the snapBack() function and verify that you used double equal signs (==) in the if ... then statement, rather than a single equals sign (=).

Canceling the selectStart Event

Pete tests the latest version of the page and notices a problem for Internet Explorer users: when the sales item snaps back, the text on the page often becomes selected (see Figure 8-29).

Content automatically selected by the snapBack() function **Figure 8-29**

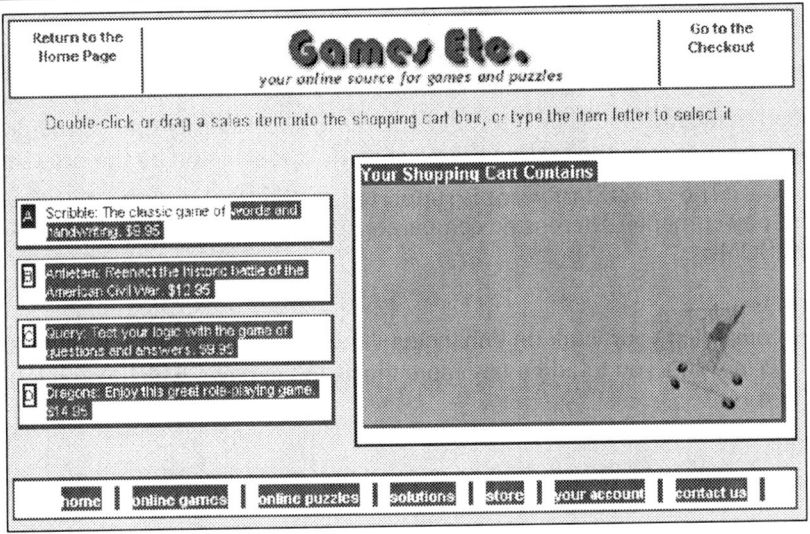

This happens because the default action of the browser is to select text on the Web page when the mouse button is held down and dragged through the page. As the sales items are snapped back, the text selection event kicks in as objects are moved across the mouse pointer.

The action of selecting text on the page is indicated in Internet Explorer by the select-Start event. If you cancel this event, then you can prevent the action of selecting text in the Web page by both the user and the browser itself. Recall from the last session that you can cancel an event by creating a function that returns the Boolean value "false." You'll do that now for this problem, inserting the following code into the document:

```
document.onselectstart=stopSelect;
function stopSelect() {
    return false;
}
```

To cancel the selectStart event:

1. Return to the **games.htm** file in your text editor.

2. At the bottom of the setUp() function, insert the following line:

   ```
   document.onselectstart=stopSelect;
   ```

3. Below the setUp() function, insert the following function. Figure 8-30 shows the revised code.

   ```
   function stopSelect() {
       return false;
   }
   ```

Figure 8-30 ▸ **Canceling text selection within the Web document**

```
function setup() {
    shop1 = document.getElementById("item1");
    shop2 = document.getElementById("item2");
    shop3 = document.getElementById("item3");
    shop4 = document.getElementById("item4");
    cart = document.getElementById("cartBox");

    assignF(shop1);
    assignF(shop2);
    assignF(shop3);
    assignF(shop4);

    document.onselectstart=stopSelect;
}

function stopSelect() {
    return false;
}
```

4. Close the file, saving your changes.

5. Reload **games.htm** in your Internet Explorer browser. Verify that as you drag your mouse pointer over the text on the page, no text is selected by the browser.

   Trouble? The selectStart event is supported only in the Internet Explorer document object model. There is no comparable event handler for the Netscape 4 or W3C DOMs.

You've completed your work on enhancing the drag-and-drop features of the Games Etc. page. Pete wants you to add a few more things to the page, which you'll look at in the next session.

Session 8.2 Quick Check

1. What is the reference for the event object in Internet Explorer? What is the reference in the DOM event model?
2. What property would you use to determine the type of event associated with the event object?
3. What properties would you use to determine the screen coordinates of an event?
4. What properties would you enter to determine the window coordinates of an event?
5. What technique can you use to ensure that a dragged item will always be on top as it moves across the Web page?
6. A function associated with the click event is called "stopClick()". What line should you add to this function to cancel the default action associated with the click event?

Session 8.3

Formatting a Dragged Object

Pete has looked over your Web page and would like it to provide users with more visual feedback. For example, when a user hovers the pointer over one of the movable objects, Pete would like the pointer to change shape to 🖑 to indicate that the object is clickable. When an object is being moved across the page, he wants the pointer to change to ✛ .

Setting the Cursor Style

Mouse pointers can be defined using an object's style properties. The syntax is

`object.style.cursor=cursorType;`

where `object` is an object in the document, and `cursorType` is a text string that identifies the type of pointer to be displayed. You can also define the pointer style in a CSS style declaration by using the syntax

`cursor: cursorType`

Figure 8-31 shows the different types of pointers you can display with either the JavaScript object property command or a style sheet declaration. In addition to the types listed in the figure, you can also specify a pointer type of "auto", which allows a user's browser to determine the appearance of the pointer for you. If you want to use a customized pointer, you can load one from a URL using the style `cursor: url( url )` where `url` is the location of the cursor image. Cursor images are stored in files with the file extensions .uri or .ani. Many browsers do not yet support customized cursors, so you should not rely on them if you need a Web page to be cross-browser compatible. In addition, many browsers support an extended list of cursor styles not shown in Figure 8-31.

Figure 8-31 **Cursor styles**

Cursor	Style	Cursor	Style
+	cursor: crosshair	↕	cursor: n-resize
↖	cursor: default	↙↗	cursor: ne-resize
↖?	cursor: help	↔	cursor: e-resize
✛	cursor: move	↖↘	cursor: se-resize
🖑	cursor: pointer	↕	cursor: s-resize
I	cursor: text	↙↗	cursor: sw-resize
⧖	cursor: wait	↔	cursor: w-resize
↖	cursor: url(url)	↖↘	cursor: nw-resize

Reference Window

Setting Cursor Styles

- To change the appearance of a mouse pointer use the cursor style

  ```
  object.style.cursor = cursorType;
  ```
  where *object* is an object on the Web page and *cursorType* is a text string of one of the cursor styles supported by CSS.
- To change the pointer using CSS, add the following style to the style declaration for an object:

  ```
  cursor: cursorType
  ```

   Pete wants to change the cursor style for each of the sales items to 🖑 . When a customer moves a sales item, he wants the cursor to change to ✛ while the object is in motion. After the customer drops the sales item, the cursor style should return to 🖑 . To make this change you'll add commands to the assignF(), grabIt(), and dropIt() functions that set the cursor style when the page loads, during the mousedown event, and after the sales item is dropped during the mouseup event.

To set the cursor style:

1. Reopen the **games.htm** file in your text editor.
2. Add the following line to the end of the assignF() function:

   ```
   object.style.cursor="pointer";
   ```

   Remember that assignF() contains the general code that sets the style for each of the four sales items.

3. Add the following line to the grabIt() function after the command to increase the z-index value of the dragItem object:

```
dragItem.style.cursor="move";
```

4. Add the following line to the start of the dropIt() function. Figure 8-32 highlights the inserted code.

```
dragItem.style.cursor="pointer";
```

Changing the cursor style   **Figure 8-32**

```
function assignF(object) {
    object.onmousedown=grabIt;
    object.style.cursor="pointer";
}

function grabIt(e) {
    dragItem=eventSource(e);
    mouseX=eventPositionX(e);
    mouseY=eventPositionY(e);

    diffX=mouseX-getXCoord(dragItem);
    diffY=mouseY-getYCoord(dragItem);

    maxZ++;
    dragItem.style.zIndex=maxZ;
    dragItem.style.cursor="move";

    applyEventF(dragItem,"mousemove",moveIt,false);
    applyEventF(dragItem,"mouseup",dropIt,false);
}

function moveIt(e) {
    mouseX=eventPositionX(e);
    mouseY=eventPositionY(e);
    placeIt(dragItem, mouseX-diffX, mouseY-diffY);
}

function dropIt(e) {
    dragItem.style.cursor="pointer";
    dropPosX=getXCoord(dragItem);
    dropPosY=getYCoord(dragItem);
    if (!withinIt(dropPosX, dropPosY, cart)) snapBack();
    removeEventF(dragItem,"mousemove",moveIt,false);
}
```

5. Save your changes to the file and reload **games.htm** in your Web browser. Verify that the cursor style for each of the sales items is now 🖑 and that the cursor style while dragging an object is ✛ (see Figure 8-33).

The pointer and move cursor styles   **Figure 8-33**

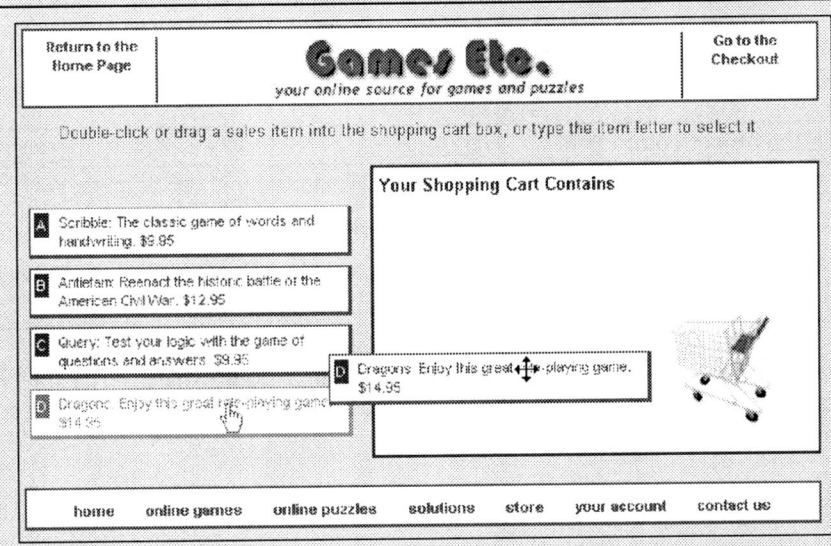

Trouble? If you are running Opera you will not see the cursor style change to the "move" pointer. Internet Explorer 4 does not support the "pointer" cursor, using the cursor style "hand" instead.

Changing the Color

The second enhancement that Pete wants you to make is to change the color of items once they've been placed into the shopping cart. Pete would like all items in the shopping cart to appear in blue, while outside the cart they should appear in red. This provides additional visual feedback to customers that sales items have been properly dropped into the shopping cart. One of the functions in the shop.js file is the colorIt function, which allows you to specify the text and border color of an object (see Figure 8-2). To change the color of the dragItem object to blue, you would use the command

```
colorIt(dragItem, "blue");
```

You'll insert the following command block into the moveIt function so that whenever a user moves an item into the shopping cart box, the item will change color:

```
if (withinIt(mouseX-diffX, mouseY-diffY, cart))
    colorIt (dragItem, "blue");
else colorIt(dragItem, "red");
```

Once again, the withinIt function determines whether the coordinates of the upper-left corner of the object fall within the shopping cart boundaries. You determine these coordinates by subtracting the values of the diffX and diffY variables from the coordinates of the current mouse position. Thus, the upper-left corner of dragItem is located at the coordinates (MouseX-diffX, MouseY-diffY). (You can refer back to Figure 8-21 for an illustration.)

To set the color of the dragged item:

1. Return to the **games.htm** file in your text editor.

2. Locate the moveIt() function and add the following lines, as shown in Figure 8-34.

```
if (withinIt(mouseX-diffX, mouseY-diffY, cart))
    colorIt (dragItem, "blue");
else colorIt(dragItem, "red");
```

Figure 8-34 Changing the object color

```
function moveIt(e) {
    mouseX=eventPositionX(e);
    mouseY=eventPositionY(e);
    placeIt(dragItem, mouseX-diffX, mouseY-diffY);
    if (withinIt(mouseX-diffX, mouseY-diffY, cart)) colorIt(dragItem, "blue");
    else colorIt(dragItem, "red");
}
```

3. Save your changes and reload **games.htm** in your Web browser. Verify that when you drag a sales item over the shopping cart box, its border color and font color change to blue.

Working with the Double-Click Event

Pete is aware that some customers do not like using drag-and-drop techniques for manipulating objects, and prefer one-step methods. Pete would like those customers to have the option of moving a sales item by double-clicking it. He suggests that you add a double-click event handler to the Web page so that if a customer double-clicks a sales item, it is placed in the sales cart; double-clicking an item in the sales cart should remove it from the cart. To complete this task, you'll create a function called snapIn(), which will be similar to the snapBack() function you created at the end of the last session. Unlike snapBack(), snapIn() will place each sales item in an appropriate spot within the shopping cart. The snapIn() function will also change the color of dragItem to blue in order to provide the visual indication that it lies within the shopping cart. The code for the function is

```
function snapIn() {
   if (dragItem==shop1) placeIt(dragItem, 300, 140);
   else if (dragItem==shop2) placeIt(dragItem, 300, 185);
   else if (dragItem==shop3) placeIt(dragItem, 300, 230);
   else if (dragItem==shop4) placeIt(dragItem, 300, 275);
   colorIt(dragItem, "blue");
}
```

Add this function to the games.htm file.

To add the snapIn() function:

1. Return to the **games.htm** file in your text editor.

2. Below the snapBack() function, insert the following function.

```
function snapIn() {
   if (dragItem==shop1) placeIt(dragItem, 300, 140);
   else if (dragItem==shop2) placeIt(dragItem, 300, 185);
   else if (dragItem==shop3) placeIt(dragItem, 300, 230);
   else if (dragItem==shop4) placeIt(dragItem, 300, 275);
   colorIt(dragItem, "blue");
}
```

   You also need to modify the snapBack() function so that it sets the color of an object placed back in its original location to red.

3. Add the following line to the end of the snapBack() function. Figure 8-35 shows the final code for both functions.

```
colorIt(dragItem, "red");
```

The snapBack() and snapIn() functions ◄ **Figure 8-35**

```
function snapBack() {
   if (dragItem==shop1) placeIt(dragItem, 10, 140);
   else if (dragItem==shop2) placeIt(dragItem, 10, 185);
   else if (dragItem==shop3) placeIt(dragItem, 10, 230);
   else if (dragItem==shop4) placeIt(dragItem, 10, 275);
   colorIt(dragItem, "red");
}

function snapIn() {
   if (dragItem==shop1) placeIt(dragItem, 300, 140);
   else if (dragItem==shop2) placeIt(dragItem, 300, 185);
   else if (dragItem==shop3) placeIt(dragItem, 300, 230);
   else if (dragItem==shop4) placeIt(dragItem, 300, 275);
   colorIt(dragItem, "blue");
}
```

Next you'll create the jumpIt() function that determines the location of the sales item. If the item is within the shopping cart, the function calls the snapBack() function to move the item back to its original location. If the item is not within the shopping cart, the function calls the snapIn() function to put it in the cart. The code for the jumpIt() function is

```
function jumpIt() {
  dragPosX=getXCoord(dragItem);
  dragPosY=getYCoord(dragItem);
  if (withinIt(dragPosX, dragPosY, cart)) snapBack();
  else snapIn();
}
```

Add this function to the games.htm file.

To create the jumpIt() function:

1. Below the assignF() function, insert the following code:

```
function jumpIt() {
  dragPosX=getXCoord(dragItem);
  dragPosY=getYCoord(dragItem);
  if (withinIt(dragPosX, dragPosY, cart)) snapBack();
  else snapIn();
}
```

2. Save your changes to the file.

Finally, you need to create an event handler to respond to a double-click event within any of the four sales items. You'll add the following line to the assignF() function (recall that the assignF() function is the general function that assigns event handlers and properties to the four sales items):

```
object.ondblclick=mouseDouble;
```

The code for the mouseDouble() function called by this event handler is

```
function mouseDouble(e) {
  dragItem = eventSource(e);
  jumpIt();
}
```

Note that the mouseDouble() function calls the cross-browser function eventSource() to accommodate the differences between the event models in determining the source of the double-click event.

To complete and test the double-click event handler:

1. Add the following command to the end of the assignF() function:

```
object.ondblclick=mouseDouble;
```

2. Below the assignF() function, insert the mouseDouble() function, as shown in Figure 8-36.

```
function mouseDouble(e) {
  dragItem = eventSource(e);
  jumpIt();
}
```

```
function assignF(object) {
    object.onmousedown=grabIt;
    object.style.cursor="pointer";
    object.ondblclick=mouseDouble;
}

function mouseDouble(e) {
    dragItem = eventSource(e);
    jumpIt();
}

function jumpIt() {
    dragPosX=getXCoord(dragItem);
    dragPosY=getYCoord(dragItem);
    if (withinIt(dragPosX, dragPosY, cart)) snapBack();
    else snapIn();
}
```

▶ **3.** Save your changes to the file and reload **games.htm** in your Web browser. Verify that as you double-click each of the four sales items, they are alternately moved into and out of the shopping cart.

Trouble? Under some browsers, the double-click action may display one of the browser's shortcut menus in addition to moving the sales item. If you double-click the letter box within a sales item, the letter box will change color, but the sales item will not move.

Working with the Mouse Button

So far in this case, you've assumed that users press the left (or primary) mouse button to move items around the page; however, this is not necessarily the case. Users can also drag and drop the sales items using the right mouse button—or even the middle button, for mice that have them. If you need to determine which mouse button a user has pressed, you can use the button property, which returns a numeric value indicating the button. In the DOM event model, the button values are 0=left, 1=middle, 2=right. In the Internet Explorer event model, these values are 0=left, 2=right, 4=middle. For Netscape 6 the values are 1=left, 2=middle, 3=right. Thus, any script you write that incorporates the mouse button has to adjust for these differences. You can determine which button values are assigned by your browser by using the demo_events.htm file from the previous session.

The right and middle mouse buttons usually have default actions associated with them. For example, the right mouse button usually displays a shortcut menu for the highlighted object. Thus, you may not wish to interfere with these default actions.

Working with Keyboard Events

Some users with disabilities are unable to work with mouse pointers and must interact with Web pages using solely their keyboards. Pete wants his Web site to be widely accessible, so he asks you to add a keyboard interface to the shopping cart page. He suggests allowing customers to select or deselect sales items by pressing the letter on the keyboard that corresponds to the item (see Figure 8-37).

Figure 8-37 | Creating an event handler for a keyboard event

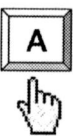
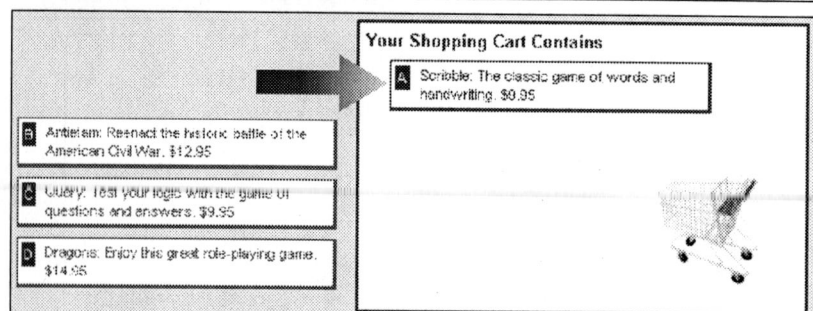

pressing the A key moves the first sales item into the shopping cart

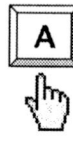
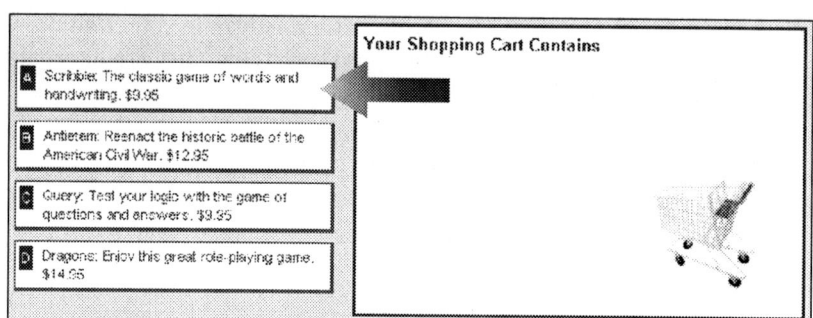

pressing the A key again takes the sales item out

Capturing a Keyboard Event

Three main keyboard events are available to work with:

- **keydown**: The user has pressed a key down.
- **keyup**: The user has released a key.
- **keypress**: The user has pressed and released a key.

For this page, you'll work with the keydown event, running a function named key-Drag() to move a sale item either into or out of the shopping cart whenever the user presses the a, b, c, or d key. Since the user is not pressing the key down within any particular object, you'll add an event handler for this event to the entire document.

To create an event handler for the key down event:

1. Return to the **games.htm** file in your text editor.

2. Add the following command to the setUp() function, as shown in Figure 8-38.

   ```
   document.onkeydown=keyDrag;
   ```

```
function setup() {
    shop1 = document.getElementById("item1");
    shop2 = document.getElementById("item2");
    shop3 = document.getElementById("item3");
    shop4 = document.getElementById("item4");
    cart = document.getElementById("cartBox");

    assignF(shop1);
    assignF(shop2);
    assignF(shop3);
    assignF(shop4);

    document.onselectstart=stopSelect;
    document.onkeydown=keyDrag;
}
```

Examining Key Codes

Now that you've created an event handler for the keydown event, your next task is to determine which key a user has pressed. Both event models use the keyCode property of the event object to return the numeric value associated with the pressed key. While no set standard yet matches a particular key code to a specific key, most of the key code values have common meanings among all browsers. Figure 8-39 lists some keyboard keys and their corresponding key code values. For example, if a user presses the letter A on the keyboard, the corresponding keycode value is 65.

Keys and keycode values | Figure 8-39

Keys(s)	Key Code Value(s)	Keys(s)	Key Code Value(s)
[0 - 9]	48 - 57	page up	33
[a - z]	65 - 90	page down	34
backspace	8	end	35
tab	9	home	36
enter	13	left arrow	37
shift	16	up arrow	38
ctrl	17	right arrow	39
alt	18	down arrow	40
pause/break	19	insert	45
caps lock	20	delete	46
esc	23	[f1 - f12]	112 - 123
space	32		

To test whether these key code values match the key codes returned by your browser, you can reopen the demo_events.htm file that you used in the second session of this tutorial and press and hold down different keys on your keyboard. The corresponding key code value for each key will be displayed on the Web page.

If you need to determine which keyboard letter a user has pressed, you do not need to go through all 26 of the key code values. You can quickly return the letter character through the String method:

```
String.fromCharCode(key)
```

where *key* is the keycode value. For example, the expression

```
String.fromCharCode(65)
```

returns the character "a" because 65 is the keycode value of that character.

Because there are differences between the two event models in how they refer to event objects, you decide to create a cross-browser function named getKeyCode() to return the keycode value. Add this function to shop.js, along with your other cross-browser functions.

To create the getKeyCode() function:

1. If necessary, reopen the **shop.js** file in your text editor.

2. At the bottom of the file, insert the following function (see Figure 8-40):

```
function getKeyCode(e) {
    if (IE) return event.keyCode;
    else if (DOM) return e.keyCode;
}
```

Figure 8-40   The getKeyCode() function

```
function eventPositionY(e) {
    if (IE) return event.clientY;
    else if (DOM) return e.clientY;
}

function getKeyCode(e) {
    if (IE) return event.keyCode;
    else if (DOM) return e.keyCode;
}
```

3. Close **shop.js**, saving your changes.

Creating the keyDrag() Function

With all of the other functions in place, you can now write the keyDrag() function. This function is similar to the mouseDouble() function you just created for the double-click event. The difference is that, instead of setting the dragItem object equal to the event source, you'll use the key code values to determine which sales item to move. The code of the keyDrag() function is

```
function keyDrag(e) {
    dragItem = null;
    key=getKeyCode(e);
    if (key==65) dragItem=shop1;
    else if (key==66) dragItem=shop2;
    else if (key==67) dragItem=shop3;
    else if (key==68) dragItem=shop4;
    jumpIt();
}
```

This script starts by setting dragItem to a null value, which ensures that the function does not inherit a dragItem setting from any other event functions that have moved a sales item. Add this function to the games.htm file.

To insert the keyDrag() function:

1. Return to **games.htm** in your text editor.

2. Below the assignF() function, insert the following code (see Figure 8-41):

```
function keyDrag(e) {
    dragItem = null;
    key=getKeyCode(e);
    if (key==65) dragItem=shop1;
    else if (key==66) dragItem=shop2;
    else if (key==67) dragItem=shop3;
    else if (key==68) dragItem=shop4;
    jumpIt();
}
```

The keyDrag() function | Figure 8-41

```
function assignF(object) {
    object.ormousedown=grabIt;
    object.style.cursor="pointer";
    object.ondblclick=mouseDouble;
}

function keyDrag(e) {
    dragItem = null;
    key=getKeyCode(e);
    if (key==65) dragItem=shop1;
    else if (key==66) dragItem=shop2;
    else if (key==67) dragItem=shop3;
    else if (key==68) dragItem=shop4;
    jumpIt();
}
```

3. Close the file, saving your changes.

4. Reopen **games.htm** in your Web browser. Verify that when you press **a**, **b**, **c**, and **d** the four sales items are alternately added to and removed from the shopping cart.

   Trouble? In some browsers, the a, b, c, or d keys may be associated with browser commands.

Modifier Keys

In addition to keyboard characters, keyboards contain modifier keys. For a PC, the **modifier keys** are Ctrl, Alt, and Shift. Modifier keys pressed along with letter keys are used as keyboard shortcuts to menu commands in many programs. For example, in many browsers, holding down the Ctrl key while pressing p runs the Print command. You can create your own key combinations to run customized functions from the keyboard. However, in doing so you must be careful not to interfere with the key combinations already reserved by a user's browser; in case of a conflict, the browser might ignore your customized keyboard shortcut.

Both event models use the following properties of the event object to determine the state of the Alt, Ctrl, and Shift keys:

```
altKey;
ctrlKey;
shiftKey;
```

Each of these properties returns a Boolean value indicating whether the modifier key is being pressed. In addition, the DOM event model also supports the event object property

```
metaKey;
```

to determine whether the Meta key is being pressed. The Meta key is a key found on a UNIX workstation and is usually equivalent to the Alt key on PC keyboards or the Command key on Macintosh keyboards. You can use modifier keys along with other events occurring within a user's Web browser. For example, you could add the following conditional expression to the grabIt() function so that a customer can grab an item for dragging only when the Shift key is being pressed:

```
function grabIt(e) {
   if (event.shiftKey || e.shiftKey) {
   commands
   }
}
```

One other difference between Macintosh and PC browsers with respect to working with keystrokes, is that the Safari browser treats the occurence of striking the arrow, page down, or page up key on the keyboard as two keydown events. To treat any of these events as a single keystroke, add the command

```
return false;
```

to the function associated with the keydown event.

You've completed your work on the Web page, having created code for several different mouse and keyboard events in order to achieve the drag-and-drop shopping cart Pete wanted for the Games Etc. Web page. He will look over your document and get back to you with any further ideas or projects. You can close any open files in your text editor or browser.

Tips for Working with Events

- Create customized cross-browser functions that resolve the differences among the event models.
- Position any objects that will be dragged and dropped using inline styles prior to running the drag-and-drop commands.
- In a drag-and-drop application, provide users with additional visual feedback that an object is being moved, such as color changes and pointer changes.
- Capture keyboard and mouse events to make your Web page more accessible to users with disabilities.

Review

Session 8.3 Quick Check

1. What style declaration would you use to display an hourglass as the pointer? What is the equivalent JavaScript command to do this?
2. What property would you use to determine which mouse button was pressed during an event? Describe how the event models differ in their interpretations of the value returned by this property.
3. What event corresponds to a user pressing and holding down a keyboard key?
4. What event object property would you use to determine which key was pressed by a user?
5. What key code value is generated when a user presses the spacebar?
6. What event object property would you use to determine whether the user is pressing the Alt key?

Tutorial Summary

In this tutorial you learned how to work with the DOM and Internet Explorer event models to capture and respond to mouse and keyboard events. The first session examined different ways of attaching event handlers to your objects and scripts. It then explored the two main event models, examining how events are propagated through the document tree. The session concluded with the task of creating cross-browser functions to capture and release functions attached to events and objects. The second session looked at the properties of the event object and demonstrated how to determine the coordinates of an event and the object that initiated it. Using these properties, you created objects that could be dragged and dropped on the Web page. The third session displayed how to work with the double-click event and examined how to determine which mouse button was pressed by the user. The third session concluded with keyboard events. You learned how to capture a keyboard action, how to determine which key was pressed by the user, and to work with modifier keys.

Key Terms

bubbling phase	event model	keypress
capture phase	event object	keyup
DOM event model	Internet Explorer event	modifier key
event bubbling	model	target phase
event listener	keydown	

Review Assignments

Data files needed for this Review Assignment: events.js, functions.js, games.css, image1. jpg through image24.jpg, logo.jpg, makepuzzle.js, puzzle.jpg, puzztxt.htm

Pete has approved your design of the monthly specials page for the Games Etc. Web site. He now wants you to finish a Web page he's been working on that displays a sliding block puzzle. In a sliding block puzzle, the puzzle pieces are laid out in a grid with one blank space. The object of the puzzle is to use the blank space to move the pieces around in the puzzle until the puzzle image is restored. A preview of the page is shown in Figure 8-42. The puzzle is divided into a 5 × 5 grid, with each piece in the grid 60 pixels wide by 60 pixels high. Each piece is formatted as a separate div element with the image set as the tile's background. Starting at the upper left of the grid and moving right and then down, the div elements have the id names piece01, piece02, and so forth. The blank space is also a div element, with the id name "blank".

Figure 8-42

Pete wants this puzzle to work with both the mouse and the keyboard. He needs you to program the following actions:

- If a user clicks a piece to the left, right, above, or below the blank space, that piece should swap positions with the blank space.
- Pieces adjacent to the blank space should display the pointer cursor, while all other pieces should display the default cursor.
- One piece in the puzzle is highlighted with a red border. A user can highlight different pieces by pressing the arrow keys on the keyboard.
- If the highlighted piece is adjacent to the blank space, a user can swap the highlighted piece with the blank space by pressing the spacebar on the keyboard.

Pete has also provided several JavaScript files that contain functions you'll be able to use in your Web page. The makepuzzle.js file contains functions to create and scramble the puzzle pieces. The events.js file contains several functions that resolve the differences between the event models in working with the event object. The functions.js file contains functions to work with the properties of objects on the Web page. Figure 8-43 summarizes the functions that you'll use in this problem. Some of these functions should be familiar to you from this and previous tutorials.

Figure 8-43

File	Function	Description
makepuzzle.js	setUpBoard()	Sets up the initial layout of the puzzle
	scramble()	Scrambles the board layout
	colorPiece(object, z, color)	Changes the border color and z-index value of a puzzle piece where *object* is the piece, *z* is the new z-index value, and *color* is the new color.
events.js	applyEventF(obj,ename,fname,cap)	Attaches an event handler for an event *ename* occurring in an object *obj*, attaching the function *fname* to it.
	removeEventF(obj,ename,fname,cap)	Removes an event handler from an object
	eventSource(e)	Returns the source of an event *e*
	getKeyCode(e)	Returns the keycode of a keyboard event *e*
functions.js	getDIV(x,y)	Returns the div element that contains the coordinates (x, y)
	swapIt(object1, object2)	Swaps the positions of *object1* and *object2*
	getXCoord(object) getYCoord(object)	Returns the x and y coordinate of *object*

To create the sliding block puzzle:

1. Use your text editor to open the **puzztxt.htm** file from the tutorial.08/review folder. Enter *your name* and *the date* in the comment section and save the file as **puzzle.htm**. Examine the contents of the file to become familiar with the order form and its elements. Also take some time to study the contents of the **functions.js**, **events.js**, and **makepuzzle.js** files to understand the customized functions you'll use in this assignment.

2. If necessary, return to the **puzzle.htm** file in your text editor. Within the init() function in the embedded script element, add the following commands:

   a. Create four variables named pieceLeft, pieceTop, pieceRight, and pieceBottom. These variables will reference the four pieces adjacent to the blank space. Set the initial value of the pieceLeft variable equal to the div element with the id "piece24". Set the initial value of the pieceTop variable equal to the div element with the id "piece20". Set the initial values of pieceRight and pieceBottom to null.

   b. Create a variable named blankPiece that represents the blank space in the puzzle. Set the value of the blankPiece variable equal to the div element with the id "blank".

   c. Call the watchPiece() function using pieceLeft as the parameter value. Call the watchPiece() function again using pieceTop as the parameter value.

3. Below the init() function, insert the watchPiece() function. The purpose of this function is to watch one of the pieces for the click event. The function has a single parameter named object. Add the following commands to the function:

   a. Use the applyEventF() function to run the mouseSwap function when the click event occurs within the object (you'll create the mouseSwap() function shortly). Set the capture parameter to false.

   b. Change the cursor style of the object to "pointer".

4. Create another function named ignorePiece(). This function is similar to the watch-Piece() function except that it detaches the click event from the piece object. Add the following commands to the function:

    a. Use the removeEventF() function to ignore the mouseSwap function when the click event occurs within the object. Set the capture parameter to false.

    b. Change the cursor style of the object to "default".

5. Add the mouseSwap() function. The purpose of this function is to swap the position of a piece clicked in the puzzle with the blank space. The mouseSwap() function has a single parameter, e, which represents the event object. Add the following commands to the function:

    a. Create a variable named pieceClicked which is equal to the source of the event. (*Hint*: Use the eventSource() function from the events.js file.)

    b. Use the swapIt() function to swap the positions of pieceClicked and blankPiece.

    c. Call the resetPieces() function.

6. Insert the resetPieces() function. The purpose of this function is to remove the event handlers from the pieces that were formerly adjacent to the blank space (now that the blank space has been moved, you will have to determine where the adjacent pieces are now located). There are no parameters for this function. Add the following commands:

    a. If pieceLeft is not equal to null, call the ignorePiece() function using pieceLeft as the parameter value. Repeat this step for the pieceTop, pieceRight, and pieceBottom variables.

    b. Call the findNewPieces() function.

7. Insert the findNewPieces() function. The purpose of this function is to determine which four pieces are now adjacent to the blank space. There are no parameters for this function. Add the following commands:

    a. Use the getXCoord() and getYCoord() functions to determine the x and y coordinates of the blankPiece. Store the values returned by these functions in variables named x and y respectively.

    b. Use the getDIV() function to locate the piece to the left of the blank space. The first parameter value is equal to x – 30. The second parameter value is equal to y + 30. Store the object returned by the getDIV() function in the pieceLeft variable.

    c. If pieceLeft is not equal to null (indicating there is a piece to the left of the blank space), call the watchPiece() function using pieceLeft as the parameter value.

    d. Repeat Steps b and c for the pieceTop, pieceRight, and pieceBottom variables. The coordinates for pieceTop should be (x + 30, y – 30); for pieceRight the coordinates are (x + 90, y + 30); and for pieceBottom the coordinates are (x + 30, y + 90).

8. Save your changes to the file. Open **puzzle.htm** in your Web browser and verify (a) that only pieces adjacent to the blank space display the pointer cursor; and (b) that clicking a piece adjacent to the blank space swaps the positions of the piece and the blank space.

9. Return to **puzzle.htm** in your text editor. Next you'll create the keyboard interface for the puzzle. Within the init() function add the following commands:

   a. Apply an event handler to the document that runs the function keyOnPiece() in response to a keydown event.

   b. Create a variable named keyPiece that represents the piece highlighted in the puzzle. Set the initial value to the div element with the id name "piece01".

   c. Use the colorPiece() function to set the z-index value of keyPiece to 2 and the border color to red.

10. Insert the function keyOnPiece(). The purpose of this function is to either move the highlighted piece or swap it with the blank space. The function has a single parameter, e, representing the event object. Add the following commands:

    a. Use the getKeyCode() function to return the key code value of the event. Store the value in a variable named key.

    b. If the left arrow key has been pressed, call the function moveKeyPiece() with the parameter value "left". (*Hint*: Refer to Figure 8-39 to determine the key code value for the left arrow key.)

    c. Repeat the previous step for the up, right, and down arrows. For the up arrow, call the moveKeyPiece() function with a parameter value of "up"; for the right arrow the parameter value is "right"; and for the down arrow the parameter value is "down".

    d. Otherwise, if the key value indicates that the spacebar has been pressed, run the swapKeyPiece() function.

    e. Return the value false from the function so that the Safari browser treats the arrow keys as single keystrokes.

11. Insert the function moveKeyPiece(). The purpose of this function is to move the highlighting from one piece to another. The function has a single parameter named direction. Add the following commands to the function:

    a. Create a variable named nextKeyPiece. This variable represents the next piece that will be highlighted in the puzzle. Set the initial value of nextKeyPiece to null.

    b. Use the getXCoord() and getYCoord() functions to retrieve the (x,y) coordinates of keyPiece. Store these values in variables named x and y respectively.

    c. If direction equals "left", use the getDIV() function to determine the position of the next piece to be highlighted. Use parameter values of x – 30, and y + 30. Store the object returned by the getDIV() function in the nextKeyPiece variable.

    d. Repeat the previous step for direction values equal to "up", "right", and "down". For "up" the coordinates of the next piece are (x + 30, y – 30); for "right" the coordinates are (x + 90, y + 30); and for "down" the coordinates are (x + 30, y + 90).

    e. If nextKeyPiece is not equal to null (meaning that there is a piece adjacent to the current piece in the direction indicated), then: (1) Call the colorPiece() function to change the z-index of keyPiece to 1 and the border color to "white"; (2) Call the colorPiece() function to change the z-index of nextKeyPiece to 2 and the border color to "red"; (3) Change the value of keyPiece to nextKeyPiece.

12. Insert the function swapKeyPiece(). The purpose of this function is to swap the high-lighted piece with the blank space, if they are adjacent. There are no parameters for this function. Add the following commands:

   a. Use the getXCoord() and getYCoord() functions to retrieve the (x,y) coordinates of keyPiece. Store these values in variables named x and y respectively.

   b. Call the getDIV() function using the parameter values x − 30 and y + 30. If the object returned by this function is equal to blankPiece, then call the swapIt() function to swap the positions of keyPiece and blankPiece.

   c. Repeat the previous step with the following coordinates: (x + 30, y − 30), (x + 90, y + 30), and (x + 30, y + 90). You must put the four If statements in an If...Else conditional structure to ensure that only one swap occurs.

   d. Call the resetPieces() function.

13. Save your changes to the file and reopen **puzzle.htm** in your Web browser. Verify that (a) pressing the arrow keys moves the highlighting from one piece to another; and (b) that pressing the spacebar when the highlighted piece is next to the blank space swaps the position of the two.

14. Submit your completed assignment to your instructor. You may try to scramble the puzzle and solve it, but it is not necessary to complete the assignment.

Apply

Use the skills you learned to create a drag-and-drop preference list

Case Problem 1

Data files needed for this Case Problem: bkgrnd.jpg, links.jpg, logo.jpg, styles.css, survey.js, survtxt.htm

Online Market Surveys   Derek Mahnaz organizes the Online Market Survey, a Web site that reports consumer preferences and opinions. Derek has asked you to create a Web page in which consumers can list their preferences for computer manufacturers. Derek envisions the Web page listing the manufacturers in separate boxes. Users would then be able to drag and drop the boxes in order of preference, with the computer manufacturers they prefer most at the top, and those least preferred at the bottom. Figure 8-44 shows a preview of Derek's page.

Figure 8-44

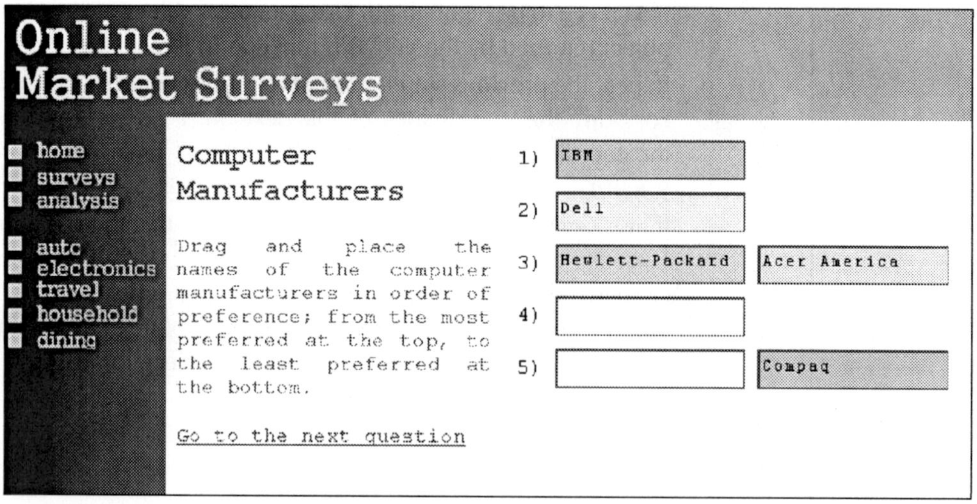

Each of the five computer manufacturer names has been placed in a separate div element, with id names of Store1 through Store5. Derek has also provided a file, survey.js, that includes some functions of use to you. The placeIt() function places objects at specific coordinates on the page. The getXCoord() and getYCoord() functions return the x and y coordinates of a page object. A link to this file has already been added to Derek's Web page.

To complete the Market Survey page:

1. Use your text editor to open the **survtxt.htm** file from the tutorial.08/case1 folder. Enter *your name* and *the date* in the comment section and save the file as **survey.htm**.

2. In the embedded script element, insert the following global variables:
   a. store, startX, startY, diffX, diffY, and maxZ. Set the initial value of maxZ to 2.
   b. Add two more global variables: one that returns a Boolean value indicating whether the user's browser supports the Internet Explorer event model, and the other that returns a Boolean value indicating whether the browser supports the DOM event model.

3. Add the following five cross-browser functions that support both event models: (a) a function to determine the source of events occurring in the Web page; (b) a function to determine the x-coordinate of the event; (c) a function to determine the y-coordinate of the event; (d) a function to attach or listen for an event occurring within an object and apply a function to that event; and (e) a function to remove an attached event function from an object.

4. Create a function named setEvents(). In this function, add event handlers to the Store1 through Store5 elements, running the selectStore() function when a user depresses the mouse button within each element.

5. Create the selectStore() function to grab a store element in preparation for dragging it across the Web page. The function should have a single parameter, e. Add the following commands to the function:
   a. Set the Store variable equal to the source of the event. Set startX equal to the x-coordinate of the Store object and startY equal to the y-coordinate of the Store object.
   b. Set mouseX equal to the x-coordinate of the event object and mouseY equal to the y-coordinate of the event object. Subtract startX from mouseX and store the difference in a variable named diffX. Subtract startY from mouseY and store the difference in diffY.
   c. Ensure that the dragged store is always on top by increasing the value of maxZ by 1 and changing the z-index value of the Store object to maxZ.
   d. Attach the moveStore() function to the Store object and run it in response to a mousemove event. Attach the dropStore() function to the Store object, running it in response to a mouseup event. Use event bubbling as the propagation method for both functions.

6. Create the moveStore() function to enable moving the Store object across the page alongside the mouse pointer. The function has a single parameter, e, representing the event object. Add the following commands:
   a. Store the x-coordinate of the event in the variable mouseX. Store the y-coordinate of the event in mouseY.
   b. Use the placeIt() function to place the Store object at the page coordinates (mouseX-diffX, mouseY-diffY).

7. Create the dropStore() function to enable dropping the Store object on the page. The function has a single parameter, e, for the event object. Add the following commands:

   a. Detach the moveStore() function from the Store object in the case of a mouse-move event.

   b. Store the current x-coordinate of the Store object in a variable named x. Store the y-coordinate of the Store object in a variable named y.

   c. Derek wants the Store object to line up neatly within the blank boxes on the page. Thus, if x falls in the range 440–590 and y falls in the range 100–130, use the placeIt() function to place the Store object at the page coordinates (440, 100). Repeat this for the other four blank boxes. If x falls in the range 440–590 and y lies within 140–170, move Store to (440,140). If x falls in the range 440–590 and y lies within 180–210, move Store to (440, 180). If x lies within 440–590 and y lies within 220–250, move Store to (440, 220). If x lies within 440–590 and y lies within 260–290, move Store to (440, 260). Otherwise, do nothing.

8. Create a function named cancelSelect() that returns the Boolean value false. Add an event handler to the setEvents() function to run the cancelSelect() function in response to the start of text selection within the document.

9. Add an event handler to the body element, running the setEvents() function when the page is loaded.

10. For the inline styles of the Store1 through Store5 div elements, add a style to change the appearance of the cursor to "pointer".

11. Save your changes to the file and load **survey.htm** in your Web browser. Verify that you can drag and drop the five computer manufacturer boxes to the boxes in the preference list and that the manufacturer names line up within the boxes. Verify that each of the manufacturer boxes displays the pointer cursor.

12. Submit your completed Web site to your instructor.

Case Problem 2

Data files needed for this Case Problem: back.jpg, badgtxt.htm, bar.jpg, corner.jpg, functions.js, image0.jpg through image9.jpg, links.jpg, logo.jpg, styles.css

Badger Aviation   Wayne Statz is the president and owner of Badger Aviation, an aviation company specializing in tours, charters, lessons, and shuttles in southern Wisconsin. He's hired you to update the company's Web page. One of the pages you'll work with contains a slideshow from one of Badger Aviation's tours of the area. Wayne would like you to create a horizontal scrollbar for the slideshow that users can navigate with either the mouse or the keyboard. Figure 8-45 shows a preview of the page you'll create for Wayne.

Figure 8-45

Much of the layout has been done for you. Your job is to create the array of images for the slideshow and program the operation of the scrollbar. The scroll button in the scroll-bar has been stored in the Web page as a div element with the id name "button". An external JavaScript file named functions.js contains two functions that you can use in completing this Web page: the placeIt() function places objects at specified coordinates on the page and the getXCoord() function contains the x-coordinate of an object on the page. You'll have to create any other functions that you need.

To complete the Badger Aviation slideshow:

1. Use your text editor to open the **badgtxt.htm** file from the tutorial.08/case2 folder. Enter *your name* and *the date* in the comment section and save the file as **badger.htm**.

2. Add an embedded script element to the document head. Within the script element do the following:

   a. Create an image array named slide. Populate the array with the 10 image files image0.jpg through image9.jpg.

   b. Create two global variables: one that indicates whether a user's browser supports the Internet Explorer event model and another that indicates whether the browser supports the DOM event model.

3. Create the following four cross-browser event functions: (a) one to attach a function to an object when an event occurs; (b) one to remove an attached event function from an object; (c) one to return the x-coordinate of an event; and (d) one to return the key code value of a keyboard event.

4. Create a function named setup() to set up the page for the operation of the horizontal scrollbar. Add the following commands to the function:
   a. Create a variable named scrollbutton that references the element with the id "button".
   b. Apply a mousedown event handler to the scrollbutton object that runs the grabIt() function.
   c. Apply a selectstart event handler to the document object that runs the stopSelect() function.
   d. Apply a keydown event handler to the document that runs the keyShow() function.
5. Create the stopSelect() function that returns the value false.
6. Create the grabIt() function used to grab the scrollbar button. The function has a single parameter, e, the event object. Add the following commands to the function:
   a. Set the x-coordinate of the event in a variable named mouseX.
   b. Calculate the difference between the mouseX and the x-coordinate of the scrollbutton object and store the value in the diffX variable.
   c. Attach or listen for the mousemove event in the scrollbutton object, running the moveIt() function in response. Set the capture parameter to "false".
   d. Attach or listen for the mouseup event in the scrollbutton object, running the dropIt() function in response. Set the capture parameter to "false".
7. Create the moveIt() function. The function has a single parameter: the event object e. Add the following commands:
   a. Store the current x-coordinate of the event in the mouseX variable.
   b. Subtract diffX from the mouseX variable and store the difference in a variable named buttonposX. This represents the current horizontal position of the scrollbar button.
   c. The scrollbar button should be prohibited from being dragged off the scrollbar. To do this, the x-coordinate of the button should always remain between 20 and 299. If the value of buttonposX is less than 20, set its value to 20. If the value of buttonposX is greater than 299, set its value to 299.
   d. Use the placeIt() function to place the scrollbutton object. The x-coordinate should be equal to buttonposX and the y-coordinate should be equal to 6.
   e. Call the function showImage() using buttonposX as the parameter value. You'll create this function later.
8. Create the dropIt() function. The function should detach the moveIt() function from the mousemove event occurring in the scrollbutton object.
9. Create the keyShow() function. The purpose of this function is to move the scrollbar button using the left and right arrows on the keyboard. The function has a single parameter, e, equal to the event object. Add the following commands to the function:
   a. Store the key code value of the pressed keyboard button in a variable named key.
   b. Store the current x-coordinate of the scrollbutton object in the buttonposX variable.
   c. If the user has pressed the left arrow key, decrease the value of the buttonposX variable by 31. If the user has pressed the right arrow key, increase the value of buttonposX by 31.
   d. If the value of buttonposX is less than 20, set its value to 20. If the value of buttonposX is greater than 299, set its value to 299.

    e. Place the scrollbutton object at the coordinates (*buttonposX*, 6).

    f. Call the function showImage() using buttonposX as the parameter value.

    g. Return the value false from the function so that the Safari browser treats the arrow keys as single keystrokes.

10. Create the showImage() function. The purpose of this function is to determine which of the 10 images to display based on the horizontal position of the scrollbar button. The x-coordinate of the scrollbar button ranges from 20 to 299, while the index numbers of images in the slide array range from 0 to 9. One aspect of this function is to convert the x-coordinate values into a corresponding index number. The function has a single parameter named x. Add the following commands to the function:

    a. Subtract 20 from the value of x and divide that difference by 31. Round the calculated value down to the next lowest integer and store the result in a variable named i. (*Hint*: Use the Math.floor() function to round the value down.) This converts the x-coordinate range into an index number.

    b. Change the source of the "photo" image in the Web document to the source of the slide[i] image.

11. Add an event handler to the body element that runs the setup() function when the page loads.

12. Add a cursor style to the inline style for the "button" element that sets the cursor image to "pointer".

13. Save your changes to the file and open **badger.htm** in your Web browser. Verify that you can navigate through the slideshow using either your mouse button or the left/right arrows on your keyboard.

14. Submit your completed Web site to your instructor.

Challenge

Explore how to create a crossword-style puzzle

Case Problem 3

Data files needed for this Case Problem: across.gif, crosstxt.htm, down.gif, functions.js, makepuzzle.js, pcglogo.jpg, styles.css

Park City Gazette   The *Park City Gazette*, edited by Kevin Webber, is the weekly newspaper of Park City, Colorado. In addition to its print offerings, the newspaper has an online version for distribution on the Web. The paper is known for its puzzles and games, so recently Kevin decided to include a puzzle in the online edition of the *Gazette*.

Kevin would like users to be able to type their answers directly into the puzzle. They should be able to navigate the puzzle by pressing the arrow keys on their keyboard, and typing a letter should move a user to the next cell. A user should also be able to toggle whether typing is entered vertically or horizontally by pressing the spacebar on the keyboard.

The current cell in the puzzle should be displayed with a yellow background. If a user enters a correct letter into a cell, the background should be changed to light green. If an incorrect letter is entered, a light red background should be displayed. Blank puzzle cells should be displayed with a white background. Figure 8-46 shows a preview of a partially completed puzzle with some correct and incorrect answers.

Figure 8-46

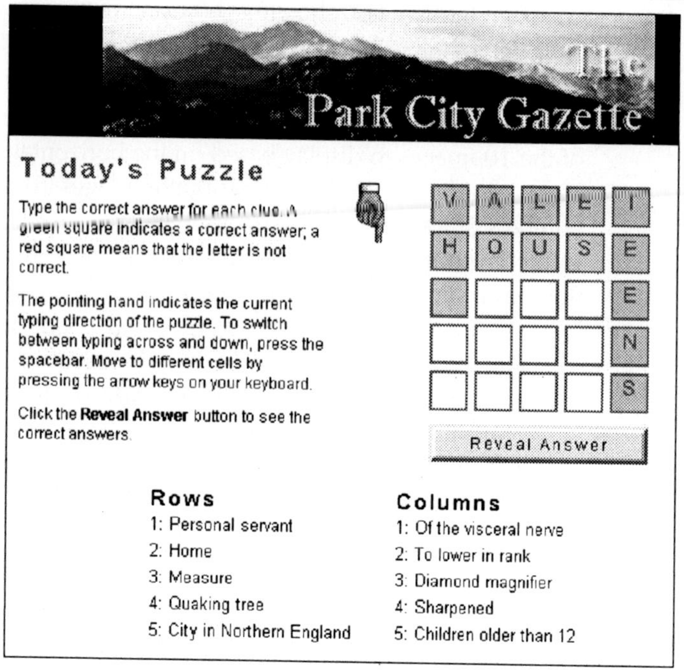

Each of the 25 cells in the puzzle is stored in a separate div element with the id "gridxy", where x represents the row number and y represents the column number. The row and column numbers start with 0 and go up to the number 4. Thus, the first cell in the puzzle has the id value "grid00", the cell in the first row and second column has the id value "grid01", and so forth. The last cell in the puzzle has an id value of "grid44". You'll need to use this information to place the letters that users type in the correct cells in the puzzle.

One of Kevin's assistants has already entered the HTML code for the puzzle page and has also produced some JavaScript code to generate the puzzle grid and its solution. These functions are in an external JavaScript file named makepuzzle.js. In addition to this file, Kevin's assistant has also created an external JavaScript file named functions.js that contains a function named writeText(*object*, *text*), which writes a text string *text* into an *object* on the Web page. You'll use this function to insert a user's guesses into the correct puzzle cells. The correct answer to the puzzle is stored in an array named "words".

To complete the *Park City Gazette* puzzle:

1. Use your text editor to open the **crosstxt.htm** file from the tutorial.08/case3 folder. Enter **your name** and **the date** in the comment section and save the file as **cross.htm**.

2. Above the init() function, create the following global variables:
   a. An image array named handImage. Set the source of the first image in the array to the across.gif file; set the source of the second image to the down.gif file.
   b. A variable that determines whether the user's browser supports the IE event model; create another variable that determines whether the browser supports the DOM event model.
   c. A variable named currentX that indicates the current row number. Set its initial value to 0. Create a variable named currentY that indicates the current column. Set its initial value to 0 as well.

d. A variable named currentCell that will be used to point to the currently high-lighted cell in the puzzle. Create a variable named currentColor that stores the color of the current cell. Set its initial value to "white".

e. A Boolean variable named across that indicates the direction of the user's typing (either across or down the puzzle grid). Set its initial value to true to indicate that letters are entered in the across direction.

f. A variable named keyNum that will be used to store the key code number of a pressed key. Do not set an initial value for this variable.

3. Within the init() function, add the following commands:

a. Set the currentCell variable equal to the element with the id "grid00". Change the background color of the currentCell object to yellow.

b. Add an event handler to the document object that runs the getKey() function when a user presses a key.

4. Add the function getKey(). The purpose of this function is to capture the key code of the pressed key and then to call the appropriate function for that key. The function has a single parameter, the event object e. Add the following commands to the function:

a. Retrieve the key code value of the pressed key and store it in the variable keyNum.

b. If the user pressed the spacebar, run the toggleDirection() function.

c. If the user pressed one of the four arrow keys, run the moveCursor() function.

d. Otherwise, run the writeGuess() function.

e. Return the value false from the function so that the Safari browser treats the arrow keys as single keystrokes.

5. Directly below the getKey() function, create the toggleDirection() function. The pur-pose of this function is to allow a user to press the spacebar to toggle the typing direction from across to down and vice versa. It will also swap the pointing hand image on the page to match the typing direction. To complete this function:

a. If the value of the across variable is true, then: (1) Change the across value to false; (2) Change the source of the second image in the document to the source of the second image in the handImage array.

b. If the value of the across variable is false, then: (1) Change the across value to true; (2) Change the source of the second image in the document to the source of the first image in the handImage array.

6. Below the toggleDirection() function, create the following functions, which will be used to update the values of the currentX and currentY variables as the cursor moves around the puzzle grid:

a. moveLeft()—In this function, decrease the value of the currentX variable by 1. If currentX is less than 0, change its value to 4.

b. moveRight()—Increase the value of currentX by 1. If currentX is greater than 4, change its value to 0.

c. moveUp()—Decrease the value of the currentY variable by 1. If currentY is less than 0, change its value to 4.

d. moveDown()—Increase the value of currentY by 1. If currentY is greater than 4, change its value to 0.

7. Directly below these four functions, create a function named moveCursor(). The pur-pose of this function is to move the active cell in response to a user pressing the arrow keys on the keyboard. Add the following commands to the function:

a. Set the background color of currentCell to the value of the currentColor variable.

b. If the value of the keyNum variable indicates that the user pressed the left arrow key, call the moveLeft() function. If the user pressed the up arrow key, call the moveUp() function. If the user pressed the right arrow key, call the moveRight() function. If the user pressed the down arrow key, call the moveDown() function.

c. Change currentCell to the element whose id is "gridxy" where x is the value of currentX and y is the value of currentY.

d. Store the current background color of currentCell in the currentColor variable.

e. Change the background color of currentCell to yellow.

Explore

8. Create a function named "writeGuess()". The purpose of this function is to write the letter typed by the user into the current cell and then to change the background color of that cell to indicate whether the user typed the correct letter. After the letter has been written, the current cell should move either to the right or down, depending on the typing direction (as indicated in the across variable). The function should, therefore, do the following:

Explore

Explore

a. Use the fromCharCode() String method to extract the letter corresponding to the value of the keyNum variable. Store the letter in a variable named outChar.

b. Use the toUpperCase() string method to change the outChar variable to an uppercase letter.

c. Use the writeText() function to write outChar to the current cell.

d. If the value of outChar is correct, change the background color of the current cell to "lightgreen". (*Hint*: To test whether the outChar letter is correct, compare outChar's value to the value of the words array item words[$y * 5 + x$] where y is the value of the current column and x is the value of the current row.) If the value is not correct, change the background color of the current cell to pink.

e. If the value of the across variable is true, then move the location of the current cell to the right using the moveRight() function; otherwise, call the moveDown() function to move down.

f. Point the currentCell object to the element with the id "gridxy" where x is the value of the currentX variable and y is the value of the currentY variable. Store the background color of currentCell in the currentColor variable. Change the background color of currentCell to yellow.

9. Add an event handler to the body element that runs the init() function when the page is loaded.

10. Add an event handler to the reveal element that runs the showAns() function when the element is clicked. (The showAns() function is a function in the makepuzzle.js file that displays the correct answer to the puzzle.) Add an inline style to the reveal element that changes the cursor style to "pointer".

11. Save your changes to the file and load the cross.htm file in your Web browser. Verify that (a) when you type letters on the keyboard, those letters are displayed in the puzzle grid; (b) the current cell is displayed with a yellow background; (c) correct letters are displayed with a light green background; (d) incorrect letters are displayed with a pink background; (e) pressing the arrow keys moves the current cell around the puzzle grid; (f) pressing the spacebar toggles the typing direction and swaps the pointing hand image; and (g) clicking **Reveal Answer** reveals the puzzle solution. (*Note*: The Opera browser will intercept keystrokes for the H and P letters and attempt to display the history list and printer dialog box. You can ignore these incidents and continue to type in the puzzle solution.)

12. Submit the completed Web site to your instructor.

Create

Create a drag-and-drop shopping cart

Case Problem 4

Data files needed for this Case Problem: *none supplied*

Produce World   Produce World, a local grocery store, is making some of its products available on the World Wide Web. Customers will be able to visit the Web site and select items for purchase. Their selections will be sent to the store, where they will be gathered and packaged for pickup by the customer. Steve Adronski, a manager at Produce World, has asked for your help in creating a Web page that will feature a drag-and-drop shopping cart. The page will display the following items for purchase:

- Bananas at $1.60/bunch
- Red Delicious Apples at $2.80/bag
- Georgia Peaches at $1.90/bag
- Blueberries at $1.49/carton
- Strawberries at $2.49/carton
- Cantaloupe at $2.00/piece
- Red Seedless Grapes at $1.59/bag
- Green Seedless Grapes at $1.59/bag

The design of the shopping cart is up to you. You can add inline graphics for each of the produce items, if you would like to locate the appropriate clip art. You may also want to create a distinctive logo for Produce World.

To complete this assignment:

1. Create a file named **produce.htm** that contains the layout and content of your Web page.
2. Create an external JavaScript file named **produce.js** that contains any specialized JavaScript functions you need for your page.
3. Add drag-and-drop capability to the produce items in the produce.htm file.
4. Display a helpful mouse cursor symbol when the user selects produce to drag.
5. If a customer fails to drop a selected produce item in the shopping cart, have the item snap back to its original spot on the page.
6. Create a button named "Total" on the page that tallies up the total number of items selected and the total cost, and then displays that information in an alert dialog box when the Total button is clicked.
7. Submit the completed Web site to your instructor.

Review

Quick Check Answers

Session 8.1

1. document.getElementById("Total").onmousedown=CalcTotal;
2. <script type="text/javacript" for="Total" event="onclick"> ... </script>
3. From the bottom of the object hierarchy to the top.
4. document.getElementById("Total").attachEvent("onclick",CalcTotal);
5. event.cancelBubble = true;
6. Events are propagated from the top of the hierarchy during the capture phase, down to the event's target, and then back up the hierarchy during the bubbling phase.
7. document.getElementById("Total").addEventListener("click",CalcTotal, *capture*) where *capture* is either true (to listen for the event in the capture phase) or false (to listen for the event in the bubbling phase).

8. *evt*.stopPropagation()

where *evt* is the event object.

Session 8.2

1. IE event model: event or *windowObject*.event

   DOM event model: the parameter of the event function
2. type
3. screenX and screenY
4. clientX and clientY
5. Increase the z-index of the object to be the maximum on the page.
6. return false;

Session 8.3

1. cursor: wait

   object.style.cursor = "wait";
2. button

   The IE event model uses 1=left, 2=middle, 4=right

   The DOM event model uses 0=left, 1=middle, 2=right
3. keydown
4. keyCode
5. 32
6. altKey

Objectives

Working with Cookies

Managing Data in a Web Site Using JavaScript Cookies

Case

Patti's Potpourri

Patti Marie runs a small home-based business called Patti's Potpourri, selling collectibles and other small items. Recently she launched a Web site that she built herself. The Web site gives general information about her business and displays some of the products she sells. She would also like her site to allow users to purchase products online. However, she has found that she doesn't have the time to program the Web site for these tasks while she is running her business. Patti has hired you to enhance the site for online shopping and has several tasks she needs you to accomplish for her. She would like returning customers to receive a personal welcome on the home page when they open the site. She would also like to enable online shopping on her existing products page. In addition, Patti wants to make sure that her site allows customers to review their order forms before they are submitted. You'll add these functions to Patti's Web site by creating and manipulating JavaScript cookies.

Student Data Files

▼tutorial.09

  ▽ **tutorial folder**

    patti_accounttxt.htm
    patti_carttxt.htm
    patti_checkouttxt.htm
    patti_confirmtxt.htm
    patti_hometxt.htm
    patti_trinketstxt.htm
    pattitxt.js
    + 11 graphic files
    + 1 style sheet

  ▽ **review folder**

    patti_account2txt.htm
    patti2txt.js
    + 1 style sheet
    + 3 graphic files

  ▽ **case1 folder**

    mc_carverfeedbacktxt.htm
    mc_carvertxt.htm
    mc_carvertxt.js
    + 1 style sheet
    + 1 graphic file

Session 9.1

Introducing Cookies

You meet with Patti to discuss her plans for updating her Web site. As the two of you look over her site together, she describes the online shopping features that she envisions for customers who visit her Web site. Open Patti's home page now.

To view Patti's existing Web site:

1. With your text editor, open the files **patti_accounttxt.htm**, **patti_carttxt.htm**, **patti_checkouttxt.htm**, **patti_confirmtxt.htm**, **patti_hometxt.htm**, **patti_trinketstxt.htm**, and **pattitxt.js**; enter *your name* and *the date* in the comment section of each file; and save the files as **patti_account.htm**, **patti_cart.htm**, **patti_checkout.htm**, **patti_confirm.htm**, **patti_home.htm**, **patti_trinkets.htm**, and **patti.js** respectively.

2. Briefly scan each file's code to become familiar with it, then close each file.

3. Open **patti_home.htm** in your browser (see Figure 9-1).

   Trouble? Some of the toolbar links lead to pages that have not yet been created, and are thus not functional.

The home page of Patti's Web site

Figure 9-1

Patti's Potpourri

Username:

Password:

[Log In]

Get a User ID

Home

Trinkets

Seasonal Items

Gift Ideas

Wooden Bowls

Cart 🛒

Contact Us

Check out our new and featured items below!

This Week's Featured Item!

This elegant, hand crafted vase is available for a limited time at Patti's Potpourri. Add a touch of class to your table setting or room. A limited edition collector's item.

[Buy Now!]

New at Patti's Potpourri!

Patti has just added new products to her Trinkets line. This keepsake box is perfect for jewelry and small collectibles. A durable, beautiful gift for that special someone in your life.

[Buy Now!]

Patti wants all users to be able to freely navigate her product listings and purchase her products. She also wants to enable users to create accounts to personalize some of the site's pages and automatically enter some user information when a user is making a purchase. Figure 9-2 describes the functions that Patti has planned for each of the pages she has created for her site.

Functions of Patti's Web pages

Figure 9-2

File	Description
patti_account.htm	Contains a form enabling user to create an account
patti_cart.htm	Displays items that user has selected for purchase
patti_checkout.htm	Shows order summary and allows user to enter shipping and billing information
patti_confirm.htm	Summarizes items ordered, shipping information, and billing information, and allows user to make changes or submit order
patti_home.htm	Home page, providing navigation links and site overview
patti_trinkets.htm	Photos and descriptions of products in Patti's trinkets collection, with associated form elements allowing user to add items to the shopping cart

The functionality that Patti wants to add to her Web site is commonly known as an **online shopping cart**, which is an electronic means for users to select items that they wish to purchase online.

Developing a Shopping Cart Application

Most of the shopping carts on Web sites today use databases as their back ends. A Web site's **back end** is the mechanism that helps the site function behind the scenes, without being visible to users who visit the site. In tandem with a database, a shopping cart's back end commonly incorporates a server-side scripting language to move data from a client's browser to a permanent storage facility, such as a database on a server.

Patti has brought you on to develop her Web site's **front end**, which is the visible part of a Web site that users see and interact with when visiting and performing transactions. Patti's Web site is a very small one that will conduct a very limited number of transactions. Her budget is also very limited, and she needs a very simple and inexpensive means of getting her Web site to support online transactions. You will build the front-end aspects of the shopping cart application for Patti's Web site, ensuring that they will support a back end when it is built later.

When developing a shopping cart application, you need to start by deciding which type of shopping cart you want to create. One option is to build a server-side shopping cart using a database application or a text file to store items. A **server-side shopping cart** is a shopping cart application that is controlled through a server. All items added to the shopping cart, including the quantity and price of each item, are stored in a program on a server. Generally, server-side shopping cart applications are managed using a database. Many of the large shopping cart applications on the Internet use this type of application.

Another option is to build a client-side shopping cart using cookies. A **client-side shopping cart** is an application that is controlled through a user's browser via JavaScript. While a client-side shopping cart is not an option for a large Web-based business such as amazon.com or eBay, it is an excellent option when working with a small Web site such as Patti's. With a client-side shopping cart, all of the processing required to support the shopping cart is done in a client's browser, meaning that you are not wasting the resources of a powerful server to handle extremely minor processing tasks. This frees the server to handle the major tasks it is designed for, such as major e-commerce transactions. Another advantage to a client-side shopping cart is that it keeps information from being vulnerable while a user is conducting transactions. As users add items to their shopping carts, the data is collected by the application. The transmission of this data to a server occurs only after a user is done shopping. Because the data is transmitted once, it minimizes the chances that the data will be intercepted by a hacker or by some other malicious means. Figure 9-3 illustrates differences in the flow of data between client-side and server-side shopping cart applications.

Figure 9-3 ▶ **Client-side and server-side shopping cart applications**

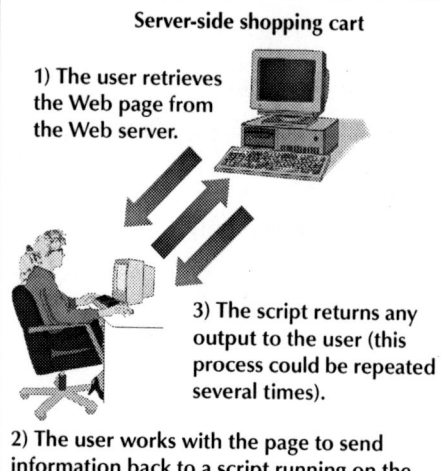

Server-side shopping cart

1) The user retrieves the Web page from the Web server.

3) The script returns any output to the user (this process could be repeated several times).

2) The user works with the page to send information back to a script running on the server.

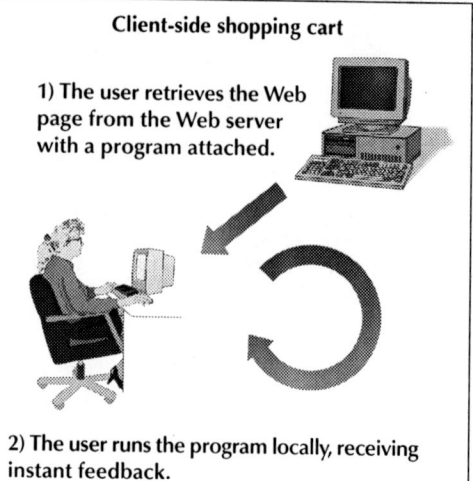

Client-side shopping cart

1) The user retrieves the Web page from the Web server with a program attached.

2) The user runs the program locally, receiving instant feedback.

Building a server-side shopping cart is an expensive proposition because of the time and technical expertise that it requires. A client-side cart, by contrast, is an affordable alternative. In addition to costing less to develop, a client-side application reduces the costs of building and supporting the server-side application needed to move and permanently store the cart's contents. Given Patti's budget limitations and the simplicity of her Web site, you and Patti agree that developing a client-side shopping cart application makes the most sense.

To create a client-side shopping cart, you need to understand how to work with JavaScript cookies.

Understanding Cookies

Each visit to a Web page by a user is known as a **session**. By default, no information is retained from one session to another, even when the user is the same. In some cases, however, it's important to carry information over from one session for use in another session. In an online shopping Web page, this often includes information on a user's account and purchasing history. To preserve information from one session to another, Web programmers use cookies. A **cookie** is a text file that stores data from a user's interaction with a specific Web site. Each cookie stores information from a particular session. Cookies were originally conceived and developed by Netscape as a workaround to allow for features not supported by HTTP, the protocol that most Web pages use. HTTP is known as a **stateless** protocol, meaning that it provides no way to track information that a user may have provided when moving from one Web page to another. Cookies implement this functionality by storing information that a user has provided in a simple file on the user's hard drive.

Cookies are **persistent**, meaning that they remain active between sessions and even after users turn off their computers. A cookie cannot be larger than 4 KB in size, and a browser's memory cannot hold more than 20 cookies from one Web site. In addition, a browser can store a maximum of 300 cookies from various Web sites. When a browser receives a cookie that puts it over this limit, it examines the currently stored cookies and identifies the one that has gone unused for the longest amount of time. It then replaces this cookie with the new cookie.

Cookies are used to store many different types of information. A cookie can store a username and password for a Web site. It can catalog the Web pages accessed when a user last visited a given Web site. Form data from a Web site also can be stored in a cookie.

Cookies can be divided into two types: client-side cookies and server-side cookies. A **client-side cookie** is initiated by a page coming from a Web server and is created in a browser's memory. All of the activity of creating, storing, and later recalling the cookie is done exclusively in the browser. A **server-side cookie**, by contrast, is created and stored on a server using server-side scripting languages such as Perl, PHP, ASP.Net, C++, and Java. The code to call a server-side cookie from the server is stored in the browser's memory. The creation of server-side cookies requires knowledge of a server-side scripting language, which is beyond the scope of this tutorial. This tutorial will focus only on client-side cookies.

Cookies have long been a topic of debate among Web developers and users. Some people contend that cookies are intrusive and can cause operating problems with a computer. Examples cited include adware programs that intrude on users and can slow down Internet browsing performance. Another argument asserts that cookies can fill a user's computer with unnecessary information that is used to track a user's movements on the Internet and that this reason is enough to warrant users to block all cookies as a means of protecting their privacy. Although a cookie can hold a lot of data because of its format as a text file, a cookie file is small in comparison to other files such as executables or images. In addition, because a cookie is just a text file, it cannot store harmful programs such as worms, viruses, or Trojan horses. In addition, it cannot be used to gain access to secure data on your computer. A cookie is also accessible only to the Web site that created it; one site cannot retrieve information from another site's cookie.

Cookies do have drawbacks for Web designers, however. For one, they cannot store data in the same way that a database does. While a database can be designed to hold a great quantity of data, a cookie is not capable of holding more than 4 KB of data. In addition, a browser stores a maximum of 20 cookies from a given Web site. As a result, the maximum storage capacity in cookies per Web site is 80 KB. For many online shopping Web sites, this is not enough to support the transactions involved with a shopping cart. Thus, cookies cannot be used to hold large amounts of the data required in online shopping applications.

Cookies can also be easily deleted by users. In addition, users have the option of limiting the numbers and types of cookies that their computers accept. This makes using cookies in certain applications, such as online shopping, an impractical choice. If you choose to use cookies, it is important to let users know that their browsers need to be set to accept cookies. It is also a good idea to include a privacy statement on a Web site that implements cookies. A **privacy statement** explains how a Web site protects the privacy of those who visit and provide information. Information contained in a company's privacy policy generally includes how the company plans to collect information about you, and how it will control, use, and share this information with other companies. Another provision in a privacy policy may include how you can decide if your information may be shared with others. You can get a feel for the approaches of different companies in this area by searching for and reading the privacy statements on Web sites that you visit regularly. Patti is currently working on a privacy statement for her Web site, which she will add at a later time.

Types of Cookies

Cookies are classified as either first-party cookies or third-party cookies. A **first-party cookie** is any cookie that is created from the Web site you are visiting. First-party cookies are commonly used to store information, such as your preferences when visiting a site. A **third-party cookie** is any cookie that is created at a different Web site and is then sent to the Web site you are currently visiting. A common use for this type of cookie is to track your Web page use for advertising or other marketing purposes. Third-party cookies can be either persistent or temporary.

Both first-party and third-party cookies can also be considered unsatisfactory cookies. An **unsatisfactory cookie** is a cookie that might allow access to personally identifiable information without your knowing about it.

A cookie can also include a compact privacy policy. A **compact privacy policy** is code that is sent to a user's browser that identifies the nature of a cookie. Based on this code, the browser can then decide whether or not to permit the cookie. Patti does not require you to develop a compact privacy policy for the cookies on her Web site at this time.

Setting Cookie Options in a Browser

Browsers allow users to control how much access to provide to cookies and when to delete them. A user can choose to delete all cookies or individual ones, and can also block out certain Web sites. Before you start building Patti's shopping cart, you should become familiar with some of the options that your users will have for controlling the cookies that Patti's Web site will use. Explore the user options for controlling cookies in common browsers by following the steps below. Because different browsers offer different options, you should follow the steps for all of the browsers to which you have access.

To examine cookie options in Internet Explorer for Windows:

1. Click **Tools** on the menu bar, then click **Internet Options**.
2. In the Internet Options dialog box, click the **Privacy tab** (see Figure 9-4).

Privacy settings in Internet Explorer | **Figure 9-4**

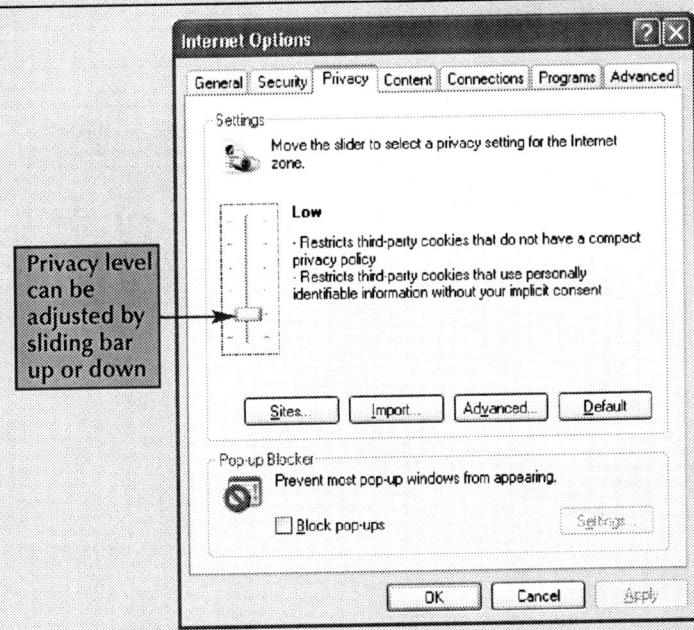

Privacy level can be adjusted by sliding bar up or down

As Figure 9-4 shows, the Privacy tab provides six privacy settings. To ensure that you will be able to work with the shopping cart you create, your privacy setting needs to be no higher than "Medium."

3. Explore the privacy level options and other settings on the Privacy tab.

Figure 9-5 explains the options for customizing cookies on the Internet Explorer Privacy tab.

Customized cookie settings in Internet Explorer | **Figure 9-5**

Setting	Description
Privacy level slider bar	Set privacy level by sliding up or down
Sites	Specify URLs of Web sites from which to allow or disallow cookies, regardless of their privacy policies; active when the privacy level is set below "Block All Cookies"
Import	Specify an external file from which to import privacy preferences
Advanced	Customize handling of first- and third-party cookies, including overriding automatic cookie handling; accepting, blocking, or prompting when a first- or third-party cookie is encountered; and allowing all session cookies
Default	Restore default privacy settings
Pop-up Blocker	Block pop-up windows from any Web site; when checked, click Settings button to specify Web sites to exempt from pop-up blocking

4. If your Privacy tab is set to "Block All Cookies," "High," or "Medium High," drag the privacy settings slider bar down until the setting reads **Medium**.

5. Click **OK** to close the Internet Options dialog box.

To examine cookie options in Netscape:

1. Click **Edit** on the menu bar, then click **Preferences**.

   Trouble? In Netscape for Macintosh, click Netscape on the menu bar, then click Preferences.

2. In the Category pane, double-click **Privacy & Security**, then click **Cookies** on the menu that opens (see Figure 9-6).

Figure 9-6	Cookie settings in Netscape

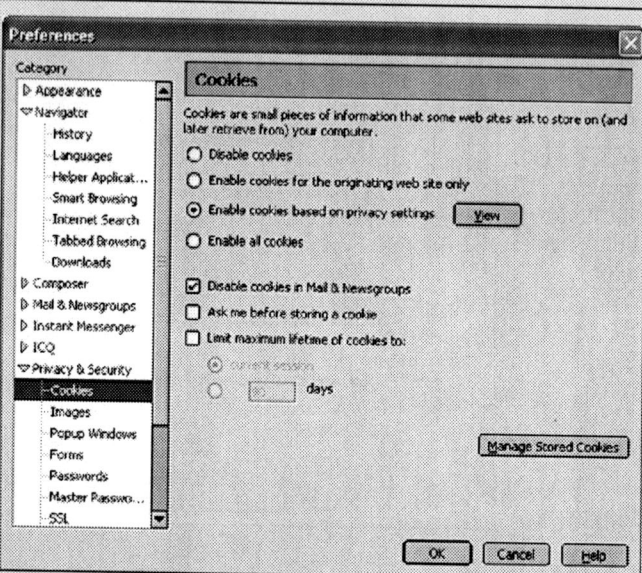

As Figure 9-6 shows, the cookie settings in the Preferences dialog box allow you to specify how the browser deals with cookies. The default setting for Cookie Acceptance Policy is "Enable cookies based on privacy settings."

3. If necessary, click the **Enable cookies based on privacy settings** option button to select it.

4. Click the **View** button to open the Privacy Settings dialog box (see Figure 9-7).

Figure 9-7	Privacy settings in Netscape

The Privacy Settings dialog box allows you to specify a privacy level for your browser. To ensure that you will be able to work with the shopping cart you create, your privacy setting needs to be no higher than "medium."

5. If the Level of Privacy section of the dialog box shows a setting of "high" or "custom," click the **medium** option button.

6. Click **OK** twice to close the Privacy Settings and Preferences dialog boxes.

To examine cookie options in Firefox:

1. Click **Tools** on the menu bar, then click **Options**.

Trouble? In Firefox for Macintosh, click Firefox on the menu bar, then click Preferences.

2. In the Options dialog box, click **Privacy** in the left pane (see Figure 9-8).

Cookie settings in Mozilla Firefox ◀ Figure 9-8

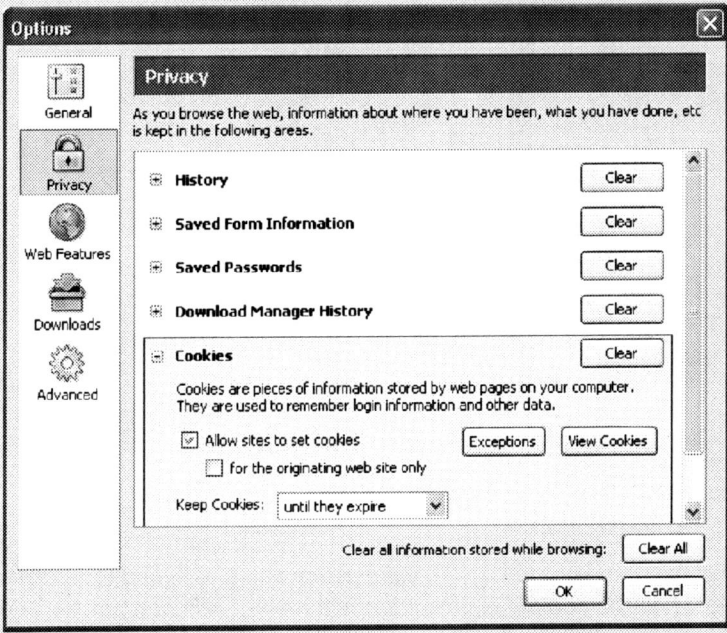

The Privacy options in Firefox allow you to specify settings for how the browser deals with cookies. The default settings are "Allow sites to set cookies" and "Keep Cookies until they expire."

3. If necessary, adjust your browser's settings to match those shown in Figure 9-8.

4. Click **OK** to close the Options dialog box.

Trouble? If you are running a browser other than Internet Explorer, Netscape, or Firefox, use the browser's Help options or a Web search engine to learn how to change the privacy settings for your browser. Change settings if necessary to ensure that the browser accepts first-party cookies.

Trouble? If you change computers or browsers at any point while completing this Tutorial, complete the above steps to ensure that the browser's privacy options are set correctly.

Creating a Cookie

Now that you have a basic understanding of how to create and work with cookies, you are ready to implement a shopping cart for Patti's Web site. Your first task is to capture a user's first name, last name, username, and password from the account page in Patti's Web site. To accomplish this, you will add code to create four cookies that will store these four pieces of data. The values in these cookies will then be used to personalize content for the site's home page and shopping cart.

Cookies play an important role in the function of a shopping cart application. The main function of a cookie in a shopping cart is to hold information about a product that a user wants to purchase. The information you want to collect for Patti's Web site using cookies includes a product's name and price, as well as the quantity that a user wants to purchase. Your pages can use the information stored in cookies at any time to summarize the items a user has selected for purchase. You can also enable a user to delete a selected item using code to delete the cookie information associated with it.

Every cookie has five distinct parts. Each part affects how a cookie behaves, how long it is active, and how it communicates with the Web server. Figure 9-9 explains each of the parts of a cookie.

Figure 9-9 **Cookie attributes**

Attribute	Description
Name	The name that identifies the cookie
Value	The value assigned to the cookie
Expires	The date when the cookie expires and should be deleted
Path	The location of files on the Web server that may access the cookie
Domain	The Web server or Web servers that may access the cookie
Secure	Optional indication that the cookie is secure and should only transmit data via the HTTPS protocol

The syntax for creating a cookie is

```
document.cookie = "name = value; expires = expiration; path = path;
domain = domain; secure";
```

where *name* is the name of the cookie, *value* is the value assigned to it, *expiration* is the date and time when the cookie expires, *path* is the path, and *domain* is its domain. The name and value properties are the only properties that must be explicitly assigned to create a cookie. All of the other properties are assigned default values if they are not specifically stated.

The name and value Properties

A cookie is a child of the document object. Each cookie stores a single piece of information as its value, which is paired with a name when the cookie is created. The JavaScript syntax to create a cookie is

```
document.cookie = "name = value";
```

where `name` is the name assigned to the cookie and `value` is its value. For example, if you wanted to create a cookie named "username" and assign it a value of "John Doe", the code would be

```
document.cookie = "username = John Doe";
```

You can also create code to dynamically generate the parameters for cookies. For example, the following code creates a cookie named input1 with a value equal to a user's input in the uname field of the form1 form:

```
username = document.form1.uname.value;
document.cookie = "input1 = "+username;
```

Patti's Web site requires four cookies to customize and personalize the Web site for users. These cookies will store a user's first name, last name, username, and password. The first name and last name data will allow you to welcome a customer to the site personally. Later on when Patti has someone work on the site's back end, the username and password will allow the Web site to verify a user's identity against an online database of user accounts. You'll create the makeCookie() function containing code to create these four cookies, allowing all of the cookies to be generated at once.

The initial code for the makeCookie() function is

```
function makeCookie(fn,ln,user,pswd) {
    document.cookie = "fn = "+fn;
    document.cookie = "ln = "+ln;
    document.cookie = "user = "+user;
    document.cookie = "pswd = "+pswd;

    window.location = "patti_home.htm";
}
```

The function will be called from an account creation form, which will pass it the four parameters corresponding to the first name, last name, username, and password information that a user enters. The function will then open the site's main page, which will be personalized with the first name and last name data.

To add code to the makeCookie() function to create cookies:

1. Open the file **patti.js** in your editor.

2. Just above the comment Helper Functions, enter the following code:

```
function makeCookie(fn,ln,user,pswd) {
    document.cookie = "fn = "+fn;
    document.cookie = "ln = "+ln;
    document.cookie = "user = "+user;
    document.cookie = "pswd = "+pswd;

    window.location = "patti_home.htm";
}
```

Figure 9-10 shows the new code in the file.

The first part of the makeCookie() function ◄ **Figure 9-10**

```
function makeCookie(fn,ln,user,pswd){
      document.cookie = "fn = "+fn;
      document.cookie= "ln = "+ln;
      document.cookie = "user = "+user;
      document.cookie= "pswd = "+pswd;

      window.location = "patti_home.htm";
}
/* Helper Functions */
```

3. Save your work.

The expires Property

In addition to the name and value, a cookie can be assigned an expiration date. This part of the cookie represents the date and time the cookie should be deleted from the browser's memory. To assign an expiration date, you use the "expires" property with the syntax

```
expires = Day, DD-Mmm-YY HH:MM:SS GMT
```

where *Day* is the day of the week, *DD* is the two-digit day of the month, *Mmm* is the three-letter English abbreviation for the month, *YY* is the last two digits of the year, *HH* is the hours (00–23), *MM* is the minutes, *SS* is the seconds, and *GMT* indicates that the time is in Greenwich mean time. For example, to set the username cookie to expire on Saturday, October 30th, 2010, at 6:30 pm GMT, you would use the code

```
document.cookie = "username = John Doe; expires = Saturday,
30-Oct-10 23:30:00 GMT";
```

At a minimum, the expiration value must include the day of the week and the date. Thus, you could set the username cookie to expire on Saturday, October 30th, 2010, using the code

```
document.cookie = "username = John Doe; expires = Saturday, 30-Oct-10";
```

If you do not include a time for the cookie to expire on a given date, the cookie expires at 00:00:01 GMT on the expiration date.

Instead of hard coding a date, Web pages that generate cookies usually set the expiration date automatically by calculating a certain length of time in the future. You can dynamically select an expiration date using the Date() method. For example, the following code creates a cookie that expires seven days from when it is created:

```
var thisday = new Date();
var expdate = new Date(thisday.getTime() + 7 * 24 * 60 * 60 * 1000);
expdate.toGMTString();
document.cookie = "username = John Doe; expires = "+expdate.
toGMTString();
```

This code converts the length of time until expiration to milliseconds, and adds it to the time value from the current date. It then converts the date and time to Greenwich mean time, which is the standard used to identify a cookie's expiration date and time.

You could create similar code to set cookies to expire in different time frames. For example, if you instead wanted a cookie to expire in a matter of hours, you would remove the number 7 from the calculation of the expdate value, and replace the value 24 with the number of hours in the future you want the cookie to expire.

If a cookie is created without an expiration date, it is considered a per session cookie. A **per session cookie** exists only for as long as the browser is communicating with the Web site. Once the user closes the browser or navigates to a new site, the cookie expires.

You decide to set all cookies generated by Patti's Web site to expire two weeks from the time they are created. To do this, you'll create a variable that stores a date and time two weeks in the future, and then add the expires property to the code for each cookie in the makeCookie() function.

To control the expiration of cookies:

1. In the patti.js file just above the makeCookie() function, enter the following code:

```
var now = new Date();
var expdate = new Date(now.getTime() + 14 * 24 * 60 * 60 * 1000);
```

2. In the makeCookie() function, enter the following code to each of the four document.cookie statements just before the closing semicolon:

```
+"; expires="+expdate.toGMTString()
```

Figure 9-11 shows the new code in the file.

specifies an expiration date 14 days from a cookie's creation

```
var now = new Date();
var expdate = new Date(now.getTime() + 14 * 24 * 60 * 60 * 1000);

function makeCookie(fn,ln,user,pswd){
    document.cookie = "fn = "+fn+";expires="+expdate.toGMTString();
    document.cookie= "ln = "+ln+";expires="+expdate.toGMTString();
    document.cookie = "user = "+user+";expires="+expdate.toGMTString();
    document.cookie= "pswd = "+pswd+";expires="+expdate.toGMTString();

    window.location = "patti_home.htm";
}

/* Helper Functions */
```

code to convert days to milliseconds

3. Save your work.

The path Property

By default, a cookie is available only to the page where it originated. In some cases, however, you want a cookie to be available to other pages on the same server. You can set the pages to which a cookie is available using the path attribute. For example, suppose you are working on a Web site that includes three different directories on its sever. If you want to make the username cookie available to all of the Web pages located in the "history" directory, you set the path property equal to /history, as in the following code:

```
document.cookie = "username = John Doe; expires = Saturday,
30-Oct-10 23:30:00 GMT; path = /history";
```

If the path property is omitted, a value of " / " is assumed and the cookie is available to all pages in the domain.

Because Patti's Web site is very simple at this point; the default path value is sufficient, and you don't need to specify this property for the cookies you're creating.

The domain Property

In some situations you may want to make a cookie available to a Web server other than the one where the cookie originated. You can use the domain property to specify the URL of the domain to which you want to make the cookie available. If no value is specified for the domain property, its value is set to the server of origin. If you wanted the username cookie to be available to the server http://www.somewhere.com, for example, you would use the code

```
document.cookie = "username = John Doe; expires = Saturday,
30-Oct-10 23:30:00 GMT; path = /history; domain =
http://www.somewhere.com";
```

When you use the path attribute along with the domain attribute, the path specifies the folder and subsequent subfolders to which the cookie should apply in the domain where the cookie originates. The domain attribute points to a server other than the one hosting the Web site that will also recognize the cookie. As with the path property, the cookies for Patti's simple Web site do not require the domain property at this time.

The secure Property

The final property you can set for a cookie is the "secure" property. This property enables you to specify that a cookie is to be transmitted over the **HTTPS protocol**, which is a set of rules that govern the transmission of information over the World Wide Web in an encrypted state. HTTPS is the HTTP protocol using Secure Sockets Layer (SSL) to encrypt data to protect it as it is transferred between servers. To set a cookie as a secure cookie, you add the parameter "secure" without a value. If you wanted to make the username cookie secure, you would use the code

```
document.cookie = "username = John Doe; expires = Saturday,
30-Oct-10 23:30:00 GMT; path = /history; domain =
http://www.somewhere.com; secure"
```

For your work on Patti's Web site, all of the cookies you create will be unsecured. You will therefore not need to work with the secure property.

Reference Window	**Creating a Cookie**

- To create a cookie, use the syntax
  ```
  document.cookie = "name = value; expires = expiration;
  path = path; domain = domain; secure";
  ```
  where *name* is the cookie's name, *value* is the cookie's value, *expiration* is the date and time (Greenwich mean time) of the cookie's expiration, *path* is the path of pages on the current server that can access the cookie, and *domain* is a nonoriginating domain that can access the cookie; the optional parameter "secure" specifies that the cookie is to be transmitted using the HTTPS protocol.

Now that you are familiar with the structure and content of cookies, as well as how to create them, you are ready to start using them to customize Patti's Web site. In the next session, you'll retrieve cookie values and display these values in a Web page.

Review	# Session 9.1 Quick Check

1. Name two differences between a client-side shopping cart and a server-side shopping cart.
2. What is the difference between client-side and server-side cookies?
3. Why is it important for a Web site to include a privacy statement?
4. What is the syntax to create a cookie named item with a value of chair and an expiration date of Monday, July 2nd, 2007, at 12:00 pm Greenwich mean time?
5. What Web pages would be able to access a cookie with a path setting of " / " but no domain name?
6. When does a per session cookie expire?
7. If a cookie is assigned an expiration date of Saturday, 10-May-08, what time on this date will it expire?

Session 9.2

Working with Cookie Values

Patti's Web site is designed so that user input is first checked using a validation script named checkForm(). This function verifies that a user has completed all of the form fields, and that the user entered the same password twice. If a user's entries fail either of these tests, the user receives an appropriate alert box. If the input tests valid, however, then Patti wants cookies to be generated based on the user input. Enter code in the check-Form() script to pass validated user input to the makeCookie() function.

To call the makeCookie() function:

1. In your text editor open the **patti.js** file and scroll down to the checkForm() function in the Helper Functions section.

2. Replace the comment "// pass valid input to makeCookie() function" with the following code:

   ```
   makeCookie(fn,ln,user,pswd);
   ```

   Figure 9-12 shows the completed code for the checkForm() function.

Code to run the makeCookie() function after validation	Figure 9-12

```
function checkForm(){
        var fn = document.login2.fn.value;
        var ln = document.login2.ln.value;
        var user = document.login2.user.value;
        var pswd = document.login2.pswd.value;
        var pswd2 = document.login2.pswd2.value;
        if((fn == "")||(ln == "")||(user == "")||(pswd == "")||(pswd2 == ""))
                {
                        alert("Please fill out all input fields on this form.");
                        return false;
                }
        else if(pswd != pswd2)
                {
                        alert("Your passwords did not match. Please try again.");
                        return false;
                }
        else
                {
                        makeCookie(fn,ln,user,pswd);
                }
}
```

Extracting Cookie Values

Once your Web site stores information in cookies, you need to extract the values from those cookies with a function in order to use the values in your Web pages. You'll use the following function, findCookie(), to extract cookie values for Patti's Web site:

```
function findCookie(val) {
   var cookie = null;
   var findVal = val + "=";
   var dc = document.cookie;
   if (dc.length > 0) {
      var start = dc.indexOf(findVal);
      if (start >= 0) {
         start += findVal.length;
         lastVal = dc.indexOf(";", start);
         if (lastVal == -1) {
            lastVal = dc.length;
         }
         cookie = (dc.substring(start, lastVal));
      } else {
```

```
        return cookie;
      }
   }
   return cookie;
}
```

This function is called with the name of a cookie passed as a parameter. The function uses the indexOf() method to extract the position value of the first character of the cookie's value, passing this number to the start variable. It does the same for the last character of the value, storing it in the lastVal variable. The function then uses these two values as parameters for the substring method to extract the cookie's value as a text string, assigning it to the cookie variable. This variable is then available for your use in personalizing Patti's home page. Add the findCookie() function to the Web site now.

To build a function to extract cookie values:

1. Return to the **patti.js** file in your editor.

2. Below the makeCookie() function, enter the following code:

```
function findCookie(val) {
   var cookie = null;
   var findVal = val + "=";
   var dc = document.cookie;
   if (dc.length > 0) {
      var start = dc.indexOf(findVal);
      if (start >= 0) {
         start += findVal.length;
         lastVal = dc.indexOf(";", start);
         if (lastVal == -1) {
            lastVal = dc.length;
         }
         cookie = (dc.substring(start, lastVal));
      } else {
         return cookie;
      }
   }
      return cookie;
}
```

Figure 9-13 shows the new code in the file.

The completed findCookie() function ◄ Figure 9-13

```
function makeCookie(fn,ln,user,pswd){
    document.cookie = "fn = "+fn+";expires="+expdate.toGMTString();
    document.cookie= "ln = "+ln+";expires="+expdate.toGMTString();
    document.cookie = "user = "+user+";expires="+expdate.toGMTString();
    document.cookie= "pswd = "+pswd+";expires="+expdate.toGMTString();

    window.location = "patti_home.htm";
}

function findCookie(val) {
    var cookie = null;
    var findval = val + "=";
    var dc = document.cookie;
    if (dc.length > 0) {
        var start = dc.indexof(findval);
        if (start >= 0) {
            start += findval.length;
            lastval = dc.indexof(";", start);
            if (lastval == -1) {
                lastval = dc.length;
            }
            cookie = (dc.substring(start, lastval));
        } else {
            return cookie;
        }
    }
    return cookie;
}

/* Helper Functions */
```

3. Save your work.

Next you need to add code that uses the findCookie() function to assign the values of the cookies you'll be using to variables. You can then use these cookie values to personalize the Web site.

To pass cookie values to variables:

1. Return to the **patti.js** file in your editor.

2. Below the findCookie() function, enter the following code:

```
fn = findCookie("fn");
ln = findCookie("ln");
user = findCookie("user");
pswd = findCookie("pswd");
```

Figure 9-14 shows the new code in the file.

Figure 9-14

Code to extract four user account values based on the findCookie() function

```
function findCookie(val) {
    var cookie = null;
    var findVal = val + "=";
    var dc = document.cookie;
    if (dc.length > 0) {
        var start = dc.indexof(findval);
        if (start >= 0) {
            start += findval.length;
            lastval = dc.indexof(";", start);
            if (lastval == -1) {
                lastval = dc.length;
            }
            cookie = (dc.substring(start, lastval));
        } else {
            return cookie;
        }
    }
    return cookie;
}

fn = findCookie("fn");
ln = findCookie("ln");
user = findCookie("user");
pswd = findCookie("pswd");

/* Helper Functions */
```

▶ **3.** Save your work.

Populating Form Fields with Cookie Values

Next you will add code that populates the username form field in the login form with the username value extracted from the corresponding cookie. This will make it easier for a returning user to log back into the site. To start, you'll assign the value of the user variable to the username field in the login form using the retrieveAccount() function:

```
function retrieveAccount() {
    document.login.username.value=user;
}
```

Next you'll add an event handler to the opening body tag to run this function when the page opens. Though Patti will eventually want this code on all of her pages, she has asked you to apply it intially to one page, patti_home.htm, so she can see how it works before rolling it out to the whole Web site. Add this code to the patti_home.htm file now.

To complete the code for the patti_account.htm file:

▶ **1.** In your editor, open the **patti_home.htm** file.

▶ **2.** In the document head section, add the following code:

```
<script type="text/javascript">
    function retrieveAccount() {
        document.login.username.value=user;
    }
</script>
```

▶ **3.** Add the following event handler to the opening <body> tag:

```
onload="retrieveAccount()"
```

Figure 9-15 shows the code entered in patti_home.htm.

Code in the patti_home.htm file that displays the username | **Figure 9-15**

```
-->
<script type="text/javascript">
   function retrieveAccount() {
      document.login.username.value=user;
   }
</script>

<script type="text/javascript" src="patti.js"></script>
<link rel="stylesheet" type="text/css" href="patti.css" />

<title>Patti's Home Page</title>
</head>

<body onload="retrieveAccount()">
<img src="logo.jpg" alt="" border="0" />
<img src="patti.jpg" alt="" border="0" />
```

4. Save your work.

Using Cookie Values to Create a Personalized Greeting

Next, you will use the cookie values to create a personalized greeting on the site's main page. The greeting will include the user's first and last name. If the user visits this page before filling out account information, the greeting will not be personalized. The code to personalize the home page is

```
<script type="text/javascript">if((fn != "")&&(ln != "")){document.
write("Hello, "+fn+" "+ln+". ")}</script>
```

To display a personalized greeting on the main page:

1. In your editor, return to the file patti_home.htm.

2. Locate the div element with the id home_page_text, then enter the following code after the opening <strong> tag:

```
<script type="text/javascript">if((fn != "")&&(ln != "")){document.
write("Hello, "+fn+" "+ln+". ")}</script>
```

Figure 9-16 shows the edited code for patti_home.htm.

Code to personalize Patti's home page | **Figure 9-16**

```
<div id="home_page_text">
<br />
<strong><script type="text/javascript">if((fn != "")&&(ln !=
"")){document.write("Hello, "+fn+" "+ln+". ")}</script>Check out our new and
featured items below!</strong>
<br /> <br />
```

3. Save your work and close patti_home.htm in your editor

4. In your browser, open **patti_account.htm**.

5. Complete the form fields with the following entries:

First Name	*your first name*
Last Name	*your last name*
User Name	*your first name*
Password	123
Confirm Password	123

See Figure 9-17.

Figure 9-17 | Completed account form

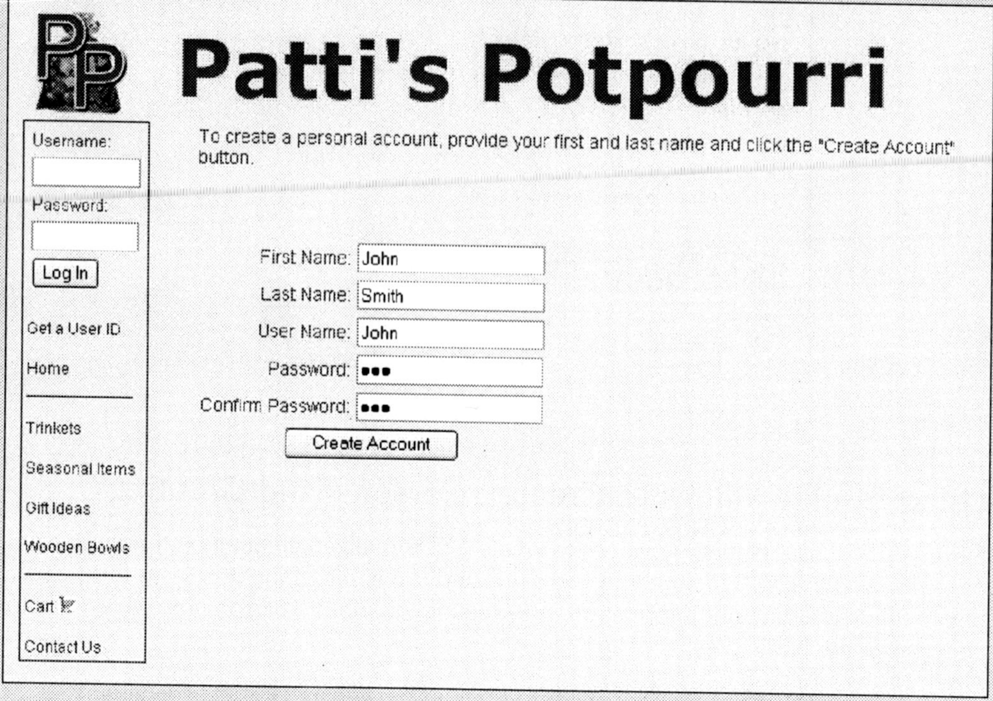

Patti's Potpourri

Username:

Password:

Log In

Get a User ID

Home

Trinkets

Seasonal Items

Gift Ideas

Wooden Bowls

Cart 🛒

Contact Us

To create a personal account, provide your first and last name and click the "Create Account" button.

First Name: John
Last Name: Smith
User Name: John
Password: ●●●
Confirm Password: ●●●

Create Account

6. Click **Create Account**.

The patti_home.htm page opens, as shown in Figure 9-18. Notice that the page is personalized, showing your first name and last name at the top of the page just below the logo. In addition, the Username field in the login form is prepopulated. This will be especially useful for returning users who must log back into the site.

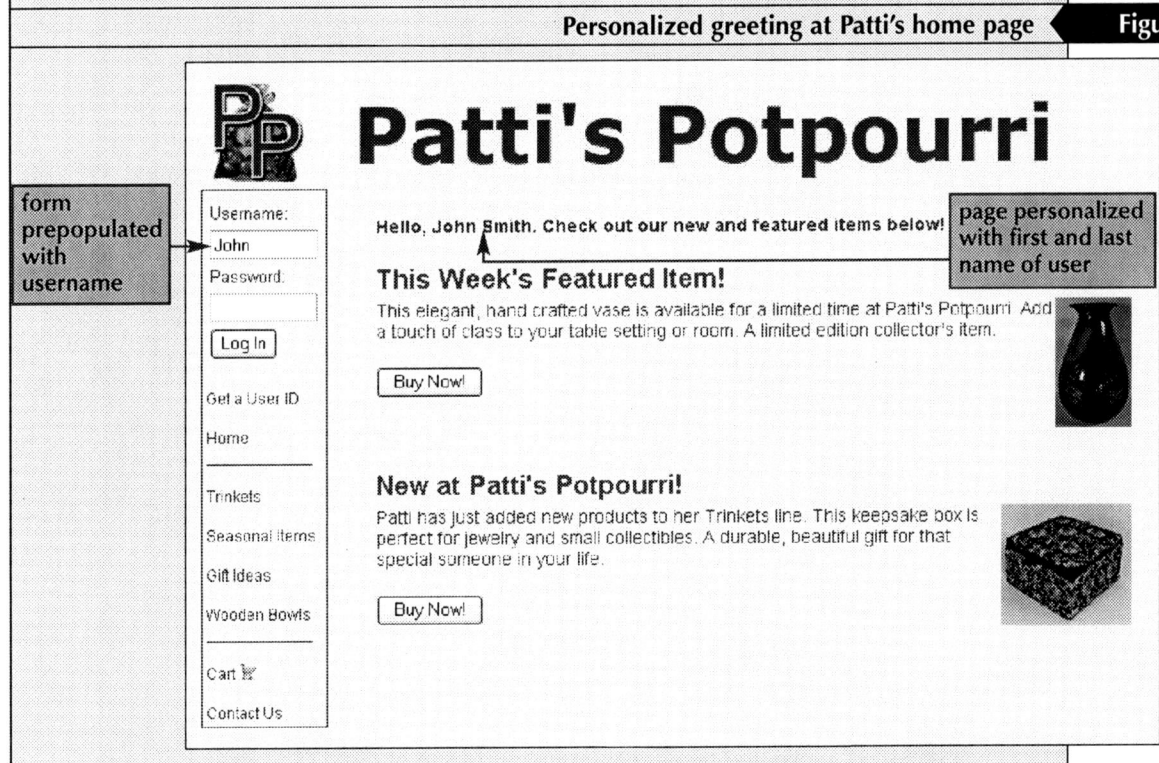

Personalized greeting at Patti's home page | Figure 9-18

Implementing a Shopping Cart

You show Patti the revised Web site and demonstrate the personalized greeting it provides for users. She is pleased with your work and thinks the personalization makes the site more professional and welcoming. She would like you to expand the site's use of cookies to add shopping cart functionality. When a user selects an item, the item's name and price information, along with the quantity the user wishes to purchase, should be placed in the cart. When the user views the cart, the user should see this information as well as the total cost for purchasing the selected items.

Patti wants users to be able to enter a quantity in a text box and then click its associated Add to Cart button to place the item and the quantity ordered in a shopping cart. She also wants a user to receive immediate feedback to confirm the item and quantity added to the shopping cart. Most of the programming to meet Patti's needs is finished. To complete the shopping cart functionality, you need to add code to create a cookie for an order placed on the page with an expiration date set to the expdate variable. The code must then generate an alert box to provide the user with verification of the item name and quantity added to the shopping cart.

One way to add information to the shopping cart would be to create a cookie for a product's name, another for the quantity ordered, another for the product number, and one more for the price for each item added to the cart—a total of four cookies for each item. Using this system, a user who orders each of the four items available for sale would generate a total of sixteen cookies, on top of the four already created when the user created an account. Because Patti may want to add more items on this page or other pages in her site, however, you need to limit the number of cookies you create. As Figure 9-19 illustrates, the scenario above leaves the site with no room to create more cookies. If Patti added one more item to sell on her Web site, there would not be enough cookies left to support the new product.

Figure 9-19 | **Shopping cart solution using all available cookies**

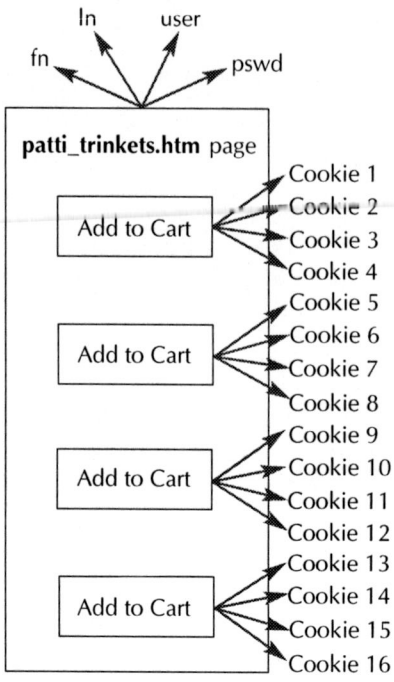

As mentioned above, the numerical limitation is one of the disadvantages of working with cookies. To get around the issue of using too many cookies in Patti's shopping cart, you can instead create a single cookie for each item placed in the shopping cart, with each cookie's value containing product name, product number, quantity, and price. As Figure 9-20 shows, this method reduces the number of cookies required to support the shopping cart from 16 to four.

Figure 9-20 | **Shopping cart solution minimizing cookie use**

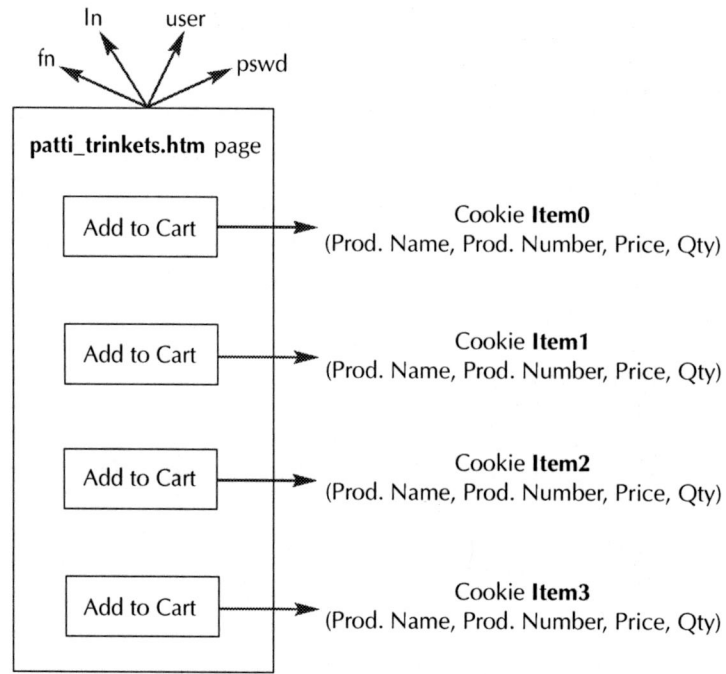

When you use cookie values containing multiple values, you can extract the data held in each cookie using arrays. Although using arrays requires more programming to add and extract data than required for creating individual cookies, you decide to store all the information for each product in a single cookie to support future expansion of Patti's product line.

To start, you will call the placeOrder() function from the patti_trinkets.htm file. The placeOrder() function, which has already been developed for you, verifies that the quantity ordered is not 0, and then calls another function to submit the order.

You will pass four parameters to this function, corresponding to the product number, the product name, the price, and the form number (the number appearing at the end of a form's name). For example, if a user places an order for Candlestick Holders, the following values are passed as parameters to the function:

- C892
- Candlestick Holders
- 27.40
- 2

Notice that the quantity ordered is not passed as a parameter. The placeOrder() function instead accesses the quantity ordered as a form value.

To add event handlers to pass parameters to the placeOrder() function:

1. Open the file **patti_trinkets.htm** in your editor.

2. In the form with the id order0, add the following event handler to the input element for the Add to Cart button:

   ```
   onclick="placeOrder('V212','Ornamental Green Vase','8.05',0)"
   ```

3. Add the following code to the button input fields for the remaining forms:

   order1: `onclick="placeOrder('B122','Keep Sake Box','14.65',1)"`

   order2: `onclick="placeOrder('C892','Candlestick Holders','27.40',2)"`

   order3: `onclick="placeOrder('V456','Blue Vase','17.95',3)"`

   Figure 9-21 shows the completed code for this page containing the event handlers.

Figure 9-21

Code to create cookies containing data on each product

```
<input type="button" value="Add to Cart"
      onclick="placeOrder('V212','Ornamental Green Vase','8.05',0)" />
   </form>
```

```
<input type="button" value="Add to Cart"
      onclick="placeOrder('B122','Keep Sake Box','14.65',1)" />
   </form>
```

```
<input type="button" value="Add to Cart"
      onclick="placeOrder('C892','Candlestick Holders','27.40',2)" />
   </form>
```

```
<input type="button" value="Add to Cart"
      onclick="placeOrder('V456','Blue Vase','17.95',3)" />
   </form>
```

▶ **4.** Save your work and close patti_trinkets.htm in your editor.

The placeOrder() function, which was already in place in the patti.js file, looks up the quantity ordered for a given item and verifies that it is greater than 0. The function then passes the order parameters to the makeOrderCookie() function. You will create the makeOrderCookie() function now. The purpose of the function is to build a single cookie whose value holds the product number, product name, product price, and quantity ordered. The code for this function is

```
function makeOrderCookie(n,id,prod,pr,q){
  document.cookie = "myitem"+n+" = "+id+","+prod+","+pr+","+q+";
    expires = "+expdate.toGMTString() +";path = /";
  alert("You have added "+q+" of the "+prod+" to your shopping cart.");
}
```

For example, if a user adds 2 Candlestick Holders to the shopping cart, the function is called with the parameters 2,C892,Candlestick Holders,27.40,2. The cookie created would be named myitem2 and would have the value "C892,Candlestick Holders,27.40,2". The script places commas in the cookie value between the product number, product name, price, and form number. The commas are helpful in extracting the individual parts of the cookie's value. Enter the code for the makeOrderCookie() function now in the external JavaScript file for Patti's Web site.

To create a cookie to hold order information from the patti_trinkets.htm page:

1. In your editor, return to the file patti.js.

2. Above the Helper Functions comment, insert the following code (see Figure 9-22):

```
function makeOrderCookie(n,id,prod,pr,q){
   document.cookie = "myitem"+n+" = "+id+","+prod+","+pr+","+q+";
      expires = "+expdate.toGMTString();
   alert("You have added "+q+" of the "+prod+" to your shopping
   cart.");
}
```

Code for the makeOrderCookie() function	Figure 9-22

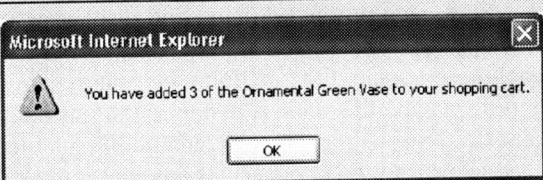

3. Save your work.

4. In your browser, open **patti_trinkets.htm**.

5. Click in the quantity input field for the product "Ornamental Green Vase."

6. Enter **3**, then click the **Add to Cart** button for this item.

   As Figure 9-23 shows, the Web page generates an alert box, confirming that you have added 3 of the Ornamental Green Vases to your cart.

Alert box generated after item information has been placed in the shopping cart	Figure 9-23

7. Click **OK**

8. Click the **Add to Cart** button for the item Keep Sake Box, then click **OK**.

Displaying Shopping Cart Contents

To complete the shopping cart, you need to enable users to view their complete orders. To do this, you'll create a script that reads the information in each of the product cookies stored in a user's browser and then displays it in a user-friendly format. Patti has already created a format for this information in the patti_cart.htm file. To read the information in each cookie and split it into its component parts, you'll use the showOrder() function, which is shown in Figure 9-24.

Figure 9-24

The showOrder() function

```
function showOrder(){
    var subTot = 0;
    var prod = new Array();
    prod[0] = findCookie("myitem0");
    prod[1] = findCookie("myitem1");
    prod[2] = findCookie("myitem2");
    prod[3] = findCookie("myitem3");

    if((prod[0] == null)&&(prod[1] == null)&&(prod[2] == null)&&(prod[3] ==
null))
            {
                document.write("<tr><td>");
                document.write("Your cart is empty.");
                document.write("</td></tr>");
            }
    for(i=0;i<=prod.length;i++)
            {
            if((prod[i] != null)&&(prod[i] != ""))
                {
                document.write("<tr><td>");
                start = prod[i].substring(0,4);
                document.write(start+"</td><td>");

                name = prod[i].indexOf(",")+1;
                name2 = prod[i].indexOf(",",name);
                prod_name = prod[i].substring(name,name2);
                document.write(prod_name+"</td><td class=right'>");

                price = prod[i].indexOf(",",name2)+1;
                price2 = prod[i].indexOf(",",price);
                prod_price = parseFloat(prod[i].substring(price,price2));
                price = prod_price.toFixed(2);
                document.write("$"+price+"</td><td class='center'>");

                quant = parseInt(prod[i].substring(prod[i].length-
1,prod[i].length));
                document.write(quant+"</td><td class='right'>");

                cost_raw = quant*prod_price;
                cost_tot = cost_raw;
                subTot += cost_tot;
                cost = cost_raw.toFixed(2);
                document.write("$"+cost+"</td><td>");
                document.write("<a href=# onclick = 'delProd("+[i]+")'>Remove
Item</a>");
                document.write("</td><td>");
                }
            }
        document.write("<tr><td colspan = '5' class='right'>The total cost of your
order is <b>$"+subTot.toFixed(2)+"</b></td></tr>");
    }
```

This function extracts substrings from the cookie value that correspond to the product number, product name, product price, and the quantity ordered, storing the results in an array. It also totals the cost of each product ordered and displays a total cost just below the list of items in the shopping cart.

After splitting up each item cookie, the function creates a dynamic table with rows and columns to support displaying this data. A **dynamic table** is a table whose content and HTML tags are generated through a script. By generating a table dynamically, it can display all of the items that a user has ordered, without empty rows or information on items that the user isn't ordering.

To finish creating Patti's shopping cart, call the showOrder() function in the patti_cart.htm file.

To finish creating Patti's shopping cart:

1. In your editor, open the file **patti_cart.htm**.

2. Scroll down to the second table in this file and locate the div element with the id "mailing_info".

3. Locate the comment "<!-- call showOrder() function -->" and replace it with the following code (see Figure 9-25):

```
<script type="text/javascript">
showOrder()
</script>
```

Competed code that calls the showOrder() function ◄ **Figure 9-25**

```
<div id="mailing_info">
<form name="order" action="patti_checkout.htm" onsubmit="return confirmForm()"
method="post">
<table border="0" cellpadding="0" cellspacing="0">
  <tr>
      <td valign="top" colspan="2">
          <table align="center" border="0" cellpadding="5" cellspacing="1">
            <tr>
               <th>Product Number</th>
               <th>Product</th>
               <th>Price</th>
               <th>Quantity</th>
               <th>Cost</th>
            </tr>
               <script type="text/javascript">
               showOrder()
               </script>
          </table>
      </td>
  </tr>
  <tr>
```

4. Close patti_cart.htm in your editor, saving your work.

5. In your browser, open the file **patti_cart.htm**.

Figure 9-26 shows the items in the shopping cart, which you added earlier. For each item, the product number, product name, price, quantity, and cost are clearly displayed. Each row also ends with a Remove Item link. Below the list of items in the shopping cart, the page displays the total cost for your order. The page also reads the cookies storing your first and last names and populates the First Name and Last Name fields with this information, saving some time in the ordering process.

Figure 9-26	Shopping cart display

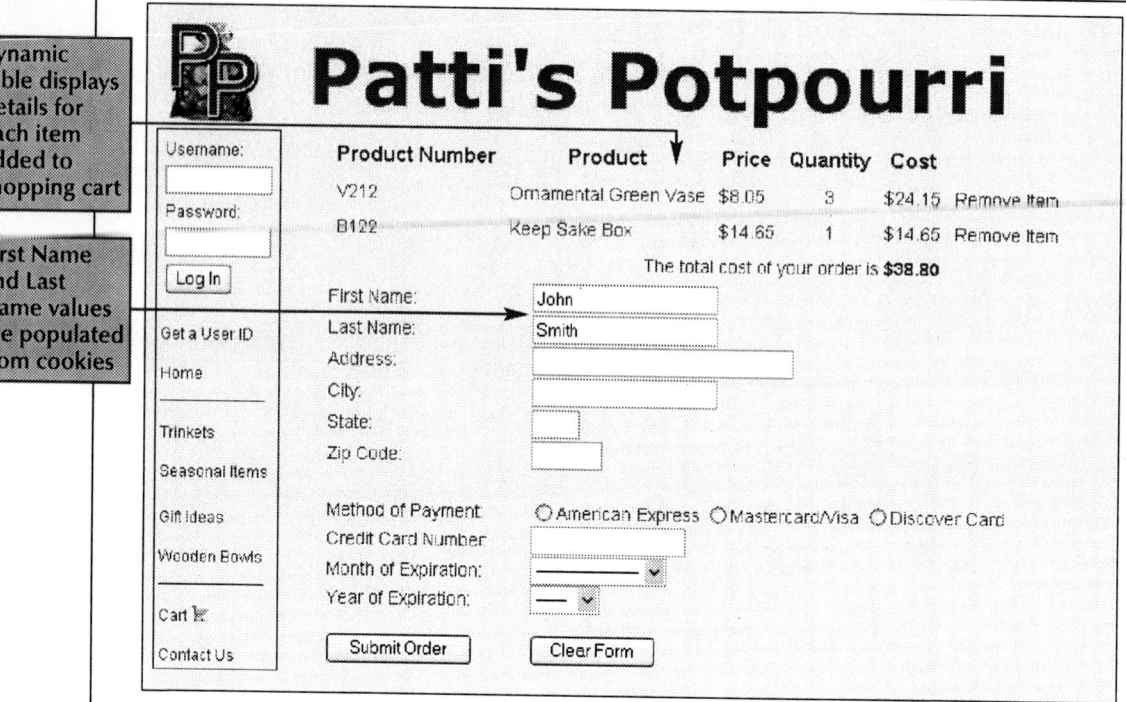

The Remove Item link for each item in the cart is not currently functional. This link is an important part of the shopping cart application, as it provides a user the opportunity to delete an item from the shopping cart should the user not want to purchase it. To finish the shopping cart page, you need to build a function to complete this task. Each Remove Item link already contains an event handler that calls the delProd() function and passes it a parameter that identifies the product that should be deleted from the cart. You'll create the delProd() function, which has the following code:

```
function delProd(prod) {
    document.cookie = "myitem"+prod+"=;expires=Thu, 01-Jan-70
       00:00: 01 GMT;"
    location.reload();
}
```

This function expires the cookie for the product that called it and reloads the Web page in the browser, updating the display of the cart contents.

To add the delProd() function to delete an item from the shopping cart:

1. Return to patti.js in your editor.

2. Above the Helper Functions comment, add the following code (see Figure 9-27):

```
function delProd(prod) {
    document.cookie = "myitem"+prod+"=;expires=Thu, 01-Jan-70
       00:00: 01 GMT;"
    location.reload();
}
```

Code for the delProd() function ◄ **Figure 9-27**

```
function makeOrderCookie(n,id,prod,pr,q){
   document.cookie = "myitem"+n+" = "+id+","+prod+","+pr+","+q+";expires = "
      +expdate.toGMTString();
   alert("You have added "+q+" of the "+prod+" to your shopping cart.");
}

function delProd(prod){
   document.cookie = "myitem"+prod+" = ;expires = Thu, 01-Jan-70 00:00:01 GMT;";
      location.reload();
}

/* Helper Functions */
```

3. Save your work, then return to your browser and refresh **patti_cart.htm**.

4. Click the **Remove Item** link for the Keep Sake Box product in the shopping cart.

As Figure 9-28 shows, the item Keep Sake Box is removed from the shopping cart, and the total cost of the order is updated.

The shopping cart page after deleting the Keep Sake Box ◄ **Figure 9-28**

You show your work to Patti. She tests the shopping cart application and is pleased with the results of her experience. She is very happy to have a working shopping cart for her Web site. In the next session, you will enhance the functionality of the shopping cart by adding simple validation.

Session 9.2 Quick Check

Review

1. What is the advantage of storing multiple pieces of information in the value of a single cookie?
2. What is one disadvantage to working with arrays?
3. What is the purpose of a dynamic table in a shopping cart application?
4. Why is it important to allow a user to remove an item from a shopping cart?

Session 9.3

Form Control Using Cookies

Patti is happy with the work you have completed so far. She has requested one addition to the shopping cart: a feedback form that allows users to verify the information they entered on the patti_cart.htm page before it is submitted to the server. Figure 9-29 shows a preview of the feedback form that you will create.

Figure 9-29 | **Preview of the form feedback page**

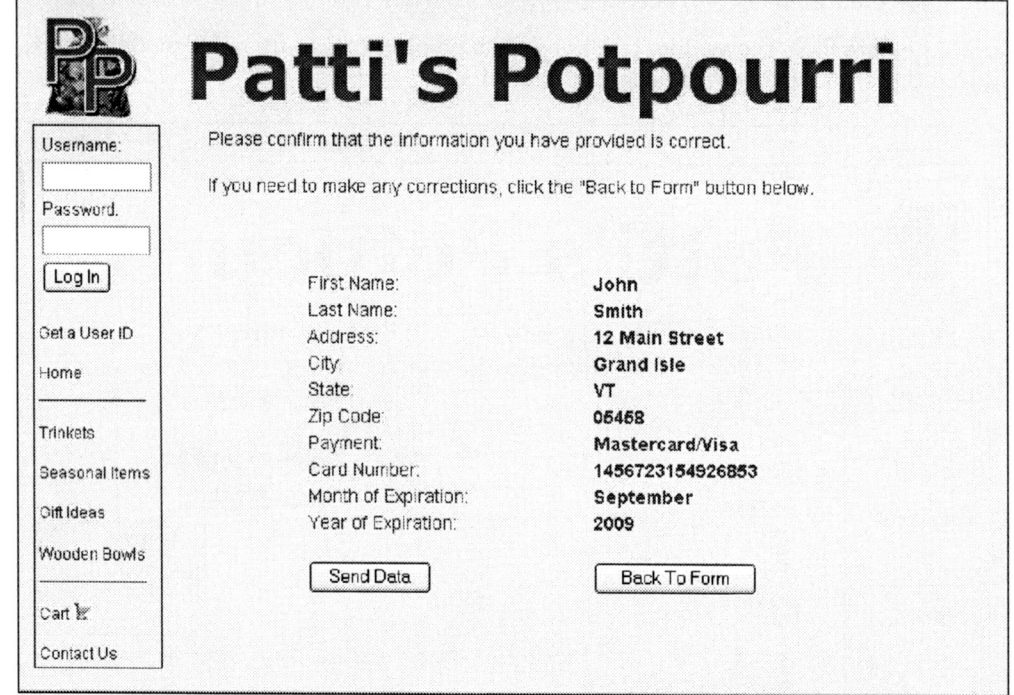

Preserving Form Data

To ensure the feedback form that you create will meet Patti's needs, you speak with Patti about her plans for her online business. She tells you that she has no intentions of expanding her online business any time soon. With this information in mind, you decide that you can use cookies to collect and store the mailing/billing data in the shopping cart page without running out of cookie storage on a user's browser. If Patti decides to expand her online business in the future, technologies other than cookies may be appropriate to support more product choices. However, for the moment, cookies offer a straightforward way to implement the functionality she has requested.

Setting up the feedback page is a two-step process. When a user clicks the Submit button on the shopping cart page, the form passes the data entered to confirmForm(), a validation script that's already been entered for you in the patti.js file. This script verifies that no fields have been left blank, and then passes the form data to the makeFormCookie() function. This function creates a separate cookie for the data that was entered in each input field. Figure 9-30 illustrates the flow of data once a user clicks the Submit button.

Process of preserving form data on Patti's Web site ◀ Figure 9-30

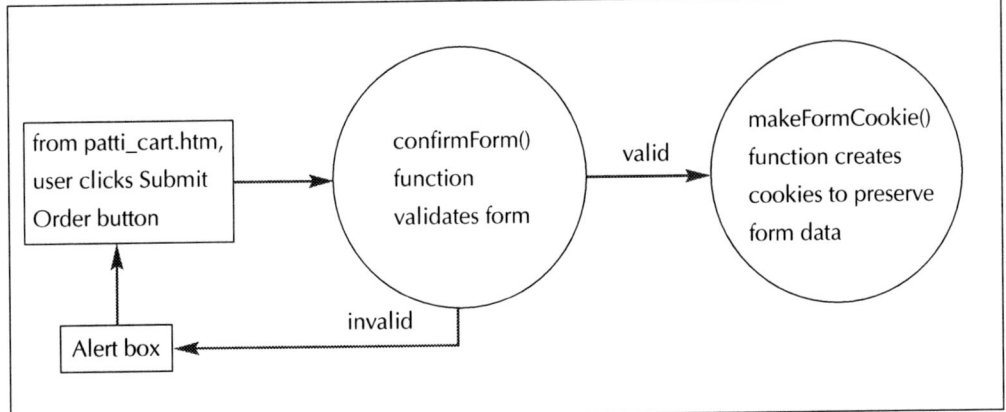

The confirmForm() script for validating form input has already been created for you. Your next task is to create the makeFormCookie() function to create one cookie for each input field in the form. The code for this function is

```
function makeFormCookie(fn,ln,c0,c1,c2,c3,c4,c5,c6,c7){
   document.cookie = "fn = "+fn+"; expires = "+expdate.toGMTString();
   document.cookie = "ln = "+ln+"; expires = "+expdate.toGMTString();
   var form = new Array();
   form[0] = c0;
   form[1] = c1;
   form[2] = c2;
   form[3] = c3;
   form[4] = c4;
   form[5] = c5;
   form[6] = c6;
   form[7] = c7;
   for(i=0;i<9;i++) {
   document.cookie = "c"+[i]+" = "+form[i]+"; expires =
    "+expdate.toGMTString();
   }
}
```

This function starts by creating cookies based on the input in the First Name and Last Name fields. Although these cookies are created when a user completes the form on the patti_account.htm page, users are not required to complete this form or set up an account to use the Web site. Thus, users may come to the shopping cart page without ever having entered their first and last names. For users who have registered or logged in, this part of the function merely writes over the existing cookie with the same information. This step in the process is important, however, as it ensures that the First Name and Last Name values entered by every user are saved in cookies.

Next, the makeFormCookie() function creates an array with the id "form" containing the values in the remaining form fields. The function concludes by creating a separate cookie for each of the values in the array, including the expiration date configured earlier.

The makeFormCookie() function performs a process known as preserving form data. **Preserving form data** refers to the process of collecting and saving form data to be used later in the functioning of a Web site during the current session or for retrieval at a later date in a future session. Add the makeFormCookie() function to Patti's Web site now.

To create the function to preserve form data:

1. Return to the patti.js file in your editor.

2. Just below the delProd() function, enter the following code:

```
function makeFormCookie(fn,ln,c0,c1,c2,c3,c4,c5,c6,c7){
    document.cookie = "fn = "+fn+"; expires = "+expdate.toGMTString();
    document.cookie = "ln = "+ln+"; expires = "+expdate.toGMTString();
    var form = new Array();
    form[0] = c0;
    form[1] = c1;
    form[2] = c2;
    form[3] = c3;
    form[4] = c4;
    form[5] = c5;
    form[6] = c6;
    form[7] = c7;
    for(i=0;i<9;i++) {
    document.cookie = "c"+[i]+" = "+form[i]+"; expires =
    "+expdate.toGMTString();
    }
}
```

3. Save your work.

Figure 9-31 shows the code for the makeFormCookie() function in the patti.js file.

Figure 9-31 **The makeFormCookie() function**

```
function delProd(prod){
    document.cookie = "myitem"+prod+" = ;expires = Thu, 01-Jan-70
00:00:01 GMT;";
    location.reload();
}

function makeFormCookie(fn,ln,c0,c1,c2,c3,c4,c5,c6,c7){
    document.cookie = "fn = "+fn+";expires = "+expdate.toGMTString();
    document.cookie = "ln = "+ln+";expires = "+expdate.toGMTString();
    var form = new Array();
    form[0] = c0;
    form[1] = c1;
    form[2] = c2;
    form[3] = c3;
    form[4] = c4;
    form[5] = c5;
    form[6] = c6;
    form[7] = c7;
    for(i=0;i<9;i++) {
        document.cookie = "c"+[i]+" = "+form[i]+";expires =
"+expdate.toGMTString();
    }
}

/* Helper Functions */
```

With the form data preserved, you can now use it to create a feedback page.

Creating a Form Feedback Page

You are now ready to create the **form feedback page** that Patti requested to allow users to review their input from the form and verify that the input is accurate. Patti has already created the page patti_checkout.htm for use in this process. She wants you to use JavaScript to display the values from the cookies you just created on this page.

In preparation for the feedback page, the array values created by the makeForm-Cookie() function need one final check. If any of the values are null, they will be rendered as "null" on the Web page. This could happen if a cookie that is supposed to hold a piece of form input did not capture this input for any reason, or if a user bookmarked the checkout page and then returned to it later. To provide a more professional look, you want to be sure that the feedback page displays blank feedback in these situations. To accomplish this, the code shown in Figure 9-32 has been added to the patti.js file. This code checks each of the array variables for null values, and changes the value to "" for any variable with a null value.

Code to change null values to empty strings ◄ **Figure 9-32**

```
if(c0 == null) {c0 = "";}
if(c1 == null) {c1 = "";}
if(c2 == null) {c2 = "";}
if(c3 == null) {c3 = "";}
if(c4 == null) {c4 = "";}
if(c5 == null) {c5 = "";}
if(c6 == null) {c6 = "";}
if(c7 == null) {c7 = "";}
```

Next you need to add code to extract the form values from the cookies created by the makeFormCookie() function. You will use the findCookie() function to extract each cookie's value, assigning the value to a variable with the same name as the cookie. Add this code now.

To create a cookie to preserve form data:

1. Return to the patti.js file in your editor.

2. Below the makeFormCookie() function, enter the following code:

```
c0 = findCookie("c0");
c1 = findCookie("c1");
c2 = findCookie("c2");
c3 = findCookie("c3");
c4 = findCookie("c4");
c5 = findCookie("c5");
c6 = findCookie("c6");
c7 = findCookie("c7");
```

Figure 9-33 shows the completed code for extracting the cookie values for the form in the shopping cart page.

Code to retrieve cookie values and pass them to individual variables ◄ **Figure 9-33**

```
        {
            document.cookie = "c"+[i]+" = "+form[i]+";expires = "+expdate.toGMTString();
        }
}

c0 = findCookie("c0");
c1 = findCookie("c1");
c2 = findCookie("c2");
c3 = findCookie("c3");
c4 = findCookie("c4");
c5 = findCookie("c5");
c6 = findCookie("c6");
c7 = findCookie("c7");

/* Helper Functions */
```

3. Save your work.

The code for the buttons on Patti's checkout Web page is already programmed with event handlers that allow the buttons to respond to user actions. If a user clicks the Back To Form button, an event handler redirects the user back to the form. The Submit button opens the Web page patti_confirm.htm. In most cases, a form directs data to a **CGI script**, which is a part of a Web site's back end that moves form data to a server for storage. However, because Patti has asked you to focus on the site's front end for now, you will not be linking the form to a CGI script at this time.

The code you have created so far obtains the shopping cart form data and makes it available to display in the Web page. Next you need to transfer these values to the feedback page. You'll do this by writing the values of the variables you just created into a table on the feedback page.

To place the variable values in the feedback page:

1. In your editor, open the file **patti_checkout.htm**.

2. In the table cell after the label First Name, insert the following code between the opening and closing <div> tags (see Figure 9-34):

   ```
   <script type="text/javascript">document.write(fn)</script>
   ```

3. Repeat Step 2 to add the following code to the remaining table cells:

Last Name:	`<script type="text/javascript">document.write(ln)</script>`
Address:	`<script type="text/javascript">document.write(c0)</script>`
City:	`<script type="text/javascript">document.write(c1)</script>`
State:	`<script type="text/javascript">document.write(c2)</script>`
Zip Code:	`<script type="text/javascript">document.write(c3)</script>`
Payment:	`<script type="text/javascript">document.write(c4)</script>`
Card Number:	`<script type="text/javascript">document.write(c5)</script>`
Month of Expiration:	`<script type="text/javascript">document.write(c6)</script>`
Year of Expiration:	`<script type="text/javascript">document.write(c7)</script>`

   Figure 9-34 shows the completed code for the table.

Code to write form data preserved in cookies ◄ Figure 9-34

```
<table align="center" width="450">
    <tr>
        <td>First Name:</td>
        <td><div class="bold_items"><script
type="text/javascript">document.write(fn)</script></div></td>
    </tr>
    <tr>
        <td>Last Name:</td>
        <td><div class="bold_items"><script
type="text/javascript">document.write(ln)</script></div></td>
    </tr>
    <tr>
        <td>Address:</td>
        <td><div class="bold_items"><script
type="text/javascript">document.write(c0)</script></div></td>
    </tr>
    <tr>
        <td>City:</td>
        <td><div class="bold_items"><script
type="text/javascript">document.write(c1)</script></div></td>
    </tr>
    <tr>
        <td>State:</td>
        <td><div class="bold_items"><script
type="text/javascript">document.write(c2)</script></div></td>
    </tr>
    <tr>
        <td>Zip Code:</td>
        <td><div class="bold_items"><script
type="text/javascript">document.write(c3)</script></div></td>
    </tr>
    <tr>
        <td>Payment:</td>
        <td><div class="bold_items"><script
type="text/javascript">document.write(c4)</script></div></td>
    </tr>
    <tr>
        <td>Card Number:</td>
        <td><div class="bold_items"><script
type="text/javascript">document.write(c5)</script></div></td>
    </tr>
    <tr>
        <td>Month of Expiration:</td>
        <td><div class="bold_items"><script
type="text/javascript">document.write(c6)</script></div></td>
    </tr>
    <tr>
        <td>Year of Expiration:</td>
        <td><div class="bold_items"><script
type="text/javascript">document.write(c7)</script></div></td>
    </tr>

    <tr>
        <td><br /><input type="submit" value="Send Data" id="submit" /></td>
        <td><br /><input type="button" value="Back To Form"
onclick="window.location='patti_cart.htm'" id="back" /></td>
    </tr>
</table>
```

▶ **4.** Save your work and close patti_checkout.htm.

The code you entered completes a table that displays the data submitted in the form for user verification. Next you need to test the feedback page.

To test the form feedback page:

▶ **1.** Return to your browser and open the file **patti_cart.htm**.

▶ **2.** Scroll down to the form and enter the following data :

Address:	12 Main Street
City:	Grand Isle
State:	VT
Zip Code:	05458
Method of Payment:	Mastercard/Visa
Credit Card Number:	1456723154926853
Month of Expiration:	September
Year of Expiration:	2009

▶ **3.** Click **Submit Order** at the bottom of the form.

The form feedback page opens, as shown in Figure 9-35.

Figure 9-35

The completed form feedback page for Patti's Web site

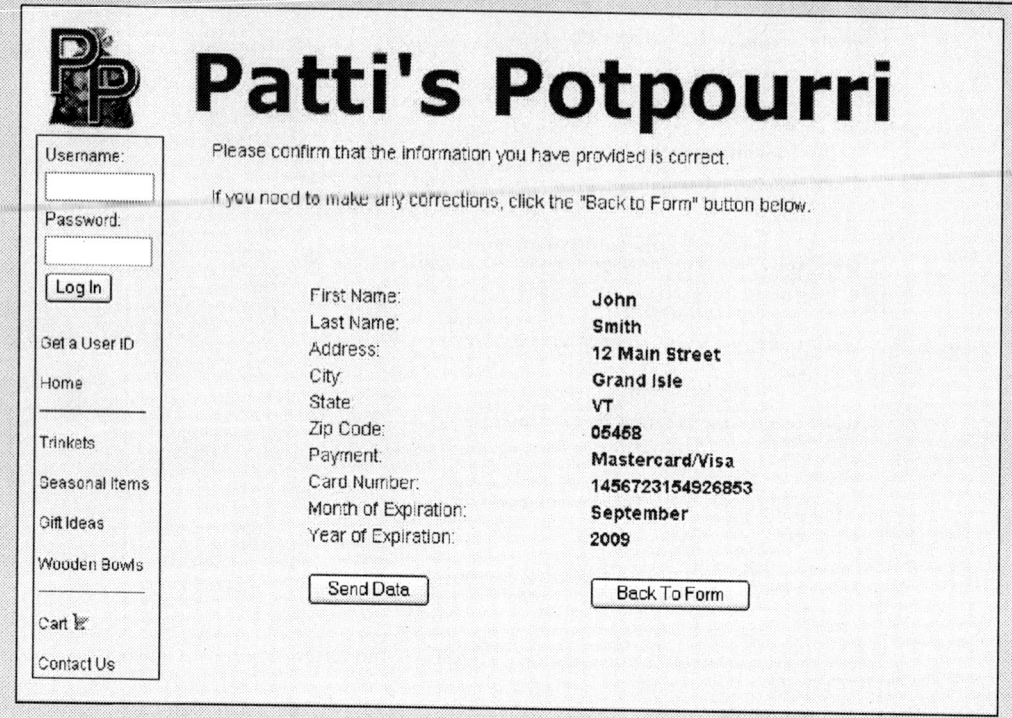

Users of Patti's Web site now have a mechanism to double-check the information that they've entered for an order before submitting the order to the server.

Deleting Cookies

You want to complete one final task before showing your work to Patti. Although the site does not yet need to work with a CGI script, you want to add some basic functionality that will be required when the time comes for one. When the form is set up to work with a CGI script, the site will need a script that deletes the cookies responsible for preserving the form data and the items ordered from Patti's Potpourri.

You can control the deletion of a cookie in two ways. The first method is to set the date and time you want the cookie deleted, and let the cookie expire at that designated time. An advantage to this approach is that you know exactly when the cookie will expire, regardless of when it is created. A disadvantage is that if the cookie is created after its expiration date, it effectively becomes a per session cookie and does not fulfill its intended function. For example, if you were to create a cookie with an expiration date of Sunday, 07-May-05, 00:00:001 GMT after this date, it would effectively become a per session cookie.

An alternative method for deleting cookies is to develop a function that deletes a cookie when it is called. A function can delete a cookie by changing the cookie's expiration date to a date before it came into existence. After this change is made, the browser reads the date, sees that it has passed, and then immediately deletes the cookie. For example, the following code deletes the cookie "username" by changing the expiration date to Thursday, January 1st, 1970, at one second past midnight:

```
document.cookie = "username = John Doe; expires = Thu, 01-Jan-70 00:00:
01 GMT;"
```

While this date is commonly used by programmers to expire cookies, you can use any date in the past to delete a cookie.

To expire cookies on Patti's Web site, you will create a function named zapOrder(), which will pass an expiration date of Thu, 01-Jan-70, 00:00:01 GMT to a variable. The function will then replace the expiration date of each cookie with the value of this variable, expiring each cookie instantly. After the user submits the order data from the feedback page, a confirmation page will open, informing the user that the order has been submitted. The zapOrder() function will be called from this page. The confirmation page will display text that tells the user that the order has been received and will be processed. The page will use the first name and the last name provided when the account was created to personalize this message. Including a confirmation page is important, as it lets users know that the ordering process is complete and nothing more is required of them. As the page is loading the data, the cookies will be deleted, except for the user's first name, last name, username, and password. This will allow users to return to the Web site and place another order without needing to log in again.

To enter a function to delete the form and item cookies:

1. In your editor, return to the file patti.js.

2. Above the Helper Functions comment, enter the following code:

```
function zapOrder(){
    deldate = "Thu, 01-Jan-70 00:00:01 GMT";
    for (i=0;i<=4;i++) {
        document.cookie = "myitem"+[i]+" = ; expires = "+deldate+";";
    }
    for (i=0;i<=10;i++) {
        document.cookie = "c"+[i]+" = ; expires = "+deldate+";";
    }
}
```

Figure 9-36 shows the completed code for the zapOrder() function.

Code for the zapOrder() function ◀ **Figure 9-36**

```
c0 = findCookie("c0");
c1 = findCookie("c1");
c2 = findCookie("c2");
c3 = findCookie("c3");
c4 = findCookie("c4");
c5 = findCookie("c5");
c6 = findCookie("c6");
c7 = findCookie("c7");

function zapOrder(){
deldate = "Thu, 01-Jan-70 00:00:01 GMT";
    for (i=0;i<=4;i++) {
        document.cookie = "myitem"+[i]+" = ; expires = "+deldate+";";
    }
    for (i=0;i<=10;i++) {
        document.cookie = "c"+[i]+" = ; expires = "+deldate+";";
    }
}

/* Helper Functions */
```

3. Save your work and close patti.js.

Next, you need to add an event handler in the confirmation page to call the zapOrder() function.

To enter code to call the zapOrder() function:

1. In your editor, open the file **patti_confirm.htm**.
2. In the <body> tag, add the event handler **onload="zapOrder()"** (see Figure 9-37).

Figure 9-37	Code in the patti_confirm.htm file that deletes cookies

```
<script type="text/javascript" src="patti.js"></script>
<link rel="stylesheet" type="text/css" href="patti.css" />

<title>Confirmation Page</title>
</head>

<body onload="zapOrder()">

<img src="logo.jpg" alt="" border="0" />
<img src="patti.jpg" alt="" border="0" />
<br />
<div id="links">
```

3. Save your work and close patti_confirm.htm in your editor.
4. Return to patti_checkout.htm in your browser, and click the **Send Data** button.

   Figure 9-38 shows the confirmation page in the browser.

Figure 9-38	The confirmation page of Patti's Web site

Patti's Potpourri

Username:

Password:

[Log In]

Get a User ID

Home

Trinkets

Seasonal Items

Gift Ideas

Wooden Bowls

Cart ⛏

Contact Us

Thank you **John Smith** for your order. Your order will be processed within 24 hours. After payment is confirmed, your order will be shipped to you immediately.

Thanks for shopping at Patti's Potpourri!

Return to Patti's home page

5. Click the **Cart** link.

   The shopping cart page opens showing no products selected and with no entries in the input fields. This confirms that your code deleted the cookies successfully.
6. Close your browser.

You have completed your work with cookies for Patti's Web site. She is happy with the functions you have developed for her site, and she is impressed with the quality of your work. She will call you in the future when she needs additional development for her Web site.

Session 9.3 Quick Check

1. What does the term "preserving form data" mean?
2. Why is it a good idea to incorporate a form feedback page in a site requiring form input from a user?
3. What is the function of a CGI script?
4. What purpose does a checkout page have in an online ordering process?
5. Describe two methods for controlling the deletion of a cookie.

Tutorial Summary

In this tutorial, you learned about different types of JavaScript cookies and their advantages and disadvantages. You learned how to control cookie privacy settings in popular browsers. You learned how to create, store, and delete cookies in a shopping cart application. You saw how you can use form input to set the value of a cookie. You also saw how you can dynamically create cookie names and then pass values to these cookies. You practiced extracting cookie values and then using them as a means of personalizing a Web page. In addition, you used cookie values to create a feedback page for users to confirm information that they have entered. Finally, you created code to delete cookies.

Key Terms

back end	form feedback page	server-side cookies
CGI script	front end	server-side
client-side cookies	HTTPS protocol	shopping cart
client-side shopping cart	online shopping cart	stateless
compact privacy policy	per session cookies	third-party cookies
cookie	persistent	unsatisfactory cookie
dynamic table	preserving form data	
first-party cookies	privacy statement	

Review Assignment

Data files needed for this Review Assignment: cart.gif, logo.jpg, patti2txt.js, patti.css, patti.jpg, patti_account2txt.htm

After becoming familiar with the enhanced features that you added to her Web site, Patti has requested a change in the site's functionality. In addition to the page customization that users see after logging in, Patti would like an alert box to open after login showing the user's full name and a greeting. She would like this greeting to inform her visitors that they can change their account information if they wish. To do this, you'll create a script and associate it with the login form at the upper-left corner of each Web page on Patti's site. Start by implementing and testing this feature on the page where users create their accounts. Figure 9-39 shows a preview of the alert box that you'll create.

Figure 9-39 | **Alert box for login page**

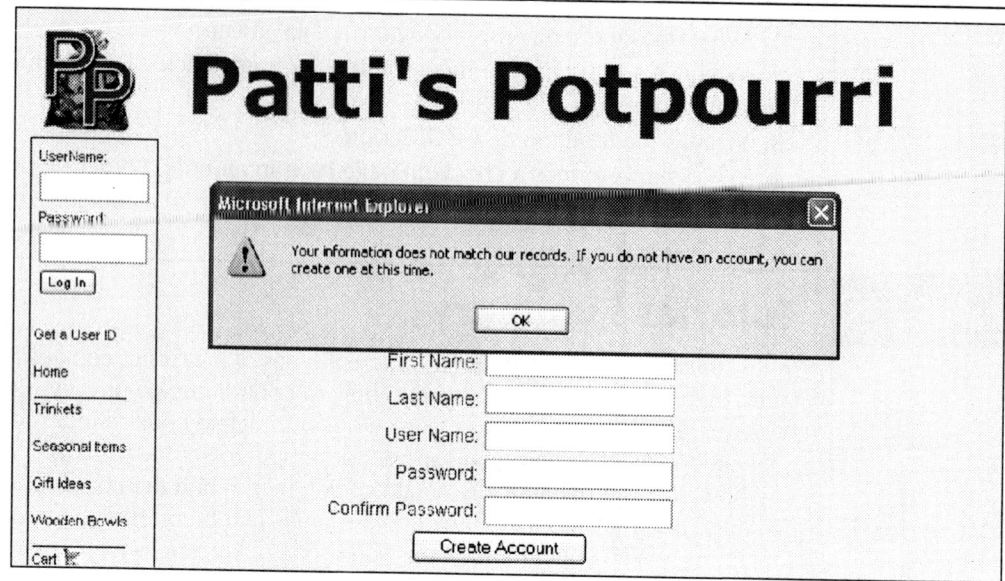

1. In your editor, open the file **patti2txt.js**. Enter *your name* and *the date* in the comment section, and then save it as **patti2.js**.
2. Below the findCookie() function, enter the code `fn = findCookie("fn");` to pass the value of the cookie "fn" to a variable of the same name. Repeat this process for the cookies with the names "ln", "pswd", and "user".
3. Create a function named showCookies():
   a. In this function, pass the value of the "username" field from the form "login" to a variable named new_user. Then pass the value of the "user_pswd" field from the form "login" to a variable named "see_pswd".
   b. Create a conditional statement that checks if the value of "new_user" is the same as the value of "user", and checks if the value of "see_pswd" is the same as the value of "pswd".
   c. If these two conditions are true, then the function should display an alert box containing the following message:
      "Hello "+fn+" "+ln+". Welcome back to Patti's Potpourri. If you wish to change your account information, please complete the form on this page."
   d. If one or both of the conditions are not true, then the function should display an alert box containing the following message:
      "Your information does not match our records. If you do not have an account, you can create one at this time."
4. Close patti2.js, saving your work.
5. Open **patti_account2txt.htm** in your editor, enter *your name* and *the date* in the comment section, and save the file as **patti_account2.htm**.
6. In the form named "login", locate the input element with the id "submit1", add the event handler **onclick="showCookies()"**, then save your work and close the file.
7. In your browser, open the page **patti_account2.htm**.

8. Fill in the Username field in the upper-left corner of the page with your *first name*. Fill in the password field with a password of **123**. Click the **Log In** button below this form.

   An alert box opens displaying the message "Your information does not match our records. If you do not have an account, you can create one at this time." Close the alert box.

9. Complete the form fields with the following entries:

   First Name   *your first name*
   Last Name   *your last name*
   User Name   *your first name*
   Password   **123**
   Confirm Password **123**

10. Click the **Create Account** button.

11. Fill in the "Username" field in the upper-left corner of the page with *your first name*. Fill in the password field with a password of **123**. Click the **Log In** button below this form.

    An alert box opens displaying a personalized greeting.

12. Close the alert box.

13. Submit your work to your instructor.

Case Problem 1

Apply

Use the skills you learned to create a verification page for a charitable donation Web site.

Data files needed for this Case Problem: mc_carver.css, mc_carver.gif, mc_carverfeedbacktxt.htm, mc_carvertxt.htm, mc_carvertxt.js.

The McCarver Philanthropic Foundation The McCarver Foundation, a small philanthropic organization, works with three local charitable organizations in the Caldwell parish of Louisiana. The mission of the foundation is to solicit funds from individuals and organizations who are looking to support these charitable groups. Reema Nasr, director of communications for the foundation, has requested your help in creating a form feedback page. When a user of the foundation's Web site wishes make a donation to one of the supported organizations, Reema would like to provide the user with a chance to verify the information provided before submitting it. To complete this task, you need to collect the form data on the foundation's donation page and make it available on a feedback page that allows a donor to confirm the data entered. Figure 9-40 shows a preview of the confirmation page you will create.

Figure 9-40

Figure 9-40   **Feedback page for the McCarver Philanthropic Donation site**

1. In. your editor, open the files **mc_carvertxt.htm**, **mc_carverfeedbacktxt.htm**, and **mc_carvertxt.js**. Enter *your name* and *the date* in the comment section of each file, and save the files as **mc_carver.htm**, **mc_carverfeedback.htm**, and **mc_carver.js** respectively.

2. Review the code already present in the file mc_carver.js. The file contains functions called findCookie() and sendForm(). The findCookie() function retrieves cookie values based on the cookie's name. The sendForm() function passes all form input to variables used to make the required cookies.

3. At the bottom of the mc_carver.js file, insert a command that uses the Date() method to capture the current date and pass it to a variable named "now". Below this, create a variable named "expdate" and set it equal to the current date plus two weeks.

4. Below the variable "expdate", add a function named createCookies(). The function should take five parameters, with the names d1, d2, d3, d4, and d5.

    a. Add code to the function to create five cookies, with the names d1, d2, d3, d4, and d5.

    b. Set the value of each cookie to the variable value of the same name. For example, the cookie d1 should be assigned the value in the variable d1. Set all of these cookies to expire according to the value held in the variable "expdate" converted to GMT.

    c. Conclude the function with code to redirect users to the page mc_carverfeedback.htm.

5. Below the createCookies() function, add code to extract the cookie value from the cookie named d1 and pass it to a variable named d1. Repeat this code for the cookies named d2 through d5.

6. Save your work and close mc_carver.js.

7. In the file mc_carverfeedback.htm, replace the six placeholder comments with document.write commands to write the value of the variable named in each comment. Be sure to include script tags around each document.write command. Save your work and close mc_carverfeedback.htm in your editor.

8. Open **mc_carver.htm** in your browser. Enter values in each field of the form, then click the Send Donation button. After reviewing the data in the feedback page, close your browser and submit your work to your instructor.

Case Problem 2

Data files needed for this Case Problem: merchant.css, merchant_accttxt.htm, merchant_thankstxt.htm, merchants.gif, merchanttxt.htm, and merchanttxt.js.

The Merchant's Market The Merchant's Market is an online grocery store that allows members to purchase fresh fruits and vegetables from local farmers. It is a nonprofit organization started by local farmers looking for ways to get their products to customers more efficiently. The market now allows its members to make purchases online, deducting the purchase amounts from their checking accounts. Before members can use this service, they must provide information about themselves and their checking accounts. Members have already provided some data, such as their mailing addresses and the names of the banks they use when paying their bills. You will build a front end to allow users to register and confirm the information they have entered. Once the confirmation page is submitted, the site should direct users to a page that assigns them a username equal to their e-mail address and a temporary password equal to the routing number of their checking accounts. They will use this information to log in to this site in future visits. Figure 9-41 shows a preview of the confirmation page you will create.

Figure 9-41 | Verification page for the Merchant's Market

Merchant's Market

Account Verification Page

First Name:	John
Last Name:	Smith
E-Mail Address:	smith@hotmail.com
Checking Account Number:	5645665546565656
Routing Number:	897878789

[Submit Request]   [Return To Form]

1. In your editor, open the files **merchant_accttxt.htm**, **merchanttxt.htm**, **merchant_thankstxt.htm**, and **merchanttxt.js**. Enter *your name* and *the date* in the comment section of each file, and save the files with the names **merchant_acct.htm**, **merchant.htm**, **merchant_thanks.htm**, and **merchant.js** respectively.
2. At the bottom of the merchant.js file, add code that uses the Date() method to pass the current date to a variable named currDate.
3. Using the currDate variable, add code to create a date that is one year from the current date, and pass it to a variable named expdate.

4. Below the expdate variable, create a function named reDirect(). Using an if statement, evaluate the content in the variable "first" to see if it is not empty. If the results returns "true", redirect the user to the file merchant_acct.htm.

5. Create a function named newCookie() that creates a cookie named "reg" and sets it equal to the value "registered". Set the cookie's expiration date to the value of the expdate variable converted to GMT.

6. Create a function named buildCookies().
   a. This function should accept five parameters: first, last, em, acct_num, and r_num.
   b. Add code to the function to create a cookie with the same name as each parameter. The value assigned to each cookie should be the value of the corresponding parameter. Set the expiration date for each cookie to one year from the current date.

7. Below the buildCookies() function, use the findCookie() function to pass the value of each cookie you created in the previous step to a variable of the same name. For example, pass the value of the cookie named "first" to a variable named "first".

8. Save your work and close merchant.js.

9. In your editor, return to the file merchant_acct.htm. Locate the form with the name "feedback". In the first table row, replace the comment tag "<!-- replace with "first" code -->" with JavaScript to write the value of the variable named "first". Be sure to enclose your JavaScript code within a script element. Repeat for the remaining comment tags in the merchant_acct.htm file.

10. Save your work and close merchant_acct.htm.

11. In your editor, return to the file merchant_thanks.htm. Replace the comment <!--replace with "em" code-->"with JavaScript to write the value of the variable "em".

12. In your browser, open the file merchant.htm.

13. Complete the form fields with the following entries:

First Name	your first name
Last Name	your last name
E-Mail Address	your e-mail address
Checking Account Number	9876543219
Routing Number	006336999

14. Click the Process Request button at the bottom of the form.

15. Save your work, close this file and close your editor. Submit the completed Web page to your instructor.

Apply

Use the skills you learned to create a login page for an online store.

Case Problem 3

Data files needed for this Case Problem: mollie.css, mollie_1.jpg, mollie_bb.jpg, mollie_prodtxt.htm, mollietxt.htm, mollietxt.js, and vase1.jpg.

Mollie's Barn Boutique Login Page Mollie Sheldon runs a boutique from her barn in Lowell, Massachusetts. She sells an eclectic assortment of antiques and craft items. She has set up a Web site for her business where users can view items in stock and make purchases. Mollie would like you to add functionality that allows users to log in and that personalizes the pages in response. You'll build a login page for Mollie's Barn Boutique, and incorporate a personalized greeting from Mollie on the main page after a user logs in. Figure 9-42 shows a preview of the personalization.

Figure 9-42	Personalized greeting at Mollie's Boutique

Mollie's Barn Boutique

Welcome jsmith123 to Mollie's Boutique!

Take a look around at our assortment of odds and ends. You'll find just the right gift for that special someone. Everything you see here is guaranteed by Mollie.

Return to Mollie's home page.

Blue Vase

Candlesticks

Memory Box

Ornamental Candlesticks

Perfume Bottle

Green Vase

1. In your editor, open the file **mollietxt.js**. Enter *your name* and *the date* in the comment section and then save the file as **mollie.js**.

2. At the bottom of the file, create a variable named "u" and assign it the value of the cookie by the same name. Create a second variable named "p" and assign it the value of the cookie by the same name.

3. Create a function named deterUser(). Use an if statement to check if the variables "u" and "p" are both equivalent to null. If so, then set the visibility of the objects with the ids "login" and "first" to "hidden". In addition, set the visibility of the object with the id "button" to "visible".

4. Create a function named valUser().
   a. Use an if statement to check if the variables "u" and "p" are both equivalent to null. If so, then redirect users to a page named mollie_prod.htm. Close the if statement.
   b. From the form with the id "enter", pass the value of the "user" field to a variable of the same name. Repeat for the "pwd" field.
   c. Use an if statement to check if the variables "user" and "pwd" are both empty.
      • If so, then the function should return "false".
      • Otherwise, it should create a variable named "today" containing the current date and a variable named "expdate" equal to the current date plus ninety days. It should also create a cookie named "u" with a value equal to the value of the "user" variable and an expiration date equal to the variable "expdate". In addition, it should create a cookie named "p" with a value equal to the value of the "pwd" variable and an expiration date equal to the variable "expdate".

5. Save your work and close this file.

6. In your browser, open the file **mollie.htm**.

7. Complete the form fields with the following entries:

Username	*your first name*
Password	**123**
Confirm Password	**123**

8. Click the **Log-In** button at the bottom of the form.
   Click the **Enter** button at the bottom of the image to enter Mollie's Boutique.
9. Click the **Return to Mollie's home page** link.
10. Submit your work to your instructor.

Apply

Use the skills you learned to create an online shopping cart.

Case Problem 4

Data files needed for this Case Problem: bowl0.jpg, bowl1.jpg, dan.css, dan.gif, dan_carttxt.htm, dantxt.htm, and dantxt.js.

The Daniel James Collection The Daniel James collection was started by renowned wood carver Daniel James. He has produced award-winning wood carvings for years. He now wants to make his showroom available on the Web. He wants to start slowly with a simple Web site selling only a couple of items. He needs you to set up a small front-end shopping cart for him. Figure 9-43 shows the shopping cart you will create.

Figure 9-43 **The shopping cart page for the Daniel James Collection**

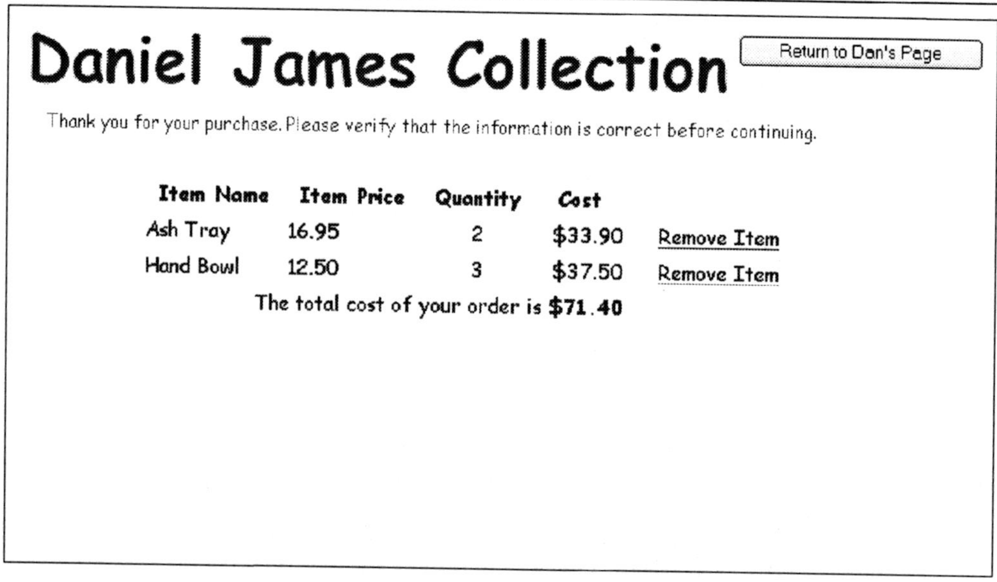

1. In your editor, open the files **dan_carttxt.htm**, **dantxt.htm**, and **dantxt.js**. Enter ***your name*** and ***the date*** in the comment section and then save them as files **dan_cart.htm**, **dan.htm**, and **dan.js** respectively. Close the file dan.htm.
2. At the end of the file dan.js, create a function named makeTable(). The function should write the opening table tag and the first row of a table to a Web page. The table should have a width of 500 pixels. The first row of the table should contain four table header cells, containing the text "Item Name", "Item Price", "Quantity", and "Cost". Be sure to close the table row.
3. Create a function named endTable() that writes a closing table tag.
4. Create a function named addCart() that accepts three parameters: "itm", "p", and "v".
   a. Use an if statement to check if the parameter "v" is equal to zero. If so, then pass the value of the input field "bowl1" from the form "item1" to a variable named "q".
   b. Use an if statement to check if the parameter "v" is equal to 1. If so, then pass the value of the input field "bowl2" from the form "item2" to a variable named "q".

c. Use an if statement to check if the parameter "v" is empty. If so, then create an alert box displaying the text "Please enter a quantity greater than zero." The function should then return "false".

d. Create a variable named currDate with a value equal to the current date. Below it, create a variable named expdate with a value equal to a date six months from the current date.

e. Create a cookie with the name "dan*v*" where *v* is the value of the variable "v". The value of the cookie should be the values held in the variables "itm", "p", and "q", separated by commas. The cookie's expiration date should equal the value of the variable expdate converted to GMT.

f. Generate an alert box displaying the text "Thank you for your purchase of the "+itm+"."

5. Create a function named seeItm().

a. Create a variable named addTot and set it equal to zero.

b. Create an array named "itm". Pass the value of the cookies dan0 and dan1 to the array.

c. Using an if statement, evaluate each element in the array "itm" to see if it is null. If both array elements are null, then write the text "Your cart is empty." and return "false". Otherwise, call the function makeTable() and loop through all of the items in the array "itm". For each item, use an if statement to confirm that the element is not null and not empty. If these conditions are both true, execute the following commands:

-   Write an opening table row tag and an opening table data tag.
-   Find the first instance of a comma in the first element of the array "itm". Pass the result to a variable named stopnow. Find the value of the item by searching the string from the very beginning to a point specified in the variable named "stopnow". Pass the results of this search to a variable named "start". Write the value of the variable "start" to the file followed by a closing table cell tag and an opening table cell tag.
-   Search the array element for a comma. After finding its numeric location in the string, add 1 to this value and pass the entire results to a variable named px. Search the element for another comma from a starting point held in the variable px. Pass the results to a variable named px2. Pull out from this string all text starting from a point designated by the value held in the variable px and ending at a point designated by the value held in the variable px2. Parse out the number, including decimal values. Pass this result to a variable named tot_px. Fix the numeric value to two decimal places and pass the result to a variable named tot_px1. Write the value of the variable tot_px1 to the file, followed by a closing table cell tag and an opening table cell tag specifying center alignment.
-   You will now extract the last value in the array element. Take the entire length of the array element and subtract 1 from it. This is the starting point to extract the substring that contains the quantity value. The end point is the entire length of the array element. Given the starting and ending points in the array element, search out the quantity value held in the array. Parse out the number and pass it to the variable quant. Write the value of the quant variable to the document followed by a closing table cell tag and an opening table cell tag specifying right alignment.

- Multiply the values in the variables quant and tot_px and pass the result to a variable named cost_raw. Fix the numeric display of the variable cost_raw to two decimal places. Pass the result of this to the variable "cost". Parse out the numeric value of "cost", including decimals, and pass this value to the variable cost_tot. Add the value of cost_tot to the existing value of addTot. Fix the value of addTot to two decimal places and pass the result to a variable named "total".

- Write a dollar sign followed by the value of the variable "cost" to the document, followed by a closing table cell tag and an opening table cell tag specifying right alignment. Next write the text link "Remove Item" with href set to # and an onclick() event handler that calls the function delItm() with the argument "+[i]+".

- Write a closing table cell tag followed by a closing table row tag. Write a new table row. The row's only cell should span four columns and should be right-aligned. The cell should contain the text "The total cost of your order is" followed by a dollar sign and the value of the "total" variable, formatted as bold. Close the else statement, then call the function endTable().

6. Create a function named delItm() with a single parameter, "itm".

   a. The function should create a cookie named "danx" where x is the value of the "itm" parameter. Set the cookie to expire immediately.

   b. Next, the function should reload the page in the browser.

7. Save your work and close dan.js.

8. In the file dan_cart.htm, replace the comment "<!-- Insert code here. -->" with a script calling the function seeItm(). Save your work and close dan_cart.htm.

9. Open **dan.htm** in your browser. Add an item to your cart, then click the View Cart button at the top of the page. View the contents of the shopping cart. Test the functionality for removing items from the cart by clicking the **Remove Item** link for the item you placed in the cart.

10. Submit your work to your instructor.

Review

Quick Check Answers
Session 9.1

1. A client-side shopping cart is controlled by the browser, and a server-side shopping cart is controlled from the server. All items added to a server-side shopping cart are stored in a program on the server, and all items in a client-side shopping cart are stored on the user's computer.

2. A server-side cookie resides on a server, and a client-side cookie resides in a browser's memory.

3. A privacy statement explains how a Web site protects the privacy of those who visit and provide information.

4. document.cookie = "item = chair; expires = Monday, 02-Jul-07 12:00:00 GMT"

5. The cookie would be accessible to any Web page on the server of origin.

6. A per session cookie expires at the end of the session in which it was generated.

7. The cookie expires at 00:00:01 GMT.

Session 9.2

1. Storing multiple pieces of information in the value of a single cookie enables you to use fewer cookies, thus expanding the amount of information that your site can store in cookies.

2. Working with arrays requires more programming to create cookies and extract cookie values.

3. The function of a dynamic table in a shopping cart application is to display all of the items that a user has ordered, without empty rows or information on items that the user isn't ordering.

4. It provides a user with the opportunity to delete an item from a shopping cart should the user not want to purchase it.

Session 9.3

1. "Preserving form data" refers to the process of collecting and saving form data to be used later in the functioning of a Web site during the current session or for retrieval at a later date in a future session.

2. By incorporating a form feedback page, you improve the quality control process of collecting accurate form data.

3. A CGI script is a server-side script that is responsible for collecting, moving, and storing data in a permanent storage facility such as a database or text file.

4. A checkout page allows the user to provide billing and delivery information.

5. You can control the deletion of a cookie in two ways. The first method is to set the date and time you want the cookie deleted, and let the cookie expire at that designated time. An alternative method for deleting cookies is to develop a function that deletes a cookie when it is called. A function can delete a cookie by changing the cookie's expiration date to a date before it came into existence.

Objectives

Session 10.1
- Learn how to create dynamic content under the Internet Explorer DOM
- Understand the methods and properties of nodes and the node tree
- Learn to create element and text nodes
- Understand how to attach nodes to a Web page document

Session 10.2
- Apply node properties and styles to create dynamic content
- Work with the properties and methods of attribute nodes
- Work with element attributes

Session 10.3
- Hide and redisplay Web page objects
- Understand how to create recursive functions to navigate a node tree
- Learn to work with the properties and methods of style sheet objects

Working with Dynamic Content and Styles

Creating a Dynamic Table of Contents

Case

MidWest University Dept. of History

Norene Somerville is a professor of history at Midwest University. One of her recent projects involves putting the text of important historic documents online for her students to download and study. The Web site she's creating will support a variety of different document formats, but Professor Somerville also wants each document to be available in HTML format on a single Web page. This format makes it easier for students to print out the complete text of a document without having to navigate an entire site or install word processing or document software. However, Norene is concerned that some of the documents are very long and would be difficult to manage if placed on a single page.

She believes that a table of contents that summarizes the different sections within a document and provides links to those sections would be a great aid to students. However, Norene doesn't have the time to create such a table of contents for each of the documents in her online library. She wants a program to automatically generate these tables of contents, and she has approached you for help in developing such a utility.

Student Data Files

▼tutorial.10

▽ tutorial folder
  treattxt.htm
  uscontxt.htm
  toctxt.js
  + 3 style sheets
  + 3 graphic files

▽ review folder
  fed10txt.htm
  keytxt.js
  + 2 style sheets
  + 3 graphic files

▽ case1 folder
  fr5txt.htm
  engfrtxt.js
  french5.js
  + 1 style sheet

▽ case2 folder
  camtxt.htm
  filttxt.js
  + 1 style sheet
  + 2 graphic files

▽ case3 folder
  clisttxt.htm
  newtxt.js
  data.js
  + 1 style sheet
  + 1 graphic file

▽ case4 folder
  temptxt.htm
  scenetxt.js
  + 1 style sheet
  + 6 graphic files

Session 10.1

Introducing Dynamic Content

You and Norene meet to discuss her proposal for the table of contents utility. Her idea is to base the table of contents on the heading elements often used to break up long HTML documents into topical sections. For example, the h1 heading usually marks a primary section in a document, h2 marks a secondary heading, and so forth. Figure 10-1 shows a sketch that Norene has made of how her table of contents script would work. The utility would search the Web page for heading elements, copying the text of each heading into the TOC. The table of contents would be organized as a nested list with higher-level headings placed at the top of the list. For example, all h1 headings would be placed at the top, h2 headings would be placed within the h1 headings, and so on.

Figure 10-1 ▶ **Converting document content into a table of contents**

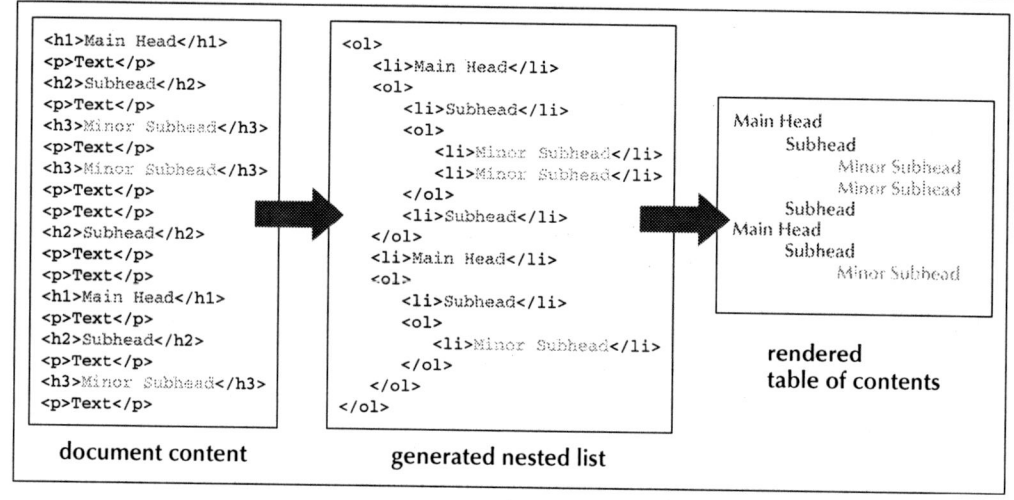

document content   generated nested list   rendered table of contents

Before starting work on the table of contents application, first examine the files that Norene has supplied for you. The sample document that she wants you to practice on is the text of the United States Constitution. This is an ideal test, since the document involves three levels of headings plus long text passages. Open this document now.

To open Norene's Web page:

▶ **1.** In your text editor, open the **uscontxt.htm** file located in the tutorial.10/tutorial folder. Enter **your name** and **the date** in the comment section and save the file as **usconst.htm**.

▶ **2.** Look through the HTML code for the document.

Note that the document contains a div element named "toc" in which you'll place the table of contents. It also includes a div element named "doc" that contains the text of the document upon which the table of contents will be based.

▶ **3.** Open **usconst.htm** in your Web browser. Figure 10-2 shows the current appearance of the page. The table of contents will be placed in the blue box on the page's left margin.

The initial constitution Web page ◄ **Figure 10-2**

All of the JavaScript code that generates the table of contents will be located in an external file. This will allow Norene to use the finished utility with other documents in her library. A file containing some initial code has been created for you. Open this file now.

To open the JavaScript file:

▶ 1. In your text editor, open the **toctxt.js** file located in the tutorial.10/tutorial folder. Enter *your name* and *the date* in the comment section and save the file as **toc.js**.

The file contains a function named makeTOC() that you'll use to generate the table of contents when the Web page is loaded in a browser. At the moment, this function contains no commands. Return to the usconst.htm file and create a link to this JavaScript file along with an event handler that runs the makeTOC() function when the page loads.

▶ 2. Return to the **usconst.htm** file in your text editor.

▶ 3. Above the closing </head> tag insert the following external script element:

```
<script src="toc.js" type="text/javascript"></script>
```

▶ 4. Add the following event handler to the body element: **onload="makeTOC()"**. Figure 10-3 shows the revised code.

Inserting the external script element ◄ **Figure 10-3**

```
<title>The Constitution of the United States</title>
<link href="history.css" rel="stylesheet" type="text/css" />
<link href="toc.css" rel="stylesheet" type="text/css" />

<script src="toc.js" type="text/javascript"></script>
</head>

<body onload="makeTOC()">
<div id="logo"><img src="hlogo.jpg" alt="Historic Documents" /></div>
<div id="logosub">Department of History<br />Midwest University</div>
<div id="doctitle"><h1>The Constitution of the United States</h1></div>
```

5. Close the file, saving your changes.

From this point on, almost all of your work will be done within the toc.js file.

Inserting HTML Content into an Element

Generating a table of contents involves working with **dynamic content**, which is content determined by the operation of a script running within the browser. Often dynamic content is determined either by users' actions or by the content of other elements on the Web page or within the Web site.

Norene wants her table of contents to display the heading "Table of Contents". While you could place an embedded script within the toc element and employ the document. write() method to insert this content, you want to create an application that is self-contained and can be applied to any document with a minimal amount of coding within each document. It would be better to add the heading to the table of contents using a function run from an external JavaScript file. One property that can be used to write content in an element is the innerHTML property. The syntax is

```
object.innerHTML = content
```

where object is a Web page object and content is a text string containing the HTML content of the object. For example, to add an h1 heading to the toc element, you would run the following commands:

```
TOC = document.getElementById("toc");
TOC.innerHTML="<h1>Table of Contents</h1>";
```

Add these commands to the makeTOC() function.

To insert a heading into the TOC:

1. Return to the **toc.js** file in your text editor.

2. Go to the makeTOC() function at the bottom of the file and insert the following commands (see Figure 10-4):

```
TOC = document.getElementById("toc");
TOC.innerHTML="<h1>Table of Contents</h1>";
```

| Figure 10-4 | Inserting HTML code into the toc element |

```
function makeTOC() {
    TOC = document.getElementById("toc");
    TOC.innerHTML="<h1>Table of Contents</h1>";
}
```

3. Save your changes to the file.

4. Reload **usconst.htm** in your Web browser. Figure 10-5 shows the table of contents with the new heading.

Inserting an h1 heading **Figure 10-5**

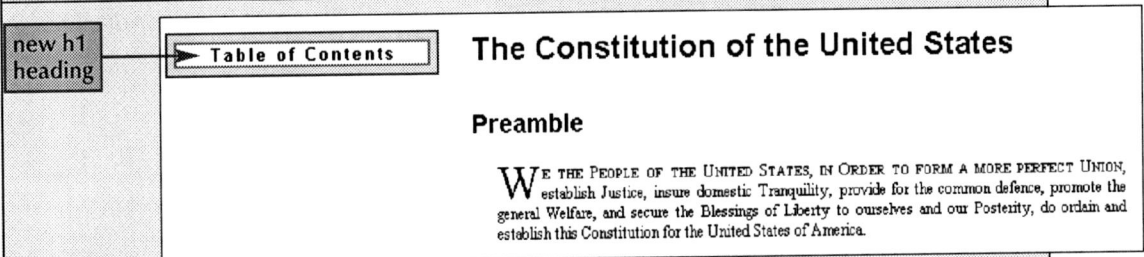

new h1 heading

Table of Contents

The Constitution of the United States

Preamble

WE THE PEOPLE OF THE UNITED STATES, IN ORDER TO FORM A MORE PERFECT UNION, establish Justice, insure domestic Tranquility, provide for the common defence, promote the general Welfare, and secure the Blessings of Liberty to ourselves and our Posterity, do ordain and establish this Constitution for the United States of America.

The styles for the table of contents and the document have already been created for you and stored in the toc.css and history.css style sheets. If you want to study the display styles that will appear as you create the table of contents throughout the course of this tutorial, you may review the contents of those two files.

Dynamic Content in Internet Explorer

The innerHTML property is not part of the official specifications for the W3C document object model. Instead, it is part of the DOM for Internet Explorer. However, since it has proven valuable and easy to use, it is supported by all browsers. The Internet Explorer DOM also supports other properties and methods to aid in the creation of dynamic content; however, these properties and methods are not as widely supported as the innerHTML property. You'll look at a few of them before studying how the W3C DOM handles dynamic content.

The innerHTML property defines the content within an HTML element. If you want to change both the content and the HTML element itself, you use the outerHTML property. The syntax for the two properties is similar:

```
object.outerHTML = content;
```

where *object* is once again the Web page object, but *content* is a text string of the HTML code for both the object and the content it contains. For example, if Norene's Web page contained the element

```
<h1 id="title">History Online</h1>
```

then the commands

```
title = document.getElementById("title");
title.outerHTML="<h2>Historic Documents</h2>";
```

would change the element to

```
<h2>Historic Documents</h2>
```

Be aware that changing the element tags in addition to the element's content can result in unforeseen errors. Running the above code removes the title element from the document hierarchy since the id attribute is not included in the new h2 element. Any subsequent part of the script that references the title element would result in an error. Thus, you should use caution whenever applying the outerHTML property, to ensure that you don't change more of an element's content than you wish.

Related to both the innerHTML and outerHTML properties are the innerText and outerText properties. These properties are used to change the text content of an element. Any text that you specify is treated by browsers as text and not as HTML code. For example, the command

```
title.innerHTML="<i>Historic Documents</i>";
```

results in the title element being displayed as

Historic Documents

By contrast, the command

```
title.innerText="<i>Historic Documents</i>";
```

results in the title element being displayed as

<i>Historic Documents</i>

In this case, the <i> tags are treated as text, rather than HTML elements.

You can use methods in the Internet Explorer DOM to insert elements at specific locations within the document tree. The syntax of the methods is

```
object.insertAdjacentHTML(position, content);
object.insertAdjacentText(position, content);
```

where *position* is a text string specifying the position in which the new HTML code or text is to be inserted relative to *object*, and *content* is the content to be inserted. The *position* parameter has four possible values:

- **BeforeBegin** inserts the content before the object's opening tag
- **AfterBegin** inserts the content directly after the object's opening tag
- **BeforeEnd** inserts the content directly before the object's closing tag
- **AfterEnd** inserts the content after the object's closing tag

For example, to insert the word "Online" at the end of the element

```
<h1 id="title">Historic Documents</h1>
```

you could run the command

```
title.insertAdjacentHTML("BeforeEnd"," Online");
```

This would change the code of the title element to

```
<h1 id="title">Historic Documents Online</h1>
```

The various properties and methods of the Internet Explorer DOM offer quick and easy ways to insert dynamic content. However, keep in mind that only the innerHTML property is supported by other browsers.

Reference Window

Dynamic Content in the IE DOM

- To change the HTML content of a page object, use the property
    `object.innerHTML="content"`
  where `object` is an object on the Web page and `content` is a text string of the object's HTML content.
- To change the HTML code of the object, including the object itself, use
    `object.outerHTML="content"`
- To change the text of a page object, use the property
    `object.innerText="content"`
  where `content` is the text (not HTML content) contained within the element.
- To change the text of a page object, including the object itself, use
    `object.outerText="content"`
- To insert HTML content at a specific location relative to a page object, use the property
    `object.insertAdjacentHTML="position, content"`
  where `position` is "BeforeBegin" (to insert `content` before the opening tag of `object`), "AfterBegin" (to insert `content` directly after the opening tag of `object`), "BeforeEnd" (to insert `content` directly before the closing tag of `object`), or "AfterEnd" (to insert `content` after the closing tag of `object`).

Working with Nodes

Dynamic content in the specifications for the W3C document object model works differently than in the Internet Explorer DOM. In the W3C DOM, objects are organized into **nodes**, with each node representing an object within the Web page and Web browser. In the W3C DOM, anything in an HTML file can be treated as a node. This includes every HTML tag and all of a tag's attributes. Even the tags in a document's head section, comment tags, and the <html> tag itself can be treated as nodes. The text within an HTML tag can also be treated as a node. For example, the tag, "<h1>Table of Contents</h1>" actually consists of two nodes: one node for the h1 element and one node for the text "Table of Contents".

The Node Tree

Nodes are arranged into a hierarchal structure called a **node tree**, which indicates the relationship between each of the nodes. Figure 10-6 shows a representation of a node tree for a simple HTML document. Notice that in the node tree, not only is each element treated as a separate node, but text within each element is treated as a node as well.

Figure 10-6	A document node tree

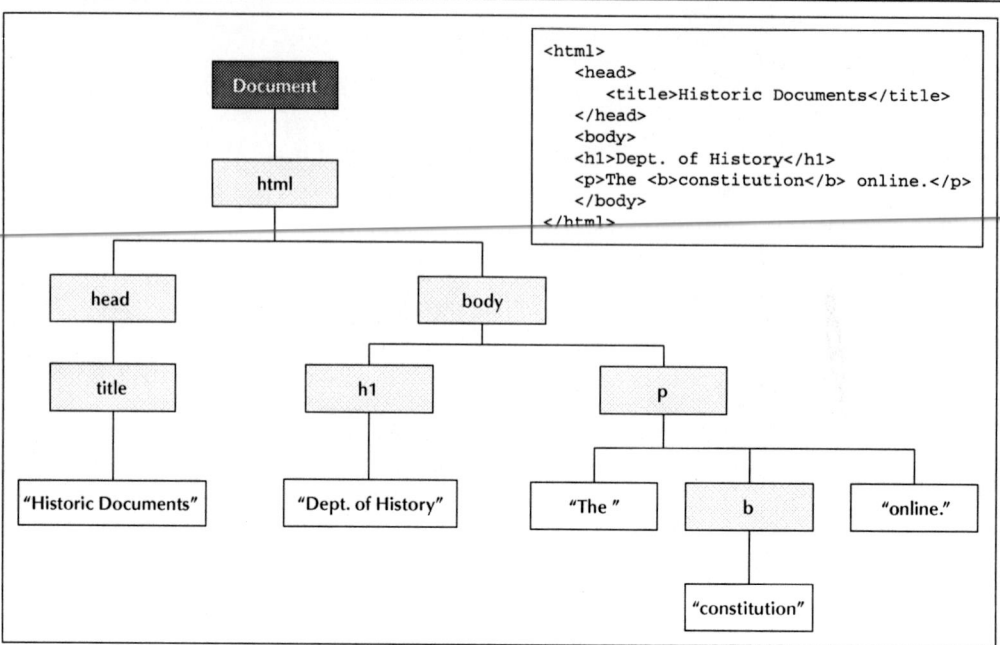

Nodes in a node tree have a familial relationship, as each node can be a parent, child, and/or sibling of other nodes. The syntax to reference a node based on its relationship with the current node is

`node.relationship`

where `node` is the currently selected node or object and `relationship` is the relationship of another node to the current node. For example, the expression

`node.parentNode`

refers to the parent of `node`. In the node tree shown in Figure 10-6, the parent of the body node is the html node, and the parent of the html node is the Document node. The parent of all nodes within a document is the **root node**. For HTML documents, the root node is the html element. A document's root node can also be referenced using the object document.documentElement. The root node is itself a child of the document node, which represents the entire document.

Each node can contain one or more child nodes. To reference the first child of the current node, use the expression

`node.firstChild`

In the node tree shown in Figure 10-6, the h1 node is the first child of the body node, and the text node "Dept. of History" is its first (and only) child. All of the child nodes are organized into the object collection

`node.childNodes`

To reference a particular object from this collection, you specify the item's index number.

`node.childNodes[i]`

where i is the index number of the child node. Thus, to reference the first child of the current node, you could also use the expression

```
node.childNodes[0]
```

For HTML files, the order of the child nodes matches the order of the elements in the file. To determine the total number of child nodes for a given node, you use the length property:

```
node.childNodes.length
```

The length of the childNodes collection for the paragraph element in Figure 10-6 would be 3 (the two text nodes and the bold element). Figure 10-7 summarizes the rest of the familial relationships in the node tree.

Node relationships   Figure 10-7

Property	Description
node.firstChild	Returns the first child of node
node.lastChild	Returns the last child of node
node.childNodes	Returns a collection containing the children of node
node.previousSibling	Returns the sibling prior to node
node.nextSibling	Returns the sibling after node
node.ownerDocument	Returns the root node of the document
node.parentNode	Returns the parent of node

Node Relationships

Reference Window

- To access the parent of a node object, use the reference
  ```
  node.parentNode
  ```
  where node is a node object in the node tree.
- To reference the first and last child of a node, use
  ```
  node.firstChild
  node.lastChild
  ```
- To reference the collection of all child nodes, use
  ```
  node.childNodes
  ```
- To reference the previous and next sibling, use
  ```
  node.previousSibling
  node.nextSibling
  ```

Node types, names, and values

There are some important differences between browsers in how they handle white space in an HTML file. The W3C DOM calls for occurrences of white space to be treated as text nodes. Thus, the HTML code

```
<h1>Table of Contents</h1>
<h2>U.S. Constitution</h2>
```

contains five nodes: 1 node for the h1 element, 1 node for the h2 element, 2 nodes for the text contained within those two elements, and a fifth node for the white space that separates the h1 and h2 elements. While Internet Explorer version 5.0 and higher supports nodes in its document object model, it does not treat occurrences of white space as text nodes. For Internet Explorer, the above code would contain only four nodes. Netscape, Opera, and most other browsers would see five nodes. This difference affects how you write program code that involves nodes, meaning that you often have to test whether the node that a program is currently working with represents a text node, an element node, or some other type of node. The following properties provide information about a node's type, name, and value:

- *node*.nodeType
- *node*.nodeName
- *node*.nodeValue

The nodeType property is an integer indicating whether the node refers to an element, a text string, a comment, an attribute, and so forth. The nodeName property is the name of the node within the document. For document elements, the nodeName property returns the name of the element in uppercase letters. The nodeValue property returns the node's value. Figure 10-8 summarizes the values of the three properties for the different nodes you would typically encounter in an HTML file.

| Figure 10-8 | Node types, names, and values |

Node	*node*.nodeType	*node*.nodeName	*node*.nodeValue
Element	1	*ELEMENT NAME*	null
Attribute	2	*attribute name*	*attribute value*
Text	3	*#text*	*text string*
Comment	8	*#comment*	*comment text*
Document	9	*#document*	null

To see how these properties compare to the sample node tree you saw earlier, Figure 10-9 displays the nodeType, nodeName, and nodeValue property values for each of the nodes from Figure 10-6.

Nodes from the sample node tree ◀ Figure 10-9

Node	*node*.nodeType	*node*.nodeName	*node*.nodeValue
Document	9	#document	null
html	1	HTML	null
head	1	HEAD	null
body	1	BODY	null
title	1	TITLE	null
"Historic Documents"	3	#text	Historic Documents
h1	1	H1	null
"Dept. of History"	3	#text	Dept. of History
p	1	P	null
"The "	3	#text	The
b	1	B	null
"constitution"	3	#text	constitution
" online"	3	#text	online

One issue you may have noticed with element nodes is that they have no value. It's tempting to think that an element node's value should be the content it contains; however, that content is already its own node. Thus, if you want to change the text contained within an element, you have to modify the value of that element's text node. For example, the title element contains the following text:

```
<h1 id="title">History Online</h1>
```

To change the text of the title to "Historic Documents Online" you could run the following code under the W3C DOM:

```
title = document.getElementById("title");
title.firstChild.nodeValue = "Historic Documents Online";
```

This code sample uses the firstChild reference since the text node is the first (and only) child of the title element.

Node Properties

- To determine the type of object a node represents, use the property
    `node.nodeType`
  where *node* is a node object in the node tree. The nodeType property returns the value 1 for elements, 2 for attributes, and 3 for text nodes.
- To return the value of a node, use
    `node.nodeValue`
  For elements, the value of the nodeValue property is null. For attributes, the value represents the attribute's value. For text nodes, the value represents the text string contained in the node.
- To return the name of a node, use
    `node.nodeName`
  For elements, the name of the node matches the name of the element in uppercase letters. For attributes, the node name matches the attribute name. For text nodes, the node name is #text.

Creating and Attaching Nodes

Norene is most interested in adding new content to the Web page. The W3C DOM supports several methods to create new nodes, which are listed in Figure 10-10.

Figure 10-10 ▶ **Methods to create nodes**

Method	Descripton
document.createAttribute(*att*)	Creates an attribute node with the name *att*
document.createComment(*text*)	Creates a comment node containing the comment text string *text*
document.createElement(*elem*)	Creates an element node with the name *elem*
document.createTextNode(*text*)	Creates a text node containing the text string *text*
node.cloneNode(*deep*)	Creates a copy of *node*. If the Boolean parameter *deep* is true, the copy extends to all descendants of the node object; otherwise, only *node* is copied.

Using these methods, you can create a wide variety of objects that can be used in a Web page document. For example, to create a text node containing the text "Historic Documents Online" you would use the following expression:

```
document.createTextNode("Historic Documents Online")
```

All of the methods described in Figure 10-10 create single nodes, with the exception of the cloneNode() method. The cloneNode() method is useful when you need to create a copy of an existing node, including any descendants of that node. The command

```
newtitle = title.cloneNode(true)
```

creates a copy of the title node, including any descendants of that node. The cloneNode() method provides a quick and easy way of creating elements and their content without having to go through the process of creating each node individually.

Creating Nodes

- To create a node for an element, use the method
  ```
  document.createElement(text)
  ```
  where *text* is the name of the element.
- To create a node for an attribute, use the method
  ```
  document.createAttribute(text)
  ```
  where *text* is the name of the attribute.
- To create a text node, use
  ```
  document.createTextNode(text)
  ```
  where *text* is the text string of the text node.
- To copy a preexisting node, use the method
  ```
  node.cloneNode(deep)
  ```
  where *node* is the preexisting node and *deep* is a Boolean value indicating whether to copy all descendants of the node (true) or only the node itself (false).

Once a node has been created, it still has to be attached to a node in the document's node tree if it is to be part of the document. Unattached nodes and node trees are known as **document fragments** and exist only in a browser's memory. You can still access document fragments and work with them in your script, but they are not displayed in a Web page document. Figure 10-11 describes several methods for attaching one node to another.

Methods to attach or remove nodes | Figure 10-11

Method	Description
node.appendChild(*new*)	Appends a *new* child node to *node*, attaching it as the last child node
node.insertBefore(*new*, *child*)	Inserts a *new* child node to *node*, placing it before the *child* node; if no *child* is specified the *new* child node is added as the last child node
node.normalized()	Traverses all child nodes of *node*; any adjacent text nodes are merged into a single text node
node.removeChild(*old*)	Removes the child node *old* from *node*
node.replaceChild(*new*, *old*)	Replaces the child node *old* with the child node *new*

Using the properties and methods described in Figures 10-10 and 10-11, you can elaborate node trees that consist of several different nodes. Figure 10-12 describes the process by which you would create the following code using those methods:

```
<p><i>Historic</i> Documents</p>
```

Figure 10-12 | **Creating and attaching nodes**

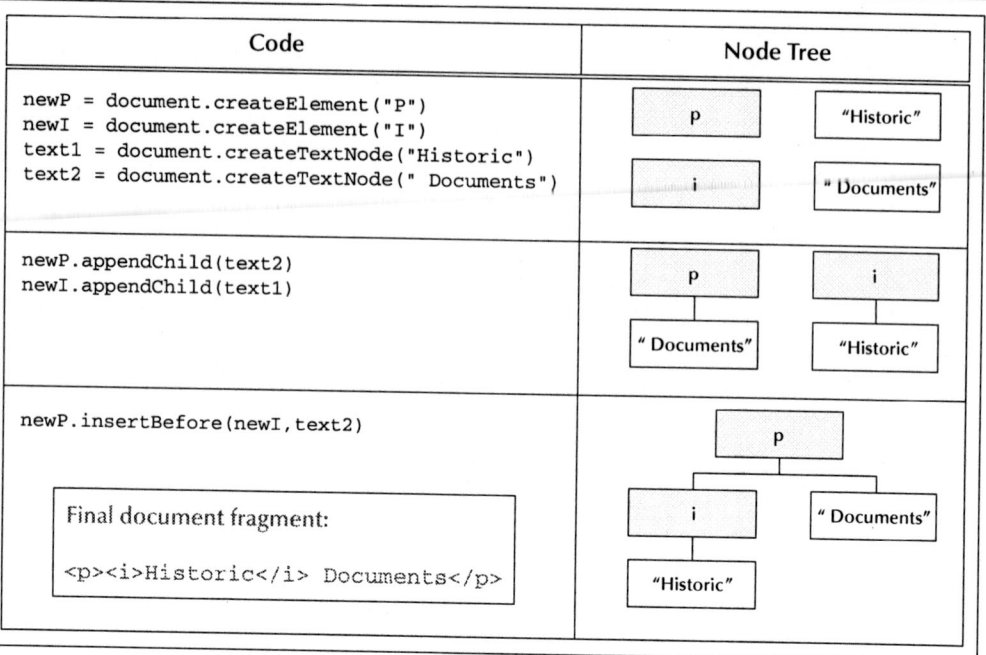

The approach shown in Figure 10-12 first uses the createElement() and createText-Node() methods to create four nodes: an element node for a paragraph, an element node for italicized text, a text node containing the text string "Historic", and a text node containing the text "Documents". The appendChild() method is then employed to attach the text nodes to the element nodes. The last line of code uses the insertBefore() method to insert the italicized text before the second text node. While at first glance this approach may seem more cumbersome than simply using the innerHTML method, the great advantage of working with nodes is that you can work with individual elements and text strings at a detail and flexibility that is not possible with other methods.

Reference Window

Attaching and Removing Nodes

- To append a new node as a child of a preexisting node, use the method
    `node.appendChild(new)`
  where *node* is the preexisting node and *new* is the new child. The new child node is appended to the end of the child nodes collection.
- To insert a new node at a specific location in the child nodes collection, use the method
    `node.insertBefore(new, child)`
  where *child* is the child node that the new node should be placed in front of.
- To remove a child node, use the method
    `node.removeChild(old)`
  where *old* is the child node to be removed.
- To replace one child node with another, use
    `node.replace(new, old)`

Now that you've seen how to create and attach nodes, you'll create a node for an ol (ordered list) element and attach it to the table of contents in Norene's Web page. Currently, the content of the toc element consists of the following elements:

```
<div id="toc">
   <h1>Table of Contents</h1>
</div>
```

You want to change this to

```
<div id="toc">
   <h1>Table of Contents</h1>
   <ol></ol>
</div>
```

The code to create the ol list element and attach it to the table of contents is therefore

```
TOCList = document.createElement("ol");
TOC.appendChild(TOCList);
```

Add this code to the makeTOC() function.

To append the ol element to the TOC:

1. Return to the **toc.js** file in your text editor.

2. Add the following commands to the makeTOC() function as shown in Figure 10-13:

   ```
   TOCList = document.createElement("ol");
   TOC.appendChild(TOCList);
   ```

Creating and attaching the ol element   Figure 10-13

```
function makeTOC() {
    TOC = document.getElementById("toc");
    TOC.innerHTML="<h1>Table of Contents</h1>";
    TOCList = document.createElement("ol");
    TOC.appendChild(TOCList);
}
```

3. Save your changes to the file.

Creating a List of Heading Elements

The next task is to populate the ordered list with list items, where the text of each list item matches the text of a heading element in the constitution document. Your code needs to do the following:

1. Examine the child nodes of the constitution document
2. For each child node, test whether it represents a heading element
3. If it is a heading element, extract the element's text and create a list item containing that same text
4. Append the list item as a new child of the ordered list in the table of contents

For simplicity's sake, assume that each heading element is a child of the "doc" element in Norene's Web page (rather than nested within other elements), and that the heading elements contain only text and no other content. For the moment, you'll place all of the text from the section headings on the same level in the table of contents, rather than at different levels as Norene requested in her sketch (Figure 10-1). You'll explore how to create nested lists in the next session.

Looping Through the Child Node Collection

There are two ways of looping through a collection of child nodes. In one approach, you use a counter variable that starts with a value of 0 and increases by 1 for each node, up to the length of the childNodes collection. The general form of this loop is

```
for (var i=0; i < node.childNodes.length; i++) {
    commands for node.childNode[i]
}
```

In this form, the child nodes in the for loop have the object reference

```
node.childNode[i]
```

where *node* is the parent node of the child nodes collection and *i* is the value of the counter variable in the for loop.

The second approach uses familial references, starting with the first child of the parent node and then moving to each subsequent sibling until no more siblings are left. The general form of this for loop is

```
for (var n=node.firstChild; n!= null; n=n.nextSibling) {
    commands for n
}
```

In this form, the current child node in the loop has the object reference

```
n
```

Note that when no next sibling is available, the value of n is equal to null and the loop stops. While both approaches yield the same results, the use of familial references is generally preferred because it does not require a browser to calculate the total length of the child nodes collection. For large documents containing thousands of nodes, this can speed up the processing time for the program. This method also gives you the flexibility to insert new nodes into a document during the for loop without having to recalculate the length of the child nodes collection.

You'll use familial references in the following function to create the list of heading elements. The initial code for the function is

```
function createList(list) {
    for (var n=historyDoc.firstChild; n!=null; n=n.nextSibling) {
    }
}
```

This function has a single parameter named list that represents an ol list element found in the table of contents. The historyDoc variable in the for loop is the history document in Norene's Web page. Add this initial version of the function to the toc.js file.

To insert the createList() function:

▶ **1.** Add the following line to the makeTOC() function:

```
historyDoc = document.getElementById("doc");
```

▶ **2.** Below the makeTOC() function, insert the following code, as shown in Figure 10-14:

```
function createList(list) {
    for (var n=historyDoc.firstChild; n!=null; n=n.nextSibling) {
    }
}
```

The initial createList() function   Figure 10-14

Matching the Heading Elements

Next you have to determine whether the current node in the for loop matches one of the heading elements Norene wants to use as section dividers. To aid you, the following code is included in the toc.js file:

```
var sections = new Array("h1","h2","h3","h4","h5","h6");
function levelNum(node) {
    for (var i=0; i<sections.length; i++) {
        if (node.nodeName==sections[i].toUpperCase()) return i;
    }
    return -1;
}
```

The sections array and the levelNum() function are two important pieces in creating your dynamic table of contents, so it's worthwhile to take some time to understand how they work. The sections variable contains an array of the elements that Norene wants to use as section dividers. The array is ordered from the element representing the highest level in the TOC (the h1 element) to the lowest (the h6 element). In the constitution document, you will need to use only elements h1 through h3; however, including the full range of headings allows you to generalize the makeTOC() function for other documents in Norene's library.

The levelNum() function uses the nodeName property to test whether a given node matches one of the elements listed in the sections array. Since element names in the nodeName property are returned in uppercase letters, you have to use the toUpperCase() String method to convert the element names in the section array to uppercase letters as well. The function goes through each item in the sections array and if a match is found, the function returns the array index number. Thus, an h1 element returns the value 0 (indicating that it represents the highest level in the TOC), an h2 element returns the value 1, and so forth. If a node object doesn't represent a section heading, the function returns the value -1. You'll apply the levelNum() function to the createList() function by adding the following if condition:

```
nodeLevel = levelNum(n);
if (nodeLevel != -1) {
    peform actions on an element node
    representing a section heading
}
```

Add this if condition to the createList() function.

To create the nodeLevel variable:

1. Within the for loop of the createList() function, insert the following code (see Figure 10-15):

```
nodeLevel = levelNum(n);
if (nodeLevel != -1) {
}
```

Figure 10-15 ▷ **Testing whether the current node is a section heading**

if nodeLevel does not equal -1 it means that the node represents one of the section headings

```
function createList(list) {
    for (var n=historyDoc.firstchild; n!=null; n=n.nextsibling) {
        nodeLevel = levelNum(n);
        if (nodeLevel != -1) {
        }
    }
}
```

2. Save your changes to the file.

Creating the List Item Elements

The final task is to create and append a list item element, basing its content on the content of the heading element. You'll use the innerHTML property to extract the content of the heading element and apply that content to the list item. The list item then needs to be added as a new child to the list in the table of contents. The code to create and attach the new list item is

```
listItem = document.createElement("li");
listItem.innerHTML = n.innerHTML;
list.appendChild(listItem);
```

Once you add these commands, you can call createList() from the makeTOC() function using the TOCList object as the parameter value. The command to populate the list in the TOC is

```
createList(TOCList);
```

Add these commands to the toc.js file.

To create the listItem object:

1. Add the following commands to the command block of the if statement in the createList() function:

   ```
   listItem = document.createElement("li");
   listItem.innerHTML = n.innerHTML;
   list.appendChild(listItem);
   ```

2. Add the following command to the makeTOC() function:

   ```
   createList(TOCList);
   ```

   Figure 10-16 highlights the new code added to the toc.js file.

Creating the list item elements ◀ **Figure 10-16**

```
function makeTOC() {
    TOC = document.getElementById("toc");
    TOC.innerHTML="<h1>Table of Contents</h1>";
    TOCList = document.createElement("ol");
    TOC.appendChild(TOCList);

    historyDoc = document.getElementById("doc");
    createList(TOCList);
}

function createList(list) {
    for (var n=historyDoc.firstChild; n!=null; n=n.nextSibling) {
        nodeLevel = levelNum(n);
        if (nodeLevel != -1) {
            listItem = document.createElement("li");
            listItem.innerHTML = n.innerHTML;

            list.appendChild(listItem);
        }
    }
}
```

3. Save your changes. If you want to take a break before starting the next session, you may also close your file.

   Next, test the makeTOC() function to verify that it displays a list of all of the heading elements in the constitution document.

4. Reload **usconst.htm** in your Web browser. As shown in Figure 10-17 the table of contents should now be populated with the titles of the h1, h2, and h3 elements in the constitution document.

Figure 10-17   The initial table of contents

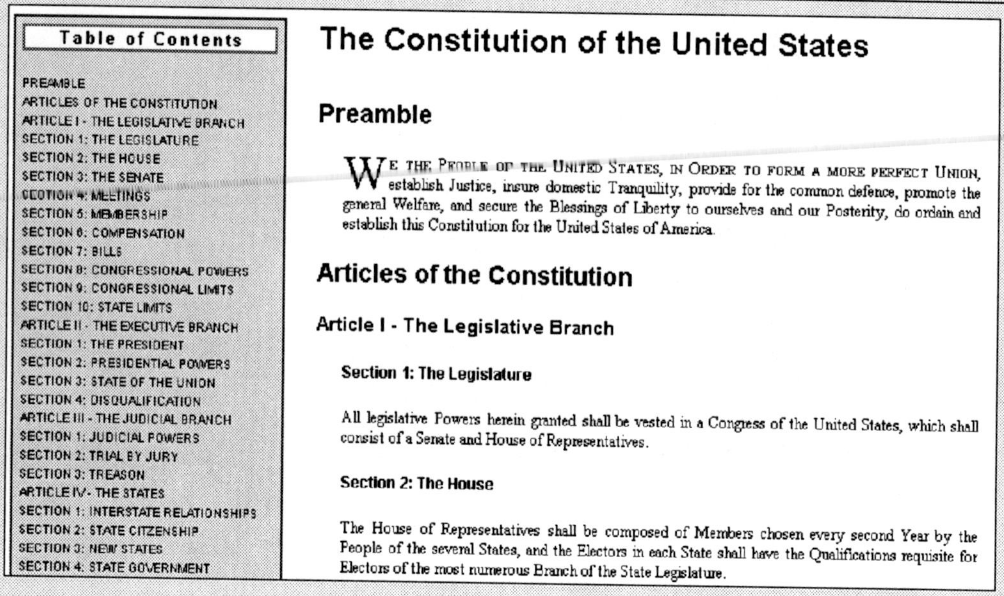

Trouble? The list items appear in uppercase letters because of a style set in the toc.css file, not because of any command in the makeTOC() function.

5. Close your Web browser if you want to take a break before starting the next session.

You've completed your initial work on the dynamic table of contents. In the next session you'll learn how to turn the table of contents into a nested list in which the text from different section headings appears at different levels. You'll also learn how to link the entries from the table of contents list to the section headings in the constitution document.

Review

Session 10.1 Quick Check

1. In the Internet Explorer DOM, what property is used to change the inner HTML content of an element?
2. What are nodes? What objects of an HTML file do they represent?
3. What property do you use to reference the parent of a node?
4. What object reference would you use to reference the third child node of an object?
5. For an element node representing a blockquote element, what value is returned by the nodeType, nodeName, and nodeValue properties?
6. What command would you enter to create a node containing the text string: "U.S. Constitution"? Give the text string the variable name docText. What command would you enter to create an h2 element? Give the h2 element the variable name mainTitle.
7. What command would you enter to place the text string you created in the previous question in the h2 element?
8. What is a document fragment?

Session 10.2

Creating a Nested List

Norene has had a chance to study the initial table of contents you created in the last session. She's pleased that the TOC was able to track all of the heading elements in the constitution document; now she wants you to make the TOC a nested list so that the h1 headings are on one level of the TOC, the h2 headings are on a second level, and so forth. Figure 10-18 shows the current HTML code created by the makeTOC() function alongside the code that Norene wants the function to generate.

The nested list ◁ Figure 10-18

```
<ol>
    <li>Preamble</li>
    <li>Articles of the Constitution</li>
    <li>The Legislative Branch</li>
    <li>The Legislature</li>
    <li>The House</li>
    <li>The Senate</li>
...
    <li>The Executive Branch</li>
    <li>The President</li>
    <li>Presidential Powers</li>
...
    <li>Amendments</li>
    <li>I. Freedom of Expression</li>
    <li>II. Right to Bear Arms</li>
...
</ol>
```

current list

```
<ol>
    <li>Preamble</li>
    <li>Articles of the Constitution</li>
    <ol>
        <li>The Legislative Branch</li>
        <ol>
            <li>The Legislature</li>
            <li>The House</li>
            <li>The Senate</li>
            ...
        </ol>
        <li>The Executive Branch</li>
        <ol>
            <li>The President</li>
            <li>Presidential Powers</li>
            ...
        </ol>
    <li>Amendments</li>
    <ol>
        <li>I. Freedom of Expression</li>
        <li>II. Right to Bear Arms</li>
        ...
    </ol>
</ol>
```

proposed nested list

As you go through Norene's proposed layout for the TOC, there are three rules that you can use to determine where to place a particular list item:

1. If the level of the list item is unchanged from the level of the previous item, simply
   append it to the current list.
2. If the level is lower than the previous heading (such as when an h3 heading follows an h2 heading) create a new ordered list and append the list item to that.
3. If the level is above the previous heading (for example, when an h1 heading follows an h3 heading), append the list item at a level higher up in the TOC.

To keep track of the level associated with each section heading in the last session, you created the nodeLevel variable, where a nodeLevel value of 0 indicates a section heading corresponding to the highest level (h1), a value of 1 indicates the next level (h2), and so forth. In addition to the nodeLevel variable, you need to create two other variables:

- **prevLevel**   The level of the previous heading element
- **newList**   An element node for a new ol (ordered list) element

The general code for the revisions that you'll make to the createList() function appears as follows:

```
function createList(list) {
    prevLevel = 0;
    for (var n=historyDoc.firstChild; n!=null; n=n.nextSibling) {
        nodeLevel = levelNum(n);
        if (nodeLevel != -1) {
            create a list item element
            if (nodeLevel = prevLevel)
                append the list item to the list
            else if (nodeLevel > prevLevel)
                append the list item to a new list
                change the prevLevel value
            else if (nodeLevel < prevLevel)
                append the list to the list of that level
                change the prevLevel value
        }
    }
}
```

You set the initial value of the prevLevel variable to 0. Each time through the loop, the code compares the level of the current section heading with the level of the previous section heading, running different commands for each of three possibilities: the levels are equal, the level of the current heading is higher than the previous heading, or the level of the current heading is lower than the previous heading. You'll look at the specific code for each of these if conditions later; for now, add this general structure to the createList() function.

To insert if conditions into the createList() function:

1. If necessary, reopen **toc.js** in your text editor.

2. Locate the createList() function and insert the following as the first line of the function:

   ```
   var prevLevel = 0;
   ```

3. Delete the line "`list.appendChild(listItem);`" and replace it with the following commands:

   ```
   if (nodeLevel == prevLevel) {
       // append listitem to the list
   }
   else if (nodeLevel > prevLevel) {
       // append listitem to a new list
       // change the prevLevel value
   }
   else if (nodeLevel < prevLevel) {
       // append listitem to the list of that level
       // change the prevLevel value
   }
   ```

   Be sure to indent your code appropriately, to make it easier to read. Figure 10-19 shows the revised text of the createList() function.

Creating the if structure for the nested list ◄ **Figure 10-19**

```
function createList(list) {
    var prevLevel = 0;
    for (var n=historyDoc.firstChild; n!=null; n=n.nextSibling) {
        nodeLevel = levelNum(n);
        if (nodeLevel != -1) {
            listItem = document.createElement("li");
            listItem.innerHTML = n.innerHTML;

            if (nodeLevel == prevLevel) {
                // append listitem to the list
            }
            else if (nodeLevel > prevLevel) {
                // append listitem to a new list
                // change the prevLevel value
            }
            else if (nodeLevel < prevLevel) {
                // append listitem to the list of that level
                // change the prevLevel value
            }
        }
    }
}
```

delete the line to append the list item →

4. Save your changes to the file.

Next enter the code for each if condition. If nodeLevel equals prevLevel, this means that the current node is at the same level in the nested list, and you simply need to append the list item to the current list. Figure 10-20 shows how creating and appending this node compares to inserting the code in an HTML document. To simplify the node tree diagram, the text nodes are omitted from the figure; remember, though, that they are also part of the node tree.

Adding a list item to a list ◄ **Figure 10-20**

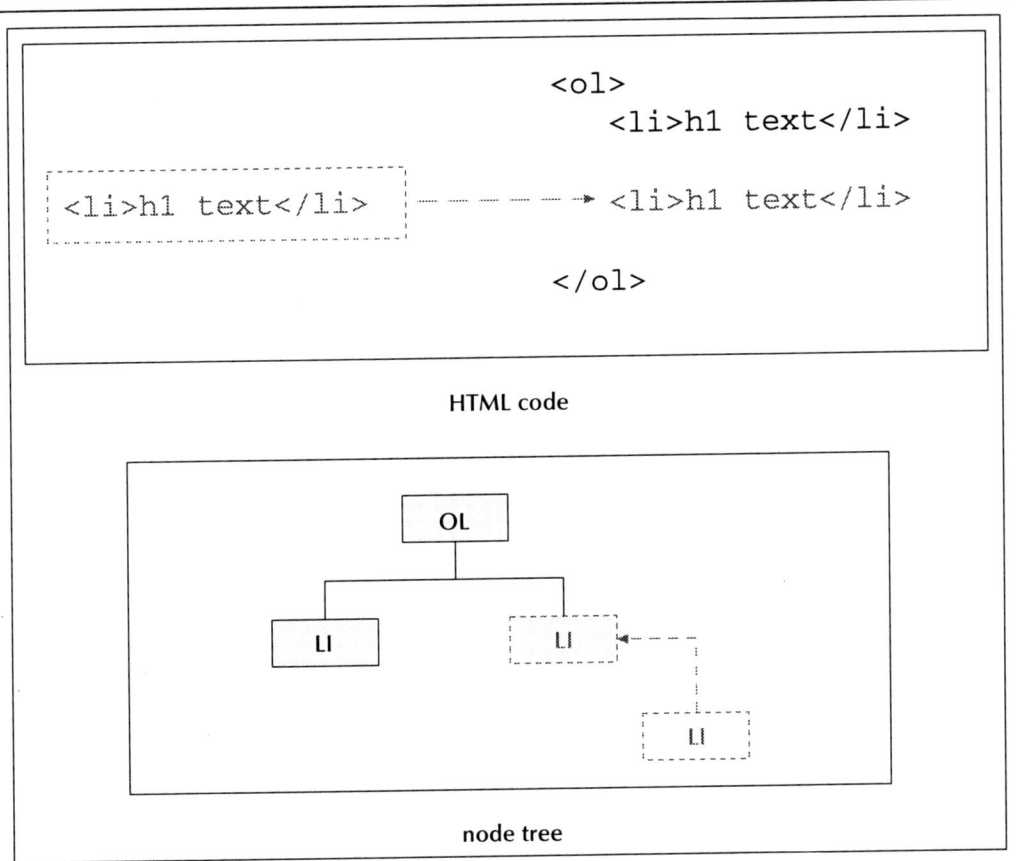

Add the command to insert the list item to the first condition in the createList() function.

To add the appendChild() command:

1. Add the following command, as shown in Figure 10-21:

```
list.appendChild(listItem);
```

Figure 10-21 ▸ **Inserting the command for the first condition**

```
function createList(list) {
    var prevLevel = 0;
    for (var n=historyDoc.firstChild; n!=null; n=n.nextSibling) {
        nodeLevel = levelNum(n);
        if (nodeLevel != -1) {
            listItem = document.createElement("li");
            listItem.innerHTML = n.innerHTML;

            if (nodeLevel == prevLevel) {
                // append listitem to the list
                list.appendChild(listItem);
            }
            else if (nodeLevel > prevLevel) {
                // append listitem to a new list
                // change the prevLevel value
            }
            else if (nodeLevel < prevLevel) {
                // append listitem to the list of that level
                // change the prevLevel value
            }
        }
    }
}
```

2. Save your changes to the file.

3. Reload **usconst.htm** in your Web browser. The table of contents should now only show the three h1 headings since they represent the headings with a level value of 0 (see Figure 10-22). No other headings are shown since the value of the prevLevel variable was set to 0 and was not changed by the code.

Figure 10-22 ▸ **Displaying only the top level headings**

Table of Contents

PREAMBLE
ARTICLES OF THE CONSTITUTION
AMENDMENTS

The Constitution of the United States

Preamble

WE THE PEOPLE OF THE UNITED STATES, IN ORDER TO FORM A MORE PERFECT UNION, establish Justice, insure domestic Tranquility, provide for the common defence, promote the general Welfare, and secure the Blessings of Liberty to ourselves and our Posterity, do ordain and establish this Constitution for the United States of America.

Articles of the Constitution

Article I - The Legislative Branch

Section 1: The Legislature

In the next if condition, you need to insert commands when the section heading is of a lower level than the previous heading (such as an h2 heading following an h1 heading). In these cases, you have to create a new ordered list and append the list item to it. The new list is then appended as a child of the current list (creating a nested list). Finally, you need to make the nested list the list object for the next time through the for loop and change the value of the prevLevel variable to the level of the current section heading. Figure 10-23 compares the HTML code with the equivalent operation in the node tree. Once again, the text nodes have been omitted to highlight the general structure of the node tree.

Appending a nested list to the node tree ◀ **Figure 10-23**

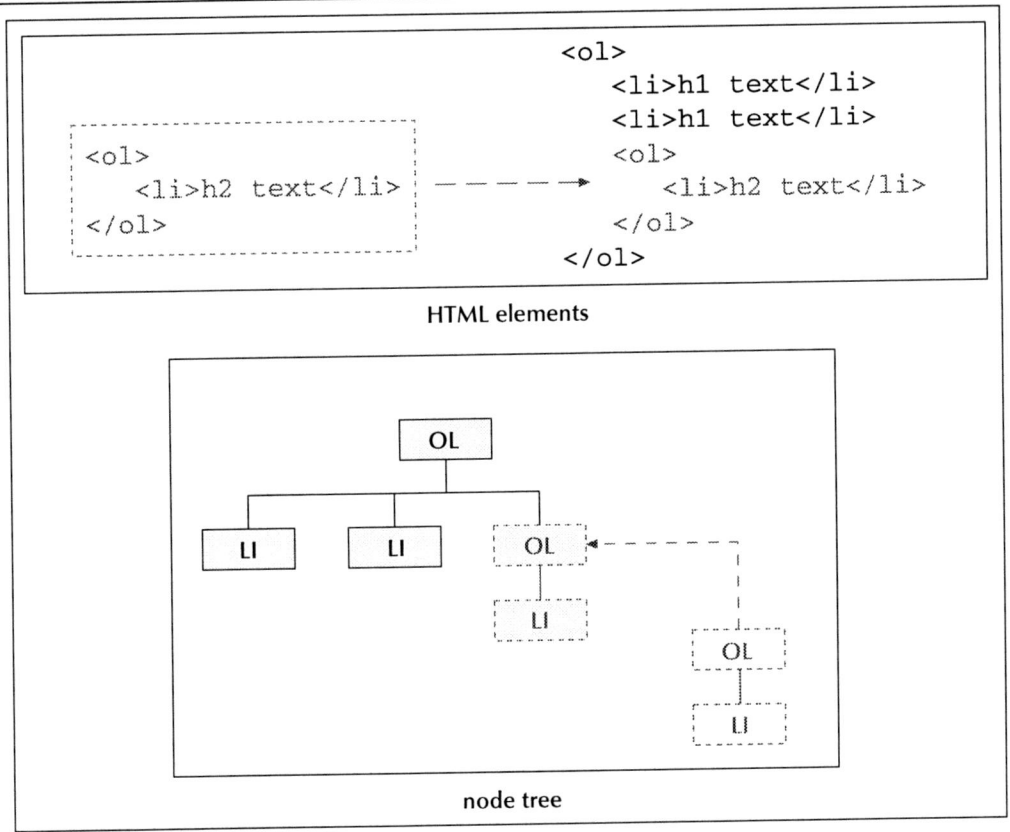

The code to change the structure of the node tree in this way is

```
newList = document.createElement("ol");
newList.appendChild(listItem);
list.appendChild(newList);
list = newList;
prevLevel = nodeLevel;
```

Add these commands to the createList() function within the second if condition.

To create the nested list:

1. Return to **toc.js** in your text editor.

2. Add the following commands to the second if condition in the createList() function, as shown in Figure 10-24:

```
newList = document.createElement("ol");
newList.appendChild(listItem);
list.appendChild(newList);
list = newList;
prevLevel = nodeLevel;
```

Figure 10-24	Inserting the command for the second condition

```
if (nodeLevel == prevLevel) {
    // append listitem to the list
    list.appendChild(listItem);
}
else if (nodeLevel > prevLevel) {
    // append listitem to a new list
    // change the prevLevel value
    newList = document.createElement("ol");
    newList.appendChild(listItem);
    list.appendChild(newList);
    list = newList;
    prevLevel = nodeLevel;
}
else if (nodeLevel < prevLevel) {
    // append listitem to the list of that level
    // change the prevLevel value
}
```

3. Save your changes to the file and reload **usconst.htm** in your Web browser. The table of contents should now appear as shown in Figure 10-25.

Figure 10-25	Nested table of contents

```
┌─────────────────────────────────┐
│        Table of Contents        │
├─────────────────────────────────┤
│                                 │
│ PREAMBLE                        │
│ ARTICLES OF THE CONSTITUTION    │
│    Article I - The Legislative Branch │
│        Section 1: The Legislature │
│        Section 2: The House     │
│        Section 3: The Senate    │
│        Section 4: Meetings      │
│        Section 5: Membership    │
│        Section 6: Compensation  │
│        Section 7: Bills         │
│        Section 8: Congressional Powers │
│        Section 9: Congressional Limits │
│        Section 10: State Limits │
│        Section 1: The President │
│        Section 2: Presidential Powers │
│        Section 3: State of the Union │
│        Section 4: Disqualification │
│        Section 1: Judicial Powers │
│        Section 2: Trial by Jury │
│        Section 3: Treason       │
│        Section 1: Interstate Relationships │
│        Section 2: State Citizenship │
│        Section 3: New States    │
│        Section 4: State Government │
│        Paragraph                │
│        Paragraph                │
│        Paragraph                │
│                                 │
└─────────────────────────────────┘
```

Trouble? The other headings are missing from the table of contents because you have not entered code to enable moving back up in the nested list. The loop can only move down at present. You'll add the commands for moving up next.

The final if condition occurs when the level of the current heading is higher than the previous heading (such as when an h1 heading follows an h3 heading). How should this occurrence be represented in the node tree? Figure 10-26 shows a nested list represented by both its HTML elements and as a node tree. Note that each ordered list element (OL) has as its parent another ordered list element, until you get to the topmost list. When you encounter a higher level section heading, such as the h1 heading, you have to append it as a child of an ordered list element higher up in the node tree.

Appending a list item to a higher level list | **Figure 10-26**

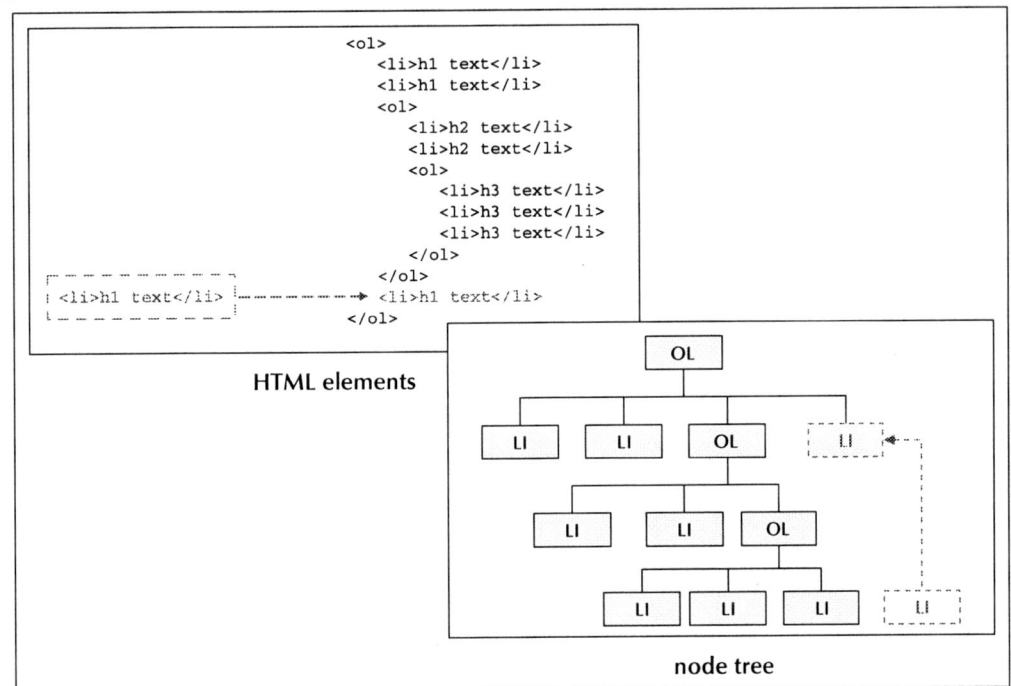

To decide which ordered list element the new list item should be appended to, you need to calculate how many levels up the node tree the item has to go. This is simply the difference between the previous level and the new level. For example, all h1 headings are on level 0 and all h3 headings are on level 2. The difference between them is 2, and thus you have to move up two levels in the TOC node tree whenever an h1 heading follows an h3 heading. To move up the node tree, you use the parentNode property to move from the list to its parent. You repeat this process for each level that you want to go up. The code for this is

```
levelUp = prevLevel - nodeLevel;
for (j=1; j<=levelUp; j++) list=list.parentNode;
```

Each time through, the for loop changes the list object to its parent. The loop stops when it has gone up the correct number of levels as indicated by the levelUp variable. Once it is at the correct level, you need to append the list item to it as a new child and change the value of the prevLevel variable so that it points to the new level in the node tree. The complete code is

```
levelUp = prevLevel - nodeLevel;
for (j=1; j<=levelUp; j++) list=list.parentNode;
list.appendChild(listItem);
prevLevel = nodeLevel;
```

Add these commands to the third if condition.

To complete the nested list:

1. Return to **toc.js** in your text editor.

2. Add the following commands to the third if condition in the createList() function, as shown in Figure 10-27:

```
levelUp = prevLevel - nodeLevel;
for (j=1; j<=levelUp; j++) list=list.parentNode;
list.appendChild(listItem);
prevLevel = nodeLevel;
```

Figure 10-27 Inserting the command for the third condition

```
if (nodeLevel == prevLevel) {
    // append listitem to the list
    list.appendChild(listItem);
}
else if (nodeLevel > prevLevel) {
    // append listitem to a new list
    // change the prevLevel value
    newList = document.createElement("ol");
    newList.appendChild(listItem);
    list.appendChild(newList);
    list = newList;
    prevLevel = nodeLevel;
}
else if (nodeLevel < prevLevel) {
    // append listitem to the list of that level
    // change the prevLevel value
    levelUp = prevLevel - nodeLevel;
    for (j=1; j<=levelUp; j++) list=list.parentNode;
    list.appendChild(listItem);
    prevLevel = nodeLevel;
}
```

3. Save your changes to the file and reload **usconst.htm** in your Web browser. The table of contents should now show all of the headings from the constitution document in a nested list (see Figure 10-28). Note that the headings displayed in the table of contents go up and down the nested list, matching the level of each heading in the constitution document.

Figure 10-28 Table of contents as a nested list

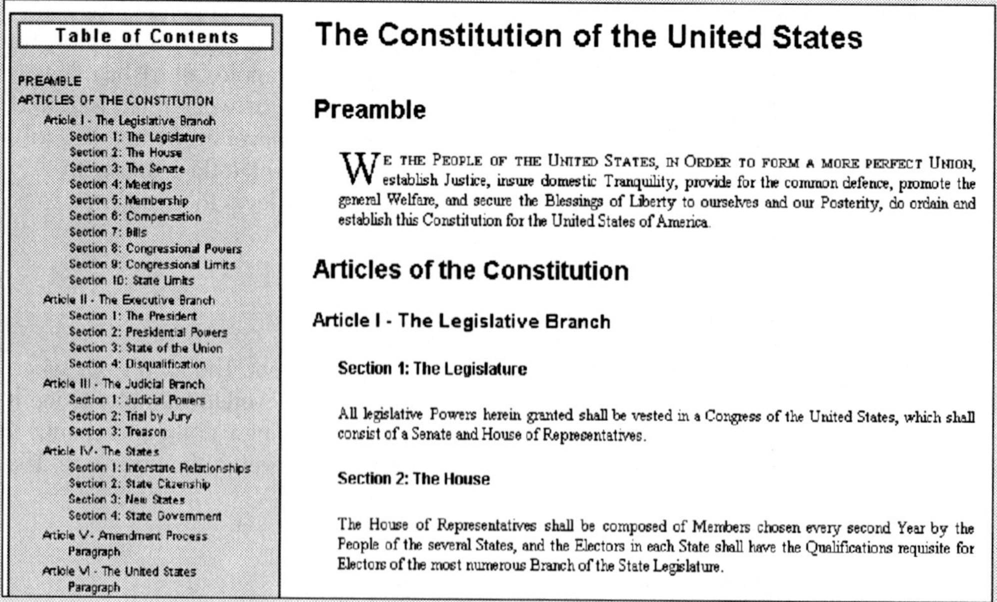

Working with Attributes

Norene stops by to check on your progress. She's thrilled with the table of contents your script has generated for her document. Since this is a hypertext document, she wonders whether the entries in the table of contents could contain links to the section headings they represent.

Once again, it's useful to write out the markup tags for the proposed change, even if you can't view those markup tags in your document. As indicated in Figure 10-29, making this change involves two steps:

1. Adding an id attribute to each section heading (if it doesn't already have one)
2. Changing the content of each list item to a link pointing to the corresponding section heading

Linking to section headings ◀ **Figure 10-29**

table of contents links
```
<ol>
    <li><a href="#head1">Preamble</a></li>
    <li><a href="#head2">Articles of the Constitution</a></li>
    <ol>
        <li><a href="#head3">Legislative Branch</a></li>
        <ol>
            <li><a href="#head4">Section 1: The Legislature</a></li>
            <li><a href="#head5">Section 2: The House</a></li>
            <li><a href="#head6">Section 3: The Senate</a></li>
    ...
```

section headings with id values
```
<h1 id="head1">Preamble</h1>
<p> ... </p>
<h1 id="head2">Articles of the Constitution</h1>
<p> ... </p>
<h2 id="head3">Legislative Branch</h2>
<p> ... </p>
<h3 id="head4">Section 1: The Legislature</h3>
<p> ... </p>
<h3 id="head5">Section 2: The House</h3>
<p> ... </p>
<h3 id="head6">Section 3: The Senate</h3>
<p> ... </p>
...
```

To create and add the id and href attributes, you first need to understand how to work with attributes in the W3C document object model.

Attribute Nodes

Attributes and their values are considered nodes and can be attached to element nodes. Unlike element and text nodes, however, they are not part of the node tree because attribute nodes are not counted as children of element nodes as text nodes are (see Figure 10-30). Thus, attribute nodes have no familial relation with any node in the node tree.

Figure 10-30	Attribute nodes

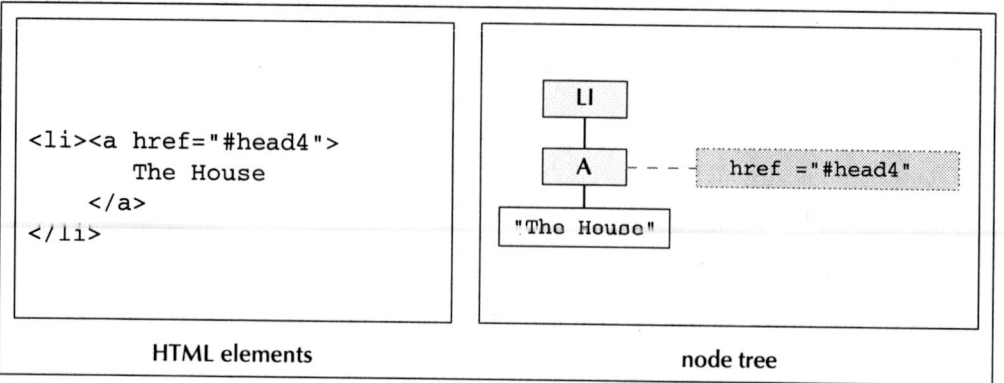

The document object model supports several methods to create, attach, and set the values of attributes. See Figure 10-31.

Figure 10-31	Methods of attribute nodes

Method	Description
document.createAttribute(*att*)	Creates an attribute node with the name *att*
node.getAttribute(*att*)	Returns the value of an attribute *att* from a *node* to which it has been attached
node.hasAttribute(*att*)	Returns a Boolean value indicating whether *node* has the attribute *att*
node.removeAttribute(*att*)	Removes the attribute *att* from *node*
node.removeAttributeNode(*att*)	Removes an attribute node *att* from *node*
node.setAttribute(*att*, *value*)	Creates or changes the *value* of the attribute *att* of *node*

To create or set an attribute for an element, you use the setAttribute() method. The following code creates a list item element and then uses the setAttribute() method to set the id value of the list item to the text string "TOChead1":

```
listItem = document.createElement("li");
listItem.setAttribute("id","TOChead1");
```

The net effect of these two commands is to create the following element:

```
<li id="TOChead1"> ... </li>
```

In some cases, you need to determine whether an element has a particular attribute, such as the id attribute. In these situations, you use the hasAttribute() method, which returns the Boolean value true if the element contains the attribute. For example, the expression

```
listItem.hasAttribute("id")
```

would return the value true if the list item had an id.

Attributes as Object Properties

For element nodes in an HTML or XHTML document, the document object model also supports a shorthand way of applying attributes as properties of an element. The general syntax is

```
elem.att
```

where *elem* is an element node and *att* is an attribute of that element. To create and set the id attribute for a list item in this shorthand form, you would enter the following commands:

```
listItem = document.createElement("li");
listItem.id = "TOChead1";
```

Rather than using the hasAttribute() method, you test whether an attribute exists by testing whether its value equals an empty text string. For example, to test whether the list-Item node has an id attribute, you can use the following expression:

```
listItem.id != ""
```

which has the Boolean value true if the id attribute is present and false if it is an empty text string or missing. In general, it's easier and more intuitive to use this shorthand form. The attribute node methods are usually reserved for working with the attributes of nodes that are not HTML elements, as would be the case if you were writing a script for an XML document.

Setting the Section Heading Ids

Now that you've learned how to work with attributes, you'll return to the next task, which is to insert ids into all of the section headings in the constitution document. You'll name each of the section headings

```
headi
```

where *i* is a variable that equals 1 for the first section heading, two for the second heading and so forth. See Figure 10-29 for an example of how the ids of the first six section headings will be numbered. You need to be careful, however, not to overwrite any preexisting ids, since it is quite possible that Norene will have already placed ids in some of the section headings. You should first test whether an id attribute already exists for an element and only insert an id if it doesn't already have one. As you create section ids, you'll store each id in a variable named sectionId; you'll use this variable later in the code to create the hypertext references for the links. The code to insert the section heading ids is

```
headNum++;
if (n.id == "") {
   sectionId = "head"+headNum;
   n.id = sectionId;
}
else sectionId = n.id;
```

Here, headNum is a counter variable that is increased each time the code encounters a section element in the constitution document. If the element has no id, an id is created for it; otherwise, the sectionId variable stores the value of the preexisting id. Add these commands to the createList() function.

To insert the section ids:

1. Return to **toc.js** in your text editor and go to the createList() function.

   First you must set the initial value of the headNum variable to 0.

2. Directly below the line "var prevLevel = 0" insert the command

   ```
   var headNum = 0;
   ```

3. At the top of the for loop, insert the following commands, as shown in Figure 10-32:

   ```
   // insert ids for the section headings
   headNum++;
   if (n.id == "") {
       sectionId = "head"+headNum;
       n.id = sectionId;
   }
   else sectionId = n.id;
   ```

Figure 10-32 Inserting section ids

```
function createList(list) {
    var prevLevel = 0;
    var headNum = 0;
    for (var n=historyDoc.firstchild; n!=null; n=n.nextsibling) {
        nodeLevel = levelNum(n);
        if (nodeLevel != -1) {

            // insert ids for the section headings
            headNum++;
            if (n.id == "") {
                sectionId = "head"+headNum;
                n.id = sectionId;
            }
            else sectionId = n.id;

            listItem = document.createElement("li");
            listItem.innerHTML = n.innerHTML;
```

4. Save your changes to the file.

Inserting Links

Now you need to revise the structure of the TOC node tree to include links. The href value for each link will be #sectionId where sectionId is the value of the sectionId variable. You'll also set the id of each list element to "TOCsectionId". This will allow you to easily match list items in the TOC with section headings in the document. You'll need this information for some of the tasks you'll do in the next session. Figure 10-33 shows the node structure of the list items with and without the links.

Changing a list item to a hypertext link | Figure 10-33

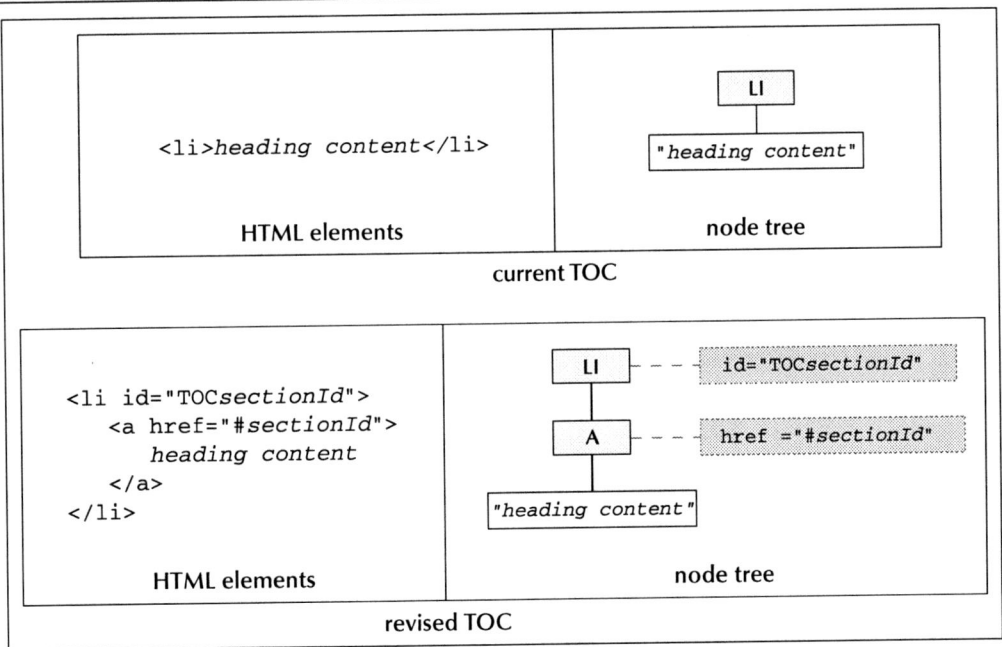

To create the new node structure, you'll replace the old commands to create the list item with the following:

```
listItem=document.createElement("li");
listItem.id="TOC"+sectionId;
linkItem = document.createElement("a");
linkItem.innerHTML = n.innerHTML;
linkItem.href="#"+sectionId;
listItem.appendChild(linkItem);
```

Insert these commands into the createList() function and then test the links in the table of contents.

To turn the list items into links:

1. Within the createList() function, delete the line "listItem.innerHTML=n.innerHTML".

2. Replace the deleted line with the following code (see Figure 10-34):

```
listItem.id="TOC"+sectionId;
linkItem = document.createElement("a");
linkItem.innerHTML = n.innerHTML;
linkItem.href="#"+sectionId;
listItem.appendChild(linkItem);
```

Figure 10-34 ▶ **Inserting links**

```
// insert ids for the section headings
headNum++;
if (n.id == "") {
    sectionId = "head"+headNum;
    n.id = sectionId;
}
else sectionId = n.id;

listItem = document.createElement("li");
listItem.id="TOC"+sectionId;

linkItem = document.createElement("a");
linkItem.innerHTML = n.innerHTML;
linkItem.href="#"+sectionId;

listItem.appendChild(linkItem);


if (nodeLevel == prevLevel) {
    // append listitem to the list
    list.appendChild(listItem);
}
```

> delete the line to place the heading content into the list item

3. Save your changes. If you plan to take a break before starting the next session you may close the file.

4. Reopen **usconst.htm** in your Web browser.

5. As shown in Figure 10-35, the entries in the table of contents should now act as links to the different sections of the constitution document. Test different links to verify that they take you to the appropriate sections of the document.

Figure 10-35 ▶ **Viewing the list of links**

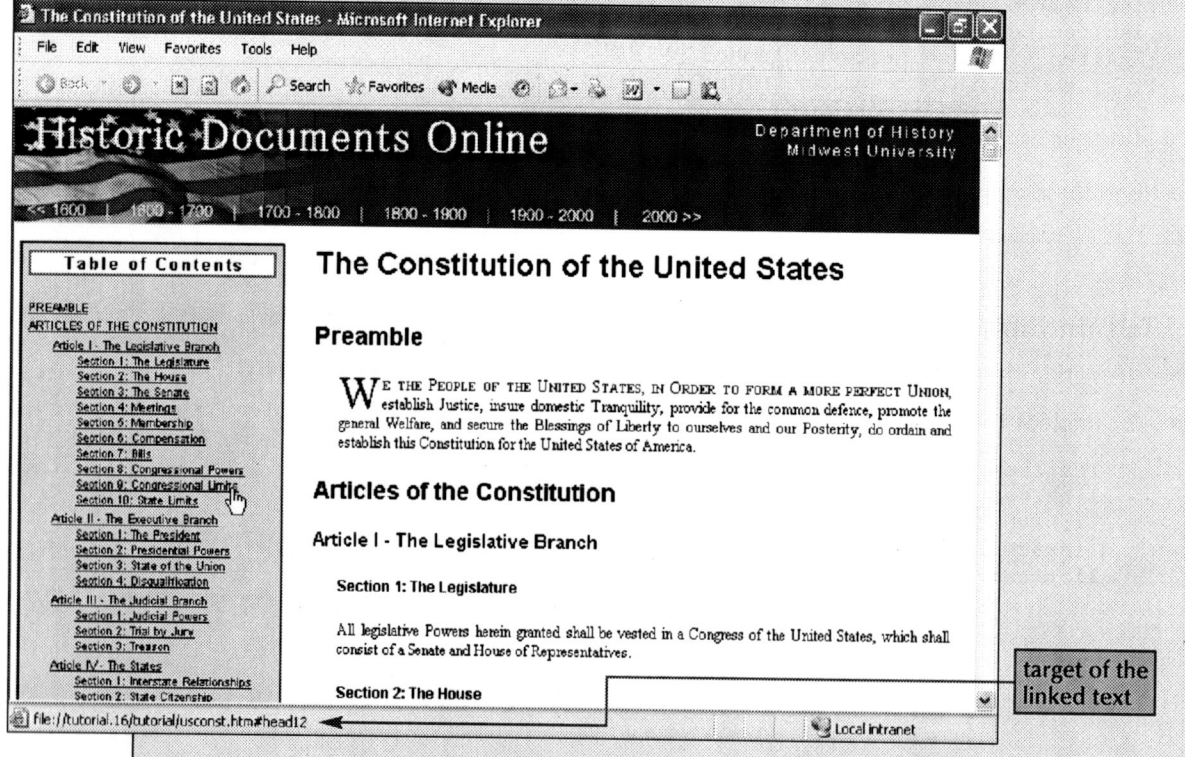

6. Close your browser if you plan to take a break before the next session.

You've completed your work in making the table of contents into a nested list of links. In the next session, you'll add more features to the table of contents, including the ability to contract and expand the table of contents and the constitution document.

Session 10.2 Quick Check

1. What code would you write to create two ul list elements, one nested inside of the other? Use the variable name topList for the upper list element and the variable named bottomList for the bottom list element.
2. In the previous question, what is the node reference to the topList object from a list item found in the bottom list?
3. Why are attribute nodes not part of the document node tree?
4. What node method would you use to determine whether an element contains the type attribute?
5. What command would you use to create an input element with the variable name CBox and a type attribute value of "checkbox"? Use an attribute node method in your answer.
6. What commands would you add to the previous question if you were to create the type attribute using a property rather than an attribute node method?
7. What property would you use in the previous question to determine whether the CBox input element had a type attribute?

Session 10.3

Expanding and Collapsing a Document

You and Norene have met again to discuss your progress on the table of contents application. Norene has seen a few other lists in which the nested entries can be alternately hidden or displayed by clicking a plus/minus box. In a **plus/minus box**, when the box shows a + symbol, it indicates that there is hidden content within and clicking the + box reveals the hidden content. When the box shows a -- symbol, it indicates that all of the items are displayed, but clicking the box will hide them (see Figure 10-36).

Expanding and contracting a list with a plus/minus box 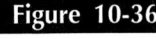 Figure 10-36

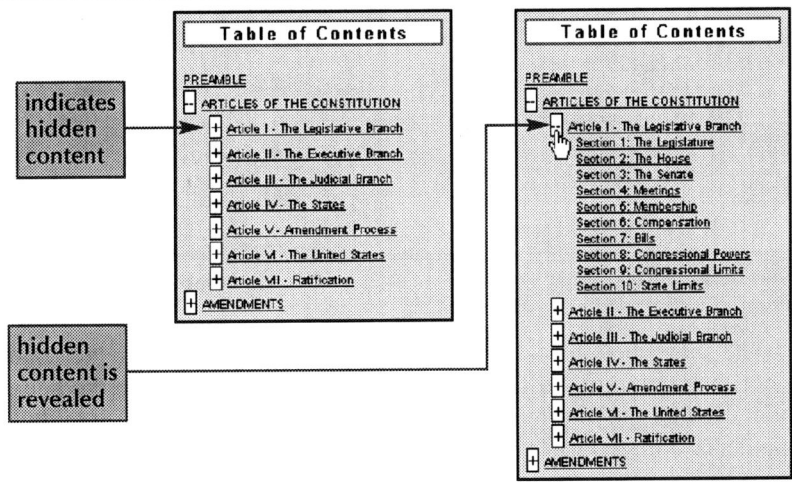

Norene asks whether you can add this feature to the table of contents so that users can expand or contract the TOC. She also wants the contents of the document to mimic the appearance of the table of contents, so that as items are hidden in the TOC they are also hidden within the document. Creating this kind of dynamic content involves several of the tools and techniques you've learned in the last few tutorials, including working with event objects and object styles.

Creating a Plus/Minus Box

The first things you'll add to the TOC are the plus/minus boxes. Since you want to treat each plus/minus box as a single object, you'll place the text of the plus/minus box within a span element. Initially the plus/minus box will display the text "--" since the TOC will open with all list items displayed to users. The commands to create the plus/minus box are

```
plusMinusBox = document.createElement("span");
plusMinusBox.innerHTML="--";
```

Next you have to determine where to place the plus/minus boxes in Norene's TOC. Since the boxes are designed to alternately hide or display nested lists, they should be placed directly before the ordered list elements containing those items. Figure 10-37 shows where you would place the plus/minus box if you were writing the HTML tags directly, and how it would be rendered on the Web page. Notice that the styles for the span element, including the background color and border, have already been placed in the toc.css file. This means that you don't have to worry about formatting your plus/minus boxes for the Web page, but you can focus instead on inserting the content.

Figure 10-37 ▷ **Placing the plus/minus box**

```
<li id="TOChead34">
    <span>--</span>
    <a href="#head34">
        Amendments
    </a>
</li>
<ul>
    <li id="TOChead35">
        <a href="#head35">
            I. Freedom of Expression
        </a>
    </li>
    <li id="TOChead36">
        <a href="#head36">
            II. Right to bear Arms
        </a>
    </li>
...
</ul>
```

HTML elements

AMENDMENTS
  I. Freedom of Expression
  II. Right to bear Arms
  III. Quartering of Soldiers
  IV. Search and Seizure
  V. Trial and Punishment
  VI. Speedy Trials
  VII. Trial by Jury
  VIII. Punishment

Rendered elements

Figure 10-38 shows how this HTML code would appear in the node tree (attribute nodes are not shown in order to simplify the diagram). As indicated in the figure, the span element used for the plus/minus box has to be inserted as the first child of any list item that precedes a nested list.

Adding the plus/minus box to the node tree ◄ **Figure 10-38**

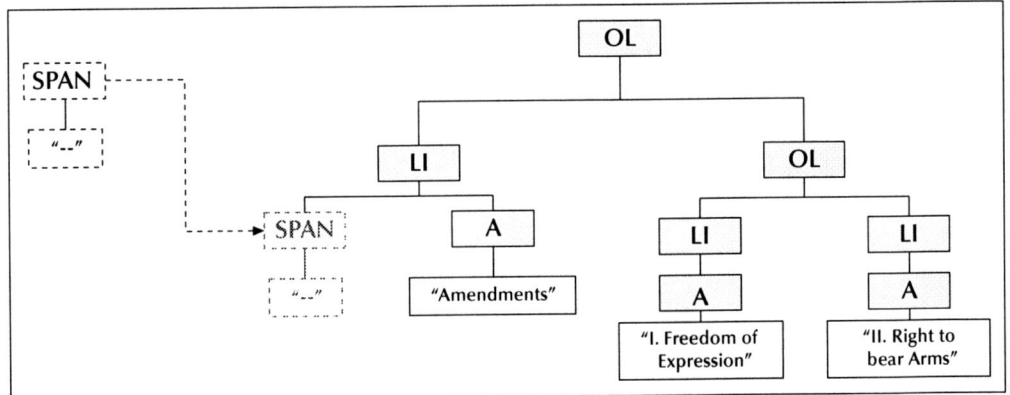

To place the box in the correct location, you create a variable for the previous list item using the previousSibling property:

```
prevListItem = list.previousSibling;
```

You then insert the plus/minus box as a child of this previous list item by using the insertBefore() method. Recall that the insertBefore() method allows you to insert new child nodes at specific locations in the child nodes collection. In this case, you want to insert the plus/minus box in front of the current first child of the previous list item. The code to insert the plus/minus box is therefore

```
prevListItem.insertBefore(plusMinusBox, prevListItem.firstChild);
```

The complete code to create and insert the plus/minus box is

```
plusMinusBox = document.createElement("span");
plusMinusBox.innerHTML="--";
prevListItem = list.previousSibling;
prevListItem.insertBefore(plusMinusBox, prevListItem.firstChild);
```

Add these commands to the createList() function in the command block in which the nested list elements are created.

To create and place the plus/minus boxes:

► **1.** If necessary, reopen **toc.js** in your text editor.

► **2.** Go to the createList() function and insert the following code at the end of the second if condition, as shown in Figure 10-39:

```
// create and place the plus-minus box
plusMinusBox = document.createElement("span");
plusMinusBox.innerHTML="--";
prevListItem = list.previousSibling;
prevListItem.insertBefore(plusMinusBox, prevListItem.firstChild);
```

| Figure 10-39 | Creating and placing the plus/minus boxes |

```
if (nodeLevel == prevLevel) {
    // append listitem to the list
    list.appendChild(listItem);
}

else if (nodeLevel > prevLevel) {
    // append listitem to a new list
    // change the prevLevel value
    newList = document.createElement("ol");
    newList.appendChild(listItem);
    list.appendChild(newList);
    list = newList;
    prevLevel = nodeLevel;

    // create and place the plus-minus box
    plusMinusBox = document.createElement("span");
    plusMinusBox.innerHTML="--";
    prevListItem = list.previousSibling;
    prevListItem.insertBefore(plusMinusBox, prevListItem.firstChild);
}
else if (nodeLevel < prevLevel) {
    // append listitem to the list of that level
    // change the prevLevel value
    levelUp = prevLevel - nodeLevel;
    for (j=1; j<=levelUp; j++) list=list.parentNode;
    list.appendChild(listItem);
    prevLevel = nodeLevel;
}
```

3. Save your changes to the file.

4. Reopen **usconst.htm** in your Web browser. As shown in Figure 10-40, plus/minus boxes should now be placed in front of the nested items within the table of contents.

| Figure 10-40 | Viewing the plus/minus boxes |

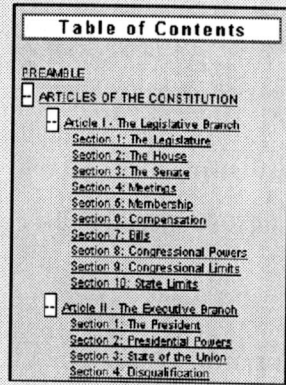

Adding Event Handlers to the Plus/Minus Boxes

When a plus/minus box is clicked, the browser should do the following:

1. Toggle the text of the box, changing a "+" to a "--" and vice-versa.
2. Alternately hide and display the contents of the nested list next to the plus/minus box.
3. Alternately hide and display the corresponding content in the constitution document.

You'll place these actions in a function named expandCollapse(). The first part of the function will toggle the display in the plus/minus box. The initial code for the expandCollapse() function is

```
function expandCollapse(e) {
    var plusMinusBox=eventSource(e);
    if (plusMinusBox.innerHTML=="--") plusMinusBox.innerHTML="+";
    else plusMinusBox.innerHTML="--";
}
```

The function has a single parameter: the event object e (for a review of event objects see the previous tutorial). In the first line of the function, the cross-browser eventSource() function is used to determine from which plus/minus box the click event originated. If the text of the plusMinusBox is "--", it is changed to "+"; otherwise, it is changed to "--". Add this function to the toc.js file and create an event handler for it.

To insert the expandCollapse() function:

1. Return to the **toc.js** file in your text editor.

2. At the end of the file, insert the following function:

   ```
   function expandCollapse(e) {
       var plusMinusBox=eventSource(e);
       if (plusMinusBox.innerHTML=="--") plusMinusBox.innerHTML="+";
       else plusMinusBox.innerHTML="--";
   }
   ```

   You also have to add an event handler to each plus/minus box to run the expand-Collapse function in response to the click event.

3. Go up to the createList() function and insert the following command, as shown in Figure 10-41:

   ```
   plusMinusBox.onclick = expandCollapse;
   ```

Creating the expandCollapse() function ◀ Figure 10-41

run the expandCollapse() function when the user clicks a plus/minus box

```
        // create and place the plus-minus box
        plusMinusBox = document.createElement("span");
        plusMinusBox.innerHTML="--";
        plusMinusBox.onclick = expandCollapse;
        prevListItem = list.previousSibling;
        prevListItem.insertBefore(plusMinusBox, prevListItem.firstChild);
    }
    else if (nodeLevel < prevLevel) {
        // append listitem to the list of that level
        // change the prevLevel value
        levelUp = prevLevel - nodeLevel;
        for (j=1; j<=levelUp; j++) list=list.parentNode;
        list.appendChild(listItem);
        prevLevel = nodeLevel;
    }

  }
 }
}

function expandCollapse(e) {
    var plusMinusBox=eventSource(e);
    if (plusMinusBox.innerHTML=="--") plusMinusBox.innerHTML="+";
    else plusMinusBox.innerHTML="--";
}
```

4. Save your changes to the file and reopen **usconst.htm** in your Web browser. Verify that each time you click a plus/minus box the content of the box changes between + and --.

Hiding and Displaying Objects

The next action of the expandCollapse() function is to alternately hide or display the nested items within the TOC. There are two different styles that you can use for hiding an object on a Web page: the visibility style and the display style. While both styles hide page elements, they differ in how other page elements are affected. With the visibility style, the hidden items still occupy their positions within the flow of a page. With the display style, the hidden items are removed from the page and the other elements flow into the space that the hidden items previously occupied (see Figure 10-42).

Figure 10-42 | **Comparing the visibility and display styles**

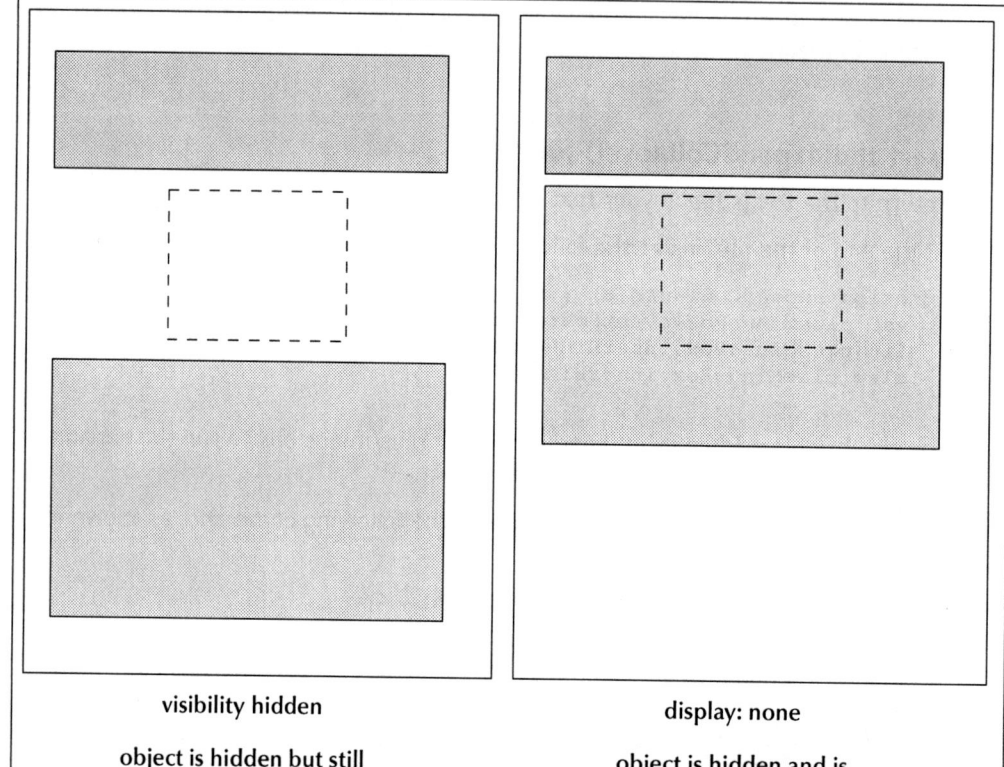

visibility hidden

object is hidden but still
is part of the page flow

display: none

object is hidden and is
removed from the page flow

For the table of contents, you'll use the display style since you want the TOC to collapse and expand as items are hidden and then redisplayed. To hide an object, you use the command

```
object.style.display = "none"
```

where `object` is the page object to be hidden. To redisplay the object, you set the display style to an empty text string. This removes the display style from the object, causing browsers to apply the default display style to the object. The command is

```
object.style.display = "";
```

In the table of contents, the only elements you need to hide and redisplay are the ordered list elements (ol). Since every nested object inherits the display status of its parent, hiding an ol element also hides any descendant elements such as list items and nested lists. To determine which ordered list to hide, you once again look at the position of the ol element relative to the plus/minus box; however, in this case you create a reference *from* the plus/minus box *to* the ol element. As indicated in Figure 10-43, to go from the plus/minus box to the ol element, you go up to the parent node (in this case the list item element) and then to the next sibling (the ol element).

The position of the plus/minus box relative to the nested list  Figure 10-43

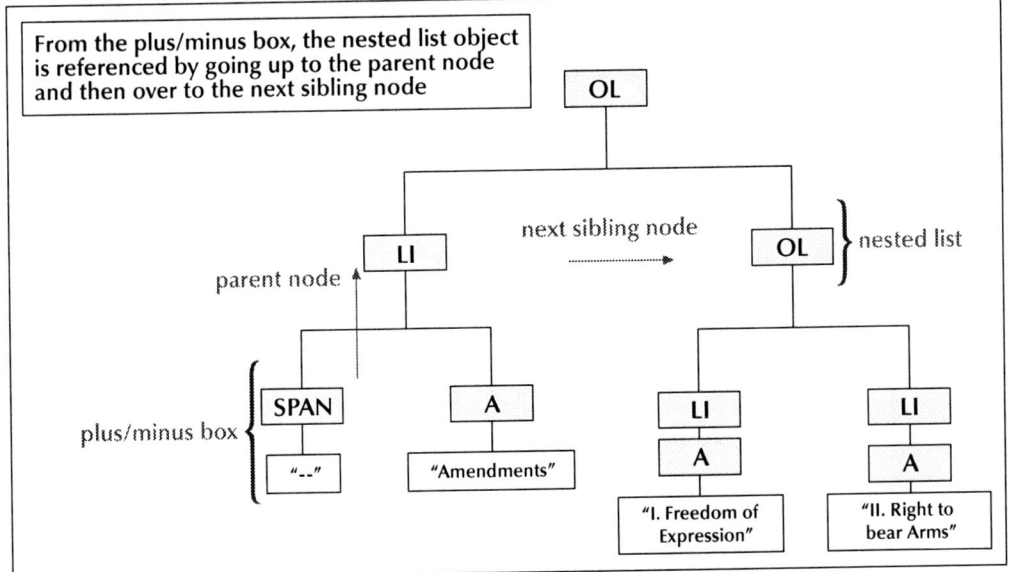

The object reference to move from the plus/minus box to a nested list is therefore

```
var nestedList = plusMinusBox.parentNode.nextSibling;
```

Next, as you did when toggling the text in a plus/minus box between + and -- , you toggle the display status of the contents of the nested list. The code is

```
if (nestedList.style.display=="") nestedList.style.display="none";
else nestedList.style.display="";
```

Add these commands to the expandCollapse() function.

To expand and collapse the nested lists in the TOC:

1. Return to the **toc.js** file in your text editor.

2. Within the expandCollapse() function, add the following code, as shown in Figure 10-44:

```
var nestedList = plusMinusBox.parentNode.nextSibling;
if (nestedList.style.display=="") nestedList.style.display="none";
else nestedList.style.display="";
```

Figure 10-44 ▶ **Expanding and collapsing the nested lists**

```
function expandcollapse(e) {
    var plusMinusBox=eventSource(e);
    if (plusMinusBox.innerHTML=="--") plusMinusBox.innerHTML="+";
    else plusMinusBox.innerHTML="--";

    var nestedList = plusMinusBox.parentNode.nextSibling;
    if (nestedList.style.display=="") nestedList.style.display="none";
    else nestedList.style.display="";
}
```

3. Save your changes to the file.

4. Reload **usconst.htm** in your Web browser. Verify that as you click the plus/minus boxes in the table of contents, the nested lists within the TOC are alternately hidden and redisplayed. Figure 10-45 shows the table of contents with a mixture of hidden and displayed nested lists.

Figure 10-45 ▶ **Table of contents with hidden lists**

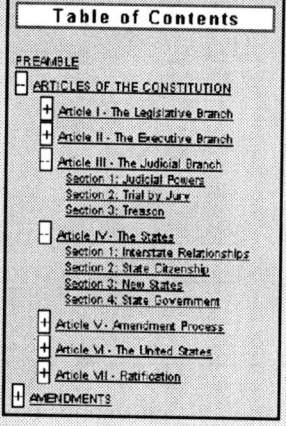

Expanding and Collapsing the Document

The final piece of the dynamic table of contents is to expand and collapse the document itself so that it mimics the appearance of the TOC. The structure of the document is fundamentally different from the structure of the TOC, however. In the TOC, different sections are nested within one another. In the document itself, by contrast, all sections are siblings, with only the section headings indicating when a section begins and ends and the element names indicating what level each section represents (see Figure 10-46). This means you have to take a fundamentally different approach in deciding which elements to hide and to display.

The structure of the TOC list and the document elements — Figure 10-46

```
<ol>
   <li>Main Head</li>
   <ol>
      <li>Subhead</li>
      <ol>
         <li>Minor Subhead</li>
         <li>Minor Subhead</li>
      </ol>
      <li>Subhead</li>
   </ol>
   <li>Main Head</li>
   <ol>
      <li>Subhead</li>
      <ol>
         <li>Minor Subhead</li>
      </ol>
   </ol>
</ol>
```

nested list

```
<h1>Main Head</h1>
<p>Text</p>
<h2>Subhead</h2>
<p>Text</p>
<h3>Minor Subhead</h3>
<p>Text</p>
<h3>Minor Subhead</h3>
<p>Text</p>
<p>Text</p>
<h2>Subhead</h2>
<p>Text</p>
<p>Text</p>
<h1>Main Head</h1>
<p>Text</p>
<h2>Subhead</h2>
<p>Text</p>
<h3>Minor Subhead</h3>
<p>Text</p>
```

document elements

Our approach is to move through the document sibling by sibling. Each time you encounter a heading element, you determine whether its corresponding entry in the TOC is currently being displayed. If it's hidden in the TOC, you hide the heading element and all subsequent siblings until you encounter the next section heading; otherwise, you display the heading element and the siblings that follow until the next section heading is encountered. The general structure of the code is

```
historyDoc = document.getElementById("doc");
for (n=historyDoc.firstChild; n!=null; n=n.nextSibling) {
   nodeLevel=levelNum(n);
   if (nodeLevel != -1) {
      set the display status for the heading
   }
   if (n.nodeType==1) {
      apply the display status to the element
   }
}
```

In this code you loop through the nodes in the document using the same structure that you used in the createList() function by starting with the first child of the doc element and moving to the next sibling node until there are no siblings left. For each node you first test whether it is a heading element by using the levelNum() function. If the value returned by the levelNum() is not equal to –1 (indicating that the node represents one of the section headings) you set the display status for the heading. Then you test whether the current node is any element node (such as a paragraph) by verifying that the value of the nodeType property is equal to 1. If it is an element node, you apply the current display status to the node and then move on to the next sibling in the document.

You'll add these commands to a function named expandCollapseDoc(). Create this function now.

To insert the expandCollapseDoc():

1. Return to the **toc.js** file in your text editor.

2. At the bottom of the file, insert the following function (see Figure 10-47):

```
function expandCollapseDoc() {
   historyDoc = document.getElementById("doc");
   for (n=historyDoc.firstChild; n!=null; n=n.nextSibling) {
      nodeLevel = levelNum(n);
      if (nodeLevel != -1) {
         //set the display status for the heading
      }
      if (n.nodeType==1) {
         //apply the display status to the element
      }
   }
}
```

Figure 10-47 Inserting the expandCollapseDoc() function

```
function expandCollapse(e) {
   var plusMinusBox=eventSource(e);
   if (plusMinusBox.innerHTML=="--") plusMinusBox.innerHTML="+";
   else plusMinusBox.innerHTML="--";

   var nestedList = plusMinusBox.parentNode.nextSibling;
   if (nestedList.style.display=="") nestedList.style.display="none";
   else nestedList.style.display="";
}

function expandCollapseDoc() {
   historyDoc = document.getElementById("doc");
   for (n=historyDoc.firstChild; n!=null; n=n.nextSibling) {
      nodeLevel = levelNum(n);
      if (nodeLevel != -1) {
         //set the display status for the heading
      }
      if (n.nodeType==1) {
         //apply the display status to the element
      }
   }
}
```

3. Save your changes to the file.

To set the display status, you first create a variable named displayStatus, setting its initial value to "" (indicating that the item will be displayed on the page).

```
displayStatus = "";
```

Then you match the heading element to its corresponding entry in the TOC. Recall that in the last session, each list item in the TOC was given an id based on the id of a section heading. If the section heading has the id *sectionId*, then the list item has the id TOC*sectionId*. You can use the getElementById() method to locate the list item for each section heading as follows:

```
TOCitem = document.getElementById("TOC"+n.id);
```

Now you need to determine whether the corresponding entry in the TOC is hidden or visible. Each list item has as its parent node an ordered list element, and the parent of that element is also an ordered list element, all the way up to the top of the TOC. If the display style of *any* of those ordered list elements is set to "none", the list item is hidden in the TOC. Thus, to determine whether the list item is hidden, you have to look at the display style of all of its parents. The following code provides a for loop that starts with the current value of the nodeLevel variable, decreasing it by one each time through the loop (as you move up to the higher levels in the TOC list); when the value of the counter is less than 0, the loop stops.

```
for (l=nodeLevel; l >= 0; l--) {
   TOCitem = TOCitem.parentNode;
   if (TOCitem.style.display == "none") {displayStatus = "none";
 break;}
}
```

Each time through the loop, you change the reference of the TOCitem variable to its parent. If the value of the display style for TOCitem is "none", you set the value of the displayStatus variable to "none" and break out of the loop (since there is no need to continue checking the higher levels in the TOC after you discover that the list item lies within a hidden list). Figure 10-48 demonstrates how this code moves up the node tree from one nested list to another.

Testing for hidden lists **Figure 10-48**

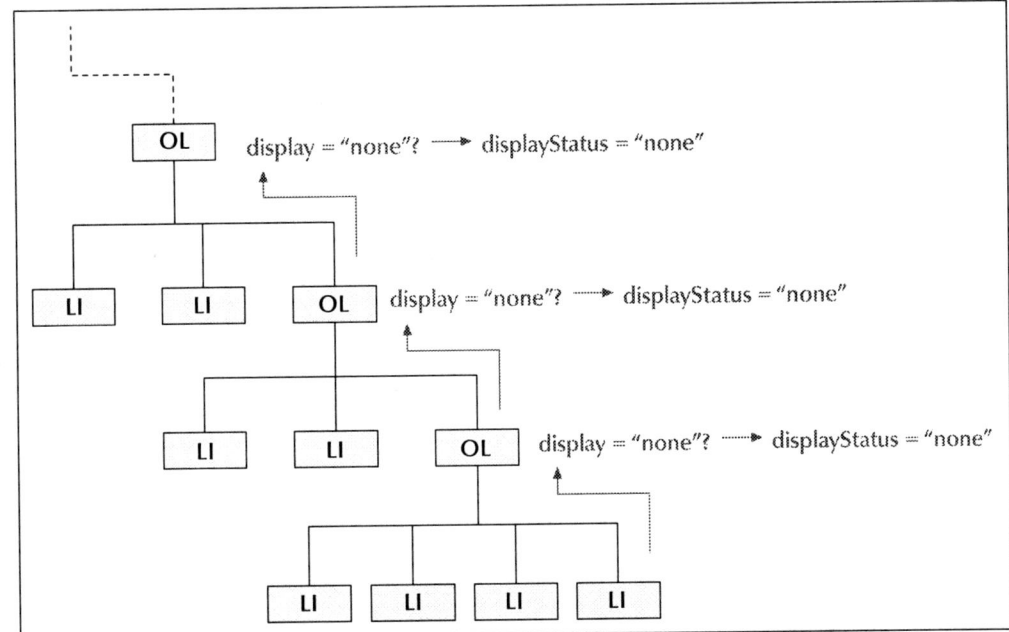

Once the value of the displayStatus variable has been determined, you apply it to the current node in the constitution document using the command

```
n.style.display = displayStatus;
```

Add these commands to the expandCollapseDoc() function.

To complete the expandCollapseDoc():

1. In the expandCollapseDoc() function, below the comment "set the display status for the heading", insert the following commands:

```
displayStatus = "";
TOCitem = document.getElementById("TOC"+n.id);
for (l=nodeLevel; l >= 0; l--) {
   TOCitem = TOCitem.parentNode;
   if (TOCitem.style.display == "none") {displayStatus = "none";
   break;}
}
```

2. Below the comment "apply the display status to the element", insert the command:

```
n.style.display = displayStatus;
```

Figure 10-49 shows the final code of the expandCollapseDoc() function.

Figure 10-49	The final expandCollapseDoc() function

```
function expandCollapseDoc() {
   historyDoc = document.getElementById("doc");
   for (n=historyDoc.firstChild; n!=null; n=n.nextSibling) {
      nodeLevel = levelNum(n);
      if (nodeLevel != -1) {
         //set the display status for the heading
         displayStatus = "";
         TOCitem = document.getElementById("TOC"+n.id);
         for (l=nodeLevel; l >= 0; l--) {
            TOCitem = TOCitem.parentNode;
            if (TOCitem.style.display == "none") {displayStatus = "none"; break;}
         }
      }
      if (n.nodeType==1) {
         //apply the display status to the element
         n.style.display = displayStatus;
      }
   }
}
```

Next, call the expandCollapseDoc() function.

3. Insert the following command, as shown in Figure 10-50:

```
expandCollapseDoc();
```

Figure 10-50	The final expandCollapse() function

```
function expandCollapse(e) {
   var plusMinusBox=eventSource(e);
   if (plusMinusBox.innerHTML=="--") plusMinusBox.innerHTML="+";
   else plusMinusBox.innerHTML="--";

   var nestedList = plusMinusBox.parentNode.nextSibling;
   if (nestedList.style.display=="") nestedList.style.display="none";
   else nestedList.style.display="";

   expandCollapseDoc();
}
```

4. Close the **toc.js** file, saving your changes.

5. Reopen the **usconst.htm** file in your Web browser. Click the different plus/minus boxes in the TOC and verify that the content displayed in the constitution document mimics the TOC. See Figure 10-51.

Historic Documents Online

Department of History
Midwest University

<< 1600 | 1600 - 1700 | 1700 - 1800 | 1800 - 1900 | 1900 - 2000 | 2000 >>

The Constitution of the United States

Preamble

WE THE PEOPLE OF THE UNITED STATES, IN ORDER TO FORM A MORE PERFECT UNION, establish Justice, insure domestic Tranquility, provide for the common defence, promote the general Welfare, and secure the Blessings of Liberty to ourselves and our Posterity, do ordain and establish this Constitution for the United States of America.

Articles of the Constitution

Article I - The Legislative Branch

Article II - The Executive Branch

Article III - The Judicial Branch

Article IV - The States

Article V - Amendment Process

Paragraph

The Congress, whenever two thirds of both Houses shall deem it necessary, shall propose Amendments to this Constitution, or, on the Application of the Legislatures of two thirds of the several States, shall call a Convention for proposing Amendments, which, in either Case, shall be valid to all Intents and Purposes, as part of this Constitution, when ratified by the Legislatures of three fourths of the several States, or by Conventions in three fourths thereof, as the one or the other Mode of Ratification may be proposed by the Congress; Provided that no Amendment which may be made prior to the Year One thousand eight hundred and eight shall in any Manner affect the first and fourth Clauses in the Ninth Section of the first article; and that no State, without its Consent, shall be deprived of its equal Suffrage in the Senate.

Article VI - The United States

Article VII - Ratification

Amendments

Testing the Dynamic TOC

You show the completed table of contents to Norene. She's very pleased with the final product. She asks whether your work can be easily applied to other documents in her library. You decide to show her by testing it on a document containing the text of a 1790 peace treaty between the United States government and the Creek Indians.

To test the TOC application on a new document:

1. Use your text editor to open the **treattxt.htm** file from the tutorial.10/tutorial folder. Enter *your name* and *the date* in the head section of the document and save it as **treaty.htm**.

2. Above the closing </head> tag, insert an external script element pointing to the toc.js file:

```
<script src="toc.js" type="text/javascript"></script>
```

3. Add the event handler **onload="makeTOC()"** to the body element.

4. Insert the following div element below the <body> tag:

```
<div id="toc"></div>
```

5. Enclose the content of the document within a div element by adding the following opening tag directly before the Preamble h1 element:

```
<div id="doc">
```

6. Add a closing **</div>** directly before the closing </body> tag at the bottom of the file. Figure 10-52 shows the revised code of the treaty.htm file.

Figure 10-52 — Revising the treaty document

```
<script src="toc.js" type="text/javascript"></script>
</head>

<body onload="makeTOC()">
<div id="toc"></div>

<div id="logo"><img src="hlogo.jpg" alt="Historic Documents" /></div>
<div id="logosub">Department of History<br />Midwest University</div>
<div id="doctitle"><h1>Treaty with the Creek Indians: 1790</h1></div>

<div id="doc">
<h1>Preamble</h1>
<p>THE parties being desirous of establishing permanent peace and friendship
between the United States and the said Creek Nation, and the citizens and
members thereof, and to remove the causes of war by ascertaining their limits,
and making other necessary, just and friendly arrangements: The President of the
United States, by Henry Knox, Secretary for the Department of War, whom he hath
constituted with full powers for these purposes, by and with the advice and
consent of the Senate of the United States, and the Creek Nation, by the
undersigned Kings, Chiefs and Warriors, representing the said nation, have
agreed to the following articles. </p>



</div>
</body>
</html>
```

7. Close the **treaty.htm** file, saving your changes.

8. Open **treaty.htm** in your Web browser and explore the functionality of the table of contents. As shown in Figure 10-53, the dynamic table of contents should be displayed on the left margin. Clicking the plus/minus boxes should collapse and expand the document contents, and clicking the entries in the TOC should move you to the corresponding sections in the treaty.

The treaty document with the dynamic TOC ◀ **Figure 10-53**

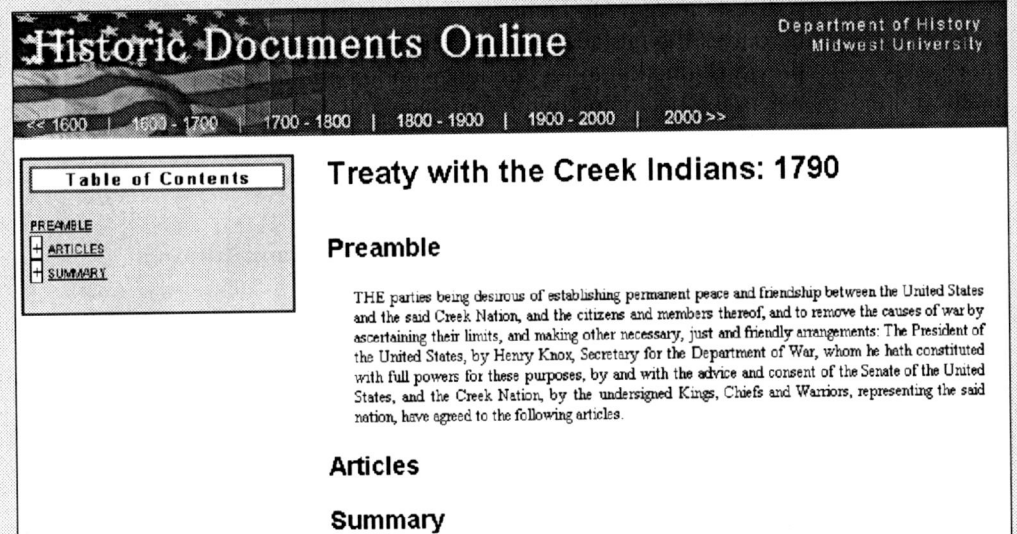

Traversing the Node Tree using Recursion

In creating the dynamic table of contents, you made several simplifying assumptions. One was that all of the section headings in each historic document would be siblings and children of the "doc" element. You did not allow for the possibility that a section heading would be further nested within another element. However, some applications that involve working with the node tree require a script to be able to traverse the entire tree, touching each node.

At first glance this may seem like a daunting task. A single node may have many child nodes, and each of those child nodes may have its own collection of child nodes, and so forth, down through several levels of the tree. The path through the node tree must be able to go down each of the branches of the tree, touching each node and not touching any node more than once. To do that, scripts employ recursion. **Recursion** is a programming technique in which a function calls itself repeatedly until a stopping condition is met. Figure 10-54 shows the general form of a recursive function.

A recursive function ◀ **Figure 10-54**

```
function fname() {
    if (stopping condition not met) {
        commands;
        fname();
    }
}
```

In this code, the function *fname()* is run as long as the stopping condition is not met. One part of the if statement's command block is a command to run the *fname()* function again. Thus, you have a series of nested function calls that create a sequence of function calls. At some point, one of the nested functions fulfills the stopping condition and you move back to the previous function in the sequence and continue from that point. Eventually you move back to the beginning of the sequence and the entire process stops. The following example of recursion is used with a function that counts the number of descendant nodes within a given node:

```
function countNodes(nodeObject) {
    for (var n=nodeObject.firstChild; n!= null; n=n.nextSibling) {
        count++;
        countNodes(n);
    }
    return count;
}
```

Figure 10-55 illustrates the behavior of this function for a small node tree. The count-Nodes() function uses a for loop to examine each child node of the node object. The loop begins with the first child of the node object, moves to the next sibling each time through the loop, and halts when there are no more siblings to go to. Each time through the loop, the value of the count variable increases by 1, keeping a running total of the number of child nodes. At the same time, each time through the loop, the function applies the countNodes() function to the current child node to determine how many child nodes it contains. When the loop is finished, the final value of the count variable is returned.

Figure 10-55	Counting the total number of child nodes

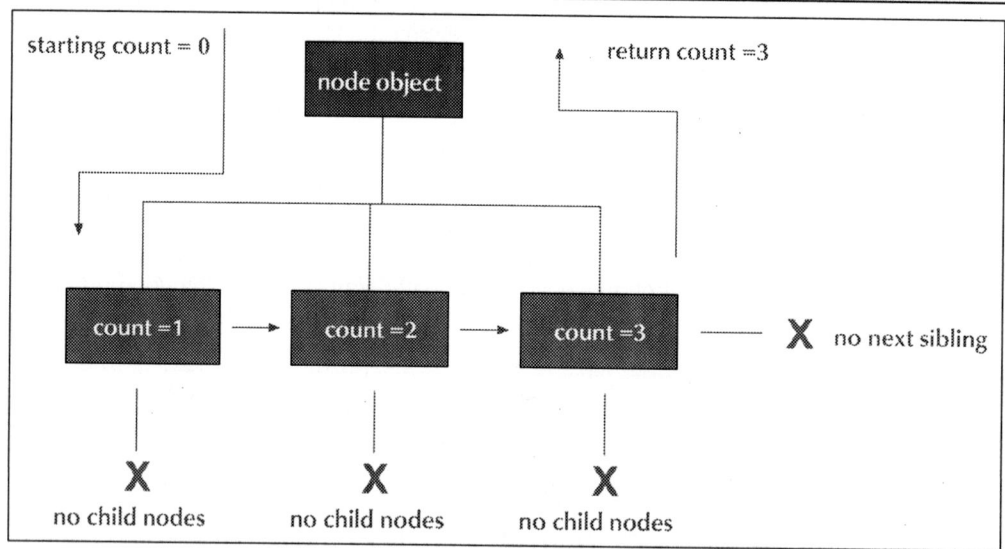

One important point to remember: the node variable, n, in this example must be entered as "var n = nodeObject.firstChild" in the for loop and not "n = nodeObject. firstChild". This is because the n variable would be treated as a global variable if it were not re-initialized with the var statement each time the recursive function is called.

Each recursive function needs a starting point, and in the case of the countNodes() function, a starting value for the count variable. The following code shows how you would call the countNodes() function using the top of the document (the html element in the case of HTML documents) as the starting node and setting the initial value of the count variable to 0:

```
function reportCount() {
    count = 0;
    return countNodes(document.documentElement);
}
```

Figure 10-56 displays the recursive action of the countNodes() function on a larger node tree. Note that the function "drills" down the node tree until it reaches the lowest node on the left-most part of the tree. From there it continues to the right and up until it returns to the root node. Whenever it encounters a node, it first counts the child nodes for the element before going to the next sibling. As it moves through the node tree, the value of the count variable increases by one at each node it encounters, eventually returning a count value of 10.

Recursion in the node counter | Figure 10-56

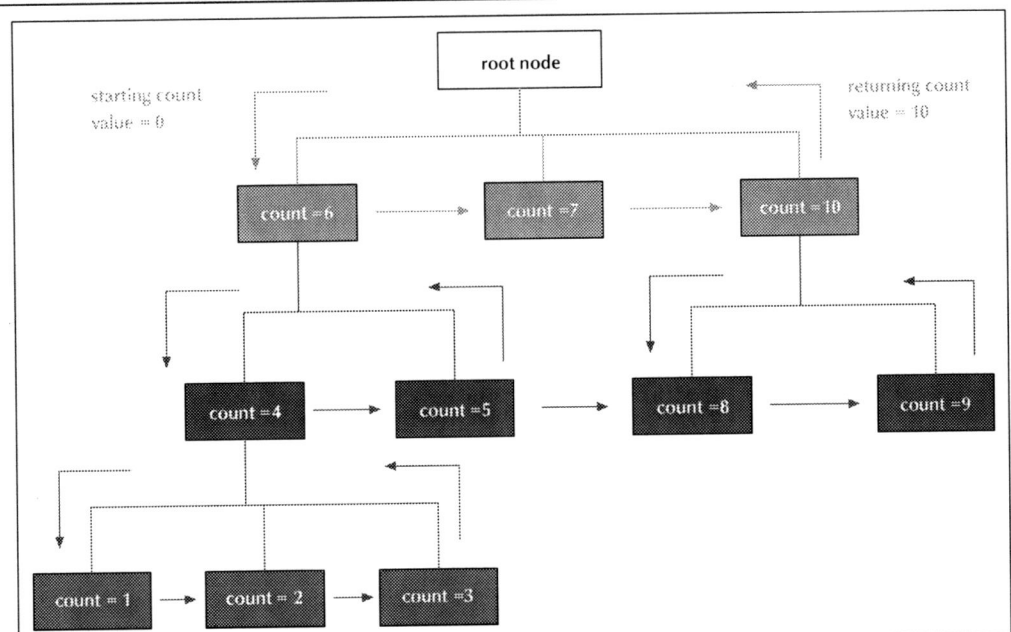

You don't need to use recursion with Norene's Web site; this technique will be useful for future projects that Norene may have for you.

Working with Style Sheets

Norene is pleased with all of the work you've done on the dynamic table of contents. She's approached you with one last problem. Norene wants to provide users with a version of each historic document that is suitable for printing. This version of the layout would contain only the historic document with none of the other features from the Web page. For example, such pages would include no table of contents box or history department logo. One way of making this revision would be to create a style sheet specifically designed for printed output (see Review 2 for a discussion of print style sheets). However, Norene would rather give users the option of choosing which version of the page to print. She asks whether you can use objects on the page that students can click to switch from one style sheet to another.

Norene has provided two icons that you can have users click to switch between the Web version of the constitution page and the printer version. You'll float these two images on the right margin of the document title. Add these images to the Web page now.

To insert the Web and printer icons:

1. Reopen **usconst.htm** in your text editor.

2. Locate the div element with the id "doctitle". Directly before the h1 element insert the following code, as shown in Figure 10-57:

```
<img src="print.jpg" alt="" style="float: right; cursor:
    pointer" />
<img src="web.jpg" alt="" style="float: right; cursor: pointer" />
```

Figure 10-57	Inserting Web and printer icons

```
<body onload="makeTOC()">
<div id="logo"><img src="hlogo.jpg" alt="Historic Documents" /></div>
<div id="logosub">Department of History<br />Midwest University</div>
<div id="doctitle">
<img src="print.jpg" alt="" style="float: right; cursor: pointer" />
<img src="web.jpg" alt="" style="float: right; cursor: pointer" />
<h1>The Constitution of the United States</h1></div>
```

3. Save your changes to the file.

4. Reload **usconst.htm** in your Web browser. As shown in Figure 10-58, the Web and printer icons now float on the right margin of the page.

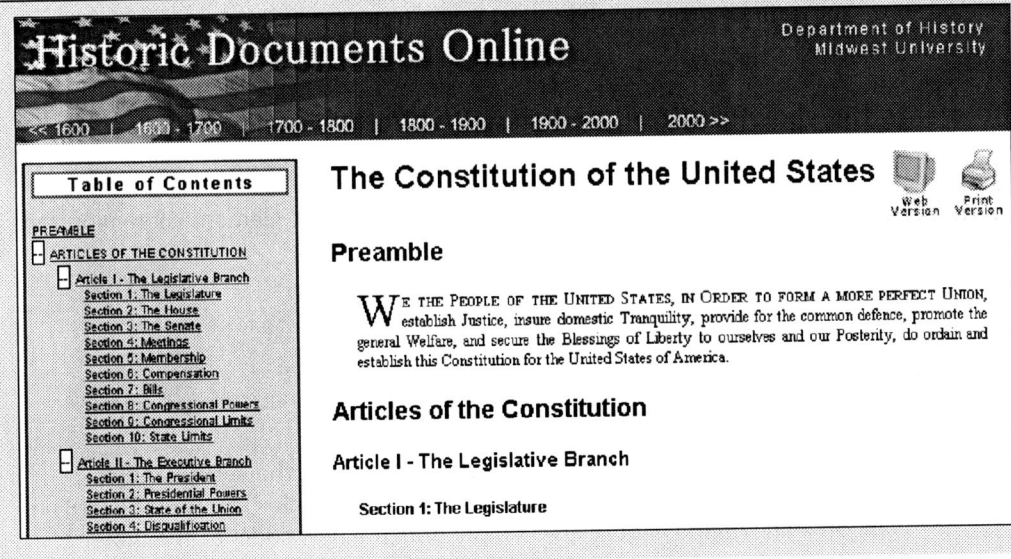

Norene has also provided an external style sheet file, print.css that defines the format of the printed version of the constitution page.

Working with the link element

So far in this tutorial you've worked only with elements found in the body of a Web page; however, elements in a document's head can be modified as well. The head of the constitution page contains a link element that loads the history.css style sheet. The code for the tag is

```
<link href="history.css" rel="stylesheet" type="text/css" />
```

You want to change this tag to

```
<link href="print.css" rel="stylesheet" type="text/css" />
```

to load the print styles for the page (and thus unload the Web version styles). You could examine the HTML code for the usconst.htm document to determine exactly where this element falls in the document node tree, but a quicker way would be to use the document.getElementsByTagName() method. Recall from Tutorial 4 that this method returns an object collection of all tags with a particular tag name. For example, to create an object collection of all the link elements in the document, you would use the expression

```
document.getElementsByTagName("link")
```

The first link element, which in this case is the link element for the history.css style sheet, has the object reference

```
document.getElementsByTagName("link")[0]
```

To change the link so that it uses the print.css style sheet instead, you change the value of the href attribute to "print.css":

```
document.getElementsByTagName("link")[0].href="print.css";
```

Use this information to add two functions to the constitution page. One, named show-PrintVer(), changes the href attribute of the first style sheet to "print.css"; the second, named showWebVer(), changes the style sheet to the history.css file.

To create the showPrintVer() and showWebVer() functions:

1. Return to the **usconst.htm** file in your text editor.

2. Above the closing </head> tag, insert an embedded script element containing the following two functions:

```
function showPrintVer() {
   document.getElementsByTagName("link")[0].href="print.css";
}
function showWebVer() {
   document.getElementsByTagName("link")[0].href="history.css";
}
```

3. Locate the img element for the print.jpg image and insert the event handler **onclick="showPrintVer()"**. Insert the event handler **onclick="showWebVer()"** in the web.jpg inline image. Figure 10-59 highlights the new code for the file.

Figure 10-59	The showPrintVer() and showWebVer() functions

```
<title>The Constitution of the United States</title>
<link href="history.css" rel="stylesheet" type="text/css" />
<link href="toc.css" rel="stylesheet" type="text/css" />

<script src="toc.js" type="text/javascript"></script>

<script type="text/javascript">
function showPrintVer() {
   document.getElementsByTagName("link")[0].href="print.css";
}
function showWebVer() {
   document.getElementsByTagName("link")[0].href="history.css";
}
</script>
</head>

<body onload="makeTOC()">
<div id="logo"><img src="hlogo.jpg" alt="Historic Documents" /></div>
<div id="logosub">Department of History<br />Midwest University</div>
<div id="doctitle">
<img src="print.jpg" alt="" style="float: right; cursor: pointer"
    onclick="showPrintVer()" />
<img src="web.jpg" alt="" style="float: right; cursor: pointer"
    onclick="showWebVer()" />
```

4. Close the file, saving your changes.

5. Reload **usconst.htm** in your Web browser. Verify that as you click the printer and Web icons, the layout of the page changes between the print version and the Web version. See Figure 10-60.

   Trouble? If you are running Internet Explorer for the Macintosh, the Web page appearance will not change.

The print version of the constitution page ◄ **Figure 10-60**

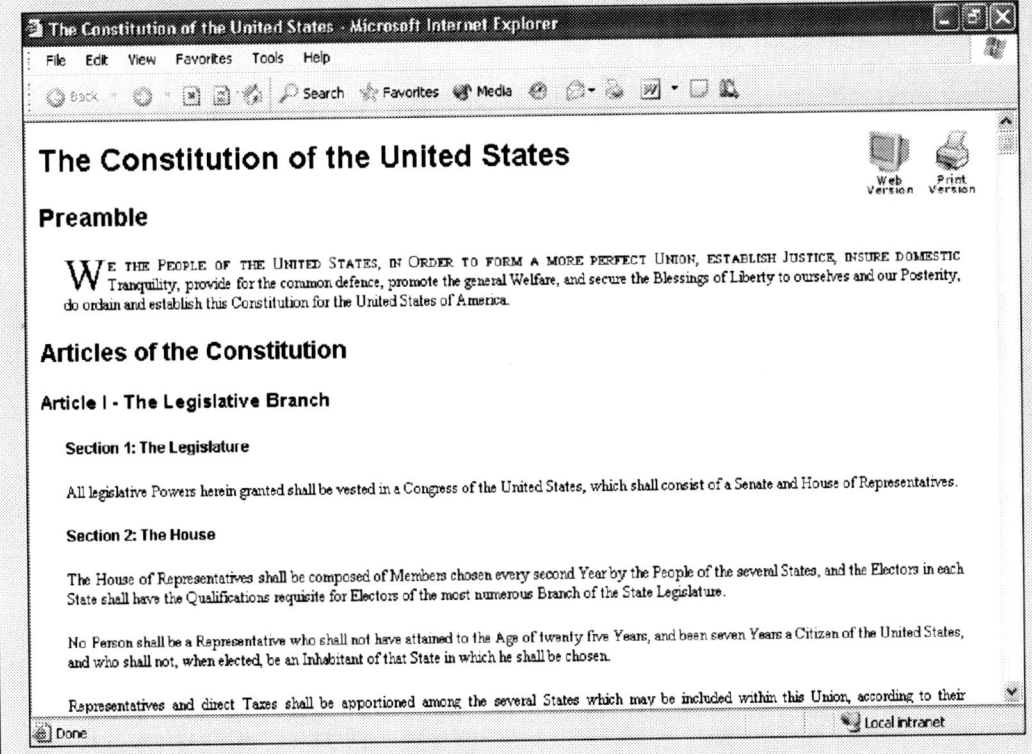

6. Close your Web browser.

The Style Sheet Collection

In addition to working with style sheets by modifying the link element, you can also work with them directly as objects in the document object model. The DOM organizes style sheets into object collections using the form

```
document.styleSheets[i]
```

where *i* is the index number of the style sheet. The first style sheet that a browser encounters has an index value of 0, the second has an index value of 1, and so forth. Figure 10-61 lists the properties of the style sheet object. Note that most of the properties are read-only, which means that they allow you to extract information about the style sheet object, but not to change, for example, the value of its href attribute.

Figure 10-61

Properties of style sheets

Property	Description
styleSheet.cssText	The text of the declarations in the style sheet (Internet Explorer DOM)
styleSheet.disabled	Returns a Boolean value indicating whether the style sheet has been disabled (true) or has been enabled (false)
styletSheet.href	The url of the style sheet. For embedded style sheets, the href value is an empty text string [read-only]
styleSheet.media	A text string containing the list of media types associated with the style sheet [read-only]
styleSheet.rules	Returns the collection of rules within the style sheet (Internet Explorer DOM)
styleSheet.cssRules	Returns the collection of rules within the style sheet (W3C DOM)
styleSheet.title	The title of the style sheet [read-only]
styleSheet.type	The MIME type of the style sheet [read-only]

You can enable style sheets or disable them using the disabled property of the style sheet object. For example, to disable the first style sheet, you use the command

```
document.styleSheets[0].disabled = true;
```

To enable the style sheet, you set the disabled property to false:

```
document.styleSheets[0].disabled = false;
```

Most browsers support the styleSheets collection, but some do not. One browser that does not recognize the styleSheets collection is Opera. If you need to support these browsers, it's best to modify the attributes of the link element instead of working with the styleSheets collection. For a more general approach, however, it's better to work with the styleSheets object collection since it includes both external and embedded style sheets.

Working with Style Sheet Rules

The style sheet object also contains an object collection for each rule in a style sheet. In the W3C DOM, the object reference to the rules collection is

```
styleSheet.cssRules
```

where *styleSheet* is a styleSheet object. For example, if the first style sheet in a Web page contains the declarations

```
<style type="text/css">
   h1 {color: red}
   h2 {color: blue}
</style>
```

then the object reference

```
document.styleSheets[0].cssRules[0]
```

refers to the style sheet declaration h1 {color: red}. Note that in the Internet Explorer DOM, style sheet rules are referenced using the object collection

```
styleSheet.rules
```

Figure 10-62 lists some of the methods you can use to create and edit the rules within your style sheets. Note that the two document object models use different methods to add and remove style sheet rules.

Methods of style sheet rules | Figure 10-62

Method	Description
styleSheet.addRule(selector, style, index)	Adds a new rule to the style sheet object where *selector* is the selector to receive the style, *style* is the text of style rule, and *index* specifies position where the rule should insert. The default *index* value is 0 which places the rule at the beginning of the style sheet. (Internet Explorer DOM)
styleSheet.deleteRule(index)	Deletes the rule with the index number *index* from the style sheet (W3C DOM)
styleSheet.insertRule(rule, index)	Inserts a new *rule* into the style sheet at index number *index* (W3C DOM)
styleSheet.removeRule(index)	Removes the rule with the index number *index* from the style sheet (Internet Explorer DOM)

Norene tells you that she doesn't require you to modify any properties of the style sheets or rules in her documents. You've completed your work on her project. She'll apply the modifications you've made to the other documents in her library and get back to you with future projects.

Tips for Working with Dynamic Content and Styles

- Use the innerHTML property as a quick and easy way of modifying the contents of element nodes. Do not use other Internet Explorer properties, since they are not well supported by other browsers.
- Use familial references rather than counter variables in for loops to increase the speed and flexibility of your program code.
- When writing scripts that modify node elements, be sure to test the active node is an element node by using the nodeType property.
- Be aware that browsers will treat white space found in HTML files differently. The Internet Explorer browser does not treat occurrences of white space as text nodes, while in the W3C DOM and in many browsers, white space is treated as a text node.
- Use attribute properties as a quick and easy way to work with the attributes of element nodes.
- Use recursive functions to navigate an entire node tree, ensuring that each node is included in the path.
- Use the getElementsByTagName() method as a quick and easy way of generating object collections for elements in your document that share a common element name.

Session 10.3 Quick Check

1. What commands would you enter to create an inline image node named imgObj and then to append it as the first child of a node named listItem?
2. What command would you use to hide and remove from the page flow a page element with the id "imgObj"?
3. What is recursion?
4. What expression would you enter to create a collection of all div elements in the document? How would you reference the second div element in the collection?
5. What expression would you enter to reference the third style sheet attached to the document?
6. What expression would you enter to reference the second rule from the document's third style sheet? Provide an answer for both Internet Explorer and W3C document object models.

Tutorial Summary

In this tutorial, you learned how to create and manage dynamic content and styles to develop a dynamic table of contents application that could be applied to a wide variety of documents. In the first session, you were introduced to the Internet Explorer DOM's approach to dynamic content and you learned how to apply the innerHTML property to insert new content into a page element. The first session also introduced the node tree, exploring how to navigate through a node tree, create new nodes, and attach them to a Web page document. Using this information, you were able to create a list of section headings from a document. In the second session, you applied what you learned about node properties and methods to create a nested list of section headings. The second session also demonstrated how to work with attribute nodes and how to work with element attributes. In the third session, you created an expandable/collapsible document by applying the display style to elements within the dynamic table of contents and within the sample document. The third session also discussed how to navigate through a node tree by using a recursive function. The session and tutorial concluded with a discussion of style sheet objects, creating a Web page in which different style sheets could be loaded and applied to a document.

Key Terms

document fragment	node tree	recursion
dynamic content	plus/minus box	root node
node		

Practice

actice the skills you
arned in the tutorial
sing the same case
enario.

Review Assignments

Data files needed for this Review Assignment: fed10txt.htm, fedpaper.css, hlogo.jpg, keytxt.js, print.css, print.jpg, web.jpg

Norene has another application for you to add to her library of historic documents. Some documents are not broken into sections, so creating a table of contents would not be appropriate. For those documents, Norene would like the Web page to display a box containing a sorted list of important keywords and phrases found in the document. Each keyword or phrase has been marked in the documents with a dfn (definition) element. The entries in the keyword list need to search the current historic document for the presence of these dfn elements and create links between the keyword list entries and the keywords in the document. Norene also wants the page to have a Web version and a print version, and she wants users to be able to easily switch between the two.

Figure 10-63 shows a preview of the page created for the tenth Federalist paper written by James Madison in 1787 on the danger of factions to the republic.

Figure 10-63

Web   Print
Version   Version

The Federalist Papers: No. 10

The Union as a Safeguard Against Domestic Faction and Insurrection From the New York Packet. Friday, November 23, 1787.

TO THE PEOPLE OF THE STATE OF NEW YORK:

AMONG THE NUMEROUS ADVANTAGES PROMISED BY A WELLCONSTRUCTED UNION, none deserves to be more accurately developed than its tendency to break and control the violence of faction. The friend of popular governments never finds himself so much alarmed for their character and fate, as when he contemplates their propensity to this dangerous vice. He will not fail, therefore, to set a due value on any plan which, without violating the principles to which he is attached, provides a proper cure for it. The instability, injustice, and confusion introduced into the public councils, have, in truth, been the mortal diseases under which popular governments have everywhere perished; as they continue to be the favorite and fruitful topics from which the adversaries to liberty derive their most specious declamations. The valuable improvements made by the American constitutions on the popular models, both ancient and modern, cannot certainly be too much admired; but it would be an unwarrantable partiality, to contend that they have as effectually obviated the danger on this side, as was wished and expected. Complaints are everywhere heard from our most considerate and virtuous citizens, equally the friends of public and private faith, and of public and personal liberty, that our governments are too unstable, that the public good is disregarded in the conflicts of rival parties, and that measures are too often decided, not according to the rules of justice and the rights of the minor party, but by the superior force of an interested and overbearing majority. However anxiously we may wish that these complaints had no foundation, the evidence, of known facts will not permit us to deny that they are in some degree true. It will be found, indeed, on a candid review of our situation, that some of the distresses under which we labor have been erroneously charged on the operation of our governments; but it will be found, at the same time, that other causes will not alone account for many of our heaviest misfortunes; and, particularly, for that prevailing and increasing distrust of public engagements, and alarm for private rights, which are echoed from one end of the continent to the other. These must be chiefly, if not wholly, effects of the unsteadiness and injustice with which a factious spirit has tainted our public administrations.

By a faction, I understand a number of citizens, whether amounting to a majority or a minority of the whole, who are united and actuated by some common impulse of passion, or of interest, adversed to the rights of other citizens, or to the permanent and aggregate interests of the community.

Keywords

creditors
debtors
electors
enlightened statesmen
faction
liberty
popular government
pure democracy
reason of man
republic
republican principle
rights of property
unequal distribution of property

Norene has already provided the source document and external style sheets that format the appearance of the document and the keyword list for both the Web and printer. Your job is to write the application that creates the content of the keyword list.

To create the keyword list:

1. Use your text editor to open the **fed10txt.htm** file from the tutorial.10/review folder. Enter *your name* and *the date* in the comment section and save the file as **fed10. htm**. Take some time to study the contents of the file, paying attention to the id names assigned to various elements in the document.

2. Insert an external script element that points to the **keywords.js** file. Add an event handler to the body element that runs the function makeKeyWordBox() when the page is loaded. Close the file, saving your changes.

3. Use your text editor to open the **keytxt.js** file from the tutorial.10/review folder. Enter *your name* and *the date* in the comment section and save the file as **keywords.js**.

4. Create a function named makeElemList(). The purpose of this function is to return an array containing a sorted list of the contents of elements with a common tag name. You'll use this function later to create a list of the keywords in the document. The function has a single parameter named elem that contains the text of the tag name. Add the following commands to the function:

   a. Store the collection of elements whose tag name equals the elem parameter in a variable named elemList. (*Hint*: Use the document.getElementsByTagName() method.)

   b. Create a new array named elemTextArr.

   c. Create a for loop that goes through each of the objects in the elemList object collection. For each object, change the text to lowercase letters and store the content of the element in the corresponding elemTextArr array item. (*Hint*: Use the toLowerCase() String method to change the content of the object to lowercase letters.)

Explore

   d. Sort the entries in the elemTextArr array using the *array*.sort() method where *array* is the name of the array.

   e. Return the elemTextArr array.

5. Create a function named setElemId(). The purpose of this function is to create and return id values for elements in the document that match a specific tag name and element content. You'll use this function later to insert matching id values between the items in the keyword list and the keywords found in the document. The function has two parameters: elem, which contains the text of the tag name, and elemText, which contains the text of the element content. Add the following commands to the function:

   a. Store the collection of elements whose tag name equals the elem parameter in a variable named elemList.

   b. Create a for loop that goes through each of the objects in the elemList object collection.

   c. Within the for loop, test whether the content of the current elemList object, converted to lowercase letters, equals the value of the elemText parameter. If it does, test whether the id of the object is equal to an empty text string. If the id is missing, create a variable named elemId equal to the text string "keyword*i*" where *i* is the value of the counter variable in the for loop, and set the id of the object to the value of the elemId variable. If the id is not missing, set the value of the elemId variable to the value of the id attribute of the object.

   d. After the for loop has run, return the value of the elemId variable.

6. Create a function named makeKeyWordBox(). The purpose of this function is to create a list of keywords from the dfn elements in the historic document. There are no parameters for this function. Add the following commands:

   a. Create a variable named historyDoc that references the element with the id "doc".

   b. Create an element node named keywordBox for a div element. Set the id of the keywordBox to "keywords". Create another element node named keywordBoxTitle for an h1 element. Set the content of the h1 element to the text "Keywords" and append keywordBoxTitle to the keywordBox node as a child node. Create an element node named ulList that stores a ul element. Append ulList as a second child of the keywordBox node.

   c. Call the makeElemList() function using the text string "dfn" as the parameter value. Store the array returned by the function in a variable named keywords.

   d. Next, create and format the items in the keyword list. For the keywords array, create a for loop that does the following for each item in the array: (1) Create an element node named newListItem that contains a list item element; (2) Create an element node named newLink that contains a hyperlink element; (3) Set the content of newLink to the value of the current item in the keywords array (*Hint*: use the reference keywords[*i*] where *i* is the value of the counter variable in the for loop); (4) Create a variable named linkId whose value is equal to the value returned by the setElemId() function. The first parameter value in the setElemId() function should be the text string "dfn". The second parameter value should be the current item in the keywords array; (5) Change the href attribute of newLink to the value of the linkId variable; (6) Append newLink to newListItem and append newListItem to ulList.

   e. Append keywordBox as the first child of the historyDoc node.

   f. Call a function named createPrintWebImages().

7. Create a function named createPrintWebImages(). The purpose of this function is to insert Web and printer icons at the top of the Web page, format the appearance and content of those icons, and apply an event handler to each icon. The function has no parameters. Add the following commands:

   a. Create a variable named historyDoc that references the element with the id name "doc" in the document.

   b. Create an element node named printImg that contains an img element. Set the source of printImg to the print.jpg file. Set the value of the alt attribute for printImg to "Printer Version". Set the cursor style of printImg to "pointer". Run the showPrintVer() function when users click on the printImg node.

   c. Repeat step b to create an element node named webImg that also contains an img element. The source of this image is the web.jpg file, the value of the alt attribute should be "Web version", the cursor style should be "pointer", and the showWebVer() function should be run when the user clicks the webImg node.

   d. Insert the printImg node before the first child of the historyDoc object. Do the same for the webImg node.

8. Create a function named showPrintVer() to switch the browser to the print.css style sheet.

9. Create a function named showWebVer() to switch the browser to the fedpaper.css style sheet.

10. Close **keywords.js**, saving your changes.

11. Open **fed10.htm** in your Web browser. Verify that a keyword box containing a list of 13 keywords from Federalist Paper #10 is generated and that the entries in the keyword letter are in lowercase letters and sorted in alphabetical order. Further verify that clicking a keyword in the list moves the browser to the keyword entry in the document. Click the Web and printer icons to confirm that you can switch from a Web view to a printer view of the document. (*Note:* If you are running Internet Explorer for the Macintosh, you will not see a change in the Web page view.)

12. Submit the completed Web site to your instructor.

Apply

Use the skills you learned to create an English to French translation page

Case Problem 1

Data files needed for this Case Problem: engfrtxt.js, fr5txt.htm, french5.js, styles.css

French 101   Professor Eve Granger teaches French 101 at a local university. She is working on a Web site containing French phrases that she wants her students to review for the weekly quiz. She's asked you to help her create the Web site. She wants a student to be able to press the mouse button down on a French phrase in the site and have the English translation appear. When the student releases the mouse button, the French phrase should reappear. Figure 10-64 shows a preview of the Web page you'll create for Professor Granger.

Figure 10-64

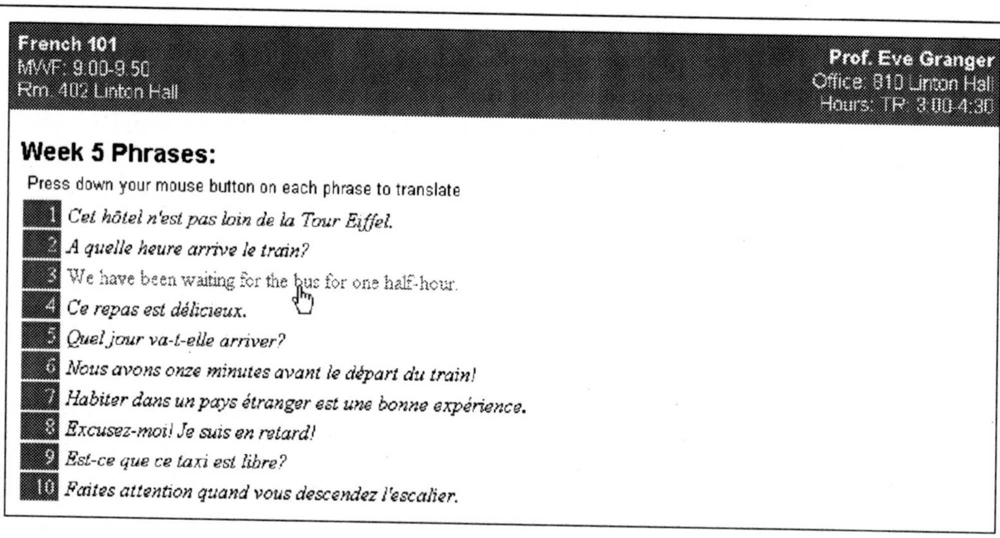

Professor Granger has already created an external script file named french5.js that contains two arrays. The french array contains 10 French phrases. The english array contains the 10 English translations of those phrases. You'll use these arrays to insert the French phrases and their translations into the Web page.

To complete this Web site:

1. Use your text editor to open the **fr5txt.htm** file from the tutorial.10/case1 folder. Enter *your name* and *the date* in the comment section and save the file as **french5.htm**.

2. Insert two external script elements that link to the french5.js and engfr.js files.

3. Insert an event handler into the body element that runs the function setUpTranslation() when the page loads.

4. Close the file, saving your changes.

5. Use your text editor to open the **engfrtxt.js** file from the tutorial.10/case1 folder. Enter *your name* and *the date* in the comment section and save the file as **engfr.js**.

6. Create a function named setUpTranslation(). The purpose of this function is to place the French phrases into the document and set up the event handlers for the mouse-down and mouseup events. Add the following commands:

    a. In Professor Granger's document the phrases are placed in paragraphs. The phrase number is placed within the first span element inside the paragraph. The phrase text is placed in the second span element within the paragraph. Create a variable named phrases that contains the object collection of all the paragraph elements in Professor Granger's document. (*Hint*: Use the document.getElementsBy-TagName() method.)

    b. Create a for loop that loops through each of the objects in the phrases collection. For each object in the collection do the following: (1) Change the inner content of the second child node of the object to french[*i*] where *i* is the value of the counter variable in the for loop; (2) Run the swapFE() function in response to a mouse-down event occurring within the object's second child node; (3) Run the swapEF() function in response to a mouseup event occurring within the object's second child node.

7. Create a function named swapFE(). The purpose of this function is to exchange the French phrase for the English translation. The function has a single parameter, the event object e. Add the following commands to the function:

    a. Store the source of the event in a variable named phrase. This variable represents the phrase that was clicked in the document. (*Note*: You will have to create a cross-browser function or insert code that will determine the source of the event.)

    b. There are 10 phrases in the document. Determine the phrase number by extracting the integer value from the previous sibling of the phrase node. (*Hint*: Use the parseInt() function applied to the inner content of the previous sibling node.) Store the phrase number in the variable phrasenum.

    c. The index values from the English and French arrays range from 0 to 9. Change the inner content of the phrase node to the value of array item english[*phrasenum* -1] where *phrasenum* is the value of the phrasenum variable.

    d. Change the font style of the phrase node to normal. Change the color of the phrase node to the color value (155, 102, 102).

8. Create a function named swapEF(). The purpose of this function is to exchange the English translation for the French phrase. Apply the same commands you used in the swapFE() function to this function, except that the phrase node should store the value of the french[*phrasenum*-1] item, the font style should be italic, and the font color should be black.

9. Close the file, saving your changes.

10. Open **french5.htm** in your Web browser. Verify that as you press the mouse button down on each phrase, the English translation appears. When you release the mouse button, the French phrase should reappear.

11. Submit the completed Web site to your instructor.

Case Problem 2

Data files needed for this Case Problem: camtxt.htm, filttxt.js, links.jpg, logo.jpg, styles.css

MicroCity   David Forrest works at MicroCity, an online store for computers and electronics. One of his jobs is to create a table listing the different digital cameras sold by MicroCity. The company carries hundreds of digital camera models and David thinks that the data table will be too long for customers to easily view. He would like to give customers the ability to filter the data table, showing only those models that match certain criteria. Customers should be able to select the criteria from a drop-down list box. Figure 10-65 shows a preview of the Web page that David wants you to help him create.

Figure 10-65

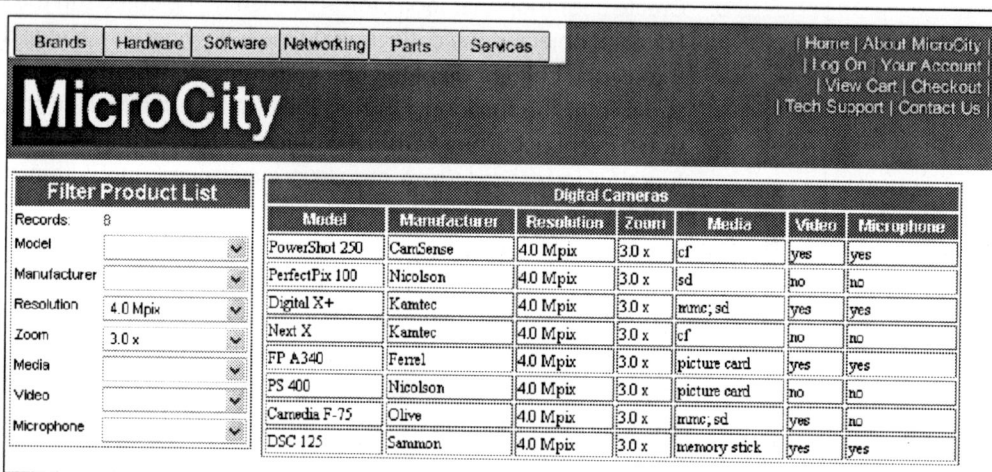

The data table contains seven columns, indicating each camera's model name, manufacturer, resolution, zoom capability, storage media, support for video, and whether it contains a microphone. The drop-down list boxes on the left contain the unique values from each of the columns in the data tables. If a customer selects a zoom value of "3.0 x" from the drop-down list box, only those cameras with that zoom feature should be displayed in the data table. Customers should be able to select more than one filter, and only those cameras satisfying all filter values should be shown. A table named "records" displays the records in the data table after filtering.

To complete this Web site:

1. Use your text editor to open the **camtxt.htm** file from the tutorial.10/case2 folder. Enter *your name* and *the date* in the comment section and save the file as **cameras.htm**.

2. In the head section, insert a script element pointing to the **filter.js** file. Add an event handler to the body element to run the function init() when the page loads. Close the file, saving your changes.

3. Use your text editor to open the **filttxt.js** file from the tutorial.10/case2 folder. Enter *your name* and *the date* in the comment section and save the file as **filter.js**.

4. Create a function named resetTable(). The purpose of this function is to reset the data table by displaying all hidden table rows. Add the following commands to the function:

   a. Use the getElementsByTagName() method to create a collection of all tr elements in the Web page. Store the object collection in the allRows variable.

   b. Create a for loop that goes through each object in the allRows collection. For each object set the display style to an empty text string (thus displaying the table row in the Web page).

5. Create the countRecords() function. The purpose of this function is to count the number of visible rows in the data table after the table headings. The total is then displayed in the table cell with the id "records". Add the following commands to the function:

   a. Create an object named headRow that points to the table row with the id "titleRow". Create a variable named rowCount, setting its initial value to 0.

   b. Create a for loop that uses familial references starting with the first sibling of headRow and moving to the next sibling until there are no siblings left. Within the for loop, test whether the node name of the current node is equal to "TR". If it is, test whether the value of its display style is equal to an empty text string. If it is (indicating that it is visible in the document) increase the value of the rowCount variable by 1.

   c. Change the inner content of the "records" table cell to the value of the rowCount variable.

6. Create the checkCell() function. The purpose of this function is to test whether a value in a cell from the data table equals the text string of a filter value. If it does not, the table row containing the table cell should be hidden. The function has two parameters: cell and filterText. The cell parameter points to the table cell object. The filterText parameter contains the text of the filter value. Add the following command to the function:

   a. Insert an if condition that tests whether the inner content of the cell object does not equal the value of the filterText parameter. If it doesn't, change the display style of the parent node of the cell object to "none".

7. Create the findCell() function. The purpose of this function is to determine in which cell in the data table row the checkCell() function should be run. The function has three parameters: row, cellNum, and filterText. The row parameter contains an object for the current table row. The cellNum contains the column number (from 1 to 7) of the cell to check for filtering. The filterText parameter contains the text string of the filter value. Add the following commands to the function:

   a. Create a variable named cellCount. Set its initial value to 0.

   b. Create a for loop that uses familial references to loop through each cell in the current table row, starting with the first child of the table row and moving to the next sibling until there are no more siblings left. Within the for loop, test whether the name of the current node is "TD". If it is, increase the value of cellCount by 1 and run the checkCell() function if cellCount equals cellNum, using the current cell node and the value of filterText as the parameter values.

8. Create the filterTable() function. The purpose of this function is to loop through each row in the data table, running the findCell() function. The function has two parameters: cellNum and filterText. Add the following commands:

   a. Create an object named headRow that points to the document object with the id "titleRow". This object represents the title row in the data table.

   b. Create a for loop that uses a familial reference to loop through each row in the data table starting with the first sibling of headRow and moving to the next sibling until there are no siblings left. If the node name of the current node equals "TR" call the findCell() function using the current node, cellNum, and filterText as the parameter values.

9. Create the filter() function. The purpose of this function is to extract the selected values from each of the selection lists in the Web page and then call the filterTable() function for each filter value. Add the following commands to the function:

   a. Call the resetTable() function to redisplay all rows in the data table.

   b. Create an object collection named allSelects containing all select elements in the document.

   c. Create a for loop that loops through each object in the allSelects collection. The loop should have a counter variable that starts with the value 0 and increases by 1 as long as it is less than the length of the allSelects collection. For each select object in the collection, extract the text of the selected option and store the text in the filterText variable, and then if filterText is not equal to an empty text string, call the filterTable() function using the value of the counter variable plus 1 as the value for the cellNum parameter and filterText as the value of the filterText parameter.

   d. After the for loop, run the countRecords() function to update the value in the "records" table cell.

10. Create the init() function. The purpose of this function is to add event handlers to all of the selection lists in the document so that they run the filter() function whenever a customer changes the selected value in a list. The function should also set the initial value of the "records" cell, displaying the total number of records in the data table. Add the following commands:

    a. Create an object collection named allSelects containing all select elements in the document.

    b. For each object in the allSelects collection, add an event handler for the onchange event that runs the filter() function.

    c. Call the countRecords() function.

11. Close the file, saving your changes.

12. Open **cameras.htm** in your Web browser. Verify that when the page opens, the total number of cameras in the data table (24) is displayed in the upper-left table cell. Select Kamtec from the Manufacturer drop-down list box and verify that five camera models are displayed in the data table. Continue to select filter values from the other drop-down list boxes, confirming that the data table is automatically updated to reflect the selected filter. To undo a filter, select the empty text string from the appropriate selection list.

13. Submit the completed Web site to your instructor.

Case Problem 3

Data files needed for this Case Problem: clisttxt.htm, data.js, lhouse.css, logo.jpg, newtxt.js

The Lighthouse Aaron Kitchen is the fundraising coordinator for The Lighthouse, a charitable organization located in central Kentucky. One of his responsibilities is to maintain a contact list of donors and the amount each has contributed to the organization. Aaron wants to create an interactive Web page that contains a table of contributors with the most recent contributors listed at the top. He wants the page to include tools that allow him to add new contributors to the table or delete old contributors from the list. Figure 10-66 shows a preview of the Web page. (*Note:* Older browsers, such as Internet Explorer for the Macintosh, do not support the splice() method. To complete the case problem you will have to use a current browser.)

Figure 10-66

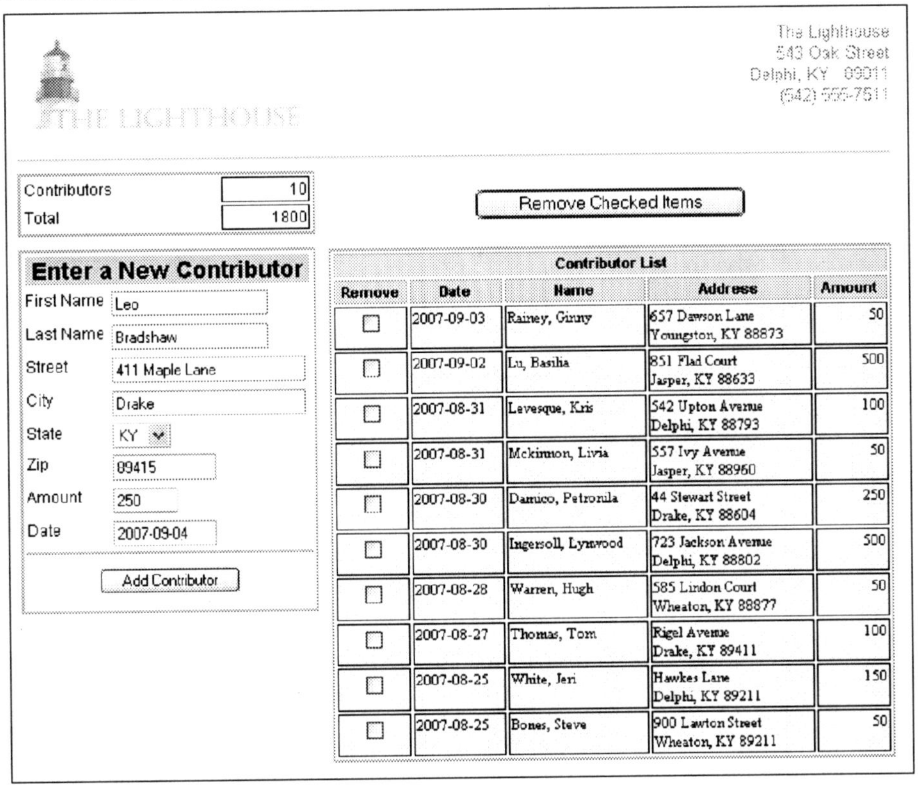

The page includes a data entry form named "donations" in which Aaron can enter a contributor's name, address, and amount and date of contribution. By clicking the Add Contributor button, the new record should be added to the table and the total number of contributors, displayed in the upper-left corner of the page, should be updated. Each row in the contributors table contains a check box. If a user selects a check box and then clicks the Remove Checked Items button, the selected contributors should be removed from the table and the total values should be updated.

Challenge

Explore how to use dynamic content to create a data entry form

Aaron has already created several JavaScript arrays containing information about current contributors and stored them in the file data.js. There are eight arrays:

- firstName: the first name of each contributor
- lastName: the last name of each contributor
- street: each contributor's street address
- city: each contributor's city of residence
- state: each contributor's state of residence
- zip: each contributor's zip code
- amount: the amount of the contribution
- date: the date of the contribution

Currently each array contains 10 entries representing 10 different contributors. You'll use the information in these arrays to populate the rows of the contributors table. As you add or remove rows from the contributors table, you'll also add or remove entries from the array. To remove an array entry, you can use the command

```
array.splice(start, deleteCount)
```

where *array* is an array, *start* is the starting index of the array items to remove, and *deleteCount* is the number of items to remove. For example, the command

```
firstName.splice(5,1)
```

removes the sixth item from the firstName array. See Tutorial 3 for more information on the splice() method.

To complete this Web site:

1. Use your text editor to open the **clisttxt.htm** file from the tutorial.10/case3 folder. Enter *your name* and *the date* in the comment section and save the file as **clist.htm**.
2. Insert two script elements in the head section that link to the **data.js** and **newdata.js** files.
3. Add an event handler to the body element that runs the function makeTable() when the page is loaded. Locate the input element for the Add Contributor button. Add an event handler that runs the function addRecord() when the button is clicked. Locate the input element for the Remove Check Items button. Add an event handler to run the removeRecords() function when the button is clicked.
4. Close the **clist.htm** file, saving your changes.
5. Open **newtxt.js** from the tutorial.10/case3 folder with your text editor. Enter *your name* and *the date* in the comment section and save the file as **newdata.js**.
6. Create the updateTotals() function. The purpose of this function is to display the total number of contributors and contributions in the table cells whose ids are "totalContr" and "totalAmt". Add the following commands to the function:
   a. Within the totalContr table cell, display the length of the amount array.
   b. Create a variable named totalContributions and set its initial value to 0.
   c. Create a for loop that loops through each entry in the amount array. Each time through the loop increases the value of the totalContributions variable by the amount in the current entry in the amount array.
   d. Within the totalAmt table cell, display the value of the totalContributions variable.

7. Create the makeTable() function. The purpose of this function is to create the contributors table by adding new table rows for each of the entries in the eight data arrays. The contributors table initially opens with an empty table row that you'll clone to create the new table rows containing contributor data. Add the following commands to the function:

   a. Create a variable named headingRow that references the table row with the id "titleRow". This row contains the titles from the contributors table. Create a second variable named blankRow that references the table row with the id "emptyRow".

Explore

   b. Use the cloneNode() method to clone the blankRow node. Set the value of the *deep* variable to true in order to copy the entire node tree. Store this document fragment in a variable named dataRow.

   c. Create a for loop that loops through the entries in the amount array. For each entry call the addRow() function using the value of the counter variable in the for loop as the parameter value in the addRow() function.

   d. Call the updateTotals() function.

8. Create the addRow() function. The purpose of this function is to add a single row to the contributors table, extracting information from the eight data arrays. The function has a single parameter named index that is equal to the array index number from which data is to be taken. Add the following commands to the function:

Explore

   a. Use the cloneNode() method to clone the dataRow document fragment you created in the makeTable() function. Set the value of the deep parameter to true. Store this document fragment in the variable newRow.

   b. Change the content of newRow's second child node to the value of the date array using the current index. Change the content of newRow's third child node to the text string "*lastName, firstName*" where *lastName* and *firstName* are the values of the lastName and firstName arrays using the current index. Change the content of newRow's third child node to the text string: "*street <br /> city, state zip*" where *street*, *city*, *state*, and *zip* are the current values from the street, city, state, and zip arrays. Change the content of newRow's fourth child node to the value of the amount array.

Explore

   c. If the value of the index variable equals 0, meaning that this is the first row being added to the contributor table, then use the replaceChild() method to replace the blankRow node with newRow. (*Hint*: Apply the replaceChild() method to the blankRow.parentNode node.) If the index variable is not equal to 0, then insert the newRow node before the next sibling of the headingRow node. (*Hint*: Apply the insertBefore() method to the headingRow.parentNode node.)

9. Create the addRecord() function. The purpose of this function is to create a new contributor record based on the values entered by the user in the Web form. Add the following commands to the function:

   a. Create a variable named recordNum equal to the length of the amount array.

   b. Set the value of first[recordNum] to the value of the fname field from the donations Web form. Set the value of last[recordNum] to the value of the lname field. Set the value of the street array item to the value of the street field and the value of the city array item to the value of the city field. Determine which state option has been selected by the user and store the text of the selected option in the state array item. Set the value of the zip, amount, and date array items to the values of the zip, amount, and date fields in the donations Web form.

    c. Call the addRow() function using the value of the recordNum variable as the parameter value.

    d. Call the updateTotals() function.

10. Create the removeRecord() function. The purpose of this function is to remove a record from each of the eight data arrays. The function has a single parameter named index that indicates the array item to remove. Add the following commands to the function:

    a. Use the splice() method to remove the item from the firstName array whose index value equals the value of the index parameter. Remove only one array item.

    b. Repeat Step a for the lastName, street, city, state, zip, amount, and date arrays.

11. Create the removeNode() function. The purpose of this function is to remove a node from a node tree and then return a reference to the node's previous sibling. You'll use it later to remove rows from the contributor table. The parameter has a single parameter named node representing the node you want to remove. Add the following commands to the function:

Explore

    a. Create a variable named prevNode referencing the node's previous sibling.

    b. Use the removeChild() method to remove the node. (*Hint:* Apply the removeChild() method to the node's parent node.)

    c. Return the prevNode variable from the function.

12. Create the removeRecords() function. The purpose of this function is to remove contributor records from the contributor table and the eight data arrays if the check box for that record has been checked in the contributor table. Add the following commands to the function:

    a. Create a variable named headerRow referencing the row with the id "titleRow".

    b. Create a variable named recordNum equal to the length of the amount array.

Explore

    c. Create a for loop that uses familial references, starting with the node variable, n, equal to the first sibling of the headerRow node and proceeding to the next sibling (the next table row) until there is no next sibling. Within the for loop, decrease the value of the recordNum variable by 1. Then, insert an if condition that tests whether the name of the current node is "TR" (a table row). If it is, insert a second if condition that tests whether the check box within the first table cell of the current row has been selected. (*Hint:* Reference the check box using the reference n.firstChild.firstChild.) If the check box has been checked, then: (1) Call the removeRecord() function using recordNum as the parameter value, and (2) Let the node counter, n, be equal to the value returned by the removeNode() function using the n as the parameter value.

    d. After the for loop has finished, call the updateTotals() function to update the contribution totals in the Web page.

13. Close **newdata.js**, saving your changes.

14. Open **clist.htm** in your Web browser. Verify that the page displays a list of 10 contributors totaling $1800 in contributions. Verify that you can enter a new contributor by inserting the contributor data into the Web form and clicking the Add Contributor button. Verify that you can remove contributor records from the arrays and the table by clicking check boxes in the table and clicking the Remove Check Items button. Check that the contributor totals are automatically updated for you.

15. Submit the completed Web site to your instructor.

Case Problem 4

Create

reate a JavaScript util-
to filter lines from an
nline play

Data files needed for this Case Problem: bio_out.jpg, globe_out.jpg, plays.css, plays_out.jpg, scenetxt.js, son_out.jpg, strat_out.jpg, tempest.jpg, temptxt.htm

The World of Shakespeare   Clare Daynes, the professor of English literature at MidWest University, continues to work on her Web site of Shakespeare's works. She would like to give students who are doing textual analysis of the plays the ability to display only those lines spoken by selected characters. She has asked you to create a utility that generates a drop-down list containing all of the characters from a particular scene, listed in alphabetical order. When a student selects a character from the list, only those lines spoken by that character should be displayed. Figure 10-67 shows a preview of a Web page that fulfills Professor Daynes's request. (*Note:* You will need a current browser that supports the array methods used in the uniqueElemText() function of this problem.)

Figure 10-67

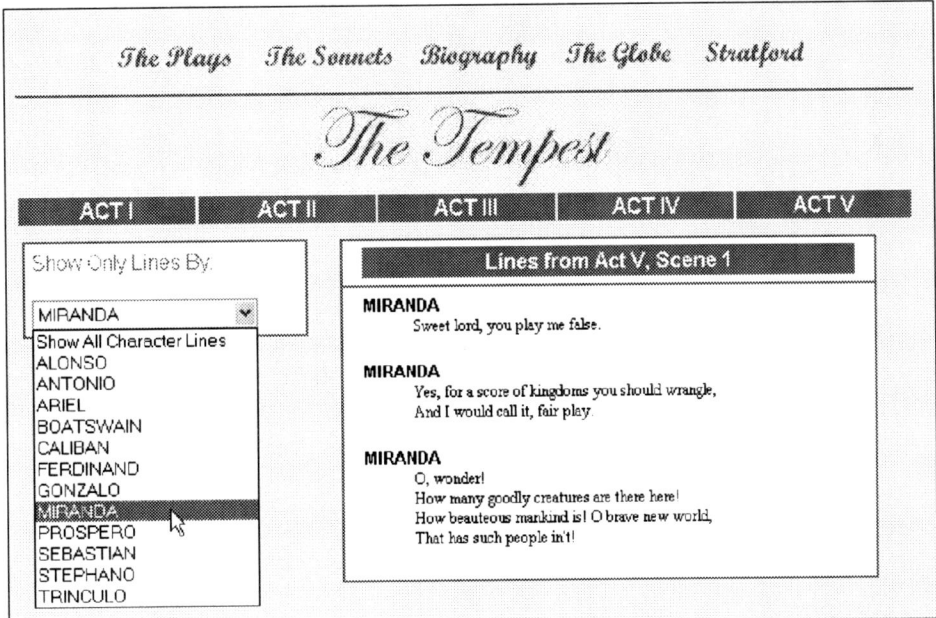

Professor Daynes has already created a Web page containing the text from the last act of *The Tempest*. The play text has been placed within a div element with the id "scenes". The character names have been placed in h3 headings within that div element with their lines following immediately after in blockquote elements. She has also created a div element with the id "characterList" in which she wants the drop-down list box to be placed. She wants the content to be automatically generated by your utility. The HTML content of the list box should be as follows:

```
<p>Show Only Lines By:</p>

<select id="cList">

    <option>Show All Character Lines</option>

    <option>Character 1</option>

    <option>Character 2</option>

...

</select>
```

where *Character 1* is the name of the first character in alphabetical order, *Character 2* is the name of the second character, and so forth. To create a list of the characters from the scene, the following function has been provided for you:

```
uniqueElemText(elemName)
```

This function returns an array containing the unique text from HTML tags whose name equals elemName, sorted in order. For example, running the command

```
characterNames = uniqueElemText("h3")
```

creates an array named characterNames containing all of the unique character names found in h3 heading elements, sorted in alphabetical order.

To complete this assignment:

1. Use your text editor to open the **temptxt.htm** file from the tutorial.10/case4 folder. Enter **your name** and **the date** in the comment section and save the file as **tempest.htm**. Create a link in the file to an external script file named scene.js.
2. Open the **scenetxt.js** file in your text editor, enter **your name** and **the date** in the comment section and save the file as **scene.js**.
3. Write a function that creates the contents of the character list box. Run the function when this page is loaded by the browser.
4. Add an event handler to the selection list you generated that runs a function to filter the contents of the scene whenever the user changes the selected character from the list.
5. Modify the function to filter the play so that it shows only the character name and succeeding lines for the selected character. All lines from other characters should be hidden. If the user selects "Show All Character Lines", the entire scene should be displayed.
6. Test your Web page in your browser. Verify that only the lines from the selected character are displayed in the Web page and that the entire scene is displayed if "Show All Character Lines" is selected.
7. Submit your completed Web site to your instructor.

Quick Check Answers
Session 10.1

1. innerHTML
2. A node is part of the document object model that represents a particular type of content. Nodes can represent any element or object, including text strings, attributes, and HTML elements placed in either the head or body section of the document.
3. parentNode
4. childNodes[2]
5. The nodeType property returns the value 1. The nodeName property returns "BLOCKQUOTE". The nodeValue property returns a null value.
6. docText = document.createTextNode("U.S. Constitution")mainTitle = document.createElement("h2");
7. mainTitle.appendChild(docText);
8. A document fragment is a collection of nodes that is not attached to the document, but instead resides in computer memory.

Session 10.2

1. topList = document.createElement("ul");bottomList = document. createElement("ul")top.List.appendChild(bottomList)
2. listItem.parentNode.parentNode;
3. Because they are not considered child nodes of the node to which the attribute has been applied.
4. hasAttribute("type")
5. CBox = document.createElement("input");CBox.setAttribute("type", "checkbox");
6. CBox.type = "checkbox";
7. CBox.type == ""

Session 10.3

1. listNode.insertBefore(imgObj, listNode.firstChild);
2. imgObj.style.display = "none";
3. Recursion is a programming technique in which a function calls itself repeatedly until a stopping condition is met.
4. document.getElementsByTagName("div");document. getElementsByTagName("div")[1]
5. document.styleSheets[2]
6. W3C DOM: document.styleSheets[2].cssRules[1]
   IE DOM: document.styleSheets[2].rules[1]

HTML and XHTML Elements and Attributes

This appendix provides descriptions of the major elements and attributes of HTML and XHTML. It also indicates the level of browser support for the Windows version of three major browsers: Internet Explorer (IE), Netscape (NS), and Opera (OP). Browser support is indicated in the columns on the right of each of the following tables. For example, a value of 4.0 in the Internet Explorer column indicates that the element or attribute is supported by the Windows version of Internet Explorer 4.0 and above. A version number with an asterisk indicates that the browser support is not extended to the more recent browser versions. For example, the entry "4.0*" in the Netscape column means that the feature is supported only in the 4.0 version of the Netscape browser and not in any other version (including later versions).

Be aware that browsers are constantly being modified, so you should check a browser's documentation for the most current information. Also, the level of browser support can vary between operating systems.

The following data types are used throughout this appendix:

• *char*	A single text character
• *char code*	A character encoding
• *color*	An HTML color name or hexadecimal color value
• *date*	A date and time in the format: *yyyy-mm-ddThh: mm:ssTIMEZONE*
• *integer*	An integer value
• *mime-type*	A MIME data type, such as "text/css", "audio/wav", or "video/x-msvideo"
• *mime-type list*	A comma-separated list of mime-types
• **option1**|option2| …	The value is limited to the specified list of *options*. A default value, if it exists, is displayed in **bold**.
• *script*	A script or a reference to a script
• *styles*	A list of style declarations
• *text*	A text string
• *text list*	A comma-separated list of text strings
• *url*	The URL for a Web page or file
• *value*	A numeric value
• *value list*	A comma-separated list of numeric values

General Attributes

Several attributes are common to many page elements. Rather than repeating this information each time it occurs, the following tables summarize these attributes.

Core Attributes

The following five attributes, which are laid out in the specifications for HTML and XHTML, apply to all page elements and are supported by most browser versions.

ATTRIBUTE	DESCRIPTION	HTML	XHTML	IE	NS	OP
class="text"	Specifies the class or group to which an element belongs	4.0	1.0	3.0	4.0	3.5
id="text"	Specifies a unique identifier to be associated with the element	4.0	1.0	3.0	4.0	3.5
style="styles"	Defines an inline style for the element	4.0	1.0	3.0	4.0	3.5
title="text"	Provides an advisory title for the element	2.0	1.0	4.0	6.0	3.0

Language Attributes

The Web is designed to be universal and has to be adaptable to languages other than English. Thus, another set of attributes provides language support. This set of attributes is not as widely supported by browsers as the core attributes are. As with the core attributes, they can be applied to most page elements.

ATTRIBUTE	DESCRIPTION	HTML	XHTML	IE	NS	OP
dir="**ltr**｜rtl"	Indicates the text direction as related to the lang attribute. A value of ltr displays text from left to right. A value rtl displays text from right to left.	4.0	1.0	5.5	6.0	7.1
lang="text"	Identifies the language used in the page content	4.0	1.0	4.0		

Form Attributes

The following attributes can be applied to most form elements or to a Web form itself, but not to other page elements.

ATTRIBUTE	DESCRIPTION	HTML	XHTML	IE	NS	OP
accesskey="*char*"	Indicates the keyboard character that can be pressed along with the accelerator key to access a form element	4.0	1.0	4.0	6.0	7.0
disabled="disabled"	Disables a form field for input	4.0	1.0	4.0	6.0	7.0
tabindex="*integer*"	Specifies a form element's position in a document's tabbing order tabbing order	4.0	1.0	4.0	6.0	7.0

Internet Explorer Attributes

Internet Explorer supports a collection of attributes that can be applied to almost all page elements. Other browsers do not support these attributes, or support them only for a more limited collection of elements.

ATTRIBUTE	DESCRIPTION	HTML	XHTML	IE	NS	OP
accesskey="*char*"	Indicates the keyboard character that can be pressed along with the accelerator key to access the page element			5.0		
contenteditable="true | false | **inherit**"	Specifies whether the element's content can be modified online by the user			5.5		
disabled="disabled"	Disables the page element for input			5.0		
hidefocus="true | **false**"	Controls whether the element provides a visual indication of whether the element is in focus			5.5		
tabindex="*integer*"	Specifies the position of the page element in the tabbing order of the document			5.0		
unselectable="on | **off**"	Specifies whether the element can be selected by the user			5.5		

Event Attributes

To make Web pages more dynamic, HTML and XHTML support event attributes that identify scripts to be run in response to an event occurring within an element. For example, clicking a main heading with a mouse can cause a browser to run a program that hides or expands a table of contents. Each event attribute has the form

`event = "script"`

where *event* is the name of the event attribute and *script* is the name of the script or command to be run by the browser in response to the occurrence of the event within the element.

Core Events

The general event attributes are part of the specifications for HTML and XHTML. They apply to almost all page elements.

ATTRIBUTE	DESCRIPTION	HTML	XHTML	IE	NS	OP
onclick	The mouse button is clicked.	4.0	1.0	3.0	2.0	3.0
ondblclick	The mouse button is double-clicked.	4.0	1.0	4.0	6.0	7.0
onkeydown	A key is pressed down.	4.0	1.0	4.0	4.0	5.0
onkeypress	A key is initially pressed.	4.0	1.0	4.0	4.0	5.0
onkeyup	A key is released.	4.0	1.0	4.0	4.0	5.0
onmousedown	The mouse button is pressed down.	4.0	1.0	4.0	4.0	5.0
onmousemove	The mouse pointer is moved within the element's boundaries.	4.0	1.0	4.0	6.0	5.0
onmouseout	The mouse pointer is moved out of the element's boundaries.	4.0	1.0	4.0	3.0	3.0
onmouseover	The mouse pointer hovers over the element.	4.0	1.0	3.0	2.0	3.0
onmouseup	The mouse button is released.	4.0	1.0	4.0	4.0	5.0

Document Events

The following list of event attributes applies not to individual elements within the page, but to the entire document as it displayed within the browser window or frame.

ATTRIBUTE	DESCRIPTION	HTML	XHTML	IE	NS	OP
onafterprint	The document has finished printing.			5.0		
onbeforeprint	The document is about to be printed.			5.0		
onload	The page is finished being loaded.	4.0	1.0	3.0	2.0	3.0
onunload	The page is finished unloading.	4.0	1.0	3.0	2.0	3.0

Form Events

The following list of event attributes applies either to the entire Web form or fields within the form.

ATTRIBUTE	DESCRIPTION	HTML	XHTML	IE	NS	OP
onblur	The form field has lost the focus.	4.0	1.0	3.0	2.0	3.0
onchange	The value of the form field has been changed.	4.0	1.0	3.0	2.0	3.0
onfocus	The form field has received the focus.	4.0	1.0	3.0	2.0	3.0
onreset	The form has been reset.	4.0	1.0	4.0	3.0	3.0
onselect	Text content has been selected in the form field.	4.0	1.0	4.0	6.0	
onsubmit	The form has been submitted for processing.	4.0	1.0	3.0	2.0	3.0

Data Events

The following list of event attributes applies to elements within the Web page capable of data binding. Note that these events are supported only by the Internet Explorer browser.

ATTRIBUTE	DESCRIPTION	HTML	XHTML	IE	NS	OP
oncellchange	Data has changed in the data source.			5.0		
ondataavailable	Data has arrived from the data source.			4.0		
ondatasetchange	The data in the data source has changed.			4.0		
ondatasetcomplete	All data from the data source has been loaded.			4.0		
onrowenter	The current row in the data source has changed.			5.0		
onrowexit	The current row is about to be changed in the data source.			5.0		
onrowsdelete	Rows have been deleted from the data source.			5.0		
onrowsinserted	Rows have been inserted into the data source.			5.0		

Internet Explorer Events

The Internet Explorer browser supports a wide collection of customized event attributes. Unless otherwise noted, these event attributes can be applied to any page element and are not supported by other browsers or included in the HTML or XHTML specifications.

ATTRIBUTE	DESCRIPTION	HTML	XHTML	IE	NS	OP
onactive	The element is set to an "active" state.			5.5		
onafterupdate	Data has been transferred from the element to a data source.			4.0		
onbeforeactivate	The element is about to be set to an "active" state.			6.0		
onbeforecopy	A selection from the element is about to be copied to the clipboard.			5.0		
onbeforecut	A selection from the element is about to be cut to the clipboard.			5.0		
onbeforedeactivate	The element is about to be "deactivated".			5.5		
onbeforeeditfocus	The element is about to become "active".			5.0		
onbeforepaste	Data from the clipboard is about to be pasted into the element.			5.0		
onbeforeunload	The page is about to be unloaded.			4.0		
onbeforeupdate	The element's data is about to be updated.			5.0		
onblur	The element has lost the focus.			5.0		
oncontextmenu	The right mouse button is activated.			5.0	6.0	
oncontrolselect	Selection using a modifier key (Ctrl for Windows, Command for Macintosh) has begun within the element.			5.5		
oncopy	Data from the element has been copied to the clipboard.			5.0		
oncut	Data from the element has been cut to the clipboard.			5.0		
ondrag	The element is being dragged.			5.0		
ondragdrop	The element has been dropped into the window or frame.			5.0		
ondragend	The element is no longer being dragged.			5.0		

ATTRIBUTE	DESCRIPTION	HTML	XHTML	IE	NS	OP
ondragenter	The dragged element has entered a target area.			5.0		
ondragleave	The dragged element has left a target area.			5.0		
ondragover	The dragged element is over a target area.			5.0		
ondragstart	The element has begun to be dragged.			5.0		
ondrop	The dragged element has been dropped.			5.0		
onerrorupdate	The data transfer to the element has been cancelled.			4.0		
onfocus	The element has received the focus.			5.0		
onfocusin	The element is about to receive the focus.			6.0		
onfocusout	The form element has just lost the focus.			6.0		
onhelp	The user has selected online help from the browser.			4.0		
oninput	Text has just been entered into the form field.			6.0		
onlosecapture	The element has been captured by the mouse selection.			5.0		
onmouseenter	The mouse pointer enters the element's boundaries.			5.5		
onmouseleave	The mouse pointer leaves the element's boundaries.			5.5		
onmousewheel	The mouse wheel is moved.			6.0		
onmove	The browser window or element has been moved by the user.			5.5		
onmoveend	Movement of the element has ended.			5.5		
onmovestart	The element has begun to move.			5.5		
onpaste	Data has been pasted from the clipboard into the element.			5.0		
onpropertychange	One or more of the element's properties has changed.			5.0		
onreadystatechange	The element has changed its ready state.			4.0		
onresize	The browser window or element has been resized by the user.			4.0		
onscroll	The scrollbar position within the element has been changed.			4.0	7.0	7.0
onselectstart	Selection has begun within the element.			4.0		
onstop	The page is finished loading.			5.0		

HTML and XHTML Elements and Attributes

The following table contains an alphabetic listing of the elements and attributes supported by HTML, XHTML, and the major browsers. Some attributes are not listed in this table, but are described instead in the general attributes tables presented in the previous section of this appendix.

ELEMENT/ATTRIBUTE	DESCRIPTION	HTML	XHTML	IE	NS	OP
`<!-- text -->`	Inserts a comment into the document (comments are not displayed in the rendered page)	2.0	1.0	1.0	1.0	2.1
`<!doctype>`	Specifies the Document Type Definition for a document	2.0	1.0	2.0	1.0	4.0
`<a> </a>`	Marks the beginning and end of a link	2.0	1.0	1.0	1.0	2.1
`accesskey="char"`	Indicates the keyboard character that can be pressed along with the accelerator key to activate the link	4.0	1.0	4.0	6.0	7.0
`charset="text"`	Specifies the character encoding of the linked document	4.0	1.0			7.0
`coords="value list"`	Specifies the coordinates of a hotspot in a client-side image map; the value list depends on the shape of the hotspot: shape="rect" "left, right, top, bottom" shape="circle" "x_center, y_center, radius" shape="poly" "x1, y1, x2, y2, x3, y3, ..."	4.0	1.0		6.0	7.0
`href="url"`	Specifies the URL of the link	3.2	1.0	1.0	2.0	2.1
`hreflang="text"`	Specifies the language of the linked document	4.0	1.0		6.1	
`name="text"`	Specifies a name for the enclosed text, allowing it to be a link target	2.0	1.0	1.0	1.0	2.1
`rel="text"`	Specifies the relationship between the current page and the link specified by the href attribute	2.0	1.0	3.0	6.0	7.0
`rev="text"`	Specifies the reverse relationship between the current page and the link specified by the href attribute	2.0	1.0	3.0	6.0	7.0
`shape="rect|circle| polygon"`	Specifies the shape of the hotspot	4.0	1.0		6.0	7.0
`title="text"`	Specifies the pop-up text for the link	2.0	1.0	4.0	6.0	3.0
`target="text"`	Specifies the target window or frame for the link	4.0	1.0	3.0	1.0	2.1
`type="mime-type"`	Specifies the data type of the linked document	4.0	1.0			7.0

ELEMENT/ATTRIBUTE	DESCRIPTION	HTML	XHTML	IE	NS	OP
`<abbr> </abbr>`	Marks abbreviated text	4.0	1.0		6.0	4.0
`<acronym> </acronym>`	Marks acronym text	3.0	1.0	4.0	6.0	4.0
`<address> </address>`	Marks address text	2.0	1.0	1.0	1.0	2.1
`<applet> </applet>`	Embeds an applet into the browser. **Deprecated**	3.2	1.0*	3.0	2.0	3.5

`align="absmiddle|`
`absbottom|baseline|`
`bottom|center`
`|left|middle`
`|right|texttop`
`|top"`
	Specifies the alignment of the applet with the surrounding text	3.2	1.0*	3.0	2.0	3.0

`alt="text"`	Specifies alternate text for the applet. **Deprecated**	3.2	1.0*	3.0	2.0	
`archive="url"`	Specifies the URL of an archive containing classes and other resources to be used with the applet. **Deprecated**	4.0	1.0*	4.0	3.0	
`code="url"`	Specifies the URL of the applet's code/class. **Deprecated**	3.2	1.0*	3.0	2.0	3.5
`codebase="url"`	Specifies the URL of all class files for the applet. **Deprecated**	3.2	1.0*	3.0	2.0	
`datafld="text"`	Specifies the data source that supplies bound data for use with the applet	4.0		4.0		
`datasrc="text"`	Specifies the ID or URL of the applet's data source	4.0		4.0		
`height="integer"`	Specifies the height of the applet in pixels	3.2	1.0*	3.0	2.0	3.5
`hspace="integer"`	Specifies the horizontal space around the applet in pixels. **Deprecated**	3.2	1.0*	3.0	2.0	4.0
`mayscript="mayscript"`	Permits access to the applet by programs embedded in the document				3.0*	
`name="text"`	Specifies the name assigned to the applet. **Deprecated**	3.2	1.0*	3.0	2.0	3.5
`object="text"`	Specifies the name of the resource that contains a serialized representation of the applet. **Deprecated**	4.0	1.0*			
`src="url"`	Specifies an external URL reference to the applet			4.0		3.5
`vspace="integer"`	Specifies the vertical space around the applet in pixels. **Deprecated**	3.2	1.0*	3.0	2.0	4.0
`width="integer"`	Specifies the width of the applet in pixels. **Deprecated**	3.2	1.0*	3.0	2.0	3.5

ELEMENT/ATTRIBUTE	DESCRIPTION	HTML	XHTML	IE	NS	OP
`<area />`	Marks an image map hotspot	3.2	1.0	1.0	2.0	2.1
`alt="text"`	Specifies alternate text for the hotspot	3.2	1.0	4.0	3.0	2.1
`coords="value list"`	Specifies the coordinates of the hotspot; the value list depends on the shape of the hotspot: shape="rect" "left, right, top, bottom" shape="circle" "x_center, y_center, radius" shape="poly" "x1, y1, x2, y2, x3, y3, ..."	3.2	1.0	1.0	2.0	2.1
`href="url"`	Specifies the URL of the document to which the hotspot points	3.2	1.0	1.0	2.0	2.1
`nohref="nohref"`	Specifies that the hotspot does not point to a link	3.2	1.0	1.0	2.0	2.1
`shape="rect|circle| polygon"`	Specifies the shape of the hotspot	3.2	1.0	1.0	2.0	2.1
`target="text"`	Specifies the target window or frame for the link	3.2	1.0*	1.0	2.0	2.1
`<b> </b>`	Marks text as bolded	2.0	1.0	1.0	1.0	2.1
`<base />`	Specifies global reference information for the document	2.0	1.0	1.0	1.0	2.1
`href="url"`	Specifies the URL from which all relative links in the document are based	2.0	1.0	1.0	1.0	2.1
`target="text"`	Specifies the target window or frame for links in the document	2.0	1.0*	1.0	1.0	2.1
`<basefont />`	Specifies the font setting for the document text. **Deprecated**	3.2	1.0*	1.0	1.0	2.1
`color="color"`	Specifies the text color. **Deprecated**	3.2	1.0*	1.0	1.0	2.1
`face="text list"`	Specifies a list of fonts to be applied to the text. **Deprecated**	3.2	1.0*	1.0	1.0	2.1
`size="integer"`	Specifies the size of the font range from 1 (smallest) to 7 (largest). **Deprecated**	3.2	1.0*	1.0	1.0	2.1
`<bdo> </bdo>`	Indicates that the enclosed text should be rendered with the direction specified by the dir attribute	4.0	1.0	5.0	6.0	4.0
`<bgsound />`	Plays a background sound clip when the page is opened			2.0		2.1
`balance="integer"`	Specifies the balance of the volume between the left and right speakers where balance ranges from -10,000 to 10,000			4.0		
`loop="integer| infinite"`	Specifies the number of times the clip will be played (a positive integer or infinite)			2.0		2.1
`src="url"`	Specifies the URL of the sound clip file			2.0		2.1
`volume="integer"`	Specifies the volume of the sound clip, where the volume ranges from -10,000 to 0			4.0		

ELEMENT/ATTRIBUTE	DESCRIPTION	HTML	XHTML	IE	NS	OP
`<big> </big>`	Increases the size of the enclosed text relative to the default font size	3.0	1.0	3.0	1.0	2.1
`<blink> </blink>`	Blinks the enclosed text on and off			4.0	1.0	7.0
`<blockquote> </blockquote>`	Marks content as quoted from another source	2.0	1.0	1.0	1.0	2.1
`align="left|center|right"`	Specifies the horizontal alignment of the content			4.0	4.0	
`cite="url"`	Provides the source URL of the quoted content	4.0	1.0		6.0	
`clear="none|left|right|all"`	Prevents content rendering until the specified margin is clear	3.0*		4.0		4.0
`<body> </body>`	Marks the page content to be rendered by the browser	2.0	1.0	1.0	1.0	2.1
`alink="color"`	Specifies the color of activated links in the document. **Deprecated**	3.2	1.0*	4.0	1.1	7.1
`background="url"`	Specifies the background image file used for the page. **Deprecated**	3.0	1.0*	1.0	1.1	2.1
`bgcolor="color"`	Specifies the background color of the page. **Deprecated**	3.2	1.0*	1.0	1.1	2.1
`bgproperties="fixed"`	Fixes the background image in the browser window			2.0		
`bottommargin="integer"`	Specifies the size of the bottom margin in pixels			2.0		7.0
`leftmargin="integer"`	Specifies the size of the left margin in pixels			2.0	6.2	7.0
`link="color"`	Specifies the color of unvisited links. **Deprecated**	3.2	1.0*	1.0	1.1	2.1
`marginheight="integer"`	Specifies the size of the margin above and below the page				4.0	4.0
`marginwidth="integer"`	Specifies the size of the margin to the left and right of the page				4.0	4.0
`nowrap="false|true"`	Specifies whether the content wraps using normal HTML line-wrapping conventions			4.0		
`rightmargin="integer"`	Specifies the size of the right margin in pixels			4.0		
`scroll="yes|no"`	Specifies whether to display a scrollbar			4.0		
`text="color"`	Specifies the color of page text. **Deprecated**	3.2	1.0*	1.0	1.1	2.1
`topmargin="integer"`	Specifies the size of the top page margin in pixels			2.0	6.2	7.0
`vlink="color"`	Specifies the color of previously visited links. **Deprecated**	3.2	1.0*	1.0	1.1	2.1

ELEMENT/ATTRIBUTE	DESCRIPTION	HTML	XHTML	IE	NS	OP
` `	Inserts a line break into the page	2.0	1.0	1.0	1.0	2.1
`clear="none|left|right|all"`	Displays the line break only when the specified margin is clear. **Deprecated**	3.2	1.0*	1.0	1.0	2.1
`<button> </button>`	Creates a form button	4.0	1.0	4.0	6.0	5.0
`datafld="text"`	Specifies the column from a data source that supplies bound data for the button			4.0		
`dataformatas="html|plaintext|text"`	Specifies the format of the data in the data source bound with the button			4.0		
`datasrc="url"`	Specifies the URL or ID of the data source bound with the button			4.0		
`name="text"`	Provides the name assigned to the form button	4.0	1.0	4.0	6.0	5.0
`type="submit|reset|button"`	Specifies the type of form button	4.0	1.0	4.0	6.0	5.0
`value="text"`	Provides the value associated with the form button	4.0	1.0	4.0	6.0	5.0
`<caption> </caption>`	Creates a table caption	3.0	1.0	2.0	1.1	2.1
`align="bottom|center|left|right|top"`	Specifies the alignment of the caption. **Deprecated**	3.0	1.0*	2.0	1.1	2.1
`valign="top|bottom"`	Specifies the vertical alignment of the caption			2.0		
`<center> </center>`	Centers content horizontally on the page. **Deprecated**	3.2	1.0*	1.0	1.0	2.1
`<cite> </cite>`	Marks citation text	2.0	1.0	1.0	1.0	2.1
`<code> </code>`	Marks text used for code samples	2.0	1.0	1.0	1.0	2.1
`<col> </col>`	Defines the settings for a column or group of columns	4.0	1.0	3.0	6.0	4.0
`align="left|right|center`	Specifies the alignment of the content of the column(s)	1.0	4.0		4.0 7.0	
`bgcolor="color"`	Specifies the background color of the column(s)			4.0		
`char="char"`	Specifies a character in the column used to align column values	4.0	1.0			
`charoff="integer"`	Specifies the offset in pixels from the alignment character specified in the char attribute	4.0	1.0			
`span="integer"`	Specifies the number of columns in the group	4.0	1.0	3.0	6.0	7.0
`valign="top|middle|bottom|baseline"`	Specifies the vertical alignment of the content in the column(s)	4.0	1.0	4.0		4.0
`width="integer"`	Specifies the width of the column(s) in pixels	4.0	1.0	3.0	6.0	7.0

ELEMENT/ATTRIBUTE	DESCRIPTION	HTML	XHTML	IE	NS	OP
`<colgroup> </colgroup>`	Creates a container for a group of columns	4.0	1.0	3.0	6.0	4.0
`align="left|right center"`	Specifies the alignment of the content of the column group	4.0	1.0	4.0		7.0
`bgcolor="color"`	Specifies the background color of the column group			4.0		
`char="char"`	Specifies a character in the column used to align column group values	4.0	1.0			
`charoff="integer"`	Specifies the offset in pixels from the alignment character specified in the char attribute	4.0	1.0			
`span="integer"`	Specifies the number of columns in the group	4.0	1.0	3.0	6.0	7.0
`valign="top|middle |bottom|baseline"`	Specifies the vertical alignment of the content in the column group	4.0	1.0	4.0		4.0
`width="integer"`	Specifies the width of the columns in the group in pixels	4.0	1.0	3.0	6.0	7.0
`<dd> </dd>`	Marks text as a definition within a definition list	2.0	1.0	1.0	1.0	2.1
`<del> </del>`	Marks text as deleted from the document	3.0	1.0	4.0	6.0	4.0
`cite="url"`	Provides the URL for the document that has additional information about the deleted text	3.0	1.0	4.0	6.1	4.0
`datetime="date"`	Specifies the date and time of the text deletion	3.0	1.0	4.0	6.1	4.0
`<dfn> </dfn>`	Marks the defining instance of a term	3.0	1.0	1.0	6.0	2.1
`<dir> </dir>`	Contains a directory listing. **Deprecated**	2.0	1.0*	1.0	1.0	2.1
`compact="compact"`	Permits use of compact rendering, if available. **Deprecated**	2.0	1.0*			
`<div> </div>`	Creates a generic block-level element	3.0	1.0	3.0	2.0	2.1
`align="left|center right|justify"`	Specifies the horizontal alignment of the content. **Deprecated**	3.0	1.0*	3.0	2.0	2.1
`datafld="text"`	Indicates the column from a data source that supplies bound data for the block			4.0		
`dataformatas="html |plaintext|text"`	Specifies the format of the data in the data source bound with the block			4.0		
`datasrc="url"`	Provides the URL or ID of the data source bound with the block			4.0		
`nowrap="nowrap"`	Specifies whether the content wraps using normal HTML line-wrapping conventions	3.0*		4.0		
`<dl> </dl>`	Encloses a definition list using the dd and dt elements	2.0	1.0	1.0	1.0	2.1
`compact="compact"`	Permits use of compact rendering, if available. **Deprecated**	2.0	1.0*	4.0	1.0	
`<dt> </dt>`	Marks a definition term in a definition list	2.0	1.0	1.0	1.0	2.1
`nowrap="nowrap"`	Specifies whether the content wraps using normal HTML line-wrapping conventions			4.0		

ELEMENT/ATTRIBUTE	DESCRIPTION	HTML	XHTML	IE	NS	OP
`<em> </em>`	Marks emphasized text	2.0	1.0	1.0	1.0	2.1
`<embed> </embed>`	Places an embedded object into the page			3.0	1.0	3.0
`align="bottom|left |right|top"`	Specifies the alignment of the object with the surrounding content			3.0	1.0	3.5
`autostart="true |false"`	Starts the embedded object automatically when the page is loaded			3.0	1.0	3.0
`height="integer"`	Specifies the height of the object in pixels			3.0	1.0	3.0
`hidden="true|false"`	Hides the object on the page			3.0	2.0	3.0
`hspace="integer"`	Specifies the horizontal space around the object in pixels				1.1	4.0
`name="text"`	Provides the name of the embedded object			4.0	4.0	
`pluginspage="url"`	Provides the URL of the page containing information on the object			3.0	2.0	3.5
`pluginurl="url"`	Provides the URL of the page for directly installing the object				4.0	
`src="url"`	Provides the location of the file containing the object			3.0	1.1	3.5
`type="mime-type"`	Specifies the mime-type of the embedded object			3.0	3.0	3.5
`units="text"`	Specifies the measurement units of the object			4.0	3.0	
`vspace="integer"`	Specifies the vertical space around the object in pixels				1.1	4.0
`width="integer"`	Specifies the width of the object in pixels			3.0	1.1	3.0
`<fieldset> </fieldset>`	Places form fields in a common group	4.0	1.0	4.0	6.0	4.0
`align="left|center |right"`	Specifies the alignment of the contents of the field set			4.0		4.0
`datafld="text"`	Indicates the column from a data source that supplies bound data for the field set			4.0		
`dataformatas="html| plaintext|text"`	Specifies the format of the data in the data source bound with the field set			4.0		
`datasrc="url"`	Provides the URL or ID of the data source bound with the field set			4.0		
`<font> </font>`	Formats the enclosed text. **Deprecated**	3.2	1.0*	2.0	1.0	2.1
`color="color"`	Specifies the color of the enclosed text. **Deprecated**	3.2	1.0*	2.0	2.0	2.1
`face="text list"`	Specifies the font face(s) of the enclosed text. **Deprecated**	3.2	1.0*	2.0	3.0	3.0
`size="integer"`	Specifies the size of the enclosed text with values ranging from 1 (smallest) to 7 (largest). A value of +integer increases the font size relative to the font size specified in the basefont element. **Deprecated**	3.2	1.0*	2.0	3.0	2.1

ELEMENT/ATTRIBUTE	DESCRIPTION	HTML	XHTML	IE	NS	OP
`<form> </form>`	Encloses the contents of a Web form	2.0	1.0	1.0	1.0	2.1
`accept="mime-type list"`	Lists mime-types that the server processing the form will handle	4.0	1.0			
`accept-charset="char code"`	Specifies the character encoding that the server processing the form will handle	4.0	1.0			
`action="url"`	Provides the URL to which the form values are to be sent	2.0	1.0	1.0	1.0	2.1
`autocomplete="on|off"`	Enables automatic insertion of information in fields in which the user has previously entered data			5.0		
`enctype="mime-type"`	Specifies the mime-type of the data to be sent to the server for processing; the default is "application/x-www-form-urlencoded"	2.0	1.0	1.0	1.0	2.1
`method="get|post"`	Specifies the method of accessing the URL specified in the action attribute	2.0	1.0	1.0	1.0	2.1
`name="text"`	Specifies the name of the form	2.0	1.0	1.0	1.0	2.1
`target="text"`	Specifies the frame or window in which output from the form should appear	4.0	1.0	3.0	2.0	2.1
`<frame> </frame>`	Marks a single frame within a set of frames	4.0	1.0*	3.0	2.0	2.1
`border="integer"`	Specifies the thickness of the frame border in pixels				4.0*	
`bordercolor="color"`	Specifies the color of the frame border			4.0	3.5	
`frameborder="1|0"`	Determines whether the frame border is visible (1) or invisible (0); Netscape also supports values of yes or no	4.0	1.0*	3.0	3.5	7.0
`longdesc="url"`	Provides the URL of a document containing a long description of the frame's contents	4.0	1.0*			
`marginheight="integer"`	Specifies the space above and below the frame object and the frame's borders, in pixels	4.0	1.0*	3.0	2.0	2.1
`marginwidth="integer"`	Specifies the space to the left and right of the frame object and the frame's borders, in pixels	4.0	1.0*	3.0	2.0	2.1
`name="text"`	Specifies the name of the frame	4.0	1.0*	3.0	2.0	2.1
`noresize="noresize"`	Prevents users from resizing the frame	4.0	1.0*	3.0	2.0	2.1
`scrolling="auto|yes|no"`	Specifies whether the browser will display a scrollbar with the frame	4.0	1.0*	3.0	2.0	2.1
`src="url"`	Provides the URL of the document to be displayed in the frame	4.0	1.0*	3.0	2.0	2.1

ELEMENT/ATTRIBUTE	DESCRIPTION	HTML	XHTML	IE	NS	OP
`<frameset> </frameset>`	Creates a collection of frames	4.0	1.0*	3.0	2.0	2.1
`border="integer"`	Specifies the thickness of the frame borders in the frameset in pixels			4.0	3.0	2.1
`bordercolor="color"`	Specifies the color of the frame borders			4.0	3.0	
`cols="value list"`	Arranges the frames in columns with the width of each column expressed either in pixels, as a percentage, or using an asterisk (to allow the browser to choose the width)	4.0	1.0*	3.0	2.0	2.1
`frameborder="1|0"`	Determines whether frame borders are visible (1) or invisible (0); Netscape also supports values of yes or no			3.0	3.5	
`framespacing="integer"`	Specifies the amount of space between frames in pixels			3.1		
`rows="value list"`	Arranges the frames in rows with the height of each column expressed either in pixels, as a percentage, or using an asterisk (to allow the browser to choose the height)	4.0	1.0*	3.0	2.0	2.1
`<hi> </hi>`	Marks the enclosed text as a heading, where *i* is an integer from 1 (the largest heading) to 6 (the smallest heading)	2.0	1.0	1.0	1.0	2.1
`align="left| center|right| justify"`	Specifies the alignment of the heading text. **Deprecated**	3.0	1.0*	1.0	1.0	2.1
`<head> </head>`	Encloses the document head, containing information about the document	2.0	1.0	1.0	1.0	2.1
`profile="url"`	Provides the location of metadata about the documenta	4.0	1.0			
`<hr />`	Draws a horizontal line (rule) in the rendered page	2.0	1.0	1.0	1.0	2.1
`align="left|center |right"`	Specifies the horizontal alignment of the line. **Deprecated**	3.2	1.0*	1.0	1.0	2.1
`color="color"`	Specifies the color of the line			3.0		
`noshade="noshade"`	Removes 3-D shading from the line. **Deprecated**	3.2	1.0*	1.0	1.0	2.1
`size="integer"`	Specifies the height of the line in pixels or as a percentage of the enclosing element's height. **Deprecated**	3.2	1.0*	1.0	1.0	2.1
`width="integer"`	Specifies the width of the line in pixels or as a percentage of the enclosing element's width. **Deprecated**	3.2	1.0*	1.0	1.0	2.1

ELEMENT/ATTRIBUTE	DESCRIPTION	HTML	XHTML	IE	NS	OP
`<html> </html>`	Encloses the entire content of the HTML document	2.0	1.0	1.0	1.0	2.1
`version="text"`	Specifies the version of HTML being used	2.0	1.1			
`xmlns="text"`	Specifies the namespace prefix for the document		1.0	5.0		
`<i> </i>`	Displays the enclosed text in italics	2.0	1.0	1.0	1.0	2.1
`<iframe> </iframe>`	Creates an inline frame in the document	4.0	1.0*	3.0	6.0	4.0
`align="bottom|left|middle|top|right"`	Specifies the horizontal alignment of the frame with the surrounding content. **Deprecated**	4.0	1.0*	3.0	6.0	6.0
`datafld="text"`	Indicates the column from a data source that supplies bound data for the inline frame			4.0		
`dataformatas="html|plaintext|text"`	Specifies the format of the data in the data source bound with the inline frame			4.0		
`datasrc="url"`	Provides the URL or ID of the data source bound with the inline frame			4.0		
`frameborder="1|0"`	Specifies whether to display a frame border (1) or not (0)	4.0	1.0*	3.0	6.0	4.0
`height="integer"`	Specifies the height of the frame in pixels	4.0	1.0*	3.0	6.0	4.0
`hspace="integer"`	Specifies the space to the left and right of the frame in pixels	4.0	1.0*	3.0	6.0	4.0
`longdesc="url"`	Indicates the document containing a long description of the frame's content	4.0	1.0*			
`marginheight="integer"`	Specifies the space above and below the frame object and the frame's borders, in pixels	4.0	1.0*	3.0	6.0	4.0
`marginwidth="integer"`	Specifies the space to the left and right of the frame object and the frame's borders, in pixels	4.0	1.0*	3.0	6.0	4.0
`name="text"`	Specifies the name of the frame	4.0	1.0*	3.0	6.0	4.0
`scrolling="auto|yes|no"`	Determines whether the browser displays a scrollbar with the frame	4.0	1.0*	3.0	6.0	4.0
`src="url"`	Indicates the document displayed within the frame	4.0	1.0*	3.0	6.0	4.0
`vspace="integer"`	Specifies the space to the top and bottom of the frame in pixels	4.0	1.0*	3.0	6.0	4.0
`width="integer"`	Specifies the width of the frame in pixels	4.0	1.0*	3.0	6.0	4.0
`<ilayer> </ilayer>`	Creates an inline layer used to display the content of external document				4.0*	
`above="text"`	Specifies the name of the layer displayed above the current layer				4.0*	
`background="url"`	Provides the URL of the file containing the background image				4.0*	
`below="text"`	Specifies the name of the layer displayed below the current layer				4.0*	

ELEMENT/ATTRIBUTE	DESCRIPTION	HTML	XHTML	IE	NS	OP
bgcolor="color"	Specifies the layer's background color				4.0*	
clip="top, left, bottom, right"	Specifies the coordinates of the viewable region of the layer				4.0*	
height="integer"	Specifies the height of the layer in pixels				4.0*	
left="integer"	Specifies the horizontal offset of the layer in pixels				4.0*	
pagex="integer"	Specifies the horizontal position of the layer in pixels				4.0*	
pagey="integer"	Specifies the vertical position of the layer in pixels				4.0*	
src="url"	Provides the URL of the document displayed in the layer				4.0*	
top="integer"	Specifies the vertical offset of the layer in pixels				4.0*	
visibility="hide|inherit|show"	Specifies the visibility of the layer				4.0*	
width="integer"	Specifies the width of the layer in pixels				4.0*	
z-index="integer"	Specifies the stacking order of the layer				4.0*	
<img> </img>	Inserts an inline image into the document	2.0	1.0	1.0	1.0	2.1
align="left|right|top|texttop|middle|absmiddle|baselines|bottom|absbottom"	Specifies the alignment of the image with the surrounding content. **Deprecated**	2.0	1.0*	1.0	1.0	2.1
alt="text"	Specifies alternate text to be displayed in place of the image	2.0	1.0	1.0	1.0	2.1
border="integer"	Specifies the width of the image border. **Deprecated**	3.2	1.0*	1.0	1.0	2.1
controls="control"	For video images, displays a playback control below the image			2.0		
datafld="text"	Names the column from a data source that supplies bound data for the image			4.0		
dataformatas="html|plaintext|text"	Specifies the format of the data in the data source bound with the image			4.0		
datasrc="url"	Provides the URL or ID of the data source bound with the image			4.0		

ELEMENT/ATTRIBUTE	DESCRIPTION	HTML	XHTML	IE	NS	OP
dynsrc="*url*"	Provides the URL of a video or VRML file		2.0		2.1	
height="*integer*"	Specifies the height of the image in pixels	3.0	1.0	1.0	1.0	2.1
hspace="*integer*"	Specifies the horizontal space around the image in pixels. **Deprecated**	3.0	1.0*	1.0	1.0	2.1
ismap="ismap"	Indicates that the image can be used as a server-side image map	2.0	1.0	1.0	1.0	2.1
longdesc="*url*"	Provides the URL of a document containing a long description of the image	4.0	1.0		6.1	
loop="*integer*"	Specifies the number of times the video will play			2.0		2.1
lowsrc="*url*"	Provides the URL of the low-resolution version of the image			4.1	1.0	
name="*text*"	Specifies the image name	4.0	1.0*	4.0	3.0	3.0
src="*url*"	Specifies the image source file	2.0	1.0	1.0	1.0	2.1
start="fileopen|mouseover"	Indicates when to start the video clip (either when the file is opened or when the mouse hovers over the image)			2.0		2.1
suppress="true|false"	Suppresses the display of the alternate text and the placeholder icon until the image file is located				4.0*	
usemap="*url*"	Provides the location of a client-side image associated with the image (not well-supported when the URL points to an external file)	3.2	1.0	1.0	2.0	2.1
vspace="*integer*"	Specifies the vertical space around the image in pixels. **Deprecated**	3.2	1.0*	1.0	1.0	2.1
width="*integer*"	Specifies the width of the image in pixels	3.0	1.0	1.0	1.0	2.1
<input> </input>	Marks an input field in a Web form	2.0	1.0	1.0	1.0	2.1
align="left|right|top|texttop|middle|absmiddle|baseline|bottom|absbottom"	Specifies the alignment of the input field with the surrounding content. **Deprecated**	2.0	1.0*	1.0	1.0	2.1
alt="*text*"	Specifies alternate text for image buttons and image input fields	4.0	1.0	4.0	4.0	4.0
checked="checked"	Specifies that the input check box or input radio button is selected	2.0	1.0	1.0	1.0	2.1
datafld="*text*"	Indicates the column from a data source that supplies bound data for the input field	4.0		4.0		
dataformatas="html|plaintext|text"	Specifies the format of the data in the data source bound with the input field	4.0		4.0		
datasrc="*url*"	Provides the URL or ID of the data source bound with the input field	4.0		4.0		

ELEMENT/ATTRIBUTE	DESCRIPTION	HTML	XHTML	IE	NS	OP
height="integer"	Specifies the height of the image input field in pixels			4.0	1.0	4.0
hspace="integer"	Specifies the horizontal space around the image input field in pixels			5.0	4.0	4.0
ismap="ismap"	Enables the image input field to be used as a server-side image map	4.0	1.1		6.0	
maxlength="integer"	Specifies the maximum number of characters that can be inserted into a text input field	2.0	1.0	1.0	1.0	2.1
name="text"	Specifies the name of the input field	2.0	1.0	1.0	1.0	2.1
readonly="readonly"	Prevents the value of the input field from being modified	2.0	1.0	1.0	1.0	2.1
size="integer"	Specifies the number of characters that can be displayed at one time in an input text field	2.0	1.0	1.0	1.0	2.1
src="url"	Indicates the source file of an input image field	2.0	1.0	1.0	1.0	2.1
type="button|checkbox|file|hidden|image|password|radio|reset|submit|text"	Specifies the type of input field	2.0	1.0	1.0	1.0	2.1
usemap="url"	Provides the location of a client-side image associated with the image input field (not well-supported when the URL points to an external file)	4.0	1.0	2.0	2.0	2.1
value="text"	Specifies the default value of the input field	2.0	1.0	2.0	2.0	2.1
vspace="integer"	Specifies the vertical space around the image input field in pixels			5.0	4.0	4.0
width="integer"	Specifies the width of an image input field in pixels			4.0	1.0	4.0
<ins> </ins>	Marks inserted text	3.0	1.0	4.0	6.0	4.0
cite="url"	Provides the URL for the document that has additional information about the inserted text	3.0	1.0	4.0	6.1	4.0
datetime="date"	Specifies the date and time of the text insertion	3.0	1.0	4.0	6.1	4.0
<isindex />	Inserts an input field into the document for search queries. **Deprecated**	2.0	1.0*	1.0	1.0	2.1
action="url"	Provides the URL of the script used to process the sindex data			1.0	4.0*	2.1
prompt="text"	Specifies the text to be used for the input prompt. **Deprecated**	3.0	1.0*	1.0	1.0	2.1

ELEMENT/ATTRIBUTE	DESCRIPTION	HTML	XHTML	IE	NS	OP
`<kbd> </kbd>`	Marks keyboard-style text	2.0	1.0	1.0	1.0	3.5
`<label> </label>`	Associates the enclosed content with a form field	4.0	1.0	4.0	6.0	4.0
`datafld="text"`	Indicates the column from a data source that supplies bound data for the label			4.0		
`dataformatas="html|plaintext|text"`	Specifies the format of the data in the data source bound with the label			4.0		
`datasrc="url"`	Provides the URL or ID of the data source bound with the label			4.0		
`for="text"`	Provides the ID of the field associated with the label	4.0	1.0	4.0	6.0	7.0
`<layer> </layer>`	Creates a layer used to display the content of external documents; unlike the ilayer element, layer elements are absolutely positioned in the page				4.0*	
`above="text"`	Specifies the name of the layer displayed above the current layer				4.0*	
`background="url"`	Provides the URL of the file containing the background image				4.0*	
`below="text"`	Specifies the name of the layer displayed below the current layer				4.0*	
`bgcolor="color"`	Specifies the layer's background color				4.0*	
`clip="top, left, bottom, right"`	Specifies the coordinates of the viewable region of the layer				4.0*	
`height="integer"`	Specifies the height of the layer in pixels				4.0*	
`left="integer"`	Specifies the horizontal offset of the layer in pixels				4.0*	
`pagex="integer"`	Specifies the horizontal position of the layer in pixels				4.0*	
`pagey="integer"`	Specifies the vertical position of the layer in pixels				4.0*	
`src="url"`	Provides the URL of the document displayed in the layer				4.0*	
`top="integer"`	Specifies the vertical offset of the layer in pixels				4.0*	
`visibility="hide|inherit|show"`	Specifies the visibility of the layer				4.0*	
`width="integer"`	Specifies the width of the layer in pixels				4.0*	
`z-index="integer"`	Specifies the stacking order of the layer				4.0*	

ELEMENT/ATTRIBUTE	DESCRIPTION	HTML	XHTML	IE	NS	OP
`<legend> </legend>`	Marks the enclosed text as a caption for a field set	4.0	1.0	4.0	6.0	7.0
`align="bottom|left |top|right"`	Specifies the alignment of the legend with the field set; Internet Explorer also supports the center option. **Deprecated**	4.0	1.0*	4.0	6.0	
`<li> </li>`	Marks an item in an ordered (ol), unordered (ul), menu (menu), or directory (dir) list.	2.0	1.0	1.0	1.0	2.1
`type="A|a|I|i |1|disc|square |circle"`	Specifies the bullet type associated with the list item: a value of "1" is the default for ordered list; a value of "disc" is the default for unordered list. **Deprecated**	3.2	1.0*	1.0	1.0	2.1
`value="integer"`	Sets the value for the current list item in an ordered list; subsequent list items are numbered from that value. **Deprecated**	3.2	1.0*	1.0	1.0	2.1
`<link />`	Creates an element in the document head that establishes the relationship between the current document and external documents or objects	2.0	1.0	3.0	4.0	3.5
`charset="char code"`	Specifies the character encoding of the external document	4.0	1.0			7.0
`href="url"`	Provides the URL of the external document	2.0	1.0	3.0	4.0	3.5
`hreflang="text"`	Indicates the language of the external document	4.0	1.0			
`media="all|aural| braille|handheld| print|projection| screen|tty|tv"`	Indicates the media in which the external document is presented	4.0	1.0	4.0	4.0	3.5
`name="text"`	Specifies the name of the link			4.0		
`rel="text"`	Specifies the relationship between the current page and the link specified by the href attribute	2.0	1.0	3.0	4.0	3.5
`rev="text"`	Specifies the reverse relationship between the current page and the link specified by the href attribute	2.0	1.0	3.0	4.0	3.5
`target="text"`	Specifies the target window or frame for the link	4.0	1.0*	4.0	7.0	
`title="text"`	Specifies the title of the external document	2.0	1.0		6.0	7.0
`type="mime-type"`	Specifies the mime-type of the external document	4.0	1.0	3.0	4.0	3.5
`<map> </map>`	Creates an element that contains client-side image map hotspots	3.2	1.0	1.0	2.0	2.1
`name="text"`	Specifies the name of the image map	3.2	1.0*	1.0	2.0	2.1

ELEMENT/ATTRIBUTE	DESCRIPTION	HTML	XHTML	IE	NS	OP
`<marquee> </marquee>`	Displays the enclosed text as a scrolling marquee			2.0	7.0	7.2
`behavior="alternate` `|scroll|slide"`	Specifies how the marquee should move			2.0	7.0	7.2
`bgcolor="color"`	Specifies the background color of the marquee			2.0		7.2
`datafld="text"`	Indicates the column from a data source that supplies bound data for the marquee			4.0		
`dataformatas="html|` `plaintext|text"`	Indicates the format of the data in the data source bound with the marquee			4.0		
`datasrc="url"`	Provides the URL or ID of the data source bound with the marquee			4.0		
`direction="down|` `left|right|up"`	Specifies the direction of the marquee			2.0	7.0	7.2
`height="integer"`	Specifies the height of the marquee in pixels			2.0	7.0	7.2
`hspace="integer"`	Specifies the horizontal space around the marquee in pixels			2.0		
`loop="integer|` `infinite"`	Specifies the number of times the marquee motion is repeated			2.0		7.2
`scrollamount=` `"integer"`	Specifies the amount of space, in pixels, between successive draws of the marquee text			2.0	7.0	7.2
`scrolldelay="integer"`	Specifies the amount of time, in milliseconds, between marquee actions			2.0	7.0	7.2
`truespeed="truespeed"`	Indicates whether the scrolldelay value should be set to its exact value; otherwise any value less than 60 milliseconds is rounded up			4.0		
`vspace="integer"`	Specifies the vertical space around the marquee in pixels			2.0		
`width="integer"`	Specifies the width of the marquee in pixels			2.0	7.0	7.2
`<menu> </menu>`	Contains a menu list. **Deprecated**	2.0	1.0*	1.0	1.0	2.1
`compact="compact"`	Reduces the space between menu items. **Deprecated**	2.0	1.0*			
`start="integer"`	Specifies the starting value of the items in the menu list			6.0	4.0	

`type="A|a|I|i`
`1|disc|square|`
`circle|none"`
	Specifies the bullet type associated with the list items	3.2	1.0*	1.0	1.0	2.1

ELEMENT/ATTRIBUTE	DESCRIPTION	HTML	XHTML	IE	NS	OP
`<meta> </meta>`	Creates an element in the document's head section that contains information and special instructions for processing the document	2.0	1.0	2.0	1.0	3.0
`content="text"`	Provides information associated with the name or http-equiv attributes	2.0	1.0	2.0	1.0	3.0
`http-equiv="text"`	Provides instructions to the browser to request the server to perform different http operations	2.0	1.0	2.0	1.0	3.0
`name="text"`	Specifies the type of information specified in the content attribute	2.0	1.0	2.0	1.0	3.0
`scheme="text"`	Supplies additional information about the scheme used to interpret the content attribute	4.0	1.0			
`<nobr> </nobr>`	Disables line wrapping for the enclosed content			1.0	1.0	2.1
`<noembed> </noembed>`	Encloses alternate content for browsers that do not support the embed element			3.0	2.0	3.0
`<noframes> </noframes>`	Encloses alternate content for browsers that do not support frames	4.0	1.0*	3.0	2.0	2.1
`<nolayer> </nolayer>`	Encloses alternate content for browsers that do not support the layer or ilayer elements				4.0*	
`<noscript> </noscript>`	Encloses alternate content for browsers that do not support client-side scripts	4.0	1.0	3.0	3.0	3.0
`<object> </object>`	Places an embedded object (image, applet, sound clip, video clip, etc.) into the page	4.0	1.0	3.0	6.0	4.0
`archive="url"`	Specifies the URL of an archive containing classes and other resources preloaded for use with the object	4.0	1.0		6.0	
`align="absbottom|absmiddle|baseline|bottom|left|middle|right|texttop|top"`	Aligns the object with the surrounding content. **Deprecated**	4.0	1.0*	3.0	6.0	
`border="integer"`	Specifies the width of the border around the object. **Deprecated**	4.0	1.0*	6.0	6.0	7.0
`classid="url"`	Provides the URL of the object	4.0	1.0	3.0	6.0	4.0
`codebase="url"`	Specifies the base path used to resolve relative references within the embedded object	4.0	1.0	3.0	6.0	4.0
`codetype="mime-type"`	Indicates the mime-type of the embedded objects' code	4.0	1.0	3.0	6.0	4.0

ELEMENT/ATTRIBUTE	DESCRIPTION	HTML	XHTML	IE	NS	OP
data="*url*"	Provides the URL of the object's data file	4.0	1.0	3.0	6.0	4.0
datafld="*text*"	Identifies the column from a data source that supplies bound data for the embedded object	4.0				
dataformatas="html|plaintext|text"	Specifies the format of the data in the data source bound with the embedded object	4.0				
datasrc="*url*"	Provides the URL or ID of the data source bound with the embedded object	4.0				
declare="declare"	Declares the object without embedding it on the page	4.0	1.0			
height="*integer*"	Specifies the height of the object in pixels	4.0	1.0	3.0	6.0	4.0
hspace="*integer*"	Specifies the horizontal space around the image in pixels	4.0	1.0	3.0	6.0	4.0
name="*text*"	Specifies the name of the embedded object	4.0	1.0	3.0	6.0	4.0
standby="*text*"	Specifies the message displayed by the browser while loading the embedded object	4.0	1.0			7.0
type="*mime-type*"	Indicates the mime-type of the embedded object	4.0	1.0	3.0	6.0	4.0
vspace="*integer*"	Specifies the vertical space around the embedded object	4.0	1.0	3.0	6.0	4.0
width="*integer*"	Specifies the width of the object in pixels	4.0	1.0	3.0	6.0	4.0
\<ol> \</ol>	Contains an ordered list of items	2.0	1.0	1.0	1.0	2.1
compact="compact"	Reduces the space between ordered list items. **Deprecated**	2.0	1.0*			
start="*integer*"	Specifies the starting value in the list. **Deprecated**	3.2	1.0*	1.0	1.0	2.1
type="A|a|I|i|1"	Specifies the bullet type associated with the list items. **Deprecated**	3.2	1.0*	1.0	1.0	2.1
\<optgroup> \</optgroup>	Contains a group of option elements in a selection field	4.0	1.0	6.0	6.0	7.0
label="*text*"	Specifies the label for the option group	4.0	1.0	6.0	6.0	7.0
\<option> \</option>	Formats an option within a selection field	2.0	1.0	1.0	1.0	2.1
label="*text*"	Supplies the text label associated with the option	4.0	1.0			
selected="selected"	Selects the option by default	2.0	1.0	1.0	1.0	2.1
value="*text*"	Specifies the value associated with the option	2.0	1.0	1.0	1.0	2.1
\<p> \</p>	Marks the enclosed content as a paragraph	2.0	1.0	1.0	1.0	2.1
align="**left**|center|right|justify"	Horizontally aligns the contents of the paragraph. **Deprecated**	3.0	1.0*	1.0	1.0	2.1

ELEMENT/ATTRIBUTE	DESCRIPTION	HTML	XHTML	IE	NS	OP
`<param> </param>`	Marks parameter values sent to an object element or an applet element	3.2	1.0	3.0	2.0	3.5
`name="text"`	Specifies the parameter name	3.2	1.0	3.0	2.0	3.5
`type="mime-type"`	Specifies the mime-type of the resource indicated by the value attribute	4.0	1.0	6.0		6.0
`value="text"`	Specifies the parameter value	3.2	1.0	3.0	2.0	3.5
`valuetype="data|ref|object"`	Specifies the data type of the value attribute	4.0	1.0	6.0		6.0
`<plaintext> </plaintext>`	Marks the enclosed text as plain text			1.0	1.0	2.1
`<pre> </pre>`	Marks the enclosed text as preformatted text, retaining white space from the document	2.0	1.0	1.0	1.0	2.1
`width="integer"`	Specifies the width of preformatted text, in number of characters. **Deprecated**	2.0	1.0*		6.0	
`<q> </q>`	Marks the enclosed text as a quotation	3.0	1.0	4.0	6.0	4.0
`cite="url"`	Provides the source URL of the quoted content	4.0	1.0		6.0	
`<s> </s>`	Marks the enclosed text as strikethrough text. **Deprecated**	3.0	1.0*	1.0	3.0	2.1
`<samp> </samp>`	Marks the enclosed text as a sequence of literal characters	2.0	1.0	1.0	1.0	2.1
`<script> </script>`	Encloses client-side scripts within the document; this element can be placed within the head or the body element or refer to an external script file	3.2	1.0	3.0	2.0	3.0
`charset="char code"`	Specifies the character encoding of the script	4.0	1.0	3.0	7.0	7.0
`defer="defer"`	Defers execution of the script	4.0	1.0	4.0		
`event="text"`	Specifies the event that the script should be run in response to	4.0		4.0		
`for="text"`	Indicates the name or ID of the element to which the event attribute refers to	4.0		4.0		
`language="text"`	Specifies the language of the script. **Deprecated**	4.0	1.0*	3.0	2.0	3.0
`src="url"`	Provides the URL of an external script file	4.0	1.0	3.0	3.0	3.0
`type="mime-type"`	Specifies the mime-type of the script	4.0	1.0	4.0	4.0	
`<select> </select>`	Creates a selection field (drop-down list box) in a Web form	2.0	1.0	1.0	1.0	2.1
`align="left|right|top|texttop|middle|absmiddle|baseline|bottom|absbottom"`	Specifies the alignment of the selection field with the surrounding content. **Deprecated**	3.0*		4.0		

ELEMENT/ATTRIBUTE	DESCRIPTION	HTML	XHTML	IE	NS	OP
datafld="text"	Identifies the column from a data source that supplies bound data for the selection field	4.0		4.0		
dataformatas="html|plaintext|text"	Specifies the format of the data in the data source bound with the selection field	4.0		4.0		
datasrc="url"	Provides the URL or ID of the data source bound with the selection field	4.0		4.0		
multiple="multiple"	Allows multiple sections from the field	2.0	1.0	1.0	1.0	2.1
name="text"	Specifies the selection field name	2.0	1.0	1.0	1.0	2.1
size="integer"	Specifies the number of visible items in the selection list	2.0	1.0	1.0	1.0	2.1
<small> </small>	Decreases the size of the enclosed text relative to the default font size	3.0	1.0	3.0	1.0	2.1
<span> </span>	Creates a generic inline elment	3.0	1.0	3.0	2.0	2.1
datafld="text"	Identifies the column from a data source that supplies bound data for the inline element			4.0		
dataformatas="html|plaintext|text"	Specifies the format of the data in the data source bound with the inline element			4.0		
datasrc="url"	Provides the URL or ID of the data source bound with the inline element			4.0		
<strike> </strike>	Marks the enclosed text as strikethrough text. **Deprecated**	3.0	1.0*	1.0	3.5	2.1
<strong> </strong>	Marks the enclosed text as strongly emphasized text	2.0	1.0	1.0	1.0	2.1
<style> </style>	Encloses global style declarations for the document	3.0	1.0	3.0	4.0	3.5
media="all|aural|braille|handheld|print|projection|screen|tty|tv|"	Indicates the media of the enclosed style definitions	4.0	1.0	4.0	4.0	3.5
title="text"	Specifies the style of the style definitions	4.0	1.0			
type="mime-type"	Specifies the mime-type of the style definitions	4.0	1.0	3.0	4.0	
<sub> </sub>	Marks the enclosed text as subscripted text	3.0	1.0	3.0	1.1	2.1
<sup> </sup>	Marks the enclosed text as superscripted text	3.0	1.0	3.0	1.1	2.1

ELEMENT/ATTRIBUTE	DESCRIPTION	HTML	XHTML	IE	NS	OP
`<table> </table>`	Encloses the contents of a Web table	3.0	1.0	2.0	1.1	2.1
`align="left|center |right"`	Aligns the table with the surrounding content. **Deprecated**	3.0	1.0*	2.0	2.0	2.1
`background="url"`	Provides the URL of the table's background image			3.0	4.0	5.0
`bgcolor="color"`	Specifies the background color of the table. **Deprecated**	4.0	1.0*	2.0	3.0	2.1
`border="integer"`	Specifies the width of the table border in pixels	3.0	1.0	2.0	1.1	2.1
`bordercolor="color"`	Specifies the table border color			2.0	4.0	
`bordercolordark= "color"`	Specifies the color of the table border's shaded edge			2.0		
`bordercolorlight= "color"`	Specifies the color of the table border's unshaded edge			2.0		
`cellpadding= "integer"`	Specifies the space between the table data and the cell borders in pixels	3.2	1.0	2.0	1.1	2.1
`cellspacing= "integer"`	Specifies the space between table cells in pixels	3.2	1.0	2.0	1.1	2.1
`cols="integer"`	Specifies the number of columns in the table			3.0	4.0	
`datafld="text"`	Indicates the column from a data source that supplies bound data for the table	4.0		4.0		
`dataformatas="html| plaintext|text"`	Specifies the format of the data in the data source bound with the table	4.0		4.0		
`datapagesize= "integer"`	Sets the number of records displayed within the table	4.0	1.1	4.0		
`datasrc="url"`	Provides the URL or ID of the data source bound with the table	4.0		4.0		
`frame="above|below |border|box| hsides|lhs|rhs| void|vside"`	Specifies the format of the borders around the table	4.0	1.0	3.0	6.0	7.1
`height="integer"`	Specifies the height of the table in pixels			2.0	1.1	2.1
`hspace="integer"`	Specifies the horizontal space around the table in pixels				2.0	
`rules="all|cols| groups|none|rows"`	Specifies the format of the table's internal borders or gridlines	4.0	1.0	3.0	7.0	7.1
`summary="text"`	Supplies a text summary of the table's content	4.0	1.0		6.1	
`vspace="integer"`	Specifies the vertical space around the table in pixels				2.0	
`width="integer"`	Specifies the width of the table in pixels	3.0	1.0	2.0	1.1	2.1

ELEMENT/ATTRIBUTE	DESCRIPTION	HTML	XHTML	IE	NS	OP
<tbody> </tbody>	Encloses the content of the Web table body	4.0	1.0	3.0	6.0	4.0
align="**left**|center |right|justify |char"	Specifies the alignment of the contents in the cells of the table body	4.0	1.0	4.0	6.0	4.0
bgcolor="*color*"	Specifies the background color of the table body			4.0	6.0	
char="*char*"	Specifies the character used for aligning the table body contents when the align attribute is set to "char"	4.0	1.0			
charoff="*integer*"	Specifies the offset in pixels from the alignment character specified in the char attribute	4.0	1.0			
valign="**baseline**| bottom|middle|top"	Specifies the vertical alignment of the contents in the cells of the table body	4.0	1.0	4.0	6.0	4.0
<td> </td>	Encloses the data of a table cell	3.0	1.0	2.0	1.1	2.1
abbr="*text*"	Supplies an abbreviated version of the contents of the table cell	4.0	1.0			
align="**left**|center |right"	Specifies the horizontal alignment of the table cell data	3.0	1.0	2.0	1.1	2.1
background="*url*"	Provides the URL of the background image file			3.0	4.0	4.0
bgcolor="*color*"	Specifies the background color of the table cell. **Deprecated**	4.0	1.0*	2.0	3.0	2.1
bordercolor="*color*"	Specifies the color of the table cell border			2.0		
bordercolordark= "*color*"	Specifies the color of the table cell border's shaded edge			2.0		
bordercolorlight= "*color*"	Specifies the color of the table cell border's unshaded edge			2.0		
char="*char*"	Specifies the character used for aligning the table cell contents when the align attribute is set to "char"	4.0	1.0			
charoff="*integer*"	Specifies the offset in pixels from the alignment character specified in the char attribute	4.0	1.0			
colspan="*integer*"	Specifies the number of columns the table cell spans	3.0	1.0	2.0	1.1	2.1
headers="*text*"	Supplies a space-separated list of table headers associated with the table cell	4.0	1.0			
height="*integer*"	Specifies the height of the table cell in pixels. **Deprecated**	3.2	1.0*	2.0	1.1	2.1
nowrap="nowrap"	Disables line-wrapping within the table cell. **Deprecated**	3.0	1.0*	2.0	1.1	2.1
rowspan="*integer*"	Specifies the number of rows the table cell spans	3.0	1.0	2.0	1.1	2.1
scope="col|colgroup |row|rowgroup"	Specifies the scope of the table for which the cell provides data	4.0	1.0			
valign="top|**middle** |bottom"	Specifies the vertical alignment of the contents of the table cell	3.0	1.0	2.0	1.1	2.1
width="*integer*"	Specifies the width of the cell in pixels. **Deprecated**	3.2	1.0*	2.0	1.1	2.1

ELEMENT/ATTRIBUTE	DESCRIPTION	HTML	XHTML	IE	NS	OP
`<textarea> </textarea>`	Marks the enclosed text as a text area input box in a Web form	2.0	1.0	1.0	1.0	2.1
`datafld="text"`	Specifies the column from a data source that supplies bound data for the text area box	4.0		4.0		
`dataformatas="html|plaintext|text"`	Specifies the format of the data in the data source bound with the text area box	4.0		4.0		
`datasrc="url"`	Provides the URL or ID of the data source bound with the text area box	4.0		4.0		
`cols="integer"`	Specifies the width of the text area box in characters	2.0	1.0	1.0	1.0	2.1
`name="text"`	Specifies the name of the text area box	2.0	1.0	1.0	1.0	2.1
`readonly="readonly"`	Specifies the value of the text area box cannot be modified	4.0	1.0	4.0	6.0	5.0
`rows="integer"`	Specifies the number of visible rows in the text area box	2.0	1.0	1.0	1.0	2.1
`wrap="off|soft|hard"`	Specifies how text is wrapped within the text area box and how that text-wrapping information is sent to the server-side program; in earlier versions of Netscape Navigator, the default value is "off" (Netscape also accepts the values "off", "virtual", and "physical".)			4.0	4.0*	
`<tfoot> </tfoot>`	Encloses the content of the Web table footer	4.0	1.0	3.0	6.0	4.0
`align="left|center|right|justify|char"`	Specifies the alignment of the contents in the cells of the table footer	4.0	1.0	4.0	6.0	4.0
`bgcolor="color"`	Specifies the background color the table body			4.0	6.0	
`char="char"`	Specifies the character used for aligning the table footer contents when the align attribute is set to "char"	4.0	1.0			
`charoff="integer"`	Specifies the offset in pixels from the alignment character specified in the char attribute	4.0	1.0			
`valign="baseline|bottom|middle|top"`	Specifies the vertical alignment of the contents in the cells of the table footer	4.0	1.0	4.0	6.0	4.0
`<th> </th>`	Encloses the data of a table header cell	3.0	1.0	2.0	1.1	2.1
`abbr="text"`	Supplies an abbreviated version of the contents of the table cell	4.0	1.0			
`align="left|center|right"`	Specifies the horizontal alignment of the table cell data	3.0	1.0	2.0	1.1	2.1
`axis="text list"`	Provides a list of table categories that can be mapped to a table hierarchy	3.0	1.0			

ELEMENT/ATTRIBUTE	DESCRIPTION	HTML	XHTML	IE	NS	OP
background="*url*"	Provides the URL of the background image file			3.0	4.0	4.0
bgcolor="*color*"	Specifies the background color of the table cell. **Deprecated**	4.0	1.0*	2.0	3.0	2.1
bordercolor="*color*"	Specifies the color of the table cell border			2.0		
bordercolordark= "*color*"	Specifies the color of the table cell border's shaded edge			2.0		
bordercolorlight= "*color*"	Specifies the color of the table cell border's unshaded edge			2.0		
char="*char*"	Specifies the character used for aligning the table cell contents when the align attribute is set to "char"	4.0	1.0			
charoff="*integer*"	Specifies the offset in pixels from the alignment character specified in the char attribute	4.0	1.0			
colspan="*integer*"	Specifies the number of columns the table cell spans	3.0	1.0	2.0	1.1	2.1
headers="*text*"	A space-separated list of table headers associated with the table cell	4.0	1.0			
height="*integer*"	Specifies the height of the table cell in pixels. **Deprecated**	3.2	1.0*	2.0	1.1	2.1
nowrap="nowrap"	Disables line-wrapping within the table cell. **Deprecated**	3.0	1.0*	2.0	1.1	2.1
rowspan="*integer*"	Specifies the number of rows the table cell spans	3.0	1.0	2.0	1.1	2.1
scope="col| colgroup|row| rowgroup"	Specifies the scope of the table for which the cell provides data	4.0	1.0			
valign="top|middle |bottom"	Specifies the vertical alignment of the contents of the table cell	3.0	1.0	2.0	1.1	2.1
width="*integer*"	Specifies the width of the cell in pixels. **Deprecated**	3.2	1.0*	2.0	1.1	2.1
\<thead> \</thead>	Encloses the content of the Web table header	4.0	1.0	3.0	6.0	4.0
align="left|center |right|justify |char"	Specifies the alignment of the contents in the cells of the table header	4.0	1.0	4.0	6.0	4.0
bgcolor="*color*"	Specifies the background color of the table body			4.0	6.0	
char="*char*"	Specifies the character used for aligning the table header contents when the align attribute is set to "char"	4.0	1.0			
charoff="*integer*"	Specifies the offset in pixels from the alignment character specified in the char attribute	4.0	1.0			
valign="baseline| bottom|middle| top"	Specifies the vertical alignment of the contents in the cells of the table header	4.0	1.0	4.0	6.0	4.0
\<title> \</title>	Specifies the title of the document, placed in the head section of the document	2.0	1.0	1.0	1.0	2.1

ELEMENT/ATTRIBUTE	DESCRIPTION	HTML	XHTML	IE	NS	OP
`<tr> </tr>`	Encloses the content of a row within a Web table	3.0	1.0	2.0	1.1	2.1
`align="left|center|right"`	Specifies the horizontal alignment of the data in the row's cells	3.0	1.0	2.0	1.1	2.1
`background="url"`	Provides the URL of the background image file for the row				4.0	
`bgcolor="color"`	Specifies the background color of the row. **Deprecated**	4.0	1.0*	2.0	3.0	2.1
`bordercolor="color"`	Specifies the color of the table row border			2.0		
`bordercolordark="color"`	Specifies the color of the table row border's shaded edge			2.0		
`bordercolorlight="color"`	Specifies the color of the table row border's unshaded edge			2.0		
`char="char"`	Specifies the character used for aligning the table row contents when the align attribute is set to "char"	4.0	1.0			
`charoff="integer"`	Specifies the offset in pixels from the alignment character specified in the char attribute	4.0	1.0			
`height="integer"`	Specifies the height of the table row in pixels			5.0	6.0	4.0
`valign="baseline|bottom|middle|top"`	Specifies the vertical alignment of the contents of the table row	3.0	1.0	2.0	1.1	2.1
`<tt> </tt>`	Marks the enclosed text as teletype or monospaced text	2.0	1.0	1.0	1.0	2.1
`<u> </u>`	Marks the enclosed text as underlined text. **Deprecated**	3.0	1.0*	1.0	3.5	2.1
`<ul> </ul>`	Contains an unordered list of items	2.0	1.0	1.0	1.0	2.1
`compact="compact"`	Reduces the space between unordered list items. **Deprecated**	2.0	1.0*			
`type="disc|square|circle"`	Specifies the bullet type associated with the list items. **Deprecated**	3.2	1.0*	1.0	1.0	2.1
`<var> </var>`	Marks the enclosed text as containing a variable name	2.0	1.0	1.0	1.0	2.1
`<wbr />`	Forces a line-break in the rendered page			1.0	1.0	
`<xml> </xml>`	Encloses XML content (also referred to as a "data island") or references an external XML document			5.0		
`ns="url"`	Provides the URL of the namespace that the XML content is bound to			5.0		
`prefix="text"`	Specifies the namespace prefix of the XML content			5.0		
`src="url"`	Provides the URL of an external XML document			5.0		
`<xmp> </xmp>`	Marks the enclosed text as preformatted text, preserving the white space of the source document; replaced by the pre element. **Deprecated**	2.0		1.0	1.0	2.1

Cascading Style Sheets

This appendix describes the selectors, units, and attributes supported by Cascading Style Sheets (CSS), Internet Explorer (IE), Netscape, and Opera. Version numbers indicate the lowest version that supports the given selector, unit, or attribute. Note that support might be incomplete. A particular version might not support all aspects of the CSS feature. You should always check your code against different browsers and browser versions to ensure that your page is being rendered correctly. Additional information about CSS can be found at the World Wide Web Consortium Web site at *www.w3.org*.

Selectors

The general form of a style declaration is:

selector {attribute1:value1; attribute2:value2; ...}

where *selector* is the selection of elements within the document to which the style will be applied; *attribute1, attribute2*, etc. are the different style attributes; and *value1, value2*, etc. are values associated with those styles. The following table shows some of the different forms that a selector can take and the corresponding support from CSS, IE, Netscape, and Opera.

Selectors	Matches	CSS	IE	NS	OP
*	All elements in the document	2.0	5.0	6.0	4.0
e	An element, e, in the document	1.0	3.0	4.0	3.5
e1, e2, e3, …	A group of elements, e1, e2, e3 in the document	1.0	3.0	4.0	3.5
e1 e2	An element e2 nested within the parent element, e1	1.0	3.0	4.0	3.5
e1 > e2	A element e2 that is a child of the parent element, e1	2.0		6.0	3.5
e1+e2	An element, e2, that is adjacent to element e1	2.0		6.0	5.0
e1.class	An element, e1, belonging to the *class* class	1.0	3.0	4.0	3.5
.class	Any element belonging to the *class* class	1.0	3.0	4.0	3.5
#id	An element with the id value *id*	1.0	3.0	4.0	3.5
[att]	The element contains the *att* attribute	2.0		6.0	4.0
[att="val"]	The element's *att* attribute equals *"val"*	2.0		6.0	4.0
[att~="val"]	The element's *att* attribute value is a space-separated list of "words," one of which is exactly *"val"*	2.0		6.0	4.0
[att|="val"]	The element's *att* attribute value is a hyphen-separated list of "words" beginning with "val"	3.0		6.0	
[att^="val"]	The element's *att* attribute begins with *"val"*	3.0		6.0	
[att$="val"]	The element's *att* attribute ends with *"val"*	3.0		6.0	
[att*="val"]	The element's *att* attribute contains the value *"val"*	3.0		6.0	
[ns|att]	References all *att* attributes in the *ns* namespace	3.0		6.0	

Pseudo-Elements and Pseudo-Classes

Pseudo-elements are elements that do not exist in HTML code but whose attributes can be set with CSS. Many pseudo-elements were introduced in CSS2 and are not widely supported by browsers.

Pseudo-Element	Matches	CSS	IE	NS	OP
e:after {content: "text"}	Text content, *text*, that is inserted at the end of an element, e	2.0		6.0	4.0
e:before {content: "text"}	Text content, *text*, that is inserted at the beginning of an element, e	2.0		6.0	4.0
e:first-letter	The first letter in the element, e	1.0	5.5	6.0	3.5
e:first-line	The first line in the element, e	1.0	5.5	6.0	3.5

Pseudo-classes are classes of HTML elements that define the condition or state of the element in the Web page. Many pseudo-classes were introduced in CSS2 and are not widely supported by browsers.

Pseudo-Class	Matches	CSS	IE	NS	OP
:canvas	The rendering canvas of the document			6.0	
:first	The first printed page of the document (used only with print styles created with the @print rule)	2.0			
:last	The last printed page of the document (used only with print styles created with the @print rule)	2.0			
:left	The left side of a two-sided printout (used only with print styles created with the @print rule)	2.0			
:right	The right side of a two-sided printout (used only with print stylescreated with the @print rule)	2.0			
:root	The root element of the document (the html element in HTML and XHTML documents)			6.0	
:scrolled-content	The content that is scrolled in the rendering viewport			6.0	
:viewport	The rendering viewport of the document			6.0	
:viewport-scroll	The rendering viewport of the document plus the scrollbar region			6.0	
e:active	The element, e, is being activated by the user (usually applies only to hyperlinks)	1.0	4.0	6.0	5.0
e:empty	The element, e, has no content			6.0	
e:first-child	The element, e, which is the first child of its parent element	2.0		6.0	7.0
e:first-node	The first occurrence of the element, e, in the document tree			6.0	
e:focus	The element, e, has received the focus of the cursor (usually applies only to Web form elements)	2.0	6.0	7.0	
e:hover	The mouse pointer is hovering over the element, e (usually applies only to hyperlinks)	2.0	4.0	6.0	4.0
e:lang(text)	Sets the language, *text*, associated with the element, e	2.0			
e:last-child	The element, e, that is the last child of its parent element	2.0		6.0	7.0
e:last-node	The last occurrence of the element, e, in the document tree			6.0	
e:link	The element, e, has not been visited yet by the user (applies only to hyperlinks)	1.0	3.0	4.0	3.5
e:not	Negate the selector rule for the element, e, applying the style to all e elements that do not match the selector rules			6.0	
e:visited	The element, e, has been already visited by the user (to only to hyperlinks)	1.0	3.0	4.0	3.5

@ Rules

CSS supports different "@ rules" designed to run commands within a style sheet. These commands can be used to import other styles, download font definitions, or define the format of printed output.

@ Rule	Description	CSS	IE	NS	OP
`@charset "encoding"`	Defines the character set encoding used in the style sheet (this must be the very first line in the style sheet document)	2.0	5.5	6.0	3.5
`@font-face {font-family: e; font-styles; src: url(url) }`	Downloads a font definition from an external file, where is the name assigned to the font, *font-styles* are CSS styles to format the font's appearance, and *url* is the location of the external font file	2.0	4.0	6.0	3.5
`@import url(url) media`	Imports an external style sheet document into the current style sheet, where *url* is the location of the external style sheet and *media* is a comma-separated list of media types (optional)	1.0	4.0	6.0	3.5
`@media media {style declaration}`	Defines the media for the styles in the *style declaration* block, where *media* is a comma-separated list of media types	2.0	4.0	6.0	3.5
`@namespace prefix url(url)`	Defines the namespace used by selectors in the style sheet, where *prefix* is the local namespace prefix (optional) and *url* is the unique namespace identifier; the @namespace rule must come before all CSS selectors			6.0	
`@page label pseudo-class {styles}`	Defines the properties of a printed page, where *label* is a label given to the page (optional), *pseudo-class* is one of the CSS pseudo-classes designed for printed pages, and *styles* are the styles associated with the page	2.0	5.5	6.0	4.0

Miscellaneous Syntax

The following syntax elements do not fit into the previous categories but are useful in constructing CSS style sheets.

Item	Description	CSS	IE	NS	OP
`style !important`	Places high importance on the preceding *style*, overriding the usual rules for inheritance and cascading	1.0	4.0	6.0	3.5
`/* comment */`	Attaches a *comment* to the style sheet	1.0	3.0	4.0	3.5

Units

Many style attribute values use units of measurement to indicate color, length, angles, time, and frequencies. The following table describes the measuring units used in CSS.

Units	Description	CSS	IE	NS	OP
Color	**Units of color**				
name	A color name; all browsers recognize 16 base color names: aqua, black, blue, fuchsia, gray, green, lime, maroon, navy, olive, purple, red, silver, teal, white, and yellow	1.0	3.0	4.0	3.5
`#rrggbb`	The hexadecimal color value, where *rr* is the red value, *gg* is the green value, and *bb* is the blue value	1.0	3.0	4.0	3.5
`#rgb`	A compressed hexadecimal value, where the *r*, *g*, and *b* values are doubled so that, for example, #A2F = #AA22FF	1.0	3.0	4.0	3.5

Units	Description	CSS	IE	NS	OP
Color	**Units of color**				
name	A color name; all browsers recognize 16 base color names: aqua, black, blue, fuchsia, gray, green, lime, maroon, navy, olive, purple, red, silver, teal, white, and yellow	1.0	3.0	4.0	3.5
#rrggbb	The hexadecimal color value, where *rr* is the red value, *gg* is the green value, and *bb* is the blue value	1.0	3.0	4.0	3.5
#rgb	A compressed hexadecimal value, where the *r*, *g*, and *b* values are doubled so that, for example, #A2F = #AA22FF	1.0	3.0	4.0	3.5
rgb(*red, green, blue*)	The decimal color value, where *red* is the red value, *green* is the green value, and *blue* is the blue value	1.0	3.0	4.0	3.5
rgb(*red%, green%, blue%*)	The color value percentage, where *red*% is the percent of maximum red, *green*% is the percent of maximum green, and *blue*% is the percent of maximum blue	1.0	3.0	4.0	3.5
Length	**Units of length**				
auto	Keyword which allows the browser to automatically determine the size of the length	1.0	4.0	4.0	3.5
em	A relative unit indicating the width and the height of the capital "M" character for the browser's default font	1.0	4.0	4.0	3.5
ex	A relative unit indicating the height of the small "x" character for the browser's default font	1.0	4.0	4.0	3.5
px	A pixel, representing the smallest unit of length on the output device	1.0	3.0	4.0	3.5
in	An inch	1.0	3.0	4.0	3.5
cm	A centimeter	1.0	3.0	4.0	3.5
mm	A millimeter	1.0	3.0	4.0	3.5
pt	A point, approximately 1/72 inch	1.0	3.0	4.0	3.5
pc	A pica, approximately 1/12 inch	1.0	3.0	4.0	3.5
%	A percent of the width or height of the parent element	1.0	3.0	4.0	3.5
xx-small	Keyword representing an extremely small font size	1.0	3.0	4.0	3.5
x-small	Keyword representing a very small font size	1.0	3.0	4.0	3.5
small	Keyword representing a small font size	1.0	3.0	4.0	3.5
medium	Keyword representing a medium-sized font	1.0	3.0	4.0	3.5
large	Keyword representing a large font	1.0	3.0	4.0	3.5
x-large	Keyword representing a very large font	1.0	3.0	4.0	3.5
xx-large	Keyword representing an extremely large font	1.0	3.0	4.0	3.5
Angle	**Units of angles**				
deg	The angle in degrees	2.0			
grad	The angle in gradients	2.0			
rad	The angle in radians	2.0			
Time	**Units of time**				
ms	Time in milliseconds	2.0			
s	Time in seconds	2.0			
Frequency	**Units of frequency**				
hz	The frequency in hertz	2.0			
khz	The frequency in kilohertz				

Attributes and Values

The following table describes the attributes and values for different types of elements. The attributes are grouped into categories to help you locate the features relevant to your particular design task.

Attribute	Description	CSS	IE	NS	OP
Aural	**Styles for Aural Browsers**				
azimuth: *location*	Defines the location of the sound, where *location* is left-side, far-left, left, center-left, center, center-right, right, far-right, right-side, leftward, rightward, or an angle value	2.0			
cue: url(*url1*) url(*url2*)	Adds a sound to an element: if a single value is present, the sound is played before and after the element; if two values are present, the first is played before and the second is played after	2.0			
cue-after: url(*url*)	Specifies a sound to be played immediately after an element	2.0			
cue-before: url(*url*)	Specifies a sound to be played immediately before an element	2.0			
elevation: *location*	Defines the vertical location of the sound, where *location* is below, level, above, lower, higher, or an angle value	2.0			
pause: *time1 time2*	Adds a pause to an element: if a single value is present, the pause occurs before and after the element; if two values are present, the first pause occurs before and the second occurs after	2.0			
pause-after: *time*	Adds a pause after an element	2.0			
pause-before: *time*	Adds a pause before an element	2.0			
pitch: *value*	Defines the pitch of a speaking voice, where *value* is x-low, low, medium, high, x-high, or a frequency value	2.0			
pitch-range: *value*	Defines the pitch range for a speaking voice, where *value* ranges from 0 to 100; a low pitch range results in a monotone voice, whereas a high pitch range sounds very animated	2.0			
play-during: url(*url*) mix repeat *type*	Defines a sound to be played behind an element, where *url* is the URL of the sound file; mix overlays the sound file with the sound of the parent element; repeat causes the sound to be repeated, filling up the available time; and *type* is auto to play the sound only once, none to play nothing but the sound file, or inherit	2.0			
richness: *value*	Specifies the richness of the speaking voice, where *value* ranges from 0 to 100; a low value indicates a softer voice, whereas a high value indicates a brighter voice	2.0			
speak: *type*	Defines how element content is to be spoken, where *type* is normal (for normal punctuation rules), spell-out (to pronounce one character at a time), none (to suppress the aural rendering), or inherit	2.0			
speak-numeral: *type*	Defines how numeric content should be spoken, where *type* is digits (to pronounce one digit at a time), continuous (to pronounce the full number), or inherit	2.0			
speak-punctuation: *type*	Defines how punctuation characters are spoken, where *type* is code (to speak the punctuation literally), none (to not speak the punctuation), or inherit	2.0			
speech-rate: *value*	Defines the rate of speech, where *value* is x-slow, slow, medium, fast, x-fast, slower, faster, or a value in words per minute	2.0			
stress: *value*	Defines the maximum pitch, where *value* ranges from 0 to 100; a value of 50 is normal stress for a speaking voice	2.0			
voice-family: *text*	Defines the name of the speaking voice, where *text* is male, female, child, or a text string indicating a specific speaking voice	2.0			
volume: *value*	Defines the volume of a voice, where *value* is silent, x-soft, soft, medium, loud, x-loud, or a number from 0 (lowest) to 100 (highest)	2.0			

Attribute	Description	CSS	IE	NS	OP
Backgrounds	**Styles applied to an element's background**				
background: color url(url) repeat attachment position	Defines the background of the element, where color is a CSS color name or value, url is the location of an image file, repeat defines how the background image should be repeated, attachment defines how the background image should be attached, and position defines the position of the background image	1.0	3.0	4.0	3.5
background-attachment: type	Specifies how the background image is attached, where type is inherit, scroll (move the image with the page content), or fixed (fix the image and not scroll)	1.0	4.0	4.0	3.5
background-color: color	Defines the color of the background, where color is a CSS color name or value; the keyword "inherit" can be used to inherit the background color of the parent element, or "transparent" can be used to allow the parent element background image to show through	1.0	4.0	4.0	3.5
background-image: url(url)	Specifies the image file used for the element's background, where url is the URL of the image file	1.0	4.0	4.0	3.5
background-position: x y	Sets the position of a background image, where x is the horizontal location in pixels, as a percentage of the width of the parent element, or the keyword "left", "center", or "right", y is the vertical location in pixels, as a percentage of the height and of the parent element, or the keyword, "top", "center", or "bottom"	1.0	4.0	4.0	3.5
background-repeat: type	Defines the method for repeating the background image, where type is no-repeat, repeat (to tile the image in both directions), repeat-x (to tile the image in the horizontal direction only), or repeat-y (to tile the image in the vertical direction only)	1.0	4.0	4.0	3.5
Block-Level Styles	**Styles applied to block-level elements**				
border: length style color	Defines the border style of the element, where length is the border width, style is the border design, and color is the border color	1.0	4.0	4.0	3.5
border-bottom: length style color	Defines the border style of the bottom edge of the element	1.0	4.0	4.0*	3.5
border-left: length style color	Defines the border style of the left edge of the element	1.0	4.0	4.0	3.5
border-right: length style color	Defines the border style of the right edge of the element	1.0	4.0	4.0	3.5
border-top: length style color	Defines the border style of the top edge of the element	1.0	4.0	4.0	3.5
border-color: color	Defines the color applied to the element's border using a CSS color unit	1.0	4.0	4.0	3.5
border-bottom-color: color	Defines the color applied to the bottom edge of the element	1.0	4.0	4.0	3.5
border-left-color: color	Defines the color applied to the left edge of the element	1.0	4.0	4.0	3.5
border-right-color: color	Defines the color applied to the right edge of the element	1.0	4.0	4.0	3.5
border-top-color: color	Defines the color applied to the top edge of the element	1.0	4.0	4.0	3.5
border-style: style	Specifies the design of the element's border (dashed, dotted, double, groove, inset, none, outset, ridge, or solid)	1.0	4.0	4.0	3.5
border-style-bottom: style	Specifies the design of the element's bottom edge	1.0	4.0	4.0	3.5
border-style-left: style	Specifies the design of the element's left edge	1.0	4.0	4.0	3.5
border-style-right: style	Specifies the design of the element's right edge	1.0	4.0	4.0	3.5
border-style-top: style	Specifies the design of the element's top edge	1.0	4.0	4.0	3.5
border-width: length	Defines the width of the element's border, in a unit of measure or using the keyword "thick", "medium", or "thin".	1.0	4.0	4.0	3.5
border-width-bottom: length	Defines the width of the element's bottom edge	1.0	4.0	4.0	3.5
border-width-left: length	Defines the width of the element's left edge	1.0	4.0	4.0	3.5

Attribute	Description	CSS	IE	NS	OP
`border-width-right: length`	Defines the width of the element's right edge	1.0	4.0	4.0	3.5
`border-width-top: length`	Defines the width of the element's top edge	1.0	4.0	4.0	3.5
`margin: top right bottom left`	Defines the size of the margins around the top, right, bottom, and left edges of the element, in one of the CSS units of length	1.0	4.0	4.0	3.5
`margin-bottom: length`	Defines the size of the element's bottom margin	1.0	4.0	4.0	3.5
`margin-left: length`	Defines the size of the element's left margin	1.0	4.0	4.0	3.5
`margin-right: length`	Defines the size of the element's right margin	1.0	4.0	4.0	3.5
`margin-top: length`	Defines the size of the element's top margin	1.0	4.0	4.0	3.5
`padding: top right bottom left`	Defines the size of the padding space within the top, right, bottom, and left edges of the element, in one of the CSS units of length	1.0	4.0	4.0	3.5
`padding-bottom: length`	Defines the size of the element's bottom padding	1.0	4.0	4.0	3.5
`padding-left: length`	Defines the size of the element's left padding	1.0	4.0	4.0	3.5
`padding-right: length`	Defines the size of the element's right padding	1.0	4.0	4.0	3.5
`padding-top: length`	Defines the size of the element's top padding	1.0	4.0	4.0	3.5
Content	**Styles to attach additional content to elements**				
`content: text`	Generates a text string to attach to the content of the element	2.0			4.0
`content: attr(attr)`	Returns the value of the *attr* attribute from the element	2.0		6.0	4.0
`content: close-quote`	Attaches a close quote using the characters specified in the quotes style	2.0		6.0	4.0
`content: counter(text)`	Generates a counter using the text string *text* attached to the content (most often used with list items)	2.0			4.0
`content: counters(text)`	Generates a string of counters using the comma-separated text string *text* attached to the content (most often used with list items)	2.0			4.0
`content: no-close-quote`	Prevents the attachment of a close quote to an element	2.0		6.0	4.0
`content: no-open-quote`	Prevents the attachment of an open quote to an element	2.0		6.0	4.0
`content: open-quote`	Attaches an open quote using the characters specified in the quotes style	2.0		6.0	4.0
`content: url(url)`	Attaches the content of an external file indicated in the *url* to the element	2.0		6.0	4.0
`counter-increment: id integer`	Defines the element to be automatically incremented and the amount by which it is to be incremented, where *id* is an identifier of the element and *integer* defines by how much	2.0			4.0
`counter-reset: id integer`	Defines the element whose counter is to be reset and the amount by which it is to be reset, where *id* is an identifier of the element and *integer* defines by how much	2.0			4.0
`quotes: text1 text2`	Defines the text strings for the open quotes (*text1*) and the close quotes (*text2*)	2.0		6.0	4.0
Display Styles	**Styles that control the display of the element's content**				
`clip: rect(top, right, bottom, left)`	Defines what portion of the content is displayed, where *top*, *right*, *bottom*, and *left* are distances of the top, right, bottom, and left edges from the element's top-left corner; use a value of auto to allow the browser to determine the clipping region	2.0	4.0	4.0	7.0
`display: type`	Specifies the display type of the element, where *type* is one of the following: block, inline, inline-block, inherit, list-item, none, run-in, table, inline-table, table-caption, table-column, table-cell, table-column-group, table-header-group, table-footer-group, table-row, or table-row-group	1.0	4.0	4.0	3.5
`height: length`	Specifies the height of the element in one of the CSS units of length	1.0	4.0	6.0	3.5
`min-height: length`	Specifies the minimum height of the element	2.0		6.0	4.0
`min-width: length`	Specifies the minimum width of the element	2.0		6.0	4.0
`max-height: length`	Specifies the maximum height of the element	2.0		6.0	4.0

Attribute	Description	CSS	IE	NS	OP
max-width: *length*	Specifies the maximum width of the element	2.0		6.0	4.0
overflow: *type*	Instructs the browser on how to handle content that overflows the dimensions of the element, where *type* is auto, inherit, visible, hidden, or scroll	2.0	4.0	6.0	4.0
overflow-x: *type*	Instructs the browser on how to handle content that overflows the element's width, where *type* is auto, inherit, visible, hidden, or scroll		5.0		
overflow-y: *type*	Instructs the browser on how to handle content that overflows the element's height, where *type* is auto, inherit, visible, hidden, or scroll		5.0		
text-overflow: *type*	Instructs the browser on how to handle text overflow, where *type* is clip (to hide the overflow text) or ellipsis (to display the ... text string)		6.0		
visibility: *type*	Defines the element's visibility, where *type* is hidden, visible, or inherit	2.0	4.0	4.0	4.0
width: *length*	Specifies the width of the element in one of the CSS units of length	1.0	4.0	4.0	3.5
Fonts and Text	**Styles that format the appearance of fonts and text**				
color: *color*	Specifies the color of the element's foreground (usually the font color)	1.0	3.0	4.0	3.5
font: *style variant weight size/line-height family*	Defines the appearance of the font, where *style* is the font's style, *variant* is the font variant, *weight* is the weight of the font, *size* is the size of the font, *line-height* is the height of the lines, and *family* is the font face; the only required attributes are *size* and *family*	1.0	3.0	4.0	3.5
font-family: *family*	Specifies the font face used to display text, where *family* is sans-serif, serif, fanstasy, monospace, cursive, or the name of an installed font	1.0	3.0	4.0	3.5
font-size: *value*	Specifies the size of the font in one of the CSS units of length	1.0	3.0	4.0	3.5
font-size-adjust: *value*	Specifies the aspect *value* (which is the ratio of the font size to the font's ex height) for the font	2.0			
font-stretch: *type*	Expands or contracts the font, where *type* is narrower, wider, ultra-condensed, extra-condensed, condensed, semi-condensed, normal, semi-expanded, extra-expanded, or ultra-expanded	2.0			
font-style: *type*	Specifies a style applied to the font, where *type* is normal, italic, or oblique	1.0	3.0	4.0	3.5
font-variant: *type*	Specifies a variant of the font, where *type* is inherit, normal, or small-caps	1.0	4.0	6.0	3.5
font-weight: *value*	Defines the weight of the font, where *value* is 100, 200, 300, 400, 500, 600, 700, 800, 900, normal, lighter, bolder, or bold	1.0	4.0	4.0	3.5
letter-spacing: *value*	Specifies the space between letters, where *value* is a unit of length or the keyword "normal"	1.0	4.0	6.0	3.5
line-height: *value*	Specifies the height of the lines, where *value* is a unit of length or the keyword, "normal"	1.0	3.0	4.0	3.5
text-align: *type*	Specifies the horizontal alignment of text within the element, where *type* is inherit, left, right, center, or justify	1.0	3.0	4.0	3.5
text-decoration: *type*	Specifies the decoration applied to the text, where *type* is blink, line-through, none overline, or underline	1.0	3.0	4.0	3.5
text-indent: *length*	Specifies the amount of indentation in the first line of the text, where *length* is a CSS unit of length	1.0	3.0	4.0	3.5
text-shadow: *color x y blur*	Applies a shadow effect to the text, where *color* is the color of the shadow, *x* is the horizontal offset in pixels, *y* is the vertical offset in pixels, and *blur* is the size of the blur radius (optional); multiple shadows can be added with effect shadow effect separated by commas	2.0			
text-transform: *type*	Defines a transformation applied to the text, where *type* is capitalize, lowercase, none, or uppercase	1.0	4.0	4.0	3.5
vertical-align: *type*	Specifies how to vertically align the text with the surrounding content, where *type* is baseline, middle, top, bottom, text-top, text-bottom, super, sub, or one of the CSS units of length	1.0	4.0	4.0	3.5

Attribute	Description	CSS	IE	NS	OP
`white-space: type`	Specifies the handling of white space (blank spaces, tabs, and new lines), where *type* is inherit, normal, pre (to treat the text as preformatted text), or nowrap (to prevent line-wrapping)	1.0	5.5	6.0	4.0
`word-spacing: length`	Specifies the amount of space between words in the text, where *length* is either a CSS unit of length or the keyword "normal" to use normal word spacing	1.0	40.	6.0	3.5
Layout	**Styles that define the layout of elements**				
`bottom: y`	Defines the vertical offset of the element's bottom edge, where *y* is either a CSS unit of length or the keyword "auto" or "inherit"	2.0	4.0	6.0	4.0
`clear: type`	Places the element only after the specified margin is clear of floating elements, where *type* is inherit, none, left, right, or both	1.0	4.0	4.0	3.5
`float: type`	Floats the element on the specified margin with subsequent content wrapping around the element, where *type* is inherit, none, left, right, or both	1.0	4.0	4.0	3.5
`left: x`	Defines the horizontal offset of the element's left edge, where *x* is either a CSS unit of length or the keyword "auto" or "inherit"	2.0	4.0	6.0	4.0
`position: type`	Defines how the element is positioned on the page, where *type* is absolute, relative, fixed, static, and inherit	1.0	4.0	4.0	3.5
`right: x`	Defines the horizontal offset of the element's right edge, where *x* is either a CSS unit of length or the keyword "auto" or "inherit"	2.0	4.0	6.0	4.0
`top: y`	Defines the vertical offset of the element's top edge, where *y* is a CSS unit of length or the keyword "auto" or "inherit"	2.0	4.0	6.0	4.0
`z-index: value`	Defines how overlapping elements are stacked, where *value* is either the stacking number (elements with higher stacking numbers are placed on top) or the keyword "auto" to allow the browser to determine the stacking order	2.0	5.0	4.0	4.0
Lists	**Styles that format lists**				
`list-style: type image position`	Defines the appearance of a list item, where *type* is the marker type, *image* is the URL of the location of an image file used for the marker, and *position* is the position of the marker	1.0	4.0	4.0	3.5
`list-style-image: url(url)`	Defines image used for the list marker, where *url* is the location of the image file	1.0	4.0	6.0	3.5
`list-style-type: type`	Defines the marker type used in the list, where *type* is disc, circle, square, decimal, decimal-leading-zero, lower-roman, upper-roman, lower-alpha, upper-alpha, or none	1.0	4.0	4.0	3.5
`list-style-position: type`	Defines the location of the list marker, where *type* is inside or outside	1.0	4.0	6.0	3.5
`marker-offset: length`	Defines the distance between the marker and the enclosing list box, where *length* is either a CSS unit of length or the keyword "auto" or "inherit"	2.0			
Outlines	**Styles to create and format outlines**				
`outline: color style width`	Creates an outline around the element content, where *color* is the color of the outline, *style* is the outline style, and *width* is the width of the outline	2.0			7.0
`outline-color: color`	Defines the color of the outline	2.0			7.0
`outline-style: type`	Defines the style of the outline, where *type* is dashed, dotted, double, groove, inset, none, outset, ridge, solid, or inherit	2.0			7.0
`outline-width: length`	Defines the width of the outline, where *length* is expressed in a CSS unit of length	2.0			7.0
Printing	**Styles for printed output**				
`page: label`	Specifies the page design to apply, where *label* is a page design created with the @page rule.	2.0			T7?

Attribute	Description	CSS	IE	NS	OP
page-break-after: *type*	Defines how to control page breaks after the element, where *type* is avoid (to avoid page breaks), left (to insert a page break until a left page is displayed), right (to insert a page break until a right page is displayed), always (to always insert a page break), auto, or inherit	2.0	4.0	7.0	3.5
page-break-before: *type*	Defines how to control page breaks before the element, where *type* is avoid left, always, auto, or inherit	2.0	4.0	7.0	3.5
page-break-inside: *type*	Defines how to control page breaks within the element, where *type* is avoid, auto, or inherit	2.0			3.5
marks: *type*	Defines how to display crop marks, where *type* is crop, cross, none, or inherit	2.0			T7?
size: *width height orientation*	Defines the size of the page, where *width* and *height* are the width and the height of the page and *orientation* is the orientation of the page (portrait or landscape)	2.0			4.0
orphans: *value*	Defines how to handle orphaned text, where *value* is the number of lines that must appear within the element before a page break is inserted	2.0			3.5
widow: *value*	Defines how to handle widowed text, where *value* is the number of lines that must appear within the element before a page break is inserted	2.0			3.5
Scrollbars and Cursors	**Styles to format the appearance of scrollbars and cursors**				
cursor: *type*	Defines the cursor image used, where *type* is n-resize, ne-resize, e-resize, se-resize, s-resize, sw-resize, w-resize, nw-resize, crosshair, pointer, move, text, wait, help, auto, default, inherit, or a URL pointing to an image file; individual browsers also support dozens of other cursor types	2.0	4.0	6.0	7.0
scrollbar-3dlight-color: *color*	Defines the *color* of the outer top and left edge of the slider		5.5		7.0
scrollbar-arrow-color: *color*	Defines the *color* of the scrollbar directional arrows		5.5		7.0
scrollbar-base-color: *color*	Defines the *color* of the scrollbar button face, arrow, slider, and slider tray		5.5		7.0
scrollbar-darkshadow-color: *color*	Defines the *color* of the outer bottom and right edges of the slider		5.5		7.0
scrollbar-face-color: *color*	Defines the *color* of the button face of the scrollbar arrow and slider		5.5		7.0
scrollbar-highlight-color: *color*	Defines the *color* of the inner top and left edges of the slider		5.5		7.0
scrollbar-shadow-color: *color*	Defines the *color* of the inner bottom and right edges of the slider		5.5		7.0
Special Effects	**Styles to create special visual effects**				
filter: *type parameters*	Applies transition and filter effects to elements, where *type* is the type of filter and *parameters* are parameter values specific to the filter		4.0		
Tables	**Styles to format the appearance of tables**				
border-collapse: *type*	Determines whether table cell borders are separate or collapsed into a single border, where *type* is separate, collapse, or inherit	2.0	5.0	7.0	4.0
border-spacing: *length*	If separate borders are used for table cells, defines the distance between borders, where *length* is a CSS unit of length or inherit	2.0		6.0	4.0
caption-side: *type*	Defines the position of the caption element, where *type* is bottom, left, right, top, or inherit	2.0		6.0	4.0
empty-cells: *type*	If separate borders are used for table cells, defines whether to display borders for empty cells, where *type* is hide, show, or inherit	2.0		6.0	4.0
speak-header: *type*	Defines how table headers are spoken in relation to the data cells, where *type* is always, once, or inherit	2.0			
table-layout: *type*	Defines the algorithm used for the table layout, where *type* is auto (to define the layout once all table cells have been read), fixed (to define the layout after the first table row has been read), or inherit	2.0	5.0	6.0	7.0

Appendix C

JavaScript

Objects, Properties, Methods, and Event Handlers

This appendix defines some of the important JavaScript objects, properties, methods, and event handlers and their compatibility with the Internet Explorer (IE) and Netscape browsers.

JavaScript Elements	Description	IE	Netscape
Anchor	An anchor in the document (use the anchor name)	4.0	4.0
Properties			
accessKey	The hotkey that gives the element focus	4.0	6.0
charset	The character set of the linked document	6.0	6.0
coords	The coordinates of the object, used with the shape attribute	6.0	6.0
hreflang	The language code of the linked resource	6.0	6.0
name	The name of the anchor	4.0	4.0
nameProp	The string holding the filename portion of the URL in the href	5.0	
shape	The string defining the shape of the object	6.0	6.0
tabIndex	The numeric value that indicates the tab order for the object	4.0	6.0
text	The anchor text	4.0	4.0
type	Specifies the media type in the form of a MIME type for the link target	6.0	6.0
Methods			
blur( )	Removes focus from the element	4.0	6.0
handleEvent (*event*)	Causes the Event instance *event* to be processed	4.0	
focus( )	Gives the element focus	4.0	6.0
Applet	A Java applet in the document	4.0	3.0
Properties			
align	Specifies alignment, for example, "left"	4.0	6.0
alt	Specifies alternative text for the applet	6.0	
altHTML	Specifies alternative text for the applet	4.0	
archive	A list of URLs		6.0
code	The URL for the applet class file	4.0	6.0
codeBase	The base URL for the applet	4.0	6.0
height	The height of the object in pixels	4.0	6.0
hspace	The horizontal margin to the left and the right of the applet	4.0	6.0
name	The name of the applet	4.0	3.0
object	The name of the resource that contains a serialized representation of the applet		
vspace	The vertical margin above and below the applet	4.0	6.0
width	The width of the object in pixels	4.0	6.0

JavaScript Elements	Description	IE	Netscape
Area	An area defined in an image map	3.0	3.0
Properties			
accessKey	The hotkey that gives the element focus	4.0	6.0
alt	Alternative text to the graphic	4.0	6.0
cords	Defines the coordinates of the object	6.0	6.0
hash	The anchor name from the URL	3.0	3.0
host	The host and domain names from the URL	3.0	3.0
hostname	The hostname from the URL	3.0	3.0
href	The entire URL	3.0	3.0
pathname	The pathname from the URL	3.0	3.0
port	The port number from the URL	3.0	3.0
protocol	The protocol from the URL	3.0	3.0
search	The query portion from the URL	3.0	3.0
shape	The shape of the object, for example, "default", "rect", "circle", or "poly"	4.0	6.0
tabIndex	Numeric value that indicates the tab order for the object	4.0	6.0
target	The target attribute of the \<area\> tag	3.0	3.0
Methods			
getSelection()	Returns the value of the current selection		3.0
Event Handlers			
onDblClick()	Runs when the area is double-clicked	4.0	4.0
onMouseOut()	Runs when the mouse leaves the area	3.0	3.0
onMouseOver()	Runs when the mouse enters the area	3.0	3.0
Array	An array object	3.0	3.0
Properties			
index	For an array created by a regular expression match, the zero-based index of the match in the string	5.5	4.0
input	Reflects the original string against which the regular expression was matched	5.5	4.0
length	The next empty index at the end of the array	4.0	3.0
prototype	A mechanism to add properties to an array object	3.0	3.0
Methods			
concat(*array*)	Combines two arrays and stores the result in a third array named *array*	4.0	4.0
join(*string*)	Stores each element in a text string named *string*	3.0	3.0
pop( )	"Pops" the last element of the array and reduces the length of the array by 1	5.5	4.0
push(*arg1, arg2, ...*)	"Pushes" the elements in the list to the end of the array and returns the new length	5.5	4.0
reverse( )	Reverses the order of the elements in the array	3.0	3.0
shift( )	Removes the first element from an array, returns that element, and shifts all other elements down one index	5.5	4.0
slice(*array, begin,end*)	Extracts a portion of the array, starting at the index number *begin* and ending at the index number *end*; the elements are then stored in *array*	4.0	4.0
sort(*function*)	Sorts the array based on the function named *function*; if *function* is omitted, the sort applies dictionary order to the array	3.0	3.0
splice(*start,howMany, [,item1[,item2 [,…]]]*)	Removes *howMany* elements from the array, beginning at index *start* and replaces the removed elements with the *itemN* arguments (if passed); returns an array of the deleted elements	5.5	4.0
toString( )	Returns a string of the comma-separated values of the array	4.0	3.0
unshift([Item1 [,item2[,…]]])	Inserts the items to the front of an array and returns the new length of the array	5.5	4.0

JavaScript Elements	Description	IE	Netscape
Button	A push button in an HTML form (use the button's name)	3.0	3.0
Properties			
accessKey	Indicates the hotkey that gives the element focus	4.0	6.0
align	Specifies the alignment of the element, for example, "right"	4.0	6.0
disabled	A Boolean indicating whether the element is disabled	4.0	6.0
enabled	Indicates whether the button has been enabled	3.0	4.0
form	The name of the form containing the button	3.0	4.0
name	The name of the button element	3.0	2.0
size	Indicates the width of the button in pixels	4.0	6.0
tabIndex	Indicates the tab order for the object	4.0	6.0
type	The value of the type attribute for the <button> tag	4.0	3.0
value	The value of the button element	3.0	2.0
Methods			
blur()	Removes focus from the button	3.0	3.0
click()	Emulates the action of clicking the button	3.0	2.0
focus()	Gives focus to the button	4.0	4.0
Event Handlers			
onBlur	Runs when the button loses the focus	3.0	3.0
onClick	Runs when the button is clicked	3.0	2.0
onFocus	Runs when the button receives the focus	4.0	4.0
onMouseDown	Runs when the mouse button is pressed	3.0	2.0
onMouseUp	Runs when the mouse button is released	3.0	2.0
Checkbox	A check box in an HTML form	3.0	2.0
Properties			
accessKey	Indicates the hotkey that gives the element focus	4.0	6.0
align	Specifies the alignment of the element, for example, "right"	4.0	6.0
checked	Indicates whether the check box is checked	3.0	2.0
defaultChecked	Indicates whether the check box is checked by default	3.0	2.0
disabled	Boolean indicating whether the element is disabled	4.0	6.0
enabled	Indicates whether the check box is enabled	3.0	4.0
form	The name of the form containing the check box	3.0	4.0
height	The height of the checkbox in pixels	5.0	
name	The name of the check box element	3.0	2.0
size	Indicates the width of the check box in pixels	4.0	6.0
status	Boolean indicating whether the check box is currently selected	4.0	
tabIndex	Indicates the tab order for the object	4.0	6.0
type	The value of the type attribute for the <input> tag	4.0	3.0
value	The value of the check box element	3.0	2.0
width	The width of the check box in pixels	5.0	
Methods			
blur()	Removes the focus from the check box	3.0	3.0
click()	Emulates the action of clicking on the check box	3.0	2.0
focus()	Gives focus to the check box	4.0	4.0
Event Handlers			
onBlur	Runs when the check box loses the focus	4.0	3.0
onClick	Runs when the check box is clicked		
onFocus	Runs when the check box receives the focus	4.0	4.0
Date	An object containing information about a specific date or the current date; dates are expressed either in local time or in UTC (Universal Time Coordinates), otherwise known as Greenwich Mean Time	3.0	2.0

JavaScript Elements	Description	IE	Netscape
Methods			
getDate()	Returns the day of the month, from 1 to 31	3.0	2.0
getDay()	Returns the day of the week, from 0 to 6 (Sunday = 0, Monday = 1, etc.)	3.0	2.0
getFullYear()	Returns the year portion of the date in four-digit format	4.0	4.0
getHours()	Returns the hour in military time, from 0 to 23	3.0	2.0
getMilliseconds()	Returns the number of milliseconds	4.0	4.0
getMinutes()	Returns the minute, from 0 to 59	3.0	2.0
getMonth()	Returns the value of the month, from 0 to 11 (January = 0, February = 1, etc.)	3.0	2.0
getSeconds()	Returns the seconds	3.0	2.0
getTime()	Returns the date as an integer representing the number of milliseconds since December 31, 1969, at 18:00:00	3.0	2.0
getTimezoneOffset()	Returns the difference between the local time and Greenwich Mean Time in minutes	3.0	2.0
getYear()	Deprecated. Returns the number of years since 1900; for example, 1996 is represented by '96'—this value method is inconsistently applied after the year 1999	3.0	2.0
getUTCDate()	Returns the UTC getDate() value	4.0	4.0
getUTCDay()	Returns the UTC getDay() value	4.0	4.0
getUTCFullYear()	Returns the UTC getFullYear() value	4.0	4.0
getUTCHours()	Returns the UTC getHours() value	4.0	4.0
getUTCMilliseconds()	Returns the UTC getMilliseconds() value	4.0	4.0
getUTCMinutes()	Returns the UTC getMinutes() value	4.0	4.0
getUTCMonth()	Returns the UTC getMonth() value	4.0	4.0
getUTCSeconds()	Returns the UTC getSeconds() value	4.0	4.0
getUTCTime()	Returns the UTC getTime() value	4.0	4.0
getUTCYear()	Returns the UTC getYear() value	4.0	4.0
setDate(*date*)	Sets the day of the month to the value specified in *date*	3.0	2.0
setFullYear(*year*)	Sets the year to the four-digit value specified in *year*	4.0	4.0
setHours(*hour*)	Sets the hour to the value specified in *hour*	3.0	2.0
setMilliseconds(*milliseconds*)	Sets the millisecond value to *milliseconds*	4.0	4.0
setMinutes(*minutes*)	Sets the minute to the value specified in *minutes*	3.0	2.0
setMonth(*month*)	Sets the month to the value specified in *month*	3.0	2.0
setSeconds(*seconds*)	Sets the second to the value specified in *seconds*	3.0	2.0
setTime(*time*)	Sets the time using the value specified in *time*, where *time* is a variable containing the number of milliseconds since December 31, 1969, at 18:00:00	3.0	2.0
setYear(*year*)	Sets the year to the value specified in *year*	3.0	2.0
toDateString()	Returns a date as a string value	5.5	
toLocaleDateString()	Returns a date as a string value	5.5	
toTimeString()	Returns a time as a string value	5.5	
toGMTString()	Converts the current date to a text string in Greenwich Mean Time	3.0	2.0
toLocaleString()	Converts a date object's date to a text string, using the date format the Web browser is set up to use	3.0	2.0
toSource	String representing the source code of the object		4.0
toString()	String representation of a Date object	4.0	2.0
toUTCString()	Date converted to string using UTC	4.0	4.0
UTC()	Milliseconds since December 31, 18:00:00, using UTC	3.0	2.0
UTC(*date*)	Returns *date* in the form of the number of milliseconds since December 31, 1969, at 18:00:00 for Universal Coordinated Time	3.0	2.0
setUTCDate(*date*)	Applies the setDate() method in UTC time	4.0	4.0

JavaScript Elements	Description	IE	Netscape
setUTCFullYear(*year*)	Applies the setFullYear() method in UTC time	4.0	4.0
setUTCHours(*hour*)	Applies the setHours() method in UTC time	4.0	4.0
setUTCMilliseconds (*milliseconds*)	Applies the setMilliseconds() method in UTC time	4.0	4.0
setUTCMinutes(*minutes*)	Applies the setMinutes() method in UTC time	4.0	4.0
setUTCMonth(*month*)	Applies the setMonth() method in UTC time	4.0	4.0
setUTCSeconds(*seconds*)	Applies the setSeconds() method in UTC time	4.0	4.0
setUTCTime(*time*)	Applies the setTime() method in UTC time	4.0	4.0
setUTCYear(*year*)	Applies the setYear() method in UTC time	4.0	4.0
`dir`	`A directory listing element in the document`	4.0	6.0
Properties			
compact	A Boolean indicating whether the listing should be compacted	6.0	6.0
`div`	`A <div> (block container) element in the document`	4.0	6.0
Properties			
align	Alignment of the element	4.0	6.0
`document`	`An HTML document (child of Window)`	3.0	2.0
Properties			
alinkColor	The color of active hypertext links in the document	3.0	2.0
all[ ]	An array of each of the HTML tags in the document	4.0	
anchors[ ]	An array of the anchors in the document	3.0	3.0
applets[ ]	An array of the applets in the document	3.0	3.0
attributes[ ]	A collection of attributes for the element		6.0
bgColor	The background color of the document	3.0	2.0
body	Reference to the <body> element object of the document	3.0	6.0
charset	A string containing the character set of the document	4.0	
characterSet	A string containing the character set of the document		6.0
childNodes[ ]	A collection of child nodes of the object	5.0	6.0
classes.*class.tag.style*	Deprecated; the *style* associated with the element in the document with the class name *class* and the tag name *tag*		4.0
cookie	A text string containing the document's cookie values	3.0	2.0
designMode	Specifies whether design mode is on or off	5.0	
dir	A string holding the text direction of text enclosed in the document	5.0	6.0
doctype	Reference to the DocumentType object for the document	6.0	6.0
documentElement	Reference to the root node of the document object hierarchy	5.0	6.0
domain	The domain of the document	4.0	3.0
embeds	An array of the embedded objects in the document	4.0	3.0
expando	A Boolean dictating whether instance properties can be added to the object	4.0	
fgColor	The text color used in the document	3.0	2.0
firstChild	Reference to the first child node of the element, if one exists	5.0	6.0
form	A form within the document (the form itself is also an object)	3.0	2.0
forms	An array of the forms in the document	3.0	2.0
ids.*id.tag.style*	Deprecated. The *style* associated with the element in the document with the id name *id* and the tag name *tag*		4.0
implementation	An object with method *hasFeature(feature, level)* that returns a Boolean indicating if the browser supports the feature given in the string *feature* at the DOM level passed in the string *level*	6.0	6.0
lastChild	Reference to the last child node of the element, if one exists	5.0	6.0
lastModified	The date the document was last modified	3.0	2.0
layers	An array of layer objects		4.0
linkColor	The color of hypertext links in the document	3.0	2.0
links	An array of the links within the document	3.0	2.0

JavaScript Elements	Description	IE	Netscape
localName	A string indicating the "local" XML name for the object		6.0
location	The URL of the document	3.0	2.0
media	The media for which the document is intended	5.5	
nextSibling	Reference to next sibling of the node		6.0
nodeName	A string containing the name of the node, the name of the tag to which the object corresponds		6.0
nodeValue	A string containing value within the node		6.0
ownerDocument	Reference to the document in which the element is contained		6.0
parentNode	Reference to the parent of the object		6.0
parentWindow	Reference to the window that contains the document		6.0
previousSibling	Reference to the previous sibling of the node		6.0
protocol	A string containing the protocol used to retrieve the document—its full name		4.0
referrer	The URL of the document containing the link that the user accessed to get to the current document	3.0	2.0
security	A string that contains information about the document's certificate		5.5
styleSheets[ ]	Collection of style sheets in the document	4.0	6.0
tags.*tag*.st*yle*	The *style* associated with the tag name *tag*		4.0
title	The title of the document	3.0	2.0
URL	The URL of the document	3.0	2.0
vlinkColor	The color of followed hypertext links	3.0	2.0
XMLDocument	Reference to the top-level node of the XML DOM exposed by the document	5.0	
XSLDocument	Reference to the top-level node of the XSL DOM exposed by the document	5.0	
Methods			
addEventListener (whichEvent, handler, direction)	Instructs the object to execute the function *handler* whenever an event of the type stated in *whichEvent* occurs; *direction* is a Boolean telling which phase to fire; use true for capture and false for bubbling		6.0
appendChild(newChild)	Appends *newChild* to the end of the node's childNodes[ ] list	5.0	6.0
attachEvent(whichHandler, theFunction)	Attaches the function *theFunction* as a handler specified by the string *whichHandler*	5.0	
clear()	Clears the contents of the document window	3.0	2.0
cloneNode(cloneChildren)	Clones the node and returns the new clone	5.0	6.0
close()	Closes the document stream	3.0	2.0
createAttribute(name)	Returns a new attribute node of a name given by string *name*	6.0	6.0
createComment(data)	Returns a new comment node with the text given by *data*	6.0	6.0
createElement(tagName)	Returns a new element object that corresponds to *tagName*	4.0	6.0
createEventObject ([eventObj])	Creates and returns a new Event instance to pass to *fireEvent()*	5.5	
createStyleSheet ([url [,index]])	Creates a new styleSheet object from the Stylesheet at the URL in the string *url* and inserts it into the document at index *index*	4.0	
createTextNode(data)	Returns a new text node with value given by *data*	5.0	6.0
detachEvent(whichHandler, theFunction)	Instructs the object to stop executing *theFunction* as a handler given the string *whichHandler*	5.0	
dispatchEvent(event)	Causes *event* to be processed by the appropriate handler; is used to redirect events		6.0
fireEvent(handler [, event])	Fires the event handler given by *handler*	5.5	
focus()	Gives focus to the document and fires *onfocus* handler	5.5	
getElementById(id)	Returns the element with *id* (or *name*) that is equal to *id*	5.0	6.0

JavaScript Elements	Description	IE	Netscape
getElementByName(name)	Gets a collection of elements with *id* (or *name*) that is equal to *name*	5.0	6.0
getElementByTagName (tagname)	Gets a collection of elements corresponding to *tagname*	5.0	6.0
getSelection()	Returns the selected text from the document		4.0
hasAttributes()	Returns a Boolean showing if any attributes are defined for the node		6.0
hasChildNodes()	Returns a Boolean showing if the node has children	5.0	6.0
insertBefore(newChild, refChild)	Inserts the node *newChild* in front of *refChild* in the *childNodes*[ ] list of *refChild*'s parent node	5.0	6.0
isSupported(feature [, version])	Returns a Boolean showing which feature and version identified in the arguments is supported		6.0
normalize()	Merges adjacent text nodes in the subtree rooted at this element	6.0	6.0
open()	Opens the document stream	3.0	2.0
recalc([forceAll])	If *forceAll* is *true*, all dynamic properties are reevaluated	5.0	
removeChild(oldChild)	Removes *oldChild* from the node's children and returns a reference to the removed node	5.0	6.0
removeEventListener (whichEvent, handler, direction)	Removes the function *handler* for the event declared in *whichEvent* for the phase stated in the Boolean *direction*		6.0
replaceChild(newChild, oldChild)	Replaces the node's child node *oldChild* with the node *newChild*	5.0	6.0
setActive()	Sets the document as the current element but does not give it focus	5.5	
write()	Writes to the document window	3.0	2.0
writeln()	Writes to the document window on a single line (used only with preformatted text)	3.0	2.0
Event Handlers			
onClick	Runs when the document is clicked	3.0	2.0
onDblClick	Runs when the document is double-clicked	3.0	2.0
onKeyDown	Runs when a key is pressed down	3.0	2.0
onKeyPress	Runs when a key is initially pressed	3.0	2.0
onKeyUp	Runs when a key is released	3.0	2.0
onLoad	Runs when the document is initially loaded	3.0	2.0
onMouseDown	Runs when the mouse button is pressed down	3.0	2.0
onMouseUp	Runs when the mouse button is released	3.0	2.0
onUnLoad	Runs when the document is unloaded	3.0	2.0
Error	This object gives information about the error that occurred during runtime	5.0	6.0
Properties			
description	Describes the nature of the error	5.0	6.0
lineNumber	The line number that generated the error	6.0	
number	The numeric value of the Microsoft-specific error number	5.0	
File, FileUpload	A file upload element in an HTML form (use the FileUpload box's name)	3.0	2.0
Properties			
accessKey	Indicates the hotkey that gives the element focus	4.0	6.0
disabled	A Boolean signifying if the element is disabled	4.0	6.0
form	The form object containing the FileUpload box	3.0	2.0
name	The name of the FileUpload box	3.0	2.0

JavaScript Elements	Description	IE	Netscape
size	The width in pixels	4.0	6.0
tabIndex	A numeric value of the width in pixels	4.0	6.0
type	The type attribute of the FileUpload box	3.0	2.0
value	The pathname of the selected file in the FileUpload box	2.0	3.0
Methods			
blur()	Removes the focus from the FileUpload box	4.0	3.0
focus()	Gives the focus to the FileUpload box	4.0	3.0
handleEvent(*event*)	Invokes the event handler for the specified *event*	4.0	3.0
select()	Selects the input area of the FileUpload box	3.0	2.0
Event Handlers			
onBlur	Runs when the focus leaves the FileUpload box	4.0	3.0
onChange	Runs when the value in the FileUpload box is changed	4.0	3.0
onFocus	Runs when the focus is given to the FileUpload box	4.0	3.0
Form	An HTML form (use the form's name)	3.0	2.0
Properties			
acceptCharset	Specifies a list of character encodings for input data to be accepted by the server processing the form	5.0	6.0
action	The location of the CGI script that receives the form values	3.0	2.0
autocomplete	Specifies whether form autocompletion is on or off	5.0	
elements[ ]	An array of elements within the form	3.0	2.0
encoding	The type of encoding used in the form	3.0	2.0
enctype	Specifies the MIME type of submitted data		6.0
length	The number of elements in the form	3.0	2.0
method	The type of method used when submitting the form	3.0	2.0
name	The name of the form	3.0	2.0
target	The name of the window into which CGI output should be directed	3.0	2.0
Methods			
handleEvent(*event*)	Invokes the event handler for the specified *event*	4.0	3.0
reset()	Resets the form	3.0	2.0
submit()	Submits the form to the CGI script	3.0	2.0
urns(*urn*)	Retrieves a collection of all elements to which the behavior of string *urn* is attached	5.0	
Event Handlers			
onReset	Runs when the form is reset	4.0	3.0
onSubmit	Runs when the form is submitted	3.0	2.0
Frame	A frame window (use the frame's name)	3.0	2.0
Properties			
document	The current document in the frame window	3.0	2.0
frames	An array of frames within the frame window	3.0	2.0
length	The length of the frames array	3.0	2.0
name	The name of the frame	3.0	2.0
parent	The name of the window that contains the frame	3.0	2.0
self	The name of the current frame window	3.0	2.0
top	The name of the topmost window in the hierarchy of frame windows	3.0	2.0
window	The name of the current frame window	3.0	2.0
Methods			
alert(*message*)	Displays an Alert box with the text string *message*	3.0	2.0
blur()	Removes the focus from the frame	4.0	3.0

JavaScript Elements	Description	IE	Netscape
clearInterval(*ID*)	Cancels the repeated execution *ID*	4.0	4.0
clearTimeout(*ID*)	Cancels the delayed execution *ID*	4.0	4.0
confirm(*message*)	Displays a Confirm box with the text string *message*	3.0	2.0
open(*URL, name, features*)	Opens a URL in the frame with the name *name* and a feature list indicated by *features*	3.0	2.0
print()	Displays the Print dialog box	4.0	4.0
prompt(*message, response*)	Displays a Prompt dialog box with the text string *message* and the default value *response*	3.0	2.0
setInterval(*expression, time*)	Runs an *expression* after *time* milliseconds	4.0	4.0
setTimeout(*expression, time*)	Runs an *expression* every *time* milliseconds	4.0	4.0
Event Handlers			
onBlur	Runs when the focus is removed from the frame	4.0	4.0
onFocus	Runs when the frame receives the focus	4.0	4.0
onMove	Runs when the frame is moved	4.0	4.0
onResize	Runs when the frame is resized	4.0	4.0
h1...h6	Heading level element in the document	4.0	6.0
Properties			
align	The alignment of the element, for example, "right"	4.0	6.0
head	Corresponds to the \<head\> element in the document	4.0	6.0
Properties			
profile	A list of the URLs for data properties and legal values	6.0	6.0
hidden	A hidden field on an HTML form (use the name of the hidden field)	3.0	2.0
Properties			
form	The name of the form containing the hidden field	3.0	2.0
name	The name of the hidden field	3.0	2.0
type	The type of the hidden field	4.0	3.0
value	The value of the hidden field	3.0	2.0
history	An object containing information about the Web browser's history list	3.0	2.0
Properties			
current	The current URL in the history list	4.0	3.0
length	The number of items in the history list	3.0	2.0
next	The next item in the history list	4.0	3.0
previous	The previous item in the history list	3.0	2.0
Methods			
back()	Navigates back to the previous item in the history list	3.0	2.0
forward()	Navigates forward to the next item in the history list	3.0	2.0
go(*location*)	Navigates to the item in the history list specified by the value of *location*; the *location* variable can be either an integer or the name of the Web page	3.0	2.0
hr	A horizontal rule element in the document	4.0	6.0
Properties			
align	Alignment of the object, for example, "right"	4.0	6.0
color	The color of the rule	4.0	
noShade	A Boolean indicating that the rule is not to be shaded	4.0	6.0
size	The size (height) of the rule in pixels	4.0	6.0
width	The width of the rule in pixels	4.0	6.0

JavaScript Elements	Description	IE	Netscape
html	Corresponds to the <html> element in the document	4.0	6.0
Properties			
version	The DTD version for the document	6.0	6.0
iframe	An inline frame element in the document	4.0	6.0
Properties			
align	The alignment of the object, for example, "right"	4.0	6.0
allowTransparency	A Boolean specifying whether the background of the frame can be transparent	5.0	
border	The width of the border around the frame	4.0	
contentDocument	The document that corresponds to the content of this frame		6.0
contentWindow	The window that corresponds to this frame	5.0	
frameBorder	String of "0" (no border) or "1" (show border)	4.0	6.0
height	The height of the frame in pixels	4.0	6.0
longdesc	The URL of a long description for the frame	6.0	6.0
marginHeight	Vertical margins in pixels	4.0	6.0
marginWidth	Horizontal margins in pixels	4.0	6.0
name	The name of the frame	4.0	6.0
width	The width of the frame in pixels	4.0	6.0
image	An inline image (use the name assigned to the image)	4.0	3.0
Properties			
align	Specifies the alignment of the object, for example, "left", "right", or "center"	4.0	6.0
alt	A string containing alternative text for the image	4.0	6.0
border	The width of the image border in pixels	4.0	3.0
complete	A Boolean value indicating whether the image has been completely loaded by the browser	4.0	3.0
height	The height of the image in pixels	4.0	3.0
hspace	The horizontal space around the image in pixels	4.0	3.0
isMap	A Boolean indicating whether the image is a server-side image map	4.0	6.0
longDesc	The URL for a more detailed description of the image	6.0	6.0
loop	An integer indicating how many times the image is to loop when activated	4.0	
lowSrc	Specifies a URL for a lower-resolution image to display		6.0
lowsrc	The value of the lowsrc property of the <img> tag	4.0	3.0
name	The name of the image	4.0	3.0
nameProp	Indicates the name of the file given in the *src* attribute of the <img>	5.0	
src	The URL of the image	4.0	3.0
style	Reference to the inline *Style* object for the element	4.0	4.0
useMap	Contains a URL to use as a client-side image map	4.0	6.0
vspace	The vertical space around the image in pixels	4.0	3.0
width	The width of the image in pixels	4.0	3.0
Methods			
handleEvent(*event*)	Invokes the event handler for the specified *event*	4.0	4.0
Event Handlers			
onAbort	Runs when the image load is aborted	4.0	3.0
onError	Runs when an error occurs while loading the image	4.0	3.0
onKeyDown	Runs when a key is pressed down	4.0	3.0
onKeyPress	Runs when a key is pressed	4.0	4.0
onKeyUp	Runs when a key is released	4.0	4.0
onLoad	Runs when the image is loaded	4.0	3.0

JavaScript Elements	Description	IE	Netscape
`implementation`	Information about the DOM technologies the browser supports (child of Document)	6.0	6.0
Methods			
hasFeature(feature [, version])	A Boolean indicating if the browser supports the feature at the DOM level given in version	6.0	6.0
`label`	A form field label in the document	4.0	6.0
Properties			
accessKey	Indicates the hotkey that gives the element focus	4.0	6.0
form	The form that encloses the label	4.0	6.0
`layer`	A document layer (use the name of the layer); deprecated in favor of the standard `<div>` element	4.0	
Properties			
above	The layer above the current layer		4.0
background	The background image of the layer		4.0
below	The layer below the current layer		4.0
bgColor	The background color of the layer		4.0
clip.bottom, clip.height, clip.left, clip.right, clip.top, clip.width	The size and position of the layer's clipping area		4.0
document	The document containing the layer		4.0
name	The value of the *name* or *id* attribute for the layer		4.0
left	The *x*-coordinate of the layer		4.0
pageX	The *x*-coordinate relative to the document		4.0
pageY	The *y*-coordinate relative to the document		4.0
parentLayer	The containing layer		4.0
siblingAbove	The layer above in the zIndex		4.0
siblingBelow	The layer below in the zIndex		4.0
src	The URL of the layer document		4.0
top	The *y*-coordinate of the layer		4.0
visibility	The state of the layer's visibility		4.0
zIndex	The zIndex value of the layer		4.0
Methods			
handleEvent(*event*)	Invokes the event handler for the specified *event*		4.0
load(*source, width*)	Loads a new URL into the layer from *source* with the specified *width*		4.0
moveAbove(*layer*)	Moves the layer above *layer*		4.0
moveBelow(*layer*)	Moves the layer below *layer*		4.0
moveBy(*x, y*)	Moves the *x* pixels in the *x*-direction, and the *y* pixels in the *y*-direction		4.0
moveTo(*x, y*)	Moves the upper-left corner of the layer to the specified (*x, y*) coordinate		4.0
moveToAbsolute(*x, y*)	Moves the layer to the specified coordinate (*x, y*) within the page		4.0
resizeBy(*width, height*)	Resizes the layer by the specified *width* and *height*		4.0
resizeTo(*width, height*)	Resizes the layer to the specified *height* and *width*		4.0
Event Handlers			
onBlur	Runs when the focus leaves the layer		4.0
onFocus	Runs when the layer receives the focus		4.0
onLoad	Runs when the layer is loaded		4.0
onMouseOut	Runs when the mouse leaves the layer		4.0
onMouseOver	Runs when the mouse hovers over the layer		4.0

JavaScript Elements	Description	IE	Netscape
`legend`	A `<legend>` (fieldset caption) element in the document	4.0	6.0
Properties			
accessKey	Indicates the hotkey	4.0	6.0
align	Specifies the alignment of the element, for example, "right"	4.0	6.0
form	The form in which the element is enclosed	4.0	6.0
`link`	A link within an HTML document (use the name of the link)	3.0	2.0
Properties			
accessKey	Indicates the hotkey that gives the element focus	4.0	6.0
charset	The character set of the linked document	6.0	6.0
coords	Defines the coordinates of the object	6.0	6.0
disabled	A Boolean indicating whether the element is disabled	4.0	6.0
hash	The anchor name from the link's URL	3.0	2.0
host	The host from the link's URL	3.0	2.0
hostname	The hostname from the link's URL	3.0	2.0
href	The link's URL	3.0	2.0
hreflang	Indicates the language code of the linked resource	6.0	6.0
media	The media the linked document is intended for		6.0
nameProp	Holds the filename portion of the URL in the *href*	5.0	
pathname	The path portion of the link's URL	3.0	2.0
port	The port number of the link's URL	3.0	2.0
protocol	The protocol used with the link's URL	3.0	2.0
search	The search portion of the link's URL	3.0	2.0
target	The target window of the hyperlinks	3.0	2.0
text	The text used to create the link	4.0	4.0
type	Specifies the media type in the form of a MIME type for the link target	6.0	6.0
Methods			
handleEvent(*event*)	Invokes the event handler for the specified *event*	4.0	4.0
Event Handlers			
onClick	Runs when the link is clicked	3.0	2.0
onDblClick	Runs when the link is double-clicked	4.0	4.0
onKeyDown	Runs when a key is pressed down	4.0	4.0
onKeyPress	Runs when a key is initially pressed	4.0	4.0
onKeyUp	Runs when a key is released	4.0	4.0
onMouseDown	Runs when the mouse button is pressed down on the link	4.0	4.0
onMouseOut	Runs when mouse moves away from the link	4.0	4.0
onMouseOver	Runs when the mouse hovers over the link	4.0	4.0
onMouseUp	Runs when the mouse button is released	4.0	4.0
`location`	The location of the document	3.0	2.0
Properties			
hash	The location's anchor name	3.0	2.0
host	The location's hostname and port number	3.0	2.0
href	The location's URL	3.0	2.0
pathname	The path portion of the location's URL	3.0	2.0
port	The port number of the location's URL	3.0	2.0
protocol	The protocol used with the location's URL	3.0	2.0
Methods			
Assign(*url*)	Assigns the URL in the string *url* to the object	3.0	2.0
reload()	Reloads the location	4.0	3.0
replace(*url*)	Loads a new location with the address *url*	4.0	3.0

JavaScript Elements	Description	IE	Netscape
map	Corresponds to a `<map>` (client-side image map) element in the document	4.0	6.0
Properties			
Areas[ ]	A collection of *areas* enclosed by the object	4.0	6.0
Name	String holding the name of the image map	4.0	6.0
Math	An object used for advanced mathematical calculations	3.0	2.0
Properties			
E	The value of the base of natural logarithms (2.7182...)	3.0	2.0
LN10	The value of the natural logarithm of 10	3.0	2.0
LN2	The value of the natural logarithm of 2	3.0	2.0
LOG10E	The base 10 logarithm of E	3.0	2.0
LOG2E	The base 2 logarithm of E	3.0	2.0
PI	The value of pi (3.1416...)	3.0	2.0
SQRT1_2	The square root of ½	3.0	2.0
SQRT2	The square root of 2	3.0	2.0
Methods			
abs(*number*)	Returns the absolute value of *number*	3.0	2.0
acos(*number*)	Returns the arc cosine of *number* in radians	3.0	2.0
asin(*number*)	Returns the arc sine of *number* in radians	3.0	2.0
atan(*number*)	Returns the arc tangent of *number* in radians	3.0	2.0
atan2()	Returns the arc tangent of the quotient of its arguments	3.0	2.0
ceil(*number*)	Rounds *number* up to the next-highest integer	3.0	2.0
cos(*number*)	Returns the cosine of *number*, where *number* is an angle expressed in radians	3.0	2.0
exp(*number*)	Raises the value of E (2.7182...) to the value of *number*	3.0	2.0
floor(*number*)	Rounds *number* down to the next-lowest integer	3.0	2.0
log(*number*)	Returns the natural logarithm of *number*	3.0	2.0
max(*number1, number2*)	Returns the greater of *number1* and *number2*	3.0	2.0
min(*number1, number2*)	Returns the lesser of *number1* and *number2*	3.0	2.0
pow(*number1, number2*)	Returns the value of *number1* raised to the power of *number2*	3.0	2.0
random()	Returns a random number between 0 and 1	3.0	2.0
round(*number*)	Rounds *number* to the closest integer	3.0	2.0
sin(*number*)	Returns the sine of *number*, where *number* is an angle expressed in radians	3.0	2.0
sqrt(*number*)	Returns the square root of *number*	3.0	2.0
tan(*number*)	Returns the tangent of *number*, where *number* is an angle expressed in radians	3.0	2.0
toString(*number*)	Converts *number* to a text string	3.0	2.0
menu	A `<menu>` (menu list) element in the document	4.0	6.0
Properties			
compact	A Boolean signifying whether the list should be compacted	6.0	6.0
navigator	An object representing the browser currently in use	3.0	2.0
Properties			
appCodeName	The code name of the browser	3.0	2.0
appName	The name of the browser	3.0	2.0
appVersion	The version of the browser	3.0	2.0
cookieEnabled	A Boolean signifying whether persistent cookies are enabled	4.0	6.0
language	The language of the browser	4.0	4.0
mimeTypes	An array of the MIME types supported by the browser	4.0	4.0
oscpu	A string containing the operating system		6.0
platform	The platform on which the browser is running	4.0	4.0

JavaScript Elements	Description	IE	Netscape
plugins	An array of the plug-ins installed on the browser	4.0	3.0
preference	Allows a signed script to get and set certain Navigator preferences		4.0
userAgent	The user-agent text string sent from the client to the Web server	3.0	2.0
Methods			
javaEnabled()	Indicates whether the browser supports Java	4.0	3.0
plugins.refresh()	Checks for newly installed plug-ins	4.0	3.0
taintEnabled()	Specifies whether data tainting is enabled	5.5	3.0
`Option`	An option from a selection list (use the name of the option or the index value from the options array)	3.0	2.0
Properties			
defaultSelected	A Boolean indicating whether the option is selected by default	4.0	3.0
disabled	A Boolean indicating whether the element is disabled	4.0	6.0
index	The index value of the option	3.0	2.0
label	Alternate text for the option as specified in the *label* attribute		6.0
selected	A Boolean indicating whether the option is currently selected	3.0	2.0
text	The text of the option as it appears on the Web page	3.0	2.0
value	The value of the option	3.0	2.0
`param`	Corresponds to an occurrence of a <param> element in the document	4.0	6.0
Properties			
name	The name of the parameter	4.0	6.0
type	The type of the value when *valueType* is "ref"	6.0	6.0
value	The value of the parameter	6.0	6.0
valueType	Provides more information about how to interpret value; usually "data", "ref", or "object"	6.0	6.0
`Password`	A password field in an HTML form (use the name of the password field)	3.0	2.0
Properties			
defaultValue	The default password	3.0	2.0
name	The name of the password field	3.0	2.0
type	The type value of the password field	3.0	2.0
value	The value of the password field	3.0	2.0
Methods			
focus()	Gives the password field the focus	3.0	2.0
blur()	Leaves the password field	3.0	2.0
select()	Selects the password field	3.0	2.0
Event Handlers			
onBlur	Runs when the focus leaves the password field	3.0	2.0
onFocus	Runs when the password field receives the focus	3.0	2.0
`plugin`	A plug-in object in the Web page	4.0	3.0
Properties			
description	The description of the plug-in	4.0	3.0
filename	The plug-in filename	4.0	3.0
length	The number of MIME types supported by the plug-in	4.0	3.0
name	The name of the plug-in	4.0	3.0
`popup`	A popup window object created by using the createPopup() method in IE	5.5	
Properties			
document	Reference to the window's document	5.5	
isOpen	A Boolean indicating if the window is open	5.5	

JavaScript Elements	Description	IE	Netscape
Radio	A radio button in an HTML form (use the radio button's name)	3.0	2.0
Properties			
accessKey	Indicates the hotkey that gives the element focus	4.0	6.0
align	A string specifying the alignment of the element, for example, "right"	4.0	6.0
alt	Alternative text for the button		6.0
checked	A Boolean indicating whether a specific radio button has been checked	3.0	2.0
defaultChecked	A Boolean indicating whether a specific radio button is checked by default	3.0	2.0
defaultValue	The initial value of the button's *value* attribute	3.0	6.0
disabled	A Boolean indicating whether the element is disabled	4.0	6.0
form	The name of the form containing the radio button	3.0	2.0
name	The name of the radio button	3.0	2.0
type	The type value of the radio button	4.0	3.0
value	The value of the radio button	3.0	2.0
Methods			
blur()	Gives the radio button the focus	3.0	2.0
click()	Clicks the radio button	3.0	2.0
focus()	Gives focus to the radio button	3.0	2.0
handleEvent(*event*)	Invokes the event handler for the specified *event*	4.0	4.0
Event Handlers			
onBlur	Runs when the focus leaves the radio button	3.0	2.0
onClick	Runs when the radio button is clicked	3.0	2.0
onFocus	Runs when the radio button receives the focus	3.0	2.0
RegExp	An object used for searching regular expressions	4.0	4.0
Properties			
global	Specifies whether to use a global pattern match	4.0	4.0
ignoreCase	Specifies whether to ignore case in the search string	4.0	4.0
input	The search string	4.0	4.0
lastIndex	Specifies the index at which to start matching the next string	4.0	4.0
lastMatch	The last matched characters	4.0	4.0
lastParen	The last parenthesized substring match	4.0	4.0
leftContext	The substring preceding the most recent match	4.0	4.0
multiline	Specifies whether to search on multiple lines	4.0	4.0
rightContext	The substring following the most recent match	4.0	4.0
source	The string pattern	4.0	4.0
Methods			
compile()	Compiles a regular search expression	4.0	4.0
exec(*string*)	Executes the search for a match to *string*	4.0	4.0
test(*string*)	Tests for a match to *string*	4.0	4.0
Reset	A reset button in an HTML form (use the name of the reset button)	3.0	2.0
Properties			
accessKey	Indicates the hotkey that gives the element focus	4.0	6.0
align	Specifies the alignment of the element, for example, "right"	4.0	6.0
alt	Alternative text for the button		6.0
defaultValue	Contains the initial value of the button	3.0	6.0
disabled	A Boolean indicating whether the element is disabled	4.0	6.0
form	The name of the form containing the reset button	3.0	2.0

JavaScript Elements	Description	IE	Netscape
name	The name of the reset button	3.0	2.0
type	The type value of the reset button	4.0	3.0
value	The value of the reset button	3.0	2.0
Methods			
blur()	Removes the focus from the reset button	3.0	2.0
click()	Clicks the reset button	3.0	2.0
focus()	Gives the focus to the reset button	3.0	2.0
handleEvent(*event*)	Invokes the event handler for the specified *event*	4.0	4.0
Event Handlers			
onBlur	Runs when the focus leaves the reset button	3.0	2.0
onClick	Runs when the reset button is clicked	3.0	2.0
onFocus	Runs when the reset button receives the focus	3.0	2.0
screen	An object representing the user's screen	4.0	4.0
Properties			
availHeight	The height of the screen, minus toolbars or any other permanent objects	4.0	4.0
availWidth	The width of the screen, minus toolbars or any other permanent objects	4.0	4.0
colorDepth	The number of possible colors in the screen	4.0	4.0
height	The height of the screen	4.0	4.0
pixelDepth	The number of bits per pixel in the screen	5.0	4.0
width	The width of the screen	4.0	4.0
Script	Corresponds to a `<script>` element in the document	4.0	6.0
Properties			
charset	The character set used to encode the script	6.0	6.0
defer	A Boolean indicating whether script execution may be deferred	4.0	6.0
src	The URL of the external script	4.0	6.0
text	The contents of the script	4.0	6.0
type	The value of the type attribute	4.0	6.0
Select	A selection list in an HTML form (use the name of the selection list)	3.0	2.0
Properties			
disabled	A Boolean indicating whether the element is disabled	4.0	6.0
form	The name of the form containing the selection list	3.0	2.0
length	The number of *options* in the selection list	3.0	2.0
multiple	A Boolean indicating whether multiple *options* may be selected	4.0	6.0
name	The name of the selection list	3.0	2.0
options[ ]	An array of options within the selection list; see the options object for more information on working with individual selection list options	3.0	2.0
selectedIndex	The index value of the selected option from the selection list	3.0	2.0
size	The number of options that are visible at one time	4.0	6.0
tabIndex	Numeric value that indicates the tab order for the object	4.0	6.0
type	The type value of the selection list	4.0	3.0
value	The *value* of the currently selected option	4.0	6.0
Methods			
add(element, before)	Adds the *option* referenced by the *element* to the list of options before the *option* referenced by *before*; if *before* is null, it is added at the end	5.5	6.0
blur()	Removes the focus from the selection list	3.0	2.0

JavaScript Elements	Description	IE	Netscape
focus()	Gives the focus to the selection list	3.0	2.0
handleEvent(*event*)	Invokes the event handler for the specified *event*	4.0	4.0
remove(index)	Removes the option at index *index* from the list of *options*	5.5	6.0
Event Handlers			
onBlur	Runs when the focus leaves the selection list	3.0	2.0
onChange	Runs when focus leaves the selection list and the value of the selection list is changed	3.0	2.0
onFocus	Runs when the selection list receives the focus	3.0	2.0
`String`	`An object representing a text string`	3.0	2.0
Properties			
length	The number of characters in the string	3.0	2.0
Methods			
anchor(*name*)	Converts the string into a hypertext link anchor with the name *name*	3.0	2.0
big()	Displays the string using the <big> tag	3.0	2.0
blink()	Displays the string using the <blink> tag	3.0	2.0
bold()	Displays the string using the <b> tag	3.0	2.0
charAt(*index*)	Returns the character in the string at the location specified by *index*	3.0	2.0
charCodeAt(position)	Returns an unsigned integer of the Unicode value of the character at index *position*	5.5	4.0
concat(*string2*)	Concatenates the string with the second text string *string2*	4.0	4.0
fixed()	Displays the string using the <tt> tag	3.0	2.0
fontColor(*color*)	Sets the color attribute of the string	3.0	2.0
fontSize(*value*)	Sets the size attribute of the string	3.0	2.0
indexOf(*string, start*)	Searches the string, beginning at the *start* character, and returns the index value of the first occurrence of the string *string*	3.0	2.0
italics()	Displays the string using the <i> tag	3.0	2.0
lastIndexOf(*string, start*)	Searches the string, beginning at the *start* character, and locates the index value of the last occurrence of the string *string*	3.0	2.0
link(*href*)	Converts the string into a hypertext link pointing to the URL *href*	3.0	2.0
match(*expression*)	Returns an array containing the matches based on the regular expression *expression*	4.0	4.0
replace(*expression, new*)	Performs a search based on the regular expression *expression* and replaces the text with *new*	4.0	4.0
search(*expression*)	Performs a search based on the regular expression *expression* and returns the index number	4.0	4.0
slice(*begin, end*)	Returns a substring between the *begin* and the *end* index values; the *end* index value is optional	4.0	4.0
small()	Displays the string using the <small> tag	3.0	2.0
split(*separator*)	Splits the string into an array of strings at every occurrence of the *separator* character	4.0	4.0
strike()	Displays the string using the <strike> tag	3.0	2.0
sub()	Displays the string using the <sub> tag	3.0	2.0
substr(*begin, length*)	Returns a substring starting at the *begin* index value and continuing for *length* characters; the *length* parameter is optional	4.0	4.0
substring(*begin, end*)	Returns a substring between the *begin* and the *end* index values; the *end* index value is optional	3.0	2.0
sup()	Displays the string using the <sup> tag	3.0	2.0
toLowerCase()	Converts the string to lowercase	3.0	2.0
toUpperCase()	Converts the string to uppercase	3.0	2.0

JavaScript Elements	Description	IE	Netscape
`style`	This corresponds to an instance of a `<style>` element in the page	4.0	6.0
Properties			
disabled	A Boolean indicating whether the element is disabled	4.0	6.0
sheet	The styleSheet object corresponding to the element		6.0
styleSheet	The styleSheet object corresponding to the element	4.0	
type	The value of the *type* attribute for the style sheet	4.0	6.0
`Submit`	A submit button in an HTML form (use the name of the submit button)	3.0	2.0
Properties			
accessKey	String indicating the hotkey that gives the element focus	4.0	6.0
alt	Alternative text for the button	6.0	
defaultValue	The initial value of the button's *value* attribute	3.0	6.0
disabled	A Boolean indicating whether the element is disabled	4.0	6.0
form	The name of the form containing the submit button	3.0	2.0
name	The name of the submit button	3.0	2.0
tabIndex	Numeric value that indicates the tab order for the object	4.0	6.0
type	The type value of the submit button	4.0	3.0
value	The value of the submit button	3.0	2.0
Methods			
blur()	Removes the focus from the submit button	3.0	2.0
click()	Clicks the submit button	3.0	2.0
focus()	Gives the focus to the submit button	3.0	2.0
handleEvent(*event*)	Invokes the event handler for the specified *event*	4.0	4.0
Event Handlers			
onBlur	Runs when the focus leaves the submit button	3.0	2.0
onClick	Runs when the submit button is clicked	3.0	2.0
onFocus	Runs when the submit button receives the focus	3.0	2.0
`Text`	An input box from an HTML form (use the name of the input box)	3.0	2.0
Properties			
accessKey	A string indicating the hotkey that gives the element focus	4.0	6.0
defaultValue	The default value of the input box	3.0	2.0
disabled	A Boolean indicating whether the element is disabled	4.0	6.0
form	The form containing the input box	3.0	2.0
maxLength	The maximum number of characters the field can contain	4.0	6.0
name	The name of the input box	3.0	2.0
size	The width of the field in characters	4.0	6.0
tabIndex	The numeric value that indicates the tab order for the object	4.0	6.0
type	The type value of the input box	4.0	3.0
value	The value of the input box	3.0	2.0
Methods			
blur()	Removes the focus from the input box	3.0	2.0
focus()	Gives the focus to the input box	3.0	2.0
handleEvent(*event*)	Invokes the event handler for the specified *event*	4.0	4.0
select()	Selects the input box	3.0	2.0
Event Handlers			
onBlur	Runs when the focus leaves the input box	3.0	2.0
onChange	Runs when the focus leaves the input box and the input box value changes	3.0	2.0

JavaScript Elements	Description	IE	Netscape
onFocus	Runs when the input box receives the focus	3.0	2.0
onSelect	Runs when some of the text in the input box is selected	3.0	2.0
Textarea	A text area box in an HTML form (use the name of the text area box)	3.0	2.0
Properties			
accessKey	Indicates the hotkey that gives the element focus	4.0	6.0
cols	The number of columns of the input area	4.0	6.0
defaultValue	The default value of the text area box	3.0	2.0
enabled	Indicates whether a text area field is enabled using a Boolean	3.0	3.0
form	The form containing the text area box	3.0	2.0
name	The name of the text area box	3.0	2.0
rows	The number of rows of the input area	4.0	6.0
tabIndex	Numeric value that indicates the tab order for the object	4.0	6.0
type	The type value of the text area box	4.0	3.0
value	The value of the text area box	3.0	2.0
Methods			
blur()	Removes the focus from the text area box	3.0	2.0
focus()	Gives the focus to the text area box	3.0	2.0
handleEvent(*event*)	Invokes the event handler for the specified *event*	4.0	4.0
select()	Selects the text area box	3.0	2.0
Event Handlers			
onBlur	Runs when the focus leaves the text area box	3.0	2.0
onChange	Runs when the focus leaves the text area box and the text area box value changes	3.0	2.0
onFocus	Runs when the text area box receives the focus	3.0	2.0
onKeyDown	Runs when a key is pressed down	4.0	4.0
onKeyPress	Runs when a key is pressed	4.0	4.0
onKeyUp	Runs when a key is released	4.0	4.0
onSelect	Runs when some of the text in the text area box is selected	3.0	2.0
window	The document window	3.0	2.0
Properties			
clipboardData	Provides access to the OS's clipboard	5.0	
defaultStatus	The default message shown in the window's status bar	3.0	2.0
directories	A Boolean specifying whether the Netscape 6 "directories" button is visible.		6.0
document	The document displayed in the window	3.0	2.0
frameElement	The *Frame* in which the window is enclosed	5.5	
frames	An array of frames within the window (see the frames object for properties and methods applied to individual frames)	3.0	2.0
history	A list of visited URLs	4.0	3.0
innerHeight	The height of the window's display area	4.0	4.0
innerWidth	The width of the widow's display area	4.0	4.0
length	The number of frames in the window	3.0	2.0
location	The URL loaded into the window	3.0	2.0
locationbar.visible	A Boolean indicating the visibility of the window's location bar	4.0	4.0
menubar.visible	A Boolean indicating the visibility of the window's menu bar	4.0	4.0
name	The name of the window	3.0	2.0
opener	The name of the window that opened the current window	4.0	3.0
outerHeight	The height of the outer area of the window	4.0	4.0
outerWidth	The width of the outer area of the window	4.0	4.0
pageXOffset	The *x*-coordinate of the window	4.0	4.0

JavaScript Elements	Description	IE	Netscape
pageYOffset	The *y*-coordinate of the window	4.0	4.0
parent	The name of the window containing this particular window	3.0	2.0
personalbar.visible	A Boolean indicating the visibility of the window's personal bar	4.0	4.0
screen	The browser's *screen* object	4.0	6.0
screenLeft	The *x*-coordinate in pixels of the left edge of the client area of the browser window	5.0	
screenTop	The *y*-coordinate in pixels of the top edge of the client area of the browser window	5.0	
scrollbars.visible	A Boolean indicating the visibility of the window's scroll bars	4.0	4.0
scrollX	How far the window is scrolled to the right		6.0
scrollY	How far the window is scrolled down		6.0
self	The current window	3.0	2.0
status	The message shown in the window's status bar	3.0	2.0
statusbar.visible	A Boolean indicating the visibility of the window's status bar	4.0	4.0
toolbar.visible	A Boolean indicating the visibility of the window's toolbar	4.0	4.0
top	The name of the topmost window in a hierarchy of windows	3.0	2.0
window	The current window	3.0	2.0
Methods			
alert(*message*)	Displays the text contained in *message* in a dialog box	3.0	2.0
back()	Loads the previous page in the window	4.0	4.0
blur()	Removes the focus from the window	4.0	3.0
captureEvents()	Sets the window to capture all events of a specified type	4.0	4.0
clearInterval(*ID*)	Clears the interval for *ID*, set with the SetInterval method	4.0	4.0
clearTimeout()	Clears the timeout, set with the setTimeout method	3.0	2.0
close()	Closes the window	3.0	2.0
confirm(*message*)	Displays a confirmation dialog box with the text *message*	3.0	2.0
createPopup(*arg*)	Creates a popup window and returns a reference to the new popup object	5.5	
disableExternalCapture	Disables external event capturing	4.0	4.0
enableExternalCapture	Enables external event capturing	4.0	4.0
find(*string, case, direction*)	Displays a Find dialog box, where *string* is the text to find in the window, *case* is a Boolean indicating whether the find is case-sensitive, and *direction* is a Boolean indicating whether the find goes in the backward direction (all of the parameters are optional)	4.0	4.0
focus()	Gives focus to the window	4.0	3.0
forward()	Loads the next page in the window	4.0	4.0
handleEvent(*event*)	Invokes the event handler for the specified *event*	4.0	4.0
moveBy(*horizontal, vertical*)	Moves the window by the specified amount in the *horizontal* and *vertical* directions	4.0	4.0
moveTo(*x, y*)	Moves the window to the *x*- and *y*-coordinates	4.0	4.0
open()	Opens the window	3.0	2.0
print()	Displays the Print dialog box	4.0	4.0
prompt(*message, default_text*)	Displays a Prompt dialog box with the text *message* (the default message is: *default_text*)	3.0	2.0
releaseEvents(*event*)	Releases the captured events of a specified *event*	4.0	4.0
resizeBy(*horizontal, vertical*)	Resizes the window by the amount in the *horizontal* and *vertical* directions	4.0	4.0
resizeTo(*width, height*)	Resizes the window to the specified *width* and *height*	4.0	4.0
routeEvent(*event*)	Passes the *event* to be handled natively	4.0	4.0
scroll(*x, y*)	Scrolls the window to the *x, y* coordinate	4.0	3.0

JavaScript Elements	Description	IE	Netscape
scrollBy(x, y)	Scrolls the window by x pixels in the x-direction and y pixels in the y-direction	4.0	4.0
scrollTo(x, y)	Scrolls the window to the x, y coordinate	4.0	4.0
setActive( )	Sets the window to be active but does not give it focus	5.5	
setCursor(type)	Changes the cursor to type		6.0
setInterval(expression, time)	Evaluates the expression every time milliseconds have passed	4.0	4.0
setTimeout(expression, time)	Evaluates the expression after time milliseconds have passed	3.0	2.0
sizeToContent( )	Resizes the window so all contents are visible		6.0
stop()	Stops the windows from loading	4.0	4.0
Event Handlers			
onBlur	Runs when the window loses the focus	4.0	3.0
onDragDrop	Runs when the user drops an object on or within the window	4.0	4.0
onError	Runs when an error occurs while loading the page	4.0	3.0
onFocus	Runs when the window receives the focus	4.0	3.0
onLoad	Runs when the window finishes loading	3.0	2.0
onMove	Runs when the window is moved	4.0	4.0
onResize	Runs when the window is resized	4.0	4.0
onUnload	Runs when the window is unloaded	3.0	2.0

JavaScript

Operators, Keywords, and Syntactical Elements

The following table lists some of the important JavaScript operators, keywords, and syntactical elements. It also identifies their compatibility with Microsoft Internet Explorer and Netscape browsers.

Operators	Description	IE	Netscape
Assignment	**Operators used to assign values to variables**		
=	Assigns the value of the variable on the right to the variable on the left ($x = y$)	3.0	2.0
+=	Adds the two variables and assigns the result to the variable on the left ($x += y$ is equivalent to $x = x + y$)	3.0	2.0
-=	Subtracts the variable on the right from the variable on the left and assigns the result to the variable on the left ($x - = y$ is equivalent to $x = x - y$)	3.0	2.0
*=	Multiplies the two variables together and assigns the result to the variable on the left ($x *= y$ is equivalent to $x = x * y$)	3.0	2.0
/=	Divides the variable on the left by the variable on the right and assigns the result to the variable on the left ($x /= y$ is equivalent to $x = x / y$)	3.0	2.0
&=	Combines two expressions into a single expression ($x \&= y$ is equivalent to $x = x \& y$)	3.0	2.0
%=	Divides the variable on the left by the variable on the right and assigns the remainder to the variable on the left ($x \%= y$ is equivalent to $x = x \% y$)	3.0	2.0
Arithmetic	**Operators used for arithmetic functions**		
+	Adds two variables together ($x + y$)	3.0	2.0
-	Subtracts the variable on the right from the variable on the left ($x - y$)	3.0	2.0
*	Multiplies two variables together ($x * y$)	3.0	2.0
/	Divides the variable the left by the variable on the right (x / y)		
%	Calculates the remainder after dividing the variable on the left by the variable on the right ($x \% y$)	3.0	2.0
++	Increases the value of a variable by 1 ($x ++$ is equivalent to $x = x + 1$)	3.0	2.0
&	Combines two expressions ($x \& y$)	3.0	2.0

Operators	Description	IE	Netscape
Arithmetic	**Operators used for arithmetic functions**		
--	Decreases the value of variable by 1 (x -- is equivalent to $x = x - 1$)	3.0	2.0
-	Changes the sign of a variable (- x)	3.0	2.0
Comparison	**Operators used for comparing expressions**		
==	Returns true when the two expressions are equal ($x == y$)	3.0	2.0
!=	Returns true when the two expressions are not equal ($x != y$)	3.0	2.0
!==	Returns true when the values of the two expressions are equal ($x !== y$)	5.0	5.0
>	Returns true when the expression on the left is greater than the expression on the right ($x > y$)	3.0	2.0
<	Returns true when the expression on the left is less than the expression on the right ($x < y$)	3.0	2.0
>=	Returns true when the expression on the left is greater than or equal to the expression on the right ($x >= y$)	3.0	2.0
<=	Returns true when the expression on the left is less than or equal to the expression on the right ($x <= y$)	3.0	2.0
Conditional	**Operators used to determine values based on conditions that are either true or false**		
(condition) ? value1 : value2	If *condition* is true, then this expression equals *value1*, otherwise it equals *value2*		
Keywords	**JavaScript keywords are reserved by JavaScript**		
infinity	Represents positive infinity (often used with comparison operators)	5.0	4.0
this	Refers to the current object	3.0	2.0
var	Declares a variable	3.0	2.0
with	Allows the declaration of all the properties for an object without directly referencing the object each time	3.0	2.0
Logical	**Operators used for evaluating true and false expressions**		
^	The XOR (exclusive OR) operator	3.0	2.0
!	Reverses the Boolean value of the expression	3.0	2.0
&&	Returns true only if both expressions are true (also known as an AND operator)		
||	Returns true when either expression is true (also known as an OR operator)	3.0	2.0
|	Returns true if the expression is false and false if the expression is true (also known as a NEGATION operator)	3.0	2.0
Syntax	**Syntactical elements**		
;	Indicates the end of a command line	3.0	2.0
/* comments */	Used for inserting *comments* within a JavaScript command line	3.0	2.0
// comments	Used to create a line of *comments*	3.0	2.0

Creating Dynamic Web Pages with Netscape 4

As JavaScript and browsers have evolved, their ability to create dynamic Web pages has also evolved. Currently, most browsers strive to match the most recent standards of HTML, XHTML, and the JavaScript language. Earlier browser versions are less successful in this regard, however. Thus, programmers must decide how compatible the Web page code they write will be with earlier browsers.

One of the landmark browser releases was Netscape version 4.0 (and later version 4.7). In this version, Netscape added support for several dynamic features, including the first model for handling events and event objects, an element for storing dynamic content, and methods for working with dynamic styles. Many of Netscape 4's features were either part of the current JavaScript and DHTML standards, or they were later adopted into the working standard. However, several features of this browser version were not adopted by the wider browser community. This forced Netscape to decide whether to continue to support the dynamic features unique to Netscape 4 in version 6.0 of their browser, or to drop those features, supporting only the current standard. In order to build a more efficient and compact browser engine, Netscape 6 and more recent releases, do not support the dynamic features of Netscape 4.

Thus, even though both Netscape 4 and more recent versions of the Netscape browser share the same name, you need to treat them as entirely different browsers when creating dynamic Web pages and working with JavaScript. Because Netscape 4 was widely used when it was first released and is still used in some areas today, it is worthwhile to explore the features of this browser version.

Working with Layers

One of the chief innovations in Netscape 4 was the introduction of the layer element. The **layer element** was designed to store content in a generic block-level element, similar to the div element. The general syntax of the layer element is

```
<layer id="id" attributes>
    content
</layer>
```

where *id* is the id of the layer, *attributes* is a list of HTML attributes that define the appearance, behavior, and placement of the layer, and *content* is the content contained within the layer. This content can contain text, inline images, and so forth. For example, the following layer element contains content for a page's heading:

```
<layer id="heading">
    <h1>Pixal Products</h1>
    <p>Quality digital cameras and peripherals</p>
</layer>
```

Setting the Layer Size

Figure E-1 describes some of the major attributes associated with the layer element.

Figure E-1 ▶ **Attributes of the layer element**

Attribute	Description
clip="*top, left, bottom, right*"	Specifies the coordinates of the viewable region of the layer
height="*value*"	Specifies the height of the layer, in pixels
left="*value*"	Specifies the horizontal offset of the layer, in pixels
pagex="*value*"	Specifies the horizontal position of the layer
pagey="*value*"	Specifies the vertical position of the layer
src="*url*"	Specifies the URL of the document displayed in the layer
top="*value*"	Specifies the vertical offset of the layer, in pixels
visibility="*option*"(hide | inherit | show)	Specifies whether the layer is hidden, shown, or inherits its visibility from the layer that contains it
width="*value*"	Specifies the width of the layer, in pixels
z-index="*value*"	Specifies the stacking order of the layer, relative to the other layers

For example, the code

```
<layer id="heading" width="200" height="150">
    <h1>Pixal Products</h1>
    <p>Quality digital cameras and peripherals</p>
</layer>
```

places the heading layer in a block that is 200 pixels wide by 150 pixels high. If there is more content than can be fit into the specified width and height, Netscape 4 increases the height of the layer to compensate. If you need to keep a layer to specified dimensions regardless of content, you add the clip property to the layer element using the syntax

```
<layer id="id" clip="top, left, bottom, right">
    content
</layer>
```

where *top*, *left*, *bottom*, and *right* are the coordinates for the clipping region within the layer. To fix the heading layer at a width of 300 pixels and a height of 100 pixels, you would use the attributes

```
<layer id="heading" width="300" height="150" clip="0,0,300,100">
```

If the content exceeds the dimensions of the layer, Netscape 4 truncates the excess content.

Displaying an External Document in a Layer

The layer element differs from the div element in its ability to display content from external documents. In that sense, layer elements act like inline frames. The syntax to link a layer to an external document is

```
<layer id="id" src="url"></layer>
```

where *url* is the URL of the external file. For example, to display the contents of the heading.htm file in the heading layer, you would use the following code:

```
<layer id="heading" src="heading.htm"></layer>
```

As with inline frames, you can specify the size of a layer element. However, a layer does not automatically display scrollbars if the content of the external document exceeds the layer size. Either the layer increases in size to match the file's content, or the layer is truncated (if you use the clip attribute).

Using Inline Layers and Working with Non-Layer Content

Netscape 4 treats layers like block level elements that float on the top-left corner of the page. If a document contains two layer elements, their content overlaps unless you: (1) place them at different locations using absolute positioning in an attached style sheet, or (2) separate their content using non-layer elements such as the br element. If you want to use relative positioning so that the layers flow alongside each other and along other Web page content, you use the **ilayer element** (ilayer stands for "inflow layer"). The syntax of the ilayer element is

```
<ilayer id="id" attributes>
    content
</ilayer>
```

The ilayer element can also be used to display content from external documents.

Working with Non-Layer Content

When browsers other than Netscape 4 encounter a layer or ilayer element, they ignore the <layer> and <ilayer> tags, but display the content of those tags. This means you can nest layer and ilayer elements within other, more standard elements. For example, the following code nests a layer element within a span element. Netscape 4 browsers recognize the div element and ignore the effects of the span element; other browsers ignore the <layer> tag, but display the span content correctly.

```
<span><layer id="heading">Pixal Products</layer></span>
```

For external documents, you can place an inline frame within a layer element as follows:

```
<layer src="heading.htm"><iframe src="heading.htm" /></layer>
```

Once again, Netscape 4 browsers recognize the external layer element and ignore the inline frame, while other browsers ignore the layer and display the inline frame.

Another way to handle non-Netscape 4 browsers is to place any content that you don't want Netscape 4 to process within a nolayer element. The syntax of the nolayer element is

```
<nolayer>
    Non-Netscape 4 content
</nolayer>
```

Netscape 4 ignores any content placed within the <nolayer> tag, but other browsers ignore the <nolayer> tags and process the content.

Working with Netscape 4 Objects

The document object model for Netscape 4 differs in several important respects from the DOMs for both Internet Explorer and the W3C. In most cases, programmers have to write separate code to perform the same actions in Netscape 4 as in the IE and W3C DOMs. It's therefore important to perform object detection to determine whether a user is running a Netscape 4 browser. Netscape 4 organizes all layers within a document in the document.layers collection. Thus, the following commands create Boolean variables to determine whether a user's browser supports the Netscape 4, Internet Explorer, or W3C DOMs:

```
var NS4DOM = document.layers ? true : false;
var IEDOM = document.all ? true : false;
var W3CDOM = document.getElementById ? true : false
```

If the active browser is Netscape 4, the NS4DOM variable has the Boolean value true; otherwise, it has the value false.

Next, you'll explore how the Netscape 4 document object model differs from the IE and W3C DOMs.

Referencing Page Objects

In the Netscape 4 DOM, a document object can be referenced using the expression

```
document.id
```

where *id* is the id value of the object. In the W3C and IE DOMs, the equivalent expression is

```
document.getElementById(id)
```

You can use the following function to resolve these cross-browser differences:

```
function getObject(id) {
    if (NS4DOM) return eval("document."+id);
    else return document.getElementById(id);
}
```

For example, to create a variable pointing to the Web page object

```
<div id="heading"> … </div>
```

you can run the command

```
headingObj = getObject("heading")
```

This command works under any of the three DOMs.

Referencing Nested Objects

There is one case for which the getObject() function does not work: when an object is nested within another page object (other than the body element). In this situation, the Netscape 4 DOM assumes that the object is a direct child of the body element. To reference such an object, you must use the expression

```
document.id1.document.id2.document.id3 …
```

where *id1*, *id2*, *id3*, etc. are the ids of objects nested within the document hierarchy. If you have a long string of nested objects, the expression to reference the element at the bottom of hierarchy can be quite long and complicated. In the IE and W3C DOMs you don't have to worry about the location of the nested object; using the expression

```
document.getElementById(id3)
```

references the object with the id *id3* no matter where it's located in the document hierarchy.

Referencing Objects by their Tag Name

Finally, the Netscape 4 DOM has a different object method for creating collections of objects with specified tag names. In the Netscape 4 DOM, the expression is

```
document.tags(tagName)
```

while in the W3C DOM it's

```
document.getElementsByTagName(tagName)
```

Thus, to create an object array of all paragraphs in a document, use

```
document.tags("p")
```

in Netscape 4 and

```
document.getElementsByTagName("p")
```

in Internet Explorer and browsers that support the W3C document object model.

Working with Object Styles

Netscape 4 differs from the Internet Explorer and W3C DOMs in how it references style attributes. In some cases the values it assigns to style attributes differ, but in all cases the syntax for referencing the style attributes is different. In the Netscape 4 DOM, style attributes are referenced using the form

```
object.attribute
```

where *object* is a reference to an object in the document and *attribute* is a style attribute. The equivalent expression in the Internet Explorer and W3C DOMs is

```
object.style.attribute
```

For example, to set the font size of an object whose id name is heading, you would run the following command for Netscape 4 browsers:

```
document.heading.fontSize="14pt";
```

For browsers using the other DOMs, you would run the command

```
document.getElementById("heading").style.fontSize="14pt";
```

The following function illustrates a general font size function that works with any of the three document object models:

```
function setFontSize(object,size) {
   if (NS4DOM) object.fontSize=size;
   else object.style.fontSize=size;
}
```

Thus, to set the font size of text within the heading element, you could run the following commands:

```
headObj=getObject("heading");
setFontSize(headObj,"14pt")
```

Stacking Objects on a Web Page

All three DOMs support the z-index style to determine the stacking order of objects on a Web page. In the Netscape 4 DOM, the expression to set the z-index value is

object.zIndex

while the W3C and Internet Explorer DOMs use

object.style.zIndex

In addition to the zIndex style property, the Netscape 4 DOM also supports two additional properties named above and below, which are used to reference objects stacked above and below another object. For example, if the subheading object is stacked below the heading object, the expression

```
document.heading.below
```

returns the subheading object. Similarly, the expression

```
document.subheading.above
```

returns the heading object. No similar property is found in either the W3C or Internet Explorer document object models.

Controlling Object Visibility

All three DOMs use the visibility style property to hide or to display objects, but they differ in the values they assign to that property. To display an object, the expressions are

Netscape 4 DOM	*object*.visibility="show"
W3C/IE DOM	*object*.style.visibility="visible"

To hide an object, the expressions are

Netscape 4 DOM	*object*.visibility="hide"
W3C/IE DOM	*object*.style.visibility="hidden"

When you hide or display objects in a dynamic Web page, you need to consider these differences if you want to support the Netscape 4 DOM.

Overflow and Clipping

Figure E-2 describes the properties used to set the width, height, content overflow, and clipping values for document objects.

Overflow and clipping attributes — **Figure E-2**

DOM	Property	Description (all measurements in pixels)
Netscape 4	*object*.width	The width of *object*
	object.height	The height of *object*
	object.clip.top	The position of the top edge of the clipping rectangle
	object.clip.right	The position of the right edge of the clipping rectangle
	object.clip.bottom	The position of the bottom edge of the clipping rectangle
	object.clip.left	The position of the left edge of the clipping rectangle
	object.clip.width	The width of the clipping rectangle
	object.clip.height	The height of the clipping rectangle
Internet Explorer and W3C	*object*.style.width	The width of *object*
	object.style.height	The height of *object*
	object.style.overflow	The way the browser handles content overflow ("visible", "hidden", "scroll", or "auto")
	object.style.clip	A text string specifying the dimensions of the clipping rectangle

As you can see, there are important differences between the document object models, especially in constructing the clipping rectangle. The Netscape 4 DOM places the clipping rectangle settings in six properties: clip.top, clip.right, clip.bottom, clip.left, clip.width, and clip.height. To set the size of the clipping rectangle, you use the following set of commands:

```
object.clip.top=top;
object.clip.right=right;
object.clip.bottom=bottom;
object.clip.left=left;
```

where *top*, *right*, *bottom*, and *left* are the coordinates of the edge of the clipping rectangle. To create the same effect in the W3C or Internet Explorer DOMs, you modify the string value of the style.clip property. The equivalent expression in those DOMs is

```
object.style.clip="rect("+top+" "+right+" "+bottom+" "+left+")";
```

When a clipping rectangle is applied to an object, you can manage the content using the style.overflow property in the W3C and Internet Explorer DOMs. There is no equivalent property to handle content overflow in the Netscape 4 DOM.

Netscape 4 Layer Methods

In addition to the different style properties, the Netscape 4 DOM includes methods for gaining greater control over the size and placement of objects on a Web page. These methods are summarized in Figure E-3.

Figure E-3 ▷ Netscape 4 layer methods

Method	Description
load(*url*, *width*)	Changes the source of the layer to the URL specified by *url*, and changes the width of the layer to *width*
moveAbove(*layer*)	Moves the layer above the *layer* object
moveBelow(*layer*)	Moves the layer below the *layer* object
moveBy(*dx*, *dy*)	Moves the layer *dx* pixels to the right and *dy* pixels down
moveTo(*x*, *y*)	Moves the layer to the (*x*, *y*) coordinates within the parent object
moveToAbsolute(*x*, *y*)	Moves the layer to the (*x*, *y*) coordinates on the Web page
resizeBy(*dx*, *dy*)	Resizes the layer by *dx* pixels horizontally and *dy* pixels vertically
resizeTo(*width*, *height*)	Resizes the layer to *width* pixels by *height* pixels

For example, the object

```
<div id="heading" style="position: absolute; left: 50px; top: 100px">
    Pixal Products
</div>
```

can be moved to the page coordinates (200, 250) under the Netscape 4 DOM using the JavaScript command

```
document.heading.moveTo(200,250)
```

By default, the moveTo() method assumes that pixels is the unit of distance.

Limits to Changing Styles

There are severe limitations on Netscape 4's dynamic content model. You cannot change the appearance of most page elements after a page is loaded. You cannot, for example, change the display style of an object to create expandable/collapsible content. Neither can you change font size, color, or font family *after* the page is loaded. Those types of modifications can only occur during the period when the page loads.

Writing Dynamic Content in the Netscape 4 DOM

The Netscape 4 DOM does not support document nodes or the node tree. To create dynamic content, you are limited to using the document.write() method. However, the Netscape 4 DOM does allow you to write HTML code into any page object that can be referenced. The general form of the command is

```
object.document.write(content)
```

where *object* is an object on the page and *content* is the HTML code you want placed in the object. Netscape 4's use of the document.write() method is similar to the innerHTML property employed by the Internet Explorer DOM. When you use the document.write() method under the Netscape 4 DOM, it opens input into the object. The document.write() method replaces whatever content was in the object, with succeeding document.write() methods adding additional lines of content. Whenever you open an input stream with the document.write() method, you must also close it. If you do not close the input stream, the new content does not appear in the browser window. The command to close an input stream is

```
object.document.close();
```

where *object* is an object on the page and *content* is the HTML code you want placed in the object. For example, the following command writes content to an element whose id is "heading":

```
document.heading.document.write("<i>Pixal Products</i>");
document.heading.document.close();
```

Note that you must include the document.close() method after the document.write() method is run.

Changing the Source of a Layer

As indicated earlier, Netscape 4 layers can also display the contents of external documents. To change the source of a layer to a new document, run the command

```
object.src="url"
```

where *object* is the layer object in the Web page and *url* is the URL of the document to be displayed in the layer. If you wanted to change the source of the layer element with the id "heading" to the file newhead.htm, for example, you could run the following command:

```
document.heading.src="newhead.htm";
```

Beyond the document.write() method and the properties and methods of the layer object, there are no other ways of creating dynamic content for Web pages under the Netscape 4 DOM.

Text Rollovers with Netscape 4

Because Netscape 4 does not allow you to change the appearance of most page objects after a Web page is loaded, text rollovers can only be created using the document.write() method. For example, the following code uses the document.write() method to change the font color during the mouseover event:

```
<head>
<script language="JavaScript">
function Over() {
    document.heading.document.write("<font color='red'>Pixal
Products</font>");
    document.heading.document.close();
}
function Out() {
    document.heading.document.write("Pixal Products");
document.Globe.document.close();
}
</script>
</head>
<body>
<layer name="heading" onmouseover="Over()" onmouseout="Out()">
    Pixal Products
</layer>
</body>
```

Exploring the Netscape 4 Event Model

As with the document object models, the syntax and structure of the Netscape 4 event model differs greatly from that employed in the Internet Explorer and W3C event models.

Event Handlers

Under the W3C and Internet Explorer event models, just about any object can be the source of an event and can have an event handler. In Netscape 4, event handlers can be added only to a select few elements. Figure E-4 lists the HTML elements that support event handlers under Netscape 4.

Figure E-4 ▶ **Netscape 4 tags that support event handlers**

Event Handler	HTML Tags
onclick	`<a>`, `<area>`, `<input (type="checkbox", "radio", "reset", "submit")>`
ondblclick	`<a>`
onkeydown	`<input (type="password", "text")>`, `<textarea>`
onkeypress	`<input (type="password", "text")>`, `<textarea>`
onkeyup	`<input (type="password", "text")>`, `<textarea>`
onmousedown	`<a>`, `<input (type="checkbox", "radio", "reset", "submit")>`
onmouseout	`<a>`, `<area>`, `<layer>`
onmouseover	`<a>`, `<area>`, `<layer>`
onmouseup	`<a>`, `<input (type="checkbox", "radio", "reset", "submit")>`, `<layer>`

Thus, if you're trying to create a cross-browser Web site that uses event handlers, you have to take into account Netscape 4's limitations. One way to get around this problem is to place those elements that do not support event handlers under the Netscape 4 event model within `<a>` tags (since the `<a>` tag supports several different event handlers). You have to include the href attribute in the `<a>` tag and set the destination of the link to "#" (the current Web page). For example, in the W3C or Internet Explorer DOM, you could add an event handler to a paragraph simply by adding the attribute to the `<p>` tag:

```
<p onmouseover="showBanner()">
   Display banner
</p>
```

In Netscape 4, you could do this with the code

```
<p><a onmouseover="showBanner()" href="#">
   Display banner
</a></p>
```

When you use this technique, you should employ a style sheet to remove the underlining from the link.

Event Propagation in Netscape 4

In the Netscape 4 event model, events propagate down from the top of a document to the lowest document elements (see Figure E-5).

Event propagation in Netscape 4 ◄ **Figure E-5**

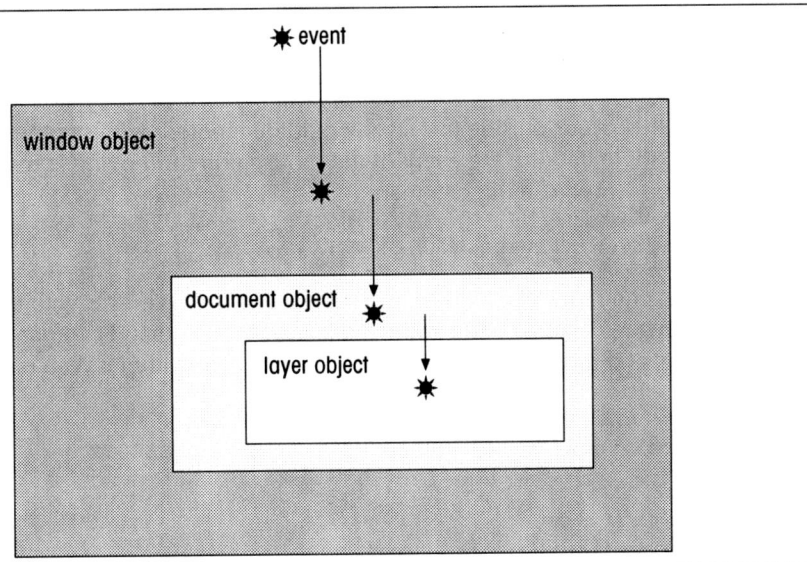

For example, the action of moving the mouse is first processed by the browser window, next by the document window, then by an object within the document, and so forth down the hierarchy of objects. If you want a Netscape 4 Web browser to take an action in response to an event, you must capture the event at a particular level of the hierarchy.

Capturing an Event

To capture an event in Netscape 4, you use the JavaScript method

```
object.captureEvents(Event.EVENT_TYPE)
```

where *object* is the object in which the event is captured, and EVENT_TYPE_ is the type of event. Note that the name of the event must be in all capital letters. Figure E-6 lists the various events that can be captured in the Netscape 4 event model.

Event types in Netscape 4 ◄ **Figure E-6**

Event.ABORT	Event.KEYDOWN	Event.MOUSEUP
Event.BLUR	Event.KEYPRESS	Event.MOVE
Event.CHANGE	Event.KEYUP	Event.RESET
Event.CLICK	Event.LOAD	Event.RESIZE
Event.DBLCLICK	Event.MOUSEDOWN	Event.SCROLL
Event.DRAGDROP	Event.MOUSEMOVE	Event.SELECT
Event.ERROR	Event.MOUSEOUT	Event.SUBMIT
Event.FOCUS	Event.MOUSEOVER	Event.UNLOAD

For example, to capture the event when a user double-clicks the mouse anywhere within the browser window, you enter the command

```
window.captureEvents(Event.DBLCLICK);
```

Here, *window* is the object and *DBLCLICK* is the event type. If you want to capture only the double-clicks within the first <layer> tag, you would capture the event at a different level in the object hierarchy:

```
document.layers[0].captureEvents(Event.DBLCLICK);
```

Any double-clicks that occur outside this layer would be ignored by this command.

Finally, if you want to capture the event of the mouse pointer moving across the Web page document, you would use the command:

```
document.captureEvents(Event.MOUSEMOVE)
```

You can capture several types of events at once by separating the events with the OR operator (represented by the | symbol). The following JavaScript command captures the mousedown, mousemove, and mouseup events occurring anywhere within a Web page document:

```
document.captureEvents(Event.MOUSEDOWN | Event.MOUSEMOVE |
Event.MOUSEUP)
```

Assigning a Function to an Event

After Netscape 4 has captured an event, a function can be assigned to run in response to that event's occurrence. For example, to run a function named "grabIt()" when a user presses the mouse pointer down anywhere within a Web document, you first capture the mousedown event and then use the object property method to assign the grabIt() function to the event. The JavaScript code would look as follows:

```
document.captureEvents(Event.MOUSEDOWN);
document.onmousedown=grabIt;
```

Releasing an Event

You can turn off event capturing in Netscape 4 by using the releaseEvents() method. For example, if you want the browser to initially capture the mousemove event, but then at a later point in your script you do not need to capture that event anymore, you can turn off the capture using the command

```
document.releaseEvents(Event.MOUSEMOVE);
```

Events can be released and then recaptured multiple times within your program code.

Routing Events to their Targets

To handle nested objects, the Netscape 4 event model allows you to route an event down the object hierarchy. For example, you might create an onclick event handler for both a Web page document and a layer object in that document. When you click the layer object, the click event starts at the top of the object hierarchy and is first captured by the document's event handler. At that point, two things happen: (1) the function associated with the event handler is run, and (2) the click event stops being propagated down the object hierarchy, never reaching the layer object.

To force the Netscape 4 browser to continue propagating such an event down the object hierarchy, you have to call the routeEvent() method at the end of the function. The code might look as follows:

```
document.captureEvents(Event.CLICK);
document.layers[0].captureEvents(Event.CLICK);
document.onclick=handleClick1;
document.layers[0].handleClick2;

function handleClick1(e) {
...
    document.routeEvent(e);
}
```

In this example, Netscape 4 runs the handleClick1() function when a user clicks any location in the document. If the user happens to click a location within the first layer object, the browser first runs the handleClick1() function, and then routes the event down the object hierarchy, running the handleClick2() function. If the routeEvent() method were not applied, this would not happen and the event propagation would stop at the document level.

Redirecting Events

Another method in Netscape 4 that you can apply to events is the handleEvent() method. While the routeEvent() method passes an event down the object hierarchy to its intended target, the handleEvent() method passes an event to a specified target. For example, the following code demonstrates how to pass the click event to the first link in a document:

```
document.captureEvents(Event.CLICK);
document.onclick=handleAllClicks;
...

function handleAllClicks(e) {

...

    document.links[0].handleEvent(e);
}
```

The effect of this code is that the first link is activated no matter where a user clicks in the document.

The Netscape 4 Event Object

In both the Netscape 4 and the W3C event models, the event object is the parameter of the function assigned to the event (unlike the Internet Explorer event model, which uses the event or window.event object). For example, in the following code:

```
function handleClick1(e) {
...
    document.routeEvent(e);
}
```

the event object is the parameter "e". The Netscape 4 event object supports many of the same properties found in the W3C event model, but there are some differences in the property names. Figure E-7 lists the properties of the Netscape 4 event object.

Figure E-7 ▶ **Properties of the Netscape 4 event object**

Description	Netscape 4 Event Property
Element in which event occurred	target
Type of event that has occurred	type
The (x, y) coordinates of the event within the entire computer screen	screenX, screenY
The (x, y) coordinates of the event within the page	pageX, pageY
The (x, y) coordinates of the event within an object on the page	layerX, layerY x, y
An integer representing the modifier key (Alt, Ctrl, or Shift) pressed by the user	modifiers
Keyboard key that caused the event	which
Mouse button that caused the event	which

For example, to determine the screen coordinates of an event in the Netscape 4 event model, you would use the object properties

```
evt.screenX
evt.screenY
```

where *evt* is the parameter in the event function.

One very useful property in both the W3C and Internet Explorer event models enables you to determine which object initiated an event. In the W3C event model, this is the currentTarget or target property, while in the Internet Explorer event model, it is the srcElement property. The Netscape 4 event model includes no such property. The target property is part of the Netscape 4 model, but it only applies to the mouseover and mouse-out events. Using the target property for any other event results in an error.

Keyboard Keys and Buttons

The Netscape 4 event model also differs from the W3C and Internet Explorer models in the way that a script determines which mouse button or keyboard key a user has pressed. In Netscape 4, the button or key is returned by the property

```
evt.which
```

where *evt* is once again the parameter of the event function. For example, to resolve the differences between browsers, you can use the following function to return the keyboard key:

```
function getKey(e) {
   if (NS4DOM) return e.which;
   else if (IEDOM) return event.keyCode;
   else if (W3CDOM) return e.keyCode;
}
```

Note that this function uses the Boolean variables NS4DOM, IEDOM, and W3CDOM. The cross-browser function that determines which mouse button was clicked has a similar structure:

```
function getButton(e) {
    if (NS4DOM) return e.which;
    else if (IEDOM) return event.button;
    else if (W3CDOM) return e.button;
}
```

Netscape 4's button values differ from those of the W3C or Internet Explorer event models. The Netscape 4 event model does not support the middle button, and as indicated in Figure E-8, the left button has a value of 1 and the right button a value of 3.

Button values in the three event models   Figure E-8

Event Model	Event Property	Left	Middle	Right
Netscape 4	e.which	1	n/a	3
Internet Explorer	event.button	1	4	2
W3C	e.button	0	1	2

If you need to capture whether a modifier key, such as the Ctrl, Shift, or Alt key, is being pressed, you need to use Netscape 4's modifiers property. The syntax of the property is

```
evt.modifiers
```

Figure E-9 shows the value of the modifiers property when different combinations of modifier keys are being pressed.

Values of the modifiers property   Figure E-9

e.modifiers Value	Modifier Key(s) Being Pressed
0	None
1	Alt
2	Ctrl
3	Alt+Ctrl
4	Shift
5	Alt+Shift
6	Ctrl+Shift
7	Alt+Ctrl+Shift

For example, if the modifiers property returns a value of 5, you know that a user is pressing both the Alt and Shift keys.

As each year passes, fewer and fewer users run the Netscape 4 browser. At the time of this writing, about 0.2% of browsers in use are Netscape 4. Creating a cross-browser page that supports Netscape 4 can be an exercise in acute frustration—particularly if you are working with the event model or with dynamic content. However, if you are designing Web sites for a population of people who typically use older browsers, such as users in developing or third world countries, then the number of Netscape 4 users among your audience may be much higher. In such cases, you may decide it's important to ensure that your Web pages support Netscape 4 and all of its features.

Debugging your JavaScript Code

Understanding Programming Errors

As you write JavaScript code you will inevitably come upon situations where your code fails to work correctly or fails to work at all. When this happens, you have to locate the source of the error and correct it in a process called **debugging**. As discussed in Tutorial 1, there are three general types of programming errors:

- **Load-time errors**: Occur when code is initially loaded by a browser

- **Run-time errors**: Occur when code is executed by a browser

- **Logical errors**: Occur when code has been successfully run, but with incorrect results

Load-time Errors

Load-time errors occur because of mistakes in the syntax of a JavaScript command or expression. Figure F-1 describes some of the more common errors of syntax that may creep into your JavaScript code.

Figure F-1 | **Common syntax errors**

Error	Example	Description

Mismatched parenthesis or braces	`if (bname == "IE") {`
	`    alert("IE Browser");`
	`else {`
	`    alert("Other Browser");`
	`}`
		Missing closing brace [}] after the first If condition

Missing quotation marks around text strings	`alert(IE Browser);`	No quotation marks around the text string
Mismatched quotation marks	`alert("IE Browser);`	No closing quotation mark around the text string
Missing + symbols when concatenating text strings	`bname = "IE";` `alert("browser = " bname);`	No + symbol used to concatenate the text string with the bname variable
Using = instead of == as a conditional operator	`if (bname = "IE")`	The = symbol is used in the if statement rather than the == symbol
Using <> instead of != as a conditional operator	`if (bname <> "IE")`	The <> symbol is not recognized by JavaScript.
Applying an unsupported property or method to an object	`verNum = 1;` `alert(verNum.length);`	The length property is not supported by numeric values
Using reserved key words	`var case = 3;`	Case can only be used in switch/case statements

When a load-time error is uncovered, the browser halts loading the script, and no further commands are processed. Depending on the browser, an error message may also appear specifying the line number and character number where the load-time error was first noticed. This does not mean that the error occurred at this location in the document (the source of the trouble could be much earlier in the script); it simply indicates the location at which the JavaScript interpreter was forced to cancel loading the script.

Run-time Errors

A run-time error is an error that results in the browser being unable to run a line of code, but only after the code has been loaded and checked by the browser for syntax errors. Run-time errors are usually the result of mistyped variable or function names. Figure F-2 lists some common sources of run-time errors.

Common run-time errors | **Figure F-2**

Error	Example	Description
Mistyping a variable name	`var bName = "IE";` `alert(bname);`	The text of the bName variable name must match both uppercase and lowercase letters

Mistyping a function name	`showbrowser();`
	`function showBrowser() {`
	`    alert(bName);`
	`}`
		The text of the showBrowser() function name must match both uppercase and lowercase letters

Referencing an object	`document.webform.bfield.value="IE";`	The bfield field in the webform form has not been loaded before it has been by loaded by the browser the browser yet

One common run-time error occurs when the script attempts to access a page object, such as a form element, that hasn't yet been loaded by the browser. The browser loads a page in the order it appears in the HTML file. It is common to place JavaScript code at the beginning of the page within the head section. This can lead to an error if the code attempts to work with an element defined within the body section of the page, since those elements are not yet processed by the browser at the time the code is loaded. One way to avoid this problem is to use an onload event handler for any code that you want processed when the page is loaded, but *after* all of the page elements have been processed by the browser. Like load-time errors, browsers often report run-time errors showing both the line and character numbers where the errors occur.

Logical Errors

After a script has been processed without any run-time or load-time errors, the script will complete without any error message being reported by the browser. However, the code may still not be mistake free. An error could exist in the logic of the code, causing different output from what you planned. For example, a date value might not be formatted correctly, a cookie value might not be correctly read, and so forth. Logical errors are often difficult to locate because there is no built-in reporting mechanism for following the changing values of JavaScript variables.

Debugging a Program

There are several techniques you can employ to quickly locate the sources of logical errors. Most of these involve reporting the values of variables while the program is running. This can be done using alert boxes, status bar messages, and writing code to a debug window.

Using Alert Boxes

The simplest way to track your code as it is being run by a browser is to insert a series of alert boxes at different parts of the script. For example, the following code uses an alert box to immediately report the value of the bName variable after it has been set by the getBrowser() function:

```
var bName = getBrowser();
alert(bName);
```

Alert boxes can also be used to indicate whether a browser has run a section of code. In the following code, alert boxes are used to indicate which of two possible results of an if condition has been met; this allows the programmer to track the logical decisions of the script as it is run by the browser:

```
if (bName == "IE") {
    alert("condition is true");
    JavaScript commands
} else {
    alert("condition is false");
    JavaScript commands
}
```

One useful technique with alert boxes in tracking the source of a logical error is to place an alert box at a location in the code where the script is still running correctly and a second alert box at a location where the code has already failed. Repeatedly run the script as you move the two alert boxes closer together to isolate the source of the trouble.

Using the Status Bar

In some scripts you will not want to use an alert box to report variable names or to notify you that a particular section in the code has been met. A less obtrusive technique is to write the debugging information to the window's status bar. For example, to write the value of the bName variable described above, you would run the following code:

```
var bName = getBrowser();
window.status = bName;
```

Note that in some browsers, such as Firefox, you are not able to write text to the status bar unless you have modified the default security settings of the browser.

Using a Debug Window

One of the limits of an alert box is that it slows down your program and doesn't handle situations in which you need to report a lot of different values. For example, the following code tracks the collection of inline images in a document. Each time through the loop, an alert box reports the source of the inline image.

```
for (i=0; i<document.images.length; i++) {
    alert(document.images[i].src);
    JavaScript commands
}
```

While this script would work fine for a Web page containing just a few images, it would not be effective for a page containing hundreds of images. Rather than use an alert box you can create your own pop-up window containing messages, variables values, and other text from the script you're running. Known as a **debug window** or a **log window**, such a tool offers a quick and versatile way of monitoring your program's actions. Unlike alert boxes, you can use a single debug window to write multiple values. The following code writes the inline image information from the previous series of alert boxes using a debug window instead:

```
debugWin = window.open("","","width=200,height=200,resize=yes,scrollbars=yes");
for (i=0; i<document.images.length; i++) {
    debugWin.document.write(document.images[i].src);
    debugWin.document.write("<br />");
    debugWin.document.close();
    JavaScript commands
}
```

Note that each time through the loop the source of the inline image is written to the debug window. A <br /> tag is also written to the window so that each debug message appears on a separate line. The code also includes the command

```
debugWin.document.close();
```

The close() method closes input to the debug window, forcing the latest piece of text to be written into the window. If there is an error in the For loop, the debug window allows you to locate exactly at what point in the loop the error occurred. Note that to use a debug window, your pop-up blocker must be configured to allow its creation.

Catching Errors

You can gain further control over how your browser responds by writing code to catch errors before they're noted by the browser running the script. One approach is to use the onerror event handler.

The onerror Event Handler

The onerror event handler is a property of the window object and specifies what action the browser should take if it encounters either a load-time or run-time error within the browser window. The syntax of the onerror event handler is

```
window.onerror=function;
```

where *function* is the name of a function to be run in response to an error occurring within the browser window. For example, the following code causes the function to display the alert box "Error was Found" in response to an error event:

```
window.onerror=showMsg;

function showMsg() {
   alert("Error was Found");
   return true;
}
```

Note that this function returns the Boolean value true. By returning a value of true from the onerror function, the error dialog box normally displayed by the browser is suppressed. Returning a value of false causes the browser to display whatever error message it usually displays, in addition to any actions indicated by the onerror function.

The function called by the onerror event handler can also support three parameters: the error message, the URL of the document containing the error, and the line number within the document at which the error occurred. The following sample error function displays the values from these three parameters:

```
window.onerror=showMsg;

function showMsg(msg, url,line) {
   alert("Error: "+msg);
   alert("From document: "+url);
   alert("At line: "+line);
}
```

The onerror event handler should be placed at the beginning of a script so that it can intercept any subsequent errors in the code.

You can suppress error messages for a particular element by adding the event handler onerror="null" as an attribute of the element's HTML tag. This is often used for catching errors associated with loading inline images into a Web page. For example, the HTML code

```
<img src="largeLogo.jpg" alt="" onerror="null />
```

prevents a browser from displaying an error message if it is unable to load the inline image graphic largeLogo.jpg.

The try...catch Structure

The other way to capture an error is with a try...catch structure. A try...catch structure looks for the occurrence of not just load-time or run-time errors, but any event that the programmer has defined as unusual. Such events are called **exceptions**. The general syntax of the try...catch structure is

```
try {
    statements that may
    contain errors or exceptions
}

catch(exception) {
    commands to run in the event of
    an error or exception
}
```

The following is an example of a simple use of the try...catch structure.

```
try {
    Document.Write("<h1>Home</h1>");
}

catch(err) {
    alert("syntax error");
}
```

When the browser runs the commands in the try() statement, any errors it notices are handled by the commands in the nearest catch statement. The try statement in this example contains a deliberate error (the method is entered as Document.Write rather than document.write), meaning that it triggers the commands in the catch() statement. In this case, the browser displays a simple alert box containing the text "syntax error." Most browsers display catch warnings in their own customized error alert dialog boxes.

One of the advantages of the try...catch structure is that catching a run-time or load-time error in this way does not result in the browser halting the execution of the script. Once the browser has run the commands specified in the catch() statement, it continues executing the remaining commands in the program.

The error Object

The catch() statement supports a single parameter that contains information about the error or exception found in the try() statement. This parameter is referred to as the **error object** or **exception object**. The error object contains useful information about the error or exception caught by the browser. Figure F-3 describes the properties and methods associated with the error object.

Properties and methods of the error object ◀ **Figure F-3**

Property	Description
error.message	The message associated with the *error* object
error.name	The name of the *error* object
error.number	The id number of the *error* object
error.description	The description of the error associated with the *error* object.

Method	Description
error.toString()	Return the text string of the error associated with the *error* object, displaying the error name followed by the error message.

The "message" and "name" properties provide useful information describing the nature of the error or exception. Earlier versions of Internet Explorer do not support these properties, but instead use the "description" and "number" properties to provide error information. The following code shows how to access these properties using the same try...catch example displayed previously:

```
try {
    Document.Write("<h1>Home</h1>");
}

catch(err) {
    alert(err.name+": "+err.message);
}
```

Browsers differ slightly in the exact content they provide for the name and message properties. Figure F-4 displays the alert boxes generated by the above code for Internet Explorer and Netscape.

Alert dialog boxes ◀ **Figure F-4**

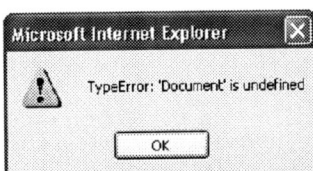

Internet Explorer

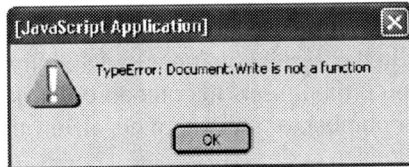

Netscape

JavaScript also allows programmers to define their own errors. The command to construct an error object is

```
new Error(message)
```

where *message* is a customized message associated with the error object. It is not necessary to specify a message. The following code demonstrates how to create an error object containing the message "Invalid input":

```
new Error("invalid input");
```

Throwing an Error or Exception

Customized error objects are often used to trap exceptions in which a user running the program makes a mistake (perhaps in entering field data) and the script needs to catch the user error before continuing. To trap these kinds of exceptions, you use a **throw command**. To help you remember the different elements involved with catching errors, you can think of the throw command as throwing an error or an exception, and the **catch() statement** as "catching" that mistake and then responding to it. The syntax of the throw command is

```
throw expression
```

where *expression* is a data value, such as a number or text string, or an error object. The throw statement essentially generates a run-time error for the browser to deal with. Throwing errors is very useful in form validation. Rather than creating a series of if...else statements, you can incorporate a series of catch() statements to deal with particular examples of invalid input.

In the following code, the browser prompts users to enter a number. If a user does not enter a number, the code throws an exception, catches it, and displays the appropriate dialog box alerting the user of his or her error.

```
number = prompt("Enter a number");

try {
    if (isNaN(number)) {
        throw new Error("invalid input");
    }
}

catch(err) {
    alert(err.message);
}
```

Note that the throw statement in this example creates a customized error object which is then used in the catch() statement to generate the error message. If a user does enter a number as prompted, no exception is noted by the browser and the commands in the catch() statement are not run.

The same catch() statement can be used for multiple errors or exceptions. In this case, you specify different values in the throw statement to determine which error or exception is caught. For example, if you prompt users to enter an order quantity, a user might make two mistakes: entering a nonnumber, or entering a negative value. You can catch both of these mistakes using the following code:

```
number = prompt("Enter a quantity to order");

try {
   if (isNaN(number)) {
      throw "That is not a number";
   } else if (number <= 0) {
      throw "You must enter a positive number";
   }
}

catch(err) {
   alert(err);
}
```

In response to an error, this code causes a browser to display one of the alert dialog boxes shown in Figure F-5. Note that in this case the expression in the throw statement is the text of the alert box rather than a customized error object. You could certainly add more throw statements to this structure to catch a wide variety of errors, including noninteger numbers, numbers greater than a specific value, and so forth.

Catching different exceptions   **Figure F-5**

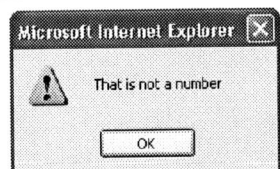

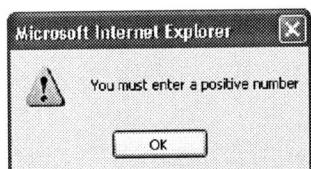

The finally Statement

The try...catch structure also allows for a **finally statement** that defines a command block to be run regardless of whether an error or exception is thrown and caught. The general syntax of the try...catch...finally structure is

```
try {
   statements that may
   contain errors or exceptions
}

catch(exception) {
   commands to be run in the event of
   an error or exception
}

finally {
   commands that are run in every
   situation
}
```

A "finally" section is a good place to put any code that a browser needs to execute regardless of any error or exceptions noted in other parts of the script. The finally section can't appear by itself and must be located somewhere after the try statement.

While JavaScript does not have the same type of debugging tools that other programming languages support, you can enlist alert boxes, debugging windows, and try...catch structures to quickly debug your programs and present error-free code to your users.

Glossary/Index

Note: Boldface entries include definitions.

D

data event, HTML and XHTML, REF 5
data type The type of data stored in a variable; JavaScript supports numeric, text, Boolean, and null data types. JVS 17–19
Date element, REF 45–47
date function, creating, JVS 60–62
date method Method that retrieves information from a date object or changes a date object's value. JVS 57–58
date object A JavaScript object that contains information about a specified date and time. JVS 56–62
   creating date and time variable, JVS 56, JVS 60–62
   retrieving date, month, and hour values, JVS 57–58
   retrieving hour, minute, and second variables, JVS 58–59
   setting date and time variables, JVS 59–60
date value
   retrieving, JVS 57–58
   setting, JVS 59–60
`<dd>` tag, REF 13
debug window A pop-up window containing debugging information and tips. , REF 86–87
debugging The process by which programming errors are located and resolved. JVS 33–38, REF 83–92
   alert boxes, REF 85–86
   common mistakes, JVS 35
   debug (log) window, REF 86–87
   error object, REF 88–90
   finally statement, REF 91–92
   onerror event handler, REF 87–88
   status bar, REF 86
   throwing errors or exceptions, REF 90–91
   tools and techniques, JVS 35–38
   try...catch structure, REF 88
declaring A process by which a variable is created and, optionally, an initial value for the variable is indicated. JVS 16, JVS 20
decrement operator (--) A unary operator that decreases the value of an expression by one. JVS 64, REF 66
definition list A list of definition terms, with each term followed by a definition description; created using the dt and dd elements. REV 11
degree symbol (°), REV 18
`<del>` tag, REF 13
deleting cookies, JVS 512–514
delimeter A character or set of characters that separates one substring from another within a larger text string. JVS 363
deprecated A feature of HTML that is no longer being developed by the W3C. REV 3
detecting image objects, JVS 221
`<dfn>` tag, REF 13
DHTML. *See* Dynamic HTML
dialog box, JVS 299–302
   alert, JVS 299
   confirm, JVS 299
   prompt, JVS 299
dir attribute, REF 2
`<dir>` tag, REF 13
dir element, REF 47
disabled attribute, REF 3
display style, elements, REV 76–78
display window, calculating size, JVS 193–197
displaying
   crop marks, REV 89
   external documents in layers, REF 69
   objects, JVS 566–568
   pop-up menu contents, JVS 234–236
`<div>` tag, REF 13
div element A generic block-level element. REF 47, REV 12
`<dl>` tag, REF 13

`<!doctype>` tag, REF 8
document element, REF 47–49
document event, HTML and XHTML, REF 4
document fragment An unattached node or node tree that resides only in the browser memory and is not part of the document node tree. JVS 539
document object model (DOM) The systematic organization of all objects within a Web document or Web browser. JVS 163–166
   development, JVS 163–166
   document tree, JVS 166
   IE, positioning objects in, JVS 180–181
   Netscape 4, REF 74–75
document tree, JVS 166
document.write() method, JVS 11–13
dollar sign ($)
   escape sequences, JVS 380
   text strings, JVS 372
DOM. *See* document object model (DOM)
DOM event model The event model developed by the W3C. JVS 425, JVS 428–430
DOM event object, JVS 434–437
DOM Level 0 The first document object model, introduced by Netscape Navigator 2.0. JVS 163–164, JVS 165
DOM Level 1 The first official DOM specification released by the W3C, providing support for nearly all elements contained with HTML or XHTML documents. Enjoys nearly universal browser support. JVS 164, JVS 165
DOM Level 2 The DOM specification providing an event model in which events could be captured and responded to. It also added a style model to work with CSS style sheets, and a range model to allow programmers to manipulate sections of text within a document. Current browsers support many, but not all, of the features of DOM Level 2. JVS 164, JVS 165
DOM Level 3 The DOM specification that provides a framework for working with document loading and saving, as well as for working with DTDs and document validation. Few browsers support the DOM Level 3 specifications at the time of this writing. JVS 164, JVS 165
domain property, cookies, JVS 489
dot (.), escape sequences, JVS 380
double-click event, JVS 453–455
Do/While loop, JVS 121
drag-and-drop feature, JVS 441–452
   calculating distance from pointer, JVS 440–441
   canceling selectStart event, JVS 447–448
   determining event coordinates, JVS 438–440
   determining event source, JVS 438
   dropIt() function, JVS 443–444
   formatting dragged items, JVS 449–452
   keeping dragged items on top, JVS 445
   moveIt() function, JVS 441–443
   returning dragged items to starting point, JVS 445–447
DropShadow filter, JVS 240, JVS 241
`<dt>` tag, REF 13
dynamic content Content determined by the operation of a script running within the browser. JVS 528–577
   attributes, JVS 555–560
   expanding and collapsing documents, JVS 561–575
   heading elements. See heading element
   inserting into elements, JVS 530–531
   Internet Explorer, JVS 531–533
   nested lists, JVS 547–554
   Netscape 4, limitations, REF 74
   nodes. See node
   recursion, JVS 575–577
   testing, JVS 573–575
   writing in Netscape 4 DOM, REF 74–75

dynamic HTML Dynamic features added to a Web page by employing aspects of HTML/XHTML, style sheets, and JavaScript. JVS 160–162
Dynamic Hypertext Markup Language (DHTML), JVS 160–162
dynamic table A table whose content and HTML tags are generated through a script. JVS 502

E

`<!-- -->` tag, REF 8
ECMA. *See* European Computer Manufacturers Association (ECMA)
ECMAScript A scripting language standard developed by the ECMA. JVS 8
element A distinct feature of a Web document, such as a paragraph, a heading, or the page's title. REV 4. *See also specific elements*
   aligning content, REV 61–62
   attributes, REV 6–7
   block-level. *See* block-level element
   body, REV 7
   character-forming, REV 13–15
   clipping content, REV 67
   content overflow, REV 66
   control, REV 28
   display style, REV 76–78
   div, REV 12
   empty, REV 5
   head, REV 7
   height, REV 66
   hiding, REV 77–78
   HTML. *See* HTML element
   inline, REV 8, REV 13–15
   inserting HTML content, JVS 530–531
   JavaScript, REF 43–63
   logical, REV 15
   meta, REV 8
   noframes, REV 44–45
   physical, REV 15
   positioning. *See* positioning element
   root, REV 7
   setting position, JVS 180
   sizing, REV 65–67
   table, REV 19
   title, REV 7–8
   width, REV 65
   XHTML. *See* XHTML element
`<em>` tag, REF 14
em unit A relative unit of length equal to the width of a capital "M". REV 57
e-mail harvester A program that scans documents, usually Web pages, looking for e-mail addresses. JVS 3
e-mail link, writing, JVS 12–13
`<embed>` tag, REF 14
embedded style A style applied to a Web page by adding the style element to the document head. REV 51–53
Emboss filter, JVS 240
empty element An element having no textual content, such as an inline image or line break. REV 5
Engrave filter, JVS 240
equal sign (=)
   assignment operator, JVS 65, REF 65
   comparison operators, JVS 78, REF 66
error
   debugging. *See* debugging
   load-time, JVS 33, REF 83, REF 84
   logical, JVS 34, REF 83, REF 85
   run-time, JVS 33–34, REF 83, REF 84–85
   throwing, REF 90–91
Error element, REF 49

error object A JavaScript object containing error information used for debugging. , REF 88–90

escape sequence A special command inside a text string that tells a JavaScript interpreter not to interpret what follows as a character. JVS 380–381

European Computer Manufacturers Association (ECMA) An international body responsible for the development of standards for client-side scripting languages like JavaScript. JVS 8

event An action that occurs within a Web browser or Web document. JVS 53, JVS 418–461

attaching and detaching, JVS 428

calculating distance from pointer, JVS 440–441

determining coordinates, JVS 438–440

determining source, JVS 438

keyboard, JVS 455–460

running scripts in response, JVS 55

tips, JVS 460

event attribute, HTML and XHTML, REF 4

event bubbling The process by which events move up through the object hierarchy from the bottom element to the top-most object. JVS 425–426

canceling, JVS 427–428

event handler A statement that tells browsers what code to run in response to a specified event. JVS 53–55, JVS 185–187, JVS 420–425

adding to plus/minus boxes, JVS 564–565

assigning, JVS 424–425

canceling actions, JVS 423

Netscape 4, REF 76

as object properties, JVS 422

as script elements, JVS 422–423

event listener A JavaScript feature that detects when a particular event has reached an object in the document hierarchy. JVS 429

event model The way that browsers work with events occurring within the browser window and Web page.

cross-browser, JVS 431–432

DOM, JVS 425, JVS 428–430

IE. See Internet Explorer event model

Netscape 4. See Netscape 4 event model

event object The JavaScript object that stores information about an event occurring within the Web browser or Web document. JVS 433–437

DOM, JVS 434–437

IE, JVS 433–434

Netscape 4, REF 79–80

ex unit A relative unit of length equal to the height of a lowercase "x". REV 57

exception Any occurrence that a programmer deems unusual when debugging program code. , REF 88

throwing, REF 90–91

exception object A JavaScript object containing an exception. , REF 88–90

exclamation point (!)

comparison operator, REF 66

logical operator, JVS 78

expanding

documents, JVS 561–575

frames, JVS 315–316

expires property, cookies, JVS 488–489

expression, tips for working with, JVS 87

Extensible Hypertext Markup Language (XHTML) A version of HTML written in the XML markup language. REV 4

attributes, REF 8–32

elements. See XHTML element

JavaScript within files, JVS 15

versions, REV 3

Extensible Markup Language (XML) A markup language used to create documents that must adhere to specific rules for content and structure. REV 4

extension Feature added to HTML by specific browsers, which may not be supported by other browsers. REV 2–3

external JavaScript file, accessing, JVS 27–30

external style A style sheet placed in a separate file (usually with the file extension .css) that is linked to a page in a Web site. REV 53–54

extracting array items, JVS 113–115

F

Fade transition, JVS 249

field A control element in which a user can enter information. REV 28

calculated, JVS 349–354

hidden, REV 37

input. See input field

field value The value of a Web form field. REV 28

`<fieldset>` tag, REF 14

File element, REF 49–50

FileUpload element, REF 49–50

filter An effect that is applied to an object or page to change its appearance. The filter style is supported only by Internet Explorer. JVS 239–247

adding to pages, JVS 244–245

applying by using styles, JVS 239–243

running with JavaScript, JVS 243–244

filter collection The collection of all filter styles associated with an object. JVS 243–244

finally statement A statement that is run regardless of whether any error or exception is caught. , REF 91–92

first-party cookie A cookie that is created from the Web site that a user is visiting. JVS 482

fixed position Placement of an element at a fixed location in the display window so that it does not scroll with other elements on a page. REV 74

FlipH filter, JVS 241

FlipV filter, JVS 241

floating element, REV 74–75

floating frame. See inline frame

font

decorative features, REV 60, REV 61

generic, REV 56

selecting, REV 56–57

size, REV 57

specific, REV 56

style, REV 59, REV 61

weight, REV 59–60, REV 61

`<font>` tag, REF 14

For loop, JVS 116–120

arrays, JVS 118–120

form, JVS 336–368, REV 28–37

appending and retrieving form data, JVS 398–400

appending data to URLs, JVS 397–398

attributes, REV 37

calculated fields, JVS 349–354

check boxes, JVS 349, REV 28, REV 32–33

control elements, REV 28

controlling using cookies, JVS 506

creating form elements, REV 29–30

form buttons, REV 28, REV 36

form feedback page, JVS 508–512

form validation. See form validation

hidden fields, REV 37

input boxes, REV 28, REV 30–31

input fields, JVS 340–342

older browsers, JVS 353–354

option buttons, JVS 346–348

option buttons (radio buttons), REV 28, REV 31–32

passing data between, JVS 397–400

populating fields with cookie values, JVS 494–495

preserving form data, JVS 506–508

referencing, JVS 337–338

referencing form elements, JVS 339–340

resetting, JVS 358

selection lists, JVS 343–346, REV 28, REV 33–35

submitting, JVS 355–357

text area boxes, REV 28, REV 35–36

text strings. See text string

this keyword, JVS 348–349

form attribute, HTML and XHTML, REF 3

form button, REV 28, REV 36

Form element, REF 50

`<form>` tag, REF 15

form event, HTML and XHTML, REF 5

form feedback page A form that provides feedback to users; often used in shopping cart applications. JVS 508–512

form validation A process by which the server or the user's browser checks a form for data entry errors. JVS 354–359

client-side, JVS 354, JVS 355

entries, JVS 387–396

passing data between forms, JVS 397–400

resetting forms, JVS 358

server-side, JVS 354, JVS 355

submitting forms, JVS 355–357

tips, JVS 400

validating entries, JVS 387–396

format, numbers, JVS 75

formatting

dragged objects, JVS 449–452

frames, REV 42–43

styles. See Cascading Style Sheets (CSSs); style

text strings, JVS 367–368

frame A section of the browser window capable of displaying the content of an entire Web page. JVS 309–321, REV 37–46

blocking, JVS 316–318

collapsing, JVS 315–316

expanding, JVS 315–316

formatting, REV 42–43

frames collection, JVS 312

frameset objects, JVS 312

framesets, REV 39–41

inline (floating), JVS 319–320, REV 45–46

links, REV 43–44

navigating between, JVS 312–313

noframes element, REV 44–45

specifying source, REV 41–42

tables, REV 25–26, REV 27

tips, JVS 321

treating as windows, JVS 313–314

Frame element, REF 50–51

`<frame>` tag, REF 15

frame-blind browser A browser that does not support frames. REV 44–45

frameset A collection of frames. REV 39–41

forcing page into, JVS 318

layout, JVS 314

`<frameset>` tag, REF 16

frameset object, JVS 312

front end The visible part of a Web site with which users interact. JVS 480

function A named collection of commands that performs an action or returns a value. JVS 20–25
  assigning to events using Netscape 4, REF 78
  calling, JVS 21–25
  pop-up menus, calling, JVS 236–238
  to return value, JVS 25–26
  variable scope, JVS 25
function name The name assigned to a function. JVS 20–21

G

generic block, REV 12
generic font A font style in a style sheet identified by its type (serif, sans-serif, monospace, cursive, or fantasy). REV 56
get method A method of sending form data by appending the data to the end of the URL specified in the action attribute of the form element. REV 37
global scope A property that indicates a variable can be used within any function or set of commands within an application. JVS 25
global variable A variable that has global scope. JVS 25
Glow filter, JVS 240, JVS 241
Gradient filter, JVS 240
GradientWipe transition, JVS 249
Gray filter, JVS 241
greater than symbol (>)
  comparison operators, JVS 78, REF 66
  HTML, REV 18
group box, REV 28

H

`<head>` tag, REF 16
head element The element in an HTML file containing information about the document, such as the document's title or list of keywords. REF 51, REV 7
heading, creating, REV 8–9
heading element, JVS 541–546
  creating list item elements, JVS 544–546
  looping through child node collection, JVS 542–543
  matching, JVS 543–544
h1...h6 element, REF 51
`<hi>` tag, REF 16
hidden element, REF 51
hidden field A Web form field that is hidden from users. REV 37
hidefocus attribute, REF 3
hiding
  elements, REV 77–78
  JavaScript code, JVS 32–33
  objects, JVS 566–568
history element, REF 51
history list, moving in, JVS 280–282
history object The object containing a list of the sites a Web browser has displayed before reaching the current page in the window. JVS 280–282
  security, JVS 284
horizontal line, creating, REV 17
hour value, retrieving, JVS 57–59
hover pseudo-class, JVS 227
`<hr />` tag, REF 16
hr element, REF 51–52
HTML. *See* Hypertext Markup Language (HTML)
HTML element, REF 8–32
  core attributes, REF 2
  core events, REF 4
  data events, REF 5
  document events, REF 4
  event attributes, REF 4

form attributes, REF 3
form events, REF 5
IE attributes, REF 3
IE events, REF 6–7
language attributes, REF 2
`<html>` tag, REF 17
HTTPS protocol A set of rules that govern the transmission of information over the World Wide Web in an encrypted state. JVS 490
Hypertext Markup Language (HTML) A markup language that describes hypertext links and other elements used in the creation of Web pages. REV 2–4, REV 4–46
  attributes, REF 8–32
  block-level elements. *See* block-level element
  class attribute, REV 15–16
  creating links, REV 16
  document heads, REV 7–8
  element attributes, REV 6–7
  elements. *See* HTML element
  embedding media clips, REV 18–19
  file structure, REV 7
  forms. *See* form
  frames. *See* frame
  horizontal lines, REV 17
  id attribute, REV 15
  images, REV 16–17
  inline elements, REV 13–15
  inserting content into elements, JVS 530–531
  opening browser windows, JVS 286
  special characters, REV 17–18
  tables. *See* table
  tags, REV 5–6
  versions, REV 3
  white space, REV 6

I

`<i>` tag, REF 17
id attribute, REF 2, REV 15
IE. *See* Internet Explorer *entries*
If statement, JVS 123–124
  nesting, JVS 124–125
If...Else statement, JVS 126–128
  multiple, JVS 127–128
`<iframe>` tag, REF 17
iframe element, REF 52
`<ilayer>` tag, REF 17–18
ilayer element, REF 69
illegal operation, numeric values, JVS 74–75
image
  background, REV 63, REV 64–65
  inline, REV 16–17
  placement, REV 63–65
image collection The collection of image objects within a document. JVS 217
image element, REF 52
image object An object that contains an inline image.
  creating, JVS 219
  detecting, JVS 221
  properties, JVS 219–220
  swapping, JVS 224–225
image rollover An effect in which the source of an inline image changes from one graphic file to another, usually in response to the mouse pointer hovering over and then leaving the image. JVS 221–226
  preloading images, JVS 222–224
  running, JVS 225–226
  swapping image objects, JVS 224–226
  testing, JVS 226

image style, REV 63–65
`<img>` tag, REF 18–19
implementation element, REF 53
increment operator (++) A unary operator that increases the value of an expression by one. JVS 64, REF 65
indentation, text, REV 59
index A number within an array that indicates the selected item. JVS 106
inline element An element displayed within a block-level element. REV 8, REV 13–15
inline frame A frame that appears as an inline element within a Web page. JVS 319–320, REV 45–46
inline image A graphic image placed within a Web page. JVS 217–218, REV 16–17
inline layer, REF 69
inline style A style applied to an element by adding the style attribute to the element's markup tag , REV 51
input box, REV 28, REV 30–31
`<input>` tag, REF 19–20
input field, JVS 340–342
  navigating between, JVS 341–342
  setting value, JVS 340–341
`<ins>` tag, REF 20
inserting array items, JVS 113–115
Inset transition, JVS 249
instance, JVS 198
Internet Explorer (IE), JVS 7, REV 2
  DOM, JVS 165
  dynamic content, JVS 531–533
  filters. *See* filter
  Microsoft Script Debugger, JVS 35
  positioning properties in DOM, JVS 180–181
  transitions. *See* transition
Internet Explorer attribute, HTML and XHTML, REF 3
Internet Explorer event, HTML and XHTML, REF 6–7
Internet Explorer event model The event model developed for Internet Explorer. JVS 425–428, JVS 430
  attaching and detaching events, JVS 428
  canceling event bubbling, JVS 427–428
  event bubbling, JVS 425–426
Internet Explorer event object, JVS 433–434
interpage transition A visual effect applied as a browser transitions from one page to another. JVS 256–257
interpreted language A programming language in which the code is executed directly without compiling. JVS 7
Invert filter, JVS 241
Iris transition, JVS 249
`<isindex />` tag, REF 20

J

Java A client-sided compiled programming language developed by Sun Microsystems in the 1990s. JVS 7
Java Interpreter An application that runs Java programs. JVS 7
JavaScript An interpreted programming language designed to work with Web pages and browsers. JVS 7
  development, JVS 7–8
  elements, REF 43–63
  keyword, REF 66
  opening browser windows, JVS 286–287
  operators, keywords, and syntactical elements, REF 65–66
  overview, JVS 2–8
  syntax, REF 66
JavaScript command, running as link, JVS 55
JScript A version of JavaScript supported by the Internet Explorer browser. JVS 8

pattern-matching The use of regular expressions to determine whether a given text string matches the pattern expressed in a regular expression. JVS 369

per session cookie A cookie that exists only for as long as a browser is communicating with a Web site. JVS 488

percent symbol (%)
    assignment operator, JVS 65, REF 65
    remainder operator, JVS 63, REF 65

permanent status bar message The default status bar message, displayed when no actions are occurring with the browser window. JVS 277–278

persistent The property of remaining active between sessions, even after users turn off their computers. JVS 481

personalized greeting, JVS 495–497

physical element An element that describes how text should appear but doesn't indicate the nature of its content. REV 15

pipe symbol (|), logical operator, JVS 78, REF 66

pixel A single point on an output device. REV 58

Pixelate filter, JVS 240

Pixelate transition, JVS 249

placement, images, REV 63–65

`<plaintext>` tag, REF 26

plugin element, REF 56

plus symbol (+)
    addition operator, JVS 63, REF 65
    assignment operator, JVS 65, REF 65
    combining text strings, JVS 14, JVS 18
    escape sequences, JVS 380
    increment operator, JVS 64, REF 65
    repetition character, JVS 379

plus/minus box A box that shows either a + or – symbol. Clicking on the + symbol displays hidden nested content. Clicking on the – symbol hides nested content. JVS 561–565
    adding event handlers, JVS 564–565
    creating, JVS 562–564

populating
    arrays, JVS 106–110
    form fields with cookie values, JVS 494–495

pop-up blocker A program that prevents a browser from automatically opening pop-up windows. JVS 291–292

pop-up element, REF 56

pop-up menu A menu that appears on a page, usually in response to a user clicking an object on the page. JVS 233–238
    calling functions, JVS 236–238
    creating, JVS 228–229
    displaying contents, JVS 234–236

pop-up window A new window opened by a Web browser's main window. JVS 285
    adding to sites, JVS 292–294
    closing automatically, JVS 298
    creating, JVS 287, JVS 304–307
    pop-up blockers, JVS 291–292
    security issues, JVS 294
    setting features, JVS 287–291

positioning element, REV 72–76
    absolute positioning, REV 72–73
    fixed positioning, REV 74
    floating elements, REV 74–75
    relative positioning, REV 73
    stacking elements, REV 75–76
    static positioning, REV 74

post method A method of sending form data by sending the data in a separate data stream, allowing the Web server to receive the data through what is called "standard input." JVS

pound symbol (#), code numbers, REV 17

`<pre>` tag, REF 26

precedence, styles, REV 55

preserving form data The process of collecting and saving form data to be used later in the functioning of a Web site during the current session, or for retrieval at a later date in a future session. JVS 506–508

print styles, REV 87–91

printer-friendly version, REV 86

privacy policy, compact, JVS 482

privacy statement A statement that explains how a Web site protects the privacy of those who visit and provide information. JVS 482

program loop A set of commands that it is executed repeatedly until a stopping condition has been met. JVS 116–121
    jumping to next iteration, JVS 140–141
    statement labels, JVS 141–142
    terminating, JVS 140
    tips, JVS 142

prompt dialog box A dialog box that displays both a message and a text box in which a user can enter text. JVS 299

property An aspect of an object that describes its appearance, purpose, or behavior
    in conditional expressions, JVS 172
    customized, JVS 199
    image objects, JVS 219–220
    objects, JVS 162, JVS 170–172
    positioning in IE DOM, JVS 180–181
    window object, JVS 276

pseudo-class A classification of an element based on its status, position, or current use in a document. REV 82
    applying styles, REV 82–83, REV 84
    CSS, REF 34
    page, REV 87–88

pseudo-element An element selected based on its content, use, or position in a document. REV 83
    applying styles, REV 83–84
    CSS, REF 34

pull-down menu A menu that is partially hidden and then revealed, usually in response to a user clicking part of the menu. JVS 229

Q

`<q>` tag, REF 26

question mark (?), repetition character, JVS 379

R

RadialWipe transition, JVS 249

radio button, REV 28, REV 31–32

Radio element, REF 57

random number, JVS 86

RandomBars transition, JVS 249

RandomDissolve transition, JVS 249

read-only A property whose value can be read, but not changed. JVS 171

recursion A programming technique in which a function calls itself repeatedly until a stopping condition is met. JVS 575–577

redirecting events using Netscape 4, REF 79

RegExp element, REF 57

registered trademark symbol, REV 18

regular expression A text string that defines a character pattern. JVS 369–389
    alternate patterns and grouping, JVS 381–384
    creating, JVS 369–370
    defining character positions, JVS 372–374
    defining character types and character classes, JVS 374–378
    escape sequences, JVS 380–381
    matching substrings, JVS 370–371
    methods, JVS 385–387
    object constructor, JVS 384–385
    repeating characters, JVS 378–379
    setting flags, JVS 371–372
    validating entries, JVS 387–396

regular expression literal The syntax used to enter the pattern for a regular expression directly in a text string. JVS 369

relative positioning Placing an element relative to its default location within its parent element. REV 73

relative unit A style unit that defines a length relative to the size of a standard character in the output device. REV 57

releasing events using Netscape 4, REF 78

repetition character, JVS 378–379

reserved target name Names reserved by browsers to identify the window or frame in which the target of a link should appear. REV 43–44

Reset element, REF 57–58

resolution, monitors, layout for, JVS 191–197

retrieving form data, JVS 398–400

reveal transition A transition in which a visual effect is applied as one object is changed into another. JVS 247–248

reversing arrays, JVS 111

rollover effect An effect applied to an element when a user's mouse pointer hovers over it and then moves off of it. REV 83

root element The element that contains all other elements in a document. REV 7

root node The topmost node in a node tree. JVS 534

rounding to specified number of digits, JVS 85–86

routing events using Netscape 4, REF 78–79

row group A group of rows within a Web table; created using the thead, tfoot, and tbody elements. REV 20–21

row size, frames, REV 40–41

@rule, CSS, REF 34

rule, tables, REV 26–27

run-time error A programming error that occurs when a browser attempts to run program code; often occurs with a misnamed variable or function. JVS 33–34, REF 83, REF 84–85

S

`<s>` tag, REF 26

`<samp>` tag, REF 26

scalable The quality of some Web pages that enables them to be rendered the same regardless of the size of the browser window. REV 58

scope The property that defines where and how a variable can be used within an application. JVS 25

screen element, REF 58

Script element, REF 58

`<script>` tag, REF 26

script element, JVS 8–10
    creating, JVS 8–9
    event handlers as, JVS 422–423
    placing, JVS 9
    statements, JVS 9–10

scripting transitions, JVS 251–252

second value, retrieving, JVS 58–59

secondary window A new window opened by a Web browser's main window. JVS 285. *See also* pop-up window

section heading ids, JVS 557–558

security
    browser windows, JVS 294
    history object, JVS 284

Select element, REF 58–59

`<select>` tag, REF 26–27

selection list, JVS 343–346, REV 28, REV 33–35

selector, REF 33, REV 78–84
    applying styles to IDs and classes, REV 81–82
    applying styles to pseudo-classes and pseudo-elements, REV 82–84
    attribute, REV 80
    contextual, REV 78–80
    CSS, REF 33

selectStart event, canceling, JVS 447–448

self keyword A reserved JavaScript keyword that refers to the current browser window. JVS 297

semicolon (;)

    command line, REF 66

    statements, JVS 10

server A computer that stores documents and other resources, making them available to a network. REV 1

server-side cookie A cookie created and stored on a server using server-side scripting languages such as Perl, PHP, ASP.Net, C++, and Java. JVS 481

server-side programming Programming that is executed on a Web server, with the results sent to the server or to the client. JVS 4–5

server-side shopping cart A shopping cart application that is controlled through a server. JVS 480

server-side validation Validation performed by a Web server. JVS 354, JVS 355

session Each visit to a Web page by a user. JVS 481

Shadow filter, JVS 240, JVS 241

single-line comment, JVS 31

size

    columns, frames, REV 40–41

    display window, calculating, JVS 193–197

    font, REV 57

    layer elements, REF 68–69

    pages, REV 88

    rows, frames, REV 40–41

    sizing elements with CSS, REV 65–67

    table borders, REV 23

    tables, REV 23–25

slash (/)

    assignment operator, REF 65

    comments, JVS 31

    division operator, JVS 63, REF 65

    escape sequences, JVS 380

    JavaScript comments, REF 66

Slide transition, JVS 249

sliding menu A menu that is partially hidden either off of a Web page or behind another object on the page; when a user clicks the visible part of the menu, the menu "slides" into a fully visible position. JVS 230

`<small>` tag, REF 27

sorting arrays, JVS 112

spacing

    table cells, REV 23–24, REV 25

    text, REV 58–59

spam Junk e-mail sent in bulk to unwilling recipients. JVS 2

spammer A person who sends spam. JVS 2

`<span>` tag, REF 27

spanning cell A cell within a Web table that spans several rows and/or columns. REV 21–23

sparse array, JVS 111

special character, REV 17–18

specific font A font style in a style sheet identified by a font name. REV 56

Spiral transition, JVS 249

stacking

    elements, REV 75–76

    objects on Web pages, REF 72

stateless protocol A protocol that provides no way to track information that a user may have provided when moving from one Web page to another. JVS 481

statement A single command line in a JavaScript program.. *See also* command; *specific commands*

    conditional. *See* conditional statement

    JavaScript, JVS 9–10

    labels, JVS 141–142

static position Placing an element in its default location on the page. REV 74

status bar A browser feature that displays messages about actions occurring within the window. JVS 277–280

    debugging programs, REF 86

    default message, JVS 277–278

    transient message, JVS 278–280

Stretch transition, JVS 249

`<strike>` tag, REF 27

String element, REF 59

string object An object containing a text string. JVS 360

    methods, JVS 362–367

Strips transition, JVS 249

`<strong>` tag, REF 27

strongly typed language A programming language in which a program must explicitly identify a variable's data type. JVS 18

style. *See also* Cascading Style Sheets (CSSs)

    applying filters using, JVS 239–243

    embedded, REV 51–53

    external, REV 53–54

    filter, creating, JVS 242

    inline, REV 51

style attribute, REF 2

    setting, JVS 179

`<style>` tag, REF 27

style element, REF 60, REV 52

style inheritance The effect by which an element adopts the styles associated with its parent. REV 55–56

style object, JVS 179–181

style sheet A collection of properties that describes how elements within a document should be rendered by the device presenting the document. JVS 578–583, REV 49. *See also* Cascading Style Sheets (CSSs)

    applying, REV 51

    calendar, JVS 104

    collections, JVS 581–582

    link element, JVS 579–581

    rules, JVS 582–583

    tips, JVS 583

`<sub>` tag, REF 27

subarray A section of an array, created using the slice() or splice() array methods. JVS 113

Submit element, REF 60

substring A portion of a longer text string. REF 27

    matching, JVS 370–371

`<sup>` tag, REF 27

Switch statement, JVS 128–129

syntax, JavaScript, REF 66

syntax rules, JVS 13–14

T

tabbed menu A menu comprised of several menus stacked on a page; clicking one menu tab brings the corresponding menu contents to the top of the stack. JVS 230–233

tabindex attribute, REF 3

table, REV 19–28

    border size, REV 23

    captions, REV 21

    cell padding, REV 24–25

    cell spacing, REV 23–24

    column groups, REV 27–28

    defining structure, REV 20

    dynamic, JVS 502

    frames, REV 25–26, REV 27

    row groups, REV 20–21

    rules, REV 26–27

    sizing, REV 23–25

    spanning cells, REV 21–23

`<table>` tag, REF 28

table element, REV 19

tag A feature in a markup language that identifies an element within a document. REV 4–6

    closing, REV 5

    comment, REV 5–6

    meta, REV 8

    one-sided, REV 5

    opening, REV 5

    two-sided, REV 4, REV 5

tag name, object, REF 71

target phase The phase in event propagation in which an event reaches the object from the which the event originated. JVS 429

`<tbody>` tag, REF 29

`<td>` tag, REF 29

testing image rollover, JVS 226

text area box, REV 28, REV 35–36

Text element, REF 60–61

`<!-- text -->` tag, REF 8

text rollover, JVS 226–227

    general, JVS 227

    hover pseudo-class, JVS 227

    Netscape 4, REF 75

text string A collection of characters stored as a single entity. JVS 17, JVS 359–368

    calculating length, JVS 360–362

    converting between numbers and, JVS 75–77

    formatting, JVS 367–368

    string object, JVS 360

    string object methods, JVS 362–367

text styles, REV 56–62

    aligning element content, REV 61–62

    combining formatting in single style, REV 62

    font size, REV 57–58

    font styles, weights, and decorative features, REV 59–61

    fonts, REV 56–57

    indentation, REV 59

    spacing, REV 58–59

Textarea element, REF 61

`<textarea>` tag, REF 30

`<tfoot>` tag, REF 30

`<th>` tag, REF 30–31

`<thead>` tag, REF 31

third-party cookie A cookie that is created at a different Web site and is then sent to the Web site that a user is currently visiting. JVS 482

this keyword A reserved JavaScript keyword that references the current selected object. JVS 199, JVS 348–349

throw command A statement that catches an exception created by a programmer. , REF 90–91

time function, creating, JVS 60–62

time value, setting, JVS 59–60

time-delayed command A command that is run after a particular amount of time has passed using the setTimeout() method. JVS 82

timed-interval command A command that is run a specified time intervals using the setInterval() method. JVS 82–84

title attribute, REF 2

`<title>` tag, REF 31

title element, REV 7–8

top keyword A reserved JavaScript keyword that refers to the object that appears at the top of the object hierarchy. JVS 313

`<tr>` tag, REF 32

tracking The amount of space between words. REV 58

Join us in discovering a new view on technology!

Whether you are opening this textbook for the first time, or referencing it long after your course is over, we hope you'll find a new perspective on technology with every use.

As the name of our series implies, the New Perspectives Series pushes the envelope when it comes to helping people learn about technology.

- **Our case-based approach was the FIRST to address both HOW and WHY technology is critical to solving problems in college and the business world.**

- **Our distance learning solutions, online companions, and testing software provide additional technology tools to enhance the overall learning experience.**

Our goal is to produce the most timely and technologically sound products in the entire college publishing industry. Because we consider you a part of our team, your feedback and questions are crucial to our success. Visit our Web site at **www.cengage.com/ct/newperspectives** and let us know what you think.

Thank you, and welcome to the New Perspectives community!

Some of the exercises in this book require that you begin by opening a Data File. Follow one of the procedures below to obtain a copy of the Data Files you need.

Instructors

- The Data Files are on the Instructor Resources CD under the category Data Files for Students, which you can copy to your school's network for student use.
- Download the Data Files via the Internet by following the instructions below.
- Contact us via e-mail at reply@course.com.
- Call Course Technology's Customer Service Department for fast and efficient delivery of the Data Files if you do not have access to a CD-ROM drive.

Students

- Check with your instructor to determine the best way to obtain copies of the Data Files.
- Download the Data Files via the Internet by following the instructions below.
- It is recommended that you store all your Data Files on a USB drive for maximum efficiency in organizing and working with the files.

Instructions for Downloading the Data Files from the Internet

1. Start your browser and enter the URL www.course.com.
2. When the course.com Web site opens, click Student Downloads, and then search for your text by title or ISBN by entering the title or ISBN in the text box and then clicking the Go button.
3. If necessary, from the Search results page, select the title of the text you are using.
4. When the textbook page opens, click the Download Student Files link, and then click the link of the compressed files you want to download.
5. If the File Download – Security Warning dialog box opens, click Save. (NOTE: If the Save As dialog box opens, select a folder on your USB drive or hard disk to download the file to. Write down the folder name listed in the Save in box and the filename listed in the File name box.)
6. The filename of the compressed file appears in the Save As dialog box (e.g., 3500-8.exe, 0361-1d.exe).
7. Click either the OK button or the Save button, whichever choice your browser gives you.
8. When a dialog box opens indicating the download is complete, click the OK button (or the Close button, depending on which operating system you are using). Close your browser.
9. Open Windows Explorer and display the contents of the folder to which you downloaded the file. Double-click the downloaded filename on the right side of the Windows Explorer window. If the Open File – Security Warning dialog box opens, click Run.
10. In the WinZip Self-Extractor window, specify the appropriate drive and a folder name to unzip the files to. Click Unzip.
11. When the WinZip Self-Extractor displays the number of files unzipped, click the OK button. Click the Close button in the WinZip Self-Extractor dialog box. Close Windows Explorer. You are now ready to open the required files.

Macintosh users should use a program to expand WinZip or PKZip archives. Students, ask your instructors or lab coordinators for assistance.